MW00465578

DAVID ALAN BARD
PRESIDING BISHOP

2019

MICHIGAN ANNUAL CONFERENCE

OF

THE UNITED METHODIST CHURCH

FIRST SESSION

Grand Traverse Resort

Traverse City, Michigan

May 30 – June 2, 2019

Bishop David Alan Bard, Presiding Bishop
Joy A. Barrett, Annual Conference Secretary

OFFICIAL MINUTES & RECORDS

VOLUME 2

— MAC Photos

CONFERENCE OFFICERS

MICHIGAN AREA EPISCOPAL OFFICE
1011 Northcrest Rd
Lansing, MI 48906-1262
517.347.4003

MICHIGAN CONFERENCE CENTER
1011 Northcrest Rd
Lansing, MI 48906-1262
517.347.4030

MICHIGAN CONFERENCE CENTER – NORTH
1161 E Clark Rd, Ste 212
DeWitt, MI 48820-8312
517.347.4030

MICHIGAN CONFERENCE CENTER – WEST
207 Fulton St E, Ste 6
Grand Rapids, MI 49503-3278
517.347.4030

MICHIGAN AREA EPISCOPAL OFFICE   517.347.4003

Resident Bishop
David A. Bard   bishop@michiganumc.org

Clergy Assistant to the Bishop   Ext. 4012
Rev. John W. Boley   jboley@michiganumc.org

Executive Assistant to the Bishop   Ext. 4011
Deana Nelson   dnelson@michiganumc.org

Executive Assistant to the Clergy Assistant to the Bishop   Ext. 4013
Jennifer Weaver   jweaver@michiganumc.org

CONFERENCE OFFICERS OF THE ANNUAL CONFERENCE

Conference Chancellor
Andrew Vorbrich   Lennon, Miller, O'Connor, Bartosiewicz, PLC

Director of Administrative Services and Treasurer
David Dobbs   ddobbs@michiganumc.org

Conference Facilitator
Susanne "Sue" Buxton   sbbuxton@sbcglobal.net

Conference Lay Leaders
Anne Soles   layleader@michiganumc.org
John Wharton   layleader@michiganumc.org

Conference Secretary
Joy Barrett   secretary@michiganumc.org

Conference Statistician
Pamela Stewart   statistician@michiganumc.org

CONFERENCE OFFICERS

DISTRICT OFFICES

CENTRAL BAY DISTRICT

3764 Fashion Square Blvd, Saginaw, MI 48603
989.793.8838

Rev. David I. Kim, District Superintendent   dkim@michiganumc.org
Teri Rice, Executive Assistant   trice@michiganumc.org

EAST WINDS DISTRICT

624 W Nepessing St, Ste 201 – Lapeer, MI 48446-2088
810.396.1362

Rev. John H. Hice, District Superintendent   jhice@michiganumc.org
Cheryl Rentschler, Executive Assistant   crentschler@michiganumc.org

GREATER DETROIT DISTRICT

8000 Woodward Ave – Detroit, MI 48202-2528
313.481.1045

Rev. Dr. Charles S.G. Boayue, Jr., District Superintendent   cboayue@michiganumc.org
Dwanda Ashford, Executive Assistant   dashford@michiganumc.org

GREATER SOUTHWEST DISTRICT

2350 Ring Rd N, Ste B – Kalamazoo, MI 49006-5428
269.372.7525

Rev. Dwayne E. Bagley, District Superintendent   dbagley@michiganumc.org
Mandana Nordbrock, Executive Assistant   mnordbrock@michiganumc.org

HERITAGE DISTRICT

900 S 7th St – Ann Arbor, MI 48103-4769
734.663.3939

Rev. Elizabeth A. Hill, District Superintendent   ehill@michiganumc.org
Dar McGee, Executive Assistant   dmcgee@michiganumc.org

MID-MICHIGAN DISTRICT

1161 E Clark Rd, Ste 216 – DeWitt, MI 48820-8312
517.347.4173

Rev. Dr. Jerome R. DeVine, District Superintendent   jdevine@michiganumc.org
Sarah Gillette, Executive Assistant   sgillette@michiganumc.org

MIDWEST DISTRICT

207 Fulton St E, Ste 6 – Grand Rapids, MI 49503-3278
616.459.4503

Rev. Dr. Margie R. Crawford, District Superintendent   mcrawford@michiganumc.org
Liz Bode, Executive Assistant   lbode@michiganumc.org

NORTHERN SKIES DISTRICT

927 W Fair Ave – Marquette, MI 49855-2611
906.228.4644

Rev. Scott A. Harmon, District Superintendent   sharmon@michiganumc.org
Diana Byar, Executive Assistant   dbyar@michiganumc.org

NORTHERN WATERS DISTRICT

1249 Three Mile Rd S – Traverse City, MI 49696-8307
231.947.5281

Rev. Jodie R. Flessner, District Superintendent   jflessner@michiganumc.org
Jill Haney, Executive Assistant   jhaney@michiganumc.org

CONFERENCE DIRECTORS   517.347.4030

DIRECTOR OF CONNECTIONAL MINISTRY   Ext. 4070
Rev. Benton R. Heisler   bheisler@michiganumc.org

DIRECTOR OF CLERGY EXCELLENCE   Ext. 4050
Rev. Dr. Jennifer Browne   jbrowne@michiganumc.org

DIRECTOR FOR CONGREGATIONAL VIBRANCY   Ext. 4090
Rev. Dirk Elliott   delliott@michiganumc.org

DIRECTOR OF ADMINISTRATIVE SERVICES AND TREASURER   Ext. 4130
David Dobbs   ddobbs@michiganumc.org

DIRECTOR OF BENEFITS AND HUMAN RESOURCES   Ext. 4110
Rev. Donald J. Emmert   demmert@michiganumc.org

DIRECTOR OF COMMUNICATIONS   Ext. 4030
Mark Doyal   mdoyal@michiganumc.org

CONFERENCE OFFICE OF CONNECTIONAL MINISTRIES   517.347.4030

Director of Connectional Ministries   Ext. 4070
Rev. Benton R. Heisler   bheisler@michiganumc.org

Executive Assistant to the Director of Connectional Ministries   Ext. 4071
Sus'ann Busley   sbusley@michiganumc.org

Associate Director for Mission and Ministry   Ext. 4076
Rev. Paul D. Perez   pperez@michiganumc.org

Associate Director for Multi-Cultural Vibrancy   Ext. 4073
Rev. Brittney D. Stephan   bstephan@michiganumc.org

Children's Initiatives Coordinator   Ext. 4077
Rev. Kathryn L. Pittenger   kpittenger@michiganumc.org

Young Adult Initiatives Coordinator   Ext. 4078
Pastor Lisa M. Batten   lbatten@michiganumc.org

Missionary for Hispanic / Latino Ministries   Ext. 4074
Sonya Luna   sluna@michiganumc.org

Disaster Response Ministries Coordinator   Ext. 4082
Nancy Money   nmoney@michiganumc.org

Events Planner   Ext. 4075
Nancy Arnold   narnold@michiganumc.org

CONFERENCE OFFICERS

Annual Conference Registrar   Ext. 4081
Sarah Vollmer   svollmer@michiganumc.org

Nominations / Journal Clerical Assistant   Ext. 4072
Katherine Hippensteel   khippensteel@michiganumc.org

Receptionist / Protection Policy Assistant   Ext. 4079
Aritha Davis   adavis@michiganumc.org

CONFERENCE OFFICE OF CLERGY EXCELLENCE   517.347.4030

Director of Clergy Excellence   Ext. 4050
Rev. Dr. Jennifer Browne   jbrowne@michiganumc.org

Executive Assistant to the Director of Clergy Excellence   Ext. 4051
Debbie Stevenson   dstevenson@michiganumc.org

Administrative Assistant to Clergy Excellence   Ext. 4052
Cheryl Poole   cpoole@michiganumc.org

CONFERENCE OFFICE OF CONGREGATIONAL VIBRANCY   517.347.4030

Director for Congregational Vibrancy   Ext. 4090
Rev. Dirk Elliott   delliott@michiganumc.org

Executive Assistant to the Director of Congregational Vibrancy   Ext. 4091
Jodi Fuller   jsmith@michiganumc.org

Associate Director for Congregational Vibrancy   Ext. 4092
Naomi García   ngarcia@michiganumc.org

Associate Director for Congregational Vibrancy   Ext. 4093
Rev. Gary G. Step   gstep@michiganumc.org

Associate Director for Lay Leadership Development   Ext. 4094
Laura Witkowski   lwitkowski@michiganumc.org

Coordinator of Youth Ministry Development   Ext. 4095
TBD

CONFERENCE OFFICE OF FINANCE AND ADMINISTRATIVE SERVICES   517.347.4030

Director of Administrative Services and Treasurer   Ext. 4130
David Dobbs   ddobbs@michiganumc.org

Treasury and Benefits Operations Manager   Ext. 4131
Becky Emmert   bemmert@michiganumc.org

Accountant
Jill Smith

Ext. 4133
jsmith@michiganumc.org

Accounts Payable
Nancy Wyllys

Ext. 4132
nwyllys@michiganumc.org

Accounts Receivable
Rich Pittenger

Ext. 4134
rpittenger@michiganumc.org

IT Specialist
Rev. Michael J. Mayo-Moyle

Ext. 4136
mmayomoyle@michiganumc.org

Benefits Executive Assistant
Jennifer Gertz

Ext. 4135
jgertz@michiganumc.org

Statistician / Ezra Database Specialist
Pamela Stewart

Ext. 4135
pstewart@michiganumc.org

CONFERENCE OFFICE OF BENEFITS AND HUMAN RESOURCES

517.347.4030

Director of Benefits and Human Resources
Rev. Donald J. Emmert

Ext. 4110
demmert@michiganumc.org

Benefits Administrator and Payroll
John Kosten

Ext. 4111
jkosten@michiganumc.org

CONFERENCE OFFICE OF COMMUNICATIONS

517.347.4030

Director of Communications
Mark Doyal

Ext. 4030
mdoyal@michiganumc.org

Executive Assistant to the Director of Communications
Kristen Gillette

Ext. 4031
kgillette@michiganumc.org

Senior Content Editor
Rev. Mariel Kay DeMoss

Ext. 4032
kdemoss@michiganumc.org

Communications Production Assistant
Valerie Mossman-Celestin, Deaconess

Ext. 4033
vmossman-celestin@michiganumc.org

Social Media Assistant
Paul Reissmann

Ext. 4034
preissmann@michiganumc.org

CHARGE LAY MEMBERS TO ANNUAL CONFERENCE

CENTRAL BAY DISTRICT

Charge	Lay Member
Arbela	Not Represented
Arenac Cnty: Christ	Stacy Sesler
Auburn	Sue Plessner
Bay City: Grace	Matt Coppess
	Not Represented
	Not Represented
Bayport, Hayes	Marge Hall
Beaverton: First	Not Represented
Bentley	Not Represented
Birch Run	Not Represented
Burt	Not Represented
Caro	Lisa Wightman
	Not Represented
Caseville	Marie Kiehl
Cass City	Connie Schwaderer
Churchill	Reid Rosebrugh
Clare	Susie Neff
	Barb Tyler
Coleman: Faith	Not Represented
Coomer, Winn	Not Represented
Elkton	Not Represented
Essexville: St Luke's	Sherry Stone
	Not Represented
Fairgrove	Not Represented
Farwell	Sue Franklin
Frankenmuth	Charles Allport
	Ann Graham
	Not Represented
Freeland	Tatyana Spaulding
Gladwin: First	Janet King
Glennie	Tabitha Reinhardt
Gordonville, Midland: Homer	Gaylia Anger
	Lori Anger
Hale: First	Chuck Hamilton
Harrison: The Gathering	Not Represented
Harrisville, Lincoln	Not Represented
Hemlock, Nelson	Sarah Vollmer
Kilmanagh, Owendale	Rhonda Powers
Kingston	Gayle Farver
Mapleton	Not Represented
Mayville	Kathy Freeland
Midland Cnty: Hope, Edenville, Dale	
	Charlie Russian
Midland: Aldersgate	Ralph Czerepinski
	Not Represented
	Not Represented

Charge	Lay Member
Midland: First	Peg Born
	Bethany Goodman
	Chuck Goodman
	Carol Harfmann
	Kathy Hoffman
	Kandis Pritchett
	Not Represented
	Not Represented
	Not Represented
	Not Represented
	Not Represented
Millington	Maury Chapin
Mio	Bob Hegel
Mt Pleasant: Chippewa Indian	Not Represented
Mt Pleasant: First	George Aultman
	John Skinner
Mt Pleasant: Leaton	Carolyn Bohlmann
Mt Pleasant: Trinity, Countryside	Dale Russell
Oscoda, Oscoda: Indian Church	Julie Burrell
Pigeon: First	Bonnie Dunstan
Pigeon: Salem	Hans Eichler
Pinconning, Garfield	Izzy Nowak
Port Austin UPC, Pinnebog	Janet Cameron
Reese	John Elsesser
Rose City: Trinity, Whittemore	Gary Gillings
	Beth Harper
Rosebush	Not Represented
Saginaw: Ames	Edith Cooper
	Not Represented
Saginaw: First	Robert Miller
	Not Represented
	Not Represented
Saginaw: New Heart	Not Represented
Saginaw: State Street	Not Represented
Saginaw: Swan Valley, Laporte	Mary Aaron
	Doris Simons
Sanford	George Farner
Sebewaing: Trinity	Rena Lorenz
Shepherd, Blanchard-Pine River	Linda Miller
St Charles	Linda Kube
Sterling, Alger, Standish: Community	
	Rose Bledsoe
Sutton-Sunshine	Not Represented
Tawas	Joe Koehn
	Ed Nagy
Vassar: First	Linda Reimus
Wagarville: Community	Cathy Kennedy
Watrousville	Not Represented

Weidman	Not Represented
West Branch: First	Ray Mcclintic
	Not Represented
Wilber	Not Represented
Wisner	Jerry Letson
Wesley Foundation: CMU	Lauren Canary

EAST WINDS DISTRICT

Applegate, Buel, Croswell: First	
	Not Represented
Armada, West Berlin	Not Represented
Atherton, Grand Blanc: Phoenix	John Howell
Attica	Harry Wilcox
Bad Axe: First	Not Represented
	Not Represented
Brown City	Cyndy Rossman
Burton: Christ	Marilyn Wykes
Byron: First, Gaines	Not Represented
Capac	Connie Tosch
Central Lakeport	Not Represented
Clarkston	Kelsey Burns
	Laura Dake
	Lou Dupree
	Pat Edwards
	Michele Ettinger
	Shelby Ettinger
	Ric Huttenlocher
	Barb Trueman
	Bob Wyatt
Clio: Bethany	Nonie Lemmon
	Elizabeth Whiting
Cole, Melvin	Julie Cramer
Columbiaville	Eva Jankowske
Davisburg	Not Represented
Davison	Mike Hall
Deckerville	Not Represented
Dryden, Leonard	Chris Hoppenworth
Durand: First	Gary Pabst
Fenton	Stacey Highfield
	Jim York
	Sandy York
	Not Represented
	Not Represented
Flint: Asbury	Not Represented
Flint: Bethel	Terry Brannon
	Jennifer Rogers
Flint: Bristol	Susan Phillips
Flint: Calvary	Greg Timmons Ii
Flint: Charity	Johnny Watkins
Flint: Court Street	Randeigh Dickinson
	David Lindsey
	Kevin Meinka
Flint: Faith	Not Represented
Flint: Hope	Peter Thoms
Flushing	Bob Halbedel
	Kris Supernaw
Forester, Port Sanilac	Not Represented
Genesee, Thetford Center	Not Represented
Goodrich	Eric Carlson
	Clint Densham
Grand Blanc	Carol Cerny
	Tom Cerny
Halsey, South Mundy	Cecil Freels
Harbor Beach, Port Hope	Judy Chasney
Holly: Calvary	Linda Parsons
Holly: Mt Bethel	Nancy Mills
Imlay City	Joyce Terry
Jeddo, Avoca	Not Represented
Lake Fenton	Not Represented
Lake Orion	Susan Montgomery
	Not Represented
	Not Represented
	Not Represented
Lapeer: Trinity	Jim Elzerman
	Debi Lobb
	Deanne Schlusler
Lennon, Duffield	Not Represented
Lexington	Lynn Geer
Linden	Joan Tyree
Marlette: First	Tom Skakle
Marysville	Scott Krauss
	Not Represented
McGregor, Carsonville	Cheri Griggs
Memphis: First, Lamb	Jamie Harper
Minden City, Shabbona	Arthur Severance
Montrose	Dee Campbell
Mt Morris: First	Deb Sprague
North Branch: First, Silverwood	Linda Fitch
North Street	Beth Burch
Omard	Not Represented
Oregon, Elba	Not Represented
Ortonville	Steve Lemmon
Otisville, Fostoria, West Deerfield	Veneita Chapin
Oxford	John Warren
Port Huron: First	Bob Bernum
	Carol Kandell
	Bob Sult
	Not Represented

Port Huron: Gratiot Park, Washington Ave
Nanette Miller
Richfield — Kristen Lepalm
Richmond: First — Glenn Quick
Romeo — Sue Coker
Carol Herm
Saint Clair: First — Bob Rhoades
Not Represented
Sandusky: First — Mary Nichol
Seymour Lake — Claudia Lowthian
Snover: Heritage — Jan Watson
Swartz Creek — Bruce Lanning
Rose Parks
Not Represented
Not Represented
Thomas — Not Represented
Ubly — Not Represented
West Forest — Not Represented
West Vienna — Max Hammel
Worth Twp: Bethel — Carol Derby
Yale — Not Represented

GREATER DETROIT DISTRICT

Algonac Trinity — Not Represented
Beverly Hills — Alice Tucker
Birmingham: Embury — Not Represented
Birmingham: First — Len Billingsley
Margaret Buccini
David Dale
Sue Dale
Dawn Dulworth
Rachael Dunlap
Phyllis Hart
Ted Mcclew
Holly Pisano
Karen Plants
Dave Ruby
Sue Ruby
Bridget Schipper
Bob Sutherland
Ellen Sutherland
Darrell White
Linda White
Not Represented
Bloomfield Hls: St Paul — Not Represented
Clawson — Ben Walker
Dearborn Hts: Stephen's — Not Represented
Dearborn: First — Rick Anderson
Jill Sestok
Dearborn: Good Shepherd — Marti Tamaroglio

Detroit: Calvary — George Campbell
Detroit: Cass Cmnty — Amanda Funk
Ben Schornack
Detroit: Central — Alex Oatley
Gary Zundel
Detroit: Centro Familiar Cristiano
Not Represented
Detroit: Conant Ave — Dianne Brown
Detroit: Ford Memorial — Not Represented
Detroit: French — Not Represented
Not Represented
Detroit: Metropolitan — Ken Davis
Jeanette Harris
Detroit: Mt Hope — Not Represented
Detroit: Resurrection — Not Represented
Detroit: Scott Memorial — Pearl Lewis
Josh Matthews
Detroit: Second Grace — Beatrice Alghali
Lewis Moore
Tracey Moore
Detroit: St Paul — Amy Heitman
Detroit: Trinity-Faith — Elsa Bailey-Draper
Downriver — Patty Molloy
Not Represented
Eastpointe: Immanuel — Linda Morrell
Farmington: First — Jill Burress
Not Represented
Farmington: Nardin Park — John Gingrich
Nancy Gingrich
Mary Glenn
Michael Kain
Mike Marks
Farmington: Orchard — Cathy Albery
Dave Albery
Lesley Bonsky
Not Represented
Ferndale: First — Bonnie Kern
Flat Rock: First — Randy Ruppel
Franklin: Community — Mark Cooper
Fraser: Christ — Not Represented
Garden City: First — Kevin Stannard
Grosse Pointe — Ben Ford
Venus Rembert-Karchin
Bob Rossbach
Harper Woods: Redeemer — Barb Davis
Hazel Park: First — Not Represented
Howarth, Paint Creek — Steffani Glygoroff
Livonia: Clarenceville — Barb Bennett
Livonia: Newburg — Susan Adams
Marie Boyd
Not Represented

Livonia: St Matthew's	Mary Beltzman	Trenton: Faith	Bob Eberhardt
	Mark Ellis		Reje Eberhardt
	Kathy Lefler		Kay Korns
Macomb: Faith	Not Represented	Trenton: First	Margaret Creekmore
Madison Hts	Deb Overla	Troy: Big Beaver	Not Represented
Madison Hts: Korean First Central			Not Represented
	Not Represented	Troy: First	Cathy Miller
Madison Hts: Vietnamese Ministry			Robin Ostergaard
	Not Represented		Isaac Verhelst
Mt Clemens: First	Lois Hill	Troy: Korean	Hoon Hopgood
	Linda Johnston		Not Represented
Mt Vernon	Not Represented		Not Represented
New Baltimore: Grace	Chuck Sullivan		Not Represented
Omo: Zion, Washington	Not Represented		Not Represented
Pontiac: Grace And Peace Cmnty			Not Represented
	Not Represented	Utica	David Miller
Pontiac: St John	Not Represented		Peggy Miller
Redford: Aldersgate	Chris Johnson	Warren: First	Not Represented
	Not Represented		Not Represented
	Not Represented	Waterford: Central	Francie Bauer
Redford: New Beginnings	Larry Chapman		Christy Painter
Riverview	Dottie Kamin		Barbara Spiece
Rochester Hls: St Luke's	Chris Ariss	Waterford: Four Towns	John Hoogacker
		Waterford: Trinity	Not Represented
		Wayne-Westland: First	Ernest Owulette
Rochester: St Paul's	Leslie Bennett	West Bloomfield	Margaret Cantrell
	Helen Fausch	Westland: St James, Detroit: Peoples	
	Betsy Fisch		Not Represented
	Ronald Fisch	Wyandotte: First	Kirk Hayhurst
	Grant Fry		Sue Hayhurst
	Sigrid Grace		
	Krista Hughes		
	Rick Kress	**GREATER SOUTHWEST DISTRICT**	
	Peter Marsh	Allegan	Mark Bolyen
	Susan Sonye		Bobby Tremaine
	Ace Watson	Almena	Jackie Coons
	Mary Watson	Arden	Not Represented
	Not Represented	Augusta: Fellowship	Shari Pearce
Romulus: Community	Carl Morris	Bangor: Simpson	Karla Vassar
Roseville: Trinity	Roxann Kohler	Battle Creek: Baseline, Bellevue	
Royal Oak: First	Bob Prud'homme		Not Represented
	Cathy Thatcher	Battle Creek: Chapel Hill	Linda Grap
	Mark Thatcher		Mike Johnson
	Not Represented		Carrie Morton
Southfield: Hope, Detroit: St Timothy		Battle Creek: Christ, Washington Heights	
	Not Represented		Diane Garfield
	Not Represented	Battle Creek: Convis Union	Not Represented
	Not Represented	Battle Creek: First	Bill Lewis
	Not Represented	Battle Creek: Maple	Not Represented
	Not Represented	Battle Creek: Newton	Sue Ratliff
Sterling Hts: First	David Lamb	Berrien Cnty: Lakeside	Bev Lawton

Berrien Springs, Pokagon	Not Represented
Bloomingdale	Not Represented
Bronson: First, Colon	Not Represented
Buchanan: Faith	Wayne Wilcox
Buchanan: First	Brenda Klingerman
Burnips, Monterey Center	Basil Kidwell
Burr Oak	Not Represented
Casco	Karl Andrews
Cassopolis	John Kelley
Centreville	Michelle Brokaw
Climax, Scotts	Bill Smith
Coldwater	Beth Griggs
	Lana Hunter
Coloma	Diane Hogue
Constantine, White Pigeon	Marti Brown
Delton: Faith	Not Represented
Dowagiac: First	Gloria Staten
Dowling: Country Chapel	Renee Foster
Edwardsburg: Hope	Marti Bartels
	Judy Denemark
	Not Represented
Fennville: Fennville, Pearl	Dana Tipken
Galesburg	Bob Doerr
Galien: Galien, Olive Branch	Not Represented
Ganges	Not Represented
Girard	Shelly Ash
Glenn	Not Represented
Gobles, Kendall	Karen Grimes
Gull Lake	Karen Morse
	Lorence Wenke
Hartford	Doug Nelson
Hinchman	Dawn Oldenburg
Hopkins, South Monterey	Earl Collier
Kalamazoo: First	John Clark
	Lisa Coe
	Fred Douglas
	Deb Search Willoughby
	Molly Williams
Kalamazoo: Milwood	Vince Wheat
Kalamazoo: Northwest	Not Represented
Kalamazoo: Sunnyside	Jo Ann Mundy
	Christy Newhouse
Kalamazoo: Westwood	Sally Mahieu
	Jill Reid
Lacota	Not Represented
Lawrence, Lawton: St Paul's	Louise Cammire
Marcellus: Marcellus, Wakelee	
	Not Represented
Martin, Shelbyville	Ruth Schrier
Mendon	Betty Taylor
New Buffalo: Water's Edge	Cookie Ferguson
Niles: Portage Prairie	Not Represented
Niles: Wesley, Morris Chapel, Niles: Grace	
	Deb Litchfield
Nottawa	Vicky Fisher
Oshtemo: Lifespring	Not Represented
Oshtemo: Oshtemo	Jan Snyder
Otsego: Otsego	Nyla Merrill
	Kay Strong
Otsego: Trowbridge	Not Represented
Parchment	Not Represented
Paw Paw	Christine Mortimer
Plainwell: First	Stacy Levine
Portage: Chapel Hill	Dar Perkins
	John Ruhrup
	Jenaba Waggy
Portage: Pathfinder	Connie Stoll
	Ron Stoll
Riverside	Not Represented
Saugatuck	Not Represented
Schoolcraft, Pleasant Valley	Judy Oliphant
Scottdale, Bridgeman: Faith	Bob Larson
Silver Creek	Gail Ward
Sodus: Chapel Hill	Margie Krieger
South Haven: First	Not Represented
St Joseph: First	Keith Foote
	Lorie Kraus
	Not Represented
Stevensville	Robin Lydic
	Ron Putt
	Jesse Robbins
Sturgis	Marcia Harrington
	Not Represented
Three Oaks	Priscilla Hellenga
Three Rivers: Center Park	Arlene Thompson
Three Rivers: First	Bob Slingerland
Three Rivers: Ninth Street	Not Represented
Townline	Mandana Nordbrock
Union City, Athens	Sandra Belmore
Vicksburg	Bob Ball
	Rachel Ball

HERITAGE DISTRICT

Adrian: First	Julie Shultz
	Not Represented
	Not Represented
Albion: First	Sally Ammerman
Allen	Not Represented
Ann Arbor: Calvary	Carol Miller

LAY MEMBERS

Charge	Lay Member	Charge	Lay Member
Ann Arbor: First	Jean Bush-Bacelis	Dundee	Louise Proctor
	Wendy Everett		Not Represented
	Em Howard	Erie	Donna Foster
	Rick Miller	Frontier	Not Represented
	Shonagh Taruza	Grass Lake	Not Represented
	Carrie Throm	Hardy	Not Represented
	Josh Warn	Hartland	Becky Toth
Ann Arbor: Korean	Not Represented	Highland	Glen Betts
	Not Represented		Not Represented
Ann Arbor: West Side	Doug Weber	Hillsdale: First	Not Represented
	Sue Weber	Hillside, Somerset Center	Not Represented
Azalia, London	Not Represented	Homer, Lyon Lake	Not Represented
Belleville: First	Ronnie Stansifer	Howell: First	Mary Lou Dell
	Not Represented		Rick Dell
Blissfield: Emmanuel	Not Represented		Sue Rice
Blissfield: First	Not Represented	Hudson: First	Not Represented
Brighton: First	Brian Everett	Ida, Samaria: Grace	Diana Smith
	Suzanne Everett	Jackson: Brookside, Trinity	Michael Austin
	John Phillips	Jackson: Calvary	Sharon Barnes
	Not Represented	Jackson: First	John Hawthorne
	Not Represented		Dawn Nesterowich-Doerr
Britton: Grace	Marsha Weber		Terri Reynolds
Camden, Montgomery, Stokes Chapel			Not Represented
	Linda Shiffler	Jackson: Zion	Not Represented
Canton: Cherry Hill, Ypsilanti: St Matthews		Lambertville	Not Represented
	Bob Simmons		Not Represented
Canton: Friendship	Not Represented		Not Represented
	Not Represented		Not Represented
Carleton	Not Represented	Lasalle: Zion, Petersburg	Dave Wahr
Chelsea: First	Jeanne Franks	Lee Center	Connie Lack
	Jeff Melvin	Litchfield, Jonesville	Shelly Snow
	Mike Steklac		Not Represented
	Edie Wiarda	Lulu	Not Represented
Clayton, Rollin Center	Esther Noffsinger	Macon	Sharon Scott
Clinton	Not Represented	Manchester: First	Anne Marie Hanna
Commerce	Ell Pizarek		Not Represented
	Jerry Sundberg	Manchester: Sharon	Diana Parr
	Not Represented	Marshall	Rachel Labram
	Not Represented		Ed Ramos
Concord	Not Represented		John Seppanen
Deerfield, Wellsville	Not Represented	Milan: Marble Mem.	Rod Hill
Denton: Faith	David Ak Korlapati		Brenda Kempher
Dexter	Vicki Aeschliman	Milford	Debbie Bonnewell
	Stephen Bringardner		Linda Fraser
	Jane Fink	Monroe: Calvary, South Rockwood	
	Karl Fink		Jim Ellerman
	Bill Gordon	Monroe: First, Heritage	Linda Luci
	Teena Gordon	Monroe: St Paul's	Cathy Butson
	Pat Wilkins		Paula Vergowven
Dixboro	Brent Howlett		Not Represented
		Morenci, Weston	Janis Wilt

Napoleon	Sherrie Snyder	Brookfield Eaton	Not Represented
New Hudson	Susanne Hardy	Carland	Not Represented
North Adams, Jerome	Ron Mcclain	Carson City	Not Represented
North Lake	Not Represented		Not Represented
North Parma, Springport	Not Represented	Charlotte: Lawrence Ave	Patty Snyder
Northville: First	Mike Betts	Chesaning: Trinity	Roni Newman
	Spencer Betts		Jill Shorkey
	Wendy Betts	Corunna: Corunna	Not Represented
	Maddie Eiler	Corunna: Northwest Venice	Dawn Stroup
	Peggy Mcmichael	Delta Mills	Not Represented
	Tracy Ortlieb	Dimondale	Not Represented
Novi	Not Represented	East Lansing: The Peoples Church	
Oak Grove	Not Represented		Susan Kilmer
Pinckney: Arise	Rich Guyon		Not Represented
Pleasant Lake	Not Represented	East Lansing: University	Sue Abent
Plymouth: First	Brad Coyle		Julie Bills
	Joy Coyle		Don Jost
	Jan Kavulich	Eaton Rapids: First	Not Represented
	Jim Quinlan		Not Represented
Pope, Griffith	Not Represented	Elsie	Ava Williams
Quincy	Not Represented	Fowlerville: First	Judy Herald
Reading	Norma Smith	Freeport, Nashville: Peace, Hastings:	
Salem Grove, Waterloo Village	Nancy Hughes	Welcome Corners	Not Represented
Saline: First	Dave Hares	Grand Ledge: First	Mary Daniels
	Sue Hares		Not Represented
	Dick Schoenfeldt	Gresham, Sunfield	Priscilla Law
	Tammy Schoenfeldt	Grovenburg	Not Represented
	Not Represented	Hastings: First	Jim Frederick
	Not Represented		Not Represented
South Lyon: First	Dave Fanning	Hastings: Hope	Not Represented
	Heather Fazio	Henderson, Chapin, Owosso: Burton	
	Patti Yerke		Lisa Chant
	Not Represented	Holt	Maynard Hamilton
Springville	Not Represented		Not Represented
Stony Creek	Dave Mongson		Not Represented
Tecumseh	Not Represented	Ithaca, Beebe	Kathy Wilson
	Not Represented	Juddville	Kay Crawford
Walled Lake	Bill Bird	Kalamo, Quimby	Not Represented
Willow	Jeanne Lochner	Laingsburg Parish: Laingsburg, Pittsburg	
Ypsilanti: First	Gerry Conti		Carrie Rathbun Hawks
	Alix Smith	Lake Odessa: Central	John Gentner
	Not Represented	Lake Odessa: Lakewood	Jo Raines
Ypsilanti: Lincoln Cmnty	Bob Seay		Tom Raines
		Lansing: Asbury	Judy Mclean
		Lansing: Central	Patricia Bell
MID-MICHIGAN DISTRICT			Pat Mort
Alma	Not Represented	Lansing: First	Not Represented
Ashley, Bannister, Pompeii	Janet Swanson	Lansing: Grace	Carol Simmons
Barry County: Woodland	Not Represented	Lansing: Mount Hope	Judy Lott
Bath, Gunnisonville	Linda Gehrls		Ron Lott
Breckenridge	Ray Rohn	Leslie, Felt Plains	Not Represented

LAY MEMBERS

Livingston Circuit: Plainfield, Trinity   Missy Noll
Maple River Parish: Maple Rapids, Lowe
    Not Represented
Mason: First   Glenn Darling
    Julia Droscha
    Deb Fennell
Millville, Williamston: Wheatfield
    Katrina Rockwell
Morrice, Bancroft   Not Represented
Mulliken   Not Represented
Munith, Stockbridge   Not Represented
Nashville: Nashville   Elnora Wallin
New Lothrop: First   Becky Warren
Okemos Cmnty Church   Lee Mcallister
    Tressa Mcallister
    Jan Merkle
Ovid United, Middlebury   Theresa Austin
Owosso: First   Earle Knapp
    Tom Moorhead
Owosso: Trinity   Not Represented
Perry, Shaftsburg   Shelly Nyquist
Portland   Connie Almy
    Not Represented
Redeemer Church: Dewitt Campus
    Not Represented
    Not Represented
    Not Represented
    Not Represented
Redeemer Church: St Johns Campus
    Not Represented
    Not Represented
Riverdale: Lincoln Road   Faith Mason
Robbins   Charlotte Kilvington
Shepardsville   Helen Squiers
St Johns: Pilgrim   Denny Pennock
St Louis: First   Amber Maclaren
Sycamore Creek: Potterville Campus
    Kathy Dobie
    Not Represented
Sycamore Creek: S Lansing Campus
    Not Represented
    Not Represented
Vernon   Not Represented
Wacousta Community   Dean Mccracken
    Not Represented
Webberville, Williamston: Crossroads
    Doug Elzerman
Williamston: Williamston   Nancy Ham

MIDWEST DISTRICT

Allendale: Valley Church   Not Represented
Alto, Browne Center   Not Represented
Amble   Dee Barringer
Barryton: Faith   Not Represented
Big Rapids: First   Amanda Hahn
    Randy Hahn
Big Rapids: Third Avenue, Paris, Rodney
    Jean Huhtala
Byron Center   Jim Brown
Caledonia   Thom Kohl
Carlisle   Amy Eckert
Cedar Springs   Keith Caldwell
Claybanks   Edie Bogart
Coopersville   Not Represented
Courtland-Oakfield, Wyoming Park
    Jeanne Bowser
    Karla Verhage
Crystal Valley, Walkerville   Not Represented
Dorr: Crosswind Cmnty   Not Represented
East Nelson   Sandy Samsel
Edmore: Faith   Cindi Scheiern
Fenwick, Palo, Vickeryville   Not Represented
Fremont   Laurene Homsher
    Not Represented
Georgetown   Doug Barry
    Holly Downer
    Cyndi Hartley
Grand Haven: Church Of The Dunes
    Bill Chappell
    Shirley Chappell
    Rich Cole
    Not Represented
Grand Rapids: Aldersgate   Al Clark
Grand Rapids: Cornerstone   Meghann Clary
    Jake Karhoff
    Betsy Weems
    Not Represented
    Not Represented
    Not Represented
    Not Represented
    Not Represented
    Not Represented
    Not Represented
Grand Rapids: Faith   Deb Hoek
Grand Rapids: First   David Bloss
    Susan Bloss
    Jill Peirce
    Ken Peirce
    Lea Tobar
    Tim Tuthill

Grand Rapids: Genesis	Susan Buchta
	Susan Gray
Grand Rapids: La Nueva Esperanza	
	Not Represented
Grand Rapids: Northlawn	Not Represented
Grand Rapids: Restoration	Not Represented
Grand Rapids: Saint Paul's	Tom Orsborn
Grand Rapids: South	Not Represented
Grand Rapids: Trinity	Bonnie Czuhajewski
	Kip Smalligan
	Not Represented
Grand Rapids: Vietnamese	Not Represented
Grandville	Not Represented
Grant Center	Not Represented
Greenville: First	Chuck Hill
	Not Represented
	Not Represented
	Not Represented
Hart	Maureen Huizing
Hesperia, Ferry	Randy Ackley
Holland: First	Al Minert
	Peg Minert
	Not Represented
	Not Represented
Holton	Char Spaulding
Ionia: Easton	George Sperry
Ionia: First, Lyons-Muir	Not Represented
Ionia: Zion	Not Represented
Kent City: Chapel Hill	Not Represented
Lakeview: New Life	Doris Shaw
	Not Represented
Leighton	Keith Pratt
Levalley, Berlin Center	Judy Huynh
Lowell: First	Emmy Vanderbilt
	Not Represented
Lowell: Vergennes	Not Represented
Marne	Not Represented
Mears, Shelby	Denise Schuitema
Mecosta: New Hope	Jean Chapin
	Art Sherwood
	Lois Sherwood
Middleville	Susan Rietman
Montague	Tom Hinken
	Michelle Vallier
Muskegon Hts: Temple	Susan Harrison
Muskegon: Central	Mary Oakes
	Not Represented
Muskegon: Crestwood	Not Represented
Muskegon: Lake Harbor	Jason Colella
	Not Represented

Muskegon: Unity	Cindy Belt
Newaygo	Jen Larsen
North Muskegon: Community	Kevin Dick
	Doug Wood
Parmelee	Not Represented
Pentwater: Centenary	Susan Macgregor
Pierson: Heritage	Holly Fahner
Ravenna	Susan Gilbert
Rockford	Steve Laninga
	Not Represented
	Not Represented
Salem Indian Mission, Bradley Indian Mission	
	Not Represented
Sand Lake, South Ensley	Mary Johnson
Sitka	Not Represented
Sparta	Jane Bosserd
Stanwood: Northland	Not Represented
Turk Lake, Belding	Not Represented
Twin Lake	Not Represented
Wayland	Nick Bayer
White Cloud	Richard Long
Wolf Lake	Pam Bryant
Wyoming: Wesley Park	Deb Hodges
	Luann Hoffman

NORTHERN SKIES DISTRICT

Bark River, Hermansville: First	Marjorie Meyers
Bergland, Ewen, Wakefield	Tom Brown
Cheboygan: St Paul's	Randy Mikula
	Not Represented
Crystal Falls: Christ, Amasa: Grace	
	Not Represented
Emmett County: New Hope	Jason Frye
Escanaba: Central	Not Represented
Escanaba: First	Sharyn Caszatt
Gladstone: Memorial	
	Laurie Kaufman De La Garza
	Not Represented
Grand Marais, Germfask, Mcmillan	
	Not Represented
Gwinn	Catherine Stephenson
Hancock: First	Robert Mcmullen
	Not Represented
Houghton: Grace	Anita Quinn
Iron Mountain: First, Quinnesec: First	
	Mark Rose
Iron Mountain: Trinity	Beth Clark
	Bruce Clark
Ironwood: Wesley	Keith Mullikin

LAY MEMBERS

Ishpeming: Wesley — Natalie Oates
Not Represented
Not Represented
Keweenaw Parish: Calumet, Mohawk-
  Ahmeek, Lake Linden — Not Represented
L'anse, Sidnaw, Zeba — Not Represented
Mackinaw City: Church Of The Straits
  — Roger Moore
Manistique: First — Janet Helmbold
Marquette: Hope — Lorna Addison
  — Susan Morgan
Menominee: First — Keith Akins
Munising, Trenary — Not Represented
Negaunee: Mitchell — Sherry Dahlin
Newberry, Engadine — Joy Morgan
Norway: Grace, Faithorn — Chris Spence
Ontonagon, Greenland, Rockland: St. Paul
  — Not Represented
Painesdale: Albert Paine Mem.
  — Not Represented
Paradise, Hulbert: Tahquamenon
  — Not Represented
Pickford — Eric Wallis
Republic, Michigamme: Woodland
  — Not Represented
Sault St Marie: Central, Algonquin
  — Raymond Bell
St Ignace — Not Represented
Stephenson — Not Represented
White Pine Community — Jane Dickow

NORTHERN WATERS DISTRICT

Alden, Central Lake — Not Represented
Alpena: First — Pat Major
  — Not Represented
Avondale — Not Represented
Baldwin: Covenant Community, Chase-Barton
  — Jan Timmer
Barnard, East Jordan — Kim Diller
Bear Lake, Arcadia — Myrna Walter
Bellaire: Community — Lindy Munn
Boyne City, Boyne Falls, Epsilon
  — Not Represented
Brooks Corners — Not Represented
Cadillac — Don Rennie
  — Not Represented
Charlevoix — Not Represented
Charlevoix: Greensky Hill — Robin Barney-Lees
Empire — Roy Pentilla

Evart, Sears — Kathy Galley
Frankfort, Elberta — Trudi Hook
Free Soil - Fountain — Not Represented
Gaylord: First — Mike Cooper
  — Nancy Ross
  — Rich Ross
Grant — Not Represented
Grawn — Fred Schlegel
Grayling: Michelson Memorial — Donna Hubbard
Harbor Springs, Alanson — Juris Brants
Harrietta — Not Represented
Hersey — Ginnie Waite
Hillman — Cheri Scramlin
Horton Bay — Not Represented
Houghton Lake — Kristy Carrick-Myers
  — Not Represented
  — Not Represented
Indian River — Mark Fielder
  — Not Represented
Kalkaska — Dee Miller
Keswick — Nancy Elmore
Kewadin: Indian Mission — Not Represented
Kewadin: Kewadin — Not Represented
Kingsley — Diane Walton
Lake Ann — Ruth Leckrone
Lake City — Jane Tinsley
Leland — Joann Hook
  — Michelle White
Ludington: St Paul — Derek Eaton
Ludington: United — Karen Disegna
  — Wayne Disegna
  — Jane Mengot
Mancelona, Alba — Judy Zimpfer
Manistee — Not Represented
  — Not Represented
Manton — Bill Oram
Marion, Cadillac: South Community
  — Not Represented
Mesick, Brethren: Epworth — Not Represented
NE Missaukee Parish: Merritt-Butterfield,
  Moorestown-Stittsville — Don Fluture
Northport Indian Mission — Wava Hofmann
Norwood — Not Represented
Old Mission Peninsula — Marge Long
Onaway, Millersburg — Chuck Abshagen
Ossineke — Jeannette Schultz
Petoskey — Sharyn Hansen
  — Michelle Mitchum
  — Janie Sielski

Pine River Parish: Leroy, Ashton, Luther
       Mike Ramsey
Reed City   Cinda Locker
       Not Represented
Roscommon: Good Shepherd
       Not Represented
Scottville   Linda Starr
Spratt   Cindy Josey
Traverse Bay   Cappy Potter

Traverse City: Central   Sue Cobb
       Carol Evans
       Amber Hassler
       Allen Horstman
       Nan Horstman
       Ali Thornton
Traverse City: Mosaic   Toinette Wicks
Unified Parish: Williamsburg, Fife Lake,
       East Boardman, South Boardman
       Debby Sieting

— MAC Photos

CONFERENCE EQUALIZATION LAY MEMBERS BY POSITION

Deaconesses & Home Missioners
    Valerie Mossman-Celestin
Diaconal Minister   Diane Griffin
UMW Conference President   Linda Darrow
UMM Conference President   *none*
Conference Co-Lay Leader   Anne Soles
Conference Co-Lay Leader   John Wharton
District Lay Leader: Central Bay   *none*
District Co-Lay Leader: East Winds
    Michael Schlusler, Bonnie Potter
District Lay Leader: Greater Detroit
    Ruby Anderson
District Lay Leader: Greater Southwest
    Wynne Hurlbut
District Lay Leader: Heritage   Max Waagner
District Lay Leader: Mid-Michigan
    Nona Spackman
District Lay Leader: Midwest   Suzanne Hewitt
District Lay Leader: Northern Skies
    John Preston
District Lay Leader: Northern Waters
    Denny Olin
Convener of Youth Ministries   *none*
Convener of Young Adult Ministries   *none*
Youth Representatives (12-18):
    Central Bay   Ethan Chu
    East Winds   Celia Peters
    Greater Detroit   Jack Day
    Greater Southwest   Savannah Hahn
    Heritage   Ashlin Jackson
    Mid-Michigan   Libby Shorkey
    Midwest   *none*
    Northern Skies   Sarina Maki
    Northern Waters   Lisa Hahn
Young Adult Representatives (18-30):
    Central Bay   Izzy Nowak
    East Winds   Ali Flores
    Greater Detroit   Samson Kobbah III
    Greater Southwest   Jenna Brevitz
    Heritage   Ellyn Sandefur
    Mid-Michigan   Kaittye Oberski
    Midwest   Jessie Cypret
    Northern Skies   Gordon Grigg III
    Northern Waters   Bethany Maciejewski
Conference Co-Director of Lay Servant
    Ministries   Jody Pratt
Conference Co-Director of Lay Servant
    Ministries   John Hart

Conference Secretary of Global Ministries
    Jackie Euper
Conference Secretary   *clergy*
Conference Chancellor   Andy Vorbrich
Annual Conference Coordinator   Nancy Arnold
Conference Treasurer   David Dobbs
Conference Parliamentarian   *none*
Associate Conference Lay Leader   *none*
Director of Connectional Ministries   *clergy*
Director for Congregational Vibrancy   *clergy*
Director of Benefits and Human Resources
    clergy
Director of Clergy Excellence   *clergy*
Director of Communications   Mark Doyal
Associate Director for Congregational
    Vibrancy   *clergy*
Associate Director for Congregational
    Vibrancy   Naomi García
Associate Director for Lay Leadership
    Development   Laura Witkowski
Youth Ministry Initiatives Coordinator
    Bridget Nelson
Associate Director for Multicultural Vibrancy
    clergy
Associate Director for Mission and Ministry
    clergy
Children's Ministry Initiatives Coordinator
    clergy
Young Adult Initiatives Coordinator   *clergy*
Missionary for Hispanic/Latino Ministry
    Sonya Luna
Committee on the Episcopacy, Chair Jay Hook
Persons Serving on General or Jurisdictional
    Agencies: *Ruby Anderson,* Taylorie Bailey,
    Suzanne Hewitt, Jackie Euper, Diana Spitnale
    Miller, Linda Schramm, Nichea VerVeer Guy,
    Laura Witkowski
General or Jurisdictional Conference
    Delegates:
    Ruby Anderson, Wayne Bank, Diane Brown,
    Laurie Dahlman, *Jackie Euper, Valerie*
    Mossman-Celestin, Anne Soles, Ruth Sutton,
    Nichea VerVeer Guy, Laura Witkowski
Conference Statistician   *clergy*
Committee on Rules, Members:
    Judy Coffey, Brenda Foltz, Dave Lundquist,
    Todd Price, Keith Radak, Jim Searls

Conference Leadership Council, Members:
Nick Arnold, Tina Campbell, Sung Yu,
Carmen Zeigler
Council on Finance & Administration,
Members:
Jim Bosserd, Renae Clevenger,
Cameron DeLong, Clayton Osburn,
Patrick Tiedt, Andy Wayne
Annual Conference Trustees:
David Apol, Michael Belt
Legislative Coordinator   *Diane Brown*
Conference Facilitator   Sue Buxton
Commission on the Annual Conference
Session, Members: Don Archambeau,
Mara Marsman, *Nichea Verveer Guy*
Committee on the Journal, Members:
Blair Hunt, Joyce Showerman, Beth Snyder
Board of Ordained Ministry, Members:
Ruby Anderson, Sharon Appling, *Laurie
Dahlman*, Annette Erbes, Cathy Hazen, Claire
Hills, Carol Hodges, Steve Lett, Kelly Ross,
Carole Wesner, *John Wharton*
Commission on Communications, Chair
Mark Doyal
Board of Justice, Chair   *clergy*

Board of Global Ministries, Chair
Brenda DuPree
Commission on Archives and History, Chair
Mary Whitman
Committee on Nominations, Chair
Committee on Human Resources, Chair *clergy*
Protection Policy Implementation Team, Chair
Judy Heriff
Board of Young People's Ministries, Chair
clergy
Board of Congregational Life, Chair   *clergy*
Cmte on Hispanic/Latino Ministry, Chair   *clergy*
Cmte on Asian American Ministry, Chair   *clergy*
Cmte on Native American Ministry, Chair
Cmte on African American Ministry, Co-Chair
clergy
Cmte on African American Ministry, Co-Chair
Simmie Proctor
Board of Pension and Health Benefits, Chair
clergy
Administrative Review Committee, Chair   *none*
Committee on Investigation, Chair   *none*
Episcopal Residence Cmte, Chair   *clergy*
Cmte on Equitable Compensation, Chair   *none*

LAY MEMBERS

— MAC Photos

EQUALIZATION AT-LARGE LAY MEMBERS
ASSIGNED BY BOARD OF LAITY

CENTRAL BAY DISTRICT
Kendall Farnum, Linda Hall, Lori Harless, Merry Henderson, Amelia Kasper, Nancy Neuroth, Michael Palmer, Teri Rice, Janet Shaffer, Jeff Temple, Margie Williams

EAST WIND DISTRICT
Ricardo Angarita Oviedo, Dj Birkinbine, Kathy Dorman, James Dover, Carolyn Elzerman, Audrey Freels, Joe Homrich, Bruce Hurd, Lawrence Iseler, Bob McCormick, Kim Offner, Gretchen Orr, Jen Peters, Cheryl Rentschler, Linda Schenburn, Monica Standel, Paul Tiedeman, Suzanne Tinka, Dawn Titus, Marie Weaver, Michele Weston

GREATER DETROIT DISTRICT
Karen Arendall, Shirley Bittings, Elizabeth Boayue, Olivia Cato, Josh Dixon, Ken Dowell, Jane Egermann, Cheryl Ellington, Alma Gipson, Laura Gotham, Lois Holman, Nadine Johnson, Jimmie Jones, Tracy Lahay, Wendi Lenard, Sherman Louis, Audrey Mangum, Daphne Mitchell, Oneika Mobley, Linda Owulette, Mike Perez, Kathy Sestok, Eric Triebwasser, Ciere Turner, Aaron Tuscherer, Jim Waldrop, Tim Yu

GREATER SOUTHWEST DISTRICT
Connor Bailey, Elizabeth Batten, Mary Blashill, Amy Brevitz, Lynda Busick, Sarah DeHaan, Linda Depta, Bernie Eash, Era Grasty, Jane Johnson, Connie Luegge, Sandy Miller, Tonya Murphy, Martha Reeves, Alice Reissmann, Donna Smith, Sue Stickle, Jean Szczypka, Cindy Thiele, Caleb Thomas, Lona Vogie

HERITAGE DISTRICT
David Aeschliman, Lisa Berlanga, Bev Clark, Marge Clute, Norm Colbry, Mary Violet Comiskey, Andrea Cortelyou, Rene Crombez, Colleen Croxall, Elisabeth Danielsons, Sue Dolato, Carol Gorham, Rick Gorham, Dick Hill, George Jonte-Crane, Bruce Lack, Aimee Luck, Dar McGee, Rochelle Miller, Joyce Mitchell, Cathy Montgomery, Connie Perrine, Esther Puckett, Jim Rutherford, Michelle Thompson, Susan Walker, Michelle Walkup, Chuck Woolley

MID-MICHIGAN DISTRICT
Carole Armstrong, Sus'ann Busley, Diana Carpenter, Marilyn Frith, Andrea Gentner, Jennifer Hahm, Shelia Huis, Tom Huis, Carol Huntington, Janell Kebler, Donna Kleiver, Jim LeBaron, David Lipps, Katie Price, Jackie Salisbury, Sharon Smith, Denny Stoneman, Wells Warren

MIDWEST DISTRICT
Carrie Albin, Matt Albin, Tamara Brubaker-Salcedo, Wendy Clark, Mary-jo Delany, Sarah DeLany, Peg Edvenson, Anne Hillman, John Huizing, Lindsay Isenhart, Emil Jensen, Cookie Kramer, Orlan Lehmann, Angela Lovegrove, Zach McNees, Laure Mieskowski, Joy Murphy, Lai Nguyen, Adele Numbi, Kirk Perry, Reba Peterson, Linda Sbraccia, Bobbie Springer, Sarah Zachow

NORTHERN SKIES DISTRICT
B. J. Ash, Kay Bashore, Liane Callow, Robin Henry, Larry Molloy, Pam Quayle, Patti Steinberg, Paula Wright

NORTHERN WATERS DISTRICT
Randie Clawson, Cynthia Corey/Montague, Katja Falker, Doris Felton, Erin Fletcher, Neil Haney, Jeanette Hayes, Elise Hitts, Julie Lawhead, Timothy Locker, George Pamp, Beth Pelkey, Susan Wirgau

LAY MEMBERS EQUALIZATION SUMMARY

Clergy Members to Annual Conference

Clergy Members to the Annual Conference are as defined in ¶¶ 32 and 602 of *The Book of Discipline of the UMC – 2016*. These numbers have been combined from the Detroit Annual Conference and West Michigan Annual Conference 2018 Journals using the Business of the Annual Conference, Part II: Pertaining to Ordained and Licensed Clergy, Question 57.

Deacons in Full Connection	54
Elders in Full Connection	885
Provisional Deacons	5
Provisional Elders	35
Associate Members & Affiliate Members with Vote	34
Full-time Local Pastors	133
Part-time Local Pastors	87
Total Clergy	1,233

Lay Members to Annual Conference

An equal number of Lay Members are invited to Annual Conference in accordance with ¶¶ 32 and 602 of *The Book of Discipline of the UMC – 2016*. Each Annual Conference determines and approves a process for equalization. The Michigan Conference outlines the process for equalization in the Standing Rules, § 5 Rules of Order, 5.2 Membership. In summary, Lay Members are gathered from local churches/charges, by virtue of their leadership office, or invited by the Board of Laity.

Members from Central Bay Churches/Charges	(13,180)	95
Members from East Winds Churches/Charges	(15,567)	109
Members from Greater Detroit Churches/Charges	(22,030)	151
Members from Greater Southwest Churches/Charges	(13,897)	105
Members from Heritage Churches/Charges	(20,596)	146
Members from Mid-Michigan Churches/Charges	(12,027)	93
Members from Midwest Churches/Charges	(16,242)	119
Members from Northern Skies Churches/Charges	(6,245)	42
Members from Northern Waters Churches/Charges	(10,042)	77
Equalization by Office		111
Equalization Invited by the Board of Laity		185
Total Laity		1,233

LAY MEMBERS

NOMINATIONS REPORT
for the
Michigan Conference
The United Methodist Church
Traverse City, MI
July 1, 2019 – June 30, 2020

(Year elected in parenthesis following name)

The Annual Conference granted the Nominations Committee to fill vacancies between Annual Conferences. – May 31, 2019.

AGENCIES RELATING TO
CHRIST-CENTERED MISSION AND MINISTRY

Annual Conference Session, Commission on the (1.1)

Eight voting members shall be nominated by the Committee on Nominations, in consultation with the Executive Team, who shall be either Clergy Members of the Annual Conference or Lay People who are members of a local church within the Annual Conference.

Members shall serve four-year terms, renewable twice, in annually staggered classes.

The Conference Secretary, Rev. Joy Barrett, shall serve as the Secretary of the Commission. Annual Conference Coordinator/Events Planner: Nancy Arnold

Class	Lay People	Clergy
2020	Nichea Ver Veer Guy (2018)	Leslee Fritz (2018)
2021	Mara Marsman (2018)	Anna Moon (2018)
2022	Don Archambeau (2018)	David Eardley (2018)
2023	Jennifer "Jen" Peters (2019)	Marsha Woolley (2018)

Commission shall elect from among its membership the following:
Chairperson: Nichea Ver Veer Guy (2018)
Vice Chairperson: Rev. Marsha Woolley (2018)
Head Usher: Mara Marsman (2018)
Worship Coordinator: Rev. Anna Moon (2018)

Executive Committee: Bishop (Bishop David A. Bard), Clergy Assistant to the Bishop (Rev. John Boley), Chairperson (Nichea Ver Veer Guy), Worship Coordinator (Rev. Anna Moon), Director of Connectional Ministries (Rev. Benton Heisler), Legislative Coordinator (Diane Brown), Director of Communications (Mark Doyal), Conference Secretary (Rev. Joy Barrett), Annual Conference Coordinator/Events Planner (Nancy Arnold).

Ex officio **with vote**: Resident Bishop (Bishop David A. Bard) or representative, Conference Lay Leader (Anne Soles/John Wharton) or representative, Conference Secretary (Rev. Joy Barrett), Chair of the Committee on Rules (Todd Price), District Superintendent designated by the Cabinet (Rev. Jodie Flessner), Legislative Coordinator (Diane Brown), Conference Facilitator (Susanne "Sue" Buxton), A Representative of the Board of Ordained Ministry (Rev. Lynn Hasley).

Ex officio **with voice, but no vote**: Director of Connectional Ministries (Rev. Benton Heisler), Director of Communications (Mark Doyal).

Given voice, **per Commission Action**: Annual Conference Registrar (Sarah Vollmer)

Communications, Commission on (1.2)

Four persons who shall be Clergy Members or Local Pastors of the Annual Conference (if clergy) or Professing Members of a local church within the Annual Conference (if laity).

Members shall serve four-year terms, renewable once, in annually staggered classes.

Members shall be nominated by the Committee on Nominations, in consultation with the Director of Communications.

The Conference Director of Communications (Mark Doyal) shall chair the commission.

Class	Laity	Clergy
2020	Oneika Mobley (2018)	
2021		Dillon Burns (2018)
2022	Clayton Hardiman (2018)	
	Vicky Prewitt (2018)	
2023		

Ex officio with vote: Bishop (Bishop David A. Bard), or Clergy Assistant to the Bishop (Rev. John Boley), at the Bishop's discretion, Conference Lay Leader (Anne Soles/John Wharton), Board Members of UM Communications residing within the bounds of the Annual Conference.

Ex officio with voice, but no vote: Senior Editor of Conference Communications (Rev. Mariel "Kay" DeMoss), IT Specialist (Rev. Michael Mayo-Moyle) or representative, Conference Director of Communications (Mark Doyal), Director of Connectional Ministries (Rev. Benton Heisler).

Journal, Committee on the (1.3)

Four people who shall be members of the Annual Conference (if clergy) or Professing Members of a local church within the Annual Conference (if laity).

Members shall serve four-year terms, renewable once, in annually staggered classes.

Members shall be nominated by the Committee on Nominations.

The Conference Secretary (Rev. Joy Barrett) shall serve as Chairperson and Secretary.
The committee shall elect from among its members a Vice Chairperson (_____).

Class	Laity	Clergy
2020	Mandana Nordbrock (2019)	
2021	Blair Hunt (2018)	
2022	Beth Snyder (2018)	
2023		

Ex officio with vote: Conference Secretary (Rev. Joy Barrett).

Ex officio with voice, but no vote: Conference Director of Communications (Mark Doyal).

Provided for Information Only: Journal Design Team – Rev. Joy Barrett, Sus'ann Busley, David Dobbs, Mark Doyal, Becky Emmert, Jennifer Gertz, Rev. Wilson "Drew" Hart, Rev. Benton Heisler, Katherine Hippensteel, Mandana Nordbrock, Beth Snyder

Provided for Information Only: Annual Conference Secretarial Support – Rev. Kathryn "Kathy" Cadarette, Pastor Carol (Abbott) Freeland, Rev. Wilson "Drew" Hart, Blair Hunt, Pastor Cheryl Mancier, Mandana Nordbrock, Joyce Showerman, Beth Snyder, Pastor Crystal Thomas

Justice, Board of (1.4)

Chairperson: Rev. George Covintree (2018)

(Chairperson of the Board is an additional member, chosen by Committee on Nominations)

Vice Chairperson: (_____)

(Convener shall serve as Vice Chairperson of the Board, chosen by the conveners)

Each Division shall elect a Convener.

Church and Society, Division of (1.4.3.1)

Four people who shall be members of the Annual Conference (if clergy) or
Professing Members of a local church within the Annual Conference (if laity).

Members shall serve four-year terms, renewable once, in annually staggered classes.

Members shall be nominated by the Committee on Nominations.

Convener shall be elected among the members: Pastor Albert Rush

Class	Laity	Clergy
2020		Corey Simon (2018)
2021	Clarice McKenzie (2018)	
2022		Albert Rush (2018)
2023	Joan Bosserd-Schroeder (2018)	

***Ex officio* with vote**: Mission Coordinator for Social Action of the Conference United Methodist Women (Alice Tucker), any Member of the General Board of Church and Society residing in the bounds of the Annual Conference, the Conference Peace with Justice Coordinator, who shall be named by the Division of Church and Society and shall serve at the division's pleasure for up to eight years.

Religion and Race, Division on (1.4.3.2)

Two Clergy Members of the Annual Conference. Two Laymen who shall be Professing Members of a local church within the Annual Conference. Two Laywomen who shall be Professing Members of a local church within the Annual Conference.

Members shall serve four-year terms, renewable once, in annually staggered classes.

Members shall be nominated by the Committee on Nominations.

Convener shall be elected among the members: Tina Campbell and Rev. Scott Manning

Class	Laity	Clergy
2020		David Huseltine (2018)
2021	Ernestine "Tina" Campbell (2018)	
2022	Kenneth "Ken" Dowell (2018)	Scott Manning (2018)
2023	Hoon-Yung Hopgood (2018)	

***Ex officio* with vote**: Any member of the General Commission on Religion and Race residing within the bounds of the Annual Conference.

Status and Role of Women, Division on the (1.4.3.3)

Two Clergy Women who shall be members of the Annual Conference. A Clergyman who shall be a member of the Annual Conference. Three Laymen who shall be Professing Members of a local church within the Annual Conference. Three Laywomen who shall be Professing Members of a local church within the Annual Conference.

Members shall serve four-year terms, renewable once, in annually staggered classes.

Members shall be nominated by the Committee on Nominations.

Convener shall be elected among the members and shall be a woman: Patricia Bostic

Class	Laity	Clergy
2020		
2021	Patricia Bostic (2018)	Eric Stone (2018)
		Carol Blair Bouse (2018)
2022	Mary Blashill (2018)	Kristine "Kristy" Hintz (2018)
2023		

Ex officio **with vote**: Any member of the General Commission on the Status and Role of Women residing within the bounds of the Annual Conference.

Disability Concerns, Division on (1.4.3.4)

Four people who shall be members of the Annual Conference (if clergy) or Professing Members of a local church within the Annual Conference (if laity).

Members shall serve four-year terms, renewable once, in annually staggered classes.

Members shall be nominated by the Committee on Nominations.

At least one member of the division shall have a physical disability.
At least one member of the division shall have a mental disability.

Convener shall be elected among the members: Pastor Coleen Wilsdon

Class	Laity	Clergy
2020		Coleen Wilsdon (2018)
2021		Amee Paparella (2018)
2022		Frederick Sampson (2018)
2023		Ellen Brubaker (2018)

Global Ministries, Board of (1.5)

Twelve people who shall be members of the Annual Conference (if clergy) or Professing Members of a local church within the Annual Conference (if laity).
Members shall serve four-year terms, renewable once, in annually staggered classes
Members shall be nominated by the Committee on Nominations.

Board will elect from its members the following:
    Chairperson: Brenda DuPree   Vice Chairperson: Rev. Julie Elmore
    Secretary: (_____)   Financial Secretary: Charles "Chuck"
                                              Woolley

Class	Laity	Clergy
2020	Jacqueline "Jackie" Euper (2018)	Julie Liske (2018)
	Wayne Bank (2018)	
2021	Richard "Dick" Kopple (2018)	Karen Williams (2018)
2022	Brenda DuPree (2018)	Julie Elmore (2018)
	Mildred Mallard (2018)	
2023	Charles "Chuck" Woolley (2018)	

Existing Task Forces: Liberia – Rev. Jon Reynolds (2018)
                             Haiti – Rev. Karl Zeigler (2018)

Ex officio **with vote**: Mission Coordinator for Education and Interpretation of the Conference United Methodist Women (Michele Weston), the Conference Secretary of Global Ministries, who shall be appointed by the Board and shall serve at its pleasure for up to eight years (Jacqueline "Jackie" Euper), Conference Disaster Response Coordinator (Rev. Robert "Bob" Miller and Dan O'Malley) selected by the Board of Global Ministries, Any Member of the General Board of Global residing within the bounds of the Annual Conference (Rev. Paul Perez), Conference VIM Coordinator (Jody Pratt), District Superintendent (Rev. David Kim).

Archives and History, Commission on (1.6)

Four Clergy Members of the Annual Conference.
Four Lay Persons who shall be Professing Members of a church within the Annual Conference.

Members shall be nominated by the Committee on Nominations

Members shall serve four-year terms, renewable once, in annually staggered classes

Commission will elect from its members the following:

Chairperson: Mary Whitman   Vice Chairperson: (_____)
Secretary: (_____)   Treasurer: (_____)

Class	Laity	Clergy
2020	Brian Lightner (2019)	William "Tom" T. Robinson (2018)
2021	William "Bill" McNitt (2018)	Melanie Young (2018)
2022	Mary Whitman (2018)	John Ross Thompson (2018)
2023	Kenneth Gackler (2018)	

Ex officio **with voice and vote:** The Archivists of the Conference Archives: Adrian College (Rebecca McNitt), Albion College (Mike VanHouten), President of the Michigan Area UMC Historical Society (Diana Spitnale Miller), Members of the General Commission on Archives and History (Diana Spitnale Miller, Linda Schramm).

AGENCIES RELATING TO BOLD AND EFFECTIVE LEADERS

Conference Leadership Council (2.1)

Four Clergy Members of the Annual Conference, at least one of whom shall be
a member of the Board of Ordained Ministry.
Five Lay People who are Professing Members of a congregation within the Annual Conference.

Members shall be nominated by the Committee on Nominations.

Members shall serve three-year terms, renewable thrice, in annually staggered classes.

In consultation with the Bishop, the Council shall elect from its voting members:

President: Rev. Amy Mayo-Moyle   Vice President: _____
Secretary: _____

Class	Laity	Clergy
2020	Sung Yu (2018)	Amy Mayo-Moyle (2018)
	Nicholas "Nick" Arnold (2018)	
2021	Carmen Zeigler (2018)	Eric Mulanda (2018)
2022	Sue Fielder (2019)	Darryl Totty (2018)
	Judith "Judy" Coffey (2019)	Megan Walther (2019)

Ex officio **with voice and vote**: Conference Lay Leader (Anne Soles/John Wharton), President of the Council on Finance and Administration (Rev. Bradley "Brad" Bartelmay), a representative of the Division on Religion and Race of the Board of Justice (Ernestine "Tina" Campbell), Any member of the Connectional Table residing within the bounds of the Annual Conference (Rev. Dr. Jerome "Jerry" DeVine and Rev. Kennetha Bigham-Tsai).

Ex officio **with voice only**: Director of Administrative Services and Conference Treasurer (David Dobbs), Director of Connectional Ministries (Rev. Benton Heisler), Director of Communications (Mark Doyal), Bishop (Bishop David A. Bard), or Clergy Assistant to the Bishop (Rev. John Boley), Dean of the Appointive Cabinet (Rev. Elizabeth Hill), Director of Benefits and Human Resources (Rev. Donald "Don" Emmert), any other Directors whose position may be created by the Conference Leadership Council (Rev. Dr. Jennifer "Jennie" Browne, Rev. Dirk Elliott).

Except for *ex officio* members listed hereinabove, Chairperson of Conference Agencies and employees of Conference Agencies shall be ineligible for membership on the Council.

Ordained Ministry, Board of (2.2)

At least twenty-five Full Clergy Members of the Annual Conference. At least one of whom shall be engaged in Extension Ministry. At least one of whom shall be age thirty-five or younger. At least two-thirds of whom shall be graduates of theological schools listed by the University Senate. A least one of whom shall be retired. At least three Clergy Persons who are either Associate Members or Local Pastors who have completed Course of Study. At least twelve Lay People who are Professing Members of a local church within the Annual Conference.

Members shall be nominated by the Bishop.

Members shall serve four-years terms (starting at the close of the Annual Conference Session following General Conference), renewable twice, with quadrennially staggered classes.

The Board shall elect from among its members:
Chairperson: Rev. Laura Speiran
Vice Chairperson: Rev. Mark Erbes
Secretary: Rev. Amy Lee Terhune
Registrar for Full and Associate Members: Rev. Timothy "Tim" Ziegler
Registrar for Provisional Members: Rev. Julie Greyerbiehl
Registrar for Local Pastors: Pastor Melody Olin
Registrar for Specialized Ministry Certification: Rev. Patricia "Pat" Catellier

2008 Quadrennia
Janet "Jan" Brown (2018)
Jennifer Jue (2018)
Laura Speiran (2018)

2012 Quadrennia
Wesley "Wes" Brun (ret) (2018)
Patricia "Pat" Catellier (2018)
Thomas "Thom" Davenport (2018)
Briony Desotell (2018)
Mark Erbes (2018)
Annelissa "Lisa" Gray-Lion (2018)
Julie Greyerbiehl (2018)
Carter Grimmett (2018)
Daniel "Dan" Hart (2019)

Lynn Hasley (ret) (2018)
Anthony Hood (2018)
William "Bill" Johnson (ret) (2018)
Rob McPherson (2018)
Sherri Swanson (2018)
Amy Lee Terhune (2018)
Mark Thompson (2018)
Christina Wright (2018)
Timothy "Tim" Ziegler (2018)

2016 Quadrennia
William "Bill" Haggard (2018)
Paul Hahm (2018)
Lindsey Hall (2018)

John "J.D." Landis (2018)
Scott Lindenberg (2018)
Megan Walther (2019)

ASSOCIATE MEMBERS OR LOCAL PASTORS / COMPLETED COURSE OF STUDY
Terri Bentley (2018)
Billie Lou Gillespie (2018)
Melody Olin (2019)

LAY PERSONS

2012 Quadrennia

Ruby Anderson (2018)
Laurie Dahlman (2018)
Catharine "Cathy" Hazen (2018)

Claire Hills (2018)
Duane Townley (2018)
John Wharton (2018)

2016 Quadrennia

Sharon Appling (2018)
Carol Hodges (2018)
Sue Pung (2019)

Kelly Ross (2018)
Jay Zylstra (2019)

Executive Committee: Chairpersons of the Order of Elders (Rev. Barry Petrucci), the Order of Deacons (Rev. Sue Pethoud), the Fellowship of Local Pastors and Associate Members (Rev. Susan "Sue" Platt), Director of Clergy Excellence (Rev. Dr. Jennifer "Jennie" Browne).

Conference Relations shall be chaired by the Vice Chairperson, Rev. Mark Erbes. The Board shall determine membership. A District Superintendent shall not be a member.

Ex officio **with voice and vote**: Chairpersons of the Order of Elders (Rev. Barry Petrucci), the Order of Deacons (Rev. Georgia Hale), the Fellowship of Local Pastors and Associate Members (Rev. Susan "Sue" Platt), a District Superintendent named by the Bishop (Rev. Scott Harmon), Director of Clergy Excellence (Rev. Dr. Jennifer "Jennie" Browne).

Nominations, Committee on (2.3)

Two persons nominated by the Annual Conference Session.
Ten persons nominated by the Conference Leadership Council.
Members shall serve four-year terms, renewable once, staggered annually.

The Committee shall elect the following from among its members:
Chairperson: Rev. Janet Larner　Vice Chairperson: Rev. Melissa Claxton
Secretary: Rev. Virginia Heller

Class	Laity	Clergy
2020	Taylorie Bailey (2018)	Janet Larner (2018)
2021	Simmie Proctor (2018)	Melissa Claxton (2018)
2022	Ruby Anderson (2018)	Michael "Mike" Conklin (2018)
	Wayne Bank (2018)	Virginia Heller (2018)
2023	Laurie de la Garza (2018)	Scott Manning (2019)

Nominated by Annual Conference Session: Beth Pelkey – Lay Member (2019)
Nominated by Annual Conference Session:

Ex Officio **with vote**: District Superintendent (Rev. Dwayne Bagley), Conference Lay Leader (Ann Soles/John Wharton), Chairperson or Representative of Rules (_____), Secretary of the Annual Conference (Rev. Joy Barrett).

Ex officio **with voice, but no vote**: Director of Connectional Ministries (Rev. Benton Heisler).

Episcopacy, Committee on the (2.4)

Six Clergy Members of the Conference.
Six Lay Persons who shall be Professing Members of a local church within the conference, one of whom shall be the Conference Lay Leader.
Three members appointed by the Resident Bishop who, if laity, shall be Professing Members of a local church within the Conference and, if clergy, shall be members of the Annual Conference.

Members shall serve four-year terms, renewable once, in annually staggered classes.

The Committee shall elect from among its members the following:
Chairperson: John Wharton   Vice Chairperson: _____
Secretary: Rev. Dr. Darryl Totty

Class	Laity	Clergy
2020	David "Dave" Howard (2018)	Carolin Spragg (2018)
2021	Karl Jennings (2018)	Darryl Totty (2018)
2022	Koom Cho (2018)	Robert "Bob" Hundley (2018)
	Craig Schroeder (2018)	Brian West (2018)
2023	Linda Darrow (2019)	Erin Fitzgerald (2019)
	Marchelle "Micki" Phelps (2019)	Megan Walther (2019)

Selected by the Bishop:
Pastor Gregory "Greg" Timmons (2018)   Rev. Elbert Dulworth (2018)
Bruce Smolenski (2018)

Conference Lay Leader: Anne Soles (2018)/John Wharton (2018)

Ex officio **with vote**: Members of the Jurisdictional Committee on the Episcopacy who reside within the bounds of the Annual Conference: Rev. Dr. Charles Boayue, Jacqueline "Jackie" Euper, Nichea Ver Veer Guy, Rev. Benton Heisler.

Protection Policy Implementation Team (2.5)

Eight adults (at least 18 years of age) who shall be members of the Annual Conference (if clergy) or Professing Members of a local church within the Annual Conference (if laity).

Members shall serve four-year terms, renewable once, in annually staggered classes.

Members shall be nominated by the Committee on Nominations.

The Team shall elect the following from among its members:
Chairperson: Judy Heriff   Vice Chairperson: Marguerite Zawislak

Class	Laity	Clergy
2020	Phyllis Hart (2018)	Daniel "Dan" Colthorp (2019)
	Marguerite Zawislak (2018)	_____
2021	Ruth Sutton (2019)	_____
2022	Judy Herriff (2018)	
2023	Michael "Mike" Darby (2018)	

AGENCIES RELATING TO VIBRANT CONGREGATIONS

United Methodist Women (3.1)

Membership shall be composed of all members of the local United Methodist Women units existing within the bounds of the Conference.

The United Methodist Women shall elect from among its members:
President: Linda Darrow   Vice President: Patricia Bostic
Secretary: Beth Mitchell   Treasurer: Julia Paradine-Rice

Ex officio **with vote**: Resident Bishop (Bishop David A. Bard), Members of the Board of Directors of the national office of the United Methodist Women residing within the bounds of the Annual Conference. Members of the United Methodist Women Program Advisory Group residing within the bounds of the Conference; Members of the North Central Jurisdiction United Methodist Women Leadership Team residing within the bounds of the Conference; District Superintendent (Rev. Scott Harmon).

United Methodist Men (3.2)

Membership of the United Methodist Men shall be made up of all men who are Professing Members of local churches within the bounds of the Annual Conference.

The United Methodist Men shall elect the following offices from among its members:

President: Donald "Don" Archambeau   Vice President: Max Waagner
Secretary: Peter Thoms   Treasurer: Raymond "Ray" McClintic

Ex officio Members: Any Members of the North Central Jurisdiction United Methodist Mem residing within the bounds of the Conference, any Members of the General Commission on United Methodist Men residing within the bounds of the Conference, Conference Lay Leader (or designated representative), Resident Bishop (Bishop David A. Bard), District Superintendent (Rev. Dr. Margie Crawford).

Laity, Board of (3.3)

Conference Lay Leader: Anne Soles (2018)/John Wharton (2018)

District Lay Leaders:
Central Bay: _____
East Winds: Bonnie Potter, Co-Leader (2018)
Greater Detroit: Ruby Anderson (2018)
Greater Southwest: Wynne Hurlbut (2018)
Heritage: Max Waagner (2018)
Mid-Michigan: Nona Spackman (2018)
Midwest: _____
Northern Skies: John Preston (2018)
Northern Waters: Denny Olin (2018)

Associate District Lay Leaders:

Michael Schlusler, Co-Leader (2018)
Kenneth Dowell (2018)

Associate Director for Lay Leadership Development: Laura Witkowski
Conference Co-Directors of Lay Servant Ministries: John Hart and Jody Pratt
President of the United Methodist Men (or representative): _____
President of the United Methodist Women (or representative): Linda Darrow, President and Marchelle "Micki" Phelps, UMW Rep
Convener of the Division of Young Adult Ministry of the Board of Young People's Ministries: _____

Convener of the Division of Youth Ministry of the Board of Young People's Ministries: _____

Conference Scouting Coordinator: Robert Sanders
Director of Connectional Ministries: Rev. Benton Heisler
District Superintendent designated by the Cabinet: Rev. Dwayne Bagley

Young People's Ministries, Board of (3.4)

Chairperson: Rev. Christina Miller-Black
(Chairperson of the Board is an additional member, chosen by Committee on Nominations.)

Vice Chairperson: _____
(Convener shall serve as Vice Chairperson of the Board, chosen by the conveners.)

Each Division shall elect a Convener.

Ex officio with voice, but no vote: A representative of the Michigan Area Board of Christian Camping (_____).

Youth Ministry, Division of (3.4.3.1)

Two clergy persons appointed in the Annual Conference,
who shall serve four-year terms, renewable once, in biennially staggered classes.

Two adult Laypersons who shall be Professing Members of a local church within the Annual Conference,
who shall serve four-year terms, renewable once, in biennially staggered classes.

Ten Youth (age 13-17) who shall be Professing Members of a local church within the Annual Conference,
who shall serve one-year terms, renewable as long as they are under age 18 at the start of a new term.

Members shall be nominated by the Committee on Nominations.

Convener shall be elected among the members: _____

Class	Laity	Clergy
2020	Daphne Mitchell (2019)	
	Rena Crowbez (2019)	
2021		
2022		
2023		Zachary "Zach" McNees (2019)

Class	Youth	Youth
	Lenah Alghali (2019)	Isabelle Nowak (2019)
	Ethan Chu (2019)	Erin Stevens (2019)
	Mary Violet Comiskey (2019)	Elizabeth Storkey (2019)
	Elise Hitts (2019)	Kayla Sweeney (2019)
	Tyler Moody (2019)	

Given Voice, **per Division Action**: Bridget Nelson, Coordinator of Youth Ministry Development (Conference Staff).

Young Adult Ministry, Division of (3.4.3.2)

Two Young Adult (age 18-30) Clergy Persons of the Annual Conference who shall be
nominated by the committee on nominations.

Four Young Adult Lay Persons (age 18-30) who shall be nominated by the committee on nominations and who
shall be Professing Members of a local church within the Annual Conference.

Members shall serve one-year terms, renewable as long as they are age 30 or under
at the start of the new term.

Convener shall be elected among the members: _____

Class	Laity	Clergy
2020		
2021		Jessica Davenport (2019)
		Scott Marsh (2019)

Given Voice, **per Division Action:** Young Adult Initiatives Coordinator, Pastor Lisa Batten (Conference Staff).

Higher Education and Campus Ministry, Division of (3.4.3.3)

Six people who shall be members of the Annual Conference (if clergy) or
Professing Members of a local church within the Annual Conference (if laity).

Members shall serve four-year terms, renewable once, in annually staggered classes.

Members shall be nominated by the Committee on Nominations.

Convener shall be elected among the members: _____

Class	Laity		Clergy
2020			Katherine Fahey (2018)
2021	Blair Hunt (2018)		
2022	Tito Kromah (2018)		Cora Glass (2019)
2023	Bonnie Garbrecht (2018)		Jeffrey "Jeff" Williams (2018)

Co-Opted Members: Rick Miller (2019), Rev. Devon Herrell (2019)

Ex officio with vote: Any Member of the General Board of Higher Education and Ministry residing within the bounds of the Annual Conference.

Given Voice, per Division Action: Young Adult Initiatives Coordinator, Pastor Lisa Batten (Conference Staff).

Congregational Life, Board of (3.5)

Chairperson: Rev. Sherry Parker
(Chairperson of the Board is an additional member, chosen by Committee on Nominations.)

Vice Chairperson:
(Convener shall serve as Vice Chairperson of the Board, chosen by the conveners.)

Each Division shall elect a Convener

Given Voice, per Board Action: Director of Congregational Vibrancy, Rev. Dirk Elliott (Conference Staff).

Congregational Vibrancy, Division of (3.5.3.1)

Four people who shall be members of the Annual Conference (if clergy) or Professing Members of a local church within the Annual Conference (if laity).

Members shall serve four-year terms, renewable once, in annually staggered.

Members shall be nominated by the Committee on Nominations.

Convener shall be elected among the members: Rev. LuAnn Rourke

Class	Laity		Clergy
2020			Michael Sawicki (2018)
2021			Matthew "Matt" Stoll (2018)
2022	Kathleen "Kathy" Lefler (2018)		
2023			LuAnn Rourke (2018)

Ex officio with vote: Any Member of Discipleship Ministries residing within the bounds of the Annual Conference, District Superintendent (Rev. David Kim).

Small Membership Church, Division on the (3.5.3.2)

Four people who shall be members of the Annual Conference (if clergy) or Professing Members of a local church within the Annual Conference (if laity).

Members shall serve four-year terms, renewable once, in annually staggered classes.

Members shall be nominated by the Committee on Nominations.

Convener shall be elected among the members: Rev. Matt Bistayi

Class	Laity		Clergy
2020			Kimberly "Kim" Metzer (2018)
2021			Matthew "Matt" Osborne (2018)
2022			Peggy Katzmark (2018)
2023			Matthew "Matt" Bistayi (2018)

Christian Unity and Interreligious Relationships, Division on (3.5.3.3)

Six persons who shall be members of the Annual Conference (if Clergy) or Professing Members of a local church within the Annual Conference (if laity), one of whom shall serve as the District Coordinator for Christian Unity and Interreligious Relationships.

Members shall serve four-year terms, renewable once, in annually staggered classes.

Members shall be nominated by the Committee on Nominations.

Convener: Rev. Rodney "Rod" Gassaway

Class	Laity	Clergy
2020	Laurie Smith Del Pino (2018)	
2021	Matthew "Matt" Packer (2018)	Dianne VanMarter (2018)
2022		Rodney "Rod" Gasaway (2018)
2023	Suzanne Hewitt (2019)	

Ex officio with vote: Any United Methodists residing within the bounds of the Annual Conference who are members of the following: The Office of Christian Unity and Interreligious Relationships of the Council of Bishops, the governing Board of the National Council of Churches of Christ in the U.S.A., the World Methodist Council, The United Methodist delegation to the most recent World Council of Churches Assembly, the United Methodist delegation to the most recent plenary meeting of Churches Uniting in Christ.

Hispanic/Latino Ministry, Committee on (3.6)

The committee shall define its membership and organize in any way it sees fit, subject to the approval of the Conference Leadership Council.

Term: Four-year term, max two terms

Chairperson: Rev. Rey Mondragon

Class	Laity	Clergy
2020	Ricardo Angarita Oviedo (2018)	Joel Walther (2018)
	Patsy Coffman (2018)	Jennifer Jue (2018)
2021	Lea Tobar (2018)	Ellen Zienert (2018)
		Sari Brown (2018)
2022	Victoria "Tori" Booker (2018)	Patricia Gandarilla (2018)
	Jorge Costales (2018)	Laura Feliciano (2018)
	Holly Downer (2018)	
2023	Audrey Mangum (2018)	Rey Mondragon (2018)
	Lawrence Iseler (2018)	

Co-Opted Members (maximum of four; may be asked to fill the following positions such as but not limited to):
Training Coordinator:
Grant Application Coordinator:
Immigration Advisor:

Ex officio with voice, but no vote: District Superintendent (Rev. Dr. Margie Crawford), Conference Treasurer (David Dobbs), Director of Connectional Ministries (Rev. Benton Heisler), Staff employed by the Conference Leadership Council and assigned to the Committee on Hispanic/Latino Ministry (Sonya Luna).

Asian-American Ministry, Committee on (3.7)

The committee shall define its membership and organize in any way it sees fit,
subject to the approval of the Conference Leadership Council.

Chairperson: Rev. Jung Eun Yum

Class	Laity	Clergy
2020		Latha Ravi (2018)
		Anna Moon (2018)
2021		Won Dong Kim (2018)
		Gunsoo Jung (2018)
2022		Jung Eun Yum (2018)
		Sang Chun (2018)
2023		

Co-opted Members: Rev. Dr. Darryl Totty (2018), Rev. Seung "Andy" Baek (2018), Rev. Dr. Jennifer Jue (2018), Prospero Tumonong (2018)

Ex officio **with voice, but no vote:** District Superintendent designated by Cabinet (Rev. David Kim), Director of Connectional Ministries or another Conference Representative (Sonya Luna).

Native American Ministry, Committee on (3.8)

"Insofar as possible, the majority of the committee's members should be Native Americans.

Taking into account the mandate of the purpose of this committee, the committee shall define its membership and organize in any way it sees fit, subject to the approval of the Conference Leadership Council."

The preliminary proposal that follows will need to be confirmed/revised by the Conference Leadership Council and the Committee on Native American Ministries/Indian Workers Conference at their next meeting:
The membership of the Committee on Native American Ministry (CONAM) shall include two persons elected by each Native American United Methodist congregation or ministry; the pastor may be a delegate or alternate, as determined by the church and at least four members at large selected by CONAM:

Executive Committee: Chairperson (Pastor Ronald "Todd" Williamson), Vice-Chairperson (Pastor George Pamp), Secretary (Valerie Maidens), Treasurer (Valerie Maidens), Cabinet Representative (Rev. Jodie Flessner, District Superintendent).

Bradley Indian Mission UMC	Oscoda UMC
Chippewa Indian UMC	Saganing Native American Mission UMC
Salem Indian Mission UMC	Zeba Indian Mission UMC
Greensky Hill Indian Mission UMC	Kewadin Indian Mission UMC
Northport Indian Mission UMC	

PaWaTing MaGedwin Kikaajik (Native American Elders Program)

Members-At-Large – Laity: Amy Alberts, Rose Bledsoe, Fran Church Pratt, Rich Guyon, Clara Lawrence

Ex Officio *Voice, but no vote (because of category)*: Bishop (Bishop David A. Bard), Cabinet Member Representative (Rev. Jodie Flessner), Director of Connectional Ministries (Rev. Benton Heisler).

African-American Ministry, Committee on (3.9)

The committee shall define its membership in any way it sees fit,
subject to the approval of the Conference Leadership Council.

Co-Chairs: Rev. Janet "Jan" Brown, Simmie Proctor
Recording Secretary: Pastor Marshall Murphy
Communications Coordinator: Dwanda Ashford

NOMINATIONS REPORT

Spiritual Formation Coordinator: Sharon Appling
Spiritual Care Coordinator: Pastor Anthony Ballah
Registrar: Gregory "Greg" Keeler

Members:

Laity	**Clergy**
Cecelia Tolliver	B. Kevin Smalls
Loretta Lee	Sandra Bibilomo
	Darryl Totty
	Esrom Shaw

Ex officio **with voice, but no vote**: District Superintendent (Rev. Dr. Charles Boayue).

ADMINISTRATIVE AGENCIES

Finance and Administration, Council on (4.1)

Six Clergy Members of the Annual Conference.
Seven Lay People who are Professing Members of a local church within the Annual Conference.
At least one of the thirteen members shall be appointed to (in the case of a Clergy Person) or
a member of (in the case of a Lay Person) a church with fewer than two hundred members.

Members shall be nominated by the Committee on Nominations.

Members shall serve four-year terms (starting at the close of the Annual Conference Session
following General Conference), renewable once, with quadrennially staggered classes.

The Council shall elect from among its members the following:
President: Bradley "Brad" Bartelmay   Vice President: Andrew "Andy" Wayne
Secretary: Susan MacGregor

Laity	**Clergy**
2016 Quadrennia	
Renae Clevenger (2018)	Geraldine "Geri" Hamlen (2018)
Cameron "Cam" DeLong (2018)	M. Christopher "Chris" Lane (2019)
Susan MacGregor (2018)	
Clayton Osborn (2018)	
2020 Quadrennia	
Jim Bosserd (2018)	Bradley "Bard" Bartelmay (2018)
Patrick Tiedt (2018)	Janet Gaston Petty (2018)
Andrew "Andy" Wayne (2018)	Donald "Don" Gotham (2019)

Ex officio **with voice and vote**: Any Member of the General Council on Finance and Administration who resides within the bounds of the Annual Conference.

Ex officio **with voice, but no vote**: Director of Administrative Services and Conference Treasurer (David
Dobb), Resident Bishop (Bishop David A. Bard), or Clergy Assistant to the Bishop (Rev. John Boley), District
Superintendent (Rev. John Hice), Director of Connectional Ministries (Rev. Benton Heisler), Director of Benefits
and Human Resources (Rev. Donald "Don" Emmert), any other Conference Directors as the Conference Lead-
ership Council shall designate, any Director level benefits officer as determined by the Board of Pension and
Health Benefits. Executive Director of the United Methodist Foundation of Michigan (Rev. David Bell).

Pension and Health Benefits, Board of (4.2)

Six Clergy Members of the Annual Conference.
Six Lay Persons who shall be Professing Members of a local church within the Annual Conference.

Members shall be nominated by the Committee on Nominations.

Members shall serve one non-renewable eight-year term, in annually staggered classes.

The Board shall elect from among its members the following:

Chairperson: Rev. Steven Buck   Vice Chairperson: _____

Secretary: _____

Director of Administrative Services/Conference Treasurer, David Dobbs

Class	Laity	Clergy
2020	Carol Kandell (2018)	David Hills (2018)
2021	Kenneth Norton (2018)	Steven "Steve" Buck (2018)
2022	Kathleen Dorman (2018)	
2023	Kevin Dick (2018)	Carol Johns (2018)
2024		Gary Glanville (2018)
2025	Al Minert (2018)	Cornelius "Neil" Davis (2018)
2026		Joel Fitzgerald (2018)
2027	Dennis Stanek (2019)	

Ex officio **with vote**: Any Board Member of Wespath Benefits and Investments residing within the bounds of the Annual Conference (Rev. Joel Fitzgerald), a District Superintendent (Rev. Dr. Jerome "Jerry" DeVine) designated by the Cabinet.

Ex officio **with voice, but no vote**: Director of Administrative Services and Conference Treasurer (David Dobbs), Director of Benefits and Human Resources (Rev. Donald Emmert), any other Conference Directors as the Conference Leadership Council shall designate, any Director level benefits officer as determined by the Board.

Administrative Review Committee (4.3)

Three Full Clergy Members of the Annual Conference.
Two additional Full Clergy Members of the Annual Conference who shall
serve as alternate committee members.
None of the foregoing shall be a District Superintendent (or a relative thereof) or
a member of the Board of Ordained Ministry (or relative thereof).

Members shall be nominated by the Bishop.

Members shall serve four-year terms, renewable once.

Class	
2020	**Full Clergy Members**
	Gerald Hagans (2018)
	Gloria Haynes (2019)
	George Lewis (2019)
	Alternate Full Clergy Members
2020	Ellen Brubaker (2018)
	Catherine "Cathee" Miles (2019)

NOMINATIONS REPORT

Trustees, Board of (4.4)

Six Clergy Members of the Annual Conference.
Six Lay Persons who are Professing Members of a local church within the Annual Conference.

All Board Members must be at least eighteen years of age.

All Board Members must fulfill any other criteria for serving on the Board of Directors of a corporation that the laws of the State of Michigan may require.

Members shall be nominated by the Committee on Nominations.

Except as otherwise required by law, members shall be elected to four-year terms, renewable once, with annually staggered classes.

The Board shall elect from among its members the following:
Chairperson: _____   Vice Chairperson: _____
Secretary: _____

Except as otherwise required by law, the Director of Administrative Services/Conference Treasurer (David Dobbs) shall serve as the Board Treasurer.

Class	Laity	Clergy
2020	David Apol (2018)	Clifford Radke (2018)
	Karl Bauman (2018)	George Lewis (2018)
2021	Michael Belt (2018)	Carolin Spragg (2018)
		Daniel "Dan" Hart (2018)
2022	Robert "Rob" Long (2018)	Matthew "Matt" Hook (2018)
2023	Jorge Costales (2018)	Joy Moore (2019)
	Jim LeBaron (2019)	

Ex officio **with vote**: District Superintendent (Rev. John Hice).

Ex officio **with voice, but no vote**: Director of Administrative Services and Conference Treasurer (David Dobbs), Director of Connectional Ministries (Rev. Benton Heisler).

Investigation, Committee on (4.5)

Four Ordained Clergy Members of the Annual Conference.
Three Lay People who are Professing Members of a local church within the Annual Conference.

Three Ordained Clergy Members of the Annual Conference shall serve as alternate members.
Six Lay People – three of whom, if possible, shall be Diaconal Ministers – who are Professing Members of a local church within the Annual Conference shall serve as alternate members.

Members shall be nominated by the Resident Bishop.

Members shall serve a one-quadrennium term.

Members of the following entities and their immediate family members shall be ineligible for members of the committee: Cabinet and Board of Ordained Ministry.

The Committee shall elect from among its members the following:
Chairperson: _____

Class	Laity	Clergy
2020	Minnie Armstrong (2019)	Richard "Rick" Blunt (2018)
	Murray Davis (2019)	G. Patrick England (2019)
	Paula Hines (2018)	Catherine "Cathi" Huvaere (2018)
	Wynne Hurlbut (2018)	Philip Tousley (2019)
	Michael Schlusler (2019)	Brian West (2019)
	Craig Schroeder (2018)	

Alternate Members:

Class	Laity	Clergy
2020	Louelle Burke (2018)	Glenn Litchfield (2018)
	Laura De La Garza (2019)	Julie Liske (2018)
	Fred Gray (2019)	
	Linda Polter (2019)	
	Max Waagner (2018)	

Rules, Committee on (4.6)

Eight Voting Members who shall be either Clergy Members of the Annual Conference or Lay People who are Members of a local church within the Annual Conference.

Members shall be nominated by the Committee on Nominations.

Members shall serve four-year terms, renewable twice, in annual staggered classes.

The Committee shall elect from among its members the following:

Chairperson: Todd Price   Vice Chairperson: _____
Secretary: _____

Class	Laity	Clergy
2020	Todd Price (2018)	
2021	C. David Lundquist (2018)	
	Herbert "Herb" Vanderbilt (2018)	
2022	James "Jim" Searls (2018)	Paula Timm (2018)
2023	Keith Radek (2019)	Richard "Rick" Blunt (2019)

Ex officio **with vote**: Legislative Coordinator selected by the Commission on the Annual Conference (Diane Brown), Annual Conference Facilitator (Susanne "Sue" Buxton), a District Superintendent (Rev. Dr. Charles Boayue) designated by the Cabinet, Annual Conference Secretary (Rev. Joy Barrett), Conference Parliamentarian (if one is appointed by the Bishop).

Ex officio, but no **vote**: Director of Connectional Ministries (Rev. Benton Heisler).

Episcopal Residence Committee (4.7)

Chairperson of the Committee on Episcopacy (or representative): John Wharton
President of Council on Finance and Administration (or representative): Bradley "Brad" Bartelmay
Chairperson of Board of Trustees (or representative): Carolin Spragg
Others may be co-opted, with voice, but without vote, as needed.

Equitable Compensation, Commission on (4.8)

Four Clergy Members of the Annual Conference, at least one of whom shall be appointed to a church with fewer than 200 members.
Four Lay Persons who shall be Professing Members of a church within the Annual Conference, at least one of whom shall be a member of a church with fewer than 200 members.

Members shall serve four-year terms, renewable once, in annually staggered classes.

Members shall be nominated by the Committee on Nominations.

The Commission shall elect from among its members the following:

Chairperson: Nancy Patera   Vice Chairperson: _____
Secretary: _____

The Director of Administrative Services/Conference Treasurer (David Dobbs) shall serve as the Treasurer of the Commission.

Class	Laity	Clergy
2020	Robert "Bob" Bernum (2018)	Gerald Hagans (2018)
2021	Molly Shaffer (2018)	Nancy Patera (2018)
2022	Barry Trantham (2018)	Karen Williams (2018)
2023		Virginia Heller (2019)

Ex officio **with vote**: A District Superintendent (Rev. Dwayne Bagley) designated by the Cabinet, a Member of the Council on Finance and Administration (Rev. Donald "Don" Gotham).

Ex officio **with voice, but no vote**: Director of Administrative Services and Conference Treasurer (David Dobbs).

Human Resources, Committee on (4.9)

Eight people who shall be members of the Annual Conference (if Clergy) or
Professing Members of a local Church within the Annual Conference (if Laity).

Members shall serve four-year terms, renewable once, in annually staggered classes.

Members shall be nominated by the Committee on Nominations.

A Chairperson chosen by the Committee on Nominations from among the Members: Rev. Ellen Zienert

A Vice-Chairperson chosen by the Committee on Human Resources from among its members: Deborah "Deb" Fennell

A Secretary chosen by the Committee on Human Resources from among its membership: _____

Class	Laity	Clergy
2020	Alice Tucker (2018)	
2021	Georgia Marsh (2018)	Ellen Zienert (2018)
2022	Deborah "Deb" Fennell (2018)	Deborah "Deb" Fennell (2018)
2023	_____	Grant Lobb (2019)
		Nancy Powers (2019)

Ex officio **with vote**: Bishop (Bishop David A. Bard), or Clergy Assistant to the Bishop (Rev. John Boley), a District Superintendent (Rev. Dr. Margie Crawford) designated by the Cabinet.

Ex officio **with voice, but no vote**: Director of Connectional Ministries (Rev. Benton Heisler), Director of Administrative Services/Conference Treasurer (David Dobbs), Director of Benefits and Human Resources (Rev. Donald Emmert), Chair of the Personnel Committee of the Council on Finance and Administration (   ).

Officers of The Annual Conference

Secretary (6.1): Rev. Joy Barrett (2017)
Four-year term, two terms maximum. Elected at first Annual Conference Session following General Conference.

Statistician (6.2): Pamela Stewart (07/15/2019)
Four-year term, two terms maximum. Elected at Annual Conference Session immediately preceding General Conference.

Facilitator (6.3): Susanne "Sue" Buxton (2018)
Four-year term, two terms maximum. Layperson.

Parliamentarian (6.4): None –
May be appointed by the Bishop at his/her discretion.

Chancellor (6.5): Andrew Vorbrich (2017)
Nominated by the Bishop, elected quadrennially.

Director of Administrative Services and Conference Treasurer (6.6): David Dobbs (2017)
Elected at first Annual Conference Session following each General Conference.

Lay Leader (6.7): Co-Leaders – Anne Soles (2018), **John Wharton** (2018)
Four-year term, one term.

AFFILIATE ENTITIES OF THE ANNUAL CONFERENCE
Elected UMC Board Members

Affiliated via the Board of Global Ministries (10.1)

Bronson Health Group (10.1.1) – Trustees of
(UMC Members are no longer a requirement, per change in their 2014 By-Laws)

Clark Retirement Community (10.1.2) – Trustees of
(Report Only, election is by Clark, per change in Clark's By-Laws.)
OFFICERS:

Chair: Steve Finney (2013)   Secretary: Beth Kelly (2015)
Vice Chair: Robert "Bob" Gillette (2013)   Treasurer: Gregg Richardson (2016)

TRUSTEES:
[Tenure: By-Law terms are limited to 9 years.]
Suzeanne Benet (2015)
Spencer Brown (2015)
Jayne Courts (2016)
Dale Grogan (2015)
Kathy Holt (2016)

Ex officio: Brian Ellis, Charles Homeyer, Brian Pangle, Carol Ann Youells.

Methodist Children's Home Society (10.1.3) – Directors
[Tenure: By-Law terms are limited to 10 years.]

Laity	Clergy
David Bennett (2011)	William "Bill" Amundsen (2008) *
Marianne Conner (2016)	Charles Boayue (2001) *
Eric Pelton (2017)	
Doug Ross (2007) *	
Carrie Russell (2014)	
Juli Stephens (2018)	
Christine Weemhoff (2000) *	

* Extended by action of the directors.

Cabinet Assignment: A District Superintendent (Rev. Dr. Charles Boayue).

United Methodist Community House (10.1.4)
Officers: President (Tamara Belton), Treasurer (Terry McCarthy)

Laity	Clergy
Taylorie Bailey	
Lillian Howell-Bell White	
Zsanara Hoskins	
Ken Miguel-Cipriano	
Marchelle "Micki" Phelps	
Karynn Sikkema	

Ex officio: Linda Darrow (UMW), Linda Burton-Collier (UMW).

United Methodist Retirement Communities, Inc. (10.1.5) – Board of Trustees

Laity
Rich Brown (2004)
Russ Ives (2009)
Dick Lundy (1983)
Stuart Main (2007)
John Nixon (2007)
Gary Vander Haagen (2007)

Clergy
Matthew "Matt" Hook (2007)

Cabinet Assignment: A District Superintendent (Rev. Elizabeth Hill).

Affiliated Via the Board of Young People's Ministries (10.2)

Adrian College (10.2.1) – Trustees of

[Tenure: By-Law terms are limited to 9 years.]

Laity
Bonnie Garbrecht (2008) *

Clergy
Russell "Russ" McReynolds (2006) *

Area Bishop: Bishop David A. Bard

* Term extended by request of the Trustees of Adrian College.

[ ] Indicate names submitted for election of two by College in coordination with Board of Higher Education and Campus Ministry.

Albion College (10.2.2) – Trustees of

[Tenure: By-Law terms are limited to 12 years.]

Laity

Clergy
Stephen "Steve" Charnley (2007)
Faith Fowler (2013)

Area Bishop: Bishop David A. Bard

[ ] Indicate names submitted for election of two by College in coordination with Board of Higher Education and Campus Ministry.

Bay Shore Evangelical Association (10.2.3) – Directors

Laity
Kerry Bailey (2011)
Justin Kuhl (2016)
Jeff Leipprandt (2015)
Susanne Niedrich (2006)
Kendal Root (2016)
Bill Schaard (2015)
Chuck Squires (2016)
Kevin Wightman (2015)

Clergy
Susanne "Susie" Hierholzer (2016)
Mark Karls (Ret) (2010)
George Lewis (2011)
Douglas "Doug" Mater (2017)
Jacquelyn "Jackie" Roe (2013)

Michigan Area United Methodist Camping (10.2.4)

Camping Board elections are effective upon conclusion of Annual Conference, 06/02/2019.

Chairperson: _____

Interim Director: Joel Wortley

Elected by the Board, per Board By-Laws: Deborah "Deb" Fennell (2018)

Elected by the Annual Conference, per Board By-Laws (no less than 60%):

	Laity	Clergy
2020	Michelle Hills (2014)	Sheryl Foster (2013)
2021	Susan Witte (2017)	David Wichert (2017)
2022	Stuart Smith (2018)	Terry Euper (2019)
	Bob Wyatt (2018)	Anita Hahn (2019)
2023	Dale Kimball (2019)	Joel Walther (2019)
	Steve Steggerda (2019)	Patricia "Patti" Harpole (2019)

Designated by the Full Cabinet *(voice, but no vote)*: District Superintendent (Rev. Dwayne Bagley).

Ex officio **with voice, but no vote:** Executive Director of Camping: Joel Wortley (interim).

Lake Louise Christian Community (10.2.5) – Board of Trustees

Tenure: By-Law terms are limited to 9 years. Elect their own chair.

Laity	Clergy
Liz Carr (2014)	Benjamin "Ben" Bower (2018)
Doug Clark (2016)	Hillary Thurston-Cox (2019)
Daphne Mitchell (2013)	
Linda Zeeb (2018)	

Affiliated via the Commission on Archives and History (10.3)

Michigan Area UMC Historical Society, Inc. (10.3) – Elected by Commission on Archives and History.

Chairperson: Diana Spitnale Miller

Laity	Clergy
Ken Gackler (2008)	Melanie Young (2012)
Sharon Scott (2007)	
Mary Whitman (2014)	
Dan Yakes (2008)	

Members At-Large: William McNitt, Lois Omundson, Rev. Lowell Peterson, Della Wilder

Ex officio **with voice and vote**: The Chairperson of the Commission on Archives and History (Mary Whitman), The Archivists of the Conference Archives – Rebecca McNitt (Adrian) and Mike VanHouten (Albion), Members of the General Commission on Archives and History residing in the Annual Conference: Diana Spitnale Miller, Linda Schramm; Member of the Historical Society of the UMC Board: Linda Schramm.

Affiliated via the Council on Finance and Administration (10.4)

Michigan Area Loan Funds (10.4.1) – *Elected by the UM Foundation of Michigan*

Laity	Clergy
Nancy Craig (2019)	Bradley "Brad" Bartelmay (2019)
Ransom Leppink (2019)	Edward "Ed" Ross (2019)
Joy Stair (2019)	
Sue Woodard (2019)	

Ex officio: Rev. David Bell, Resident Agent.

United Methodist Foundation of Michigan (10.4.2) – *12 Directors elected by the UM Foundation of Michigan*

Class	Laity	Clergy
2019	Lauren Frey (2011)	Gary Glanville (2014)
		Bradley "Brad" Bartelmay (2015)
		Mary McInnes (2019)
2020	Ransom Leppink (2012)	
	Nancy Craig (2014)	
	Joy Stair (2012)	
	Sue Woodard (2011)	
2021	Steven Peters (2019)	Edward "Ed" Ross (2015)
	To Be Named	Joel Fitzgerald (2018)

Ex officio: Rev. David Bell, President and Executive Director; Bishop David A. Bard, Resident Bishop; David Dobbs, Conference Treasurer.

Disaster Response Team

Team Chairperson: Rev. Robert Miller
Disaster Response Coordinator: Dan O'Malley
Disaster Recovery Coordinator: Nancy Money
Conference Emotional and Spiritual Care Coordinator: _____
Conference Communications Director: Mark Doyal
Conference Finance Officer: David Dobbs
Conference VIM Coordinator: Jody Pratt

District Disaster Response Coordinators
    Central Bay: _____
    East Winds: Robert McCormick
    Greater Detroit: Dwanda Ashford, Don Archambeau
    Greater Southwest: Rev. David "Dave" Morton
    Heritage: Rev. Robert Miller
    Mid-Michigan:
    Midwest: Rev. Lyle Ball, Janet Ball
    Northern Skies: Terri Branstrom
    Northern Waters: Dave Stockford

Ex officio with voice, but no vote: District Superintendent (Rev. Dwayne Bagley) and Director of Connectional Ministries (Rev. Benton Heisler).

Justice for Our Neighbors (JFON) – Michigan Board

Elected by Annual Conference, no less than 60% of Board:

Rev. Paul Perez, Chair	C. David Lundquist
Kristine Faasse	LouAnn McKimmy
Hoon-Yung Hopgood	Joan VanDessel
Sonya Luna	

Elected by Board:
    Trace Bauman
    Mani Khavajian

DISTRICT COMMITTEES
Provided for Information Only

District Boards of Church Location and Building

Central Bay District – Rev. David Kim, District Superintendent

Laity
Karl Bauman, Chair (2018)
Randy Hock (2018)
Darlene Levia (2018)

Clergy
Jon Gougeon (2018)
James "Jim" Payne (2018)

East Winds District – Rev. John Hice, District Superintendent

Laity
Bob Bernum (2018)
Kathy Dorman (2018)
Peter Plum (2018)
Doris Sain (2018)
Dayna Wright (2018
Robert Wyatt (2018), Co-Chair

Clergy
Barbara Benjamin (2018)
Jerry Griggs (2018), Co-Chair
David Reed (2018)

Greater Detroit District – Rev. Dr. Charles Boayue, District Superintendent

Laity
Don Archambeau (2018)
John Lawrence (2018)
Pearl Lewis (2018)
Eugene Paik, Chair (2018)
Lynn Van De Putte (2018)

Clergy
Jean Snyder, Chair (2018)
Jonathan Combs (2018)
Jinny Song (2018)

Greater Southwest District – Rev. Dwayne Bagley, District Superintendent

Laity
Wynne Hurlbut (2018)
Mark Crawford (2018)
Nate Hawthorne (2018)
Donald Weaver (2018)

Clergy
Ronald "Ron" VanLente (2018)

Heritage District – Rev. Elizabeth Hill, District Superintendent

Laity
Nicolas Dever (2018)
Jim Jacobs (2018)
Doug Parr (2019)

Clergy
Peter "Pete" Harris (2019)
Robert Hughes (2018)
Robert "Bob" Stover (2018)
James Walker (2019)

Mid-Michigan District – Rev. Dr. Jerome DeVine, District Superintendent

Laity
James LeBaron, Chair (2018)
William Blanchett (2018)
Darcy Bozen (2018)
Deborah Federau (2018)
Dick Rice (2018)

Clergy
Jeanne Randels (2018)

Midwest District – Rev. Dr. Margie Crawford, District Superintendent

Laity

David Apol, Chair (2018)
Dennis Bekken (2018)
John Faas (2018)
Louann Hoffman (2018)
Susan MacGregor (2018)
Steve Meredith (2018)

Clergy

Gregory "Greg" Buchner (2018)
Diane Gordon (2018)
Michael "Mike" Ramsey (2018)

Northern Skies District – Rev. Scott Harmon, District Superintendent

Laity

Donald Balmer (2018)
Larry Rogers (2018)
Pat Waeghe (2018)

Clergy

James "Jim" Mathews (2018)
Theodore "Ted" Trudgeon (2018)

Northern Waters District – Rev. Jodie Flessner, District Superintendent

Laity

Tom Bowman (2018)
Lyle Matteson (2018)
Ann Porter (2018)

Clergy

John Scott, Chair (2018)
Eugene Baughan (2018)
Patricia Haas (2018)
George Spencer (2018)

District Committees on Ordained Ministry

Central Bay District

Ordained Ministry Representative: Rev. David Wichert
District Superintendent: Rev. David Kim

Laity

Mary Fox (2019)
Larry Wyman, Sr. (2019)

Clergy

Joseph Beaven (2019)
Timothy Dibble (2019)
Ernesto Mariona (2018)
Robert "Rob" Richards (2018)
Amy Lee Terhune (2019)

East Winds District

Ordained Ministry Representative: Rev. Jennifer Jue (2018), Rev. Susan Platt (2018)
District Superintendent: Rev. John Hice

Laity

Tom Cerny (2018)
Bonnie Potter (2018)
Bernie Schneider (2018)

Clergy

Bo Rin Cho (2018)
Richard "Rick" Dake (2018)
Ann Emerson (2018), Vice-Chair
Patricia Hoppenworth (2018)
Maurice Horne (2018)
John Huhtala (2018), Co-Chair
Joel Walther (2018), Secretary
Catherine Huvaere (2018)
Dennis Irish (2018)
Charles Jacobs (2018)
Jeffrey Jaggers (2018), Co-Chair

Clergy

Jennifer Jue (2018)
Grant Lobb (2018)
Susan Platt (2018)
Tara Sutton (2019)
Philip Tousley (2018)

Karen Williams (2018)
Christine Wyatt (2018)
Susan Youmans (2018)

Greater Detroit District

Ordained Ministry Representative: _____
District Superintendent: Rev. Dr. Charles Boayue

Laity	Clergy	Clergy
Ruby Anderson (2018)	*Steven McCoy, Chair (2018)*	Gregory Mayberry (2018)
Don Archambeau (2018)	*Hilda Harris, Vice Chair (2018)*	Amy Mayo-Moyle (2018)
Grace Epperson (2018)	Melanie Carey (2018)	Jeffery Nelson (2018)
Carole Wesner (2018)	Suzanne Goodwin (2018)	Latha Ravi (2018)
	Donald "Don" Gotham (2018)	B. Kevin Smalls (2018)
	Carter Grimmett (2018)	Weatherly Verhelst (2018)
	Jack Mannschreck (2018)	Joy Wong (2018)
	Judith May (2018)	

Greater Southwest District

Ordained Ministry Representative: Laurie Dahlman (2018)
District Superintendent: Rev. Dwayne Bagley

Laity	Clergy
Laurie Dahlman (2018)	*David Hills, Chair (2018)*
Fred Douglas (2018)	Martin "Marty" Culver (2018)
Wynne Hurlbut (2018)	Julie Elmore (2018)
	Ronald Hansen (2018)
	Mona Joslyn (2018)
	Karen Wheat (2018)

Heritage District

Ordained Ministry Representative: _____
District Superintendent: Rev. Elizabeth Hill

Laity	Clergy
Lynne Pauer (2018)	*Nancy Lynn, Chair (2018)*
Ken Kneisel (2019)	Loretta Job (2018)
Max Waagner, Lay Leader (2018)	Ronald "Ron" Brooks (2018)
John Wharton (2018)	Annelisa Gray-Lion (2018)
	Paul Gruenberg (2018)
	Rob McPherson (2018)
	Marsha Woolley (2018)
	Timothy "Tim" Ziegler (2018)

Mid-Michigan District

Ordained Ministry Representative: Pastor Terri Bentley (2018), Rev. Mark Erbes (2018)
District Superintendent: Rev. Dr. Jerome "Jerry" DeVine

Laity	Clergy
Kathy Dobie, Recording Sec. (2018)	*Cynthia Skutar, Chair (2018)*
Fred Olmsted (2018)	Terri Bentley (2018)
	Patricia Brook (2019)
	Mark Erbes (2018)
	Kathy Pittenger (2019)
	Nancy Powers, Registrar-Local Pastors (2018)
	Kathleen Smith (2018)
	Irene Vittoz, Registrar-Candidates (2018)
	Ellen Zienert (2018)

Midwest District

Ordained Ministry Representative: Rev. William "Bill" Johnson (2018)
District Superintendent: Rev. Dr. Margie Crawford

Laity
AnnMarie Buchner (2018)
Daniel "Dan" Davis (2018)

Clergy
Susan Hagans, Chair (2018)
William "Bill" Johnson, Registrar (2018)
Mark Miller (2018)
Nancy Patera (2018)
J. "Lynn" Pier-Fitzgerald (2018)
Ryan Wieland (2018)

Northern Skies District

Ordained Ministry Representative: Rev. Scott Lindenberg (2018)
District Superintendent: Rev. Scott Harmon (Executive Secretary)

Laity
Anine Bessolo, At-large (2018)
Kelly Ross (2019)

Clergy
Geraldine "Geri" Hamlen, Chair (2018)
Christopher Hintz, Vice Chair (2018)
James "Jim" Balfour, At-large (2018)
Albert Barchue, At-large (2018)
Scott Lindenberg, At-large (2018)
Peggy Paige, Registrar (2018)

Northern Waters District

Ordained Ministry Representative: Rev. James Mitchum (2018)
District Superintendent: Rev. Jodie Flessner

Laity
Debie Horn (2018)
Allen Horstman (2018)
Denny Olin (2018)

Clergy
Dale Ostema, Chair (2018)
Deborah "Deb" Johnson (2019)
Yoo Jin Kim (2019)
James Mitchum (2018)
Melody Olin (2018)

District Committees on District Superintendency

Central Bay District

District Superintendent: Rev. David Kim
District Lay Leader: _ _ _ _ _ _ _ (2018)

Laity
Linda Doane (2018)
Al Gonzalez (2018)
Cathy Kelley (2018)
Madison Meyer (2018)

Clergy
Ernesto Mariona, Chair (2018)
Robert "Rob" Richards (2018)

East Winds District

District Superintendent: Rev. John Hice
District Lay Leader: Michael Schlusler (2018)

Laity
Lois Bunton, DS Appointee (2018)
James Dover (2018)
Susie Hagenstein (2018)
Bruce Hurd (2018)
Debra Lobb, DS Appointee (2018)
Michael Schlusler (2018)
Dayne Walling, At-large (2018)

Clergy
Sari Brown, At-large (2018)
Julius Del Pino (2018), Secretary
Janine Plum (2018), Chair

Greater Detroit District

District Superintendent: Rev. Dr. Charles Boayue
District Lay Leader: Ruby Anderson (2018)

Laity
Ruby Anderson (2018)
Don Archambeau (2018)
Christopher Brown (2018)
Suzanne Goodwin (2018)
Cherlyn McKanders (2018)
Dale Milford (2018)

Clergy
Judith May, Chair (2018)
Carter Grimmett, Vice Chair (2018)
Diana Goudie (2018)
Lynn Hasley (2018)

Greater Southwest District

District Superintendent: Rev. Dwayne Bagley
District Lay Leader: Wynne Hurlbut (2018)

Laity
Michelle Brokaw (2018)
Lisa Coe (2018)
Marlene Cutler (2018)
Larry Edris (2018)
John Graves (2018)
Wynne Hurlbut (2018)
Karen Scheetz (2018)
Donna Smith (2018)
Deb Search Willoughby (2018), Chair

Clergy
David Haase (2018)

Heritage District

District Superintendent: Rev. Elizabeth Hill
District Lay Leader: Max Waagner (2018)

Laity
Jane Case (2018)
Vicky Engelbert (2018)
Wendy Everett (2018)
John Phillips (2018)
Max Waagner (2018)
John Wharton (2018)

Clergy
Robert Miller, Chair (2018)
Mary Loring (2018)
Bradley "Brad" Luck (2018)

Mid-Michigan District

District Superintendent: Rev. Dr. Jerome "Jerry" DeVine
District Lay Leader: Nona Spackman (2018)

Laity
Dean McCracken (2019)
Marilyn Rothert (2018)
Nona Spackman (2018)

Clergy
Deborah Thomas, Chair (2018)
Russell "Russ" McReynolds (2018)
Molly Turner (2018)

Midwest District

District Superintendent: Rev. Dr. Margie Crawford
District Lay Leader:

Laity
Deborah "Deb" Hodges (2018)
John Huizing (2018)
Sydney Judnich (2018)
Linda Sbraccia (2018)

Clergy
Dean Prentiss, Chair (2018)
Jennifer Wheeler (2018)

Northern Skies

District Superintendent: Rev. Scott Harmon
District Lay Leader: John Preston (2018)

Laity
Janet Helmbold (2018)
Dawn Payne (2018)
John Preston (2018)

Clergy
David "Dave" Wallis, Chair (2018)
Kristine "Kristi" Hintz (2018)

Northern Waters District

District Superintendent: Rev. Jodie Flessner
District Lay Leader: Denny Olin (2018)

Laity
Brian Highway, Chair (2018)
Chuck Corwin (2019)
Valerie Maidens (2018)
Denny Olin (2018)

Clergy
Daniel "Dan" Bowman (2018)
John "Jack" Conklin (2018)
Daniel Hofmann (2018)

Please e-mail any corrections/updates by June 17, 2019 to:

Janet Larner at jmlarner@gmail.com and Sus'ann Busley at sbusley@michiganumc.org.
Please do NOT turn in paper corrections to the Conference Secretary's Office at Annual Conference.
Please Include page number, agency, person's name, and explanation of the correction or change – i.e., "delete" or "add."
If the person is to be added, specify whether they are clergy/laity, male/female, and the beginning year of service.
If you are interested in serving where vacancies exist, please contact:
Janet Larner at jmlarner@gmail.com and Sus'ann Busley at sbusley@michiganumc.org.
Thank you!

NOMINATIONS REPORT

DISTRICT SUPERINTENDENTS' AGENCY ASSIGNMENTS
AND CABINET RESPONSIBILITIES
2019-2020

Cabinet Roles

Dean ....Rev. Elizabeth A. Hill
Secretary...Rev. John H. Hice
Assistant Secretary ....Rev. Dr. Margie R. Crawford
Chains...Rev. David I. Kim / Rev. Scott A. Harmon
Inquiries...Rev. David I. Kim
Hospitality ....Rev. Jodie R. Flessner
Prayer Cards...Rev. Dr. Margie R. Crawford
Inclusiveness ....Rev. Dr. Margie R. Crawford

Agency Liaison Assignments

African-American Ministry..........................Rev. Dr. Charles S.G. Boayue, Jr.
Annual Conference Session ....Rev. Jodie R. Flessner
Asian-American Ministry...Rev. David I. Kim
Camping and Retreat Ministries ....Rev. Dwayne E. Bagley
Children's Home Society ....Rev. Dr. Charles S.G. Boayue, Jr.
Disaster Response ....Rev. Dwayne E. Bagley
Equitable Compensation ....Rev. Dwayne E. Bagley
Finance and Administration (CF&A).................................Rev. John H. Hice
Global Ministries..Rev. David I. Kim
Hispanic/Latino ....Rev. Dr. Margie R. Crawford
Human Resources ....Rev. Dr. Margie R. Crawford
Incapacity/Disability ....Rev. Dr. Jerome R. DeVine
Leadership Council ....Rev. Elizabeth A. Hill
Native American Ministry ....Rev. Jodie R. Flessner
New Church Development ....Rev. David I. Kim
Nominations/Board of Laity ....Rev. Dwayne E. Bagley
Ordained Ministry ....Rev. Scott A. Harmon
Pension and Health Benefits ....Rev. Dr. Jerome R. DeVine
Rules Committee.....................................Rev. Dr. Charles S.G. Boayue, Jr.
Trustees ....Rev. John H. Hice
UM Men ....Rev. Dr. Margie R. Crawford
UM Retirement Communities..Rev. Elizabeth A. Hill
UM Women..Rev. Scott A. Harmon

DAILY PROCEEDINGS

FIRST DAY – MORNING SESSION

Thursday, May 30, 2019

The Michigan Annual Conference Opening Worship and Memorial Service opened at 10:00 a.m. at the Grand Traverse Resort, Acme, Michigan, in the Governor's Hall. A ceremony of Baptismal Remembrance was celebrated by all. Bishop David Bard preached. Worship leaders: Ruby Anderson, David Kim; liturgical movement: Kristine Hintz, Weatherly Burkhead-Verhelst, Beth Titus. Clergy, diaconal ministers, clergy spouses, children of clergy and laity who passed away since the last annual conference session were memorialized by a reading of the names. The naming of the saints was led by Bishop Bard. Those memorialized were:

- **Clergy**: Emerson W. Arntz, Rex E. Bean, Leo E. Bennett, Young Bong Yoon, William D. Carr, Douglas K. Olsen, Bernard R. Randolph, Michael L. Raymo, Marvin R. Rosa, J. Christ Schroeder, Ward N. Scovel, Jr., Gerald M. Sever, Jr., Robert E. Smith, Mark E. Spaw, Susan Bennett Stiles, Harold M. Taber, James F. Thomas, Joyce A. Thomas, Brian K. William, Gregory R. Wolfe, Paton M. Zimmerman, Francis Anderson, Harold Derks, Earl Downing, Jaunita Ferguson, Bert Hosking, Richard Kuhn, Sally LaFrance, Gary Lyons, Sharon Kay Rush-Osmond, Don Weatherup, Robert Bough, Bruce Denton, and David Yundy
- **Clergy Spouses**: Marilyn Joyce Ackerman, Barbara A. Parr Burton, Marge J. Dahringer, Joanne Dayringer, Irma Eidens, Grovenor "Kip" Grimes, Elizabeth Haering, Ruth P. Hoover, Mary Lou Jury, William H. Pope, Jr., Lois Powell, Loring Rossman, Linda Schweizer, Blanche Taylor, Betty Wallace, Helen L. Whittern, Vickie Wojewski, Nancy Steele, Karleen Pettis, and Betty Luce.
- **Children of Clergy:** Andrew Garth Brook, Chloe Rose Ostema, Jon Youqiang Surgeon Rider, and Tendai Barbara Mumbiro.
- **Laity**: Kayte Aspray, Samuel Carter, Sr., Shirley Joan Chapin, Carroll J. Christopher, Kenneth Halter, Carmen Arlene Misner, Pat Proctor, Jackie Washington, and Morris C. Taber.

Communion was served by the ordinands and retirees from both conferences. An offering was received which will benefit our covenant partners, The Methodist Church of Haiti (45% to Grace Children's Hospital & Pediatric Clinic) and The Liberia Annual Conference (45% to Bishop Judith Craig Children's Village). A 10% tithe of the offering will go the Michigan Disaster Relief and Recovery Fund.

Announcements were made by Nichea Ver Veer Guy, Commission on the Annual Conference Session chairperson, and Brittney Stephan, Associate Director for Multicultural Vibrancy.

The session was recessed at 12:06 p.m. for lunch with a prayer for the meal by Brittney Stephan.

FIRST DAY – CLERGY SESSION

Thursday, May 30, 2019

Clergy session was called to order at 1:45 p.m. in the Michigan Ballroom of the Grand Traverse Resort, Acme, Michigan, by Bishop Bard.

Announcements were given by Laura Speiran, chairperson of the Board of Ordained Ministry.

Enabling Motions:
> Motion: Speiran moved that all Provisional Members, Associate Members, Full-time and Part-time Local Pastors, Affiliate Members, and all clergy from other denominations appointed to serve among us be granted voice, but not vote in this clergy session. *Motion adopted.*
>
> Motion: Speiran moved that according to Discipline Paragraph 602.1-6, and our own conference structure document, paragraph 5.4.3.2.2, that all lay members of the Board of Ordained Ministry be allowed voice and vote in this clergy session. *Motion adopted.*
>
> Motion: Speiran moved to allow conference lay staff, Debbie Stevenson, Jennifer Weaver, Deana Nelson, and Mark Doyal, voice but no vote in this clergy session. *Motion adopted.*
>
> Motion: Speiran moved that Rev. Boehm's son, who is here to assist him, be allowed in the room with no voice and no vote. *Motion adopted.*

Episcopal Greeting: Bishop Bard greeted the clergy.

A Liturgy to Remember our Baptism was led by Laura Speiran, Sue Platt, Georgia Hale, Barry Petrucci, chairpersons of the Orders, Fellowship, and the Board of Ordained Ministry.

Hymn: "Come, Holy Ghost, Our Hearts Inspire"

Order of Elders and Deacons, Fellowship of Local Pastors and Associate Members: Barry Petrucci (Elders), Georgia Hale (Deacons), and Sue Platt (Fellowship of Local Pastors & Associate Members) reported.
> Motion: Steve Charnley moved the adoption of the following statement of affirmation: We, the 2019 Clergy Session of the Michigan Conference of the United Methodist Church, stand in solidarity with our Board of Ordained Ministry in their lament regarding the decisions of the 2019 Special Session of General Conference. We affirm their intention to do their sacred work of examining and ultimately recommending candidates for commissioning and ordination who demonstrate gifts and graces for vital ministry, without regard to their sexual orientation or gender identity. With our Board, we affirm and honor that God calls all to healthy human relationships and that these relationships are critical to effective ministry.

Greg Buechner requested a vote count.
> Amendment: Charles Boayue moved the insertion of ", a majority of the voting members of " immediately following, "We" in the opening sentence.

Motion: Greg Buechner moved to suspend the rules to immediately call the question. *Motion adopted* by the required two-thirds vote.

Boayue Amendment was *adopted*.

Charnley motion, as amended, was *adopted*. Yes: 298; No:125.

Motion: Speiran moved the election of Barry Petrucci as the next Order of Elder chairperson. *Motion adopted*.

Motion: Speiran moved the election of Sue Pethoud as the next Order of Deacons chairperson. *Motion adopted*.

Hymn: "The Servant Song"

Ordained and Licensed Clergy Status Action Items

Motion: Charles Boayue read the statement from the Cabinet in response to question **#17**.

Motion: Speiran moved the adoption of question **#18a**. *Motion adopted* as presented by the corrected addendum.

Motion: Jodie Flessner, registrar for local pastors, moved the adoption of question **#20**. *Motion adopted* by the required three-quarter vote.

Information: Flessner presented question **#21a** [with corrections].

Motion: Flessner moved the adoption of **#21b** [information made by the Board of Ordained Ministry to extend Eric Johnson by one year to complete the course of study]. *Motion adopted*.

Motion: Flessner moved the adoption of **#21d**. *Motion adopted*.

Motion: Flessner moved the full adoption of question **#21**. *Motion adopted* by required three-quarter vote.

Motion: Mark Erbes, chair of Conference Relations Committee, moved the adoption of question **#25**. *Motion adopted*.

Motion: Erbes moved the adoption of question **#26b**. *Motion adopted* by the required two-thirds vote.

Motion: Rick Dake moved that each of those to be commissioned and ordained be introduced individually and voted on as a class by the Clergy Session. *Motion adopted*.

Motion: Tim Ziegler moved the adoption of question **#27**. *Motion adopted* by the required three-quarter vote.

Motion: Julie Greyerbiehl, Provisional Registrar, moved the adoption of question **#28a**. A video was shown of those to be elected as provisional members as deacons of The United Methodist Church. Introductions were made and a vote was taken for the whole class. *Motion adopted* by the required three-quarter vote. *Motion adopted* by the required three-quarter vote.

Motion: Greyerbiehl moved the adoption of questions **#28b**. A video was shown of those to be elected as provisional members and Elders of The United Methodist Church. Introductions were made and a vote was taken for the whole class. *Motion adopted* by the required three-quarter vote.

Motion: Greyerbiehl moved the adoption of question **#29d**.*Motion adopted*.

Motion: Ziegler moved the adoption of question **#32a** and **33a**. The candidates to be elected as members in full connection, and ordained as Deacons, were introduced and a vote was taken for the whole class. *Motions adopted* by the required two-thirds vote.

Motion: Zeigler moved the adoption of question **#32b** and **34a**. Candidates to be elected as members in full connection, and ordained as Elders, were introduced and votes taken for the whole class. *Motions adopted* by the required two-thirds vote.

Motion: Mark Erbes moved the adoption of question **#42b.** *Motion adopted.*

Motion: Erbes moved the adoption of question **#44a.** *Motion adopted.*

Motion: Erbes moved the adoption of question **#46a.** *Motion adopted.*

Motion: Erbes moved the adoption of question **#50a(1).** *Motion adopted.*

Motion: Erbes moved the adoption of question **#50a(2)**. *Motion adopted* with the required two-thirds vote.

Motion: Erbes moved the adoption of question #**52**. *Motion adopted.*

Motion: Erbes moved the adoption of question **#53a** and **53c**. *Motion adopted.*

Motion: Erbes moved the adoption of question **#54a**. *Motion adopted.*

Motion: Erbes moved the adoption of question **#72a** [as corrected]. *Motion adopted* by the required two-thirds vote.

Motion: Erbes moved the adoption of **#76c**. *Motion adopted* with the required two-thirds vote.

Jenny Brown gave announcements and instructions for the Saturday celebration of ministry.

Lynn Hasley and Lindsey Hall gave instructions for the Service of Recognition, Commissioning, and Ordination.

Recognition Items: Speiran recognized and thanked Jeremy Williams for accompanying our singing.

Recognition of Retirees: Erbes and Speiran presented the names of those retiring this year, the names of which are found in questions **#44a, 53a, 53c, 54a, & 56a**. Note: The number of years of active service represented by this years' retirees is 628!

Naming of the Saints: Erbes and Speiran presented the names of the clergy who have died since the previous annual conference, the names of which are found in question **#48c, 48c, 48d, & 48e**. Bishop Bard prayed.

Information Items: Speiran and Erbes presented questions **18b, 18c, 19a, 19b, 19c, 22, 24a, 24b, 29a, 41, 43a(2), 43b, 43c(2), 49** [amended], **50a(5), 58, 59, 63, 72b, 76a, 79, 80,** and **81** for information, with additions and corrections to the written report.

Motion to adopt the full report: Speiran moved the adoption of the full clergy report. *Motion adopted.*

Speiran announced the next Michigan Annual Conference will be held at the Grand Traverse Resort in Acme, Michigan, from May 28-31, 2020.

Adjournment of the clergy session was called at 4:10 p.m. with a benediction by Bishop Bard.

Ruling of Law Request: Following the adjournment of the clergy session, Peter Harris requested of Bishop David A. Bard a ruling of law on the motion made by Steve Charnley. This request is in accord with Paragraph 2609.6; Bishop Bard has thirty days in which to offer a ruling. All such rulings are referred to the Judicial Council for review. (see note below)

Note: *Bishop Bard's ruling is located at the end of the Daily Proceedings section.*

FIRST DAY – AFTERNOON LAITY SESSION

Thursday, May 30, 2019

The Michigan Annual Conference Laity Session was called to order at 1:30 p.m. by John Wharton and Anne Soles, Conference Co-Lay Leaders.

Bishop Bard welcomed the laity to Annual Conference and introduced Wharton and Soles.

Board of Ordained Ministry: Thom Davenport discussed the role of the Board of Ordained Ministry and the discernment process to ministry. A short video was shown from the Michigan Annual Conference Board of Ordained Ministry Recruitment Committee. Davenport highlighted the programs available to those in the discernment process.

Wharton discussed the purpose and goals of the Laity Session.

Wharton and Soles introduced the District Lay Leaders: John Preston (Northern Skies), Dennis Olin (Northern Waters), Nona Spackman (Mid-Michigan), Bonnie Potter and Mike Schlusler (East Winds), Wynne Hurlburt (Greater Southwest), Max Waagner (Heritage) and Ruby Anderson (Greater Detroit). Laity from each district were invited to stand.

Wharton and Soles introduced the following chairpersons: Mara Marsman (Head Usher), John Walls (United Methodist Men), Linda Darrow (United Methodist Women), and Denny Olin (Grace Patrol).

Wharton and Soles introduced Diane Brown (Legislative Coordinator), Nancy Arnold (Conference Events Planner), Laura Witkowski (Associate Director for Lay Leadership Development), Sue Buxton (Conference Facilitator), and David Dobbs (Conference Treasurer).

Wharton shared the qualifications of the Equalization Members (two-year membership to the local church and four years of active participation).

Wharton discussed the purpose of Annual Conference by sharing the stated purpose statement.

Wharton discussed the different color badges and voting privileges. Soles discussed the need for overflow rooms for visitors and guests.

Wharton discussed the role and responsibilities of the laity at Annual Conference.

Wharton discussed the North Central Jurisdiction structure.

Brown discussed the role of the Legislative Committees and gave instructions on when legislative committees start and where the rooms were located. Brown discussed the voting process on the resolutions as some resolutions are automatically assigned to the entire Annual Conference due to Rules of Order instead of the Legislative Committees. Clarification was given that members to Annual Conference needed to print off the legislative booklet as these would not be provided.

Brown discussed the Consent Calendar and the Legislative Report, which will be available at noon on Friday. Brown discussed the various situations that may occur with the Consent Calendar and legislative items.

Wharton discussed the new process of using electronic devices for voting.

The lay nominees to General Conference were called to the front of the room and introduced themselves to the laity.

Wharton discussed what makes a lay leader bold and effective with examples of key characteristics.

A panel discussion took place with some of the District Lay Leaders. The panel consisted of Soles, Waagner, Thomas, and Schlusler. These District Lay Leaders discussed the training sessions they attended, their individual responsibilities and experiences, and the role of a District Lay Leader in regard to other laity and clergy. Individual laity asked questions of the panel and gave remarks with their experience as a local church lay leader.

Wharton closed the Laity Session in prayer at 3:39 p.m.

FIRST DAY – AFTERNOON SESSION

Thursday, May 30, 2019

Bishop Bard called the business session to order at 4:37 p.m.

Nichea Ver Veer Guy, Chair on the Commission of Annual Conference, welcomed members to Annual Conference and introduced Sam McLellan, Tribal Chairman of the Grand Traverse Band of Ottawa and Chippewa Indians. McLellan welcomed members of Annual Conference to Grand Traverse Resort and offered greetings from the Native American Community. Bishop Bard presented McLellan with a gift.

Bishop Bard directed members to page 101 and 102 of the Program Book where there is information regarding the sins and injustices against the Native American Community.

Organization of Conference: Nichea Ver Veer Guy, Chair of the Commission on Annual Conference, spoke.

Motion: Ver Veer Guy moved that the voting bar of the Michigan Annual Conference, which begins its journey as one conference, be designated as the marked areas inside the outer perimeter of the chairs in the Governor's Hall. The designated areas on the back outer edges will be available to visitors as non-voting areas. **Motion adopted.**

Motion: Ver Veer Guy moved that the episcopal office staff, communications staff, and connectional ministries staff, who are not already members of Annual Conference, special guests, courtesy seating for those assisting persons with Disabilities, and Bishop's wife Julie Bard be given a seat in the bar area. **Motion adopted.**

Motion: Ver Veer Guy moved that the Michigan Annual Conference Agenda as found in the Program Book be accepted, with the authority given to the Commission on Annual Conference Executive Committee in consultation with the Bishop to make necessary adjustments. **Motion adopted.**

Ver Veer Guy discussed the new accomodations available to members. Ver Veer Guy directed members of the Conference to the Safety and Security Guidelines in the Program Book and discussed the process of enacting these guidelines should the need arise.

Rules of Order: Todd Price, MAC Standing Rules Chairperson, reported.

Motion: Price moved that the Plan of Organization as a whole, with the Rules of Order as they appear within the Michigan Conference Legislation Book and changes on the screen, and with the provisions of the 2016 Book of Discipline of The United Methodist Church, be the by-laws of the Michigan Annual Conference. On matters of procedure, when these rules and the Discipline are silent, Robert's Rules of Order Newly Revised version be used at the 2016 General Conference shall be effective. **Motion adopted.**

General Conference Delegation Report: Charles Boayue and Nichea Ver Veer Guy reported. A Michigan delegation General Conference Video was shown. Bishop Bard praised the delegation for their openness with him in the General Conference process as Bishops are not involved in the delegation process. Bishop Bard spoke about the events at General Conference and encouraged members to be open to opposing views. John Boley gave instructions for voting for 2020 General Conference delegates, and introduced the 2020 General Conference delegate nominees.

Historical Reports: Benton Heisler reported and expressed appreciation to various persons who are responsible for making sure the historical reports are done.

Personal Privilege: George Coventree addressed the Camping report, expressing great concern for the current state of our conference camps. He requested the conference leadership to do a full study of our conference camps and report their findings to the 2020 session of the Michigan Annual Conference.

Motion: Benton Heisler moved the acceptance of the 2019 Historical Report. **Motion adopted.**

Legislative Committee: Diane Brown, Legislative Coordinator, gave instructions pertaining to legislation sections.

A prayer for the dinner meal was offered by Kathy Pittenger, Children's Initiatives Coordinator.

Business session was adjourned at 5:56 p.m.

SECOND DAY – MORNING SESSION

Friday, May 31, 2019

Worship at Grand Traverse Resort: The Michigan Annual Conference Worship opened at 8:30 a.m. at Grand Traverse Resort, Acme, Michigan, in the Governor's Hall. The theme was Wisdom and Courage. Laura Witkowski preached the sermon "Ordinary Courage." The worship service was based on Matthew 14:22-33. Worship Leaders were Sandra Bibilomo and Lea Tobar.

Worship ended at 9:30 a.m. A 30 minute was called by the order of the day.

The Corporate Business Session reconvened at 10:00 a.m. by Bishop Bard In the Governor's Hall. He announced that the opening worship special offering totaled $35,329.09. This offering will benefit Grace Children's Hospital & Pediatric Clinic in Haiti (45%), Bishop Judith Craig Children's Village in Liberia (45%), and the Michigan Disaster Relief and Recovery Fund (10%).

United Methodist Foundation: David Bell spoke to the house about what the United Methodist Foundation of Michigan can offer churches.

Motion: Albert Rush moved to change the color of the clergy card provides full voice and voting rights from white another color. **Motion adopted.**

Training session: Leslee Fritz guided the house through a time of electronic voting device training.

Motion: Mary Ivanov moved to suspend the rules to limit additional nominations. **Motion adopted.**

Motion: Mary Ivanov moved to limit nominations from the floor to previous to the first ballot **Motion adopted.**

Point of Privilege: Bishop Bard announced the sudden death of Deb Ferris, wife of Rev. John Ferris. He offered prayer

Motions: The following persons were nominated from the conference floor as General Conference delegate nominees

Laity:
- Bob Hegel moved: Lisa McCormick, Bob McCormick, Bill Gordon, John
- Preston, Michael Cooper, and Howard Burdett
- Pat Tiedt moved: Laurie Dahlman
- Anita Hahn moved: Laity: Lisa Hahn & Isabella Nowak
- Susan Hitts moved: laity Elise Hitts
- Neil Davis moved: laity: Joshua Matthews

Clergy:
- J.D. Landis moved: Charles Boayue
- Gary Step moved: Dirk Elliott
- Tom Anderson moved: Margie Bryce, Cori Conran, Les Longden, Andy Baek, Dan Bowman

General Conference Delegate Ballot #1: John Warton prayed before laity ballot #1. John Hice prayed before clergy ballot #1. Laity and clergy voted for 4 delegates for 2020 General Conference.

Pension and Benefits Resolutions: Don Emmert, Director of Conference Benefits and Human Resources, reported.

Motion: Emmert moved the adoption of R#2019-1, "Authorize CBOPHB to Manage Benefits Claims." **Motion adopted.**

Motion: Emmert moved the adoption of R#2019-2, "Establish the Housing/Rental Allowance for Retired or Clergy on Medical Leave." **Motion adopted**.

Motion: Emmert moved to refer R#2019-3, "2020 Comprehensive Benefit Funding Plan," to the Board of Pensions and Health Benefits. **Motion adopted.**

Motion: Emmert moved the adoption of R#2019-4, "Establish Past Service Rate." **Motion adopted.**

Bishop Bard encouraged everyone present to take advantage of the health screenings being offered during this annual conference session.

John Buxton Award: John Wharton and Anne Soles presented the award to Don Emmert.

Report on Ballot #1

Clergy: Number of ballots cast: 568; valid: 568; needed for election: 285; no election. Candidates with fewer than 10 votes were not listed.

Kennetha Bigham-Tsai:	276
Paul Perez:	265
Joy Barrett:	242

Megan Walther: 193
Matt Hook: 120
Benton Heisler: 113
Tara Sutton: 112
Thomas Anderson: 107
Charles Boayue: 93
Jowl Fitzgerald: 55
Anita Hahn: 71
Elbert Dulworth: 37
Sherri Swanson: 37
Christina Wright: 36
Dirk Elliott: 35
Carter Grimmett: 35
Steven McCoy: 28
Bradley Bartlemay: 27
Margie Bryce: 27
Les Longden: 24
Jill Zundel: 23
Dan Bowman: 21
Andy Baek: 19
John Weiler: 16
Cori Conran: 15
Nancy Lynn: 10

Laity: Number of ballots cast: 833; valid: 833; needed for election: 419; 1 election. Candidates with fewer than 10 votes were not listed.

Elected

Laura Witkowski: **419**

Diane Brown: 372
Nichea VerVeer Guy: 347
Jennifer Peters: 323
Ruby Anderson: 316
Andrew Wayne: 181
Robert Hegel: 116
Lisa Hahn: 114
Jacqueline Euper: 75
Hoon-Yung Hopgood: 68
Anne Soles: 64
Joshua Matthews: 62
Max Waagner: 59
Ruth Sutton: 55
Isabella Nowak: 53
Elise Hitts: 50
Gordon Grigg III: 46
William Tolentino, Jr.: 41
Laurie Dahlman: 40

Steven Lett:	39
George Jonte-Crane:	38
Brenda DuPree:	32
Lisa McCormick:	31
Laurie Kaufman Delagarza:	29
Bob McCormick:	29
John Preston:	20
Howard Burdett:	19
Bill Gordon:	18
Michael Cooper:	16

Announcements were made by Nichea VerVeer Guy. She presented a gift to Jen Peters for all her work for the annual conference.

The business session recessed at 12:00 p.m. for lunch. Sonya Luna, Missionary for Hispanic/Latino Ministry, offered the prayer before the meal.

SECOND DAY – AFTERNOON SESSION

Friday, May 31, 2019

Business session was reconvened at 1:33 by Nichea VerVeer Guy.

Becca Farnum shared a time of teaching.

A Mission Intern video was shown.

Bishop Bard called the business session to order at 2:20 p.m. and offered some prayer concerns. A time of silence was observed and prayer offered in memory of the late Bishop Judith Craig and others.

General Conference Delegate Ballot #2: Anne Soles prayed before laity ballot #2. Margie Crawford prayed before clergy ballot #2. Laity voted for 3 delegates and clergy for 4 delegates for 2020 General Conference.

Legislation Work: Diane Brown, Legislative Coordinator, reported.

Consent Calendar was presented by Brown.
 Motion: Brown moved the acceptance of the Consent Calendar. **Motion adopted.**
   #5- Hire & Support Returning Neighbors
   #6- Redefining What It Means to be "Handicap Accessible"
   #7- Covenant of Ministry Partnership with Liberia Annual Conference
   #8- Reaffirmation of Michigan Conf Support for Camping Ministry
   #10- A Call to Reunite Families Separated at the Border
   #11- Revise Ministry Shares Calculation – Adoption Merger Churches
   #12- Revise Ministry Shares Calculation – Merged Churches

#13- Older Adult Ministries Team
#14- Guidelines for Equitable Compensation Support
#15- 2020 Minimum Salary Schedule

General Conference Resolutions:

GCR#2019-1 - *Be at Peace Among Yourselves*

Bishop Bard ruled that GCR#2019 was out of order as presented in the Program Book.

Amendment: Jeff Nelson moved to strike first "no" and insert, "We, the 2019 Michigan Annual Conference, encourage the Council of Finance and Administration to expend "no", strike "shall be expended" and insert at end of the first paragraph, "As such, we ask that conference members refrain from filing complaints that would result in such harm."

Bishop Bard invited the House to indicate whether or not to consider the Nelson amendment. The House affirmed its support with a 54% yes vote. The matter was then postponed for further review when Judicial Council Decision 1292 was cited.

Report on Ballot #2

Clergy: Number of ballots cast: 504; valid: 504; needed for election: 253; 3 elections. Candidates with fewer than 10 votes were not listed.

Elected

Kennetha Bigham-Tsai:	**294**
Paul Perez:	**289**
Joy Barrett:	**276**

Megan Walther:	239
Benton Heisler:	125
Matt Hook:	115
Tara Sutton:	102
Thomas Anderson:	102
Charles Boayue:	61
Joel Fitzgerald:	24
Anita Hahn:	43
Elbert Dulworth:	37
Sherri Swanson:	22
Carter Grimmett:	20
Dirk Elliott:	18
Christina Wright:	15
Steven McCoy:	14
Jill Zundel:	13
Andy Baek:	12
Margie Bryce:	10
Les Longden:	10
Dan Bowman:	10

Laity: Number of ballots cast: 804; valid: 804; needed for election: 403; no elections. Candidates with fewer than 10 votes were not listed.

DAILY PROCEEDINGS

Diane Brown:	399
Nichea VerVeer Guy:	386
Jennifer Peters:	371
Ruby Anderson:	301
Andrew Wayne:	143
Max Waagner:	140
Lisa Hahn:	93
Robert Hegel:	84
Jacqueline Euper:	48
Hoon-Yung Hopgood:	43
Anne Soles:	40
Joshua Matthews:	40
Ruth Sutton:	39
Gordon Grigg III:	23
Isabella Nowak:	20
Elise Hitts:	19
Steven Lett:	16
William Tolentino, Jr.:	16
Laurie Dahlman:	15
Brenda DuPree:	13
Lisa McCormick:	13
George Jonte-Crane:	12
Bob McCormick:	12

Camp Report: Paula Timm, chairperson of the Michigan Area United Methodist Camping Board, reported. A video was shown. Trish Farrell, Director of Judson Collins, spoke to what is happening at Judson Collins Camp.

A 22 minute break was called at 3:43 p.m. by Bishop Bard.

The business session reconvened at 4:05 p.m. with a Mission Intern video. John Boley shared some announcements.

General Conference Delegate Ballot #3: Naomi Garcia prayed before laity ballot #3. Elizabeth Hill prayed before clergy ballot #3. Laity voted for 3 delegates and clergy for 1 delegate for 2020 General Conference.

Council on Finance and Administration: David Dobbs, Director of Administrative Services and Conference Treasurer reported. Dobbs discussed the work done over the last year with the creation of the new Conference. For 2018, of 736 churches in the conference, 425 churches paid 100% of their Ministry Shares (57.74%); 82 churches paid 0% (11.14%). 15 churches have already paid their full 2019 Ministry Shares! Dobbs presented a certificate to Ron Iris, Conference Statistician, whose term is ending. A new staff position, Ezra Database Specialist and Conference Statistician, has been created. An overview of the 2020 annual conference budget was presented. This budget is lower than both last year's and the previous year's budgets. The budget covers (from highest to lowest cost) conference benevolences, clergy support, administration of the conference, general church administration, world service fund.

Nominations Report: Janet Larner, Chair of the Nominations Committee, presented the report to the Conference.

Nominations: Beth Pelkey and Scott Manning were nominated from the floor to be members of the Nominations Committee. Both persons have agreed to fill the position.

Motion: Larner moved to approve the Nominations Report with the understanding the Committee on Nominations will continue to fill vacancies throughout the year. **Motion adopted**.

Report of Ballot #3

Clergy: Number of ballots cast: 429; valid: 429; needed for election: 215; 1 election. Candidates with fewer than 10 votes were not listed.

Elected:

Megan Walther:	**228**

Benton Heisler:	91
Charles Boayue:	26
Matt Hook:	24
Tara Sutton:	16
Thomas Anderson:	13
Anita Hahn:	11

Laity: Number of ballots cast: 795; valid: 795; needed for election: 399; 3 elections. Candidates with fewer than 10 votes were not listed.

Elected:

Diane Brown:	**488**
Nichea VerVeer Guy:	**431**
Jennifer Peters:	**435**

Ruby Anderson:	327
Andrew Wayne:	150
Max Waagner:	143
Lisa Hahn:	56
Robert Hegel:	49
Jacqueline Euper:	28
Hoon-Yung Hopgood:	17
Anne Soles:	18
Joshua Matthews:	15
Ruth Sutton:	23
Gordon Grigg III:	10
Elise Hitts:	12
William Tolentino, Jr.:	11
Laurie Dahlman:	12

Jurisdictional Conference Delegate Ballot #4: Judy Coffey prayed before laity ballot #4. David Kim prayed before clergy ballot #1. Laity voted for 4 delegates and clergy for 4 delegates for 2020 Jurisdictional Conference.

The business session was closed at 5:05 p.m. by Bishop Bard.

Michigan Annual Conference Corporate Session was called to order at 5:05 p.m. by Brent Webster. The following is a brief summary of action taken by the former West Michigan Board of Trustees:

- Sold the former Christ UMC in Lansing for $300,000.00
- Approved major repairs to the Episcopal Residence in DeWitt
- Completed the sale of the Grand Rapids Conference Center
- Worked with the Chancellor's Office to resolve the property line dispute at the Lake Michigan Camp
- Made repairs to the DCM parsonage in Grand Rapids to get it ready to sell
- Acquired a parsonage in DeWitt for the DCM
- Sold the former Vermontville UMC to the Village of Vermontville
- Transferred the title of the former Christ UMC in Traverse City to the Mosaic Church

Here is a brief summary of their activity of the Detroit Conference Board of Trustees:

- Sold the former Flint Faith UMC
- Sold the former Marquette Laurium UMC
- Sold the former conference parsonage in Fort Gratiot
- A parsonage was purchased for the Benefits Officer in DeWitt

The two boards met as one for the annual risk management review with Church Mutual Insurance Company. The first official board meeting of the Michigan Board of Trustees took place in January. At that meeting we did the following:

- Reviewed the list of conference owned properties that the board is responsible to maintain.
- Heard reports on the properties that are being held by the trustees for sale.
- Reviewed the outstanding work that needs to be done at the Ministry Center and the Ministry Center North. Work that needs to be done might be called "cosmetic" in nature.
- Discussed the process for annual review of all conference owned parsonages (better known as the white glove inspections).

The following is a list of properties being held by the Trustees to sell:

- Lakeville land 25x80 foot strip in the hands of our attorney.
- Kalamazoo: Stockbridge Ave. United Methodist Church

We have sold the following properties:

- The former Tricklewood parsonage that was the home of the West Michigan Conference Director of Connectional Ministries.
- The former Unionville United Methodist Church
- The former Flint Eastwood United Methodist Church.

We have renewed the mortgage for the Ministry Center for another five years. The Trustees are negotiating the disposal of the former Trowbridge United Methodist Church.

<u>Motion</u>: On behalf of the Cabinet, John Boley and Charles Boayue moved that in accordance with paragraph 2549 of the 2016 Book of Discipline, that these 9 churches be closed as of the following dates. **Motion adopted.** Bishop Bard offered prayer.

1. Saginaw: State Street UMC: June 30, 2019
2. Midland: Mapleton UMC: June 30, 2019
3. Flint: Faith UMC: August 15, 2018
4. Dearborn Heights: Stephen's UMC: December 31, 2018
5. Trowbridge UMC: December 31, 2018
6. Litchfield UMC: June 30, 2019
7. Grovenburg UMC: June 30, 2018
8. Quimby UMC: June 30, 2018
9. Alto UMC: December 31, 2018

General Conference 2019 passed two different petitions permitting the disaffiliation of local congregations from the United Methodist Church. Both petitions are now in effect. The petitions provide a process for disaffiliation, including payment of ministry shares and other obligations, before the trust clause can be released. These petitions place a significant responsibility on the Conference Board of Trustees to establish additional policies and procedures for disaffiliation, using guidance and templates from the General Council on Finance and Administration, which have been published and received very recently. Every disaffiliation agreement ultimately must be approved by the Annual Conference. The Michigan Conference Board of Trustees have special meetings coming up in the very near future to perform these responsibilities. Further information about progress and decisions of the Board of Trustees will be disseminated through Conference Communications.

Corporate Session was adjourned at 5:28 p.m.

Business Session was reconvened at 5:28 p.m. by Bishop Bard.

Report on Ballot #4

<u>Clergy</u>: Number of ballots cast: 485; valid: 485; needed for election: 243; no elections. Candidates with fewer than 10 votes were not listed.

Charles Boayue:	218
Joel Fitzgerald:	211
Christina Wright:	206
Benton Heisler:	162
Donald Gotham:	155
Tara Sutton:	136
Matt Hook:	120
Thomas Anderson:	98
Bradley Bartlemay:	86
Anita Hahn:	68
John Weiler:	54
Sherri Swanson:	50
Jill Zundel:	47
Elbert Dulworth:	40

Carter Grimmett:	32
Steven McCoy:	29
Dirk Elliott:	24
Andy Baek:	16
Dan Boman:	16
Margie Bryce:	11
Les Longden:	11
Nancy Lynn:	10

Laity: Number of ballots cast: 814; valid: 814; needed for election: 408; 1 election. Candidates with fewer than 10 votes were not listed.

Elected
Ruby Anderson: **425**

Hoon-Yung Hopgood:	317
Andrew Wayne:	293
Max Waagner:	269
Lisa Hahn:	260
Ruth Sutton:	222
Anne Soles:	220
Brenda DuPree:	166
Robert Hegel:	160
George Jonte-Crane:	124
Laurie Kaufman Delagarza:	122
Jacqueline Euper:	94
Gordon Grigg III:	71
Joshua Matthews:	66
Elise Hitts:	48
Steven Lett:	43
Isabella Nowak:	41
William Tolentino, Jr.:	38
Laurie Dahlman:	31
Bob McCormic:	18
Lisa McCormick:	16
John Preston:	12
Howard Burdett:	10

Jurisdictional Conference Delegate Ballot #5: Diane Brown prayed before laity ballot #5. Neil Davis prayed before clergy ballot #5. Laity voted for 3 delegates and clergy for 4 delegates for 2020 Jurisdictional Conference.

General Conference Legislation

GCP#2019-1 *Add Domestic Violence to the List of Chargable Offenses*
Christina Wright, on behalf of the Board of Ordained Ministry, spoke to the nature of the petition.
GCP#2019-1 was adopted.

Report on Ballot #5

Clergy: Number of ballots cast: 443; valid: 443; needed for election: 223; 3 elections. Candidates with fewer than 10 votes were not listed.

Elected

Charles Boayue:	**276**
Joel Fitzgerald:	**250**
Christina Wright:	**245**

Donald Gotham:	218
Benton Heisler:	158
Tara Sutton:	121
Matt Hook:	75
Bradley Bartlemay:	63
Thomas Anderson:	46
Anita Hahn:	38
John Weiler:	31
Sherri Swanson:	28
Jill Zundel:	20
Carter Grimmett:	17
Elbert Dulworth:	13
Dirk Elliott:	13
Steven McCoy:	12

Laity: Number of ballots cast: 745; valid: 745; needed for election: 373; 1 election. Candidates with fewer than 10 votes were not listed.

Elected

Hoon-Yung Hopgood: 408

Andrew Wayne:	307
Lisa Hahn:	274
Ruth Sutton:	268
Max Waagner:	263
Brenda DuPree:	117
Robert Hegel:	114
Anne Soles:	95
Jacqueline Euper:	60
Gordon Grigg:	24
George Jonte-Crane:	53
Joshua Matthews:	35
Laurie Kaufman Delagarza:	31
Eilise Hitts:	20
Isabella Nowak:	19
Laurie Dahlman:	10
Steven Lett:	10
William Tolentino Jr:	16
Bob McCormick:	13

Announcements were given by Nichea VerVeer Guy.

Business Session was closed at 6:15 p.m. by Lisa Batten, Young Adult Initiatives Coordinator.

THIRD DAY – MORNING SESSION

Saturday, June 1, 2019

Worship at Grand Traverse Resort: The Michigan Annual Conference Worship opened at 8:30 a.m. at Grand Traverse Resort, Acme, Michigan, in the Governor's Hall. The theme was Wisdom, Courage, and love. The Rev. Dr. Jennifer Browne preached the sermon "What's a Nice Girl Like You Doing in a Place Like This?" based on Esther 4:12-14. The liturgist was Darryl Totty.

Worship ended at 9:34 a.m. A 30 minute was called by the order of the day.

A Mission Intern video was shown.

Kristen Grauer, Foreign Service Officer, U.S. Department of State, (and P.K. from the West Michigan Annual Conference) shared a time of teaching at 10:00 a.m., during which she talked about how the skills she learned growing up in the church prepared her for her professional work as a U.S. Diplomat.

The Corporate Business Session reconvened at 11:04 a.m. by Bishop Bard in the Governor's Hall. The Bishop led the House in a moment of prayer in response to yesterday's mass shooting in Virginia.

Withdrawn GC/JC Nominees: Benton Heisler (clergy), Jackie Euper (laity), and Laurie Dahlman (laity) self-withdrew their names from the list of nominees for General/Jurisdictional Conference.

Jurisdictional Conference Delegate Ballot #6: Don Archambeau prayed before ballot #6. Laity voted for 2 delegates and clergy for 1 delegate for 2020 Jurisdictional Conference.

Legislation Work: Diane Brown, Legislation Coordinator, reported.
    GCR#2019-1 - *Be at Peace Among Yourselves*
        Bishop Bard ruled both this petition AND the Nelson amendment out of order. *[Note: see the Friday afternoon daily proceedings for the original petition and amendment.]*

    GCR#2019-2 - *Aspirations for the Michigan Annual Conference.*
        Alex Plum spoke to the nature of the resolution.
        Keith Lenard requested a "rule of law on the 'Aspirations for the Michigan Annual Conference' GCR#2019-2 to know if it violates paragraph 2702a,b,d,e, 304.3, 310.2d, and Judicial Council decisions 1120, 1292, and the understanding of paragraphs 103 and 104 which the resolution disseminates doctrine contrary to Article XXI in light of decision 1185."
        Bishop Bard said he would review GCR#2019-2 and make a ruling within the time allotted by the Book of Discipline. (see note below)
        <u>Motion</u>: Mark Thompson moved to suspend the rules to allow for calling the question. **Motion adopted**.
    GCR#2019-2 adopted.

Note: *Bishop Bard's ruling is located at the end of the Daily Proceedings section.*

Announcements were made by Nichea Ver Veer Guy. John Reynolds introduced Richlain K. Quire, wife of Bishop Samuel J. Quire Jr. of the Liberian Annual Conference. She presented a gift to Bishop Bard from the Liberian Annual Conference.

The business session adjourned at 12:00 p.m. for lunch with a prayer from Darryl Totty.

THIRD DAY – AFTERNOON SESSION

Saturday, June 1, 2019

Celebrating the Journey of Ministry was called together by Laura Speiran, Chair of the Michigan Conference Board of Ordained Ministry, at 1:30 p.m. in the Governor's Hall at the Grand Traverse Resort in Acme, Michigan. She acknowledged and recognized individuals for their work on the Board of Ordained Ministry.

Jeff Nelson read a poem he wrote for the retirees.

Recognition of 2019 Retirees: (673 years of active service)
    Deacon:
        Loretta M. Job
    Local Pastors:
        Dale C. Barber, Carole A. Brown, Nickolas K. Genoff, Donald J. Graham, Rosaline D. Green, Dale A. Hotelling, Donna J. Keyte, Margaret A. Martinez, Ralph A. Posnik, Jr., Cecelia L. Sayer, Calvin "Herb" Wheelock, and Mark E. Zender.
    Honorable Location:
        C. David Hainer and Robert "Mel" Vostry
    Elders:
        Maureen V. Baker, Eric S. Beck, Colon R. Brown, Linda J. Burson, Kathryn S. Cadarette, Michelle A. Gentile, John D. Landis, Douglas E. Mater, John M. Mehl, Robert S. Moore-Jumonville, Rebecca K. Morrison, James C. Noggle, Merlin H. Pratt, Douglas E. Ralston, Stephen E. Rhoades, Terrill M. Schneider, Theodore A. Trudgeon, Edmond G. Taveirne, Barbara E. Welbaum, and Randy J. Whitcomb
    Dillon Burns performed a 'slam' he composed for the new leaders coming into the MAC.

Recognition of:
    License to Preach Graduates and Local Pastors in their first appointment:
        Helen Alford, Frederick J. Bowden, Lawrence J. French, Julie A. Krauss, Zachary McNees, Gregory E. Timmons, Bradley R. Vasey, BJ Ash, Zella M. Daniel, Cari A. Godbehere, William Lass, Carol A. Middel, Douglas A. Tipkein, Charlene Wagner, Ann C. Birchmeier, Robert P. Demyanovich, Douglass Hasse, Duane Lindsey, Victoria I. Prewitt, and Craig H. Van Beek.

Those serving among us from other annual conferences:
>Jonathan Bratt Carle, Jessica Davenport, Laura Feliciano, and Cesar G. Rodriguez

Those to be commissioned as Provisional Deacons:
>Alexander James Plum and LuAnne Marie Stanley Hook

Those to be commissioned as Provisional Elders:
>Nicholas Eric Bonsky, Kimberly Mae Bos, Leslee Jean Fritz, Julia Renee Humenik, Elizabeth Ann Hurd, Kayla Marie Roosa, Amy Norette Triebwasser, Ruth Anne Irish VanderSande, and Joan Elizabeth VanDessel

Jeremy Peters read a poem he wrote.

Recognition of:

Local Pastors who have completed Course of Study School/lAssociate Members:
>Lyle J. Ball, Kathryn Leydorf-Keck, Colleen A. Wierman, Brian K. Johnson, Jaqueline L. Raineri, Todd W. Shafer, Beverley J. Williams, Bruce Malicoat, Walter P. Reichle, and Ronald L. Worley

New Associate Members:
>Anne W. Riegler and Theodore A. Trudgeon

Those to be ordained Deacon:
>Sarah Barrett-Nadeau Alexander and Cora Elizabeth Glass

Those to be ordained Elder
>Joel Thomas Pier Fitzgerald, Jeremiah J. Mannschreck, Eun Sik Poy, Jonathan Earle Reynolds, Scott Leonard Sherrill, and Devin Robert Smith

Kelsey Burns read a poem she composed.

Recognition of:

Chaplains, Extension Ministers, and Deacons in appointments beyond the local church were invited to stand and be recognized.

Celia Peters read a poem she wrote.

School for Pastoral Ministry: Jeanne Garza, dean for the School for Pastoral Ministry, reported. This year's School for Pastoral Ministry will take place August 20-21 at the Kellogg Center in East Lansing. Theme: Healing. Featured speakers will be Rev. Junius B. Dotson and Rev. Kennetha Bigham-Tsai.

Recognition of:

Holder of the Conference Cane: Arthur L. Spafford

Sarah Alexander (deacon) and Eun Sik Poy (Cloud) (elder) symbolically received their respective stoles from Eric Beck and Anne Reigler in recognition as the *new leaders* of our annual conference.

A break was called at 3:20 p.m. by Bishop Bard in the order of the day.

Business session resumed at 4:15 p.m. in the Governor's Hall by Bishop Bard. Bridget Nelson, Youth Ministry Initiatives Coordinator, introduced herself and the youth lay members and briefly explained the nature of her work.

Report on Ballot #6

<u>Clergy</u>: Number of ballots cast: 422; valid: 422; needed for election: 212;
no elections. Candidates with fewer than 10 votes were not listed.

Bradley Bartelmay:	210
Donald Gotham:	67
Tara Sutton:	40
Matt Hook:	35
Anita Hahn:	18
Thomas Anderson:	15

<u>Laity</u>: Number of ballots cast: 790; valid: 790; needed for election: 396;
no election. Candidates with fewer than 10 votes were not listed.

Lisa Hahn:	376
Ruth Sutton:	327
Andrew Wayne:	258
Max Waagner:	211
Brenda DuPree:	62
Anne Soles:	56
Robert Hegel:	45
Gordon Grigg:	26
Joshua Matthews:	20
George Jonte-Crane:	18
Laurie Kaufman Delagarza:	16
Isabella Nowak:	11
William Tolentino, Jr:	10

Jurisdictional Conference Delegate Ballot #7: David Lundquist prayed before laity ballot #7. Jeff Nelson prayed before the clergy ballot #7. Laity voted for 2 delegates and clergy for 1 delegate for 2020 Jurisdictional Conference.

Legislation Work: Diane Brown, Legislation Coordinator, reported.

GCR#2019-3 - *Conduct a Poll*

Amy Mayo-Moyle, chair of Conference Leadership Council, spoke to the nature and purpose of the resolution.

<u>Motion</u>: Jessica Davenport called the question. Tara Sutton prayed. **Motion adopted.**

<u>Vote #1</u>: Shall the House take the poll? 72% (843) yes; 28% (322) no.

<u>Vote #2</u>: Results of the poll: 69% (789) option #1; 31% (350) option #2

Report on Ballot #7

<u>Clergy</u>: Number of ballots cast: 379; valid: 379; needed for election: 191;
1 election. Candidates with fewer than 10 votes were not listed.

<u>Elected</u>
Brad Bartelmay: 258

Donald Gotham:	62
Tara Sutton:	16
Matt Hook:	14

Laity: Number of ballots cast: 738; valid: 738; needed for election: 370; 2 elections. Candidates with fewer than 10 votes were not listed.

Elected:

Lisa Hahn:	**433**
Ruth Sutton:	**401**

Andrew Wayne:	236
Max Waagner:	179
Brenda DuPree:	44
Anne Soles:	38
Robert Hegel:	25
Gordon Grigg III:	14
Joshua Matthews:	11

Alternate Delegate Ballot #8: Mary Violet Comiskey prayed before laity ballot #8. Gary Step prayed before the clergy ballot #8. Laity voted for 2 delegates and clergy for 2 delegates for 2020 Jurisdictional Conference.

Announcements were given by Nichea Ver Veer Guy.

Business session adjourned for dinner at 5:37 p.m. Greg Timmons, Executive Director of Flint Recovery, gave an update on the Flint water crisis and offered a prayer for the meal.

THIRD DAY – EVENING SESSION

Saturday, June 1, 2019

The business session reconvened at 7:00 p.m. by Bishop Bard in the Governor's Hall.

Report on Ballot #8

Clergy: Number of ballots cast: 392; valid: 392; needed for election: 197; 1 election. Candidates with fewer than 10 votes were not listed.

Elected

Sherry Swanson:	**198**

John Weiler:	180
Donald Gotham:	103
Tara Sutton:	85
Matt Hook:	58
Anita Hahn:	40
Elbert Dulworth:	20
Jill Zundel:	17
Steven McCoy:	16
Thomas Anderson:	14
Dirk Elliott:	14

<u>Laity</u>: Number of ballots cast: 422; valid: 422; needed for election: 212; no elections. Candidates with fewer than 10 votes were not listed.

Andrew Wayne:	303
Brenda DuPree:	295
Max Waagner:	281
Gordon Grigg III:	238
Anne Soles:	75
Joshua Matthews:	35
Robert Hegel:	29
George Jonte-Crane:	25
Laurie Kaufman Delagarza:	23
Elise Hitts:	22
Isabella Nowak:	21
Steven Lett:	12
William Tolentino, Jr.:	10
Lisa McCormick:	10

Alternate Delegate Ballot #9: Janell Kebler prayed before laity ballot #8. Christopher Grimes prayed before the clergy ballot #9. Laity voted for 2 delegates and clergy for 1 delegate for 2020 Jurisdictional Conference.

Legislation Work: Diane Brown, Legislative Coordinator, reported:

 R#2019-9 - *Recognize the Unborn Baby*

  Legislative Committee Chair, Andy Wayne, reported on the actions of the legislative committee:

   <u>Amendment #1</u>: SUBSTITUTE MOTION – The Michigan Conference recognizes the unborn baby as potentially fully human from the moment of conception, but agrees with ¶161.k in the *2016 Book of Discipline*.

   Vote on Substitute: Yes: 42, <u>No: 78</u> [substitute failed]

   <u>Amendment #2</u>: Line 26 – replace "fully human from" with "being created by God at"

   Vote on Amendment: Yes: 39, <u>No: 62</u> [amendment failed]

   Final Action: Yes: 43 <u>No: 72</u>

   Consent Calendar: NO

 <u>Vote to consider resolution</u>: House affirmed the consideration, 34% yes 66% no.

 <u>Motion</u>: Don Gotham moved to suspend the rules to limit speeches to 1 for and 1 against. **Motion adopted.**

 Mike Cooper, author of R#2019-9, spoke to rationale of Resolution. Keith Reinhardt prayed.

R#2019-9 was not adopted.

Report on Ballot #9

 <u>Clergy</u>: Number of ballots cast: 275; valid: 275; needed for election: 139; 1 election. Candidates with fewer than 10 votes were not listed.

Elected
Matt Weiler: **163**

Donald Gotham: 55
Tara Sutton: 18
Matt Hook: 13
Anita Hahn: 10

Laity: Number of ballots cast: 422; valid: 422; needed for election: 212; 1 election. Candidates with fewer than 10 votes were not listed.

Elected
Brenda DuPree: **350**

Andrew Wayne: 293
Gordon Grigg III: 232
Max Waagner: 218
Anne Soles: 31
Isabella Nowak: 16
Elise Hitts: 15
Joshua Matthews: 12

Alternate Delegate Ballot #10: D.J. Birkinbine prayed before laity ballot #10. Laity voted for 1 delegate for 2020 Jurisdictional Conference.

Legislation Work: Diane Brown, Legislative Coordinator, reported:
GCP#2019-2 – *Create Central Conference in North America.*
Ray McGee, the author, withdrew the petition from consideration. Bishop Bard ruled it in order.
GCP#2019-3 – *Create Central Conference in North America.*
Ray McGee, the author, withdrew the petition from consideration. Bishop Bard ruled it in order.
GCP#2019-4 - *Create Central Conference in North America.*
Ray McGee, the author, spoke to the nature and purpose of the petition.
Motion: Cookie Kramer called the question. **Motion adopted.**
Tatania Splauding prayed.
GCP#2019-4 was adopted.

Report on Ballot #10

Laity: Number of ballots cast: 661; valid: 661; needed for election: 331; no elections. Candidates with fewer than 10 votes were not listed.

Andrew Wayne: 284
Gordon Grigg III: 263
Max Waagner: 57
Anne Soles: 14

Point of Privilege: Jerry Bukoski prayed for the current plight of farmers who are victims of natural disasters, and for those who are unable to plant due to the fact that an overabundance of rain has kept them from getting into their fields.

DAILY PROCEEDINGS

Alternate Delegate Ballot #11: Bethany Maciejewski prayed before laity ballot #11. Laity voted for 1 delegate for 2020 Jurisdictional Conference.

Point of Privilege: Margie Crawford asked the House to recognize the American Sign Language interpreters who signed during all the business sessions of annual conference.

A 5-minute break was called by Bishop Bard at 8:30 p.m.

The business session reconvened at 8:37 p.m. with some announcements by Bishop Bard.

Report on Ballot #11

Laity: Number of ballots cast: 652; valid: 652 needed for election: 327; no elections. Candidates with fewer than 10 votes were not listed.

Andrew Wayne:	302
Gordon Grigg III:	291
Max Waagner:	22
Anne Soles:	12

Alternate Delegate Ballot #12: Greg Timmons II prayed before laity ballot #11. Laity voted for 1 delegate for 2020 Jurisdictional Conference.

Paul Perez, Associate Director for Mission and Ministry, talked about "EngageMI," the mission engagement program book for the Michigan Annual Conference, and some upcoming events.

Report on Ballot #12

Laity: Number of ballots cast: 602; valid: 602; needed for election: 302; no elections. Candidates with fewer than 10 votes were not listed.

Gordon Grigg III:	286
Andrew Wayne:	285
Max Waagner:	14

Alternate Delegate Ballot #13: Audrey Mangum prayed before laity ballot #13. Laity voted for 1 delegate for 2020 Jurisdictional Conference.

Mark Doyal, Director of Communications, thanked all the UM Communications workers who have worked this annual conference. He talked about the new conference website, the MAC Facebook page, and "mifaith." Gary Henderson, United Methodist Communications Chief Relationship Officer, presented an "epikoinania" award to Mark Doyal for excellence in communication arts. Mark thanked his entire Communications team for all their hard work.

George Howard, Director of Connectional Engagement at the General Board of Global Ministries, greeted the conference and showed a video celebrating the 200th anniversary of the GBGM. He highlighted the work of John Stewart, a missionary in the Wyandotte Indian Mission in upper Sandusky, Ohio. He spoke of the ways the GBGM connects the local church to global mission. He thanked the MAC for our support of and contribution to UMCOR over the past year.

Report on Ballot #13

Laity: Number of ballots cast 598: 598; valid: 300 needed for election; 1 election. Candidates with fewer than 10 votes were not listed.

Elected
Gordon Grigg III: 325

Andrew Wayne: 256

Linda Darrow, President of Michigan Conference United Methodist Women, talked about the upcoming event, "Mission u." A UMW video was shown.

Motion: Ray McGee requested a Declaratory Decision on whether a ceremony celebrating a homosexual union and/or performing a same sex wedding are "distinctively connectional". As paragraph 16, article IV states, "General Conference shall have full legislative power over all matters distinctively connectional" and in utilizing this constitutionally granted authority, prohibits the performance of these ceremonies in paragraph 341.6. In addition, as listed, the performing of these ceremonies as a chargeable offense as found in paragraph 2702.1.b. Therefore, if the performing of these ceremonies is deemed to not be "distinctively connectional", has the General Conference exceeded its constitutionally granted power in prohibiting them? **Motion adopted.**

Dirk Elliot, Director of Congregational Vibrancy, talked about the characteristics of a vibrant congregation, and encouraged churches to make use of our conference vibrancy team: Naomi Garcia, Gary Step, Laura Witkowski, Bridget Nelson, and Jodi Fuller.

Harry Denman Evangelism Award: Dirk Elliot presented the award to Matt Bistayi, Valley Church.

Hess "Doc" Hall, Director of Older Adult Spiritual Formation Programs at Disciples Ministries, brought greetings from the General Board of Discipleship.

One Matters Award: Gary Step, Associate Director for Congregational Vibrancy, presented the One Matters Award to Ryan Wenburg, Hartford UMC.

Julia Droscha, a youth delegate, addressed the House and shared the dreams and hopes of the youth of our conference as it pertains to the future of The United Methodist Church.

Business session adjourned at 10:06 p.m. by Bishop Bard.

FOURTH DAY – MORNING SESSION

Sunday, June 2, 2019

Worship at Grand Traverse Resort: The Michigan Annual Conference Worship opened at 9:00 a.m. at Grand Traverse Resort in Acme, Michigan, in the Governor's Hall. The theme was Wisdom, Heart, and Courage and was based on Matthew 6:31-34 and Hebrew 12:1-2.

CFA Report: David Dobbs, Director of Administrative Services and Treasurer, presented the 2020 MAC budget.

Budget Motion: Dobbs moved to approve the 2020 Michigan Area Conference Budget, including the following items. **Motion adopted.**
1. The amount of $14,700,910 shall be the Conference budget for 2020 which is a decrease of .84% from prior year.
2. The amount of $3,720,000 shall be the Benefits budget for 2020 which is a decrease of 3.12% from prior year.
3. The salary of District Superintendents and Directors shall be $87,394, an increase of 2% and housing allowance will remain at $20,000.
4. The Support Staff wages will increase 2% for those eligible.

Cabinet/Dean's Report: Charles Boayue, Jr., Dean of the Cabinet, reported. See page 330 for full text of Boayue's report.

The historical examinations of candidates into full connectional and ordination as full elder or full deacon. Laura Speiran, chair of the Michigan Annual Conference Board of Ordained Ministry, introduced the historical questions and called the candidates to the stage. Bishop Bard conducted the historic examination of the candidates. John Boley offered prayer for these candidates.

Bishop Bard recognized his Executive Assistant, Deana Nelson.

A 15-minute break was called by the order of the day at 10:15 a.m.

Worship reconvened at 10:36 a.m.

Point of Personal Privilege: Jim Balfour asked for the MAC to send greetings to Thomas Brown, a "product" of the Marquette District, who today is being consecrated as a bishop in the diocese of Maine.

Bishop Bard brought greetings from Bishop Lori Haller of the Iowa Annual Conference.

Bishop Bard recognized and thanked Anita Hahn, Northern Waters District Superintendent, whose term is ending at the end of June. Hahn recognized and thanked her colleagues for their support and guidance during her eight years as District Superintendent.

Bishop Bard introduced Reverend Jodie Flessner as the new Northern Waters District District Superintendent.

Setting of Appointments for the Michigan Annual Conference was led by Bishop Bard with corrections made by John Boley and the District Superintendents. District Lay Leaders welcomed the clergy to their respective district. Ricardo Angarita-Oviedo, Margie Crawford, and Suzanne Hewitt blessed the appointments for the coming year.

Rev. Elizabeth Hill, new Dean of the Cabinet, led the Conference in prayer.

Bishop Bard recognized Nichea Ver Veer Guy, Chair on the Commission for Annual Conference, for her work.

Conference Youth presented Bishop Bard with tools for ministry.

Announcements were given by Nichea Ver Veer Guy.

Motion: Nichea Ver Veer Guy moved that on behalf of the Commission on Annual Conference, the adjournment of this conference at the end of ordination. **Motion adopted.**

The conference adjourned *sine die* at 11:21 a.m. (conference officially adjourned following the Recognition, Commissioning, and Ordination service). Anna Moon prayer before the meal.

FOURTH DAY – AFTERNOON SESSION
SERVICE OF COMMISSIONING AND ORDINATION

Sunday, June 2, 2019

Service of Recognition, Commissioning, and Ordination was held at Grand Traverse Resort and Conference Center at 2:00 p.m., led by Bishop David Bard and members of the MAC Cabinet.

- John Boley introduced the ecumenical guest, the Rev. Katherine A. Finegan, Bishop of the Northern Great Lakes Synod of the Evangelical Lutheran Church in America (ELCA).
- Susan E. Platt, chair, Fellowship of Local Pastors and Associate Members introduced those that have completed the Course of Study.
- Persons to be **commissioned, transferred, and ordained were** presented by the Conference Lay Leaders and the Chairs and Members of the Board of Ordained Ministry. Bishop Bard performed the General Examination.
- Bishop Bard preached the sermon, "Toto, We're Not in Kansas Anymore, or The Oz of Leadership," based on Psalm 78:72 and Colossians 3:12-17.
- An offering was taken with the gifts supporting the Ministerial Education Fund.
- Bishop Bard performed the Examination of all candidates for commissioning, associate members, deacons, and elders. After being ordained, deacons and elders were presented.

- An *invitation to ministry* was extended to anyone who thinks they may be hearing a call to ministry to come forward and be greeted by members of the Boards of Ordained Ministry.
- Bishop Bard concluded the Ordination Service at with a final blessing.

Persons recognized as local pastors who have completed course of study: Lyle J. Ball, Brian K. Johnson, Kathryn L. Leydorf-Keck, Bruce W. Malicoat, Jaqueline L. Raineri, Walter P. Reichle, Todd W. Shafer, Colleen A. Wierman, Beverly J. Williams, and Ronald L. Worley.

Persons commissioned as Provisional Deacons: LuAnne Marie Stanley Hook and Alexander James Plum

Persons commissioned as Provisional Elders: Nicholas Eric Bonsky, Kimberly Mae Bos, Leslee Jean Fritz, Julia Renee Humenik, Elizabeth Ann Hurd, Kayla Marie Roosa, Amy Norette Triebwasser, Ruth Anne Irish VanderSande, and Joan Elizabeth VanDessel.

Person Transferred and commissioned as an Elder: Hillary Thurson-Cox and Taegyu Shin

Persons Recognized as Associate Members: Anne Wallace Riegler and Theodore Arthur Trudgeon

Persons ordained on behalf of Liberia Annual Conference: Lucinda Eastman

Persons ordained Deacons: Sarah Barrett-Nadeau Alexander and Cora Elizabeth Glass

Persons ordained Elders: Joel Thomas Pier Fitzgerald, Jeremiah John Mannschreck, Eun Sik Poy, Jonathan Earle Reynolds, Scott Leonard Sherrill, and Devin Robert Smith, and Lucinda Eastman (ordained an Elder on behalf of the Liberia Annual Conference of The United Methodist Church).

David A. Bard,
Presiding Bishop

Joy A. Barrett,
Conference Secretary

Bishop's Ruling of Law
Affirmation of the Board of Ordained Ministry Process
Bishop David Alan Bard, Michigan Area

On Thursday May 30, 2019 during the clergy session of the Michigan Annual Conference, a resolution was introduced by Rev. Steve Charnley, which in its amended form reads:

We, a majority of the voting members of the 2019 Clergy Session of the Michigan Conference of The United Methodist Church, stand in solidarity with our Board of Ordained Ministry in their lament regarding the decisions of the 2019 Special Session of General Conference. We affirm their intention to do their sacred work of examining and ultimately recommending candidates to commissioning and ordination who demonstrate gifts and graces for vital ministry, without regard to their sexual orientation or gender identity. With our Board, we affirm and honor that God call all to healthy human relationships and that these relationships are critical to effective ministry.

The motion carried by hand-written ballot: 298 "yes" and 125 "no."

This resolution reflects a statement issued by the Board of Ordained Ministry on March 13, 2019, the text of which follows:

In honor of the ministry we share and in lament regarding the decisions of the 2019 Special Session of General Conference of The United Methodist Church, we, the Michigan Conference Board of Ordained Ministry, are compelled to reaffirm how we fulfill our discernment responsibilities since our inception as a Conference board. It is the central call of the Conference Board of Ordained Ministry to credential persons to licensed and ordained ministry within the denomination. As that gathered body within the Michigan Conference, we take seriously our call to listen for the movement of the Holy Spirit in calling and equipping people for ministry. We affirm that the Spirit moves in the lives of all people, calling some to professional ministry, including LGBTQIA+ individuals. As such, we reaffirm our Spirit-led intention to hear the call, readiness, and effectiveness of candidates for ministry without regard to sexual orientation or gender identity. We will continue to recommend candidates for commissioning and ordination who demonstrate gifts and graces for vital ministry, trusting that the clergy session will recognize the integrity of the Board's work and approve them for ministry. Likewise, we affirm the Bishop's authority to consecrate, commission, and ordain all qualified candidates for ministry, celebrating with the Conference the gifts they bring and the ways in which God has called them to be in ministry with us.

We honor that God calls all to healthy human relationships. Such vital relationships are critical to effective ministry. It is the Board's work to assess the wholeness and holiness of those relationships. Because we are called to love God and each other fully, we will not engage in or tolerate the harassment of others by asking questions not directly related to the practice of effective ministry.

As the Michigan Conference Board of Ordained Ministry, our compass has been, and will continue to be, the indicators given by the Holy Spirit of authentic call, of evidenced readiness, and well-demonstrated effectiveness in the work of ministry. We offer this public statement in the certain hope that our siblings in professional ministry will celebrate with us the task we share.

As the clergy session was closing, the Rev. Peter Harris asked for a ruling of law, later submitted in writing: **Is the resolution affirmed at our clergy session and the Board of Ordained Ministry statement upon which it is based, in direct violation of Judicial Council rulings, particularly ruling 1344?**

Ruling by Bishop Bard

Judicial Council decision 1344 clearly states that "The Board of Ordained Ministry is mandated... to examine all applicants as to their fitness for the ordained ministry, and make full inquiry as to the fitness of the candidate..... The Board's examination must include all paragraphs relevant to the election of pastoral ministry, including those provisions set forth in paragraphs that deal with issues of race, gender, sexuality, integrity, indebtedness, etc."

The challenge in ruling on the statement approved at clergy session is to ascertain both its intent and its effect. This is made more difficult by the ambiguity in the language. When the resolution affirms examining and recommending candidates "without regard to their sexual orientation or gender identity" does it intend that issues of behavior and practice will not be addressed? This resolution could be read that way. Its intent, therefore, would be to circumvent the *Disciplinary* requirements and its effect would be to encourage an incomplete examination of candidates. On the other hand, the resolution begins with a lament. Its intent could be primarily an expression of disappointment and a resolution to treat persons fairly, particularly LGBTQ persons. In this case its precise effects cannot be determined hypothetically, but only in the subsequent actions of the Board over which the clergy session retains rights and obligations to inquire about the depth and breadth of the Board's examination.

A bishop is to "uphold the discipline and order of the Church," and simultaneously "be the shepherd of the whole flock" (¶403.1e and f). Particularly in this time of heightened emotion, anxiety and tension within The United Methodist Church, there is something to be said for leaning into the pastoral while upholding discipline and order, offering some space for expressiveness while being clear about the parameters imposed by The Book of Discipline.

Therefore, I rule that the resolution approved at the clergy session, based on the statement issued by the Board of Ordained Ministry, is not a direct violation of Judicial Council decisions. However, this in no way gives permission to the Board of Ordained Ministry to ignore its "duty to conduct a careful and thorough examination and investigation, not only in terms of depth but also of breadth of scope" (JCD 1344), nor absolves the clergy session of its right and obligation to inquire of the Board whether or not it has, in point of fact, engaged its work thoroughly. The bishop also must ascertain and discern whether or not persons recommended by the Board and approved by the clergy session are duly eligible for commissioning and ordination.

Bishop's Ruling of Law
Aspirations for the Michigan Annual Conference
Bishop David Alan Bard, Michigan Area

On Saturday, June 1, 2019 during the plenary session of the Michigan Annual Conference, the following resolution, duly submitted to the conference in accord with our rules, was debated and voted upon:

Faced with the uncertainty after the 2019 Special Session of General Conference, United Methodists in Michigan look to Jesus' model of gracious welcome and evangelical inclusion to guide us. As we look forward to how the global church restructures and new Methodisms emerge, the Michigan Annual Conference aspires to live into an expression of Methodism that:

- *includes LGBTQIA people in the full life and membership of The United Methodist Church;*
- *creates time and space for reflection, forgiveness, and reconciliation among our siblings who believe differently as we move into the future;*
- *organizes itself in faithful, just and equitable structures that resist oppression, while acknowledging and undoing its complicity in systems of racial and economic inequity; and*
- *spends our time and financial resources on mission for the sake of the Gospel of Jesus Christ, especially with vulnerable communities in Michigan and around the world, and not on church trials, investigations, or bringing charges against clergy based on sexual orientation, gender identity, and/or gender expression or related actions.*

The vote was to approve the resolution: 819 in favor and 377 opposed.

Rev. Keith Lenard was later recognized and made the following request for a ruling of law: *I would like a Rule of Law on the 'Aspirations for the Michigan Annual Conference' (GCR 2019-2) to know if it violates Paragraphs 2702 a,b,d,e, 304.3, 310.2d and Judicial Council Decisions 1120, 1292, and the understanding of paragraphs 103 and 104 which this resolution disseminates doctrine contrary to Article XXI in light of Decision 1185, Wesley's Notes on the New Testament: Romans 1:27-32, 1 Corinthians 6:9, 1 Timothy 1:8-10, and 2 Peter 2:7, John Wesley's sermon "A Caution Against Bigotry," which states "These monsters might almost make us overlook the works of the devil that are wrought in our own country. But alas! we cannot open our eyes ever here, without seeing them on every side. Is it a small proof of his power, that common swearers, drunkards, whoremongerers, adulterers, thieves [sic], robbers, sodomites, murderers, are still found in every part of our land?" This alludes to "Do no harm" in the General rules which links to this sermon "by avoiding evil of every kind especially that which is most seriously practiced." This resolution disseminates by aspirational cause a false doctrine and is contrary to United Methodism, historical Methodism since its beginning, and the first General Conference of 1808.*

Ruling by Bishop Bard

Judicial Council decision 886 clearly states that annual conferences "may not legally negate, ignore, or violate provisions of the *Discipline.* However, the Judicial Council in decision 1052 stated that "Annual Conferences are free to express their ideal and opinions as long as they do not attempt to negate, ignore, or contradict the *Discipline*," and in decision 1120 affirmed that "an annual conference may adopt a resolution on human sexuality that is aspirational in nature." In subsequent decisions (e.g. 1340), the Judicial Council has continued to affirm that annual conferences may adopt resolutions that are aspirational in nature.

Aspirational statements are future-oriented. They look to and express a yearning for something new or different. By their very nature, then, aspirational statements may express a hope for a United Methodist Church different from the current church as defined by *The Discipline*. As long as aspirational statements are forward-looking, and do not encourage an abrogation of the current *Discipline* as a means to creating something new, citing *Disciplinary* paragraphs as an argument against the adoption of such statements seems contradictory. To adopt a future-oriented statement looking toward a United Methodist Church that includes LGBTQIA people in its full life and membership and in which resources are not spent on church trials, investigations, or bringing charges against clergy based on sexual orientation, gender identity, and/or gender expression or related actions in ways perhaps currently precluded by *The Discipline*, that does not in any way negate or encourage the negation of the current *Discipline*, is the very essence of an aspirational statement. Paragraphs 2702.1 a, b, d; 304.3; 310.2d are not violated by the adoption of this resolution. As the nature of this adopted resolution is aspirational, there is no violation of Judicial Council decisions 1120 or 1292.

Does this resolution disseminate doctrines contrary to the established standard of doctrine of The United Methodist Church (¶2702.1e)? Having argued that aspirational resolutions, by their very nature, look toward a different future, one might simply contend that the same principle applies to doctrinal statements. Furthermore, "While the Church considers its doctrinal affirmations a central feature of its identity and restricts official changes to a constitutional process, the Church encourages serious reflection across the theological spectrum" (¶105). However, one can conceive of an aspirational resolution whose intent and language are so contrary to core Wesleyan theological convictions, as understood in ¶103 and ¶104, that ¶2702.1e could be appropriately invoked. The resolution, "Aspirations for the Michigan Annual Conference" is not such a resolution.

Article XXI, cited in the request for a ruling of law, is not germane to the resolution. This section of our Articles of Religion is clearly intended to distinguish churches in the Wesleyan movement from those Christian traditions in which abstinence from marriage is a requirement for all clergypersons.

In reading the sections of Wesley's <u>Explanatory Notes on the New Testament</u> cited in the request for a ruling of law, one does not see Wesley highlight for special attention words or phrases related to human sexuality.

Furthermore, citing individual texts from Wesley's <u>Explanatory Notes</u> or <u>Standard Sermons</u> in the manner of the request for a ruling of law, raises significant issues. In Wesley's <u>Explanatory Notes</u>, for example, Wesley, in commenting on Revelation 13 writes, "This beast is the Romish papacy, as it came to a point six hundred years since, stands now, and will for some time longer." We would not consider such a statement part of our core doctrinal convictions. In the sermon referenced in the request for a ruling of law, "A Caution Against Bigotry," just prior to the section cited in the request, Wesley offers a portrait of "the natural religion of the Creeks, Cherokees, Chickasaws, and all other Indians bordering on our southern settlements" that includes torture and the killing of old and young. We would not consider such statements part of our core doctrinal convictions.

To be sure, "Wesley's *Sermons* and *Notes* were understood specifically to be included in our present existing established standards of doctrine" (¶103). However, these documents are not doctrinal statements in the way the Articles of Religion or Confession of Faith are doctrinal statements. Wesley himself "was not a systematic theologian" (Robert W. Burtner and Robert E. Chiles, <u>John Wesley's Theology</u>, 8). "He seems never to have felt the impulse to produce anything resembling a comprehensive exposition of his theological ideas" (Albert C. Outler, <u>John Wesley</u>, 27). The use of Wesley's *Sermons* and *Notes* as doctrinal standards, then, might best be in continuing to define and refine distinctive Wesleyan emphases in our United Methodist theology (¶102) and to use these as living sources for engaging in our theological task as encouraged in ¶105.

In conclusion, the resolution, "Aspirations for the Michigan Annual Conference" is not a violation of ¶2702.1e.

— MAC Photos

CORPORATE SESSION 2019

May 31, 2019

This report is a combination of the West Michigan Board of Trustees for the last seven months of 2018, the Detroit Board of Trustees for the same period, and the Michigan Board of Trustees for the first five months of 2019.

The three boards have had and continue to have outstanding members who faithfully serve the conference and seek to care for conference owned property whether that be the property of a closed church, a conference owned parsonage, or one of many sites used by the conference to conduct business and ministry.

The following is a brief summary of action taken by the former West Michigan Board of Trustees:

1. Sold the former Christ UMC in Lansing for $300,000.00
2. Approved major repairs to the Episcopal Residence in DeWitt
3. Completed the sale of the Grand Rapids Conference Center
4. Worked with the Chancellor's Office to resolve the property line dispute at the Lake Michigan Camp
5. Made repairs to the DCM parsonage in Grand Rapids to get it ready to sell
6. Acquired a parsonage in DeWitt for the DCM
7. Sold the former Vermontville UMC to the Village of Vermontville
8. Transferred the title of the former Christ UMC in Traverse City to the Mosaic Church

The Detroit Conference Board of Trustees was just as busy. Here is a brief summary of their activity:

1. Sold the former Flint Faith UMC
2. Sold the former Marquette Laurium UMC
3. Sold the former conference parsonage in Fort Gratiot
4. A parsonage was purchased for the Benefits Officer in DeWitt

The two boards met as one for the annual risk management review with Church Mutual Insurance Company.

The first official board meeting of the Michigan Board of Trustees took place in January. At that meeting we did the following:

1. Reviewed the list of conference owned properties that the board is responsible to maintain.
2. Heard reports on the properties that are being held by the trustees for sale.
3. Reviewed the outstanding work that needs to be done at the Ministry Center and the Ministry Center North. Work that needs to be done might be called "cosmetic" in nature.
4. Discussed the process for annual review of all conference owned parsonages (better known as the white glove inspections).

The following is a list of properties being held by the trustees to sell:

1. Lakeville land 25x80 foot strip in the hands of our attorney
2. Kalamazoo Stockbridge Ave UMC

We have sold the following properties:

1. The former Tricklewood parsonage that was the home of the West Michigan Conference Director of Connectional Ministries.
2. The former Unionville UMC
3. The former Flint Eastwood UMC

We have renewed the mortgage for the Ministry Center for another five years.

The trustees are negotiating the disposal of the former Trowbridge UMC.

Motion for the Closing of Churches at the 2019 Corporate Session
May 31, 2019

Clergy Assistant to the Bishop: Rev. John Boley:

"Very Truly, I tell you, unless a grain of wheat falls into the earth and dies, it remains just a single grain; but if it dies, it bears much fruit." John 12:24

Sisters and brothers in Christ, the churches that have been named here today have provided vital ministry to our annual conferences. They have provided nurture to members, ministry to their communities and have fostered ecumenical and interfaith relationships. They have made disciples of Jesus Christ for the transformation of the world.

However, over time, these churches have declined in worship attendance, giving, and leadership engagement and have been affected by other situations that impact their ability to do ministry in The United Methodist Church. After conducting ministry assessments, the Bishop, the Cabinet and the applicable District Board of Church Location and Building have determined that these churches no longer serve the purpose for which they were organized. The members may transfer their membership to other United Methodist churches, and the appropriate bodies are handling disposition of church buildings and other assets. These churches have left a legacy in ministry. We trust that even in death and transition, the seeds that they have planted will bear fruit for the kingdom of God.

Dean of the Cabinet: Rev. Charles Boayue:

We are closing nine churches in the Michigan Conference this year. As always, it is with both a sense of joy and sorrow – sorrow for the ending of a congregation's ministry, but joy for all the ministry of the past and the way in which lives have been touched.

(Charles presents the short blurb about each of these congregations):

1. Saginaw: State Street UMC – Central Bay District
2. Midland: Mapleton – Central Bay District.
3. Flint: Faith UMC – East Winds District
4. Dearborn Heights Stephens UMC – Greater Detroit District
5. Trowbridge UMC – Greater Southwest District
6. Litchfield UMC – Heritage District
7. Grovenburg UMC – Mid-Michigan District
8. Quimby UMC – Mid-Michigan District
9. Alto UMC – Midwest District

Dean of the Cabinet: Rev. Charles Boayue

Mr. Chair (Rev. Brent Webster), to the 2019 Michigan Annual Conference Corporate session, in accordance with paragraph 2549 of the 2016 Book of Discipline, the Cabinet moves that these 9 churches be closed as of the following dates:

1. Saginaw: State Street UMC – June 30, 2019
2. Midland: Mapleton – June 30, 2019
3. Flint Faith UMC – August 15, 2018
4. Dearborn Heights Stephens UMC – December 31, 2018
5. Trowbridge UMC – December 31, 2018
6. Litchfield UMC – June 30, 2019
7. Grovenburg UMC – June 30, 2018
8. Quimby UMC – June 30, 2018
9. Alto UMC – December 31, 2018

Rev. Brent L. Webster, Trustee Chair:

This motion is prayerfully before the Michigan Annual Conference body. If you would affirm the closure of these churches on the dates indicated, please raise your placards.

If you would not affirm this motion, same sign.

The motion is approved.

Bishop Bard offers a closing prayer.

As most of you know, General Conference 2019 passed two different petitions permitting the disaffiliation of local congregations from the United Methodist Church. Both petitions are now in effect. The petitions provide a process for disaffiliation, including payment of ministry shares and other obligations, before the trust clause can be released. These petitions place a significant responsibility on the Conference Board of Trustees to establish additional policies and procedures for disaffiliation, using guidance and templates from the General Council on Finance and Administration, which have been published and received very recently. Every disaffiliation agreement ultimately must be approved by the Annual Conference.

This is to inform you that the Conference Board of Trustees is on it. We have special meetings coming up in the very near future to perform these responsibilities. Further information about progress and decisions of the Board of Trustees will be disseminated through Conference Communications.

Is there any other business to be brought before the corporate session?

I will entertain a motion to adjourn. We are adjourned.

Rev. Brent L. Webster, Chairperson
Michigan Conference Board of Trustees

CERTIFICATE OF ORDINATION AND COMMISSIONING

This is to certify that on Sunday, June 2, 2019
at Grand Traverse Conference Center, Acme, Michigan

I commissioned as Provisional Deacons of The United Methodist Church:
LuAnne M. Stanley Hook   Alexander J. Plum

I commissioned as Provisional Elders of The United Methodist Church:
Nicholas E. Bonsky   Kimberly M. Bos   Leslee J. Fritz
Julia R. Humenik   Elizabeth A. Hurd   Kayla M. Roosa
Amy N. Triebwasser   Ruth A. Irish VanderSande   Joan E. Van Dessel

I received by transfer and commissioned as Provisional Elders
of The United Methodist Church:
Hillary Thurston-Cox   Taegyu Shin

I ordained as Deacons of The United Methodist Church:
Sarah B. Alexander   Cora E. Glass

I ordained as Elders of The United Methodist Church:
Joel T. Fitzgerald   Jeremiah J. Mannschreck   Eun Sik Poy
Jonathan E. Reynolds   Scott L. Sherrill   Devin R. Smith

I ordained as an Elder on behalf of the Liberia Conference
of The United Methodist Church:
Lucinda Eastman

David A Bard

Bishop David A. Bard
Michigan Conference of The United Methodist Church

All Commission (Left to Right)
Julia Humenik, Joan VanDessel, Kimberley Bos, Nicolas Bonsky,
Amy Triebwasser, Elizabeth Hurd, Ruth Anne VanderSande, Kayla Roosa,
Leslee Fritz, Alexander Plum, LuAnne Hook.

ORDINANDS PHOTOS

All Ordination (Left to Right)
Cora Glass, Jonathan Reynolds, Eun Sik Poy, Devin Smith,
Jeremiah Mannschreck, Scott Sherrill, Joel Fitzgerald, Sarah Alexander.

— MAC Photos

Associate Members ("Recognized" Left to Right)
Anne Riegler, Theodore Trudgeon.

Commissioned Deacons (Left to Right)
Alexander Plum, LuAnne Hook.

— MAC Photos

ORDINANDS PHOTOS

Commission Elders (Left to Right)
Julia Humenik, Joan VanDessel, Kimberley Bos, Nicolas Bonsky,
Amy Triebwasser, Elizabeth Hurd, Ruth Anne VanderSande,
Kayla Roosa, Leslee Fritz.

Course of Study ("Recognized as Finished" Left to Right)
Brian Johnson, Jaqueline Raineri, Colleen Wierman, Todd Shafer.

— MAC Photos

Ordained Deacon (Left to Right)
Cora Glass, Sarah Alexander.

Ordained Elders (Left to Right)
Jonathan Reynolds, Eun Sik Poy, Devin Smith, Jeremiah Mannschreck, Scott Sherrill, Joel Fitzgerald.

Transferred (Left to Right)
Hillary Thurston-Cox, Taegyu Shin.

— MAC Photos

THE UNITED METHODIST CHURCH
THE BUSINESS OF THE ANNUAL CONFERENCE

The Minutes of the **Michigan Annual Conference**
Held in Traverse City, Michigan, May 30 – June 2, 2019
Bishop David Alan Bard, Presiding
Date When Organized January 1, 2019 – First Session

PART I ORGANIZATION AND GENERAL BUSINESS

1. Who are elected for the quadrennium (¶¶603.7, 619)?

   Secretary?   **Joy Barrett**
   - Mailing Address: 128 Park St., Chelsea, MI 48118
   - Telephone: 734-475-8119 ext. 18
   - Email: secretary@michiganumc.org

   Statistician?   **Pamela Stewart**
   - Mailing Address: 1161 E Clark Rd Suite 212, DeWitt 48820
   - Telephone: 517-347-4030
   - Email: pstewart@michiganumc.org

   Treasurer?   **David Dobbs**
   - Mailing Address: 1161 East Clark Rd Suite 212; DeWitt, MI 48820
   - Telephone: 517-347-4030
   - Email: ddobbs@michiganumc.org

2. Is the Annual Conference incorporated (¶603.1)? Yes

3. Bonding and auditing:
   What officers handling funds of the conference have been bonded, and in what amounts (¶¶618, 2511)?

Name	Position	Amount Bonded
David Dobbs	Conference Treasurer	$3,000,000.00
	Officers, Directors & Trustees	$2,000,000.00

   Have the books of said officers or persons been audited (¶¶617, 2511)? (See report, page 219 of Journal.)

4. What agencies have been appointed or elected?
   a) Who have been elected chairpersons for the mandated structures listed?

Structure	Chairperson	Mailing Address	Phone No.	Email
Council on Finance & Administration (¶611)	Brad Bartelmay	57 W Tenth St Holland, MI 49423	616-396-5205	bradbartelmay @gmail.com
Board of Ordained Ministry (¶635)	Laura Speiran	660 Waldon Rd, Clarkston MI 48346	248-625-1611	lauraspeiran@ gmail.com
Board of Pensions (¶639)	Steven Buck	6446 Prairie Dunes Dr Grand Blanc 48439	810-444-7089	sjbuck@comcast.net
Board of Trustees of the Annual Conference (¶2512)	Jim LeBaron	13401 Peacock Rd Laingsburg 48848	517-641-8042	jlebaronllc@aol.com
Committee on Episcopacy (¶637)	John Wharton	7409 Steeplechase Ct Saline MI 48176	734-429-5258	jwharton@comcast.net
Administrative Review Committee (¶636)	John Boley	1011 Northcrest Rd Okemos MI 48906	517-347-4003	jboley@michiganumc. org

b) Indicate the name of the agency (or agencies) and the chairperson(s) in your annual conference which is (are) responsible for the functions related to each of the following general church agencies (¶610.1):

General Agency	Conference Agency	Chairperson	Mailing Address	Phone No.	Email
General Board of Church and Society	Division on Church and Society	George Covintree	29835 Rock Creek Rd Southfield MI 48076	248-905-3448	georgecovintree@me.com
General Board of Discipleship	Conference Leadership Council	Amy Mayo-Moyle	30450 Farmington Rd Farmington Hills MI 48334	248-626-3620	amayomoyle@yahoo.com
General Board of Global Ministries	Board of Global Ministries	Brenda Dupree	8165 Holcomb Clarkston MI 48348	248-202-4746	bkdupree@comcast.net
General Board of Ordained Ministry	Board of Ordained Ministry	Laura Speiran	660 Waldon Rd Clarkston MI 48346	248-625-1611	lauraspeiran@gmail.com
Higher Education and Campus Ministry	Division of Higher Education and Campus Ministry	Jeff Williams	220 Church St Wayland 49348	269-944-9231	jeffwrev@gmail.com
General Commission on Archives and History	Commission on Archives and History	Mary Whitman	9155 Greenway Ct N222 Saginaw MI 48609	989-781-9223	librawhitman@yahoo.com
General Commission on Christian Unity and Interreligious Concerns	Division on Christian Unity & Interreligious Relationships	Rodney Gasaway	36522 Ann Arbor Trail Livonia MI 48150	743-578-6256	rodney@newburgumc.org
General Commission on Religion and Race	Division on Religion and Race	George Covintree	29835 Rock Creek Rd Southfield MI 48076	248-905-3448	georgecovintree@me.com
General Commission on the Status and Role of Women	Division on the Status and Role of Women	George Covintree	29835 Rock Creek Rd Southfield MI 48076	248-905-3448	georgecovintree@me.com
United Methodist Communications	Director of Communications	Mark Doyal	1011 Northcrest Rd Lansing MI 48906	517.347.4030	mdoyal@michiganumc.org

c) Indicate the conference agencies and chairpersons which have responsibilities for the following functions:

General Agency	Name of Agency	Chairperson	Mailing Address	Phone No.	Email
Criminal Justice and Mercy Ministries ¶657?	Board of Justice	George Covintree	29835 Rock Creek Rd Southfield MI 48076	248-905-3448	georgecovintree@me.com
Disability Concerns (¶653)?	Division on Disability Concerns	George Covintree	29835 Rock Creek Rd Southfield MI 48076	248-905-3448	georgecovintree@me.com

Equitable Compensation (¶625)?	Commission on Equitable Compensation	Nancy Patera	6232 Sunset Beach Lake Odessa 48849	616-902-6973	nancypatera@ me.com
Laity (¶631)?	Board of Laity	Anne Soles	PO Box 467 Pentwater MI 49449	231-869-4059	Annesoles @charter.net
		John Wharton	7409 Steeplechase Ct Saline MI 48176	734-429-5258	jwharton@com cast.net
Native American Ministry (¶654)?	Committee on Native American Ministry	Ronald Todd Williamson	1146 Nicolson St, Wayland 49348	616-262-0358	revrtwilliamson @gmail.com
Small Membership Church (¶645)?	Division on Small Member-ship Church	Dirk Elliott	1161 East Clark Rd Suite 212 DeWitt MI 48820	517-347-4030	delliott@ michiganumc. org

d) Indicate the president or equivalent for the following organizations.

Organization	Name of Agency	Chairperson	Mailing Address	Phone No.	Email
Conference United Methodist Women (¶647)	Conference United Methodist Women	Linda Darrow	232 N Cooley St Mt. Pleasant MI 48858	989-763-8750	darrowlinda@ gmail.com
Conference United Methodist Men (¶648)	Conference United Methodist Men	Don Archambeau	28270 Elmira St Livonia 48150	734-422-2227	Donarcham beau@gmail. com
Conference Council on Youth Ministry (¶649)	Youth Ministry Development Coordinator	TBD			
	Board of Young People's Ministry, chair	Christina White	225 W Court St Flint MI 48502	810-235-4651	pastorchristym. b@gmail.com
Conference Council on Young Adult Ministry (¶650)?	Young Adult Initiatives Coordinator	Lisa Batten	1011 Northcrest Rd Lansing MI 48906	517-347-4030	lbatten@mich igan.org
	Board of Young People's Ministry, chair	Christina White	225 W Court St Flint MI 48502	810-235-4651	pastorchristym. b@gmail.com

e) Have persons been elected for the following district boards and committees? Answer yes or no.
(1) District Boards of Church Location & Building (¶2518.2)? Yes
(2) Committees on District Superintendency (¶669)? Yes
(3) District Committees on Ordained Ministry (¶666)? Yes

f) What other councils, boards, commissions, or committees have been appointed or elected in the annual conference?

Structure	Chairperson	Mailing Address	Phone	Email
Conference Leadership Council	Amy Mayo-Moyle	30450 Farmington Rd Farmington Hills MI 48334	248-626-3620	amayomoyle@ yahoo.com
Protection Policy Team	Judy Herriff	5651 Bunker Rd Eaton Rapids MI 48827		jherriff@gmail. com

Michigan Area UM Camping Board	Joel Wortley	2307 W Maple Rapids Rd St Johns MI 48879	517-881-6466	Executivedirector @umcamping.org
Conference Disaster Response Team	Dan O'Malley, Coordinator	9356 Enchantment Dr, Alto MI 49302	616-868-6193	dano.omalley@ gmail.com
	Robert Miller, Chair	1401 Palmer Street Plymouth MI 48170	810-623-0985	pastorbobmiller@ comcast.net
Children's Initiative Coordinator	Kathy Pittenger	1011 Northcrest Rd Lansing MI 48906	517-347-4030	kpittenger@mich iganumc.org
Committee on Hispanic/Latino Ministries	Sonya Luna	1011 Northcrest Rd Lansing MI 48906	517-347-4030	sluna@michigan umc.org
Committee on Asian-American Ministry	Jung Eun Yum	315 W Larkin St PO Box 466 Midland MI 48640	989-835-6797	jeyum@hotmail. com
Committee on African-American Ministry	Jan Brown	1100 E Samaria Rd Erie MI 48133	313-303-1533	januk99@gmail. com
	Simmie Proctor	73486 8th Ave South Haven MI 49090	269-637-6053	simmiepr@ hotmailcom
Comte on Native American Ministry	Ronald Todd Williamson	1146 Nicolson St, Wayland 49348	616-262-0358	revrtwilliamson@ gmail.com
Board of Congregational Life	Sherry Parker-Lewis, chair	400 E Grand River Ave Brighton MI 48116	810-229-8561	sherry@brighton fumc.org
Congregational Vibrancy, Division	Dirk Elliott	1161 E Clark Rd Ste 212 DeWitt MI 48820	517-347-4030	delliott@michi ganumc.org
Committee on Human Resources	Ellen Zienert	517 W Shiawassee Lansing MI 48933	517-515-9500	ekzienert@ gmail.com
Annual Conference Session Commission	Nichea Ver Veer Guy	125 Baynton NE Grand Rapids MI 49503	616-456-7168	orangecelt00 @aol.com
Rules of Order Committee	Todd Price	9921 Seltzer Livonia MI 48150	734-834-4030	pencollector@ me.com
Conf Nominating Committee (CNC)	Janet Larner	175 North Dr Shepherd MI 48883	989-828-5866	jmlarner@ gmail.com
Committee on Journal	Joy Barrett	128 Park St Chelsea MI 48118	734-475-8819	jbarrett@chelsea umc.org
United Methodist Foundation of MI	Ransom Leppink	PO Box 365 Lakeview MI 48850	989-352-6430	leppinks@ hotmail.com

5. Have the secretaries, treasurers, and statisticians kept and reported their respective data in accordance to the prescribed formats? (¶606.8)? Yes

6. What is the report of the statistician? (See report, page 689 of Journal.)

7. What is the report of the treasurer? (See report, page 689 of Journal.)

8. What are the reports of the district superintendents as to the status of the work within their districts? (See report, page 330 of Journal.)

9. What is the schedule of minimum base compensation for clergy for the ensuing year (¶¶342, 625.3)? (See legislation, page 326 of Journal.)

10. What amount has been apportioned to the pastoral charges within the conference to be raised for the support of the district superintendents for the ensuing year (¶614.1a)? $2,126,446

11. a) What amount has been apportioned to the pastoral charges within the conference to be raised for the support of the pension and benefit programs of the conference for the ensuing year (¶¶614.1d, 1507)? $3,720,000

     b) What are the apportionments to this conference for the ensuing year?
         (1) For the World Service Fund? $1,918,093
         (2) For the Ministerial Education Fund? $ 647,843
         (3) For the Black College Fund? $ 258,419
         (4) For the Africa University Fund? $ 57,833
         (5) For the Episcopal Fund? $ 568,025
         (6) For the General Administration Fund? $ 227,758
         (7) For the Interdenominational Cooperation Fund? $ 50,666

12. What are the findings of the annual audit of the conference treasuries? (See report, page 219 of Journal)

13. Conference and district lay leaders (¶¶603.9, 660):
     a) Conference co-lay leaders:
         Anne Soles, 217 Old State Rd, PO Bo 467, Pentwater MI 49449   annesoles@charter.net
         John Wharton, 7409 Steeplechase Ct, Saline MI 48176   jwharton@comcast.net

     b) Associate conference lay leaders: NA

     c) District and associate district lay leaders:

CENTRAL BAY:	TBD	
EAST WINDS	Michael Schlusler	mschlusler@gmail.com
Associate:	Bonnie Potter	mpotter60@charter.net
GREATER DETROIT:	Ruby Anderson	rbydandrs@aol.com
Associate:	Kenneth Dowell	ken@dowell.ws
GREATER SOUTHWEST:	Wynne Hurlbut	wynne_hurlbut@frontier.com
HERITAGE:	Max Waagner	max.waagner@gmail.com
MIDWEST:	TBD	
MID-MICHIGAN:	Nona Spackman	nspackman12@gmail.com
NORTHERN WATERS:	Denny Olin	dennyolin@gmail.com
NORTHERN SKIES:	John Preston	johncarterpreston@gmail.com

14. List local churches which have been:
     a) Organized or continued as New Church Starts (¶259,1-4, continue to list congregations here until listed in questions 14.c, d, or e)

GCFA #	Church Name	District	Mailing Address	Phone Number	Date
004793	Madison Heights: Vietnamese Ministry	Greater Detroit	500 W Gardenia Ave Madison Hts, MI 48071	?	07/01/2016
005992	Detroit: French	Greater Detroit	1803 E 14 Mile Rd Birmingham, MI 48009	?	07/01/2018
582123	Traverse City: Mosaic	Northern Waters	1249 Three Mile Rd S Traverse City, MI 49696-8307	231-946-3048	07/01/2017
581061	Detroit: Centro Familiar Cristiano	Greater Detroit	1270 Waterman St. Detroit, MI 48209	734-482-8374	02/01/2016
582635	Grand Rapids: Restoration	Midwest	2730 56th St SW S Wyoming, MI 49418	616.589.4793	01/01/2018

b)   Organized or continued as Mission Congregations (¶259,1-4, continue to list congregations here until listed in questions 14.c, d, or e)

GCFA #	Church Name	District	Mailing Address	Phone Number	Date
582761	Harrison: The Gathering	Central Bay	PO Box 86, Harrison, MI 48625-0086	989-539-1445	07/01/2004
597886	Mt Pleasant: Chippewa Indian	Central Bay	3490 S Leaton Rd, Mt Pleasant, MI 48858	517-773-0414	?

c)   Organized or continued Satellite congregations (¶247.22, continue to list here until listed in questions 14.a, c, d, or e)

GCFA #	Church Name	Parent Church	District	Mailing Address	Date Launched
582282	Bay City: Grace - East Campus	Bay City: Grace 580897	Central Bay	4267 2 Mile Rd, Bay City, MI 48706-2332	07/01/2016
589330	Saginaw: Kochville	Midland: Aldersgate 589330	Central Bay	6030 Bay Rd, Saginaw, MI 48604-8703	09/01/2018
582293	Birmingham: First - Berkley 1St Campus	Birmingham: First 581881	Greater Detroit	1589 W Maple, Birmingham, MI 48009-4607	07/01/2015
582316	Detroit: Cass Cmnty - World Bldg Campus	Detroit: Cass Cmnty 582145	Greater Detroit	3901 Cass Ave, Detroit, MI 48201-1721	07/01/2017
582065	Redford: Aldersgate - Brightmoore Campus	Redford: Aldersgate 580501	Greater Detroit	10000 Beech Daly Rd, Redford, MI 48239	07/02/2012
582362	Troy: Korean – Troy Hope Campus	Troy: Korean 582830	Greater Detroit	42693 Dequindre, Troy, MI 48085-3960	07/01/2008
581527	Brighton: First - Whitmore Lake: Wesley Campus	Brighton: First 580306	Heritage	400 E Grand River, Brighton, MI 48116	01/01/2019
582453	Friendship - Shelby Twp Campus	Canton: Friendship 580476	Heritage	1240 Beck Rd, Canton, MI 48187-4811	01/01/2017
582338	Ann Arbor: First - Green Wood Campus	Ann Arbor: First 580226	Heritage	120 S State St, Ann Arbor, MI 48104-1606	06/07/1990
599806	Dewitt: Redeemer - St Johns: First Campus	Dewitt: Redeemer 598868	Mid-Michigan	13980 Schavey Rd, Dewitt, MI 48820-9013	07/01/2018
582373	Lansing: Sycamore Crk - Potterville Campus	Lansing: Sycamore Crk 583971	Mid-Michigan	1919 S Pennsylvania Ave, Lansing, MI 48910-3251	07/01/2017
005888	Grand Rapids: Cornerstone - Heritage Hill Campus	Grand Rapids: Cornerstone 599134	Midwest	1675 84th St SE, Caledonia, MI 49316-7939	07/01/2016
582418	Grand Rapids: Cornerstone - S Wyoming Campus	Grand Rapids: Cornerstone 599134	Midwest	1675 84th St SE, Caledonia, MI 49316-7939	07/01/2016
582087	Marquette: Hope - Connection Center Campus	Marquette: Hope 005753	Northern Skies	111 E Ridge, Marquette, MI 49855-4208	07/01/2016

| 582258 | Marquette: Hope - Skandia Campus | Marquette: Hope 005753 | Northern Skies | 111 E Ridge, Marquette, MI 49855-4208 | 07/01/2016 |
| 582384 | Free Soil-Fountain - Fountain Campus | Free Soil – Fountain 600600 | Northern Waters | PO BOX 173, Free Soil, MI 49411-0173 | 06/01/2013 |

d)   Organized as Chartered (¶259.5-10, continue to list here until listed in questions 14.d or e)

GCFA #	Church Name	District	Mailing Address	Phone Number	Date Chartered
0					

e)   Merged (¶¶2546, 2547)

    (1)   United Methodist with United Methodist

District	GCFA #	Name of First Church	GCFA #	Name of Second Church	GCFA #	Name of Merged Church	Date Merged
East Winds	587843	Port Huron: Washington Avenue	587808	Port Huron: Gratiot Park	587808	Port Huron: Gratiot Park	01/01/2019
Central Bay	589545	Poseyville	589740	Midland: Aldersgate	589330	Midland: Aldersgate	08/01/2018
Central Bay	589886	Sterling	589864	Standish: Community	589864	Standish: Beacon of Light	04/01/2019

    (2)   Other mergers (indicate denomination)

District	GCFA #	Name of First Church	GCFA #	Name of Second Church	GCFA #	Name of Merged Church	Date Merged
0							

f)   Discontinued or abandoned (¶¶229, 341.2, 2549) (State which for each church listed.)

    (1)   New Church Start (¶259.2,3)

GCFA #	Church Name	District	Location	Date Closed
0				

    (2)   Mission Congregation (¶259.1a)

GCFA #	Church Name	District	Location	Date Closed
0				

    (3)   Satellite Congregation

GCFA #	Church Name	District	Location	Date Closed
582327	ARENAC CNTY: CHRIST - Trinity Campus	Saginaw Bay	Twining	1-30-2018
582395	MILLVILLE - Village Church Campus	Mid-Michigan	Dansville, MI	10/31/2017

    (4)   Chartered Local Church (¶259.5)

GCFA #	Church Name	District	Location	Date Closed
581380	Dearborn Hts: Stephen's	Greater Detroit	Dearborn Heights	12/31/2018
581983	Dearborn Hts: Warren Valley	Greater Detroit	Dearborn Heights	06/30/2018
602962	Otsego: Trowbridge	Greater Southwest	Otsego	12/31/2018
589784	Saginaw: State Street	Central Bay	Saginaw	06/30/2019
589272	Mapleton	Central Bay	Freeland	06/30/2019
596244	Litchfield	Heritage	Litchfield	06/30/2019

599258	Quimby	Mid-Michigan	Hastings	6/30/2018
598607	Alto	Midwest	Alto	12/31/2018
595728	Grovenburg	Mid-Michigan	Holt	6/30/2018
584122	Flint: Faith	East Winds	Flint	08/15/2018
585968	Laurium	Northern Skies	Laurium	6/30/2018

g)   Relocated and to what address

GCFA #	Church Name	District	Mailing Address	Physical Location	Date Relocated
0					

h)   Changed name of church? (Example: "First" to "Trinity")

GCFA #	Former Name	New Name	Address	District
589864	STANDISH: Community	STANDISH: Beacon of Light	201 S Forest St Standish, MI48658-9528	Central Bay

i)   Transferred this year into this conference from other United Methodist conference(s) and with what membership (¶¶41, 260)?

GCFA #	Name	Membership	Sending Conference
0			

j)   What cooperative parishes in structured forms have been established? (¶206)

GCFA #	Parish Name	Charge Name	Church Name	District
586768	Bad Axe Coop Parish		Bad Axe, Minden City, Ubley	East Winds
586781	Brown City Coop Parish		Brown City, Omard	East Winds
587444	Marysville Coop Parish		Marysville, Central Lakeport	East Winds
588005	Sandusky Coop Parish		Sandusky, Deckerville	East Winds
N/A	God's Country Coop Parish:		Grand Marais, Germfask, McMillan, Newberry, Engadine, Paradise, Hulbert: Tahquamenon	Northern Skies
N/A	Flat River Coop Parish		Turk Lake, Belding, Ionia: Easton	Midwest
599464	Maple River Parish		Lowe, Maple Rapids	Mid-Michigan
586713	Water's Edge Coop Parish		New Baltimore, Algonac Trinity	Greater Detroit

k)   What other changes have taken place in the list of churches?

15.   Are there Ecumenical Shared Ministries in the conference? (¶207, 208)

a)   Federated church (Membership is denomination specific.)

GCFA #	Name	District	Other Denomination(s)
601012	Church of the Straits	Northern Skies	Presb.

b)   Union Church (Membership Unified.)

GCFA #	Name	District	Other Denomination(s)
596404	Okemos Community Church	Mid-Michigan	Congregational
599214	E. Lansing: Peoples Church	Mid-Michigan	Am. Bapt., U.C.C., Presb.

| 599726 | Ovid United Church | Mid-Michigan | U.C.C. |
| 587724 | Port Austin UPC | Central Bay | UPC |

c) Merged Church (Membership separate, church related only to one denomination.)

GCFA #	Name	District	Other Denomination(s)
0			

d) Yoked Parish (Different denomination churches share pastor)

GCFA #	Name	District	Other Denomination(s)
0			

16. What changes have been made in district and charge lines (please list the GCFA # beside church name)?

Moved from Circuit to single Station:

600303 ~ BEAR LAKE
600314 ~ ARCADIA
586085 ~ Mohawk-Ahmeek
586917 ~ SHABBONA
587808 ~ PORT HURON: GRATIOT PK
586735 ~ OMO: ZION
588062 ~ WASHINGTON
597534 ~ BLANCHARD-PINE RIVER

601991 ~ KENDALL
601570 ~ BRIDGMAN: FAITH
589625 ~ ROSE CITY: TRINITY
589900 ~ WHITTEMORE
588506 ~ ALGER
584884 ~ OWOSSO: BURTON
597501 ~ GREENVILLE: FIRST
598243 ~ SHEPHERD

Moved to new multiple point Charge: (GCNo. for Lead Church)

586974 ~ Saginaw: Swan Valley, LaPorte, Hemlock, Nelson
588107 ~ Yale, Cole, Melvin
583960 ~ Flint: Bristol, Burton: Christ
584634 ~ Lake Fenton, Lennon, Duffield
587626 ~ Oxford, Thomas
602858 ~ Hinchman, Scottdale
581128 ~ Britton: Grace, Macon
596244 ~ Jonesville, Napoleon

584485 ~ Henderson, Chapin, Owosso: Trinity
582910 ~ Turk Lake, Belding, Ionia: Easton
586484 ~ White Pine: Community, Bergland, Ewen
586063 ~ Menominee: First, Stephenson
585822 ~ Ironwood: Wesley, Wakefield
585684 ~ Houghton: Grace, Painesdale: A. Paine Memorial
585467 ~ Calumet, Lake Linden

Moved to new multiple station Circuit:

597534 ~ BLANCHARD-PINE RIVER and 598243 ~ SHEPHERD
601980 ~ Gobles and 601375 ~ Almena

PART II – PERTAINING TO ORDAINED AND LICENSED CLERGY

(Note: A (**v**) notation following a question in this section signifies that the action or election requires a majority vote of the clergy session of the annual conference. If an action requires more than a simple majority, the notation (**v 2/3**) or (**v 3/4**) signifies that a two-thirds or three-fourths majority vote is required. Indicate credential of persons in Part II: FD, FE, PD, PE, and AM when requested.)

17. Are all the clergy members of the conference blameless in their life and official administration (¶604.4 and ¶605.7, The Book of Discipline of The United Methodist Church, 2016)

    We take very seriously the call to moral excellence in the lives of clergy, knowing that only by the grace of God can any of us be blameless in our life and official administration. All persons stand in need of the grace of God and of the love and forgiveness of the Christian community.

    In signing below and submitting this statement to the Board of Ordained Ministry, we the district superintendents, attest that all the clergy members of the conference are blameless in their life and official administration, or are involved in supervisory or complaint processes, and in signing below the Bishop David A. Bard attests the same for the district superintendents.

    Herein signed, Rev. Dwayne Bagley, Rev. Dr. Charles S. G. Boayue, Jr., Rev. Dr. Margie Crawford, Rev. Dr. Jerome DeVine, Rev. Anita Hahn, Rev. Scott A. Harmon, Rev. John H. Hice, Rev. Elizabeth A. Hill, Rev. David I. Kim, Bishop David A. Bard

18. Who constitute:
    a) The Administrative Review Committee (¶636)? (**v**)

Clergy Name, Year Appointed, District	Clergy Alternate Name, Year Appointed, District
Gerald F. Hagans (Ret) ('18) [MW]	Ellen A. Brubaker (Ret) ('18) [MW]
Gloria Haynes (Ret) ('19) [CB]	Catherine J. Miles (Ret) ('19) [EW]
George H. Lewis (FE) ('19) [HD]	
Thomas P. Macaulay (Ret) ('19) [EW]	

    b) The Conference Relations Committee of the Board of Ordained Ministry (¶635.1d)?
    2019–2020

Name	Position
Ms. Ruby Anderson (Lay)	
Ms. Laurie Dahlman (Lay)	
Rev. Mark Erbes (FE)	CRC Chair, BOM Vice-Chair
Rev. Anthony Hood (FE)	
Rev. Bill Johnson (RE)	Transfers
Rev. Laura Speiran (FD)	BOM Chair
Rev. Sherri Swanson (FE)	
Rev. Amy Terhune (FE)	

    c) The Committee on Investigation (¶2703)? **2019–2020**

Clergy Name, Year Appointed, District	Professing Member Name, Year Appointed, District
1. Richard W. Blunt ('18) (MM)	1. Paula Hines ('18) (MW)
2. Cathi M. Huvaere ('18) (EW)	2. Wynne Hurlbut ('18) (GS)
3. Patrick England ('19) (GS)	3. Craig Schroeder ('18) (GS)
4. Philip Tousley ('19) (EW)	4. Minnie Armstrong ('19) (EW)
5. Brian West ('19) (MM)	5. Murray Davis ('19) (GD)
	6. Michael Schlusler ('19) (EW)

Clergy Alternate Name, Year Appointed, District	Professing Member Alternate Name, Year Appointed, District
1. Glenn C. Litchfield ('18) (GS)	1. Louelle Burke ('18) (NW)
2. Julie A. Liske ('18) (MW)	2. Max Waagner ('18) (HD)
	3. Laura De La Garza ('19) (NS)
	4. Linda Polter ('19) (HD)
	5. Fred Gray ('19) (CB)

19. Who are the certified candidates (¶ ¶ 310, 313, 314)?
(NOTE: Everyone who wants to become an LP, PE, or PD must first become a certified candidate.)
a)   Who are currently certified as candidates for ordained or licensed ministry?

Name	District	Date Certified
Helen Alford	Central Bay	05.14.2018
Ray Francis	Central Bay	01.15.2019
Sean M. Griffin	Central Bay	04.14.2016
Douglas Hasse	Central Bay	10.16.2017
Carla Long	Central Bay	03.14.2016
Scott W. Marsh	Central Bay	05.25.2016
Duane Thomas	Central Bay	04.20.2017
Kelsey Burns	East Winds	04.25.2017
Frederick J. Bowden	East Winds	12.27.2017
Julia A. Cramer	East Winds	05.17.2019
Michelle Ettinger	East Winds	03.21.2019
Stacey Highfield	East Winds	03.21.2019
Julie Krauss	East Winds	04.18.2018
Duane Lindsey	East Winds	02.15.2018
Carol Ann Middel	East Winds	04.18.2018
Gregory Timmons	East Winds	02.15.2018
Joyce Vanderlip	East Winds	04.20.2017
Rachael Dunlap	Greater Detroit	06.19.2015
Steffani Glygoroff	Greater Detroit	12.13.2018
La Tonya Johnson	Greater Detroit	04.02.2017
Nadine Johnson	Greater Detroit	05.18.2017
Michelle King	Greater Detroit	12.18.2015
Sean LaGuire	Greater Detroit	02.21.2019
Audrey Mangum	Greater Detroit	05.17.2018
George Marck	Greater Detroit	05.09.2019
Robert Prud'homme	Greater Detroit	05.18.2017
Lawrence J. French	Greater Southwest	02.27.2018
Katelyn Hiscock	Greater Southwest	10.09.2018
Ashlei K. Horn	Greater Southwest	04.17.2018
Brian Lightner	Greater Southwest	04.09.2019
Dawn Oldenburg	Greater Southwest	04.09.2019
Paul C. Reissmann	Greater Southwest	05.25.2016
Douglas A. Tipken	Greater Southwest	04.17.2018
Craig H. VanBeek	Greater Southwest	04.17.2018
Jenaba R. Duymovic Waggy	Greater Southwest	08.09.2016

Beatrice S. Alghali	Heritage	05.18.2017
Jonathon Brenner	Heritage	12.01.2016
Elisabeth Danielsons	Heritage	05.09.2016
Crystal Fox	Heritage	11.15.2018
Denise Kasischke	Heritage	01.31.2019
David Korlapati	Heritage	11.15.2018
Reeve Segrest	Heritage	01.31.2019
Shonagh Taruza	Heritage	06.07.2018
Bradley R. Vasey	Heritage	12.07.2017
Paula Vergowven	Heritage	05.02.2019
Sarah Wheatley	Heritage	03.22.2018
Diana Carpenter	Mid-Michigan	02.18.2016
Zella Daniel	Mid-Michigan	04.20.2017
Cari A. Godbehere	Mid-Michigan	02.26.2018
Haley Hansen	Mid-Michigan	06.17.2019
Charlene Wagner	Mid-Michigan	02.15.2018
Angela M. Lovegrove	Midwest	08.10.2017
Zachary McNees	Midwest	02.28.2019
BJ Ash	Northern Skies	05.14.2018
Victoria (Vicky) I. Prewitt	Northern Skies	05.14.2018
Erica N. Thomas	Northern Skies	05.14.2018
Cynthia Montague	Northern Waters	04.25.2019
Troy Trombley	Northern Waters	09.20.2018

b)   Who have had their candidacy for ordained or licensed ministry accepted by a District Committee on Ordained Ministry in another annual conference? (Include name of accepting conference.)

Name	Receiving Conference	Date Originally Certified	Date Accepted by District in Other Conf.
Jessica M. Davenport	Michigan Conference	Illinois Great River Conf-2012	08.14.2018 (GSD)
Stephanie Norton	Michigan Conference	Alabama-West FL Conf-2015 Great Plains Conf-2016	04.09.2019 GSD)
Taylor Pryde	Western North Carolina Conference	12.08.2016 (WMC)	4.18.2019 (EWD)

c)   Who have been discontinued as certified candidates for licensed or ordained ministry?

Name	District	Date Certified	Date Disc'd
Allen Bower	Greater Detroit	06.18.2015	05.09.2019
Raymond Johnson	Central Bay	02.08.2018	06.30.2018
Joshua J. Lee	Greater Southwest	08.15.2017	04.09.2019

(Note: Once a candidate is appointed as FL or PL, they are no longer listed as a certified candidate (except the first year they are appointed when they would need to be listed in 19 and in 20 or 21).

BUSINESS OF THE A/C

Students appointed as Local Pastors (¶318.3) are the only people who are allowed to be listed as a candidate in one conference while being listed as an LP in a different conference. ¶318.3 stipulates that students appointed as local pastors can serve in either a full or part-time capacity).

20. Who have completed the studies for the license as a local pastor, are approved, but are not now appointed? (¶315 —Indicate for each person the year the license was approved.): (3/4v)

Name	District	Year License Approved
Jack E. Balgenorth	Greater Southwest	2014
Ann Birchmeier	Heritage	2019
John M. Brooks	Greater Southwest	2015 (8 COS)
Kyle J. Bucholz	Heritage	2015
Scott A. Clark	East Winds	2013
Everett L. Harpole	Greater Southwest	2015 (6 COS)
Rochelle J. Hunter	Greater Detroit	2013
David Kang	Greater Detroit	2018
Trevor J. McDermont	Greater Southwest	2016 (13 COS)
Julius Nagy	Heritage	2014 (4 COS)
Noreen S. Shafer	Northern Waters	2010 (7 COS)
Charmaine Shay	East Winds	2015 (4 COS)
Ronald D. Slager	Greater Southwest	*2015
Daniel J. Wallington	Central Bay	2015 (0 COS)
Donna Zuhlke	Greater Detroit	2014 (6 COS)

21. Who are approved and appointed as: (Indicate for each person the first year the license was awarded. Indicate what progress each has made in the course of study or the name of the seminary in which they are enrolled. Indicate with an asterisk those who have completed the five-year course of study or the M.Div. (¶319.4)? PLEASE NOTE: Persons on this list must receive an episcopal appointment. (3/4 v)

a) Full-time local pastors? (¶318.1)

Name	First Year License Awarded	Number of Courses of Study Completed or Year Completed
CENTRAL BAY		
Joseph L. Beavan	2010	*2017
Martin T. Cobb	1999	*M.Div. MTSO
Carmen Cook	2014	13 COS
Robert Demyanovich	2019	0 COS
Cindy Gibbs	2008	*2014
Jon W. Gougeon	2002	*2010
Mark A. Harriman	2014	7 COS
Nathan Jeffords	2012	M.Div. ATS
Brenda K. Klacking	2000	*2005
Scott W. Marsh	2019	M.Div. G-ETS
Heather Nowak	2017	M.Div. MTSO
Penny L. Parkin	2014	12 COS
Patrick R. Poag	2004	*M.Div. ATS
Robert G. Richards	1993	*2010
Melene Wilsey	2017	5 COS
Donald L. Wojewski	2004	*2012

EAST WINDS

Lisa Jo Clark	2000	*2012
Curtis B. Clarke	2011	*2018
Billie Lou Gillespie	2000	*2007
Maurice R. Horne, Sr. *(Ext. Ministry)*	1999	*2010
Esther A. Irish	2008	*2017
Brian K. Johnson	2011	*2018
Betty Kay Leitelt	2006	*2017
Duane, A. Lindsey	2019	0 COS
Tommy McDoniel	2010	*M.Div. G-ETS
Penelope R. Nunn	2014	9 COS
Patrick D. Robbins	1998	*2008
Christopher G.L. Titus	2010	M.Div. UTS
Thomas Waller	2015	6 COS
Karen B. Williams	2002	*2012

GREATER DETROIT

Se Jin Bae	2015	*M.Div. RT
Anthony Ballah	2016	M.Div. G-ETS
Jonathan Combs	2009	*2016
Patricia Gandarilla	2012	*2012 Basic and Advanced COS
Markey Gray	2016	*M.Div. PTS
Christopher Grimes	2014	*M.Div. G-ETS
Marvin Herman	2007	*2015
Carolyn A. Jones	2016	5 COS
Keith Lenard, Jr.	2014	*M.Div. ATS
Marshall Murphy	2011	*M.Div. G-ETS
Jacqueline Raineri	2012	*2018
Albert Rush	2012	17 COS

GREATER SOUTHWEST

Lisa M. Batten	2009	MA G-ETS *(¶ 344.1.d)*
Ellen D. Bierlein	2018	0 COS
Brian R. Bunch	1993	*M.Div. ESR
Daniel R. Colthorp	2018	15 COS
Jessica M. Davenport	2012	*M.Div. WTS
Richard J. Foster	2012	11 COS
Lawrence J. French	2018	0 COS
Samuel C. Gordy	2012	9 COS
Wayne E. McKenney	1995	*M.Div. AMBS
John D. Messner	2008	*Completed COS
Stephanie Norton	2019	M.Div. ATS
James Palaszeski	2014	5 COS
Kellas D. Penny III	2013	*M.Div. ATS
Margaret Mallory Sandlin	2017	*M.Div. G-ETS
David E. Small	*1982*	*Retired, HL (¶ 358.2)*
Scott B. Smith	2013	M.Div. UTS
Robert L. Snodgrass II	2014	5 COS
Crystal C. Thomas	2013	M.Div. UTS
Douglas A. Tipken	2019	0 COS

Craig H. VanBeek	2019	0 COS
Matthew J. West	2018	0 COS
Beverley J. Williams	2012	*2018
Janet S. Wilson	2018	0 COS

HERITAGE

Carol Abbott Freeland	2014	4 COS
Nicolas R. Berlanga	2013	5 COS
Ian Boley	2016	*M.Div.
Deborah S. Cole	2015	14 COS
Michael C. Desotell	2014	M.Div. G-ETS
Robert W. Dister	2012	*2018
Robert Fuchs	2016	8 COS
Donna Galloway	2014	8 COS
Suzanne L. Hutchison	2014	12 COS
Todd Jones	2016	15 COS
Mark E. Mitchell	1995	*M.Div. AMBS
Patricia A. Pebley	2012	*M.Div. UTS
Nathan Starkey	2014	13 COS
Katherine Waggoner	2011	*M.Div.

MID-MICHIGAN

Mark D. Aupperlee	2018	4 COS
Terri L. Bentley	2002	*Completed COS
Theresa A. Fairbanks	2016	1 COS
Suzanne K. Goodwin	2019	MA G-ETS (¶ 309.2)
Scott Herald	2016	7 COS
Karen L. Jensen-Kinney	2015	12 COS
Martin A. Johnston	2016	4 COS
Peggy A. Katzmark	2007	*2013
Matthew D. Kreh	2015	12 COS
Ian S. McDonald	2012	*2018
Kimberly S. Metzer	2017	6 COS
Heather L. Nolen	2017	M.Div. G-ETS
Steven C. Place	2011	13 COS
Jon L. Pohl	2006	*Completed COS

MIDWEST

Daniel L. Barkholz	2016	12 COS
Carleton R. Black	2011	16 COS
Jeffrey J. Bowman	1995	*Completed COS
Terri L. Cummins	2010	*2016
Gerald A. Erskine	2014	5 COS
Julie E. Fairchild	2015	*M.Div. MTSO
Laura Feliciano	2009	*M.Div. VUDS
Alejandro D. Fernandez	2015	10 COS
Thomas C. Fifer	2018	*M.Div. DDS
Kevin K. Guetschow	2010	*2016
Zachary D. McNees	2019	0 COS
Daniel D. Nguyen	2012	M.Div. G-ETS
Nancy J. Patera	2007	*Completed COS

Michael J. Ramsey	2010	18 COS
Marcus V. Schmidt	2016	4 COS
Anthony C. Shumaker	2002	*Completed COS
Edwin D. Snook	2002	M.Div. UTS
Donna J. Sperry	2014	M.Div. MTSO
Ronald "Todd" Williamson	2017	2 COS

NORTHERN SKIES

Timothy Bashore	2013	7 COS
Eric M. Falker	2014	M.Div. UTS
Nelson Hall	1999	*2018
John P. Murray	2015	*M.Div. ATS
Matthew Osborne	2012	*2018
Victoria Prewitt	2019	0 COS
Nathan Reed	2011	*2018
Walter P. Reichle	2012	*2018
Irene R. White	1996	*2004

NORTHERN WATERS

Sean T. Barton	2017	15 COS
Bradley E. Bunn	2017	17 COS
Susan E. Hitts	2017	0 COS
Richard Hodgeson	2013	7 COS
Lisa Kelley	2013	18 COS
Michael P. Kelley	2004	*2012
Bryan K. Kilpatrick	2014	*M.Div. G-ETS
Scott R. Loomis	2012	18 COS
Joshua M. Manning	2014	9 COS
Zelphia Mobley	2015	*M.Div. CST
Melody Lane Olin	2006	*Completed COS
Craig A. Pahl	2000	*Completed COS
Daniel J.W. Phillips	2015	*M.Div. G-ETS
Todd W. Shafer	2010	*2018
Jeremy J. Wicks	2011	15 COS
Colleen A. Wierman	2011	*2018

b)　Part-time local pastors? (¶318.2) (fraction of full-time in one-quarter increments)

Name	First Year License Awarded	Fraction of Full Time to be Served	Number of Courses of Study Completed or Year Completed
CENTRAL BAY			
Helen Alford	2019	1/2	0 COS
William C. Cleland	2014	3/4	5 COS
Doug Hasse	2019	1/4	0 COS
Eric Johnson	2007	1/2	14 COS
Cheryl L. Mancier	2007	1/2	18 COS
Clifford Radtke	2006	3/4	*2012
Keith Reinhardt	2014	1/4	5 COS

EAST WINDS

Anika Bailey	2018	1/2	M.Div. MTSO
Nancy J. Bitterling	2000	1/4	Retired ¶ 320.5, *M.Div. G-ETS
Frederick J. Bowden	2019	1/4	0 COS
Leah Caron	2016	1/4	M.Div. UTS
Donald R. Derby	2001	1/4	Retired ¶ 320.5, *Completed COS
Jerry D. Griggs	1998	3/4	*2010
Patricia A. Hoppenworth	2002	3/4	*2007
James E. Huff, Jr.	2005	1/2	*2007
Ronald G. Hutchinson	1998	3/4	*2011
Julie A. Krauss	2019	1/2	0 COS
Shelly A. Long	2016	1/2	M.Div. UTS
Bruce Malicoat	2006	3/4	*2018
Carol Ann Middel	2019	1/2	0 COS
Eric J. Miller	2014	1/2	6 COS
Ronald Rouse	2013	1/2	17 COS
Ellen O. Schippert	2007	3/4	*2012
Gregory E. Timmons	2019	1/2	0 COS
Brian Willingham	2014	3/4	3 COS

GREATER DETROIT

Mary Ellen Chapman	2002	1/2	Retired ¶ 320.5, *Completed COS
Willie Council	2014	1/2	12 COS
Rosaline D. Green	2017	1/2	Retired ¶ 320.5, 2 COS
Kenneth Johnson	2017	1/4	0 COS
Laurie M. Koivula	2014	1/2	13 COS
Cherlyn McKanders	2017	3/4	*M.Div.
Dale R. Milford	2015	1/4	4 COS
Myra Moreland	2018	1/4	2 COS
Nhan Duc Nguyen	2019	3/4	0 COS
Rhonda Osterman	2012	1/2	10 COS
John Pajak	2009	1/2	18 COS
Esrom Shaw	2013	1/4	5 COS
Dianne H. VanMarter	2002	1/2	Retired ¶ 320.5, *M.Div.

GREATER SOUTHWEST

Scott M. Bouldrey	2003	1/4	*M.Div. MTSO
Sara L. Carlson	2015	1/4	M.Div. AMBS
Jodi M. Cartwright	2017	3/4	M.Div. G-ETS
David L. Haase	2008	1/4	*Completed COS
Jason E. Harpole	2014	1/4	8 COS
Andrea L. Johnson	2018	1/2	3 COS
George W. Lawton	1999	1/4	Retired ¶ 320.5, *Completed COS
Brenda L. Ludwig (IN Conf)	1999	3/4	Retired ¶ 320.5, *Completed COS
O'Ryan Rickard	2003	1/4	Retired ¶ 320.5, *M.Div. – AMBS
James C. Robertson	2014	1/4	1 COS

HERITAGE

Beatrice S. Alghali	2019	1/2	0 COS
Mary Barrett	2016	3/4	0 COS
Lawrence J. Embury	2015	1/2	4 COS
William Lasse	2019	1/4	0 COS
Donald E. Lee	*2002*	*1/4*	*Retired ¶ 357.1*
Timothy R. Puckett	2011	1/2	*M.Div. ATS
Bradley R Vasey	2017	1/2	0 COS
Kelly Vergowven	2017	1/2	0 COS
Kenny Walkup Jr.	2015	3/4	8 COS

MID-MICHIGAN

Jerry J. Bukoski	2014	1/4	6 COS
Paul A. Damkoehler	2008	1/2	M.Div. ATS
Zella M. Daniel	2019	1/2	0 COS
Monique R. French	2014	1/2	*M.Div. UTS
Cari Godbehere	2019	1/4	0 COS
Judith A. Hazle	2012	1/4	10 COS
Mark Huff	2017	1/2	1 COS
Kathryn L. Leydorf-Keck	2007	3/4	*2018
Kathleen Smith	*2002*	*1/2*	*Retired ¶ 320.5, *Completed COS*
Charlene Wagner	2019	1/4	0 COS
Coleen Wilsdon	2017	1/2	4 COS

MIDWEST

Mona J. Dye	*2007*	*1/2*	*Retired ¶ 320.5, *Completed COS*
William F. Dye	*2003*	*1/2*	*Retired ¶ 320.5, *Completed COS*
Paul E. Hane	*2003*	*1/2*	*Retired ¶ 320.5, *Completed COS*
Andrew B. Hollander	2017	3/4	1 COS
Jan Marie Johnson (Ext. Ministry)	2010	1/4	Western Theology Grad (¶ 316.1,344.1.d)
Eric L. Magner	2017	3/4	0 COS
Darryl L. Miller	2007	1/4	7 COS
Banza Mukalay	2018	1/2	0 COS
Larry W. Nalett	*1993*	*1/2*	*Retired ¶ 320.5, *Completed COS*
Gary L. Peterson	*2008*	*1/4*	*Retired ¶ 320.5, *Completed COS*
David O. Pratt	*1997*	*1/4*	*Retired ¶ 320.5, *Completed COS*
Jennifer J. Wheeler	2013	1/4	M.Div. AMBS
Inge E. Whittemore	2016	1/2	4 COS
Ronald L. Worley	2004	1/4	*2018

NORTHERN SKIES

Donald E. Bedwell	*2002*	*1/2*	*Retired ⸗ 320.5, *Completed COS*
Christine J. Bergquist	1990	1/2	*2003
Rosemary R. DeHut	2002	1/4	*2011
Ryan C. Edwardson	2016	1/2	*M.Div. DDS
Sandra J. Kolder	*2004*	*3/4*	*Retired ⸗ 320.5, *Completed COS*
Peter LeMoine	2018	1/2	0 COS
Michelle K. Merchant	2016	1/2	1 COS

NORTHERN WATERS

Lyle J. Ball	2010	3/4	*2018
Lemuel O. Granada	2002	1/4	13 COS
Howard H. Harvey	2017	1/4	M.Div. MTSO
Randell J. Hitts	2017	1/2	5 COS
Jonathan D. Mays	2015	1/2	0 COS
Michael R. Neihardt	2013	1/4	2 COS
Richard D. Roberts	2015	1/4	0 COS
Jeffrey A. Swainston	2017	3/4	3 COS

c)   Students from other annual conferences or denominations serving as local pastors and enrolled in a school of theology listed by the University Senate (¶318.3, 4)?   None

d)   Students who have been certified as candidates in your annual conference and are serving as local pastors in another annual conference while enrolled in a school of theology listed by the University Senate (¶318.3)

Name	Serving Conference	Enrolled Seminary
Naylo Hopkins	Susquehanna	Wesley Theological Seminary
Jennifer C. Ward	Susquehanna	Wesley Theological Seminary

e)   Persons serving as local pastors while seeking readmission to conference membership (¶¶365.4, 367, 368.3)? (If not in this conference indicate name of conference where serving.)   **None**

22.   Who have been discontinued as local pastors (¶320.1)?

Name	Date Discontinued	District
Dale C. Barber	03.31.2019	East Winds
Russell D. Morgan	07.01.2018	Central Bay
Michael A. Pinto	04.09.2019	Greater Southwest
James Reinker	11.01.2018	Greater Detroit

23.   Who have been reinstated as local pastors (¶320.4) (v)?   None

24.   What ordained ministers or provisional members from other Annual Conferences or Methodist denominations are approved for appointment in the Annual Conference while retaining their conference or denominational membership (¶¶331.8, 346.1)? (List alphabetically; indicate Annual Conference or denomination where membership is held. Indicate credential.)

a) Annual Conferences

Name	Clergy Status	Home Conference
J. Albert Barchue	OE	Liberia
Daniel M. Bilkert	ROE	East Ohio
Jonathan E. Bratt Carle	OE	Tennessee
Linda J. Farmer-Lewis	ROE	Wisconsin
Victoria Hadaway	OE	Northern Illinois
Thomas L. Hoffmeyer	OE	Indiana
Manohar "Mantu" A. Joshi	OE	California-Nevada Conference
Timothy L. Kobler	OE	Holston
Steven W. Manskar	OE	Minnesota
Gertrude Mukalay	OE	North Katanga, Democratic Republic of Congo
John Kabala Ilunga Ngoie	OE	North Katanga, Democratic Republic of Congo
Andrew R. Phillips	OE	North Carolina
Mark J. Roberts	OE	Alabama-West Florida
Benjamin Kevin Smalls	OE	Baltimore Washington
Brittney Stephan	OP	Indiana
Lawrence J. Wiliford	ROE	Upper New York
Terry S. Wiliford	ROE	Upper New York

b) Other Methodist Denominations

Name	Clergy Status	Denomination
Diane Covington	OF (Ret)	Christian Methodist Episcopal
Joshua A. Henderson	OE	Wesleyan Church
Travis Heystek	OE	Wesleyan Church
Daeki Kim	OE	Indiana
Eung Yong Kim	OE	Korea Methodist Church
David Nellist	OE	British Methodist
Vaughn Thurston-Cox	OE	Free Methodist

25. What clergy in good standing in other Christian denominations have been approved to serve appointments or ecumenical ministries within the bounds of the Annual Conference while retaining their denominational affiliation (¶¶331.8, 346.2)? (v) (Designate with an asterisk those who have been accorded voting rights within the annual conference. Indicate credential.)

Name	Clergy Status	Denomination
Thomas C. Hartley	OF	Presbyterian Church USA
Derl G. Keefer	OF	Church of the Nazarene
Julie Kline	OE	United Church of Christ
Frederick G. Sampson III	OF	National Baptist Convention
Stephen Spina	OF	Presbyterian Church USA
Mack C. Strange	OF	Southern Baptist

26. Who are affiliate members? (List alphabetically; indicate annual conference or denomination where membership is held.)
     a)   With vote (¶586.4b [v])?   **None**
     b)   Without vote (¶¶334.5, 344.4)? (**v 2/3**)

Name	Conference/ Denomination	First Year of Affiliation
David S. Bell	East Ohio	2011
Carol B. Cooley	West Ohio	2000
David A. Newhouse	Northern Illinois	2016
Joseph A. Perez	New York	1996
P. Kay Welsch	Wisconsin	2013

NOTE: If your conference has admitted or ordained persons as a courtesy to another conference, list these persons in Question 40 only. If persons have been admitted or ordained by another annual conference as a courtesy to your conference, list these persons in Questions 27-39, whichever are appropriate, giving the date and name of the accommodating conference.

27. Who are elected as associate members? ¶322 (3/4v) (List alphabetically – see note preceding Question 27):

Name	District	Course of Study Complete
Anne W. Riegler	Midwest	*Completed COS
Theodore A. Trudgeon	Northern Skies	*2014

28. Who are **elected** as provisional members and what seminary are they attending, if in school? (under ¶¶322.4, 324, 325)
     a)   Provisional Deacons under the provisions of ¶¶ 324.4a, c or ¶324.5 (**3/4v**)

Name	Seminary
LuAnne M. Stanley Hook	Garrett-Evangelical Theological Seminary
Alexander J. Plum	Garrett-Evangelical Theological Seminary

     b)   Provisional Elders under the provisions of ¶¶324.4a, b or ¶324.6 (3/4v); ¶ 322.4 (**3/4 v**) (*indicates graduate of this school)

Name	Seminary
Nicholas E. Bonsky	Methodist Theological School in Ohio
Kimberly M. Bos	*Garrett-Evangelical Theological Seminary
Leslee J. Fritz	*Garrett-Evangelical Theological Seminary
Julia R. Humenik	*Garrett-Evangelical Theological Seminary
Elizabeth A. Hurd	Boston University School of Theology
Kayla M. Roosa	*Garrett-Evangelical Theological Seminary
Taegyu Shin	*Methodist Theological University, South Korea
Hillary Thurston-Cox	*Asbury Theological Seminary
Amy N. Triebwasser	Methodist Theological School in Ohio
Ruth A. Irish VanderSande	*Asbury Theological Seminary
Joan E. VanDessel	*Garrett-Evangelical Theological Seminary

29. Who are **continued as** provisional members, in what year were they admitted to provisional membership, and what seminary are they attending, if in school (¶326 **v**)?

a)   In preparation for ordination as a deacon or elder? (¶326)

Name	Clergy Status	Date
Barbara Benjamin	PE	2018
Robert Blanchard	PE	2018
Sari Brown	PE	2016
Dillon Burns	PE	2017
Christopher Butson	PE	2018
Matthew Chapman	PE	2017
Jeffrey O. Cummings	PE	2016
Tania J. Dozeman	PE	2018
Elise Low Edwardson	PE	2017
Katherine L. Fahey	PE	2016
Michelle Forsyth	PE	2018
Rodney Gasaway	PD	2017
Amanda M. Hall (Leave of Absence)	PD	2015
Cydney M. Idsinga	PE	2015
Sean K. Kidd	PE	2018
Won Dong Kim	PE	2015
YooJin Kim	PE	2018
Mary K. Loring	PE	2015
Heather A. McDougall Molner	PE	2014
Tiffany M. Newsom	PE	2017
Marva Pope	PE	2015
Beth A. Reum (Medical Leave)	PE	2011
Corey Simon	PE	2018
Jinny Song	PD	2016 G-ETS
Brian E. Steele	PE	2017
Linda J. Stephan	PE	2018
Mary A. Sweet	PE	2015
Michael Vollmer	PE	2016

b)   Provisional deacons who became provisional elders? (v) **None**
c)   Provisional elders who became provisional deacons? (v) (Indicate year) **None**
d)   Provisional members who transferred from other conferences or denominations? (¶347.1)
      (v)

Name	Clergy Status	Previous Denomination
David Reed	PE – Received 2017	Missionary Church
Joonshik Yoo	PE – Received 2013	Korean Methodist

30. What ordained clergy, coming from other Christian denominations, have had their orders recognized (¶347.6): **(v) A person's orders may be recognized when they are transferring their membership into your annual conference from another Christian denomination. A person who is listed in Q.30 must also be listed in either Q. 31 a or b, depending on the transfer status.**

31. What ordained clergy have been received from other Christian denominations (¶347.3): (List alphabetically—see note preceding Question 27):
     a)   As provisional members (¶347.3c)? **(v) None**
     b)   As local pastors (¶347.3)? **(v) None**

32. Who are elected as members in full connection? (List alphabetically-see note preceding Question 27. **Anyone appearing on this question must also be listed somewhere in questions 33-34 or 36, unless the clergy's orders from another denomination were recognized on question 30 in a previous year.) (3/4 v)**:

   a)   Deacons
   Name
   Sarah B.N. Alexander
   Cora E. Glass

   b)   Elders
   Name
   Joel T. Fitzgerald
   Jeremiah J. Mannschreck
   Eun Sik Poy
   Jonathan E. Reynolds
   Scott L. Sherrill
   Devin R. Smith

33. Who are ordained as deacons and what seminary awarded their degree? Or, if their master's degree is not from a seminary, at what seminary did they complete the basic graduate theological studies? (List alphabetically-see note preceding Question 27)
   a)   After provisional membership (¶330)? **(3/4 v)**

Name	**Seminary**
Sarah B.N. Alexander	Methodist Theological School in Ohio
Cora E. Glass	Garrett-Evangelical Theological Seminary

   b)   Transfer from elder? (¶309) **(v 3/4)**   **None**

34. Who are ordained as elders and what seminary awarded their degree?

   a)   After provisional membership? (¶335) (v 3/4)

Name	**Seminary**
Joel T. Fitzgerald	Vanderbilt University
Jeremiah J. Mannschreck	Garrett-Evangelical Theological Seminary
Eun Sik Poy	Asbury Theological Seminary
Jonathan E. Reynolds	Garrett-Evangelical Theological Seminary
Scott L. Sherrill	Princeton Theological Seminary
Devin R. Smith	United Theological Seminary

   b)   Transfer from deacon? (¶309) **(v 3/4)**   **None**

35. What provisional members, previously discontinued, are readmitted (¶364)? **(v)**   **None**

36. Who are readmitted (¶¶365-367 [v], ¶368 **[v 2/3]**): **None**

37. Who are returned to the effective relationship after voluntary retirement (¶357.7): **(v)** **None**

38. Who have been received by transfer from other annual conferences of The United Methodist Church (¶¶347.1, 416.5, 635.2n)? (List alphabetically. Indicate credential. See note preceding Question 27.): **(v)** **None**

39. Who are transferred in from other Methodist denominations (¶347.2)? (List alphabetically. Indicate credential.) **None**

40. Who have been ordained as a courtesy to other conferences, after election by the other conference? (See note preceding Question 27. Such courtesy elections or ordinations do <u>not</u> require transfer of conference membership.)
    a)   Deacons? **None**
    b)   Elders? **None**

41. Who have been transferred out to other annual conferences of The United Methodist Church (¶416.5)? (List alphabetically. Indicate credential. See note preceding Question 27.)

Name	Date Transferred	Conference
Susan D. Martin	07.01.2018	Indiana Conference

42. Who are discontinued as provisional members (¶327)? **(v)**.
    a)   By expiration of eight-year time limit (¶ 327) **None**
    b)   By voluntary discontinuance (¶ 327.6) **(v)**

Name	Clergy Status	Date of Discontinuance
Stephen F. Lindeman	PE	07.01.2018

    c)   By involuntary discontinuance (¶ 327.6) **(v)**   **None**
    d)   By reaching Mandatory Retirement Age (¶ 327.7)   **None**

43. Who are on location?
    a)   Who has been granted honorable location (¶358.1)?
        (1)   This year? **(v)**   **None**
        (2)   Previously?

Name	Year Originally Granted	Charge Conf. Membership	Year of Most Recent Report
Robert J. Easlick	2004	Fenton	2018
Mary E. Isaacs Frost	1989	First UMC Oviedo, FL	2017
Melvin F. Hall	1986	South Bend, IN: First	2017
Clinton McKinven-Copus	2007	Ludington UMC	2018
Brian Rafferty	2016	Lansing: Mt. Hope UMC	2018
Rodney E. Rawson	1979	Davison UMC	2018
Donald C. Schark	1995	Menominee: First	2018
Timothy T. Tuthill	2017	Grand Rapids: First UMC	2018
Michelle Wisdom-Long	2011	Kalamazoo: First UMC	2018

    b)   Who on honorable location are appointed ad interim as local pastors? (¶358.2) (Indicate date and appointment.)

Name	Appointment	Year Originally Granted
David E. Small	Paw Paw – 07.01.2016	1999

    c)   Who has been placed on administrative location (¶359)?
        (1)   This year? **(v)**   **None**
        (2)   Previously?

Name	Year Originally Granted	Charge Conf. Membership	Year of Most Recent Report
Valerie M. Hill	1999	Greenville	

44. Who have been granted the status of honorable location–retired (¶358.3)?
     a)   This year? **(v)**

Name	Clergy Status	Year H.L. Originally Granted	Charge Conference Membership
C. David Hainer	FE	1996	Bowne Center UMC, Alto
Robert "Mel" Vostry	FE	1991	Palmer, Alaska

     b)   Previously?

Name	Clergy Status	Year H.L. Originally Granted	Charge Conference Membership
Gordon B. Boyd	FE	2015	
William H. Brady	FE	1976	
Hayden K. Carruth, Jr	FE	1992	Ypsilanti: St. Matthews UMC
Jon M. Clapp	FE	1981	Clarkston: First
Thomas A. Crossman	FD	1991	St. Paul/St. Andrew, New York NY
Bruce W. Dempsey	FE	1993	Muskegon Heights: Temple
David L. Draggoo	FE	1986	Laingsburg UMC
James "Kyle" Elliott	FE	1964	Birmingham, AL: Riverchase
Ronald F. Ellis	FE	1971	Livonia: St. Matthew's
Harold G. Ford	FE	1974	Birmingham: First
Leon W. Herndon	FE	2010	Metropolitan UMC
Mary E. Howard	FE	1978	Richardson, TX: First
Michael Edward Long	FE	1998	Traverse City: Traverse Bay
Terry L. MacArthur	FE	1985	Portage: Chapel Hill
Laurie J. McKinven-Copus	FE	2005	Ludington UMC
Charles D. McNary	FE	1977	Bangor Simpson UMC
Thurlan E. Meredith	FE	1993	Northlawn UMC, Grand Rapids
Allen C. Myers	RHL	1980	Trinity UMC, Grand Rapids
Louis E. Otter II	FE	1971	
Edward F. Otto	FE	1978	First UMC, Chicago IL
Robert L. Porter	FE	1980	Ferndale: First UMC
David P. Rahn	FE	1988	Grand Blanc UMC
Paul K. Scheibner	FE	1983	Good Shepherd of the North, Roscommon
Carl G. Silvernail	FE	1969	Kingston
Donald R. Silvis	FE	1972	Lowell UMC
David E. Small	FE	1999	Paw Paw UMC
Philip P. Steele	FE	1971	Milwood UMC, Kalamazoo
Charles E. Strawn	FE	1979	None available in Amsterdam
Ronald W. Tallman	FE	1981	Hope UMC, Greenwood Village CO
Bertran W. Vermeulen	FE	1984	Fremont UMC
George W. Versteeg	FE	1976	
Harvard J. Warren	FE	1972	Bradenton, FL
Harold V. Whited	FE	1964	
Lawrence C. Whiting	FE	1981	None
Galen E. Wightman	FE	1969	Washington, D.C.: Foundry UMC
Kenneth B. Woodside	FE	1991	Southfield: Hope

45. Who have had their status as honorably located and their orders terminated (¶358.2)? **(v)**
None

46. Who have had their conference membership terminated?
a)   By withdrawal to unite with another denomination (¶360.1, .4)? **(v)**

Name	Date of Termination	Appointment
Ut Van To	11.06.2018	Vietnamese Missionary

b)   By withdrawal from the ordained ministerial office (¶360.2, .4)? **(v) None**
c)   By withdrawal under complaints or charges (¶¶360.3, .4; 2719.2)? **None**
d)   By termination of orders under recommendation of the Board of Ordained Ministry (¶358.2, 359.3)? **(v) None**
e)   By trial (¶2713)? **None**

47. Who have been suspended under the provisions of ¶362.1d, ¶2704.2c or ¶2711.3? (Give effective dates. Indicate credential.)   **None**

48. Deceased (List alphabetically)
a)   What associate members have died during the year?
Active: **None**
Retired:

Name	Date of Birth	Date of Death
Emerson W. Arntz	09.04.1942	06.04.2018
Bernard R. Randolph	10.02.1915	07.21.2018
Gerald M. Sever, Jr.	09.01.1946	06.19.2018

b)   What provisional members have died during the year? (Indicate credential.)
Active: **None**
Retired: **None**

c)   What elders have died during the year?
Active:

Name	Date of Birth	Date of Death
Mark E. Spaw	05.24.1957	03.08.2019
Donald S. Weatherup	09.14.1961	05.13.2019
Brian K. William	12.02.1975	04.16.2019

Retired:

Name	Date of Birth	Date of Death
Francis F. Anderson	11.03.1926	10.18.2018
Bruce M. Denton	10.12.1950	05.05.2019
Juanita J. Ferguson	07.08.1943	11.18.2018
Richard C. Kuhn	06.12.1936	12.08.2018
Douglas K. Olsen	05.24.1947	07.15.2018
Marvin R. Rosa	06.18.1937	02.11.2019
Ward N. Scovel, Jr.	12.15.1935	10.13.2018
Susan B. Stiles	11.04.1951	08.31.2018
Harold M. Taber	12.12.1929	08.18.2018
James F. Thomas	06.01.1933	06.01.2018
Gregory R. Wolfe	02.10.1948	04.15.2019
Young B. Yoon	12.29.1924	07.24.2018
Paton M. Zimmerman	05.22.1925	11.27.2018

d) What deacons have died during the year?
    Active: **None**
    Retired:

Name	Date of Birth	Date of Death
William D. Carr	02.17.1938	11.08.2018

e) What local pastors have died during the year?
    Active: **None**
    Retired:

Name	Date of Birth	Date of Death
Rex E. Bean	08.08.1923	08.19.2018
Sharyn K. Osmond	02.19.1951	04.19.2019

49. What provisional or ordained members (elders and deacons) have received appointments in other Annual Conferences of The United Methodist Church while retaining their membership in this Annual Conference (¶¶331.8, 346.1)?

Name	Clergy Status	Conference Where Appointed	Appointment	Year
Susan D. Amick	FD	North Georgia	Decatur First UMC	2019
Thomas Beagan	FE	Western Pennsylvania	Charter Oak UMC	
Eric Burton-Krieger	FE	Indiana	Central-Indianapolis St. Luke's	2015
Catherine Christman	FE	Wisconsin	South West-Stoughton	2016
Rebecca L. Farrester	FE	Oregon-Idaho	Columbia-Milwaukie St. Paul	2016
Chul-Goo Lee	FE	Florida	South Florida Korean UMC	
April McGlothin-Eller	FD	North Georgia	Newnan Office of the UM Children's Home	2017
Vince McGlothin-Eller	FD	North Georgia	Newnan First UMC	2019
Todd J. Query	FD	Virginia	York River-Ext Min and Wellspring	2015
Jonathan D. VanDop	FE	North Texas	West Texas VA Health System	2018
Joonshik Yoo	PE	West Ohio	Korean Church of Dayton	

50. Who are the provisional, ordained members or associate members on leave of absence and for what number of years consecutively has each held this relation (¶353)? (Indicate credential. Record Charge Conference where membership is held.)

a) Voluntary?
    (1) Personal, 5 years or less (¶353.2a 3) (v)

Name	Status	Date Effective	Years	Charge Conference
Kenneth Dunstone	FE	07.01.2017	2	
Tyson G. Ferguson	FE	07.01.2016	3	
Donald R. Ferris-McCann	FE	07.01.2016	3	Elsie
Margaret R. Garrigues	FE	09.01.2016	3	Ann Arbor: First
Amanda Hall	PD	07.01.2017	2	Rochester: St. Paul's
Janice T. Lancaster	FD	03.31.2017	2	Northlawn
Jane R. Lippert	FE	09.01.2015	3	Traverse City Central
Donna J. Minarik	FE	07.01.2019	0	Mason: First UMC
Amee A. Paparella	FE	02.28.2018	1	
Colleen R. Treman	FD	07.01.2016	3	Kalamazoo First

(2)   Personal, more than 5 years (¶353.2a 3) (v 2/3)

Name	Status	Date Effective	Years	Charge Conference
Jennifer L. Bixby	FE	09.15.2006	13	
Michael Coffey	FE	04.30.2012	7	
Christopher D. Cowdin	FE	05.01.2003	16	Troy: First

   (3)   Family, 5 years or less (¶353.2b 3) **(v)**   **None**
   (4)   Family, more than 5 years (¶353.2b 3) **(v 2/3)**   **None**
   (5)   Transitional (¶353.2c)

Name	Status	Date Effective	Years	Charge Conference
Gregory W. Lawton	FD	01.01.2019	0	Georgetown UMC

  b)   Involuntary? (¶354)? **(2/3 v)**   **None**

51.   Who are granted sabbatical leave (¶351)? **(v)**   **None**

52.   Who have been granted medical leave due to medical or disabling conditions (¶356)? **(v)**

Name	Status	Date Effective	Charge Conference
Mary S. Brown	FE	12.01.2016	Montague
Marshall Dunlap	FE	02.01.2016	
Nickolas Genoff	PL	01.01.2019	
David J. Goudie	FE	09.01.2017	
Faith Green-Timmons	FE	04.01.2018	Flint: Calvary
Emily K. Hansson	FE	01.01.2019	Centreville UMC
Tracy N. Huffman	FE	07.01.2019	Monroe: St. Paul
Lynda B. Liles	FD	07.01.2011	Rochester: St. Paul's
Jane D. Logston	FE	09.01.2018	Bear Lake/Arcadia
Theresa "Little Eagle" Oyler-Sayles	FE	04.15.2009	
Beth A. Reum	PE	01.15.2016	Berrien Springs
Colin P. Stover	FE	01.01.2011	Lapeer: Trinity
Thomas L. Taylor	FE	02.01.2013	
T. Bradley Terhune	FE	09.01.2018	Kochville/Mapleton
Tamara S.M. Williams	FE	07.01.2017	N Muskegon Community

53.   What members in full connection have been retired (¶357): (**List** alphabetically. If retiring in the interim between conference sessions (¶357.2d), indicate the effective date of retirement.) (**Under ¶357.1, no vote required; under ¶357.2, v; under ¶357.3, 2/3 v**)
Deacons
a)   This year?

Name	Date Effective
Loretta M. Job	07.01.2019

b)   Previously?

Name	Date Effective
Grace Ann Beebe	2017
Jane A. Berquist	2006
Dorothy M. Blakey	1999
Pamela L. Buchholz	2013
Charlotte A. Cowdin	2003

Murphy S. Ehlers	2018
Catherine M. Freeman	2014
Annelissa M. Gray-Lion	2018
Joyce Hanlon	2001
Janet A. Lee	2002
Pamela J. Mathieu	2012
Judith Y. Mayo	2014
Dorothy D. Mercer	2003
Catherine J. Miles	2017
Betsy Myers	2002
Johncie K. Palmer	2008
Jaye A. Reisinger	2018
Carolyn Wik	2014
Christine Wyatt	2015

Elders

c)   This year?

Name	**Date Effective**
Maureen V. Baker	07.012019
Eric S. Beck	07.01.2019
Colon R. Brown	07.01.2019
Linda J. Burson	02.04.2019
Kathryn S. Cadarette	07.01.2019
Michelle A. Gentile	07.01.2019
John D. Landis	07.01.2019
Douglas E. Mater	07.01.2019
John M. Mehl	06.01.2019
Robert S. Moore-Jumonville	04.01.2019
Rebecca K. Morrison	07.01.2019
James C. Noggle	04.01.2019
Douglas E. Ralston	07.01.2019
Stephen E. Rhoades	07.01.2019
Edmond G. Taveirne	11.15.2018
Barbara E. Welbaum	07.01.2019
Randy J. Whitcomb	01.01.2019

d)   Elders Previously?

	Name	**Year**		**Name**	**Year**
1.	Joseph H. Ablett	1985	13.	Wayne H. Babcock	2003
2.	Gordon E. Ackerman	2001	14.	Eugene K. Bacon	2016
3.	Craig L. Adams	2010	15.	Thomas G. Badley	2002
4.	Pegg Ainslie	1997	16.	Paul F. Bailey	2001
5.	Terry W. Allen	2006	17.	Theron E. Bailey	1994
6.	Andrew A. Allie	2009	18.	Wilson C. Bailey	2007
7.	Jana Lynn Almeida	2016	19.	Melanie J. Baker	2016
8.	David D. Amstutz	2018	20.	Peggy J. Baker	2018
9.	William J. Amundsen	2003	21.	James R. Balfour II	2010
10.	J. Leon Andrews	1992	22.	Glenn C. Ball	1996
11.	Richard C. Andrus	1999	23.	Martha C. Ball	2002
12.	Joy E. Arthur	1991	24.	Alfred T. Bamsey	2000

25.	James W. Barney	2005
26.	Marilyn B. Barney	2008
27.	Wayne C. Barrett	2011
28.	B. Gordon "Gordie" Barry	2015
29.	Ralph T. Barteld	1997
30.	Jack M. Bartholomew	1995
31.	William P. Bartlett	2011
32.	Joseph R. Baunoch	2004
33.	William M. Beachy	2014
34.	Norman R. Beckwith, Sr.	2008
35.	Gary L. Bekofske	2014
36.	John K. Benissan	2011
37.	Kenneth W. Bensen	2003
38.	Evans C. Bentley	2018
39.	Elwood J. Berkompas	1995
40.	Bruce L. Billing	2011
41.	Joseph J. Bistayi	2005
42.	Eugene A. Blair	2012
43.	Paul F. Blomquist	1996
44.	James W. Boehm	1998
45.	Gilbert R. Boersma	2011
46.	Benjamin Bohnsack	2006
47.	Sylvia A. Bouvier	2006
48.	Keith A. Bovee	1994
49.	Dianne M. Bowden	2013
50.	Benjamin H. Breitkreuz	2008
51.	Kenneth J. Bremer	2017
52.	Robert D. Brenner	2013
53.	J. Melvin Bricker	1995
54.	Patricia L. Bromberek	2011
55.	Patricia L. Brook	2018
56.	Wayne W. Brookshear	1983
57.	Dale E. Brown	2014
58.	Janet J. Brown	2018
59.	Lawrence P. Brown	2014
60.	Tom Brown II	1997
61.	Ellen A. Brubaker	2001
62.	Wesley L. Brun	2006
63.	Vivian C. Bryant	2003
64.	Steven J. Buck	2013
65.	Donald L. Buege	2017
66.	Tommy Burdette	2016
67.	Ray W. Burgess	2000
68.	Bonnie D. Byadiah	1997
69.	William A. Cargo	2011
70.	Donna J. Cartwright	2003
71.	H. Reginald Cattell	1994
72.	Lynn F. Chappell	2009
73.	Kathy R. Charlefour	2014
74.	Victor D. Charnley	2013
75.	Richard C. Cheatham	1998
76.	David A. Cheyne	2005
77.	David E. Church	1995
78.	Saundra J. Clark	2013
79.	William V. Clegg, Jr.	2011
80.	William M. Clemmer	2014
81.	Leonard A. Clevenger	2015
82.	James D. Cochran	1998
83.	Bufford "Buff" W. Coe	2017
84.	Roger L. Colby	2008
85.	David C. Collins	2011
86.	Michael T. Conklin	2012
87.	Frederick P. Cooley	2000
88.	Kathryn M. Coombs	2002
89.	Oscar W. Cooper, Jr.	1989
90.	George E. Covintree, Jr.	2015
91.	Ramona E. Cowling	2002
92.	Lawson D. Crane	2009
93.	Wallace "Pete" Crawford	2015
94.	Doris Crocker	1998
95.	Anthony N. Cutting	2011
96.	Billie R. Dalton	2013
97.	Reva H. Daniel	2005
98.	Robert Davis	1997
99.	Gary C. Dawes	2014
100.	Donald J. Daws	1997
101.	Alan W. DeGraw	2000
102.	Lynn A. DeMoss	1997
103.	Jerry P. Densmore	2014
104.	Isabell M. Deppe (Involuntary)	2000
105.	David A. Diamond	2006
106.	James A. Dibbet	2011
107.	William D. Dobbs	2015
108.	Robert D. Dobson	1991
109.	William R. Donahue, Jr.	2014
110.	Linda J. Donelson	2015
111.	Paul G. Donelson	2015
112.	William H. Doubblestein	2006
113.	David L. Dryer	2006
114.	Paula Jane Duffey	2005
115.	Robert Duggan	2005
116.	Daniel M. Duncan	2014
117.	Susan Defoe Dunlap	2013
118.	Mary M. Eckhardt	2010
119.	Eldon K. Eldred	2003
120.	Joe D. Elenbaas	2010
121.	John W. Ellinger	2007
122.	Hydrian Elliott	2011
123.	John W. Elliott	2014
124.	Gene Patrick England	2018
125.	Janet M. Engler	2015
126.	Richard R. Erickson	2006

127.	Terry A. Euper	2010	178. A. Theodore Halsted, Jr.	1992
128.	Thomas J. Evans	2013	179. John N. Hamilton	2016
129.	Haldon D. Ferris	2002	180. Frederick G. Hamlin	1994
130.	John C. Ferris	2012	181. Eric S. Hammar	1991
131.	Raymond D. Field	2003	182. Claudette I. Haney	2005
132.	Harold F. Filbrandt	1994	183. Randall R. Hansen	2014
133.	Garrison "Fred" Finzer	2012	184. Ronald W. Hansen	2011
134.	Frederick H. Fischer	1996	185. Alan J. Hanson	2013
135.	John W. Fisher	2013	186. John "Jack" E. Harnish	2013
136.	David L. Flagel	2013	187. Duane M. Harris	2018
137.	David L. Fleming	2014	188. Hilda L. Harris	2004
138.	George W. Fleming	2002	189. Caroline F. Hart	2018
139.	Barbara J. Flory	2011	190. Pauline S. Hart	2008
140.	Carolyn Floyd	2008	191. Thomas E. Hart	2002
141.	Valerie A. Fons	2017	192. Robert D. Harvey	1999
142.	Tat-Khean Foo	2003	193. Lynn Hasley	2016
143.	James E. Fox	1995	194. Robert C. Hastings	2004
144.	Thomas P. Fox	2012	195. Timothy S. Hastings	2012
145.	Nancy K. Frank	2015	196. Carl L. Hausermann	2001
146.	Barbra L. Franks	2007	197. Ronda L. Hawkins	2014
147.	Bea B. Fraser-Soots	2015	198. Wayne A. Hawley	2007
148.	Lynda F. Frazier	2015	199. Geoffrey L. Hayes	2009
149.	Lillian T. French	2010	200. Stanley L. Hayes	1999
150.	Donald R. Fry	2008	201. Gloria Haynes	2015
151.	Charles W. Fullmer	1997	202. Leonard B. Haynes	1998
152.	Elizabeth Gamboa	2008	203. Lyle D. Heaton	2016
153.	Charles F. Garrod	1995	204. Constance L. Heffelfinger	2016
154.	Roger F. Gedcke	2010	205. Keith W. Heifner	2006
155.	George F.W. Gerritsen	2000	206. Robert J. Henning	2011
156.	Max L. Gibbs	2009	207. John R. Henry	2011
157.	Jack e. Giguere	1999	208. Theodore W. Hepner	2002
158.	David G. Gladstone	2012	209. William A. Hertel	2001
159.	Daniel L. Gonder	2018	210. Timothy R. Hickey	2000
160.	Diane L. Gordon	2018	211. Duane J. Hicks	1997
161.	Diana Kay Goudie	2009	212. Howard Higgins	2015
162.	Robert F. Goudie	2003	213. John W. Hinkle	1999
163.	Michael Grajcar, Jr.	1991	214. Robert L. Hinklin	2001
164.	James C. Grant	1999	215. Lawrence E. Hodge	2000
165.	Ronald B. Grant	2012	216. Harris J. Hoekwater	2018
166.	Joseph M. Graybill	2011	217. Jacqueline Holdsworth	2011
167.	Patricia A. Green	2013	218. Laurence E. Hubley	2002
168.	James E. Greer II	2013	219. John C. Huhtala, Sr.	2009
169.	George R. Grettenberger	1992	220. James R. Hulett	1998
170.	A. Ray Grienke	1999	221. Gerald S. Hunter	2015
171.	Robert C. Grigereit	1999	222. Joel W. Hurley	1998
172.	Kathleen A. Groff	2008	223. David M. Hurst	1998
173.	James M. Gysel	2011	224. Joseph D. Huston	2009
174.	Gerald F. Hagans	2006	225. James L. Hynes	2000
175.	Susan J. Hagans	2006	226. Roger W. Ireson	2001
176.	William E. Haggard	2018	227. Ronald L.F. Iris	2006
177.	Gary T. Haller	2017	228. Andrew Jackson	2006

229. Charles R. Jacobs	2010	
230. James D. Jacobs	2011	
231. James P. James	2007	
232. Jerry L. Jaquish	2012	
233. Curtis E. Jensen	2010	
234. Carol J. Johns	2015	
235. Deborah M. Johnson	2014	
236. Jane Ellen Johnson	2016	
237. Mark G. Johnson	2015	
238. William C. Johnson	2012	
239. David L. Johnston	2009	
240. Jack E. Johnston	2012	
241. Mark G. Johnston	2012	
242. Donald W. Joiner	2010	
243. Charles Jones	1997	
244. Margaret Zee Jones	2006	
245. Robert E. Jones	2009	
246. Emmett Kadwell, Jr.	2011	
247. Pamela S. Kail	2012	
248. Mark A. Karls	2014	
249. Thomas F. Keef	2014	
250. Ron L. Keller	1998	
251. James G. Kellerman	2013	
252. Dwayne L. Kelsey	2000	
253. O. Jay Kendall	2012	
254. Robert L. Kersten	1995	
255. Charles W. Keyworth	2017	
256. David E. Kidd	1997	
257. Susan M. Kingsley	2016	
258. Bruce R. Kintigh	2018	
259. Dean A. Klump	2007	
260. David G. Knapp	2009	
261. Kenneth A. Kohlmann	2001	
262. Norman C. Kohns	2005	
263. Robert I. Kreger	2013	
264. James P. Kummer	2016	
265. Kathleen S. Kursch	2017	
266. Sally J. LaFrance	2004	
267. Frederick LaMere	2002	
268. D. Keith Laidler	1997	
269. Wayne T. Large	2003	
270. Jean M. Larson	2010	
271. Mary G. Laub	2010	
272. Melvin L. Leach	2015	
273. Hoon K. Lee	2013	
274. John Hyung Lee	2011	
275. Jung Kee Lee	2013	
276. S. Douglas Leffler	1994	
277. Ben B. Lester	2011	
278. Alger T. Lewis	1999	
279. Bradford K. Lewis	2010	
280. Eugene A. Lewis	2003	
281. Kendall A. Lewis	1990	
282. Barbara Lewis-Lakin	2015	
283. Donald L. Lichtenfelt	1994	
284. Olaf R. Lidums	2007	
285. Johnny S. Liles	2004	
286. Paul B. Lim	2000	
287. Donna J. Lindberg	2004	
288. David M. Liscomb	1998	
289. Carl Q. Litchfield	2017	
290. David L. Litchfield	2006	
291. Glenn C. Litchfield	2016	
292. Calvin D. Long	2018	
293. Leicester R. Longden	2013	
294. John D. Lover	2000	
295. Paul E. Lowley	2000	
296. Carole S. Lyman	2010	
297. Frank W. Lyman Jr.	2010	
298. Gary V. Lyons	1996	
299. Elizabeth A. Macaulay	2018	
300. Thomas P. Macaulay	2010	
301. Francis R. MacCanon	1988	
302. Mary Lynch Mallory	2009	
303. Paul J. Mallory	2014	
304. Charles R. Marble	2000	
305. Beverly L. Marr	2017	
306. Edrye A. Eastman Maurer	2016	
307. Jeffrey R. Maxwell	2016	
308. Judith A. May	2016	
309. William R. Maynard	2009	
310. Robert J. Mayo	2013	
311. Paul D. Mazur	1990	
312. William P. McBride	2016	
313. Marvin H. McCallum	2002	
314. Kenneth D. McCaw	2000	
315. J. Patrick McCoy	2014	
316. Allen D. McCreedy	2000	
317. Brent L. McCumons	2011	
318. Ginethea D. McDowell	2002	
319. Martin A. McEntarfer	1992	
320. A. Faye McKinstry	2014	
321. David R. McKinstry	2010	
322. Sandra B. Hoffman McNary	2007	
323. John W. McNaughton	2003	
324. Russell F. McReynolds	2007	
325. David W. Meister	2016	
326. Paul J. Melrose	2011	
327. Douglas K. Mercer	2000	
328. Patricia A. Meyers	2014	
329. Kevin L. Miles	2017	
330. Dale M. Miller	2016	

331. Duane E. Miller	2011	382. Ralph H. Pieper II	2012
332. Sylvester Miller III	2003	383. J. "Lynn" Pier-Fitzgerald	2017
333. David H. Minger	2006	384. Thomas M. Pier-Fitzgerald	2016
334. Daniel J. Minor	2011	385. Robert B. Pierce	2007
335. Frederick B. Moore, Sr.	2008	386. Keith I. Pohl	1993
336. John L. Moore	1995	387. Gerald A. Pohly	1996
337. Richard D. Moore	2015	388. Karen B. Poole	2006
338. Richard A. Morrison	2007	389. Linda Jo Powers	2015
339. Harold S. Morse	2011	390. Carl E. Price	1998
340. John D. Morse	2012	391. W. Cadman Prout	1981
341. David L. Morton	2001	392. Blaine B. Rader	2004
342. Meredith T. Moshauer	1997	393. Jeanne M. Randels	2014
343. David G. Mulder	2018	394. David E. Ray	2012
344. Elias N. Mumbiro	2015	395. Kenneth B. Ray	2010
345. Marjorie H. Munger	2013	396. Wayne G. Reece	2000
346. Nanette Myers-Cabeen	2014	397. Kenneth C. Reeves	2006
347. John E. Naile	2014	398. Jeffrey D. Regan	2013
348. David B. Nelson	1998	399. James L. Rhinesmith	1969
349. Lance E. Ness	2017	400. Clifford Rice	2002
350. Frederick D. Neumann	2017	401. Philip A. Rice	2002
351. Ross N. Nicholson	1990	402. Richard M. Riley	2014
352. Sharon G. Scott Niefert	2001	403. William A. Ritter	2005
353. R. Ivan Niswender	1994	404. Archie T. Roberts	1997
354. Karen Y. Noel	2018	405. Stanley "Joe" Robertson	2002
355. Arthur V. Norris	2001	406. Beatrice K. Robinson	2007
356. Bruce L. Nowacek	2016	407. William Tom Robinson	2004
357. Gordon W. Nusz	2003	408. Edward C. Ross	2012
358. Dorothy Okray	2007	409. Robert H. Roth, Jr.	2018
359. William W. Omansiek	2010	410. Edwin A. Rowe	2013
360. Karen K. Orr	2014	411. Gregory E. Rowe	2016
361. Donna J. Osterhout	2016	412. Larry W. Rubingh	2012
362. James E. Paige, Jr.	2008	413. James L. Rule	2012
363. Margaret "Peggy" Paige	2012	414. Meredith Rupe	2006
364. Wade S. Panse	2012	415. James Russell Rupert	2009
365. John G. Park	2011	416. Donald A. Russell	1996
366. Gerald R. Parker	1994	417. William P. Sanders	2003
367. James F. Parker	1994	418. Gary L. Sanderson	1999
368. Roger A. Parker	2008	419. Donald A. Scavella, Sr.	2005
369. Cynthia M. Parsons	2018	420. John G. Schleicher	2006
370. Edward L. Passenger	1999	421. Margery A. Schleicher	2007
371. Margaret A. Passenger	2005	422. Leonard R. Schoenherr	2013
372. J. Douglas Paterson	2018	423. W. Thomas Schomaker	2004
373. Paul E. Patterson	1990	424. William D. Schoonover	1992
374. Mark R. Payne	2016	425. James P. Schwandt	2008
375. William V. Payne	1996	426. Robert B. Secrist	1991
376. Richard A. Peacock	2008	427. David A. Selleck	2015
377. Douglas L. Pedersen	2005	428. Gerald L. Selleck	2018
378. A. Edward Perkins	2006	429. Richard A. Selleck	1996
379. Susan M. Petro	2014	430. Priscilla J. Seward	2003
380. Warren D. Pettis	1998	431. Merton W. Seymour	1999
381. Janet Gaston Petty	2012	432. Philip M. Seymour	2011

433. Jane B. Shapley	1996	484. John Ross Thompson	2010
434. Maurice D. Sharai, Jr.	2005	485. R. John Thompson	2010
435. Isaac Yong-Cheol Shin	2010	486. Ronald J. Thompson	1995
436. Gary R. Shiplett	2000	487. Dorothy J. Thon	2017
437. Anthony J. Shipley	2007	488. Duane G. Thon	2007
438. Larry R. Shrout	1998	489. Phylemon D. Titus	2002
439. Robert J. Sielaff	2018	490. Karen Hien Thi Vo To	2018
440. Webley J. Simpkins	1994	491. William J. Torrey	1993
441. Jay K. Six	2016	492. Gerald L. Toshalis	2006
442. Edward H. Slate	2012	493. Kenneth L. Tousley	1995
443. Harold J. Slater	2010	494. Raymond J. Townsend	2009
444. Dennis E. Slattery	2012	495. Ted P. Townsend	1998
445. Linda J. Slaughter-Titus	2010	496. Douglas R. Trebilcock	2006
446. Stephen C. Small	2004	497. Keith R. Treman	2015
447. Betty A. Smith	2004	498. Saul C. Trinidad	2013
448. Charles W. Smith	2011	499. Michael J. Tupper	2016
449. James A. Smith	1993	500. Arthur R. Turner	2006
450. Jerome K. Smith	2011	501. Molly C. Turner	2012
451. Russell L. Smith	1994	502. Richard A. Turner	1995
452. William M. Smith	2005	503. James E. Tuttle	2016
453. Dorraine S. Snogren	1990	504. Diane E. Vale	1990
454. David P. Snyder	2014	505. Oscar Ventura	2009
455. Jean R. Snyder	2002	506. William A. Verhelst	2006
456. G. Charles Sonquist, Jr.	2002	507. Douglas W. Vernon	2010
457. Harlan E. Sorensen	2006	508. Rony S. Veska	2013
458. Joseph L. Spackman	2013	509. Alonzo E. Vincent	2013
459. Arthur L. Spafford	1991	510. Paul T. Wachterhauser	2009
460. Sandra Lee Spahr	2006	511. Glenn M. Wagner	2017
461. Gordon E. Spalenka	1993	512. Lynn W. Wagner	2002
462. Carolin S. Spragg	2013	513. Daniel J. Wallace	1997
463. Lynette Stallworth	2002	514. Joyce E. Wallace	2013
464. Robert W. Stark	2008	515. Suzanne B. Walls	2016
465. Ethel Z. Stears	1999	516. Lowell F. Walsworth	2002
466. Jerry L. Stewardson	2003	517. Robert E. Walton	2002
467. Carlyle F. Stewart III	2014	518. Maurice E. Walworth, Jr.	2006
468. Linda D. Stoddard	2016	519. George F. Ward	2006
469. Arthur R. Stone	2006	520. Kenneth E. Ward	2005
470. David A. Stout	2007	521. Robert P. Ward	1993
471. Robert P. Stover	2012	522. Grant A. Washburn	1995
472. Dana R. Strall	2017	523. Brent L. Webster	2012
473. Michael P. Streevy	2010	524. Roy "LaVere" Webster	1995
474. David R. Strobe	2013	525. Harold E. Weemhoff, Jr.	2015
475. Donald B. Strobe	1990	526. Glenn R. Wegner	2004
476. David T. Strong	1998	527. Stephan Weinberger	2016
477. Verne Carl Summers	1992	528. Edward C. Weiss, Jr.	1994
478. Royal J. Synwolt	1991	529. James D. Weiss	1993
479. Thomas E. Tarpley, Sr.	2015	530. Karen A. (Mars) Welch	2008
480. Roy G. Testolin	2013	531. Gerald L. Welsh	1994
481. Wayne N. Thomas	2010	532. Robert L. Wessman	1999
482. J. Todd Thompson	2010	533. Charles H. West	2009
483. James M. Thompson	2006	534. Margaret Rodgers West	2009

535.	Karen S. Wheat	2015	546. Chong Y. Won	2015
536.	Robert A. White	2016	547. Gregory B. Wood	2015
537.	Theodore D. Whitely, Sr.	2015	548. Robert D. Wright	2015
538.	Bobby Dale Whitlock	2009	549. William R. Wright	2017
539.	Myron K. Williams	1994	550. William A. Wylie-Kellermann	2017
540.	Richard K. Williams	2001	551. Deborah A. Line Yencer	2018
541.	Sondra B. Willobee	2017	552. Richard A. Youells	1995
542.	Margaret Halls Wilson	2009	553. Lee F. Zachman	2010
543.	Richard D. Wilson	2008	554. Karl L. Zeigler	2010
544.	Douglas E. Wingeier	2000	555. Ellen K. Zienert	2018
545.	David A. Winslow	2008		

54. What associate members have been retired (¶357): (List alphabetically. If retiring in the interim between conference sessions (¶357.2d), indicate the effective date of retirement.)
(Under ¶357.1, no vote required; under ¶357.2, v; under ¶357.3, 2/3 v)
a) This year?

Name	**Year**
Merlin H. Pratt	2019
Terrill M. Schneider	2018
Theodore A. Trudgeon	2019

b) Previously?

Name	**Year**	**Name**	**Year**
John R. Allan	1998	James M. Mathews	2003
Eugene L. Baughan	2002	Clyde E. Miller	1987
Elaine M. Buker	1997	Walter H. Miller	2004
John T. Charter	1999	Gerald E. Mumford	1993
Jane A. Crabtree	2003	Harold V. Phillips	2017
Jean Arthur Crabtree	1994	Darlene Kay Pratt	2016
Walter David	1992	James A. Rencontre	1997
Roy G. Forsyth	1991	Randall E. Roose	1993
Marcos A. Gutierrez	2010	Nicholas W. Scroggins	2010
Patricia A. Harpole	2017	Howard Seaver	2012
Catherine W.J. Hiner	2009	Brian K. Sheen	2004
Dale F. Jaquette	1992	Charles R. VanLente	2010
Geraldine M. Litchfield	2014	Nola R. Williams	2000
Michael W. Luce	2012		

55. What provisional members have been previously retired (¶358, 2008 *Book of Discipline*)?

Name	**Clergy Status**	**Year**
Carol L. Bourns	PE	2007

56. Who have been recognized as retired local pastors (¶320.5):
a) This year? * **indicates completed COS or M.Div**

Name	**COS or M.Div.**	**Date Effective**
Carole A. Brown	M.Div.	07.01.2019
Donald J. Graham	*COS	07.01.2019
Rosaline D. Green	2 COS	07.01.2019
Dale A. Hotelling	*2012	01.01.2019
Donna J. Keyte	*COS	07.01.2019
Margaret A. Martinez	M.Div.	07.01.2019

Ralph A. Posnik, Jr.	*COS	07.01.2019
Cecelia L. Sayer	*2013	07.01.2019
Calvin "Herb" Wheelock	*2011	07.01.2019
Mark E. Zender	*2016	07.01.2019

b)   Previously? (*Those with an asterisk have completed the Course of Study)

Name	Year	Name	Year
L. Cecile Adams	2013	Daniel W. Harris	2003
*Sheila F. Baker	2014	Patricia A. Harton	2010
James E. Barnett	2013	*Jacque Hodges	2017
*Donald E. Bedwell	2011	*Clare Walter Huyck	2015
Virginia B. Bell	2005	*Raymond A. Jacques	2008
*Leo "Bud" Elwood Bennett	1993	*Thomas H. John, Sr.	2012
*Nancy J. Bitterling	2018	Charles B. Jones	1997
Betty M. Blair	2009	*J. Robert Keim	2011
*Nancy L. Boelens	2009	Margaret Kivisto	2013
*Peggy Ann Boltz	2014	*Sandra J. Kolder	2017
*Connie R. Bongard	2015	Robert I. Kreger	2013
*Debra K. Brown	2015	*Suzanne P. Kornowski	2011
*Richard B. Brown	2010	Jeanne N. Laimon	2015
Ronald A. Brown	1994	*Bonny J. Lancaster	2006
*Ellen F. Burns	2010	*George W. Lawton	2007
*Linda J. Burton-Collier	2014	Ruth A. McCully	2009
*Roberta W. Cabot	2014	James B. Montney	2012
David Gunnar Carlson	2010	*Dianne Doten Morrison	2016
*Linda J. Carlson	2009	*Larry W. Nalett	2004
*Mary Ellen Chapman	2016	*Lawrence A. Nichols	2016
*Robert D. Chapman	2012	Judith A. Nielsen	2007
*Paulette G. Cheyne	2008	*Gary L. Peterson	2016
*Esther Cox	1988	Kathy Phillips	2016
*Martin H. Culver	2011	*David O. Pratt	2016
Bonita Davis	2008	*Jean B. Rencontre	2008
*Merlin Delo	1997	*O'Ryan Rickard (¶ 327.7)	2013
*Donald R. Derby	2018	*John F. Ritter	2001
*Judy K. Downing-Siglin	2001	*Carolyn A. Robinson-Fisher	2011
*Richard J. Duffey	2005	*Deanna M. Sailor-Petit	2006
*Mona J. Dye	2017	*Jeffrey J. Schrock	2016
*William F. Dye	2017	*William Schuman	2001
James A. Fegan	2005	Allen F. Schweitzer	2000
*Edna M. Fleming	2011	Edward C. Seward	2004
*David C. Freeland	2017	*Connie E. Shatz	2012
Richard A. Fritz	2014	*Alice J. Sheffield	2012
*Linda L. Fuller	2018	*Michael J. Simon	2017
*Joyce F. Gackler	2012	*Kathleen Smith	2012
*Sandra J. Gastian	2011	*Mary E. Spencer	2009
*Sue J. Gay	2007	*Cherrie A. Sporleder	2013
*Carl E. Greene	2011	*Robert A. Srock	2012
*Sueann K. Hagan	2017	Bruce Steinberg	2018
*Paul E. Hane	2018	John R. Sternaman	2002
*Carolyn G. Harris	2013	*James W. Stilwell	2017

*Diane E. Stone	2010	*Irene L. Vittoz	2018
*Stanley Patrick Stybert	2010	*Donald R. Wendell	2009
*Kenneth E. Tabor	2010	*Betty J. Whitely	2007
*Clarence VanConant	2010	*Henry Williams	2012
Earleen A. VanConant	2000	Roberta L. Willson	2014
*Sandra K. VandenBrink	2013	*Donald Woolum	2003
*Herbert J. VanderBilt	2017	*David L. Youngs	2006
*Dianne H. Van Marter	2015	*Gayle Sue (Berntsen) Zaagman	2014

57. What is the number of clergy members of the Annual Conference? 1,233

     a)   By appointment category and conference relationship?

         (NOTES:

         (1)   Where applicable, the question numbers on this report form corresponding to each category have been placed in parenthesis following the category title. Where these question numbers appear, the number reported in that category should agree with the number of names listed in the corresponding questions.

         (2)   For the three categories of Appointments to Extension Ministries, report as follows:

¶344.1a, c): the number of clergy members appointed within United Methodist connectional structures, including district superintendents, or to an ecumenical agency.

¶344.1b): the number of clergy members appointed to extension ministries, under endorsement by the Division of Chaplains and Related Ministries of the General Board of Higher Education and Ministry.

¶344.1d): the number of clergy members appointed to other valid ministries, confirmed by a two-thirds vote of the Annual Conference.

Note: Report those in extension ministry in one category only.

See the Discipline paragraphs indicated for more detailed description of these appointment categories.)

Note: Those approved to serve as a local pastor, but not currently under appointment, are not counted as clergy members of the conference.

Categories	Deacons in Full Connection	Elders in Full Connection	Provisional Deacons	Provisional Elders	Associate Members & Affiliate Members with Vote	Full–time Local Pastors	Part–time Local Pastors
Pastors and deacons whose primary appointment is to a Local Church (¶¶331.1c, 339) (74)	12	243	4	36	5	130	78
Deacons (in full connection and provisional) serving Beyond the Local Church (¶331.1a, b) (77a,b)	17	XXXXX XXXXX XXXXX	0	XXXXX XXXXX XXXXX	XXXXX XXXXX XXXXX	XXXXX XXXXX XXXXX	XXXXX XXXXX XXXXX
Appointments to Extension Ministries (¶316.1; 344.1a, c) (76a)	XXXXX XXXXX XXXXX	23	XXXXX XXXXX XXXXX	0	0	3	0
Appointments to Extension Ministries (¶316.1; 344.1b) (76b)	XXXXX XXXXX XXXXX	9	XXXXX XXXXX XXXXX	0	0	0	0
Appointments to Extension Ministries (¶316.1; 344.1d) (76c)	XXXXX XXXXX XXXXX	10	XXXXX XXXXX XXXXX	0	0	1	0
Appointments to Attend School (¶331.3) (78)	0	0	0	0	0	XXXXX XXXXX	XXXXX XXXXX
Appointed to Other Annual Conferences (49)	4	5	0	1	0	XXXXX XXXXX	XXXXX XXXXX
On Leave of Absence (50a1, a2)	2	10	1	0	0	XXXXX XXXXX	XXXXX XXXXX
On Family Leave (50a3. a4)	0	0	0	0	0	XXXXX XXXXX	XXXXX XXXXX
On Sabbatical Leave (51)	0	0	0	0	0	XXXXX XXXXX	XXXXX XXXXX
On Medical Leave (52)	1	12	0	1	0	0	1
On Transitional Leave (50a5)	1	0	0	0	0	XXXXX XXXXX	XXXXX XXXXX
Retired (53, 54, 55)	20	571	0	1	31	XXXXX XXXXX	XXXXX XXXXX
Total Number, Clergy Members	57	883	5	39	36	134	79
Grand Total, All Conference Clergy Members	1233						

b)   By gender and racial/ethnic identification? (NOTE: See the instruction for item 57 for guidelines to assist in the racial/ethnic identification count.)

Clergy Demographics

Categories	Deacons in Full Connection		Elders in Full Connection		Provisional Deacons		Provisional Elders		Associate Members & Affiliate Members with Vote		Full–time Local Pastors		Part–time Local Pastors	
	Male	Female	Male	Female	Male	Female	Male	Female	Male	Female	Male	Female	Male	Female
Asian	0	0	23	4	0	1	4	0	0	0	2	0	1	1
Black	0	1	31	14	0	0	0	1	0	0	6	2	6	3
Hispanic	1	0	3	0	0	0	0	0	1	0	2	2	0	0
Native American	0	0	0	1	0	0	0	0	0	0	0	0	0	0
Pacific Islander	0	0	0	0	0	0	0	0	0	0	0	0	1	0
White	9	45	607	201	3	1	12	22	25	10	74	43	39	28
Multi-Racial	0	0	0	0	0	0	0	0	0	0	2	1	0	0
Grand Total-All Conference Clergy Members*	10	46	664	220	3	2	16	23	26	10	86	48	47	32

PART III CERTIFICATION IN SPECIALIZED MINISTRY
Note: Indicate credential of persons in Part III: FD, FE, PD, PE, AM, FL, PL, and LM.

58. Who are the candidates in process for certification in specialized ministry?

Name	Clergy/Lay Status	Specialized Ministry
Kathryn L. Pittenger	FD	Christian Education
Andrew Schleicher	FD	Christian Education
Kathryn L. Pittenger	FD	Children's Ministry
Mary Hagley	FD	Youth Ministry
Diana Carpenter	Lay	Spiritual Formation
Julie Lawhead	Lay	Spiritual Formation

59. Who is certified in specialized ministry? (List the areas of specialized ministry. Indicate by an asterisk those certified this year.)

Name	Clergy/Lay Status	Specialized Ministry
Pamela Buchholz	RD	Christian Education
M. Kay DeMoss	FD	Christian Education
I. Naomi Garcia	Laity	Christian Education
Diane Griffin	Diaconal	Christian Education
Colleen T. Treman	FD	Christian Education
Daniel R. Colthorp	FL	Youth Ministry
Michele Ettinger	Lay	Youth Ministry
Brian Johnson	FL	Youth Ministry
Sue Pethoud	FD	Youth Ministry
Mark R. Babb	FD	Music Ministry
John Potter	Lay	Music Ministry
Susan D. Amick	FD	Spiritual Formation
Lisa M. Batten	FL	Spiritual Formation
Annelissa Gray-Lion	RD	Spiritual Formation
Sueann K. Hagan	RL	Spiritual Formation
Jennifer J. Jue	FE	Spiritual Formation
Nancy LeValley	Laity	Spiritual Formation
Jack Mannschreck	FE	Spiritual Formation
Philip Tousley	FE	Spiritual Formation
Christine E. Wyatt	RD	Spiritual Formation
Andrew Schleicher	FD	Christian Communications

60. Who are transferred in as a certified person in specialized ministry? **None**

61. Who are transferred out as a certified person in specialized ministry? **None**

62. Who have been removed as a certified person in specialized ministry? **None**

PART IV CERTIFIED LAY MINISTRY
(¶¶268, and 666.10 *The Book of Discipline*)

63. Who are certified as lay ministers (¶¶268, and 666.10)? (List alphabetically, by district)

Name	District	Certified / Re-Certified
Sharon Appling	Greater Detroit	2018
Steven P. Beukema	Greater Southwest	2017
Patricia Bird	Greater Southwest	2015 / 2018
Bu Ki Cho	Greater Southwest	2017
Jon Clark	Greater Southwest	2017
Linda S. Depta	Greater Southwest	2016 / 2017
Wynne L. Hurlbut	Greater Southwest	2017
Kevin Kahmark	Greater Southwest	2016 / 2017
Alexander Miller *(DSA 2014)*	Greater Southwest	2014 / 2017
Simmie N. Proctor	Greater Southwest	2017
Marcia Tucker	Greater Southwest	2016 / 2017
Donald A. Weaver	Greater Southwest	2017
Richard Vorel	Greater Southwest	2017
Lois Fennimore *(DSA 2011)*	Heritage	2011 / 2017
Christine L. Pease *(DSA 07.01.2014)*	Heritage	2017
Mickey Ann Cousino *(DSA 09.01.2015)*	Mid-Michigan	2017
Joseph Keith Caldwell	Midwest	2015 / 2018
Gary Zinger *(DSA 07.01.2017)*	Midwest	2014 / 2018
Nancy LeValley	Northern Waters	2011 / 2018
Donna Stone	Northern Waters	2009 / 2018

PART V DIACONAL MINISTERS
(Paragraph numbers in questions 64-71 refer to *The 1992 Book of Discipline*)

64. Who are transferred in as diaconal ministers (¶312)? **None**

65. Who are transferred out as diaconal ministers (¶312)? **None**

66. Who have had their conference relationship as diaconal ministers terminated by Annual Conference action (¶313.3)? (**Under ¶313.3a, no vote; under ¶313.3b, 2/3 v**) None

67. What diaconal ministers have died during the year?
    a)   Effective: **None**
    b)   Retired: **None**

68. What diaconal ministers have been granted leaves of absence under ¶313.1a, c, d) (disability, study/sabbatical, or personal leave): (**v**) **None**

69. What diaconal ministers have been granted an extended leave (¶313.1e): **None**

70. Who have returned to active status from extended leave (¶313.1e)? (**v**)? **None**

71. Who have taken the retired relationship to the Annual Conference as diaconal ministers (¶313.2): **(Under ¶313.2b, 2/3 v)**
   a)   This year? **None**
   b)   Previously?

Name	Date Effective
Barbara A. Brooks	2007
Janice E. Caldwell	1999
Jane Case	2011
Thelma M. Childress	1994
Daphna Lee Flegal	2018
Margaret L. Foster	1999
George W. Gish	2003
Mary Levack Quick	2002
Beverly W. Rice	1997

PART VI APPOINTMENTS AND CONCLUDING BUSINESS

72. Who are approved for less than full-time service?
   a)   What associate members and elders (full and provisional) are approved for appointment to less than full-time service, what is the total number of years for which such approval has been granted to each, and for what fraction of full-time service (in one-quarter, one-half, or three-quarter increments) is approval granted (¶¶338.2, 342.2, 1506)? **(2/3 v; after 8 years 3/4 v):**

Name	Current Appointment	Years	Fraction of Full-Time Service
John W. Ball	Lake Orion	0	3/4
Charles D. Farnum	Director, CMU Wesley	5	1/4
Steve Khang	Ann Arbor Korean	5	3/4
Shawn P. Lewis-Lakin	Birmingham: First UMC	0	3/4
Marva Pope	Wayne: First UMC	1	1/2
Latha Ravi	Cass Community	0	1/4
Heidi Reinker	Trenton: First	3	3/4
Linda "Lyne" K. Stull-Lipps	Riverdale: Lincoln Road	3	3/4
Beth Titus	Nardin Park	5	1/2
Susan J. Trowbridge	Battle Creek: First UMC	5	1/2
Melanie S. Young	Ovid UMC/Middlebury	1	3/4

   b)   What deacons in full connection and provisional deacons are approved for appointment to less than full-time service (¶331.7)?

Name	Current Appointment	Years	Fraction of Full-Time Service
Mark R. Babb	Sturgis: First UMC	0	1/2
Patricia L. Catellier	Portage: Chapel Hill	2	1/4
Mariel Kay DeMoss	MI Area Communications	4	3/4
Mary Hagley	Dixboro UMC	6	1/2
Georgia N. Hale	Grand Rapids: Genesis	4	1/4
Todd J. Query	Virginia/York River	4	1/2 and 1/4
Laura Speiran	Clarkston UMC	5	3/4
Cara Beth Ann Weiler	Kalamazoo: Sunnyside	10	1/2 and 1/4
Alicea Williams	Mount Clemens: First	3	1/2

73. Who have been appointed as interim pastors under the provisions of ¶338.3 since the last session of the annual conference, and for what period of time? **None**

74. What elders, deacons (full connection and provisional), associate members, local and supply pastors are appointed to ministry to the local church and where are they appointed for the ensuing year? (Attach a list.)

75. What changes have been made in appointments since the last annual conference session? (Attach list. Include and identify Appointments Beyond the Local Church (Deacons) and Appointments to Extension Ministries (Elders). Give effective dates of all changes.)

76. What elders (full connection and provisional), associate members, and local pastors are appointed to extension ministries for the ensuing year? (Attach a list)
    a) Within the connectional structures of United Methodism (¶344.1a, c)?

Name	Clergy Status	Date Effective	Extension Ministry Assignment	Charge Conference
Maurice R. Horne, Sr.	FL	2018	Flint Mission Zone Minister of Outreach	Lincoln Park

b) To ministries endorsed by the Board of Higher Education and Ministry (¶344.1b)?
c) To other valid ministries under the provisions of ¶344.1d? **(2/3 v)**

Name	Clergy Status	Date Effect.	Extension Ministry Assignment	Charge Conference
John W. Ball	FE	2019	Celebrate Hope Consultant	Lake Orion
Margaret E. Bryce	FE	2019	Adj Prof Ministry Consultant at Ashland Theological Seminary	
David G. Elmore	FE	2016	Chaplain for Ascension at Home/Reverence Hospice, Portage	Coldwater
Emmanuel J. Giddings, Sr.	FE	2006	Director of Alfalit International/ Liberia Literacy Program	
Melody Johnson	FE	2002	Corporate Chaplain, Porter Hills Retirement Community	Birmingham: First
Nathaniel W. Johnson	FE	2016	Spectrum Health Delivery System, Manager of Pastoral Care and Bereavement	Grand Rapids: Vergennes
Joy J. Moore	FE	2019	Luther Seminary, Associate Professor of Biblical Preaching	Flint: Bethel
Kenneth J. Nash (345)	FE	2016	Wesleyan Church of Hamburg, Hamburg, NY	Grand Rapids: Cornerstone
Matthew R. Schlimm	FE	2019	Professor of Old Testament, University of Dubuque Theological Seminary	Kalamazoo: Westwood
Barbara L. Smith-Jang	FE	2003	Pastoral Counselor, Taejon Christian International School, Taejon South Korea	Grand Ledge: First
Alice Fleming Townley (¶345)	FE	2010	Parish Associate, Okemos Presbyterian Church, Okemos	East Lansing: University
Jonathan D. VanDop	FE	2019	West Texas Veteran's Health Administration	Coopersville

77. Who are appointed as deacons (full connection and provisional) for the ensuing year? (Attach a list.)
    a) Through non-United Methodist agencies and settings beyond the local church (¶331.1a)?
    b) Through United Methodist Church-related agencies or schools within the connectional structures of The United Methodist Church (¶331.1b)?

78. Who are appointed to attend school (¶416.6)? (List alphabetically all those whose prime appointment is to attend school.)

79. Where are the diaconal ministers appointed for the ensuing year (¶310) **[1992 Discipline]**?

Name	**Appointment**
Diane Griffin	Howell: First UMC – Director of Educational Ministries
Matthew Packer	Fenton UMC Chancel Choir Director and Music Coordinator

80. What other personal notations should be made? (Include such matters as changes in pension credit (¶1506.5), corrections or additions to matters reported in the "Business of the Annual Conference" form in previous years, and legal name changes of clergy members and diaconal ministers.)
    Carol Abbott Freeland
    Margaret A. Martinez-Ventour to Margaret A. Martinez
    Heather McDougall Molner

81. Where and when shall the next Conference Session be held (¶603.2, 3)?
    Grand Traverse Resort in Acme, Michigan, May 28-31, 2020

— MAC Photos

— MAC Photos

APPOINTMENTS
Appointments by District

DM – Diaconal Minister
PD – Provisional Deacon
PM – Provisional Member
FD – Deacon in Full Connection
DP – Deacon from other denomination serving UM probation
OD – Deacon Member of Other Annual Conference
PE – Provisional Elder
FE – Elder in full connection
EP – Elder/full minister from other denomination serving UM probation
OE – Elder member of other annual conference

OF – Full member of other denomination
AF – Affiliated Member
AM – Associate Member
FL – Full Time Local Pastor
PL – Part Time Local Pastor
SP – Student Local Pastor
RA – Retired Associate Member
RE – Retired Full Member
RD – Retired Deacon
RP – Retired Provisional Member

RL – Retired Local Pastor
RLA – Retired Local Pastor Under Appointment
OR – Retired Member of Other Conference
HL – Honorable Location
HLOC – Honorable Location Other Conference
DSA – District Superintendent Assignment (name)
CLM – Certified Lay Minister
++ – Ad Interim Appointment
*Home Address

CENTRAL BAY DISTRICT

District Superintendent: David I. Kim FE2
Executive Assistant: Teri Rice

DS Email: dkim@michiganumc.org
Office Email: trice@michiganumc.org

Office: (989) 793-8838
3764 Fashion Square Blvd, Saginaw 48603

CHARGE		PASTOR	ADDRESS	TELEPHONE CHURCH	HOME
Alger	DSA1	Janet Shaffer	7786 W. Newberry St., Box 123, Alger 48610	(989) 836-2291	
			*120 Anna Dr, Tawas City 48763-9208		989-362-6536
Arbela	RE2	Gloria Haynes	Box 252, 8496 Barnes, Millington 48746	(989) 793-5880	
			*2152 Village West Dr., S, Lapeer 48466		(734) 626-0070
Arenac County: Christ	AM1	James A. Payne	3322 E. Huron Rd., Box 145, AuGres 48703	(989) 876-7449	
		(part-time ½)	*124 N. Chestnut, PO Box 167, Sterling 48659		(989) 654-9001
Auburn	FE2	Robert D. Nystrom	207 S. Auburn, Auburn 48611	(989) 662-6314	
			*201 S. Auburn, Auburn 48611		(269) 535-2481

CENTRAL BAY DISTRICT

CENTRAL BAY DISTRICT

CHARGE	PASTOR	ADDRESS	CHURCH	HOME
BAY CITY Grace	Eric D. Kieb	FE5	4267 S. Two Mile Rd, Bay City 48706 *2161 Niethammer Dr. Bay City 48706	(989) 684-1101	(989) 671-8951
Bay Port Hayes	Matthew Chapman	PE4	838 Second St., Bay Port 48720 7001 Filion Rd., Pigeon 48755 *838 Second St., Bay Port 48720	(989) 656-2151	(989) 656-2151
Beaverton: First	Lynn F. Chappell	RE5	150 West Brown, Beaverton 48612 *148 W Brown, Beaverton 48612	(989) 435-4322	(989) 435-9403
Bentley	Merry Henderson	DSA1	7209 N. Main St., PO Box 1, Rhodes 48652 *10601 Carr Rd, Saint Charles 48655	(989) 846-0398	(989) 447-1874
Birch Run	Rey Mondragon (LTFT ¾)	FE5	Box 277, 12265 Church St., Birch Run 48415 *8196 Poellet, Birch Run 48415	(989) 624-9340	(734) 645-8991
Blanchard-Pine River	Janet M. Larner	FE3	7655 West Blanchard Road, Blanchard 49310-9109 *175 North Dr, Shepherd 48883-9070	(989) 561-2864	(989) 245-8846
Burt	Rey Mondragon (LTFT ¼)	FE3	Box 96, 2799 Nichols Rd., Burt 48417 *8196 Poellet, Birch Run 48415	(989) 770-9948	(734) 645-8991
Caro	Anthony Tomasino	FE4	670 Gilford, Caro 48723 *208 W. Burnside, Caro 48723	(989) 673-2246	(989) 673-4355
Caseville	Donald L. Wojewski	FL2	6490 Main St., Box 1027, Caseville 48725 *6474 Main, Box 1027, Caseville 48725	(989) 856-4009	(989) 856-2626
Cass City	Robert P. Demyanovich	FL2	5100 N. Cemetery, Box 125, Cass City 48726 *6339 Brenda Dr., Cass City 48726	(989) 872-3422	(248) 636-5679
Churchill	Brenda K. Klacking (part-time ½)	FL7	501 E. State Rd., West Branch 48661 *1005 W. Eighth St., Mio 48647	(989) 345-0827	(989) 826-5521
Clare	John G Kasper	FE7	105 E Seventh Street, Clare 48617-1301 *714 S Rainbow Dr, Clare 48617-9605	(989) 386-2591	(989) 386-7683
Coleman: Faith	Scott W. Marsh	FL1	310 Fifth St., Box 476, Coleman 48618 *209 E. Jefferson St, Coleman 48618	(989) 465-6181	(231-760-0601

CHARGE	PASTOR		ADDRESS	CHURCH	HOME
Coomer Winn	Raymond W Francis	CLM/DSA4	8187 S Winn Rd (5410 S Vandecar Rd), Mt Pleasant 48858 8187 S Winn Rd, Mt Pleasant 48858	(989) 866-2566 (989) 866-2417	(989) 330-9135
Elkton	Won D. Kim	PE3	*812 W Center St, Alma 48801-2140 150 South Main St., Box 9, Elkton 48731 *134 S. Main St., Elkton 48731	(989) 375-4113	(989) 375-4185
Essexville: St. Luke's	Eric A. Stone	FE11	206 Scheurmann St., Essexville 48732 *212 Hart St., Essexville 48732	(989) 893-8031	(989) 894-2453
Fairgrove	Penny Parkin (part-time ½)	FL6	5116 W. Center, Box 10, Fairgrove 48733 *2024 Liberty, Fairgrove 48733	(989) 693-6564	(989) 600-8086
Farwell	Martin T Cobb	FL3	PO Box 709, 281 E Ohio Street, Farwell 48622-0709 *511 N Superior St, Farwell 48622	(989) 588-2931	
Frankenmuth	Ryan L. Wenburg	FE1	346 East Vates, Frankenmuth 48734 *326 East Vates, Frankenmuth 48734	(989) 652-6858	(989) 598-5438
Freeland	Kayla Roosa	PE3	205 E. Washington, Box 207, Freeland 48623 *7801 N. River Road, Freeland 48623	(989) 695-2101	(989) 573-8357
Gladwin: First	Carmen L. Cook	FL2	309 S. M-18, Gladwin 48624 *1271 Chatterton, Gladwin 48624	(989) 426-9619	(989) 426-2698
Glennie	Keith Reinhardt	PL4	5094 Bamfield Rd., Box 189, Glennie 48737 *7620 Spruce, Hale 48739	(989) 735-3951	(989) 710-1976
Gordonville Midland: Homer	Ernesto Mariona	FE2	76 E. Gordonville Rd., Midland 48640 507 S. Homer Rd., Midland 48640 *8225 Beaver Rd, Saint Charles 48655	(989) 631-4388 (989) 835-5050	(248) 760-9590
Hale: First	Melvin L. Leach	RE2	201 West Main St., Box 46, Hale 48739 *7540 O'Connor, Box 334, Hale 48739	(989) 728-9522	(586) 212-2802
Harrison: The Gathering	Cheryl L Mancier	PL4	PO Box 86, 426 N First St. Suite 106, Harrison 48625-0086 *4338 Bay Rd, Gladwin 48624-8767	(989) 539-1445	(989) 426-9886

CENTRAL BAY DISTRICT

CENTRAL BAY DISTRICT

CHARGE	PASTOR		ADDRESS	CHURCH	HOME
Harrisville	Eric L. Johnson	PL2	107 W Church St., Harrisville 48740	(989) 724-5450	
Lincoln			101 East Main St., Lincoln 48742	(989) 736-6910	(810) 335-1276
			*216 5th St, Harrisville 48740		
Hope	Patrick R. Poag	FL15	5278 North Hope Rd., Hope 48628	(989) 689-3811	
Edenville			455 W. Curtis Rd., Box 125, Edenville 48620	(989) 689-6250	
Dale			4688 S. Freeman Rd, Box 436, Beaverton 48612	(989) 435-4829	
			*5302 N. Hope Rd., Hope 48628		(989) 689-4788
Kilmanagh	William C. Cleland	PL6	2009 S. Bay Port Rd., Bay Port 48720	(989) 453-3520	
Owendale			7370 Main St., Box 98, Owendale 48754	(989) 678-4172	(989) 975-1500
			*129 S. Silver St., Bad Axe 48413		
Kingston	Mark A. Harriman	FL2	PO Box 196, 3453 Washington St., Kingston 48741	(989) 683-2832	(989) 683-2929
			*3442 Washington St., Box 243, Kingston 48741		
Mayville	Nathan J. Jeffords	FL1	601 East Ohmer, PO Box 189, Mayville 48744	(989) 843-6151	(989) 781-0860
			*860 E. Brown Rd, Mayville 48744		
MIDLAND					
Aldersgate	Michael T. Sawicki	FE7	2206 Airfield Lane, Midland 48642	(989) 631-1151	
Saginaw: Kochville Campus *(became satellite campus 9/1/18)*			6030 Bay Rd., Saginaw 48604	(989) 792-2321	(989) 492-4464
			*415 Coolidge Dr., Midland 48642		
First	Anita K. Hahn	FE1	315 W. Larkin St., Box 466, Midland 48640	(989) 835-6797	(989) 708-8894
			*3217 Noeske, Midland 48640		
Associate	Jung Eun Yum	FE6	315 W. Larkin St., Box 466, Midland 48640	(989) 835-6797	(989) 486-9307
			*1010 Pepperidge Ct. Midland 48642		
Millington	John J. Britt	FE5	Box 321, 9020 State, Millington 48746	(989) 871-3489	(989) 871-3341
			*4851 W. Main St., Millington 48746		
Mio	Brenda K. Klacking	FL6	1101 W. Eighth St., Mio 48647	(989) 826-5598	(989) 826-5521
	(part-time ½)		*1005 W. Eighth St., Mio 48647		

CHARGE	PASTOR		ADDRESS	CHURCH	HOME
MT. PLEASANT					
Chippewa Indian	TO BE SUPPLIED		3490 S Leaton Rd, Mt Pleasant 48858-7995		
			*3490 S Leaton Rd, Mt Pleasant 48858-7995		(989) 621-8867
First	Julie A. Greyerbiehl	FE2	400 S Main Street, Mount Pleasant 48858-2598	(989) 773-6934	(517) 655-2321
			*1109 Glenwood Dr, Mt Pleasant 48858-4325		
Leaton	Deborah A. Line Yencer	RE2	6890 E Beal City Road, Mt Pleasant 48858	(989) 773-3838	(248) 425-4684
			*17429 Summit Ct, Barryton 49305		
Trinity	TO BE SUPPLIED		202 S Elizabeth St, Mt Pleasant 48858-2820	(989) 772-5690	
Countryside			202 S. Elizabeth St (4264 S Leaton Rd), Mt Pleasant 48858	(989) 773-0359	
			*250 S Crawford Rd, Mt Pleasant 48858-9053		
Oscoda	William R. Seitz	FE9	120 W. Dwight, Oscoda 48750	(989) 739-8591	(989) 739-5213
Oscoda Indian Church			7994 Alvin Rd., Mikado 48750		
			*108 W. Dwight St, Oscoda 48750		
PIGEON					
First	Cindy Gibbs	FL5	7102 Michigan Ave., Box 377, Pigeon 48755	(989) 453-2475	(989) 453-3232
			*7090 Scheurer St., Box 377, Pigeon 48755		
Salem	David K. Stewart Sr.	FE7	23 Mabel, Box 438, Pigeon 48755	(989) 453-2552	(989) 453-2317
			*7065 Clabuesch St., Box 438, Pigeon 48755		
Pinconning	Heather Nowak	FL2	314 Whyte St., Pinconning 48650	(989) 879-3271	
Garfield			701 N. Garfield Road, Linwood 48634	(989) 879-6992	
			*		
Port Austin	Clifford L. Radtke	PL2	8625 Arch, Box 129, Port Austin 48467	(989) 738-5322	
Pinnebog			4619 Pinnebog Rd., Kinde 48445		(269) 545-2275
			*114 Washington St., Port Austin 48467		
Reese	Jon W. Gougeon	FL11	9859 Saginaw St., PO Box 7, Reese 48757	(989) 868-9957	(989) 868-9957
			*1968 Rhodes, Reese 48757		
Rose City: Trinity	Helen Alford	PL1	125 West Main St., PO Box 130, Rose City 48654	(989) 685-2350	989-473-2220
			*3950 Rose City Rd, Lupton 48635		

CENTRAL BAY DISTRICT

CENTRAL BAY DISTRICT

CHARGE	PASTOR		ADDRESS	CHURCH	HOME
Rosebush	Joseph L Beavan	FL6	PO Box 187, 3805 School Street, Rosebush 48878-0187	(989) 433-2957	(989) 433-5509
SAGINAW			*3272 E Weidman Rd, Rosebush 48878-9715		
Ames	David A. Wichert	FE1	801 State St., Saginaw 48602	(989) 754-6373	(989) 401-6622
			*1477 Vancouver, Saginaw 48638		
First	Amylee B. Terhune	FE4	4790 Gratiot Road, Saginaw 48638	(989) 799-0131	(989) 793-5880
			*4674 Village Drive, Saginaw 48638		
New Heart	Melene E. Wilsey	FL4	1802 W. Michigan Ave., Saginaw 48602	(989) 792-4689	(989) 839-4798
			*1304 W. Stewart, Midland 48640		
Swan Valley	Robert G. Richards	FL1	9265 Geddes Rd., Saginaw 48609	(989) 781-0860	
LaPorte			3990 Smith's Crossing, Freeland 48623	(989) 695-9692	
Hemlock			406 W. Saginaw, Box 138, Hemlock 48626	(989) 642-5932	
Nelson			5950 S Hemlock Rd, Hemlock 48626	(989) 642-8285	
			*16344 Nothern Pintail Trail, Hemlock 48626		(989) 642-4560
St. Charles	Karen J. Sorden	FE3	301 W. Belle, Box 87, St. Charles 48655	(989) 865-9091	(989) 865-8144
			*510 Christy Drive, St. Charles 48655		
Sanford	Lisa L. Cook	FE6	2560 W. River Rd., Sanford 48657	(989) 687-5353	(989) 701-7240
			*2550 N. West River Rd., Sanford 48657		
Sebewaing: Trinity	Pamela A. Beedle-Gee	FE2	513 Washington, Sebewaing 48759	(989) 883-3350	
			*525 Washington, Sebewaing 48759		
Shepherd	Janet M. Larner	FE3	PO Box 309, 107 W Wright Ave, Shepherd 48883-0309	(989) 828-5866	(989) 245-8846
			*175 North Dr, Shepherd 48883-9070		
Standish: Beacon of Light	James A. Payne (part-time ½)	AM1	201 S. Forest, Standish 48658	(989) 846-6277	(989) 654-9001
			*124 N. Chestnut, PO Box 167, Sterling 48659		
Sutton-Sunshine	Penny Parkin (part-time ½)	FL3	2996 N. Colwood Rd., Caro 48723	(989) 673-6695	(989) 600-8086
			*2024 Liberty, Fairgrove 48733		
Tawas	Kris S. Kappler	FE2	20 East M-55, Tawas City 48763	(989) 362-4288	(859) 858-8233
			*801 W. Franklin St., East Tawas 48730		

CHARGE	PASTOR		ADDRESS	CHURCH	HOME
Vassar: First	Scott Sherrill	FE4	139 N. Main, Box 71, Vassar 48768	(989) 823-8811	(906) 370-5937
			*706 Cork Pine Lane, Vassar 48768		
Wagarville: Community	Douglas E. Hasse	PL2	2478 W. Wagarville Rd., Gladwin 48624		(989) 598-0716
			*5943 Weiss St # 58, Saginaw 48603		
Watrousville	William P. Sanders	RE6	4446 W. Caro Rd., Caro 48723	(989) 673-3434	(989) 693-6564
			*6116 Slocun Ave, Unionville 48767		
Weidman	Cynthia S.L. Greene	FE1	PO Box 98, 3200 N Woodruff Rd., Weidman 48893-0098	(989) 644-3148	
			*9532 W Saint Charles Rd, Sumner 48889-8729		
West Branch: First	Timothy C. Dibble	FE6	2490 W. State Rd., West Branch 48661	(989) 345-0210	(989) 345-0688
			*2458 W. State Rd., West Branch 48661		
Whittemore	Gary Gillings	DSA1	Box 155, 110 North St., Whittemore 48770	(989) 756-2831	(989) 756-3981
			*205 W State St, Whittemore 48770		
Wilber	Keith Reinhardt	PL6	3278 N. Sherman Rd., East Tawas 48730	(989) 362-7860	
			*7620 Spruce, Hale 48739		
Wisner	In Boem Oh	PE4	5375 N. Vassar Rd., Akron 48701	(989) 691-5277	(989) 710-1976
			*5363 N. Vassar Rd., Akron 48701		

NAME	POSITION		ADDRESS	OFFICE	HOME

APPOINTMENTS TO EXTENSION MINISTRIES LOCATED IN THE CENTRAL BAY DISTRICT:
(further information at end of appointment section)

Charles Farnum	Director, Wesley Foundation – Central Michigan University				
	(LTFT ¼)	FE14	1400 S Washington St, Mt Pleasant 48858-4268		(989) 545-1761
Timothy Hastings	Chaplain, St. Mary's of Michigan Medical Center, Saginaw				
		RE16	*1908 Stark St., Saginaw 48602		(989) 752-7898
David I. Kim	District Superintendent, Central Bay District Office			(989) 793-8838	
		FE2	3617 Mackinaw Street Ste 1, Saginaw 48602	(989) 835-7511	
Lisa M. McIlvenna	Executive Director	FE12	315 W. Larkin, Midland 48640		(248) 224-4296
	Fresh Aire Counseling Services		*614 Fisher St., Saginaw 48604		

CENTRAL BAY DISTRICT

EAST WINDS DISTRICT

EAST WINDS DISTRICT

| District Superintendent | John H. Hice FE2 | Office: (810) 396-1362 |
| Executive Assistant | Cheryl Rentschler | 624 West Nepessing Ste 201, Lapeer 48446 |

DS Email: jhice@michiganumc.org
Office Email: crentschler@michiganumc.org

CHARGE	PASTOR		ADDRESS	TELEPHONE CHURCH	HOME
Applegate	Ellen O. Schippert	PL1	4792 Church, Box 1, Applegate 48401		
Buel			2165 E. Peck Rd., Croswell 48422		
Croswell: First			13 North Howard St., Croswell 48422	(810) 679-3595	(810) 990-5460
			*7350 Lakeshore Rd N, Palms 48465		
Armada	Christopher G.L. Titus	FL1	23200 E. Main, Box 533, Armada 48005	(586) 784-5201	(586) 784-9484
West Berlin			905 Holmes Rd., Box 91, Allenton 48002	(810) 395-2409	
			*23234 E. Main St., Box 533, Armada 48005		
Atherton	Sang Y. (Abraham) Chun	FE4	4010 Lippincott Blvd., Burton 48519	(810) 742-5644	(734) 856-3151
Grand Blank: Phoenix			4423 S. Genesse Rd., Grand Blanc 48439	(810) 743-3370	
			*6105 Wilderness Point, Grand Blanc 48439		
Attica	Ronald Rouse	PL7	27 Elk Lake Rd., Attica 48412	(810) 724-0690	(248) 379-2509
			*26789 Dayton Rd., Richmond 48062		
BAD AXE COOPERATIVE PARISH					
Bad Axe: First	Philip Tousley	FE1	216 East Woodworth, Bad Axe 48413	(989) 269-7671	
Minden City			PO Box 126, 3346 Main St. Minden City 48456		
Ubly			4496 Pike St., Ubly 48475		(989) 269-8403
			*1165 Thompson Dr., Bad Axe 48413		
BROWN CITY COOPERATIVE PARISH					
Brown City	Patrick D. Robbins	FL1	7043 Lincoln, PO Box 39, Brown City 48416	(810) 346-2010	
Omard			2055 Peck Rd., Brown City 48416	(810) 346-3448	(810) 346-2555
			*6931 George St., Brown City 48416		

CHARGE	PASTOR		ADDRESS	CHURCH	HOME
Byron: First	Barbara S. Benjamin	PE2	Box 127, 101 S Ann, Byron 48418	(810) 266-4976	
Gaines			117 Clinton St., Box 125, Gaines 48436	(989) 271-9131	(810) 370-1157
			*10214 Bath Rd., Byron 48418		
Capac	Lisa J. Clark	FL20	14952 Imlay City Rd., Capac 48014	(810) 395-2112	(810) 247-0946
			*211 W. Mill, Capac 48014		
Clarkston	Richard L. Dake	FE15	6600 Waldon Rd., Clarkston 48346	(248) 625-1611	(248) 625-1727
			*6599 Church St., Clarkston 48346		
Associate	Megan Jo Crumm Walther	FE3	6600 Waldon Rd., Clarkston 48346	(248) 625-1611	(734) 751-6836
Deacon	Laura Speiran	FD6	*7228 Chapel View Dr., Clarkston 48346	(248) 625-1611	(734) 678-6186
	(LTFT ¾)		6600 Waldon Rd., Clarkston 48346		
Clio: Bethany	Catherine M. Huvaere	FE3	*7801 Hoffman, Waterford 48327	(810) 686-5151	(616) 550-2570
			353 E. Vienna St., Box 327, Clio 48420		
			*10480 Varna, Clio 48420		
Columbiaville	Esther A. Irish	FL7	4696 Pine, PO Box 98, Columbiaville 48421	(810) 793-6363	(810) 793-4175
			*4350 Golden Glow Dr., Columbiaville 48421		
Davisburg	Thomas C. Hartley, Sr.	OF2	803 Broadway, Davisburg 48350	(248) 634-3373	(248) 698-4502
	(LTFT ¼)		*711 Oxhill Drive, White Lake 48386		
Davison	Bo Rin Cho	FE3	207 E. Third St., Davison 48423	(810) 653-5272	(517) 775-5436
			*819 Alana Court, Davison 48423		
Dryden	Patricia A. Hoppenworth	PL12	5400 W. Main St., Box 98, Dryden 48428	(810) 796-3341	
Leonard			245 E. Elmwood, Box 762, Leonard 48367	(248) 628-7983	
			*1421 Poplar, LL, Port Huron 48060		(810) 734-1171
Durand: First	Aaron Kesson	FE3	10016 E. Newburg Rd, Durand 48429	(989) 288-3880	(989) 288-4364
	(LTFT ½)		*302 Hampton, Durand 48429		
Fenton	Jeffrey L. Jaggers	FE6	119 S. Leroy St., Fenton 48430	(810) 629-2132	(810) 354-8430
			11310 Greenview, Fenton 48430		
Associate	Michelle Forsyth	PE5	119 S. Leroy St., Fenton 48430	(810) 629-2132	(810) 288-8900
			*514 Mill Pond Dr., Fenton 48430		
Diaconal	Matthew J. Packer	DM3	*6020 Creekside Dr., Swartz Creek 48473		(810) 610-3692

EAST WINDS DISTRICT

EAST WINDS DISTRICT

CHARGE	PASTOR		ADDRESS	CHURCH	HOME
FLINT					
Asbury	Tommy McDoniel	FL9	1653 Davison Rd., Flint 48506	(810) 235-0016	
			*2050 Covert Rd. Burton 48529		(248) 705-4401
Bethel	Andrew A. Allie	RE1	1309 N. Ballenger, Flint 48504	(810) 238-3843	(810) 444-8331
			*5424 Sycamore Ln, Flint 48532		
Bristol	Brian K. Willingham	PL1	G-5285 Van Slyke Rd., Flint	(810) 238-9244	
Burton: Christ			4428 Columbine Ave., Burton 48529	(810) 743-1770	(810) 513-1407
			*1884 Springfield St., Flint 48503		
Calvary	Gregory Timmons	PL2	2111 Flushing Rd., Flint 48504	(810) 238-7685	(810) 250-4304
Charity	Frederick Bowden	PL2	*2327 Limestone Lane, Flushing 48433	(810) 789-2961	(313) 443-4300
			4601 Clio Rd., Flint 48504		
Court Street	Jeremy T. Peters	FE5	*25151 Dequindre Rd Lot 17, Madison Hts 48071	(810) 235-4651	(810) 407-8333
			225 W. Court St., Flint 48502		
Deacon	Christina M. White	FD2	*1827 Overhill, Flint 48503	(810) 235-4651	(810) 664-7033
	(LTFT ½)		225 W. Court St., Flint 48502		
	Carol M. Blair Bouse	FE7	5307 Worchester Dr, Swartz Creek 48473	(810) 732-4820	(810) 867-4033
Hope			G-4467 Beecher Rd., Flint 48532		
			*601 Leland, Flushing 48433		
Flushing	Jeremiah J. Mannschreck	FE2	413 E. Main St., Flushing 48433	(810) 659-5172	(810) 659-6231
			*1159 Clearview Dr., Flushing 48433		
Forester	Anika Bailey	PL2	2481 N. Lakeshore Rd., Carsonville 48419		
Port Sanilac			7225 Main St., Box 557, Port Sanilac 48469		(313) 543-9434
			*7209 Main, Port Sanilac 48469		
Genesee	Karen B. Williams	FL10	7190 N. Genesee Rd., Box 190, Genesee 48437	(810) 640-2280	
Thetford Center			G-11394 N. Center Rd., Genesee 48437	(810) 687-0190	(810) 547-1706
			*7472 Roger Thomas Dr., Mt Morris 48458		
Goodrich	Joel L. Walther	FE3	8071 S. State Road, Goodrich 48438	(810) 636-2444	(734) 625-4077
			*7228 Chapel View Dr., Clarkston 48346		

CHARGE	PASTOR		ADDRESS	CHURCH	HOME
Grand Blanc	Julius Del Pino	FE4	515 Bush Ave., Grand Blanc 48480	(810) 694-9040	
			*12110 Francesca Dr., Grand Blanc 48439		(810) 694-1615
Halsey	Tara R. Sutton	FE4	10006 Halsey Rd., Grand Blanc 48439	(810) 694-9243	
South Mundy			10018 S. Linden Rd., Grand Blanc 48439		(810) 694-9243
			*10030 Halsey Rd., Grand Blanc 48439		
Harbor Beach	Sari Brown	PE3	PO Box 25, 253 S. First St., Harbor Beach 48441		
Port Hope			PO Box 25, 4521 Main St., Port Hope 48468		(989) 479-6053
			*PO Box 25, 247 First St., Harbor Beach 48441		
HOLLY					
Calvary	Clifford J. Schroeder III	FE8	15010 N. Holly Rd., Holly 48442	(248) 634-9711	
			*3464 Quick Rd., Holly 48442		(248) 245-8155
Mt. Bethel	Leah Caron	PL2	3205 Jossman Rd., Holly 48442	(248) 627-6700	
			*735 Vivian Ln, Oxford 48371		(248) 520-0884
Imlay City	Marcel A. Lamb	FE7	210 North Almont Ave., Imlay City 48444	(810) 724-0687	
			*280 Bancroft St., Imlay City 48444		(810) 721-7149
Jeddo	Julie Krauss	PL2	8533 Wildcat Rd., Box 7, Jeddo 48032		
Avoca			8905 Avoca Rd, Box 233 Avoca 48006		(810) 385 3601
			*880 Crystal Ln, Marysville 48040		
Lake Fenton	Duane A. Lindsey	PL1	2581 N. Long Lake Rd., Fenton MI 48430	(810) 629-5161	
Lennon			1014 Oak St., PO Box 19, Lennon 48449	(810) 621-3676	
Duffield			7001 Duffield Rd., Box 344 Durand 48429		
			*11494 Torrey Rd, Fenton 48430-9730		
Lake Orion	Lawrence A. Wik	FE6	140 East Flint, Lake Orion 48362	(248) 693-6201	(810) 635-2304
			*3691 Hi Crest, Lake Orion 48360		(248) 391-0930
Associate	John W. Ball (LTFT ¾)	FE7	140 East Flint, Lake Orion 48362	(248) 693-6201	
			*2647 Orbit Dr, Lake Orion 48360		(248) 393-1520
Lapeer: Trinity	Grant R. Lobb	FE8	1310 North Main St., Lapeer 48446	(810) 664-9941	
			*804 Fourth St., Lapeer 48446		(810) 664-2213

EAST WINDS DISTRICT

EAST WINDS DISTRICT

CHARGE	PASTOR		ADDRESS	CHURCH	HOME
Lexington	Susan M. Youmans	FE2	5597 Main St., Lexington 48450	(810) 359-8215	
Linden	Michelle N. Forsyth (LTFT ¼)	PE2	*7051 Greenbush Ln, Lexington 48450		(248) 912-4660
			201 S. Bridge St., Box 488, Linden 48430	(810) 735-5858	
			*11494 Torrey Rd., Fenton 48430		(810) 208-0988
Marlette: First	George Ayoub	FE2	3155 Main St., Marlette 48453	(989) 635-2075	
			*3169 Main St., Marlette 48453		(989) 635-2436
MARYSVILLE COOPERATIVE PARISH					
Marysville Central Lakeport	Curtis B. Clarke	FL1	721 West Huron Blvd., Marysville 48040	(810) 364-7391	(313) 570-4442
			3597 Milwaukee, Lakeport 48059	(810) 385-9446	(989) 280-5553
			*683 18th St., Marysville 48040		
McGregor Carsonville	Jerry D. Griggs	PL22	2230 Forester Rd., Deckerville 48427	(810) 657-9168	(810) 378-5686
			3953 Sheldon, Carsonville 48419		
			*5800 Paldi, Peck 48466		
Memphis: First Lamb	James E. Huff Jr.	PL16	81265 Church St., PO Box 29, Memphis 48041	(810) 392-2294	(810) 392-8031
			1209 Cove Rd., Wales 48027		
			*34750 Maple, PO Box 29, Memphis 48041		
Montrose	Harold V. Phillips	RA4	158 E. State St., Box 3237, Montrose 48457	(810) 639-6925	(810) 639-6924
			*12012 Vienna Rd., Montrose 48457		
Mt. Morris: First	Ralph H. Pieper II	RE2	808 E. Mt. Morris St., Mt. Morris 48458	(810) 686-3870	(586) 260-7538
			*3373 Brookgate Dr., Flint 48507		
North Branch: First Silverwood	Ronald G. Hutchinson	PL12	4195 Huron St., Box 156, North Branch 48461	(810) 688-2610	(810) 614-7928
			2750 Clifford Rd., Box 61, Silverwood 48760	(989) 761-7599	
			*3049 Burnside Rd., North Branch 48461		
North Street	David A. Reed	PE5	4580 North Rd., Clyde 48049	(810) 385-4027	(810) 385-8366
			*4584 North Rd., Clyde 48049		
Oregon Elba	Jeanne H. Wisenbaugh	DSA2	2985 German Rd., Columbiaville 48421	(810) 793-6828	(810) 732-8123
			154 S. Elba Rd., Lapeer 48446	(810) 664-5780	
			*1457 Weserrace Dr, Flint 48532		

CHARGE	PASTOR		ADDRESS	CHURCH	HOME
Ortonville	Brian K. Johnson	FL5	93 Church St., Box 286, Ortonville 48462	(248) 627-3125	
			*319 Sherman Ct., Ortonville 48462		(248) 627-3347
Otisville	Betty "Kay" Leitelt	FL10	Box 125, 200 W. Main St., Otisville 48463	(810) 631-2911	
Fostoria			Box 67,7435 Willits Rd., Fostoria 48435	(989) 795-2389	
West Deerfield			PO Box 185, 383 Otter Lake Rd. Fostoria 48435	(810) 793-2116	
			*9622 Hammil Rd., Otisville 48463		(810) 631-8395
Oxford	Jennifer J. Jue	FE1	21 E. Burdick St., Oxford 48371	(248) 628-1289	
Thomas			504 First St., Box 399, Oxford 48371	(248) 628-7636	
			*91 Cross Timbers Dr., Oxford 48371		(248) 628-1022
PORT HURON					
First	LuAnn L. Rourke	FE3	828 Lapeer Ave., Port Huron 48060	(810) 985-8107	
			*3014 E. Woodland Dr., Port Huron 48060		(810) 987-5333
Gratiot Park	Eric J. Miller	PL2	811 Church St., Port Huron 48060	(810) 985-6206	
			*48212 Cardinal, Shelby Twp. 48317		(586) 206-4527
Richfield	Shelly Ann Long	PL4	10090 E. Coldwater, PO Box 307, Davison 48423	(810) 653-3644	
			*11564 Kings Coach Rd., Grand Blanc 48439		(248) 417-1196
Richmond: First	Tom Waller	FL2	69495 Main St., Box 293, Richmond 48062	(586) 727-2622	
			*35675 Pound Rd., Richmond 48062		(586) 727-6555
Romeo	Trevor A. Herm	FE3	280 North Main St., Romeo 48065	(586) 752-9132	
			*289 North Bailey St., Romeo 48065		(810) 275-3277
St. Clair: First	John N. Grenfell III	FE2	415 North Third St., Saint Clair 48079	(810) 329-7186	
			*3202 S Shoreview, Fort Gratiot 48059		(734) 787-7539
SANDUSKY COOPERATIVE PARISH					
Sandusky: First	Susan E. Platt	AM2	68 Lexington St., Sandusky 48471	(810) 648-2606	
			*155 Bella Ave., Sandusky 48471		(989) 802-2684
Deckerville	TO BE SUPPLIED		3354 Main St., Deckerville 48427	(810) 376-2029	
			*		
Seymour Lake	Janine Plum	FE5	3050 Sashabaw, Oxford 48371	(248) 628-4763	
			*3191 Clipper Court, Oxford, 48371-5405		(810) 624-1404

EAST WINDS DISTRICT

EAST WINDS DISTRICT

CHARGE	PASTOR		ADDRESS	CHURCH	HOME
Shabbona	Nancy J. Bitterling	RLA1	4455 Decker Rd., Decker 48426	(989) 872-8094	
			*3610 Bluff Rd, Port Austin 48467		(989) 738-04752
Snover: Heritage	Penelope R. Nunn	FL2	3329 W. Snover Rd.,PO Box 38, Snover 48472	(810) 672-9101	
			*1571 N. Main St., Box 65, Snover 48472		(810) 672-9233
Swartz Creek	Gary R. Glanville	FE5	7400 Miller Rd., Swartz Creek 48473	(810) 635-4555	
			*4187 Mountain Ash Court, Swartz Creek 48473		(810) 287-9861
Associate	Aaron B. Kesson	FE3	7400 Miller Rd., Swartz Creek 48473	(810) 635-4555	
	(LTFT ½)		*302 Hampton, Durand 48429		(517) 930-1543
West Forest	Bruce E. Malicoat	PL14	7297 E. Farrand Rd., Millington 48746	(989) 871-3456	
West Vienna	Billie Lou Gillespie	FL14	129 E. Vates, Frankenmuth 48734	(810) 686-7480	
			5485 W. Wilson Rd., Clio 48420		(810) 686-4025
			*5445 W. Wilson Rd., Clio 48420		
Worth Township: Bethel	Donald R. Derby	RLA2	8020 Babcock Rd., Box 143, Croswell 48422	(810) 327-1440	
			*1014 St Joseph Ln, Marysville 48040		(810) 990-5544
Yale	Dennis E. Irish	FE1	2 South Main St., Yale 48097	(810) 387-3962	
Cole Associate	Julia A. Cramer	DSA1	7015 Carson Rd., Yale 48097	(810) 387-4400	
Melvin			1171 E. Main St., Melvin 48454		
			* (Irish) 1 Park Avenue, Yale 48097		(810) 300-3963
			*(Cramer) 7656 Washington St, Melvin 48454-970		(810) 304-2310

NAME	POSITION	ADDRESS	OFFICE	HOME
APPOINTMENTS TO EXTENSION MINISTRIES LOCATED IN THE EAST WINDS DISTRICT: (further information at end of appointment section)				
Ann Emerson	Director, Lake Huron Retreat Center			
	FD20	8794 Lakeshore Dr., Lakeport 48059	(810) 327-6272	(810) 327-6468
John H. Hice	District Superintendent, East Winds District Office			
	FE2	624 West Nepessing Ste 201, Lapeer 48446	(810) 396-1362	
Maurice R. Horne, Sr.	Flint Mission Zone Minister of Outreach			
	FL2	1201 Lincoln Avenue, Flint 48507	(810) 239-3427	
Christina M. White	East Winds District Coordinator of Disciple Formation (LTFT ½)			
	FD2	624 W Nepessing, Ste 201, Lapeer 48446	(810) 396-1362	

EAST WINDS DISTRICT

GREATER DETROIT DISTRICT

GREATER DETROIT DISTRICT

District Superintendent	Charles S.G. Boayue FE2	Office: (313) 481-1045
Executive Assistant	Dwanda Ashford	8000 Woodward Avenue, Detroit 48202
	DS Email: cboayue@michiganumc.org	
	Office Email: cboayue@michiganumc.org	

				TELEPHONE	
CHARGE	PASTOR		ADDRESS	CHURCH	HOME
Beverly Hills	Anthony Ballah	FL5	20000 W. 13 Mile Rd., Beverly Hills 48025	(248) 646-9777	(248) 327-6276
			*30700 Old Stream, Southfield 48076		
BIRMINGHAM					
Embury	Jean R. Snyder	RE2	1803 E. 14 Mile Rd., Birmingham 48009	(248) 644-5708	(248) 650-5888
			*1582 Millecoquins Ct., Rochester 48307		
First	Elbert P. Dulworth	FE4	1589 W. Maple, Birmingham 48009	(248) 646-1200	(248) 258-0903
			*1043 Chesterfield, Birmingham 48009		
Senior Associate	Shawn Lewis-Lakin	FE3	1589 W. Maple, Birmingham 48009	(248) 646-1200	
	(LTFT ¾)		*154 S. Cranbrook Cross Road, Bloomfield Hills 48301		
Associate	Lindsey Hall	FE7	1589 W. Maple, Birmingham 48009	(248) 646-1200	(402) 586-5106
			*130 Arlington, Birmingham 48009		
Associate	Susanne E. Hierholzer	FE1	1589 W. Maple, Birmingham 48009	(248) 646-1200	(989) 326-0766
			*361 Pleasant St, Birmingham 48009		
Associate	Zack Dunlap	PE5	1589 W. Maple, Birmingham 48009	(248) 646-1200	(734) 272-5667
			*3485 Kipling, Berkley 48072		
Deacon	Sarah Alexander	FD1	1589 W. Maple, Birmingham 48009	(248) 646-1200	(734) 649-7043
			*8925 Sudbury St. Livonia 48150		
Bloomfield Hills: St. Paul	Frederick G. Sampson, III	OF7	165 E. Square Lake Rd., Bloomfield Hills 48302	(248) 338-8233	(248) 338-9528
			*208 Barrington Rd., Bloomfield Hills 48302		
Clawson	Michael R Perez, Jr.	DSA1	205 N. Main, Clawson 48017	(248) 435-9090	(586) 252-7257
			*442 Marias Ave, Clawson 48017		

CHARGE	PASTOR		ADDRESS	CHURCH	HOME
DEARBORN					
First	David Nellist	OE2	22124 Garrison, Dearborn 48124	(313) 563-5200	(313) 562-8220
Deacon	Carl T.S. Gladstone (LTFT ½)	FD1	*301 S. Silvery Lane, Dearborn 48124	(313) 563-5200	(586) 295-3055
Good Shepherd	Robert J. Sielaff	RE2	22124 Garrison, Dearborn 48124 *542 W Grand Blvd, Detroit 48216-1439 1570 Mason, Dearborn 48124 *42054 Baintree Circle, Northville 48168	(313) 278-4350	
DETROIT					
Calvary	Will Council	PL6	15050 Hubbell, Detroit 48227 *7796 Surrey Dr., Romulus 48174	(313) 835-1317	(734) 641-8711
Cass Community	Faith E. Fowler	FE26	3901 Cass Ave., Detroit 48201 *2245 Wabash, Detroit 48216	(313) 833-7730	(313) 408-1980
Associate	Jonathan E. Reynolds	FE2	3901 Cass Ave., Detroit 48201 *130 Arlington, Birmingham 48009	(313) 833-7730	(248) 891-2788
Associate	Latha Ravi (LTFT ¼)	FE1	3901 Cass Ave., Detroit 48201 *533 Hill St, Rochester 48307	(313) 833-7730	(248) 464-4600
Deacon	Sue Pethoud	FD3	3901 Cass Ave., Detroit 48201 *4529 Pleasant Valley Rd., Brighton 48114	(313) 833-7730	(810) 278-1235
Central	Jill Hardt Zundel	FE6	23 E. Adams, Detroit 48226 2013 Hyde Park, #33, Detroit 48207	(313) 965-5422	(313) 393-8899
Centro Familiar Cristiano	Patricia Gandarilla-Becerra (part-time ½)	FL8	1270 Waterman, Detroit 48209 *8961 Niver, Allen Park 48101	(313) 843-4170	(402) 699-1325
Conant Avenue	Willie Smith	FE5	18600 Conant, Detroit 48234 *16876 Braile, Detroit 48219	(313) 891-7237	(313) 566-7226
Ford Memorial	Donald Beasley	DSA4	16400 W. Warren, Detroit 48228 *13969 Fielding, Detroit	(313) 584-0035	(313) 475-3415

GREATER DETROIT DISTRICT

GREATER DETROIT DISTRICT

CHARGE	PASTOR		ADDRESS	CHURCH	HOME
French *(New Church Start)*	Gertrude M. Mukalay (LTFT ¾)	OE2	1803 E 14 Mile Rd, Birmingham 48009 *1858 Estates Dr, Detroit 48206		
	John K. Ilunga Ngoie (LTFT ¼)	OE2	1803 E 14 Mile Rd, Birmingham 48009 *1858 Estates Dr, Detroit 48206		
Metropolitan	Janet Gaston Petty	FE4	8000 Woodward Ave., Detroit 48202 26110 Hendrie Blvd, Huntington Woods 48070	(313) 875-7407	(248) 546-9749
Mt. Hope	Esrom Shaw	PL7	15400 E. Seven Mile Rd., Detroit 48206 1685 W. Boston, Detroit 48206	(313) 371-8540	(313) 868-1352
Resurrection	Carolyn A. Jones (part-time ½)	FL1	8150 Schaefer, Detroit 48228 *2466 Edison, Detroit 48206	(313) 582-7011	(313) 573-0043
St. Paul	Kenneth M. Johnson	PL2	8701 W. Eight Mile Rd., Detroit 48221 *30700 Old Stream, Southfield 48076	(313) 342-4656	(248) 327-6276
Scott Memorial	Cornelius Davis, Jr.	FE4	15361 Plymouth, Detroit 48227 *531 New Town-Victoria Park, Detroit 48215	(313) 836-6301	(313) 331-8075
Second Grace	Darryl E. Totty	FE5	18700 Joy Rd., Detroit 48228 *29193 Northwestern Hwy, #388, Southfield 48034	(313) 838-6475	(313) 215-3841
Trinity-Faith	Markey C. Gray	FL2	19750 W. McNichols, Detroit 48219 *23470 Meadow Park, Redford 48239	(313) 533-0101	(313) 533-8423
Downriver	Jacqueline L. Raineri	FL2	15740 Racho Blvd., Trilium Academy, Taylor 48195 *20433 Foxboro, Riverview 48192	(734) 765-7729	(810) 338-2373
Eastpointe: Immanuel	Albert Rush	FL8	23715 Gratiot, Eastpointe 48021 *22839 Linwood Eastpointe 48021	(586) 776-7750	(586) 871-2025
Faith Macomb	Dianne H. VanMarter	RLA5	56370 Fairchild Rd., Macomb 48042 *20100 Cushing, Detroit 48205	(586) 749-3147	(810) 488-0608
FARMINGTON First	Anthony R. Hood	FE4	33112 Grand River, PO Box 38, Farmington 48326 25766 Livingston Circle, Farmington Hills 48335	(248) 474-6573	(248) 474-7568

CHARGE	PASTOR		ADDRESS	CHURCH	HOME
Nardin Park	Melanie L. Carey	FE4	29887 W. 11 Mile Rd., Farmington Hills 48336	(248) 476-8860	(248) 476-8860
Associate	Beth D. Titus	FE6	*25109 Lyncastle Ln., Farmington Hills 48336		(586) 665-4333
	(LTFT ½)		29887 W. 11 Mile Rd., Farmington Hills 48336	(248) 476-8860	
Orchard	Amy E. Mayo Moyle	FE5	*6771 Kestral Ridge, Brighton 48116		(517) 918-2215
			30450 Farmington, Farmington Hills 48334	(248) 626-3620	
Associate	Nicholas Bonsky	PE1	*32979 Thorndyke Court, Farmington Hills 48334		(586) 944-3292
			30450 Farmington, Farmington Hills 48334	(248) 626-3620	
Ferndale: First	Robert D. Schoenhals	FE7	*29221 Aranel St, Farmington Hills 48334		(248) 542-5598
			22331 Woodward, Ferndale 48220	(248) 545-4467	
Flat Rock: First	Amy Triebwasser	PE3	*657 W. Oakridge, Ferndale 48220		
			28400 Evergreen, Flat Rock 48134	(734) 782-2565	
Franklin: Community	David Huseltine	FE4	*29451 Evergreen, Flat Rock 48134		(248) 761-4327
			26425 Wellington, Franklin 48025	(248) 626-6606	
Fraser: Christ	Kevin J. Harbin	FE5	*2423 Ogden W., Farmington Hills 48323		(586) 293-4194
			34385 Garfield, Fraser 48026	(586) 293-5340	
Garden City: First	Jonathan Combs	FL5	*34355 Garfield, Fraser 48026		(734) 422-5375
	(part-time ¾)		6443 Merriman Rd., Garden City 48135	(734) 421-8628	
Grosse Pointe	Ray McGee	FE4	*31515 Windsor, Garden City 48135		(313) 881-1129
			211 Moross Rd., Grosse Pte Farms 48236	(313) 886-2363	
Associate	Keith A. Lenard, Jr.	FL3	*64 Moross Rd., Grosse Pte Farms 48236		(734) 778-0835
			211 Moross Rd., Grosse Pte Farms 48236	(313) 866-2363	
Harper Woods: Redeemer	Marshall C. Murphy	FL3	*414 Champine, Grosse Pte Farms 48236		
			20571 Vernier Rd., Harper Woods 48225	(313) 884-2035	
Hazel Park: First	Frederick G. Sampson, III	OF4	*20572 Anita, Harper Woods 48225		(248) 338-9528
			315 E. Nine Mile Rd., Hazel Park 48030	(248) 546-5955	
Howarth	Marvin L. Herman	FL2	*208 Barrington Rd., Bloomfield Hills 48302		
			550 E. Silverbell Rd., Lake Orion 48360	(248) 373-2360	(810) 908-0373
Paint Creek			4420 Collins Rd., Rochester 48306	(248) 652-1583	
			*137 Stratford Ln, Lake Orion 48362		

GREATER DETROIT DISTRICT

GREATER DETROIT DISTRICT

CHARGE	PASTOR		ADDRESS	CHURCH	HOME
LIVONIA					
Clarenceville	Donald R. Sperling	FE10	20300 Middlebelt Rd., Livonia 48152	(248) 474-3444	
			*34184 Haldane, Livonia 48152		(248) 615-1435
Newburg	Steven E. McCoy	FE7	36500 Ann Arbor Trail, Livonia 48150	(734) 422-0149	
			*33652 Trillium Court, Livonia 48150		(734) 424-4593
Deacon	Rodney Gasaway (LTFT ½)	PD3	36500 Ann Arbor Trail, Livonia 48150	(734) 422-0149	(734) 578-6256
St. Matthew's	Jeremy P. Africa	FE5	*36522 Ann Arbor Trail, Livonia 48150 30900 W. Six Mile Rd., Livonia 48152	(734) 422-6038	
			*31000 W Six Mile, Livonia 48152		(734) 855-4882
MADISON HEIGHTS					
Korean First Central	Daeki Kim	OE2	500 W. Gardenia Ave., Madison Heights 48071	(248) 545-5554	
			*30150 Shoreham St., Southfield 48076		
Madison Heights	Rhonda Osterman	PL8	246 E. Eleven Mile Rd., Madison Heights 48071	(248) 544-3544	
			*12998 DeCook Dr., Sterling Hts. 48313		(586) 243-9240
Vietnamese Ministry	Nhan Duc Nguyen	OF4	246 E. Eleven Mile Rd., Madison Heights 48071		
			*38108 Charwood Dr., Sterling Heights 48312		(714) 501-0323
Mount Clemens: First	Daniel J.C. Hart	FE1	57 S.B. Gratiot Ave., Mt. Clemens 48043	(586) 468-6464	
			*110 Belleview St., Mt. Clemens 48043		(586) 863-3646
Deacon	Aliicea Lynn Williams (LTFT ½)	FD4	57 S.B. Gratiot Ave., Mt. Clemens 48043	(586) 468-6464	(810) 694-8318
Mount Vernon	Cherlyn McKanders	PL3	*21515 Bay Hills Dr., Macomb 48044 3000 28 Mile Rd., Washington 48094	(248) 650-2213	(248) 881-8541
			*59989 Whitman N Apt D, Washington 48094-2261		
Omo: Zion	Mary Ellen Chapman	RLA1	63020 Omo Rd., Box 344, Richmond 48062	(810) 233-2824	(586) 291-6552
			*19059 Carmelo Dr N, Clinton Township 48038		
PONTIAC					
Grace & Peace Community	Laura M. Koivula	PL1	451 W Kennett, Pontiac 48340	(248) 334-3280	
			*1851 Birchcrest Rd., Waterford 48328		(248) 559-3053
St. John	Lester Mangum	FE7	620 University Dr., Pontiac 48342	(248) 338-8933	
			*622 University Dr., Pontiac 48342		(248) 217-9071

CHARGE	PASTOR		ADDRESS	CHURCH	HOME
REDFORD					
Aldersgate	Benjamin J. Bower	FE4	10000 Beech Daly Rd., Redford 48239	(313) 937-3170	
			*11328 Arnold, Redford 48239		(313) 531-7487
Assoc. Brightmoore Campus	Jonathan Combs (part-time ¼)	FL5	12065 W. OuterDr. Detroit 48223.	(313) 937-3170	
			*31515 Windsor, Garden City 48135		(734) 422-5375
New Beginnings	Diane Covington	OF5	16175 Delaware, Redford 48240	(313) 255-6330	
			*18261 University Pk. Dr., Livonia 48152		(248) 943-0534
Riverview	Carol A. Middel	PL1	13199 Colvin, Riverview 48193	(734) 284-2721	
			*42018 Woodbrook Dr, Canton 48188-2612		(734) 397-2332
Rochester: St. Paul's	David A. Eardley	FE7	620 Romeo St., Box 80307, Rochester 48308	(248) 651-9361	
			*632 Romeo St., Rochester 48307		(248) 651-9770
Associate	Erin L. Fitzgerald	FE2	620 Romeo, Box 80307, Rochester 48308	(248) 651-9361	
			*632 Romeo Rd, Rochester 48307		(616) 510-7941
Associate	Carter Grimmett	FE3	620 Romeo, Box 80307, Rochester 48308	(248) 651-9361	
			*598 Jacob Way, #103, Rochester 48307		(313) 303-1230
Rochester Hills: St. Luke's	Scott E. Manning	FE4	3980 Walton Blvd., Rochester Hills 48309	(248) 373-6960	
			*6161 Mission Dr., West Bloomfield 48324		(248) 366-1937
Romulus: Community	Carolyn A. Jones (part-time ½)	FL2	11160 Olive St., Romulus 48174	(734) 941-0736	
			*2466 Edison, Detroit 48206		(313) 573-0043
Roseville: Trinity	Stephen Euper	FE8	18303 Common, Roseville 48066	(586) 886-2363	
			*30455 Progress, Roseville 48066		(586) 776-1459
Royal Oak: First	Jeffrey S. Nelson	FE4	320 W. Seventh, Royal Oak 48067	(248) 541-4100	
			*3113 Marion Dr, Royal Oak 48073		(248) 629-7185
Associate	Myra Moreland	PL2	320 W. Seventh, Royal Oak 48067	(248) 541-4100	
			*		
Deacon	Caleb Williams	FD4	320 W. Seventh, Royal Oak 48067	(248) 541-4100	
			*24819 Resselaer St, Oak Park 48237		(231) 313-9005

GREATER DETROIT DISTRICT

GREATER DETROIT DISTRICT

CHARGE	PASTOR		ADDRESS	CHURCH	HOME
Southfield: Hope	Benjamin Kevin Smalls	OE2	26275 Northwestern Hwy., Southfield 48076 *	(248) 356-1020	
Associate	Reggie A. White (LTFT ¼)	OF1	26275 Northwestern Hwy., Southfield 48076 *5704 N. Pinnacle, West Bloomfield 48322	(248) 356-1020	(301) 512-4075
Associate	Rosaline D. Green	RLA3	26275 Northwestern Hwy., Southfield 48076 *	(248) 356-1020	
Associate	Christopher Grimes	FL3	26275 Northwestern Hwy., Southfield 48076 *29476 Briar Bank Ct, Southfield 48034	(248) 356-1020	(248) 470-4042
Associate	Dale R. Milford	PL1	26275 Northwestern Hwy., Southfield 48076 *14314 Artesian St, Detroit 48223	(248) 356-1020	(313) 399-4530
St. Timothy	Benjamin Kevin Smalls	OE2	15888 Archdale, Detroit 48227 *29229 Utley Rd, Farmington Hills 48334	(313) 837-4070	(248) 626-4368
Associate	Reggie A. White (LTFT ¼)	OF1	15888 Archdale, Detroit 48227 *5704 N. Pinnacle, West Bloomfield 48322	(313) 837-4070	(301) 512-4075
Sterling Heights	Joel T. Fitzgerald	FE2	11333 16½ Mile, Sterling Heights 48312 *632 Romeo Rd, Rochester 48307	(586) 268-3130	(616) 848-9759
TRENTON Faith	Wayne A. Price	FE1	2530 Charlton, Trenton 48183 *1641 Edsel Drive, Trenton 48183	(734) 671-5211	(269) 330-6768
First	Heidi C. Reinker (LTFT ¾)	FE4	2610 W. Jefferson, Trenton 48183 *2604 Lenox Rd., Trenton 48183	(734) 676-2066	(734) 676-0041
TROY Big Beaver	Gregory M. Mayberry	FE4	3753 John R, Troy 48083 *2050 Fairfield, Troy 48085	(248) 689-1932	(248) 689-2839
First	Weatherly Burkhead Verhelst	FE5	6363 Livernois, Troy 48098 *6339 Vermoor, Troy 48098	(248) 879-6363	(989) 598-6506

CHARGE	PASTOR		ADDRESS	CHURCH	HOME
Korean	Eung Yong Kim	OE1	42693 Dequindre, Troy 48085	(248) 879-2240	
Associate	Tae Gyu Shin	PE4	42693 Dequindre, Troy 48085 *	(248) 879-2240	
Associate	Se Jin Bae	PE5	42693 Dequindre, Troy 48085	(248) 879-2240	(248) 841-1595
Associate Hope Campus	Anna Moon	FE7	*1940 Flagstone Circle, Rochester 48307	(248) 879-2240	
Deacon	Jinny Song	PD4	*17377 Averhill Blvd., Macomb 48042 42693 Dequindre, Troy 48085	(248) 879-2240	
Utica	Donald D. Gotham	FE9	*3200 Olde Franklin Dr., Farmington 48334 8650 Canal Rd., Sterling Hts. 48314	(586) 731-7667	(586) 739-2726
Warren: First	Melissa J. Claxton	FE2	*8506 Clinton River Rd., Sterling Hts. 48314 5005 Chicago Rd., Warren 48092	(586) 264-4701	(586) 264-2212
Washington	Cherlyn E. McKanders	PL1	*32006 Wellston, Warren 48093 58430 Van Dyke, Box 158, Washington 48094	(586) 781-9662	(248) 881-8541
WATERFORD Central	Jack L. Mannschreck	FE7	*59989 Whitman N Apt D, Washington 48094-2261 3882 Highland Rd., Waterford 48328	(248) 681-0040	(248) 683-2986
Deacon	Cora E. Glass	FD2	*3720 Shaddick, Waterford 48328 3882 Highland Rd., Waterford 48328	(248) 681-0040	(248) 410-2645
Four Towns	Sean LaGuire	DSA1	*4011 Shaddick, Waterford 48328 6451 Cooley Lake Rd., Waterford 48327	(248) 682-0211	(313) 926-2498
Trinity	Michael R. Perez, Jr.	DSA1	*11318 Sioux, Redford 48239-2372 6440 Maceday Dr., Waterford 48329	(248) 623-6860	(586) 252-7257
			**442 Marias Ave, Clawson 48017		

GREATER DETROIT DISTRICT

GREATER DETROIT DISTRICT

CHARGE	PASTOR		ADDRESS	CHURCH	HOME
WATER'S EDGE COOPERATIVE PARISH					
Algonac: Trinity	John J. Pajak	PL5	424 Smith St., Algonac 48001	(810) 794-4379	
			*1421 Michigan St., Algonac 48001		
New Baltimore: Grace	Brian Steele	PE2	49655 Jefferson, New Baltimore 48047	(586) 725-1054	(586) 648-6242
			*33840 Hooker Rd., New Baltimore 48047		
Wayne: First	Marva C. Pope	FE2	3 Town Square, Wayne 48184	(734) 721-4801	(248) 629-0746
	(LTFT ½)		*3017 Flora Lane, Wayne 48184		
West Bloomfield	Monica L. William	FE1	4100 Walnut Lake Rd., West Bloomfield 48323	(248) 851-2330	(248) 851-0149
			*5553 Fox Hunt Lane, West Bloomfield 48322		
Westland: St. James	Rahim O. Shabazz	FE2	30055 Annapolis, Westland 48186	(734) 729-1737	
Detroit: People's			19370 Greenfield Rd., Detroit 48235	(313) 342-7868	
			*3722 Heritage Parkway, Dearborn 48124		
Wyandotte: First	Dianna L. Rees	FE7	72 Oak, Wyandotte 48192	(734) 282-9222	(313) 570-6292
			*2210 20th St., Wyandotte 48192		(734) 284-3224

NAME	POSITION	ADDRESS	OFFICE	HOME
	APPOINTMENTS TO EXTENSION MINISTRIES LOCATED IN THE GREATER DETROIT DISTRICT:			
	(further information at end of appointment section)			
Charles S.G. Boayue	District Superintendent, Greater Detroit District Office		(313) 481-1045	
	FE2　　8000 Woodward Avenue, Detroit 48202			
Carl T.S. Gladstone	Director of Motor City Wesley, Young Leaders Initiative Board (LTFT ½)		(313) 718-2275	
	FD1　　8000 Woodward, Detroit 48202			(586) 295-3055
	*542 W Grand Blvd. 48216			
Lisa M. McIlvenna	Samaritan Counseling Center FE11　　29887 W. 11 Mile Rd, Farmington Hills 48336		(248) 474-4701	(248) 879-3220
	*5601 Houghton, Troy 48098			
Alexander J. Plum	Director, Henry Ford Health Systems, Global Health Initiatives		(313) 833-7730	
	PD1　　3901 Cass Ave, Detroit 48201-1721			
	APPOINTMENT TO LOCAL CHURCH FOR DEACON TO MISSIONAL WORK (331.5)			
Susan Pethoud	Detroit: Cass Community Social Services		(313) 833-7730	(810) 278-1235
	FD5　　3901 Cass Ave. Detroit 48201			

GREATER DETROIT DISTRICT

GREATER SOUTHWEST DISTRICT

GREATER SOUTHWEST DISTRICT

District Superintendent	Dwayne E Bagley FE2	DS Email: dbagley@michiganumc.org	Office: (269) 372-7525
Executive Assistant	Mandana Nordbrock	Office Email: mnordbrock@michiganumc.org	2350 Ring Road North, Ste B, Kalamazoo 49006

				TELEPHONE	
CHARGE	PASTOR		ADDRESS	CHURCH	HOME
Allegan	Robert K Lynch	FE8	409 Trowbridge St., Allegan 49010-1230	(269) 673-4236	
			*1310 South M 40, Allegan 49010		(269) 673-2512
Arden	O'Ryan Rickard	RLA11	6891 M 139, Berrien Springs 49103	(269) 429-4931	
			*6148 Avon St, Portage 49024-2630		(269) 235-1700
Augusta: Fellowship	Scott M Bouldrey	PL3	PO Box 337, 103 N. Webster, Augusta 49012	(269) 731-4222	
			*109 N Webster St, Augusta 49012-9679		(269) 275-2633
Bangor: Simpson	Mona K Joslyn	FE4	507 Joy St., Bangor 49013-1123	(269) 427-7725	
			*9177 South Gullway, Richland 49083		(269) 484-4060
BATTLE CREEK					
Baseline	Margaret K. Sandlin	FL2	9617 E Baseline Rd, Battle Creek 49017	(269) 963-7710	
Bellevue			122 W Capital Ave, Bellevue 49021	(269) 763-9421	
			*523 Sherwood Rd, Bellevue 49021		(989) 387-1494
Chapel Hill	Chad M. Parmalee	FE7	157 Chapel Hill Drive, Battle Creek 49015-4631	(269) 963-0231	
			*192 Brentwood Dr, Battle Creek 49015-4512		(517) 281-0362
Associate	Janet S. Wilson	FL2	157 Chapel Hill Drive, Battle Creek 49015-4631	(269) 963-0231	
			*20515 Bedford Rd N, Battle Creek 49017-8869		(269) 317-5591
Christ	Crystal C. Thomas	FL2	65 Bedford Road N, Battle Creek 49037	(269) 965-3251	
Washington Heights			153 N. Wood St, Battle Creek 49037	(269) 968-8773	
			*15 N Woodlawn Ave, Battle Creek 49037		(269) 282-0697
Convis Union	Andrea L. Johnson	PL2	18990 12 Mile Rd, Battle Creek 49014-8496	(269) 965-3787	
			*PO Box 79, Battle Creek 49016-0079		(269) 317-1937

GREATER SOUTHWEST DISTRICT

CHARGE	PASTOR		ADDRESS	CHURCH	HOME
First	Susan J. Trowbridge (LTFT ½)	FE1	111 E Michigan Ave, Battle Creek 49014-4012	(269) 963-5567	(517) 667-8414
Maple	Linda D Stoddard	RE12	*PO Box 151, 329 S Main St, Vermontville 49096-0151 342 Capital Ave NE, Battle Creek 49017	(269) 964-1252	(269) 965-1671
Newton	Connor James Bailey	DSA1	*126 Heather Ridge, Battle Creek 49017 8804 F Drive South, Ceresco 49033	(269) 979-2779	(269) 312-3153
Berrien County: Lakeside	George W Lawton	RLA13	*3727 Greenleaf Cir Apt 211, Kalamazoo 49008 PO Box 402, Union Pier 49129-0402	(269) 469-8468	(269) 469-8468
Berrien Springs Pokagon	William Walters	DSA2	*8000 Warren Woods Rd #79, Three Oaks 49128-8519 310 West Mars, Berrien Springs 49103 31393 Kansas St, Dowagiac 49047-9708	(269) 471-7220 (269) 683-8515	(269) 479-5561
Bloomingdale	Carol A Newman	DSA8	*609 Rynearson St, Buchanan, MI 49107 PO Box 9, Bloomingdale 49026-0009	(269) 521-3323	(269) 628-2414
Bridgman: Faith	Ashlei K. Horn	DSA2	*20584 Meadow Dr, Gobles 49055-9666 PO Box 414, 9156 Red Arrow Hwy, Bridgman 49106	(269) 465-3696	(269) 364-8545
Bronson: First Colon	Samuel C Gordy	FL2	*29680 County Road 687, Bangor 49013 312 E. Chicago St, Bronson 49028 PO Box 646, 224 N. Blackstone, Colon 49040	(517) 369-6555 (269) 432-2783	(269) 330-6054
BUCHANAN Faith	Edward H Slate	RE8	*330 E Cory St, Bronson 49028 728 North Detroit Street, Buchanan 49107-1243	(269) 695-3261	(269) 262-0011
First	Ellen D. Bierlein	FL2	*1358 Honeysuckle Ln, Niles 49120-4665 132 S Oak Street, Buchanan 49107-1559	(269) 695-3282	(269) 695-3896
Burnips Monterey Center	Craig H VanBeek	FL3	*304 Pontiac Court, Buchanan 49107-1273 PO Box 30 4237 30th St, Burnips 49314-0030 PO Box 30, (3022 130th Ave, Hopkins) Burnips 49314	(616) 896-8410 (616) 896-8410	(616) 299-6668
Burr Oak	Carl Q. Litchfield	RE2	*4290 Summer Creek Dr, Dorr 49323-9512 PO Box 91, 105 S. Fourth St., Burr Oak 49030	(269) 489-2985	(269) 275-5296
			*27435 Michigan Ave, Mendon 49072		

GREATER SOUTHWEST DISTRICT

CHARGE	PASTOR		ADDRESS	CHURCH	HOME
Casco	Jodi M. Cartwright	PL1	880 66th Street, South Haven 49090-9523	(269) 227-3328	
			*870 66th St, South Haven 49090		(517) 282-9642
Cassopolis	Wade S Panse	RE5	PO Box 175, 209 South Rowland St, Cassopolis 49031	(269) 445-3107	(269) 449-5335
Centreville	Michael W. Vollmer	PE1	*1218 Riverwood Terrace, St. Joseph 49085-2118		
			305 E Main Street, Centreville 49032	(269) 467-8645	
			*304 E Market St, Centreville 49032		(989) 607-0019
Climax	Beverley J Williams	FL4	PO Box 125, 133 East Maple, Climax 49034-0125	(269) 746-4023	
Scotts			PO Box 112, 8458 Wallene, Scotts 49088	(269) 626-9757	
			*331 Prairie Drive, Climax 49034-9034		(269) 746-8728
Coldwater	Julie Yoder Elmore	FE3	26 Marshall St, Coldwater 49036	(517) 279-8402	
			*20 Parsons Ct, Coldwater 49036-1118		(517) 607-6977
Coloma	Christine M. Beaudoin	FE2	PO Box 670, 144 South Church St, Coloma 49038	(269) 468-6062	(480) 659-1472
			*331 Tannery Dr, Coloma 49038-9709		
Constantine	Tiffany M Newsom	PE3	285 White Pigeon St., Constantine 49042-1063	(269) 435-8151	
White Pigeon			PO Box 518, 204 N Kalamazoo St, White Pigeon 49099	(269) 483-9054	
			*265 White Pigeon St, Constantine 49042		(517) 917-5705
Delton: Faith	Brian R Bunch	FL8	PO Box 467, 503 S Grove, Delton 49046-0467	(269) 623-5400	
			*146 Bush St, Delton 49046-9798		(269) 623-5335
Dowagiac First	Christopher M. Momany	FE1	PO Box 393, 326 N Lowe, Dowagiac 49047-0393	(269) 782-6157	(248) 462-5317
			*207 Michigan Ave, Dowagiac 49047		
Dowling: Country Chapel	Richard J Foster	FL4	PO Box 26, Dowling 49050-0026	(269) 721-8077	
			*3400 Lacey Rd, Dowling 49050-0749		(269) 721-3400
Edwardsburg: Hope	Scott K Otis	FE3	PO Box 624, 69941 Elkhart Rd., Edwardsburg 49112-0624		(269) 663-5321
			*20624 Starbrick Rd, Edwardsburg 49112-9275		(616) 307-9765
Fennville	Douglas A. Tipken	FL2	PO Box 407, 5849 124th Ave, Fennville 49408-0407	(269) 561-5048	
Pearl			PO Box 407, Fennville 49408	(269) 561-5048	
			*687 W Fennville St, Fennville 49408-8404		(269) 873-0014

CHARGE	PASTOR			ADDRESS	CHURCH	HOME
Galesburg	Leonard E Davis		OR4	PO Box 518, 111 W Battle Creek St, Galesburg 49053	(269) 665-7952	
Galien	Cynthia L. Veilleux		DSA2	*10998 Pleasant Lake Rd, Delton 49046	(269) 545-2275	(269) 623-4412
Olive Branch				PO Box 266, 208 N Cleveland Ave, Galien 49113-0266		
				PO Box 266, 2289 Olive Branch Rd, Galien 49113-0266		(517) 741-9041
Ganges	Marcia A Tucker		DSA6	*72 Sycamore Bnd, Union City 49094-9704	(269) 543-3581	
				PO Box 511, 2218 68th Street, Fennville 49408-0511		(269) 857-4797
Girard	Matthew J. West		FL2	*6948 Colver, Fennville 49408-9619	(517) 279-9418	
				990 Marshall Rd., Coldwater 49036		(269) 967-4444
Glenn	TO BE SUPPLIED			*199 Highfield Rd, Marshall 49068	(269) 227-3930	
				PO Box 46, Glenn 49416-0046		(269) 637-3087
Gobles	Lawrence J. French		FL1	*77020 County Road 380, South Haven 49090-9417	(269) 628-2263	
Almena				PO Box 57, 210 E Exchange St, Gobles 49055-0057	(269) 668-2811	(269) 254-8104
				27503 County Rd 375, Paw Paw 49079-9425		
				*31880 Jefferson Ave, Gobles 49055-9659		
Gull Lake	Leonard R. Schoenherr	Co-Pastor	RE4	8640 Gull Rd, Richland 49083-9647	(269) 629-5137	(269) 903-2182
				*4500 Mountain Ash Lane, Kalamazoo 49004-3781		
Co-Pastor	Michael J Tupper		RE1	8640 Gull Rd, Richland 49083-9647	(269) 629-5137	(269) 303-3743
				*45554 West St, Lawrence 49064		
Hartford	Stephanie E. Norton		FL1	425 East Main Street, Hartford 49057-1160	(269) 621-4103	(269) 532-4741
				*143 Paras Hill Dr, Hartford 49057-1164		
Hinchman	Dawn Marie Oldenburg		DSA2	8154 Church St, Berrien Springs 49103-9798	(269) 471-5492	
Scottdale				4276 Scottdale Rd., St. Joseph 49085-9366	(269) 429-7270	(269) 208-9673
				*9862 Vineyard St, Bridgman, MI 49106		
Hopkins	Andrew R Phillips		OE2	PO Box 356, 322 N Maple St, Hopkins 49328-9558	(269) 793-7323	
South Monterey				PO Box 356, Hopkins 49328	(269) 793-7323	(919) 259-4681
				*86 E 13th St #3, Holland 49423		

GREATER SOUTHWEST DISTRICT

GREATER SOUTHWEST DISTRICT

CHARGE	PASTOR		ADDRESS	CHURCH	HOME
KALAMAZOO					
First	Stephen MG Charnley	FE6	212 South Park Street, Kalamazoo 49007-4704	(269) 381-6340	
			*471 W South St #403, Kalamazoo 49007-4676		(269) 312-8633
Associate	Manohar Avina Joshi	OE1	212 South Park Street, Kalamazoo 49007-4704	(269) 381-6340	
	(LTFT ½)		*1720 Embury Rd, Kalamazoo 49008-2246		(503) 799-6679
Associate	Julie A. Kline	OF1	212 South Park Street, Kalamazoo 49007-4704	(269) 381-6340	
			*1724 Nichols Rd, Kalamazoo 49006		(269) 330-8502
Milwood	Billie R Dalton	RE3	3919 Portage Road, Kalamazoo 49001	(269) 381-6720	
			*6585 San Gabriel Dr, Kalamazoo 49009		(269) 615-6945
Northwest	Mark J Roberts	OE2	3140 N 3rd Street, Kalamazoo 49009	(269) 290-1312	
	(LTFT ¼)		*22980 64th Ave, Mattawan 49071		(406) 217-2237
Sunnyside	John Matthew Weiler	FE11	2800 Gull Road, Kalamazoo 49048-1384	(269) 349-3047	
			*3279 Cardinal Hills Trail, Kalamazoo 49004-6614		(269) 599-2274
Deacon	Cara Beth Ann Weiler	FD11	2800 Gull Road, Kalamazoo 49048-1384	(269) 349-3047	
	(LTFT ¼)		*3279 Cardinal Hills Trail, Kalamazoo 49004-6614		
Westwood	Sean K. Kidd	PE1	538 Nichols Road, Kalamazoo 49006-2946	(269) 344-7165	
			*1003 Greenway Terrace, Kalamazoo 49006-2616		(616) 401-8576
Deacon	Sandra V Bibilomo	FD9	538 Nichols Road, Kalamazoo 49006-2946	(269) 344-7165	
	(LTFT ¼)		*2021 March St, Kalamazoo 49001-3957		(269) 369-8803
Kendall	Glenn C. Litchfield	RE1	PO Box 57, 26718 County Road 388, Gobles 49055-0057	(269) 628-2263	
			*61470 County Road 657, Lawton 49065-9609		(269) 436-0023
Lacota	Michael A Pinto	DSA13	PO Box 7, 01160 CR 681, Lacota 49063-0007	(269) 253-4382	
			*2321 Tamarack, Kalamazoo 49006-1426		(269) 342-2747
Lawrence	Wayne E McKenney	FL6	PO Box 276, 122 S Exchange St, Lawrence 49064-0276	(269) 674-8381	
Lawton: St Paul's			PO Box 456, 63855 N. M-40, Lawton 49065-0456	(269) 624-1050	
			*45520 24th St, Mattawan 49071-8769		(269) 669-7062
Marcellus	John D Messner	FL12	PO Box 396, 197 W Main St, Marcellus 49067-0396	(269) 646-5801	
Wakelee			15921 Dutch Settlement, Marcellus 49067-9530	(269) 646-2049	
			*224 Davis St, Marcellus 49067-9361		(269) 646-7791

CHARGE	PASTOR		ADDRESS	CHURCH	HOME
Martin	Corey M. Simon	PE1	PO Box 154, 969 E Allegan, Martin 49070-0154	(269) 672-7097	
Shelbyville			PO Box 154, 938 124th Ave, Shelbyville 49344-9745 *948 Lee St, Martin 49070	(269) 672-7097	(231) 622-2070
Mendon	Carl Q Litchfield	RE2	PO Box 308, 320 W Main St, Mendon 49072-0308 *27435 Michigan Ave, Mendon 49072	(269) 496-4295	(269) 275-5296
NILES					
Portage Prairie	Scott B. Smith	FL1	2450 Orange Road, Niles 49120-8786 *3310 Chicago Rd, Niles 49120-8717	(269) 695-6708	(269) 357-3693
Wesley	Robert L Snodgrass II	FL6	302 Cedar Street, Niles 49120-2612	(269) 683-7250	
Morris Chapel			1730 Holiday, Niles 49120-8007	(269) 684-5194	
Grace			501 Grant Street, Niles 49120-2955 *16270 Lewis Rd, Vandalia 49095-9555	(269) 683-8770	(574) 261-5139
Nottawa	Alexander (Sandy) Miller	DSA17	PO Box 27, 25838 M-86, Nottawa 49075 *61616 Filmore Rd, Sturgis 49091-9318	(269) 467-7134	(269) 467-7134
OSHTEMO					
LifeSpring	Jason E Harpole	PL4	1560 S 8th Street, Oshtemo 49009-9327 *205 Amos Ave, Portage 49002-0415	(269) 353-1303	(269) 388-8312
Oshtemo	John W Fisher	RE7	PO Box 12, 6574 Stadium Dr, Oshtemo 49077-0012 *3506 East Shore Dr, Portage 49002-6603	(269) 375-5656	(269) 327-3277
Otsego	Joseph D Shaler	FE19	PO Box 443, 223 E Allegan St, Otsego 49078-0443 *411 Walden Dr, Otsego 49078-9652	(269) 694-2939	(269) 806-9087
Parchment	Thomas A Davenport	FE4	225 Glendale Blvd, Parchment 49004-1319 *1227 Grand Ave, Kalamazoo 49006-3254	(269) 344-0125	(269) 762-3159
Paw Paw	David E Small	FL/RHL4	420 W Michigan Ave, Paw Paw 49079-1043 *52333 Ackley Terrace, Paw Paw 49079-9567	(269) 657-7727	(269) 303-8062
Plainwell: First	Kathy E Brown	FE10	PO Box 85, 200 Park St., Plainwell 49080-0085 *714 E Gun River Dr, Plain-well 49080-9533	(269) 685-5113	(269) 312-1378

GREATER SOUTHWEST DISTRICT

GREATER SOUTHWEST DISTRICT

CHARGE	PASTOR		ADDRESS	CHURCH	HOME
PORTAGE					
Chapel Hill	Barry T Petrucci	FE19	7028 Oakland Dr, Portage 49024-4148	(269) 327-6643	
Deacon	Patricia L. Catellier (LTFT ¼)	FD5	*5300 Bronson Blvd, Portage 49024-5746 7028 Oakland Dr., Portage 49024-4148	(269) 327-6643	(269) 276-0482
Pathfinder	Donald W Wolfgang	FE4	*7146 Oakland Drive, Portage 49024-4150 8740 S Westnedge Ave, Portage 49002-6232	(269) 327-6761	(269) 382-0708
Riverside	David L Haase	PL6	*8731 Newhouse, Portage 49024 PO Box 152, (4401 Fikes Rd Benton Harbor) Riverside 49084	(269) 849-1131	(912) 674-8155
Saugatuck	Emmett H Kadwell Jr	RE9	*211 W Saint Joseph St, Watervliet 49098-9214 PO Box 647, 250 Mason St, Saugatuck 49453-0647	(269) 857-2295	(269) 463-3536
Schoolcraft	Julia R Humenik	PE5	*2794 6th St, Shelbyville 49344-9559 PO Box 336, 342 N Grand Ave, Schoolcraft 49087-0336	(269) 679-4845	(231) 912-0806
Pleasant Valley			PO Box 517, 9300 West XY Ave, Schoolcraft 49087-0517	(269) 679-5352	
Silver Creek	Sara Louise Carlson	PL4	*318 Willow Ct, Schoolcraft 49087-9735 31994 Middle Crossing Rd, Dowagiac 49047-9354	(269) 782-7061	(269) 679-4501
Sodus: Chapel Hill	Brenda E. Gordon	FE2	*4229 Mahoney St, Portage 49002-6570 4071 Naomi Road, Sodus 49126-9768	(269) 927-3454	(269) 329-1072
South Haven	Ronald D. VanLente	FE2	*4033 Naomi Rd, Sodus 49126-9768 429 Michigan, South Haven 49090-1333	(269) 637-2502	(269) 925-4528
St. Joseph: First	Daniel R. Colthorp	FL2	*12320 76th St, South Haven 49090-8430 2950 Lakeview Ave, St. Joseph 49085	(269) 983-3929	(269) 468-9378
Deacon	James W Kraus Jr	FD19	*5835 Demorrow Rd, Stevensville 49127 2950 Lakeview Ave, St. Joseph 49085	(269) 983-3929	(269) 369-8475
Stevensville	David F Hills	FE5	*2820 Willa Dr, St Joseph 49085-2555 5506 Ridge Rd, Stevensville 49127-1025	(269) 429-5911	(269) 983-5798
			*1418 Lake Blvd #1, St. Jo-seph 49085-1691		(989) 330-3730

CHARGE	PASTOR		ADDRESS	CHURCH	HOME
Sturgis	Susan J. Babb	FE1	200 Pleasant Ave., Sturgis 49091	(269) 651-5990	(989) 287-1770
			*1332 Rolling Ridge Ln, Sturgis 49091-1751		
Deacon	Mark R Babb	FD1	200 Pleasant Ave., Sturgis 49091	(269) 651-5990	(989) 287-1956
	(LTFT ½)		*1332 Rolling Ridge Ln, Sturgis 49091-1751		
Three Oaks	Brenda L. Ludwig	RLA2	2 Sycamore Street E, Three Oaks 49128-1146	(269) 756-2053	(812) 508-5780
			*8000 Warren Woods Rd #81, Three Oaks 49128		
THREE RIVERS					
Center Park	Derl G. Keefer	OF1	18662 Moorepark Rd., Three Rivers 49093	(269) 279-9109	(816) 519-1473
	(LTFT)		*318 E St, Three Rivers 49093		
First	Heather A. McDougall	PE1	215 N Main St, Three Rivers 49093-1504	(269) 278-4722	(269) 352-4857
	(LTFT ¼)		*61644 Windridge Ct, Centreville 49032-9560		
Ninth Street	Edward C Ross	RE3	704 9th St, Three Rivers 49093-1206	(269) 278-2065	(269) 382-0870
			*4231 Persian Dr, Kalamazoo 49006		
Townline	James C Robertson	PL6	41470 24th Ave, Bloomingdale 49026-9760	(269) 521-4559	(269) 838-3500
			*55130 County Rd 384, Grand Junction 49056-9725		
Union City	James Palaszeski	FL2	PO Box 95, 200 Ellen St, Union City 49094-0095	(517) 741-7028	(989) 912-5738
Athens			PO Box 267, 123 Clark St, Athens 49011	(269) 729-9370	
			*72 Sycamore Bend, Union City 49094		
Vicksburg	Gregory P Culver	FE3	217 S Main Street, Vicksburg 49097-1212	(269) 649-2343	(231) 651-9309
			*7794 TS Ave E, Scotts 49088-9748		

GREATER SOUTHWEST DISTRICT

GREATER SOUTHWEST DISTRICT

APPOINTMENTS TO EXTENSION MINISTRIES LOCATED IN THE GREATER SOUTHWEST DISTRICT:
(further information at end of appointment section)

NAME	POSITION	ADDRESS	OFFICE	HOME
Dwayne E Bagley	District Superintendent, Greater Southwest District Office			
	FE2	2350 Ring Road North, Suite B, Kalamazoo 49006	(269) 372-7525	(269) 370-2800
Lisa M Batten	Young Adult Initiatives Coordinator, Michigan Conference			
	FL2	1810 N Drake Rd, Kalamazoo 49006	(517) 347-4030	(269) 491-1799
Sandra V Bibilomo	Representative Payee, Guardian Finance and Advocacy Services			
	FD8	1000 S Burdick, Kalamazoo 49001	(269) 364-6759	(269) 369-8803
Jessica M Davenport	Director & Campus Pastor, Wesley Foundation of Kalamazoo			
	FL2	2350 Ring Road North, Kalamazoo 49006	(269) 344-4076	(309) 262-3469
David G. Elmore	Chaplain, Ascension at Home Hospice			
	FE1	5220 Lovers Ln, Ste 140, Portage 49002	(800) 343-1396	(517) 817-8855
Heather A McDougall	Chaplain, Beacon Health System			
	PE4			(269) 352-4857
Cara Beth Ann Weiler	Social Worker, Southwest Michigan Childen's Trauma Assessment Center			
	FD11	Unified Clinics – WMU, 1000 Oakland Dr, Kalamazoo 49008	(269) 387-7073	(269) 578-6335

APPOINTMENT FROM OTHER CONFERENCES:

Mark J. Roberts	Chaplain, Borgess Medical Center, Kalamazoo (3/4 time)			
(Alabama-West Florida Conf.)	OE2	1521 Gull Rd, Kalamazoo 49048	(406) 217-2237	

HERITAGE DISTRICT

		Office: (734) 663-3939
District Superintendent	Elizabeth A. Hill FE2	DS Email: ehill@michiganumc.org
Executive Assistant	Dar McGee	Office Email: dmcgee@michiganumc.org
		900 S. 7th Street, Ann Arbor 48103

				TELEPHONE	
CHARGE	PASTOR		ADDRESS	CHURCH	HOME
Adrian: First	Wilson (Drew) A. Hart	FE6	1245 W. Maple Ave., Adrian 49221	(517) 265-5689	
			*4580 S. Clubview Dr., Adrian 49221		(734) 904-9775
Albion: First	Leslee J. Fritz	PE3	600 E. Michigan, Albion 49224	(517) 629-9425	(517) 629-6531
			*11184 29 Mile Rd, Albion 49224-9735		
Allen	Larry W Rubingh	RE3	PO Box 103, 167 W Chicago Rd, Allen 49227	(517) 200-8416	(517) 812-6636
			*2480 N Portage Rd, Jackson 49201		
ANN ARBOR					
Calvary	Mary K. Loring	PE1	1415 Miller Rd., Ann Arbor 48103	(734) 769-0869	
			*700 Newport Pl., Ann Arbor 48103		(616) 307-0369
First	Nancy S. Lynn	FE2	120 S. State St., Ann Arbor 48104	(734) 662-4536	(734) 730-2421
			*3475 Glazier Way, Ann Arbor 48105		
Associate	Nicolas R Berlanga	FL2	120 S. State St., Ann Arbor 48104	(734) 662-4536	(734) 983-8677
			*1507 Warwick, Ann Arbor 48103		
Korean	Joonshik Yoo	PE1	1526 Franklin St., Ann Arbor 48103	(734) 662-0660	
			*1811 Avondale, Ann Arbor 48103		
Associate	Steve H. Khang (LTFT ¾)	FE13	1526 Franklin St., Ann Arbor 48103	(734) 662-0660	(734) 482-0460
			*4131 Inglewood Dr, Ypsilanti 48197		
West Side	Timothy R. Ziegler	FE7	900 S. Seventh St., Ann Arbor 48103	(734) 663-4164	(734) 645-3623
			*3023 Appleridge Dr, Ann Arbor 48103		
Azalia	Beatrice S. Alghali	PL1	9855 Azalia Rd., Box 216, Milan 48160	(734) 529-3731	
London			11318 Plank Rd., Milan 48160	(734) 439-2680	
			*22492 Pontchartrain Dr, Southfield 48034-2127		(248) 281-3157

HERITAGE DISTRICT

CHARGE	PASTOR		ADDRESS	CHURCH	HOME
Belleville: First	James J. Walker	FE13	417 Charles St., Belleville 48111	(734) 697-9288	
			*455 High St., Belleville 48111		(734) 697-7398
BLISSFIELD					
Emmanuel	Devin R. Smith (LTFT ½)	FE5	215 E. Jefferson St., Blissfield 49228	(517) 486-3020	
			*302 E. Jefferson St., Blissfield 49228		(517) 486-2752
First	Gunsoo Jung	FE1	201 W. Adrian St., Blissfield 49228	(517) 486-4040	
			*403 Brenot Ct., Blissfield 49228		(517) 486-3805
Brighton: First	Sherry L. Parker-Lewis	FE12	400 E. Grand River, Brighton 48116	(810) 229-8561	
			*7608 Brookview Ct., Brighton 48116		(810) 229-7831
Associate	Robert Fuchs	FL3	400 E. Grand River, Brighton 48116	(810) 229-8561	
			*3082 Park Dr., Brighton 48116		(810) 227-8979
Whitmore Lake Campus			9318 Main St., Box 431, Whitmore Lake 48189	(734) 449-2121	
Britton: Grace	Ruth VanderSande	PE1	9250 E. Monroe, Britton 49229	(517) 451-8280	
Macon			11964 Macon Hwy., Clinton 49236	(517) 423-8270	
			*7645 Clinton-Macon Rd., Clinton 49236		(810) 335-3962
Camden	Frederick G Cain	RE7	PO Box 272, 201 S Main St, Camden 49232	(517) 368-5406	
Montgomery			PO Box 272, 201 S Main St, Camden 49232	(517) 269-4232	
Stokes Chapel			PO Box 272, 201 S Main St, Camden 49232	(517) 368-5406	
			*PO Box 155, 201 S Main St, Camden 49232		(517) 797-5530
CANTON					
Cherry Hill	Michael Desotell	FL6	321 S. Ridge Rd., Canton 48188	(734) 495-0035	
St. Matthew's			1344 Borgstrom, Ypsilanti 48198	(734) 483-5876	
			*1110 Ruth, Ypsilanti 48198		
Friendship	Michael K. Norton	FE23	1240 Beck Rd., Canton 48187	(734) 710-9370	(734) 730-6746
			*1237 Lotz Rd. South, Canton 48188		(734) 722-0183
Carleton	Taek H. Kim	FE8	11435 Grafton Rd., Box 327, Carleton 48117	(734) 654-2833	
			*1424 Monroe St., Box 327, Carleton 48117		(734) 654-2001

CHARGE	PASTOR		ADDRESS	CHURCH	HOME
Chelsea: First	Joy A. Barrett	FE16	128 Park St., Chelsea 48118	(734) 475-8119	(734) 475-8449
Deacon	Rodney Gasaway (LTFT ½)	PD1	*10 Sycamore Dr., Chelsea 48118	(734) 475-8119	(734) 578-6256
Clayton	Robert W. Dister	FL8	128 Park St., Chelsea 48118		
			*36522 Ann Arbor Trail, Livonia 48150	(517) 445-2641	(517) 445-4009
Rollin Center			3387 State St., PO Box 98, Clayton 49235		
			3988 Townley Rd., Box 98, Manitou Beach 49253		
Clinton	Robert P. Blanchard	PE2	*3282 State St., PO Box 98, Clayton 49235	(517) 456-4972	(734) 244-6409
			10990 Tecumseh-Clinton Rd., Clinton 49236		
Commerce	Andrew H. Lee	FE1	*6830 Close Dr, Tecumseh 49286	(248) 363-3935	(248) 977-0400
			1155 N Commerce Rd., Commerce Township 48382		
Concord	Robert M Hughes	FE4	*840 Morella, Commerce Twp. 48382	(517) 524-6156	(517) 677-6381
			PO Box 366, 119 S. Main St., Concord 49237-0366		
Deerfield	Bradley R. Vasey	PL1	*361 Calhoun St, Union City 49194-9359	(517) 447-3420	(419) 704-1884
			110 Williams St., Box 395, Deerfield 49238	(517) 486-4777	
Wellsville			2509 S. Wellsville, Blissfield 49228		
Denton: Faith	Arthur D. Korlapati	DSA2	*4322 Corey Hwy, Blissfield 49228	(734) 483-2276	(248) 444-6529
			6020 Denton Rd., Belleville 48111		
Dexter	Matthew J. Hook	FE17	*7338 Talbot Drive Apt 102, Lansing 48917	(734) 426-8480	(734) 426-8420
			7643 Huron River Dr., Dexter 48130		
Deacon	Thomas Snyder	FD6	*7605 Grand Ave., Dexter 48130	(734) 426-8480	(734) 476-8954
			7643 Huron River Dr., Dexter 48130		
Dixboro	E. Jeanne Garza	FE1	*8650 Huron River Dr., Dexter 48130	(734) 665-5632	(269) 503-2099
			5221 Church Rd., Ann Arbor 48105		
Deacon	Mary Hagley (LTFT ½)	FD7	*3350 Oak Dr, Ann Arbor 48105	(734) 665-5632	(734) 652-5389
			5221 Church Rd., Ann Arbor 48105		
Dundee	Bradley S. Luck	FE2	*2929 Brandywine Dr., Ann Arbor 48103	(734) 529-3535	(734) 625-6693
			645 Franklin, Dundee 48131		
			*241 Sidney St., Dundee 48131		

HERITAGE DISTRICT

HERITAGE DISTRICT

CHARGE	PASTOR		ADDRESS	CHURCH	HOME
Erie	Janet J. Brown	RE2	1100 E. Samaria Rd., Erie 48133	(734) 856-1453	
Frontier	Donald Lee	RLA3	*23470 Meadow Park, Redford 48239		(313) 533-8423
			PO Box 120, 9925 Short St, Frontier 49239-0120	(269) 233-0631	
Grass Lake	Lawrence J. Williford	OR1	*PO Box 127, 106 E Maple St, Camden 49232-0127		(517) 398-3082
			449 E Michigan Ave, Grass Lake 49240-9501	(517) 522-8040	
Hardy	John H. Schneider Jr.	FE7	*4273 Indian Trl, Jackson 49201		(585) 409-3546
			6510 E. Highland Rd., Howell 48843	(517) 546-1122	
Hartland	Paul Gruenberg	FE8	6520 E. Highland Dr., Howell 48843		(517) 579-2526
			10300 Maple St., Hartland 48353	(810) 632-7476	
Highland	Thomas C. Anderson	FE4	*1403 Odette, Hartland 48353		(810) 991-1023
			680 W. Livingston Rd., Highland 48357	(248) 887-1311	
Hillsdale: First	Rob A. McPherson	FE2	*650 W. Livingston Rd., Highland 48357		(248) 887-1311
			45 N Manning, Hillsdale 49242	(517) 437-3681	
Hillside	Patricia A Pebley	FL6	*1079 Markris Dr, Hillsdale 49242-2036		(269) 845-5221
Somerset Center			6100 Folks Rd, Horton 49246	(517) 563-2835 (517) 688-4330	
			PO Box 277, 12095 E Chicago Rd, Somerset Center 49282		(517) 563-8920
Homer	Robert P Stover	RE8	*6094 Folks Rd, Horton 49246-9657		
			101 E Adams St, Homer 49245	(517) 568-4001	
Lyon Lake			8493 17 Mile Rd, Marshall 49068	(269) 789-0017	
Howell: First	George H. Lewis	FE10	*105 E Adams St, Homer 49245-1101		(517) 568-1126
			1230 Bower St., Howell 48843	(517) 546-2730	
Diaconal	Diane M. Griffin	DM	*7608 Brookview Ct., Brighton 48116		(810) 229-7831
			1230 Bower St., Howell 48843	(517) 546-2730	
Hudson: First	Carol J. (Abbott) Freeland	FL2	*247 S. Mill St., Pinckney 48169		(734) 878-9414
			420 W. Main St., Hudson 49247	(517) 448-5891	
Ida	Robert J. Freysinger	FE1	*428 W. Main St., Hudson 49247		(517) 306-6236
			Box 28, 8124 Ida East, Ida 48140	(734) 269-6127	
Samaria: Grace			Box 37, 1463 Samaria Rd., Samaria 48177	(734) 856-6430	
			*3276 Lewis Ave, Ida 48140-9708		(517) 812-0762

CHARGE	PASTOR		ADDRESS	CHURCH	HOME
JACKSON					
Brookside	Ronald K Brooks	FE7	4000 Francis, Jackson 49203	(517) 782-5167	
Trinity			1508 Greenwood Ave, Jackson 49203-4048	(517) 782-7937	(517) 782-2706
			*217 Mohawk, Jackson 49203		
Calvary	Terry Wiliford	OR1	925 Backus St, Jackson 49202-3203	(517) 782-0543	(585) 645-4554
			*4273 Indian Trl, Jackson 49201		
First	Tonya M. Arnesen	FE1	275 W Michigan Ave, Jackson 49201	(517) 787-6460	(586) 292-1036
Zion	TO BE SUPPLIED		*1734 Malvern Dr, Jackson 49203-5341	(517) 769-2570	
			7498 Cooper St, Jackson 49201		
			*		
Jonesville	Mary A Sweet	PE1	203 Concord Rd, Jonesville 49250-9824	(517) 849-9565	
Napoleon			PO Box 337, 210 Nottawasepee, Napoleon 49261	(517) 536-8609	(231) 881-7367
			*969 Adams St, Litchfield 49252-9779		
Lambertville	James E. Britt	FE2	8165 Douglas Rd., Box 232, Lambertville 48144	(734) 847-3944	(810) 282-8081
			*8116 Michelle Ln., Lambertville 48144		
Associate	Devin R. Smith (LTFT ½)	FE5	8165 Douglas Rd., Box 232, Lambertville 48144	(734) 847-3944	(517) 486-2752
			*302 E. Jefferson St., Blissfield 49228		
LaSalle: Zion	Carter L. Cortelyou	FE2	1607 Yargerville Rd., LaSalle 48145	(734) 243-5940	(248) 506-5406
Petersburg			152 Saline St., PO Box 85, Petersburg 49270	(734) 279-1118	
			*1607 Yargerville., LaSalle 48145		
Lee Center	James M Gysel	RE6	22392 24 Mile Road, Olivet 49076-9533	(517) 857-3447	(269) 209-4795
			*3239 Nighthawk Lane, Battle Creek 49015-7640		
Lulu	William Lass	PL2	2810 Lulu Rd., Ida 48140	(734) 625-4997	(734) 735-1669
			*5423 N Stoney Creek Rd, Monroe 48162		
MANCHESTER					
Manchester	Dillon S. Burns	PE3	501 Ann Arbor Rd., Manchester 48158	(734) 428-8495	(734) 428-4780
			*330 Ann Arbor St., Manchester 48158		

HERITAGE DISTRICT

HERITAGE DISTRICT

CHARGE	PASTOR		ADDRESS	CHURCH	HOME
Sharon	Peter S. Harris	FE13	Box 543, 19980 Pleasant Lk. Rd., Manchester 48158	(734) 428-0996	
			*16181 Wellwood Ct., Tipton 49287		(517) 431-3908
Marshall	Melany A Chalker	FE7	721 Old US 27N, Marshall 49068-9609	(269) 781-5107	(517) 403-8528
Milan: Marble Memorial	Jacquelyn A. Roe	FE2	*762 N Kalamazoo Ave, Marshall 49068-1071		
			8 Park St., Milan 48160	(734) 439-2421	
			*835 Faith Ct., Milan 48160		(906) 553-1953
Milford	Douglas J. McMunn	FE9	1200 Atlantic St., Milford 48381	(248) 684-2798	(248) 685-1737
Deacon	Sheryl A. Foster (LTFT ½)	FD12	*350 Cabinet St., Milford 48381		
			1200 Atlantic St., Milford 48381	(248) 628-1002	
			*5821 Selske Dr., Brighton 48116		(248) 318-5613
MONROE					
Calvary	Stephen K. Perrine	FE13	790 Patterson Dr., Monroe 48161	(734) 242-0145	
South Rockwood			6311 S. Huron River Dr., South Rockwood 48033	(734) 379-3131	
			*23435 Oak Glen, Southfield 48033		(248) 827-7110
First	Katherine C. Waggoner (part-time ¾ + ¼)	FL9	312 Harrison, Monroe 48161	(734) 242-3000	
Heritage			4010 N. Custer Rd., Monroe 48161	(734) 242-9747	(517) 447-3915
St.Paul's	Melodye S. VanOudheusden	FE1	*310 Carey St., Deerfield 49238		
			201 S. Monroe St., Monroe 48161	(734) 242-3000	
			*212 Hollywood Dr., Monroe 48162		(517) 250-1879
Morenci	Donna Galloway (part-time ½ + ½)	FL6	110 E. Main St., Morenci 49256	(517) 458-6923	
Weston			4193 Weston Rd., Box 96, Weston 49289	(517) 436-3492	
			*111 E. Main St., Morenci 49256		(517) 458-6687
New Hudson	Seung H. (Andy) Baek	FE2	56730 Grand River, Box 803, New Hudson 48165	(248) 437-6212	(248) 437-6367
			*56799 New Hudson Rd, Box 803 New Hudson 48165		
North Adams	Timothy R Puckett	PL6	PO Box 62, 228 E Main St, North Adams 49262	(517) 287-5190	
Jerome			8768 Jerome Rd N, Jerome 49249		(517) 936-5835
			*10445 Folks Rd, Hanover 49241-9777		

CHARGE	PASTOR		ADDRESS	CHURCH	HOME
North Lake	Todd Wesley Jones	FL4	14111 N. Territorial, Chelsea 48118	(734) 475-7569	
			*14130 Wagon Wheel Ct., Chelsea 48118		(734) 475-9348
North Parma	Mark E. Mitchell	FL2	11970 Devereaux, PO Box 25, Parma 49269-0025	(517) 531-4619	
Springport			127 W Main St, PO Box 1004, Springport 49284-1004	(517) 857-2777	(517) 414-0180
			*258 Green St, Springport 49284		
Northville: First	Marsha M. Woolley	FE7	777 W. 8 Mile Rd., Northville 48167	(248) 349-1144	(248) 349-1143
			*20490 Lexington Blvd., Northville 48167		
Associate	TO BE SUPPLIED		777 W 8 Mile Rd., Box 55, Northville 48167	(248) 349-1144	
			*		
Novi	June M. Marshall-Smith	FE13	41671 W. Ten Mile Rd., Novi 48375	(248) 349-2652	(248) 349-6117
			*40755 Oakwood Dr., Novi 48375		
Oak Grove	Paula M. Timm	FE9	6686 Oak Grove Rd., Oak Grove 48855	(517) 546-3942	(989) 712-0013
			*6893 Sanford Rd., Howell 48855		
Pinckney: Arise	Reed P. Swanson	FE2	11211 Dexter-Pinckney Rd., Pinckney 48169	(734) 878-1928	(586) 202-1894
			*11267 Dexter-Pinckney Rd., Pinckney 48169		
Pleasant Lake	Christine L Pease	CLM/DSA6	PO Box 83, 4815 E Territorial Rd, Pleasant Lake 49272-0083		(517) 543-5618
			*340 Pleasant St, Charlotte 48813-1626		
Plymouth: First	Robert A. Miller, Jr.	FE2	45201 N. Territorial Rd., Plymouth 48170	(734) 453-5280	(810) 623-0985
			*1401 Palmer St., Plymouth 48170		
Associate	Suzanne L. Hutchison	FL2	45201 N. Territorial Rd., Plymouth 48170	(734) 453-5280	(810) 923-1649
			*44698 Maidstone, Canton 48187		
Pope	Lawrence J. Embury	PL2	10401 Townley Rd, Springport 49284-0228	(517) 857-3655	
Griffith			9537 S Clinton Trail, Eaton Rapids 48827-8544	(517) 663-6262	(517) 206-2952
			*PO Box 86, 1855 Sarossy Lake Rd, Grass Lake 49240-0086		
Quincy	Richard D Wilson	RE3	32 W. Chicago St., Quincy 49082-1144	(517) 639-5035	(269) 781-4082
			*548 East Dr, Marshall 49068-1363		

HERITAGE DISTRICT

HERITAGE DISTRICT

CHARGE	PASTOR		ADDRESS	CHURCH	HOME
Reading	Deborah Sue Cole	FL6	PO Box 457, 312 E Michigan St, Reading 49274	(517) 283-2443	
			*317 First Street, Reading 49274		(517) 283-2775
Salem Grove	Mary Barrett	PL4	3320 Notten Rd., Grass Lake 49240		
Waterloo: Village			8110 Washington St, Grass Lake 49240-9241	(734) 475-1171	(517) 521-3939
Saline: First	Thomas H. Zimmerman	FE4	*305 N. Howard, PO Box 530, Webberville 48892		
			1200 N. Ann Arbor St., Saline 48176	(734) 429-4730	(419) 262-5575
South Lyon: First	Mary Ann McInnes	FE3	*3020 Aspen Lane, Ann Arbor 48108		
			640 S. Lafayette, South Lyon 48178	(248) 437-0760	(586) 515-0013
Associate	Kenny Ray Walkup, Jr.	PL5	*650 S. Lafayette, South Lyon 48178		
			640 S. Lafayette, South Lyon 48178	(248) 437-0760	(248) 361-6658
Springville	Evans C. Bentley	RE2	*1115 Paddock, South Lyon 48178		
			10341 Springville Hwy., Onsted 49265	(517) 467-4471	(734-552-5064
Stony Creek	Nathaniel Starkey	FL3	*1109 N River Ct, Tecumseh 49286		
			8635 Stony Creek Rd., Ypsilanti 48197	(734) 482-0240	(734) 482-8113
Tecumseh	Mark A. Miller	FE10	*5493 Willis Rd., Ypsilanti 48197		
			605 Bishop Reed Dr., Tecumseh 49286	(517) 426-2523	(517) 423-3767
Walled Lake	Ian Boley	FL4	*808 Derby Dr., Tecumseh 49286		
			313 Northport St., Walled Lake 48390	(248) 624-2405	(989) 400-1268
Willow	Kelly Vergowven	PL3	*1977 Meadow Ridge Dr., Commerce Twp. 48390		
			36925 Willow Rd., Box 281, New Boston 48164	(734) 654-9020	(734) 497-3560
YPSILANTI			*8833 Surfwood Dr., Monroe 48162		
First	Briony P. Desotell	FE6	209 Washtenaw Ave., Ypsilanti 48197	(734) 482-8374	(734) 730-6747
Lincoln Community	Christopher A. Butson	PE1	*1110 Ruth, Ypsilanti 48198		
			9074 Whittaker Rd., Ypsilanti 48197	(734) 482-4446	(734) 735-4892
			*9066 Whittaker Rd., Ypsilanti 48197		

NAME	POSITION	ADDRESS		OFFICE	HOME
APPOINTMENTS TO EXTENSION MINISTRIES LOCATED IN THE HERITAGE DISTRICT:					
(further information at end of appointment section)					
Elizabeth A. Hill	District Superintendent, Heritage District Office				
		FE2	900 S. 7th Street, Ann Arbor 48103	(734) 663-3939	
Roy Testolin	Pastoral Counselor, Heritage Interfaith Counseling Center				
		RE21	*12884 E Dr S, Marshall 49068	(269) 979-5180	(269) 781-9257
Teresa J. Zimmerman	Associate Director Spiritual Life, Chelsea Retirement Community				
		FD3	805 W. Middle St., Chelsea 48118	(734) 433-1000	(734) 428-0576
Christina L. Wright	Associate Director, Dept of Spiritual Care, Michigan Medicine U of M				
		FD1	1500 E Medical Center Dr, Ann Arbor 48109	(734) 936-4041	
APPOINTMENT FROM OTHER CONFERENCES:					
Timothy L. Kobler	Chaplain/Director, University of Michigan Wesley Foundation				
(Holston Conf.)		OE2	602 E Huron, Ann Arbor 48104	(734) 668-6881	

HERITAGE DISTRICT

MID-MICHIGAN DISTRICT

MID-MICHIGAN DISTRICT

| District Superintendent | Jerome R. DeVine FE2 | DS Email: jdevine@michiganumc.org |
| Executive Assistant | Sarah Gillette | Office Email: sgillette@michiganumc.org |

Office (517) 347-4173
1161 E Clark Rd Ste 216, DeWitt 48820

| | | | | TELEPHONE | |
CHARGE	PASTOR		ADDRESS	CHURCH	HOME
Alma	Deborah S Thomas	FE7	501 Gratiot Ave, Alma 48801-1708	(989) 463-4305	
			*627 Woodworth Ave, Alma 48801		(989) 463-1485
Ashley	Zella M Daniel	PL2	PO Box 7, 112 N New St, Ashley 48806-5114	(989) 862-4392	
Bannister			103 Hanvey St, Bannister 48807-5140	(989) 862-4392	
Pompeii			PO Box 125, 135 Burton St, Pompeii 48874	(989) 838-4159	
			*2415 E Tobias, Clio 48420		(810) 869-8815
Barry County: Woodland	Kathleen Smith	RLA5	203 N Main St, Woodland 48897-9638	(269) 367-4061	
			*7500 Bayne Rd, Woodland 48897-9632		(269) 367-4123
Bath	Matthew D Kreh	FL5	PO Box 308, 13777 Main St, Bath 48808-0308	(517) 641-6551	
Gunnisonville			2031 E Clark Rd, Bath 48808-9413	(517) 482-7987	
			*2025 Cumberland Rd, Lansing 48906-3771		(517) 440-8178
Breckenridge	Cleoria M. French	PL1	PO Box 248, Breckenridge 48615	(989) 842-3632	
			*5245 Pheasant Run Dr., Apt #3, Saginaw 48638		(810) 814-6487
Brookfield: Eaton	Cari A. Godbehere	PL2	PO Box 430, 7681 Brookfield, Charlotte 48813-0430	(517) 543-4225	
			*14929 Nichols Rd, Bath 48808-9717		(517) 420-3903
Carland	Charlene Wagner	PL2	4002 Carland Rd., Elsie 48831		
			*587 N Baldwin Rd, Owosso 48867		(989) 494-7763
Carson City	Ian S. McDonald	FL1	PO Box 298, 119 E Elm Street, Carson City 48811	(989) 584-3797	
			*121 S Abbott St, Carson City 48811		(906) 322-5318
Charlotte: Law Avenue	Gary S Wales	FE7	PO Box 36, Charlotte 48813-0036	(517) 543-4670	
			*1072 N Stonehill Dr, Charlotte 48813		(517) 231-6775

CHARGE	PASTOR		ADDRESS	CHURCH	HOME
Chesaning: Trinity	Timothy S.Woycik	FE8	1629 W. Brady, Chesaning 48616	(989) 845-3157	(989) 845-2227
			*1701 W. Brady Rd., Chesaning 48616		
CORUNNA					
Corunna	Stephen Spina	OF3	200 W. McArthur, Corunna 48817	(989) 743-5050	(715) 374-0078
			*225 W. Corunna Rd., Corunna 48817		
Northwest Venice	Norman R. Beckwith Sr.	RE6	6001 E. Wilkinson Rd, Corunna 48817		(989) 661-2377
			*18517 W Brady Rd., Oakley 48649		
Delta Mills	Joseph L Spackman	RE7	6809 Delta River Dr, Lansing 48906-9002	(517) 321-8100	(517) 694-8346
			*3806 Comice Falls Dr Apt 6, Holt 48842-8809		
DeWitt: Redeemer	Rodney J Kalajainen	FE32	13980 Schavey Rd, DeWitt 48820-9013	(517) 669-3430	(517) 669-9140
			*2155 Longwoods Dr, DeWitt 48820-8182		
Associate	Timothy W Trommater	FE3	13980 Schavey Rd, DeWitt 48820-9013	(517) 669-3430	(517) 783-3803
			*139 W Brunswick Dr, DeWitt 48820-9107		
St. Johns Campus	Kalajainen / Trommater		200 E State Street, St Johns 48879-1552	(989) 224-6859	
Dimondale	Linda Farmer-Lewis	OR1	PO Box 387, 6801 Creyts Rd, Dimondale 48821-0387	(517) 646-0641	(517) 581-5595
			*6747 Creyts Rd, Dimondale 48821-9409		
EAST LANSING					
Peoples Church	Andrew Pomerville		200 W Grand River Ave, East Lansing 48823-4212	(517) 332-5073	
University	William C Bills	FE4	1120 S Harrison Rd, East Lansing 48823-5201	(517) 351-7030	(616) 706-6050
			*405 Green Meadows Dr, Lansing 48917		
Eaton Rapids: First	Martin M DeBow	FE6	600 S Main St, Eaton Rapids 48827-1426	(517) 663-3524	(517) 663-8256
			*702 State St, Eaton Rapids 48823-1603		
Elsie	Ava R. Williams	DSA2	PO Box 189, 160 W Main St, Elsie 48831-0189	(989) 862-5239	(202) 524-9579
			*		
Fowlerville: First	Scott Herald	FL4	201 S. Second, Box 344, Fowlerville 48836	(517) 223-8824	(734) 545-2276
			*18521 Daymon Dr., Gregory 48137		

MID-MICHIGAN DISTRICT

MID-MICHIGAN DISTRICT

CHARGE	PASTOR		ADDRESS	CHURCH	HOME
Freeport	Mickey Ann Cousino	DSA5	PO Box 142, 193 Cherry St, Freeport 49325-0142	(616) 765-5316	
Nashville: Peace			6043 E M-79 Hwy, Nashville 49073	(517) 852-1993	
Hastings: Welcome Corners			3185 N M-43 Hwy, Hastings 49058-7944	(269) 945-2654	(616) 765-5322
			*1713 W Sisson Rd., Hastings 49058-9534		
Grand Ledge: First	Cynthia A Skutar	FE7	411 Harrison St, Grand Ledge 48837-1575	(517) 627-3256	(517) 627-7347
			*912 E Scott St, Grand Ledge 48837-2053		
Gresham	Heather L Nolen	FL3	4800 Lamie Highway, Charlotte 48813-8873	(517) 652-1580	
Sunfield			PO Box 25, 227 Logan St, Sunfield 48890-0025	(517) 566-8448	(734) 846-3491
			*235 Dunham St, Sunfield 48890-9772		
HASTINGS					
First	Bryce E Feighner	FE3	209 W Green St, Hastings 49058-2229	(269) 945-9574	
			*220 N Chester Rd., Charlotte 48813-9547		(517) 588-1619
Hope	Kimberly S Metzer	FL3	PO Box 410, 2920 S M-37 Hwy, Hastings 49058-0410	(269) 945-4995	
			*121 W North St, Hastings 49058-1027		
Henderson	Steffani Glygoroff	DSA1	218 E. Main, Henderson 48841	(989) 723-5729	
Chapin			19848 S. Chapin Rd., Elsie 48831	(989) 661-2497	
Owosso: Trinity			720 S. Shiawassee St., Owosso 48867	(989) 723-2664	(248) 805-3597
			*302 E Main St, Henderson 48841		
Holt	Mark R Erbes	FE6	PO Box 168, 2321 Aurelius Rd, Holt 48842-0168	(517) 694-8168	
			*1951 Heatherton Dr, Holt 48842-1570		(517) 694-8277
Ithaca	Gary L Simmons	FE5	327 E Center Street, Ithaca 48847-1501	(989) 875-4313	
Beebe			327 E Center Street, (2975 N Baldwin) Ithaca 48847		
			*601 N Union St, Ithaca 48847-1311		
Juddville	Wallace "Peter" Crawford	RE4	3907 N. Durand Rd., Box 152, Corunna 48817	(810) 638-7498	(517) 388-2286
			*4934 Center St., Millington 48746		(989) 882-3084
Kalamo	Jerry J Bukoski	PL6	1475 S Ionia Rd, Vermontville 49096	(810) 986-0240	
			*1069 S Ionia Rd, Vermontville 49096-8576		(517) 588-8415

CHARGE	PASTOR		ADDRESS	CHURCH	HOME
LAINGSBURG PARISH					
Laingsburg	Brian G. West	FE2	210 Crum St., Laingsburg 48848	(517) 651-5531	
Pittsburg			2960 Grand River, Owosso 48867		(517) 651-5266
			*214 Crum St., Laingsburg 48848		
LAKE ODESSA					
Central	Dominic A Tommy	FE3	PO Box 485, 912 4th Ave, Lake Odessa 48849-0485	(616) 374-8861	(616) 374-8294
			*455 Sixth Ave, Lake Odessa 48849		
Lakewood	Steven C Place	FL3	10265 E Brown Rd, Lake Odessa 48849-9207	(269) 367-4800	(269) 367-4161
			*10121 E Brown Rd, Lake Odessa 48849-9207		
Associate	Kathleen Smith	RLA5	10265 E Brown Rd, Lake Odessa 48849-9207	(269) 367-4800	(269) 367-4123
			*7500 Bayne Rd, Woodland 48897-9632		
LANSING					
Asbury	Jon L Pohl	FL3	2200 Lake Lansing Rd, Lansing 48912-3614	(517) 484-5794	(231) 748-4330
			*2412 Post Oak Ln, Lansing 48912		
Central	Mark E Thompson	FE3	215 N Capitol Ave, Lansing 48933-1372	(517) 485-9477	(269) 591-0731
			*2828 Woodview Dr, Lansing 48911-1727		
First	Lori J Sykes	FE8	3827 Delta River Dr, Lansing 48906-3477	(517) 321-5187	(517) 721-1676
			*3727 Delta River Dr, Lansing 48906-3476		
Grace	Paul SungJoon Hahm	FE4	1900 Boston Blvd, Lansing 48910-2456	(517) 482-5750	(517) 484-0227
			*2915 S Cambridge Rd, Lansing 48910		
Mt Hope	Robert B Cook	FE8	501 E Mt Hope Ave, Lansing 48910-9136	(517) 482-1549	(517) 449-4826
			*1707 Woodside Dr, East Lansing 48823-2957		
Associate	Eric Mulanda Nduwa	FE5	501 E Mt Hope Ave, Lansing 48910-9136	(517) 482-1549	(847) 868-6687
			*545 N. Dexter Dr. Lansing 48910-3410		
Deacon	Nancy Fancher (LTFT ½)	FD2	501 E Mt Hope Ave, Lansing 48910-9136	(517) 482-1549	(517) 371-3311
			*1317 W Saginaw St, Lansing 48915-1957		

MID-MICHIGAN DISTRICT

MID-MICHIGAN DISTRICT

CHARGE	PASTOR		ADDRESS	CHURCH	HOME
Sycamore Creek	Thomas F Arthur	FE11	1919 S Pennsylania Ave, Lansing 48910-3251	(517) 394-6100	
Associate	Mark D. Aupperlee	FL2	*5058 Glendurgan Ct, Holt 48842-9438		(517) 889-5540
			1919 S Pennsylania Ave, Lansing 48910-3251	(517) 394-6100	
Potterville Campus	Arthur / Aupperlee		*420 Ardson Rd, E Lansing 48823-3284		(517) 643-1161
			105 N Church St, Potterville 48876-5119	(517) 645-7701	
Leslie	Paul A Damkoehler	PL2	401 S Main St, Leslie 49251-9402	(517) 589-9211	
Felt Plains			401 S Main St (3523 Meridian Rd), Leslie 49251	(517) 589-9211	
			*2417 Pattengill Ave, Lansing 48910-2627		(517) 375-8049
Livingston Circuit:					
Plainfield	Mark Huff	PL3	17845 M-36, Gregory 48137	(517) 851-7651	
Fowlerville: Trinity			8201 Iosco Rd., Fowlerville 48836	(517) 223-9601	
			*8233 Iosco Rd.,, Fowlerville 48836		(517) 223-3150
MAPLE RIVER PARISH					
Maple Rapids	Kathryn L Leydorf-Keck	PL13	330 S Maple Ave, Maple Rapids 48853	(989) 224-4460	
Lowe			5485 W Lowe Rd, St. Johns 48879-9789		
			*10886 S Woodbridge Rd, Bannister 48807-9765		(517) 282-4446
Mason: First	Suzanne K. Goodwin	FD1	201 E Ash St, Mason 48854-1775	(517) 676-9449	
			*616 Hall Blvd, Mason 48854-1704		(248) 318-4869
Millville	Theresa A Fairbanks	FL2	1932 N M-52, Stockbridge 49285-9625	(517) 851-8785	
Williamston: Wheatfield			520 E Holt Rd, Williamston 48895-9463	(517) 851-7853	
			*1956 N M 52, Stockbridge 49285		(231) 510-1935
Morrice	Coleen Wilsdon	PL3	204 Main, Box 301, Morrice 48857	(517) 625-7715	
Bancroft			101 S. Beach St., Box 175, Bancroft 48414	(989) 634-5291	
			*8452 E. Cole Rd., Durand 48420		(989) 413-9850
Mulliken	Vaughn W Thurston-Cox	OE4	400 Charlotte St, Mulliken 48861-9772	(517) 649-8382	
			*9590 Looking Glass Brook Dr, Grand Ledge 48837-9268		(517) 250-3924

CHARGE	PASTOR		ADDRESS	CHURCH	HOME
Munith	Stephan Weinberger	RE1	PO Box 189, 224 N Main St, Munith 49259-0189	(517) 596-2441	
			*3880 Lone Pine Dr Apt 3, Holt 48842-8796		(517) 242-5020
Nashville	Karen Jensen-Kinney	FL5	PO Box 370, 210 Washington St, Nashville 49073-0370	(517) 852-2043	(517) 852-0685
			*540 Chapel Dr, Nashville 49073		
New Lothrop: First	Stephen Spina	OF3	7495 Orchard, Box 247, New Lothrop 48460	(810) 638-5702	(715) 374-0078
			*225 West Corunna Ave., Corunna 48817		
Okemos: Community Church	Richard W Blunt	FE6	PO Box 680, 4734 Okemos Rd, Okemos 48805-0680	(517) 349-4220	(517) 721-1301
			*2441 S Wild Blossom Ct, East Lansing 48823-7203		
Ovid: United Church	Melanie S Young	FE2	PO Box 106, 131 West Front Street, Ovid 48866	(989) 834-5958	(231) 301-2055
	(LTFT ¾)		*141 W Front St, Ovid 48866-9601		
Middlebury			PO Box 7, 8100 W. Hibbard Rd., Ovid 48866	(989) 834-2573	(810) 208-0648
			*9921 Belcrest Blvd., Fenton 48430		
OWOSSO					
Burton	TO BE SUPPLIED		510 N. Baldwin Rd., Owosso 48867	(989) 723-3981	
			*		
First	Deane B. Wyllys	FE2	1500 N. Water St., Owosso 48867	(989) 725-2201	
			*1415 N. Water St., Owosso 48867		(248) 860-7385
Perry	Nancy G Powers	FE8	PO Box 15, 131 Madison St, Perry 48872-0015	(517) 675-1567	
Shaftsburg			PO Box 161, 12821 Warner Rd, Shaftsburg 48882-0161		
			*PO Box 142, 121 S Madison St, Perry 48872-0142		(517) 625-3444
Portland	Letisha M Bowman	FE5	310 E Bridge St, Portland 48875-1439	(517) 647-4649	(517) 647-6460
			*309 Grape St, Portland 48875-1134		
Riverdale: Lincoln Road	Linda K Stull-Lipps	FE4	9479 W Lincoln Rd, Riverdale 48877-9739	(989) 463-5704	(269) 830-1136
	(LTFT ¾)		*9437 W Lincoln Rd, Riverdale 48877		
Robbins	Peggy A Katzmark	FL6	6419 Bunker Rd, Eaton Rapids 48827-9108	(517) 663-5226	(517) 663-8417
			*827 S Waverly Rd, Eaton Rapids 48827		
St. Johns: Pilgrim	Andrew L Croel	FE6	2965 W Parks Road, St Johns 48879-9286	(989) 224-6865	(989) 224-4423
			*2917 W Parks Rd, St. Johns 48879-9286		

MID-MICHIGAN DISTRICT

MID-MICHIGAN DISTRICT

CHARGE	PASTOR		ADDRESS	CHURCH	HOME
St Louis: First	Terri L Bentley	FL12	116 S Franklin Street, St. Louis 48880-1737	(989) 681-3320	(989) 681-2486
			*116 N East St, St Louis 48880-1721		
Shepardsville	Judith A Hazle	PL8	6990 East Winfield Road, Ovid 48866-8607	(989) 834-5104	(989) 640-1436
			*1795 W Centerline Rd, St Johns 48879-9275		
Stockbridge	Stephan Weinberger	RE1	219 E Elizabeth St, Stockbridge 49285-9666	(517) 851-7676	(517) 242-5020
			*3880 Lone Pine Dr Apt 3, Holt 48842-8796		
Vernon	Norman R. Beckwith, Sr.	RE5	202 E. Main St., PO Box 155, Vernon 48476	(989) 288-4187	(989) 661-2377
			*18571 W Brady Rd., Oakley 48649		
Wacousta Communty	Hillary Thurston-Cox	PE4	9180 Herbison Rd, Eagle 48822-9718	(517) 626-6623	(517) 566-2066
			*235 Dunham St, Sunfield 48890-9772		
Webberville	Martin A Johnston	FL3	4215 E Holt Rd, Webberville 48892-8208	(517) 521-3631	(517) 521-3434
Williamston: Crossroads			5491 N Zimmer Rd, Williamston 48895-9181	(517) 655-1466	
Williamston	Linda J Stephan	PE2	*120 E Beech St, Webberville 48892-9702	(517) 655-2430	(616) 617-9419
			211 S Putnam St, Williamston 48895-1309		
			*733 Orchard Dr, Williamston 48895-1074		

NAME	POSITION		ADDRESS	OFFICE	HOME

APPOINTMENTS TO EXTENSION MINISTRIES LOCATED IN THE MID-MICHIGAN DISTRICT:
(further information at end of appointment section)

Kennetha J Bigham-Tsai	Chief Connectional Ministries Officer of the Connectional Table				
	FE2	*6137 Horizon Dr, East Lansing 48823-2227			(517) 242-2442
John W Boley	Clergy Assistant to the Bishop, Michigan Area Episcopal Office				
	FE4	1011 Northcrest Rd, Lansing 48906-1262		(517) 347-4003	(989) 400-0355

CHARGE	PASTOR	ADDRESS	CHURCH	HOME
Jennifer Browne	Director of Clergy Excellence, Michigan Conference	FE2 161 E Clark Rd Ste 212, DeWitt 48820	(517) 347-4030	(517) 898-4575
William W Chu	Director, Wesley Foundation – Michigan State University	FE9 1118 S. Harrison, East Lansing 48823	(517) 332-0861	(517) 996-2207
M Kay DeMoss	Senior Writer & Content Editor, MI Conference Communications Team	FD5 1011 Northcrest Rd, Lansing 48906	(517) 347-4030	(231) 670-5921
Jerome R. DeVine	District Superintendent, Mid-Michigan District Office	FE2 1161 E Clark Rd Ste 216, DeWitt 48820	(517) 347-4173	
Dirk Elliott	Director of Congregational Vibrancy, Michigan Conference	FE2 161 E Clark Rd Ste 212, DeWitt 48820	(517) 347-4030	(810) 965-2349
Donald J Emmert	Director of Benefits & Human Resources, Michigan Conference	FE2 161 E Clark Rd Ste 212, DeWitt 48820	(517) 347-4030	
Nancy Fancher	Executive Director, Maple Valley Community Center of Hope	FD3 1317 W Saginaw St, Lansing 48915-1957	(517) 862-5497	(517) 371-3311
Paul D Perez	Associate Director for Mission & Ministry, Michigan Conference	FD2 1011 Northcrest Rd, Lansing 48906	(517) 347-4030	(810) 347-6363
Kathryn L. Pittenger	Children's Initiatives Coordinator, Michigan Conference	FD2 161 E Clark Rd Ste 212, DeWitt 48820	(517) 347-4030	(248) 505-5848
Alice Fleming Townley	Parish Associate, Okemos Presbyterian Church	FE10 2258 Bennett Rd, Okemos 48823	(517) 507-5117	(517) 324-5432
Benton R Heisler	Director of Connectional Ministries, Michigan Conference	FE2 1011 Northcrest Rd, Lansing 48906	(517) 347-4030	(616) 430-0417
Michael J Mayo-Moyle	IT Specialist, Michigan Conference	FE2 161 E Clark Rd Ste 212, DeWitt 48820	(517) 347-4030	(810) 444-9439

APPOINTMENT FROM OTHER CONFERENCES:

CHARGE	PASTOR	ADDRESS	CHURCH	HOME
Brittney D. Stephan (Indiana Conf.)	Associate Director for Multi-Cultural Vibrancy	OP2 1161 E Clark Rd, Ste 212, DeWitt 48820	(517) 357-4030	

MID-MICHIGAN DISTRICT

MIDWEST DISTRICT

MIDWEST DISTRICT

District Superintendent	Margie R. Crawford	FE2	DS Email: mcrawford@michiganumc.org		Office (616) 459-4503
Executive Assistant	Elizabeth M Bode		Office Email: lbode@michiganumc.org	207 Fulton St E Suite 6, Grand Rapids 49503	

				TELEPHONE	
CHARGE	PASTOR		ADDRESS	CHURCH	HOME
Allendale: Valley	Matthew J Bistayi	FE11	5980 Lake Michigan Dr, Ste B, Allendale 49401-9576	(616) 892-1042	
			*10811 Lance Ave, Allendale 49401-7317		(616) 892-6240
Associate	Zach D. McNees (part-time ½)	FL1	5980 Lake Michigan Dr, Ste B, Allendale 49401-9576	(616) 892-1042	
Bowne Center	Robert D Wright	RE4	*1141 Northlawn St NE, Grand Rapids 49505		(269) 986-0108
			12051 84th St. SE, Alto 49302	(616) 868-6778	
Amble	Andrew B Hollander	PL3	*10187 Mulberry Dr, Middleville 49333		(269) 205-2609
			PO Box 392, 15207 Howard City Edmore Rd, Howard City 49329 (231) 796-1061		
			*15488 Gates Rd, Howard City 49329		(231) 580-6304
Barryton: Faith	TO BE SUPPLIED		95 E Marion Ave, Barryton 49305-5115	(989) 382-5431	
			*		
BIG RAPIDS					
First	Devon R. Herrell	FE1	304 Elm Street, Big Rapids 49307-1814	(231) 796-7771	
			*14080 Wildwood Dr, Big Rapids 49307-8782		(231) 649-2302
Third Avenue	Morgan William (Bill) Davis	DSA1	226 N Third Ave, Big Rapids 49307	(231) 796-4157	
Paris			109 Lincoln, Paris 49338	(231) 796-4157	
Rodney			PO Box 14, 12135 Charles St, Rodney 49342	(231) 796-4157	
			*1764 Kettle Lake Rd, Kalkaska 49646		
Byron Center	Jeffrey O Cummings	PE4	2490 Prescott SW, Byron Center 49315	(616) 878-1618	
			*8650 Meadow Haven Dr SW, Byron Center 49315-9243		(616) 878-9739
Caledonia	Elizabeth A. Hurd	PE1	250 Vine St, Caledonia 49316	(616) 891-8669	
			*260 Vine St, Caledonia 49316		(616) 891-8167

CHARGE	PASTOR		ADDRESS	CHURCH	HOME
Carlisle	Gary M Zinger	CLM/DSA3	1084 76th St SW, Byron Center 49315	(616) 878-1836	
			*6559 Burlingame Ave SW, Byron Center 49315		(616) 890-2744
Cedar Springs	William C. Johnson	FE2	PO Box K, 140 S Main St, Cedar Springs 49319	(616) 696-1140	(616) 366-2421
			*4390 Summerlane Ave NE, Grand Rapids 49525-2421		
Claybanks	Gary L Peterson	RLA4	PO Box 104, 9197 S 56th Ave, Montague 49437-9485	(231) 923-0573	(231) 893-5210
			*8054 S 56th Ave, Montague 49437		
Coopersville	Cori Lynn Conran	FE8	105 68th Ave N, Coopersville 49404-9704	(616) 997-9225	(269) 986-0732
			*422 Harrison St., Coopersville 49404-1136		
Courtland-Oakfield	Kimberly A DeLong	FE3	10295 Myers Lake Ave NE, Rockford 49341-9511	(616) 866-4298	(616) 443-5210
Wyoming Park			2244 Porter St SW, Wyoming 49519-2222	(616) 532-7624	
			*4934 Brownstone Dr NE, Rockford 49341-7780		
Crystal Valley	David O Pratt	RLA2	PO Box 125, Walkerville 49459	(231) 873-5422	
Walkerville			PO Box 125, Walkerville 49459	(231) 873-4236	
			*409 3rd St, Ludington 49431		(810) 404-0085
Dorr: CrossWind Community	Kevin K Guetschow	FL3	1683 142nd Ave, Dorr 49323-9426	(616) 681-0302	(269) 365-2926
			*4380 Tracy Trail, Dorr 49323		
East Nelson	Inge E Whittemore	PL4	9024 18 Mile Rd NE, Cedar Springs 49319-9217	(616) 696-0661	(616) 897-6525
			*590 Wildview, Lowell 49331-9331		
Edmore: Faith	Daniel L Barkholz	FL3	833 S First Street, Edmore 48829-9396	(989) 427-5575	(269) 903-9665
			*320 S Maple St, Edmore 48829-7300		
Fenwick	Gerald A Erskine	PL6	PO Box 241, 235 W Fenwick Rd, Sheridan 48884-0241	(989) 291-5547	
Palo			PO Box 241, 8445 Division St., Sheridan 48884-0241	(989) 291-5547	
Vickeryville			PO Box 241, 6850 S Vickeryville Rd, Sheridan 48884	(989) 291-5547	
			*10963 Sundog Trail, Perrinton 48871-9745		(989) 682-4779

MIDWEST DISTRICT

MIDWEST DISTRICT

CHARGE	PASTOR		ADDRESS	CHURCH	HOME
FLAT RIVER COOPERATIVE PARISH					
Turk Lake	Donna Jean Sperry	FL4	8900 W Colby Road, Greenville 48838-9502	(616) 754-3718	
Belding			301 South Pleasant, Belding 48809-1647	(616) 794-1244	
Ionia: Easton		FL6	4970 Potters Rd, Ionia 48846-9541	(616) 527-6529	(586) 255-6228
			*319 Pearl St, Ionia 48846-1339		
Fremont	Julie E Fairchild	FL3	351 Butterfield St, Fremont 49412	(231) 924-0030	(740) 692-5565
			*352 Butterfield, Fremont 49412		
Georgetown	Sherri L Swanson	FE2	2766 Baldwin St, Jenison 49428	(616) 669-0730	(269) 405-0002
Deacon	Mariel Kay DeMoss	FD2	*6105 Balcom Ln, Allendale 49401		
			2766 Baldwin St, Jenison 49428	(616) 669-0730	
Deacon	Gregory W Lawton	FD2	*1520 Sherman St SE, Grand Rapids 49506		(231) 670-5921
	Louis W Grettenberger	FE3	*10 N 160th Ave, Holland 49424		(616) 805-5407
Grand Haven: Church			717 Sheldon Road, Grand Haven 49417-1860	(616) 842-7980	
of the Dunes			*633 Hillock Ct, Grand Haven 49417-1805		(616) 883-9806
GRAND RAPIDS					
Aldersgate	James E Hodge	FE7	4301 Ambrose Ave NE, Grand Rapids 49525-6122	(616) 363-3446	
			*5160 Windcrest Ct SW, Wyo-ming 49418		(616) 308-9925
Cornerstone	Bradley P Kalajainen	FE30	1675 84th St SE, Caledonia 49316	(616) 698-3170	(616) 891-8443
			*7810 Golf Meadows Dr SE, Caledonia 49316-8462		
Assoc. Heritage Hill Campus	Alejandro D Fernandez	FL5	1675 84th St SE, Caledonia 49316	(616) 698-3170	(616) 891-5611
			*10160 Alaska Ave SE, Cale-donia 49316-9512		
Assoc. South Wyoming Campus	Marcus V Schmidt	PL4	1675 84th St SE, Caledonia 49316-7939	(616) 698-3170	(616) 443-9257
			*5482 Fieldstone Dr SW, Wyoming 49418		
Faith	Daniel M Bilkert (LTFT ½)	OR2	2600 Seventh St NW, Grand Rapids 49504	(616) 453-0693	(419) 606-0640
			*2239 Ducoma St NW, Grand Rapids 49504		

CHARGE	PASTOR		ADDRESS	CHURCH	HOME
First	Robert L Hundley	FE7	227 Fulton St E, Grand Rapids 49503-3236	(616) 451-2879	(616) 427-3749
Associate	Joan E. VanDessel	PE1	*3035 Grenada Dr SE, Grand Rapids 49546		
			227 Fulton St E, Grand Rapids 49503-3236	(616) 451-2879	(616) 818-9295
Genesis	James Thomas Boutell	FE2	*2005 Collingwood Ave SW, Wyoming 49519-1647		
			3189 Snow Ave, Lowell 49331	(616) 974-0400	(616) 678-7664
Deacon	Georgia Noel Hale (LTFT ¼)	FD5	*1805 Forest Lake Dr, SE, Grand Rapids 49546		(616) 678-7664
			1601 Galbraith Ave SE Ste 304, Grand Rapids 49546-6479	(616) 974-0400	
Iglesia Metodista Unida La Nueva Esperanza	Laura E Feliciano (part-time ¾)	FL2	*272 S Ball Creek Rd, Kent City 49330-9452		
			1005 Evergreen St. SE, Grand Rapids 49507-2008	(616) 560-4207	(615) 218-8187
Northlawn	Zach D. McNees (part-time ½)	FL1	*324 Griswold SE, Grand Rapids 49507-3136		
			1157 Northlawn NE, Grand Rapids 49505-3723	(616) 361-8503	(269) 986-0108
Restoration	Banza Mukalay	PL2	*1141 Northlawn St NE, Grand Rapids 49505		
			2730 56th St SW, South Wyoming 49418	(616) 589-4793	(616) 589-4793
St Paul's	Virginia L Heller	FE2	*4217 Norman Dr SE, Grand Rapids 49508		
			3334 Breton Rd SE, Grand Rapids 49512-2710	(616) 949-0880	(269) 274-9416
South	Mack C Strange	OF13	*3509 Bromley SE, Kentwood 49512		
			4500 S Division Ave, Grand Rapids 49548-4307	(616) 534-8931	(616) 532-9226
Trinity	Steven W Manskar	OE2	*5103 Marlowe SE, Grand Rapids 49508		
			1100 Lake Dr SE, Grand Rapids 49506-1538	(616) 456-7168	(615) 948-0650
Deaconess	Anne M Hillman	DC2	*2128 Monroe Ave NW, Grand Rapids 49505		
			1100 Lake Dr SE, Grand Rapids 49506-1538	(616) 456-7168	(616) 866-9316
Vietnamese	Daniel Dung Nguyen	FL8	*128 Maple St, Rockford 49341-1226		
			212 Bellevue St SE, Wyoming 49548-3337	(616) 534-6262	(616) 288-3007
Grandville	Ryan B Wieland	FE4	*497 Harp St SE, Kentwood 49548-4378		
			3140 S Wilson, Grandville 49418-1273	(616) 538-3070	(616) 258-2001
Grant Center	Meredith P Rupe	RE2	*2000 Frontier Ct. SW, Wyo-ming 49519		
			15260 21 Mile Road, Big Rapids 49307-8852	(231) 796-8006	(906) 282-9142
			*620 Birch Circle Dr E, Boyne Falls 49713		

MIDWEST DISTRICT

MIDWEST DISTRICT

CHARGE	PASTOR		ADDRESS	CHURCH	HOME
Greenville: First	Donald E Spachman	FE6	204 W Cass Street, Greenville 48838-1758	(616) 754-8532	
			*405 W Grant St, Greenville 48838-2209		(616) 712-6024
Hart	Steven R Young	FE5	308 S State St, Hart 49420-1227	(231) 873-3516	
			*3818 Melody Lane, Hart 49420-9500		(231) 873-4766
Hesperia	Paul E Hane	RLA9	187 E South Ave, Hesperia 49421-9273	(231) 854-5345	
Ferry			2215 Main St, Shelby 49455-8220	(231) 854-5345	
			*231 E South Ave, Hesperia 49421-9105		(231) 854-6132
Holland: First	Bradley S Bartelmay	FE3	57 West 10th St, Holland 49423-3130	(616) 396-5205	
			*6105 Balcom Ln, Allendale 49401		(269) 266-2221
Associate	Tania J Dozeman	PE2	57 West 10th St, Holland 49423-3130	(616) 396-5205	
			*66 Crosswind Dr, Holland 49424		(616) 566-4165
Deacon	Luanne M. Stanley-Hook	PD1	57 West 10th St, Holland 49423-3130	(616) 396-5205	
			*6618 Butternut Dr, West Olive 49460-7501		(616) 994-0085
Holton	Matthew T Stoll	FE2	9530 Holton-Duck Lake Rd, Holton 49425-9772	(231) 821-2323	
			*8670 Ward St, Holton 49425-7531		(231) 821-0374
IONIA					
First	Jonathan Bratt Carle	OP3	105 E Main Street, Ionia 48846-1614	(616) 527-1860	
Lyons-Muir Church			1074 Olmstead Road, Muir 48860-9627	(989) 855-2247	
			*2536 Union Ave SE, Grand Rapids 49507-3527		(901) 417-2844
IONIA PARISH					
LeValley	Nancy J Patera	FL3	4018 Kelsey Highway, Ionia 48846-9431	(616) 527-1480	
Berlin Center			4018 Kelsey Hwy, Ionia 48846 (3042 Peck Lake Rd, Saranac)	(616) 527-1480	
			*6232 Sunset Beach, Lake Odessa 48849		(616) 902-6973
Zion	Larry Nalett	RLA2	423 W Washington Street, Ionia 48846-1570	(616) 527-1910	
			*620 N Rich St, Ionia 48846-1238		(616) 527-2025
Kent City: Chapel Hill	Michael J Ramsey	FL3	14591 Fruit Ridge Ave NW, Kent City 49330-9751	(616) 675-7184	
			*14555 Fruit Ridge Ave, Kent City 49330-9751		(616) 293-9831

CHARGE	PASTOR		ADDRESS	CHURCH	HOME
Lakeview: New Life	Timothy B. Wright	FE1	6584 M 46, Six Lakes 48886-9755	(989) 352-7788	(989) 352-6728
			*8544 Howard City-Edmore Rd, Lakeview 48850		
Leighton	David L. McBride	FE14	4180 Second St, Caledonia 49316-9220	(616) 891-8028	(616) 891-1646
			*4180 Second St, Caledonia 49316-9220		
LOWELL					
First	James Bradley Brillhart	FE6	621 E Main St, Lowell 49331-1719	(616) 897-5936	(616) 897-8267
			*640 Shepard Dr, Lowell 49331-8642		
Deacon	Cheryl A Mulligan (LTFT ¼)	FD6	621 E Main St, Lowell 49331-1719	(616) 897-5936	(616) 340-7995
			*3170 Buttrick Ave SE, Ada 49301-9216		
Vergennes	Thomas C Fifer	FL2	10411 Bailey Dr NE, Lowell 49331-9779	(616) 897-6141	(616) 560-3914
			*2445 Almont Ave SE, Grand Rapids 49507		
Marne	Cydney M. Idsinga	PE2	PO Box 85, 14861 Washington, Marne 49435-0085	(616) 677-3957	(616) 677-3991
			*14861 Washington St, Marne 49435-5102		
Mears	Anne W Riegler	AM3	PO Box 100, 1990 N Joy St, Mears 49436	(231) 873-0875	(231) 631-0573
Shelby			68 E Third St, Shelby 49455-1166	(231) 861-2020	
			*5181 Hancock St, Montague 49437-1617		
Mecosta: New Hope	Carman J. Minarik	FE1	7296 9 Mile Road, Mecosta 49332-9722	(231) 972-2838	(248) 921-2714
			*3955 9 Mile Rd, Remus 49340-9712		
Middleville	Anthony C Shumaker	FL8	PO Box 400, 111 Church St, Middleville 49333-0400	(269) 795-9266	(269) 650-5112
			*1497 120th Ave, Hopkins 49328-9626		
Montague	Michael A Riegler	FE3	8555 Cook St, Montague 49437-1516	(231) 894-5789	(231) 631-4712
			*5181 Hancock St, Montague 49437-1617		
MUSKEGON					
Central	Mark D Miller	FE7	1011 Second Street, Muskegon 49440-1231	(231) 722-6545	(231) 766-8989
			*1354 Hendrick Rd, Norton Shores 49441-5738		
Crestwood	Jennifer J Wheeler	PL3	1220 Creston, Muskegon 49442	(231) 773-9696	(231) 881-7367
			*1510 Calvin Ave, Muskegon 49442-4115		

MIDWEST DISTRICT

MIDWEST DISTRICT

CHARGE	PASTOR		ADDRESS	CHURCH	HOME
Lake Harbor	Mary Letta-Bement Ivanov	FE6	4861 Henry St, Muskegon 49441-5436 *1322 Clayton Ave, Muskegon 49441-4305	(231) 798-2181	(231) 780-3951
Unity	Ronald L Worley	PL6	1600 North Getty St, Muskegon 49445-2618 *PO Box 254, 76 W Muskegon St NW, Kent City 49330-0254	(231) 744-1972	(616) 485-4441
Muskegon Heights: Temple	Jeffrey J Bowman	FL8	2500 Jefferson St, Muskegon Heights 49444-1444 *1205 Yorkshire Dr, Muskegon 49441-5358	(231) 733-1065	(231) 798-9309
Newaygo	Eric L Magner	PL3	PO Box 366, 101 W State Road, Newaygo 49337-0366 *PO Box 366, 104 State Rd, Newaygo 49337	(231) 652-6581	(231) 750-3488
North Muskegon: Community	Jeremy PH Williams	FE3	1614 Ruddiman Dr, North Muskegon 49445-3040 *2317 Marquard Ave, North Muskegon 49445-3228	(231) 744-4491	(517) 554-1836
Parmelee	William V Clegg Jr	RE8	PO Box 237, 9266 W Parmelee Rd, Middleville 49333-0237 *4593 N Camrose Court, Wyoming 49519-4977	(269) 795-8816	(616) 366-2486
Pentwater: Centenary	William E Haggard	RE2	PO Box 111, 82 S Hancock, Pentwater 49449-0111 *124 S Rutledge St, Pentwater 49449-9576	(231) 869-5900	(231) 301-2055
Pierson: Heritage	Terri L Cummins	FL4	19931 W Kendaville Rd, Pierson 49339-9713 *18985 W Coral Rd, Howard City 49329	(231) 937-4310	(231) 903-5139
Ravenna	Carleton R Black	FL9	PO Box 191, 12348 Stafford St, Ravenna 49451-0191 *3482 Lo Al Dr, Ravenna 49451-9405	(231) 853-6688	(231) 853-6111
Rockford	Gregory L. Buchner	FE1	159 Maple St, Rockford 49341-1250 *PO Box 894, 1105 West Pickard, Mt Pleasant 48804	(616) 866-9515	(989) 621-7782
Salem Indian Mission Bradley Indian Mission	R Todd Williamson	FL5	3644 28th St, Hopkins 49328 695 128th Ave, Shelbyville 49344 *1146 Nicolson St, Wayland 49348	(269) 397-1780	
Sand Lake South Ensley	Darryl L Miller	PL13	PO Box 97, 65 W Maple St, Sand Lake 49343-0097 PO Box 97, Sand Lake 49343 *1568 Solon, Cedar Springs 49319-9438	(616) 636-5673 (616) 636-5659	(616) 262-0358
Sitka	TO BE SUPPLIED		9606 S. Dickinson Rd., Holton 49425-9425 *	(231) 744-1767	(616) 696-4057

CHARGE	PASTOR		ADDRESS	CHURCH	HOME
Sparta	Phillip J Friedrick	FE3	54 E Division St, Sparta 49345 *1960 Skyview Dr, Sparta 49345-9756	(616) 887-8255	(231) 670-7796
Stanwood: Northland	Gary D Bondarenko	FE6	PO Box 26, 6842 Northland Dr, Stanwood 49346-0026 *PO Box 26, 18835 Fillmore Rd, Stanwood 49346-0026	(231) 629-4590	(231) 823-2514
Twin Lake	William E Dye	RLA2	PO Box 352, 5940 S Main St, Twin Lake 49457-0352 *550 Western Ave Apt 424, Muskegon 49440	(231) 828-4083	(231) 429-1891
Wayland	Jeffrey C Williams	FE6	200 Church St, Wayland 49348-1203 *220 Church St, Wayland 49348-1203	(269) 792-2208	(269) 944-9231
White Cloud	Edwin D Snook	FL8	PO Box 188, 1125 Newell St, White Cloud 49349-0188 *718 E Pine Hill Ave, White Cloud 49349-9146	(231) 689-5911	(231) 689-6774
Wolf Lake	Mona J Dye	RLA2	378 Vista Terrace, Muskegon 49442-1848 *550 Western Ave Apt 424, Muskegon 49440	(231) 788-3663	(231) 429-1892
Wyoming: Wesley Park	Dean N Prentiss	FE9	1150 32nd St SW, Wyoming 49509-2875 *2664 Borglum Ave NE, Grand Rapids 49505-3616	(616) 988-6738	(616) 514-7124

MIDWEST DISTRICT

MIDWEST DISTRICT

APPOINTMENTS TO EXTENSION MINISTRIES LOCATED IN THE MIDWEST DISTRICT:
(further information at end of appointment section)

NAME	POSITION	ADDRESS	OFFICE	HOME
Janet Carter	Chaplain, Pine Rest Christian Mental Health Services			
	FD	300 68th St SE, Grand Rapids 49508	(616) 281-6363	(616) 260-9604
Margie Crawford	District Superintendent, Midwest District Office			
	FE2	207 Fulton St E Suite 6, Grand Rapids 49503	(616) 459-4503	
Kimberly M. Bos	Director, Wesley Foundation – Ferris State University (LTFT 1/2)			
	PE1	628 S Warren Ave, Big Rapids 49307-2210	(231) 796-8315	(231) 557-0574
Jan Johnson	Chaplain, Mercy Health Partners			
	FL	PO Box 358, 1500 E Sherman Blvd, Muskegon 49443-0358	(231) 672-3629	
Nathaniel Johnson	Manager of Pastoral Care & Bereavement for Spectrum System			
	FE	Pastoral Care MC163, 100 Michigan St NE, Grand Rapids 49503	(616) 391-3096	(616) 710-9703
Julie Liske	Executive Director, Circles Grand Rapids			
	FD	920 Cherry St SE, Grand Rapids 49506-1472	(616) 299-0115	
Cheryl Mulligan	Respiratory Therapist, Helen DeVos Pediatric Pulmonary Clinic			
	FD	35 Michigan St NE, Ste 3003, Grand Rapids 49503	(616) 267-2200	
Laura E Feliciano	New Church and Hispanic-Latino Committee Staff, Michigan Conference			
	FL2	1005 Evergreen St SE, Grand Rapids 49507-2008	(616) 514-1327	(615) 218-8187
Gary Step	Associate Director of Congregational Vibrancy, Michigan Conference			
	FE2	6666 Crown Point Drive, Hudsonville 49426-9014	(517) 347-4030	(231) 420-2676

APPOINTMENT FROM OTHER CONFERENCES:

NAME	POSITION	ADDRESS	OFFICE	HOME
David Bell	President and Executive Director, United Methodist Foundation of Michigan			
(East Ohio Conference)	AF	840 W Grand River Ave, Brighton 48116	(810) 534-3001	(888) 451-1929

NORTHERN SKIES DISTRICT

District Superintendent	Scott A. Harmon	FE2	DS Email: sharmon@michiganumc.org	Office: (906) 228-4644
Executive Assistant	Diana Byar		Office Email: dbyar@michiganumc.org	927 W. Fair Avenue, Marquette 49855

				TELEPHONE	
CHARGE	PASTOR		ADDRESS	CHURCH	HOME
Bark River	Christine J. Bergquist	PL30	3716 "D" Rd., Bark River 49807		
Hermansville: First			W 5494 Second St., Hermansville 49847		(906) 466-2839
			*1290 10th Rd., Bark River 49807		
Cheboygan: St. Paul's	John D. Bailey	FE3	531 E. Lincoln Ave., Cheboygan 49721	(231) 627-9710	(231) 627-9710
			*568 O'Brien Dr., Cheboygan 49721		
Crystal Falls: Christ	Victoria I. Prewitt	FL2	500 Marquette Ave., Box 27, Crystal Falls 49920	(906) 875-3123	(906) 875-6134
Amasa: Grace			PO Box 144, 209 Pine St., Amasa 49903		
			*110 Elm Grove, Crystal Falls 49920		
ESCANABA					
Central	Elise Rodgers Low Edwardson	PE4	322 S. Lincoln, Escanaba 49829	(906) 786-0643	(906) 789-1874
			*1814 22nd Ave., Escanaba 49829		
First	Ryan C. Edwardson	PL4	302 S. Sixth St., Escanaba 49829	(906) 786-3713	(906) 789-1874
			*1814 22nd Ave South, Escanaba 49829		
Gladstone: Memorial	Cathy L. Rafferty	FE1	1920 Lakeshore Dr., Gladstone 49837	(906) 428-9311	(906) 420-8096
			*1006 Lakeshore Dr., Gladstone 49837		
GOD'S COUNTRY COOPERATIVE PARISH	Devin T. Lawrence	DSA1			
Grand Marais			N 14226 M-77, PO Box 268, Grand Marais 49839	(906) 494-2751	
Germfask			1212 Morrison St., PO Box 135, Germfask 49836	(906) 586-3162	
McMillan			7406 Co. Rd. 415, PO Box 54, McMillan 49853	(906) 293-8933	
			*719 Garden Ave, Manistique 49854-1615		(906) 202-3231

NORTHERN SKIES DISTRICT

NORTHERN SKIES DISTRICT

CHARGE	PASTOR		ADDRESS	CHURCH	HOME
Newberry	Timothy G. Callow	FE7	110 W. Harrie St., Newberry 49868	(906) 293-5711	
Engadine			13970 Park Ave., PO Box 157, Engadine 49827	(906) 477-9989	(906) 293-5497
			*PO Box 157, N6828 Elm St., Engadine 49827		
Paradise	Mary D. Brooks	DSA7	7087 N. M-123, PO Box 193, Paradise 49768	(906) 492-3585	
Hulbert:Tahquamenon			10505 W 6th St., PO Box 91, Hulbert 49748		
			*207 W Ave. B, Newberry 49868		(906) 293-1966
Gwinn	Ronald A. Fike	FE6	251 W. Jasper, Box 354, Gwinn 49841	(906) 346-6314	(906) 346-3441
Hancock: First	Scott P. Lindenberg	FE4	*252 W. Carbon, PO Box 352, Gwinn 49841	(906) 482-4190	(906) 482-1404
			401 Quincy, Box 458, Hancock 49930		
Houghton: Grace	Charles A. Williams	FE1	*1631 Portage Dr., Hancock 49930	(906) 482-2780	(906) 482-1751
Painesdale: Albert Paine Memorial			201 Isle Royale, Houghton 49931		
			156 Iroquois St., Painesdale 49955		
			*807 Oak Grove Pkwy., Houghton 49931		
IRON MOUNTAIN					
First	Walter P. Reichle	FL8	106 Fourth St., Iron Mountain 49801	(906) 774-3586	
Quinnesec			677 Division, PO Box 28, Quinnesec 49876	(906) 774-7971	(906) 828-1228
			*901 Fairbanks St.,Iron Mountain 49801		
Trinity	Geraldine G. Hamlen	FE6	808 Carpenter Ave., Iron Mountain 49801	(906) 774-2545	(906) 774-0064
			*421 Woodward, Kingsford 49802		
Ironwood: Wesley	Keith P Mullikin	DSA1	500 E. McLeod Ave., PO Box 9, Ironwood 49938	(906) 932-3900	
Wakefield			706 Putnam St., Wakefield 49968	906-988-2533	(906) 285-9847
			*600 Garvey, Ironwood 49938		
Ishpeming: Wesley	Matthew L. Osborne	FL2	PO Box 342, 801 Hemlock, Ishpeming 49849	(906) 486-4681	(906) 475-9337
			*220 Shoreline Dr., Negaunee 49866		
KEWEENAW PARISH					
Calumet	James M. Mathews	RA1	57235 Calumet Ave., Calumet 49913	(906) 337-2720	
Lake Linden			53237 N. Hecla St., Lake Linden 49945	(906) 296-0148	(906) 337-0539
			*26350 Wyandotte, Laurium 49913		

NORTHERN SKIES DISTRICT

CHARGE	PASTOR		ADDRESS	CHURCH	HOME
L'Anse	Nathan T. Reed	FL1	304 N. Main, L'Anse 49946	(906) 524-7939	
Sidnaw			S 121 W. Milltown Rd., Sidnaw 49961		
Zeba			16024 Zeba Rd., L'Anse 49946	(906) 524-6967	(906) 524-7936
			*227 N. Front, L'Anse 49946		
Mackinaw City: Church of the Straits	David M. Wallis	FE14	PO Box 430, 307 N. Huron, Mackinaw City 49701	(231) 436-8682	(231) 436-5484
			*309 East Jamet, PO Box 718, Mackinaw City 49701		
Manistique: First	Donald E. Bedwell	RLA8	190 N. Cedar St., Manistique 49854	(906) 341-6662	(906) 341-5812
			*141 New Delta, Manistique 49854		
Marquette: Hope	Kristine K. Hintz *co-pastor*	FE6	111 E. Ridge St., Marquette 49855 (Main campus)	(906) 225-1344	(906) 226-3683
			927 W. Fair, Marquette 49855 (Connection Center)	(906) 942-7310	
			189 Kreiger Dr, Skandia, 49885 (Skandia Campus)		
			*619 Mesnard, Marquette 49855		
	Christopher P. Hintz *co-pastor*	FE4	111 E. Ridge St., Marquette 49855 (Main Campus)	(906) 225-1344	(906) 226-3683
			927 W. Fair, Marquette 49855 (Connection Center)	(906) 942-7310	
			189 Kreiger Dr, Skandia, 49885 (Skandia Campus)		
			*619 Mesnard, Marquette 49855		
Menominee: First	John P. Murray	FL1	601 Tenth, PO Box 323, Menominee 49858	(906) 864-2555	(814) 366-0239
Stephenson			S 111 Railroad St., Box 205, Stephenson 49887	(906) 753-6363	
			*1801 17th Ave., Menominee 49858		
Mohawk-Ahmeek	Larry Molloy	DSA1	PO Box 76, 120 Stanton Ave., Mohawk 49950		(906) 284-4221
			*226 Fourth St, Eagle Harbor 49950		
Munising	Sandra J. Kolder	RLA9	312 S. Lynn, Munising 49862	(906) 387-3394	(906) 586-9696
Trenary			PO Box 201, N 1133 E.T. Rd., Trenary 49891	(906) 446-3599	
			*PO Box 130, W18394 H-42 Rd., Curtis 49820		
Negaunee: Mitchell	J. Albert Barchue	OE4	207 Teal Lk Ave., Box 190, Negaunee 49866	(906) 475-4861	(906) 475-6524
			*1013 Hungerford, Negaunee 49866		
New Hope of Emmett County	Michelle Merchant	PL5	PO Box 72, 4516 N US 31, Levering 49755-0072	(231) 537-2000	(231) 564-0723
			*3224 Hill Road NW, Rapid City 49676-9585		

NORTHERN SKIES DISTRICT

CHARGE	PASTOR		ADDRESS	CHURCH	HOME
Norway: Grace	Irene R. White	FL9	130 O'Dill Dr., Norway 49870	(906) 563-8917	
Faithorn			W8601 Blum Rd., Vulcan 49892		
			*725 Norway St., Norway 49870		(906) 563-9877
Ontonagon	Nelson L. Hall	FL2	109 Greenland, PO Box 216, Ontonagon 49953	(906) 884-4556	
Greenland			1002 Ridge Rd., Greenland 49929	(906) 883-3141	
Rockland: St. Paul			50 National Ave., PO Box 339, Rockland 49960	(906) 886-2851	
			*1101 Pine St., Ontonagon 49953		(906) 884-2789
Pickford	Timothy Bashore	FL6	115 E. Church St., Box 128, Pickford 49774	(906) 647-6195	
			230 W. Townline Rd., Pickford 49774		(906) 647-7231
Republic	Peter LeMoine	PL2	216 S. Front St., PO Box 395, Republic 49879	(906) 376-2389	(906) 390-0521
Woodland			HRC 1, Box1125, Michigamme 49861	(906) 323-6151	(906) 376-2085
			*356 Maple St., Republic 49879		
St. Ignace	Eric M. Falker	FL1	615 W. U.S. 2, PO Box 155, St. Ignace 49781	(906) 643-8088	
			*90 Spruce St., St. Ignace 49781		(906) 376-2085
SAULT STE. MARIE					
Central	Victoria L. Hadaway	OE2	111 E. Spruce St., Sault Ste. Marie 49783	(906) 632-8672	
Algonquin			1604 W. 4th Ave., Sault Ste. Marie 49783	(906) 632-8672	
			*1513 Augusta, Sault Ste. Marie 49783		(906) 632-3125
White Pine	Rosemary R. DeHut	PL1	9 Tamarack, PO Box 158, White Pine 49971	(906) 885-5419	
Bergland			108 Birch St., PO Box 142, Bergland 49910		
Ewen			621 M28, PO Box 272, Ewen 49925		
			*22358 Norwich Trail, Ontonagon 49953		(906) 884-2871

NAME	POSITION		ADDRESS	OFFICE	HOME

APPOINTMENTS TO EXTENSION MINISTRIES LOCATED IN THE NORTHERN SKIES DISTRICT:
(further information at end of appointment section)

Scott A. Harmon	District Superintendent, Northern Skies District Office				
	FE2	927 W. Fair Avenue, Marquette 49855		(906) 228-4644	

NORTHERN WATERS DISTRICT

| District Superintendent | Jodie R. Flessner FE1 | | DS Email: jflessner@michiganumc.org | Office: (231) 947-5281 |
| Executive Assistant | Jill Haney | | Office Email: :jhaney@michiganumc.org | 1249 Three Mile Rd S, Traverse City 49696-8307 |

| | | | | TELEPHONE | |
CHARGE	PASTOR		ADDRESS	CHURCH	HOME
Alden	Daniel W Biteman	FE10	PO Box 130, 9015 Helena Street, Alden 49612-0130	(231) 331-4132	
Central Lake			PO Box 213, 8147 W State Rd, Central Lake 49622		(231) 409-8015
			*PO Box 157, 9022 Franklin, Alden 49612-0157		
Alpena: First	Seok Nam Lim	FE2	167 S. Ripley Blvd., Alpena 49707	(989) 354-2490	(989) 356-1846
			*1320 Hobbs Dr., Alpena 49707		
Arcadia	Kenneth D. VanderLaan	DSA1	PO Box 72, 3378 Division, Arcadia 49613	(231) 864-3680	(231) 923-6476
			*5763 W 9th St, Mears 49436		
Avondale	TO BE SUPPLIED		PO Box 388, 6976 14 Mile Rd, Evart 49631		
Baldwin: Covenant Community	Lyle J Ball	PL5	PO Box 250, 5330 S M-37, Baldwin 49304-0250	(231) 745-3232	
Chase: Barton			PO Box 104, 6957 S Depot St, Chase 49623-5111	(231) 832-5069	(231) 972-7335
			*6874 5 Mile Rd, Blanchard 49310-9474		
Barnard	Craig A Pahl	FL6	PO Box 878, East Jordan 49727-0878	(231) 547-5269	
East Jordan			PO Box 878, 201 4th St, East Jordan 49727-0878	(231) 536-2161	(231) 536-7596
			*PO Box 238, 305 Esterly, East Jordan 49727-0238		
Bear Lake	Cynthia Corey	DSA2	PO Box 157, 7861 Main St, Bear Lake 49614-0157	(231) 864-3680	(231) 645-1244
			*8340 Zosel St, Onekama 49675		
Bellaire: Community	Daniel J.W. Phillips	FL1	PO Box 235, 401 N Bridge St, Bellaire 49615-0235	(231) 533-8133	(810) 986-0240
			*4046 Grass Lake Rd, Bellaire 49615-9398		
Boyne City	Eun Sik Poy	FE5	324 S Park St, Boyne City 49712-1528	(231) 582-9776	
Boyne Falls			3057 Mill St, Boyne Falls 49713-5100	(231) 582-9776	
Epsilon			8251 E Mitchell Rd, Petoskey 49770-8831	(231) 347-6608	(231) 347-5382
			*4979 Boyne City Rd, Boyne City 49712		

NORTHERN WATERS DISTRICT

CHARGE	PASTOR		ADDRESS	CHURCH	HOME
Brooks Corners	Douglas Mochama Obwoge	DSA1	5951 30th Ave, Sears 49679-8077	(231) 734-2733	
			*5951 30th Ave, Sears 49679-8077		(231) 734-2733
Cadillac	Thomas E. Ball	FE13	PO Box 37, 1020 E Division St, Cadillac 49601-0037	(231) 775-5362	(231) 775-1851
			*114 Barbara St, Cadillac 49601-2446		
Associate	Travis Heystek	OF2	PO Box 37, 1020 E Division St, Cadillac 49601-0037	(231) 775-5362	(540) 819-5712
			*210 Blodgett St, Cadillac 49601		
CHARLEVOIX					
Charlevoix	Randell J Hitts	PL3	104 State St, Charlevoix 49720-1343	(231) 547-2654	(231) 622-3565
			*1206 State St, Charlevoix 49720-1625		
Greensky Hill	Jonathan D Mays	PL7	8484 Green Sky Hill Rd, Charlevoix 49720-9686	(231) 547-2028	(231) 459-8067
			*409 Prospect St, Charlevoix 49720-1020		
Empire	Melody Lane Olin	FL1	PO Box 261, 10050 W Michigan St, Empire 49630-0261	(231) 326-5510	(231) 970-2048
			*PO Box 261, 10205 Aylsworth Rd, Empire 49630-0261		
Evart	Jean M. Smith	AM1	PO Box 425, 619 N Cherry St, Evart 49631-0425	(231) 734-2130	(231) 734-2003
Sears			5951 30th Ave, 4897 Pratt St, Sears 49679	(231) 734-2733	
			*8543 Seven Mile Rd, Evart 49631-8407		
Frankfort	Barbara J Fay	AM10	PO Box 1010, 537 Crystal Ave, Frankfort 49635	(231) 352-7427	(231) 352-4724
Elberta			PO Box 405, 555 Lincoln Ave, Elberta 49628	(231) 352-4311	
			*320 Maple Street, Frankfort 49635		
Free Soil-Fountain	Richard D Roberts	PL7	PO Box 173, 2549 E Michigan St, Free Soil 49411-9680	(231) 690-4591	(231) 233-8954
			*2415 E Michigan St, Free Soil 49411-9679		
Gaylord: First	Daniel J. Bowman	FE6	215 South Center, Box 617, Gaylord 49734	(989) 732-5380	
			*915 Five Lakes Rd., Gaylord 49735		(810) 441-1600
Grant	TO BE SUPPLIED		PO Box 454, Interlochen 49643 (10999 Karlin Rd, Buckley 49620)	(231) 269-3981	
			*		
Grawn	Sean T Barton	FL2	PO Box 62, Grawn 49637 (1260 S West Silver Lake Rd, TC 49685)	(231) 943-8353	(269) 908-7313
			*1222 S West Silver Lake Rd, Traverse City 49685-8532		

CHARGE	PASTOR		ADDRESS	CHURCH	HOME
Grayling: Michelson Memorial	Richard E. Burstall	FE6	400 Michigan Ave., Grayling 49738	(989) 348-2974	(989) 348-9697
			*142 Barbara St., Grayling 49738		
Harbor Springs	Susan E Hitts	FL4	343 East Main St, Harbor Springs 49740-1513	(231) 526-2414	(231) 548-5774
Alanson			7330 Chicago St, Alanson 49706-9231	(231) 548-5709	
			*1881 Ellinger Rd, Alanson 49706		
Harrietta	Travis Heystek	OF2	PO Box 13, 116 N Davis St, Harrietta 49638	(231) 389-0267	(540) 819-5712
			*210 Blodgett St, Cadillac 49601		
Hersey	Lemuel O Granada	PL8	PO Box 85, 200 W Second Street, Hersey 49639-0085	(231) 832-5168	(231) 723-2763
			*351 2nd St, Manistee 49660-1747		
Hillman	Lisa Kelley	FL7	96 State St, PO Box 638, Hillman 49746	(989) 742-3014	(989) 727-3624
	(part-time ½)		*7770 Scott Rd., Hubbard Lake 49747		
Horton Bay	Michael R Neihardt	PL3	4961 Boyne City Rd, Boyne City 49712-9217	(231) 582-9262	(231) 392-5258
			*2347 Shawn Rd, Kalkaska 49646		
Houghton Lake	George R. Spencer	FE4	7059 W. Houghton Lake Dr., Houghton Lake 48629	(989) 422-5622	(989) 422-4365
			*316 Superior, Houghton Lake 48629		
Indian River	Todd W Shafer	FL3	PO Box 457, 956 Eagles Nest Rd, Indian River 49749-9707	(231) 238-7764	(231) 258-6916
			*5954 Berry Lane, Indian River 49749-9487		
Kalkaska	Yong Choel Woo	FE1	2525 Beebe Rd, Kalkaska 49646	(231) 258-2820	(231) 258-5995
			*2301 Shawn Rd NW, Kalkaska 49646		
Keswick	Patricia Ann Haas	FE9	3376 S Center Hwy, Suttons Bay 49682-9253	(231) 271-3755	(231) 271-4117
			*3400 S Center Hwy, Suttons Bay 49682-9252		
Kewadin	Howard Harvey	PL5	PO Box 277, 7234 Cairn Hwy, Kewadin 49648	(231) 264-9640	(231) 709-5481
			*701 Chippewa St, Apt 6, Elk Rapids 49629-9438		
Kewadin Indian Mission	George Pamp	DSA3	PO Box 227, 7250 Cairn Hwy, Kewadin 49648	(231) 347-9861	(231) 838-9375
			*851 W Conway, Harbor Springs 49740-9585		
Kingsley	Colleen A Wierman	FL6	PO Box 395, 113 W Blair Street, Kingsley 49649-0395	(231) 263-5278	(231) 263-4145
			*8658 Hency Rd, Kingsley 49649-9736		

NORTHERN WATERS DISTRICT

NORTHERN WATERS DISTRICT

CHARGE	PASTOR		ADDRESS	CHURCH	HOME
Lake Ann	Joshua Manning	FL3	6583 First St, Lake Ann 49650	(231) 275-7236	
			*6596 First St, Lake Ann 49650-9549		(334) 320-9603
Lake City	Russell K. Logston	FE1	PO Box - Drawer P, 301 E John St, Lake City 49651	(231) 839-2123	
			*133 N Park St, Lake City 49651-9702		(231) 839-7542
Leland	Daniel B Hofmann	FE6	PO Box 602, 106 N 4th St, Leland 49654-0602	(231) 256-9161	
			*PO Box 1134, 4840 Golfview Dr, Leland 49654-1134		(231) 994-2159
LUDINGTON					
St Paul	Bradley E Bunn	FL3	3212 W Kinney Rd, Ludington 49431-9780	(231) 843-3275	
			*3257 W Kinney Rd, Ludington 49431-9780		(404) 625-6802
United	Dennis B Bromley	FE7	5810 Bryant Road, Ludington 49431-1504	(231) 843-8340	
			*914 Seminole Dr, Ludington 49431-1584		(231) 425-4386
Mancelona	Bryan K Kilpatrick	FL3	PO Box 301, 117 E Hinman St, Mancelona 49659	(231) 587-8461	
Alba			PO Box 301, Mancelona 49659 (5991 Barker St, Alba 49611)	(231) 587-8461	
			*406 Sunnyside St, Mancelona 49659-9771		
Manistee	John A Scott	FE5	387 First St, Manistee 49660-1749	(231) 723-6219	
			*819 Elm St, Manistee 49660-2035		(231) 723-3304
Manton	Jeff Swainston	PL3	PO Box B, 102 N Michigan Ave, Manton 49663	(231) 824-3593	
			*PO Box 77, 102 N. Michigan, Manton, MI 49663-0902		(616) 813-8746
Marion	James J Mort	FE13	PO Box C, 216 W Main St, Marion 49665	(231) 743-2834	
Cadillac South Community			PO Box C, Marion 49665 (11800 47 Mile Rd, Cadillac 49601)	(231) 775-3067	
			*205 Flemming St, Marion 49665		(231) 743-0062
Mesick	Anika Kasper	DSA1	PO Box 337, 121 S Alvin St, Mesick 49668	(231) 885-1699	
Brethren: Epworth			PO Box 177, 3939 High Bridge Rd, Brethren 49619	(231) 477-5486	
			*3851 N 15 Rd, Mesick 49668		(231) 885-1179
NE MISSAUKEE PARISH					
Merritt-Butterfield	Hyun-Jun Cho	FE1	428 S Merritt Rd, Merritt 49667-9762	(231) 328-4598	
Moorestown-Stittsville			4509 E Moorestown Rd, Lake City 49651-9438	(231) 328-4598	
			*7037 E Houghton Lake Rd, Merritt 49667-9786		(231) 301-2692

CHARGE	PASTOR		ADDRESS	CHURCH	HOME
Northport Indian Mission	Mary Wava Hofmann	DSA1	PO Box 401, 8626 N Manitou Trail, Northport 49670	(231) 941-2360	(231) 994-2159
			*4840 E. Golfview Dr, Leland 49654		
Norwood	TO BE SUPPLIED		667 4th St, Norwood Village, Charlevoix 49720	(517) 262-4595	
Old Mission Peninsula	Zelphia J. Mobley	FL1	16426 Center Rd, Traverse City 49686-9775	(231) 223-4393	(586) 441-2274
			*14432 Peninsula Dr, Traverse City 49686		
Onaway	Yoo Jin Kim	PE2	3647 North Lynn St., PO Box 762, Onaway 49765	(989) 733-8811	(989) 733-8434
Millersburg			5484 Main St., Box 258, Millersburg 49759		
			*3653 N. Elm, Box 762, Onaway 49765		
Ossineke	Michael P. Kelley	FL8	13095 US-23, PO Box 65, Ossineke 49766	(989) 471-2334	(989) 727-8202
			*7770 W. Scott Rd., Hubbard Lake 49747		
Petoskey	James P Mitchum	FE23	1804 E Mitchell Road, Petoskey 49770-9686	(231) 347-2733	(231) 374-4747
			*900 Jennings Ave, Petoskey 49770-3139		
PINE RIVER PARISH	Scott R Loomis	FL8	PO Box 38, 310 West Gilbert St, LeRoy 49655-0038	(231) 768-4972	(231) 768-4512
LeRoy			PO Box 38, 20862 11 Mile Rd, LeRoy 49655-0038	(231) 832-8347	
Ashton			PO Box 175, 315 State St, Luther 49656-0175	(231) 797-0073	
Luther			*PO Box 234, 400 W Gilbert St, LeRoy 49655-0234		
Reed City	Kristen I. Coristine	FE1	503 S Chestnut, Reed City 49677-1301	(231) 832-9441	(231) 675-4172
			*219 S State St, Reed City 49677-1140		
Roscommon: Good Shepherd	Thomas L Hoffmeyer	OE1	149 W. Robinson Lake Rd., Roscommon 48653	(989) 275-5577	(989) 821-6056
of the North			*303 Rising Fawn Trail, Roscommon 48653		
Scottville	Richard Hodgeson	FL3	114 W State St, Scottville 49454	(231) 757-3567	(231) 757-4781
			*301 W Maple Ave, Scottville 49454-1327		
Spratt	Lisa Kelley	FL7	7440 M-65 South, Lachine 49743	(989) 742-3014	(989) 727-3624
	(part-time ½)		*7770 Scott Rd., Hubbard Lake 49747		

NORTHERN WATERS DISTRICT

CHARGE	PASTOR		ADDRESS	CHURCH	HOME
TRAVERSE CITY					
Central	Dale P Ostema	FE13	222 Cass St, Traverse City 49684-5734	(231) 946-5191	
			*1713 Indian Woods Dr, Traverse City 49686-3031		(231) 933-4026
Associate	M Christopher Lane	FE11	222 Cass St, Traverse City 49684-5734	(231) 946-5191	
			*10160 E Pickwick Ct, Traverse City 49684		(231) 947-5594
Mosaic (New Church Start)	Jeremy J Wicks	FL3	1249 Three Mile Rd. S, Traverse City 49696	(231) 946-3048	
			*PO Box 395, 449 N. Brownson St, Kingsley 49649		(517) 851-1494
Traverse Bay	Kathryn Snedeker	FE4	1200 Ramsdell St, Traverse City 49684-1451	(231) 946-5323	
			*7364 Williams Court, Elk Rapids 49629		(989) 239-9267
UNITED PARISH					
Williamsburg	John 'Jack' J Conklin	FE3	PO Box 40, 5750 Williamsburg Rd, Williamsburg 49690	(231) 267-5792	
Fife Lake			PO Box 69, 206 Boyd St, Fife Lake 49633-0069	(231) 879-4270	
East Boardman			PO Box 69, 2082 Boardman Rd SW, South Boardman 49680	(231) 879-6055	
South Boardman			PO Box 112, 5488 Dagle St, South Boardman 49680-0112	(231) 879-6055	
			*124 Boyd St, Fife Lake 49633-9031		(231) 920-2908

NAME	POSITION		ADDRESS	OFFICE	HOME
APPOINTMENTS TO EXTENSION MINISTRIES LOCATED IN THE NORTHERN WATERS DISTRICT:					
(further information at end of appointment section)					
Jodie R. Flessner	District Superintendent, Northern Waters District Office				
		FE1	1249 Three Mile Rd S, Traverse City 49696	(231) 947-5281	
Kathryn M Steen	Lead Hospital Chaplain, Munson Medical Center				
		FE12	1105 Sixth Street, Traverse City 49684-2349	(231) 935-7163	
APPOINTMENTS TO OTHER VALID MINISTRIES					
Russell K. Logston	St John's Lutheran Church (Para 345)				
		FE1			(231) 421-5138

MEMBERS OF THE MICHIGAN ANNUAL CONFERENCE APPOINTED TO OTHER CONFERENCES

(Paragraph 346.1, *Book of Discipline*)

PASTOR	CHARGE	ADDRESS	CHURCH	HOME
FLORIDA CONFERENCE				
Chul-Goo Lee FE7	Korean American UMC, 4905 W. Prospect Rd., Ft. Lauderdale FL 33309		(954) 739-8581	
INDIANA CONFERENCE				
Eric Burton-Krieger FE5	Indianapolis St. Luke's UMC (Assoc.), 100 W 86th St, Indianapolis IN 46260-2391		(317) 846-3404	(615) 934-0068
OREGON-IDAHO CONFERENCE				
Rebecca L Wieringa FE4	Milwaukie St. Paul's UMC, 11631 SE Linwood Ave, Milwaukie OR 97222-2754		(503) 654-1705	(269) 615-4527
ROCKY MOUNTAIN CONFERENCE				
Sandra L Spahr RE7	Avondale UMC, 233 Highway 50 East, PO Box 237, Avondale CO 81022			(719) 568-5858
WESTERN PENNSYLVANIA CONFERENCE				
Thomas M Beagan FE8	Charter Oak UMC, 405 Frey Rd., Pittsburgh, PA 15235		(412) 372-1341	
WEST OHIO CONFERENCE				
Yong Choel Woo FE6	Madisonville Korean, 32 Wesley Blvd., Worthington, OH 43085		(614) 844-6200	
WISCONSIN CONFERENCE				
Catherine Christman FE4	Stoughton UMC, 525 Lincoln Ave, Stoughton WI 53589		(608) 873-3273	(608) 205-2214

APPOINTMENTS TO OTHER CONFERENCES

APPOINTMENTS BEYOND THE LOCAL CHURCH
APPOINTMENTS TO EXTENSION MINISTRIES
2019-2020

Appointment to Extension Ministries
(¶316.1 *The Book of Discipline 2016*)

(Lisa M. Batten) Young Adult Initiatives Coordinator

(Jessica M. Davenport) Executive Director & Campus Pastor, Wesley Foundation of Kalamazoo

(Laura E. Feliciano) Conference Staff, New Church and Hispanic–Latino Committee (PT ¼)

(Maurice R. Horne, Sr.) Flint Mission Zone Minister of Outreach

(Jan M. Johnson) Palliative Care Chaplain, Mercy Health / Trinity Health. Montague - Missional C.C.

Appointment Beyond the Local Church
(¶331.1 a., b. *The Book of Discipline 2016*)

Susan D. Amick (FD) Chaplain, Wesley Woods Senior Living, Atlanta, GA. Decatur First - Missional C.C.

Grace Ann Beebe (RD) Consultant, Disability Awareness and Accessibility Concerns. Trenton: Faith - Missional C.C.

Christina L. Miller-Black (FD) (LTFT ½) East Winds District Coordinator of Disciple Formation. Flint: Court Street – Missional C.C.

Janet S. Carter (FD) Manager of Pastoral Services, Pine Rest Christian Mental Health Services. Grand Rapids: First - Missional C.C.

M. Kay DeMoss (FD) Senior Content Editor, Michigan Conference Communications (LTFT ¾). Georgetown - Missional C.C.

Ann E. Emerson (FD) Director, Lake Huron Retreat Center. Lexington - Missional C.C.

Nancy V. Fancher (FD) (LTFT ½) Maple Valley Community Center of Hope. Lansing Mt Hope - Missional C.C.

Carl T.S. Gladstone (FD) (LTFT ½) Director of Motor City Wesley, Young Leaders Initiative Board. Dearborn: First - Missional C.C.

Julie A. Liske (FD) Chaplain Director, Circles Grand Rapids. Wyoming: Wesley Park - Missional C.C.

April K. McGlothin-Eller (FD) Church Engagement Manager, Newnan Office of the UM Children's Home of North Georgia Conference. Royal Oak: First - Missional C.C.

APPOINTMENTS

Vincent W. McGlothin-Eller (FD) Associate Pastor, Newnan First UMC, La-Grange, North Georgia. Royal Oak: First - Missional C.C.

Paul D. Perez (FD) Associate Director for Mission and Ministry. Northville - Missional C.C.

Sue A. Pethoud (FD) Church & Community Liaison, Cass Community Social Services. Cass Community - Missional C.C.

Kathryn L. Pittenger (FD) Children's Initiatives Coordinator. DeWitt: Redeemer - Missional C.C.

Todd J. Query (FD) (LTFT ½) Freelance Curriculum Writer / Contributor, Sparkhouse, Augsburg Fortress Publishers and (LTFT ¼) Wellspring UMC, Virginia Conference. Albion First - Missional C.C.

Andrew J. Schleicher (FD) Senior Project Specialist, Marketing & Advertising, United Methodist Communications, Nashville, TN. Denton: Faith - Missional C.C.

Cara B. Weiler (FD) (LTFT ½) Southwest Michigan Children's Trauma Center. Sunnyside- Missional C.C.

Christina L. Wright (FD) Associate Director, Department of Spiritual Care, Michigan Medicine, University of Michigan. Royal Oak First - Missional C.C.

Teresa J. Zimmerman (FD) Associate Director of Spiritual Life, Chelsea Retirement Community. Manchester - Missional C.C.

Appointment Beyond the Local Church
(¶331.4a *The Book of Discipline 2016*)

Sandra V. Bibilomo (FD) (LTFT ¾) Representative Payee of Guardian Finance and Advocacy Services. Westwood - Missional C.C.

Cheryl A. Mulligan (FD) Field Clinical Specialist, RespirTech Medical. Lowell First – Missional C.C.

Alexander J. Plum (PD) Director, Henry Ford Health Systems, Global Health Initiatives. Cass Community – Missional C.C.

Appointment to Attend School
(¶338.4 *The Book of Discipline 2016*)

Appointment within the Connectional Structure
(¶344.1.a *The Book of Discipline 2016*)

John H. Amick, Director, Sustainable Development, UMCOR/Global Ministries, Atlanta, GA

Dwayne E. Bagley, Greater Southwest District Superintendent

Kennetha J. Bigham-Tsai, Chief Connectional Ministries Officer, Connectional Table

Jeremy P. Benton, Director & Campus Minister, Wesley Foundation of Greenville, Greenville, NC. Ortonville C.C.

Charles S.G. Boayue, Greater Detroit District Superintendent

John W. Boley, Clergy Assistant to Bishop

Kimberly M. Bos (PE), Director, Wesley Foundation at Ferris State University

Jennifer Browne, Director of Clergy Excellence

William W. Chu, Campus Pastor at Wesley Foundation at MSU. E. Lansing University C.C.

Margie R. Crawford, Midwest District Superintendent

Jerome R. DeVine, Mid-Michigan District Superintendent

Dirk Elliott, Director of Congregational Vibrancy Fenton C.C.

Donald J. Emmert, Director of Benefits and Human Resources

Katherine L. Fahey (PE), Director of Admissions & Recruitment, Garrett-Evangelical Theological Seminary.

Charles D. Farnum, Executive Director (LTFT ¼)
Wesley Foundation at CMU. Mt Pleasant: First C.C.

Jodie R. Flessner, Northern Waters District Superintendent

Scott A. Harmon, Northern Skies District Superintendent

Benton R. Heisler, Director of Connectional Ministries. Cornerstone C.C.

John H. Hice, East Winds District Superintendent

Elizabeth A. Hill, Heritage District Superintendent

David I. Kim, Central Bay District Superintendent

Michael J. Mayo-Moyle, IT Specialist. Farmington: Orchard C.C.

Jon R. Powers, Chaplain, Ohio Wesleyan University, Delaware, OH. Grand Rapids: Trinity C.C.

Gary G. Step, Associate Director for Congregational Vibrancy. Valley C.C.

Appointment to Extension Ministries
(¶344.1.b, c *The Book of Discipline 2016*)

Adam W. Bissell, Chaplain/Spiritual Care Coordinator, The Good Samaritan Society Prescott Hospice, Prescott AZ. Eastpointe: Immanuel C.C.

Herbert Lee Griffin, Jr., Chaplain/Wing Chaplain, U.S. Marine Corps. Battle Creek: Washington Heights C.C.

Timothy Hastings, (RE) Chaplain, St. Mary's of Michigan. Saginaw: Ames C.C.

Jayme L. Kendall, Staff Chaplain, United States Air Force. Indian River C.C.

Kristen J. Leslie, Professor of Pastoral Theology and Care, Eden Theology Seminary. Adrian: First C.C.

Heather A. McDougall, (PE) (LTFT ¾) Chaplain, Beacon Health System. Cornerstone C.C.

Lisa M. McIlvenna, Executive Director/Pastoral Counselor, Fresh Aire Samaritan Counseling Center. Midland: First C.C.

Stacy R. Minger, Associate Professor of Preaching, Asbury Theological Seminary, Wilmore, KY. Girard C.C.

Matthew R. Schlimm, Professor of Old Testament, University of Dubuque Theological Seminary, Dubuque, IA. Westwood C.C.

Kathryn M. Steen, Lead Staff Hospital Chaplain, Munson Medical Center, Traverse City. Traverse City: Central C.C.

Roy G. Testolin, (RE) Pastoral Counselor, Heritage Interfaith Counseling Center, Battle Creek. Battle Creek: First C.C.

Randy J. Whitcomb (RE), Chaplain, In House Hospice Solutions.
Bloomfield Hills: St. Paul's C.C.

Steven L. Woodford, Readjustment Counselor, Veterans Administration.
Bay City: Grace C.C.

Appointment to Extension Ministries
(¶344.1.d *The Book of Discipline 2016*)

John W. Ball, (LTFT ¼) Consultant, Celebrate Hope.

Margaret E. Bryce, Adjunct Professor of Practical Theology, Ashland Theological Seminary, Detroit.

David G. Elmore, Chaplain, Ascension Home Hospice. Coldwater C.C.

Alice M. Fleming-Townley, Associate Pastor, Presbyterian Church of Okemos (¶345 *The Book of Discipline 2016*). East Lansing University C.C.

Valerie A. Fons, (RE) Chaplain, Bread and Water and L.A.U.N.C.H. Wisconsin Conference. St Joseph: First C.C.

Emmanuel J. Giddings, Director, Afalit International/Liberia Literacy Program.

Melody P. Johnson, Director of Pastoral Care, Porter Hills Retirement Communities & Services, Grand Rapids. Birmingham: First C.C.

Nathaniel W. Johnson, Manager, Pastoral Care & Bereavement, Spectrum Health Delivery System. Vergennes C.C.

Russell K. Logston, Pastor, St. John's Lutheran Church (¶345 *The Book of Discipline 2016*). Lake City C.C.

Joy J. Moore, Associate Professor of Biblical Preaching, Luther Seminary, Saint Paul MN.

Kenneth J. Nash, Lead Pastor, Watermark Wesleyan, New York, (¶345 *The Book of Discipline 2016*) Grand Rapids C.C.

Barbara L. Smith-Jang, Pastoral Counselor/Parent Liaison, Taejon Christian International School, Daejeon South Korea.   East Lansing: University C.C.

Jonathan D. VanDop, Chaplain, West Texas Veteran's Health Administration, San Antonio TX

Appointment from Other Conferences
(¶346.1 *The Book of Discipline 2016*)

East Ohio Conference:
David S. Bell, President and Director United Methodist Foundation of Michigan. Brighton: First C.C.

Alabama-West Florida:
Mark J. Roberts, Chaplain, Borgess Medical Center, Kalamazoo (3/4 time) (¶344.1.d *The Book of Discipline 2016*)

Indiana Conference:
Brittney D. Stephan, (PE), Associate Director for Multi-Cultural Vibrancy

Holston Conference:
Timothy Kobler, Wesley Foundation Director at University of Michigan

Appointment of Deaconesses
(¶1913 *The Book of Discipline 2016*)

Valerie Mossman-Celestin, Haitian Artisans for Peace International

---

Bold	- A New Appointment
+	- Clergy from Other Annual Conference or Christian Denomination
Italicized	- District Change
( )	- Local Pastor
(AM)	- Associate Member
C.C.	- Charge Conference
{DSA}	- D. S. Assignment
(HL)	- Honorable Location
(LTFT)	- Less Than Full Time (Full or Provisional Member)
(OF)	- Full Member other Denomination
(OR)	- Retired Member of Other A.C.
(PT)	- Part Time (Local Pastor)
(PD)	- Provisional Deacon
(FD)	- Full Deacon
(RD)	- Retired Deacon
(PE)	- Provisional Elder
(RA)	- Retired Associate Member
(RE)	- Retired Full Elder
(RL)	- Retired Local Pastor
(SP)	- Student Local Pastor
[CLM]	- Certified Lay Minister
TBS	- To Be Supplied

APPOINTMENTS

**MICHIGAN AREA HEADQUARTERS OF THE
UNITED METHODIST CHURCH AND AFFILIATE**

REPORT ON CONSOLIDATED FINANCIAL STATEMENTS

YEARS ENDED DECEMBER 31, 2018 AND 2017

CONTENTS

2

Maner Costerisan PC
2425 E. Grand River Ave.
Suite 1
Lansing, MI 48912-3291
T: 517 323 7500
F: 517 323 6346
www.manercpa.com

INDEPENDENT AUDITOR'S REPORT

To the Board of Directors
Michigan Area Headquarters of the
 United Methodist Church and Affiliate

Report on the Financial Statements

We have audited the accompanying consolidated financial statements of Michigan Area Headquarters of the United Methodist Church and affiliate which comprise the consolidated statements of financial position as of December 31, 2018 and 2017, and the related consolidated statements of activities and changes in net assets, functional expenses and cash flows for the years then ended, and the related notes to the consolidated financial statements.

Management's Responsibility for the Financial Statements

Management is responsible for the preparation and fair presentation of these consolidated financial statements in accordance with accounting principles generally accepted in the United States of America; this includes the design, implementation, and maintenance of internal control relevant to the preparation and fair presentation of consolidated financial statements that are free from material misstatement, whether due to fraud or error.

Auditor's Responsibility

Our responsibility is to express an opinion on these consolidated financial statements based on our audits. We conducted our audits in accordance with auditing standards generally accepted in the United States of America. Those standards require that we plan and perform the audit to obtain reasonable assurance about whether the consolidated financial statements are free from material misstatement.

An audit involves performing procedures to obtain audit evidence about the amounts and disclosures in the financial statements. The procedures selected depend on the auditor's judgment, including the assessment of the risks of material misstatement of the consolidated financial statements, whether due to fraud or error. In making those risk assessments, the auditor considers internal control relevant to the entity's preparation and fair presentation of the consolidated financial statements in order to design audit procedures that are appropriate in the circumstances, but not for the purpose of expressing an opinion on the effectiveness of the entity's internal control. Accordingly, we express no such opinion. An audit also includes evaluating the appropriateness of accounting policies used and the reasonableness of significant accounting estimates made by management, as well as evaluating the overall presentation of the consolidated financial statements.

3

We believe that the audit evidence we have obtained is sufficient and appropriate to provide a basis for our audit opinion.

Opinion

In our opinion, the consolidated financial statements referred to above present fairly, in all material respects, the financial position of the Michigan Area Headquarters of the United Methodist Church and affiliate as of December 31, 2018 and 2017, and the changes in their net assets and their cash flows for the years then ended in accordance with accounting principles generally accepted in the United States of America.

Maner Costerisan PC

May 21, 2019

AUDITOR'S REPORT

MICHIGAN AREA HEADQUARTERS OF THE
UNITED METHODIST CHURCH AND AFFILIATE
CONSOLIDATED STATEMENTS OF FINANCIAL POSITION
DECEMBER 31, 2018 AND 2017

	2018	2017
ASSETS		
Cash and cash equivalents	$ 798,324	$ 644,820
Accounts receivable	104	2,574
Property and equipment, less accumulated depreciation	869,011	894,533
Total assets	$ 1,667,439	$ 1,541,927
LIABILITIES AND NET ASSETS		
Liabilities:		
Accounts payable	$ 13,027	$ 32,053
Accrued wages and related	128,440	92,340
Accrued interest	2,556	2,735
Long-term debt	727,180	772,291
Total liabilities	871,203	899,419
Net assets:		
Without donor restrictions	796,236	642,508
Total liabilities and net assets	$ 1,667,439	$ 1,541,927

See notes to consolidated financial statements.   5

MICHIGAN AREA HEADQUARTERS OF THE
UNITED METHODIST CHURCH AND AFFILIATE
CONSOLIDATED STATEMENT OF ACTIVITIES AND CHANGES IN NET ASSETS
YEAR ENDED DECEMBER 31, 2018

	Michigan Area Episcopal Office Fund	Bequest Fund	Bishop's Emergency Fund	Building and Maintenance Fund	Total
SUPPORT AND OTHER REVENUE:					
General Conference Finance and Administration					
Episcopal Fund	$ 86,252	$ -	$ -	$ -	$ 86,252
Detroit Annual Conference	494,677	-	-	-	494,677
West Michigan Annual Conference	400,431	-	-	-	400,431
Investment return, net	764	17	17	-	798
Total support and other revenue	982,124	17	17	-	982,158
EXPENSES:					
Program services:					
Office of the Assistant to the Bishop	380,602	-	-	-	380,602
Office of the Bishop	116,310	-	-	-	116,310
Management and general	331,518	-	-	-	331,518
Total expenses	828,430	-	-	-	828,430
CHANGE IN NET ASSETS	153,694	17	17	-	153,728
NET ASSETS - beginning of year	607,936	13,273	13,547	7,752	642,508
NET ASSETS - end of year	$ 761,630	$ 13,290	$ 13,564	$ 7,752	$ 796,236

See notes to consolidated financial statements.　　6

MICHIGAN AREA HEADQUARTERS OF THE
UNITED METHODIST CHURCH AND AFFILIATE
CONSOLIDATED STATEMENT OF ACTIVITIES AND CHANGES IN NET ASSETS
YEAR ENDED DECEMBER 31, 2017

	Michigan Area Episcopal Office Fund	Bequest Fund	Bishop's Emergency Fund	Building and Maintenance Fund	Total
SUPPORT AND OTHER REVENUE:					
General Conference Finance and Administration					
Episcopal Fund	$ 84,143	$ -	$ -	$ -	$ 84,143
Detroit Annual Conference	462,432	-	-	-	462,432
West Michigan Annual Conference	384,636	-	-	-	384,636
Investment return, net	805	25	25	-	855
Other income	-	-	-	10,000	10,000
Total support and other revenue	932,016	25	25	10,000	942,066
EXPENSES:					
Program services:					
Office of the Assistant to the Bishop	487,381	-	-	-	487,381
Office of the Bishop	73,563	-	-	-	73,563
Management and general	179,183	-	-	6,539	185,722
Total expenses	740,127	-	-	6,539	746,666
CHANGE IN NET ASSETS	191,889	25	25	3,461	195,400
NET ASSETS - beginning of year	416,047	13,248	13,522	4,291	447,108
NET ASSETS - end of year	$ 607,936	$ 13,273	$ 13,547	$ 7,752	$ 642,508

See notes to consolidated financial statements.   7

MICHIGAN AREA HEADQUARTERS OF THE
UNITED METHODIST CHURCH AND AFFILIATE
CONSOLIDATED STATEMENT OF FUNCTIONAL EXPENSES
YEAR ENDED DECEMBER 31, 2018

	Program services				
	Office of the Assistant to the Bishop	Office of the Bishop	Total	Management and general	Total
Salaries and benefits	$ 296,514	$ 62,081	$ 358,595	$ 174,202	$ 532,797
Payroll taxes	5,282	4,413	9,695	10.221	19,916
Called clergy	-	-	-	3,222	3,222
Contracted services	-	-	-	34,949	34,949
Mortgage loan interest	11,399	8,866	20,265	11,399	31,664
Building maintenance	4,861	3,781	8,642	4,861	13,503
Dues and subscriptions	1,558	273	1,831	1,739	3,570
Postage	401	1,770	2,171	401	2,572
Supplies and office printing	8,997	6,998	15,995	8,997	24,992
Telephone	5,185	2,263	7,448	25,838	33,286
Travel and parking	19,247	1,881	21,128	4,282	25,410
Computer and technology	4,367	3,396	7,763	4,367	12,130
Office equipment	11,021	8,572	19,593	11,021	30,614
Depreciation	11,770	9,155	20,925	11,770	32,695
Miscellaneous	-	2,861	2,861	24,249	27,110
	$ 380,602	$ 116,310	$ 496,912	$ 331,518	$ 828,430

See notes to consolidated financial statements.   8

**MICHIGAN AREA HEADQUARTERS OF THE
UNITED METHODIST CHURCH AND AFFILIATE
CONSOLIDATED STATEMENT OF FUNCTIONAL EXPENSES
YEAR ENDED DECEMBER 31, 2017**

| | Program services | | | | |
	Office of the Assistant to the Bishop	Office of the Bishop	Total	Management and general	Total
Salaries and benefits	$ 462,189	$ 59,616	$ 521,805	$ -	$ 521,805
Payroll taxes	14,806	4,197	19,003	-	19,003
Called clergy	-	-	-	9,837	9,837
Contracted services	-	-	-	14,056	14,056
Mortgage loan interest	-	-	-	33,758	33,758
Building maintenance	-	-	-	16,155	16,155
Dues and subscriptions	1,449	595	2,044	1,345	3,389
Postage	-	955	955	-	955
Supplies and office printing	376	3	379	11,778	12,157
Telephone	2,226	2,993	5,219	5,084	10,303
Travel and parking	6,335	2,757	9,092	10,600	19,692
Computer and technology	-	-	-	7,870	7,870
Office equipment	-	-	-	10,370	10,370
Building fund	-	-	-	6,539	6,539
Depreciation	-	-	-	32,409	32,409
Miscellaneous	-	2,447	2,447	25,921	28,368
	$ 487,381	$ 73,563	$ 560,944	$ 185,722	$ 746,666

See notes to consolidated financial statements.   9

MICHIGAN AREA HEADQUARTERS OF THE
UNITED METHODIST CHURCH AND AFFILIATE
CONSOLIDATED STATEMENTS OF CASH FLOWS
YEARS ENDED DECEMBER 31, 2018 AND 2017

	2018	2017
INCREASE (DECREASE) IN CASH AND CASH EQUIVALENTS:		
Cash flows from operating activities:		
Increase in net assets	$ 153,728	$ 195,400
Adjustments to reconcile increase in net assets to net cash provided (used) by operating activities:		
Depreciation	32,695	32,409
Accounts receivable	2,470	3,055
Accounts payable	(19,026)	11,856
Accruals	35,921	46,355
Total adjustments	52,060	93,675
Net cash provided (used) by operating activities	205,788	289,075
Cash flows from investing activities:		
Purchase of fixed assets	(7,173)	(6,728)
Cash flows from financing activities:		
Repayment of long-term debt	(45,111)	(39,519)
NET INCREASE (DECREASE) IN CASH AND CASH EQUIVALENTS	153,504	242,828
CASH AND CASH EQUIVALENTS, beginning of year	644,820	401,992
CASH AND CASH EQUIVALENTS, end of year	$ 798,324	$ 644,820
SUPPLEMENTAL CASH FLOW INFORMATION:		
Cash paid for interest	$ 31,485	$ 36,493

See notes to consolidated financial statements.   10

AUDITOR'S REPORT

MICHIGAN AREA HEADQUARTERS OF THE
UNITED METHODIST CHURCH AND AFFILIATE
NOTES TO CONSOLIDATED FINANCIAL STATEMENTS

NOTE 1 - SUMMARY OF SIGNIFICANT ACCOUNTING POLICIES

Principles of consolidation - the accompanying consolidated financial statements include the accounts of the Michigan Area Headquarters of the United Methodist Church and the Michigan Area United Ministry Center (collectively Headquarters).

Basis of accounting - Headquarters' consolidated financial statements are prepared on the accrual basis of accounting, which is in accordance with accounting principles generally accepted in the United States of America.

Net assets, revenues, gains and losses are classified based on the existence or absence of donor or grantor imposed restrictions. Accordingly, net assets and changes therein are classified and reported as follows:

Net assets without donor restrictions - Net assets available for use in general operations and not subject to donor or grantor restrictions

Net assets with donor restrictions - Net assets subject to donor (or grantor) imposed restrictions. Some donor restrictions are temporary in nature, such as those that will be met by the passage of time or other events specified by the donor. Other donor restrictions are perpetual in nature, where the donor stipulates that resources are maintained in perpetuity. Gifts of long-lived assets and gifts of cash restricted for the acquisition of long-lived assets are recognized as revenue when the assets are placed in service. Donor restrictions are released when a restriction expires, that is, when the stipulated time has elapsed, or when the stipulated purpose has been accomplished.

Fund accounting - To facilitate observance of limitations and restrictions placed on the use of available resources, the accounts are maintained in accordance with the principles of fund accounting. Funds are established according to the nature and purpose of resources available to Headquarters. The assets, net assets and financial activity of Headquarters are recorded in the following self-balancing fund groups:

      ➢   Michigan Area Episcopal Office Fund - includes resources without donor restrictions available for current operations.

      ➢   Bequest Fund - includes resources without donor restrictions, originating from a bequest without restrictions, to be used at the Bishop's discretion.

      ➢   Bishop's Emergency Fund - includes resources without donor restrictions, originating from board designations of under spent budgets, to be used at the Bishop's discretion.

      ➢   Building and Maintenance Fund - includes resources without donor restrictions, originating from the Detroit Annual Conference and West Michigan Annual Conference, to be used for major maintenance and building projects at Headquarters.

11

MICHIGAN AREA HEADQUARTERS OF THE
UNITED METHODIST CHURCH AND AFFILIATE
NOTES TO CONSOLIDATED FINANCIAL STATEMENTS

NOTE 1 - SUMMARY OF SIGNIFICANT ACCOUNTING POLICIES (Concluded)

Functional allocation of expenses - The costs of providing program and other activities have been reported in the statement of activities and changes in net assets. The statement of functional expenses presents the natural classification of expenses that are allocated to program or supporting functions of the Headquarters. Allocated expenses primarily consist of payroll and related, telephone, travel and general expenses based on salary and wage analysis and management's estimated use of resources. Fund raising costs have not been segregated on the basis of immateriality.

➢ Office of the Assistant to the Bishop - includes expenses for the Clergy Assistant to the Bishop and other program expenses, which support activities throughout the state of Michigan.

➢ Office of the Bishop - includes general office operations and expenses specific to the Bishop or the Bishop's executive assistant, which support activities throughout the state of Michigan.

Cash and cash equivalents include all highly liquid investments purchased with an original maturity of three months or less.

Accounts receivable are stated at the amount management expects to collect from outstanding balances. Based on management's assessment of the credit history with clients having outstanding balances and current relationships with them, management has concluded that realization losses on balances outstanding at year-end will be immaterial. Balances still outstanding after management has used reasonable collection efforts are written off through a charge to bad debt expense and a credit to accounts receivable.

Property and equipment is recorded at cost. Depreciation is computed over the useful life of the assets using the straight-line method. The Headquarters capitalizes all equipment purchased with a useful life exceeding one year and a cost greater than $500.

Revenue recognition - Revenue is recognized when earned. Program service fees, payments under cost-reimbursable contracts, fees and payments received in advance are deferred to the period the related services are performed or expenditures are incurred. Gifts and contributions are recognized when cash, securities or other assets, or an unconditional promise to give is received. Conditional promises to give are recognized when the conditions on which they depend have been substantially met.

Net investment return or loss is included in the statement of activities and changes in net assets and consists of interest and dividend income, realized and unrealized gains and losses, less related expenses.

12

**MICHIGAN AREA HEADQUARTERS OF THE
UNITED METHODIST CHURCH AND AFFILIATE
NOTES TO CONSOLIDATED FINANCIAL STATEMENTS**

NOTE 2 - NATURE OF ORGANIZATION, RISKS AND UNCERTAINTIES

The Michigan Area Headquarters of the United Methodist Church is a non-profit religious organization. The Michigan Area Methodist Ministry Center is a non-profit religious corporation. The purpose of Headquarters is to provide funding for the Bishop's activities, which are carried out throughout the state of Michigan. Headquarters is exempt from income taxes under the provisions of Section 501(c)(3) of the Internal Revenue Code.

Headquarters is required to disclose significant concentrations of credit risk regardless of the degree of such risk. Financial instruments that potentially subject the Headquarters to concentrations of credit risk consist principally of cash and cash equivalents. The Headquarters places its cash and cash equivalents with FDIC insured financial institutions. Although such cash balances may have exceeded the federally insured limits at certain times during the year and at year-end, they are, in the opinion of management, subject to minimal risk.

Headquarters is funded primarily though reimbursements from the General Conference Finance and Administration Episcopal Fund, the Detroit Annual Conference and the West Michigan Annual Conference, all of which are related organizations.

Headquarters evaluates events and transactions that occur after year end for potential recognition or disclosure in the consolidated financial statements. These subsequent events have been considered through May 21, 2019, which is the date the consolidated financial statements were available to be issued.

Tax positions are taken based on interpretation of federal, state, and local income tax laws. Management periodically reviews and evaluates the status of uncertain tax positions and makes estimates of amounts, including interest and penalties, ultimately due or owed. No amounts have been identified, or recorded, as uncertain tax positions. Federal, state and local tax returns generally remain open for examination by various taxing authorities for a period of 3 to 4 years.

The process of preparing consolidated financial statements requires the use of estimates and assumptions regarding certain types of assets, revenues, and expenses. The costs of providing the various programs and other activities have been summarized on a functional basis in the consolidated statement of activities and changes in net assets. Accordingly, certain costs have been allocated among programs and supporting services based on management estimates.

13

MICHIGAN AREA HEADQUARTERS OF THE
UNITED METHODIST CHURCH AND AFFILIATE
NOTES TO CONSOLIDATED FINANCIAL STATEMENTS

NOTE 3 - LIQUIDITY AND AVAILABILITY

The Headquarters regularly monitors the availability of resources required to meet its operating needs and other contractual commitments, while also striving to maximize the investment of its available funds. For purposes of analyzing resources available to meet general expenditures over a 12-month period, the Headquarters considers all expenditures related to its ongoing activities as well as the conduct of services undertaken to support those activities to be general expenditures.

The following reflects the Headquarters' financial assets as of December 31, 2018, which are deemed available for general expenditures within one year of the date of the statement of financial position:

Cash and cash equivalents	$ 798,324
Accounts receivable	104
Financial assets available to meet cash needs for general expenditures within one year	$ 798,428

In addition to financial assets available to meet general expenditures over the next 12 months, the Headquarters operates with a balanced budget and anticipates collecting sufficient revenue to cover general expenditures.

NOTE 4 - RETIREMENT BENEFITS

Headquarters sponsors a defined contribution pension plan covering substantially all of its employees. Headquarters contributes 6.5% of each participant's annual wages. Employer contributions and costs totaled approximately $16,400 and $16,000 for the years ended December 31, 2018 and 2017, respectively.

14

MICHIGAN AREA HEADQUARTERS OF THE
UNITED METHODIST CHURCH AND AFFILIATE
NOTES TO CONSOLIDATED FINANCIAL STATEMENTS

NOTE 5 - LEASES

Headquarters has use of two copiers under operating leases. The first copier has a monthly cost of $216 with the lease expiring in March 2020. The second copier has a monthly cost of $333 with the lease expiring in February 2023. Lease payments to be made under these agreements are as follows:

Year ending December 31,	
2019	$ 6,588
2020	4,644
2021	3,996
2022	3,996
2023	666

NOTE 6 - PROPERTY AND EQUIPMENT

Property and equipment consists of the following at December 31:

	2018	2017
Land and building	$ 919,731	$ 919,731
Furniture and fixtures	60,990	60,990
Office equipment	48,497	41,324
	1,029,218	1,022,045
Less accumulated depreciation	160,207	127,512
Net property and equipment	$ 869,011	$ 894,533

**MICHIGAN AREA HEADQUARTERS OF THE
UNITED METHODIST CHURCH AND AFFILIATE
NOTES TO CONSOLIDATED FINANCIAL STATEMENTS**

NOTE 7 - LONG TERM DEBT

Long term debt consists of the following at December 31:

	2018	2017
Mortgage payable (Michigan Area Loan Fund) - original balance of $825,000, payable in monthly installments of $6,413 including interest at 4.74%, collateralized by the building, final maturity of August 2019.	$ 647,180	$ 692,291
Note payable (West Michigan Conference) - original balance of $40,000, payable in one lump sum at maturity, no interest accumulated, unsecured, final maturity of January 2019.	40,000	40,000
Note payable (Detroit Annual Conference) - original balance of $40,000, payable in one lump sum at maturity, no interest accumulated, unsecured, final maturity of January 2019.	40,000	40,000
	727,180	772,291
Less current portion	727,180	45,111
Total long-term debt	$ -	$ 727,180

Maturities of long term debt are due as follows:

Year ending December 31,	
2019	$ 727,180

**MICHIGAN AREA HEADQUARTERS OF THE
UNITED METHODIST CHURCH AND AFFILIATE
NOTES TO CONSOLIDATED FINANCIAL STATEMENTS**

NOTE 8 - RELATED PARTY TRANSACTIONS

The Detroit Annual Conference processes payroll transactions for Headquarters at no charge. The value of these services has not been determined but is not considered significant to the financial statements.

At December 31, 2018 and 2017, Headquarters had the following included in accounts receivable from related parties:

	2018	2017
Detroit Annual Conference	$ -	$ 112
West Michigan Annual Conference	-	425
	$ -	$ 537

At December 31, 2018 and 2017, Headquarters maintained the following liabilities owed to the West Michigan Conference and Detroit Annual Conference for services performed:

	2018	2017
Detroit Annual Conference:		
Accounts payable	$ 7,077	$ 18,628
Accrued wages and related	122,288	43,715
	$ 129,365	$ 62,343
West Michigan Conference:		
Accrued wages and related	$ -	$ 42,821

In December 2014, the West Michigan Conference and the Detroit Conference each advanced the Headquarters $40,000 to finance the completion of the Ministry Center. These loans are payable January 2019 from amounts raised from special donations (see Note 7).

In August 2013, the Michigan Area United Methodist Ministry Center entered into an $825,000 mortgage agreement, the proceeds of which were used for the acquisition of office space for the use by Headquarters. Headquarters has entered into an agreement with the Detroit Annual Conference and the West Michigan Annual Conference to provide support for the mortgage payments. Based on this agreement, Headquarters anticipates receiving support for the entire amount of the mortgage commitment (see Note 7).

**MICHIGAN AREA HEADQUARTERS OF THE
UNITED METHODIST CHURCH AND AFFILIATE
NOTES TO CONSOLIDATED FINANCIAL STATEMENTS**

NOTE 9 - MICHIGAN UNITED METHODISTS VOTE TO BECOME ONE

In a live state-wide web address held on June 10, 2015, Michigan Area Bishop Deborah Lieder Kiesey, announced that the Detroit Annual conference and the West Michigan Annual Conference have voted to create a single organizational body in Michigan by January 1, 2019. The decision will impact over 140,000 professing members in the state, attending nearly 850 local churches.

NOTE 10 - NEW ACCOUNTING STANDARD

In August 2016, the FASB issued ASU No. 2016-14, *"Presentation of Financial Statement of Not-for-Profit Entities" (Topic 958)*. The ASU amends the current reporting model for nonprofit organizations and enhances their required disclosures. The major changes include: (a) requiring the presentation of only two classes of net assets now entitled "net assets without donor restrictions" and "net assets with donor restrictions", (b) modifying the presentation of underwater endowment funds and related disclosures, (c) requiring the use of the placed in service approach to recognize the expirations of restrictions on gifts used to acquire or construct long-lived assets absent explicit donor stipulations otherwise, (d) requiring that all nonprofits present an analysis of expenses by function and nature in either the statement of activities, a separate statement, or in the notes and disclose a summary of the allocation methods used to allocate costs, (e) requiring the disclosure of quantitative and qualitative information regarding liquidity and availability of resources, (f) presenting investment return net of external and direct internal investment expenses, and (g) modifying other financial statement reporting requirements and disclosures intended to increase the usefulness of nonprofit financial statements. In addition, ASU 2016-14 removes the requirement that not-for-profit entities that chose to prepare the statements of cash flows using the direct method must also present a reconciliation (the indirect method). The Organization adopted ASU No. 2016-14 for the year ending December 31, 2018. The December 31, 2017 comparative information has been reclassified to conform to the current year presentation.

18

**DETROIT ANNUAL CONFERENCE
OF THE UNITED METHODIST CHURCH**

REPORT ON FINANCIAL STATEMENTS
(with supplementary information)

YEAR ENDED DECEMBER 31, 2018
(with comparative totals for the year ended December 31, 2017)

CONTENTS

Maner Costerisan PC
2425 E. Grand River Ave.
Suite 1
Lansing, MI 48912-3291
T: 517 323 7500
F: 517 323 6346
www.manercpa.com

INDEPENDENT AUDITOR'S REPORT

To the Council on Finance and Administration
Detroit Annual Conference
 of the United Methodist Church

Report on the Financial Statements

We have audited the accompanying financial statements of Detroit Annual Conference of the United Methodist Church which comprise the statements of assets, liabilities and net assets - modified cash basis as of December 31, 2018 and 2017, and the related statement of support, revenue and other receipts, expenses, other disbursements and changes in net assets - modified cash basis and functional expenses - modified cash basis for the year ended December 31, 2018, and the related notes to the financial statements.

Management's Responsibility for the Financial Statements

Management is responsible for the preparation and fair presentation of these financial statements in accordance with the modified cash basis of accounting described in Note 1; this includes determining that the modified cash basis of accounting is an acceptable basis for the preparation of the financial statements in the circumstances. Management is also responsible for the design, implementation, and maintenance of internal control relevant to the preparation and fair presentation of financial statements that are free from material misstatement, whether due to fraud or error.

Auditor's Responsibility

Our responsibility is to express an opinion on these financial statements based on our audits. We conducted our audits in accordance with auditing standards generally accepted in the United States of America. Those standards require that we plan and perform the audit to obtain reasonable assurance about whether the financial statements are free from material misstatement.

An audit involves performing procedures to obtain audit evidence about the amounts and disclosures in the financial statements. The procedures selected depend on the auditor's judgment, including the assessment of the risks of material misstatement of the financial statements, whether due to fraud or error. In making those risk assessments, the auditor considers internal control relevant to the entity's preparation and fair presentation of the financial statements in order to design audit procedures that are appropriate in the circumstances, but not for the purpose of expressing an opinion on the effectiveness of the entity's internal control. Accordingly, we express no such opinion. An audit also includes evaluating the appropriateness of accounting policies used and the reasonableness of significant accounting estimates made by management, as well as evaluating the overall presentation of the financial statements.

3

We believe that the audit evidence we have obtained is sufficient and appropriate to provide a basis for our audit opinion.

Opinion

In our opinion, the financial statements referred to above present fairly, in all material respects, the assets, liabilities and net assets of Detroit Annual Conference of the United Methodist Church as of December 31, 2018 and 2017, and its support, revenue and other receipts, expenses, other disbursements and changes in net assets for the year ended December 31, 2018, in accordance with the modified cash basis of accounting as described in Note 1.

Report on Summarized Comparative Information

We have previously audited the Detroit Annual Conference of the United Methodist Church's 2017 financial statements, and we expressed an unmodified audit opinion on those audited financial statements in our report dated May 22, 2018. In our opinion, the summarized comparative information presented in the statement of support, revenue and other receipts, expenses, other disbursements and changes in net assets - modified cash basis and in the statement of functional expenses - modified cash basis for the year ended December 31, 2017, is consistent, in all material respects, with the audited financial statements from which it has been derived.

Basis of Accounting

We draw attention to Note 1 of the financial statements, which describes the basis of accounting. The financial statements are prepared on the modified cash basis of accounting, which is a basis of accounting other than accounting principles generally accepted in the United States of America. Our opinion is not modified with respect to this matter.

Report on Supplementary Information

Our audits were conducted for the purpose of forming an opinion on the financial statements as a whole. The supplementary information, as identified in the table of contents, is presented for purposes of additional analysis and is not a required part of the financial statements. Such information is the responsibility of management and was derived from and relates directly to the underlying accounting and other records used to prepare the financial statements. The information has been subjected to the auditing procedures applied in the audits of the financial statements and certain additional procedures, including comparing and reconciling such information directly to the underlying accounting and other records used to prepare the financial statements or to the financial statements themselves, and other additional procedures in accordance with auditing standards generally accepted in the United States of America. In our opinion, the information is fairly stated in all material respects in relation to the financial statements as a whole.

Maner Costerisan PC

May 21, 2019

4

DETROIT ANNUAL CONFERENCE OF THE UNITED METHODIST CHURCH
STATEMENTS OF ASSETS, LIABILITIES AND NET ASSETS - MODIFIED CASH BASIS
DECEMBER 31, 2018 AND 2017

	2018	2017
ASSETS		
Cash and cash equivalents	$ 1,250,284	$ 1,802,361
Investments	8,619,865	10,634,290
Receipts in transit	562,312	844,607
Due from affiliated church organizations, less allowance for doubtful accounts of $120,000 and $104,397 in 2018 and 2017, respectively	263,902	257,176
Notes and loans receivable	207,000	208,000
Property and equipment - net	2,209,082	1,761,059
TOTAL ASSETS	$ 13,112,445	$ 15,507,493
LIABILITIES AND NET ASSETS		
LIABILITIES:		
Assets held on behalf of others	$ 419,197	$ 614,061
NET ASSETS:		
Without donor restrictions	11,798,459	13,827,940
With donor restrictions	894,789	1,065,492
Total net assets	12,693,248	14,893,432
TOTAL LIABILITIES AND NET ASSETS	$ 13,112,445	$ 15,507,493

See notes to financial statements.   5

DETROIT ANNUAL CONFERENCE OF THE UNITED METHODIST CHURCH
STATEMENT OF SUPPORT, REVENUE AND OTHER RECEIPTS, EXPENSES,
OTHER DISBURSEMENTS AND CHANGES IN NET ASSETS - MODIFIED CASH BASIS
YEAR ENDED DECEMBER 31, 2018
(with comparative totals for the year ended December 31, 2017)

	2018 Without donor restrictions	With donor restrictions	Total	2017
SUPPORT, REVENUE AND OTHER RECEIPTS:				
Support and revenue:				
Apportionments	$ 5,850,264	$ -	$ 5,850,264	$ 5,870,549
Special offerings / mission and ministry	-	175,845	175,845	248,744
Investment return, net	(576,628)	(5,959)	(582,587)	1,321,100
Other income	1,701,433	3,190	1,704,623	1,366,395
Assets released from restrictions	343,779	(343,779)	-	-
Total support and revenue	7,318,848	(170,703)	7,148,145	8,806,788
Other receipts:				
Pension apportionments	1,701,155	-	1,701,155	1,739,285
Past years pension apportionments	35,491	-	35,491	11,975
Insurance reimbursements	8,487,254	-	8,487,254	8,722,742
Total support, revenue and other receipts	17,542,748	(170,703)	17,372,045	19,280,790
EXPENSES AND OTHER DISBURSEMENTS:				
Expenses:				
Salaries	2,196,255	-	2,196,255	1,919,363
Health insurance	404,315	-	404,315	394,756
Pension and post-employment benefit expense	66,257	-	66,257	46,503
Other employee costs	167,209	-	167,209	150,082
Training and continuing education	31,874	-	31,874	30,311
Travel, meeting and moving expenses	484,570	-	484,570	400,697
Operating and administrative expenses	1,470,298	-	1,470,298	1,467,588
Parsonage and building expenditures	48,487	-	48,487	33,379
Remittances to general church	1,555,648	-	1,555,648	1,635,400
Conference benevolence	3,152,328	-	3,152,328	2,512,089
Contribution to camping ministries	-	-	-	4,247,763
Depreciation	59,138	-	59,138	53,275
Total expenses	9,636,379	-	9,636,379	12,891,206
Other disbursements:				
Remittances to board of pensions	1,164,991	-	1,164,991	1,144,412
Health insurance	8,770,859	-	8,770,859	8,440,665
Total expenses and other disbursements	19,572,229	-	19,572,229	22,476,283
CHANGE IN NET ASSETS	(2,029,481)	(170,703)	(2,200,184)	(3,195,493)
NET ASSETS - beginning of year	13,827,940	1,065,492	14,893,432	18,088,925
NET ASSETS - end of year	$ 11,798,459	$ 894,789	$ 12,693,248	$ 14,893,432

See notes to financial statements.   6

DETROIT ANNUAL CONFERENCE OF THE UNITED METHODIST CHURCH
STATEMENT OF FUNCTIONAL EXPENSES - MODIFIED CASH BASIS
YEAR ENDED DECEMBER 31, 2018
(with comparative totals for the year ended December 31, 2017)

	Program services					
	Connectional ministry and administration	Conference leadership team	Mission and ministry	General church apportionments	New church development	Pension and health benefits
Salaries	$ -	$ 579,996	$ -	$ -	$ 72,662	$ -
Health and life insurance	-	94,930	-	-	-	87,865
Pension and post-employment benefits	-	2,933	-	-	-	12,882
Other employee costs	-	90,529	-	-	-	-
Training and continuing education	-	895	-	-	-	-
Travel, meeting and moving	270,817	54,271	-	-	-	-
Operating and administrative	-	160,249	-	-	-	-
Parsonage and building	-	-	-	-	-	-
Remittances to general church	-	-	-	1,232,872	-	-
Conference benevolence	-	711,010	463,701	-	497,291	5,773
Contributions	-	-	-	-	-	-
Depreciation	-	-	-	-	-	-
	$ 270,817	$ 1,694,813	$ 463,701	$ 1,232,872	$ 569,953	$ 106,520

See notes to financial statements.   7

DETROIT ANNUAL CONFERENCE OF THE UNITED METHODIST CHURCH
STATEMENT OF FUNCTIONAL EXPENSES - MODIFIED CASH BASIS
YEAR ENDED DECEMBER 31, 2018
(with comparative totals for the year ended December 31, 2017)

	Program services					
	Other designated activity	Total	Management and general	Total	2017
Salaries	$ 246,182	$ 898,840	$ 1,297,415	$ 2,196,255	$ 1,919,363
Health and life insurance	10,104	192,899	211,416	404,315	394,756
Pension and post-employment benefits	196	16,011	50,246	66,257	46,503
Other employee costs	10,224	100,753	66,456	167,209	150,082
Training and continuing education	-	895	30,979	31,874	30,311
Travel, meeting and moving	-	325,088	159,482	484,570	400,697
Operating and administrative	-	160,249	1,310,049	1,470,298	1,467,588
Parsonage and building	-	-	48,487	48,487	33,379
Remittances to general church	-	1,232,872	322,776	1,555,648	1,635,400
Conference benevolence	1,417,249	3,095,024	57,304	3,152,328	2,512,089
Contributions	-	-	-	-	4,247,763
Depreciation	-	-	59,138	59,138	53,275
	$ 1,683,955	$ 6,022,631	$ 3,613,748	$ 9,636,379	$ 12,891,206

See notes to financial statements.   8

DETROIT ANNUAL CONFERENCE OF THE UNITED METHODIST CHURCH
NOTES TO FINANCIAL STATEMENTS

NOTE 1 - SUMMARY OF SIGNIFICANT ACCOUNTING POLICIES

Basis of accounting - The books and records of the Conference are maintained on the modified cash basis of accounting. Under this method, income is recognized when received and expenses are recorded at the time of payment except for the recognition of certain assets and liabilities related to the timing of local church contributions at year end, amounts due from/to various organizations resulting from apportionments and/or special offerings and reimbursements of health insurance premiums, investments, notes and loans receivable, property and equipment and cash held on behalf of others in an agency capacity. Additionally, certain amounts held on the Conference's behalf at Wespath Benefits and Investments are not included in these financial statements and related cash flows attributable to local churches are reported as other receipts and disbursements. See Note 10.

Financial statement presentation - The statements of support, revenue and other receipts, expenses, other disbursements and changes in net assets - modified cash basis and functional expenses – modified cash basis include certain prior-year summarized comparative information in total but not by net asset class. Such information does not include sufficient detail to constitute a presentation in conformity with the modified cash basis of accounting. Accordingly, such information should be read in conjunction with the Conference's prior year financial statements from which the summarized information was derived.

Fund accounting - To facilitate observance of limitations and restrictions placed on the use of available resources, the accounts are maintained in accordance with the principles of fund accounting. Funds are established according to the nature and purpose of resources available to the Detroit Annual Conference of the United Methodist Church. The assets, liabilities, net assets and financial activity of the Conference are recorded in the following self-balancing fund groups:

> ➢ Connectional Ministry and Administration Fund - resources available for current operations in supervision and administration of the mission and ministry of the Detroit Annual Conference of the United Methodist Church.

> ➢ Conference Leadership Team Fund - resources available for distribution to the programs of mission and ministry of the Detroit Annual Conference of the United Methodist Church program agencies.

> ➢ Mission and Ministry Fund - resources to allow churches direct involvement in the charities promoted by Conference agencies. Member churches select individual charities to fund from a listing prepared by the Conference.

9

DETROIT ANNUAL CONFERENCE OF THE UNITED METHODIST CHURCH
NOTES TO FINANCIAL STATEMENTS

NOTE 1 - SUMMARY OF SIGNIFICANT ACCOUNTING POLICIES (Continued)

➤ General Church Apportionments Fund - resources available for providing financial support for the programs of the general church agencies, including recruitment and education of ordained ministers, support of seven United Methodist black colleges in the United States, support of the United Methodist Africa University in Zimbabwe, resources for the General Church agencies including the General Council on Finance and Administration, the General Board of Global Ministries, the General Board of Discipleship, the General Board of Church and Society and the Connectional Table, through the World Service Fund as well as funding for administration through the General Church Administration and Interdenominational Cooperation funds.

➤ New Church Development Fund - resources available for new church development as well as loan funds administered by the Conference Board of Global Ministries.

➤ Pension and Health Benefits Fund - resources available for support, relief, assistance and pensioning of clergy, lay workers for the various units of the Conference and their families.

➤ Plant Fund - property and equipment owned and used directly in the operation of the Conference.

➤ Other Designated Funds - resources for purposes related to Conference programs, including Trustee funds (arising from the sales of parsonages) and the WMRP fund (related to communications).

Cash and cash equivalents include all highly liquid investments purchased with an original maturity of 3 months or less.

Investments are recorded at fair value and consist of various equity securities, U.S. treasury notes, certificates of deposit, mutual funds and pooled funds. Net investment return or loss is recorded in the statement of support, revenue and other receipts, expenses, other disbursements and changes in net assets - modified cash basis and consists of interest and dividend income, realized and unrealized gains and losses, less investment expenses.

Receipts in transit include contributions collected by local churches during the years ended December 31, 2018 and 2017, but not received by the Conference until after year end.

Notes and loans receivable consist of outstanding principal for loans the Conference provided to local churches to help finance capital expenditures.

10

DETROIT ANNUAL CONFERENCE OF THE UNITED METHODIST CHURCH
NOTES TO FINANCIAL STATEMENTS

NOTE 1 - SUMMARY OF SIGNIFICANT ACCOUNTING POLICIES (Concluded)

Property and equipment are capitalized at cost. Donated assets are recorded at fair value at date of donation. Parsonages are recorded at original cost plus the cost of subsequent additions. Depreciation is computed over the estimated useful life of assets using the straight-line method. Additions to property and equipment over $1,000 are capitalized. Cost of maintenance and repairs are charged to expense when incurred. The useful lives adopted for the purpose of computing depreciation are:

Parsonages and improvements	20 to 40 years
Conference center furniture and equipment	5 to 7 years

Assets held on behalf of others consist of cash held in an agency capacity.

Functional allocation of expenses - The costs of providing program and other activities have been reported in the statement of support, revenue and other receipts, expenses, other disbursements and changes in net assets - modified cash basis. The statement of functional expenses – modified cash basis presents the natural classification of expenses that are allocated to program or supporting functions of the Conference. Allocated expenses primarily consist of payroll and related, travel and meetings, operating and administrative and various other expense classifications necessary to support the day-to-day operations of the Conference. Employee driven expenses are allocated based on salary and wage analysis. All other allocated expenses utilize management's estimated use of resources.

Net assets, revenues, gains and losses are classified based on the existence or absence of donor or grantor imposed restrictions. Accordingly, net assets and changes therein are classified and reported as follows:

Net assets without donor restrictions - Net assets available for use in general operations and not subject to donor or grantor restrictions. The Conference has no designated net assets without donor restriction.

Net assets with donor restrictions - Net assets subject to donor (or grantor) imposed restrictions. Some donor restrictions are temporary in nature, such as those that will be met by the passage of time or other events specified by the donor. Other donor restrictions are perpetual in nature, where the donor stipulates that resources are maintained in perpetuity. Gifts of long-lived assets and gifts of cash restricted for the acquisition of long-lived assets are recognized as revenue when the assets are placed in service. Donor restrictions are released when a restriction expires, that is, when the stipulated time has elapsed, or when the stipulated purpose has been accomplished (See Note 12).

DETROIT ANNUAL CONFERENCE OF THE UNITED METHODIST CHURCH
NOTES TO FINANCIAL STATEMENTS

NOTE 2 - ORGANIZATION, RISKS AND UNCERTAINTIES

The Detroit Annual Conference of the United Methodist Church (the Conference) is a Michigan non-profit corporation. The purpose of the Conference is to administer the collective ministries of local churches that make up its membership. The member churches are located in the Upper Peninsula of Michigan and the eastern half of the Lower Peninsula of Michigan. Using apportionments received from its member churches, the Conference provides support for various missions, educational programs and summer youth camps. The Conference is exempt from income taxes under provisions of Section 501(c)(3) of the Internal Revenue Code.

The Conference is required to disclose significant concentrations of credit risk regardless of the degree of such risk. Financial instruments which potentially subject the Conference to concentrations of significant credit risk consist of cash and cash equivalents, and investments. The Conference places its cash with various FDIC insured financial institutions and thereby limits the amount of credit exposure to any one financial institution. Credit risk with respect to investments is limited due to the wide variety of companies and industries. Although such investments and cash balances may exceed the federally insured limits at certain times during the year and at year-end they are, in the opinion of management, subject to minimal risk. The Conference maintains a diversified investment portfolio which is subject to market risk.

Investments are disclosed in Notes 5 and 6 and consist largely of amounts invested in various funds by the United Methodist Foundation of Michigan (UMF) as well as Wespath Benefits and Investments (WBI).

UMF Balanced Fund - The primary investment objective of the Fund is to provide for long term capital growth. The Fund operates as a "fund of funds" through which participants are invested primarily in the Stock Fund and Bond Fund. The Fund will be allocated approximately 35% to 65% in the Stock Fund and approximately 35% to 65% in the Bond Fund. The Fund seeks to achieve its investment objectives by investing in a diversified portfolio of common stocks, bonds and money market instruments.

UMF Stock Fund - The Fund seeks to achieve long-term capital appreciation through investments in stocks and other securities, with primary emphasis on U.S. large capitalization companies and secondary emphasis on global and international equities and on U.S. small and middle capitalization companies. The Fund is subject to the general investment restrictions and the socially responsible investment criteria as adopted by the UMF Foundation.

UMF Bond Fund - The Fund's primary objective is to achieve a high level of current income, with capital appreciation as a secondary objective, by investing in investment-grade debt securities. The Fund invests in U.S. Treasury and agency securities, municipal securities, corporate bonds, mortgaged backed securities, preferred shares and other fixed income securities rated as investment grade by a Nationally Recognized Statistical Rating Organization. The Fund is subject to the general investment restrictions and the socially responsible investment criteria as adopted by the UMF Foundation.

DETROIT ANNUAL CONFERENCE OF THE UNITED METHODIST CHURCH
NOTES TO FINANCIAL STATEMENTS

NOTE 2 - ORGANIZATION, RISKS AND UNCERTAINTIES (Concluded)

UMF Money Market Investment Account - The Fund's objective is to seek maximum current income consistent with liquidity and the maintenance of a portfolio of high quality short-term money market securities. The Fund attempts to achieve its objective by investing in a diversified portfolio of U.S. dollar denominated money market securities. These securities primarily consist of short term U.S. Government securities, U.S. Government agency securities, and securities issued by U.S. Government sponsored enterprises and U.S. Government instrumentalities, commercial paper and repurchase agreements and variable and floating rate obligations.

WBI Short Term Investment Fund - The Fund seeks to maximize current income consistent with preservation of capital. The Fund seeks to achieve its investment objective through the exposure to short-term fixed income securities in the sweep account. The Fund exclusively holds cash and cash equivalents in the form of units of the sweep account. The sweep account holds U.S. government bonds, agency bonds, corporate bonds, securitized projects, dollar denominated international fixed income securities, commercial paper, certificates of deposit, and other similar types of investments. The performance objective of the Fund is to slightly outperform its performance benchmark, the Bank of America Merrill Lynch 3-Month Treasury Bill Index.

WBI Multiple Asset Fund - The Fund seeks to maximize long-term investment returns, including current income and capital appreciation, while reducing short-term risk by investing in a broad mix of investments. The performance objective of the Fund is to outperform the investment returns of its performance benchmark (35% Russell 3000 Index, 30% MSCI ACWI excluding USA IMI, 25% Bloomberg Barclays U.S. Universal Index excluding Mortgage Backed Securities, and 10% Inflation Protection Fund Custom Benchmark by 0.8% on average per year (net of fees) over a market cycle (5 to 7 years).

The process of preparing financial statements requires the use of estimates and assumptions regarding certain types of assets, revenues, and expenditures. Such estimates primarily relate to unsettled transactions and events as of the date of the financial statements. Accordingly, upon settlement, actual results may differ from estimated amounts.

Tax positions are taken based on interpretation of federal, state and local income tax laws. Management periodically reviews and evaluates the status of uncertain tax positions and makes estimates of amounts, including interest and penalties, ultimately due or owed. No amounts have been identified, or recorded, as uncertain tax positions. Federal, state and local tax returns generally remain open for examination by the various taxing authorities for a period of 3 to 4 years.

The Conference evaluates events and transactions that occur after year end for potential recognition or disclosure in the financial statements. These subsequent events have been considered through May 21, 2019, which is the date the financial statements were available to be issued.

DETROIT ANNUAL CONFERENCE OF THE UNITED METHODIST CHURCH
NOTES TO FINANCIAL STATEMENTS

NOTE 3 - MICHIGAN UNITED METHODISTS VOTE TO BECOME ONE

In a live state-wide web address held on June 10, 2015, Michigan Area Bishop Deborah Lieder Kiesey, announced that the Detroit Annual Conference and the West Michigan Annual Conference have voted to create a single organizational body in Michigan by January 1, 2019. The decision will impact over 140,000 professing members in the state, attending nearly 850 local churches.

NOTE 4 - LIQUIDITY AND AVAILABILITY

The Conference regularly monitors the availability of resources required to meet its operating needs and other contractual commitments, while also striving to maximize the investment of its available funds. For purposes of analyzing resources available to meet general expenditures over a 12-month period, the Conference considers all expenditures related to its ongoing program service activities as well as the conduct of services undertaken to support those activities to be general expenditures.

The following reflects the Conference's financial assets as of December 31, 2018, which are deemed available for general expenditures within one year of the date of the statement of assets, liabilities and net assets – modified cash basis.

Financial assets:	
Cash and cash equivalents	$ 1,250,284
Investments	8,619,865
Receipts in transit	562,312
Due from affiliated church organizations, net	263,902
Notes receivable, current portion	40,000
Total financial assets	10,736,363
Contractual or donor-imposed restrictions:	
Less: net assets with donor restrictions	(894,789)
Financial assets available to meet cash needs	
for general expenditures within one year	9,841,574
Funds budgeted for future pension and benefit obligations	(2,580,053)
	$ 7,261,521

In addition to financial assets available to meet general expenditures over the next 12 months, the Conference operates with a balanced budget and anticipates collecting sufficient revenue to cover general expenditures not covered by donor-restricted resources. The Conference is substantially supported by contribution revenue. Because a donor's restriction may require resources to be used in a particular manner or in a future period, the Conference must maintain sufficient resources to meet those requirements. Therefore, certain financial assets may not be available for general expenditure within one year. The Conference structures its financial assets to be available as its general expenditures, liabilities and other obligations come due.

14

AUDITOR'S REPORT

DETROIT ANNUAL CONFERENCE OF THE UNITED METHODIST CHURCH
NOTES TO FINANCIAL STATEMENTS

NOTE 5 - INVESTMENTS

The Conference invests certain amounts with the United Methodist Foundation of Michigan (the Foundation). The Foundation was formed as a nonprofit organization by member churches of the Annual Conferences of West Michigan and Detroit. It is governed and monitored by its own independent commission. The Foundation's primary purpose is to broaden the financial base of member churches by assisting in and receiving planned and deferred gifts, assisting in the set-up and marketing of endowment funds, and the generation of market-level returns on invested monies through the use of investment pools.

The Conference also invests funds with Wespath Benefits and Investments, which is a not-for-profit administrative agency of The United Methodist Church, responsible for the general supervision and administration of investments and benefit services according to the principles of The United Methodist Church.

Investments at December 31 consist of the following:

	2018	2017
Direct investments:		
Equity securities	$ 2,310,822	$ 2,582,646
United States Treasury Notes	65,500	65,500
Mutual funds - Equity	264,011	858,358
Mutual funds - Fixed income	964,729	314,260
Money market	239,960	188,351
United Methodist Development Fund - certificates of deposit	345,798	339,025
Pooled funds managed by the Foundation:		
UMF Balanced Fund	283,687	490,516
UMF Stock Fund	1,284,049	2,366,280
UMF Bond Fund	281,255	490,417
Pooled funds managed by Wespath Benefits and Investments:		
Short Term Investment Fund	1,428	9,111
Multiple Asset Fund	2,578,626	2,929,826
Total investments	$ 8,619,865	$ 10,634,290

Investment return, net from cash deposits and investments consist of the following for the year ended December 31:

	2018	2017
Interest and dividends, net	$ 86,779	$ 83,230
Realized and unrealized gain (loss)	(669,366)	1,237,870
Total investment return, net	$ (582,587)	$ 1,321,100

15

DETROIT ANNUAL CONFERENCE OF THE UNITED METHODIST CHURCH
NOTES TO FINANCIAL STATEMENTS

NOTE 6 - FAIR VALUE MEASUREMENTS

Accounting standards establish a hierarchy that prioritizes the inputs to valuation techniques giving the highest priority to readily available unadjusted quoted prices in active markets for identical assets (Level 1 measurements) and the lowest priority to unobservable inputs (Level 3 measurements) when market prices are not readily available or reliable. The three levels of the hierarchy are described below:

Level 1:   Quoted prices in active markets for identical securities.

Level 2:   Prices determined using other significant observable inputs. Observable inputs are inputs that other market participants may use in pricing a security. These may include quoted prices for similar securities, interest rates, prepayment speeds, credit risk and others.

Level 3:   Prices determined using significant unobservable inputs. In situations where quoted prices or observable inputs are unavailable or deemed less relevant (for example, when there is little or no market activity for an investment at the end of the period), unobservable inputs may be used. Unobservable inputs reflect the Conference's own assumptions about the factors market participants would use in pricing an investment, and would be based on the best information available.

The asset or liability's fair value measurement level within the fair value hierarchy is based on the lowest level of any input that is significant to the fair value measurement. Valuation techniques used need to maximize the use of observable inputs and minimize the use of unobservable inputs.

Following is a description of the valuation methodologies used to determine how an asset is measured at fair value. There have been no changes in the methodologies used at December 31, 2018 and 2017.

Mutual funds: Valued at the daily closing price as reported by the fund. Mutual funds held by the Conference are open-end mutual funds that are registered with the Securities and Exchange Commission. These funds are required to publish their daily net asset value (NAV) and to transact at that price. The mutual funds held by the Conference are deemed to be actively traded.

Equity securities: Valued at the price reported on the active market on which the individual securities are traded.

U.S. government securities and certificates of deposit: Valued using pricing models maximizing the use of observable inputs for similar securities.

Pooled Funds: Reported by the United Methodist Foundation (UMF) and Wespath Benefits and Investments to the Conference, these pooled funds represent the allocable share of the underlying investments. These investments include numerous securities that are combined with the investment portfolios of other organizations held by the UMF and Wespath Benefits and Investments. As such, these investments are valued at the net asset value of the units held by the Conference and are excluded from the fair value hierarchy.

16

DETROIT ANNUAL CONFERENCE OF THE UNITED METHODIST CHURCH
NOTES TO FINANCIAL STATEMENTS

NOTE 6 - FAIR VALUE MEASUREMENTS (Concluded)

The preceding methods described may produce a fair value calculation that may not be indicative of net realizable value or reflective of future fair values. Furthermore, although the Conference believes its valuation methods are appropriate and consistent with other market participants, the use of different methodologies or assumptions to determine the fair value of certain financial instruments could result in a different fair value measurement at the reporting date.

The following is a market value summary by the level of the inputs used in evaluating the Conference's assets carried at fair value at December 31. The inputs or methodology used for valuing securities may not be an indication of the risk associated with investing in those securities.

	2018	2017
Level 1:		
Direct investments:		
Equity securities	$ 2,310,822	$ 2,582,646
U.S. Treasury Notes	65,500	65,500
Mutual funds - Equity	264,011	858,358
Mutual funds - Fixed income	964,729	314,260
Certificates of deposit	345,798	339,025
Total investments measured at fair value	3,950,860	4,159,789
Money market funds at cost	239,960	188,351
Investments measured at net asset value	4,429,045	6,286,150
Total investments	$ 8,619,865	$ 10,634,290

NOTE 7 - PROPERTY AND EQUIPMENT

Property and equipment consist of the following at December 31:

	2018	2017
Parsonages:		
Conference	$ 2,246,032	$ 1,794,183
Area	213,878	213,878
Conference center furniture and equipment	543,725	488,413
	3,003,635	2,496,474
Less accumulated depreciation	794,553	735,415
Net property and equipment	$ 2,209,082	$ 1,761,059

17

DETROIT ANNUAL CONFERENCE OF THE UNITED METHODIST CHURCH
NOTES TO FINANCIAL STATEMENTS

NOTE 7 - PROPERTY AND EQUIPMENT (Concluded)

	2018	2017
Conference parsonages:		
Marquette District Superintendent - Marquette	$ 316,523	$ 316,523
Crossroad's District Superintendent - Flint	218,010	218,010
Ann Arbor Superintendent - Ann Arbor	278,372	278,372
Detroit Renaissance District Superintendent - Farmington Hills	425,617	425,617
Bluewater District Superintendent - Fort Gratiot	305,327	305,327
Saginaw Bay District Superintendent - Midland	250,334	250,334
Director of Human Resources and Benefits - Parsonage	451,849	-
Total conference parsonages	$ 2,246,032	$ 1,794,183
Area parsonages:		
15160 Duxbury Lane, DeWitt Township	$ 213,878	$ 213,878

The area parsonages are owned jointly with the Council of Finance and Administration of the West Michigan Annual Conference. The above amount represents the Detroit Annual Conference of the United Methodist Church's share, which approximates 58% of the original cost basis of the property.

Land included in the parsonages listed above amounted to approximately $155,300 for the years ended December 31, 2018 and 2017.

NOTE 8 - NOTES AND LOANS RECEIVABLES

Financing receivables consist of the following at December 31:

	2018	2017
Interest-free advances to Conference officials.	$ 1,000	$ 2,000
Note receivable (MI Area Headquarters) - original balance of $40,000, receivable in one lump sum at maturity, no interest accumulated, unsecured, final maturity January 2019.	40,000	40,000
Land procurement loan receivable from Canton Friendship United Methodist Church, with annual interest payments of $7,470 at 4.5%, maturity to be determined.	166,000	166,000
	$ 207,000	$ 208,000

18

DETROIT ANNUAL CONFERENCE OF THE UNITED METHODIST CHURCH
NOTES TO FINANCIAL STATEMENTS

NOTE 8 - NOTES AND LOANS RECEIVABLES (Concluded)

Maturities of financing receivables at December 31 are as follows:

Years ending December 31,	
2019	$ 40,000
2020	-
2021	-
2022	-
2023	-
Thereafter	167,000
	$ 207,000

Notes receivable are carried at unpaid principal balances, less an allowance for doubtful collection. Management periodically evaluates the adequacy of the allowance based on past experience and potential adverse situations that may affect the borrower's ability to repay. It is management's policy to write off a loan only when they are deemed permanently uncollectible. As of December 31, 2018 and 2017, management believes that no allowance is necessary.

The classification of notes receivable regarding age and interest accrual status at December 31 are as follows:

	2018			2017		
	Principal	Interest	Total	Principal	Interest	Total
Current	$ 207,000	$ -	$ 207,000	$ 208,000	$ -	$ 208,000
Past due:						
30 - 59 days	-	-	-	-	-	-
60 - 89 days	-	-	-	-	-	-
≥ 90 days	-	74,700	74,700	-	67,230	67,230
Total past due	-	74,700	74,700	-	67,230	67,230
Total financing receivables	$ 207,000	$ 74,700	$ 281,700	$ 208,000	$ 67,230	$ 275,230

Past due interest has not been accrued under the modified cash basis of accounting.

19

DETROIT ANNUAL CONFERENCE OF THE UNITED METHODIST CHURCH
NOTES TO FINANCIAL STATEMENTS

NOTE 9 - LEASES

The Conference leases office space in Dewitt, Michigan set to expire December 31, 2022. The Conference also leases a copier set to expire March 2022. The future minimum lease payments for the Detroit Annual Conference are as follows:

Year ending December 31,	
2019	$ 50,896
2020	52,300
2021	53,754
2022	51,528

Beginning January 1, 2019, the West Michigan Annual Conference and the Detroit Annual Conference will join to become a single organizational body located in Dewitt, Michigan. Lease obligations for both conferences will transfer to the new organization. The West Michigan Annual Conference leases office space for approximately $24,000 per year in Grand Rapids, Michigan which is set to expire December 31, 2022.

NOTE 10 - PENSION AND OTHER POST-EMPLOYMENT BENEFITS

From 1982 through 2006, the conference contributed to the Ministerial Pension Plan that was administered by Wespath Benefits and Investments to fund clergy retirement benefits. Wespath Benefits and Investments has taken the position that the Conference is responsible for funding any shortfall in benefits. Beginning January 1, 2019, the West Michigan Annual Conference and the Detroit Annual Conference will join to become a single organizational body and pension obligations for both conferences will transfer to the new organization. As a result, the combined total estimated actuarial liability based on the actuarial calculation as of January 1, 2017 is projected to be $129,842,074 in 2019. The expected combined contribution for both organizations for 2019 is $0. Amounts reported as remittances to the board of pensions represent payments made to Wespath Benefits and Investments for the purpose of providing pensions and other post-employment benefits to Conference clergy. Amounts on deposit with Wespath Benefits and Investments at December 31, 2018 and 2017 were approximately $121,000,000 and $134,000,000, respectively, which were invested in diversified investment funds and are available to provide for future post-employment benefits

The Conference participates in a voluntary multi-employer defined contribution pension plan that covers substantially all Conference lay employees. The Conference contributes 6.5% of each participant's annual wages. Contributions made by the Conference approximated $85,000 and $72,000 for the years ended December 31, 2018 and 2017, respectively.

DETROIT ANNUAL CONFERENCE OF THE UNITED METHODIST CHURCH
NOTES TO FINANCIAL STATEMENTS

NOTE 10 - PENSION AND OTHER POST-EMPLOYMENT BENEFITS (Concluded)

Additionally, the Conference has an interest in a clergy defined benefit pension plan for service prior to 1982 that is frozen. The Plan is administered by Wespath Benefits and Investments and management believes that the plan is fully funded.

Effective January 1, 2007, the Conference adopted the Clergy Retirement Security Program (CRSP-DB). This program is an amendment and restatement of the previous clergy pension program. Regular contributions made by the Conference approximated $795,000 and $1,073,000 for the years ended December 31, 2018 and 2017, respectively. The Conference was also required to make additional contributions of $1,728,312 for the year ended December 31, 2018. Beginning January 1, 2019, the West Michigan Annual Conference and the Detroit Annual Conference will join to become a single organizational body and pension obligations for both conferences will transfer to the new organization. The combined expected contribution based on the most recent actuarial calculation as of January 1, 2017 was projected to be $2,873,999 for 2019.

The Conference's policy is to fund all costs of qualified retirees' (clergy and lay employees) health care coverage expense when paid. No expenses were required in 2017 as the coverage was considered fully funded. Based on the most recent actuarial calculation dated October 23, 2017, the post-employment medical benefit liability is projected to reflect an estimated overfunded amount of $25,514,000 as of January 1, 2017.

NOTE 11 - RELATED PARTY TRANSACTIONS

The Conference conducts essentially all transactions, other than purchases of goods and services and sales of certain property, with affiliated congregations. Certain administrative expenses are reimbursed by related organizations. The Conference also processes payroll transactions for affiliated organizations at no charge. The value of these services has not been determined but is not considered significant to the financial statements.

In December 2014, the Conference advanced $40,000 to the Michigan Area Headquarters (Headquarters) to finance the completion of the Ministry Center. This loan matures in 2019 with no interest.

Additionally, the Conference has recorded amounts receivable from Headquarters to reimburse for operational costs incurred by the Conference in the amounts of $129,365 and $94,189, for the years ended December 31, 2018 and 2017, respectively.

DETROIT ANNUAL CONFERENCE OF THE UNITED METHODIST CHURCH
NOTES TO FINANCIAL STATEMENTS

NOTE 11 - RELATED PARTY TRANSACTIONS (Concluded)

In August 2013, the Michigan Area United Methodist Ministry Center and the Michigan Area Headquarters entered into an $825,000 mortgage agreement, the proceeds of which were used for the acquisition of office space for Headquarters. The Conference has entered into an agreement with Headquarters and the West Michigan Annual Conference of the United Methodist Church to provide support to Headquarters for the mortgage payments. Payments are to be sufficient to repay the underlying mortgage note plus interest at 4.74% per annum. The Conference's estimated portion of remaining payments is as follows:

Year ending December 31,	Principal	Interest	Total commitment
2019	$ 323,590	$ 10,011	$ 333,601

NOTE 12 - NET ASSETS

Net assets activity with donor restriction were available for the following purposes at December 31, 2018:

	December 31, 2017	Inflows	Outflows	December 31, 2018
Subject to expenditure for specific purpose:				
LeBlanc Fund - restricted for pension benefits; for clergy in cases of disability, divorce or death	$ 596,221	$ -	$ -	$ 596,221
Mission and Ministry Fund - contributions restricted by local churches	269,771	175,845	(343,779)	101,837
Detroit flood relief - contributions restricted by local churches	59,574	3,190	-	62,764
Total purpose restricted net assets	925,566	179,035	(343,779)	760,822
Endowment fund:				
Reed Fund School of Ministry - restricted endowment for inspirational speakers	76,417	(5,959)	-	70,458
Original gifts in perpetuity subject to spending policy and appropriations:				
Reed Fund School of Ministry	63,509	-	-	63,509
Total endowment net assets	139,926	(5,959)	-	133,967
Total net assets with donor restriction	$ 1,065,492	$ 173,076	$ (343,779)	$ 894,789

22

DETROIT ANNUAL CONFERENCE OF THE UNITED METHODIST CHURCH
NOTES TO FINANCIAL STATEMENTS

NOTE 12 - NET ASSETS (Concluded)

Net assets activity with donor restriction were available for the following purposes at December 31, 2017:

	December 31, 2016	Revenue	Expenses	December 31, 2017
Subject to expenditure for specific purpose:				
LeBlanc Fund - restricted for pension benefits; for clergy in cases of disability, divorce or death	$ 596,221	$ -	$ -	$ 596,221
Mission and Ministry Fund - contributions restricted by local churches	249,416	248,744	(228,389)	269,771
Detroit flood relief - contributions restricted by local churches	88,706	7,842	(36,974)	59,574
Total purpose restricted net assets	934,343	256,586	(265,363)	925,566
Endowment fund:				
Reed Fund School of Ministry - restricted endowment for inspirational speakers	57,075	19,342	-	76,417
Original gifts in perpetuity subject to spending policy and appropriations:				
Reed Fund School of Ministry	63,509	-	-	63,509
Total endowment net assets	120,584	19,342	-	139,926
Total net assets with donor restriction	$ 1,054,927	$ 275,928	$ (265,363)	$ 1,065,492

23

DETROIT ANNUAL CONFERENCE OF THE UNITED METHODIST CHURCH
NOTES TO FINANCIAL STATEMENTS

NOTE 13 - ENDOWMENTS

Endowments consist of funds established for a variety of purposes and may include both donor-restricted funds and funds internally designated to function as endowments. Net assets associated with endowment funds, both donor restricted and funds designated by the Conference, are reported based on the existence or absence of donor-imposed restrictions.

The Conference has interpreted the Michigan Uniform Prudent Management of Institutional Funds Act (MUPMIFA) as permitting the preservation of the historical value of the original gift of the donor-restricted endowment funds absent explicit donor stipulations to the contrary. As a result of this interpretation, the Organization classifies as net assets with donor restrictions (a time restriction in perpetuity) (a) the original value of gifts donated to the donor restricted endowment, (b) the original value of subsequent gifts to the donor restricted endowment, and (c) accumulations to the donor restricted endowment made in accordance with the direction of the applicable donor gift instrument at the time the accumulation is added to the fund. Investment income from the donor restricted endowment is classified as net assets with donor restrictions (a purpose restriction) until those amounts are appropriated for expenditure by the Organization in a manner consistent with the donor stipulated purpose within the standard of prudence prescribed by MUPMIFA. Donor-restricted amounts not retained in perpetuity are subject to appropriation for expenditure by the Conference in a manner consistent with the standard of prudence prescribed by MUPMIFA. In accordance with MUPMIFA, the Conference considers the following factors in making a determination to appropriate or accumulate donor-restricted endowment funds.

1. The duration and preservation of the fund.
2. The purposes of the donor-restricted endowment fund.
3. General economic conditions.
4. The possible effect of inflation and deflation.
5. The expected total return from income and the appreciation of investments.
6. Other resources of the Conference
7. The investment policies of the Conference.

The Conference's investment and spending practices for endowment assets attempt to provide a predictable stream of funding to programs supported while seeking to maintain the purchasing power of the endowment assets.

The Conference has adopted an endowment spending policy that directs it to budget the anticipated amount of endowment income and distribute based on budgeted amounts to the beneficiaries or programs specified by the endowment agreements.

From time to time, certain donor-restricted endowment funds may have fair values less than the amount required to be maintained by donors or by law (underwater endowments). The Conference has interpreted MUPMIFA to permit spending from underwater endowments in accordance with prudent measures required under law. There were no such deficiencies for the years ended December 31, 2018 and 2017, respectively.

24

DETROIT ANNUAL CONFERENCE OF THE UNITED METHODIST CHURCH
NOTES TO FINANCIAL STATEMENTS

NOTE 13 - ENDOWMENTS (Concluded)

Endowment net assets composition as of December 31, 2018 and 2017:

	Accumulated investment gains	Original gift in perpetuity by donor	Total
Endowment net assets January 1, 2017	$ 57,075	$ 63,509	$ 120,584
Investment return:			
Interest and dividends, net	3,478	-	3,478
Realized and unrealized gain (loss)	15,864	-	15,864
Total investment return, net	19,342	-	19,342
Endowment net assets December 31, 2017	76,417	63,509	139,926
Investment return:			
Interest and dividends, net	4,402	-	4,402
Realized and unrealized gain (loss)	(10,361)	-	(10,361)
Total investment return, net	(5,959)	-	(5,959)
Endowment net assets December 31, 2018	$ 70,458	$ 63,509	$ 133,967

NOTE 14 - CONTINGENCIES

From time to time the Conference is involved in various legal proceedings that have arisen in the ordinary course of business. The Conference is party to various local congregation loan obligations and may be contingently liable upon default. Management believes that the outcome of any contingent liabilities, either individually or in the aggregate, will not have a material adverse effect on the Conference's financial position or future results of operations.

Effective January 1, 2007 the Conference became primarily self-insured, up to certain limits, for health claims through Blue Cross Blue Shield of Michigan. The plan includes all participating Conference employees as well as affiliated congregation clergy. The Conference has purchased stop-loss insurance, which will reimburse the Conference for individual policy claims that exceed $100,000 annually. Claims are expensed as paid. The amount of claims incurred but not reported attributable to the Conference has not been determined. The total expense under the program was approximately $404,000 and $395,000 for Conference employees for the years ended December 31, 2018 and 2017, respectively. The Conference is reimbursed for stop loss premiums and claims paid for affiliates covered under the Plan.

DETROIT ANNUAL CONFERENCE OF THE UNITED METHODIST CHURCH
NOTES TO FINANCIAL STATEMENTS

NOTE 15 - CONTRIBUTION TO CAMPING MINISTRIES

Effective January 1, 2017, the Detroit Annual Conference along with the West Michigan Conference have elected to transfer all assets held on behalf of their camping and outdoor ministries to Michigan Area United Methodist Camping. The goal of the conferences is to centralize the camping and outdoor ministries program under one organization to focus on marketing and providing quality year-round camp and retreat facilities and programs that offer and promote Christian faith for people of diverse backgrounds and ages. Michigan Area United Methodist Camping (a non-profit organization) was incorporated May 2016 as a charitable, nonprofit provider under Section 501(c)3 of the Internal Revenue Code.

The following summarizes the items contributed to Michigan Area United Methodist Camping for the year ended December 31, 2017:

Cash and cash equivalents	$ 717,496
Investments	988,116
Property and equipment	2,542,151
Total contribution expense	$ 4,247,763

NOTE 16 - NEW ACCOUNTING STANDARD

In August 2016, the FASB issued ASU No. 2016-14, *"Presentation of Financial Statement of Not-for-Profit Entities" (Topic 958)*. The ASU amends the current reporting model for nonprofit organizations and enhances their required disclosures. The major changes include: (a) requiring the presentation of only two classes of net assets now entitled "net assets without donor restrictions" and "net assets with donor restrictions", (b) modifying the presentation of underwater endowment funds and related disclosures, (c) requiring the use of the placed in service approach to recognize the expirations of restrictions on gifts used to acquire or construct long-lived assets absent explicit donor stipulations otherwise, (d) requiring that all nonprofits present an analysis of expenses by function and nature in either the statement of activities, a separate statement, or in the notes and disclose a summary of the allocation methods used to allocate costs, (e) requiring the disclosure of quantitative and qualitative information regarding liquidity and availability of resources, (f) presenting investment return net of external and direct internal investment expenses, and (g) modifying other financial statement reporting requirements and disclosures intended to increase the usefulness of nonprofit financial statements. In addition, ASU 2016-14 removes the requirement that not-for-profit entities that chose to prepare the statements of cash flows using the direct method must also present a reconciliation (the indirect method). The Conference adopted ASU No. 2016-14 for the year ending December 31, 2018. The December 31, 2017 comparative information has been reclassified to conform to the current year presentation.

SUPPLEMENTARY INFORMATION

27

DETROIT ANNUAL CONFERENCE
COMBINING STATEMENT OF SUPPORT, REVENUE
AND OTHER RECEIPTS, EXPENSES, OTHER DISBURSEMENTS AND
CHANGES IN NET ASSETS - MODIFIED CASH BASIS
YEAR ENDED DECEMBER 31, 2018
(with comparative totals for the year ended December 31, 2017)

	2018				
	Connectional ministry and administration fund	Conference leadership team fund	Mission and ministry fund	General church apportionments fund	New church development fund
SUPPORT, REVENUE AND OTHER RECEIPTS:					
Support and revenue:					
Apportionments	$ 3,061,756	$ 1,557,058	$ -	$ 1,231,450	$ -
Special offerings/Ministry Jubilee	-	-		-	
Investment return, net	(3,755)	10,381	-	-	(121,187)
Other income	69,816	-	-	-	537,174
Net assets released from restrictions	-	-	343,779	-	-
Total support and revenue	3,127,817	1,567,439	343,779	1,231,450	415,987
Other receipts:					
Pension apportionment	-	-	-	-	-
Past years pension apportionments	-	-	-	-	-
Insurance reimbursements	-	-	-	-	-
Total support, revenue and other receipts	3,127,817	1,567,439	343,779	1,231,450	415,987
EXPENSES AND OTHER DISBURSEMENTS:					
Expenses:					
Salaries	1,138,404	579,996	-	-	72,662
Health insurance	211,416	94,930	-	-	-
Pension and post-employment benefit expense	50,246	2,933	-	-	-
Other employee costs	66,456	90,529	-	-	-
Training and continuing education	16,140	895	-	-	-
Travel, meeting and moving expenses	420,886	54,271	-	-	-
Operating and administrative expenses	936,928	160,249	-	-	-
Parsonage and building expenditures	48,487	-	-	-	-
Remittances to general church	322,776	-	-	1,232,872	-
Conference benevolence	57,304	711,010	463,701	-	497,291
Contributions	-	-	-	-	-
Depreciation	-	-	-	-	-
Total expenses	3,269,043	1,694,813	463,701	1,232,872	569,953
Other disbursements:					
Remittances to Board of Pensions	-	-	-	-	-
Health insurance	-	-	-	-	-
Total expenses and other disbursements	3,269,043	1,694,813	463,701	1,232,872	569,953
CHANGE IN NET ASSETS	(141,226)	(127,374)	(119,922)	(1,422)	(153,966)
NET ASSETS - beginning of year	459,977	1,393,592	(442,186)	-	1,284,262
NET ASSETS - end of year	$ 318,751	$ 1,266,218	$ (562,108)	$ (1,422)	$ 1,130,296

28

		2018					
Pension and health benefits fund	Plant fund	Other designated funds	Total without donor restrictions	With donor restrictions	Total	2017
$ -	$ -	$ -	$ 5,850,264	$ -	$ 5,850,264	$ 5,870,549
-	-	-	-	175,845	175,845	248,744
(380,852)	-	(81,215)	(576,628)	(5,959)	(582,587)	1,321,100
-	-	1,094,443	1,701,433	3,190	1,704,623	1,366,395
-	-	-	343,779	(343,779)	-	-
(380,852)	-	1,013,228	7,318,848	(170,703)	7,148,145	8,806,788
1,701,155	-	-	1,701,155	-	1,701,155	1,739,285
35,491	-	-	35,491	-	35,491	11,975
8,487,254	-	-	8,487,254	-	8,487,254	8,722,742
9,843,048	-	1,013,228	17,542,748	(170,703)	17,372,045	19,280,790
159,011	-	246,182	2,196,255	-	2,196,255	1,919,363
87,865	-	10,104	404,315	-	404,315	394,756
12,882	-	196	66,257	-	66,257	46,503
-	-	10,224	167,209	-	167,209	150,082
14,839	-	-	31,874	-	31,874	30,311
9,413	-	-	484,570	-	484,570	400,697
373,121	-	-	1,470,298	-	1,470,298	1,467,588
-	-	-	48,487	-	48,487	33,379
-	-	-	1,555,648	-	1,555,648	1,635,400
5,773	-	1,417,249	3,152,328	-	3,152,328	2,512,089
-	-	-	-	-	-	4,247,763
-	59,138	-	59,138	-	59,138	53,275
662,904	59,138	1,683,955	9,636,379	-	9,636,379	12,891,206
1,164,991	-	-	1,164,991	-	1,164,991	1,144,412
8,770,859	-	-	8,770,859	-	8,770,859	8,440,665
10,598,754	59,138	1,683,955	19,572,229	-	19,572,229	22,476,283
(755,706)	(59,138)	(670,727)	(2,029,481)	(170,703)	(2,200,184)	(3,195,493)
12,743,427	700,572	(2,311,704)	13,827,940	1,065,492	14,893,432	18,088,925
$ 11,987,721	$ 641,434	$ (2,982,431)	$ 11,798,459	$ 894,789	$ 12,693,248	$ 14,893,432

**COUNCIL OF FINANCE AND ADMINISTRATION OF THE
WEST MICHIGAN ANNUAL CONFERENCE OF THE
UNITED METHODIST CHURCH**

REPORT ON FINANCIAL STATEMENTS
(with supplementary information)

YEAR ENDED DECEMBER 31, 2018
(with comparative totals for the year ended December 31, 2017)

Maner
Costerisan
Certified Public Accountants
Business & Technology Advisors

C O N T E N T S

2

Maner Costerisan PC
2425 E. Grand River Ave.
Suite 1
Lansing, MI 48912-3291
T: 517 323 7500
F: 517 323 6346
www.manercpa.com

INDEPENDENT AUDITOR'S REPORT

To the Council of Finance and Administration of the
West Michigan Annual Conference of the United Methodist Church

Report on the Financial Statements

We have audited the accompanying financial statements of the Council of Finance and Administration of the West Michigan Annual Conference of the United Methodist Church which comprise the statements of assets, liabilities and net assets - modified cash basis as of December 31, 2018 and 2017, and the related statements of support, revenue and other receipts, expenses, other disbursements, and changes in net assets - modified cash basis and functional expenses - modified cash basis for the year ended December 31, 2018, and the related notes to the financial statements.

Management's Responsibility for the Financial Statements

Management is responsible for the preparation and fair presentation of these financial statements in accordance with the modified cash basis of accounting described in Note 1; this includes determining that the modified cash basis of accounting is an acceptable basis for the preparation of the financial statements in the circumstances. Management is also responsible for the design, implementation, and maintenance of internal control relevant to the preparation and fair presentation of financial statements that are free from material misstatement, whether due to fraud or error.

Auditor's Responsibility

Our responsibility is to express an opinion on these financial statements based on our audit. We conducted our audit in accordance with auditing standards generally accepted in the United States of America. Those standards require that we plan and perform the audit to obtain reasonable assurance about whether the financial statements are free from material misstatement.

An audit involves performing procedures to obtain audit evidence about the amounts and disclosures in the financial statements. The procedures selected depend on the auditor's judgment, including the assessment of the risks of material misstatement of the financial statements, whether due to fraud or error. In making those risk assessments, the auditor considers internal control relevant to the entity's preparation and fair presentation of the financial statements in order to design audit procedures that are appropriate in the circumstances, but not for the purpose of expressing an opinion on the effectiveness of the entity's internal control. Accordingly, we express no such opinion. An audit also includes evaluating the appropriateness of accounting policies used and the reasonableness of significant accounting estimates made by management, as well as evaluating the overall presentation of the financial statements.

3

We believe that the audit evidence we have obtained is sufficient and appropriate to provide a basis for our audit opinion.

Opinion

In our opinion, the financial statements referred to above present fairly, in all material respects, the assets, liabilities and net assets of the Council of Finance and Administration of the West Michigan Annual Conference of the United Methodist Church as of December 31, 2018 and 2017, and its support, revenue and other receipts, expenses, other disbursements and changes in net assets for the year ended December 31, 2018, in accordance with the basis of accounting as described in Note 1.

Report on Summarized Comparative Information

We have previously audited the Council of Finance and Administration of the West Michigan Annual Conference of the United Methodist Church's 2017 financial statements, and our report dated May 22, 2018, expressed an unmodified opinion on those audited financial statements. In our opinion, the summarized comparative information presented in the statement of support, revenue and other receipts, expenses, other disbursements and changes in net assets - modified cash basis and in the statement of functional expenses - modified cash basis for the year ended December 31, 2017 is consistent, in all material respects, with the audited financial statements from which it has been derived.

Basis of Accounting

We draw attention to Note 1 of the financial statements, which describes the basis of accounting. The financial statements are prepared on the modified cash basis of accounting, which is a basis of accounting other than accounting principles generally accepted in the United States of America. Our opinion is not modified with respect to that matter.

Report on Supplementary Information

Our audit was conducted for the purpose of forming an opinion on the financial statements as a whole. The supplementary information, as identified in the table of contents, is presented for purposes of additional analysis and is not a required part of the financial statements. Such information is the responsibility of management and was derived from and relates directly to the underlying accounting and other records used to prepare the financial statements. The information has been subjected to the auditing procedures applied in the audits of the financial statements and certain additional procedures, including comparing and reconciling such information directly to the underlying accounting and other records used to prepare the financial statements or to the financial statements themselves, and other additional procedures in accordance with auditing standards generally accepted in the United States of America. In our opinion, the information is fairly stated in all material respects in relation to the financial statements as a whole.

Maner Costerisan PC

May 21, 2019

4

COUNCIL OF FINANCE AND ADMINISTRATION OF THE
WEST MICHIGAN ANNUAL CONFERENCE OF THE UNITED METHODIST CHURCH
STATEMENTS OF ASSETS, LIABILITIES AND
NET ASSETS - MODIFIED CASH BASIS
DECEMBER 31, 2018 AND 2017

	2018	2017
ASSETS		
Cash and cash equivalents	$ 1,221,396	$ 1,285,066
Investments	22,491,345	24,210,155
Receipts in transit	561,929	174,995
Notes and loans receivable	128,476	254,302
Property and equipment - net	1,291,509	772,720
TOTAL ASSETS	$ 25,694,655	$ 26,697,238
LIABILITIES AND NET ASSETS		
LIABILITIES:		
Assets held on behalf of others	$ 1,416,528	$ 1,573,552
NET ASSETS:		
Without donor restrictions	23,553,682	24,514,857
With donor restrictions	724,445	608,829
Total net assets	24,278,127	25,123,686
TOTAL LIABILITIES AND NET ASSETS	$ 25,694,655	$ 26,697,238

See notes to financial statements.   5

**COUNCIL OF FINANCE AND ADMINISTRATION OF THE
WEST MICHIGAN ANNUAL CONFERENCE OF THE UNITED METHODIST CHURCH
STATEMENT OF SUPPORT, REVENUE AND OTHER RECEIPTS, EXPENSES,
OTHER DISBURSEMENTS AND CHANGES IN NET ASSETS - MODIFED CASH BASIS
YEAR ENDED DECEMBER 31, 2018
(with comparative totals for the year ended December 31, 2017)**

	2018			
	Without donor restrictions	With donor restrictions	Total	2017
SUPPORT, REVENUE AND OTHER RECEIPTS:				
Support and revenue:				
Ministry shares	$ 5,031,073	$ 7,008	$ 5,038,081	$ 5,361,057
Special offerings	-	879,359	879,359	1,368,498
Investment return, net	(1,355,410)	(6,641)	(1,362,051)	2,669,582
Registration fees	19,438	-	19,438	192,765
Other income	1,331,369	158,908	1,490,277	619,218
Net assets released from restrictions	923,018	(923,018)	-	-
Total support and revenue	5,949,488	115,616	6,065,104	10,211,120
Other receipts:				
Pension billings	2,386,433	-	2,386,433	1,780,436
Insurance billings	4,758,399	-	4,758,399	4,525,155
Total support, revenue and other receipts	13,094,320	115,616	13,209,936	16,516,711
EXPENSES AND OTHER DISBURSEMENTS:				
Expenses:				
Salaries	1,419,056	-	1,419,056	1,454,047
Health and life insurance	1,776,215	-	1,776,215	1,780,108
Pension and post-employment benefit expense	152,044	-	152,044	183,660
Other employee costs	141,997	-	141,997	140,041
Training and continuing education	43,689	-	43,689	45,192
Travel, meeting and moving expenses	366,524	-	366,524	643,606
Operating and administrative expenses	689,112	-	689,112	763,796
Parsonage and building expenditures	50,437	-	50,437	45,752
World Service	659,423	-	659,423	784,582
Programs and conference benevolence	1,925,684	-	1,925,684	2,369,486
Depreciation and amortization	33,526	-	33,526	35,152
Contribution to camping ministries	-	-	-	2,954,332
Remittances to General Conference	837,607	-	837,607	820,561
Total expenses	8,095,314	-	8,095,314	12,020,315
Other disbursements:				
Remittances to Board of Pensions	765,818	-	765,818	619,732
Health and life insurance	5,194,363	-	5,194,363	4,413,544
Total expenses and other disbursements	14,055,495	-	14,055,495	17,053,591
Change in net assets	(961,175)	115,616	(845,559)	(536,880)
Net assets - beginning of year	24,514,857	608,829	25,123,686	25,660,566
Net assets - end of year	$ 23,553,682	$ 724,445	$ 24,278,127	$ 25,123,686

See notes to financial statements.   6

COUNCIL OF FINANCE AND ADMINISTRATION OF THE
WEST MICHIGAN ANNUAL CONFERENCE OF THE UNITED METHODIST CHURCH
STATEMENT OF FUNCTIONAL EXPENSES - MODIFIED CASH BASIS
YEAR ENDED DECEMBER 31, 2018
(with comparative totals for the year ended December 31, 2017)

	Program services				
	Connectional ministry and administration	World Service and Conference Benevolence	Six Lanes and Advance Specials	Ministerial Education and Black College	Pension and Health Benefits and Life Insurance
Salaries	$ -	$ 395,902	$ -	$ -	$ -
Health and life insurance	-	89,955	-	-	1,439,300
Pension and post-employment benefit	-	29,415	-	-	-
Other employee costs	-	16,874	-	-	15,477
Training and continuing education	-	13,161	-	-	-
Travel, meeting and moving expenses	264,227	74,471	-	-	-
Operating and administrative expenses	-	110,338	-	-	-
Parsonage and building expenditures	-	-	-	-	-
World Service	-	659,423	-	-	-
Programs and conference benevolence	-	653,452	714,073	59,862	-
Depreciation and amortization	-	-	-	-	-
Contribution to camping ministries	-	-	-	-	-
Remittances to General Conference	-	31,787	108,623	313,525	-
	$ 264,227	$ 2,074,778	$ 822,696	$ 373,387	$ 1,454,777

See notes to financial statements.   7

COUNCIL OF FINANCE AND ADMINISTRATION OF THE
WEST MICHIGAN ANNUAL CONFERENCE OF THE UNITED METHODIST CHURCH
STATEMENT OF FUNCTIONAL EXPENSES - MODIFIED CASH BASIS
YEAR ENDED DECEMBER 31, 2018
(with comparative totals for the year ended December 31, 2017)

	Program services					
	New Church Development	Other program activity	Total	Management and general	Total	2017
Salaries	$ 115,997	$ 95,762	$ 607,661	$ 811,395	$ 1,419,056	$ 1,454,047
Health and life insurance	26,820	21,870	1,577,945	198,270	1,776,215	1,780,108
Pension and post-employment benefit	17,715	8,897	56,027	96,017	152,044	183,660
Other employee costs	10	16,728	49,089	92,908	141,997	140,041
Training and continuing education	2,653	25,510	41,324	2,365	43,689	45,192
Travel, meeting and moving expenses	-	-	338,698	27,826	366,524	643,606
Operating and administrative expenses	10,385	389,499	510,222	178,890	689,112	763,796
Parsonage and building expenditures	-	-	-	50,437	50,437	45,752
World Service	-	-	659,423	-	659,423	784,582
Programs and conference benevolence	199,400	15,792	1,642,579	283,105	1,925,684	2,369,486
Depreciation and amortization	-	-	-	33,526	33,526	35,152
Contribution to camping ministries	-	-	-	-	-	2,954,332
Remittances to General Conference	-	-	453,935	383,672	837,607	820,561
	$ 372,980	$ 574,058	$ 5,936,903	$ 2,158,411	$ 8,095,314	$ 12,020,315

See notes to financial statements.   8

COUNCIL OF FINANCE AND ADMINISTRATION OF THE
WEST MICHIGAN ANNUAL CONFERENCE OF THE UNITED METHODIST CHURCH
NOTES TO FINANCIAL STATEMENTS

NOTE 1 - SUMMARY OF SIGNIFICANT ACCOUNTING POLICIES

Basis of accounting - The books and records of the Council are maintained on the modified cash basis of accounting. Under this method, income is recognized when received and expenses are recorded at the time of payment except for the recognition of certain assets and liabilities related to the timing of local church contributions at year end, reimbursement of health insurance premiums, payroll deductions, investments, property and equipment, notes and loans receivable and assets held on behalf of others in an agency capacity. Additionally, certain amounts held on the Council's behalf at Wespath Benefits and Investments are not included in these financial statements and related cash flows attributable to local churches are reported as other receipts and disbursements. See Note 10.

Financial statement presentation - The statements of support, revenue and other receipts, expenses, other disbursements and changes in net assets - modified cash basis and functional expenses - modified cash basis include certain prior-year summarized comparative information in total but not by net asset class. Such information does not include sufficient detail to constitute a presentation in conformity with the modified cash basis of accounting. Accordingly, such information should be read in conjunction with the Council's prior-year financial statements from which the summarized information was derived.

Net assets - Net assets, revenues, gains and losses are classified based on the existence or absence of donor or grantor imposed restrictions. Accordingly, net assets and changes therein are classified and reported as follows:

Net assets without donor restrictions - Net assets available for use in general operations and not subject to donor or grantor restrictions.

Net assets with donor restrictions - Net assets subject to donor (or grantor) imposed restrictions. Some donor restrictions are temporary in nature, such as those that will be met by the passage of time or other events specified by the donor. Other donor restrictions are perpetual in nature, where the donor stipulates that resources are maintained in perpetuity. Gifts of long-lived assets and gifts of cash restricted for the acquisition of long-lived assets are recognized as revenue when the assets are placed in service. Donor restrictions are released when a restriction expires, that is, when the stipulated time has elapsed, or when the stipulated purpose has been accomplished (See Note 12).

COUNCIL OF FINANCE AND ADMINISTRATION OF THE
WEST MICHIGAN ANNUAL CONFERENCE OF THE UNITED METHODIST CHURCH
NOTES TO FINANCIAL STATEMENTS

NOTE 1 - SUMMARY OF SIGNIFICANT ACCOUNTING POLICIES (Continued)

Fund accounting - to facilitate observance of limitations and restrictions placed on the use of available resources, the accounts are maintained in accordance with the principles of fund accounting. Funds are established according to the nature and purpose of resources available to the Council. The assets, liabilities, net assets and financial activity of the Council are recorded in the following self-balancing fund groups:

➢ Connectional Ministry and Administration fund - resources available for current operations in supervision and administration of the mission and ministry of the West Michigan Annual Conference of the United Methodist Church.

➢ World Service and Conference Benevolence fund - resources available for distribution to the United Methodist denominational programs and the West Michigan Annual Conference of the United Methodist Church program agencies.

➢ Six Lanes and Advanced Specials fund - resources to allow churches direct involvement in the causes promoted by the Council agencies. Member churches select individual causes to fund from a listing prepared by the Council.

➢ Ministerial Education and Black College fund - resources available for providing financial support for the recruitment and education of ordained ministers and to provide financial support to traditionally black colleges related to the Church.

➢ Pension and Health Benefits and Life Insurance fund - resources available for support, relief, assistance and pensioning of clergy, lay workers for the various units of the Council and their families.

➢ Plant fund - property and equipment owned and used directly in the operation of the Council.

➢ Loan Program funds - resources used to assist local churches and camps in financing capital expenditures.

➢ New Church Development fund - resources available for new church development.

➢ Other funds - resources for designated purposes related to other programs the Council supports.

COUNCIL OF FINANCE AND ADMINISTRATION OF THE
WEST MICHIGAN ANNUAL CONFERENCE OF THE UNITED METHODIST CHURCH
NOTES TO FINANCIAL STATEMENTS

NOTE 1 - SUMMARY OF SIGNIFICANT ACCOUNTING POLICIES (Concluded)

Cash and cash equivalents includes all highly liquid investments purchased with an original maturity of 3 months or less.

Investments are recorded at fair value and consist of various debt and equity securities. Investments in money market funds are recorded at cost. Net investment return or loss is included in the statement of support, revenue and other receipts, expenses, other disbursements and changes in net assets - modified cash basis and consists of interest and dividend income, realized and unrealized gains and losses, less investment expenses.

Receipts in transit include contributions collected by local ministries during the years ended December 31, 2018 and 2017, but not received by the Council until after year end.

Notes and loans receivable consists of outstanding principal for loans the Council provided to local churches to help finance capital expenditures.

Property and equipment is capitalized at cost. Donated assets are recorded at fair value at date of donation. Parsonages are recorded at original cost plus the cost of subsequent additions. Depreciation is computed over the estimated useful life of assets using the straight-line method. Additions to property and equipment over $1,000 are capitalized. Cost of maintenance and repairs are charged to expense when incurred. The useful lives adopted for the purpose of computing depreciation are:

Parsonages and improvements	30 to 40 years
Furniture, equipment and vehicles	5 to 7 years

Assets held on behalf of others includes cash held in an agency capacity.

Functional allocation of expenses - The costs of providing program and other activities have been reported in the statement of support, revenue and other receipts, expenses, other disbursements and changes in net assets - modified cash basis. The statement of functional expenses - modified cash basis presents the natural classification of expenses that are allocated to program or supporting functions of the Council. Allocated expenses primarily consist of payroll and related and various other expense classifications necessary to support the day-to-day operations of the Council. Employee driven expenses are allocated based on salary and wage analysis. All other allocated expenses utilize management's estimated use of resources.

11

COUNCIL OF FINANCE AND ADMINISTRATION OF THE
WEST MICHIGAN ANNUAL CONFERENCE OF THE UNITED METHODIST CHURCH
NOTES TO FINANCIAL STATEMENTS

NOTE 2 - ORGANIZATION, RISKS AND UNCERTAINTIES

The Council of Finance and Administration of the West Michigan Annual Conference of the United Methodist Church (the Council) is a Michigan non-profit corporation. The purpose of the Council is to develop and administer a comprehensive and coordinated plan of fiscal and administrative policies, procedures, and management services for the annual conference. The member churches are located in the western half of the Lower Peninsula of Michigan. Using ministry shares and special offerings received from its member churches, the Council contributes to denominational ministries and provides support for various missions, educational programs and summer youth camps. The Council is exempt from income taxes under provisions of Section 501(c)(3) of the Internal Revenue Code.

The Council is required to disclose significant concentrations of credit risk regardless of the degree of such risk. Financial instruments which potentially subject the organization to concentrations of significant credit risk consist of cash and cash equivalents, and investments. The Council places its cash with FDIC insured financial institutions and thereby limits the amount of credit exposure to any one financial institution. Credit risk with respect to investments is limited due to the wide variety of companies and industries. Although such investments and cash balances may exceed the federally insured limits at certain times during the year and at year-end they are, in the opinion of management, subject to minimal risk. The Council maintains a diversified investment portfolio which is subject to market risk.

Investments are disclosed in Notes 5 and 6 and consist largely of amounts invested in various funds by the United Methodist Foundation of Michigan (UMF) as well as Wespath Benefits and Investments (WBI).

UMF Pooled Trust Fund - The fund is available for exclusive investment by the UMF arising from charitable contributions made through charitable remainder trusts, other charitable trusts, funds operating as charitable trusts, or gift annuity contracts. The primary investment objective of the fund is to provide for long term capital growth. The UMF also may consider investments in securities of other United Methodist organizations based primarily upon their religious affiliation and the desire of the UMF to support their ministry. The fund seeks to achieve its investment objectives by investing in a diversified portfolio of common stocks, bonds and money market instruments.

UMF Stock Fund - The fund seeks to achieve long-term capital appreciation through investments in stocks and other securities, with primary emphasis on U.S. large capitalization companies and secondary emphasis on global and international equities and on U.S. small and middle capitalization companies. The fund is subject to the general investment restrictions and the socially responsible investment criteria as adopted by the UMF.

COUNCIL OF FINANCE AND ADMINISTRATION OF THE
WEST MICHIGAN ANNUAL CONFERENCE OF THE UNITED METHODIST CHURCH
NOTES TO FINANCIAL STATEMENTS

NOTE 2 - ORGANIZATION, RISKS AND UNCERTAINTIES (Continued)

UMF Bond Fund - The fund's primary objective is to achieve a high level of current income, with capital appreciation as a secondary objective, by investing in investment-grade debt securities. The Fund invests in U.S. Treasury and agency securities, municipal securities, corporate bonds, mortgage back securities, preferred shares and other fixed income securities rated as investment grade by a Nationally Recognized Statistical Rating Organization. The fund is subject to the general investment restrictions and the socially responsible investment criteria as adopted by the UMF.

UMF Money Market Investment Account - The fund's objective is to seek maximum current income consistent with liquidity and the maintenance of a portfolio of high quality short-term money market securities. The fund attempts to achieve its objective by investing in a diversified portfolio of U.S. dollar denominated money market securities. These securities primarily consist of short term U.S. Government securities, U.S. Government agency securities, and securities issued by U.S. Government sponsored enterprises and U.S. Government instrumentalities, commercial paper and repurchase agreements.

WBI Short Term Investment Fund - The fund seeks to maximize current income consistent with preservation of capital. The fund seeks to achieve its investment objective through the exposure to short-term fixed income securities in the sweep account. The fund exclusively holds cash and cash equivalents in the form of units of the sweep account. The sweep account holds U.S. government bonds, agency bonds, corporate bonds, securitized projects, dollar denominated international fixed income securities, commercial paper, certificates of deposit, and other similar types of investments. The performance objective of the fund is to slightly outperform its performance benchmark, the Bank of America Merrill Lynch 3-Month Treasury Bill Index.

WBI Fixed Income Fund - The fund seeks to earn current income by investing in a broad mix of fixed-income instruments. The performance objective of the fund is to outperform the performance benchmark (Barclays Capital U.S. Universal Index, excluding Mortgage-Backed Securities) by 0.50% (net of fees) over a market cycle (5 to 7 years). The fund is primarily composed of a broad range of fixed-income instruments, such as U.S. and non-U.S. government bonds, agency bonds, corporate bonds, mortgage-backed securities and asset-backed securities.

WBI International Equity Fund - The fund seeks to attain long-term capital appreciation from a diversified portfolio of non-U.S. domiciled, publicly owned companies, and to a lesser extent, international privately-owned companies, private real estate and equity index futures. The performance objective of the fund is to outperform the investment returns of its performance benchmark, the MSCI All Country World Index (ACWI) by 0.75% on average per year over a market cycle (5 to 7 years).

WBI U.S. Equity Fund - The fund seeks to earn long-term capital appreciation from a broadly diversified portfolio of U.S. listed equities and traded on a regulated U.S. equity exchange. The performance objective of the fund is to match the investment returns of its performance benchmark, the Russell 3000 Index, by 0.35% on average per year over a market cycle (5 to 7 years).

13

COUNCIL OF FINANCE AND ADMINISTRATION OF THE
WEST MICHIGAN ANNUAL CONFERENCE OF THE UNITED METHODIST CHURCH
NOTES TO FINANCIAL STATEMENTS

NOTE 2 - ORGANIZATION, RISKS AND UNCERTAINTIES (Concluded)

WBI U.S. Equity Index Fund - The fund seeks to earn long-term capital appreciation from a passively managed broadly diversified portfolio of U.S. listed equities. The performance objective of the fund is to match the investment returns of its performance benchmark, the Russell 3000 Index, over a market cycle (5 to 7 years).

WBI Multiple Asset Fund - The fund seeks to maximize long-term investment returns, including current income and capital appreciation, while reducing short-term risk by investing in a broad mix of investments. The performance objective of the fund is to outperform the investment returns of its performance benchmark (35% Russell 3000 Index, 30% MSCI ACWI excluding USA IMI, 25% Barclays U.S. Universal Index excluding Mortgage Backed Securities, and 10% Inflation Protection Fund Custom Benchmark by 0.8% on average per year (net of fees) over a market cycle (5 to 7 years).

The process of preparing financial statements requires the use of estimates and assumptions regarding certain types of assets, revenues, and expenditures. Such estimates primarily relate to unsettled transactions and events as of the date of the financial statements. Accordingly, upon settlement, actual results may differ from estimated amounts.

Tax positions are taken based on interpretation of federal, state and local income tax laws. Management periodically reviews and evaluates the status of uncertain tax positions and makes estimates of amounts, including interest and penalties, ultimately due or owed. No amounts have been identified, or recorded, as uncertain tax positions. Federal, state and local tax returns generally remain open for examination by the various taxing authorities for a period of 3 to 4 years.

The Council evaluates events and transactions that occur after year end for potential recognition or disclosure in the financial statements. As of May 21, 2019, which is the date the financial statements were available to be issued, there were no subsequent events which required recognition or disclosure.

NOTE 3 - MICHIGAN UNITED METHODISTS VOTE TO BECOME ONE

In a live state-wide web address held on June 10, 2015, Michigan Area Bishop Deborah Lieder Kiesey, announced that the Detroit Annual Conference and the West Michigan Annual Conference have voted to create a single organizational body in Michigan by January 1, 2019. The decision will impact over 140,000 professing members in the state, attending nearly 850 local churches.

14

**COUNCIL OF FINANCE AND ADMINISTRATION OF THE
WEST MICHIGAN ANNUAL CONFERENCE OF THE UNITED METHODIST CHURCH
NOTES TO FINANCIAL STATEMENTS**

NOTE 4 - LIQUIDITY AND AVAILABILITY

The Council regularly monitors the availability of resources required to meet its operating needs and other contractual commitments, while also striving to maximize the investment of its available funds. For purposes of analyzing resources available to meet general expenditures over a 12-month period, the Council considers all expenditures related to its ongoing program service activities as well as the conduct of services undertaken to support those activities to be general expenditures.

The following reflects the Council's financial assets as of December 31, 2018, which are deemed available for general expenditures within one year of the date of the statement of assets, liabilities and net assets - modified cash basis:

Financial assets	
Cash and cash equivalents	$ 1,221,396
Investments	22,491,345
Receipts in transit	561,929
Notes and loans receivable, current portion	52,576
Total financial assets	24,327,246
Contractual or donor-imposed restrictions:	
Less: net assets with donor restrictions	(724,445)
Financial assets available to meet cash needs	
for general expenditures within one year	23,602,801
Funds budgeted for future pension and benefit obligations	(20,235,972)
	$ 3,366,829

In addition to financial assets available to meet general expenditures over the next 12 months, the Council operates with a balanced budget and anticipates collecting sufficient revenue to cover general expenditures. The Council also maintains a line of credit available to meet short-term needs. The Council is substantially supported by contribution revenue. Because a donor's restriction may require resources to be used in a particular manner or in a future period, the Council must maintain sufficient resources to meet those requirements. Therefore, certain financial assets may not be available for general expenditure within one year. The Council structures its financial assets to be available as its general expenditures, liabilities and other obligations come due.

NOTE 5 - INVESTMENTS

The Council invests certain amounts with the United Methodist Foundation of Michigan (UMF). The UMF was formed as a nonprofit organization by member churches of the West Michigan Annual Conference and Detroit Annual Conference. It is governed and monitored by its own independent commission. The UMF's primary purpose is to broaden the financial base of member churches by assisting in and receiving planned and deferred gifts, assisting in the set-up and marketing of endowment funds, and the generation of market-level returns on invested monies through the use of investment pools.

15

COUNCIL OF FINANCE AND ADMINISTRATION OF THE
WEST MICHIGAN ANNUAL CONFERENCE OF THE UNITED METHODIST CHURCH
NOTES TO FINANCIAL STATEMENTS

NOTE 5 - INVESTMENTS (Continued)

The Council also invests funds with Wespath Benefits and Investments, which is a not-for-profit administrative agency of The United Methodist Church, responsible for the general supervision and administration of investments and benefit services according to the principles of The United Methodist Church.

Investments at December 31 consist of the following:

	2018	2017
Direct investments:		
Mutual funds:		
Consumer goods	$ -	$ 1,957
Common stocks:		
Basic materials	284,493	288,752
Financials	1,531,938	1,721,497
Industrial goods	768,207	520,298
Health care	1,838,639	1,287,619
Technology	2,333,394	2,452,998
Consumer goods	1,203,114	998,946
Conglomerates	82,231	264,789
Services	634,456	1,295,374
REITs	494,206	322,123
Utilities	247,945	446,067
Retail services	87,601	96,340
Energy	483,149	1,071,510
Food and beverages	548,072	602,236
Insurance	239,854	489,265
Corporate bonds	2,069,712	2,113,322
Money market	633,734	495,036
Government and agency securities	2,516,216	2,594,956
Pooled funds managed by the Foundation:		
UMF Pooled Trust Fund	10,734	12,057
UMF Stock Fund	828,716	1,152,666
UMF Bond Fund	498,716	658,973
Pooled funds managed by		
Wespath Benefits and Investments:		
Short Term Investment Fund	861,261	571,491
Fixed Income Fund	633,009	869,348
International Equity Fund	245,375	200,093
U.S. Equity Fund	531,055	482,636
U.S. Equity Index Fund	52,324	55,072
Multiple Asset Fund	2,833,194	3,144,734
Total investments	$ 22,491,345	$ 24,210,155

16

COUNCIL OF FINANCE AND ADMINISTRATION OF THE
WEST MICHIGAN ANNUAL CONFERENCE OF THE UNITED METHODIST CHURCH
NOTES TO FINANCIAL STATEMENTS

NOTE 5 - INVESTMENTS (Concluded)

Investment return, net from cash deposits and investments consist of the following for the year ended December 31:

	2018	2017
Interest and dividends, net	$ 99,254	$ 394,734
Realized and unrealized gain (loss)	(1,461,305)	2,274,848
Total investment return, net	$ (1,362,051)	$ 2,669,582

NOTE 6 - FAIR VALUE MEASUREMENTS

Accounting standards establish a hierarchy that prioritizes the inputs to valuation techniques giving the highest priority to readily available unadjusted quoted prices in active markets for identical assets (Level 1 measurements) and the lowest priority to unobservable inputs (Level 3 measurements) when market prices are not readily available or reliable. The three levels of the hierarchy are described below:

Level 1: Quoted prices in active markets for identical securities.

Level 2: Prices determined using other significant observable inputs. Observable inputs are inputs that other market participants may use in pricing a security. These may include quoted prices for similar securities, interest rates, prepayment speeds, credit risk and others.

Level 3: Prices determined using significant unobservable inputs. In situations where quoted prices or observable inputs are unavailable or deemed less relevant (for example, when there is little or no market activity for an investment at the end of the period), unobservable inputs may be used. Unobservable inputs reflect the Council's own assumptions about the factors market participants would use in pricing an investment, and would be based on the best information available.

From time to time, changes in valuation techniques may result in reclassification of an investment's assigned level within the hierarchy.

The asset or liability's fair value measurement level within the fair value hierarchy is based on the lowest level of any input that is significant to the fair value measurement. Valuation techniques used need to maximize the use of observable inputs and minimize the use of unobservable inputs. The following is a description of valuation methodologies used to determine how an asset is measured at fair value. There have been no changes in the methodologies used at December 31, 2018 and 2017.

COUNCIL OF FINANCE AND ADMINISTRATION OF THE
WEST MICHIGAN ANNUAL CONFERENCE OF THE UNITED METHODIST CHURCH
NOTES TO FINANCIAL STATEMENTS

NOTE 6 - FAIR VALUE MEASUREMENTS (Continued)

Mutual funds: Valued at the daily closing price as reported by the fund. Mutual funds held by the Council are open-end mutual funds that are registered with the Securities and Exchange Commission. These funds are required to publish their daily net asset value (NAV) and to transact at that price. The mutual funds held by the Council are deemed to be actively traded.

Equities: For its investments with asset managers that hold public common, preferred stocks, and other equity securities, the Council has position-level transparency into individual holdings. These investments are priced using nationally recognized pricing services based on observable market data.

Corporate bonds: The bonds held by the Council generally do not trade in active markets on the measurement date. Therefore these investments are valued using inputs including yields currently available on comparable securities of issuers with similar credit ratings, recent market price quotations (where observable), bond spreads, and fundamental data relating to the issuer.

Government Securities: Government securities consist of treasury notes and various other government agency securities. These are valued using pricing models maximizing the use of observable inputs for similar securities.

Unit investment trusts: Unit investment trusts consist of open-ended pooled funds. The fair value of these investments is determined by each manager using either in-house or third-party securities valuation firms. The securities valuation firms generate fair value amounts based on numerous inputs and other information received from the underlying partnership. As such, these investments are valued at the net asset value of the units (ownership percentage) held by the Conference and are excluded from the fair value hierarchy.

Limited partnerships: The limited partnerships consist of pooled investment and private equity funds. The fair value of these investments is determined by each manager using either in-house or third-party securities valuation firms. The securities valuation firms generate fair value amounts based on numerous inputs and other information received from the underlying partnership. As such, these investments are valued at the net asset value of the units (ownership percentage) held by the Conference and are excluded from the fair value hierarchy.

Pooled funds: Reported by the United Methodist Foundation (UMF) and Wespath Benefits and Investments to the Conference, these pooled funds represent the allocable share of the underlying investments. These investments include numerous securities that are combined with the investment portfolios of other organizations held by the UMF and Wespath Benefits and Investments. As such, these investments are valued at the net asset value of the units held by the Conference and are excluded from the fair value hierarchy.

COUNCIL OF FINANCE AND ADMINISTRATION OF THE
WEST MICHIGAN ANNUAL CONFERENCE OF THE UNITED METHODIST CHURCH
NOTES TO FINANCIAL STATEMENTS

NOTE 6 - FAIR VALUE MEASUREMENTS (Concluded)

The preceding methods described may produce a fair value calculation that may not be indicative of net realizable value or reflective of future fair values. Furthermore, although the Council believes its valuation methods are appropriate and consistent with other market participants, the use of different methodologies or assumptions to determine the fair value of certain financial instruments could result in different fair value measurements.

The following is a market value summary by the level of the inputs used in evaluating the Council's assets carried at fair value at December 31. The inputs or methodology used for valuing securities may not be an indication of the risk associated with investing in those securities.

	2018	2017
Level 1:		
Mutual funds:		
Consumer goods	$ -	$ 1,957
Common stocks:		
Basic materials	284,493	288,752
Financials	1,531,938	1,721,497
Industrial goods	768,207	520,298
Health care	1,838,639	1,287,619
Technology	2,333,394	2,452,998
Consumer goods	1,203,114	998,946
Conglomerates	82,231	264,789
Services	634,456	1,295,374
Energy	483,149	1,071,510
Retail services	87,601	96,340
REITs	494,206	322,123
Utilities	247,945	446,067
Food and beverages	548,072	602,236
Insurance	239,854	489,265
Level 2:		
Corporate bonds	2,069,712	2,113,322
Government and agency securities	2,516,216	2,594,956
Total investments measured at fair value	15,363,227	16,568,049
Money market funds at cost	633,734	495,036
Investments measured at net asset value	6,494,384	7,147,070
Total investments	$ 22,491,345	$ 24,210,155

**COUNCIL OF FINANCE AND ADMINISTRATION OF THE
WEST MICHIGAN ANNUAL CONFERENCE OF THE UNITED METHODIST CHURCH
NOTES TO FINANCIAL STATEMENTS**

NOTE 7 - PROPERTY AND EQUIPMENT

Property and equipment consist of the following at December 31.

	2018		2017	
Parsonages:				
Conference	$	1,070,346	$	518,031
Area		209,469		209,469
Conference center furniture and equipment		605,236		605,236
Conference offices furniture, equipment and vehicles		149,402		149,402
Area office furniture and equipment		41,690		41,690
		2,076,143		1,523,828
Less accumulated depreciation		784,634		751,108
Net property and equipment	$	1,291,509	$	772,720
Conference parsonages:				
DCM	$	599,093	$	256,981
Grand Traverse Superintendent		261,050		261,050
Midwest District Superintendent		210,203		-
Total conference parsonages	$	1,070,346	$	518,031
Area parsonages:				
15160 Duxbury Lane, DeWitt Township	$	209,469	$	209,469

The area parsonages are owned jointly with the Detroit Annual Conference. The above amount represents the Council of Finance and Administration of the West Michigan Annual Conference's share, which approximates 42% of the original cost basis of the property.

Land included in the parsonages listed above amounted to approximately $220,000 and $125,000 at December 31, 2018 and 2017.

**COUNCIL OF FINANCE AND ADMINISTRATION OF THE
WEST MICHIGAN ANNUAL CONFERENCE OF THE UNITED METHODIST CHURCH
NOTES TO FINANCIAL STATEMENTS**

NOTE 8 - NOTES AND LOANS RECEIVABLE

Notes and loans receivable consist of the following, as of December 31.

	2018	2017
Note receivable from the Millville UMC, with monthly payments of $2,153, including interest of 3% maturing December 2020.	$ -	$ 74,412
Note receivable from the Climax/Scotts UMC, with monthly payments of $845, including interest of 3% maturing June 2019.	3,376	14,774
Note receivable from the Valley UMC, with monthly payments of $971, including interest of 3% maturing April 2027.	85,100	94,028
Note receivable from the Courtland-Oakfield UMC, with monthly payments of $1,402, including interest of 3% paid off in 2018	-	31,088
Note receivable from the Michigan Area Headquarters with interest of 0%, the entire balance is due January 2019, unsecured.	40,000	40,000
	$ 128,476	$ 254,302

Maturities of financing receivables at December 31 are as follows:

Years ending December 31,	
2019	$ 52,576
2020	9,480
2021	9,768
2022	10,065
2023	10,371
Thereafter	36,216
	$ 128,476

COUNCIL OF FINANCE AND ADMINISTRATION OF THE
WEST MICHIGAN ANNUAL CONFERENCE OF THE UNITED METHODIST CHURCH
NOTES TO FINANCIAL STATEMENTS

NOTE 8 - NOTES AND LOANS RECEIVABLE (Concluded)

Notes receivable are carried at unpaid principal balances, less an allowance for doubtful collection. Management periodically evaluates the adequacy of the allowance based on past experience and potential adverse situations that may affect the borrower's ability to repay. It is management's policy to write off a loan only when they are deemed permanently uncollectible. As of December 31, 2018 and 2017, management believes that no allowance is necessary.

The classification of notes receivable regarding age and interest accrual status at December 31 are as follows:

	2018			2017		
	Principal	Interest	Total	Principal	Interest	Total
Current	$ 128,476	$ -	$ 128,476	$ 254,302	$ -	$ 254,302

NOTE 9 - LEASES

The Council leases office space in Grand Rapids, set to expire December 31, 2022. The future minimum lease payments for the Council are as follows:

Year ending December 31,	
2019	$ 24,205
2020	24,931
2021	25,679

Beginning January 1, 2019, the West Michigan Annual Conference and the Detroit Annual Conference will join to become a single organizational body located in Dewitt, Michigan. Lease obligations for both conferences will transfer to the new organization. The Detroit Annual Conference leases office space for approximately $50,000 per year in Dewitt which is set to expire December 31, 2022.

22

COUNCIL OF FINANCE AND ADMINISTRATION OF THE
WEST MICHIGAN ANNUAL CONFERENCE OF THE UNITED METHODIST CHURCH
NOTES TO FINANCIAL STATEMENTS

NOTE 10 - PENSION AND OTHER POST-EMPLOYMENT BENEFITS

From 1982 through 2006, the Council contributed to the Ministerial Pension Plan (MPP) that was administered by Wespath Benefits and Investments to fund clergy retirement benefits. Wespath Benefits and Investments has taken the position that the Council is responsible for funding any shortfall in benefits. Beginning January 1, 2019, the West Michigan Annual Conference and the Detroit Annual Conference will join to become a single organizational body and pension obligations for both conferences will transfer to the new organization. As a result, the combined total estimated actuarial liability based on the actuarial calculation as of January 1, 2017 is projected to be $129,842,074 in 2019. The expected combined contribution for both organizations for 2019 is $0.

The Council participates in a voluntary multi-employer defined contribution pension plan that covers substantially all Council lay and clergy employees. The Council contributes between 9% and 12% of each participant's annual wages. Contributions made by the Council approximated $45,000 and $55,000 for each of the years ended December 31, 2018 and 2017, respectively.

Additionally, the Council participates in a defined benefit pension plan that is frozen (Pre-1982 Plan). The Plan is administered by Wespath Benefits and Investments. The Council's plan assets exceeded the estimated actuarial plan liability based on the actuarial calculation as of January 1, 2017 by $4,505,476 or 105% for 2019. The Council's plan assets exceeded the estimated actuarial plan liability based on the most recent actuarial calculation as of January 1, 2018 by $5,868,884 or 107% for 2020.

Effective January 1, 2007, the Council adopted the Clergy Retirement Security Program (CRSP-DB). This program is an amendment and restatement of the previous clergy pension program. Regular contributions made by the Council approximated $370,000 and $375,000 for the years ended December 31, 2018 and 2017, respectively. The Council was also required to make additional contributions of $1,322,786 and $1,400,963 for the years ended December 31, 2018 and 2017, respectively. Beginning January 1, 2019, the West Michigan Annual Conference and the Detroit Annual Conference will join to become a single organizational body and pension obligations for both conferences will transfer to the new organization. The combined expected contribution based on the most recent actuarial calculation as of January 1, 2017 was projected to be $2,873,999 for 2019.

The Council's policy is to fund the majority of costs of qualified retirees' (clergy and lay employees) health care coverage. Such costs are expensed when paid and amounted to approximately $1,195,000 and $1,168,000 for the years ended December 31, 2018 and 2017, respectively. Based on the most recent actuarial calculation dated December 27, 2017, the post-employment medical benefit liability is projected to reflect an estimated unfunded amount of $6,163,000 as of January 1, 2017.

**COUNCIL OF FINANCE AND ADMINISTRATION OF THE
WEST MICHIGAN ANNUAL CONFERENCE OF THE UNITED METHODIST CHURCH
NOTES TO FINANCIAL STATEMENTS**

NOTE 11 - RELATED PARTY TRANSACTIONS

The Council conducts essentially all transactions, other than purchases of goods and services and sales of certain property, with affiliated congregations. Certain administrative expenses are reimbursed by related organizations. The Council also processes payroll transactions for affiliated organizations at no charge. The value of these services has not been determined but is not considered significant to the financial statements.

In August 2013, the Michigan Area United Methodist Ministry Center and the Michigan Area Headquarters entered into an $825,000 mortgage agreement, the proceeds of which were used for the acquisition of office space for Headquarters. The Council has entered into an agreement with the Headquarters and the Detroit Annual Conference of the United Methodist Church to provide support to the Headquarters for the mortgage payments. Payments are to be sufficient to repay the underlying mortgage note plus interest at 4.74% per annum. The Council's estimated portion of remaining payments is as follows:

Year ending December 31,	Principal	Interest	Total commitment
2019	$ 323,590	$ 10,011	$ 333,601

24

**COUNCIL OF FINANCE AND ADMINISTRATION OF THE
WEST MICHIGAN ANNUAL CONFERENCE OF THE UNITED METHODIST CHURCH
NOTES TO FINANCIAL STATEMENTS**

NOTE 12 - NET ASSETS

Net assets activity with donor restrictions are available for the following purposes at December 31, 2018:

	2017	Inflows	Outflows	2018
Subject to expenditures for specified purpose:				
New Church Investment fund - restricted for development of new churches	$ 183,462	$ (4,641)	$ -	$ 178,821
Special offerings - contributions designated by local churches	265,747	208,419	(219,750)	254,416
Ministerial training - restricted for the training of clergy	149,013	834,856	(703,268)	280,601
Total purpose restricted net assets	598,222	1,038,634	(923,018)	713,838
Endowment fund:				
Original gifts in perpetuity subject to spending policy and appropriations:				
World service	10,607	-	-	10,607
Total net assets with donor restrictions	$ 608,829	$ 1,038,634	$ (923,018)	$ 724,445

25

COUNCIL OF FINANCE AND ADMINISTRATION OF THE
WEST MICHIGAN ANNUAL CONFERENCE OF THE UNITED METHODIST CHURCH
NOTES TO FINANCIAL STATEMENTS

NOTE 12 - NET ASSETS (Concluded)

Net assets activity with donor restrictions are available for the following purposes at December 31, 2017:

	2016	Inflows	Outflows	2017
Subject to expenditures for specified purpose:				
New Church Investment fund - restricted for development of new churches	$ 71,291	$ 112,171	$ -	$ 183,462
Campgrounds - restricted for the upkeep and running of camps	790,193	-	(790,193)	-
Special offerings - contributions designated by local churches	171,500	333,261	(239,014)	265,747
Ministerial training - restricted for the training of clergy	144,017	1,149,512	(1,144,516)	149,013
Total purpose restricted net assets	1,177,001	1,594,944	(2,173,723)	598,222
Endowment fund:				
Original gifts in perpetuity subject to spending policy and appropriations:				
World service	10,607	-	-	10,607
Total net assets with donor restrictions	$ 1,187,608	$ 1,594,944	$ (2,173,723)	$ 608,829

26

COUNCIL OF FINANCE AND ADMINISTRATION OF THE
WEST MICHIGAN ANNUAL CONFERENCE OF THE UNITED METHODIST CHURCH
NOTES TO FINANCIAL STATEMENTS

NOTE 13 - ENDOWMENTS

Endowments consist of funds established for a variety of purposes and may include both donor-restricted funds and funds internally designated to function as endowments. Net assets associated with endowment funds, both donor restricted and funds designated by the Council, are reported based on the existence or absence of donor-imposed restrictions.

The Council has interpreted the Michigan Uniform Prudent Management of Institutional Funds Act (MUPMIFA) as permitting the preservation of the historical value of the original gift of the donor-restricted endowment funds absent explicit donor stipulations to the contrary. As a result, when directed by the gift instrument, the Council classifies as net assets with donor restrictions (a time restriction in perpetuity) (a) the original value of gifts donated to the donor restricted endowment, (b) the original value of subsequent gifts to the donor restricted endowment, and (c) accumulations to the donor restricted endowment made in accordance with the direction of the applicable donor gift instrument. Investment income from the donor restricted endowment is classified as net assets with donor restrictions (a purpose restriction) until those amounts are appropriated for expenditure by the Council in a manner consistent with the donor stipulated purpose within the standard of prudence prescribed by MUPMIFA. In accordance with MUPMIFA, the Organization considers the following factors in making a determination to appropriate or accumulate donor restricted endowment funds:

1. The duration and preservation of the fund.
2. The purposes of the donor-restricted endowment fund.
3. General economic conditions.
4. The possible effect of inflation and deflation.
5. The expected total return from income and the appreciation of investments.
6. Other resources of the organization.
7. The investment policies of the Council.

The Council's investment and spending practices for endowment assets attempt to provide a predictable stream of funding to programs supported while seeking to maintain the purchasing power of the endowment assets.

From time to time, certain donor-restricted endowment funds may have fair values less than the amount required to be maintained by donors or by law (underwater endowments). We have interpreted MUPMIFA to permit spending from underwater endowments in accordance with prudent measures required under law. There were no such deficiencies for the years ended December 31, 2018 and 2017, respectively

27

COUNCIL OF FINANCE AND ADMINISTRATION OF THE
WEST MICHIGAN ANNUAL CONFERENCE OF THE UNITED METHODIST CHURCH
NOTES TO FINANCIAL STATEMENTS

NOTE 13 - ENDOWMENTS (Concluded)

Endowment net assets composition as of December 31, 2018 and 2017:

	With donor restrictions		
	Accumulated investment gains	Original gift in perpetuity by donor	Total
Endowment net assets January 1, 2017	$ 790,193	$ 10,607	$ 800,800
Appropriated for expenditure	(790,193)	-	(790,193)
Endowment net assets December 31, 2017	-	10,607	10,607
Appropriated for expenditure	-	-	-
Endowment net assets December 31, 2018	$ -	$ 10,607	$ 10,607

NOTE 14 - CONTINGENCIES

From time to time the Council is involved in various legal proceedings that have arisen in the ordinary course of business. Management does not believe that the outcome of these proceedings, either individually or in the aggregate, will have a material adverse effect on the Council's financial position or future results of operations.

Effective September 1, 2009 the Council became primarily self-insured, up to certain limits, for health claims through Professional Benefits Services. The plan includes all participating Council employees as well as affiliated congregation clergy. The Council has purchased stop-loss insurance, which will reimburse the Council for individual policies that exceed $100,000 annually. Claims are expensed as paid. The total claims expense under the program was approximately $4,975,000 and $4,500,000 for Council employees for the years ended December 31, 2018 and 2017, respectively. The Council is reimbursed for stop loss premiums and claims paid for affiliates covered under the plan. The total amount of claims incurred but not reported attributable to the Council has not been determined, however, claims incurred in December estimated in the amount of $143,000 were paid in 2019.

**COUNCIL OF FINANCE AND ADMINISTRATION OF THE
WEST MICHIGAN ANNUAL CONFERENCE OF THE UNITED METHODIST CHURCH
NOTES TO FINANCIAL STATEMENTS**

NOTE 15 - CONTRIBUTION TO CAMPING MINISTRIES

Effective January 1, 2017, the West Michigan Conference along with the Detroit Annual Conference have elected to transfer all assets held on behalf of their camping and outdoor ministries to Michigan Area United Methodist Camping. The goal of the conferences is to centralize the camping and outdoor ministries program under one organization to focus on marketing and providing quality year-round camp and retreat facilities and programs that offer and promote Christian faith for people of diverse backgrounds and ages. Michigan Area United Methodist Camping (a non-profit organization) was incorporated May 2016 as a charitable, nonprofit provider under Section 501(c)3 of the Internal Revenue Code.

The following summarizes the items contributed to Michigan Area United Methodist Camping:

Cash and cash equivalents	$ 508,725
Investments	799,576
Property and equipment	1,646,031
Total contribution expense	$ 2,954,332

NOTE 16 - NEW ACCOUNTING STANDARD

In August 2016, the FASB issued ASU No. 2016-14, *"Presentation of Financial Statement of Not-for-Profit Entities" (Topic 958)*. The ASU amends the current reporting model for nonprofit organizations and enhances their required disclosures. The major changes include: (a) requiring the presentation of only two classes of net assets now entitled "net assets without donor restrictions" and "net assets with donor restrictions", (b) modifying the presentation of underwater endowment funds and related disclosures, (c) requiring the use of the placed in service approach to recognize the expirations of restrictions on gifts used to acquire or construct long-lived assets absent explicit donor stipulations otherwise, (d) requiring that all nonprofits present an analysis of expenses by function and nature in either the statement of activities, a separate statement, or in the notes and disclose a summary of the allocation methods used to allocate costs, (e) requiring the disclosure of quantitative and qualitative information regarding liquidity and availability of resources, (f) presenting investment return net of external and direct internal investment expenses, and (g) modifying other financial statement reporting requirements and disclosures intended to increase the usefulness of nonprofit financial statements. In addition, ASU 2016-14 removes the requirement that not-for-profit entities that chose to prepare the statements of cash flows using the direct method must also present a reconciliation (the indirect method). The Organization adopted ASU No. 2016-14 for the year ending December 31, 2018. The December 31, 2017 comparative information has been reclassified to conform to the current year presentation.

SUPPLEMENTARY INFORMATION

30

**COUNCIL OF FINANCE AND ADMINISTRATION OF THE
WEST MICHIGAN ANNUAL CONFERENCE OF THE UNITED METHODIST CHURCH
COMBINING STATEMENT OF SUPPORT, REVENUE AND OTHER RECEIPTS, EXPENSES,
OTHER DISBURSEMENTS AND CHANGES IN NET ASSETS - MODIFIED CASH BASIS
YEAR ENDED DECEMBER 31, 2018
(with comparative totals for the year ended December 31, 2017)**

	2018				
	Connectional Ministry and Administration fund	World Service and Conference Benevolence fund	Six Lanes and Advance Specials fund	Ministerial Education and Black College fund	Pension and Health Benefits and Life Insurance fund
SUPPORT, REVENUE AND OTHER RECEIPTS:					
Support and revenue:					
Ministry shares	$ 2,457,456	$ 1,956,274	$ -	$ 387,098	$ -
Special offerings	-	-	-		-
Investment return, net	(485,498)	(1,884)	-	-	(836,258)
Registration fees	90	18,605	-	-	-
Other income	965,354	32,137	-	-	61,963
Net assets released from restrictions	-	7,665	822,696	-	-
Total support and revenue	2,937,402	2,012,797	822,696	387,098	(774,295)
Other receipts:					
Pension billings	-	-	-	-	2,386,433
Insurance billings	56,861	-	-	-	4,701,538
Total support, revenue and other receipts	2,994,263	2,012,797	822,696	387,098	6,313,676
EXPENSES AND OTHER DISBURSEMENTS:					
Expenses:					
Salaries	811,395	395,902	-	-	-
Health and life insurance	198,270	89,955	-	-	1,439,300
Pension and post-employment benefit expense	96,017	29,415	-	-	-
Other employee costs	92,908	16,874	-	-	15,477
Training and continuing education	2,365	13,161	-	-	-
Travel, meeting and moving expenses	264,227	74,471	-	-	410
Operating and administrative expenses	75,861	110,338	-	-	103,006
Parsonage and building expenditures	50,437	-	-	-	-
World Service	-	659,423	-	-	-
Programs and conference benevolence	283,105	653,452	714,073	59,862	-
Depreciation and amortization	-	-	-	-	-
Contribution to camping ministries	-	-	-	-	-
Remittances to general conference	383,672	31,787	108,623	313,525	-
Total expenses	2,258,257	2,074,778	822,696	373,387	1,558,193
Other disbursements:					
Remittances to Board of Pensions	-	-	-	-	765,818
Health and life insurance	-	-	-	-	5,194,363
Total expenses and other disbursements	2,258,257	2,074,778	822,696	373,387	7,518,374
Change in net assets before transfers	736,006	(61,981)	-	13,711	(1,204,698)
Transfers	-	-	-	-	-
Change in net assets	736,006	(61,981)	-	13,711	(1,204,698)
Net assets - beginning of year	1,419,215	471,147	-	(3,424)	20,686,494
Net assets - end of year	$ 2,155,221	$ 409,166	$ -	$ 10,287	$ 19,481,796

31

		2018					
Plant fund	Loan Program funds	New Church Development fund	Other funds	Total without donor restrictions	With donor restrictions	Totals	2017
$ -	$ -	$ 230,245	$ -	$ 5,031,073	$ 7,008	$ 5,038,081	$ 5,361,057
-	-	-	-	-	879,359	879,359	1,368,498
-	(31,770)	-	-	(1,355,410)	(6,641)	(1,362,051)	2,669,582
-	-	-	743	19,438	-	19,438	192,765
-	3,893	22,293	245,729	1,331,369	158,908	1,490,277	619,218
-	-	-	92,657	923,018	(923,018)	-	-
-	(27,877)	252,538	339,129	5,949,488	115,616	6,065,104	10,211,120
-	-	-	-	2,386,433	-	2,386,433	1,780,436
-	-	-	-	4,758,399	-	4,758,399	4,525,155
-	(27,877)	252,538	339,129	13,094,320	115,616	13,209,936	16,516,711
-	-	115,997	95,762	1,419,056	-	1,419,056	1,454,047
-	-	26,820	21,870	1,776,215	-	1,776,215	1,780,108
-	-	17,715	8,897	152,044	-	152,044	183,660
-	-	10	16,728	141,997	-	141,997	140,041
-	-	2,653	25,510	43,689	-	43,689	45,192
-	-	23,540	3,876	366,524	-	366,524	643,606
-	23	10,385	389,499	689,112	-	689,112	763,796
-	-	-	-	50,437	-	50,437	45,752
-	-	-	-	659,423	-	659,423	784,582
-	-	199,400	15,792	1,925,684	-	1,925,684	2,369,486
33,526	-	-	-	33,526	-	33,526	35,152
-	-	-	-	-	-	-	2,954,332
-	-	-	-	837,607	-	837,607	820,561
33,526	23	396,520	577,934	8,095,314	-	8,095,314	12,020,315
-	-	-	-	765,818	-	765,818	619,732
-	-	-	-	5,194,363	-	5,194,363	4,413,544
33,526	23	396,520	577,934	14,055,495	-	14,055,495	17,053,591
(33,526)	(27,900)	(143,982)	(238,805)	(961,175)	115,616	(845,559)	(536,880)
-	-	-	-	-	-	-	-
(33,526)	(27,900)	(143,982)	(238,805)	(961,175)	115,616	(845,559)	(536,880)
1,202,702	1,287,941	(32,212)	(517,006)	24,514,857	608,829	25,123,686	25,660,566
$ 1,169,176	$ 1,260,041	$ (176,194)	$ (755,811)	$ 23,553,682	$ 724,445	$ 24,278,127	$ 25,123,686

— MAC Photos

CFA FINANCIAL POLICY

Financial Policies

as Presented by the
Council on Finance and Administration

The following index is provided as a quick method to access this important document.

Note: For other specific rules of a financial nature please check the following:
    Board of Equitable Compensation
    Board of Pension & Health Benefits

CFA FINANCIAL POLICY

Stewardship Recommendation

The members of the Annual Conference strongly urge each local church to conduct an every-member commitment program as outlined by Discipleship Ministries or some other effective means of involving the congregation in the needs and program of the church. (Resources are also available through Discipleship Ministries of the United Methodist Church.)

Ministry Shares Calculation

Ministry Shares represent the connectional commitment of the United Methodist Church. All United Methodist churches share in support of the programs and ministries of the UMC as it offers Christ through district, conference, or worldwide activities. The Ministry Share components addressed through these policies include ministries managed by the Michigan Conference, the Ministerial Pension Fund, Church World Service, and the Episcopal Fund.

1. For the purpose of establishing a uniform system of financing the Conference, all Ministry Shares made by the Conference and Districts shall be based on the Grade Figure System employed by the Conference for the common budget.

2. The Council on Finance and Administration shall apportion the amount comprising the annual budget among the churches of the Michigan Annual Conference for the fiscal year (January through December.) These Ministry Shares shall be based on the Grade Figure System and in conformity with the requirements of *The Book of Discipline of The United Methodist Church* and rules adopted by the Annual Conference.

3. The Grade Figure System has been chosen because it allows Ministry Shares for the local church to be based upon the financial relationship of the local church to the total of the churches in the Conference. Each church is expected to assume its portion of the common budget. Giving in addition to Ministry Shares, such as designated special day offerings, authorized General and Conference Advance Specials, etc. is to be made in keeping with the *Discipline* affirmation that "payment in full [of the World Service apportionment] by local churches is the first benevolent responsibility of the church (¶812)."

4. The grade figure for the common budget shall be determined by the current operating expense budget (lines 40 - 47 of the Local Church Report) plus non-United Methodist benevolent giving (line 38 of the Local Church Report), except that in any year when the Ministry Shares are paid in full, the non-United Methodist benevolent giving amount will be excluded from the calculation. Annual variances in the resulting calculation will be moderated by using a four-year rolling average of these numbers. (Note: the line numbers can change based upon changes to the Statistical Report.)

5. Steps in determining the grade figure for the common budget:
   a. For each local church, for each of the four most recent years reported, find the sum of lines 40 through 47 of the Local Church Report (plus line 38 non UMC benevolences – unless ministry shares are paid in full). For each year that Ministry Shares were paid in full, exclude the amount from Line 38. Add the four annual sums and find the simple average.
   b. Divide the simple average by the Conference total (simple average) for the same lines.
   c. Example:

Local church total 2017 = $89,750	Conference total 2017 = $57,147,624
Local church total 2016 = $86,317	Conference total 2016 = $58,487,020
Local church total 2015 = $71,725	Conference total 2015 = $56,025,720
Local church total 2014 = $75,726	Conference total 2014 = $51,369,385
Sum divided by four = $80,879	Sum divided by four = $55,757,437

Local church average $80,879 divided by Conference average $55,757,437 equals grade figure of .001451; multiply by the total common budget to calculate the Ministry Shares.

6. Benefits Ministry Shares provide funding for the following areas: contributions for the denomination's retirement plan; premiums for the denomination's welfare plan; all expenses related to operations of the Conference Benefits Office and Conference Board of Pension & Health Benefits. Therefore, every local church will be administered a Benefits Ministry Share in connectional support of these conference ministries. The calculation for Benefits Ministry Shares shall be separate from the grade figure for the common budget and shall be based upon the annual compensation paid by each local church to it Appointed Clergyperson or District Superintendent Assignment. The Conference Benefits Office will bill the Benefits Ministry Share to each local church monthly.

7. Steps in calculating the Benefits Ministry Shares billing:
    a. For the purpose of Benefits Ministry Shares calculations, compensation includes base cash salary plus housing if provided. Twenty-five (25) percent of the base cash salary is added to the salary to determine compensation if a parsonage is provided. If a housing allowance is provided, the actual amount of the housing allowance is added to the salary to determine total compensation.
    b. A fixed percentage of total compensation is used to calculate Benefits Ministry Shares. The fixed percentage will be established annually by CFA in collaboration with the Conference Board of Pensions and Health Benefits.
    c. A reduced percentage will be used in situations of Retired Clergy Appointments, District Superintendent Assignments (DSA), or temporary situations of no appointment/assignment.
    d. Benefits Ministry Share amounts will be adjusted the first of the month following a change in compensation or appointment status.
    e. Example with Benefits Ministry Share percentage fixed at 12%:
        1. Compensation = $40,000 salary plus parsonage
           Local church Benefits Ministry Share compensation is $40,000 + 25% of $40,000 or $50,000 x 12% = $6,000 annually, billed $500 monthly
        2. Compensation = $27,000 salary plus $15,000 housing allowance
           Local church Benefits Ministry Share compensation is $27,000 + $15,000 or $42,000 x 12% = $5,040 annually, billed $420 monthly
        3. Compensation = $34,000 salary with no housing
           Local church Benefits Ministry Share is $34,000 x 12% = $4,080 annually, billed $340 monthly
        4. Compensation = $18,000 with no housing for a DSA
           Benefits Ministry Share percentage is reduced to 4% to reflect the DSA
           Local church Benefits Ministry Share is $18,000 x 4% = $720 annually, billed $60 monthly

8. Overpayment of a church's Benefits Ministry and Common Budget Ministry Shares will be carried over to that church's Benefits Ministry and Common Budget Ministry Shares for the following year.

9. Special policies are further set out below for churches without a 4-year history:
    a. Calculation of Ministry Shares for new churches: a new church will be assigned Ministry Shares by the Conference and the District 20% of its "full" amount during the first calendar year after the effective charter year. During the second calendar year, the Ministry Shares will be at 40%; during the third year 60%, fourth year 80%; fifth year and thereafter 100%. Prior to the end of the year of their chartering, new church starts are expected to send a tithe (10%) of their giving receipts to the Conference on a quarterly basis.

b. Calculation of Ministry Shares for merged churches: the statistics of the merging churches will be added together before calculating the Ministry Shares of the newly formed church for the ensuing year. Reasons for departure from this procedure will be reviewed by CF&A upon appeal, and adjustments may be made on a case-by-case basis.

c. Calculation of Ministry Shares for vital merger churches: a new classification of merged churches will be "Vital Mergers." Those mergers fulfilling the Vital Merger qualifications will be considered a new church start by the New Church Development Committee. As part of the Vital Merger process, the congregations involved will create a proposed budget for the merged church which will go into effect on the date the merged church begins worshipping and meeting as one congregation. This budget will be developed in consultation with, and given approval by, the District Superintendent and the District Committee on Church Building and Location. This budget will then be forwarded to the Conference Treasurers office to be used to formulate Ministry Share figures for the newly merged church. A new total base figure will be calculated for the merged church based on the formula outlined in paragraph 6. This new total base figure will be in effect until the actual financial records of the merged church are reported for the first full year of its existence and can be used to calculate a total base figure based on actual expenditures. The Vital Merger church will be assigned Ministry Shares by the Conference and District at 25% of its "full" amount during the first calendar year after the merger. During the second calendar year, the Ministry Shares will be 50%; 75% for the third calendar year; and 100% for the fourth calendar year and thereafter. The church must submit to the District Superintendent and Conference Treasurer's offices and the Board of Pensions a plan for managed debt repayment for any conference pension or health care arrearages.

d. Calculation of Ministry Shares for adoption merger churches: a new classification of merged churches will be "Adoption Mergers." In an Adoption Merger, a larger, healthy congregation (known as the parent congregation) agrees to partner with a smaller, usually struggling congregation (known as the partner congregation), assuming leadership and all assets and liabilities of the partner church, with the intention that the partner church is absorbed by the parent church but remains open and the church becomes a multi-site congregation. The adoption will be approved by the New Start Team, the District Superintendent, and the District Committee on Church Building and Location. The Ministry Shares for churches involved in the Adoption will be calculated as follows: 1) the year the Adoption becomes effective the Ministry Shares calculation will be calculated on the parent church only, using the standard calculation of a four-year rolling average, 2) the second year the Ministry Shares will be calculated on the parent church's expenses for the four preceding years, which will include one year of the combined expenses of both campuses, 3) the third year the Ministry Shares will be calculated on the parent church's expenses for the four preceding years, which will include two years of the combined expenses, 4) the fourth year the Ministry Shares will be calculated on the parent church's expenses for the four preceding years, which will include three years of the combined expenses. The church must submit to the District Superintendent, the Conference Treasurer's office and the Director of Benefits and Human Resources a plan for managed debt repayment for any conference pension or health care arrearages.

10. As Ministry Shares are received during the year, the World Service apportionment from the General church shall be paid at the level of receipts.

11. The portion of the Ministry Share for each local church designated for the Episcopal Fund shall be paid in the same proportion as the church pays its pastor. (¶818.3 of *The Book of Discipline of The United Methodist Church 2016*)

12. Funds received in excess of expenses for the Conference fiscal year shall be placed in the reserves of the respective Ministry Share funds and maintained by the Conference Treasurer.

13. During the Conference fiscal year, the Council on Finance and Administration, by a two-thirds (2/3) vote of its members, may use for the benefit of, or distribute to, Conference agencies and causes from the respective funds, such amounts as the Council by its action, upon concurrence with the Bishop, shall determine are required for use or distribution before the next session of the Annual Conference.

Section I - **Administration**

A. **Local Church Contributions**

1. All ministry shares apportioned to individual churches for the conference fiscal year shall be divided in ten (10) monthly installments. A statement will be sent from the treasurer's office 12 times a year.

2. All contributions, whether apportioned or un-apportioned, for Michigan Conference agencies and institutions, and for all benevolent causes of The United Methodist Church, shall be sent to the Conference Treasurer for distribution.

B. **Clergy Support Items**

1. Travel Reimbursement - Churches shall reimburse pastors of local congregations for travel expenses using a voucher system based on reimbursement equivalent to the IRS allowance for business mileage.

2. Expense Reimbursement - Churches may reimburse pastors of local congregations for professional expenses as defined by IRS code. A voucher system shall be used for such reimbursement.

3. Utilities - Churches shall pay all utilities in full for their parsonages, including heat, electricity, water, sewage, and basic telephone service.

4. Annual Conference – The Michigan Conference recommends that the local church pay living expenses for their clergy and lay members who attend Annual Conference. Such expenses should be paid at the rate specified for registration, meals and lodging as shown on the Annual Conference registration materials.

5. Health Insurance

    a. Enrollment in the conference active group health care plan in most situations will be mandatory for all eligible participants. Enrollment of eligible dependents is optional at the discretion of the participant.

    b. Each charge or conference-approved group shall share with the participant the full cost of conference group health insurance covering the pastor/conference lay employee and his/her dependents according to the approved premium sharing schedule.

    c. Even if a pastor is enrolled as a dependent in a spouse's health care plan, the church will be expected to share a portion of the cost of the conference active group health care.

    d. In the case of health benefits coverage for dependents when there is a legal separation or divorce, please refer to the conditions established by the healthcare policy of the Conference Board of Pension & Health Benefits.

    e. At the time of a pastoral move, the insurance should be paid to the end of the billing period by the church from which the pastor is moving.

    f. If a pastor chooses to be enrolled as a dependent on a spouse's health insurance plan, the pastor must have a signed waiver of coverage placed in the file in the

Benefit's office. Joining the active conference group health care plan during the open enrollment period is always an option. Enrollment since the last previous open enrollment period is a prerequisite to receiving certain retirement benefits.

6. Effective dates for salary and Clergy Retirement Security Plan/Comprehensive Protection Plan (CRSP/CPP) Payments for Ministerial Appointment Changes

   a. The salary shall be paid through June 30 when an appointment change is made at the session of Annual Conference. Salary payments for mid-year appointments will coincide with the effective date of the appointment.

   b. Payment on CRSP/CPP billing from the General Board of Pension and Health Benefits shall be made for the entire month of June for those appointment changes made during the session of Annual Conference. CRSP/CPP payments for mid-year appointments with an effective date of the first of the month shall be made for the previous month for the outgoing pastor and for the current month for the incoming pastor. Payments for appointment changes effective the 15th of a month shall be made for half of the current month for the outgoing pastor and half of the current month for the incoming pastor.

7. United Methodist Personal Investment Plan (UMPIP) - This is the pastor's recommended contribution (at least three percent) to his/her own personal retirement account. The local church is not required to contribute to this. Where churches do, however, it shall be considered as part of the total cash salary and so reported.

C. Cabinet Level Salaries

The salaries of District Superintendents, Director of Connectional Mission and Ministries, Director of Conference Benefits and Human Resources Services, Director of Administrative Services and Conference Treasurer, Director of Communications, Director of Clergy Excellence, and the Director of Congregational Vibrancy shall be set by Council of Finance & Administration. Council of Finance & Administration shall consider the best information available, including, but not limited to, the denominational average compensation, Conference average compensation, the average salary of the top 10 highest paid pastors, and the US Consumer Price index or inflation rate.

Section I – Travel Expense Policies

A. Conference travel

Expenses incurred due to travel on behalf of the Michigan Conference of the United Methodist Church may be reimbursed. All persons who are entitled to travel and other expense reimbursements must complete and submit an expense reimbursement form on a regular basis. Expenses within the appropriate budget limits will be reimbursed. Each form should include detailed explanations of trip expenses and mileage. Receipts for all expenses exceeding $10 must be attached to the report. According to IRS regulations, reimbursed expenses which are inadequately supported or un-documented may be considered additional compensation and thus be taxable to the recipient.

1. Who May Request Travel Reimbursement – Any Conference employee or member of a Commission, Board, or agency who has traveled for a required Conference purpose may request travel reimbursement. Such amounts must be reasonable. Expenses relating to commuting will not be reimbursed.

2. Information and Documentation Requirements

   a) Airlines – Receipt from airline must be provided. Electronic tickets may be documented with the emailed receipt from the airline company. Air travel insurance is not a reimbursable expense.

b) Auto Expenses – Includes parking fees, tolls, car rental (see below), taxicab, shuttles and other expense incurred in ground transportation; all of which are eligible to be reimbursed. No police or court fines or tickets for parking violations will be reimbursed.

c) Car Rental – Rental cars are reimbursable where common carriers are not available or feasible due to scheduling needs, or actual rental cost including gas and other charges are less than the standard mileage rate or common carrier cost.

d) Dates of Travel – The expense report should clearly indicate the dates of travel for each trip.

e) Incidentals – Tips for baggage handling, porters, bellhops, restaurant service, and business telephone charges are reimbursable. Incidentals should not exceed $10 per day.

f) Lodging – Lodging should be obtained at the most reasonable rate available for the location. A copy of the bill should be submitted with the expense report. Actual cost will be reimbursed when a copy of the bill is submitted. Entertainment expenses are not reimbursable.

g) Meals – Meals are reimbursable when travel begins prior to or ends after the normal meal time. Reimbursement will not be made for alcoholic beverages. Generally, meals should not exceed $40 per day. The maximum daily meal allowance begins when you leave your office. The trip ends when you arrive back at your office but excludes personal travel during the total trip.

h) Mileage – Miles traveled on Conference business will be reimbursed at the appropriate rate approved by the Internal Revenue Service. Total miles per trip should be itemized for each day reported. Mileage to be reimbursed is the round-trip miles from the primary office location unless the trip originates from home in a different city in which case the mileage to be reimbursed **is the lesser** of the round-trip miles from the primary office location or the home location. Odometer readings are not required but may be reported. Commuting miles and miles incurred for personal business enroute for Conference business are not reimbursable. A group mileage report may be completed for committee meetings where there are no other expenses which require receipts to be attached to the report. Any expense reimbursement requiring a receipt must be reported separately by individuals.

i) Purpose – The business purpose of each trip must be clearly documented on the travel expense report. Confidential information need not be disclosed but should be maintained in a personal log or diary for your own records. Group meal receipts must document all individuals included in the expense.

j) Receipts – Receipts must be submitted for all expenses exceeding $10. The receipt should report individual items purchased. The original detailed receipts and the credit card authorization receipt showing the partial card number and any tip amounts must accompany any requisition submitted for expenses paid by credit card. Please submit original receipts only. If costs are being shared by another organization and receipts are required for that entity, a copy of the shared items and corresponding expense report submitted to the second organization may be submitted.

k) Registration Fees – Evidence of fees paid must be submitted.

l) Spouse Expenses – Spousal travel expenses will only be reimbursed in situations where their presence is required by the Conference on Conference business. To avoid any perception that personal expenses are being reimbursed, Board minutes or other written documentation should document a spouse's required presence.

3. Who May Approve Expense Reports

The Bishop may approve travel reimbursement of District Superintendents; the Director of Connectional Ministries may approve travel reimbursement request for Associate Directors and Treasurer. The Treasurer may approve reimbursement requests by any employee of the Conference and the Bishop. No individual may approve a reimbursement to themselves.

Group Mileage Reports may be approved by an officer of the committee, Director of Connectional Ministries or Treasurer. The individual approving the group travel should not be listed as a payee for travel on the same report.

4. Timing of Check Requests and Processing

Forms for each month should be received in the Treasurer's Office as soon as feasible after the month's travel is completed. Travel expense reimbursement requests will be processed in the normal processing schedule. Forms which are incomplete or improperly filled out may result in a delay in processing the check or may be returned for further information.

5. Travel and other expense advances are issued only in very rare instances, except for District Superintendents and conference staff. Upon signing a promissory note, an advance may be obtained, which will be due and payable when the person leaves the staff position.

6. Conference personnel who draw travel allowance by voucher shall receive reimbursement equivalent to the federal IRS allowance for business mileage. This is designed to cover the cost of automobile operation.

7. All others drawing travel expenses from conference funds shall receive reimbursement equivalent to the federal IRS allowance for moving and medical care mileage for car and travel and $.02 per mile per passenger up to five people. This is designed to cover out-of-pocket expenses (i.e. gas and oil).

B. Travel expense by conference agencies

1. The travel expense of authorized representatives of conference agencies attending meetings convened by conference agencies drawing their full budget from the conference shall be paid by the agency which calls the meeting.

2. Dependent reimbursement cost necessary for dependents (children, sick or elderly) may be distributed from the Administrative budget for a member of any board, commission or committee meeting. The amount reimbursed shall not exceed $40 per day, per member.

3. Travel to non-United Methodist agencies - The travel expenses of authorized conference representatives attending meetings convened by non-United Methodist agencies within the state of Michigan, shall be paid by the conference, as provided in Part 1 of this section, to the extent the expenses are not borne by the convening agency.

Section III – **Moving Expense Policy**

A. Eligible Persons and Moves

1. No moving expenses will be approved until the Appointment Status Sheet is received by the Conference Treasurer's office.

2. All pastors under active appointment within the Michigan Conference structure are eligible to receive moving expense benefits. This will include local church pastors, district superintendents, staff members of conference or district councils, boards, and agencies, treasurers, bishop's assistants, superintendents or directors of parish development, conference-approved evangelists, and campus ministers.

3. Seminary students and pastors from outside the Michigan Conference who are accepting appointment in the conference are eligible for moving expense benefits as provided in this code up to a limit of 750 miles.

4. The conference will pay for one retirement move for pastors who have retired or plan to retire from Episcopal appointment in the conference. The move must be taken within five years of the retirement date. The designation of a retirement move must be declared in writing before the moving expenses are incurred. A move within the state of Michigan shall be paid in accordance with the provisions of this code. A move outside the state shall be paid up to the cost equivalent of 600 miles beyond the state border. Pastors called out of retirement and assigned to a charge will be granted an additional retirement move.

5. A disability move or the move of the surviving spouse of an eligible pastor shall be paid in accordance with the policy for retiring pastors. The conference shall pay for the move out of the parsonage or other approved housing, to another residence in the event of an eligible pastor's death, in accordance with the policy for retiring pastors.

6. When a separation or pending divorce action makes a move advisable, the spouse of a pastor is entitled to reimbursement for one move. Benefits are the same as those available to a surviving spouse of a deceased pastor.

7. Moves within a charge from one parsonage to another are the responsibility of the local charge unless ordered by the cabinet.

8. Pastors not eligible for moving expense benefits include those:

    a. under appointment outside the structure of the conference.

    b. on sabbatical, leave of absence, or location.

    c. who no longer have membership in the annual conference.

B. Policy for Moves

1. Interstate moves – Moves to or from states other than Michigan. Interstate moves are very competitive, and 2 or 3 estimates should be obtained before choosing a moving company to get the lowest rate available. Most movers will provide a "Not to Exceed" estimate.

2. Intrastate moves - Moves greater than 40 miles within the State of Michigan. These moves are regulated by State Law and the cost is based solely on weight and distance. Multiple estimates are not required.

3. Local zone moves (40 miles outside of corporate limits) - Local zone moves are not regulated as are other moves within the state. Therefore, 2 or 3 estimates should be obtained to get the lowest rate available. Charges will be based on an hourly rate times the number of employees involved. Most movers will provide "Not To Exceed" estimates if asked.

4. Family travel - Family travel for pastors covered by this policy will be paid upon request, for one car, at the IRS rate (except the first 100 miles), plus tolls. One overnight lodging will be paid for moves of more than 350 miles upon presentation of receipts.

5. Expenses covered by this code:

    a. Normal state tariff provision for loading, transporting and unloading of household goods up to a maximum weight of 20,000 pounds, including professional books and equipment. Reasonable additional weight will be allowed for clergy couples to enable movement of professional books and equipment for each clergy person. Handwritten weight certificates will not be accepted.

    b. Up to $150 will be paid by the conference to cover needed packing materials, including wardrobes and dish packs. Mattress boxes will be provided.

    c. One extra pickup and one extra delivery for each clergy person defined as the church office or local storage unit within 15 miles of the clergy member's housing.

    d. Reasonable charges for necessary handling of special items such as a piano or freezer.

    e. Standard liability insurance of 60 cents per pound which is furnished by the moving company, at no extra charge, under basic tariff provisions.

NOTE: It is now required that the householder sign a release statement on the Bill of Lading on the day of the move to release the shipment to a value of 60 cents per pound per article. Failure to do this will allow the moving company to charge a premium for insurance to cover the shipment at a value of up to $1.50 per pound.

    f. Where there are medically recognized physical limitations, up to $1,000 additional shall be allowed for packing. A physician's authorization must be provided. Contact the Conference Treasurer for authorization.

    g. Storage charges are the responsibility of the local church if the parsonage is not ready for occupancy. The conference will pay only to the place of storage.

    h. When a moving company has been selected and an estimate given, contact the treasurer's office for authorization to be given to the mover. Because Michigan in-state moves are regulated by tariff, only one estimate is needed if items 1 and 2 above do not apply to the move.

6. Expenses NOT covered by this code:

    a. Moving of items other than normal household goods and books, such as boats, trailers, autos, building materials, firewood, fishing shanties, dog houses, etc.

    b. Packing and/or unpacking services, except as noted in 5.f.

    c. Full value insurance beyond standard liability insurance provided by the moving company.

    d. Charges for waiting time, extra labor, connecting and disconnecting appliances.

    e. Consequential damages resulting from any part or aspect of the move.

    f. Emotional or pain and suffering damages arising directly or indirectly, from any part or aspect of the move.

C. Miscellaneous Policies

1. No moving company shall employ a pastor or an immediate member of his/her family to solicit business at any time for the purpose of receiving a commission or other consideration.

2. No company shall be allowed to establish an office at the seat of the conference for the purpose of soliciting business.

3. Each pastor is advised to request a copy of his/her inventory sheet from the mover at the time of loading and that it be signed by both the pastor and the moving company.

4. Pastors may want to check with their moving company or home insurance company and request an all-risk policy that would cover all damages in the moving of their household goods from one residence to another.

D. Administration

1. The Conference Treasurer shall administer the Moving Expense Fund.

2. Pastors anticipating a move shall consult with the Conference Treasurer's office to review the guidelines of this code.

3. The pastor shall be responsible for contacting a moving company and for scheduling the loading and unloading of household goods.

4. A written estimate of the cost of moving services shall be made by the moving company and a copy shall be sent to the conference treasurer's office in advance of the move.

5. A letter of authorization shall be sent from the Conference Treasurer's office in advance of the move.

6. Billing for the cost of moving expenses covered by this code shall be made directly to the Conference Treasurer's office. Moving expenses not covered by this code shall be billed directly to the pastor.

7. Provision for payment of any unusual expenses which are not defined by this code shall be arranged through consultation with the Conference Treasurer prior to the move.

8. Requests for exception to the provisions of this code shall be made to the Conference Treasurer in advance of the move. The Treasurer shall review and decide on each exception after consultation with the cabinet and/or CFA, as necessary.
9. **Pursuant to IRS rules, employer paid moves are considered taxable to the employee. The treasurer's office will provide 1099-MISC to the employee in accordance with the IRS rules.**

Approved Moving Companies
(Listed Alphabetically)

1.** Corrigan Moving Systems
     United Van Lines

     4204 Holiday Dr.
     Flint 48507
     810-235-9700 / 800-695-0540

     7409 Expressway Court St
     Grand Rapids 49548
     616-455-4500
     www. Corriganmoving.com

2. Escanaba Moving Systems
     United Van Lines
     2601 Danforth
     Escanaba 49829
     906-786-8205

3. Frisbie Moving and Storage
     United Van Lines
     14225 Schaefer Hwy
     Detroit 48227
     313-837-0808

4. Guindon Moving & Storage Co.
     1600 3rd Ave. N.
     Escanaba 49829
     800-562-1075 / 906-786-6560

5. Palmer Moving & Storage
     North American Van Lines
     24660 Dequindre
     Warren 48091-3332
     800-521-3954

6.** Rose Moving & Storage
     Allied Van Lines
     41775 Ecorse Road, #190
     Belleville, MI 48111
     800-521-2220
     www.rosemoving.com

7. Stevens Worldwide Van Lines
     Clergy Move Center
     527 Morley Drive
     Saginaw 48601
     989-755-3000 / 800-678-3836
     www.stevensworldwide.com

8. Taylor Moving & Storage
     8320 Hilton Rd.
     Brighton, MI 48114
     810-229-7070 / 800-241-7122
     www.taylormoving-storage.com

** These companies are "Preferred Movers" and may offer additional services. Please contact the movers directly to find out what additional services they may be able to offer.

Section IV – **Investment Policy**

A.   **Statement of Purpose**

The purpose of this Investment Policy (IP) is to provide governance and oversight to investments of conference funds under the control and responsibility of the Michigan Conference Council of Finance & Administration. The intent is to facilitate and not hinder conference agencies in the execution of their duties related to the management of their investment portfolios and in the use of their funds as provided in the *2016 Book of Discipline of The United Methodist Church.* In recognition of its fiduciary responsibilities and the mandate of the *2016 Book of Discipline of The United Methodist Church (613.5)*, the Council of Finance & Administration has developed this IP governing investment of their respective conference funds.

B.   **Delineation of Responsibilities**

1. Under the *2016 Book of Discipline of The United Methodist Church (612.1)*, the purpose of the Council of Finance & Administration shall be to develop, maintain, and administer a comprehensive and coordinated plan of fiscal and administrative policies, procedures, and management services for the conference. Accordingly, the Council of Finance & Administration is responsible for establishing principles, policies, standards and guidelines for the investment of all monies, assets and properties of the conference.

2. The Council of Finance & Administration is ultimately responsible for the financial integrity and oversight of conference financial resources. Under this IP all operational and implementation of policy decisions may be delegated to the Investment Committee.

3. The Council of Finance & Administration shall at least once per year review the IP, the effectiveness of the Investment Committee and the overall results of the investments and will acknowledge in writing that they have done so.

C.   **Members of the Investment Committee**

The Conference Investment Committee shall be a sub-committee of Council of Finance & Administration and be composed of five Council of Finance & Administration members selected by Council of Finance & Administration. The members' individual terms shall not exceed eight years and shall be staggered to provide for continuity and experienced leadership. The chairperson and other offices shall be nominated by the Committee from among its members and approved by the Council of Finance & Administration.

Responsibilities of the Investment Committee:

1. To define and develop investment goals, and other operational guidelines.

2. To recommend to the Council of Finance & Administration the selection and discharge of the Investment Managers.

3. To monitor and evaluate the performance results and risk posture of the Investment Manager(s).

4. To provide semi-annually to the Council of Finance & Administration a written account of the investment results, accounting summary and any significant developments.

5. To provide annually to the Council of Finance & Administration a written annual evaluation of the Investment Managers.

6. To require all portfolios will be managed with the aim of maximizing funds available for mission in a manner consistent with the preservation of capital, the

Policies Relative to Socially Responsible Investments and the Social Principles of The United Methodist Church.

7. To establish effective communication procedures between the Committee, Council of Finance & Administration, the staff and the outside service providers.

8. To monitor and control investment expenses.

9. To delegate the execution and administration of certain Committee responsibilities as appropriate to the Conference Treasurer who serves as its staff.

10. To carry out any other duties required for the legal operations of the investments, including but not limited to hiring outside vendors to perform various services.

11. To report to the Council of Finance & Administration any significant deviations from this policy for prior approval before they are implemented.

D. **Investment Managers**

To achieve its investment objectives and to ensure alignment with United Methodist Policies Relative to Socially Responsible Investments and Social Principles, the Investment Managers of Conference Funds, shall be The United Methodist Foundation of Michigan and Wespath Benefits and Investments.

E. **Investment Performance Benchmarks**

The investment performance of total portfolios and asset class components will be measured against the published benchmark for the respective investment funds, as well as, against commonly accepted performance benchmarks. Consideration shall be given to the extent to which the investment results are consistent with the investment objectives and guidelines as set forth in this IP. The standard of care when making decisions is the Prudent Expert Standard, defined as:

"...the care, skill, prudence and diligence under the circumstances then prevailing that a prudent person acting in a like capacity and familiar with such matters would use in the conduct of an enterprise of a like character and with like aims."

F. **Responsibilities of Investment Managers**

The Investment Managers shall provide the Investment Committee quarterly or as necessary the following written reports:

1. the portfolio's complete holdings;

2. a review of the investment performance measured against the respective benchmarks;

3. a commentary on investment results in light of the current investment environment on the goals and guidelines;

4. a review of the key investment decisions and the rationale for these decisions;

5. a discussion of the manager's outlook and what specific decisions this outlook may indicate;

6. any recommendations as to changes in goals and guidelines in light of material and sustained changes in the capital market; and any significant change in the manager's investment outlook, ownership or key employees.

G. **Socially Responsible Investment Guidelines**

As an Annual Conference of The United Methodist Church we are committed to implementation of the socially responsible investment policies in *2016 Book of Discipline of The United Methodist Church (717)*. (We encourage all of our congregations to be socially responsible investors.)

"Sustainable and Socially Responsible Investments-In the investment of money, it shall be the policy of The United Methodist Church that all general boards and agencies, including Wespath Benefits and Investments, and all administrative agencies and institutions, including hospitals, homes, educational institutions, annual conferences, foundations, and local churches, make a conscious effort to invest in institutions, companies, corporations, or funds with policies and practices that are socially responsible, consistent with the goals outlined in the Social Principles. All United Methodist institutions shall endeavor to seek investments in institutions, companies, corporations, or funds that promote racial and gender justice, protect human rights, prevent the use of sweatshop or forced labor, avoid human suffering, and preserve the natural world, including mitigating the effects of climate change. In addition, United Methodist institutions shall endeavor to avoid investments in companies engaged in cored business activities that are not aligned with the Social Principles through their direct or indirect involvement with the production of anti-personnel weapons and armaments (both nuclear and conventional weapons), alcoholic beverages or tobacco; or that are involved in privately operated correctional facilities, gambling, pornography or other forms of exploitative adult entertainment. The boards and agencies are to give careful consideration to environmental, social, and governance factors when making investment decisions and actively exercise their responsibility as owners of the companies in which they invest. This includes engaging with companies to create positive change and hold them accountable for their actions, while also considering exclusion if companies fail to act responsibly."

H.   **Target Asset Allocations and Rebalancing Guidelines**

The purpose of allocating among asset classes is to ensure the proper level of diversification and risk for each portfolio. The primary considerations in the asset allocation decision process are:

1.   maintaining inflation-adjusted purchasing power;
2.   growing the corpus of the funds to meet future obligations;
3.   achieving a minimum return in excess of inflation but with minimal annual fluctuations in the corpus; and,
4.   maintaining the longevity of the assets and their distributions while taking into consideration that there may be no additional contributions.

I.   **General Investment Policies**

a.   Not less than 30% nor more than 70% of the market value of the assets of the fund shall be in equity securities, unless otherwise determined by the Investment Committee.

b.   Not more than 20% of the market value of the assets of the fund shall be in cash or cash equivalents, unless otherwise determined by the Investment Committee.

c.   No more than 10% of the market value of the assets are in the securities of any one issuer, except for securities of the U.S. Government or its agencies.

d.   No more than 20% of the market value of the equity assets are in the equity issues of companies in any one industry.

e.   Periodically market conditions may cause the portfolio's investments in various equities (mutual funds) to temporarily vary from the established industry allocation policy.

J.   **General Investment Policies**

a.   Fixed-Income securities may be held only is such securities are issued by the U.S. Treasury or any agency of the U.S. Government, or are corporate bonds rated in one of the top two letter classifications by Moody's or Standard and Poor's. Convertible securities will be considered as equity securities.

b.   Short-term securities may be held only if such securities are issued by the U.S. Treasury or an agency of the U.S. Government; are commercial paper rated P-1 by Moody's, A-1 by Standard and Poor's or F-1 by Fitch's; or are certificates of deposit of U.S. banks which have or whose holding companies have a Standard and Poor's rating of A+ or better.

    c. No direct investments shall be made in foreign currency denominated securities, including American Depository Receipts except as follows: Investments may be made in common stocks, bonds and American Depository Receipts of those foreign securities listed on the New York, American or NASDAQ exchanges. Investments in a foreign securities pooled fund operated by a U.S. based money manager is also permitted provided that all transactions are in dollars.

    d. Investments shall not be made in commodities, real estate (except Real Estate Investment Trusts [REITS]), commodity contracts, financial futures, oil, gas mineral leases, mineral rights or royalty contracts.

    e. Margin transactions, short sales, options, put, calls, straddles, and/or spreads shall not be used.

    f. Investments shall not be made in the securities of an issuer which, together with any predecessor, has been in operation for less than three years.

    g. Investments shall not be made in securities for which market quotations are not readily available.

    h. Investments shall not be made in securities for the purpose of exercising control or management.

    i. Private placements of debt or equity will not be purchased.

    j. Investments shall not knowingly be made in securities of companies which have significant interest in the following activities: alcoholic beverages, tobacco, or gambling.

    k. Investments shall not knowingly be made in voting securities of companies which derive more than 15% of revenue from military contracts including both domestic and foreign customers. In the case of nonvoting securities, the limit shall be 5% of revenue.

    l. Investments shall not knowingly be made in companies which derive more than 3% of revenue from nuclear weapons contracts.

    m. Investments shall not be made if such investments will result in income which would require the filing of federal, state or local tax returns.

K. **Amendments and Revisions**

Amendments or changes to this IP may be made by the Council of Finance & Administration and incorporated directly into the policy as a revision and restatement or acknowledged and noted in an addendum until such time as the IP is revised and restated.

L. **Investment of Other Conference Funds**

The Conference Board of Pensions and Health Benefits and the Board of Trustees are given separate authority and responsibility in *2016 Book of Discipline of The United Methodist Church* for the management and investment of funds under their control. In carrying out their investment responsibilities, they may, if they determine, engage the services of the Investment Managers under this Policy to manage their funds, provided such funds shall be maintained in separate accounts. They shall also acknowledge that the responsibilities of the Investment Committee and Investment Managers and other investment guidelines as outlined in the Policy shall apply to their separate funds.

Section V – Miscellaneous Policies

A. **Conference-Wide Appeal for Funds**

No proposal for apportionments or conference-wide appeals for funds shall be recognized from the conference floor until it has first been submitted to the Council on

Finance and Administration prior to completion by the Council of its annual budget recommendation to the conference [See ¶614.5 a-c of *The 2016 Book of Discipline*.]

B. **World Service Apportionment**
1. Special attention should be given to the *2016 Book of Discipline* which reads in part: "The World Service Fund is basic in the financial program of The United Methodist Church. World Service on apportionment represents the minimum needs of the general agencies of the church. Payment in full of these apportionments by local churches and annual conferences is the first benevolent responsibility of the church." (¶812 of *The 2016 Book of Discipline*).
2. Likewise, attention is called to ¶820.5 which reads: "Churches and individuals shall give priority to the support of the World Service and conference benevolences and other apportioned funds."

C. **General Church Apportionments** - Recognizing the importance of ministries supported by the General Church apportionments, the Michigan Conference shall make every effort to support all apportioned items at 100%. If the level of receipts in any year is insufficient to do so, the CFA shall use general reserve funds to achieve the 100% goal, at the discretion of the Council of Finance & Administration. The Episcopal Fund shall be paid at 100%.

The Michigan Conference will continue to make monthly remittance on General Church Apportionments and challenges its churches to do the same. Interpretive, educational and motivational assistance will be given to local church leaders in an effort to improve understanding of and support for all Ministry Shares.

D. **Presentation of Proposed Budgets** - The budgets of all conference boards, commissions, committees, institutions and agencies seeking support from the conference or from churches, groups or individual members of the churches of the conference, shall present their proposed budget for the ensuing year to the Council on Finance and Administration for recommendation to and approval by the annual conference.
Conference program budgets will be processed by the Conference Leadership Council.

The following limitations shall apply only to those conference boards, commissions, committees, institutions, and agencies which receive their total budget support from the conference through Ministry Shares, fees, or gifts.
1. No annual conference agency expense of the budget under Connectional Ministry and Administration shall exceed the annual amount budgeted except as authorized by the conference Council on Finance and Administration.
2. Gifts and Bequests
   a) No board, agency or commission may accept gifts or bequests that will obligate that board, agency or commission beyond its present budget.
   b) If the receipt of such gifts or bequests could obligate the annual conference in the future, it cannot be received or accepted until it has been approved by the board, agency or commission, the Council on Finance and Administration, and the Annual Conference.
   c) If the acceptance of such a gift or bequest must be determined prior to a session of the annual conference, approval may be given by a two-thirds vote each of the Board of Trustees and the Council on Finance and Administration voting separately.
3. Within the budget approved by the Annual Conference, the various conference boards, commissions, committees, institutions and agencies are individually given the task of distributing this in ways consistent with their assigned responsibilities.

4. No funds shall be shifted between budget areas of administration, program, and projects without the approval of the Council of Finance & Administration.

5. No program should be initiated or continued unless there is a reasonable assurance of adequate funds on a continuing basis to allow the program to be successful.

E. **Auditing Requirements** - All agencies receiving financial support from conference benevolences, or from any other authorized conference-wide appeal, shall make audited reports (as defined in the *2016 Book of Discipline*) to the Council on Finance and Administration concerning all such receipts and the disbursement thereof in such detail and at such times as the Council may direct. Furthermore, the books of the Conference Treasurer shall be audited annually as defined in the *2016 Book of Discipline of The United Methodist Church.*

F. **Bonding of Treasurers** - The conference contracts for fidelity bonds covering financial personnel of the conference agencies located in the conference headquarters and the conference treasurer as required by the *2016 Book of Discipline of The United Methodist Church.* In addition, a fidelity bond is provided for each conference trustee and for related staff up to $1,000,000 by the General Council on Finance and Administration through the General Church Insurance Program.

G. **Control System** -The Council on Finance and Administration shall have a system of control in the disbursement of funds apportioned for conference staff, boards and agencies to ensure that they remain within their allocated budget. During the first six months of the fiscal year, the conference treasurer's office will honor vouchers presented for expenditures up to 70% of the amount approved by the annual conference for that board or agency. For the remainder of the year, spending by a board or agency may not exceed that board or agency's prorated amount of Ministry Shares receipts to date not yet expended, with the exception of salaries and like expenses. Exceptions will be made only with the approval of the appropriate supervising council or its executive committee (Conference Leadership Council or the Council on Finance and Administration) as documented in its minutes.

There shall be no carrying forward of budgeted funds from Ministry Shares receipts from one year to the next by any agency or board of the conference without approval of the Council on Finance and Administration. The following exceptions have been approved:

a. A fund of up to $10,000 may be accumulated for transitional activities at the time of a change of bishop, administered by the Episcopacy Committee.

b. A fund of up to $25,000 may be accumulated for maintenance of conference-owned properties, administered by the Board of Trustees.

c. A fund of up to $25,000 may be accumulated for counseling needs, administered by the Conference Treasurer at the direction of the Episcopal Office, for victims of clergy sexual misconduct.

d. A fund of up to $14,000 may be accumulated for district office equipment, to be administered by the Cabinet, and $7,500 for equipment for the Conference Treasurer's office.

H. **Housing/Furnishing Allowance** - An amount of the salaries of the District Superintendents, Director of Connectional Mission and Ministries, Director of Conference Benefits and Human Resources Services, Director of Administrative Services and Conference Treasurer, Director of Communications, Director of Clergy Excellence, Director of Congregational Vibrancy, Associate Directors, assistant to the bishop and director of the United Methodist Foundation (if listed under the appointments) may be designated by that person and approved by CFA as a fair housing/furnishing allowance for Internal Revenue Service Section 107 purposes.

I.　**Conflict of Interest** - Michigan Conference officials, employees and/or members of the various boards and commissions of the conference shall not, during their time of service, receive any compensation or have any financial interest in any contract or in any firm or corporation which provides goods or services (excluding publicly held companies where the official employee or member owns less than 1 percent of the voting stock thereof) or in any contract for the supply of goods or services or the procurement of furnishings or equipment, interest in any construction project of the conference, site procurement by the conference, or any other business whatsoever unless approved in writing in advance by the official's or employee's immediate supervisor and/or the board or commission upon which the member participates after full disclosure of the conflict including the amount of compensation and/or benefit the official, employee, or member will receive.

The term "official" "employee" or "member of the board or commission" shall include the official's, employee's or member's immediate family. Immediate family shall be defined as any person residing with the official, employee or member and their mother, father, and/or sons or daughters.

J.　**Depositories** – Depositories for the funds of Central Treasury shall be determined by the Council of Finance & Administration upon recommendation by the Conference.

K.　**Interest Earnings** – All interest earned on General Funds carried in Central Treasury shall be accumulated in a General Funds Interest Account. (This does not include funds in Central Treasury which are being held for specific purposes and have been designated as Interest Earning Funds by the Council.) At the end of each fiscal year, this General Interest Account shall be transferred and accumulated in the Conference Contingency Fund to be administered by the Council of Finance & Administration.

L.　**Policy on Electronic Mail and Internet Usage.** Conference employees are provided with e-mail and Internet access for the purpose of furthering the business of the Michigan Conference. All computing equipment provided to employees for their use remains the property of the Michigan Conference, and use thereof is subject at any time to monitoring by management without notice.

Use of conference e-mail accounts is limited to business purposes. As such, they may not be used to solicit participation in any non-conference-sponsored activities. Employees who engage in personal use of conference e-mail do so at their own risk and expense. The Michigan Conference will neither assume nor share any responsibility for any harassment, defamation, copyright violation, or other violations of civil or criminal law that may occur as a result of personal and/or inappropriate e-mail use. Responsibility for such incidents shall rest solely with the person who engages in such activities. Employees are prohibited from accessing other employees' files without the express consent of appropriate management personnel. Employees are also prohibited from using conference computer equipment and e-mail accounts to forward chain letters, jokes, or "spam."

Employees are reminded that e-mail communications should be drafted with the same thought and concern that would be devoted to other types of written communications, such as letters or memoranda.

The conference reserves the right at any time and without notice to access and disclose all messages, sent from and received by conference e-mail accounts.

Employee access to the Internet on conference-owned computer equipment is strictly limited to business purposes. Employees are expressly prohibited from accessing any illegal websites. Accessing websites with racist, pornographic, defamatory, sexist, or otherwise offensive content is strictly prohibited. Employees who download copyrighted material in violation of the Copyright Act of 1976, 17 U.S.C. §101, *et seq.*, are reminded that they are subject to federal criminal prosecution. The Michigan Conference will not assume any responsibility for any civil or criminal prosecutions of employees in connection with improper Internet activity, nor will the Detroit Annual Conference bear any portion of any legal fee's employees may incur in connection with such improper activity.

The use of chat rooms with conference-owned computer equipment is strictly prohibited.

Conference employees are urged to exercise caution in opening e-mail attachments from unknown persons due to the risk of computer worms and viruses. Any conference employees who knowingly allow conference computer equipment to become infected by a virus or worm shall be subject to disciplinary action, up to and including immediate termination. Such employees may also be held legally and financially liable for these actions. The Detroit Annual Conference reserves the right to commence civil litigation or to press criminal charges in such circumstances.

Violation of any conference rule regarding e-mail and Internet usage may result in disciplinary action, up to and including immediate discharge from employment.

CFA FINANCIAL POLICY

Special Offerings

The annual conference recommends:

A.   The support of general and conference Advance Specials as particularly approved by the annual conference (see *Jubilee/Spotlight Book*).

B.   The special days designated in the *Discipline* and by the Michigan Conference with offerings for:

1. Christian Education Sunday
2. World Communion Sunday
3. Rural Life Sunday
4. United Methodist Student Day
5. Human Relations Day
6. One Great Hour of Sharing
7. Native American Sunday
8. Golden Cross Sunday
9. Peace With Justice Sunday
10. Disability Awareness Sunday (without offering)

Calendar

The following dates are established:

A. **January 10, 2020**   Last day for submitting payments to the conference treasurer for credit on the previous conference fiscal year.

B. **January 24, 2020**   Deadline for all boards, commissions, committees, and agencies to submit their budget requests for the ensuing conference fiscal year to the Council on Finance and Administration

C. **January 27, 2020**   Last day for receiving pastor's annual report by the conference statistician and treasurer.

2020 Michigan Conference Budget

	2018-Combined Budget	2019 - Michigan Budget	2020 - Michigan Budget	Increase/ (Decrease)
A) Clergy Support Budget				
1) District Superintendents	$ 2,611,429	$ 2,102,743	$ 2,126,446	23,703
2) Episcopal Fund	$ 575,310	$ 562,632	$ 568,025	5,393
3) Ministerial Education Fund	$ 656,151	$ 641,692	$ 647,843	6,151
4) Episcopal Residence Committee	$ 7,500	$ 7,500	$ 7,500	-
5) Equitable Compensation Committee	$ 151,200	$ 125,000	$ 120,000	(5,000)
6) Clergy Advocacy	$ 2,000	$ 2,000	$ 2,000	-
7) Abuse Prevention Team	$ 10,500	$ 10,500	$ 10,500	-
8) Clergy Moving Expense Fund	$ 410,000	$ 350,000	$ 300,000	(50,000)
Sub-total Clergy Support Budget	$ 4,424,090	$ 3,802,067	$ 3,782,314	(19,753)
Provision for Unpaid Ministry Shares	$ 800,198	$ 601,976	$ 597,042	(4,934)
Total Clergy Support Budget	$ 5,224,288	$ 4,404,043	$ 4,379,356	(24,687)
B) Administration Budget				
1) Council on Finance & Administration	$ 2,700	$ 2,000	$ 2,000	-
2) Treasurer's Office	$ 743,461	$ 684,164	$ 734,900	50,736
3) Jurisdictional Conference	$ 36,723	$ 36,723	$ 36,723	-
4) General Conference Delegation	$ 4,500	$ 20,000	$ 28,000	8,000
5) General Church Administration	$ 230,679	$ 225,596	$ 227,758	2,162
6) Area Administration	$ 605,232	$ 556,453	$ 556,453	-
7) Operations	$ 206,018	$ 332,783	$ 312,783	(20,000)
8) Conference Secretary	$ 18,300	$ 18,300	$ 18,300	-
9) Conference Statistician	$ 3,600	$ 3,600	$ -	(3,600)
10) Conference Trustees	$ 145,795	$ 1,000	$ 1,000	-
11) Committee on Archives & History	$ 38,342	$ 40,586	$ 45,000	4,414
12) Committee on Human Resources	$ 3,000	$ 5,000	$ 5,000	-
13) Legal Fees	$ 55,000	$ 55,000	$ 55,000	-
14) Contingency Funds	$ 53,500	$ 50,000	$ 50,000	-
Sub-total Administration Budget	$ 2,146,850	$ 2,031,205	$ 2,072,917	41,712
Provision for Unpaid Ministry Shares	$ 397,630	$ 343,926	$ 351,459	7,533
Total Administration Budget	$ 2,544,480	$ 2,375,131	$ 2,424,376	49,245
C) Conference Benevolences Budget				
1) *Agencies Relating to Christ-Centered Mission and Ministry*				
a) Commission on Annual Conference Session	$ 334,500	$ 325,000	$ 275,000	(50,000)
b) Commission on Communications	$ 347,126	$ 396,000	$ 427,000	31,000
c) Committee on Journal	$ 11,220	$ 11,220	$ 11,220	-
d) Board of Justice	$ 6,950	$ 15,000	$ 15,000	-
e) Board of Global Ministries	$ 118,567	$ 210,000	$ 210,000	-
f) Engage Program Promotion	$ 7,000	$ -	$ -	-

				Change
2) Agencies Relating to Bold and Effective Leaders				
a) Conference Leadership Council	5,750	10,000	10,000	-
b) Board of Ordained Ministry	163,232	95,279	66,500	(28,779)
c) Committee on Nominations	6,000	7,500	7,500	-
d) Committee on the Episcopacy	2,000	2,000	2,000	-
e) Protection Policy	3,500	5,000	5,000	-
f) Clergy Excellence Program Funds	-	-	15,000	15,000
3) Agencies Relating to Vibrant Congregations				
a) United Methodist Men	-	-	-	-
b) United Methodist Women	-	-	-	-
c) Board of Laity	9,000	10,000	10,000	-
d) Board of Young People's Ministry	269,250	350,000	363,000	13,000
e) Board of Congregational Life	557,500	581,000	533,000	(48,000)
f) Committee on Hispanic/Latino Ministry	67,000	39,000	39,000	-
g) Committee on Asian-American Ministry	7,000	47,000	47,000	-
h) Committee on Native American Ministry	102,757	115,000	115,000	-
i) Committee on African-American Ministry	3,000	66,000	66,000	-
j) Racial & Ethnic Local Churches	118,000	-	-	-
4) Administrative Expenses/Compensation	1,214,600	2,147,841	2,172,000	24,159
5) World Service Fund	1,942,691	1,899,882	1,918,093	18,211
6) Pathways Funding	135,000	-	-	-
7) MI Area Camping	470,000	400,000	300,000	(100,000)
8) Contigency Funds	15,000	25,000	25,000	-
9) Assets Released from Restrictions	-	-	-	-
Sub-total Conference Benevolences Budget	5,916,643	6,757,722	6,632,313	(125,409)
Provision for Unpaid Ministry Shares	957,417	925,303	897,947	(27,356)
Total Conference Benevolences Budget	6,874,060	7,683,025	7,530,260	(152,765)
D) Other Apportioned Causes				
1) Black College Fund	261,732	255,965	258,419	2,454
2) Africa University Fund	58,575	57,284	57,833	549
3) Interdenominational Fund	51,316	50,185	50,666	481
Sub-total Other Apportioned Caused	371,623	363,434	366,918	3,484
Provision for Unpaid Ministry Shares	33,423	-	-	-
Total Other Apportioned Causes	405,046	363,434	366,918	3,484
Total Conference Common Budget	15,047,874	14,825,633	14,700,910	(124,723)
E) Benefits Ministry Shares Budget				
1) Pension/Welfare Payments to Wespath	1,260,000	3,128,220	3,020,000	(108,220)
2) Benefits Office	500,000	711,780	700,000	(11,780)
Total Benefits Ministry Shares Budget	1,760,000	3,840,000	3,720,000	(120,000)

2019 MICHIGAN ANNUAL CONFERENCE
IMPLEMENTATION OF RESOLUTIONS

Resolution	Page	Follow up agency/person
R #1 – Authorize CBOPHB Health Insurance Benefits Claims	322	The Michigan Conference Board of Pension & Health Benefits
R #2 – Housing/Rental Allowance for Retired or Clergy on Disability	322	The Michigan Conference Board of Pension & Health Benefits
R #3 – Comprehensive Benefits Funding Plan	323	The Michigan Conference Board of Pension & Health Benefits
R #4 – Establish Past Service Rate	323	The Michigan Conference Board of Pension & Health Benefits
R #5 – Hire and Support Returning Neighbors	323	Michigan Area Board of Justice
R #6 – Redefining What it means to be "Handicap Accessible"	323	Hershey United Methodist Church
R #7 – Covenant of Ministry Partnership with Liberia Annual Conference	323	Michigan Conference Liberia Ministry Partnership
R #8 – Reaffirmation of Michigan Conf. Support for Camping Ministry	324	MI Area UM Camping
R #10 – A Call to Reunite Families Separated at the Border	324	Michigan Board of Justice
R #11 – Revise Ministry Shares Calc. – Adopt. Merger Churches	324	MI Conf. Council on Finance and Admin; MI Conf. New Start Team/Bd. of Conf. Life
R #12 – Revise Ministry Shares Calc. – Merged Churches	325	MI Conf. Council on Finance and Administration
R #13 – Older Adult Ministries Team	325	MI Conf. Congregational Vibrancy
R #14 – Guidelines for Equitable Compensation Team	325	MI Conf. Comm. on Equitable Compensation
R #15 – 2020 Minimum Salary Schedule	326	MI Conf. Comm. on Equitable Compensation
GENERAL CONFERENCE RESOLUTIONS AND PETITIONS		
GCP #4 – Add Domestic Violence to List of Chargeable Offenses	328	Conference Secretary
GCP #4 – Create Central Conference in North America	328	Conference Secretary
GCR #2 – Aspirations for the Michigan Annual Conference	328	Conference Leadership Council
GCR #3 – Conduct a Poll	329	Conference Leadership Council

2019 RESOLUTIONS

R #1 – Authorization for CBOPHB to address claims

It was resolved by the Michigan Conference:

The Michigan Conference Board of Pension and Health Benefits moves to:

Authorize The Conference Board of Pension and Health Benefits (CBOPHB) to negotiate, compromise, or submit to arbitration any claims for benefits that may arise under the Michigan Conference Health Care Plan, the Michigan Conference Lay Employee Welfare Plan (death and disability), the United Methodist Retirement Plans (Pre-82, Ministerial Pension Plan, Clergy Retirement Security Program, United Methodist Personal Investment Plan), the United Methodist Clergy Welfare Plan (Comprehensive Protection Plan); and for that purpose to retain legal counsel as needed. The CBOPHB will be considered the final appeal and have final authority to decide any issue in the event of a dispute or disagreement by a participant.

R #2 – Establish the Housing/Rental allowance for retired clergy or clergy on medical leave

It was resolved by the Michigan Conference:

The Michigan Conference Board of Pension and Health Benefits moves to establish the Housing/Rental Allowance for retired or clergy on medical leave status in the Michigan Conference as follows:

1. An amount equal to 100% of the pension/disability payments received during the year 2020 is hereby designated as a rental/housing allowance for each retired and disabled ordained or licensed minister of The United Methodist Church who is or was a member of the Michigan Conference at the time of his or her retirement or disability;

2. This rental/housing allowance shall apply to each retired and disabled ordained or licensed minister who has been granted the retired relationship or placed on medical leave by the Michigan Conference and whose name and relationship to the conference is recorded in the Journal of the Michigan Conference or in other appropriate records maintained by the conference;

3. The pension/disability payment to which this rental/housing allowance applies shall be the pension/disability payment resulting from all service of such retired and disabled ordained or licensed ministers from all employment by any local church, annual conference or institution of The United Methodist Church, or from any other employer who employed the minister to perform services related to the ministry and who elected to make contributions to the pension and welfare funds of The United Methodist Church for such retired minister's pension or disability benefits;

4. The amount of the housing/rental allowance that may be excluded is limited to the lesser of: a) the amount designated as the housing/rental allowance, or b) the amount actually expended for housing/rent, or c) the fair rental value of housing, if required by law.

R #3 – 2020 Comprehensive Benefit Funding Plan

It was resolved by the Michigan Conference:

The Michigan Conference Board of Pension & Health Benefits moves to approve the 2020 Comprehensive Benefit Funding Plan as affirmed in the "letter of opinion" from Wespath Benefits & Investments.

[NOTE: Due to Wespath's timeline, their review and "letter of opinion" cannot be completed by the conference deadline for submitting resolutions. The "letter of opinion" will be available online and in the final printed materials once it is received from Wespath.]

R #4 – Establish Past Service Rate

It was resolved by the Michigan Conference:

The Michigan Conference Board of Pension and Health Benefits moves to establish the 2020 Past Service Rate (PSR) for the Ministers' Reserve Pension Fund (Pre-82) at $843 in the Michigan Conference(s) prior to 1982. The surviving spouse benefit shall remain at 85 percent.

R #5 – Hire & Support Returning Neighbors

It was resolved by the Michigan Conference:

Taking on our role as a "Healing Community," one of the tasks of United Methodists is to welcome our neighbors returning from incarceration in prisons and county jails. In this regard, we urge our United Methodist brothers and sisters and congregations to contact and implore our legislators to pass legislation, lifting a ban on professional and trade licensing for parolees returning to our neighborhoods.

R #6 – Redefining what it means to be "Handicap Accessible"

It was resolved by the Michigan Conference:

The Michigan Conference calls upon all congregations to evaluate and increase the level of accessibility in their church as well as the parsonage in accordance with the Americans with Disabilities Act of 1990. The Conference will assist by making churches aware of financial assistance for upgrades to meet current regulations and standards. In so doing, churches should particularly be mindful to assess the need for automatic door openers and ramps so that persons with limited mobility are not hindered in their attempts to enter our churches or parsonages.

R #7 – Covenant of Ministry Partnership with Liberia Annual Conference

It was resolved by the Michigan Conference:

The Michigan Conference approve the Michigan Conference Liberia Ministry Partnership task force working with the Liberia Annual Conference to develop a new *Covenant of Ministry* and *Working Understandings* to guide our continuing work together. The new covenant would update and replace the previous covenant of 1998 between the Detroit Annual Conference and the Liberia Annual Conference and would be brought before both the Liberia Annual Conference and Michigan Annual Conference in 2020 for approval.

R #8 – Reaffirmation of Michigan Conference Support for Camping Ministry

It was resolved by the Michigan Conference:

The Michigan Area Conference United Methodist Camping moves that Michigan Conference churches, ministries, laity and clergy be challenged and encouraged to support Michigan Conference United Methodist Camps through prayer, volunteer service, promotion and financial gifts.

Further, be it resolved that clergy understand the support of camping ministry, as volunteer and advocate, is part of their pastoral service and their time devoted as volunteer staff to the camping ministry will not be counted as vacation.

Be it further resolved that clergy and laity help recruit persons to be on paid or volunteer staff for our camps as needed, contact being made through the Michigan Area Camping office or a camp Site Director.

Be it further resolved that each local church be encouraged to hold a camp promotion Sunday to encourage participation and celebrate our Michigan Area United Methodist camps.

R #10 – A Call to Reunite Families Separated at the Border

It was resolved by the Michigan Conference:

The Michigan Conference strongly encourages all area United Methodists, local congregations and ministry groups to contact President Trump's administration, the Department of Homeland Security (DHS), and the Department of Justice (DOJ) to:
- Immediately terminate its family separation and "zero tolerance" prosecution policies that rip families apart and prevent family reunification.
- Make every effort to protect and unite children and their families.
- Respect international and U.S. law and ensure asylum seekers have an opportunity to seek protection.

R #11 – Revise Ministry Shares Calculation – Adoption Merger Churches

It was resolved by the Michigan Conference:

The Council on Finance & Administration and New Start Team/Board of Congregational Life of the Michigan Conference of The United Methodist Church jointly recommend the following change to the Ministry Shares Calculation.

Calculation of Ministry Shares for <u>adoption merger churches</u>: a new classification of merged churches will be "Adoption Mergers." In an Adoption Merger, a larger, healthy congregation (known as the parent congregation) agrees to partner with a smaller, usually struggling congregation (known as the partner congregation), assuming leadership and all assets and liabilities of the partner church, with the intention that the partner church is absorbed by the parent church, but remains open and the church becomes a multi-site congregation. The adoption will be approved by the New Start Team, the District Superintendent, and the District Committee on Church Building and Location. The Ministry Shares for churches involved in the Adoption will be calculated as follows: 1) the year the Adoption becomes effective the Ministry Shares calculation will be calculated on the parent church only, using the standard calculation of a four-year rolling average, 2) the second year the Ministry Shares will be calculated on the parent church's expenses for the four preceding years, which will include one year of the combined expenses of both campuses,

3) the third year the Ministry Shares will be calculated on the parent church's expenses for the four preceding years, which will include two years of the combined expenses, 4) the fourth year the Ministry Shares will be calculated on the parent church's expenses for the four preceding years, which will include three years of the combined expenses. The church must submit to the District Superintendent, the Conference Treasurer's office and the Director of Benefits and Human Resources a plan for managed debt repayment for any conference pension or health care arrearages. This action is retroactive to 2019 Ministry Shares.

R #12 – Revise Ministry Shares Calculation – Merged Churches

The Council on Finance & Administration of the Michigan Conference of The United Methodist Church recommends the following change to the Ministry Shares Calculation.

Calculation of Ministry Shares for merged churches: the statistics of the merging churches will be added together before calculating the Ministry Shares of the newly formed church for the ensuing year. Reasons for departure from this procedure will be reviewed by CF&A upon appeal, and adjustments may be made on a case-by-case basis after the merger of the churches is finalized.

R #13 – Older Adult Ministries Team

It was resolved by the Michigan Conference:

Be it resolved that the Board of Congregational Life will establish an Older Adult Ministries Team. The Older Adult Ministries Team will be accountable to the Board of Congregational Life. The Older Adult Ministries Team will align and coordinate the ministries of the team in order to fulfill the core purpose and goals of the team in ways consistent with the Board and Conference values and boundaries.

The Older Adult Ministries Team will not have a position on the Board of Congregational Life, which would be representative governance, but instead will be an autonomous group related to the Board of Congregational Life. The budget for the Older Adult Ministries Team will be allocated from the budget of the Board of Congregational Life. A member of the Congregational Vibrancy Team will be the staff member relating to the Older Adult Ministries Team.

R #14 – Guidelines for Equitable Compensation Support

It was resolved by the Michigan Conference:

The Commission on Equitable Compensation moves the Conference Guidelines for Equitable Compensation Support for 2020.
1. Local congregations shall conduct an annual stewardship campaign. Congregations receiving Equitable Compensation support are expected to participate in ongoing stewardship education and planning through programs such as the Stewardship Academy offered through the United Methodist Foundation of Michigan, the Vital Church Initiative (VCI) or a Paragraph 213 Review as provided in ¶213 of the United Methodist Book of Discipline.
2. Local congregations receiving Equitable Compensation grants shall annually counsel with the District Superintendent concerning levels of pastoral support.
3. Churches should be grouped, where feasible, in a denominational or ecumenical grouping so as to provide an average attendance of at least 134 under the

care of one pastor. The 134 figure is calculated using average giving, salary packages, church expenses, and ministry share totals as submitted in Tables I, II, and III.

4.   Multi-church charges that become single-point charges will not be eligible for financial assistance from the Commission unless the church seeking assistance has an average attendance of at least 134.

5.   Local congregations requesting equitable compensation support shall voucher pastors' travel and business expenses according to the guidelines of the Council on Finance and Administration.

6.   Local congregations may receive Equitable Compensation support for up to four consecutive years, reducing the original grant amount by 25% each year. Equitable Compensation funds shall not be used to fund more than the Conference minimum salary.

7.   Congregations receiving Equitable Compensation shall pay Ministry Shares in full.

8.   Churches receiving or applying for Equitable Compensation that have planned or are planning to enter into building or remodeling projects that require permission of the District Board of Church Location and Building, or which exceed 10% of the total annual budget of the local congregation, shall not proceed with proposed projects and/or related capital campaigns until such time as a plan for ending Equitable Compensation support has been presented and approved by the Commission on Equitable Compensation and the district superintendent. Exceptions to this guideline shall be given greater consideration when proposed projects are related to building accessibility.

9.   Exceptions to these guidelines may be considered upon recommendation of the Bishop and the Cabinet.

R #15 – 2020 Minimum Salary Schedule

It was resolved by the Michigan Conference:

The Commission on Equitable Compensation recommends the following Minimum Salary Schedule be adopted for 2020.

In addition, the Commission asks that churches budget a mandatory minimum of $1,500 for professional expenses and continuing education, exclusive of mileage reimbursements, for each full-time clergy person under appointment. In cases of less than full time appointment, it is recommended that the budgeted amount be prorated in accordance with the appointment (i.e., ½ Time = $750, etc.)

In accordance with ¶625.3 of the 2016 Book of Discipline, the Minimum Salary Schedule reflects the mandatory minimum cash salary which pastors shall be paid based on their status and years of service. While not mandatory, local congregations are strongly encouraged to give consideration to paying pastors with more than 10 years of service an additional 2.8% of the tenth year minimum for each additional year of service they have completed. As examples: A Full Member with 15 years of service must be paid a minimum of $47,684, but the congregation is encouraged to consider paying an additional $4771, for a total of $52,455 based on 5 additional years' service. A Local Pastor with 20 years of service must be paid a minimum $40,763, but the congregation is encouraged to consider paying an additional $8157, for a total of $48,920 based on 10 additional years' service.

Counting Years of Service To Determine Minimum Compensation

Pastors serving under appointment full or part time will have years of service counted equally for the purpose of moving through the salary schedule. Pastors serving more than six months under appointment in a year will be credited with a full year's service for the purpose of moving through the salary schedule. Pastors serving six months or less under appointment in a year will remain in the year of the salary schedule they are in. When an additional full year of service is completed, pastors will move to the next year in the salary schedule. For salary schedule purposes, years of service are carried over equally from one category to another as clergy status changes.

Years	Local Pastor 2019	2020	Associate Member 2019	2020	Provisional Member 2019	2020	Full Member 2019	2020
1	$36,375	$37,394	*	*	$40,593	$41,730	**	**
2	$36,739	$37,768	*	*	$40,997	$42,145	**	**
3	$37,104	$38,143	*	*	$41,403	$42,562	$43,313	$44,526
4	$37,467	$38,516	*	*	$41,810	$42,981	$43,755	$44,980
5	$37,832	$38,891	$39,539	$40,646	$42,215	$43,397	$44,194	$45,431
6	$38,197	$39,267	$39,931	$41,049	$42,620	$43,813	$44,629	$45,879
7	$38,560	$39,640	$40,324	$41,453	$43,025	$44,230	$45,025	$46,286
8	$38,924	$40,014	$40,721	$41,861	$43,432	$44,648	$45,505	$46,779
9	$39,289	$40,389	$41,123	$42,274	$43,838	$45,065	$45,946	$47,232
10	$39,653	$40,763	$42,463	$43,652	$44,244	$45,483	$46,385	$47,684

Recommended (Years 11-40)

Years	Local Pastor 2019	2020	Associate Member 2019	2020	Provisional Member 2019	2020	Full Member 2019	2020
11	$40,446	$41,578	$43,312	$44,525	$45,129	$46,393	$47,313	$48,638
12	$41,240	$42,395	$44,162	$45,399	$46,014	$47,302	$48,241	$49,592
13	$42,033	$43,210	$45,012	$46,272	$46,900	$48,213	$49,169	$50,546
14	$42,827	$44,026	$45,861	$47,145	$47,785	$49,123	$50,097	$51,500
15	$43,620	$44,841	$46,711	$48,019	$48,670	$50,033	$51,026	$52,455
16	$44,414	$45,658	$47,561	$48,893	$49,556	$50,944	$51,954	$53,409
17	$45,207	$46,473	$48,410	$49,765	$50,441	$51,853	$52,882	$54,363
18	$46,001	$47,289	$49,260	$50,639	$51,326	$52,763	$53,810	$55,317
19	$46,795	$48,105	$50,110	$51,513	$52,212	$53,674	$54,738	$56,271
20	$47,588	$48,920	$50,959	$52,386	$53,097	$54,584	$55,667	$57,226
21	$48,382	$49,737	$51,809	$53,260	$53,982	$55,493	$56,595	$58,180
22	$49,175	$50,552	$52,659	$54,133	$54,868	$56,404	$57,523	$59,134
23	$49,969	$51,368	$53,508	$55,006	$55,753	$57,314	$58,451	$60,088
24	$50,762	$52,183	$54,358	$55,880	$56,639	$58,225	$59,379	$61,042
25	$51,556	$53,000	$55,208	$56,754	$57,524	$59,135	$60,308	$61,997
26	$52,349	$53,815	$56,057	$57,627	$58,409	$60,044	$61,236	$62,951
27	$53,143	$54,631	$56,907	$58,500	$59,295	$60,955	$62,164	$63,905
28	$53,937	$55,447	$57,756	$59,373	$60,180	$61,865	$63,092	$64,859
29	$54,730	$56,262	$58,606	$60,247	$61,065	$62,775	$64,020	$65,813
30	$55,524	$57,079	$59,456	$61,121	$61,951	$63,686	$64,949	$66,768
31	$56,317	$57,894	$60,305	$61,994	$62,836	$64,595	$65,877	$67,722
32	$57,111	$58,710	$61,155	$62,867	$63,721	$65,505	$66,805	$68,676
33	$57,904	$59,525	$62,005	$63,741	$64,607	$66,416	$67,733	$69,630
34	$58,698	$60,342	$62,854	$64,614	$65,492	$67,326	$68,661	$70,584
35	$59,492	$61,158	$63,704	$65,488	$66,378	$68,237	$69,590	$71,539

36	$60,285	$61,973	$64,554	$66,362	$67,263	$69,146	$70,518	$72,493
37	$61,079	$62,789	$65,403	$67,234	$68,148	$70,056	$71,446	$73,446
38	$61,872	$63,604	$66,253	$68,108	$69,034	$70,967	$72,374	$74,400
39	$62,666	$64,421	$67,103	$68,982	$69,919	$71,877	$73,302	$75,354
40	$63,459	$65,236	$67,952	$69,855	$70,804	$72,787	$74,231	$76,309

GENERAL CONFERENCE PETITIONS & RELATED BUSINESS

GCP #1 – Add Domestic Violence to List of Chargeable Offenses

It was resolved by the Michigan Conference:

¶ 2702.1 A bishop, clergy member of an annual conference (¶ 370), local pastor, clergy on honorable or administrative location, or diaconal minister may be tried when charged (subject to the statute of limitations in ¶ 2702.4) with one or more of the following offenses:or (l) fiscal malfeasance; or (m) domestic violence.

Additionally:

For the purposes of this provision, domestic violence--also called intimate partner violence (IPV), domestic abuse, or relationship abuse--shall be defined as a pattern of behaviors used by one partner to maintain power and control over another partner in an intimate relationship. Domestic violence includes behaviors that physically harm, arouse fear, prevent a partner from doing what they wish or force them to behave in ways they do not want. It includes the use of physical and sexual violence, threats and intimidation, emotional abuse, and economic deprivation. Many of these different forms of domestic violence/abuse can be occurring at any one time within the same intimate relationship.

GCP #4 – Create Central Conference in North America ¶ 28

It was resolved by the Michigan Conference:

"There shall be central conferences for the work of the Church with such duties, powers, and privileges as are hereinafter set forth. The number and boundaries of the central conferences shall be determined by the Uniting Conference. Subsequently the General Conference shall have authority to change the number and boundaries of the central conferences. The central conferences shall have the duties, powers, and privileges hereinafter set forth".

GCR #2 – Aspirations for the Michigan Annual Conference

It was resolved by the Michigan Conference:

Faced with uncertainty after the 2019 Special Session of General Conference, United Methodists in Michigan look to Jesus's model of gracious welcome and evangelical inclusion to guide us. As we look forward to how the global church restructures and new Methodisms emerge, the Michigan Annual Conference aspires to live into an expression of Methodism that:

- includes LBGTQIA people in the full life and membership of the United Methodist Church;

LEGISLATION

- creates time and space for reflection, forgiveness, and reconciliation among our siblings who believe differently as we move into the future;
- organizes itself in faithful, just, and equitable structures that resist oppression, while acknowledging and undoing its complicity in systems of racial and economic inequity; and
- spends our time and financial resources on mission for the sake of the Gospel of Jesus Christ, especially with vulnerable communities in Michigan and around the world, and not on church trials, investigations, or bringing charges against clergy based on sexual orientation, gender identity, and/or gender expression or related actions.

GCR #3 – Conduct a Poll

It was resolved by the Michigan Conference:

The 2019 Michigan Annual Conference of The United Methodist Church will conduct a non-binding straw poll on the following question: If the Michigan Conference of The United Methodist Church were offered the opportunity to choose a direction for its future, should that direction be: (1) a United Methodist Conference whose policies allow for but do not require clergy to officiate at same-gender weddings, allow for consideration for ordained ministry of persons regardless of sexual orientation, and in which appointments are made with consideration given to the full range of contextual realities; or (2) a United Methodist Conference whose policies include the current <u>Book of Discipline</u> language on "homosexuality," same gender marriage and LGBTQIA+ ordination along with enhanced enforcement of these policies determined constitutional by the Judicial Council. If agreed to, this non-binding straw poll will be taken without further debate.

The taking of the straw poll was approved.

The conference supported item #1 by a vote of 789 (69%) to 350 (31%).

— MAC Photos

CABINET DEAN'S REPORT

"The Mission Imperative"
By Rev. Dr. Charles S.G. Boayue, Jr.
June 2019
Michigan Conference – The United Methodist Church

Bishop & Mrs. Bard; Fellow Members and Guests of the Michigan Conference; I greet you in the precious name of Jesus Christ, our risen Savior and Lord. I am grateful for the privilege to have been Dean of the Bishop's Cabinet this memorable year. It is a joy to serve alongside our Bishop, and these extraordinary superintendents.

This is a unique year to give the Dean's Report and, in some ways, a unique kind of a dean – a dean born outside this country who brings a unique set of eyes, ears, and perspective to any conversation. In this one year, 2019, the Michigan Conference came into being and the denomination is deeply involved in conversations about schism. At a time like this, what would you expect me to say about the Michigan Conference and the work of your Cabinet? While I could spend this time lamenting all the sad commentaries on the collective behaviors and divisive rhetoric that characterize the current climate across our Church, I would like to take another approach.

Yes, we are not of one mind on human sexuality. Sometimes we think too highly of our minds. Truth is we differ on a range of issues, including race, gender, ethnicity, justice, equality, and guns. Yet, your Cabinet hopes that, despite deep differences, we can still be one in the mission of God. The mission of God is an equal opportunity employer. Progressives, traditionalists, centrists, liberals, conservatives, old, young, women, men, children, youth, young adults, red, yellow, black, and white are all invited to participate in God's mission! The Apostle Paul, in the 12th chapter of Hebrews, invites them to lay aside their pre-occupations and set their priority straight. Without clarity of purpose, they would soon be consumed by their divisions. His reminder: you cannot run the race without focus. Put *"first things first"* to avoid *"majoring in the minors while minoring in the majors."* The race is the mission. Participation requires patient endurance because God gets to call the shots, not us! And people who have wielded power for too long struggle to understand this.

We implore you not to be fearful of the future, but to put your hands in the hands of the One who holds the future. Schisms or not, of one thing we can be certain, that *"neither death, nor life, nor angels, nor principalities, nor powers, nor things present, nor things to come, nor height, nor depth, nor any other creature, shall be able to separate us from the love of God, which is in Christ Jesus our Lord." [Romans 8: 38-39 KJV]*. This Dean's Report is a reminder that *"crowns and thrones may perish, kingdoms rise and wane, but the Church of Jesus constant will remain."* Your Cabinet is committed to God's mission as the Church's primary purpose and joins you in conviction that God will bring to completion the good work begun in us.

We became one conference in Michigan for the sake of God's mission, not our own. And in every district across this conference, congregations and individuals are making disciples of Jesus Christ for the transformation of the world! From the **Greater Southwest District's** 103 congregations where faithful disciples labor day and night to bring hope to the hopeless and salvation to the lost, to the **Central Bay District** where children, youth, and young adults are being shaped for the long journey of life under the protection of God, Michigan United Methodists are on the move to spread scriptural holiness throughout the land.

The 94 churches of the **East Winds District**, organized into 14 Mission Zones, sent a VIM Team to engage hurricane recovery work in Puerto Rico in January 2019, and operate three significant mission sites: Flint Water Recovery and NVEST (which move homeless to housing); South Flint Soup Kitchen; and Blue Water Free Store and Ministry Center.

Building upon two historic Methodist Colleges within the boundaries of the **Heritage District**, ten mission zones (each with ten churches), have been established. A day-long work camp, *"Heritage Goes to Camp,"* was held at Judson Collins Retreat Center. Young and older adults came together to clean the campsite and build closer relationships. To assist smaller-member churches with opportunities for their youth, the Heritage District will send a 30-member team of youth and adults on a week-long mission trip to Cass Community Social Services in Detroit this summer.

The **Mid-Michigan District** vision, *"creating the spaces and leaders through which God's hospitality and wholeness can thrive in communities!"* is being realized through three core values: engaging local churches in transformational Christ-Centered Mission and Ministry in their communities; identifying, equipping, supporting and deploying Bold & Effective Leaders; and creating and partnering with processes that form Vibrant Congregations. Missional hub charge conferences, lay leadership forums, clergy praxis sessions, and multiple community engagement ministries are beginning to form across the district.

From Salem Bradley Indian Mission in the South to Pentwater and Barryton Faith in the North, the **Midwest District** seeks to reach new people who hunger for the Lord's presence in their lives. Many churches are active in Kid's Hope, food banks and inviting those who are hungry to share a meal under their roof. Pastors participate in Reach Networks, building relationships and discovering new opportunities for mission. Churches meet to share mission goals. Flat River Outreach Ministries (F.R.O.M.) is one example of how churches work collaboratively with other agencies to help persons in need. Churches realize that the harvest is plenty; but the workers are few.

With focus on Dream, Engage, Inspire, Repeat, the **Northern Waters District** continues to help the local church build effective relationships to make a difference in the lives of the people God has called us to serve. The district seeks to live by the words of John 1:14 from the Message, *"The Word became flesh and blood and moved into the neighborhood."*

The **Northern Skies District** celebrates Pickford UMC for increasing worship attendance from 90 to 187 in five years; God's Country Cooperative Parish for purchasing, renovating and soon dedicating a local school in Newberry to be its Mission Center; and the Ministry of Pam Quayle, District Administrative Assistant for 25 years of faithful service to the churches of the Marquette and Northern Skies Districts, as she retires this year. The district faces challenges like the Father's Day Floods of 2018 on the Keweenaw and the challenges of navigating a large geography. Connectional support and the use of Zoom technology as a meeting platform have brought people together.

The **Greater Detroit District** vision is *"Preparing People for the next revival."* As the population, cultural, and industrial center of the State where Michigan meets the world, the annual district conferences bring together 500 local church leaders for training, fellowship, and ministry celebrations. There is excitement for New Church starts at French UMC in Birmingham, Centro Familiar Cristiano in Melvindale, Vietnamese Ministry of Madison Heights, Berkeley: First, Open Door Worship at Rochester: St. Paul's, new worship community at Cass Avenue, building expansion projects at Troy: Korean and at Royal Oak: First, as well as the re-population and redevelopment of the City of Detroit. We are discovering the increasing need for more ways to reach people with the saving Word of God.

Although we see *"in a mirror dimly"* [1 Corinthians 13:12], let's keep the mission alive – alive in young people crying out for time-out from our prolonged doctrinal blood-baths; alive in daily struggles of small membership churches to connect with persons who long for meaning, purpose, direction, and fulfillment in life. The mission is alive in J-FON offices where immigrants seek help to establish stable lives. The mission is alive where large-membership churches stretch their resources to assist those living on the margins, and wherever the Church reminds the world that red and yellow, black and white are all precious in God's sight! The mission is alive because it is God's mission. Bishop Desmond Tutu once said that *"mission is to the Church as burning is to fire. A church that is not in mission is not the Church."* Whether the UMC splinters into pieces or stays together, one thing is certain – God mission is the same yesterday, today and tomorrow until Christ comes in final victory.

Friends, the world gains nothing from our endless bloodbaths over doctrinal orthodoxy and ecclesiastical control. This broken world hungers and thirsts for relevance, meaning, purpose, direction, fulfillment, life, salvation, and destiny. The Church's mission is make a straight path in the deserts of this world for our God! The hungry and thirsty need the love of God which far surpasses human understanding. This they cannot be satisfied by traditionalism or progressivism. This world needs a faithful Church – anointed by the Holy Spirit to lower mountains of injustice, exalt valleys of dried bones, level playing fields for all people, smoothen crooked places, proclaim release to captives, give sight to the blind, heal broken hearts, set at liberty the oppressed, and declare the acceptable year of God's favor!

This mission is imperative because without it the journey leads nowhere worthy of the travel. Sinners still need a Savior; the sick, healing; the lost, redemption; the oppressed, liberty; and the perishable, imperishability! The mission drives faithful people to justice that rolls like mighty waters and righteousness like ever-flowing streams! It beckons the dispossessed to lift their eyes to the hills; admonishes the learned to *"lean not [their] own understanding;"* encourages the sinner to flee from the wrath that is coming; reminds the sojourner *"this world is not our home;"* and whispers to the ostracized *"God so love the world that God gave God's only begotten son, that whosoever believeth in Him should not perish but have eternal life!"* God's mission is necessary, urgent, indispensable, and imperative as long as *our imprisoned spirits* lay fast bound in sin and nature's night; as long as we (in the name of traditionalism, progressivism, or any other *isms*) continue to demonize each other while claiming to be brothers and sisters of the same household of faith. One philosopher wondered *"what is the greatest distance a person would have to travel in this life to attain ultimate fulfillment?"* Some said it is the distance from the Earth to the farthest reaches of the galaxies. The philosopher disagreed with this assertion by concluding that *the greatest distance one would have to travel in this life to attain ultimate fulfillment is the distance from the head to the heart.*

Our mission as United Methodists is participation in God's redemptive, restorative, and salvific mission to welcome back home, to that ultimate fulfillment, all who are lost. Sisters and Brothers, we are *"treading where the saints have trod. We are not divided, all one body we. One in hope and doctrine, one in charity."* Let us remain caught up in this amazing mission, realizing that it ain't over till God says, *"It's over!"* Amen!

MEMOIRS

A. Associates Members

1. Active
None

2. Retired

EMERSON W. ARNTZ – Born September 4, 1942. Rev. Arntz served: 1979 Ubly, Argyle; Feb. 15, 1982 Riley Center, Berville, West Berlin; 1986 Melvindale; 1987 Lakeville, Leonard; Nov. 1, 1992 Jeddo, Central-Lakeport; 2000 Jeddo, Applegate; 2002 South Central Cooperative Parish; Lake Fenton (parish director); 2009 Retired. Died June 4, 2018.

Emerson William Arntz was a husband, father, grandfather, preacher, teacher and friend. He faithfully served churches in the Detroit Annual Conference for 34 years, until his retirement in 2009. Emerson was an intelligent but humble man, who lived out his faith daily. Em was an avid reader, talented wood carver, great listener and proud "Spartan". He loved to travel, play cards and spend time with family. He is survived by his wife, Ellen; his children, Jillynn (Joe) Keppler, Jeremy (Nicole) Arntz, Paul (Shona) Spratt, and Michael (Kate) Spratt; and his grandchildren, Jordan, Alaina, Justin, Jaiden, Jack, Jamison, Gabriel, Julia Maya and Isabelle.

BERNARD R. RANDOLPH – Born October 2, 1915. Rev. Randolph served: 1948 Sanford-Averill; 1952 Mt. Pleasant/Deerfield Center; 1954 Hesperia/East Denver; 1959 Big Rapids Circuit; 1964 Houghton Lake Parish; 1966 Wayland; 1970 Benton Harbor: Grace; 1971 Ludington: St Paul; 1974 Stanwood: Northland; 03/01/75 Whitehall/Claybanks; 1976 Elk Rapids/Kewadin; 1978 Retired. Died July 21, 2018. As the holder of the West Michigan Conference Cane, he was recognized by the Michigan Conference as the oldest living Elder in West Michigan.

GERALD M. SEVER, JR. – Born September 1, 1946. Rev. Sever served: 1994 Wellsville; 1996 Deerfield, Wellsville; 1999 Laingsburg; 2006 incapacity leave; 2012 Retired. Died June 19, 2018.

Minister in the Village Missions and United Methodist Churches, Gerald Sever dearly loved sharing his love of the Lord and exemplified that love in all that he did. He especially enjoyed working in small, rural churches helping them to grow. He ministered for 46 years in New Hampshire, New York, Pennsylvania and Michigan. In addition to his ministerial duties, Gerald also served as a volunteer fire fighter; and as chaplain for the fire departments and hospitals in the communities where he served.

B. Provisional Members

1. Active
None

2. Retired
None

C. Members in Full Connection
1. Active

BRIAN K. WILLIAM – Born December 12, 1975. Rev. William transferred 2009 to Detroit Conference. 2009 Birmingham: First (assoc.) (LTFT ½); 2012 West Bloomfield. Died April 16, 2019.

Brian K. William, age 43, passed peacefully in his sleep and went to be with the Lord on April 16, 2019. Brian was a devoted husband, father, pastor, and friend. Brian was born December 12, 1975 in Changhua, Taiwan to Raymond and Nancy William and grew up primarily in Corvallis, Oregon. Brian always had a great interest in the world and its peoples. But it was his love of God that led him to attend Garrett-Evangelical Theological Seminary where he studied to become a pastor. He first served at the United Methodist Church in Burlington, IL. He next served at Birmingham First UMC where he helped run the contemporary service and missions, and then West Bloomfield UMC as their lead Pastor. There he focused on growing and caring for the multicultural congregation, creating community ties between the diverse religions and peoples, mentoring young people and other pastors, and leading and serving in missionary work from Detroit to Jeremie, Haiti. Brian met the love of his life, Monica, in 1998. His wife and children were the most important things in his life, as he was to theirs. To them he was a goofball, hugger, movie fan, lunch maker, bad 'dad joke' teller, chauffer & social director, short-order cook, soccer coach, photographer, Lego League coach, dream-maker and biggest fan. He was quirky, loving, accepting, intelligent, silly, curious, personable, kind, an out-of-the-box thinker, a mentor, and a friend to all.

2. Retired

FRANCIS F. ANDERSON – Born November 3, 1926. Rev. Anderson served: 1957 New Buffalo/Berrien County: Lakeside; 1958 Marcellus; 1961 Portage (Assoc); 1962 Kalamazoo Chapel Hill Parish; 12/09/62 White Cloud; 1966 Lansing: Central (Assoc); 1970 Jackson Haven; 1972 GBGM, World Division, Methodist Church in the Caribbean and the Americas, Belize; 1975 GBGM, MCCA, Trinidad; 09/01/78 Napoleon; UM 1980 MCCA, Savanna- La-Mar, Jamaica; 1986 GBGM, MCCA, Duncans, Jamaica; 11/01/89 Appointed in Other Annual Conferences (¶331.8, ¶346.1) Detroit Conference, Hudson; 1991 Retired. Died October 18, 2018.

YOUNG BONG YOON – Born December 29, 1924. Rev. Bong Yoon served: 1951 Sinyangri; 1954 Military Chaplain; 1961 Board of Evangelism; 1964 General Secretary, Korean Conf.; 1968 Bishop's Assistant; 1974 Korean Methodist Church; 1978 Trans. to Detroit Conf., Troy: Korean; 1995 Retired. Died July 24, 2018.

JUANITA J. FERGUSON – Born July 8, 1943. Rev. Ferguson served: 1963 Wellsville; 1965 Detroit: Cass Avenue (assoc.); 1973 Springville; 1978 Detroit: Ford Memorial; 1986 Detroit: Redford; 1990 Birmingham: First (assoc.); 1993 Detroit West District Superintendent; 1997 Beverly Hills; 1998 Waterford: Trinity; 2003 School, Chicago Theological Seminary; 2005 Essexville; 2009 Retired. Died November 18, 2018.

Juanita Ferguson born July 8, 1943, died on November 18, 2018 at the age of 75. She served Wellsville; Detroit: Cass Avenue (assoc.); Springville; Detroit: Ford Memorial; Detroit: Redford; Birmingham: First (assoc.); as the Detroit West District Superintendent; Beverly Hills; Waterford: Trinity; Chicago Theological Seminary and Essexville. Juanita loved the city and people of Detroit. The city was her domain, and she loved to be in some form of ministry in the city. She was uniquely qualified in terms of gospel preacher and servant to where she lived. You could find her riding around on her bicycle delivering food, and helping anyone she could in her gentle, caring way. She loved the Detroit Tigers not just for the sport, but for the community engagement. She served God and the people of the Detroit Annual Conference as one of the first clergywomen in the conference. People who came to know her loved her, from camping to urban ministry. Those that knew her remember her with great heart and fondness. One dear friend recalls her as "one of the most gifted people in the history of the conference." She was well admired, respected, endearing, and greatly missed.

BERT HOSKING – Born March 7, 1923. Rev. Hosking served: 1959 Detroit: Messiah; 1966 Bay City: Fremont Avenue, Delta College Wesley Foundation; 1969 Bay City: Fremont Avenue; 1971 Detroit: Trinity; Jul. 1975 Executive Director, Retirement Homes of the Detroit Annual Conference; 1979 Canton: Cherry Hill; 1986 Retired. Died May 17, 2018.

RICHARD C. KUHN – Born June 12, 1936. Rev. Kuhn served: 09/01/71 Leland/Keswick; [Transferred from Minnesota Conf 1972] 1980 Frankfort/ Elberta; 1982 Buchanan: Faith/Morris Chapel; 1987 St Louis: First; 1998 Retired. Died December 8, 2018.

Richard Charles Kuhn wrote, "As I wrap up my 81st year, I look back with satisfaction on my life." With a Master of Divinity from Boston University, he joined the Minnesota Annual Conference, serving churches at Eden Prairie, Hamline, Nashauk/Pengilly. There he met and married Beth. On voluntary location with the Conference, he moved to Traverse City, Michigan, where he was a Human Resources Specialist for the Economic Development District. Later he became Director of Law Enforcement Planning in Region 10. During that time the couple built their first apartment building. He joined the West Michigan Conference in 1971 till 1998, serving Leland/Keswick, Frankfort/Elba, Buchanan Faith/Morris Chapel, and First UMC in St. Louis. He led Lay Witness Missions, the Emmaus Community, Keryx church camps and prison Bible studies. He brought members, baptized, married, and buried countless believers saying, "The Best is yet to be!" He loved God, his family, and his life. "I am so very grateful that God gave me the Compass who has faithfully guided my life. I've not always followed the Compass as I should have, nonetheless God has blessed me abundantly. See you in the Kingdom ahead!" –Rich

SALLY A. LAFRANCE – Born June 26, 1936. Rev. LaFrance served: 1999 Transferred from West Ohio Conf; 10/01/99 Climax/Scotts; 2001 Old Mission Peninsula (Ogdensburg); 2002 Twin Lake; 10/01/04 Retired. Died September 15, 2018.

GARY V. LYONS – Born April 12, 1939. 1972 Transferred from Detroit Conf; 1972 Vermontville/Gresham; 04/05/76 Chaplain, US Navy; 1996 Retired. Died February 17, 2019.

DOUGLAS K. OLSEN – Born May 24, 1947. Rev. Olsen served: 1972 Detroit: Waterman, Simpson; 1976 Ferndale: First (assoc.); 1981 Stony Creek; 1996 Ann Arbor: Calvary; 2008 Dundee; 2015 Retired. Died July 15, 2018.

Douglas Karl Olsen was born in Ann Arbor on May 24, 1947 to Donald and Marie Olsen. He graduated from Eastern Michigan University with a degree in business administration and earned a Master of Divinity degree from the Methodist Theological School in Ohio. It was there he met his future wife Sandy whom he married on September 9, 1972. Doug retired from the ministry in 2015 from the Dundee United Methodist Church. Prior to that, he served congregations in Detroit, Ferndale, Ypsilanti and Ann Arbor. He was active in the Ann Arbor District and the Detroit Annual Conference. He chaired the district Building and Church Location Committee, was a member of the conference journal committee, and served on the conference secretarial staff. Following a 5 ½ month battle with brain cancer, he went home to his Lord on July 15, 2018. He is survived by his wife Sandy, two children Kristen and James, and his sister Susan Weber.

MICHAEL L. RAYMO – Born April 5, 1948. Rev. Raymo served: 1980 Dearborn: First (assoc.); 1985 Sterling Heights; 1988 Chaplain, Army; June 1, 2014 Retired. Died May 1, 2018.

Michael Lawrence Raymo was born on April 5, 1948 in Detroit, Michigan. He attended the United States Military Academy at West Point and served his country for 23 years. Mike married his high school sweet heart, Muriel, in 1971 and enjoyed nearly 47 years as husband and wife. He has two sons, Michael and Mark, and two daughters in "love," Tara and Farrah. He also has two grandsons, two granddaughters and another grandson to be born In August. Prior to Mike being in the military, he was the associate minister at Dearborn First United Methodist Church and the pastor at Sterling Heights United Methodist Church. Mike passed away on May 1, 2018. He touched many lives and was given a "Quilt of Valor" made by one of his colleagues from the Veterans' Administration Hospital in Birmingham, Alabama. Mike is remembered and loved by his family, as well as by the many people whom he touched through his "Word for the Day" devotions.

MARVIN R. ROSA – Born June 18, 1937. Rev. Rosa served: 1964 Rosebush/Center; 1967 Augusta/Hickory Corners; 02/15/72 Grand Rapids: Trinity (Assoc); 1979 Clare; 1986 District Superintendent, Grand Traverse District; 1992 Big Rapids: First; 03/31/93 Leave of Absence; 1996 Frankfort/Elberta; Retired 1999. Died February 11, 2019.

Marvin was born to Russell and Jean Rosa on June 18, 1937 in Lake Ann. He attended a one room grade school and graduated from Honor High School. On July 27, 1957 he married Annette Haywood. He attended NMC in Traverse City while serving as Lay Assistant to Rev. Donn Doten. He graduated from CMU while serving Rosebush/Center Churches. He commuted weekly to Garrett-Evangelical Theological Seminary while serving Augusta/Hickory Corners Churches graduating with a Master of Divinity. He served churches in Grand Rapids, Clare, Big Rapids, and Frankfort/Elba. He was District Superintendent for the Grand Traverse District, and he and Annette did a pastor exchange in England... a great experience! Marvin loved music, sang, played piano, and danced. He also liked his collection of antique John Deere tractors. He is survived by his wife Annette, 4 sons, 18 granchildren, and many more family members.

WARD N. SCOVEL, JR. – Born December 15, 1935. Rev. Dr. Scovel served: 1978 Muskegon: Central (Assoc); 1980 Battle Creek: Birchwood; 1984 Wyoming Park; 1989 Paw Paw; 1995 Leave of Absence; 03/01/98 Retired. Died October 13, 2018.

Ward Scovel was born December 15, 1935 in Berwyn, IL, to parents Ward Scovel, Sr., and Verna Scovel. What an amazing soul with such a huge spirit! After becoming an ordained minister, Ward received the prestigious Peace Award from the West Michigan Conference of the UM Church. He earned his Ph.D in Death and Dying. After 25 years in ministry, he served as a Hospice Chaplain for 16 years, sharing his near-death experience with his patients to alleviate their fear of dying. Following the death of their two sons, Steve and Carl, he and his wife co-facilitated Survivor of Suicide groups. Ward is survived by Mary A. (Sennema) Scovel, his wife of 62 years; daughters, Marcia Sprague, Kathy (Richard) Rodrigue; grandchildren, Kayla and Devi Sprague; his brother Don (Jan) Scovel, brother-in-law, David Sennema and sister-in-law, Carol Derks, and many nieces and nephews. Ward Norman Scovel made his transition on October 13, 2018.

MARK E. SPAW – Born May 24, 1957. Rev. Spaw served: 1983 Hartland (1995-1996 with Hardy); 1999 Trenton: Faith; 2010 Ann Arbor District Superintendent; 2018 medical leave. Died March 8, 2019.

Mark Edward Spaw died 3/8/19 at age 61. Loving son of Robert Jesse and Mildred Ann Spaw. Brother to Bob (Sue), Dorothy (Craig) and Kathy. Loving Uncle to 10 Nieces/Nephews and 16 great nieces/nephews. Attended Detroit Public Schools. Received B.S., Wayne State and Master of Divinity degree - Garrett-Evangelical Theological Seminary. Pastor at Hartland UMC, Trenton UMC and district superintendent of Ann Arbor District. Mark loved being a pastor – it was thoroughly enmeshed in his soul – it wasn't just a profession or vocation. He was proud to serve two long-term appointments, and only two appointments, before becoming a district superintendent. He loved being a DS and always advocated for his Ann Arbor District congregations and clergy. He was proud to have served as DS under three different bishops. Mark had high expectations for both clergy and congregation in our mission of making disciples for Jesus Christ for the transformation of the world. His transition to medical leave/retirement was difficult, but he loved his family and their support. Mark leaves a great legacy of passion for the church and its disciple-making, a great sense of humor, a keen mind, and a forthrightness that challenged and supported others in positive ways.

SUSAN BENNETT STILES – Rev. Susan Stiles, 66, passed away on August 31, 2018. Born in Michigan, Susan attended Fenton High School, graduated from Michigan State University and from Garrett-Evangelical Theological Seminary. She spent her entire career pastoring several United Methodist congregations in Michigan. Susan Stiles was preceded in death by her husband, Rev. David Stiles. She loved her family, daughter Mary Gardner; son-in-law, Keith Gardner; and granddaughter, Beckett Waverly Gardner.

HAROLD M. TABER – Born February 12, 1929. Rev. Taber served: 1949 Springport Parish (Assoc); 1952 Shepherd/Pleasant Valley; 1956 Shepherd/Indian Mission; 1958 Wacousta Community; 1960 Casnovia/Kent City: Chapel Hill; 1962 Houghton Lake Parish; 1964 Middleville; 1966 Middleville/Freeport; 1969 Jackson: Trinity; 1972 Lane Boulevard; 1975 Scottville; 01/25/76 Medical Leave/Granted Disability; 1977 Burr Oak; 1978 Medical Leave/Granted Disability; 1980 Retired. Died August 18, 2018.

Harold M. Taber died on August 18, 2018, in Grand Rapids. While serving pastorates he introduced the West Michigan Conference to audio recording of annual conference sessions and the use of media resources for School of Christian Mission and Pastor's School. He also served the United Methodist Conference as secretary for the Board of Missions and Board of Ministry and in its camping ministries as dean, registrar, and counselor for various camps. He is the son of the late Rev. Marcius and Mearl Taber and brother of Rev. Margery (Gordon) Schleicher, who survives him. Also surviving him are his wife of 69 years, Miriam; daughters, Sally Taber (Dean Tousley) and Norma Taber; son Paul (Kathye) Harrington-Taber; sister, Carolyn (Werner) Klisch; sister-in-law, Ann Taber; and five grandchildren, two great-grandchildren and numerous nieces and nephews.

JAMES F. THOMAS (AND JOYCE A. THOMAS, DIACONAL MINISTER) – JAMES F. THOMAS : Born June 1, 1933. Rev. James Thomas served: 1954 Decatur, IN: Calvary; 1955 Kewanna Circuit, IN; 1958 Wanatah, IN: Zion; 1960 Porter, IN: First; 1964 Parma, OH (Minister of Education), (E OH Conf); 1968 Boardman: First (Minister of Education); 1972 Farmington Hills: Nardin Park & Orchard (Minister of Education; 1980 Farmington Hills: Orchard (assoc.); 1982 Grand Blanc; Jan. 1, 1990 Saginaw: First; Sep 1, 1994 Swartz Creek; 2000 Retired. Died June 2, 2018.

James and Joyce Thomas served faithfully in the United Methodist and Evangelical United Brethren denominations for 60 years as an ordained elder and consecrated diaconal, respectively. They served churches in the conferences of Indiana, East Ohio, Detroit, and Desert Southwest (retired). Their passion for Christian Education guided their ministry in each location and was the principal focus of their work as a Minister of Education and Director of Christian Education. In addition, Joyce worked as a Hospital Chaplain in Flint and Saginaw. A car accident on May 31st, 2018 tragically claimed both of their lives. Their tireless service to God and the Church has touched many lives.

GREGORY R. WOLFE – Born February 10, 1948. Rev. Wolfe served: 1973 CPE Program, Milledgeville State Hospital; 1974 Potterville/West Benton; 10/16/78 Keeler/Silver Creek; 11/16/83 Grass Lake; 1994 Clare; 2003 Portland; 2008 Kalkaska; 2013 Retired; 2013 Napoleon (LTFT ¾). Died April 15, 2019.

Greg was the love of my life and I was his "Sweetie." It was a blessing and a joy to serve Christ together. Each appointment brought new challenges: new opportunities to grow leaders, to make new friends, and to be blessed by the people of God. Greg spent his life loving people, and being the best son, husband, Dad, and Poppa he could. He had a quick wit, great sense of humor, and unfailing faith in God. He loved to make music – lots and lots of music. Through his preaching, people were blessed, encouraged, grew in their faith, and were given hope for eternal life. He was down to earth, genuine, caring, and fun. Great hugs were his specialty – and always that SMILE! We all experienced God through Greg's servant heart. He shared the love of Jesus with everyone who knew him. Now he lifts his voice with the angels.

PATON M. ZIMMERMAN – Born May 22, 1925. Rev. Zimmerman served: 1981 Ann Arbor: Glacier Way; Feb 1. 1990 Warren: Wesley; 1995 Retired. Died November 27, 2018.

Paton Zimmerman was born in Beirut, Syria of the Ottoman Empire. His parents returned the family to the United States in 1938. Following high school, he enrolled in GMI in Flint, where in 1947 he received a BS in Mechanical Engineering. Employed by GM until 1977 when he began attending Wesley Theological Seminary in Washington, DC. He was licensed first as a Local Pastor in 1977, Ordained a Deacon in 1978, and subsequently an Ordained Elder in 1983. In his active pastoral ministry, he served a 3-point charge in Maryland, and churches in Ann Arbor and Warren, MI until his retirement in 1995. Since 2002, he had lived with his daughter, Elizabeth, ultimately residing for the past 13 years in North Carolina.

D. Deacons in Full Connection
1. Active
None

2. Retired
None

E. Local Pastors
1. Active
None

2. Retired

REX E. BEAN – Born August 8, 1923. Rev. Bean served Chase: Barton 1982; Retired 1987. Died August 19, 2018.

Rex was a loving husband, father, and grandfather. He served God his entire life. He started out as an educator but was called into the ministry. He attended Garrett-Evangelical Theological Seminary and served South Haven and Chase-Barton UMC. After retiring he and his wife Margaret went back to their hometown of Muskegon and continued their ministry by helping at Temple UMC in Muskegon Heights. They then moved to Clark Retirement Community in Grand Rapids, where they continued to serve God daily until their deaths. They were true disciples of Christ!

LEO E. BENNETT – Born September 19, 1926. Rev. Bennett served: 1956 South Cadillac; 1961 Alden and Kewadin Indian Mission; 1965 Cedar Springs; 1970 Wayland; 1979 Lawrence; 1986 Hinchman and Oronoko; 1989 Jackson: First (Associate Pastor). He retired in 1993. Died October 31, 2018.

Leo (Bud) Elwood Bennett passed away peacefully on October 31, 2018, at American House, Holland. He was born in Jackson, Michigan on September 19, 1926, son of Lewis and Leona (Kast) Bennett. He graduated from Lansing Technical High School in 1943. From October 1943 - April 1946 Leo served in the United States Navy, SF 2c USNR onboard the USS Denver (CL-58) and received a Purple Heart in the Pacific Theater. He married the love of his life Joyce "Dolly" Jean Bement on June 28, 1947. Leo attended Garrett-Evangelical Theological Seminary in Illinois and was ordained into the United Methodist Ministry. Leo and Joyce served church appointments in the West Michigan Conference. Upon retirement they made their home in Holland, Michigan. Leo enjoyed traveling with his "Dolly" in their motor home, wintering in Arizona. Leo was preceded in death by his wife; parents, brothers Lewis (Hazel) Bennett, Lynne Bennett, Lyle Bennett; sisters Lorraine (Lester) Burch, Leah (Wilfred) Orton, daughter-in-law Michelle Bennett. Surviving are sister: Rev. Loyce Thrush of Cottage Grove, Minnesota; sons Terry (Linda) Bennett of Grand Rapids, Michigan; Dennis "DK" Bennett of Bluffton, South Carolina; granddaughters, Morgaine (Harry) Bell of Hardwick, Vermont; Amy (Gerald) Sebolt of Grand Rapids, Michigan; and Krista (Charles) Savinsky, of Wayland, Michigan, great grandchildren Kassandra Bell, Zachary and Nathan Savinsky.

F. Diaconal Ministers

JOYCE A. THOMAS, DIACONAL MINISTER (and REV. JAMES F. THOMAS) – Joyce Thomas served: 1981 Methodist Children's Home Society; 1988 Davison; 1990 PT Chaplain, Saginaw General Hospital; 1998 Retired. Died June 2, 2018

James and Joyce Thomas served faithfully in the United Methodist and Evangelical United Brethren denominations for 60 years as an ordained elder and consecrated diaconal, respectively. They served churches in the conferences of Indiana, East Ohio, Detroit, and Desert Southwest (retired). Their passion for Christian Education guided their ministry in each location and was the principal focus of their work as a Minister of Education and Director of Christian Education. In addition, Joyce worked as a Hospital Chaplain in Flint and Saginaw. A car accident on May 31st, 2018 tragically claimed both of their lives. Their tireless service to God and the Church has touched many lives.

G. Clergy in good standing from another denomination

H. Other Clergy

HAROLD M. DERKS – Born May 17, 1927. Died February 9, 2019. Harold F. Derks was born 91 years ago in Grand Rapids, and he died February 9, 2019. Harold spent most of his life in West Michigan. He graduated from Central High School and served in the Army as an MP at Los Alamos, New Mexico. Afterward, he went to GRJC and Michigan State College on the GI bill, becoming a civil engineer. Later, he attended Garrett Evangelical Theological Seminary and became an ordained Methodist minister. The Derks family moved to Holland, MI, in 1963 where Harold was appointed as the Associate Minister at First Methodist Church. He returned to engineering in a couple years becoming Holland's City Engineer and then working for the State of Michigan Department of Transportation as the Contracts Administrator. He is survived by his wife of 64 years, Carol Sennema Derks, and his three children and seven grandchildren.

WILLIAM D. CARR – Born February 17, 1938. Rev. Carr served: 1983 Belding; 10/16/83 Galien: Olive Branch; 04/16/86 Indiana Conference, Hamilton Grove, New Carlisle; 10/15/88 Personal Leave; 1989 Bear Lake; 1989 Arcadia; 1993 Honorable Location; 03/01/03 Honorable Location – Retired. Died November 8, 2018.

EARL W. DOWNING – Born June 25, 1928. Rev. Downing served: 1974 Executive Director, Detroit Baptist Children's Home; 1979 leave of absence; 1984 Honorable Location; 1993 Honorable Location, Retired. Died December 6, 2018.

Born June 25, 1928 – Detroit MI. Died December 6, 2018 – Brighton, MI Married Gloria Klepser February 10, 1951 Earl served as a minister in the Detroit area and Ohio (1950–1962) and as director of children's homes in OH, IA, NE and MI, (1962-1979). In 1993 Earl retired from the MI Dept. of Social Services. Earl also held positions in social welfare agencies regarding youth, alcoholism, and mental health. Earl led mission trips with Volunteers in Mission to Poland and Russia and received 'Volunteer of the Year Award' (2002). He loved the performing arts with acting roles in local community theaters (Tevye from 'Fiddler' was his favorite) and singing with community choral groups. Earl's infectious "roll up your sleeves" and "can do" positive attitude evaluated the lives of everyone around him. The world was a better place with Earl, and he is missed by his family and friends. Alumni: Mackenzie High ('46), Wayne State University (BA '51 & MSW '62) and the Oberlin Graduate School of Theology (MDIV '54).

J. CHRIS SCHROEDER – Born June 2, 1944. Rev. Schroeder served: 1976 Central Lake; 1976 Alden; 1982 Sebewa Center; 1982 Sunfield; 11/16/84 Sunfield; 01/01/92 Leave of Absence; 1998 Honorable Location; 2011 Honorable Location – Retired. Died January 19, 2019.

On January 19, 2019, Chris Schroeder, age 73 passed into eternity after a battle with Parkinsons' Disease. He is survived by his wife Carolyn, 4 children - Kristen (Ed) Lamber, Rebecca (Skye) Shansby, Katharine (Todd) Broberg, Dave (and Callie) Schroeder; 8 grandchildren - Mikala, Katelyn, and Kiarra Lambert, Lily, Eleanor, Peter and Margeret Broberg, and Grace Schroeder; and sister RoxAnne (Lee) Evison, brothers Alan and Steve (Connie) Schroeder. Born in Charlotte, MI he graduated from Michigan State University and then served his country as an engineer with the CIA. He was then called by God to attend seminary and went on to pastor four churches in Alden and Sunfield, MI before he and Carolyn went to Eastern Europe as missionaries. He and Carolyn spent their retirement serving in Madison Square Church as Elder and Prayer Servant and leading retreats for hurting pastors and spouses with PastorCare and Shepherd's Heart Ministries.

ROBERT E. SMITH – Died June 30, 2018. Robert was a Local Pastor at the time he served Barryton, Hastings, and Barry County Woodland.

I. **Missionaries**
   None

J. **Missionaries Spouses**
   None

K. **Deaconesses**
   None

L. **Certified Candidate for Ordination**
   None

M. **Clergy Spouses**

MARILYN JOYCE ACKERMAN – Marilyn Joyce Ackerman of Wixom, formerly of Clawson and Frankenmuth, was born January 27, 1936 in Detroit, Michigan to Truman Thomas Huey and Mildred Fern (nee: Burkett) Sanders. She died August 22, 2018 at the age of 82. Mrs. Ackerman is the beloved wife of 60 years to Reverend Gordon Earl Ackerman. She is the loving mother of Kim (Michael) VanErp, Lisa Ackerman and the late Cheryl (the late Scott) Schlosser. Grandmother of Ariel, Shelbie and Dakota. She is also survived by her dear friend Shirley Ann Klockenga. She was a devoted, faithful and loving wife, mother and grandmother and she will be dearly missed by all that knew and loved her.

BARBARA A. PARR BURTON – Born February 18, 1934, Barbara A. Parr-Burton (Baldwin), age 85, went to be with her Lord on Tuesday, May 7, 2019. She will be greatly missed by her friends and family, especially the grandchildren whom she adored. Barbara was the surviving spouse of Rev. M. Clement Parr who served in the Detroit Conference.

MARGE J. DAHRINGER – Marjorie J. Dahringer, age 83, was born August 23, 1935 in Bad Axe, MI and passed away, September 6, 2018, surrounded by her family. Marge was a member of Howell First United Methodist Church and was married to the late Rev. Ed Dahringer. Marge graduated from Saginaw General Hospital and worked as a RN for Ypsilanti State Hospital, Pediatric Nursing Director of Beyer Hospital, also in Ypsilanti, and was the school nurse for Brighton Elementary schools. She enjoyed quilting, sewing and traveling, but most of all boat rides and sunsets on Lake Chemung. Her greatest joy was her family and she will be remembered as a loving mother, grandmother and sister.

JOANNE DAYRINGER – Born October 27, 1929 – Died December 25, 2018. Loving wife of 60 years to the late Rev. Leon E. Dayringer. Joanne was an elementary teacher for 20 years. After she retired she traveled in a 5th wheel for several years before moving to Arizona. After 15 years she moved back to Michigan to live at Clark Retirement Community and to be near her 4 children, 9 grandchildren and 7 great grandchildren. She was an accomplished seamstress and loved to quilt, knit and find new crafts to do. She loved to spend time with family, and her grandchildren, even when they were wild and crazy. She will be deeply missed.

IRMA EIDENS – Born May 4, 1919 – Died July 24, 2018. Irma was born in Kuldiga, Latvia to Otto and Rozalija Benke. On October 6, 1940 in Kuldiga, Latvia she married Eduard Eidins. The family moved to America on May 26, 1948 and in 1955 she received her final citizenship papers. She loved flowers, spending time with grandchildren and singing. Irma was very thoughtful and always took the time to send notes and cards to family and friends on their birthdays and other special times. Being a pastor's wife, she had the opportunity to serve alongside her husband at several churches throughout his career. She was a member of the United Methodist Church of Cadillac where she was active in the choir and women's circles.

GROVENOR "KIP" GRIMES – Died January 5, 2019. Kip graduated from Cooley High School, went to Ferris and then transferred to Michigan State, where he earned his civil engineering degree. He later earned his masters and became a professional engineer. He worked his entire career at MDOT, in later years becoming in charge of public transportation for the State of Michigan. While he loved his career, he considered just as important his role as helpmate to his wife of 47 years, Pastor Lynn Grimes. He was constantly on stage-building duty, running sound boards, filling in various roles in Lynn's plays (Wise Man), and just helping her wherever and whenever he could. He was a lifetime member of the United Methodist Church, beginning at Metropolitan in Detroit and ending at Holt. Kip had two sons: Christopher (Leigh) and Matthew (Laura) and the light of his life, three grandchildren: Kaden, Maddox, and Ella. He loved sailing at Torch Lake, the family cottage, woodworking, was a master gardener (roses were his specialty), attending grandchildren events, and any MSU game… especially hockey and basketball. Three years ago, he married longtime friend Rebecca Hilbert. Shortly after, he was diagnosed with pancreatic cancer which he fought with the determination he had exhibited in everything he had undertaken in his whole life.

ELIZABETH HAERING – Died February 25, 2019, at age 92. Spouse of Rev. Emil Haering, who passed in 2010.

RUTH P. HOOVER – Born July 14, 1921 – Died January 19, 2019. She was the spouse of Rev. Russell Hoover (2004). While raising her children and teaching piano, Ruth served as a pastor's wife for some 35 years at Wynn, Eagle, North Muskegon, Breckenridge, Jackson, and also at Leslie Congregational Church and Grass Lake Federated Church. They were active members of the congregation at Brookside Methodist Church. Ruth and Russell together managed Hoover Music on Wisner Street in Jackson. Ruth is survived by three sons, and one daughter; eight grandchildren and fourteen great-grandchildren.

MARY LOU JURY – Mary Lou Jury of Chelsea, MI, age 98, died Saturday, September 1, 2018 at Chelsea Retirement Community. She was born March 15, 1920 in Detroit, Michigan, the daughter of Fred Palmer & Mary (Costello) Todd. Mary Lou taught Church school, sang in the choir, led small exercise & discussion groups. She worked on many committees in the ministers' wives' groups. She worked for Blue Cross & Blue Shield and a library during her early life, then focused on being a mom and minister's wife. She was active at Chelsea Retirement Community and volunteered in their Thrift Shop and Gift Shop. On June 26, 1943, she married Rev. John S. Jury at the Metropolitan Methodist Church in Detroit, and he preceded her in death on Feb. 8, 2003. Survivors include two sons, Theodore John (Elaine) Jury of Utica, MI and Stephen Todd Jury of Flushing, MI; two grandchildren, Matthew & Andrew Jury of Denver, CO; and many nieces & nephews. She was preceded in death by five brothers, Stayton Todd, David F. Todd, J. Beecher Todd, Fred P. Todd, Jr., Wesley R. Todd.

WILLIAM H. POPE, JR. - Born March 9, 1950, died January 8, 2019. Spouse of Rev. Marva Pope, currently serving Wayne-Westland FUMC.

LOIS POWELL - Lois Powell, aged 94, of Kalamazoo, Michigan went home to be with the Lord on April 10, 2019. Lois was born July 8, 1924 to the late Robert and Estella (Humphrey) Shimmons in Sterling, Michigan. Lois was raised by her step-mother, Lena (Sandy) Shimmons, and brought to Spring Arbor College, where she met the love of her life, the late Rev. Henry Powell in 1942. Together they

MEMOIRS

served numerous Free Methodist and Detroit Conference United Methodist congregations, including Pontiac: Elmwood, Davisburg: Mt. Bethel, Ida, North Branch, and Midland: Homer, until his retirement after 40 years of service. Henry and Lois enjoyed spending time at their rustic cabin in Grayling, Michigan and eventually owned a home in Lakeland, FL. After Henry's death, Lois remained in Lakeland for ten years before moving back to Michigan. She enjoyed many activities and trips with the Portage Senior Center and her dear friend, Bill Perrin. Lois eventually moved to The Fountains of Bronson Place and delighted in all the people, activities and desserts. Lois was the quintessential pastor's wife and was most passionate about making a difference in the lives of children. She lovingly taught Sunday School and VBS, and "fostered" many a child when they needed a place to stay. She was a devout Christian and continued leading and participating in Bible studies into her tenth decade.

LORING ROSSMAN - Loring was born on September 26, 1931 and passed away on May 5, 2018. He was the spouse of Rev. Dorothy Myers who preceded him in death on July 12, 2011. Loring was a resident of Gaines, Michigan at the time of passing. He was a graduate of Fenton High School in 1950 and a veteran of the U.S. Army, serving during the Korean War.

LINDA SCHWEIZER - Linda of Grand Blanc, was born June 14, 1941 and went to be with our Lord on July 22, 2018. She was the spouse of Rev. Allen Schweizer. Linda was born in Detroit, MI. She is survived by her husband Allen; three children, 8 grandchildren and I great grandchild.

BLANCHE TAYLOR - Born June 22, 1926, died August 7, 2018. Blanche Taylor grew up in a family of clergy. Born in Ohio to Rev. and Mrs. C.D. Osborn, her childhood filled with love, ministry, and music prepared her for life as a pastor's wife. Her marriage to Larry Taylor in 1948 began a shared ministry that lasted for over 50 years. As Larry served appointments throughout Michigan, Blanche taught Sunday School, sang in and directed choirs, and served as a nurturing anchor at home to their three children, Dan, Sue, and Annette. Following Larry's death in 1999, Blanche continued her ministry by directing the choir at Clark Retirement Community and playing piano for weekly prayer services, even to the last weeks of her life. Her ministry of kindness to all, faith by example, and a listening ear blessed her family, and all those who knew her.

BETTY WALLACE - A wife, a mother, a grandma too, this is the legacy we have from you. You taught us to love and how to fight, you gave us strength, you gave us insight. A stronger person would be hard to find, and in your heart, you were always kind. You fought for us all in one way or another, not just as a wife, not just as a mother. For all of us you gave your all and now the time has come for you to rest. So go in peace, you've earned your sleep, your love in our hearts, we'll eternally keep.

HELEN L. WHITTERN - Helen L. Whittern, 97, of Hudson, passed away Tuesday, January 15, 2019, at Drews Place at Village Green in Hillsdale. She was born February 15, 1921, in Wright Township. She married Rev. Keith Whittern on December 24, 1942, and he preceded her in death on October 1, 1957. Helen was a 1938 graduate of Waldron High School. She obtained a degree in Education from Taylor University in Indiana in 1942, later earned her Master's Degree in Education at the University of Michigan in 1960, and completed Doctoral studies at Ball State University in Muncie, IN in 1970. Surviving Helen are two children; ten grandchildren; 28 greatgrandchildren; four great-great grandchildren; a daughter-in-law; and three sisters-in-laws.

VICKIE WOJEWSKI - Vicki was born May 24, 1959 in Mt. Clemens, MI and died Friday, February 1, 2019 in Caseville, MI. She was the spouse of pastor Donald Louis Wojewski. Vickie was a 1977 graduate of Brablec High School in Roseville, MI. She studied graphic arts at South Macomb Community College. Vickie was employed by General Motors and Ford Motors as a Technical Illustrator. She and Don had lived in the Imlay City and Almont area for 20+ years before the ministry began taking them to different parts of Michigan. She was an active part of Don's ministry. Music was a very important part of her life; playing the flute and saxophone during many church worship services. She also used her graphic art talents as a secretary for the churches to which she and Don were assigned. She is survived by her husband: Donald and two daughters.

N. Child of the Parsonage

ANDREW GARTH BROOK – Died April 5, 2019 at age 38. Andrew was the son of Rev. Patricia and Roger Brook. As a son, brother, husband, father, teacher, coach, colleague, and friend, Andy always found his people. He found them, he cared for them and he loved them; and in return Andy became deeply and widely loved. It turns out the equation is simple. Be honest, be kind to those you know and those you don't, and above all be good, and people from all points will know you as friend and family. Andy was many things, but most of all a dear and devoted husband to Anne and a loving and amazing father to Penelope and Finnian. Now they will learn Andy's story, will know his soul, and will carry on his legacy. The world is a better place for having had Andy in it, and it will better for the lives he touched and will continue to be better for his beautiful children he leaves behind.

CHLOE ROSE OSTEMA – Chloe was born on September 21, 1995 in Charlevoix, MI to Dale and Debbie Ostema. She died March 20, 2019. Chloe was the beloved sister of Jay and Alison. Chloe graduated from Traverse City Central High School in 2014 and Western Michigan University in 2019. She earned her Bachelor's Degree in Psychology and was in the process of planning for her Master's Degree in Clinical Mental Health Counseling and was accepted into the programs at Western and Andrews University. Chloe was a bright light in this world and had a radiant smile. She loved being with her family and friends. Her favorite places included local beaches, Sleeping Bear Dunes, and the mountains of New

Hampshire where family resides. Chloe was a gifted artist and crafted beautiful pieces of jewelry. She had a deep faith in God and was a follower of Jesus.

JON YOUQIANG SURGEON RIDER – January 10, 1995 - March 27, 2019. Jon was born in Shenzhen China on January 10, 1995. He attended Marcellus and Jackson schools and graduated from Big Rapids High School in 2014. Jon resided in many locations in Michigan, Texas, and California. However, he found his heart's home in Glendale, Colorado. Jon worked in a variety of occupations such as tower technician, sales representative, computer installation, delivery, and Uber. Jon was a collector of many things. He appreciated the beauty in gemstones and rocks, and frequently gifted them to his loved ones. Jon bought and re-sold collectables; he was talented in creating a profit doing this. He often shared music with his sister and debated philosophy with his mother. He took great pride in his Chinese heritage and continued learning about his culture and traditions. Jon was a natural with children, especially babies, and one of his dreams was to help children with cleft palate.

O. Diaconal Ministers' Spouses
None

P. Lay Persons (Professionally Related to the Conference)

KAYTE ASPRAY – Katharine Ellen (Serumgard) "Kayte" Aspray, 72, of Bay City, died Friday, June 15, 2018, at Saginaw Covenant Cooper Hospital with her family by her side. She was born May 5, 1946 in Elmhurst and grew up in Yonkers, New York before moving to the Bay City area. She graduated from SUNY at Geneseo with a Bachelor's degree in 1968 and a Master's in 1969. Her career began at WUCM-TV at Delta College as the first female TV producer in the Tri-Cities area. Kayte retired as the Associate Academic Dean from Northwood University in 2012 after 39 years with the school. Kayte was a public service advocate. She served on the Bay City School, President of the Board for Bay County Habitat for Humanity; Secretary of the United Methodist Church's Global Ministry from 2001 – 2016; and Chair of the Detroit Conference Liberia Task Force 2015 - 2017. Kayte is survived by her two sons.

SAMUEL CARTER, SR. – Samuel Carter, Sr., was born in Mississippi on October 19, 1943. Sam was called home to his Heavenly Father on January 2, 2019. Sam was a lifelong Christian and served faithfully in many capacities. He began his faith journey at Mt. Gideon CME Church in Mississippi as a child, with his final church home being First United Methodist Church of Ferndale, Michigan. Sam was a well-respected leader in the church, and served as a Lay Leader and Lay Speaker, Sunday School superintendent, and church trustee for many years. He was especially passionate about his role as the chair of the General Commission on Religion and Race of the Methodist Church, and worked hard to build awareness, understanding and tolerance among people of all backgrounds. Throughout his life, Sam's faith in God and his love for his family were constant, unwavering fixtures. His smile, warmth and sincerity will be fondly remembered by his family and friends. He is survived by wife, Charlestein "Dot" Lovette, four children and many loving family and friends.

SHIRLEY JOAN CHAPIN – Shirley Joan Chapin was a wonderful mother and wife. She believed that we all should "Live Simply so Others may Simply Live". Joan worked tirelessly as a Peace Advocate for the United Methodist Church for 35 years. She served with the United Methodist Women, Women's Division and Board of Global Ministries. Joan actively worked for Peace and Justice for all, from standing with the Puerto Rican's on the Island of Vieques to denouncing the hate of the KKK in her own home town. She also had the amazing ability to cook love into a pot of homemade bean soup! It is her family's hope that Joan's love will continue to vibrate through the United Methodist Church via the work of the United Methodist Women, Women's Division, the Board of Global Ministries and all who knew her.

CARROLL J. CHRISTOPHER – Carroll J. "Chris" Christopher, age 89, of Novi, formerly of Troy, died January 15, 2019. He was born June 3, 1929 in Columbus, OH. He served many years as the treasurer of the Board of Ordained Ministry and was very active in his church. Surviving are his wife, Kimberly; 4 children and 2 grandchildren.

KENNETH HALTER – Kenneth Halter, age 88 years, of Grand Blanc, passed away on March 25, 2019 at Brookdale Memory Care. Kenneth was born on October 16, 1930 in Eaton Rapids, MI, to the late Gladwin and Beatrice Halter. He graduated from General Motors Institute with a Bachelor's degree in Business Administration. He worked at Buick for 40 years. He was a member of the Grand Blanc UMC, where he served as a lay preacher. He also was Detroit Conference Lay Leader, president of the Flint Jaycee's, life member of the Flint Masonic Lodge, life member of the Flint Rotary, where he received the Paul Harris Fellow Award, and member of the Grand Blanc Chamber of Commerce. He served as president on both the Buick Retirees and Flint Men's Retirees. Served as an Army M.P. in the Korean War. He is survived by his wife, Joyce (Kosal) Halter; children Susan and Tony Rizzo of Oxford; Lynda and Jeff Volker of Grand Blanc; grandchildren Matthew and Lisa Rizzo, Kimberly Rizzo, Joseph Volker, and Thomas Volker whom he loved very much. He was preceded in death by his children Steven Halter and Patti Halter.

CARMEN ARLENE MISNER – Misner, Carmen Arlene - Age 76, of Flint, died November 3, 2018. Carmen was born August 24, 1942 in Ann Arbor, the daughter of Rev. Emeral Everett and Norma Arlene (Raymer) Price. She married Earl Misner in Mt. Pleasant on August 14, 1965. Carmen was proud of her Native American heritage and actively helped serve the Native community throughout Michigan. She worked with the United Methodist Indian Mission churches throughout the state and across church conferences. Carmen was a member of Asbury United Methodist Church and sang in the choir. She served the congregation as both lay leader and lay speaker. In addition, she served the United Methodist Church as a whole, attending various conferences and committees throughout the state and country.

One of the accomplishments serving the church that she was most proud of brought together her love for the Native community and her love of her faith. She worked tirelessly to help enable Native members of the United Methodist Church in

Michigan to become lay speakers and lay leaders for their congregation and to pursue being ordained as ministers.

Carmen is survived by: her sons Michael and Jonathan Misner, both of Flint; nephews Todd (Sarah) Price, Jeff Price; nieces Cheryl (Brent) Hamelink, Lesa Price (Larry) Betz. She was preceded in death by her husband Earl and brother David.

 PAT PROCTOR – Patricia Ann Proctor, age 87 of Fremont, passed away Friday, June 8, 2018. Pat had been very active in the United Methodist Women where she had served as a National Officer holder and had traveled the world with the United Methodist Women. She had been a Sunday School Teacher and Youth Group Leader for 25 years at the Fremont United Methodist Church as well. Pat had been the janitor at the Fremont United Methodist Church for 25 years until her retirement and had been a homemaker raising her family prior. Family always came first with Pat. Pat is survived by her 6 children, 27 grandchildren, numerous great and great great grandchildren. Pat was preceded in death by her husband Darrell and her son Michael.

MORRIS C. TABER – Morris C. Taber was an active member of First Ypsilanti UMC and for many years was lay delegate to the Detroit Annual Conference, where he also served on mission boards. For several years he and his wife Ann coordinated multiple Volunteer in Mission projects to Old Mutare and Africa University in Zimbabwe. In Zimbabwe they also started several school libraries, facilitated scholarships for students, and organized shipments of books and school and medical supplies. He was also a tireless community activist, frequently donating his time and resources to causes such as Cass Community Social Services in Detroit and Justice for Our Neighbors. He is the son of the late Rev. Marcius Taber, brother of the late Rev. Harold Taber, and brother of Rev. Margery Schleicher, who survives him. Also, surviving him is his wife Ann, sons Mark (Colleen) and Steve (Julie) Taber, and sister Carolyn (Werner) Klisch.

ROLL OF DECEASED CLERGY MEMBERS

For Roll of Deceased prior to July 1, 2018, consult West Michigan Conference or Detroit Conference Minutes of 2018 and before.

Name	Date of Death	Place of Death	Age	Conference & Admission Date
Dennis G. Buwalda	*12/21/2017**	*Holt, MI*	*74*	*West Michigan 1968*
* correction of death date in previous entry: 2017, not 2018				
James G. Simmons	4/24/2018	Chelsea, MI	90	Detroit 1952
Gilson M. Miller	4/25/2018	Heber City, UT	70	Detroit 1971
Michael L. Raymo	5/1/2018	Hoover, AL	70	Detroit 1978
Bert Hosking	5/17/2018	Louisville, KY	95	Detroit 1956
James F. Thomas	6/2/2018	Grand Rapids, MI	82	N. Indiana 1952
Amerson W. Arntz	6/4/2018	Macomb Township, MI	75	Detroit 2000
Gerald M. Sever, Jr.	6/19/2018	Grand Blanc, MI	71	Detroit 1997
Douglas K. Olsen	7/15/2018	Dundee, MI	71	Detroit 1970
Bernard R. Randolph	7/21/2018	Mecosta, MI	102	West Michigan 1956
Young Bong Yoon	7/24/2018	Moreno Valley, CA	93	Korea 1951
Harold M. Taber	8/18/2018	Grand Rapids, MI	89	West Michigan 1950
Susan Bennett Stiles	8/31/2018	Charlotte, NC	66	Detroit 1975
Sally A. LaFrance	9/15/2018	Spring Lake, MI	82	West Ohio 1995
Ward N. Scovel, Jr.	10/13/2018	Penn Valley, CA	82	West Michigan 1976
Francis F. Anderson	10/18/2018	Holt, MI	92	West Michigan 1960
Juanita J. Ferguson	11/18/2018	Detroit, MI	75	Detroit 1972
Paton M. Zimmerman	11/27/2018	Southfield, MI	93	Detroit 1978
Richard C. Kuhn	12/8/2018	Perrinton, MI	82	Minnesota 1959
Marvin R. Rosa	2/11/2019	Lake Ann, MI	81	West Michigan 1968
Gary V. Lyons	2/17/2019	Gallatin, TN	79	Detroit 1972
Mark E. Spaw	3/8/2019	Farmington Hills, MI	61	Detroit 1982
Gregory R. Wolfe	4/15/2019	Napoleon, MI	71	West Michigan 1973
Brian K. William	4/16/2019	West Bloomfield, MI	43	Detroit 2004
Bruce M. Denton	5/5/2019	Lake Orion, MI	68	Detroit 1973
Donald S. Weatherup	5/13/2019	Canton, MI	57	Detroit 2002
Ross Neil Nicholson	6/29/2019	Marquette, MI	86	Detroit 1959
Charles F. Garrod	7/25/2019	Grand Rapids, MI	89	West Michigan 1957
George R. Grettenberger	7/28/2019	Okemos, MI	89	West Michigan 1954
Kenneth D. McCaw	9/5/2019	Grand Rapids, MI	85	West Michigan 1962

HISTORICAL SESSIONS OF THE ANNUAL CONFERENCE

For the listing of previous sessions of the former Detroit Annual Conference and West Michigan Annual Conference of The United Methodist Church, please refer to each conference's 2018 Journal, pages 322 and 298 respectively.

For information regarding previous sessions of the former Conferences of Evangelical United Brethren Church, refer to the Journal of the 107th Annual Session of the Michigan Conference (EUB) pages 25 and 26 dated May 20-23, 1968.

No.	Date Began	Place	Bishop	Secretary
1	May 30, 2019	Traverse City, MI	David A. Bard	Joy A. Barrett

— MAC Photos

CONFERENCE CANE

The Michigan Conference Cane replaces the two canes previously awarded by the Detroit and West Michigan Conferences. It will be used in ceremonies to honor the oldest living clergy person who has been under appointment to the Conference (and predecessor Michigan Area conferences) for a minimum of thirty (30) years. The thirty years need not be continuous, and the recipient need not be a resident of the state of Michigan at the time the award is made. The Commission on Archives and History sponsors the presentation. The current holder of the conference cane is Arthur L. Spafford.

The body of the cane is made of wood from the church in Adrian where the Detroit Conference was organized. There are inserts representing different historical periods, including: wood from the first Methodist Episcopal Church erected in Michigan in 1818 at River Rouge; wood from the desk of Reverend Seth Reed, who joined the Michigan Conference in its earliest years and died at the age of 100; wood from a tree near the resting place of Barbara Heck, a pioneering Methodist woman in America; wood from the church where Judson Collins, our first missionary to China, was converted; and wood from the pulpit used by Robert Strawbridge, pioneer of Methodism on the American continent.

The Detroit and West Michigan conferences both began the tradition of presenting canes to a senior member in 1904, during the celebration of the centennial of the first two visits to Michigan by Methodist preachers. Over the years, fifty-nine retired ministers received these cane awards (28 in West Michigan and 31 in Detroit). Recipients have included ministers not only from the United Methodist Church, but also some who began their careers in the Methodist Episcopal Church, Methodist Protestant Church, Evangelical Church, United Brethren in Christ, and the former Lexington Conference (a segregated African-American conference). The two older canes have been retired to the Conference archives.

Detroit Conference Cane holders and year presented:
David A. Curtis, 1904; Francis A. Blades, 1904; Seth Reed, 1905; Phillip I. Wright, 1924; David Casler, 1928; David B. Millar, 1929; James E. Jacklin, 1941; Samuel Graves, 1944; George Tripp, 1948; Thomas Mott, 1950; Carl S. Risley, 1951; David N. Earl, 1953; Edwin D. Dimond, 1954; James T.M. Stephens, 1959; H. Addis Leeson, 1960; Richard C.G. Williams, 1964; Charles Bragg, 1966; William A. Gregory, 1967; Frank Purdy, 1971; Henry I. Voelker, 1973; Russell D. Hopkins, 1975; Benjamin F. Holmes, 1984; Myron R. Everett, 1990; George M. Jones, 1993; Walter C.B. Saxman, 1998; Ira L. Wood, 2002; Alvin Burton, 2003; Konstantin Wipp, 2005; William D. Rickard, 2013; Donald O. Crumm, 2014; Arthur L. Spafford, 2014

West Michigan Conference Cane holders and year presented:
John H. Pitezel, 1904; Riley C. Crawford, 1906; Lorin M. Bennett, 1911; Daniel S. Haviland, 1912; Thomas T. George, 1917; John K. Stark, 1919; John Graham, 1920; James H. Potts, 1921; Leander S. Matthews, 1942; William D. Rowland, 1949; Howard D. Skinner, 1950; August H. Coors, 1953; Harley H. Harris, 1955; Charles P. Ostrom, 1964; Albert T. Cartland, 1965; Grant L. Jordan, 1971; Floyd M. Barden, 1974; Lloyd A. Mead, 1975; Alvin G. Doten, 1980; Edward F. Rhoades, 1986; Richard D. Wearne, 1988; Harley L. Lane, 1989; Glenn M. Frye, 1991; Wayne M. Palmer, 1996; Chester J. Erickson, 1999; William A. Blanding, 2005; H. James Birdsall, 2007; Bernard R. Randolph, 2008 (died 2018)

SURVIVING SPOUSES

Amstutz, Jean – 4495 Calkins Rd., Apt 109, Flint, MI 48532-3574 ....(810) 230-0514
Anderson, Virginia A – 4090 Tall Oaks Dr, Grand Ledge, MI 48837 ....(517) 627-7895
Anderson, Winona – Great Lakes Christian Homes, 2050 S Washington Rd
    Apt 1012, Holt, MI 48842-8634..(517) 694-3084
Arntz, Ellen – 47280 Savannah Dr, Macomb, MI 48044-2792 ....(586) 468-6464
Atherton, Tom – 10400 Smith Rd., Gaines, MI 48436..(989) 271-8757
Atkins, Gertrude – 6206 S. Friends Ave., Whittier, CA 90601-3726
Baggs, Betty L – Timberline Lodge, 3770 Colwood Road, Caro, MI 48723 ....(989) 672-2525
Bamberger, Fern – 2439 Winona Street, East Tawas, MI 48730 ....(989) 362-5810
Bank, Dorothy – 255 Mayer Rd., 266 Loehe Haus, Frankenmuth, MI 48734 ....(989) 652-4266
Bates, Barbara (Joyce) – 2525 N Elm St Apt 38, Miami, OK 74354-1421
Bates, Wanda – 6321 Noel Dr., Brentwood, TN 37027
Baumgart, Gloria – 3871 England Dr, Shelbyville, MI 49344 ....(269) 672-2152
Beach, Barbara – 200 Fairway West, Nicholasville, KY 40356-9414
Becker, Jeanne – 2985 Hillcrest Drive, New Era, MI 49446.......................................(231) 861-5799
Beeker, Carol – 17425 Bunker Hill, Mt., Clemens, MI 48044 ....(586) 263-1712
Beers, Helen – 553 Gidley Ave Apt H, Grand Haven, MI 49417-2358 ....(616) 844-4272
Benner, Joan – 21660 Meadow Lane, Franklin, MI 48025-4850................................(248) 723-0676
Benton, Katherine – 8530 Elkwood St., Byron Center, MI 49315...............................(616) 878-1405
Betts, Shirley – 501 King St. #114, Eaton Rapids, MI 48827 ....(517) 663-1626
Beynon, Hester W – 212 Chandler, Flint, MI 48503-2140
Blankenburg, Marilyn Jean – 9459 Orchard Street, PO Box 394, New Lothrop,
    MI 48460-0247 ....(810) 638-5722
Blue, Joan – 12198 SW Torch Lake Dr, Rapid City, MI 49676-9330 ....(231) 322-4420
Boal, Linda – 320 W. Main St, Marquette, MI 49855...(231) 871-0781
Bolitho, Mabel – 2315 40th St., R.F.D.#2, Hudsonville, MI 49426-9626
Bollinger, Evelyn – 201 Bedford Trail, Apt. 132, Sun City Center, FL 33573
Bough, Carolyn – 7341 Villamuer Rd, West Bloomfield, MI 48322-3307 ....(248) 788-1431
Bourns, Carol Lynn – 144 W 4th St Apt 403, Clare, MI 48617-1483 ....(989) 544-2719
Bowen, Barbara – 9387 Oakley Rd., St. Charles, MI 48655
Bracken, Claudia – 54 S. Avery, Waterford, MI 48328-3400 ....(248) 894-5902
Braid, Judith – 1850 Helena Ave., Hartland, MI 48353...(248) 887-4312
Branstner, Virginia – 210 E Sherwood Rd, Williamston, MI 48895-9323
Braun, Carol – 2730 Clyde Road, Ionia, MI 48846..(616) 527-0034
Bray, Jeannette – 16806 Lochmoor Circle W., Northville, MI 48167 ....(734) 667-4802
Breithaupt, Kathy – 18829 Lakewood Circle, Lake Ann, MI 49650 ....(231) 620-5508
Brooks, Alice –
Brooks, Kimberly – 216 Fifth St., Harrisville, MI 48740
Brooks, Nancy – 3845 Longfore Drive, Bay City, MI 48706
Brown, Esther – 162 Lakewood Dr, East Leroy, MI 49058 ....(269) 979-9303
Browne, Llwewellyn – 20100 Murray Hill, Detroit, MI 48235
Buker, Elaine M. – 10100 Hillview Dr. Apt.1213, Pensacola, FL 32514 ....(850) 607-7743
Bunce, Barbara – 717 Petoskey St., Gaylord, MI 49735
Burgess, Eula Jean – 422 Seaman Street, St Louis, MI 48880 ....(989) 681-4129
Burkey, Beth – 45182 W Park Dr Apt 46, Novi, MI 48377-1302
Burton-Collier, Linda J – 2574 127th Ave, Allegan, MI 49010-9250 ....(269) 793-7340
Butters, Pamela – 2204 2nd St, Connellsville, PA 15425-5313
Buwalda, Carol – 3983 Sierra Hts, Holt, MI 48842-7701 ....(517) 663-4418

ADDRESSES

Cameron, Doris J – 1103 SW 11th Street, Boca Raton, FL 33486..............................(561) 395-5827
Carr, Carolyn – 5536 Ivy Path, Stevensville, MI 49127 ....(263) 686-0290
Cermak, Adele – 10540 N Shore Dr, PO Box 839, Northport, MI 49670......................(231) 386-5204
Chappell, Marilyn – 2401 Stobbe St, Saginaw, MI 48602-4081
Christler, Betty – 801 W. Middle St. DH 461, Chelsea, MI 48118..............................(810) 338-9696
Christler, Bonnie – 2500 River Rd. #15, Marysville, MI 48040 ....(810) 841-5296
Cobb, Betty – 6711 Embassy Blvd, 106, Port Rickey, FL 34668-4739......................(813) 842-3447
Cole, Susan – 25 Arrowhead Estates Ln, Chesterfield, MI 63017-1824 ....(636) 536-2585
Coleman, Marge – 235 Gateway Dr. #507, Clare, MI 48817
Collins, Mary – PO Box 17, Northport, MI 49670 ....(231) 386-5169
Collins, Olo R – 15827 Maddelein, Detroit, MI 48205-2535
Collver, Joanne – 5619 Bayshore Rd. #135, Palmetto, FL 34221-9232
Conn, Judith – 1738 E Front St, Traverse City, MI 49686 ....(231) 995-5294
Cook, Anne – 1013 Castle Drive, Weidman, MI 48893 ....(989) 644-5903
Cowing, Della – 3800 Shamrock Drive, Charlotte, NC 28215
Cozadd, Donna Marie – 44 Jasmine Ave., Palmetto, FL 34221
Cozadd, Fay – 2450 S. Ridgewood #10, Edgewater, FL 32141
Crawford, Shirley – 3849 William Hume Dr, Zephyrhills, FL 33541-2351 ....(813) 788-0534
Crotser, Doris Lee – 109 N. 2nd Street, Lawrence, MI 49064-9697 ....(269) 674-4249
Crum, Grace – 2000 32nd St. SE, Grand Rapids, MI 49508 ....(616) 284-5445
Crumm, Barbara – 12640 Holly Rd., Apt B211, Grand Blanc, MI 48439....................(810) 771-7319
Damberg, Marion – 495 McBride St, Dundee, MI 48131-1120....................................(734) 529-2157
Daniels, Gail – 4282 Occidental Hwy., Adrian, MI 49221 ....(517) 266-9377
Darling, Thomas – 44013 Winthrop Dr., Novi, MI 48375-8375....................................(248) 348-9039
Dennis, Barbara – 11444 Clark Rd, Davisburg, MI 48350..(810) 625-5981
Denton, Jeannine – 2401 Canoe Circle Dr, Lake Orion, MI 48360 ....(586) 482-9372
Dickins, Sally – 102 Hitchcock St., Aplena, MI 49707 ....(989) 356-4982
Diehl, Ruth – Core Bldg., Po Box 126, Cokesbury Village, Hockessin, DE 19707
Dimmick, Ann – 944 Grindle Drive, Lowell, MI 49331 ....(616) 897-5326
Doane, Helen Jeanne – 801 W. Middle St. #361, Chelsea, MI 48118
Douglas, Gertrude – 2700 Magnolia Ave., LaVerna, CA 91750
Dunstan, Bonnie – 5760 Pine Dr, Caseville, MI 48725 ....(989) 856-3263
Eckert, Mary – 1300 Benjamin Ave. SE, Grand Rapids, MI 49506 ....(616) 245-7108
Eddy, Ginger – 8020 Erie Ave, Chanhassen, MN 55317-9752 ....(952) 974-2092
Elford, Coral – 225 Capel St. #108, Sarnia, CANADA
Ellison, Nancy – 15081 Ford Rd Apt PT413, Dearborn, MI 48126-4692....................(313) 561-5576
Emelianov, Jenella – 3942 Tamarack Dr, Port Huron, MI 48060-1564
Engerbretson, Mrs. Otto – Flan unit-sompson Hs, Belmount Monument Rd.,
    Philadelphia, PA 19131
Evan, Edna – 575 E. Lincoln, Apt. #8, Birmingham, MI 48009
Everett, Annabelle – 4465 35th Terrace, N., St. Petersburg, FL 33713
Fassett, Mary Lou – 1551 Franklin SE Apt 2028, Grand Rapids, MI 49506...............(616) 285-4795
Faust, Wilma – 8881 Bever Road, Delton, MI 49046..(269) 623-5520
Ferrigan, Debbie – 169 Helen St, Montrose, MI 48457-9426
Finkbeiner, Betty – 1551 Franklin St SE Apt 2017, Grand Rapids, MI 49506 ....(616) 887-2189
Foldesi, Deb – 582 W Deerfield Road, Mt Pleasant, MI 48858..................................(989) 772-2548
Francis, Donna – 1551 Franklin SE Apt 4001, Grand Rapids, MI 49506 ....(616) 245-7402
Francis, Lois – 11 Pontiac St., Oxford, MI 48371
Franke, Charles – 2555 Amelia Lane, Lansing, MI 48917 ....(517) 322-0484
Fraser-Soots, Bea Barbara – 33762 Colony Park Dr, Farmington Hills, MI
    48331-2732 ....(248) 320-5108

Frederick, Jody – 28450 Tiffin Dr, Chesterfield, MI 48047-6203 ....(586) 598-9887
Freeland, Carol Joan – 428 W Main Street, Hudson, MI 49247...................................(989) 683-2929
Frey, Kenneth – 3907 Grodi Rd, Erie, MI 48133-9763 ....(734) 848-3411
Frick, Bonnie – 116 Wilmen Rd, Quincy, MI 49082 ....(517) 639-4496
Fry, Betty Jean – 4253 Embassy Dr SE, Grand Rapids, MI 49546 ....(616) 956-5653
Furness, Jerie – 618 W. Corunna Ave., Corunna, MI 48817-1200.............................(863) 655-1610
Gamber, Joanne – 1208 N Peniel Ave, Avon Park, FL 33825-2336...........................(863) 453-3172
Gierman, Adrianne – c/o Kristen Reed, 5324 Stanford Rd, Jacksonville, FL 32207
Gilroy, Grace – 39 Park Ave, Battle Creek, MI 49017-5615 ....(269) 965-8830
Gjerstad, Flo – 5165 Spinning Wheel Dr., Grand Blanc, MI 48439-8439
Gladding, Irene – 15177 W Center Lake Dr, Tustin, MI 49688..................................(231) 829-3661
Glasgow, Joan M – 1351 Arch Road, Eaton Rapids, MI 48827 ....(517) 663-1612
Glasgow, Marion – 225 E Bort St, Long Beach, CA 90805-2234
Goodwin, Alice – 23708 Nilan Dr, Novi, MI 48375...(313) 475-0727
Graham, Jean – 748 Clark Crossing, Grand Rapids, MI 49506 ....(616) 248-0639
Grant, Gertrude – 25671 Sherwood Rd., Warren, MI 48091-4157
Grauer, Patricia – 11442 East River Dr, DeWitt, MI 48820....................................(517) 669-3483
Grenfell, Jeannine – 2966 Sylvan Dr, Fort Gratiot, MI 48059-2853
Grettenberger, Diane – 1931 Osage Dr, Okemos, MI 48864 ....(517) 347-4604
Griffith, Nan – 29518 Westbrook Pkwy, Southfield, MI 48076-5073.........................(810) 559-0333
Griner, Beth – 6533 S. Betsie River Road, Interlochen, MI 49643-9508 ....(231) 276-9960
Guilliat, Eva – Box 144, Hillman, MI 49746-9746
Hanna, Anne Marie – 341 Lafayette, PO Box 787, Manchester, MI 48158.................(734) 428-8212
Hansen, Beth – 1551 Franklin St SE Apt 4005, Grand Rapids, MI 49506 ....(616) 776-1281
Hart, Katherine – 6813 15th Avenue Dr W, Bradenton, FL 34209-4443
Hartley, Beatrice – 519 Round Tree, Sarasota, FL 33578
Haskell, Janet –
Hatch, Lois – 536 Poplar St, Ishpeming, MI 49849-1041 ....(906) 485-4355
Helm, Charlene – 7372 Main St., Box 98, Owendale, MI 48754
Higgins, Marie – 68 Reservour, Holden, MA 01520-1520
Hilliard, Viola – 801 W. Middle St. DH-467, Chelsea, MI 48118
Hinkston, Kay – 226 Greenview, Cadillac, MI 49601-9601
Hippensteel, Johanna – 695 E Girard Road, Quincy, MI 49082 ....(517) 278-2118
Hocking, Hettie – 42 Smith St, Mount Clemens, MI 48043-2338
Hodgson, Ariel – 873 W. Avon Rd., #210, Rochester Hills, MI 48307-2705
Hoff, Mary – 850 W Huron River Dr, Belleville, MI 48111-4298
Hoffmaster, M. Jean – 9236 Tallapoosa Highway, Cedartown, GA 30125
Hollies, Charles – 1403 W. Broadway Ave. PMB 418, Apache Junction, AZ 85220....(517) 780-4503
Hoon, Fannie – 228 The Western Way, Princeton, NJ 08540
Host, Margery H – 6136 Co Rd 413, McMillan, MI 49853..(906) 293-1670
Houk, Anna Belle – 4585 S Lakeshore Dr, Ludington, MI 49431 ....(231) 845-7510
Huddleson, Janet – 15822 Lavender Pl, Broomfield, CO 80023-9412.......................(303) 807-8118
Imms, Carolyn – 65 Harbor Oaks Dr, Fruitland Park, FL 34731 ....(352) 728-1052
Iseminger, Phyllis – 815 N Washington, Battle Creek, MI 49017 ....(269) 965-3407
James, Phyllis – C/o Kathryn Mccurdy, Romeo, MI 48065
Janka, Mildred – 09780 Meadows Trail, Boyne Falls, MI 49713
Jensen, Yvonne – 349 Ardussi St, Frankenmuth, MI 48734
Johns, Marlene – 3127 Heather Glynn Drive, Mulberry, FL 33860 ....(863) 425-9691
Johnson, Elouise – 3317 Sir Thomas Drive #24, Silver Springs, MD 20904..............(301) 890-3478
Johnson, Judy – 9459-32 Mission Gorge Rd, Santee, CA 92071 ....(619) 749-7859
Jones, Ruth – 540 Georgetown Dr Apt 36, Traverse City, MI 49684-4479.................(231) 645-1761

ADDRESSES

Jones, Shirley – 910 Fairmead Rd Apt B, Plainfield, IN 46168-2415
Jongeward, Elaine – 574 Belltower Ave, Deltona, FL 32725 .... (386) 574-0373
Jorgensen, Lenna (Daniel) – 3420 Nathan Ct, Rocklin, CA 95677-2351
Karlzen, Martha Jane – PO Box 3, Charlotte, MI 48813 .... (517) 541-0653
King, Wilma – 15190 Imlay City Rd Apt 2, Mussey, MI 48014-2401
Kline, Tina – 28955 Pujol St Apt 10-B, Temecula, CA 92590-2837 .... (951) 506-0609
Kline-Hunt, Janet W – 7630 W St Andrews Circle, Portage, MI 49024 .... (269) 373-1588
Kolb, Dena – RR 5 Box 5032, Grayling, MI 49738-8713
Kramer-Schurman, Donna – 696 N. State Route 741, Lebanon, OH 45036
Kraushaar, Doris – 5621 Blue Grass Lane, Saline, MI 48176-8176
Krichbaum, Susan – 24082 Bingham Pointe Dr., Bingham Farms, MI 48025
Kuhn, Mary Beth – 10143 Lakeside Dr, Perrinton, MI 48871-9647 .... (989) 682-4814
Kye, Yang Ja – 14715 San Jacinto Dr, Moreno Valley, CA 92555-6366 .... (951) 242-8484
LaFrance, David – 15132 Snowberry Ct, Spring Lake, MI 49456-2814 .... (616) 850-2157
Lamb, Ollie – 801 W Middle St # DH 372, Chelsea, MI 48118-1341
Lantz, Melinda – Hubbard Manor, Apt.#912, 22077 Beech St., Dearborn, MI 48124
Laphew, Geneva V. – 19438 Beech Daly Rd, Detroit, MI 48240-1321
Leach, Marie – 2025 Charter Oaks Dr, Clearwater, FL 33763-4209
Leach, Peggy – 3398 Crestwood Dr, Salt Lake City, UT 84109-3202
Lemmons, Barbara – 410 3rd Ave S, #D9, Hurley, WI 54534-1527 .... (715) 561-3310
Lester, Maridelle – 3128 N. Harding Ave., Indianapolis, IN 46208-4800
Lewis, Ann – 6393 Little Lake Geneva Road, Keystone Heights, FL
Lindley, Shirley – 454 Hickory Court, Leipsic, OH 45856-5856
Lovejoy, Lorraine – 224 SR 13, Wesley Manor, Jacksonville, FL 32223
Lowes, Carol – 27145 County Road 364, Mattawan, MI 49071-9558 .... (269) 668-6526
Luciani, Carolyn – 801 W Middle St Apt 560, Chelsea, MI 48118-1374 .... (734) 475-5926
Lutz-Sempert, Joyce – 7651 W. Chelsea Ct, PO Box 5066, Homosassa Springs, FL 34447
Magnuson, Edla – 714 Parkvies, Saint Paul, MN 55117-4156
Mahan, Marcia – 1555 N. Main St., Frankfort, IN 46041
Malstrom, Esther – c/o Joseph Malstrom, 1392 Van Buren St., St. Paul, MN 55101-5101
Mannino, Barbara – 8732 Huckleberry Lane, Lansing, MI 48917 .... (517) 449-3413
Marbly, Mayme S. – 8328 S Indiana Ave, Chicago, IL 60619-4727
Marshall, Esther – 2611 Wildwood Dr Apt 519, Brunswick, GA 31520-4250
Martin, Martha – 1368 Grayton St, Grosse Pointe Park, MI 48230-1128 .... (313) 885-3974
Martin, Mary – Balmoral Skilled Nursing Home, 5500 Fort St., Trenton, MI 48183
Matson, Jacqueline – 5792 Leisure South Dr SE, Kentwood, MI 49548 .... (616) 437-3022
Matthews, Edith – 18190 W. Outer Dr., Dearborn, MI 48128-1349
Maurer, Edrye A. Eastman – 10101 Jackson Square, Decatur, GA 30030 .... (269) 459-5223
McCaw, Jeanne – 4211 Embassy Dr SE, Grand Rapids, MI 49546-2438 .... (616) 975-1875
McKanders, Cherlyn – PO Box 158, Washington, MI 48094-0158 .... (313) 640-8498
McLellan, Virginia – 4640 Shaw Road, Harrisville, MI 48740 .... (989) 724-6248
McLennan, Mary – 241 Bravado Lane, Palm Beach Shores, FL 33404
McNally, Bessie – 1852 Union Ave, Benton Harbor, MI 49022-6264
McVety, Elizabeth – 1932 Stimson Rd, Brown City, MI 48416-8181 .... (810) 346-3384
Mecartney, Nancy – 801 W. Middle St., Apt. Dh 175, Chelsea, MI 48118
Meines, Noreen – 11279 Whispering Creek Dr, Allendale, MI 49401 .... (616) 895-5297
Meredith, Gertrude A. – 1701 Mallery, Flint, MI 48501
Michael, Helen – 170 Grove, Coopersville, MI 49404
Middleton, Betty – 344 Persimmon Way, Harrodsburg, KY 40330
Milano, Regina – 12 1/2 Applegrove Dr, Nicholasville, KY 40356
Miles, Louise K. – 5915 Cartago Dr, Lansing, MI 48911-6480 .... (989) 777-1248

Miles, Marilyn – 309 Fieldstone Dr., Hemlock, MI 48626-9104 ....(989) 642-3075
Miller, Beth – 175 Timber Lakes Est, Heber City, UT 84032-9694
Miller, Deborah Reid – 554 Faraday Dr SE, Grand Rapids, MI 49548-8500...............(616) 350-2991
Miller, Phyllis – 37644 Pinata Avenue, Zephyr Hills, FL 33541 ....(813) 788-1676
Millet, Edna – 776 Newberry Rd, Nashville, TN 37205-1129 ....(313) 582-8483
Minor, Eleanore – 5722 E Brenda Ln, Kalamazoo, MI 49004
Mirmak, Letha – 804 Maurice, Alton, IL 62002-1957
Mitchell, Coral – C/o Mrs. H. Mccoy, 1702 Francis, Jackson, MI 49201
Mitchell, Hazel – 16631 Mendota, Detroit, MI 48221
Mohr, Phyllis – 4070 York Ln, Jackson, MI 49201
Moore, Tamara – 33250 Bernice Ave, Paw Paw, MI 49079-9504 ....(269) 657-6445
Morse, Lorna – 833 S Ausable Trl, Grayling, MI 49738-9166 ....(989) 348-7037
Mosher, Sharry – 510 Village W Apt B, Midland, MI 48642-9343...............................(810) 627-3055
Mulder, Lydia – 219 Highland, Dearborn, MI 48128 ....(313) 278-8634
Murphy, Patricia – 1892 Jasper Place, Ocala, FL 34472 ....(352) 694-1892
Myers, Beth – 262 Pennbrook, Battle Creek, MI 49017 ....(269) 274-9120
Myers, Linda – 7463 Navajo Valley Dr., Byron Center, MI 49315
Myette, Ruth – 211 1/2 S. Spruce St, Traverse City, MI 49684 ....(231) 946-5993
Nachtrieb, Evelyn – 1616 W Glendale Ave # 380, Phoenix, AZ 85021-8948
Nelson, Juanita – 1145 College Ave, Columbus, OH 43209-2858
Nicholson, Patricia – 392 Shot Point Dr, Marquette, MI 49855-9554 ....(906) 343-6506
Noordhof, Barbara – 14297 Leonard Rd, Spring Lake, MI 49456...............................(616) 935-9718
Olde, Grace – 4137 Morehouse Raod, West Lafayette, IN 47906
Olsen, Robert – 175 Cherry Street, Freeport, MI 49325 ....(616) 765-3838
Olsen, Sandy – 557 McBride St, Dundee, MI 48131-8131 ....(734) 529-5389
Osborne, Pearl E. – 6830 E 19th Ave, Denver, CO 80220-1725
Osmond, Rick – 2051 Alice St, Farwell, MI 48622-9746 ....(989) 588-6293
Page, Mildred – 8111 E Broadway Blvd Apt 307, Tucson, AZ 85710-3929 ....(520) 495-5880
Palmer Turner, Johncie – 1039 Crestwood Ln, Jackson, MI 49203 ....(517) 769-2329
Patton, Louine – Sayre Christain Village, 580 Greenfield Dr., #107A, Lexington, KY 40517
Paulson, Gerrie – 1414 Woodcock Pass, Alger, MI 48610
Penzien, Jo – 7414 Wall Ct, Dexter, MI 48130-1338
Petersen, Elsie – Masonic Pathways, 1200 Wright Ave #233, Alma, MI 48801-1133 ...(989) 875-4665
Pillow, Lorraine – 5133 Hoffman Street, PO Box 68, Elkton, MI 48731-0068
Porter, Nancy Hicok – 9514 Bluewater Hwy Rt #3, Lowell, MI 49331-9298
Preston, Sally – 4491 E Park Dr, Bay City, MI 48706-2549..(989) 667-4438
Price, Martha – 5057 Woodlands Ct, Flint, MI 48532-4078
Pumfery, Carole – 21345 52nd St, Grand Junction, MI 49056-9755...........................(269) 427-5513
Quick, Mary Levack – 1941 Wellesley Dr, Detroit, MI 48203-1428 ....(313) 891-2861
Raymo, Muriel – 1215 Riverford Dr, Vestavia Hills, AL 35216-6191 ....(205) 985-4912
Reese, Carin – 3592 Windsor Woods Dr, Wayland, MI 49348-1463
Reese, Janice – 3302 SE Alder St, Hillsboro, OR 97123-7435..................................(503) 648-6134
Regier, Hinako – 30 Seven Star Lane, Concord, MA 1742
Reinhart, Ruth – 9136 Flamingo Circle, N. Ft. Myers, FL 33903................................(239) 652-9188
Reyner, Beverly – 4500 Killarney Park Dr, Burton, MI 48529-1832 ....(810) 744-4265
Rhoads, Annie Ruth Callis – 3800 Shamrock Dr., Charlotte, NC 28215
Rice, Birdie – 2662 Columbus Street, Detroit, MI 48206..(313) 871-7918
Rice, Dorotohy – 478 4th St Apt 202, Beaver, PA 15009-2235
Rice, Shan – 10333 W. Olive Ave. #146, Peoria, AZ 85345
Rice, Susan – 533 Kern Rd, Fowlerville, MI 48836-9251
Richards, Helen – 3700 E Allen Rd, Howell, MI 48855-8224

Richards, Ruth – 733 Gilead Shores Dr, Bronson, MI 49028
Richie, Alice – 208 Freeman Forest Dr, Newnan, GA 30265-3399 ....(770) 683-9506
Ritchie, Dorothy – PO Box 274, Hesperia, MI 49421-0274
Ritchie, Florence K. – 129 Smachbar Bldg., Champaign, IL 61820
Robinson, Carole – 1710 14th St, Wyandotte, MI 48192-3612
Rosa, Annette – 19558 Maple, PO Box 123, Lake Ann, MI 49650-0123
Rothfuss, Jackie (Jacqueline) – 2049 Rowland Ave SE #8, Grand Rapids, MI 49546....(616) 202-7206
Ruotsalainen, Jenny – PO Box 1268, Twentynine Palms, CA 92277-0980
Sailor, Clara – 119 Broad St N, Battle Creek, MI 49017....................................(269) 963-2197
Salisbury, Marylin – 1551 Franklin SE #4004, Grand Rapids, MI 49506....................(616) 246-6360
Schloop, Patricia – 1551 Franklin SE Apt 2022, Grand Rapids, MI 49506 ....(616) 246-1006
Schroeder, Carolyn – 2019 Ter Van Dr NE, Grand Rapids, MI 49505-6369
Scovel, Mary A – 14176 Lake Wildwood Dr, Penn Valley, CA 95946-9592
Scranton Bassett, Vivian – 1551 Franklin SE Apt. 3025, Grand Rapids, MI 49506 ....(616) 247-0950
Seitz, Oneida – 10590 Wadsworth Rd., Reese, MI 48757
Selberg, Linda – 640 S Lafayette St, Dearborn, MI 48124-1594
Sever, Diane – 13011 Murray St, Grand Blanc, MI 48439
Shamblen, Audrey – Centerline Park Towers #8-18, 8033 E 10 Mile Rd, Centerline, MI 48015
Sheppard, Sandy – 7420 Majestic Wood Dr, Linden, MI 48451-8836.......................(989) 823-8996
Sheridan, Nancy – 604 Ames Ct., Bay City, MI 48708
Shields, Ida – 6851 Goldenrod Ave NE, Rockford, MI 49341-9436............................(616) 874-2113
Siders, Vesta – 904 Piper Dr, Saginaw, MI 48604-1833 ....(989) 753-8806
Silvernail, Florence – 3832 Perrine Rd, Rives Junction, MI 49277-9642 ....(517) 569-3715
Simmons, Charlotte – 801 West Middle #373, Chelsea, MI 48118 ....(734) 433-9879
Skinner, Bill – 460 S Edgar Rd, Mason, MI 48854-9744 ....(517) 676-1529
Smith, Beverly – 514 E Roselawn Dr, Logansport, IN 46947-2134...........................(269) 679-4646
Smith, Diana – 10275 Strasburg Rd., Erie, MI 48133
Smith, Dorothy J. – 3341 Woodwind Dr NE, Grand Rapids, MI 49525-9752 ....(616) 719-2131
Smith, Jennella – 3942 Tamarack Dr, Port Huron, MI 48060-1564
Smith, Phyllis – Beacon Hill, 1845 Boston SE Apt 308, Grand Rapids, MI
    49506-4400...(616) 805-3560
Snow, Dorothy – 501 Leorie Street, North Muskegon, MI 49445 ....(231) 744-2659
Soderholm, David – 216 5th St, Harrisville, MI 48740-9673 ....(231) 450-0901
Stine, Jean – 9270 Jones Road, Bellevue, MI 49021 ....(269) 763-2706
Stone, Helen – 1428 Roosevelt Dr, Venice, FL 34293-6853................................(248) 835-1301
Strait, Janet Sue – 1402 Suncrest Dr. NE, Grand Rapids, MI 49503........................(616) 245-1099
Stricker, Edith – c/o Jacqueline Wisman, 1218 West E St., North Platte, NE 69101
Stubbs, Caroline – 104 E Mechanic, Yale, MI 48097-3454
Sundell, Jennifer – 3289 Hitching Post Rd Apt 40, Dewitt, MI 48820-9664 ....(616) 527-9656
Sursaw, Margaret – 37737 Hixford Pl Apt G-20, Westland, MI 48185-3365
Sutton, Helen – 1000 Manhattan Ave., Dayton, OH 45406
Syme, Judy – 250 Marcell Dr NE Apt 6, Rockford, MI 49341-1380
Taber, Miriam – 1551 Franklin St SE Apt 3305, Grand Rapids, MI 49506 ....(616) 475-0717
Taylor, Josephine – c/o Gilford Taylor, 17682 Cooley Ave., Detroit, MI 48219
Teague, Lillie Mae – 331 Franklin Blvd, Pontiac, MI 48340-8340
Tester, Lydia – 455 S. College Drive, Heston, KS 67062-8105
Thomas, Ann – 1890 Ashley Dr, Ypsilanti, MI 48198-9412
Thornton, June – 512 Englewood Drive, Roscommon, MI 48653
Timm, Ann – 5110 Autumn Ln, North Street, MI 48049-4459....................................(810) 987-5124
Timmons, Doris – 8822 Richfield Ave., Livonia, MI 48150 ....(734) 953-9208
Tingland, Edith R. – 4447 Wisner, Saginaw, MI 48601

Tomlinson, Karan – 36 Rockhampton Ridge, Battle Creek, MI 49014 ....(269) 968-4930
Trebilcock, Leanne – 30077 Fox Run Dr, Beverly Hills, MI 48025-4720 ....(248) 566-3021
Trevarthen, Amanda – 2501 Broadway, Huntington Park, CA 90255-6343
Truran, Donna – 5884 Augusta Lane, Grand Blanc, MI 48439-9472 ....(231) 955-0257
Turner, Johncie Kay (Palmer) – 1039 Crestwood Ln, Jackson, MI 49203 ....(517) 769-2329
Van Wormer, Dennis – 3013 Oakwood Dr, Port Huron, MI 48060
Vandlen, Gerry – 1551 Franklin St SE Apt 3027, Grand Rapids, MI 49506 ....(616) 475-0125
Vaught, Helen – 1641 S Broadway St, Hastings, MI 49058-2561 ....(269) 945-9392
Vuurens, Florence – 2685 Forest Hills Drive, Muskegon, MI 49441-3441 ....(231) 828-4341
Wagner, Noreen – 3534 Conger St., Port Huron, MI 48060
Walker, Lorna – 2753 E. Waterview Dr., Avon Park, FL 33825-6015 ....(863) 314-6502
Wangdahl, Agnes – 1252 Doubleday Drive, Arnold, MD 21012
Ward, Olive – 3202 Meridian Rd, Leslie, MI 49251-9520
Weatherup, Shelley – 40460 Cinnamon Cir, Canton, MI 48187-4588
Weeks, Martha – 429 Center St, PO Box 404, Manistique, MI 49854-1111 ....(906) 341-3423
Wehrli, Kitty – 32805 Garfield Rd, Fraser, MI 48026-3848
Westfall, Geraldine – 1001 Lynn, Kalamazoo, MI 49008-2952
White, Joanne – 158 LaSiesta, Edgewater, FL 32141-2141 ....(904) 428-0900
White, Sharon – 745 Clark Crossing SE, Grand Rapids, MI 49506 ....(616) 425-0045
Whyte, Blanche – 17387 Plainview, Detroit, MI 48219-8219......................................(313) 538-1194
William, Monica – 4100 Walnut Lake Rd, West Bloomfield, MI 48323........................(248) 851-0149
Williams, Virginia – 36615 Cherry St, Newark, CA 94560
Wolfe, Sue – 245 Highland Dr, Jackson, MI 49201 ....(517) 926-6041
Wong, Patricia – 326 - 5th Street, Ann Arbor, MI 48103-6209...................................(734) 741-8160
Wood, Judith – 1842 Live Oak Court, Avon, IN 46123
Wood, Una – 4300 Martin Rd., Box 462, Capac, MI -
Woodward, Eva D. – 1609 - 21st Ave. West, Braderton, FL 33505
Yarlott, Irene – 2946 Creek Park Dr NE, Marietta, GA 30062 ....(770) 321-5310
Yearby, Joan – 250675 Meadowbrook Rd, Novi, MI 48375
Yoh, Mary – 5026 Village Gardens Drive, Sarasota, FL 34234 ....(616) 392-3942
Young, Harry – 700 N. LeRoy, Fenton, MI 48430

— MAC Photos

ELECTED LAYPERSONS ON CONFERENCE COMMITTEES

Alberts, Amy – 6929 Curtis Rd, PO Box 102, Hale 48739-9006 (989) 728-5772 ......amyfaithalberts@juno.com

Anderson, Ruby – 25180 Thorndyke, Southfield 48033 (248) 352-9246 ....rbydandrs@aol.com

Angarita-Oviedo, Ricardo – 247 S 1st Street, Harbor Beach 48441 (734) 680-5185 .....vida7plena@gmail.com

Apol, David – 3246 Wayburn Ave SW Frnt Apt, Grandville 49418-1913 (616) 292-6687 .....apoldavid@aol.com

Appling, Sharon – 882 Rivard Blvd, Grosse Pointe 48230-1257 (313) 671-8974 ....sea0704@comcast.net

Archambeau, Don – 28270 Elmira St, Livonia 48150-3289 (734) 422-2227.........donarchambeau@gmail.com

Armstrong, Minnie – 18107 Baldwin Rd., Holly 48442-9392 (810) 877-0511 ....minibstrong1975@gmail.com

Arnold, Nancy – 350 Riviera Terrace, Waterford 48328 (248) 682-6140....................narnold@michiganumc.org

Arnold, Nicholas – 350 Riviera Terrace, Waterford 48328 ....NJAbaconator@aol.com

Ashford, Dwanda – 8000 Woodward Ave, Detroit 48202-2528 (313) 481-1045......drdoffice@michiganumc.org

Bailey, Taylorie – 16855 Rosemont, Detroit 48219-4117 (313) 531-0751 ....etbailey77@sbcglobal.net

Ball, Janet – 6874 5 Mile Rd, Blanchard 49310-9474 (231) 250-1084 ....ljball6@hotmail.com

Bank, Wayne – 6551 Lakeshore Rd, Lexington 48450-9619 (586) 945-7975 ....waynebank@sbcglobal.net

Baumann, Karl – 5010 N. Magrudder Rd., Coleman 48618-9581 (989) 465-1557 ....karlbauman@hotmail.com

Belt, Michael – 918 Dykstra Rd, North Muskegon 49445-2010 (231) 747-9176.......michael.belt@comcast.net

Belton, Tamara – 904 Sheldon SE, Grand Rapids 49503 (616) 452-3226 ....tmrhrdn@aol.com

Bennett, David – 2471 Veltema Dr, Holt 48842-9740 (517) 694-0517.....................bennettd41@ameritech.net

Bernum, Robert – 3209 Monticello Dr, Port Huron 48060-1855 (810) 984-2771 ....BBernum@comcast.net

Beyer, James – ....jbeyer@umcampingboard.org

Blashill, Mary – 07909 M-43, South Haven 49090-9703 (269) 767-6060 ....maryblashill@gmail.com

Bledsoe, Rose – 1106 Nine Mile Road, Sterling 48659-9772 (989) 324-8514 ....bledsoerm@gmail.com

Booker, Victoria – Beverly Hills United Methodist Church, 20000 W. 13 Mile Rd., Beverly Hills 48025
....director@jfonsemi.org

Bosserd, Jim – 3631 13 Mile Rd NW, Sparta 49345-9794 (616) 887-7805....................Bosserdjim@gmail.com

Bostic, Patricia – 4106 W. 13 Mile, Apt.D, Royal Oak 48073 (248) 677-4940.........................pbostic02@att.net

Braddock, Mildred – PO Box 231, Southfield 48037-0231 (248) 910-1731 .....mildred.braddock@sbcglobal.net

Brown, Diane – 4512 Cottonwood Dr., Ann Arbor 48108 (734) 662-0469.........................dlb4512@yahoo.com

Burke, Louella – 2004 W Hansen Rd, Scottville 49454-9613 (231) 845-1789..................aburke9534@aol.com

Burton-Collier, Linda – 2574 127th Ave, Allegan 49010-9250 (269) 793-7340 .....lindaburtoncollier@gmail.com

Busley, Sus'ann – 555 S Williamston Rd, Dansville 48819 (517) 623-6239 ....sbusley@michiganumc.org

Buxton, Susanne – 350 N Main St Unit 814, Royal Oak 48067 (248) 548-7567 ....sbbuxton@sbcglobal.net

Campbell, Ernestine – 20300 Westmoreland Rd., Detroit 48219 (313) 529-5686 ....ecampbe16@yahoo.com

Carr, Liz – 2267 Sunset Bluff Dr, Holland 49424-2386 (317) 847-3661................................Lizcarr@charter.net

Carter, Ethel – 2280 Southgate Dr SE, Kentwood 49508 (616) 452-3226 ....ethel2280@gmail.com

Chappell, Shirley – 719 S Griffin, Grand Haven 49417-2225 (616) 846-4197 ....shirley2billchapel@att.net

Cho, Koom – ....mathchampion@gmail.com

Christian, Howard – PO Box 163, Goodrich 48438-0163 (810) 636-7223 ....howard102742@yahoo.com

Chu, Ethan – 733 Orchard Dr, Williamston 48895-1074 ....ethanichu@gmail.com

Clawson, Randie – 384 Lind Dr., Traverse City 49696-1183 (231) 929-7808.........randie.clawson@yahoo.com

Clevenger, Renae – 2302 Longfellow Ln., Midland 48640-2419 (989) 430-8562.........renaeclev76@gmail.com

Coffey, Judith – 128 Forest Lawn Dr, Cadillac 49601-9734 (231) 775-6095.................jcoffeyumc@yahoo.com

Coffman, Patsy – 206 S Swegles St, St Johns 48879-8879 (989) 224-7692 ....patsymcoffman@gmail.com

Comiskey, Mary – 1321 Beamer Rd, Blissfield 49228 (517) 918-8252

Costales, Jorge – 9841 Woodlawn Dr, Portage 49002-7217 (269) 324-0697 ....chumyc@aol.com

Coyle, Joy – 6720 Spring Creek, Plymouth 48170-7624 (248) 486-6686 ....brcoyle@aol.com

Craig, Nancy – 1428 Safire Court, East Lansing 48823-6357 (517) 351-1391........................craign@msu.edu

Dahlman, Laurie – 1228 Southern Ave, Kalamazoo 49001-4339 (269)343-1490 ....ladmsu1@gmail.com

Darby, Michael – 5133 Scott Rd., Mr. Morris 48458-9724 (810) 610-8500 ....1stnaturalsolutions@gmail.com

Darrow, Linda – 232 N. Cooley St., Mt. Pleasant 48858-1311 (989) 763-8750 ....darrowlinda@gmail.com

Davis, Murray – 26225 Fordson Hwy, Redford 48239-2140 (313) 937-3453....................mbdavisinc@aol.com de la Garza, Laurie – 1306 Michigan Ave., Gladstone 49837 (906) 428-4623 ....laurie.kdlg@sbcglobal.net

DeLong, Cameron – 4934 Brownstone Drive NE, Rockford 49341 (616) 866-3191 ....cdelong@wnj.com

Dick, Kevin – 606 W Sunset Dr, Muskegon 49445-3066 (231) 719-8006................................kevin@j-fins.com

Dobbs, David – 612 State Street, Eaton Rapids 48827 (517) 663-4947 ....ddobbs@michiganumc.org

Donley, Lee – 1977 N 2700 East Rd, Moweaqua, IL 62550-8567 ....leedonley2@aol.com

Dorman, Kathleen – 2596 Vatter Rd., Snover 48472-9757 (810) 404-9630 ....khdflame@icloud.com

Dosca, Steve – 3883 Starchief St, Kalamazoo 49048-6119 (269) 345-5683 ....stevekazoomi@yahoo.com

Dowell, Kenneth – 19080 San Jose Blvd., Lathrup Village 48076-3324 (248) 559-7047...........ken@dowell.ws

Downer, Holly – 3733 Bantam Dr, Hudsonville 4942-8669 (616) 669-6794...............Holly@grmetroministry.org

Doyal, Mark – 525 University Dr, East Lansing 48823-3046 (517) 927-5920............mdoyal@michiganumc.org

DuPree, Brenda – 8165 Holcomb, Clarkston 48348-4313 (248) 625-5141....................bkdupree@comcast.net

Emmert, Becky – 1161 E Clark Road Ste 212, DeWitt 48820 (800) 334-0544 ....bemmert@michiganumc.org

Emmons, Susan – 2226 Anderson Dr SE, Grand Rapids 49506-4032 (269) 308-3802

Erbes, Annette – 1951 Heatherton Dr, Holt 48842-1570 (517) 694-8277 ....merbes@earthlink.net

Euper, Jacqueline – 11463 S State Rd., Morrice 48857 (517) 625-2920................................tjeuper@tm.net

Fennell, Deborah – 3409 Rolfe Rd, Mason 48854-9749 (517) 676-1887 ....debontheweb@wowway.com

Fielder, Sue – 2010 Maca Vista Dr, Indian River 49749-9727 (231) 238-4751 ....sue.irumc@gmail.com

Fox, Kathleen – 1626 Lake Dr Apt 189, Haslett 48840-8421 ....strox@rocketmail.com

Francis, Merna – 2924 N 33rd St, Galesburg 49053-8502 (269) 665-9430

Franklin, Susan – 2392 Fern Ct, Farwell 48622-9789 (989) 339-0491.................................Lsfbflat@gmail.com

Freeland, Kathy – 6125 Fourth, PO Box 195, Mayville 48744-0195 (989) 843-5247 ....ksfdaf@sbcglobal.net

Gackler, Kenneth – 410 Johnson St., Caledonia 49316-9724 (616) 891-5682 ....gackler@iserv.net

Garbrecht, Bonnie – 153 Garrison Ave, Battle Creek 49017 (269) 964-9828 ....garbrechtab@comcast.net

Garrigues-Cortelyou, Isaac – 318 Edmund Ave, Royal Oak 48073-2648 (248) 585-0352
....isaaccordonbleu@gmail.com

Gillette, Robert – 4091 12 Mile Road, Rockford 49341-9190 (616) 866-0934 ....gillette@wuattorneys.com

Gray, Fred – 2100 Norwood Dr., Midland 48640 (989) 631-0763 ....hhs69@aol.com

Grimmett, Toni – 60 W. Bethune, Detroit 48202 (313) 303-1230 ....citydancer1@sbcglobal.net

Gulliver, Bruce – 4107 Brockway, Saginaw 48638-4776 (989) 792-7116 ....gulliverbag@cavtel.net

Guy, Nichea – (616) 456-7168 ....orangecelt00@aol.com

Guyon, Rich – 3289 Outback Tr., Pinckney 48169-8876 (734) 751-7719......................rich.guyon@charter.net

Hahn, Lisa – 3317 Noeske St, Midland 48640 ....funny.laugh.88@gmail.com

Halsted, Kirk – 12 Orchard Terrace, Burnt Hills, NY 12027 (518) 365-3716 ....kirk.halsted@gmail.com

Hardiman, Clayton – ....chardiman@muskegonchronicle.com

Hart, Phyllis – 1894 Chatham Dr., Troy 48084-1414 (248) 649-2396...jophhart@att.net

Hazen, Catharine – 2150 Teggerdine Rd, White Lake 48386 (248)698-9326 ....cathzen@comcast.net

Herriff, Judy – 5651 Bunker Rd, Eaton Rapids 48827-9104 ....jherriff@gmail.com

Hewitt, Suzanne – 2250 Knapp St NE, Grand Rapids 49505-4414 (616) 361-9565 ....suzmckhew@att.net

Hills, Claire – 1418 Lake Blvd. #1, St. Joseph 49085-1691 ....cbhills@gmail.com

Hills, Michele – 12300 W Michigan, Parma 49269-9575 (517) 745-8455........secretary@umcampingboard.org

Hines, Paula – 925 35th St. SW, Wyoming 49509-3538 (616) 235-7001 ....paulahines@gmail.com

Hitts, Elise – 1881 Ellinger Rd., Alanson 49706 (231) 548-5774 ....21hitelie@rayder.org

Hodges, Carol – 222 N Kalamazoo Mall Apt 320, Kalamazoo 49007 ....carolhodges.kalamazoo@gmail.com

Holt, Kathy – 2376 Belle Glade Ct, Fenton 48430 (810) 750-1931 ....kathleenholt@charter.net

Hopgood, Hoon-Yung – PO Box 30036, Lansing 48909 (855) 347-8006 ..senhhopgood@senate.michigan.gov

Howard, David – 314 McCormick Place, Dexter 48130-8702 (734) 253-2126................dchoward@provide.net

Huizing, John – 40 N. Plum Street, Hart 49420-9674 (231) 873-0418.....................huizingathart@charter.net

Hunt, Blair – 2110 Palm Dale Dr SW, Wyoming 49519-9668 (269) 341-0467................blair.r.hunt@gmail.com

Hurlbut, Wynne – 36146 Cherry St, Gobles 49055-9652 (269) 628-2944..............wynne_hurlbut@frontier.com

Iseler, Lawrence – 5606 Minden Rd N, Port Hope 48468-9707 (989) 428-4229 ....mciseler70@gmail.com

Ives, Russ – ....russives@comcast.net

Jennings, Karl – 8711 Pebble Creek Dr., Pinckney 48169-8577 (517) 404-0058.........karl@borekjennings.com

Johnson, Armentha – 2084 Eastcastle Dr SE, Grand Rapids (616) 452-3226 ....J.Armentha@yahoo.com
Jones, Ruth – 540 Georgetown Dr Apt 36, Traverse City 49684 (231) 645-1761 ...tcgrannynanny@yahoo.com
Kandell, Carol – 1122 River Rd., Marysville 48040-1579 (810) 364-6891 ....carolkandell@comcast.net
Keeler, Gregory – 25170 Circle Dr, Southfield 48075-6120 (248) 350-3659 ....tron_9990@yahoo.com
Kimball, Dale – 118 Buckingham Ln, Battle Creek 49017-3146 (269) 565-0569 ....kimballd@live.com
Knapp, Earle – 820 W Corunna Ave Apt 7A, Corunna 48817-1265 (301) 980-6947 ....earl.d.knapp@me.com
Kolasa, Renard – 39395 W. 12 Mile Rd., Suite 200, Farmington Hills 48333
Kopple, Richard – 3804 Lawndale Dr., Midland 48642-6641 (989) 837-0434 ....WZQ4J6@aol.com
Kroeze, Jenny – 640 Seminole Dr, Fremont 49412-1746 (231) 924-4814 ....jennyk48g@gmail.com
Lawrence, Clara – 20222 Sunset Street, Livonia 48152 (248) 863-7705................claralaw4peace@gmail.com
Leavitt, Waltha Gaye – 8524 E. Colby Rd., Crystal 48818-9729 (989) 640-0238 ....wally@cmsinter.net
LeBaron, Jim – 13401 Peacock Rd, Laingsburg 48848-9296 (517) 641-8042 ....jlebaronllc@aol.com
Lee, Loretta – 142 Greenwood Ave, Battle Creek 49037 (269) 317-7377 ....weatherBY2000@sbcglobal.net
Lefler, Kathleen – 18934 Wayne Rd, Livonia 48152-2852 (248) 888-9456 ....kathyD0453@aol.com
Leipprandt, Jeff – 7171 Filion Rd., Pigeon 48755 ....jeff.leipprandt@gmail.com
Lenz, Peter – 3790 Pinto Rd, Kalamazoo 49004-9109 (269) 345-4864 ....phlenz@chartermi.net
Leppink, Ransom – PO Box 365, Lakeview 48850-0365 (989) 352-6430 ....leppinks@hotmail.com
Lett, Steven – 6780 Betsie River Rd, Interlochen 49643-9795 (517) 372-4204 ....slett@wlklaw.com
Lightner, Brian – 62574 52nd Ave, Hartford 49057-9707 (269) 308-2637................brianrplightner1@gmail.com
Litchfield, Dorie – 61470 County Road 657, Lawton 49065-9609 (269) 436-0023 ......creator.dorie@gmail.com
Long, Robert – 10 Sycamore Dr., Chelsea 48118-9415 (734) 475-8449 ....rlquizzy@gmail.com
Luna, Sonya – 1467 Collegewood St, Ypsilanti 48197-2021 (734) 961-7314 ....sluna@michiganumc.org
Lundquist, C David – 5920 Wood Valley Rd, Kalamazoo 49009 (616) 372-4772 ......dlundquist@ameritech.net
Machesky, Lisa – Baldwin Avenue Center, PO Box 420700, Pontiac 48340 (248) 642-6343
....lmachesky@umcampingboard.org
Maidens, Valerie – 1639 Black Bark Ln, Traverse City 49686 (231) 941-2360...............vjmaidens@yahoo.com
Mallard, Mildred – 18525 Division, Marshall 49068-9774 (269) 781-4689.....................Abcboutique@aol.com
Mangum, Audrey – 3591 W Outer Dr, Detroit 48221-1661 (912) 432-3001 ....amangumsav@gmail.com
Marsh, Georgia – 212 Chauncey Court, Marshall 49068 (269) 781-2501...........georgiamarsh212@gmail.com
Marsman, Mara – 1675 84th St SE, Caledonia 49316-7939 (616) 890-1810 ....maram@cornerstonemi.org
Maynard, Kathy – (989) 727-3677 ....K2maynard@frontier.com
McCarthy, Terry – 1765 3 Mile NE, Grand Rapids (616) 452-3226 ....terry@mccarthycolortech.com
McClintic, Raymond – 3781 Peninsular Dr, Gladwin 48624-9742 (989) 426-7019 ...raymcclintic@hotmail.com
McCormick, Robert – 13185 Wilkes Rd, Yale 48097-3615 ....mccor1958@gmail.com
McKenzie, Clarice – 396 Ford St., Bitely 49309-9679 (727) 536-1888 ....cjmckum@gmail.com
McNitt, Rebecca – 110 S. Madison St., Adrian 49221 (517) 265-5161...................dcumcarchives@adrian.edu
McNitt, William – 3400 LaSalle Dr., Ann Arbor 48108-1990 (734) 971-7045..................mmcnitt@umich.nedu
Mentzer, Mitsy – 1262 Westwood Dr., Adrian 49221-1361 (517) 263-7496...................mmentzer@mentz.com
Miller, Diana – 3352 W. River Dr., Gladwin 48624-9730 (989) 426-2644 ....diana@ddmiller.net
Minert, Al – 104 E. 29th Street, Holland 49423-5126 (616) 396-3751 ....apminerthm@att.net
Mitchell, Beth – 3813 Rockwood Dr, Kalamazoo 49004 (269) 343-6806............bmitchell@lewisreedallen.com
Mitchell, Daphne – 29926 Robert Dr., Livonia 48150-3046 (734) 425-5926 ....daphnehmyd@aol.com
Mobley, Oneika – 21420 Indian Creek Dr, Farmington Hills 48335 (313) 728-9496 .....Mobley318@yahoo.com
Mowery, M. Kay – 2151 Primrose Lane, Flint 48532 (810) 820-6493 ....mkmowery@comcast.net
Muntz, Janet – 6164 Koepfgen Rd., Cass City 48726-9408 (989) 872-2346 ....stitchinjan@airadvantage.net
Nelson, Bridget – 3113 Marion Dr, Royal Oak 48073-3237 (248) 632-2504 ....bnelson@michiganumc.org
Niedrich, Susanne – 8926 Reese Rd, Birch Run 48415-9754 (989) 624-4939.........susanneandbob@aol.com
Nordbrock, Mandana – 3412 Willow Lake Dr, Apt 302, Kalamazoo 49008 (269) 720-6152
....mnordbrock@michiganumc.org
Norton, Kenneth – 748 Bowers Rd, Bronson 49028-9227 (517) 369-1803..............klnorton@kendalefarm.com
Olin, Denny – 10205 Aylsworth Rd, PO Box 223, Empire 49630 (231) 223-4141 ....dennyolin@gmail.com
O'Malley, Dan – 9356 Enchantment Dr, Alto 49302-9500 (616) 915-6301 ....dano.omalley@gmail.com

Osburn, Clayton – 5785 Marble Dr., Troy 48085-3918 (248) 879-6371.............................clayosburn@aol.com
Packer, Matthew – 329 Windy Bluff, Flushing 48433-2646 (810) 635-8267.....................mpack65@yahoo.com
Paik, Eugene – 2253 Chalgrove Dr, Troy 48098-2298 (248) 766-0379 ....eugenepaik@me.com
Pangle, Brian – Clark Retirement Community, 1551 Franklin St SE, Grand Rapids 49506-8203
    (616) 452-1568...brian.pangle@clarkretirement.org
Paradine-Rice, Julia – 4114 Sanctuary Dr, Alma 48801-9237 (989) 576-0675......................juliapr@charter.net
Pelkey, Beth – 7011 Long Rapids Rd, Alpena 49707-9768 (989) 379-3386....................bethpelkey@juno.com
Pelton, Eric – 3260 Kernway Ct, Bloomfield Hills 48304-2402 (248) 594-7293 ....epelton@kohp.com
Peters, Jennifer –   (810) 288-7363 ....jpeters@michiganumc.org
Phelps, Marchelle "Micki" – 19622 Syracuse St, Detroit 48234-2557 ....marchellephelps@gmail.com
Polter, Linda – 413 Giles Ave., Blissfield 49228-1224 (517) 486-2947..........................linda.polter@emich.edu
Potter, Bonnie – 5140 Scott Rd., Mt Morris 48458-9724 (810) 687-2318.....................mpotter60@charter.net
Pratt, Fran – 2644 Seymour Drive, Shelbyville 49344-9523 (269) 792-4145 ....fechurchp@gmail.com
Pratt, Jody – 2984 5th St, Shelbyville 49344-9733 (616) 292-4908 ....prattgji09@gmail.com
Preston, John – 16931 Baraga Plains Rd, Baraga 49908 (906) 353-6439 ....johncarterpreston@gmail.com
Price, Todd – 9921 Seltzer, Livonia 48150-3293 (734) 834-4030...................................pencollector@me.com
Proctor, Cheryl – 104 Tuttle Park Dr, Sherwood 49089-9715 (517) 741-3125 ....seldominn_1@juno.com
Proctor, Simmie – 73486 8th Ave, South Haven 49090-9769 (269) 637-6053 ....simmiepr@hotmail.com
Pung, Susan – 4325 Water's Edge Dr, Mt Pleasant 48858 (989) 817-8884.................susanepung@yahoo.com
Radak, Keith – 834 Courtland, Ypsilanti 48197 (734) 483-8124 ....kradak@provide.net
Rietman, Susan – 15 Market St, Middleville 49333-9270 (269) 795-7644............susan.rietman@sbcglobal.net
Root, Kendall – 2206 Airfield Ln, Midland 48642 (989) 835-8232...................................knjroot@yahoo.com
Ross, Kelly – 5628 N Helen Lake Rd, Ishpeming 49849-8615 (906) 376-8086.............pinkgiraffe@hughes.net
Russell, Carrie – 16622 Woodside St, Livonia 48154-2060 (734) 632-0247........................ca.russell@att.net
Sanders, Robert – 5597 Eugene Drive, dimondale 78821-9724 (810) 621-5214.............bob.scout@lentel.com
Schlusler, Michael – 1576 Ru-Lane Drive, Lapeer 48446-1364 (810) 664-9899 ....mschlusler@gmail.com
Schramm, Linda – 244 S. Elk St., Sandusky 48471-1358 (810) 648-4696 ....lars@greatlakes.net
Schroeder, Craig – 7517 W Hickory Rd, Hickory Corners 49060-9710 (269) 760-4604........ccraigls5@aol.com
Schroeder, Joan – 7515 W Hickory Rd, Hickory Corners 49060-9710 (269) 760-4602 ....joanlbs@gmail.com
Scott, Mel – 1038 Michigan Road, Port Huron Twp 48060-7826 (810) 937-2497 ....rmscott411@yahoo.com
Scott, Sharon – 214 E Michigan Ave, Clinton 49236-9782 (517) 456-7198....................sascott2@comcast.net
Searls, James – 53 East Central, Zeeland 49464 (616) 772-4306 ....jrs@macatawa.org
Seidler, Justin – Stockwell-Mudd Library Albion College, 611 E Porter St, Albion 49224-1831
    (517) 629-0487...jseidler@albion.edu
Shaffer, Molly – 33053 Crystal Springs St, Dowagiac 49047-9326 (269) 684-6347 ....orcf@aol.com
Shelby, Pete – 1730 Probert Rd, Jackson 49203-5382
Showerman, Joyce – 600 S Main St, Eaton Rapids 48827-1426 (517) 663-5284.........jshowerman@fumer.org
Smith, Stuart – 7486 Hunters Ridge Dr, Jackson 49201 (517) 536-0363 ....smith4osu@comcast.net
Smith-Del Pino, Laurie – 12110 Francesca Dr, Grand Blanc 48439 (248) 366-1937......laurieowl@hotmail.com
Smolenski, Bruce – 76 Union Ave SE Apt 202, Grand Rapids 49503 (586) 850-6540...........bmsmo@mail.com
Snyder, Beth – 8650 Huron River Dr., Dexter 48130-9606 (734) 663-4164 ....westside@westside-umc.org
Snyder, Patricia – 807 S Sheldon, Charlotte 48813-2157 (517) 231-1301...........dpsnyder807@peoplepc.com
Soles, Anne – 217 Old State Rd, PO Box 467, Pentwater 49449 (231) 869-7651..........annesoles@charter.net
Spackman, Nona – 3806 Cornice Falls Dr Apt 6, Holt 48842 (517) 694-8346...........nspackman12@gmail.com
Squires, Chuck – 55 Auch St, Sebewaing 48759-1604 (989) 883-3751
Stair, Joy – 2756 Aspen Court, Ann Arbor 48108 (734) 327-8370..joystair@aol.com
Stanek, Dennis – 7238 Lake Bluff O.75 Ln, Gladstone 49837-2411 (906) 428-2407 ....dstanek@nmu.edu
Steggerda, Steve – 8507 S. Maple, Zeeland 49464 (616) 748-9989 ....steggs76@gmail.com
Stephens, Juli – 19206 Berkley, Detroit 48221 (248) 5636161..julis1111@aol.com
Stevenson, Debbie – 4585 Round Lake Rd, Laingsburg 48848-9485 (517) 420-7032
    ....dstevenson@michiganumc.org

Stewart, Pamela – 1161 E Clark Rd, Dewitt 48820-7930 (616) 299-6484....pstewart@michiganconference.org
Stickle, Suzanne (Sue) – 10970 Dutch Settlement Rd, Marcellus 49067-9457 (269) 646-9425
....suzannestickle@gmail.com
Stockford, Dave – 8544 Gedman Rd, Mancelona 49659-9513 (231) 587-8694.........dsstockford@freeway.net
Street, Brenda – 578 Michigan Ave, Pontiac 48342-1755 (248) 335-3603 ....bstreet992157@gmail.com
Sutton, Ruth – 2335 N. Meridian Rd., Sanford 48657-9554 (989) 687-5646....................suttonr1@charter.net
Swinger, Connie – 255 Brown St SW, Grand Rapids 49507-1533 (616) 452-3532.........connieswinger@att.net
Taylor, Richard – 5339 N Genesee Rd, Flint 48506-4528 (810) 767-7679...................rtaylor06@sbcglobal.net
Thiele, Cindy – 319 River Street, Allegan 49010-1150 (269) 673-4514 ....cindahthiele@gmail.com
Thompson, Karen – 19118 Kenny Drive, Big Rapids 49307 (231) 796-6824 ....karen@umfmichigan.org
Thoms, Peter – 1213 Carter Dr., Flint 48532-2715 (810) 732-7719 ....psthoms59@gmail.com
Tiedt, Patrick – 5755 30th Ave, Sears 49679-8078 (231) 734-2932.................................patiedt@hotmail.com
Tobar, Lea – 2430 Highridge Ln SE, Grand Rapids 49546-7536 (616) 940-0406.................flt62@hotmail.com
Tolliver, Cecelia – ....cecelia@umc-de.org
Townley, Duane – 6112 Siebert St., Midland 48640-2722 (989) 835-7564 ....dttown@aol.com
Trantham, Barry – 3158 N. McKinley Rd, Flushing 48433 (810) 659-5354..........barrytrantham@sbcglobal.net
Tucker, Alice – 22289 Woodwill St., Southfield 48075-8305 (313) 618-3173 ....fayerich@comcast.net
Tumonong, Prospero – 1908 Firethorn Ct. SE, Grand Rapids 49546 (616) 883-6397.........ptumonong@att.net
Turner, Ciere – 18600 Conant Ave., Detroit 48234 (313) 729-1225................................sturnerv@yahoo.com
Vanderbilt, Herbert – 2204 Gee Dr, Lowell 49331-9505 (616) 897-8642....................hvanderbilt@comcast.net
Vollmer, Sarah – 304 E Market St, Centreville 49032-9671 (815) 600-4785 ....svollmer@michiganumc.org
Vorbrich, Andrew – Comerica Building, 151 S Rose St Ste 900, Kalamazoo 49007-4719
　　　(269) 343-1906 ....AVorbrich@LennonMiller.com
Waagner, Max – 928 Sunburst Rd, Jackson 49203-3887 (517) 787-2924.................max.waagner@gmail.com
Wagenknecht, Sherry – 4033 Douglas Rd., Ida 48140-9714 (734) 269-2578...............wagen88@hotmail.com
Walls, John – 225 Munger Rd, Holly 48442-9158 (248) 459-6850...............................vim.jewalls@yahoo.com
Wayne, Andrew – 32800 Cadillac St., Farmington Hills 48336-4248 (248) 615-1205 ....acwayne@hotmail.com
Weemhoff, Christine – , , ...cweem@sbcglobal.net
Wesner, Carole – 6642 Guildford Dr., Shelby Twp. 48316-3330 (586) 731-0870......carole.wesner@gmail.com
Weston, Michele – 5158 Sandalwood Circle, Grand Blanc 48439-4267 (810) 694-6266 ...mweston38@att.net
Wharton, John – 7409 Steeplechase Ct., Saline 48176-9031 (734) 429-5258 ....jwharton@comcast.net
Whitman, Mary – 9155 Greenway Ct., N222, Saginaw 48609 (989) 781-9223..........librawhitman@yahoo.com
Wilder, Della – 6130 Garfield Rd, Freeland 48623-8619 (989) 695-5808...........................dellaw@yahoo.com
Witkowski, Laura – 1164 Treeway Dr NW, Sparta 49345 (616) 540-3795 ....lwitkowski@michiganumc.org
Witte, Susan – 5961 Sunfish Lake Ave NE, Rockford 49341 (616) 446-1570.......switte@umcampingboard.org
Woodard, Sue – 3815 Delano Dr, Eaton Rapids 48827-9623 (517) 628-2628...........suecwoodard@gmail.com
Woolley, Charles – 20490 Lexington Blvd, Northville 48167-1338 (734) 646-6245 ....cbwoolley@gmail.com
Wortley, Joel – 220 East Scott, Grand Ledge 48837 (517) 881-6466 ....ExecutiveDirector@umcamping.org
Wyatt, Robert – 8181 Deerwood, Clarkston 48346 (248) 625-5326
Yakes, Dan – 409 Mill Pond Road, Whitehall 49461-9603 (231) 894-9279 ....yakesd@iserv.net
Youells, Carol Ann – 740 Clark Crossing SE, Grand Rapids 49506 (616) 243-3759.........gryouells@gmail.com
Yu, Sung – ....sungyu0063@gmail.com
Zawislak, Marguerite – 3932 Wayfarer Dr., Troy 48083-6418 (248) 524-9323..............mozawislak@gmail.com
Zeeb, Linda – 13084 Torrey Rd, Fenton 48430 (810) 252-6091...................................zeeblinda@yahoo.com
Zeigler, Carmen – 33076 Mazara, Fraser 48026-5012 (810) 241-1296 ....carmenszeigler@gmail.com
Zylstra, Jay – 5842 Julie St, Hudsonville 49426-9552 (616) 667-0911 ....jay.zylstra@gmail.com

PASTORAL RECORD

This Pastoral Record indicates appointments, including clergy of other annual conferences and denominations serving within the Michigan Conference, but is **not necessarily a pension record**. The date given before/after each appointment represents the initial year of that appointment, with changes occurring immediately following Annual Conference unless otherwise noted. The record is maintained by the Ezra Database Specialist. Correspondence can be sent to pstewart@michiganumc.org.

The Michigan Conference has been transitioning database systems. Please know we are still in the process of cleaning the data and verifying data syncs. If you find significant errors in a record, please email the above address. Thank you for your patience while we transition.

Membership status codes:

AF = Affiliated Member
AM = Associate Member
CC = Certified Candidate
DM = Diaconal Minister (consecrated under
    provisions of 1992 or earlier Discipline)
DR = Retired Diaconal Minister (consecrated
    under provisions of 1992 or earlier Discipline)
FD = Deacon in Full Connection
FL = Full Time Local Pastor
NL = Local Pastor (Approved but Not Appointed)
OA = Associate Member of Other Conference
OD = Deacon Member of Other Conference
OE = Elder Member of Other Conference
OF = Other Denomination
OR = Retired Member of Other Conference
PD = Provisional Deacon
PL = Part Time Local Pastor
RD = Retired Deacon in Full Connection
RHL = Retired Honorable Location
RP = Retired Provisional Member
DSA = District Superintendent Assignment

AL = Administrative Location
BH = Bishop

FE = Elder in Full Connection
HL = Honorable Location

PE = Provisional Elder
RA = Retired Associate Member
RE = Retired Elder
RL = Retired Local Pastor
SP = Student Local Pastor

Retired status is also indicated with an asterisk (*) before the name.

Pertaining to the former West Michigan Conference clergy, D stands for year of ordination as Deacon, FE for the year of ordination as Elder, PE for the year of Provisional Elder, PD for the year of Provisional Deacon, R for the year of Retirement.

The following pertains to how the former Detroit Conference clergy are shown:
    Last name, first name (spouse)   email address
    [(Membership Status) "X" year; "Y" year]. Appointment service record; **present appointment**

Codes for "x" or "y" are in the Detroit Conference, unless otherwise noted:

F	Full Member	P	Probationary Member
FD	Deacon/Full Connection	PD	Provisional Deacon
FE	Elder/Full Connection	PE	Provisional Elder
FL	Full-time Local Pastor	PL	Part-time Local Pastor
LD	Local Deacon	SP	Student Local Pastor
LE	Local Elder	T	Received on Trial (probationary member,
LP	Local Pastor		1968 and prior)

"P," "F," and "T" are exclusive to the former Detroit Conference.
"D" is exclusive to the former West Michigan Conference.

*Ablett, Joseph H. (Wilma)   jwablett@yahoo.com [10-2301]
[(RE) T 1950; F 1956]. 1950 Minooka, IL; 1952 Deer Park, MD; 1956 Saginaw: Kochville; 1963 Oscoda; 1969 Escanaba; 1971 Marysville; 1980 Auburn; **1985 Retired**. Home: 1003 Tulip Court, Pemberville, OH 43450 (419-833-1320)

*Ackerman, Gordon Earl   ackermange@sbcglobal.net
[(RE) T 1962; F 1964]. 1959 E.U.B. IL Conf.; 1960 Symerton, IL; 1962 North Detroit; 1964 Detroit: Rice; Sep. 1966 Detroit: West Outer Drive; Oct. 1969 Frankenmuth; 1983 Tecumseh; 1988 Clawson; **2001 Retired**. Home: 2686 Blue Heron Lane, Wixom 48393

*Adams, L. Cecile Adams (Donald Ott)   1pastorcecile@gmail.com
[(RL) PL 2010]. 2010 Laporte, Mapleton; **2013 Retired**. Home: S77W 12929 D212, Muskego, WI 53150 (912-658-0253)

*Adams, Craig L (RE) (Robin) – (D-1973, FE-1977, R-2010)
Wolf Lake 1975; Saugatuck/Ganges 1979; Horton Bay 1984; Ionia: Zion 1994; Weidman 09/16/1999; Carlisle 2006; Mt Pleasant: Trinity/Countryside/Leaton 12/01/2009; Retired 2010; Grand Rapids: Northlawn 2018-2019
          craigadams1@me.com
          (H) 5073 Rum Creek Ct SE, Grand Rapids 49508-5280 (616) 514-7474

Africa, Jeremy Paul (Kaura)   jafrica@stmatthewslivonia.com
[(FE) PE 2005; FE 2008]. Jun 1, 2005 Plymouth: First (assoc.); 2006 Midland: First (assoc.); 2010 Goodrich; **2015 Livonia: St. Matthew's**. 30900 W. Six Mile Rd., Livonia 48152 (734-422-6038). Home: 31000 W. Six Mile Rd., Livonia 48152 (734-855-4882)

*Ainslie, Pegg (RE) – (D-1975, FE-1978, R-1997)
Okemos Community Church (Assoc) 11/01/1991; Lansing: Central (Assoc) 1993; Retired 1997
          (H) 2000 Pleasant Grove Rd, Lansing 48910-2437 (517) 574-4175

Alexander, Sarah Barrett-Nadeau (Matthew)   sarahbalexander@gmail.com
[(FD) PD 2016; FD 2019]. May 23, 2016 Young Leaders Initiative Motown Mission Director; **2019 Birmingham: First Director of Young Adult & High School Ministries (¶331.1c)**. 1589 W Maple Rd, Birmingham 48009-4607 (248-646-1200). Home: 8925 Sunbury, Livonia 48150

PASTORAL RECORDS

Alford, Helen alfordartist@gmail.com
[(PL) PL 2019]. **2019 Rose City: Trinity** (LTFT ½). 125 W Main St, Rose City
48654-2502 (989-685-2350). Home: 163 Hayes St., Rose City 48654-9590

Alghali, Beatrice S. sierraintl@peoplepc.com
[(PL) PL 2019]. **2019 Azalia/London** (LTFT ½). (A) 9855 Azalia Rd, PO Box 216,
Azalia 48110 (734-529-3731), (L) 11318 Plank Rd, Milan 48160-9163 (734-439-
2680). Home: 22492 Pontchartrain Dr, Southfield 48034-2127 (248-281-3157)

*Allan, John Richard (Karen Jean)
[(RA) LD 1964; LE 1966]. 1960 Farwell; Jan. 1966 Croswell; 1979 Marlette. **Aug
31, 1998 Retired**. 7227 W. Marlette, Marlette 48453 (989-635-7227)

*Allen, Terry Wayne (Sandra) revtwa@yahoo.com
[(RE) P 1971; F 1974]. 1973 Birmingham: Embury (assoc.); 1974 Flint: Flint Park;
Jan. 1976 Hemlock, Nelson; 1978 Regional Director, Pacific Northwest Area for
Church World Service/CROP; 1980 Southfield: Hope; 1983 Ferndale: First; 1989
Executive Director, United Methodist Foundation of the Detroit Annual Confer-
ence; 1990 Troy: First; 1997 Ypsilanti: First; 2000 Detroit: Metropolitan (assoc);
2002 Livonia: Newburg; Sep 1, 2005 leave of absence; **2006 Retired**. 586 River-
bank Circle, Zeeland 49464 (616-239-1503)

*Allie, Andrew Amadu (Madeir Boothe) A.Allie@comcast.net
[(RE) P 1976; F 1977]. 1976 Detroit: Westlawn; 1977 Detroit: Peoples; Feb. 1981
Pontiac: St. John's; May 1, 1992 Detroit: Scott Memorial; 2001 Flint District Su-
perintendent; 2009 Pontiac: St. John; **Dec 31, 2009 Retired**; 4/1-6/30/2012
Crossroads District Superintendent; Apr 1-Jun 20, 2018 Flint: Bethel; **2019 Flint:
Bethel** (interim). 1309 N Ballenger Why, Flint 48504 (810-238-343). Home: 5424
Sycamore Lane, Flint 48532 (810-732-6653)

*Almeida, Jana Lynn (RE) (Gabriel) – (D-1996, FE-1999, R-2016)
Vicksburg (Assoc) 1995; Grand Ledge: First 1997; Mt Pleasant: Trinity/ Coun-
tryside 10/16/1999; UM Connectional Structures (¶344.1a,c) Conference Ministry
Consultant (LTFT ½) 2004; Transitional Leave (¶354.2c.2) 01/01/2010;
Riverdale: Lincoln Road (LTFT ¾) 2010; Retired 2016
janalynn@me.com
(H) 1509 Tallywood Dr, Sarasota, FL 34237-3228 (616) 430-0414

Amick, John Harvey (Susan) jamick@umcor.org
[(FE) PE 2006; FE 2010]. 2006 Allen Park: Trinity; 2007 Redford: New Beginnings; 2008 Rochester: St. Paul's (assoc.); 2012 Flint: Hope; 2013 Deputy General Secretary, International Disaster Relief, UMCOR; **2016 Senior Director,
Disaster Relief UMCOR**. GBGM 458 Ponce de Leon, Atlanta, GA 30308 (615-
916-2225). Home: 221 Missionary Drive, Decatur, GA 30030 (248-613-9296)

Amick, Susan D (John) susan.amick@emory.edu
[(FD) PD 2014; FD 2018]. 2014 Office of Christian United and Interreligious Relationships, UM Council of Bishops; Aug. 1, 2014 Transitional Leave; 2016 Chaplaincy – Emory Spiritual Health/Missional; 2018 Chaplin, Wesley Woods Sr.
Living (¶331.4b), Missional: Grace UMC; **2019 Chaplin, Wesley Woods Sr. Living (¶331.4b), Missional: Decatur: First**. 1825 Clifton Rd., NE, Atlanta, GA
30329. Home: 221 Missionary Drive, Decatur, GA 30030 (248-613-9294)

PASTORAL RECORDS

Amstutz, David DeWayne (Carrie) therevdav777@gmail.com
[(FE) P 1976; F 1979]. 1977 Riley Center, Berville, West Berlin; 1981 North Street; Mar. 1, 1987 New Baltimore: Grace; 1990 Lambertville; 1997 Marysville; Feb 15, 1999 leave of absence; 1999 Davisburg; 2001 Riverview; 2012 Gladwin: First; **2018 Retired**. Home: 312 McIntosh, Almont 48003 (989-246-0137)

*AMUNDSEN, WILLIAM J (RE) (Catherine) – (D-1967, FE-1970, R-2003)
Edwardsburg: Hope 1969; Mesick/Harrietta 1972; Grand Rapids: Trinity (Assoc) 1979; Lowell: First 05/01/1982; Grand Ledge: First 1993; Retired 2003
  (H) 735 Maycroft Rd, Lansing 48917 (517) 285-9640 wjamundsen@juno.com

Anderson, Thomas Craig (Karen) anderson810@gmail.com
[(FE) P 1981; F 1986]. 1984 Deerfield, Petersburg; Jan. 1, 1990 Seven Churches United Group Ministry: Durand; 1995 Houghton: Grace; Aug 1, 2009 Houghton Lake.; **2016 Highland**. 680 W. Livingston Rd., Highland 48357 (248-887-1311). Home: 650 W. Livingston Rd., Highland 48357

*ANDREWS, JOHN L (RE) (Arlene) – (D-1959, FE-1962, R-1992)
Blanchard 1951; Riverdale 1955; Oshtemo 1960; Coloma 1962; Jackson Calvary 1968; Big Rapids: First 1972; UM Connectional Structures (¶344.1a,c) Grand Traverse District Superintendent 08/16/1980; Grandville 1986; Marshall 1989; Retired 1992

jlandrews1929@sbcglobal.net
  (H) 741 Clark Crossing SE, Grand Rapids 49506-3310 (616) 245-1589

*Andrus, Richard C. (Jean) rjandrus@avci.net
[(RE) P 1973; F 1976]. Sep. 1967 Morrice, Bennington; 1972 Jasper, Weston; 1975 Bayport, Hayes; 1979 New Baltimore: Grace; Feb. 1, 1987 Warren: Wesley; Jan. 16, 1990 Warren: First (assoc.); 1992 Mt. Clemens: First; **1999 Retired**. Home: 3551 Wilson St., New Baltimore 48047 (586-716-2123)

Arnesen, Tonya Morris (David) Revtonya95@comcast.net
[(FE) P 1995; F 1997]. 1995 Plymouth: First (assoc); Jun 1, 2000 New Baltimore: Grace; 2006 Detroit: Metropolitan; 2011 Dixboro; **2019 Jackson: First**. 275 W Michigan Ave, Jackson 49201 (517-787-6460). Home: 19734 Malvern Dr, Jackson 49203

*Arthur, Joy Eldon (Dorothy)
[(RE) T N. IN, 1955; F N. IN, 1959]. 1953 Alexandria Circuit; 1958 DeSoto; 1961 Muncie: College Avenue; 1964 trans. to Detroit Conf., Saginaw: Jefferson Avenue (assoc.); 1969 Highland Park: First; 1973 Belleville; Sep. 1982 Detroit East District Superintendent; 1988 Coleman: Faith, Geneva: Hope; 1990 Coleman: Faith; **Jan. 1, 1991 Retired**. Home: 183 Spring St., Midland 48640 (989-631-1039)

ARTHUR, THOMAS F (FE) (Sarah) – (PE-2009, FE-2012)
Lansing: Sycamore Creek 2009; Lansing: Sycamore Creek/Potterville 09/01/2016; Lansing: Sycamore Creek 12/08/2016

tomarthur@sycamorecreekchurch.org
  (H) 5058 Glendurgan Ct, Holt 48842-9438 (517) 889-5540
Sycamore Creek: 1919 S Pennsylvania Ave, Lansing 48910-3251
(517) 394-6100

Aupperlee, Mark D (FL) – (FL-2018)
Lansing: Sycamore Creek (Assoc.) 01/01/2018
markaupperlee@sycamorecreekchurch.org
(H) 420 Ardspm Rd, E Lansing 48823-3284 (517) 643-1161
Sycamore Creek: 1919 S Pennsylvania Ave, Lansing 48910-3251
(517) 394-6100

AYOUB, GEORGE H (FE) (Elizabeth) – (D-1984, FE-1987)
Appointed To Extension Ministries (¶344.1b,c) Masonic Pathways Senior Living Services, St. Johns 09/24/1999; (Transferred to WMC 2014) UM Connectional Structures (¶344.1a,c) Executive Director of Camps 03/01/2014; UM Connectional Structures (¶344.1a,c) Interim Executive Director of Camp, Michigan Area 2015; UM Connectional Structures (¶344.1a,c) Executive Director of Camping, Michigan 2018; Transitional Leave 08/01/2018; Appointed in Other Annual Conferences (¶331.8, ¶346.1) Detroit Conference, Marlette: First Oct. 1, 2018
a.georgepastor@gmail.com
(H) 3169 Main St., Marlette 48453
Marlette: First: 3155 Main St, Marlette 48453 (989) 635-2075

BABB, MARK R (FD) (Susan) – (D-1991, FE-1993, FD-2002)
Coldwater (Deacon) 2002; (Transferred from West Ohio Conf. 2005) Coldwater (Deacon FT) and Albion College, Music Dept Manager (LTFT) 09/01/2005; Coldwater (Deacon LTFT) and Albion College, Music Dept Manager (LTFT) 01/01/2006; Albion College (LTFT ½) 2006; St. Paul UCC, Director Of Music Ministries, Waterloo, IL 01/20/2008; Transitional Leave 06/01/2009; University of Phoenix, Associate Faculty (LTFT ½), Westminster Presbyterian Church, Choir Director (LTFT ¼) and Jackson: First Spiritual Formation Consultant (LTFT ¼) 06/01/2010; University Of Phoenix, Associate Faculty (LTFT ½) Director of Music Federated Church Of Grass Lake (LTFT ¼) and Jackson: First Spiritual Formation Consultant (LTFT ¼) 2013; Transitional Leave 2015; University Of Phoenix, Adjunct Faculty (LTFT ½) 2016; Lakeview: New Life (Deacon) Music And Worship Leader (LTFT ¼ - Missional Service) 11/15/2016; Sturgis: First as Administrativie Assistant (deacon) (¶331.1c)
lighthousemusician@gmail.com
(H) 1332 Rolling Ridge Ln, Sturgis 49091-8701 (989) 287-1770
Sturgis: First: 200 Pleasant St, Sturgis 49091-1751 (269) 651-5990

BABB, SUSAN J (FE) (Mark) – (D-1993, FE-1995)
Transferred from West Ohio Conf. 2004; Jackson: First (Assoc) 01/16/2004; Lakeview: New Life 2015; Sturgis: First 2019
pastorsueb@gmail.com
(H) 1332 Rolling Ridge Ln, Sturgis 49091-8701 (989) 287-1770
Sturgis: First: 200 Pleasant St, Sturgis 49091-1751 (269) 651-5990

*BABCOCK, WAYNE H (RE) (Lois) – (D-1972, FE-1976, R-2003)
Townline/Bloomingdale 09/01/1969; Scottdale/Bridgman: Faith 1972; Marcellus/Wakelee 01/01/1975; Kingsley/Grant 1978; Webberville/Bell Oak 1983; Webberville 01/16/1987; Berrien Springs 1991; Lawrence 1998; Retired 01/01/2003
way.loisbabcock@gmail.com
(H) 32052 County Road 687, Bangor 49013-9476 (269) 427-2681

PASTORAL RECORDS

*Bacon, Eugene Kalman (Karen) ekbacon@chartermi.net
[(RE) P 1976; F 1980]. 1978 Flushing (assoc.); 1982 Flint: Bristol, Dimond; 1988 Madison Heights; Jul 1, 1995 Hancock: First; 2006 Alpena; **2016 Retired**. Home: 100 N. Brooke St., Alpena 49707 (989-657-1468)

*Badley, Thomas G. (Darlene) tdbadley65@att.net
[(RE) T 1968; F 1971]. 1965 Rea, Cone, Azalia; 1968 Macon; 1970 Harbor Beach, Port Hope; Nov. 1973 Rochester: St. Paul (assoc.); 1975 Pontiac: Aldersgate, Elmwood; 1978 Roseville; 1984 Hancock; 1988 Clio: Bethany; 1997 Livonia: Newburg; **2002 Retired**. Home: 6219 Square Lake Dr., Kimball 48074 (810-985-6522)

Bae, Se Jin (Mi Hyang Jeong)
[(OE) Florida]. **Mar 1, 2015 Troy: Korean (assoc)**. 42693 Dequindre, Troy 48084 (248-879-2240). Home: 1940 Flagstone Circle, Rochester 48307 (248-841-1595)

BAEK, SEUNG HO "Andy" (FE) (Hehyoung "Sarah") – (D-1987, FE-1993)
Transferred from Wisconsin Conf. 1997; Grand Rapids Suhbu Korean New Church Ministry 07/16/1997; Appointed to Extension Ministries (¶344.1b,c) GBGM New Church Ministry-Suhbu Korean Congregation 2001; Suhbu Korean UMC (Re-named Church of All Nations 2006) 2005; Church of All Nations/ Oakdale 2006; Schoolcraft 2008; Appointed in Other Annual Conferences (¶346.1) West Ohio Conf, Columbus Korean 2010; Union City (¾ Time)/ Athens (¼ Time) 2012; Appointed in Other Annual Conferences (¶331.8, ¶346.1) Detroit Conference, Ann Arbor District, Dundee 2015; 2018 New Hudson
baekandy@hotmail.com
(H) 56799 New Hudson Rd., PO Box 803, New Hudson 48165 (248-437-6367)
New Hudson: 56730 Grand River, PO Box 803, New Hudson 48165
(248-437-6212)

BAGLEY, DWAYNE E (FE) (Michele) – (D-1998, FE-2001)
Webberville 1995; Albion: First 2002; Mason: First 2009; UM Connectional Structures (¶344.1a,c), Kalamazoo District Superintendent 2016; UM Connectional Structures (¶344.1a,c), Greater Southwest District Superintendent 01/01/2019
dbagley@michiganumc.org
(H) 7228 Bolingbrook Dr, Portage 49024 (269) 370-2800
(O) 2350 Ring Rd North Suite B, Kalamazoo 49006 (269) 372-7525

Bailey, Anika puppetpower28@aol.com
[(PL) PL 2018]. **2018 Forester/Port Sanilac**. (PS) 7225 Main St., PO Box 557, Port Sanilac 48469, (F) 2481 N. Lakeshore Rd., Carsonville 48419. Home: 7209 Main, Port Sanilac 48469 (313-543-9434)

Bailey, John D. (Karen) Jbailey57@hotmail.com
[(FE) FL 1999; PE 2000, FE 2003]. 1996 Custer/South Liberty, W. OH Conf.;1999 Ossineke, Hubbard Lake; Jan 1, 2005 Ossineke; 2005 Seven Churches United Group Ministry: Gaines, Duffield; 2010 Clio: Bethany; 2015 Romeo; **2017 Cheboygan: St. Paul's**. 531 E. Lincoln Ave., Cheboygan 49721 (231-627-2424). Home: 578 O'Brien Dr., Cheboygan 49721 (231-627-9710)

*BAILEY, PAUL F (RE) (Lynn) – (D-1962, FE-1967, R-2001)
Transferred to West MI Conf 1978; Associate Director, MiCAP 1978; Honorable Location 1979; Transferred to N NY Conf 1984; Transferred to Detroit Conf 1988; Transferred to West MI Conf. 1995; Potterville/West Benton 1995; Retired 05/01/2001; Ionia: Easton 04/13/2003-09/01/2004
pfbpadre@gmail.com
(H) 2500 Breton Woods Dr SE Apt 1065, Grand Rapids 49512-9156
(517) 930-3743

*BAILEY, THERON E (RE) (Cheryl) – (D-1961, FE-1963, R-1994)
Kewadin 1955; Union City 1957; Ogdensburg/UM Connectional Structures (¶344.1a,c) Wesley Foundation 1964; Hart/Mears 1966; Wyoming Wesley Park 12/15/1969; Sabbatical Leave 09/01/1977; Empire (Ad Interim) 08/01/1978; Lansing: First 09/15/1978; UM Connectional Structures (¶344.1a,c) Conf Staff Program Coordinator 03/01/1982; Grand Rapids: Saint Paul's 1989; Retired 1994
te97ce@comcast.net
(H) 3086 Slater Ave SE, Kentwood 49512-1989 (616) 956-5678

*Bailey, Wilson Charles (Noreen) wilson.bailey@att.net
[(RE) PE 1999; FE 2002]. 1999 Deerfield, Wellsville; Sep 1, 1999 Wisner; 2005 leave of absence; **Sep 30, 2007 Retired**. Home: 4901 Squirrel Run, Farwell 48622 (989-588-4695)

*Baker, Maureen Vickie (Robert) revbakerm@yahoo.com
[(RE) PL Dec 1, 2002; PE 2007; FE 2010; RE 2019]. Dec 1, 2002 Applegate; 2007 Brown City; 2013 Lexington; 2017 Mount Clemens: First; **2019 Retired**. Home: 1804 Sunflower Circle, Sebring, FL 33872 (810-488-2390)

*BAKER, MELANIE J (RE) – (D-1984, FE-1987, R-2016)
Empire 1985; Leave Of Absence 1988; North Adams/Jerome 10/01/1988; Battle Creek: Birchwood 1995; Sabbatical Leave 2003; Lansing: First 2004; Alma 07/15/2012; Personal Leave 2013; Retired 2016
MBSmicah68@aol.com
(H) 3813 ½ W Willow St, Lansing 48917-1752 (517) 204-5870

*BAKER, PEGGY J (RE) (Forrest) – (D-1999, FE-2003, R-2018)
Comstock 1999; Outland Harper Creek (New Church Start) 2006; Battle Creek: Baseline/Bellevue 2011; Retired 2018
pegbkr@gmail.com
(H) 8039 Allison Ln, Battle Creek 49014 (269) 387-1494

*BAKER, SHEILA F. (RL) (Keith P) – (PL-2005, RL-2014)
Riverside (DSA 07/01-12/01/04) (LTFT PT) 12/01/2004; Breedsville (LTFT PT) 2005; Townline (LTFT PT) 2005; Kalamazoo: Northwest (¼ Time 01/03/08) (LTFT PT) 2007; Otsego: Trowbridge (LTFT PT) 2012; Retired 02/02/2014
(H) 27399 22nd Ave, Gobles 49055-9224 (269) 628-4882

*Balfour, James Robert, II (Mary) mjbalf@gmail.com
[(RE) P 1970; F 1974]. 1973 Royal Oak: First (assoc.); 1975 Rose City, Churchill; 1982 Marquette: Grace, Skandia; Sep. 15, 1986 school; 1988 Leave of Absence; 1989 Pastoral Counselor/Administrator, Preventive & Rehabilitative Center, Burns Medical Center; 2002 St. Ignace; **2010 Retired**. Home: N 7014 K-1 Dr., Stephenson 49887 (906-298-0352)

*Ball, Glenn Charles (Margaret Ann)
[(RE) T Mich 1956; F Mich 1961]. 1954 Bingham, Solon; 1956 Horton Bay, North Bay; 1958 Adamsville, Kessington; 1961 Grand Rapids: Northlawn; 1966 Caro; 1972 Onaway, Millersburg; 1983 Frankenmuth; **1996 Retired**. Home: 255 Mayer Rd., #375L, Frankenmuth 48734 (989-652-4375)

Ball, John W. (Cyndi)   john.ball@lakeorionumc.org
[(FE) PE 1999; FE 2002]. 1999 Mayville; 2007 Leave of Absence; Apr 15, 2009 Elkton (assoc); 2009 Brighton: First (assoc.); 2013 Lake Orion (assoc); **2019 Lake Orion (assoc) (LTFT ¾), Celebrate Hope Consultant (¶344.1d) (LTFT ¼)**. 140 East Flint, Lake Orion 48362 (248-693-6201). Home: 2647 Orbit Dr., Lake Orion 48362 (248-393-1520)

BALL, LYLE J (Janet) – [(PL) PL-2010]
Chase Barton/Grant Center (DSA) 2010; Chase: Barton/Grant Center (PTLP ½) 11/01/10; Baldwin: Covenant Community (PTLP ½) and Chase Barton (PTLP ¼) 2015

ljball6@hotmail.com
(H) 6874 5 Mile Rd, Blanchard 49310-9474 (231) 972-7335
Baldwin: 5330 PO Box 250, S M-37, Baldwin 49304-6820 (231) 745-3232
Chase Barton: PO Box 104, 6957 S Depot St, Chase 49623 (231) 832-5069

*Ball, Martha C.
[(RE) P 1983; F 1987]. 1984 Wayne: First (assoc.); Nov. 1, 1985 Britton: Grace; April 1, 1991 Henderson Settlement, Kentucky District, Red Bird Missionary Conf. Jul 16, 1993 Hudson: First (LTFT ½); Jan 15, 1996 Oneida: First, Oneida, TN; 1997 leave of absence; **2002 Retired**. Home: 4298 Hillside, Ann Arbor 48105 (734-213-0443)

BALL, THOMAS E (Kelly) – [FE] (D-1982, FE-1986]
Girard/Ellis Corners 1984; Climax/Scotts 12/01/1988; Farwell 1994; Howard City: Heritage 2000; Cadillac 2007

tebpastor@yahoo.com
(H) 114 Barbara St, Cadillac 49601-2446 (231) 775-1851
Cadillac: PO Box 37, 1020 E Division St, Cadillac 49601-0037 (231) 775-5362

Ballah, Anthony (Miatta Buxton-Ballah)   ajballa@gmail.com
[(FL) FL Nov, 2016]. Apr 16, 2016 Detroit: St. Paul, Beverly Hills; **2018 Beverly Hills**. 20000 W. 13 Mile Rd., Beverly Hills 48025 (248-646-9777). Home:30700 Old Stream, Southfield 48076 (248-327-6276)

*Bamsey, Alfred Thomas (Karen)   bamsey@sbcglobal.net
[(RE) T 1958; F 1961]. 1961 Grosse Pointe (assoc.); 1964 Detroit: Bethany; 1969 Troy: First; 1976 Detroit West District Superintendent; 1982 Conference Program Director; 1990 Ann Arbor: First; **2000 Retired**. 1736 Weatherstone Dr., Ann Arbor 48108 (734-997-0421)

Barchue, J. Albert   revbarchue@yahool.com [09/23/16]
[(OE)]. **2016 Negaunee: Mitchell**. 207 Teal Lake Ave., Box 190 Negaunee 49866 (906-475-4861). Home: 1013 Hungerford, Negaunee 49866 (906-475-6524)

BARKHOLZ, DANIEL L (Mary Beth) – [(FL) CC-2013, FL-2016]
Fennville/Pearl 2016; Edmore: Faith 2017

pastordanbarkholz@gmail.com
(H) 320 S Maple St, Edmore 48829-7300 (269) 903-9665
Edmore: Faith: 833 S 1st St, Edmore 48829-9396 (989) 427-5575

*Barnett, James E. (Valerie) jvbarnett@umich.edu
[(RL) PL 2002; FL 2005]. Jan 1, 2002 Washington; Jun 1, 2002 Washington, Mt. Vernon; Jan 1, 2002 Washington; Jan 1, 2006 Washington/Mount Vernon (LTFT ¾). Nov 1, 2006 Washington/Mount Vernon (LTFT ½); Jan 1, 2007 Mount Vernon; 2007 Applegate; **2013 Retired**. 12275 Jeddo Rd., Yale 48097 (810-387-2431)

*BARNEY, JAMES W (Marilyn) – [(RE) D-1972, FE-1975, R-2005]
Transferred from New Hampshire Conf 1979; Munith/Pleasant Lake 1979; Quincy 1983; Wayland 1987; Constantine 09/15/1991; Somerset Center 1998; Retired 08/31/2005

deriter2@charter.net
(H) 1713 Linden Trail, Kalamazoo 49009-2821 (269) 251-1187

*BARNEY, MARILYN B (James) – [(RE) D-1985, FE-1990, R-2008]
Burnips/Monterey Center 1987; Three Rivers: Ninth Street/Jones 10/01/1991; Hillside 1998; Retired 2008

deriter2@charter.net
(H) 1713 Linden Trail, Kalamazoo 49009-2821 (269) 251-1021

Barrett, Joy Anna (Robert Long) jbarrett@chelseaumc.org
[(FE) P 1982; F 1985]. 1983 Gordonville; 1988 Sterling Heights; 1993 Saginaw: State Street; 1998 Ann Arbor District Superintendent; **2004 Chelsea**. 128 Park St. Chelsea 48118 (734-475-8119). Home: 10 Sycamore Dr., Chelsea 48118 (734-475-8449)

BARRETT, MARY J – [(PL) DSA-2016, PL-2016]
Waterloo Village (DSA) 2016; Waterloo Village (PTLP) 11/15/2016; Waterloo Village (PTLP) 2017 and Appointed in Other Annual Conferences (¶331.8, ¶346.1) Detroit Conf Salem Grove (PTLP) 2017

marybarrett29@yahoo.com
(H) PO Box 530, 305 N Howard, Webberville 48892-5156 (517) 521-3939
Waterloo Village: 8110 Washington St, Grass Lake 49240-9241 (734) 475-1171
Salem Grove: 3320 Notten Rd, Grass Lake 49240-9137 (734) 475-2370

*BARRETT, WAYNE C (Linda) – [(RE) D-1972, FE-1975, R-2011]
Snow 1969; Bloomingdale/Townline 1972; Muskegon: Central (Assoc) 11/01/1974; Plainfield 1978; Plainfield/UM Connectional Structures (¶344.1a,c) Director of United Methodist Foundation 02/01/1982; Executive Director, United Methodist Foundation (Re-named United Methodist Foundation of MI 2006) 1982; Retired 2011

wayne@umfmichigan.org
(H) 1517 Heathfield NE, Grand Rapids 49505-5761 (616) 458-9975
(O) 3347 Eagle Run Dr. NE, Ste B, Grand Rapids 49525 (1-888-451-1929)

*BARRY, B GORDON (Susan) – [(RE) D-1982, FE-1985, R-2015]
Remus/Halls Corner/Mecosta 1982; New Buffalo/Berrien County: Lakeside 1985; New Buffalo/Bridgman: Faith 1988; Lowell: First 1993; Stevensville 06/06/2003; Retired 2015

gordiebarry@gmail.com
(H) 5798 Whites Bridge Road, Belding 48809 (616) 244-3233

*Barteld, Ralph Thomas　　　　　　　　rtbarteld@att.net [9/23/16]
[(RE) T 1967; F 1970]. 1958 Lakeville; 1959 Forrester; 1966 Essex, Mt. Olive (Ohio); 1970 Mayville, Silverwood, Fostoria; Feb. 1979 Cheboygan; 1985 Escanaba: Central; 1991 Marysville; **1997 Retired**. Home: 735 Sixth Street, Marysville 48040 (810-388-0281)

BARTELMAY, BRADLEY S (Sherri Swanson) – [(FE) FL-1990, D-1996, FE-2002]
Stevensville (Assoc) 1990; New Buffalo/Bridgman: Faith 1993; New Buffalo: Water's Edge (Church Name Changed To Water's Edge UMC 1/1/12) 05/01/2000; Holland First 2017

bradbartelmay@gmail.com
(H) 2600 7th St NW, Grand Rapids 49504-4689 (269) 266-2221
Holland First: 57 W 10th St, Holland 49423-3130 (616) 396-5205

*Bartlett, William Peter (Lee Ann)　　　　bartlettwmpeter@gmail.com
[(RE) SP 1985; P 1991; F 1994]. 1985 Lake Linden, Painesdale; 1987 Middletown, Ohio: Pleasant Ridge (W. OH Conf.); 1992 Stephenson, Hermansville: First; 1996 God's Country Cooperative Parish: Newberry (Parish Director); 2001 Onaway, Millersburg; **2011 Retired**. Home: PO Box 6, Ironwood 49938 (906-285-6109)

*BARTHOLOMEW, JACK M (RE) (Mildred) – (SP-1969, D-1975, FE-1979, R-1995)
Quincy/Fisher Hill 1969-1974; Elk Rapids/Kewadin 1978; Hastings: Hope 02/16/1983; Lansing Calvary 02/15/1986; Stanwood: Northland 1992; Retired 1995

jbart96@att.net
(H) 1133 Yeomans St #96, Ionia 48846-1953 (616) 527-8852

*BARTON, SEAN, T (FL) – (FL-2017)
Grawn/Grant 2017; Grawn 2018

sean_barton@ymail.com
(H) 1222 S West Silber Lake Rd, Traverse City 49685-8532 (269) 908-7313
Grawn: PO Box 62 (1260 S West Silver Lake Rd, TC 49685) Grawn, 49637-0062
(231) 943-8356

Bashore, Timothy (Kay)
[(FL) PL Nov, 2013; FL 2014]. Nov 9, 2013 Bethel (Worth Twp.); **2014 Pickford**. 115 E. Church St., Box 128, Pickford 49774 (906-647-6195). Home: 230 W. Townline Rd., Pickford 49774 (906-647-7231)

BATTEN, LISA M (FL) (Jim) – (FL-2009)
UM Connectional Structures (¶344.1a,c) Director Wesley Foundation of Kalamazoo 11/15/2009; Young Adult Intiatives Coordinator 07/15/2018

lbatten@michiganumc.org
(H) 1810 N Drake Rd, Kalamazoo 49006 (269) 344-4076
(O) 1810 N Drake Rd, Kalamazoo 49006 (517) 347-4030 ext. 4078

*BAUGHAN, EUGENE L (RA) (Philis) – (PL-1974, FL-1987, AM-1993, RA-2002)
NE Missaukee Parish: Moorestown-Stittsville/Merritt-Butterfield 1974; Springport/
Lee Center 1987; Brooks Corner/Sears 1991; Barnard/East Jordan/Norwood
1997; Retired 2002; Kewadin 11/01/2009-2015
reverendgeneb@aol.com
(H) 400 Heartland Dr, Traverse City 49684-7159 (231) 943-0354

*Baunoch, Joseph Robert (Betty) docjoe@att.net
[(RE) P 1984 (N. IN); F 1987 (N. IN)]. 1981 Saratoga, Mt. Zion; 1983 Elkhart:
First (assoc.); 1985 Elkhart: Albright; 1990 Whiting/Centenary; 1993 Chaplain,
St. Mary Medical Center, Hobart, IN; 1996 Samaritan Counseling Center, Mun-
ster, IN: Wheeler; 1999 Portage: First; 2002 trans to Detroit conf., 2002 Oxford;
2004 Retired. Home: 33765 Regal, Fraser 48026 (810-841-4745)

*BEACHY, WILLIAM M (RE) (Barbara) – (D-1982, FE-1985, R-2014)
Transferred from West Ohio Conf 2001; Lansing: Trinity 2001; Retired 2014
wbeachy@comcast.net
(H) 230 E Knight St, Eaton Rapids 48827-1323 (517) 441-9456

Beagan, Thomas Michael tombeagan@thelogosministry.org
[(FE) P 1982; F 1985; FL 1992; F 1993]. 1983 Utica (assoc); 1986 Leave of Ab-
sence; 1988 Honorable Location; 1992 Northville (assoc.); 1993 reinstated
Northville (assoc); **2000 CEO/Executive Director, Logos Associates**. 1405
Frey Rd., Pittsburgh, PA 15235 (412-372-1341). Home: 6790 Stephanie Ct., Del-
mont, PA 15626 (724-327-4653)

Beaudoin, Christine M (FE) (Michael) – PL-2013, (PE-2014, FE-2017)
2013 Salem Grove; Sep 1, 2015 Velda Rose; 2018 Coloma
cmbeau81@aol.com
(H) 331 Tannery Dr, Coloma 49038 (480) 659-1472
Coloma: PO Box 670, 144 S Church St, Coloma 49037-0670 (269) 468-6062

BEAVAN, JOSEPH L (FL) (Darcy) – (FL-2010)
Brooks Corners/Sears/Barryton: Faith 01/15/2010; Rosebush 2014
icmkck@yahoo.com
(H) 3272 E Weidman Rd, Rosebush 48878-9715 (989) 433-5509
Rosebush: PO Box 187, 3805 School Rd, Rosebush 48878-0187
(989) 433-2957

*BECK, ERIC S (RE) (Heather) – (D-1979, FE-1983, R-2019)
Eaton Rapids: First (Assoc) 12/01/1980; Muskegon: Unity 1983; Union City
1986; Kalamazoo: Westwood 08/01/1995; Lake Odessa: Central 2007; Jackson:
First 2012; Retired 2019
revdrebeck@gmail.com
(H) 376 Vansickle, Charlottee 48813 (517)c962-2451 (517) 962-2451

*Beckwith, Norman Richard, Sr. (Christina) NBeckwithSr@msn.com
[(RE) P 1967; F 1970]. 1967 Homersville, OH; 1970 Lapeer: Trinity (assoc); 1972
Denton: Faith; 1976 Erie; 1981 trans. W. OH, Peebles; 1984 South Salem; 1987
Union Plains; 1988 Stryker; 1994 trans. to Detroit Conf., Bay Port, Hayes; 1998
Owosso: Trinity; **2008 Retired**. Home:18571 W. Brady Rd., Oakley 48649 (989-
277-1289)

*Bedwell, Donald Eugene (Polly)　　　　　　car54mhpd@hotmail.com
[(RL) PL Dec. 1, 2002]. Dec 1, 2002 Ishpeming: Salisbury; 2004 Manistique: First; **2011 Retired**. Home:141 New Delta, Manistique 49654 (906-341-5812)

*Beebe, Grace Ann　　　　　　beebega@aol.com
[(RD) PD 2004; FD 2007]. 2004 Consultant, Disability Awareness and Accessibility Concerns; 2015 Trenton: Faith; **2017 Retired**. Home: 2225 Emeline, Trenton 48183 (734-676-3863)

Beedle-Gee, Pamela A. (John)　　　　　　pastorpam@live.com
[(FE) PE 2003; FE 2006]. 2003 Grosse Pointe (assoc); 2009 Garden City: First; 2014 Clinton; **2018 Sebewaing: Trinity**. 513 Washington, Sebewaing 48759 (989-883-3350). Home: 525 Washington, Sebewaing 48759

*BEKOFSKE, GARY L (RE) (Nancy) – (D-1972, FE-1976, R-2014)
Tranferred from Eastern Pennsylvania Conf 1989; Hillsdale: First 06/01/1989; Lansing: Grace 1996; Montague 2005; Muskegon: Central 08/16/2009; Delton: Faith 2010; Pentwater: Centenary 2012; Retired 2014
garyleeb@hotmail.com
(H) 733 W Elmwood Ave, Clawson 48017-1283 (248) 435-5027

BELL, DAVID S (AF) (Ethel) – (AF-2009)
[East Ohio Conf] Vice President of Stewardship of the United Methodist Foundation of MI 09/01/2007; President and Executive Director, United Methodist Foundation of MI 2011
david@umfmichigan.org
(H) 5527 Timber Bend Drive, Brighton 48116 (248) 435-5027 (810) 534-3001
(O) 840 W Grand River Ave, Brighton 48116 (888) 451-1929

*Bell, Virginia B. (Jack)　　　　　　vbellagain@yahoo.com
[(RL) PL 2001] 2001 God's Country Cooperative Parish: Paradise, Hulbert: Tahquamenon; Jan 1, 2002 God's Country Cooperative Parish: Paradise, Hulbert: Tahquamenon; **Oct 30, 2005 Retired**. Home: PO Box 198, Paradise 49768 (906-492-3202)

*Benissan, John Kodzo (Janis)　　　　　　benissanjk@gmail.com
[(RE) P N. IL, 1979; F N. IL, 1981]. 1978 Harvey: Wesley Memorial; Aug. 1984 trans. to Detroit Conf., Detroit: Henderson Memorial; 1987 Saginaw: New Church Development; 1998 Cooperative Ministries of Northwest Flint: Flint: Trinity; 2003 Beverly Hills; Aug 1, 2008 Flat Rock; **2011 Retired**. Home: 15919 Petros Drive, Brownstown 48173 (734-379-1746)

Benjamin, Barbara S (Raymond)　　　　　　mrsbenjix@aol.com
[(PE) PL 2012; FL 2016; PE 2018]. Aug 1, 2012 Richfield; 2014 Richfield, Elba; 2016 Byron: First, Lennon; **2018 Bryon: First, Gaines**. (BF) Box 127, 101 S. Ann, Byron 48418 (810-266-4976), (G) 117 Clinton St., PO Box 125, Gaines 48436 (989-271-9131). Home: 10214 Bath Rd., Byron 48418 (810-433-1096)

*BENSEN, KENNETH W (RE) (Sandra) – (D-1990, FE-1992, R-2003)
Lansing: Faith 05/01/1987; Retired 2003
kbensen@gmail.com
(H) 502 W Calle Artistica, Green Valley, AZ 85614-6149 (517) 819-7511

*Bentley, Evans Charles (Betsy) evansbentley27@gmail.com
[(RE) P 1980; F 1982; RE 2018]. 1980 Birmingham: First (assoc.); 1983 Manchester: Sharon; Jan. 15., 1988 Morenci; 1995 Flat Rock: First; 2004 Monroe: St. Paul's; **2018 Retired; 2018 Springville**. 10341 Springville Hwy., Onsted 49265 (517-467-4471). Home: 1109 N River Ct, Tecumseh 49286 (734-552-5064)

BENTLEY, TERRI L (FL) (Tom) – (FL-2002)
Stevensville (Assoc) 05/31/2002; St Louis: First 02/01/2008
pastorterrib@sbcglobal.net
(H) 116 N East St, Saint Louis 48880-1721 (989) 681-2486
St Louis: First: 116 S Franklin St, Saint Louis 48880-1737 (989) 681-3320

Benton, Jeremy (Rachel) revjeremybenton@gmail.com
[(FE) PE 2008; FE 2011]. 2008 Morrice, Pittsburg, Bancroft; 2011 Ortonville; **2013 Campus Minister, Wesley Foundation of Greenville, SC**. 501 E. 5th Street, Greenville, SC 27858 (252-758-2030). Home: 606A Spring Forest Road, Greenville, SC 27834 (252-412-6214)

Bergquist, Christine J. (Gary) 1chris1cross1@att.net
[(PL) PL 1990]. 1990 Bark River; **2009 Bark River, Hermansville: First**. (BR) 3716 D Rd., Bark River, 49807, (H) W 5494 Second St., Hermansville 48847. Home: 1290 10th Rd., Bark River 49807 (906-466-2839)

*Berkompas, Elwood Jay (Donna Lindberg) woodyberk@charter.net
[(RE) P Mich., 1954; F Mich., 1957]. 1956 Adamsville; 1957 Adamsville, Kessington; 1958 Grand Rapids: Northlawn; 1962 Detroit: Trinity; 1965 Monroe: First; 1972 Detroit: Zion; 1976 Troy: First; 1982 Ann Arbor: West Side; **1995 Retired**. Home: 1530 W. Ridge St., Apt. #47, Marquette 49855 (906-273-1026)

Berlanga, Nicolas Rey (Lisa) nick@phfum.org
[(FL) PL 2012; FL 2015]. Dec 9, 2012 Melvindale: New Hope; Feb 15, 2014 Plymouth: First (assoc); 2018 Ann Arbor: First (assoc.); **2018 Ann Arbor: First** (assoc.). 120 S. State, Ann Arbor 48104 (734-662-4536). Home: 1507 Warwick Ct., Ann Arbor 48103 (734-983-8677)

*Berquist, Jane A. (George) jgberquist@aol.com
[(RD) CE CRT Assoc. CE, 1993; CON 1994; DFM 1997; RD 2006]. 1994 Royal Oak: First; 1995 Farmington Hills: Nardin Park (deacon); **2006 Retired**. Home: 26375 Halstead, #198, Farmington Hills 48331 (248-473-0184)

BIBILOMO, SANDRA V (FD) (Jimoh) – (PD-2008, FD-2011)
Benton Harbor Peace Temple (Deacon LTFT ¼) and Deacons Appointed w/in UM Connectional Structure (¶331.1b) Executive Director Harbor Harvest Urban Ministries 2008; Deacons Appointed w/in UM Connectional Structure (¶331.1b) Executive Director Harbor Harvest Urban Ministries (LTFT ¾) and Battle Creek: Washington Heights (Interim LTFT ¼) 2009; Deacons Appointed w/in UM Connectional Structure (¶331.1b) Executive Director Harbor Harvest Urban Ministries (LTFT ¾) and Kalamazoo: Westwood (Deacon LTFT ¼) 2011; Kalamazoon Westwood (Deacon LTFT ¼) 01/01/2012; Deacons Appointed Beyond the Local Church (¶331.6) Guardian Finance and Advocacy Services Representative Payee (LTFT ¾) and Kalamazoo Westwood (Deacon LTFT ¼) 2012
sandra.douglas73@yahoo.com
(H) 2021 March St, Kalamazoo 49001-3957 (269) 369-8803
Westwood: 538 Nichols Rd, Kalamazoo 49006-2946 (269) 344-7165

Bierlein, Ellen D (FL) – (FL-2018)
Buchanan: First 2018
PastorEllenB@BuchananFirstUMC.org(H) 304 Pontic Court, Buchanan 49107
(269) 695-3896
Buchanan: First: 132 S Oak St, Buchanan 49107 (269) 695-3282

BIGHAM-TSAI, KENNETHA J (FE) (Kee Tsai) – (PE-2006, FE-2009)
East Lansing: University (Assoc) 2006; Kalamazoo: Milwood 2011; UM Connectional Structures (¶344.1a,c) Lansing District Superintendent 2013; UM Connectional Structures (¶344.1a,c) Chief Connectional Officer of the Connectional Table 01/22/2018

kbighamtsai@umc.org
(H) 6137 Horizon Dr, East Lansing 48823-2227 (517) 347-4173

*Bilkert, Daniel M (OR) – (OR 2018)
East Ohio Conference, Grand Rapids: Faith 2018; Grand Rapids: Faith (LTFT ½) 2019

dgbilkert@gmail.com
(H) 2239 Ducoma St NW, Grand Rapids 49504 (419) 606-0640
GR: Faith: 2600 7th St NW, Grand Rapids 49504 (616) 453-0693

*Billing, Bruce Lee (Linda) clgbbrewski@aol.com
[(RE) P 1974; F 1978]. 1977 Otisville, West Forest; 1982 Howarth, Paint Creek; 1993 Burton: Atherton; 2001 Atherton, Phoenix; **2011 Retired**; Feb. 1, 2018-June 30, 2018 Mt. Morris: First. Home: 5231 Sandalwood Circle, Grand Blanc 48439 (810-694-0992)

BILLS, WILLIAM C (Julie) – [(FE) D-1990, FE-1993]
Burr Oak 07/16/1988; Marshall (Assoc) 1991; Martin/Shelbyville 1994; Georgetown 2007; East Lansing: University 2016

bbills@eluumc.org
(H) 405 Green Meadows Dr, Lansing 48917 (616) 706-6050
EL: University: 1120 S Harrison Rd, East Lansing 48823-5201 (517) 351-7030

Bissell, Adam Winthrop (Shannon) adamwbissell@yahoo.com
[(FE) FL 2000; PE 2002, FE 2005]. 1997-1998 Flushing (assoc); 2000 Brighton: First (assoc); 2003 Eastpointe: Immanuel; 2007 leave of absence; Feb 1, 2008 Chaplain, Lifepath Hospice, Tampa, FL; Nov 1, 2008 leave of absence; Jun, 2009 Bereavement Coordinator, Hospice of the Pines (AZ Conf.). **June, 2013 Support Services Manager/Chaplain** Good Samaritan Society Prescott Hospice. 1065 Ruth St., Prescott, AZ 86301 (928-710-5532). Home: 7444 N. Pinnacle Pass Dr., Prescott Valley, AZ 86315 (928-592-5681)

*BISTAYI, JOSEPH J (Cheryl) – [(RE) D-1970, FE-1973, R-2005]
Transferred from Detroit Conf 1978; Portage: Chapel Hill 10/01/1978; Battle Creek: Chapel Hill 1985; UM Connectional Structures (¶344.1a,c) Conference Staff Person for Spiritual Formation 1993; Georgetown 08/16/1999; Retired 2005
joecheryl@prodigy.net
(H) 47049 Manhattan Circle, Novi 48374-1832 (616) 550-4374

PASTORAL RECORDS

BISTAYI, MATTHEW J (Shellie) – [(FE) FL-2002, PE-2007, FE-2015]
Brandywine Trinity 01/01/1999; Kalamazoo: First (Assoc) 05/31/2002; Bronson: First 2006; Allendale: Valley Church 2009
mbistayi@valleychurchallendale.org
(H) 10811 Lance Ave, Allendale 49401-7317 (616) 892-6240
Valley Church: 5980 Lake Michigan Dr, Ste B, Allendale 49401-9576
(616) 892-1042

BITEMAN JR, DANIEL W (Kellie Lynn) – [(FE) FL-1983, D-1988, FE-1996]
Fife Lake/South Boardman 1983; Dewitt: Redeemer (Assoc.) 1987; Lane Boulevard 1988; Grawn 1996; Lawton: St Paul's 2006; Alden/Central Lake 2010
dbiteman@outlook.com
(H) PO Box 157, 9022 Franklin, Alden 49612-0157 (231) 409-8015
Alden: PO Box 130, 9015 Helena, Alden 49612-0130 (231) 331-4132
Central Lake: PO Box 213, Central Lake 49622

*Bitterling, Nancy J. (Curtis) njbit1@yahoo.com
[(RL) SP 2000, FL 2002, PL 2013, RL 2018]. 2000 Niles: Grace; May 31, 2002 Riverdale Lincoln Road; 2010 Nashville; 2013 Port Austin, Pinnebog; **2018 Retired; 2019 Shabbona** (LTFT ¼). 4455 Decker Rd., Decker 48426-9717 (989-872-8094). Home: 3610 Bluff Rd, PO Box 533, Port Austin 48467 (989-738-6322)

Bixby, Jennifer Lynn jennifer777@wwnet.com
[(FE) PE 2000; FE 2003]. 2000 Northville: First (assoc). 2004 leave of absence; Aug 1, 2004, Chaplain, US Navy; **Sep 15, 2006 Leave of Absence**. Home: 3034 S. Navel Ave., Yuma, AZ 85365 (928-269-6422)

BLACK, CARLETON R (Barbara) – [(FL) FL-2012]
Ravenna (DSA ½ Time) 2011; Ravenna PTLP ¾) 11/12/11; Ravenna (FTLP) 2012
carl.black77@gmail.com
(H) 3482 Lo Al Dr, Ravenna 49451-9405 (231) 853-6111
Ravenna: PO Box 191, 12348 Stafford St, Ravenna 49451-0191 (231) 853-6688

*Blair, Betty Montei (Coulson) bcbean@greatlakes.net
[(RL) FL 2002]. 2002 Lexington; **Jun 30, 2009 Retired**. 5674 Gov. Sleeper Ct., Lexington 48450 (810-359-3419)

*Blair, Eugene A. (Dawn) jabulaney3@gmail.com
[(RE) P W. OH 1982; F W. OH 1985]. 1980 Columbus: Hilltop; Toledo: New Horizon; 1986 Dean of the Chapel, UPPER ROOM; 1992 Methodist Church of Kenya, West; 1993 Columbus: Livingston Avenue; 1995 Northern Illinois Conference Staff, Congregational Development; Jan 1, 2004 transf to Detroit Conference; Jan 1, 2004 Associate Council Director, in American Spiritual Formation; 2009 Flint District Superintendent; 2011 Crossroads District Superintendent; **Apr 1, 2012 Retired**. Home: 3631 Meadow Grove Trail, Ann Arbor 48108 (734-748-0287)

*BLAKEY, DOROTHY M (RD) – (DM-1994, FD-1997, RD-1999)
Holland: First (Deacon) (LTFT ¼) 1997; Retired 1999
dorothy.m.blakey@gmail.com
(H) 5054 Maple Creek SE, Kentwood 49508-4953 (616) 455-8503

Blanchard, Josheua Edwin (Amanda)   josh_blanchard@hotmail.com
[(FL) FL 2009 OK Conf; FL 2011 (Detroit Conf); PE 2014; FL 2017]. 2009 OK
Conference; 2011 transfer to Detroit Conf. 2011 Onaway, Millersburg; 2014 Mid-
land: Homer, Gordonville; [August 31, 2018 surrender of credentials].

Blanchard, Robert   reverendblanchard@gmail.com
[(PE) PE 2018]. 2018 Clinton. 10990 Tecumseh Clinton Rd, Clinton 49236 (517-
456-4972). Home: 6830 Close Dr, Tecumseh 49286

*Blomquist, Paul Frederick (Beatrice)   SagePaul@comcast.net
[(RE) T MI, 1957; F MI, 1959]. 1955 Niles: First (assoc.); 1957 Coloma; 1962
trans to N. Eng. Conf., Pittsfield; 1964 trans. to Detroit Conf., Ferndale: First
(assoc.); 1966 Troy: Big Beaver; 1969 Warren: First; 1973 Flint District Superintendent; 1979 Port Huron: First; 1985 Farmington: Orchard; **1996 Retired**.
Home: 5578 Hummingbird Lane, Clarkston 48346 (248-620-1713)

BLUNT, RICHARD W (FE) (Natalie) – (D-1985, FE-1988)
Ogdensburg (Old Mission Peninsula) 1986; Manton 1993; Reed City 02/01/1999;
Lowell: First 2008; Okemos Community Church 2014

                                                        rickblunt@hotmail.com
          (H) 2441 S Wild Blossom Ct, East Lansing 48823-7203 (517) 721-1301
               Okemos Community: PO Box 680, 4734 Okemos Rd, Okemos 48864
                                                              (517) 349-4220

Boayue, Charles S.G., Jr. (Elizabeth)   cboayue@michiganumc.org
[(FE) FL 1990; P 1991; F 1993]. 1990 Detroit: Metropolitan (assoc.). 1991 Detroit:
Metropolitan (assoc.-LTFT), Jefferson Avenue (LTFT); 1993 Associate Council
Director: Urban Missioner; 1999 Detroit: Second Grace; 2015 Detroit Renais-
sance District Superintendent; **Jan. 1, 2019 Greater Detroit District Superin-
tendent**. 8000 Woodward Ave., Detroit 48202 (313-481-1045). Home: 35361
Stratton Hill Court, Farmington Hills 48331

*BOEHM, JAMES W (RE) – (D-1966, D-1973, FE-1976, R-1998)
Gobles/Kendall 04/01/1967-09/01/1969; Withdrew 1970; Readmitted 1973;
Transferred from Detroit Conf 1975; Newaygo 1975; Plainwell: First 1984; UM
Connectional Structures (¶344.1a,c) Kalamazoo District Superintendent 1989;
Okemos Community Church 1996; Retired 09/01/1998

                                                      catherynboehm@hotmail.com
               (H) PO Box 663, 73 N Eldridge Rd, Beulah 49617-0663 (231) 882-7074

*BOELENS, NANCY (RL) – (FL-2000, PL-2007, RL-2009)
Bath/Gunnisonville 1998; Wayland 06/06/2003-11/01/2006; Sitka 11/1/2006-
7/1/2008; Muskegon: Unity 11/01/2006-1/1/2009; Personal Leave 1/1/2009-
4/12/2009; Retired 4/12/2009; Salem Indian Mission / Bradley Indian Mission
2013-12/15/2015

                                                      boelensnancy5@gmail.com
               (H) 1875 Parkcrest Dr. SW, Apt. 2, Wyoming 49519 (616) 914-9300

PASTORAL RECORDS

***BOERSMA, GILBERT R** (RE) (Sara Jayne) – (D-1982, FE-1984, R-2011)
Frontier/Osseo 1982; Middleville/Freeport (Assoc) 1985; Wolf Lake 01/01/1989; Other Valid Ministries (¶344.1d) Pastoral Care Coordinator, Hospice Of Oceana & Muskegon Counties 02/01/1995; Clergy Appointed to Attend School, CPE Residency Program, Bronson Medical Center 1997; Appointed to Extension Ministries (¶344.1b,c) Chaplain, Hackley Hospital 06/15/1998; Appointed to Extension Ministries (¶344.1b,c) Manager, Spiritual Care Services, Hackley Hospital 2004; Transitional Leave 04/17/2009; Muskegon: Unity (LTFT ¼) 2009; Retired 10/31/2011
(H) 3364 Davis Rd, Muskegon 49441 (231) 557-5640 boersma49@gmail.com

***Bohnsack, Benjamin** (Marcia) bohnsack@sandriverfriends.com
[(RE) P 1969; F 1971]. 1970 Livonia: Newburg (assoc.); 1973 Hardy; 1980 Marquette: First; 1988 Brighton: First; 1997 Farmington: Nardin Park; **2006 Retired**.
3140 State Highway M-28 East, Marquette 49855 (906-343-6638)

Boley, Ian (Jessica Korpela)
[(FL) FL 2016]. **2016 Walled Lake**. 313 Northport St., Walled Lake 48390 (248-624-2405). Home: 1977 Meadow Ridge Rd., Walled Lake 48390 (989-400-1268)

BOLEY, JOHN W (FE) (Diane) – (D-1991, FE-1994)
Mancelona/Alba 06/16/1992; Lansing: Central 1997; Mt Pleasant: First 2002; Kalamazoo: First 2010; UM Connectional Structures (¶344.1a,c) Kalamazoo District Superintendent 2014; UM Connectional Structures (¶344.1a,c) Clergy Assistant to the Bishop 2016
jboley@michiganumc.org
(H) 2717 Frederick Ave, Kalamazoo 49008-2151 (989) 400-0355
(O) 1011 Northcrest Rd, Lansing 48906-1262 (517) 347-4030

***BOLTZ, PEGGY A.** (RL) – (FL-1995, RL-2014)
Marcellus 08/01/1995; Shelby 2002; Lawton: St Paul's 2010; Oshtemo 2011; Bellaire: Community 2013; Retired 07/16/2014

BONDARENKO, GARY D (FE) (Lisa) – (D-1989, FE-1993)
Charlotte: Lawrence Ave (Assoc) 07/16/1988; Boyne City/Boyne Falls 06/16/1991; East Lansing: Aldersgate 2000; Wayland 11/15/2006; Stanwood: Northland 2014
bondo5@sbcglobal.net
(H) PO Box 26, 18835 Fillmomre Rd, Stanwood 49346-0026 (231) 823-2514
Stanwood: Northland: PO Box 26, 6842 Northland Dr, Stanwood 49346 (231) 629-4590

***BONGARD, CONNIE R.** (RL) (Frank) – (FL-1992, RL-2015)
Leaton 05/01/1992; Mt Pleasant: First (Assoc) 08/01/1994; Edmore: Faith 07/16/1997; Farwell 01/01/2007; Retired 2015
rev_crab@hotmail.com
(H) 1007 Lincoln Dr., Weidman 48893 (989) 506-6659

Bonsky, Nicholas
[(PE) PE 2019]. **2019 Farmington: Orchard** (assoc.). 30450 Farmington Rd, Farmington Hills 48334 (248-626-3620). Home: 29221 Aranel, Farmington Hills 48334 (586-944-3292)

Bos, Kimberly Mae (PE)
UM Connectional Structures (¶344.1a,c) Director of Wesley Foundation at Ferris state University 2019

kimberly.bos@garrett.edu
(H) 14610 Tomahawk Ln, Big Rapids 49307-9505 (231) 557-0574
FSU Wesley Foundation: 628 S Warren Ave, Big Rapids 49307-2210
(231) 796-8315

*BOURNS, CAROL LYNN (RP) – (D-1992, RP-2007)
North Evart/Sylvan (¼ Time) 09/01/1991; Leave of Absence 01/01/1995; Medical Leave 1997; Retired 2007

fpm-dave@hotmail.com
(H) 144 W 4th St Apt 403, Clare 48617-1483 (989) 544-2719

Bouse, Carol Marie Blair (Allen) cmbblogos@aol.com
[(FE) P 1995; F 1997]. 1995 Owendale, Gagetown; Oct 1, 1996 Fenton (assoc); 2001 Lake Orion (assoc); 2002 Dearborn: Mt. Olivet; 2006 Bay City: Christ; **2013 Flint: Hope**. G-4467 Beecher Rd., Flint 48532 (810-732-4820)

BOUTELL, JAMES (TOMMY) T (FE) (Shelly) – (PL-2008, PE-2010, FE-2016)
Olivet (PTLP) 2008; Marne 2010; Grad Rapids: Genesis 2018

tomboutell@yahoo.com
(H) 1805 Foreste Lake Dr, SE, Grand Rapids 49546 (616) 678-7664
GR: Genesis: 3189 Snow Ave, Lowell 49331 (616) 974-0400

*Bouvier, Sylvia Ann (Carl) sylvia13bouvier@gmail.com
[(RE) P 1985; F 1987]. 1985 Lakeville, Leonard; 1987 Pontiac: Aldersgate; 1987 Oakland County Jail Chaplain; May 1, 1989 Pontiac United Ministries Association, parish director; 1992 Flint: Oak Park; 1998 Howarth, Paint Creek; **2006 Retired**. 143 NE Naranja Ave., Port Saint Lucie, FL 34983 (615-427-8562)

*BOVEE, KEITH A (RE) – (D-1956, FE-1958, R-1994)
Frontier 1952; Centreville 1954; Muskegon: Central (Assoc) 1957; North Muskegon 1959; Lowell: First 1963; St Johns: First 1965; Voluntary Location 1968; Left Appointment 1974; Marne 1982; Ionia: First 1985; Shelby 1991; Retired 1994

keith6451@att.net
(H) 1551 Franklin St SE, 3010 Manor, Grand Rapids 49506-8203 (616) 805-3682

*BOWDEN, DIANNE M (RE) (Jeff) – (PE-2002, FE-2005, R-2013)
Nashville 01/16/2002; Muskegon: Crestwood 2007; Medical Leave 05/01/2008; Retired 2013

Pastordi46@gmail.com
(H) 2310 Avenal Ct, Murfreesboro, TN 37129-6612 (615) 410-3399

Bower, Benjamin J. R. (Mallory) Missing changes with statuses?
[(FE) FL 2013; PE 2014; FE 2017]. 2013 Trenton: First; **2016 Redford: Aldersgate**. 10000 Beech Daly Rd., Redford 48239 (313-937-3170). Home: 11328 Arnold, Redford 48239 (313-531-7487)

Bowden, Frederick J fbowdencharity@gmail.com
[(PL) PL Jan 1, 2019]. Aug. 1, 2018 Flint: Charity (DSA); **Jan. 1, 2019 Flint: Charity** (LTFT ¼). 4601 Clio Rd, Flint 48504 (810-789-2961). Home: 25151 Dequindre Rd, Lot 17, Madison Hts, 48071 (313-443-4300)

Bowman, Daniel James (Celina)   preacherdb@gmail.com
[(FE) PL 1991; P 1993; F 1995]. May 16, 1991 LaSalle: Zion; Jan 1, 1995 Lapeer: Trinity (assoc); Sep 1, 1998 Marlette: First; **2014 Gaylord: First**. 215 South Center, Box 617, Gaylord 49734 (989-732-5380). Home: 915 Five Lakes Rd., Gaylord 49735 (989-635-2075)

BOWMAN, LETISHA M (FE) (Brian) – (PL-2007, PE-2011, FE-2014)
Saugatuck (DSA) 2005; Saugatuck (PTLP) 2007; Grand Rapids: First (Assoc) 2011; Portland 2015

pastortish@gmail.com
(H) 309 Grape St, Portland 48875-1134 (517) 647-6460
Portland: 310 E Bridge St, Portland 48875-1439 (517) 647-4649

BOWMAN SR, JEFFREY J (FL) (Cheryl) – (FL-2000)
Vermontville/Gresham 1995; White Cloud 2002; Muskegon Heights: Temple 2012

pjbowman400@att.net
(H) 1205 Yorkshire Dr, Muskegon 49441-5358 (231) 798-9309
Temple: 2500 Jefferson St, Muskegon Heights 49444-1444 (231) 733-1065

BRATT CARLE, JONATHAN E (PE) – (PE-2017)
[Tennessee Conference] Ionia First/Lyons-Muir 2017

jonathan.brattcarle@gmail.com
(H) 2536 Union Ave SE, Grand Rapids 49507-35274 (901) 417-2844
Ionia First: 105 E Main St, Ionia 48846-1614 (616) 527-1860
Lyons-Muir: 1074 Olmstead Rd, Muir 48860-9627 (989) 855-2247

*Breitkreuz, Benjamin H. (Sharlene)
[(RE) 1977 trans. from American Baptist Assn.; F 1982]. 1978 Indiana University Hospital, Chaplain; Director of Dept. of Pastoral Care, Parkland Memorial Hospital; Jan 1, 1993 Department of Pastoral Care and Education, Medical University of South Carolina; 1997 Community Donation Coordinator, Transplant Center; 2000 leave of absence; Aug 1, 2001 Chaplain, Clinical Pastoral Educator, Bon Secours, St. Francis Xavier Hospital (335.1); Sep 1, 2002 leave of absence; 2004 Chaplain, Clinical Pastoral Educator; Jan 1, 2007 voluntary leave of absence; **2008 Retired**. Home: 22 D Foxwood Dr., Morris Plains, NJ 07950

*BREMER, KENNETH J (RE) (Vicky) – (D-1990, FE-1995, R-2017)
Holton 06/01/1992; St Johns: Pilgrim 2006; Rockford 2014, Retired 2017
(H) 1527 G Hidden Creek Circle Dr, Grand Rapids 49505 (989) 980-0903

*Brenner, Robert Dale (Joyce)   revrdbrenner@gmail.com
[(RE) PL 2000; PE 2002, FE 2005]. 2000 Denton: Faith; Sep 1, 2002 Carleton; 2010 Farmington: First; **2013 Retired**. Home: 25766 Livingston Circle, Farmington Hills 48335 (248-474-7568)

*BRICKER, J MELVIN (RE) – (D-1966, FE-1968, R-1995)
Kalamazoo: First (Assoc) 1966; Frankfort/Elberta 1971; Rockford 1980; Grandville 1989; Retired 1995
(H) 1216 Oakmont Dr #8, Walnut Creek, CA 94595 (925) 482-0555

BRILLHART, JAMES (BRAD) B (FE) (Julia) – (D-1999, FE-2004)
Hesperia/Ferry 1999; Howard City: Heritage 2007; Lowell: First 2014
thewayofxp@gmail.com
(H) 640 Shepard Dr, Lowell 49331-8642 (616) 897-8267
Lowell: First: 621 E Main St, Lowell 49331-1719 (616) 897-5936

Britt, James Edward (Denise)   jbritt@norwaymi.com
[(FE) P 1986; F 1989]. 1986 Owosso: Central; 1990 Algonac: Trinity; 1992 West
Vienna; 2001 Livonia: Clarenceville; Aug 16, 2006 Norway Grace, Faithhorn;
2011 Flint: Calvary; **2018 Lambertville**. 8165 Douglas Rd., Box 232, Lambertvlle
48144 (734-847-3944). Home: 8116 Michelle Ln, Lambertville 48144 (810-282-
8081)

Britt, John Joseph (Janine)   rev_jjb@yahoo.com
[(FE) P 1982; F 1984]. 1982 Warren: First (assoc.); Nov. 1982 Sterling, Alger,
Bentley; 1990 Mio, Curran Sunnyside; 2005 Pigeon: First; **2015 Millington**. Box
321, 9020 State, Millington 48746 (989-871-3489). Home: 4851 W. Main St.,
Millington 48746 (989-871-3341)

*BROMBEREK, PATRICIA L (RE) (Glen Brown) – (FL-2002, PE-2004, FE-2009,
R-2011)
Niles: Grace 2002; Center Park 2004; Newaygo 2006; Newaygo (LTFT ¾)
02/01/2011; Retired 2011

plbromberek@hotmail.com
(H) 348 Lyon Lake Rd, Marshall 49068-8206 (231) 519-5956

BROMLEY, DENNIS B (FE) (JoAnn) – (D-2000, AM-2000, PE-2014, FE-2016)
Epsilon/Levering (DSA) 1993; Epsilon/ Levering/11/16/1993; Epsilon/Levering/
Pellston 09/01/1997; Clare 2003; Ludington United 2013
pastord@ludingtonumc.org
(H) 914 Seminole Dr, Ludington 49431-1584 (231) 425-4386
Ludington United: 5810 Bryant Rd, Ludington 49431-1504 (231) 843-8340

*BROOK, PATRICIA L (RE) (Roger) – (PE-2001, FE-2004, R-2018)
Dewitt: Redeemer (Assoc) 1999; Marne 02/01/2002; Hillsdale: First 2010; Re-
tired 2018; Carson City (LTFT ¼) 08/01/2018-06/30/2019
(H) 1653 Dr, E Lansing 48823 (517) 607-5770 plb331@gmail.com

BROOKS, RONALD K (FE) (Penny) – (D-1985, FE-1988)
Center Eaton/Brookfield 1985; Nashville 1988; Lawrence 05/16/1991; Lansing:
Mount Hope (Assoc) 1998; Lansing: Mount Hope 1999; Lawton: St Paul 2000;
Carson City 2006; Voluntary Leave of Absence 2008; Lansing: Central 2009;
Jackson: Brookside 2013; Jackson: Brookside/Trinity 2015
revbrooks.ron@gmail.com
(H) 217 Mohawk, Jackson 49203-5351 (517) 782-2706
Jackson: Brookside: 4000 Francis St, Jackson 49203-5436 (517) 782-5167
Jackson: Trinity: 1508 Greenwood Ave, Jackson 49203-4048 (517) 782-7937

*Brookshear, Wayne Walker (Margie)
[(RE) T 1958; F 1960]. 1956 Lennon; 1960 Pontiac: St. Luke's, Oakland Univer-
sity Wesley Foundation; 1968 Detroit: St. Mark's; 1972 Milford; **1983 Retired**.
Home: 450 Gordon Circle, Key Largo, FL 33037 (305-453-3126)

*Brown, Carole A. carolebrown@intouchmi.com
[(RL) PL Apr 1, 2005; FL 2006; RL 2019]. Apr 1, 2005 Oregon; 2006 Owosso: Burton, Carland; 2011 Mayville; **2019 Retired**. 3001 Oklahoma Ave., Flint 48506 (989-277-2306)

*Brown, Colon Robert (Lisa) cbrown1@mac.com
[(RE) P, N. IN, 1987; F N. IN, 1991; RE 2019]. 1985 Michigan City; 1987 Mishawaka; 1992 trans. to Detroit Conf., Burton: Burton; Dec 15, 1995 Grand Blanc: Phoenix; 1997 Associate Council Director, Director of Congregational Development; 2005 Associate Executive Director, United Methodist Union; Feb 1, 2006 incapacity leave; **Retired 2019**. Home: 2109 Breeze Dr., Holland 49424 (616-820-4053)

*Brown, Dale E. (Margaret) dalemargebr@gmail.com
[(RE) P 1971; F 1974]. 1973 AuGres, Turner, Twining; Mar. 1979 Mayville, Fostoria, Silverwood; Jan. 8, 1984 Hardy; 1989 Birch Run; 1999 Bay City: Fremont Avenue; 2002 Macon; Mar 1, 2004 Macon (LTFT ¾); 2007 Capac: First, Zion Community; 2011 Menominee: First; **2014 Retired**. Home: 4622 Weswilmar Dr., Holt 48842 (517-742-7067)

*Brown, Debra Kay (Dennis) pastordebi2000@yahoo.com
[(RL)] PL Oct 1, 2000]. Oct 1, 2000 Cole; 2002 Cole, Melvin; Aug 1, 2010 Kingston; 2014 medical leave; **Mar 15, 2015 Retired**. Home: 2357 Snover Rd., Deckerville 49427 (810-366-0430)

*Brown, Janet Jacqueline januk99@gmail.com
[(RE) PE 2007; FE 2010, RE 2018]. 2007 Detroit: Trinity Faith; **2018 Retired; 2018 Erie**. 1100 E. Samaria Rd., Erie 48133 (734-856-1453). Home: 23470 Meadow Park, Redford 48239 (313-533-8423)

BROWN, KATHY E (FE) – (D-1985, FE-1987)
Traverse City: Central (Assoc) 1985; Litchfield 1990; Hastings: First 02/01/2001; Plainwell: First 2010

kathyebrown935@gmail.com
(H) 714 E Gun River Dr, Plainwell 49080-9533 (269) 312-1378
Plainwell: First: PO Box 85, 200 Park St, Plainwell 49080-0085 (269) 685-5113

*BROWN, LAWRENCE P (RE) (Beverly) – (D-1988, FE-1992, R-2014)
Somerset Center/Moscow Plains 1989; Somerset Center 01/01/1993; Lakeview Asbury/Belvidere 1996; Lakeview: New Life 01/01/1998; Ionia: First 2006; Retired 2014

Larrybev@outlook.com
(H) 564 Indiana Ave, South Haven 49090-1245 (517) 526-7958

BROWN, MARY S (FE) (Carl) – (FD-1994, FE-1997)
Baldwin/Luther (¶426.1) 1995; Transferred from Detroit Conf 1996; Baldwin/Luther 1996; Bellaire: Community 10/16/1998; Traverse City Christ and Kewadin 2009; Grawn 11/01/2009; Montague 2014; Medical Leave 12/01/2016
(H) 16843 Shawano Dr, Sand Lake 49343 (231) 357-4506
pastormaryb@gmail.com

*Brown, Richard B. (Randi) richardblackstock.brown@gmail.com
[(RL) PL 2000; FL 2003]. Mar 16, 2000 Calumet, Mohawk-Ahmeek, Lake Linden, Laurium (assoc); 2003 Vernon, Bancroft; 2005 Kingston, Clifford; Dec 1, 2009 Kingston. **2010 Retired**. Home: 4257 Mill Ridge Circle, Eau Claire, WI 54703

*Brown, Ronald Alex (Joan)
[(RL) PL 1987]. 1987 Keego Harbor: Trinity; **1994 Retired**. Home: 294 Draper, Pontiac 48341 (248-681-8470)

Brown, Sari (Ricardo Angarita Oviedo)　　　　　revsaribrown@gamil.com
[(PE) PE 2016]. 2016 Grosse Pointe (assoc.); **2017 Harbor Beach, Port Hope**. (HB) PO Box 25, 253 S. First St., Harbor Beach 48441, (PH) PO Box 25, 4521 Main St., Port Hope 48468. Home: PO Box 25, 247 First St., Harbor Beach 48441 (989-479-6053)

*Brown, Tom, II　　　　　tborwn@albion.edu
[(RE) T 1957; F 1959]. 1959 Dearborn: First (assoc.); 1960 St. Clair Shores: Good Shepherd; 1965 River Rouge: Epworth; 1968 Iron Mountain: Trinity; 1973 Roseville; 1978 Hemlock, Nelson; 1984 Warren: Wesley; Dec. 1, 1986 Flint: Oak Park; 1992 Burton: Emmanuel; **1997 Retired**. Home: 801 W Middle St, Apt 177, Chelsea 48118 (517-629-9606)

BROWNE, JENNIFER (FE) (Eric Strand) – (D-1998, FE-2008)
Reed City (Assoc) 01/15/1997; Transferred from United Church of Christ 1998; Clergy Appointed To Attend School (¶416.6) 12/01/1998; UM Connectional Structures (¶344.1a,c) Albion College, Assistant to the President (¶335.1a LTFT ½) 2000; Leave of Absence 03/01/2003; Appointed in Other Annual Conferences (¶337.1) (Assoc) Detroit Conference, Brighton First 2003; Grand Rapids: First (Assoc) 2006; East Lansing: University 2011; Georgetown 2016; UM Connectional Structures (¶344.1a,c), Conference Director of Clergy Excellence
jbrowne@michiganumc.org
(H) 434 Creston Ave, Kalamazoo 49001-4203 (517) 898-4575
(O) 1161 E Clark Rd, DeWitt 48820 (517) 347-4030 ext. 4050

*BRUBAKER, ELLEN A (RE) (John Ross Thompson) – (D-1974, FE-1976, R-2001)
Transferred from Detroit Conf 1975; Traverse City: Central (Assoc) 1975; Traverse City: Central (Assoc) / Ogdensburg (Re-named Old Mission Peninsula 1978; Belding 1981; UM Connectional Structures (¶344.1a,c) Grand Rapids District Superintendent 1983; Church of the Dunes 1989; Grand Rapids: Aldersgate 1992; Retired 12/31/2001; Grand Rapids: Trinity (Assoc) (LTFT 1/8) 2015-9/1/2016
johnellen5@comcast.net
(H) 4114 Sawkaw Dr NE, Grand Rapids 49525-1858 (616) 822-5383

*Brun, Wesley LeRoy　　　　　wesbrun@gmail.com
[(RE) P MO E., 1963; F, MO E, 1965]. 1965 school (Yale); 1966 Monroe City, Florida (Missouri); 1968 St. Louis: Grace (assoc); 1974 Pastoral Counseling Center, Lutheran General Hospital, Park Ridge, IL; 1986 Executive Director, Samaritan Counseling Center of Southeastern Michigan (1999 trans to Det Conf); **2006 Retired**. H: 41120 Fox Run Rd #308, Novi 48337 (248-956-7889)

*Bryant, Vivian C. (William)　　　　　revvcb@yahoo.com
[(RE) P 1997 on recognition of orders AME; FE 2000]. 1997 Southfield: Hope (assoc); **Jun 30, 2003 Retired**. Home: 313 Castlemere Ct., Murfreesboro, TN 37130 (615-605-7636)

Bryce, Margaret E. (Craig) drmbryce@gmail.com
[(FE) PL 2008, PE 2012 (Church of the Nazarene); FE 2014]. Aug 1, 2008 Attica; 2013 Downriver; Jul 1-31, 2018 leave of absence; **Aug 1, 2018 Adjunct Professor of Practical Theology, Ashland Theological Seminary, Detroit Campus**. Home: 824 Inverness Dr, Oxford 48371

*Buchholz, Pamela Leigh (Fredric) pam06@charter.net
[(RD) PD 2006; FD 2009]. 2006 Midland: First, Minister of Christian Education (deacon); **Sep 1, 2013 Retired**. Home: 256 E. Youngs Ct., Midland 48640 (989-835-3203)

BUCHNER, GREGORY L (FE) (AnnMarie) – (FL-1999, PE-2005, FE-2008)
Three Oaks (DSA) 11/15/1997; Wakelee (DSA) 1998; Wakelee 11/16/1999; Rosebush 2005; Ovid United Church 2008; Mecosta: New Hope 2013; Rockford 2019

pastorgreg.ncd@gmail.com
(H) 1105 West Pickard, PO Box 894, Mt Pleasant MI 48804-0894 (989) 621-7782
Rockford: 159 Maple St, Rockford 49341-1250 (616) 866-9515

*Buck, Steven J. (Susan) sjbuck@comcast.net
[(RE) trans. from Wesleyan Methodist, 1977; F 1979]. 1977 Yale, Greenwood; Jan. 15, 1982 Royal Oak: First (assoc.); 1988 Marquette: First; 1993 Flint: Court Street; 2008 Northville: First; **2013 Retired**. 6446 Prairie Dunes Dr., Grand Blanc 48439 (810-444-7089)

*BUEGE, DONALD L (RE) (Cynthia) – (D-1977, FE-1981, R-2017)
Vergennes/Lowell: First (Assoc) 1979; Mesick/Harrietta 09/01/1980; Keeler/ Silver Creek 01/01/1984; Evart/Avondale 1990; Avondale/North Evart/Sylvan (LTFT ¼) 2000; Leslie/Felt Plains (LTFT ¾) 01/15/2006; Fife Lake Parish: Fife Lake/East Boardman/South Boardman 2014; Retired 2017

dbuege76@gmail.com
(H) 124 Boyd St, Fife Lake 49633-9031 (231) 879-6055

*BUKER, ELAINE M (RA) – (FL-1981, AM-1985, D-1985, RA-1997)
Big Rapids: Third Avenue/Paris/Rodney 09/01/1981; Mendon 1986; Portland 1992; Retired 1997

emarieb@gmail.com
(H) 10100 Hillview Dr. Apt.1213, Pensacola, FL 32514-5448 (850) 607-7743

BUKOSKI, JERRY J (PL) (Sandra) – (PL-2014)
Barry-Eaton Cooperative Ministry: Quimby (DSA) (LTFT ¼) 2013; Barry-Eaton Cooperative Ministry: Quimby (PTLP ¼) 2014; Kalamo/Quimby (PTLP 45%) 2015; Kalamo (LTFT ¼) 2018

jerry.bukoski@gmail.com
(H) 1069 S Ionia Rd, Vermontville 49096-8576 (517) 588-8415
Kalamo: 1475 S Ionia Rd, Kalamo 49096 (810) 986-0240

BUNCH, BRIAN R (FL) (Kendra) – (FL-1997)
Brooks Corners and Sears 1997; Brooks Corners/Barryton-Chippewa Lake/Sears 03/01/2002; NE Missaukee Parish: Merritt-Butterfield/ Moorestown-Stittsville 08/01/2005; Delton: Faith 2012

brbunch@mei.net
(H) 146 Bush St, Delton 49046-9798 (269) 623-5335
Delton: Faith: PO Box 467, 503 S Grove St, Delton 49046-0467 (269) 623-5400

Bunn, Bradley (FL) – (CC-2017, DSA-2017, FL-2017)
Ludington: St. Paul (DSA) 2017; Ludington: St. Paul (FL) 2017
bunnbrad5@gmail.com
(H) 3257 W Kinney Rd, Ludington 49431-9780 (404) 625-6802
Ludington: St. Paul: (O) 3212 W Kinney Rd, Ludington 49431-9780
(231) 843-3275

Burdette, Tom Glenn (Gail)   tburd@med.umich.edu
[(FE) P 1975; F 1979]. 1977 Ypsilanti: First (assoc.); 1983 Lincoln Community;
Nov. 1, 1985 Chaplain, M. J. Clark Home, Grand Rapids; Dec. 1, 1986 Staff
Chaplain, University of Michigan Health System' **Dec 2, 2016 Retired**. Home:
8424 Crestshire, Ypsilanti 48197 (734-484-6004)

*BURGESS, RAY W (RE) (Martha) – (D-1961, FE-1965, R-2000)
Transferred from Detroit Conf 01/01/1970; UM Connectional Structures
(¶344.1a,c) Wesley Foundation Director, Ferris State College 01/01/1970; Grand
Rapids: South 1979; Sturgis 1988; Muskegon: Central 1993; Retired 2000
mrburgess2@nmo.net
(H) 10915 Pioneer Trail, Boyne Falls 49713-9217 (231) 549-3066
(S): 8701 S Kolb 7-232, Tuscon, AZ 85706-9607 (520) 574-6692

Burns, Dillon Selby   pastordillionburns@gmail.com
[(PE) PE 2017]. **2017 Manchester: First**. 501 Ann Arbor St., Manchester 48158
(734-428-8495). Home: 330 Ann Arbor St., Manchester 48158 (734-428-4780)

*Burns, Ellen Florence (William)   burns2444@att.net
[(RL) PL 1996, FL 2000]. 1996 Eastern Thumb Cooperative Parish: Minden City,
Forester; 2000 Decker, Argyle, Shabbona, Ubly; Jan 1, 2006 Parish Director,
DASU Parish (Decker, Argyle, Shabbona, Ubly); **2010 Retired**. Home: 60
Chippewa St., Port Sanilac 48469 (810-404-2444)

*BURSON, LINDA J (RE) (Douglas Rose) – (D-1987, FE-1990, RE-2019)
Transferred from New York Conf 1997; Homer/Lyon Lake 1997; Leave of Absence 1/1/2000; UM Connectional Structures (¶344.1a,c) Conference Staff Ministry Consultant 8/1/2000; Leave of Absence 2008; Kalamazoo: Sunnyside
3/1/2009; Personal Leave 2009; Appointed in Other Annual Conferences
(¶331.8, ¶346.1) Mallory, Tennessee Conf 2017; Retired 02/04/2019
LindaJBurson@gmail.com
(H) 240 Cullom Way, Clarksville, TN 37043 (931) 302-6760

Burstall, Richard Erich   gvnit2god@yahoo.com
[(FE) PL May 15, 2005, FL 2005, PE 2008; FE 2013]. May 15, 2005 Azalia, London; 2007 Morenci; 2010 Britton: Grace; **2014 Grayling: Michelson Memorial**.
400 Michigan Ave., Grayling 49738 (989-348-2974). Home: 142 Barbara St.,
Grayling 49738 (989-348-9697)

*BURTON-COLLIER, LINDA J. (Earl Collier) – [(RL) PE-2005, FL-2010, RL-2014]
White Pigeon (DSA 07/01/01-07/01/02) 2002; Hopkins 2005; South Monterey
2005; Retired 2014
lindaburtoncollier@gmail.com
(H) 2574 127th Ave, Allegan 49010-9250 (269) 793-7340

PASTORAL RECORDS

BURTON-KRIEGER, ERIC M (Meagan) – [(FE) PE-2012, FE-2015]
Appointed in Other Annual Conferences (¶331.8, ¶346.1) Tennessee Conference, Brentwood (Assoc.) 2012; Appointed in Other Annual Conferences (¶331.8, ¶346.1) Indiana Conference, Indianapolis St. Luke's (Assoc.) 2015
eric.burton.krieger@gmail.com
(H) 520 N Rangeline Rd, Carmel, IN 46032 (615) 934-0068
St. Luke's: 100 W 86th St, Indianapolis, IN 46260-2391 (317) 846-3404

Butson, Christopher A. christopherbutson@live.com
[(PE) PL Aug 1, 2014; PE 2-18]. Jan 1, 2014 Azalia, London (LTFT ½); **2019 Ypsilanti: Lincoln Community**. 9074 Whittaker Rd., Ypsilanti 48197 (734-482-2226). Home: 9066 Whittaker Rd., Ypsilanti 48197 (734-657-2490)

***Byadiah, Bonnie D.** (Cleg Bordeaux)
[(RE) P 1980; F 1983]. 1981 Caro (assoc.); 1983 Burton; 1992 Pontiac Cooperative Parish: First; **1997 Retired**. Home: 664 Nichols, Auburn Hills 48326 (248-852-2711)

***CABOT, ROBERTA W.** – [(RL) FL-2001, PL-2010, FL-2011, RL-2014]
Wolf Lake 11/15/2001 (PTLP 05/10/10); Bear Lake 2011; Arcadia 2011; Retired 2014
(H) Kingdom Life Healing Ministries, 28 Caberfae Hwy, Manistee 49660
(231) 557-0166

***CADARETTE, KATHRYN S** (David) – [(RE) D-1994, FE-1996, RE-2019]
Horton Bay 1994; Horton Bay/Greensky Hill Indian Mission 02/01/1998; Leave of Absence 2000; Harbor Springs/Alanson 2003; Reed City 2011; Retired 2019
kathycad60@gmail.com
(H) 5925 Horton Bay Rd N, Boyne City 49712-9236 (231) 675-2172

***CAIN, FREDERICK G** – [(OR) D-1976, OE-1980, OR-2013]
[Indiana Conference, Retired Elder] Camden/Montgomery/Stokes Chapel (LTFT ½) 2013
revfgcain@yahoo.com
PO Box 155, 201 S Main St, Camden 49232-0155 (517) 797-5530

Callow, Timothy G.
[(FE) FL 2013; PE 2014; FE 2017]. **2013 God's Country Cooperative Parish: Newberry, Engadine**. (N) 110 W. Harrie St., Newberry 49868 (906-293-5711), (E) 13970 Park ave., PO Box 157, Enadine 49827 (906-477-9989). Home: PO Box 157, N6828 Elm St., Engadine 49827 (906-293-5497)

Carey, Melanie Lee (Jonathan) Revmelaniecarey@yahoo.com
[(FE) P 1990; F 1993]. 1991 Hudson: First; 1993 Livonia: Newburg (assoc); 2000 Ypsilanti: First; 2011 Detroit Renaissance District Superintendent; 2015 Clergy Assistant to the Bishop; **2016 Farmington Hills: Nardin Park**. 29887 W. 11 Mile Rd., Farmington Hills 48336 (248-476-8860). Home: 25109 Lyncastle Ln., Farmington Hills 48336 (248-477-8891)

***Cargo, William Abram** (Alice Jo) waCargo@chartermi.net
[(RE) P 1971; F WIS., 1975]. 1973 Waukaw, Elo, Eureka (Wisconsin); 1974 Admin. Sec. Office Pres, Union Seminary, NY; 1975 school, Nunnelly, Bethel, TN; 1976 Trans. to Detroit Conf., Detroit: Jefferson Avenue; 1981 Riverview; 1988 Oscoda, Oscoda Indian Church; 2006 Grayling: Michelson Memorial; **2011 Retired**. 816 S. Gondola Dr., Venice, FL 34293 (615-739-1595)

*CARLSON, DAVID 'GUNNAR' (RL) (Normajean) – (PL-2007, RL-2010)
Grass Lake (LTFT PT) 2007; Retired 2010; Montague 12/1/2016-2017; Grass Lake (LTFT ¼) 12/1/2018-6/30/2019

dgcarlson1947@comcast.net
(H) 2185 Moon St, Muskegon 49441-1551 (231) 755-8168

*CARLSON, LINDA J. (RL) (Ted) – (PL-1993, FL-1999, RL-2009)
Jackson Calvary (Assoc.) (LTFT PT) 1993; Manton 02/16/1999; Retired 2009
(H) 1720 SE 72nd Ave, Portland, OR 97215-3510

CARLSON, SARA LOUISE (PL) – (PL-2015)
Kalamazoo: Stockbridge Ave (LTFT ¼) 2015; Silver Creek (LTFT ¼) 2/01/2016

sara.carlson@wmich.edu
(H) 4229 Mahoney St, Portage 49002-6570 (269) 329-1072
Silver Creek: 31994 Middle Crossing Rd, Dowagiac 49047-9354 (269) 782-7061

Caron, Leah caron.leagh@yahoo.com
[(PL) PL 2018] **2018 Holly: Mt. Bethel**. 3205 Jossman Rd. Holly 48442 (248-627-7600). Home: 735 Vivian Ln, Oxford 48371 (248-520-0884)

CARTER, JANET S (FD) (Lee Copenhaver) – (PD-2005, FD-2009)
Deacons Appointed Beyond the Local Church (¶331.1a) Chaplain, Heartland Home Health Care & Hospice and Pine Rest Christian Mental Health Services 2005; Deacons Appointed Beyond the Local Church (¶331.1a) Chaplain, Pine Rest Christian Mental Health Services (¶331.1a) 10/23/2006; Deacons Appointed Beyond the Local Church (¶331.1a) Chaplain, Pine Rest Christian Mental Health Services (¶331.1a) and Grand Rapids: First (Deacon) 2009; Deacons Appointed Beyond the Local Church (¶331.1a) Chaplain, Pine Rest Christian Mental Health Services (¶331.1a) 2011

labarnabas@hotmail.com
(H) 669 Braeside Dr, Byron Center 49315-8075 (616) 260-9604
(O) 300 68th St SE, Grand Rapids 49508 (616) 281-6363 Ext. 2117

CARTWRIGHT, JODI M (PL) – (CC-2016, PL-2017)
Dowagiac: First (LTFT ¾) 2017; Casco (LTFT ¾) 2019

jodicartwright5@gmail.com
(H) 870 66th St, South Haven 49090-9523 (517) 282-9642
Casco: 880 66th St, South Haven 49090-9523 (269) 227-3328

CATELLIER, PATRICIA L (FD) – (PD-2010, FD-2014)
Deacons Appointed w/in UM Connectional Structure (¶331.1b) Chaplain, Borgess Medical Center (LTFT ½) 2010; Transitional Leave 09/01/2015; Portage: Chapel Hill (Deacon) (LTFT ¼) 01/01/2016

pcatellier7711@charter.net
(H) 7146 Oakland Dr, Portage 49024-4150 (269) 382-0708
Portage: Chapel Hill: 7028 Oakland Dr, Portage 49024-4148 (269) 327-6643

*Cattell, H. Reginald (Dorothy)
[(RE) Trans. from Missouri, Nov. 1972]. 1972 Imlay City, Attica; 1974 Imlay City, Goodland, E. Goodland; 1975 Hazel Park; Feb. 1979 Detroit: Zion; Nov. 1, 1983 Swartz Creek; **Sep 1, 1994 Retired**. Home: 29 St. Thorman Terrace, St. Thomas, Ontario (519-637-3937)

CHALKER, MELANY A (FE) (Darryl) – (FL-2004, PE-2005, FE-2008)
Appointed in Other Annual Conferences (¶346.1) Detroit Conference, Springville 2005; Concord 2006; Marshall 2013

pastormelany@gmail.com
(H) 762 N Kalamazoo Ave, Marshall 49068-1071 (517) 403-8528
Marshall: 721 Old US 27N, Marshall 49068-9609 (269) 781-5107

*Chapman, Mary Ellen (James)   pastor@wowway.com
[(RL) FL Mar, 2002]. Mar 1, 2002 Hazel Park; 2010 Lincoln Community; **2016 Retired; Sep 3,** 2018 Omo: Zion, Washington (LTFT ½); **Omo: Zion** (LTFT ¼). 63030 Omo Rd., PO Box 344, Richmond 48062 (810-233-2824). Home: 19059 Carmelo Dr., N, Clinton Township 48038 (586-291-6552)

Chapman, Matthew (Abigail)
[(PE) FL 2016; PE 2017]. **2016 Bay Port, Hayes**. (BP) 838 Second St., Bay Port 48720 (989-656-2151), (H) 7001 Filion Rd., Pigeon 48755. Home: 838 Second St., Bay Port 48720 (989-656-2151)

*Chapman, Robert David (Sandy)   rsmbchap@yahoo.com
[(RL) PL 1995; RL 2012]. 1995 Avoca, Ruby; disability leave; 2001 Port Huron: Gratiot Park; 2009 Port Huron: Gratiot Park and Port Huron: Washington Ave; **2012 Retired**. Home: 4458 Atkins Rd., Port Huron 48060 (810-982-2049)

*Chappell, Lynn Francis (Caren)   chappell_2@charter.net
[(RE) P 1972; F 1975]. 1974 Sterling, Alger, Bentley; 1981 Wisner; 1984 Whittemore, Prescott; 1989 Kingston, Deford; 1996 Pickford; May 1, 2003 Gladwin; **2009 Retired; 2009 Beaverton: First**. 150 West Brown, Beaverton 48612 (989-435-4322). Home: 9723 E. Townline Lake Rd. Harrison 48625-9033 (989-329-0317)

*Charlefour, Kathy Ruth (John)   revkrc@gmail.com
[(RE) PL 2001; PE 2002; FE 2005]. 2001 Monroe: East Raisinville Frenchtown; Sep 1, 2002 Monroe: East Raisinville Frenchtown (LTFT ¾) Carleton (assoc) (LTFT ¼). Nov 1, 2005 Dearborn: Good Shepherd. **2014 Retired**. Home: 43314 Hanford, Canton 48187 (734-788-3022)

CHARNLEY, STEPHEN MG (Cynthia) – [(FE) D-1978, FE-1982]
Transferred from Wisconsin Conf 1988; Newaygo 1988; Gull Lake 1994; Greenville: First 2008; Greenville: First, Turk Lake/Belding Cooperative Parish 2013; Kalamazoo: First 2014

(H) 471 W South St #403, Kalamazoo 49007-4676 (269) 312-8633
Kalamazoo: First: 212 S Park St, Kalamazoo 49007-4704 (269) 381-6340

*CHARNLEY, VICTOR D – [(RE) D-1979, FE-1981, RE-2013]
Church of the Dunes (Assoc) 1978; Received from American Baptist Church 1979; Church of the Dunes (Assoc) 1979; Battle Creek: Trinity 1984; Muskegon: Crestwood 1995; Mecosta: New Hope 2004; Retired 2013

pastvic@yahoo.com
(H) 1361 Overseas Highway Lot A13, Marathon FL, 33050 (616) 512-5936

*CHARTER, JOHN T (Murelann) – [(RA) AM-1972, RA-1999]
Battle Creek: Calvary 1972; Homer/Lyon Lake/Marengo 1973; Homer/Lyon Lake 1975; Mendon 1978; Niles: Grace 1981; Battle Creek: Christ 11/16/1992; Retired 1999

(H) 6600 Constitution Blvd Apt 215, Portage 49024-8900 (269) 353-4014

*Cheatham, Richard C. (Diane)   drrc@sbcglobal.net
[(RE) T 1964; F 1966]. 1961 Napoleon; 1967 Ann Arbor: Glacier Way; May 1974 Detroit: St. James; 1977 Brighton; 1988 Franklin: Community; **Jul 31, 1998 Retired**. Home: 6331 Penwoods, San Antonio, TX 78240

*CHEYNE, DAVID A – [(RE) D-1973, FE-1975, R-2005]
Mulliken 09/04/1972; Sand Lake/South Ensley 1975; Hersey/Grant Center 1977; Alden/Central Lake 1982; Webberville 1991; Hillside 1995; Three Oaks 1998; Baldwin: Covenant Cmnty/Luther 01/16/1999; Pine River Parish: Leroy/Ashton 1999; Sodus: Chapel Hill 2003; Retired 2005

david.cheyne@sbcglobal.net
(H) 1551 Franklin St. SE, Apt, 4003, Grand Rapids 49506-3397 (517) 339-2514

*CHEYNE, PAULETTE G. – [(RL) PL-1992, FL-1995, RL-2008]
Bell Oak / Williamston: Wheatfield (DSA 07/01/91; PTLP ½ 09/01/92; PTLP ¾ 01/01/95) (LTFT PT) 09/01/1992; Parmelee (Assoc.) 06/01/1995; Freeport / Middleville (Assoc) 06/01/1995; Winn / Coomer 2005; Blanchard-Pine River 2005; Comstock 2006; Aldersgate 11/15/2006-4/1/2008; Delta Mills 2007-4/1/2008; Delta Mills (LTFT ¼) 04/01/2008-2013; Retired 04/01/2008

paulettecheyne@gmail.com
(H) 3041 E Frost Rd, Williamston 48895-9739 (517) 896-3787

CHO, BO RIN (Koom) – [(FE) D-1990, OE-2004, FE-1992] East Lansing: Korean 03/01/2004; Transferred from Minnesota Conf 2013; Lansing: Asbury 2014; Appointed in Other Annual Conferences, Detroit, Davison 2017

borincho@comcast.net
(H) 819 Alana Ct, Davison 48423-1249 (517) 775-5436
Davison: 207 E 3rd St, Davison 48423-1405 (810) 653-5272

Cho, Hyun Jun (Kyung Ran)   pastor.hjcho@gmail.com
[(FE)]. 2010 (Korean Methodist) FE 2016]. 2010 Ann Arbor: Korean; **Aug. 1, 2019 NE Missaukee Parish: Merritt-Butterfield, Moorestown-Stittsville. (**MB) 428 S Merritt Rd, Merritt 49667-9762 (231) 328-4598; (MS) 4509 E Moorestown Rd, Lake City 49651-9438 (231) 328-4598. Home: 7037 E Houghton Lake Rd, Merritt 49667-9786 (231) 301-2692

CHRISTMAN, CATHERINE M (Michael) –
[(FE) PL-2007, FL-2008, PE-2009, FE-2014] Nashville (PTLP) 2007; Nashville (FTLP) 4/1/08; Nashville 2009; Appointed in Other Annual Conferences (¶346.1) Detroit Conference, Midland: First (Assoc) 2010;, Vassar: First 2013; Appointed in Other Annual Conferences (¶331.8, ¶346.1) Wisconsin Conference, Stoughton 2016

cchristman2006@hotmail.com
(H) 520 N Van Buren St, Stoughton, WI 53589 (231) 342-3728
Stoughton: 525 Lincoln Ave, Stoughton, WI 53589 (608) 873-3273

CHU, WILLIAM W (Julie Greyerbiehl) –
[(FE) PE-2005, FE-2008] Burr Oak (Student Local Pastor) 2001; LP w/o Appointment - Garrett-Evangelical Theological Seminary Coordinator of Educational Technologies 2003; Elk Rapids/ Kewadin/Williamsburg 2005; Elk Rapids/Kewadin/Williamsburg (Co-Pastor) 2008; Coloma/Watervliet 2009; East Lansing: University (Assoc) (½ Time) and UM Connectional Structures (¶344.1a,c) MSU Wesley Foundation, Director (½ Time) 2011; East Lansing: University (Assoc) (¼ Time) and UM Connectional Structures (¶344.1a,c) MSU Wesley Foundation, Director (¾ Time) 2013; UM Connectional Structures (¶344.1a,c) MSU Wesley Foundation, Director 01/01/2016

wmwchu@gmail.com
(H) 1109 Glenwood, Mt Pleasant 48858 (517) 992-5038
MSU Wesley: 1118 S Harrison, East Lansing 48823 (517) 332-0861

Chun, Sang Yoon (Jinah) saychun@netzero.com
[(FE) P 1988; F 1990]. 1988 Reese, Watrousville; 1992 Elkton; 1996 Korean United Methodist Church of Greater Washington (Virginia Conference), (para 426.1); 1999 Birch Run; 2005 Monroe: First; 2007 Ida, Samaria: Grace; **2016 Atherton, Phoenix.** (A) 4010 Lippincott Bovd., Burton 48519 (810-742-5644), (P) 4423 S. Genesse Rd., Grand Blanc 48439 (810-743-3370). Home: 6105 Wilderness Point, Grand Blanc 48439 (734-856-3151)

*Church, David E. (Winona) wecdec@sbcglobal.net
[(RE) T 1955; F 1960]. 1958 Grass Lake; 1962 Houghton; 1968 Wesley Foundation, Oakland University, Rochester: St. Luke's; 1969 Rochester: St. Luke's; 1970 Walled Lake; 1978 Dearborn: Mt. Olivet; 1988 Livonia: Newburg. 1992 Highland; **1995 Retired.** Home: 717 W. Middle St., Chelsea 48118 (734-475-8667)

Clark, Lisa J. (Hollis) plisaj@gmail.com
[(PL) PL 2000]. Oct 1, 2000 Capac: First and Zion Community (assoc); 2008 Capac: Zion Community (assoc.), Ruby; 2011 Capac: First, Capac: Zion Community; **2016 Capac.** 14952 Imlay City Rd., Capac 48018 (810-395-2112). Home: 211 W. Mill St., Capac 48018 (810-247-0946)

*Clark, Saundra Jean (Mike) *FE — is correct* revsonie@gmail.com
[(RE) ~~PE~~ 2003; FE 2006]. 2003 God's Country Cooperative Parish: Newberry, Engadine; **2013 Retired.** Home: PO Box 343, Powers 49874-0343 (906- 203-1314) *ordained in 2006*

[handwritten margin note: "this worng is correc"]

Clarke, Curtis B. (Rita) cbclarke95@gmail.com
[(FL) FL 2011]. Nov 12, 2011 Armada/West Berlin; **2019 Marysville, Central Lakeport.** (M) 721 W Huron Blvd, Marysville 48040 (810-364-7391), (CL) 3597 Milwaukee Rd., Lakeport 48059. Home: 683 18th St, Marysville 48040 (313-570-4442)

CLAXTON, MELISSA J (FE) (Edward) – (SP-2009, FL-2010, PE-2011, FE-2016) North Parma (Student Local Pastor) 2009; Springport/North Parma 2010; Appointed in Other Annual Conferences (¶331.8, ¶346.1) Detroit Conference, Warren: First 2018

claxton517@yahoo.com
(H) 32006 Wellston, Warren 48093
Warren: First: 5005 Chicago Rd, Warren 48092 (586) 264-4701

*CLEGG JR, WILLIAM V (RE) (Joni) – (D-1981, FE-1986, R-2011)
Haslett Mission 01/16/1984; Haslett Aldersgate 1985; Wyoming: Wesley Park 1994; Retired 2011; Parmelee (¼ Time) 11/11/2012

wvcleggjr@gmail.com
(H) 4593 N Camrose Court, Wyoming 49519-4977 (616) 366-2486
Parmelee: PO Box 237, 9266 W Parmalee Rd, Middleville 49333-0237
(269) 795-8816

Cleland, William C. (Deb) bcleland@comcast.net
[(PL) PL Dec 1, 2014]. 2014 Gagetown, Owendale; **2017 Owendale, Kilmanagh**. (O) 7370 Main St., Box 98, Owendale 48754 (989-678-4172), (K) 2009 S. Bay Port Rd., Bay Port 48720 (989-453-3520). Home: 129 S. Silver St., Bad Axe 48413 (989-975-1500)

*Clemmer, William Michael (Susan) wmclemmer@hotmail.com
[(RE) P 1981; F 1983]. 1979 Samaria, Lulu; Jan 1, 1981 Deerfield, Petersburg; 1984 Asst. Admin., Chelsea Retirement Home; Feb 1, 1987 Detroit: Metropolitan (assoc ½ Time); 1988 leave of absence; 1989 honorable location; 1994 readmitted; Sep 1, 1994 Azalia, London; Feb 1, 2003 incapacity leave; Feb 16, 2003 disability leave; 2005 Deerfield, Wellsville; **Jan 1, 2014 Retired**. Home: 15300 Dixon, Dundee 48131 (734-529-3213)

*Clevenger, Leonard A. (Renae) revlenmod21@gmail.com
[(RE) PL Nov 15, 2007; PE 2010; FE 2013]. Nov 15, 2007 Mapleton; 2010 Bloomfield Hills: St. Paul; 2013 Bay City: Grace; **2015 Retired;** Oct 1, 2018-2019 Mapleton (LTFT ¼). Home: 2302 Longfellow Lane, Midland 48640 (989-631-7277)

COBB, MARTIN T (FL) (Jessica) – (SP-1999, FL-2001, PE-2007, FL-2015)
Burr Oak 1999; Middleton/Maple Rapids/Christian Crossroads Cooperative Parish 2001; Old Mission Peninsula 2006; Litchfield/Quincy 2010; Fremont 2013; Farwell 2017

pastorcobb@gmail.com
(H) 511 N Superior St, Farwell 48622 (231) 215-3596
Farewell: PO Box 709; 281 E Ohio St, Farwell 48622-0709 (989) 588-2931

*Cochran, James D. (Theresa)
[(RE) P W. MI, 1963; F W. MI, 1965]. 1963 Lexington Conf: Scott Methodist, Maysville, KY; 1963 Trans. to W. MI Conf., Grand Rapids: St. Paul (Co-Pastor); 1965 Grand Rapids: Church of the Redeemer; 1968 Trans. to Detroit Conf., Detroit: Central (assoc.); 1970 Detroit West District Superintendent; 1976 school; 1980 Trans. to W. MI Conf., Conference Staff: Program Coordinator; 1986 Flint: Court St. (assoc.); 1987 Trans. to Detroit Conf.; 1988 Detroit: Conant Avenue; 1992 Dixboro; **1998 Retired**. Home: 8203 Berkshire Dr., Ypsilanti 48198 (734-483-5939)

*COE, BUFFORD W (RE) (Lisa) – (D-1974, FE-1978, R-2017)
Transferred from Detroit Conf 1994; Hastings: First 1994; Vicksburg 10/15/2000; Retired 2017

buffordc@aol.com
(H) 1751 Grovenberg Ct, Vicksburg 49097-7776 (269) 626-4610

Coffey, Michael
[(FE) AF 2007 Missouri Conf., FE 2008 transfer to Detroit Conf., from Missouri Conf.] 2007 Executive Director, Bay Shore Camp; **Apr 30, 2012 voluntary leave of absence**.

*Colby, Roger L. (Dorothy)   rlcolby@comcast.net
[(RE) P 1969; F 1976]. 1975 Genesee, Thetford Center; 1980 Coleman: Faith, Geneva: Hope; 1986 Houghton Lake; 1992 Flint: Central; 1998 Grand Blanc; **2008 Retired**. Home: 6444 Kings Pointe Dr., Grand Blanc 48439 (810-694-6873)

COLE, DEBORAH S (FL) – (DSA-2014, FL-2015)
Reading (DSA) 09/01/2014; Reading 2015

deb.cole@readingumc.com
(H) 317 First Street, Reading 49274-9752 (517) 283-2775
Reading: PO Box 457, 312 Michigan St, Reading 49274-0457 (517) 283-2443

Collazo, Luis   lddl@att.net
[(OE)]. **2008 Detroit: El Buen New Creations Ministry**. 1270 Waterman, Detroit 48209 (313-843-4170). Home: 29220 Hemlock Dr., Farmington Hills 48336 (248-895-8699)

*Collins, David Clark (Roberta)   pastordave@comcast.net
[(RE) P 1983; F 1987]. June 1, 1980 Bradfordsville Circuit (Louisville Conf.); June 1, 1984 North Lake, Salem Grove; Nov. 1, 1985 Lincoln Community; 1991 Saginaw: West Michigan Avenue, Sheridan Avenue; 1997 Montrose; 2006 Elkton; Apr 15, 2009 incapacity leave; **2011 Retired**. Home: 10195 W. Stanley Rd., Flushing 48433 (810-487-1949)

COLTHORP, DANIEL R (FL) (Kristina) – (CC-2008, PD-2016, FL-2018)
St Joseph: First (Deacon) Minister Of Youth & Children's Ministries 2016-2018; St Joseph: First 2018

dancolthorp@sjfirstumc.org
(H) 5835 Demorrow Rd, Stevensville 49127-1244 (269) 369-8475
St Joseph First: 2950 Lakeview Ave, Saint Joseph 49085 (269) 983-3929

Combs, Jonathan   JSCombs_99@yahoo.com [11/8/16]
[(FL) PL 2009 FL 2016]. Nov 7, 2009 Oak Park: Faith; **2015 Redford: Aldersgate: Brightmoore Campus (LTFT ¼), Garden City (LTFT ¾)**. (B) 12065 W. Outer Dr., Detroit 48223 (313-937-3170), (GC) 6443 Merriman, Garden City 48135 (734-421-8628). Home: 18261 University Pk. Dr., Livonia 48152 (248-943-0534)

*COMER, MICHAEL P (OR) (Anne) – (D1972-, FE-1975, OE-1982, OR-2009)
North Central New York Conference; Pastoral Counselor, Samaritan Center of Battle Creek 1982; Pastoral Counselor (Private Practice) 1989; Police Psychologist, Michigan State Police 3/17/2002; Police Psychologist Michigan State Police and Psychologist with the Michigan Department of Natural Resources 2011-2013

(H) 5153 Oak Hills Dr, Eaton Rapids 48827 (517) 663-1571

CONKLIN, JOHN J (JACK) (Pattie) – [(FE) FL-2002, AM-2008, PE-2014, FE-2016]
Mesick/Harrietta (DSA) 2001; Mesick/Harrietta 12/01/2001; Scottville 2009; Williamsburg/Fife Lake Boardman Parish: Fife Lake, East Boardman, South Boardman 2017 (2018 Williamsburg, Fife Lake, East Boardman, South Boardman formed Unified Parish)

jack49668@gmail.com
(H) 124 Boyd St, Fife Lake 49633-9031 (231) 757-4781
Williamsburg: PO Box 40, 5750 Williamsburg Rd, Williamsburg 49690-9639
(231) 267-5792
Fife Lake: PO Box 69, 206 Boyd St, Fife Lake 49633-9019 (231) 879-4270
East Boardman: PO Box 69, 2082 Boardman Rd SW, S Boardman 49680
(231) 879-6055
South Boardman: PO Box 112, 5488 Dagle St, S Boardman 49680-0112
(231) 879-6055

*CONKLIN, MICHAEL T (RE) (Deborah) – (D-1979, FE-1983, R-2012)
Pokagon 1981; Boyne City/Falls 1983; Centreville 1989; Coopersville 08/01/1997; Jackson Calvary 1999; Lowell: First 2003; Courtland-Oakfield 2008; Middleville/ Snow 2009; Retired 2012; Battle Creek: First (Assoc) (Ltft ¼) 2016; Battle Creek: First 2017-2018

conklinmichael4@gmail.com
(H) 125 Heather Ridge Rd, Battle Creek 49017-4529 (616) 204-8125

Cook, Carmen (Todd) cook.carmen34@gmail.com [11-16/16]
[(FL) FL 2014]. 2014 Onaway, Millersburg; **2018 Gladwin: First**. 1300 Bartlett Drive, Gladwin 48624 (989-426-9619). Home: 1271 Chatterton, Gladwin 48624

Cook, Lisa L. (Ron) revlisacook@gmail.com
[(FE) PM 1997; FM 2000]. 1997 Tawas (assoc.); May 1, 2000 Saginaw: Kochville; 2004 Northville: First (assoc); 2009 West Branch: First; **2014 Sanford**. 2560 W. River Rd., Sanford 48657 (989-687-5353). Home: 2550 N. West River Rd., Sanford 48657 (989-701-7240)

COOK, ROBERT B (FE) (Lisa Richey) – (FL-2001, PE-2003, FE-2006)
Grand Rapids: Trinity (Assoc) 05/31/2001; Leave of Absence 2006; Muskegon Heights: Temple 09/01/2006; Lansing: Mount Hope 2012

rob.cook@mounthopeumc.org
(H) 1707 Woodside Dr, East Lansing 48823-2957 (517) 449-4826
Lansing: Mount Hope: 501 E Mount Hope Ave, Lansing 48910-9136
(517) 482-1549

*Cooley, Frederick Paul (Margot) fredpc@comcast.net
[(RE) P 1962; F 1965] 1965 Mayfield Village, OH; 1969 Brook Park, OH; 1975 Garfield Heights, OH; Aug. 1979 Trans. from E. OH Conf., Bay Port, Hayes; 1984 Mt. Clemens: First (assoc.); 1988 Hancock: First; 1995 Wayne: First; **Aug 1, 2000 Retired**. 915 Egret Dr, Chelsea 48118 (734-751-0296)

*COOMBS, KATHRYN M (RE) (James) – (D-1977, FE-1983, R-2002)
Transferred from Iowa Conf 1977; Quincy 1977; Leave of Absence 1979; Watervliet 12/01/1981; Ionia: Zion/Easton 09/16/1984; Ionia: Easton (LTFT ¾) 11/01/1986; Leave of Absence 1990; Empire 1991; Elk Rapids/Kewadin 1998; Frankfort/Elberta 1999; Leave of Absence 03/01/2002; Retired 2002; Northport Indian Mission (DSA) 2003-2005; Traverse City: Christ (DSA) 2010-2011
kathryn.coombs4@gmail.com
(H) 11127 Oviatt Rd, Honor 49640-9592 (231) 326-5852

*Cooper, Oscar William, Jr. (Ruth)   billcooperlogos@sprynet.com
[(RE) T 1961; F 1963]. 1961 Ypsilanti: First; 1965 Manchester; 1969 Manchester: Sharon; 1970 Elkton; 1974 Port Huron: First; 1979 Warren: First; 1985 Saginaw: Ames; **1989 Retired**. Home: 4742 Westbury Drive, Fort Collins, CO 80526 (970-377-0233)

Coristine, Kristen I. [Parks] (Chris)   kristencoristine@gmail.com
[(FE) FL 2010; PE 2015; FE 2018]. 2010 Columbiaville (¾), Flint District Project Director; 2013 Blissfield: First; **2019 Reed City**. 114 W State St, Reed City 49677 (231-832-9441). Home: 219 S State St, Reed City 49677 (231-675-4172)

Cortelyou, Carter Louis (Andrea)   clcortelyou@gmail.com
[(FE) P 1990; F 1992]. 1990 South Central Cooperative Ministry: Linden, Argentine; Sep 1, 1994 Rose City: Trinity, Churchill; 1998 Manchester: Sharon; 2007 Otisville, West Forest; 2010 Birmingham: Embury, Royal Oak: St. John's, Waterford: Trinity; 2013 New Hope; 2014 Wayne: First; **2018 LaSalle, Petersburg**. (L) 1607 Yargerville Rd., LaSalle 48145 (734-243-5940), (P) 152 Saline St., PO Box 85, Petersburg 49270 (734-279-1118). Home: 1607 Yargerville., LaSalle 48145 (248-506-5406)

Council, Will (Denice)   pastorwillcouncil@gmail.com
[(PL) PL Dec 1, 2014]. **2014 Detroit: Calvary**. 15050 Hubbell, Detroit 48227 (313-835-1317). Home: 7796 Surrey Dr., Romulus 48174 (734-641-8711)

*Covington, Diane
[OR] 2015 Redford: New Beginnings; **2018 Retired; 2018 Redford: New Beginnings** (LTFT ½). 16175 Delaware, Redford 48240 (313-255-6330). Home: 18261 University Pk. Dr., Livonia 48152 (248-943-0534)

*Covintree, George E., Jr. (Winifred)   georgecoventree@me.com
[(RE) SP, S. NE, 1985; P 1989; F 1991]. 1985 Rockland, MA: Heatherly; 1989 Waterford: Central (assoc.); Sep 1, 1993 Detroit: Redford; 1997 Pontiac: Baldwin Avenue; 2005 Berkley: First; 2010 Livonia: St. Matthew's; **2015 Retired**. 29835 Rock Creek Rd., Southfield 48076 (248-905-3448)

*Cowdin, Charlotte A. (Douglas)   cowdinatthelake@comcast.net
[(RD) CRT, 1984; CON (CE), 1990, FD 2000]. 1980 Clarkston; Feb. 1, 1991 Leave of Absence. 1992 Study Leave. Aug 1, 1994 Coordinator of Diaconal Ministry Education, Ecumenical Theological Seminary; Jan 1, 1995 (LTFT) Retreat Leader Consultant in CE; **May 1, 2003 Retired**. Home: 6132 Wildrose Lane, Lakeport 48059 (810-385-3852)

Cowdin, Christopher Douglas   christop_cowdin@sbcglobal.net
[(FE) P 1988; F 1991]. 1989 Utica (assoc.); 1996 Family Leave; Jan. 1, 1999
Warren: Wesley (LTFT ¾); 2002 Eastpointe: Immanuel (assoc), Parish Director,
Eastside Covenant Cooperative Parish; 2002 Troy: Fellowship (LTFT ¾); **May
1, 2003 leave of absence**. Home: 3099 Cherry Creek Lane, Sterling Heights
48314 (586-731-3599)

*Cowling, Ramona Elizabeth   ramonacowling2224@comcast.net
[(RE) P 1984; F 1988]. 1985 McMillan, Engadine, Germfask; 1987 Inkster: Christ;
1989 Disability Leave; 1993 Macon; Sep 1, 1997 disability; **2002 Retired**. Home:
1131 N. Maple, #2, Ann Arbor 48103 (734-585-5156)

*COX, ESTHER (RL) – (FL-1969, RL-1988)
Hastings: Welcome Corners 1969; Quimby 1970; Not Appointed 1975; Retired
1988

*CRABTREE, JANE A (RA) (Jean) – (D-1994, AM-2000, RA-2003)
North Evart/Sylvan 01/16/1988; Turk Lake 1990; Lake City 1996; Fennville/ Pearl
2000; Family Leave 2002; Retired 07/16/2003; Olivet (DSA) 7/1/2010-
12/12/2010

                                        janecrabtree90@yahoo.com
           (H) 2538 N Mundy Ave, White Cloud 49349-9422 (231) 689-3415

*CRABTREE, JEAN ARTHUR (RA) (Jane) – (FL-1955, D-1962, E-1964, AM-
1969, RA-1994)
Stanwood: Northland 09/01/1955; Fenwick Circuit: Fenwick/Orleans/ Vickeryville
1959; Howard City 1962; Newaygo 1967; Hartford 1972; Mesick/ Harrietta 1979;
Parma/North Parma 09/01/1980; Barryton/Chippewa Lake 1984; Six Lakes/Mill-
brook 1990; Six Lakes (LTFT ¾) 1993; Retired 03/31/1994; North Evart/Sylvan
1996; Fennville/Pearl (Assoc) 2000; Avondale/North Evart/ Sylvan (DSA)
11/05/2006-07/01/2007; Olivet (DSA) 2010-2/12/2010

                                        janecrabtree90@yahoo.com
           (H) 2538 N Mundy Ave, White Cloud 49349-9422 (231) 689-3415

*Crane, Lawson D. (Beverly)   lawsonandbev@frontier.net
[(RE) P 1971; F 1974]. 1968 Clayton, Rollin Center; Feb. 1, 1976 Oak Grove;
1986 Pickford; 1993 Auburn; **2009 Retired**. 1334 Beamer, Blissfield 49228 (517-
486-2082)

Crawford, Margie R. – [(FE) PE-2005; FE-2009]
2005 Flint: Court Street (assoc.) 2005; St. Clair Shores: First 2008; St. Clair:
First 2011; (serving in West Michigan Conference 2018) Grand Rapids District
Superintendent 2018; **Midwest District Superintendent Jan 1, 2019**
                                        mcrawford@michiganumc.org
                    (H) 1630 Millbank St SE, Grand Rapids 49508
           (O) 207 Fulton St E, Ste 6, Grand Rapids 49503 (616) 459-4503

*Crawford, Wallace Peter (Alice Kay)   walcrawford@charter.net
[(RE) P 1985; F 1988]. 1986 Decker, Argyle, Shabbona; May 1, 1991 Saginaw:
Swan Valley; 1996 Elkton; 2006 Millington; **2015 Retired**. Home: 4934 Center
St., Millington 48746 (989-882-3084)

*Crocker, Doris (Wesley)　　　　　　　　　dorisandwesley@gmail.com
[(RE) SP 1990; P 1991; F 1993]. 1990 Wyandotte: First (assoc.); 1991 Samaria: Grace, Lulu; **1998 Retired**. Home: 6295 Monroe Ct., Belleville 48111 (734-547-5722)

Croel, Andrew L (FE) (Anne) – (PE-2005, FE-2008)
Dimondale/Grovenburg 2005; Carson City 2008; St Johns: Pilgrim 2014
　　　　　　　　　　　　　　　　　　　pastorandycroel@yahoo.com
　　　　　　(H) 2917 W Parks Rd, St. Johns 48879-9286 (989) 224-4423
St Johns Pilgrim: 2965 W Parks Rd, Saint Johns 48879-9286 (989) 224-6865

CULVER, GREGORY P (FE) – (D-2000, FE-2006)
Muskegon: Central (Assoc) 07/20/1999; Frankfort/Elberta 2002; Charlevoix 2010; Horton Bay 2016; Vicksburg 2017
　　　　　　　　　　　　　　　　　　　　　gpculver@mac.com
　　　　　　(H) 7794 TS Ave E, Scotts 49088-9748 (231) 651-9309
　　　　Vicksburg: 217 S Main St, Vicksburg 49097-1212 (231) 649-2343

*CULVER, MARTIN H. (RL) (Barbara) – (FL-1991, RL-2011)
Keswick (DSA) 1991; Keswick 08/01/1991; Ionia: First 2000; Kalamazoo: Milwood 2006; Lane Boulevard (DSA) 03/18/2007-03/25/2008; Retired 2011; Center Park (LTFT ¼) 2011; Center Park/Three Rivers: First (Part Time) 2017; Center Park (LTFT ¼) 2018-2019
　　　　　　　　　　　　　　　　　　pastormartyc@charter.net
　　　　　　(H) 511 Landsdowne Ave, Portage 49002 (269) 615-1360

CUMMINGS, JEFFREY O (PE) (Bridget) – (PL-2013, PE-2016)
Galien/Olive Branch (DSA ¾ Time) 1/1/2012; Galien/Olive Branch (PTLP ¾) 2013; Byron Center 2016
　　　　　　　　　　　　　　　　　　cummings.jeffrey91@gmail.com
　　　　　　(H) 8650 Meadowhaven Dr, Byron Center 49315 (269) 588-9081

CUMMINS, TERRI L (FL) – (FL-2010)
Shelby 2010; Shelby/Claybanks 2014; Pierson: Heritage 2016
　　　　　　　　　　　　　　　　　　　　tlcummins5@aol.com
　　　　　　(H) 18985 W Coral Rd, Howard City 49329 (231) 903-5139
Pierson: Heritage: 19931 W Kendaville Rd, Pierson 49339-9713 (231) 937-4310

*Cutting, Anthony Navaro (Joan)　　　　　　anthonlycutting@gmail.com
[(RE) P 1985; F 1986]. 1985 Trans. to Detroit Conf. from Free Methodist, Detroit: St. Timothy's; 1986 Detroit: Second Grace; 1993 Bay City: First; **2011 Retired**. 1659 Honeychuck Ln, Kent, OH 44240 (330-986-6203)

CONRAN, CORI LYNN [CYPRET] – [(FE) PE-2012, FE-2015]
Coopersville 2012
　　　　　　　　　　　　　　　　　　pastorcori@coopersvilleumc.org
　　　　　　(H) 422 Harrison St, Coopersville 49404-1136 (269) 986-0732
　　　Coopersville: 105 68th Ave N, Coopersville 49404-9704 (616) 997-9225

Dake, Richard Lee (Laura)　　　　　　　　rdake@clarkstonumc.org
[(FE) P 1979; F 1982]. 1980 Springville; Feb 1., 1985 Ypsilanti: St. Matthew's; Sep 1, 1992 Chelsea: First; **2004 Clarkston**. 6600 Waldon Rd., Clarkston 48346 (248-625-1611). Home: 6599 Church St., Clarkston 48346 (248-625-1727)

*DALTON, BILLIE R (Georgia) – [(RE) SP-1965, FL-1971, D-1985, FE-1989, R-2013]
Pompeii/Perrinton/Newark 09/01/1965; Mt Pleasant: First (Assoc) 1970; Lawton/ Almena 1987; South Haven: First 1995; Kalamazoo: Sunnyside (LTFT ¾) 2004; Kalamazoo: Sunnyside (Full Time) 2006; Kalamazoo: Sunnyside (LTFT ¾) 2007; Battle Creek: First 03/01/2009; Retired 2013 09/01/2013; Battle Creek: First (LTFT ½) 09/01/2013-3/4/2014; Kalamazoo Milwood (Part Time) 2017
billierdalton@milwoodunitedmethodistchurch.org
(H) 6585 San Gabriel Dr, Kalamazoo 49009 (269) 615-6945
Milwood: 3919 Portage St, Kalamazoo 49001 (269) 381-6720

DAMKOEHLER, PAUL A (PL) (Paula) – (FL-2008, PL-2015)
Webberville 01/01/2008; United Church of Ovid 2013; Leslie (PTLP ¼) 2015; Felt Plains (LTFH ¼) 2018
pdamkoehler@gmail.com
(H) 2417 Pattengill Ave, Lansing 48910-2627 (517) 375-8049
Leslie: 401 S Main St, Leslie 49251-9402 (517) 589-9211
Felt Plains: 3523 Meridian Rd, Leslie 49251

*DANIEL, REVA HAWKE (RE) (Jerry) – (PL-1984, D-1987, FE-1990, R-2005)
Pokagon (PTLP) 1984; Transferred from Detroit Conf 1988; Three Rivers: Ninth Street/Jones 1988; Leslie/Felt Plains 10/01/1991; Baldwin/Luther 05/01/1993; Jonesville/Allen 1995; West Mendon 1997; Hopkins/South Monterey 2001; Retired 2005
revarev@live.com
(H) 1140 138th Ave, Wayland 49348-9754 (616) 550-2645

Daniel, Zella Marie (PL) – (DSA-2017; PL-2019)
Ashely / Bannister / Pompeii (DSA) 10/03/2017; Ashely / Bannister / Pompeii (LTFT ½) 01/01/2019
zella.daniel@ge.com
(H) 2415 E Tobias, Clio 48420 (810) 869-8815
Ashley: 112 N New St, Ashley 48806-5114 (989) 862-4392
Bannister: 103 E Hanvey St, Bannister 48807-5140 (989) 862-4392
Pompeii: 135 Burton St, PO Box 125, Pompeii 48874-0125 (989) 838-4159

DAVENPORT, Jessica M (FL) – (FL-2018)
UM Connectional Structures (¶344.1a,c) Executive Director & Campus Pastor, Kalamazoo Wesley Foundation
Jessica.mae.davenport@gmail.com
(H) 1227 Grand Ave, Kalamazoo 49006-3254 (309) 262-3469
(O) 2350 Ring Rd N, Kalamazoo 49006 (269) 344-4076

DAVENPORT, THOMAS A (FE) (Elyse Connors) – (D-1987, FE-1991)
UM Connectional Structures (¶344.1a,c) Director, WMU Wesley Foundation 2002; Bangor: Simpson 2007; Transferred from Detroit Conf 2011; Parchment 2016
pastorthomm@hotmail.com
(H) 1227 Grand Ave, Kalamazoo 49006-3254 (269) 762-3159
Parchment: 225 Glendale Blvd, Parchment 49004-1319 (269) 344-0125

*David, Walter wwdavid@fmuth.com
[(RA) AM 1967]. 1967 Sterling Township; 1969 Sterling Heights; 1973 Escanaba: First, Bark River; Aug. 1978 Mt. Morris; 1986 Saginaw: Jefferson Avenue; **1992 Retired.** Home: 327 Nickless, Frankenmuth 48734 (989-652-3979)

*Davis, Bonita C.
[(RL) PL Sep 16, 2007]. Sep 7, 2007 LaPorte; **2008 Retired.** Home: 2200 Cleveland Ave., #2330, Midland 48640 (989-488-2787)

DAVIS JR, CORNELIUS (NEIL) (FE) (Lela Brown-Davis) – (FL-1999, PE-2002, FE-2005)
[Northern Illinois Conference, Rust Memorial 1998]; Plainfield 1999; Lansing: Faith Connections (New Church Start) 2002; Lansing: Faith Connections (¼ Time), Lansing: New Church Start ¾ Time) 2003; Faith UMC/South Lansing Ministries 2005; UM Connectional Structures (¶344.1a,c) Kalamazoo District Superintendent 2008; Appointed in Other Annual Conferences (¶331.8, ¶346.1) Detroit Conference, Southfield Hope 2014; Personal Leave 09/22/2015; Appointed in Other Annual Conferences (¶331.8, ¶346.1) Detroit Conference, Farmington First (interim) 02/01/2016; Appointed in Other Annual Conferences (¶331.8, 346.1) Detroit Conference, Detroit: Scott Memorial 2016
Frontedge7@yahoo.com
(H) 531 New Town-Victoria Park, Detroit 48125 (517) 712-4066
Scott Memorial: 15361 Plymouth Rd, Detroit 48227-2003 (313) 836-6301

*DAVIS, LEONARD E (OR) – (OR-2016)
[retired elder of Wesleyan Church] Galesburg (LTFT ¼) 2016
(H) 10998 Pleasant Lake Rd, Delton 49046 (269) 623-4412
Galesburg: PO Box 518, 111 W Battle Creek St, Galesburg 49053-0518
(269) 665-7952

*Davis, Robert F. (Sue) bobsue58@icloud.com
[(RE) T 1959; F 1962]. 1962 Detroit: Aldersgate (assoc); 1964 Whitmore Lake; 1967 Veterans' Administration; 1968 Holly; 1973 Warren: First; 1979 Conference Staff: Parish Developer; Jan 1, 1987 trans to W. MI Conf: Conference Staff: Coordinator of New Church Development; 1993 trans to Detroit Conf., Lake Orion; **1997 Retired.** Home: 09844 Meadows Trail, Boyne Falls 49713 (231-549-2530)

*Dawes, Gary Carl (Barbara)
[(RE) P 1982; F 1986]. Dec. 1, 1983 Saginaw: First (assoc.); Oct. 18, 1987 Saginaw: Kochville; Dec 1, 1992 Ypsilanti: St. Matthew's; 1996 Berkley; 2005 Adrian: First; **2014 Retired** Home: 30011 Barwell Rd., Farmington Hills 48334 (248-893-7512)

*Daws, Donald J. dzdaws@pocketmail.com
[(RE) P 1972; F 1976]. 1965 Glennie, Curran; 1973 Byhalia, OH; 1975 LaSalle; 1980 Imlay City, E. Goodland, W. Goodland, Lum; 1989 Cass City: Salem. Jan. 16, 1992 Coleman: Faith; **Aug 1, 1997 Retired.** 23661 Wilmarth Ave., Farmington 48335

DEBOW, MARTIN M (FE) (Cynthia) – (D-1985, FE-1988)
Grovenburg 1986; Coopersville 1990; Robbins 1997; Lansing: Asbury 2008; Eaton Rapids: First 2014
marty@fumer.org
(H) 702 State St, Eaton Rapids 48823-1603 (517) 663-8256
Eaton Rapids First: 600 S Main St, Eaton Rapids 48827-1426 (517) 663-3524

*DeGraw, Alan Wilford (Judith)   jadegraw@sbcglobal.net
[(RE) T 1964; F 1966]. 1964 Chicago: St. Stephens (assoc.); 1966 Oak Grove; 1967 Calumet; Jan. 1972 Essexville: St. Luke's; Feb. 1975 Pontiac: Central (assoc.); 1978 Allen Park: Trinity, Detroit: Simpson; 1980 Allen Park: Trinity; 1983 Vassar; 1991 Flat Rock: First; 1995 Oak Grove; **2000 Retired**. Home: 2574 Kerria Dr., Howell 48855 (517-540-0715)

DeHut, Rosemary Ruth   rrdehut@up.net
[(PL) PL Aug 1, 2002; FL 2008; PL Sept 1, 2018]. Aug 1, 2002 White Pine; 2008 White Pine, Ironwood: Wesley; Sept 1, 2018 White Pine Community; **2019 White Pine Community, Bergland, Ewen** (LTFT ¼). (WPC) 9 Tamarack, PO Box 158, White Pine 49971 (906-885-5419), (B) 108 Birch, PO Box 142, Bergland 49910-0142 (906-988-2533), (E) 621 M28, Ewen 49925 (906-988-2533). Home: 22358 Norwich Trail, Ontonagon 49953 (906-884-2871)

*DELO, MERLIN KEITH (RL) (Juanita) – (FL-1964, RL-1997)
Sethton / Middleton 1964; Hesperia / Ferry 1966; East Jordan 1986; Retired 1997

(H) 2706 S Maple Island Rd, Fremont 49412-9372 (231) 924-4182

DELONG, KIMBERLY A (FE) (Cameron) – (PL-1998, CC-2003, PD-2009, FD-2012, FE-2016)
Muskegon: Unity (Part Time) 1998; Grand Rapids: First (Deacon-Director of Education LTFT ½) 2009; Turk Lake/Belding 08/15/2012; Greenville: First, Turk Lake/Belding Cooperative Parish (Deacon LTFT ½) 2013; Big Rapids: Third Avenue/Paris/Rodney (Para. 315.4) 2015; Wyoming Park/Courtland-Oakfield 2017
kim.delong.1113@gmail.com
(H) 4934 Brownstone Dr NE, Rockford 49341-7780 (616) 443-5210
Wyoming Park: 2244 Porter St SW, Wyoming 49519-2222 (616) 532-7624
Courtland-Oakfield: 10295 Myers Lake Ave NE, Rockford 49341 (616) 866-4298

Del Pino, Julius E. (Laurie Smith)   jdelpino01@comcast.net
[(FE) P Cal. Pacific 1970; F Cal. Pacific 1976]. 1998 trans. from California-Pacific Conf.; 1998 Detroit: Metropolitan; Jan 1, 2004 incapacity leave; 2005 Dearborn: First; 2008 Rochester Hills: St. Luke's; **2016 Grand Blanc**. 515 Bush Ave., Grand Blanc 48439 (810-694-9040). Home: 12110 Francesca Dr., Grand Blanc 48439 (810-694-1615)

*DEMOSS, LYNN A (RE) (M. Kay) – (D-1961, FE-1963, R-1997)
Coleman/North Bradley 1963; Fremont 1966; Albion: First 1969; Muskegon: Central 1979; Grand Rapids: First 04/16/1988; Lansing: Central 1993; Retired 1997

puzisha4lynn@att.net
(H) 1520 Sherman Court SE, Grand Rapids 49506-2715 (231) 670-0993

DEMOSS, MARIEL KAY (FD) (Lynn) – (DM-1985, D-1997)
Kalamazoo: First Coordinator Of Education and Lay Development 1985; Editor/Publisher, Michigan Christian Advocate 1987; Editor/Publisher, Blodgett Press 1995; Deacons Appointed Beyond the Local Church(¶331.1a) Mission to Area People, Coordinator Of Volunteers, Muskegon Heights 1997; Deacons Appointed Beyond The Local Church(¶331.1a) Editor/Publisher, Blodgett Press 1998; Deacons Appointed Beyond the Local Church(¶331.1a) Editor/Publisher, Blodgett Press (LTFT ½) and Minister of Education, Muskegon Central (LTFT ½) 01/01/2003; Minister of Adult Education, Muskegon Central (LTFT ¼) and Deacons Appointed w/in UM Connectional Structure (¶331.6) Conference Secretary Of Global Ministries (LTFT ¼) 2005; Muskegon: Central (Deacon) Minister Of Discipleship (LTFT ½) 2009; Muskegon: Central (Deacon) Minister Of Discipleship (LTFT ½) and Deacons Appointed w/in UM Connectional Structure (¶331.1b) Conference Web-Editor (LTFT ¼) 2012; Muskegon: Central (Deacon) Minister Of Discipleship (LTFT ¼) and Deacons Appointed w/in UM Connectional Structure (¶331.1b) Area Communications Team (LTFT ½) 2013; Deacons Appointed Within Um Connectional Structure (¶331.1b) Senior Writer & Content Editor, MI Area Communications Team Annual Conference (LTFT ½) 2015; Deacons Appointed Within UM Connectional Structure (¶331.1b) Senior Writer & Content Editor, MI Area Communications Team Annual Conference (LTFT ½) and Missional: Grand Rapids: Trinity (Deacon) (Part Time) 2016; Deacons Appointed Within UM Connectional Structure (¶331.1b) Senior Writer & Content Editor, MI Area Communications Team Annual Conference (LTFT ½) and Missional: Georgetown (Part-Time) 10/22/2018; Senior Content Editor, MI Conference Communications Team (LTFT ¾) and Missional: Georgetown 01/01/2019
kdemoss@michiganumc.org
(H) 1520 Sherman Court SE, Grand Rapids 49506-2715 (231) 670-5921
(O) 1011 Northcrest Rd, Lansing 48906 (517) 347-4030 x4032

Demyanovich, Robert P PastorRobertPaul@gmail.com
[(FL) FL Jan 1, 2019]. 2018 Cass City (DSA); **Jan 1, 2019 Cass City**. 5100 Cemetery Rd, PO Box 125, Cass City, 48726-0125 (989-872-3422). Home: 6339 Brenda Dr, Cass City 48726 (248-636-5679)

*Densmore, Jerry P. JDAgape@aol.com
[(RE) FE IN]. 2001 trans to Detroit Conf. 2001 Croswell: First; 2009 Hemlock, Nelson; **2014 Retired**. Home: 3470 Williamson Rd, Saginaw 48601 (989-777-7025)

*DEPPE, ISABELL M (RE) – (D-1984, FE-1992, R-2000)
Transferred from New York Conf 1990; Center Eaton/Brookfield 1990; Potter Park 1991; Sabbatical Leave (¶ 349) 01/01/1998; Vicksburg 1998; Involuntary Retirement 09/01/2000
(H) 11492 Fordyce Rd, Farwell 48622-9204 (989) 588-3467

*Derby, Donald Raymond (Carol) revderb@gmail.com
[(RL) PL Nov 1, 2002, FL Oct 1, 2008; RL 2018]. Nov 1, 2002 Whittemore; 2005 St. Clair Shores: First; 2008 Hillman, Spratt; 2013 Heritage; **2018 Retired; 2018 Worth Twp: Bethel** (LTFT ¼). 8020 Babcock Rd., Box 143, Croswell 48422 (810-327-1440). Home: 1014 St Joseph Ln, Marysville 48040 (810-990-5544)

Desotell, Briony Erin Peters (Michael) pastorbri@hotmail.com
[(FE) PE 2006; FE 2009]. 2006 Oscoda, Oscoda Indian Mission; **2014 Ypsilanti: First**. 209 Washtenaw, Ypsilanti 48197 (734-482-8374). Home: 1110 Ruth, Ypsilanti 48198 (734-483-0460)

Desotell, Michael C.   pastormikedesotel@gmail.com
[(FL) PL 2014; FL 2017]. 2014 Ypsilanti: St. Matthew's; **2016 Ypsilanti: St. Matthew's, Canton: Cherry Hill**. (Y) 1344 Borgstrom, Ypsilanti 48198 (734-483-5876), (CH) 321 S. Ridge Rd., Canton 48188 ((734-495-0035). Home: 1110 Ruth, Ypsilanti 48198 (734-730-6746)

DeVine, Jerome (Ruth)   jdevine@michiganumc.org
[(FE) PD N. Dak, 1984; FE, Peninsula-Delaware, 1987; transf to W.MI, 1999]. 1981 Cambridge, MD, Grace; Wilmington, DE, 1985 St. Paul's: (assoc.); Newark, DE, Kingswood; 1993 Coordinator for Mission Leaders, General Board of Global Ministries; 1995 Chestertown, MD, First; 1999 transf to W. MI Conf., Ministry Consultant; 2004 Albion District Superintendent; 2009 Director of Connectional Ministries. 2014 transf to Detroit Conference; **Feb 1, 2018 Lansing District Superintendent; Jan 1, 2019 Mid-Michigan District Superintendent**. 1161 E Clark Rd Ste 216, DeWitt 48820 (517-347-4173). Home: 16170 Pleasant St, Linden 48451

*Diamond, David Arthur (Barbara)   ddiamond@columbus.rr.com
[(RE) P 1971; F 1974]. 1973 Detroit: Strathmore (assoc.); 1976 Pontiac: Baldwin Avenue; 1980 Mio; 1986 Oak Grove; 1988 Rochester: St. Paul (assoc); 1994 Utica; 2003 Alpena; **2006 Retired**. Home: 503 Adams St, Decatur GA 30030-5209 (404-747-2605)

*DIBBET, JAMES A (RE) (Gloria) – (FL-1999, PE-2001, FE-2004, R-2011)
St Johns: Salem/Greenbush/Lowe 1999; Sodus: Chapel Hill 2005; Retired 2011
(H) 220 Whitetail Dr, Prudenville 48651-9522 (989) 400-2055

Dibble, Timothy C. (Fiona)   revtcd@yahoo.com
[(FE) LP 1997; PE 1998; FE 2000]. 1997 West Marquette County Parish: White Pine, Bergland, Ewen, Trout Creek Presbyterian; 2000 British Methodist Church; 2005 Ortonville; 2011 Ypsilanti: First; **2014 West Branch: First**. 2490 W. State Rd., West Branch 48661 (989-345-0210). Home: 2458 W. State Rd., West Branch 48661 (989-345-0688)

Dister, Robert W. (Patricia)   dister.r@gmail.com
[(FL) FL 2012]. **2012 Clayton, Rollin Center**. (C) 3387 State St., Clayton 49235 (517-445-2641), (RC) 3988 Townley Rd., Manitou Beach 49253. Home: 3282 State St., PO Box 98, Clayton 49235 (517-445-4009)

*Dobbs, William D. (Janice)   bjdobbs2863@gmail.com
[(RE) P 1973; F 1978 West Michigan]. 1972 West Mendon (DSA); 1973 West Menden, 1978 Lansing: Calvary; 1983 Ludington: United; 1991 East Lansing: University; 1996 Holland: First; 2005 Central District Superintendent (renamed Heartland District, 2009); 2010 Clergy Assistant to the Bishop; **2015 Retired**. Home: 1619 Harbour Blue St, Ruskin, FL 33570 (517-898-9791)

*Dobson, Robert Dale (Ethel)   rdejdobson@charter.net
[(RE) T 1965; F 1967]. Jan. 1965 Kingsley (OH); 1966 Director, Wesley Foundation, Michigan Technological University; 1968 Marquette: First (assoc.); Feb. 1972 Taylor: West Mound; 1976 Menominee; 1986 Leave of Absence; **1991 Retired**. Home: 224 Shoreline Dr., Negaunee 49866 (906-475-5752)

*Donahue, William Richard, Jr. (Nancy)   donahuebill@comcast.net
[(RE) P 1977; F 1981]. 1978 Grace Church, Piqua, OH (student assist.); 1979 Utica (assoc.); 1982 Livingston Circuit: Plainfield, Trinity; Jan. 1, 1988 Hale; Jun 1, 1993 Dexter; 2003 Utica; 2011 Fenton; Mar 11, 2014 medical leave; **May 1, 2014 Retired**. Home: 10139 Kress, Pinckney 48169 (586-651-0550)

*Donelson, Linda Jeanne (Paul)   linda@umcs.org
[(RE) P IA, 1973; F IA, 1976]. 1975 Hope Parish; 1978 Leave of Absence; 1982 Strawberry Point (LTFT 1/3); 1984 West Bend, Mallard (LTFT ¾); 1986 Kumrur, Loebster City, Asbury; 1987 Leave of Absence; 1989 Trans. to Detroit Conf., South Central Cooperative Ministry: Linden, Argentine; 1990 Owosso: Central (LTFT ¾); 1992 Dundee; 1997 Birmingham: Embury; Oct 1, 2000 medical disability; **2015 Retired**. Home: 37273 Woodsman Trail, Detour Village 49275 (989-872-2945)

*Donelson, Paul Gregory (Linda)   donelson@umcs.org
[(RE) P 1973; F IA, 1976]. 1974 Trans. to Iowa Conf., Hope Parish; 1978 Strawberry Point; 1984 West Bend; 1987 Trans. to W. MI Conf., Centerville; 1989 Trans. to Detroit Conf., Caring Covenant Group Ministry: Richfield, Otter Lake. 1990 Corunna; 1992 Saline: First (assoc.); 1995 Monroe: Calvary; 1997 Pontiac Cooperative Parish: Pontiac: First, St. James; Apr 19, 2000 Pontiac: First, Aldersgate; 2000 Roseville; 2001 Roseville, Warren: Wesley; Oct 1, 2001 Ishpeming: Wesley; 2006 Cass City; 2010 Blissfield: First; 2013 Birch Run (¾), Burt (¼); **2015 Retired**. Home: 37273 Woodsman Trail, Detour Village 49275 (989-928-8825)

*DOUBBLESTEIN, WILLIAM H (RE) (Karen) – (D-1978, FE-1982, R-2006)
Grandville (Assoc) 1974; Galien/Olive Branch 1980; Springport/Lee Center 10/16/1983; Byron Center 1987; Dowagiac: First 2004; Retired 2006
william_doubblestein@yahoo.com
(H) 3350 100th St, Byron Center 49315-9707 (616) 481-3881

*DOWNING, JUDY K. (RL) – (FL-1988, RL-2001)
Kendall / Gobles (DSA) 1987; Kendall / Gobles 1988; Marshall (Assoc) 1998; Ionia: Easton 1999; Lyons-Muir 07/20/1999; Retired 05/31/2001
(H) 5959 Barnhart Rd, Ludington 49431-8601 (231) 425-3314

Dozeman, Tania J (PE) (Karen) – (CC-2015, PE-2018)
Holland: First (Assoc.) 2018
taniadozeman@gmail.com
(H) 66 Crosswind Dr, Holland 49424 (616) 566-4165
Holland: First 57 W 10th St, Holland 49423 (616) 396-5205

*DRYER, DAVID L (RE) (Tudie) – (D-1963, FE-1966, R-2006)
Osseo 1963; Mendon 1966; Pine River Parish: Leroy/Ashton/Luther 04/01/1968; Dansville/Vantown 1974; Hesperia/Ferry 1980; Lake City 1985; Battle Creek: Trinity 1996; Retired 2006; Battle Creek: Birchwood 01/01/2007-06/30/2007
ddryerdeerrange@comcast.net
(H) 2150 Gethings Road, Battle Creek 49015-9607 (269) 441-0456

*DUFFEY, PAULA JANE (RE) (Richard) – (D-1992, FE-1994, R-2005)
Maple Hill (PTLP) 11/01/1980-1988; Winn/Blanchard/Pine River/Coomer (FTLP) 1990; Blanchard/Pine River/Coomer (LTFT ¾) 1994; Blanchard/Pine River/Coomer 1996; Calvary Lansing 1998; Retired 2005; Grant Center (LTFT <¼) 08/01/2015-2016

dopper1921@aol.com
(H) 13599 Deaner Rd, Howard City 49329-9510 (989) 330-0251

*DUFFEY, RICHARD J. (RL) (Jane) – (PL-1980, NL-1988-1994, RL-2005)
Maple Hill (LTFT PT) 11/01/1980; Not Appointed 1988; Six Lakes (LTFT PT) 1994; Lakeview: New Life (Co-Pastor) 01/01/1998; Grovenburg (LTFT PT) 1998; Retired 2005

(H) 13599 Deaner Rd, Howard City 49329-9510 (231) 762-4473

*Duggan, Robert (June)   duggan3434@twc.com
[(RE) P 1989, on recognition of orders, Presbyterian Church, USA; F 1992, on recognition of orders, Presbyterian Church, USA]. Jun. 1964 (ordained Presbytery of New York City) Weston, WV: First Presbyterian; Mar. 1969 Detroit: St. James United Presbyterian; Jul. 1977 Paris, IL; Jan. 1, 1983 Sandusky: Presbyterian; Mar. 1987 Sagola: Grace (Interim), Florence, WI; Sep. 1988 Republic, Woodland; 1989 Trans. to Detroit Conf. from Presbyterian Church; 1990 Redford: Rice Memorial; Dec 1, 1994 Wyandotte: Glenwood; **2005 Retired**. Home: 5801 Holly Oak Ct., Louisville, KY 40291 (502-290-1754)

Dulworth, Elbert P. (Dawn)   dulworth@cablespeed.com
[(FE) PE 2000; FE 2003]. 2000 Crystal Falls: Christ, Amasa: Grace; 2004 Marquette: First (Intentional Interim ¶329.3); 2006 Laingsburg; 2012 Marquette District Superintendent; **Jun 11, 2017 Birmingham: First**. 1589 W. Maple, Birmingham 48009 (248-646-1200). Home: 1043 Chesterfield Birmingham 48009 (248-258-0903)

*DUNCAN, DANIEL M (RE) (Mary Whittaker) – (D-1983, FE-1988, R-2014)
Transferred from Detroit Conf 1986; Snow/Vergennes 1986; Muskegon: Central (Assoc) 1989; Fremont 1994; Church of the Dunes 2003; Retired 2014

danduncan56@gmail.com
(H) 909 Warren Place, Kalamazoo 49006-2268 (616) 502-5092

*Duncan, Jean-Pierre (Noreen)   gracepastorjp@yahoo.com
[(OR)]. 2014 New Baltimore: Grace; New Cooperative: New Baltimore Grace (parish director); **2018 Retired**. Home: 2282 18th St, Wyandotte 48192 (570-407-1304)

Dunlap, Marshall Grant (Susan DeFoe Dunlap)
[(FE) P 1981; F 1985]. 1983 Detroit: Thoburn; 1986 Detroit: Mt. Hope (LTFT); 1989 Trenton: Faith (LTFT ½); Jan 1, 1999 Conference Pension Officer (LTFT), Trenton: Faith (co-pastor) (LTFT ½); 1999 Royal Oak: First (co-pastor) (LTFT ½), Conference Pension Officer (LTFT ½); 2003 Royal Oak: First (co-pastor) (LTFT ¾); Conference Pension Officer (LTFT ¼). Nov 1, 2005 Royal Oak: First; 2008 Harper Woods Redeemer (LTFT ¾); Deaborn: First (co-pastor) (LTFT ¼); 2011 Retired; 2013, returned from voluntary retirement (para 358.7), Farmington: First; **Feb 1, 2016 medical leave**

*Dunlap, Susan DeFoe (Marshall)   RevSDunlap@aol.com
[(RE) P 1974; F 1977]. 1976 Denton: Faith; 1983 Detroit: Mt. Hope; 1986 Detroit: Mt. Hope (LTFT); 1989 Trenton: Faith (LTFT ½); 1999 Royal Oak: First (co-pastor); 2008 Dearborn: First (co-pastor) (LTFT ¾); 2011 Dearborn: First; **2013 Retired**.

Dunlap, Zachary L. (Rachel)   zld@comcast.net
[(FE) PL 2011; PE 2013; FE 2016]. 2011 Allen Park: Trinity; Jan 1, 2013 Blissfield: Emmanuel (½), Lambertville (assoc) (½); **2015 Birmingham: First (associate) (Path One Internship)**. 1589 W. Maple, Birmingham 48009 (248-646-1200)

Dunstone, Kenneth Curtis (Tracy)   dusntone@gmail.com
[(FE) P 1996; FE 1999]. 1996 Stephenson, Hermansville: First; Dec 16, 1999 US Army Chaplain (para 335.1b) 10th Mountain Division, Fort Drum; Jan 1, 2003 school (para 416.6); **2017 leave of absence**. Home: 6015 S. Main St., Sandy Creek, NY 13145 (315-350-3953)

* DYE, MONA J (RL) (William) – (PL-2007, FL-2011, RL-2017)
Fountain (PTLP) 12/01/2007; Fountain/Free Soil (PTLP) 2009; Ashley/Bannister /Greenbush 2011; Ashley/Bannister 2015; Ashley/Bannister/Pompeii 2016-2018; Retired 10/01/2017; Wolf Lake (LTFT ½) 2018
billmona3@msn.com
(H) 550 Western Ave Apt 424, Muskegon 49440 (231) 429-1892
Wolf Lake: 378 Vista Terrace, Muskegon 49442 (231) 788-3663

*DYE, WILLIAM F. (RL) (Mona) – (FL-2003, PL-2012, FL-2015, RL-2017)
Empire 2/1/2003; Bear Lake / Arcadia 2006; Vickeryville / Palo / Fenwick 2011; Pompeii / Middleton / North Star / Perrinton 7/15/2012; Breckenridge 9/1/2015; Retired 2017; Twin Lake (LTFT ½) 2018
billmona3@gmail.com
(H) 550 Western Ave Apt 424, Muskegon 49440 (231) 429-1891
Twin Lake: 5940 S Main St, PO Box 352, Twin Lake 49457 (231) 828-4083

Eardley, David Anthony (Sara)   reveardley@hotmail.com
[(FE) P 1992; F 1995]. 1993 Britton: Grace; 1997 Ann Arbor: First (assoc); 2001 Bay City: Christ; 2006 Frankenmuth; **2013 Rochester: St. Paul's**. 620 Romeo St., Box 80307, Rochester 48308 (248-651-9361). Home: 1450 Oakstone Dr, Rochester Hills 48309 (248-651-9770)

*Eckhardt, Mary Margaret (Robert)   revmme@earthlink.net
[(RE) P 1976; F 1979]. April 1978 Lake Orion (assoc.); 1981 Lake Orion (assoc.) (LTFT ½); 1983 Leave of Absence; 1985 Lake Orion (assoc.) (LTFT ¼); 1988 Thomas (LTFT ½), Lake Orion (assoc.) (LTFT ¼); Nov 1, 1992 Thomas, Lakeville; 2002 leave of absence; Sep 1, 2002 Livonia: St. Matthew's; **2010 Retired**. Home: 2660 Creekstone Circle, Maryville, TN 37804

Ehlers, Murphy Schieman (David)   murphyehlers@aol.com
[(FD) CRT, 1997; CON (CE) 1998; FD 2001]. 1998 Human Sexuality Consultant; Nov 1, 1998 Franklin: Community; 2001 Flint: Court Street; Feb 2, 2002 leave of absence; 2002 Retreat and Educational Ministries (LTFT ½), Rochester Hills: St. Luke's (LTFT ½); Dec 1, 2002 Retreat and Educational Ministries (LTFT ½), Warren: First (assoc); Feb 15, 2007 family leave; Oct 1, 2011 Detroit: Second Grace (deacon). Nov 30, 2015 transitional leave; Jan 1, 2016 Clawson; **Dec 31, 2017 Retired**. Home: 3425 Hawk Woods Circle, Auburn Hills 48336 (248-371-9010)

PASTORAL RECORDS

*ELDERS, MARCIA L (OR) (David) – (OF-2003, OR-2017)
[Reformed Church of America] Wyoming: South Wyoming (LTFT ¼) 2003; Wyoming: South Wyoming (LTFT ½) 10/01/2006; Wyoming: South Wyoming (LTFT ¾) 01/01/2009; Grand Rapids: Cornerstone South Wyoming Campus (LTFT ¾) 01/01/2015; Hastings: Hope (LTFT ¾) 2015; Retired 2017
revmom436@aol.com
(H) 3246 Wayburn Ave SW, Grandville 49418-1913 (616) 292-6712

*ELDRED, ELDON K (RE) (Rhea) – (D-1966, FE-1968, R-2003)
Perrinton/Pompeii 1963; Farwell 12/01/1967; Edmore 1969; Sparta 1973; Fremont 03/01/1979; Appointed to Extension Ministries (¶344.1b,c) District Superintendent, Albion District 03/01/1987; Church of the Dunes 1992; Retired 2003
eldon616@gmail.com
(H) 130 Woodslee Court, Norton Shores 49444-7795 (616) 402-3169

*ELENBAAS, JOE D (RE) (Mary) – (D-1986, FE-1988, R-2010)
Transferred from Minnesota Conf 2000; Ludington 2000; Medical Leave 11/30/2006; Retired 2010
moonlitpines@yahoo.com
(231) 499-8578

*ELLINGER, JOHN W (RE) (Sally) – (D-1968, FE-1971, R-2007)
Transferred from New York Conf 1972; Jackson: First (Assoc) 01/15/1972; Kalamazoo: Sunnyside 1976; Lansing: Grace 1981; Albion: First 1985; Holland: First 1990; UM Connectional Structures (¶344.1a,c) District Superintendent, Lansing District 1996; Traverse City: Central 2002; Retired 2007; Traverse City: Christ 12/01/2009-6/1/2010
johnwe1@charter.net
(H) 1819 Timberlane Dr, Traverse City 49686-2050 (231) 631-9237

Elliott, Dirk (Tricia) delliott@michiganumc.org
[(FE) transferred from West Ohio Conf. 2018]. 2011 Director of New Faith Communities and Congregational Development; 2018 trans to Detroit Conf; **2018 Conference Director of Congregational Vibrancy**. 1161 E Clark Rd, Ste 212, DeWitt 48820 (517-347-4030 ext. 4090). Home: 6831 Oak Leaf Trail, Linden 48451 (810-965-2349)

*Elliott, Hydrian (Emma) dopnh@gfn.org
[(RE) P 1980; F 1985]. 1982 Detroit: East Grand Boulevard; 1985 Detroit: Conant Avenue (assoc.); Feb. 27, 1986 Chaplain, Navy, USN Reserve, Station Chaplain, Naval Training Center, San Diego, CA; Nov 15, 1993 Detroit: Resurrection; Jan 16, 1998 Detroit: Trinity-Faith; May 1, 2000 Westland: St. James; 2003 Flint: Charity, Dort-Oak Park Ministry; **2011 Retired**. Home: 18425 South Drive, Apt 1531, Southfield 48076 (313-671-6272)

*Elliott, John Wilson (Carla) johnwelliott@comcast.net
[(RE); P 1972; F 1975]. 1974 Mt. Clemens: First (assoc.); 1977 North Lake; 1982 Bay City: First (assoc.); 1984 Poseyville; Mar. 1, 1986 Goodrich; Sep 1, 1994 St. Ignace; Apr 16, 2002 incapacity leave; **2014 Retired**. Home: 3517 Lorna Rd., Apt. 3, Rocky Ridge Retirement Center
Vestavia Hills, AL 35216-5999 (205-989-9230)

ELMORE, DAVID G (FE) (Julie) – (PE-2009, FE-2012, OE-2013, FE-2015)
Concord 2013; Transferred from Alaska Missionary Conf 2015; Personal Leave
2016; Ascension at Home Hospice Chaplain (¶344.1d), Missional: Coldwater 2019
dgelmore@gmail.com
(H) 20 Parsons Ct, Coldwater 49036-1118 (517) 817-8855
(O) Ascension at Home Hospice, 5220 Lovers Ln, Ste 140, Portage 49002
(800) 343-1396

ELMORE, JULIE YODER (FE) (David G.) – (FE-2012, OE-2013, FE-2015)
Litchfield/Quincy 2013; Transferred from Alaska Missionary Conf 2015; Coldwa-
ter 2017
jyelmore@gmail.com
(H) 20 Parsons Ct, Coldwater 49036-1118 (517) 607-6977
Coldwater: 26 Marshall St, Coldwater 49036-1625 (517) 279-8402

Embury, Lawrence J (PL) – (PL-2015)
Griffith 2015; Pope/Griffith (LTFT ½) 2018
frn89sdka@frontier.com
(H) 1855 Sarossy Lake Rd, PO Box 86, Grass Lake 49240-0086
(517) 206-2952
Griffith: 9537 S Clinton Tr, Eaton Rapids 48827 (517) 663-6262
Pope: 10401 Townley Rd, Springport 49284-0228 (517) 857-3655

Emerson, Ann E. annbythelakeshore@comcast.net
[(FD) PD 1998 W. OH; FD Det., 1999]. 1998 New Albany (West Ohio); 1999
trans to Detroit; **1999 Director Lake Huron Adult Retreat Center**. 8794
Lakeshore Dr., Burtchville 48059 (810-327-6272). Home: phone (810-327-6468)
[local church appointment: Lexington]

Emmert, Donald Joseph (Becky) demmert@michiganumc.org
[(FE) P 1983; F 1986]. 1984 Ontonagon, Greenland, Rockland; Feb. 16, 1990
Pinconning; 1995 New Baltimore: Grace; Jun 1, 2000 North Central Macomb
Regional Ministry: Mt. Vernon (assoc); 2001 Treasurer's Office Staff; 2003 Con-
ference Benefits Administrator (LTFT ¾), Associate Treasurer (LTFT ¼); 2006
Conference Benefits Officer; Jan 1, 2017 Michigan Area Benefits Officer; **2018
Director of Benefits and Human Resources**. 1161 E Clark Rd, Ste 212, DeWitt
48820 (517-347-4030 ext. 4110)

*England, Gene Patrick (Lisa) pastorpat1982@gmail.com
[(RE) P 1980; F 1984; RE 2018]. 1982 Detroit: Redford (assoc.); Sep. 1, 1985
Caring Covenant Group Ministry: Otisville, West Forest; Mar. 1988 Caring
Covenant Group Ministry, Parish Director; 1993 Hale; 2008 Grand Blanc; 2016
Lambertville; **2018 Retired**. Home: 2963 Bayberry Ct, Holland 49424 (810-
265-8677)

*Engler, Janet M. jengler@aol.com
[(RE) FL 2001; PE 2002, FE 2005]. 1998 Mt. Zion (VA Conf.); 2000 Manassas:
Grace (assoc), (VA Conf.); 2001 Memphis: First, Lamb; 2004 Monroe: Calvary;
2006 Burton: Christ; Mar 1, 2009 disability leave; 2011 New Lothrop, Juddville;
2013 Mt. Morris: First; **Oct 1, 2015 Retired**. Home: 261 Fox Haven Dr Unit 5,
Somerset KY 42501-3160 (586-255-9132)

ERBES, MARK R (FE) (Annette) – (D-1996, FE-2000)
Appointed in Other Annual Conferences West Ohio Conference, Faith Community (Assoc), Xenia OH (¶426.1-*1992 Discipline*) 1996; Mt Pleasant: First (Assoc) 1997; Constantine 2001; Muskegon: Lake Harbor 2007; Holt 2014
pastormark@acd.net
(H) 1951 Heatherton Dr, Holt 48842-1570 (517) 694-8277
Holt: PO Box 168, 2321 Aurelius Rd, Holt 48842-0168 (517) 694-8168

*ERICKSON, RICHARD R (RE) (Jayne) – (D-1969, FE-1973, R-2006)
Barry County: Woodland 1972; Woodland/Hastings: Welcome Corners 1975; Jackson: First (Assoc) 1976; Manistee 1982; UM Connectional Structures (¶344.1a,c) Director, Wesley Foundation, Michigan State University 1990; Retired 2006
rrerickson1301@gmail.com
(H) 3028 Hamlet Circle, East Lansing 48823-6388 (517) 420-5841

ERSKINE, GERALD A (PL) – (DSA-2014, PL-2014)
Fenwick/Palo/Vickeryville (DSA) 2014; Fenwick/Palo/Vickeryville (PTLP ¼) 11/10/2014
geralderskine@hotmail.com
(H) 10963 Sundog Trail, Perrinton 48871-9745 (989) 682-4779
Fenwick: 235 W Fenwick Rd, Sheridan 48884-0241 (989) 291-5547
Palo: 8445 Division St, Palo 48870 (989) 291-5547
Vickeryville: PO Box 241, 6850 S Vickeryville Rd, Sheridan 48884-0241
(989) 291-5547

Euper, Stephen   steveeuper@gmail.com
[(FE) PE 2005; FE 2008]. 2005 Ossineke; 2010 New Hope; Aug 9, 2010 incapacity disability leave; **2012 Eastside Covenant Cooperative Parish: Roseville: Trinity**. 18303 Common, Roseville 48066 (586-776-8828). Home: 30455 Progress, Roseville 48066 (586-776-1459)

*Euper, Terry A. (Jackie)   tjeuper@tm.net
[(RE) P 1969; F 1973]. 1972 Morrice, Bennington, Pittsburg; 1976 Troy: Big Beaver; 1989 Saginaw Bay District Superintendent; 1994 Lapeer: Trinity; 2003 Clergy Assistant to the Bishop; **2010 Retired**. Home: 11463 S. State Rd., Morrice 48857 (517-625-2920)

*EVANS, THOMAS J (Judy) – [(RE) D-1974, FE-1977, R-2013]
Comstock/Portage (Assoc) 1976; Comstock 10/01/1980; Leland/Keswick 1984; Leland 1988; Eaton Rapids: First 02/01/1994; Ludington 2007; Retired 2013; Hastings First (49%) 01/01/2017-06/30/2017
pastortom1948@yahoo.com
(H) 8630 Lake Drive, Springport 49284-9313 (231) 233-6355

FAHEY, KATHERINE L – [(PE) CC-2013, PE-2016] UM Connectional Structures (¶344.1a,c) Director of Residential Ministries, Garrett-Evangelical Theological Seminary 2016
katherinelfahey@gmail.com
(H) 4524 N Wolcott Ave Apt 3A, Chicago, IL 60640 (269) 277-4894

FAIRBANKS, THERESA – [(FL) CC-2016, PL-2016, FL-2018]
Crystal Valley/Walkerville (DSA) 06/01/2015; Crystal Valley/Walkerville (PTLP ½) 11/015/2016; Millville/Williamston: Wheatfield 2018

pastort8296@gmail.com
(H) 1956 N M 52, Stockbridge 49285 (231) 510-1935
Millville: 1932 N M 52, Stockbridge 49285 (517) 851-7853
Williamston: Wheatfield: 520 E Holt Rd, Williamston 48895

FAIRCHILD, JULIE E – [(FL) CC-2014, FL-2017] Fremont 2017
juliefairchild1957@gmail.com
Fremont: 351 Butterfield St, Fremont 49412-1717 (231) 924-2456

FALKER, ERIC M (Katja) – [(FL) FL-2014] Bellaire: Community (DSA) 09/24/2014; Bellaire: Community (FTLP) 11/10/2014; Saint Ignace 2019

emfalker@gmail.com
(H) 90 Spruce St, St Ignace 49781-1654 (906) 376-2085
St. Ignace: 615 W US Highway 2, PO Box 155, Saint Ignace 49781-0155
(906) 643-8088

FANCHER, NANCY V – [(FD) PD-2013, FD-2017] Peace (DSA) 03/16/2005; Peace (PTLP) 11/15/2005; LP w/o Appointment 03/31/2006; Transitional Leave 2013-06/20/2014; Nashville (¼) and Vermontville (¼) and Woodland (¼) (Deacon) (Missional Service: Maple Valley Community Center of Hope – Deacon) July 1-31/2014; Nashville (½) and Vermontville (¼) (Deacon) (Missional Srvice: Maple Valley Community Center of Hope – Deacon) 08/01/2014; Other Valid Ministries (¶344.1d) Missional Service: Maple Valley Community Center (LTFT ½) 2015; Deacons Appointed Beyond the Local Church(¶331.1a) Executive Director of Maple Valley Community Center of Hope (LTFT ½) 2017 and Misisonal Service: Lansing Grace (LTFT ½) 2017; Missional Service: Director of Children's Ministry Lansing: Mt Hope (LTFT ½) 2018

fancher11@yahoo.com
(H) 1317 W Saginaw St, Lansing 48915-1957 (517) 371-3311
Lansing: Mt Hope: 501 E Mt Hope Ave, Lansing 48915 (517) 482-1549

*FARMER-LEWIS, LINDA J (Bill Lewis) – [(OR) D-1981, FE-1985, OE-2011, OR-2017 (Wisconsin Conf)] Munith/Pleasnat Lake 1983; Jaskcon: First (assoc.) 1986; Homer/Lyon Lake 1987; Lansing: Trinity (Assoc) 1992; Deanof the Chapel, Albion College 1994; Leland (¶346.1) 2011; Lansing Central 2013; Retired 2017; Battle Creek: First (LTFT ¾) 2018; Dimondale (LTFT ½) 2019

farmlewis@aol.com
(H) 6747 Creyts Rd, Dimondale 48821-9409 (517) 783-9003
Dimondale: 6801 Creyts Rd, PO Box 387, Dimondale 48821 (517) 646-0641

FARNUM, CHARLES D (FE) (Kendall) – (D-1997, FE-2002)
Middleton/Maple Rapids 1997; Battle Creek: Maple 2001; Leave of Absence 07/01-16/2006; UM Connectional Structures (¶344.1a,c Director, Wesley Foundation Central Michigan University (LTFT ½) and Mt Pleasant: First (Assoc) (LTFT ½) 07/16/2006; UM Connectional Structures (¶344.1a,c) Director, Wesley Foundation Central Michigan University (LTFT ¾) 2007; UM Connectional Structures (¶344.1a,c) Director, Wesley Foundation Central Michigan University (FT) 1/1/2008; UM Connectional Structures (¶344.1a,c) Director, Wesley Foundation Central Michigan University (LTFT ¼) 1/1/2014

charlie.farnum@gmail.com
(H) 1160 Glen Ave, Mt Pleasant 48858-3705 (989) 545-1761
CMU Wesley: 1400 S Washington St, Mt Pleasant 48858-4268 (989) 400-7214

FAY, BARBARA JO (AM) (Fred) – (FL-1997, PL-2007, AM-2009)
Ganges (FTLP) 1997; LP w/o Appointment 12/31/2004; Plainwell: First (Assoc) (PTLP) 2007; Frankfort/Elberta 2010

barbf55@sbcglobal.net
(H) 320 Maple Street, Frankfort 49635 (231) 352-4724
Elberta: PO Box 405, 555 Lincoln Ave, Elberta 49628 (231) 352-4311
Frankfort: PO Box 1010, 537 Crystal Ave, Frankfort 49635-1010 (231) 352-7427

*Fegan, James A.   lorpman@aol.com
[(RL) FL 12/1/2001]. Dec 1, 2001 Stephenson, Hermansville; Jun 16, 2002 Iron River: Wesley; 2004 Republic, Woodland; **2005 Retired**. Home: 8825 M5 Rd., Gladstone 49837

FEIGHNER, BRYCE E (FE) (Eileen) – (PL-2004, PE-2007, FE-2013)
Kalamo (¼ Time) 2004; Kalamo (LTFT ½) 1/1/2007; Kalamo (LTFT ¼) and Quimby (LTFT ¼) 2011; Barry-Eaton Cooperative Ministry: Gresham (LTFT ½) 2013; Hastings: First 2017

brycefeighner@yahoo.com
(H) 935 N Taffee Dr, Hasting 49058-1142 (517) 588-1619
Hastings First: 209 W Green St, Hastings 49058-2229 (269) 945-9574

Feliciano, Laura (FL) – (CC-???, FL-2018)
Grand Rapids: Iglesia Metodista Unida La Nueva Esperanza and Conference Staff, New Church and Hispanic-Latino Committee (¶361.1) 2018

laurafeliciano@yahoo.com
(H) 324 Griswold St SE, Grand Rapids 49507 (615) 218-8187
La Nueva Esperanza: 1005 Evergreen St SE, Grand Rapids 49507 (616) 514-1327

Ferguson, Tyson Geoffrey (Erin)   tferguson@stpaulsc.org
[(FE) FL 2002; PE 2003; FE 2008]. 2002 Saline: First (assoc); 2004 Director, Penn State University Wesley Foundation; 2010 Vassar: First; 2013 Campus Minister, Wesley Foundation, Middle Tennessee State University; **2016 leave of absence**.

FERNANDEZ, ALEJANDRO (ALEX) D (FL) (Bethann) – (PL-2015, FL-2016)
Grand Rapids: Cornerstone (Assoc) Campus Pastor (LTFT ½) 01/01/2015; Grand Rapids: Cornerstone (Assoc) Campus Pastor, Heritage Hill Campus 02/29/2016

alexf@cornerstonemi.org
(H) 10160 Alaska Ave SE, Caledonia 49316-9512 (616) 891-5611
Cornerstone: Heritage Hill: 48 Lafayette Ave SE, Grand Rapids 49503 (616) 698-3170

*Ferris, Haldon Dale (Kathryn Snedeker)   revdoc3@aol.com
[(RE) P MI, 1960; F MI, 1967]. 1959 Cloverdale; 1962 Pipestone; 1966 Portage Prairie; 1968 Trans. to Detroit Conf., Livonia: St. Matthew's (assoc.); 1971 Romulus, New Boston; 1974 Dixboro; 1985 Sanford; 1988 Dearborn: Mt. Olivet; Jun 16, 1996 Saginaw: First (co-pastor); **2002 Retired**. Home: 7364 Williams Ct., Elk Rapids 49629

*Ferris, John Clair ferris.1637@comcast.net
[(RE) P 1973; F 1977] 1976 Livonia: Newburg: (assoc.); Apr. 1979 Detroit: Rice Memorial; 1986 Highland Park: First; 1990 Pontiac Cooperative Parish: Waterford: Trinity (Parish Director); 1998 Dixboro; 2006 Flint: Hope; **2012 Retired**. Home: 3766 River Birch, #10, Flint 48532 (810-733-3233)

FERRIS-MCCANN, DONALD R (FE) (Lisa) – (D-1983, FE-1986)
Mason: First (Assoc) 1984; Frankfort/Elberta 04/01/1989; Cassopolis 1993; Lake Odessa: Central 2000; Battle Creek: First 2007; Medical Leave 02/01/2009; Elsie (LTFT ¾) 2013; Elsie/Salem 5/1/2014; Leave Of Absence 2016
(H) 7346 Robert Lane, Falls Church, VA 22042 (989) 640-6969

*FIELD, RAYMOND D (RE) – (D-1980, FE-1986, R-2003)
Eagle (LTFT ¼) 1988; Eagle LTFT ½) 1989; Transferred from Detroit Conf 1990; Eagle (LTFT ¼) 1990; Bath/Gunnisonville 1993; Herperia/Ferry 1998; Hopkins/South Monterey 1999; Hersey 2001; Retired 05/01/2003
ray_field2003@yahoo.com
(H) 526 Togstad Glen, Madison, WI 53711-1425 (231) 578-2634

Fifer, Thomas C (FL) – (CC-2013, FL-2018)
Vergennes 2018
thomas.fifer@gmail.com
(H) 2445 Almont Ave SE, Grand Rapids 49507 (616) 560-3914
Lowell: Vergennes: 10411 Bailey Dr NE, Lowell 49331-9779 (616) 897-6141

Fike, Ronald A. (Gayle) basketlifter@yahoo.com
[(FE) PL 2010; PE 2013; FE 2016]. 2010 Springville; **2014 Gwinn**. 251 W. Jasper, Box 354, Gwinn 49841 (906-346-6314). Home: 252 W. Carbon, PO Box 655, Gwinn 49841 (906-346-3441)

*FILBRANDT, HAROLD F (RE) (Marian) – (D-1959, FE-1962, R-1994)
Twelve Corners Church 1950; Lacota/Casco 1955; Gobles/Kendall 1959; Frankfort 12/01/1964; Ludington First 1967; Marshall 1974; St Joseph First 02/16/1983; Holland: First 04/01/1987; Fremont 1990; Retired 1994; Glenn (LTFT ¼) 2014 – 12/31/2018
harold77020@comcast.net
(H) 77020 County Road 380, South Haven 49090-9417 (269) 637-3087

*Finzer, Garrison Fred (Lois) pastorfred2351@yahoo.com
[(RE) PL 1994; PE 1997; FE 1999]. Jul 15, 1994 Rochester Hills: First; 1996 Dexter (assoc); 2000 Seven Churches United Group Ministry: Byron: First; 2006 Hartland; **2012 Retired**. Home: 1665 Carlson Lane, SW, Marietta, GA 30064

*FISCHER, FREDERICK H (RE) – (D-1958, FE-1961, R-1996)
Suttons Bay (EUB) 1958; Maple Hill (EUB) 1962; Berrien Springs/Arden (EUB) 05/10/1965; Rosebush/Leaton 01/01/1970; Leave of Absence 1978; Williamston Center/Wheatfield 1980; Elsie/Duplain 1985; Elsie 01/01/1990; Retired 1996; Leslie/Felt Plains (LTFT 49%) 09/14/2014-2015
fischbones@frontier.com
(H) 3123 E Grand River Rd, Williamston 48895-9161 (517) 655-4896

PASTORAL RECORDS

*FISHER, JOHN W (RE) (Corinne) – (D-1975, FE-1980, R-2013)
Niles: Wesley (Assoc) 1977; Schoolcraft/Pleasant Valley 1978; Casco 1980; North Muskegon 1986; Kalamazoo: Sunnyside 1992; South Haven: First 2004; Retired 2013; Oshtemo (LTFT ½) 2013

revjwfisher@hotmail.com
(H) 3506 East Shore Dr, Portage 49002-6603 (269) 214-0276
Oshtemo: PO Box 12, 6574 Stadium Dr, Kalamazoo 49009-0012
(269) 375-5656

Fitzgerald, Erin Lea Brodhagen (Joel) – [(FE) (PE-2012, FE-2016]
Grand Rapids: Saint Paul's 2012; Rochester: St Paul's (Assoc.) 2018

erin.lb.fitzgerald@gmail.com
(H) 632 Romeo Rd, Rochester 48307
Rochester: St Paul's: 620 Romeo Rd, PO Box 80307, Rochester, 48308
(248) 651-9361

Fitzgerald, Joel Thomas Pier (Erin) – [(FE) (FL-2012, PE-2016, FE-2019]
Wyoming Park 2012; Hopkins/South Monterey 2017; Sterling Heights 2018

pierfitz@gmail.com
(H) 632 Romeo Rd, Rochester 48307 (616) 848-9759
Sterling Heights: 1133 16 1/2 Mile Rd, Sterling Heights 48312 (586) 268-3130

*FLAGEL, DAVID L (RE) (Rebecca) – (D-1975, FE-1977, R-2013)
North Adams/Jerome 09/01/1975; Coopersville 1980; Ionia Parish LeValley/ Berlin Center 03/01/1989; Lake Odessa: Lakewood 2003; Retired 2013

drflagel@yahoo.com
(H) 13566 Hill Country Dr SE, Lowell 49331-8551 (616) 821-7743

*Fleming, David L. (Lani)   DavidLFleming@gmail.com
[(RE) LP 1995, PE 1996; FE 1998]. 1995 Seven Churches United Group Ministry: Gaines, Duffield; 1999 Memphis: First, Lamb; 2001 Heritage; 2003 New Lothrop, Juddville; 2011 Davisburg; **Feb 15, 2014 Retired**. Home: 2622 San Rosa Drive, St. Clair Shores 48081 (586-776-2019)

*FLEMING, EDNA M. (RL) (George) – (PL-1995, NL-2002, RL-2011)
Charlotte: Lawrence Ave (Assoc) (LTFT PT) 1995; Not Appointed 2002; Retired 2011

(H) 793 68th St, South Haven 49090-9667 (269) 637-4406

*FLEMING, GEORGE W (RE) (Edna) – (D-1963, FE-1965, R-2002)
Turk Lake (EUB)/Greenville (Assoc) 1965; Sodus: Chapel Hill 08/01/1975; Charlotte 1987; Retired 2002

gandefleming@gmail.com
(H) 793 68th St, South Haven 49090-9667 (269) 637-4406

FLESSNER, JODIE R (FE) – (D-1993, FE-1997)
Pompeii/ Perrinton/North Star 1994; Pompeii/ Perrinton/North Star/Christian Crossroads Cooperative Parish 2001; Pine River Parish:Leroy/Ashton 2003; Caledonia 2012; UM Connectional Structures (¶344.1a,c) District Superintendent, Northern Waters District 2019

jflessner@michiganumc.org
(H) 4505 Stone Ridge Ct, Traverse City 49684-7106
(O) 1249 3 Mile Rd S, Traverse City 49696-8307 (231) 947-5281

*FLORY, BARBARA J (RE) (Robert) – (D-1989, FE-1992, R-2011)
Concord 01/01/1990; Holt (Assoc)/Alaiedon Township New Church Start 1998; Lansing: Sycamore Creek 2000; UM Connectional Structures (¶344.1a,c) New Church Development (LTFT ½) 2009; Retired 2011
barbflory@gmail.com
(H) 4517 Weswilmar Dr, Holt 48842-1645 (517) 694-7114

*FLOYD, CAROLYN C (RE) – (FD-1992, FE-1995, R-2008)
West Mendon 1990; Mancelona/Alba 1997; St Johns: First 2000; Perry/ Shaftsburg 2003; Retired 2008; Appointed in Other Annual Conferences (¶331.8, ¶346.1) Detroit Conf, Eastpointe Immanuel (LTFT ½) 01/01/2012-June 30/2012; Appointed in Other Annual Conferences (¶331.8, ¶346.1) Detroit Conf, Algonac Trinity (LTFT ¼) and Marine City (LTFT ¼) 2013; (Marine City closed 02/01/2014) Appointed in Other Annual Conferences (¶331.8, ¶346.1) Detroit Conf, Algonac Trinity (LTFT ¼) 02/01/14-6/1/2014
k_kid@sbcglobal.net
(H) 3437 Gratiot Ave, Port Huron 48060-2244 (810) 982-1629

*FONS, VALERIE (RE) (Joseph Ervin) – (FL-1995, D-1998, FE-2002, R-2017)
Bell Oak/Webberville 1995; Galien/Olive Branch 1999; Pokagon (LTFT ½) 2001; Family Leave 2003; Other Valid Ministries (¶344.1d) Bread & Water LLC and L.A.U.N.C.H. (Lake Adventures Uniting Nature & Children With Hospitality) WI 10/01/2009; Retired 02/14/2017; Other Valid Ministries (¶344.1d) Bread & Water LLC and L.A.U.N.C.H. (Lake Adventures Uniting Nature & Children With Hospitality) WI 02/14/2017
breaduponthewaters@gmail.com
(H) 987 Townline Rd, Washington Island, WI 54246 (920) 847-2393
(O) 1275 Main Rd, Washington Island, WI 54246-9009 (920) 535-0077

*Foo, Tat-Khean (Kim)   tkfkgf@sbcglobal.net
[(RE) P Malaysian Conf., 1967; F 1974]. Sep 18, 1972 Henderson, Chapin; 1973 Trans. to Detroit Conf.; 1976 Waterford: Trinity; 1990 Walled Lake; 1996 Dearborn: Mt. Olivet; Oct 1, 2002 leave of absence; **Apr 1, 2003 Retired**. Home: 32 Blair Lane, Dearborn 48120 (313-336-1988)

Forsyth, Michelle (Robert)   fumc.mnforsyth@gmail.com
[(PE) FL 2015, PE 2018]. 2015 Fenton (assoc.); **2018 Fenton (assoc.) (LTFT ¾), Linden** (LTFT ¼). (F) 119 S. Leroy St., Fenton 48430 (810-629-2132). (L) 201 S. Bridge St., PO Box 488, Linden 48430 (810-735-5858). Home: 514 Mill Pond Dr., Fenton 48430 (810-288-8900)

FOSTER, RICHARD J (FL) (Renee) – (PL-2012, FL-2013)
Williamston Crossroads (DSA LTFT ¼) 08/01/2012; Williamston Crossroads (PTLP ¼) 11/10/2012; M-52 Cooperative Ministry: Webberville (LTFT ¾)/ Williamston Crossroads (LTFT ¼) 2013; [M-52 Cooperative Ministry re-named Connections Cooperative Ministry 2015] Dowling: Country Chapel 2016
rjfoster0206@ymail.com
(H) 3400 Lacey Rd, Dowling 49050-9749 (269) 721-3400
Country Chapel: PO Box 26, 9275 S M 37 Hwy, Dowling 49050 (269) 721-8077

Foster, Sheryl A.   sherylafoster@gmail.com
[(FD) PD 2008; FD 2015]. 2008 Milford, Pastoral Assistant (½), Milford High School; **2015 Milford (deacon)**. 1200 Atlantic, Milford 48381 (248-684-2798). Home: 5821 Felske Drive, Brighton 48116 (248-318-5613)

Fowler, Faith Ellen   ccumcac@aol.com
[(FE) P 1986; F 1988]. 1986 Detroit: Ford Memorial; **Jul 1, 1994 Detroit: Cass Community**. 3901 Cass Avenue, Detroit 48201 (313-833-7730) (shelter: 11850 Woodrow Wilson, Detroit 48206, 313-883-2277). Home: 2245 Wabash, Detroit 48216 (313-408-1980)

*FOX, JAMES E (RE) (Helen) – (D-1965, FE-1968, R-1995)
Leaton Community 1961; Rosebush/Center 1962; Grand Rapids Epworth/ Westgate 1964; Lansing: Trinity 1968; Shelby 11/15/1971; Wyoming: Wesley Park 09/01/1977; Three Rivers: First 05/01/1985; Fennville/Pearl 1990; Hastings: Hope 1992; Retired 1995; Barry County: Woodland 07/22/2008-2011
                                                            jfox@broadstripe.net
                    (H) 1112 N Hanover St, Hastings 49058-1330 (269) 945-0190

*FOX, THOMAS P (RE) (Kathleen) – (D-1986, FE-1992, R-2012)
Mesick/Harrietta 1986; Reading 1992; Portage Prairie 1999; Portage Prairie (LTFT ¾) 01/01/2008; Homer/Lyon Lake 2008; Retired 2012
                                                        preacher1947@yahoo.com
                    (H) 1626 Lake Dr Apt 189, Haslett 48840-8421 (517) 331-2287

*Frank, Nancy Kathleen (Daniel)   NKFrank@msn.com
[(RE) P 1991; F 1993]. 1991 Norway: Grace, Faithorn; Nov 1, 1994 Fenton (assoc); 1996 Saginaw: Swan Valley; 2000 Dearborn: Good Shepherd; Oct 1, 2005 incapacity leave; **2015 Retired**. Home: 4605 Robindale Dr., Knoxville, TN 37921

*Franks, Barbara L.
[(RE) P KY, 1976; F KY, 1979]. 1976 school; 1978 Mt. Olivet, KY; 1980 Tower, Dayton, KY (LTFT ½), Director, United Methodist Advisory Council of Northern Kentucky (LTFT ½); 1984 Tower, Dayton, KY; 1986 Maysville: Scott; 1987 Director, Ida Spence United Methodist Mission, Covington, KY; 1989 Trans. to Detroit Conf., Rose City: Trinity, Churchill. Sep 1, 1994 LaPorte, Mapleton; Oct 1, 1996 God's Country Cooperative Parish: Paradise, Hulbert; 1998 Bay Port, Hayes; 2000 Hardy; 2005 leave of absence; **2007 Retired**. Home: 1720 Fairlawn Dr., Lot 22, Howell 48855 (517-579-4383)

*Fraser-Soots, Bea Barbara   beasoots@gmail.com
[(RE) P 1991; F 1993]. 1991 Detroit: Cass Community (assoc.); 1994 Detroit: Zion; 1997 Detroit: Mt. Hope; Sep 1, 1997 Washington, Davis; Jan 1, 1999 Ferndale: Campbell Memorial (LTFT ¼); 2000 Detroit: Redford; 2005 sabbatical leave;2006 Pontiac: Grace & Peace Community, Four Towns; 2014 Garden City: First; **Mar 2, 2015 Retired**. Home: 20225 True Vista Circle, Monument, CO 80132 (248-320-5108)

*Frazier, Lynda Frances (Kevin)   lynfrazier1120@gmail.com
[(RE) PE 2006; FE 2010]. 2005 Gordonville (LTFT ¼); Jun 20, 2010 leave of absence; 2012 Freeland; Feb 15, 2014 leave of absence; **Dec 1, 2015 Retired**. Home: 1105 Tanwood Ct., Midland 48462 (989-835-8290)

Freeland, Carol Joan [Abbott] (David)   pastorcjabbott@frontier.com
[(FL) PL 2014; FL 2015]. 2014 Iron River: Wesley; 2015 Kingston; **2018 Hudson: First**. 420 W. Main St., Hudson 49247 (517-448-5891). Home: 428 W. Main St., Hudson 49247

Freeland, David C. (Carol)   davecf@gmail.com
[(FL) PL 1998; FL 2000] Jan 1, 2000 Peck, Buel, Melvin (co-pastor); 2002 Port Austin, Pinnebog/Grindstone; 2013 Livingston Circuit: Plainfield, Trinity; **2017 Retired**. Home: 5250 Swaffer Rd., Millington 48746 (810-569-3669)

*Freeman, Catherine M. (Tom)   cathyfreeman27@yahoo.com
[(RD) PD 2008; FD 2011; RD 2014]. 2008: Dixboro; Sept 29, 2008 Dixboro: Pastoral Assistant (½), Project Manager Avalon Housing; 2010 Dixboro (½), Ann Arbor Women's Group (½); **2014 Retired**. Home: 3381 Alan Mark, Ann Arbor 48105 (734-665-8471)

French, Cleoria Monique Renee [Turner] (Cedric)
monique.turner21@gmail.com
[(PL) FL 2015, PL 2019] 2015 Saginaw: State Street; **2019 Breckenridge**. 125 3rd St., PO Box 248, Breckenridge 48615-0248 (989-842-3632). Home: 5245 Pheasant Run Dr., Apt #3, Saginaw 48638 (810-814-6487)

FRENCH, Lawrence James (FL) – (PL-2019, FL-2019)
Kalamazoo: Milwood (Assoc.) (LTFT ½) 01/01/2019; Gobles, Almena 2019
                    pastorlarryfrench@gmail.com
(H) 31880 Jefferson Ave, Gobles 49055-9659 (616) 551-9280
Gobles: 210 E Exchange St, PO Box 57, Gobles 49055-0057 (269) 628-2263
Almena: 27503 County Road 375, Paw Paw 49079-9425 (269) 668-2811

*FRENCH, LILLIAN T (RE) (Michael) – (PE-2002, FE-2005, R-2010)
Dimondale 11/16/1999; St Louis: First 2002; Jackson Calvary 01/01/2008; Retired 09/01/2010
                    LillianFrench@msn.com
(H) 4151 Lancashire Dr, Jackson 49203-5198 (517) 990-0395

FREYSINGER, ROBERT J (FE) (Marion Robin) – (D-1981, FE-1985)
Center Eaton/Brookfield 10/16/1982; Lane Boulevard 1985; Napoleon 1988; Millville 2004; Millville (LTFT ¾) and Stockbridge (LTFT ¼) 2011; Kalkaska 2013; Appointed in Other Annual Conferences (¶331.8, ¶346.1) Detroit Conf, Fowlerville First 2015; Battle Creek: Newton (LTFT ¼) 2016; Ida/Samaria: Grace 2019
                    pastorrjf913@yahoo.com
(H) 3276 Lewis Ave, Ida 48140 (517) 812-0762
Ida: 8124 Ida E, PO Box 28, Ida 48140-0028 (734) 269-6127
Samaria: Grace: 1463 Samaria, PO Box 37, Samaria 48177-0037
                    (734) 269-6127

FRIEDRICK, PHILLIP J (FE) (Gail) – (D-1984, FE-1988)
Appointed in Other Annual Conferences (¶331.8, ¶346.1) Highland Park (Assoc), Dallas, TX 1984-1985; Galien/Olive Branch 1986; Battle Creek: Birchwood 1991; Alma 1995; N Muskegon: Community 07/15/2012; Sparta 2017
(H) 1960 Skyview Dr, Sparta 49345-9756 (231) 670-7796
Sparta: 54 E Division St, Sparta 49345-1326 (616) 887-8255

FRITZ, LESLEE (PE) – (CC-2016, PL-2017, PE-2019)
Albion: First (PTLP ¾) 2017; Alboin: First 2019
                    fritzleslee@yahoo.com
(H) 11184 29 Mile Rd, Albion 49224-9735 (517) 629-6531
Albion: 600 E Michigan Ave, Albion 49224-1849 (517) 629-9425

*FRITZ, RICHARD A. (RL) (Marjean) – (FL-2009, RL-2014)
Monterey Center / Burnips 2008; Retired 2014
(H) 589 Peterson, Muskegon 49445-2145

*FRY, DONALD R (RE) (Anna) – (D-1967, FE-1970, R-2008)
Waterloo Village/First 1969; Sonoma/Battle Creek: Newton 1970; Ionia Parish: LeValley/Berlin Center 1971; Marne 1973; White Pigeon 11/22/1977; Marion/Cadillac: South Community 1981; Newaygo 1994; Three Rivers: First 2000; Ovid United 2006; Retired 2008; Dansville (LTFT ¼) 2008-2011
anna_don@charter.net
(H) 775 N Pine River St, Ithaca 48847-1115 (517) 749-9304

Fuchs, Robert F. (Susan)   bob@brightonfumc.org
[(FL) FL 2017]. **Jan 1, 2017 Brighton (assoc.) Campus Pastor - Whitmore Lake Campus**. 400 E. Grand River, Brighton 48116 (810-229-8561). Home: 3082 Park Dr., Brighton 48116 (810-571-0185)

*Fuller, Linda L. (Gale)   urmy2@greatlakes.net
[(RL) FL 2000, RL 2018]. 2000 Worth Twp.: Bethel; 2010 Caseville; **2018 Retired**. Home: 254 N Howard Ave, Croswell 48422 (989-856-4009)

*FULLMER, CHARLES W (RE) (Margaret) – (D-1957, FE-1959, R-1997)
Lyon Lake/Marengo Fall 1956; Lyon Lake 1957; Kalamazoo: First (Assoc) 1959; Grand Rapids: Valley 1962; Reed City 1966; Ionia: First 1970; Grandville 1977; Petoskey 1986; Appointed to Extension Ministries (¶344.1b,c) Chaplain, Clark Retirement Community 03/01/1994; Retired 1997; Amble 08/01/1999-10/31/2001
cwfmjf3235@gmail.com
(H) 733 Clark Crossing SE, Grand Rapids 49506-3310 (562) 607-2375
(S) PO Box 239, Lakeview 48850-0239 (989) 352-7002

*GACKLER, JOYCE F. (RL) (Ken) – (PL-2005, RL-2012)
Plainfield 06/01/2005; Retired 2012
joycef2@msn.com
(H) 410 Johnson St, Caledonia 49316-9724 (616) 891-5682

Galloway, Donna   donagalloway@msn.com
[(FL) FL Aug 1, 2014]. Aug 1, 2014 Morenci; **2016 Morenci, Weston** (M) 110 E. Main St., Morenci 49256 (517-458-6923). (W) 4193 Weston Rd., Box 96, Weston 49289 (517-436-3492). Home: 111 E. Main St., Morenci 49256 (517-458-6687)

*Gamboa, Elizabeth M. (Stephan)   gamboapersephone@aol.com
[(RE) (FE, PA)]. 2000 trans to Detroit Conf., Flint: Bristol, Dimond; 2003 Mt. Morris: First; **2008 Retired**. Home: 1601 W. 34th St., N., Wichita, KS 67204

Gandarilla-Becerra, Patricia   carpagabe@gmail.com
[(FL) FL 2012]. 2012 Detroit: El Buen, Alpha and Omega Faith Community; 2015 Ypsilanti: First (assoc), Detroit: El Buen Pastor, Revive, 50 Communities of Faith; 2016 Ypsilanti: First, New Church Development (¶344.1a,c) Detroit: Centro Familiar Cristo; **Feb 1, 2016 Detroit: Centro Familiar Cristiano** 1270 Waterman, Detroit 48209 (313-843-4170). Home: 8961 Niver, Allen Park 48101 (313-551-4003)

PASTORAL RECORDS

Garrigues, Margaret Ruth "Peggy" revpeggyg@gmail.com
[(FE) P 1990; F 1992; HL 2000; FE 2009]. 1990 Howell: First (Assoc.); 1992 Fenton (Assoc.), LTFT 1/2; Sep 1, 1994 Wagarville: Community/Wooden Shoe; 1995 family leave; 1998 Chelsea: First (assoc); 2000 Honorable Location; 2009 Fostoria, West Deerfield (LTFT ½); (2009 readmitted) 2010 Clawson; 2013 Berkley (½), Clawson (½); Jan 1, 2015 Clawson; Oct 1, 2015 Clawson (LTFT ½); Mar 16, 2016 Clawson (LTFT ¼); **Sep 1, 2016 voluntary leave of absence**.

GARZA, E JEANNE [Koughn] (FE) – (D-1996, FE-1998)
UM Connectional Structures (¶344.1a,c) Director, Wesley Foundation, Ferris State University 2003; [Transferred from Iowa Conf 2004] Traverse Bay (Assoc) 2008; Hillside/Somerset Center 2009; Sturgis 2014; Dixboro 2019
pstrig@gmail.com
(H) 3350 Oak Dr, Ann Arbor 48105-9734 (517) 745-2490
Dixboro: 5221 Church Rd, Ann Arbor 48105-9429 (734) 665-5632

Gasaway, Rodney Glenn (Janice)
[(PD) PD 2017]. 2017-Jan 31, 2018 Joy Southfield, Director Community & Economic Dev.; **Feb 1, 2018 Livonia: Newburg, Adult Education Program and Outreach (½); Jan 13, 2019 Chelsea: First, Director of Adult Ministries (½)**. 36500 Ann Arbor Trail, Livonia 48150 (734-422-0149).

*GASTIAN, SANDRA J. (RL) – (PL-1991, RL-2011)
Athens (LTFT ½) 08/01/1991; Retired 01/01/2011
(H) 416 22nd St, Springfield 49037-7858 (269) 964-9050

*GAY, SUE J. (RL) (David) – (FL-1994, PL-2005, RL-2007)
Augusta: Fellowship (DSA 6/1/93-7/1/94) 1994; Augusta: Fellowship (LTFT PT) 01/01/2005; Retired 2007
(H) 4222 NE 129 Pl, Portland, OR 97230-1406

*Gedcke, Roger Franklin (Donna) drgedcke@gmail.com
[(RE)]. 1968 Detroit: Bethel; 1969 Ferndale: St. Paul's; 1972 Ontonagon County Larger Parish; 1979 North Branch, Clifford; 1997 Clio: Bethany; **2010 Retired**. Home: 13078 Golfside Ct., Clio 48420 (810-547-1538)

Genoff, Nickolas Kelly (Tina) ngenoff@rocketmail@gmail.com
[(PL) FL Jan 1, 2004; PL 2013]. Jan 1, 2004 Port Huron: Washington Ave; 2007 Port Huron: Washington Avenue, Avoca; 2009 Croswell: First, Avoca; 2013 Applegate, Buel, Croswell: First; **Jan 1, 2019 Medical Leave**. Home: 184 S Elk, Sandusky 48471 (810-990-9853)

Gentile, Michelle Annette (Randy Whitcomb) arejayrev@aol.com
[(FE) P 1984; F 1987]. 1985 Dearborn: First (assoc.); 1988 Denton: Faith; 1990 disability leave; **2019 Retired**. Home: 2772 Roundtree Dr., Troy 48083 (248-229-8383)

*Gerritsen, Georg F.W. (Barbara) flyingdutchman@tir.com
[(RE) P 1972; F 1974]. 1972 Howarth, Thomas; 1978 Saginaw: West Michigan Avenue; 1980 Monroe: Calvary; 1985 Jeddo, Central-Lakeport; 1988 Caring Covenant Group Ministry: Oregon, Elba; 1996 Port Huron: Gratiot Park, Washington Avenue; **Jan 1, 2000 Retired**. Home: 2915 16th Ave., Port Huron 48060 (810-987-2864)

PASTORAL RECORDS

Gibbs, Cindy (Jim)   cindygibbs1957@gmail.com
[(FL) PL Jan 1, 2008; FL 2010]. Jan 1, 2008 Churchill; 2010 Romulus; **2015 Pigeon: First**. 7102 Michigan Ave., PO Box 377, Pigeon 48755 (989-453-2475). Home: 7090 Scheurer St., PO Box 377, Pigeon 48755 (989-453-3232)

*Gibbs, Max L. (Jean)
[(RE) P 1977; F 1980]. 1978 Pontiac: Central (assoc.); 1980 Flint: Oak Park (assoc.); 1982 Akron, Unionville; 1983 Director, Camp Reynoldswood, IL; 1987 Minister of the Word, Uniting Church in Australia; Feb. 1, 1990 Deerfield, Petersburg; 1991 Deckerville, Minden City; 1996 Akron; Oct 1, 1996 disability leave; **2009 Retired**. Home: 5671 Galbraith Line Rd, Croswell 48422-8959 (810) 404-9726

Giddings Sr., Emmanuel J.   enw@earthlink.net
[(FE) P 1993 (on recognition of orders, Liberia Annual Conference); F 1994]. 1992 Detroit: Central (assoc.); 1995 Detroit: Conant Avenue; 1997 St. Clair Shores: Good Shepherd; Oct 1, 1999 Associate Council Director: Urban Missioner.; Jan 1, 2003 leave of absence; **Sep 1, 2006 Director of Afalit International/Liberia Literacy Program, Liberian Conference** para 344.1

*Giguere, Jack Eugene (Joyce)   je.giguere@hotmail.com
[(RE) T 1959; F 1962]. 1959 Baltimore: Brooklyn (assoc.) (Baltimore Conf.); 1962 Clarkston (assoc.); 1965 Bad Axe; 1971 Flushing; 1980 Livonia: Newburg; 1984 Ann Arbor District Superintendent; 1989 Grosse Pointe; **1999 Retired**. Home: (summer) PO Box 1313, Bay View 49770 (231-347-8277); (winter) 410-A Goldsborough St., Easton, MD 21601

Gillespie, Billie Lou (Roger Brown)   spiritdancer1216@gmail.com
[(FL) FL 2000]. 2000 Henderson, Chapin; **Oct 15, 2006 West Vienna**. 5485 W. Wilson Rd., Clio 48420 (810-686-7480). Home: 5445 W. Wilson Rd., Clio 48420 (810-686-4025)

Gladstone, Carl Thomas Stroud (Anna)   carl@motorcitywesley.org
[(FD) PD 2004; FD 2007]. 2004 Birmingham: First (deacon) (LTFT ¾); 2007 Birmingham: First (deacon); Director, Young Leaders Initiative; Jan 1, 2010 Youth Leaders Initiative (½), Jurisdictional Coordinator Youth and Young Adult Ministries (½); Jan 1, 2016 Discipleship Ministries: Regional Staff; **2019 Dearborn: First Director of Youth & Adult Ministries & Missional and Young Leaders Initiative** (deacon) (LTFT ½); **2019 Director of Motor City Wesley** (LTFT ½) (Para 331.1a). (DF) 22124 Garrison St, Dearborn 48124-2207 (313-563-5200), (MCW) 8000 Woodward, Detroit 48202 (313-757-0471). Home: 542 W. Grand Blvd, Detroit 48216 (586-295-3055)

*Gladstone, David G.   dgladstone@lakelouisecommunity.org
[(RE) SP 1989; P 1990; F 1993]. 1989 Detroit: Metropolitan (assoc.); 1991 Eastpointe: Immanuel; 1997 Warren: First; 2003 Port Huron: First; **2012 Retired**; 2017-2018 Lexington. Home: 10850 Pioneer Trl, Boyne Falls 49713 (231-549-2728)

Glanville, Gary R. (Lisa)   drg@umc-sc.org
[(FE) P 1980; F 1983]. 1981 Saginaw: Ames (assoc.); 1983 Saginaw: Swan Valley; Mar. 1, 1987 Utica (assoc.); 1989 Ann Arbor: Calvary; 1996 Romeo; **2015 Swartz Creek**. 7400 Miller Rd., Swartz Creek 48473 (810-635-4555). Home: 7469 Lennon Rd., Swartz Creek 48473 (810-635-9110)

Glass, Cora Elizabeth glass.cora@gmail.com
[(FD) PD 2016; FD 2019]. 2016 Wesley Foundation, Resident Director of Intentional Living and Director of Discipleship Ministries/ Area Board of Higher Education and Campus Ministry Fund Developer; July 31, 2017 Garrett-Evangelical Theological Seminary, Assistant Director of Annual Giving and Alum Relations (¶331.1b); **2018 Waterford: Central, Director of Life-Long Faith Formation**. 3882 Highland Rd., Waterford 48328 (248-681-0040). Home: 4011 Shaddick, Waterford 48328 (248-410-2645)

GODBEHERE, CARI A (PL) – (DSA-2018; PL-2019)
Brookfield Eaton (DSA) (LTFT ¼) 2018; Brookfield Eaton (PL) (LTFT ¼) 01/01/2019
(H) 14929 Nichols Rd, Bath 48808-9717 (517) 420-3903
Brookfield Eaton: 7681 Brookfield Rd, Charlotte 48813-9120
(517) 543-4225

*Gonder, Daniel L. (Pamela) revdonnow@att.net
[(RE) PL 2006; PE 2010; FE 2013, RE 2018]. 2006 Fairgrove; Mar 1, 2010 Fairgrove, Watrousville; 2013 Tawas; **2018 Retired; 2018-2019 Grant** (W. Mich.) (LTFT ¼). 10999 Karlin Rd, Buckley 49620 (231-269-3981). Home: PO Box 24, Interlochen 49643 (989) 415-0537 (989-415-0537)

Goodwin, Suzannne Kuenzli (James)
[(FD) PD 2007; FD 2011]. 2007 Farmington: Orchard (deacon) (¾ Time), 2011 deacon full-time; **2019 Mason: First**. 201 E Ash St, Mason 48854 (517-676-9449). Home: 616 Hall Blvd, Mason 48854 (248-318-4869)

GORDON, BRENDA E (FE) – (D-2000, FE-2007)
Hinchman/Oronoko 2000; Empire 2006; Berrien Springs/Pokagon 2014; Berrien Springs/Pokagon and Hinchman/Oronoko 2017; Sodus: Chapel Hill 2018
begordon68@hotmail.com
(H) 4033 Naomi Rd, Sodus 49126 (269) 925-4528
Sodus: Chapel Hill: 4071 Naomi Rd, Sodus 49126 (269) 927-3454

*GORDON, DIANE L (RE) (Tom) – (FL-2003, PE-2004, FE-2007, R-2018)
Ashley/Bannister 2003; Battle Creek: Trinity 2006; Muskegon: Central 2010; Mt Pleasant: First 2013; Retired 2018
PastorDiane7@me.com
(H) 114 Lillybell Ct, Spring Lake 49456 (231) 457-3744

*GORDON, LINDA R (OR) (Bruce) – (OR-2014)
[Illionis Great Rivers Conf, Retired AM 2011] Hinchman/Oronoko (LTFT ½) 2014-2017
yes2six@gmail.com
(H) 116 S Detroit St, Buchanan 49107-1003 (269) 815-6094

GORDY, SAMUEL C. (FL) (Elizabeth) – (PL-2015, FL-2018)
Morris Chapel (PTLP ¼) 03/11/2012; Kalamazoo: Northwest (PTLP ¼) 2013; Bronson: First (PTLP ½) 2015; Bronson: First/Colon 2018
sgordy1962@gmail.com
(H) 330 E Cory St, Bronson 49028-1504 (269) 330-6054
Bronson: First: 312 E Chicago St, Bronson 49028-1318 (517) 369-6555
Colon: 224 N Blackstone Ave, PO Box 646, Colon 49040-0646
(269) 432-2783

Gotham, Donald D. (Laura)   dongotham@sbcglobal.net
[(FE) P 1994; F 1997]. 1995 Sutton-Sunshine, Bethel; Oct 1, 1996 Sutton-Sunshine, Bethel, Akron; 1997 Sandusky: First; Sep 1, 2004 Saint Clair: First; **2011 Utica**. 8650 Canal Rd., Sterling Heights 48314 ((586-731-7667). Home: 8506 Clinton River Rd., Sterling Heights 48314 (586-739-2726)

Goudie, David J (Andee)   pastordavidgoudie@gmail.com
[(FE) PE 1999; FE 2002]. 1999 Monroe: Calvary; 2004 Utica (assoc); Aug 1, 2009 Houghton: Grace; 2013 Hale: First; **Medical Leave Sept 1, 2017**. Home: 16296 Picton Ct., Clinton Twp., 48038

***Goudie, Diana Kay** (Robert)   dianagoudie09@comcast.net
[(RE) PL 1983; SP 1988; P 1991; F 1993]. 1983 Milan: Marble Memorial (assoc.) (LTFT). Sep. 1, 1991 Azalia, London; Sep 1, 1994 Redford: Aldersgate (co-pastor); 2003 Redford: Redford Aldersgate; **2009 Retired**. Home: 19710 W. 13 Mile Rd., #108, Beverly Hills 48085 (248-220-4046)

***Goudie, Robert F.** (Diana)   bobgoudie09@comcast.net
[(RE) T 1964; F 1966]. 1966 Detroit: St. James (assoc.); 1970 Waterford: Trinity; Apr. 1976 Monroe: First; 1983 Milan: Marble Memorial; Sep 1, 1994 Redford: Aldersgate (co-pastor); **2003 Retired**. Home: 19710 W. 13 Mile Rd., #108, Beverly Hills 48085 (248-220-4046)

Gougeon, Jon W. (Kitty)   pastorjon@sch-net.com
[(FL) (FL) 2003]. 2003 Sterling, Alger, Garfield; **Mar 1, 2010 Reese**. 9859 Saginaw St., PO Box 7, Reese 48757 (989-868-9957). Home: 1968 Rhodes, Reese 48757 (989-868-9957)

***Grajcar, Michael, Jr.** (Sharon)
[(RE) T Pitts., 1961; F 1964]. 1959 Renaker, Sadieville, KY; 1960 Sinking Spring, OH; 1963 Trans. to Detroit Conf., Linden; 1969 Troy: Big Beaver; 1976 Holly: Calvary; 1982 Pontiac: St. James; 1988 Riverview; 1989 Onaway, Millersburg; **1991 Retired**. Home: 17867 St. Pierre, Arcadia 49613

***GRAHAM, DONALD J.** (RL) (Judy) – (FL-2001, RL 2019)
Ionia: Zion 2001; Colon/Burr Oak 2007; Martin/Shelbyville 2012; Muskegon Lakeside 2014; Casco 2016; Retired 2019

                              pastordongraham@gmail.com
                (H) 4457 Marshall Rd, Muskegon 49441-5124 (269) 503-0354

GRANADA, LEMUEL O (PL) (Colleen) – (PL-2002, NL-2007, PL-2012)
Fountain (DSA) 2002; Fountain 11/15/2002; Brethren Epworth 2003; Fountain 2005; LP w/o Appointment 11/30/2007; Hersey (PTLP ¼) 07/29/2012
                              LGranada@charter.net
                (H) 351 2nd St, Manistee 49660-1747 (231) 723-2763
        Hersey: PO Box 85, 200 W 2nd St, Hersey 49639-0085 (231) 832-5168

***GRANT, JAMES CLYDE** (RE) – (D-1958, FE-1959, R-1999)
Almena/Glendale 1957; Dowagiac: First 1960; Grand Rapids: Second 1966; Kalamazoo Oakwood 1972; Byron Center 03/01/1975; Otsego 1985; Leave of Absence 03/06/1992; Otsego 08/01/1992; Marion/Cadillac: South Community 1994; Retired 06/23/1999
                (H) 1029 Wedgewood Drive, Plainwell 49080-1291 (269) 685-0079

PASTORAL RECORDS

*GRANT, RONALD B (RE) (Carol) – (D-1973, FE-1976, R-2012)
Concord 1975; UM Connectional Structures (¶344.1a,c) Director, Wesley Foundation WMU 1982; Leave of Absence 08/15/1992; Other Valid Ministries (¶344.1d) Limited License Psychologist, New Directions Counseling Kalamazoo 02/01/1995; Retired 11/01/2012

msu2kzoo@hotmail.com
(H) 1815 Quail Cove Dr, Kalamazoo 49009-1893 (269) 375-0321

Gray, Markey C
[(FL) FL 2018] **2018 Detroit: Trinity Faith**. 19750 W McNichols Rd, Detroit 48219 (313-533-0101). Home: 23470 Meadow Park, Redford 48239

*Gray-Lion, Annelissa Marie   lgraylion@gmail.com
[(RD) PD 2006; FD 2013; RD 2018]. Jan 1, 2007 Chelsea: First (deacon); 2009 leave of absence; 2012 Chelsea: First (deacon); **2018 Retired**. Home: 258 Harrison St, Chelsea 48118 (734-945-2097)

*GRAYBILL, JOSEPH M (RE) (Sue) – (D-1982, FE-1984, R-2011)
Transferred from Free Methodist Church 1982; Dansville/Vantown 1980; Edmore: Faith 04/01/1987; Leland 1997; Retired 2011

sueandjoegraybill@gmail.com
(H) 386 York View Lane NW, Comstock Park 49321 (231) 342-2222

*Green, Patricia A.   pgreen5188@att.net
[(RE) PL 1986; SP 1990; P 1992; F 1995]. 1986 Detroit: North Detroit; 1990 Second UMC, First UMC (associate youth pastor), North Vernon, IN, under para 426.1; 1992 Ebenezer, Madison, IN, under para. 426.1; 1993 Brighton: First (assoc); 1995 Erie; 1999 Madison Heights; 2008 Milan: Marble Memorial; **2013 Retired**. 24353 Tamarack Tr., Southfield 48075 (248-809-6644)

*Green, Rosaline D.   rgreen@hopeumc.org
[(RL) FL 2017; RL 2019] Dec 1, 2017 Southfield: Hope (assoc); **2019 Retired; 2019 Southfield: Hope** (assoc) (LTFT ½). 27275 Northwestern Hwy., Southfield (248-356-1020). Home: 29476 Briar Bank Ct, Southfield 48034 (248-470-4042)

*GREENE, CARL E. (RL) (Deanna) – (PL-2005, RL-2011)
Brethren: Epworth (DSA 7/1-11/11/05) (LTFT PT) 11/11/2005; Grant (LTFT PT) 03/15/2006; Retired 2011
(H) 3021 Glen Malier Drive, Beulah 49617-9478 (231) 375-1006

GREENE, CYNTHIA S L (FE) – (D-1993, FE-1995)
Transferred from Origon-Idaho Conf 1998; Lansing: Trinity (Assoc) 05/01/1998; Byron Center 2003; Ithaca/Beebe 2010; Lake Odessa: Lakewood 2015; Rockford 2017; Weidman 2019

cingreene01@gmail.com
(H) 9532 W Saint Charles Rd, Sumner 48889-8729
Weidman: 3200 N Woodruff Rd, PO Box 98, Weidman 48893-0098
(989) 644-3148

*Greer, James Edward, II (Madeline)   JEGreer@aol.com
[(RE) P 1982; F 1985]. 1983 Rochester: St. Paul's (assoc.); 1987 Farmington: Orchard (assoc.); 1990 New Baltimore: Grace; 1995 Bloomfield Hills: St. Paul; Nov 16, 2000 Franklin: Community; **2013 Retired**. Home: 106 Chota Hills Trace, Loudon, TN 37774 (248-227-7599)

Grenfell, John Nicholas, III (Shelley)　　　　　john@pfumc.org
[(FE) P 1987; F 1989]. Jan. 1, 1987 God's Country Cooperative Parish: Grand Marais, Germfask; Feb. 1, 1992 Menominee: First; 1994 school; 1995 Menominee: First; 1998 Belleville: First; 2007 Plymouth: First; **2018 St. Clair: First**. 415 N 3rd St, St Clair 48079 (810-329-7186). Home: 3202 S Shoreview, Fort Gratiot 48059

GRETTENBERGER, LOUIS W (FE) (Karen) – (D-1987, FE-1989)
Manton 1987; Traverse City: Christ 1993; Sparta 2009; Grand Haven Church of the Dunes 2017

louis.grettenberger@gmail.com
(H) 633 Hillock Ct, Grand Haven 49417-1805 (231) 883-9806
Church of the Dunes: 717 Sheldon Rd, Grand Haven 49417-1860 (616) 842-7980

GREYERBIEHL, JULIE A (FE) (William W Chu) – (FL-2005, PE-2009, FE-2013)
Elk Rapids/ Kewadin/Williamsburg (Assoc) 2005; Elk Rapids/Kewadin/ Williamsburg (Co-Pastor) 2008; Silver Creek/Keeler 2009; Williamston 2011; Mt Pleasant: First 2018

pastorjulieg@gmail.com
(H) 1109 Glenwood Dr, Mt Pleasant 48858 (517) 655-2321
Mt Pleasant: First: 400 S Main St, Mt Pleasant 48858 (989) 773-6934

*GRIENKE, A RAY (RE) (Beverly) – (D-1969, FE-1971, R-1999)
Transferred from South Indiana Conf 1971; Battle Creek: Sonoma/Newton 1971; Boyne City/Boyne Falls 01/15/1974; Kent City: Chapel Hill 1981; Carson City 1985; Retired 08/16/1999

rgrienke@juno.com
(H) 1920 Wank Ave, St Joseph 64507 (616) 676-0538

GRIFFIN JR, HERBERT L (FE) (Ellainia) – (D-1991, FE-1993)
Battle Creek: Washington Hts (Assoc) 1990; Appointed to Extension Ministries (¶344.1b,c) Chaplain/Wing Chaplain, US Navy, US Marine Corps 1993

herbertgriffin911@yahoo.com
(H) 11334 Village Ridge Rd, San Diego, CA 92131-3900 (858) 397-2532

*Grigereit, Robert Charles (Carolyn)　　　　　cgrigereit@aol.com
[(RE) P W. MI, 1960; F W. MI, 1962]. 1960 Deerfield: Bethlehem; 1962 Ludington: Zion; 1965 Ludington: Grace, Zion; 1967 Ludington: St. Paul; 1967 Grand Rapids: Griggs Street; 1968 Trans. to Detroit Conf., Ann Arbor: Calvary; 1976 Garden City; 1987 Midland: First (assoc.); **1999 Retired**. Home: 7355 S. Shugart Rd., Traverse City 49684 (231-946-8551)

Griggs, Jerry Dwight (Cherie)　　　　　mcrgegorumc@airadvantage.net
[(PL) PL 1998]. 1998 Eastern Thumb Cooperative Parish: McGregor, Carsonville; **2004 McGregor, Carsonville**. (M) 2230 Forest R., Deckerville 48427; (C) 3953 Sheldon, Carsonville 48419 (810-657-9168). Home: 5791 Paldi, Peck 48466 (810-378-5686)

Grimes, Christopher　　　　　christopher_michael_grimes@yahoo.com
[(FL) FL 2015]. 2013 Detroit: St. Timothy; 2015 Westland: St. James; **2017 Southfield: Hope (assoc)**. Northwestern Hwy., Southfield (248-356-1020).

Grimmett, Carter Mansfield (Toni)　　　　　　cartergrimmett@att.net
[(FE) PL 2003, PE 2007; FE 2010]. Dec, 2002 Detroit: Conant Avenue; Sep 1, 2003 Westland: St. James (LTFT ½); Jan 1, 2006 Westland: St. James (LTFT ¾); Mar 1, 2007 Westland: St. James, Inkster: Christ; 2008 Detroit: People's; Nov 1, 2013 Detroit Peoples, Calvary; 2014 St. Clair Shores: Good Shepherd; **2017 Rochester: St. Paul**. 620 Romeo St., PO Box 80308, Rochester 48308 (248-651-9361). Home: 598 Jacob Way, #103, Rochester 48307 (313-303-1230)

*Groff, Kathleen A. (Joseph)　　　　　　　　kthgrff@gmail.com
[(RE) P 1997; FE 1999]. 1997 Farmington: Nardin Park (assoc); Sep 1, 2002 Dundee; **2008 Retired**. 2011 Newaygo (LTFT ¾); 1/1/2014 Newaygo (LTFT 45%); 5/8/2014-2017 Newaygo (LTFT ¾). Home: 2524 Windbreak Ln, Lansing 48910 (989-339-7887)

Gruenberg, Paul (Lyent)　　　　　　PastorPaul@HartlandUMC.org
[(FE) PE 2003; FE 2006]. 2003 Pickford; **2012 Hartland**. 10300 Maple St., Hartland 48353 (810-632-7476). Home: 1403 Odetta, Hartland 48353 (810-991-1032)

GUETSCHOW, KEVIN K (FL) (Karen) – (FL-2010)
Kent City: Chapel Hill 2010; Dorr Crosswind Community 2017
keving@crosswindcc.org
(H) 4380 Tracy Trail, Dorr 49323-9469 (616) 227-5567
Crosswind Community: 1683 142nd Ave, Dorr 49323-9426 (616) 681-0302

Gutierrez, Dora (Marcos)　　　　　　　marcosdorag@yahoo.com
[(PL) PL Sep 1, 1998]. Sep 1, 1998 New Creations Ministries 2003 El Buen Pastor/New Creations Ministries; **Jan 1, 2005 without appointment**. Home: 11550 Willow, Southgate 48195 (734-284-8052)

*Gutierrez, Marcos A. (Dora)　　　　　　marcosdorag@yahoo.com
[(RA) P 1980 Puerto Rico Conf.; AM 1999]. 1966 Villa Fontana Carolina; 1967 San Juan Apostor, Villa Palmeras; 1968 Los Angeles Carolina; 1969 Villa Palmeras; 1975 Patillas; 1983 Caguas; 1985 trans to Wisconsin Conference, Madison; Sep 1, 1998 Detroit: El Buen New Creations Ministry; (Aug 16, 1998 trans to Detroit Conference); Apr 15, 2005 incapacity leave; **2010 Retired**. Home: 11550 Willow, Southgate 48195 (734-284-8052)

*GYSEL, JAMES M (RE) (Shari) – (D-1977, FE-1981, R-2011)
Quincy 1979; Lansing: Central (Assoc) 1983; Battle Creek: Chapel Hill 1993; Retired 2011; Lee Center (LTFT ¼) 2014
jamesgysel@mac.com
(H) 3239 Nighthawk Lane, Battle Creek 49015-7640 (269) 209-4795
Lee Center: 22386 24 Mile Rd, Olivet 49076-9533 (517) 857-3447

HAAS, PATRICIA A (FE) – (PL-2003, PE-2011, FE-2014)
Pokagon 2003; Keswick 2011
pastorphaas@gmail.com
(H) 3400 S Center Hwy, Suttons Bay 49682-9252 (231) 271-4117
Keswick: 3376 S Center Hwy, Suttons Bay 49682-9253 (231) 271-3755

HAASE, DAVID L (PL) (Linda) – (PL-2008)
Townline (DSA) (¼ Time) and Breedsville (DSA) (¼ Time) 01/03/2008; Townline (PTLP ¼) and Breedsville (PTLP ¼) 2008; Riverside (PTLP ¼) and Coloma (Assoc) (PTLP ¼) 2014; Riverside (PTLP ¼) 01/01/2016
davehaase55@gmail.com
(H) 211 W Saint Joseph St, Watervliet 49098-9214 (269) 463-3536
Riverside: PO Box 152 (4401 Fikes Rd, Benton Harbor), Riverside 49084
(269) 849-1131

Hadaway, Victoria L. vickie.31.hadaway@gmail.com
[(OE) Northern Illinois] **2018 Sault Ste. Marie: Central, Algonquin.** (SSM) 111 E. Spruce St., Sault Ste. Marie 49783 (906-632-8672), (A) 1604 W. 4th Ave., Sault Ste. Marie 49783 (906-632-8672). Home: 1513 Augusta, Sault Ste. Marie 49783 (906-632-3125)

*HAGAN, SUEANN K. (RL) (Lloyd) – (FL-2003, RL-2017)
Chase: Barton / Grant Center 10/16/2003; Battle Creek: Convis Union 2006; Retired 2017
sueannhagan@yahoo.com
5987 Heron Pond Dr, Port Orange FL 32128

*HAGANS, GERALD F (RE) (Susan) – (D-1983, FE-1986, R-2006)
Appointed in Other Annual Conferences (¶331.8, ¶346.1) Gordon/Pitsburg, West Ohio Conf 1981-1984; Muskegon: Central (Assoc) 1984; Constantine 1989; Muskegon Heights: Temple 08/01/1991; Retired 09/01/2006; Sitka (LTFT ¼) 11/15/2009-6/30/2019
francis1491@aol.com
(H) 1249 Lakeshore Dr #305, Muskegon 49441-1648 (231) 755-1767

*HAGANS, SUSAN J (RE) (Gerald) – (D-1986, FE-1989, R-2006)
Muskegon: Unity (LTFT) 1986; Muskegon: Unity 1987; Holland: First (Assoc) 11/15/1988; Muskegon: Lake Harbor 1995; UM Connectional Structures (¶344.1a,c) District Superintendent, Grand Rapids District 2000; Retired 2006; Wolf Lake (LTFT 45%) 09/07/2014-08/31/2017
susanj1491@aol.com
(H) 1249 Lakeshore Dr #305, Muskegon 49441-1648 (231) 750-0135

*HAGGARD, WILLIAM E (RE) (Robin) – (D-1980, FE-1984, R-2018)
Lake Ann 1982; Cedar Springs/East Nelson 1989; Traverse City Asbury 1995; Lansing: Mount Hope 2002; UM Connectional Structures (¶344.1a,c) District Superintendent, Grand Rapids District 2012; Retired 2018; Pentwater: Centenary 2018
billh5955@comcast.net
(H) 124 S Rutledge St, Pentwater 49449 (616) 430-9964
Pentwater: Centenary 82 S Hancock, PO Box 111, Pentwater 49449
(231) 869-5900

Hagley, Mary K. (Jeffrey) revmaryhagley@gmail.com
[(FD) PD 2011; FD 2016]. Plymouth: First (assoc). 2011 Transitional leave; **2013 Dixboro (Deacon; LTFT ½).** 5221 Church St., Ann Arbor 48105. Home: 2929 Brandywine Dr., Ann Arbor 48104 (734-652-5389)

Hahm, Paul Sungjoon (Jennifer)
[(FE) FL 2011; PE 2014; FE 2017]. 2011 Wayne: First; 2013 Brighton: First (assoc); 2015 Resident—Discipleship Ministries Urban Village Church, Chicago, Northern Illinois Conference; **2016 Lansing: Grace**

Paul.hahm@gmail.com
(H) 2915 S Cambridge Rd, Lansing 48911-1024 (517) 484-0227
Lansing Grace: 1900 Boston Blvd, Lansing 48910-2456 (517) 482-5750

HAHN, ANITA K (FE) (Kevin) – (D-1998, FE-2001)
Whitehall/Claybanks 1998; Lakeview: New Life 2006; UM Connectional Structures (¶344.1a,c) District Superintendent, Grand Traverse District 2011; UM Connectional Structures (¶344.1a,c) District Superintendent, Northern Waters District 01/01/2019; Midland: First 2019

glue4evr@yahoo.com
(H) 3217 Noeske St, Midland 48640-3348 (989) 708-8894
Midland: First: 315 W Larkin St, Midland 48640-5152 (989) 835-6797

HALE, GEORGIA N (FD) (Dwayne Glisson) – (PD-2012, FD-2017)
Transferred from Great Plains Conf 2015; Missional Appointment: Grand Rapids Genesis (Deacon) Serving Coordinator/Bridges Program (Unpaid Position) 2015

gnhale@sprintmail.com
(H) 272 S Ball Creek Rd, Kent City 49330-9452 (616) 678-7664
Grand Rapids Genesis: 3189 Snow Ave, Lowell 49331 (616) 974-0400

Hall, Amanda (Chris)   mandymmcneil@gmail.com
[(PD) PD 2015]. 2015 leave of absence (family leave); **2017 personal leave**. 2030 Chester Blvd, #241, Richmond 47374

Hall, Lindsey (Jon Reynolds)   lhall@fumcbirmingham.org
[(FE) FL 2013; PE 2014; FE 2017]. Apr 1, 2013 Birmingham: First (assoc); 2016 Birmingham: First (assoc) (LTFT ½); **2019 Birmingham: First (assoc)**. 1589 W. Maple, Birmingham 48009 (248-646-1200). Home: 130 Arlington, Birmingham 48009 (402-586-5106)

HALL, NELSON L (FL) – (PL-1999, FL-2018)
Baldwin/Luther (DSA) 1999; Baldwin/Luther 11/16/1999; Marcellus: Wakelee 2005; Augusta: Fellowship (PTLP ½) 2007; Gobles/Kendall 2013; Kalamazoo: Northwest (PTLP ¼) 2015; **Ontonagon, Greenland, Rockland: St. Paul 2018**.

nelsonlhall@gmail.com
(H) 1101 Pine, Ontonagon 49953 (906) 884-2789
Ontonagon: PO Box 216, 109 Greenland Rd., Ontonagon 49953-0216
(906) 884-4556
Greenland: 1002 Ridge Rd., Greenland 49953 (906-883-3141)
Rockland: St. Paul: 50 National Ave., PO Box 339, Rockland 49960
(906-886-2851)

*HALLER, GARY T (RE) (Laurie) – (D-1979, FE-1983, R-2017)
Traverse City: Central (Assoc)/Ogdensburg 1981; Traverse City: Central 01/01/2982; Pentwater: Centenary 1985; Grand Rapids: First (Co-Pastor) 1993; Appointed in Other Annual Conferences (¶331.8, ¶346.1) Detroit Conference, Birmingham First (Senior Pastor) 2013, Retired 2017

ghaller273@aol.com
(H) 4521 NW 167th St, Clive, IA 50325 (616) 308-7762

*Halsted, Alfred Theodore, Jr.   athalsted@aol.com
[(RE) T S.India, 1950; F 1956]. 1948 Gosport, IN; 1949 Missionary in S. India Conf.; 1952 school; 1954 Stamford Circuit, CT; 1956 Dixboro; 1960 Dexter; 1965 Hemlock, Nelson; 1970 Marlette; Nov 1, 1975 Lincoln Park: First; 1980 Redford; 1986 Marquette District Superintendent. **1992 Retired**. Home: 2030 Chester Blvd., #241, Richmond, IN 47374 (765-935-9956)

*Hamilton, John Norman (Linda)   johnhamiltonusaf@hotmail.com
[(RE) P 1978; F 1982]. 1980 Adrian: First (assoc.); Apr. 1981 Stephenson, Hermansville; 1986 Caseville; 1990 Blissfield: Emmanuel; 1995 Onaway, Millersburg Jun 16, 2001 Saulte Ste. Marie: Central; Algonquin; 2004 incapacity leave; 2014 medical leave; **2016 Retired**. 1580 Track Iron Dr., Gladwin 48624 (989-329-0382)

Hamlen, Geraldine Gayle   pastorimtrinity@gmail.com
[(FE) PE 2006; FE 2009]. 2006 Gwinn; **2014 Iron Mountain: Trinity**. 808 Carpenter Ave., Iron Mountain, 49801 (906-774-2545). Home: 421 Woodward, Kingsford 49802 (906-774-0064)

*HAMLIN, FREDERICK G (RE) – (D-1982, FE-1987, R-1994)
Benton Harbor: Grace 1978-1982; Watervliet 11/20/1984; Byron Center 1985; Camden/Montgomery/Stokes Chapel 1987; Retired 1994; Saugatuck 1996-1998
                                                    fredandjoan@frontier.com
                        (H) PO Box 458, Douglas 49406-0458 (269) 543-4790

*Hammar, Eric S.
[(RE) T 1952; F 1955]. 1953 Stephenson; 1957 White Pine; 1958 Ishpeming: Wesley; 1967 Farmington: Orchard; 1977 Saginaw Bay District Superintendent; 1983 Northville; **1991 Retired**. Home: 6356 Richalle, Brighton 48116 (810-229-3367)

*HANE, PAUL E (RL) (Julie Spurlin-Hane) – (FL-2003, RL-2018)
North Adams/Jerome (DSA) 2002; North Adams/Jerome 06/01/2003; Hesperia/Ferry 2011; Retired 2018; Hesperia/Ferry (LTFT ½)
                                                    haulpane@yahoo.com
                    (H) 231 E South Ave, Hesperia 49421-9105 (231) 854-6132
                Hesperia: 187 E South Ave, Hesperia 49421-9273 (231) 854-5345
                    Ferry: 2215 Main St, Shelby 49455-8220 (231) 854-5345

*HANEY, CLAUDETTE I KERNS (RE) – (D-1991, FE-1993, R-2005)
Harbor Springs/Alanson 1990; Homer/Lyon Lake 04/16/1993; Lawton/Almena 1995; Lawton 1996; Cassopolis 2000; Retired 2005
                                                    haney1@cox.net
                    (H) 51 Las Yucas, Green Valley, AZ 85614 (520) 829-6002

*HANLON, JOYCE (RD) (Charles) – (Consecrated-1992, D-1997, RD-2001)
Deacons Appointed Beyond the Local Church(¶331.1a) Psychotherapist, Psychology Assoc of GR 1992; Deacons Appointed w/in UM Connectional Structure (¶331.1b) GR Reflections Counseling & Consultant Services 1995; Retired 2001
                                                    cjlon@att.net
                        (H) 7797 Teakwood, Jenison 49428-7716 (616) 457-2901

*HANSEN, RANDALL R (RE) (Susan) – (FE-1982, R-2014)
Albion: First (Assoc) 1983-1985; Fennville/Pearl 07/16/1992; Transferred from Uruguay Evangelical Methodist Conf 1993; Fennville: Pearl 07/16/1992; Fennville/Pearl 1993; Muskegon: Central 2000; Montague 08/16/2009; Medical Leave 2014; Retired 10/20/2014

rshansen50@hotmail.com
(H) 1319 Chicago Ave Unit #301, Evanston, IL 60201 (847) 868-8029

*HANSEN, RONALD W (RE) (Jan) – (D-1977, FE-1980, R-2011)
Fennville/Pearl 1978; Ovid United 02/01/1984; Leave of Absence 1993; Hartford 1999; Retired 2011; Kalamazoo: Northwest (LTFT ¼) 2012-2013; Portage First (Pathfinder) (LTFT ¾) 2015-2016

revronhansen@gmail.com
(H) 7615 Andrea Lane, Portage 49024-4901 (269) 208-5410

*Hanson, Alan J. (Judy)   drajhanson@sbcglobal.net [6/10/08]
[(RE) P 1970; F 1973]. 1972 Marquette: First (assoc.); 1973 Morenci; 1981 school; 1984 Associate Staff Counselor, Fayetteville Family Life Center, North Carolina Baptist Hospital; 1985 school; Aug, 1986 Executive Director, Samaritan Counseling Center, Toledo, OH; Sep 1, 2001 Macon; 2002 Bloomfield Hills: St. Paul; 2007 Wyandotte: First; **2013 Retired**. 802 Bailey Dr., Papillion, NE 68046 (419-377-6406)

HANSSON, EMILY K [SLAVICEK] (FE) – (FL-2010, PE-2012, FE-2016)
Girard 09/01/2010; Centreville 2014; Medical Leave 01/01/2019

pastor.emilysb@gmail.com
(H) 705 E Osterhout Ave, Portage 49032 (269) 743-7487

Harbin, Kevin J. (Ellen)   keharbin@juno.com
[(FE) P 1996; FE 1999]. 1996 school (Asbury); Jan 1, 1997 Fairgrove, Gilford; 1999 St. Charles, Brant; 2002 Imlay City; 2011 Swartz Creek; **2015 Fraser: Christ**. 34385 Garfield, Fraser 48026 (586-293-5340). Home: 34355 Garfield, Fraser 48026 (586-293-4194)

Harmon, Scott A. (Bron)   sharmon@michiganumc.org
[(FE) P 1996; FE 1998]. 1996 Iron Mountain: Trinity (assoc) (LTFT ¼); Quinnesec: First; 1998 Negaunee: Mitchell; 2002 Birmingham: First (assoc); 2003 Escanaba: Central; 2013 Frankenmuth; **2017 Marquette District Superintendent; Jan 1, 2019 Northern Skies District Superintendent**. 927 W. Fair Avenue, Marquette 49855 (906-228-4644). Home: 2916 Parkview, Marquette 49855 (906-228-2976)

*Harnish, John E. (Judy)   jackharnish1@gmail.com
[(RE) P W. PA, 1970; F 1973]. 1974 Trans. to Detroit Conf., Washington, Davis; Dec. 1979 Dexter; 1990 Flint: Court Street; Jul 1, 1993 General Board of Higher Education; 2000 Ann Arbor: First; 2005 Birmingham: First; **2013 Retired**. 7341 Deadstream Rd., Honor 49640 (231-325-2948)

HARPOLE, JASON E (PL) (Sharla) – (PL-2014)
Breedsville (PTLP ¼) 2014; Oshtemo: Lifespring (LTFT ¼) 2016

PastorJHarpole@gmail.com
(H) 205 Amos Ave, Portage 49002-0415 (269) 388-8312
Oshtemo: Lifespring: 1560 S 8th St, Kalamazoo 49009-9327 (269) 353-1303

*HARPOLE, PATRICIA A (RA) (Everett) – (FL-1993, NL-1994, AM-2002, RA-2017)
Brandywine Trinity 1993; LP w/o Appointment 04/17/1994; Transferred to Ohio Conf 01/01/1999; Transferred from Ohio Conf 05/01/2002; Townline/Breedsville 11/01/2002; Dowling: Country Chapel 2004; Oshtemo: Lifespring 2009; Indian River 2014; Retired 2017

patti.harpole@gmail.com
(H) 2461 Bay Pointe, St Joseph 49085 (269) 806-2814

Harriman, Mark A. (Karen) time691@hotmail.com
[(FL) PL Dec 1. 2014; FL 2018]. Dec 1, 2014 Bethel (Worth Twp.); 2016 Bethel (Worth Twp.), Port Sanilac, Forester; **2018 Kingston**. PO Box 196, Kinston 48741 (989-683-2832). Home: 3442 Washington St, Kingston 48741 (989-683-2929)

*HARRINGTON, SALLY K (OR) – (OR-2012)
[South German Methodist Conf, RE] Galesburg (LTFT ½) 11/1/2010-2012; Sonoma/Newton (LTFT ½) 2012-2014; Newton 2014-03/31/2016

RevSallyH@gmail.com
(H) 32 Spaulding Ave W, Battle Creek 49037-1846 (269) 548-7803

*Harris, Carolyn G. (Daniel) grannyharris@yahoo.com
[(RL) PL 1995; RL 2013]. Jun 1, 1995 Monroe: East Raisinville Frenchtown (co-pastor). 1998 Salem Grove (co-pastor); 2003 Salem Grove; **2013 Retired**. Home: 5229 W. Michigan Ave. #198, Ypsilanti 48197 (734-528-9657)

*Harris, Daniel Wayne (Carolyn) papaw@peoplepc.com
[(RL) PL 1987]. 1987 Monroe: East Raisinville Jun 1, 1995 Monroe: East Raisinville Frenchtown (co-pastor). 1998 Salem Grove (co-pastor); **2003 Retired**. Home: 5229 W. Michigan Ave., #198, Ypsilanti 48197 (734-528-9657)

*Harris, Duane Marshall (Lynn) dmh8181@gmail.com
[(RE) P 1984; F 1988; R 2018]. 1986 Sutton, Sunshine; Nov. 1, 1988 Midland: First (assoc.); 1997 Essexville; 2005 Owosso: First; 2009 Auburn; **2018 Retired**. Home: 213 Meadow Ln, Midland 48640 (989-600-9150)

*Harris, Hilda L. divabish831@gmail.com
[(RE) SP 1992; P 1994; F 1996]. 1992 River Rouge: John Wesley; 1993 Detroit: St. Timothy's; 1995 Southfield: Hope (assoc); 1997 Detroit: Calvary; **Sep 1, 2004 Retired**. Home: 12654 Santa Rosa, Detroit 48238 (313-933-3342)

Harris, Peter Scouton (Jan) revpharris@aol.com
[(FE) P 1982; F 1987]. 1984 Owosso: First (assoc.); 1986 Flint: Eastwood; 1989 Lincoln Park: Dix; 1996 Stony Creek; **2007 Manchester: Sharon**. Box 543, 19980 Pleasant Lake Rd., Manchester 48158 (734-428-0996). Home: 16181 Wellwood Ct., Tipton 49287 (517-431-3908)

*Hart, Caroline F. (James) revchart@me.com
[(RE) PE 1999; FE 2002; RE 2018]. 1999 Warren: First (assoc); 2008 Coleman: Faith; **2015** Gladstone: Memorial; **2018 Retired**. Home: 3542 Madison Ave, Orion Twp 48359 (586-899-6421)

Hart, Daniel Joseph Charnley "JC" (Autumn)   daniel.hart@garrett.edu
[(FE) PE 2012; FE 2015]. 2012 Grosse Pointe (assoc.); Apr 1, 2016 Birmingham: First (assoc); **2019 Mt. Clemens: First**. 57 SB Gratiot Ave, Mt Clemens 48043-5545 (586-468-6464). Home: 110 Belleview St., Mt. Clemens 48043-2240 (586-863-3646)

*Hart, Pauline Sue (Thomas)   Harts1mi@sbcglobal.net
[(RE) P 1983; F 1986]. 1984 Detroit: Waterman-Preston; 1989 Bloomfield Hills: St. Paul; 1995 South Lyon: First (co-pastor); 2002 disability leave; **2008 Retired**. Home: 302 Wellington Dr. South Lyon 48178 (248-437-1608)

*Hart, Thomas Everett (Pauline)   Harts1mi@sbcglobal.net
[(RE) T Balt Conf., 1967; F 1970]. Nov. 1970 Trans. to Detroit Conf., Livingston Circuit: Plainfield, Trinity; 1975 Vernon, Bancroft; Sep. 1980 Manchester; 1984 West Bloomfield; 1991 Detroit: St. Timothy's; 1995 South Lyon: First (Co-pastor); **Sep 1, 2002 Retired**. Home: 302 Wellington Dr. South Lyon 48178 (248-437-1608)

Hart, Wilson Andrew (F. Caroline)   revdrewhart@gmail.com
[(FE) PE 1992; FE 1995; HL 2009; FE 2014]. 1993 Lake Orion (assoc); May 1, 1996 Mackinaw City: Church of the Straits; 2001 Millington; 2006 leave of absence; 2009 Honorable Location; **2014 Adrian: First**.1245 W. Maple, Adrian 49221 (517-265-5689). Home: 4580 Clubview Dr., Adrian 49221 (734-904-9775)

Hartley, Sr., Thomas C.
[(OF) DSA 2018, Presbyterian Church USA, OF 20196]. Davisburg (DSA) (LTFT ¼); **2019 Davisburg**. 803 Broadway, Davisburg 48350-2452 (248-634-3373). Home: 711 Oxhill Dr, White Lake 48386 (248-698-4502)

*Harton, Patricia A. (Bruce)   pbharton@comcast.net
[(RL) PL Feb 1, 2006]. Feb 1, 2006 Mt. Bethel; **2010 Retired**. Home: 10415 Lee Ann Ct., Brighton 48114 (810-588-6303)

*Harvey, Robert Dale (Ruth Ann)
[(RE) SP 1990; P 1993; F 1996]. 1990 Caring Covenant Group Ministry: Richfield, Otter Lake; Jul 1, 1994 Bay City: Fremont Avenue; **1999 Retired**. Home: 12 Sovey Court, Essexville 48732 (989-891-9335)

*Hasley, Lynn Marie (Gary)   lynnhasley@gmail.com
[(RE) PE 2004; FE 2008]. 2004 Birmingham: First (assoc); Oct 1, 2008 Eastpointe: Immanuel. Jan 9, 2012 Sabbatical leave; Jan 1, 2013 Farmington: Orchard (assoc); 2013 Franklin: Community; **2016 Retired**. Home: 6690 West Ridge Drive., Brighton 48116 (248-227-6119)

Hasse, Doug   dshasse@aol.com
[(PL) Pl Jan 1, 2019]. Sept 1, 2017 Wagarville: Community (DSA); **Jan 1, 2019 Gladwin: Wagarville Community** (LTFT ¼). 2478 Wagarville Rd, Gladwin 48624-9762 (989-426-2971). Home: 5943 Weiss St, # 58, Saginaw 48603-2720 (989-598-0716)

*Hastings, Robert Curtis (Phyllis)   Hastybob@concentric.net
[(RE) T 1965; F 1967]. 1965 Grosse Pointe (assoc.); 1967 Flint: Graham, Dimond; 1968 Highland Park: St. Paul's; 1970 Centerline; Apr. 1975 Essexville: St. Luke's; 1980 Saginaw: Kochville; 1983 Hazel Park; Aug. 1, 1987 Sabbatical Leave; Aug. 1, 1988 Dearborn Heights: Stephens; 1994 Saginaw: Jefferson Avenue; **2004 Retired**. Home: 1441 Cedar St, Saginaw 48601-2659 (989-777-2365)

*Hastings, Timothy Stewart (Deborah)   Thastings@stmarysonfmichigan.org
[(RE) P 1980; F 1982]. 1980 Saginaw: First (assoc.); 1983 Manistique; 1986 Pigeon: Salem; 1990 Saginaw: Ames (assoc.). Sep 1, 1993 leave of absence; Sep 1, 1994 school; 1996 Chaplain: St. Luke's Hospital (Saginaw); Dec 1, 1997 La-Porte, Mapleton; Sep 1, 2000 LaPorte, Mapleton (LTFT ¾) Dec 1, 2003 Mapleton; 2004 Chaplain, St. Mary's of Michigan, Saginaw; **2012 Retired**. Home: 1908 Stark St., Saginaw 48602 (989-752-7898)

*HAUSERMANN, CARL L (RE) (Marcia) – (D-1964, FE-1967, R-2001)
Galien 1964; Grand Rapids: First (Assoc) 1967; Coloma/Riverside 1971; Ionia: First 1977; Jackson Calvary 1983; Portage: Chapel Hill 1989; Retired 2001
clhauser@charter.net
(H) 1551 Franklin Street SE, Apt 2814, Grand Rapids 49506

*Hawkins, Ronda L.   revonda@beesky.com
[(RE) P 1995; F 1997]. 1995 Hardy; Jun 1, 2000 incapacity leave; **2014 Retired**. 1223 Mountain Ash Dr., Brighton (810-220-5854)

*Hawley, Wayne Alton (Pamela)   whawley@austin.rr.com
[(RE) P 1977; F 1979 (E. PA. Conf)]. 1983 Trans. to Detroit Conf. from E. PA, Harbor Beach, Port Hope; 1991 North Lake; 2001 Ida, Samaria: Grace; **2007 Retired**. 401 N. Hill St, Bernet, TX 78611 (830-637-9132)

*HAYES, GEOFFREY L (RE) (Pamela) – (D-1970, FE-1974, R-2009)
Grand Rapids: First (Assoc) 1973; Lansing: Asbury 1978; Stevensville 1987; Surrender of Credentials 03/23/2004; Re-admitted 1998; Grand Rapids: Faith 1998; Retired 2009

geoffhayes@att.net
(H) 112 Woodruff Ct, Cary, NC 27518 (919) 233-6950

*HAYES, STANLEY L (RE) (Joyce) – (D-1963, FE-1965, R-1999)
Leaton 1959; Grand Traverse Larger Parish 1964; Kingsley Circuit 1965; East Jordan 10/15/1966; Cedar Springs 1970; Cedar Springs/East Nelson 1972; Evart/ Avondale 10/15/1975; Fennville/Pearl 04/01/1984; Breckenridge 1990; Grass Lake 1994; Retired 1999; Kalkaska 10/01/1999; Old Mission Peninsula (Ogdensburg) 2002

sjhayes239@charter.net
(H) PO Box 67, 316 N Main St, Fife Lake 49633-0067 (231) 879-3884

*Haynes, Gloria   glorev0070@gmail.com
[(RE) P 1990; F 1993]. 1991 Port Sanilac, Forester, McGregor; 1996 Brown City: First, Immanuel; Jan 1, 1997 Brown City; Oct 1, 1998 South Central Cooperative Ministry: Lake Fenton (parish director); 2002 Thomas, Lakeville; 2005 Lapeer: Trinity (assoc.); 2009 Pigeon: Salem; 2012 Riverview; Feb 15, 2014 Riverview (LTFT ¾), Melvindale: New Hope (LTFT ¼); **2015 Retired; 2018 Arbela** (LTFT ¼). 8496 Barnes Rd, PO Box 252, Millington 48746-0252 (989-793-5880). Home: 2152 Village West Dr., S, Lapeer 48466

*HAYNES, LEONARD B (RE) (Birute) – (D-1970, FE-1973, R-1998)
Riverside 1970; Kingscreek 1972; Appointed to Extension Ministries (¶344.1b,c)
Pine Rest Christian Hospital 1975; Appointed to Extension Ministries (¶344.1b,c)
Bethesda Hospital 1976; Transferred from West Ohio Conf 1979; Appointed to
Extension Ministries (¶344.1b,c) Chaplain, Director of Pastoral Care, Bronson
Methodist Hospital 1979; Leave of Absence 03/24/1983-06/15/1983; Hinchman/
Oronoko 1983; Shepherd/Pleasant Valley 1986; Calvary Lansing 1992; Leave
of Absence 03/01/1998; Retired 1998

Truckermanlen@comcast.net
(H) 13630 W Meath Dr, Homer Glen, IL 60491-9137 (708) 828-7653

HAZLE, JUDITH A (PL) (Stuart) – (LM-2009, PL-2012)
Shepardsville (CLM ¼ Time) 08/01/2009; Shepardsville (PTLP ¼) 11/10/2012
pastorjudy777@gmail.com
(H) 1795 W Centerline Rd, St Johns 48879-9275 (989) 640-1436
Shepardsville: 6990 Winfield Rd, Ovid 48866-8607 (989) 834-5104

*HEATON, LYLE D (RE) (Sylvia) – (D-1978, FE-1982, R-2016)
Barryton 1979; Barryton/Chippewa Lake 1980; Middleton/Maple Rapids 1984;
Delta Mills 1990; Wacousta Community 01/01/1999; Lansing: Christ 2013; Mul-
liken/Sunfield 01/01/2016; Retired 2016

lyledheaton@gmail.com
(H) 4747 W Stoll Rd, Lansing 48906-9384 (517) 580-5058

*HEFFELFINGER, CONSTANCE L (Randy Wedeven) – [(RE) D-1976, FE-1980,
R-2016] Transferred from East Ohio Conf 1977; Fremont (Assoc) 1978; Barry
County: Woodland/Hastings: Welcome Corners 1981; Saugatuck/Ganges 1984;
Saugatuck (LTFT ½) 01/01/1990; Medical Leave 09/01/1995; Retired 2016
constance.heffelfinger@gmail.com
(H) 199 W 20th St, Holland 49423-4180 (616) 393-0919

*HEIFNER, KEITH W (Becky) – [(RE) D-1971, FE-1973, R-2006] Maplewood 1977;
Transferred from Missouri East Conf 1980; Appointed to Extension Ministries
(¶344.1b,c) Counselor, Samaritan Counseling Center Ad Interim 1980; Appointed
to Extension Ministries (¶344.1b,c) Pastoral Counselor, Samaritan Counseling
Center, Battle Creek 1981; Appointed to Extension Ministries (¶344.1b,c) Director, Samaritan Center of South Central MI, Battle Creek 1986; Appointed to Extension Ministries (¶344.1b,c) Pastoral Counselor, Battle Creek Pastoral
Counseling 01/01/1990; Big Rapids: First 1993; Marshall 1996; Parma/North
Parma 1999; Galesburg 2003; Retired 2006

Heifskb@yahoo.com
(H) 4985 Sandra Bay Dr Apt 101, Naples, FL 34109-2686 (239) 287-0828
(S) 3164 Brimstead Dr, Franklin, TN 37064-6224

HEISLER, BENTON R (Linda) – [(FE) D-1985, FE-1988]
St Joseph First (Assoc) 1986; Charlevoix/Greensky Hill 08/16/1988; Lansing:
Asbury 11/16/1992; Mt Pleasant: First 1997; District Superintendent, Lansing
District 2002; Director of Connectional Ministries, West MI Conf 01/01/2009 and
Detroit Conf. 02/01/2018; Director of Connectional Ministries, Michigan Confer-
ence 01/01/2019

bheisler@michiganumc.org
(H) 11670 Hidden Spring Trl, Dewitt 48820
(O) 1011 Northcrest Rd, Lansing 48906 (517) 347-4030 ext. 4070

HELLER, VIRGINIA L (FE) – (D-1996, FE-1999)
Muskegon: Central (Assoc) 1996; Keeler/Silver Creek 1998; Battle Creek Baseline/Bellevue 2004; Portage: Chapel Hill (Assoc) 2011; Leland 2013; South Haven: First 2014; Grand Rapids: St. Paul's 2018

pastorgini54@yahoo.com
(H) 3509 Bromley SE, Kentwood 49512 (269) 274-9416
GR: St Paul's: 3334 Breton Rd SE, Grand Rapids 49512-2710 (616) 949-0880

HENDERSON, JOSHUA (OF) (Emily) – (OF-2016)
NE Missaukee Parish: Merritt-Butterfield (LTFT ½) and Moorestown-Stittsville (LTFT ½) 09/01/2016; NE Missaukee Parish: Merritt-Butterfield and Moorestown-Stittsville 01/01/2017-07/31/2019

*Henning, Robert James (Barbara)
[(RE) P 1985; F 1988]. 1985 Trans. to Detroit Conf. from Free Methodist Church, New Lothrop, Juddville; Jul. 2, 1990 Assistant Coordinator of Prison Education Program and Assistant Professor of Interdisciplinary Studies, Spring Arbor College; 1996 Stockbridge (W MI Conference); 2007 Ludington: St. Paul (W MI conference) (para 337.1); **2011 Retired**. 140 Morgan St., Oberlin, OH.

*Henry, John R. (Robin)   outreach@up.net
[(RE) P W. OH, 1973; F 1976]. 1975 Trans. to Detroit Conf., Stephenson, Hermansville; Mar. 1981 L'Anse, Sidnaw, Zeba; 1986 Canton: Cherry Hill; 1988 Alaska Missionary Conference, Fairbanks, AK: St. Paul's; 1989 Pastor-Missionary, East Anchorage UMC; 1997 North Star UMC; 2004 L'Anse, Sidnaw, Zeba; **2011 Retired**.14876 State Hwy. M-38 Pelkie 49958 (906-338-2430)

*Hepner, Theodore Warren   BaronTed@aol.com
[(RE) P 1962; F 1965]. 1965 Detroit: Trinity; 1968 Chaplain, Army, US Army Garrison, Fort Riley, Kansas; 1969 Chaplain, Vicenze, Italy; 1973 H.Q. John F. Kennedy Center for Military Assistance, Fort Bragg, NC; 1974 HW 7th Special Forces Group (ABN), Fort Bragg, NC; 1975 US Army Chaplain (Colonel) 82D Airborne Division, Fort Bragg, NC; Aug. 1987 Stuttgart, Germany, Greater Stuttgart Military Command; 1990 Office of the Command Chaplain. 1992 Director of Endorsement & Administration, 1996 Section of Chaplains & Related Ministries; **2002 Retired**. Home: 1015 Wyndham Hill Lane, Franklin, TN 37064 (615-791-5887)

Herald, Scott
[(FL) FL 2017]. **2016 Fowlerville: First**. 201 S. Second, Box 344, Fowlerville 48836 (517-223-8824). Home: 18521 Daymon Dr., Gregory 48137 (734-545-2276)

Herm, Trevor Allen (Carol)   tcherm@comcast.net
[(FE) P 1984; F 1988]. Jan. 1, 1986 Port Huron: First (assoc.); 1989 Yale, Greenwood; 1994 Burton: Christ; 2004 Richmond: First; 2010 Cheboygan: St Paul's; **2017 Romeo**. 280 North Main St., Romeo 48065 (586-752-9132). Home: 289 North Bailey St., Romeo 48065 (810-275-3277)

Herman, Marvin L.   Hmarvherman@aol.com
[(FL) PL 2007; FL 2018]. Oct 1, 2007 Flint: Bristol (LTFT ½); **2018 Howarth, Paint Creek**. (H) 550 E. Silverbell Rd., Lake Orion 48360 (248-373-2360), (PC) 4420 Collins Rd., Rochester 48306 (248-652-1583). Home: 137 Stratford Ln, Lake Orion 48362

HERRELL, DEVON R (FE) – (PE-2005, FE-2008)
Traverse Bay (Assoc) 2005; Lake Ann 06/15/2008; South Haven: First 2013; UM Connectional Structures (¶344.1a,c) Director, Wesley Foundation, Ferris State University 2014; UM Connectional Structures (¶344.1a,c) Director, Wesley Foundation, Ferris State University (LTFT ½) 2014 and Big Rapids: Third Ave/ Paris/Rodney (LTFT ½) 2017; Big Rapids: First 2019

devonherrell@gmail.com
(H) 14080 Wildwood Dr, Big Rapids 49307-8782 (231) 649-2302
Big Rapids: First: 304 Elm St, Big Rapids 49307-1814 (231) 796-7771

*HERTEL, WILLIAM A (RE) (Janet) – (D-1963, FE-1966, R-2001)
Allen 1961; Niles (Assoc) 1964; White Cloud/East Denver 1966; White Cloud 1968; Grand Rapids: Saint Paul's 1969; Lake Odessa: Central 1974; Traverse City: Asbury 09/16/1980; Lansing: Asbury 1987; Delton: Faith 1990; Retired 2001

wjhertel@gmail.com
(H) 2531 Vista Point Ct NW, Grand Rapids 49534-2627 (931) 260-7697

Heystek, Travis (OF) (Hannah) – (OF-2018)
Harrietta 2018; Cadillac (Assoc.) 2018

travis.heystek@gmail.com
(H) 210 Blodgett St, Cadillac 49601-2004 (540) 819-5712
Harrietta: 116 N Davis St, PO Box 13, Harrietta 49638-0013 (231) 389-0267
Cadillac: 1020 E Division St, PO Box 37, Cadillac 49601-0037 (231) 775-5362

Hice, John H. (Laura) jhice@michiganumc.org
[(FE) P 1976; F W MI 1980)]. 1977 Kalamazoo: Millwood (assoc); 1978 trans. to W. MI. conf.; 1979 Hartford; 1987 Traverse City: Asbury; 1995 Grand Rapids District Superintendent; 2000 transf to Detroit Conf., Northville: First; 2008 Royal Oak: First; **2016 Crossroads District Superintendent; Jan 1, 2019 East Winds District Superintendent**. 624 W Nepessing, Ste 201, Lapeer 48446 (810-396-1362). Home: 5420 Misty Creek Court, Flint 48532 (810-820-9545)

*Hickey, Timothy Roy (Betty Lou) timandbettylou@gmail.com
[(RE) T 1960; F 1962]. 1960 Sandhill Circuit, Jackson Springs, NC; 1962 Saginaw: Jefferson Avenue; 1964 school; 1965 Ypsilanti: First (assoc.); 1967 Waterford: Trinity; 1969 Birmingham: Embury; 1973 Rochester: St. Paul's; **Oct 1, 2000 Retired**. Home: Hammock Dunes, 15 Avenue de la Mer, #2505, Palm Coast, FL 32137 (386-447-1319)

*Hicks, Duane James (Susan)
[(RE) P 1975; F 1980]. 1978 Rochester: St. Paul's (assoc.); 1981 Detroit: St. Andrew's; Jan. 1, 1982 Centerline: Bethel; 1986 Detroit: Rice Memorial; 1990 school, Walden University, Minneapolis, MN; 1991 Insight Recovery Center; 1995 Mental Health/Substance Abuse Therapist, Genesee Regional Medical Center; **1997 Retired**. Home: 8201 Sawgrass Trail, Grand Blanc 48439 (810-695-2729)

Hierholzer, Susanne E. (Craig) susiethepastor@yahoo.com
[(FE) PE 2013; FE 2016]. 2013 St. Ignace; **2019 Birmingham: First (assoc.)**. 1589 W Maple Rd, Birmingham 48009-4607 (248-646-1200). Home: 361 Pleasant St, Birmingham 48009-4435

*Higgins, Howard (Elouise)
[(RE)] **Retired**. Home: 107 Cedar Park Dr, Linn, MO 65051

Hill, Elizabeth A. (Richard)   ehill@michiganumc.org
[(FE) PE 2006; FE 2009]. 2006 Birmingham: Embury, Royal Oak: St. John's 2010 Gladstone: Memorial; 2015 Blue Water District Superintendent; **2018 Ann Arbor District Superintendent; Jan 1, 2019 Heritage District Superintendent**. 900 S 7th, Ste 1, Ann Arbor 48103 (734-663-3939). Home: 2935 Atterberry, Ann Arbor 48103

HILLS, DAVID F (FE) (Claire) – (D-1992, FE-1994)
Big Rapids: Third Avenue/Paris/ Rodney 1992; Climax/Scotts 1994; Coloma/ Watervliet 08/01/1999; Delton: Faith 2007; UM Connectional Structures (¶344.1a,c) District Superintendent, Heartland District 2010; Stevensville 08/01/2015

dfhills@gmail.com
(H) 1418 Lake Blvd #1, St. Joseph 49085-1691 (989) 330-3730
Stevensville: 5506 Ridge Rd, Stevensville 49127-1025 (269) 429-5911

*Hiner, Catherine Wanita Jean   umcrev@yahoo.com
[(RA) PL 1991; FL 1994; Deacon, AM 1998]. 1991 Ubly; 1993 Memphis: First, Lamb; 1999 Eastern Thumb Cooperative Parish, Port Sanilac, Deckerville, (Parish Director); 2004 Jeddo, Buel; **2009 Retired**. Home: 870 Marseilles, Upper Sandusky, OH 43351(419-429-9909)

*Hinkle, John W. (Ginger)   jwhinkle@aol.com
[(RE) T W. OH, 1959; F W. OH, 1962]. 1958 Donnelsville, Pitchin Charge; 1960 Springfield: Northridge; 1962 West Unity; 1967 Norwood: First; 1972 Toledo: St. Paul's; 1977 Leave of Absence; 1978 Trans. to Detroit Conf., Detroit: St. Timothy's (assoc.); 1981 Flat Rock: First; 1989 Saginaw: Ames; 1994 Saline: First; **1999 Retired**. Home: 1302 Catalani Lane, The Villages, Lady Lake, FL 32162 (352-750-0001)

*HINKLIN, ROBERT L (RE) (Christine) – (D-1963, FE-1966, R-2001)
Jasper (EUB) 1966; Jasper/Weston 1968; Napoleon 1969; Grand Rapids Plainfield/Epworth 1972; Georgetown 02/01/1976; Lansing: Mount Hope 1984; Portage: First 03/01/1987; Grandville 1998; Retired 2001; Fennville/Pearl 2002
rhinklin@aol.com
(H) 20131 Balleylee Ct, Estero, FL 33928 (239) 719-0029

HITTS, RANDALL J (PL) (Susan) – (DSA-2016, CC-2017, PL-2017)
Harbor Springs/Alanson (DSA Co-Pastor) 2016; Charlevoix (PTLP ½ Time) 2017
rjhitts@aol.com
(H) 1206 State St, Charlevoix 49720-1625 (231) 622-3565
Charlevoix: 104 State St, Charlevoix 49720-1343 (231) 547-2654

Hintz, Christopher P. (Kristine)   chintz@mqthope.com
[(FE) PE 1997, FE 2000 (W. OH.). Trans to Detroit Conference 2016]. 2014 Marquette: Grace, Skandia; **2016 Marquette: Hope**. 111 E. Ridge, Marquette 49855 (906-225-1344). Home: 619 Mesnard, Marquette 49855 (906-226-3683)

Hintz, Kristine Kim (Christopher)   khintz@mqthope.com
[(FE) P 1994; FE 1997; HL 2011; FE 2014]. 1995 Brighton: First (assoc.); 2000 family leave; 2003 Milan: Marble Memorial; Oct 1, 2007 leave of absence; 2011 Honorable Location; 2014 Marquette: First; **2016 Marquette: Hope**. 111 E. Ridge, Marquette 49855 (906-225-1344). Home: 619 Mesnard, Marquette 49855 (906-226-3683)

HITTS, SUSAN E (FL) (Randall) – (DSA-2016, CC-2017, FL-2017)
Harbor Springs/Alanson (DSA Co-Pastor) 2016; Harbor Springs/Alanson 2017
missburtlake@aol.com
(H) 1881 Ellinger Rd, Alanson 49706 (231) 548-5774
Harbor Springs: 343 E Main St, Harbor Springs 49740-1513 (231) 526-2414
Alanson: 7330 Chicago St, Alanson 49706-9231 (231) 548-5709

HODGE, JAMES E (FE) (Kathleen) – (D-1984, FE-1986)
Somerset Center/Moscow Plains 1984; Bangor: Simpson 1989; Bangor: Simpson/ Breedsville 1990; Shelby 1994; Grandville (Assoc) 2001; Caledonia 2005; Voluntary Leave Of Absence 2012; Grand Rapids: Aldersgate 2013
contemporaryjim@gmail.com
(H) 5160 Windcrest Ct SW, Wyoming 49418-9738 (616) 308-9925
GR Aldersgate: 4301 Ambrose Ave NE, Grand Rapids 49525-6122
(616) 363-3446

*HODGE, LAWRENCE E (RE) (Ruth) – (D-1965, FE-1966, R-2000)
Bloomingdale/Townline 1960; Keeler 1963; Elk Lake Parish 1966; Muskegon: Central (Assoc) 11/01/1968; Battle Creek: Birchwood 1971; Muskegon: Crestwood 1980; Hillside 1983; Ionia: First 1991; Retired 2000
(H) 9947 Huntington Rd, Battle Creek 49017-9750 (269) 969-9483

*Hodges, Jacque (Clifford) nomadgm@aol.com
[(RL) PL Dec. 2012]. Dec 1, 2011 Port Huron: New Beginnings; 2014 Mt. Vernon; Lakeville; **2017 Retired**. Home: 3494 Serenade Cmns NW, Kennesaw, GA 30152 (586-786-4909)

Hodgeson, Richard
[(FL) FL Nov 21, 2013]. Nov 21, 2013 Saginaw: Kochville; Mapleton; 2017 Scottville
richard.hodgeson@aol.com
(H) 301 W Maple Ave, Scottville 49454-1327 (231) 757-4781
Scottville: 114 W State St, Scottville 49454-1136 (231) 757-3567

*HOEKWATER, HARRIS J (RE) (Jane) – (FD-1980, FE-1985, R-2018)
Perry/Shaftsburg 1983; Sunfield 01/15/1992; Concord 1998; Pentwater: Centenary 2006; St Joseph: First 2012; Retired 2018
hoekster73@yahoo.com
(H) 2515 Tower Rd, Vanderbilt 49795 (269) 932-5390

Hoffmeyer, Thomas Leo
[(OE) OE Indian Conf Apr 1, 2019]. Apr 1, 2019 Roscommon: Good Shepherd of the North. 149 W Robinson Lake Rd, Roscommon 48653 (989-275-5577). Home: 303 Rising Fawn, Roscommon 48653 (989-821-6056)

HOFMANN, DANIEL B (FE) (Mary) – (D-1993, FE-1996)
Appointed in Other Annual Conferences (¶426.1) Ithaca, Arcanum, OH, West Ohio Conf (LTFT ¾) 1993; Ravenna 1994; Delton: Faith 2001; Eaton Rapids: First 2007; Leland 2014
rotsap@lelandcumc.com
(H) PO Box 1134, 4840 Golfview, Leland 49654-1134 (231) 994-2159
Leland: PO Box 602, 106 N 4th St, Leland 49654-0602 (231) 256-9161

*Holdsworth, Jacqueline Elaine   jackieholdsworth@gmail.com
[(RE) P 1981; F 1983]. 1981 Port Huron: First (assoc.); 1983 Allen Park: Trinity; 1991 Ann Arbor: West Side (assoc.)/Dexter (assoc.); Sep 1, 1992 Ann Arbor: West Side (assoc); 1995 Monroe: St. Paul's (co-pastor) 2003 Monroe: St. Paul's; 2004 Novi; Mar 1, 2007 incapacity leave; **May 1, 2011 Retired**. Home: 16631 29 Mile Rd., Albion 49224 (517-629-5088)

Hollander, Andrew Benjamin (PL) – (DSA-2017, PL-12/01/2017)
Amble 2017 (DSA) (PT); Amble (LTFT 45%) 12/01/2017; Amble (LTFT ¾) 2018
                                          andyhollander122@yahoo.com
                     (H) 15488 Gates Rd., Howard City 49329 (231) 580-6304
          Amble: (O) 15207 Howard City Edmore Rd., Howard City 49329-9516
                                                          (231) 796-1061

Hood, Anthony R.   drarhood@yahoo.com
[(FE) FL 1999; PE 2001; FE 2004]. Oct 1, 1999 Southfield: Hope (assoc); 2002 Highland Park: Berea-St. Paul; 2005 Detroit: Scott Memorial; **2016 Farmington: First**. 33112 Grand River, Farmington 48326 (248-474-6573). Home: 25766 Livingston Circle, Farmington Hills 48335 (248-474-7568)

Hook, Matthew James (Leigh)   matt@dexterumc.org
[(FE) P 1994; F 1996]. 1994 Christ UMC, Memphis, TN; Aug 16, 1995 Birmingham: First (assoc); 2002 school (Beeson Program, Asbury Theological Seminary); **2003 Dexter**. 7643 Huron River Dr., Dexter 48130 (734-426-8480). Home: 7605 Grand Ave., Dexter 48130 (734-426-8420)

Hoppenworth, Patricia Ann (Chris)   revhopp@gmail.com
[(FL) FL Dec 1, 2002]. Dec 1, 2002 Marine City; Jan 1, 2005 Marine City (LTFT ¾); Jan 1, 2008 Marine City (LTFT ½); **2008 Dryden, Leonard**. (D) 5400 W. Main St., Box 98, Dryden 48428 (810-796-3341), (L) 245 E. Elmwood, Box 9, Leonard 48367 (248-628-7983). Home: 1421 Poplar, LL, Port Huron 48060 (810-734-1171)

Horne, Sr., Maurice R. (Mae)   pastorhorne55@yahoo.com
[(FL) PL 1999; FL 2006]. 1999 Eastside Covenant Cooperative Parish: Detroit: Mt. Hope; 2004 Saginaw: Jefferson Avenue, Calvary; Jan 1, 2006 Saginaw: Jefferson Avenue; 2009 Flint: Lincoln Park; **Jan 1, 2018 Flint Mission Zone Minister of Outreach**. Home: 1201 Lincoln Ave., Flint 48507 (810-234-1498)

*HOTELLING, DALE A. (RL) (Beth) – (FL-1996, PL-2005, FL-2008, PL-2011, NL-8/31/2012, RL-2019)
Old Mission Peninsula (DSA) 1995; Old Mission Peninsula Ogdensburg 06/18/1996; Kalamazoo: First (Assoc) 07/16/2000; Not Appointed 2004; Um Connectional Structures (¶344.1A,C) Conference Ministry Consultant 01/01/2005; Muskegon: Crestwood 2008; Not Appointed 2010; White Pines New Church (LTFT ½) 2011; Not Appointed 08/31/2012; Retired 01/01/2019
                                          dale.hotelling@gmail.com
                     (H) 3256 Dorais Dr NE, Grand Rapids 49525-2805

*HUBLEY, LAURENCE E (RE) – (FE-1991, R-2002)
Colon 11/01/1985, Transferred from Free Methodist 1991; Hillside 1991; Hastings: Hope 1995; Wolf Lake 2000; Medical Leave 2001; Retired 06/01/2002
                                          l_hubley@yahoo.com
     (H) 17283 Rosy Mound Ln, Apt 315, Grand Haven 49417-7653 (269) 501-6887

Huff, Jr., James E. (Darlene) huff11@aol.com
[(PL) PL Jan 1, 2005]. **Jan 1, 2005 Memphis: First, Lamb**. (M) 81265 Church St., PO Box 29, Memphis 48041 (810-392-2294), (L) 1209 Cove Rd., Wales 48027. Home: 24750 Maple, PO Box 29, Memphis 48041 (810-392-8031)

Huff, Mark W. (Aurora) mawihu11@aol.com
[(PL) PL Nov 12, 2017]. **Nov 12, 2017 Livingston Circuit: Plainfield, Trinity** (LTFT ½). (P) 17845 M-36, Gregory 48137 (517-851-7651), (T) 8201 Iosco Rd., Fowlerville 48836 (517-223-3803). Home: 8233 Iosco Rd., Fowlerville 48836 (248-825-2887)

Huffman, Tracy Nichols (Robert) revtracyhuffman@gmail.com
[(FE) P 1994; F 1997]. 1995 Clarkston (assoc); 1999 Ann Arbor: West Side; 2013 Dearborn: First; 2018 Monroe: St. Paul's; **2019 Clergy Medical Leave ¶356**. Home: 400 Illinois Dr., Tecumseh 49286-7544 (734-276-3656)

HUGHES, ROBERT M (FE) (Becky) – (PE-2006, FE-2009)
Union City 2004; Reading 2012; Leave of Absence 07/13/2014; Allen 2015; Leave of Absence/Concord (DSA) (LTFT ½) 2016; Concord 2019
rhughes36@yahoo.com
(H) 361 Calhoun St, Union City 49094-9359 (517) 677-6381
Concord: 119 S Main St, PO Box 366, Concord 49237-0366 (517) 524-6156

*Huhtala, John Collins, Sr. (Karen) jhuhtala2625@comcast.net
[(RE) T 1965; F 1968]. 1968 Samaria; 1969 Manchester: Sharon (assoc.); 1970 Hemlock, Nelson; Jan. 1976 Marquette: First (assoc.), Conf. Staff, Marquette District Specialist; 1980 Sault Ste. Marie: Central, Algonquin. 1992 Port Huron: First; 1996 Flint District Superintendent; 2001 Director of Connectional Ministries; **2009 Retired**. Home: 819 St. Paul St., Marysville 48040 (810-364-8485)

*HULETT, JAMES R (RE) (Linda) – (D-1964, FE-1967, R-1998)
Transferred from North Dakota Conf 1978; Lake Odessa: Lakewood 1978; Sparta 1985; Vicksburg 1998; Retired 1998
(H) 674 Gardenview Ct SW, Byron Center 49315-8346 jcottage@localnet.com

HUMENIK, JULIA R (PE) – (FL-2015, PE-2019)
Schoolcraft/Pleasant Valley 2015
jrhumenik@gmail.com
(H) 318 Willow Ct, Schoolcraft 49087-9735 (269) 679-4501
Schoolcraft: PO Box 336, 342 N Grand Ave, Schoolcraft 49087-0336
(269) 679-4845
Pleasant Valley: PO Box 517, 9300 West XY Ave, Schoolcraft 49087-0517
(269) 679-5352

HUNDLEY JR, ROBERT L (FE) (Ruth (Pigeon) – (PL-1980, D-1982, FE-1989)
Center Eaton/Brookfield 1980; East Lansing: University (Assoc) 08/01/1982; Other Valid Ministries (¶344.1d) Director of Pastoral Care, Michigan Capital Medical Center 09/01/1990; Lansing: First 1996; Mason: First 2000; UM Connectional Structures (¶344.1a,c) District Superintendent, Lansing District 2009; Grand Rapids: First 2013
bobh@grandrapidsfumc.org
(H) 3035 Grenada Dr SE, Grand Rapids 49546-5721 (616) 427-3749
Grand Rapids First: 227 Fulton St E, Grand Rapids 49503-3236 (616) 451-2879

*Hunter, Gerald Stanley (Tracey)
[(RE) P 1989; F 1992]. 1990 Denton: Faith; May 15, 1995 Leave of Absence; 1995 Pinconning; 1999 Hartland; Oct 2, 2000 General Board of Global Ministries: Field and Finance Representative (337.1); 2002 New Hudson; **Oct 15, 2015 Retired.** 10/01-10/30/2018 Grass Lake (LTFT ¼)

boomerchinde@sbcglobal.net
(H) 11357 Weatherwax Dr., Jerome 49249 (517-688-5323)

Hurd, Elizabeth Ann (PE) – (PE-2019)
Caledonia 2019

pastor.elizabeth@caledoniaumc.org
(H) 260 Vine St, Caledonia 49316-8334 (810) 488-6300
Caledonia: 250 Vine St, Caledonia 49316-8334 (616) 891-8669

*Hurley, Joel W. (Donna)   joelhccjl@gmail.com
[(RE) F 1974]. 1974 Trans. to Detroit Conf. from Free Methodist; Aug. 1974 Kingston, Deford; 1978 Elkton; 1983 Associate Director: Marquette District, Munising; 1986 Gladwin. 1992 Saginaw: Jefferson Avenue; 1994 Honorable Location; 1995 Roscommon: Good Shepherd of the North; **Jun 4, 1998 Retired.** Home: 6945 E. Main St., #1101, Mesa, AZ 85207 (408-982-0546)

*Hurst, David M. (Susan)   dhurst@beaumonthospitals.com
[(RE) P, E. PA 1961; F, E. PA 1964]. 1960 Landonburg, PA; 1963 West Grover, PA; 1967-70 Chaplain, Haverford State Hospital, PA; 1980 Executive Director, Pastoral Care Services of Southeastern Michigan; Nov. 1, 1983 Leave of Absence; 1986 Executive Director, Dearborn Pastoral Counseling Center; Jul. 1, 1990 Hospital Chaplain, Supervisor of Programs in Clinical Pastoral Education, William Beaumont Hospital, Royal Oak; **1998 Retired.** Home: 2305 Pittsfield, Ann Arbor 48104 (734-677-3612)

Huseltine, David Earl (Elizabeth Deacon)   davidhuseltine@gmail.com
[(FE) P 1986; F 1989]. 1987 Melvindale: First; Nov. 15, 1989 Melvindale: First, Detroit: Woodmere; 1990 Farmington: Orchard (assoc.); 1994 Royal Oak: St. John's; 2001 Tawas; 2004 Flat Rock: First; Aug 1, 2008 Beverly Hills; 2010 Beverly Hills, Berkley: First; 2013 Troy: Big Beaver; **2016 Franklin Community.** 26425 Wellington, Franklin 48025 (248-626-6606). Home: 2423 Ogden W., Farmington Hills 48323 (248-761-4327)

*HUSTON, JOSEPH D (RE) – (D-1970, FE-1973, R-2009)
Camden Charge 09/01/1970; Concord 1972; Transferred to Detroit Conf 1975; Transferred from Detroit Conf 1977; Robbins/Grovenburg 10/15/1977; Grand Rapids: Saint Paul's 02/16/1982; Holt 1989; UM Connectional Structures (¶344.1a,c) District Superintendent, Central District 1999; Georgetown 2005; Lansing: Central 2007; Retired 2009; Dimondale (¼ Time)/Grovenburg (¼ Time) 2009; Dimondale (½ Time) 2017-Feb 1, 2019

jdhuston56@gmail.com
(H) 3032 Kay Dr SE, Grand Rapids 49508-1596 (517) 646-6530

Hutchinson, Ronald Glenn (Tammy)   ronhutchinson50@aol.com
[(PL) PL 1998]. 1998 Silverwood; **Apr 16, 2008 Silverwood, North Branch (LTFT).** (S) 2750 Clifford Rd, Silverwood 48760-9782 (989-761-7599), (NB) 4195 Huron St., PO Box 156, North Branch 48461 (810-688-2610). Home: 3049 Burnside Rd., North Branch 48461 (810-614-7928)

Hutchison, Suzanne L. (David)   suzy.hutchison@yahoo.com
[(FL) FL 2014]. 2014 Richmond: First; **2018 Plymouth: First (assoc.)**. 45201 N. Territorial, Plymouth 48170 (734-453-5280). Home: 44698 Maidstone, Canton 48187 (810-923-1649)

HUVAERE, CATHERINE (CATHI) M (FE) – (D-1996, FE-2002)
Marne 1993; Grand Rapids: Aldersgate 02/01/2002; Grand Rapids: Saint Paul's 2005; Niles: Wesley 2012; Clio: Bethany 2017
camahu93@gmail.com
(H) 10480 Varna St, Clio 48420-1952 (810) 550-2570
Clio Bethany: PO Box 327, 353 E Vienna St, Clio 48420-1424 (810) 686-5151

*HUYCK, CLARE (RL) – (FL-2007, RL-2015, RLA-2015, RL-2017)
Perrinton / Pompeii / Middleton / North Star (DSA) 7/1/2007-11/10/2007; Perrinton / Pompeii / Middleton / North Star (DSA) 11/10/2007-2012; Sunfield / Sebewa Center 2012-2013; Sunfield / Mulliken 2013-2015; Retired 2015; Allen 2016-2017
pastorclare@gmail.com
(H) 6812 Cooper Rd, Jackson 49201 (517) 795-5465

*HYNES, JAMES L (RE) (Bernadine) – (D-1966, FE-1968, R-2000)
Transferred from Detroit Conf 1986; Wacousta Community 1986; Leave of Absence 1992; Nashville 1994; Retired 2000
hyneshome@sbcglobal.net
(H) 1551 Franklin St SE Apt 3025, Grand Rapids 49506-3396 (616) 943-0979

IDSINGA, CYDNEY M. (PE) – (PE-2015)
Girard 2014; Marne 2018
cydinga@gmail.com
(H) 14861 Washington, Marne 49435 (616) 677-3991
Marne: 14861 Washington, PO Box 85, Marne 49435-0085 (616) 677-3957

Ilonga Ngoie, John Kabala (Gertrude M. Mukalay)
[(OE) OE 2017, North Katanga Conf, Democratic Republic of Congo] **2018 Detroit: French** (New Church Start) (LTFT ¼). 1803 E 14 Mile Rd, Birmingham 48009. Home: 1858 Estates Dr, Detroit 48206

*Ireson, Roger W. (Judy)   rwireson@aol.com
[(RE) T 1963; F 1966]. 1962 Putnamville, IN; 1963 Zion, IL, Assistant Pastor: Memorial Church; 1966 school (England); 1970 Franklin (assoc.); 1975 Bloomfield Hills: St. Paul's; 1979 Detroit: St. Timothy's; Jan. 1, 1988 General Secretary, Board of Higher Education and Ministry; **2001 Retired**. Home: 4200 Jackson Ave, Apt 4008, Austin TX 78731-6065 (615-207-3042)

*Iris, Ronald Lewis Figgins (Carla)
[(RE) P 1970; F 1974; RE-2006; AF-2013]. 1970 Rushsylvania, OH (W. OH); 1972 Hartland; 1975 Melvindale; 1980 Manchester: Sharon; 1983 Elkton; 1985 Millington, Arbela. Sep. 1, 1991 Gwinn; 1995 Allen Park: Trinity; **2006 Retired**. 12/01/2013-2015 Crystal Valley/Walkerville (LTFT ¼)
DRRoniris@aol.com
(H) 2774 W Victory Dr, Ludington 49431-9534 (231) 843-8352

Irish, Dennis Eric (Sherri)   deirishph1@yahoo.com
[(FE) FL 1/1/04; PE 2008; FE 2011]. Jan 1, 2004 Algonac: Trinity; 2008 Algonac: Trinity, Marine City; 2011 New Hope; 2013 Brown City; **2019 Yale, Cole, Melvin**. (Y) 2 South Main St., Yale 48097 (810-387-3962), (C) 7015 Carson Rd., Yale 48097 (810-387-4400), (M) 1171 E. Main, Melvin 48454. Home: 1 Park Avenue, Yale 48097 (810-387-4333)

Irish, Esther   irishe67@yahoo.com
[(FL) PL 2008; FL 2017]. 2008 Flint: Dimond; **2013 Caring Covenant Group Ministry: Columbiaville**. 4696 Pine, PO Box 98, Columbiaville 48421 (810-793-6363). Home: 4350 Golden Glow Dr., Columbiaville 48421 (810-793-4175)

IVANOV, MARY LB (FE) (Ivan) – (PE-2001, FE-2004)
Ravenna 2001; Cedar Springs 2008; Muskegon: Lake Harbor 2014
                                    mary_ivanov@hotmail.com
            (H) 1322 Clayton Ave, Muskegon 49441-4305 (231) 780-3951
Muskegon: Lake Harbor: 4861 Henry St, Muskegon 49441-5436 (231) 798-2181

*JACKSON, ANDREW (RE) (Phyllis) – (D-1997, FE-1999, R-2006)
Grand Rapids: Saint Paul's (Assoc) (Part Time) 02/01/1987; Carlisle (Part Time) 1994; Carlisle 1997; Retired 2006; Carlisle (LTFT ½) 12/01/2009-2010; Alto/ Bowne Center (LTFT ¾) 2014-2016
                                    chaplainjackson@comcast.net
            (H) 978 Amber View Dr SW, Byron Center 49315-9740 (616) 878-1284

*Jacobs, Charles Richard (Ann)   ca.jacobs@comcast.net
[(RE) P 1967; F 1970]. 1969 Ypsilanti: First (assoc.); 1972 Davisburg; 1976 Harper Woods; 1980 Hancock; 1984 Novi; 1997 Howell: First; **2010 Retired**. Home: 115 Victoria Ct., St. Clair 48079 (810-637-8166)

*Jacobs, James Douglas (Joanna)
[(RE) P W. PA, 19; F 1977]. 1975 Trans. to Detroit Conf., Port Huron: First (assoc.); Feb. 1977 Brown City: First, Immanuel; 1980 Birch Run; 1989 Monroe: First; Sep 1, 1999 school; Jun 1, 2000 Director of Pastoral Care, Mercy Memorial Hospital System, Monroe; **2011 Retired**. Home: 1109 N. Roessler, Monroe 48162 (734-384-0719)

*Jacques, Raymond Allen (Doris)   paparay384@yahoo.com
[(RL) FL 1992]. Mar. 1, 1992 Port Austin, Pinnebog, Grindstone City; 1997 Sutton-Sunshine, Bethel, Akron; 2001 Midland: Homer; **2008 Retired**. Home: 384 W. Island Dr., Beaverton 48612 (989-689-3489)

Jaggers, Jeffrey Lee (Keri Lynn)   revjagg@gmail.com
[(FE) P 1988; F 1992]. Jan. 1., 1990 Port Huron: First (assoc.); 1994 Snover: Heritage; 1998 Grayling: Michelson Memorial; 2004 Flushing; **2014 Fenton**. 119 S. Leroy St., Fenton 48430 (810-629-2132). Home: 11310 Greenview, Fenton 48430 (810-354-8463)

*James, James Price (Norma Jane)   captjimjames@comcast.net
[(RE) P 1983; F 1986]. 1984 Henderson, Chapin; May 1, 1989 Elkton; 1992 Reese, Watrousville; 1996 Lincoln Park: Dix; 2000 Lincoln Park: Dix, Taylor: West Mound; 2005 Caring Covenant Ministry: Otisville, West Forest; **2007 Retired**.

*JAQUETTE, DALE F (RA) (Betty) – (D-1986, AM-1986, RA-1992)
Pompeii/Perrinton/North Star 08/16/1981; Reading 04/16/1990; Retired 1992
betjaq@atlantic.net
(H) 504 Palm Ave, Wildwood, FL 34785-9428 (352) 330-1670

*JAQUISH, JERRY L (RE) (Joy) – (D-1981, FE-1984, R-2012)
Epsilon/Levering 1981; Leave of Absence 1987; White Cloud 1988; Manistee 2002; Retired 2012
jerryjaquish@yahoo.com
(H) PO Box 144, 956 N Thornapple Ave, White Cloud 49349-0144
(231) 689-0079

Jeffords, Nathan
[(FL) FL 2012]. 2012 Byron; 2016 Rose City: Trinity, Whittemore; **2019 Mayville**. 610 East Ohmer, PO Box 189, Mayville 48744 (989-843-6151). Home: 860 E. Brown Rd., Mayville 48744 (989-781-0860)

*JENSEN, CURTIS EUGENE (RE) (Anne) – (D-1970, FE-1975, R-2010)
Mt Pleasant: First (Assoc) 1972; Mancelona/Alba 1975; Berrien Springs 1983; Buchanan: First 1987; Pentwater: Centenary 01/16/1996; Lake Odessa: Lakewood 2001; Hillsdale: First 2003; Retired 2010
annecurtjensen@gmail.com
(H) 915 Meadowbrook Dr, Mt Pleasant 48858-9595 (517) 425-1606

JENSEN-KINNEY, KAREN L (David Kinney) – [(FL) FL-2015] Nashville / Vermontville (DSA) 2015; Nashville/Vermontville 12/01/2015; Nashville 2018
karenkinney66@gmail.com
(H) 540 Chapel Dr, Nashville 49073-9781 (517) 852-0685
Nashville: PO Box 370, 210 Washington St., Nashville 49073-9581
(517) 852-2043

*Job, Loretta M. (Larry)   loretta@brightonfumc.org
[(RD) PD 2007; FD 2010; RD 2019]. 2007 Brighton: First (deacon); 2018 Personal Leave of Absence; **2019 Retired**. Home: 208 Sisu Knoll, Brighton 48116 (810-229-4604)

*JOHN, SR., THOMAS H. (RL) (Phyllis) – (FL-1998, RLA-2012-2015, RL-2012)
Kewadin: Indian Mission 1998; Northport Indian Mission 2005; Retired 2012
(H) 313 Davis St. Apt. 1, Traverse City 49686 (231) 632-4920

*Johns, Carol J.   Caroljohns@orchardumc.org
[(RE) P 1970; F 1973]. 1972 Saginaw: First (assoc.); Oct. 1978 Bay City: Christ; 1985 Owosso: First; 1996 Farmington: Orchard; **2015 Retired**.

JOHNSON, Andrea L (PL) – (PL-2018)
Battle Creek: Convis Union (LTFT ½) 01/01/2018
pastorandreajohnson@gmail.com
(H) PO Box 79, Battle Creek 49016-0079 (269) 317-1937
Battle Creek: Convis Union: 18990 12 Mile Rd, Battle Creeek 49014
(269) 965-3787

Johnson, Brian Keith (Jenny)   pastorbrian1908@fmail.com
[(FL) FL Jan 1, 2013]. Jan 1, 2013 Bay Port Hays; **2016 Ortonville**. 93 Church St. Box 286, Ortonville 48462 (248-627-3125). Home: 319 Sherman Ct., Ortonville 48462 (248-627-3347)

*JOHNSON, DEBORAH M (RE) – (D-1979, FE-1983, R-2014)
Manton 1981; Marne 1985; Hudsonville, Organizing Pastor 09/01/1990; Lansing: Asbury 1997; Sturgis 2008; Retired 07/08/2014

debjohn386@aol.com
(H) 22849 110th Ave, Tustin 49688-8626 (231) 825-2580

Johnson, Eric L. (Karen)   dadj@hotmail.com
[(PL) PL 2007; FL 2012; PL 2018]. 2007 Port Sanilac; 2012 Sandusky: First; 2013 Seven Churches United Group Ministry: Gaines, Duffield; **2018 Harrisville, Lincoln** (LTFT ½). (H) 217 N State St, Harrisville 48740 (989-724-5450). (L) PO Box 204, Lincoln 48742-0204 (989-736-6910). Home: 216 5th St, Harrisville 48740

JOHNSON, JAN M. (James) – [(FL) FL-2010] Appointed to Extension Ministries (¶344.1b,c) Chaplain, Mercy Health Partners 11/13/2010

johnjm@mercyhealth.com
(H) 1541 Fifth St, Muskegon 49444-1849 (231) 343-8268
(O) PO Box 358, 1500 E Sherman Blvd, Muskegon 49443-0358 (231) 672-3629

*JOHNSON, JANE ELLEN (RE) (Charles) – (FL-2000, PE-2001, FE-2005, R-2016)
Farwell 2000; Lansing: Grace 01/01/2007; Retired 2016

JaneEllen@hotmail.com
(H) 4014 Grandview Terrace SW, Grandville 49418-2490 (616) 259-9896

Johnson, Kenneth M.   kennjohn07@yahoo.com
[(PL) PL 2018]. **2018 Detroit: St. Paul** (LTFT ¼). 8701 W 8 Mile Rd, Detroit 48228 (313-342-4656).

*JOHNSON, MARK G (RE) (Johnie) – (D-1983, FE-1985, R-2015)
Fenwick/Palo/Vickeryville 03/16/1982; Lawrence 1986; Kent City: Chapel Hill 05/01/1991; Hillsdale: First 1996; Ionia Parish: LeValley/Berlin Center 2003; Bath/Gunnisonville 2007; Retired 2015; LeValley/Berlin Center 12/01/2016-2017; Breckenridge 2017-2019

mark123johnson@gmail.com
(H) 2396 Houghton Hollow Dr, Lansing 48911-8419 (517) 898-6960
Breckenridge: PO Box 248, 125 3rd St, Breckenridge 48615-0248
(989) 842-3632

Johnson, Melody Pierce Hurley   mjohnson@porterhills.org
[(FE) P N. IL, 1974; F W. NC, 1976]. 1974 school (Duke); 1975 school, C.P.E., NC Baptist Hospital; 1976 Haw River Parish (assoc.); 1978 Greensboro: Morehead; 1984 Director of Religious Life, Epworth Heights; Sep 1, 1994 transf to Detroit Conf., Sep 1, 1994 Birmingham: First (assoc); 1998 Epworth Heights Assembly: Director of Religious Life (para. 335.1A), Epworth Heights Assembly, Ludington; **2002 Corporate Chaplain, Porter Hills Presbyterian Retirement Community**. 3600 Fulton St E, Grand Rapids 49546 (616-954-1799). Home: 2018 N Cross Creek Ct SE, Grand Rapids 49508-8869 (616-682-0253)

PASTORAL RECORDS

JOHNSON, NATHANIEL W (FE) (Lisa) – (D-1990, FE-1993)
Transferred from North Indiana Conf 1991; Belding 1991; Vergennes 09/01/1996; Appointed to Extension Ministries (¶326.1,3) Pastoral Counselor, CPE, Bronson Methodist Hospital, Kalamazoo 2010; Leave of Absence 09/06/2011; Appointed to Extension Ministries (¶344.1d) Chaplain, Heartland Home Care And Hospice, Spiritual Care 10/04/2011; Other Valid Ministries (¶344.1d) Chaplain, Heartland Home Health Care & Hospice (LTFT ¾) and Other Valid Ministries (¶344.1d) Chaplain, Spectrum United Memorial Hospital, Greenville (LTFT ¼) 07/09/2012; Other Valid Ministries (¶344.1d) Chaplain, Pediatrics/NICU, Helen DeVos Children's Hospital, Grand Rapids 10/10/2012; Appointed to Extension Ministries (¶344.1b,c) Chaplain, Helen DeVos Children's Hospital & Spectrum Health United Hospital, Grand Rapids 2014; Appointed to Extension Ministries (¶344.1b,c) Manager of Pastoral Care & Bereavement for Spectrum Health System 10/16/2016

pastorthan@aol.com
(H) 2821 Boynton Ave NE, Ada 49301-8210 (616) 710-9703
(O) Spectrum Health, 100 Michigan St NE, Grand Rapids 49503 (616) 391-3096

*JOHNSON, WILLIAM C (RE) (Judy) – (D-1972, FE-1975, R-2012)
Jonesville/Allen 1974; Holland: First (Assoc) 1977; Grand Rapids: Aldersgate 1981; Marshall 1992; Wyoming Park 1996; Retired 2012; Courtland-Oakfield (LTFT 45%) 11/01/2016-2017; Cedar Springs (LTFT 45%) 01/01/2018

bjinside@gmail.com
(H) 4390 Summerlane Ave NE, Grand Rapids 49525-2421 (616) 366-2421
140 S Main St, PO Box K, Cedar Springs 49319 (616) 696-1140

*JOHNSTON, DAVID L (RE) (Ann Marie) – (D-1975, FE-1976, RE-2009)
Bellevue/Kalamo 1977, DeWitt Redeemer 05/01/1983; Lansing Grace 1985; Jackson Brookside 1992; Personal Leave 06/24/2005; Retired 2009

johnston254@comcast.com
(H) 122 Bingham Dr, Brooklyn 48230-8926 (517) 784-1346

*Johnston, Jack Edson
[(RE) P Neb., 1977; F Neb., 1979]. 1977 Ogallola (assoc.); 1978 Bradshaw, Lushton; 1981 Indianola, Garden Prairie; 1983 Springview, Long Pine; 1987 Eddyville, Oconto, Miller; 1989 Trans. to Detroit Conf., Lake Linden, Larium; 1992 Hillman, Spratt; Nov 1, 2005 leave of absence; 2006 Seven Churches United Group Ministry: Byron; 2010 Ossineke; **2012 Retired**.

*Johnston, Mark Gordon (Jane Ann) mjohnston159@yahoo.com
[(RE) P W. MI, 1978; F W. MI, 1982]. 1980 Ashley, Bannister; 1982 Camp Director, Judson Collins; 1983 Trans. to Detroit Conf., Director, Manager, Judson Collins Camp; Feb 1, 1996 Hudson: First; 2008 Chesaning: Trinity; **2012 Retired**. Home: 15950 Wellwood Rd., Tipton 49287 (989-280-9188)

JOHNSTON, MARTIN A (FL) – (PL-2016, FL 2017)
Frontier (DSA) 09/01/2017; Frontier (PTLP) 11/15/2016; Connections Cooperative Ministry: Webberville/Williamston: Crossroads 2017

pastormartyj@yahoo.com
(H) 120 E Beech St, Webberville 48892-9702 (517) 521-3434
Webberville: 4215 E Holt Rd, Webberville 48892-8208 (517) 521-3631
Williamston: Crossroads: 5491 Zimmer Rd, Williamston 48895-9181
(517) 655-1466

*Joiner, Donald Wesley (Catherine)   djoiner@gbod.org
[(RE) T 1968; F 1971]. 1970 Melvindale; 1975 Flint: Atherton; Jan. 1978 Staff Consultant, Evangelism and Stewardship; Nov. 1, 1985 Gen. Bd. of Discipleship, Director of Stewardship; Nov 1, 1999 Operations Officer and Director of Fund Development, Discipleship Ministries; **Apr 1, 2010 Retired**. Home: 1225 Chloe Dr., Gallatin, TN 37066 (615-206-8659)

Jones, Carolyn   jonescat1@juno.com
[(FL) FL 2016; PL 2018; FL 2019]. Nov 15, 2016 Howarth, Paint Creek; 2018 Dearborn Heights: Stephens (LTFT ¾); Dec. 1, 2018 Romulus: Community (LTFT ½), Dearborn Heights: Stephens (LTFT ½); Jan 1, 2019 Romulus: Community (LTFT ½); **2019 Romulus: Community, Detroit: Resurrection**. (DR) 11160 Olive St, Romulus 48174 (734-941-0736); (DR) 8150 Schaefer Hwy, Detroit 48228-2796 (313-582-7011. Home: 2466 Edison, Detroit 48206 (313-573-0043)

*Jones, Charles B. (Jewel)
[(RL) FL 1986]. 1986 Detroit: Resurrection; Oct 1, 1993 disability leave; **1997 Retired**. Home: 8367 Carlin, Detroit 48228 (313-581-7147)

*JONES, MARGARET ZEE (RE) (John "Jack") – (PE-2002, FE-2005, R-2006)
Other Valid Ministries (¶335.1.D) Chaplain and Bereavement Coordinator, McLaren-Ingham Visiting Nurse and Hospice Services 09/01/2002; Other Valid Ministries (¶335.1.D) Chaplain and Bereavement Coordinator, McLaren-Ingham Visiting Nurse and Hospice Services and Retired (¶344.1.a) 06/24/2006
                                          margaretzeejones@comcast.net
            (H) 599 Pebblebrook Ln, East Lansing 48823-2159 (517) 351-0728

*JONES, ROBERT E (RE) (Carol) – (D-1970, FE-1973, R-2009)
Frontier/Osseo 1971; Mendon 11/15/1973; Grand Rapids: First (Assoc) 1978; Montague 1983; Lansing: Christ 1992; Big Rapids: First 1996; Scottville 2004; Retired 2009
                                              jonesr5648@gmail.com
            (H) 5648 Nancy Dr SW, Wyoming 49418-9788 (616) 719-3935

Jones, Todd Wesley
[(FL) FL 2017]. **2016 North Lake**. 14111 North Territorial Rd., Chelsea 48118 (734-475-7569). Home: 14130 Wagon Wheel Ct., Chelsea 48118 (734-475-9348)

Joshi, Manohar "Mantu" Avinash (OE)
[Califonia-Nevada] Kalamazoo: First (assoc) (LTFT ½) 2019
                                              mjoshi@umc-kzo.org
            (H) 1720 Embury Rd, Kalamazoo 49008-2246 (503) 799-6679
        Kalamazoo: First: 212 S Park St, Kalamazoo 49007-4704 (269) 381-6340

JOSLYN, MONA K (FE) – (D-1998, FE-2001)
Nottawa (DSA) / Leonidas (DSA) 10/01/1994; Waterloo First/Waterloo Village 08/01/1997; Bronson: First 1998; Galesburg 2006; Gull Lake 2010; Voluntary Personal Leave of Absence 2015; Bangor: Simpson 2016
                                              mojoslyn2@gmail.com
            (H) 28760 Hillside Dr, Bangor 49013-9756 (269) 484-4060
        Bangor: Simpson: (O) 507 Joy St, Bangor 49013-1123 (269) 427-7725

PASTORAL RECORDS

JUE, JENNIFER J (FE) (Erik Wong) – (PE-2007, FE-2010)
Napoleon 2007; Wayne First 2013; Oxford 2014; Oxford, Thomas 2019
jenjue@prodigy.net
(H) 91 Cross Timbers Dr, Oxford 48371-4701 (248) 628-1022
Oxford: 21 E Burdick St, Oxford 48371-4923 (248) 628-1289
Thomas: 504 1st St, Oxford 48371-1504

Jung, Gun Soo gsj0925@yahoo.com
[(FE) Iowa Conf; transfer to Detroit Conf., 2016]. Oct 1, 2013 Madison Heights:
Korean First Central; 2018 Keweenaw Parish: Calumet, Mohawk-Ameek, Lake
Linden; **2019 Blissfield: First**. 201 W. Adrian, Blissfield 49228 (517-486-4040).
Home: 403 Brenot Ct., Blissfield 49228 (515-250-6456)

*KADWELL JR, EMMETT H (RE) (Mary) – (D-1973, FE-1978, R-2011)
Ashley/Bannister 1975; Empire 10/01/1978; Stanwood: Northland 1982; Lake
Odessa: Central 1992; Niles: Wesley 01/01/2000; Reed City 2008; Retired 2011;
Saugatuck (LTFT ¼) 09/01/2011

pastor_emmett@yahoo.com
(H) 2794 6th St, Shelbyville 49344-9559 (231) 912-0806
Saugatuck: PO Box 647, 250 Mason St, Saugatuck 49453-0647 (269) 857-2295

*Kail, Pamela Sue reverend2kail@yahoo.com
[(RE) P 1990; F 1993]. 1991 Ravenna (W. MI Conf., under para. 426.1) Jul 1,
1994 school; 1995 Ironwood: Wesley, Wakefield; 1998 Dearborn: First (assoc);
2001 Ypsilanti: St. Matthew's; 2009 South Central Cooperative Ministry: Lake
Fenton, Mt. Bethel; **2012 Retired**. Home: 307 N. Monroe, Albion 49224

KALAJAINEN, BRADLEY P (FE) (Colleen) – (D-1982, FE-1984)
Freeport/Middleville/Parmalee (Assoc) 01/01/1981; Freeport 1982; Grand
Rapids: First (Assoc) 1985; Grand Rapids: Cornerstone 1990
BradK@cornerstonemi.org
(H) 7810 Golf Meadows Dr SE, Caledonia 49316-8462 (616) 891-8443
Grand Rapids: Cornerstone: 1675 84th St SE, Caledonia 49316-7939
(616) 698-3170

KALAJAINEN, RODNEY J (FE) (Janet) – (D-1979, FE-1981)
St Johns Parish 1978; Shepardsville/Price 1978; Mt Pleasant: First (Assoc) 1981;
Battle Creek: Birchwood 1984; DeWitt: Redeemer 1988
rod@dewittredeemer.org
(H) 2155 Longwoods Dr, Dewitt 48820-8182 (517) 669-9140
DeWitt: Redeemer: 13980 Schavey Rd, Dewitt 48820-9013 (517) 669-3430

*KALISZEWSKI, CHARLES R (OR) – (OR-2016)
[East Ohio Conference] Pierson: Heritage 03/01/2016; Carson City 2016
revchuckkal@hotmail.com
(H) 2816 Meadowwood St, Mt Pleasant 48858 (989) 317-8421
Carson City: PO Box 298, 119 E Elm St, Carson City 48811 (989) 584-3797

Kappler, Kris Stewart (Sarah)
[(FE) FL 1991; P 1993; F 1995]. 1991 Harbor Beach, Port Hope; 1997 Missionary, OMS International, Inc.; **2018 Tawas**. 20 East M-55, Tawas City 48763 (989-
362-4288). Home: 801 W. Franklin St., Tawas City 48763 (859-858-8233)

*Karls, Mark A. (Sandy)   pastorkarls@msn.com
[(RE) P 1979; F 1983]. 1978 Norway, Faithorn; 1983 Pigeon: Salem; 1986 Wisner; 1997 Saginaw: Ames; **2014 Retired**. 74 W. Corral, Saginaw 48638 (989-598-5438)

KASPER, JOHN G (FE) (Deb) – (FL-2000, PE-2005, FE-2008)
Hersey (DSA) 08/01/1994; Hersey 1995; Galien/Olive Branch 2001; Dowagiac: First 2006; Clare 2013

             pastorjohn@clareumc.org
(H) 714 S Rainbow Dr, Clare 48617-9605 (989) 386-7683
Clare: 105 E 7th St, Clare 48617-1301 (989) 386-2591

KATZMARK, PEGGY A (FL) – (PL-2007, FL-2014)
Omard 2007; Omard, Peck 2011; Robbins 2014

             pastorpeggy@robbinsumc.org
(H) 827 S Waverly Rd, Eaton Rapids 48827-9758 (517) 663-8417
Robbins: 6419 Bunker Rd, Eaton Rapids 48827-9108 (517) 663-5226

*Keef, Thomas Frank (Claudia)   Keefguys@comcast.net
[(RE) P 1976; F 1978]. 1977 Detroit: Aldersgate (assoc.); 1980 Utica: Hope, New Haven: Faith; 1982 Utica: Hope, Mount Vernon; 1988 Burton: Christ; 1994 Millington, Arbela; Jan 1, 1996 Millington; 2001 Clawson; 2010 Richmond: First; **2014 Retired**. 12409 Pine Mesa, Canadian Lake 49346 (231-972-5132)

*Keefer, Derl G. (OF) – (OF-2018)
[Retired Chruch of Nazarene] Three Rivers: First (LTFT ¼) 2018; Three Rivers: Center Park (¶346.1) (LTFT ¼) 2019

             derlkeefer@gmail.com
(H) 318 E St, Three Rivers 49093 (816) 519-1473
Center Park: 18662 Moorepark Rd, Three Rivers 49093-9677 (269) 279-9109

*KEIM, J. ROBERT (RL) (Judi) – (FL-2000, PL-2009, RL-2011)
Sturgis (Assoc.) (PTLP 7/1/09-12/31/11) 12/16/1999; Retired 12/31/2011
(H) 344 Hazelwood Ct., Muskegon 49442-1486 (269) 467-7541

*KELLER, RON L (RE) (Patricia) – (FL-1956, D-1959, FE-1962, R-1998)
Battle Creek: Washington Heights 09/01/1956; Appointed in Other Annual Conferences (¶331.8, ¶346.1) Northeast Ohio Conference, Republic 1958; Union City 1962; Battle Creek: Birchwood 1966; Rockford 1970; UM Connectional Structures (¶344.1a,c) Conference Staff Director 1973; Kalamazoo: Milwood 01/01/1982; Muskegon: Central 1988; Battle Creek: First 1993; Retired 1998; Kalamazoo: First Interim 01/01/2000-6/1/2000

             kelleron4@hotmail.com
(H) 5201 Woodhaven Ct #507, Flint 48532 (810) 820-7021

*Kellermann, James Garfield (Polly Strosahl)   kelstrowater@comcast.net
[(RE) P 1975; F 1978]. 1977 Redford (assoc.); 1980 Melvindale; 1985 Burton: Emmanuel; 1992 Bay City: Christ; Nov 1, 2000 Waterford: Central; **2013 Retired**. Home: 2149 Lakeside Place, Green Bay, WI 54302 (248-390-2416)

Kelley, Lisa (Michael)   pastorlisakelley@outlook.com
[(FL) FL 2013]. **2013 Hillman, Spratt**. (H) 96 State St., PO Box 638, Hillman 49746 (989-742-3014), (S)7440 M-65, South, Lachine 49743 (989-742-3014). Home: 7770 W. Scott Rd., Hubbard Lake 49747 (989-727-3624)

Kelley, Michael P. (Lisa)   pastormikekelley@yahoo.com
[(FL) PL Dec 1, 2004; FL 2009]. Dec 1, 2004 Mapleton; 2006 Mapleton, Burt; 2007 Burt, Saginaw: West Michigan Avenue; 2009 Jeddo, Buel; **2012 Ossineke**. 13095 US-23, PO Box 65, Ossineke 49766 (989-471-2334). Home: 7770 W. Scott Rd., Hubbard Lake 49747 (989-727-3624)

*Kelsey, Dwayne Lee (Ruth)   dlkelc@wowway.com
[(RE) P 1975; F 1977]. 1976 Plymouth (assoc.); 1978 Howarth, Thomas; Oct. 15, 1981 Flint: Lincoln Park; 1987 Caring Covenant Group Ministry: Davison; 1991 Romeo; 1996 Dearborn: Good Shepherd; **Jan 1, 2000 Retired**. Home: 89 Randolph Rd., Rochester Hills 48309

KENDALL, JAYME L (FE) – (PE-2004, FE-2008)
Elsie 2004; Appointed to Extension Ministries (¶344.1.c) Chaplain, MI Army National Guard 07/11/2005; Appointed in Other Annual Conferences (¶331.8, ¶346.1) Pastoral Counselor, CPE, Covenant Counseling and Family Resource Center, Snellville, GA 06/01/2007; Appointed in Other Annual Conferences (¶331.8, ¶346.1) Chaplain, Abbey Hospice, Social Circle, GA 09/01/2008; Appointed to Extension Ministries (¶344.1d) Chaplain, United States Air Force, Kirtland Air Force Base 06/01/2010
                                                   jayme.abq@icloud.com
        (H) 3311 8th St NE Apt 208, Minot, ND 58703-0005 (505) 319-7873
        (O) 230 Missile Ave, Minot AFB ND 58705-5000 (701) 723-2456

*KENDALL, O JAY (RE) (Janis) – (D-1984, FE-1986, R-2012)
Transferred from Central Illinois Conf 1993; NE Missaukee Parish: Moorestown-Stittsville/Merritt-Butterfield 09/01/1993; Leave of Absence 2005; Indian River (Assoc) (LTFT ¼) 2007; Retired 09/01/2012
        (H) PO Box 2038, 3300 M 68 Hwy, Indian River 49749-2038 (231) 238-0816

*KERSTEN, ROBERT L (RE) – (D-1963, FE-1968, R-1995)
Stanwood/Higbee 10/01/1960; Burr Oak 1962; Napoleon 1967; Transferred to Detroit Conf 1969; Transferred from Detroit Conf 1987; Barry County: Woodland/Hastings: Welcome Corners 1987; Vermontville/Gresham 1991; Retired 1995
        (H) 1601 W Queen Creek Rd, Chandler, AZ 85248 (623) 910-0134

Kesson, Aaron Bertel (Maria)   pastoraaronumc@gmail.com
[(FE) FL 2008; PE 2011; FE 2014]. 2008 Blissfield: Emmanuel (LTFT ¾); Lambertville (assoc) (LTFT ¼); 2012 Manchester; Mar 14, 2012 Chaplain Army Reserve (¶344.1b); **2017 Durand, Swartz Creek (assoc)**. (D) 100016 E. Newburg Rd., Durand 48429 (989-288-3880), (SW) 7400 Miller Rd., Swartz Creek 48473 (810-635-4555). Home: 302 Hampton, Durand 48429 (989-288-4364)

*KEYTE, DONNA J (RL) (Steven) – (PL-2003, RL-2019)
Lacota 09/01/2003; Almena (LTFT ½) 01/01/2006; Almena (PTLP ¼) 01/01/2007; Almena (PTLP ½) 01/01/2008; Retired 2019
        (H) 7632 Sandyridge St, Portage 49024 (269) 329-1560 djkeyte@yahoo.com

*Keyworth, Charles Wesley (Della Jane)   ckeyworth@fumcmid.org
[(RE) P 1983; F 1986]. Piqua, OH: Grace (student associate); 1984 Republic, Woodland; 1988 Gordonville; Sep 1, 1994 St. Charles, Brant; 1999 Midland: First (assoc); **2017 Retired**. Home: 630 Wood Run Dr., Marysville, OH 43040 (989-859-5654)

Khang, Steve Hongsup   steverkhang@gmail.com
[(FE) PE 2007; FE 2010]. 2007 Ann Arbor: Korean (assoc); 2009 Ann Arbor: Korean (assoc) (LTFT), Ypsilanti: St. Matthews (LTFT); **2014 Ann Arbor: Korean (assoc) (LTFT)**. 1526 Franklin St, Ann Arbor 48103-2437 (734-483-5876). Home: 4131 Inglewood Dr, Ypsilanti 48197-6624 (734-482-0460)

*Kidd, David Earl (Ada)   adkidds@gmail.com
[(RM) T 1961; F 1964]. 1960 Broadway, E. Baltimore Parish (Baltimore Conf.); 1962 Kensington, MD (Baltimore Conf.): St. Paul's, Minister of Education; 1964 Wesley Foundation, Flint; 1966 Wesley Foundation, Wayne State University; 1974 Flint: Trinity; Oct. 1980 Detroit: Central; 1990 Ypsilanti: First; **1997 Retired**. Home: 2767 Del Mar Drive, Okemos 48864 (517-351-7510)

KIDD, SEAN K (PE) (Christine) – (FL-2014, PE-2018)
Pokagon (DSA) (LTFT ½) 2011; Martin/Shelbyville 2014; Kalamazoo: Westwood 2019

seankidd1970@gmail.com
(H) 1003 Greenway Ter, Kalamazoo 49006-2616 (616) 401-8576
Kalamazoo: Westwood: 538 Nichols Rd, Kalamazoo 49006-2946 (269) 344-7165

Kieb, Eric Douglas (Lisa)   edkieb@sbcglobal.net
[(FE) FL 2001; PE 2003; FE 2006]. 2001 Owosso: First (assoc); 2003 Negaunee: Mitchell; 2010 Roscommon: Good Shepherd of the North; **2015 Bay City: Grace**. 4267 S. Two Mile Rd., Bay City 48708 (989-684-1101). Home: 2161 Neithammer Dr., Bay City 48706 (989-671-8951)

KILPATRICK, BRYAN K (FL) (Ashley) – (FL-2014)
Brooks Corners/Barryton: Faith/Sears 2014; Mancelona/Alba 2017
bkilpatrickministry@gmail.com
(H) 406 Sunnyside St, Mancelona 49659-9771
Mancelona: PO Box 301, 117 E Hinman St, Mancelona 49659-0301
(231) 587-8461
Alba: 5991 Barker St, Alba 49611

Kim, Daeki   skydk033@gmail.com
[(OE) OE 2018, Indiana Conf.] **2018 Madison Heights: Korean First Central**. 500 W Gardenia Ave, Madison Heights 48071. Home: 30150 ShorehamSt, Southfield 48076

Kim, David Inho (Julie)   dkim@michiganumc.org
[(FE) FL 2008; PE 2013, FE 2015]. 2008 Troy: Korean (assoc.); **2016 Saginaw Bay District Superintendent; Jan 1, 2019 Central Bay District Superintendent**. 3764 Fashion Square Blvd, Saginaw 48603 (989-793-8838). Home: 6120 Londonberrie, Midland 48640

Kim, Eung Yong   eykim11@gmail.com
[(OE) OE 2019]. **Jan 1, 2019 Troy: Korean**. 42693 Dequindre Rd, Troy 48085 (248-879-2240). Home: 974 Hillsborough Dr., Rochester Hills 48307 (248-525-5979)

Kim, Taek Han (Jamie)   revtaekkim@gmail.com
[(FE) PE 2002, FE 2005]. 2002 Birmingham: First (assoc); 2004 Walled Lake; **2012 Carleton**. 11435 Grafton Rd., Box 327, Carleton 48117 (734-654-2833). Home: 1424 Monroe St., Box 327, Carleton 48117 (734-654-2001)

PASTORAL RECORDS

Kim, Won Dong (Jessie)　　　　　　　　coolgod80@hotmail.com
[(PE) FL 2014; PE 2015]. 2014 Troy: Korean (assoc.); 2015 Goodrich; **Jan 1, 2017 Elkton**. 150 South Main St., Box 9, Elkton 48731 (989-375-4113). Home: 134 S. Main St., Elkton 48731 (989-375-4185)

Kim, Yoo Jin　　　　　　　　　　　　yjphaha@bu.edu
[(PE) PL 2016; FL Sept 1, 2018 PE 2018]. 2016 Madison Heights: Korean Central (assoc); Sept 1, 2016 Madison Heights: Korean Central (assoc) (LTFT ½), Clawson (LTFT ½); **2018 Onaway, Millersburg**. (O) 3647 N. Lynn St., PO Box 762, Onaway 49765 (989-733-8811), (M) 5484 Main St., Box 258, Millersburg 49759 (989-733-6946). Home: 3653 N. Elm, PO Box 762, Onaway 49765

*Kingsley, Susan M.　　　　　　　　　Kings2ley@yahoo.com
[(RE) FL Sep 1, 1999; PE 2000; FE 2003] Sep 1, 1999 Midland: First (assoc); 2008 Owosso: Trinity; **2016 Retired**. Home: 4110 Belaire St., Midland 48642 (989-859-6223)

*KINTIGH, BRUCE R (RE) (Paula) – (D-1979, FE-1983, R-2018)
Shepardsville/Price 1981; Kingsley/Grant 1988; Hart 1993; Battle Creek: Christ 01/01/1999; Girard/Ellis Corners 2007; [Ellis corners Closed 12/31/2007] Girard 01/01/2008; Battle Creek: Trinity 2010; Battle Creek: Birchwood/Trinity 2012; Retired 2018
b_kintigh@comcast.net
(H) 17102 11 Mile Rd, Battle Creek 49014-8942 (269) 209-3633

*Kivisto, Margaret A. (Jeffrey)　　　　　　pmkiv2004@att.net
[(RL) PL Aug 1,2004]. Aug 1, 2004 Linden, Argentine; Jan 1, 2009 Linden (LTFT ¾); **2013 Retired**. Home: 7144 Brentwood Dr., Brighton 48116 (810-227-6371)

Klacking, Brenda K.　　　　　　　　Brendakk@hotmail.com
[(FL) PL 2000; FL 2013]. 2000 Glennie, Curran: Sunnyside; 2008 Whittemore. Wilber; 2013 Whittemore, Wilber, Churchill; **2014 Churchill, Mio**. (C) 501 E State Rd, PO BOX 620, West Branch 48661 (989-312-0105), (M) 1101 W. Eighth St., Mio 48647 (989-826-5598). Home: 1005 W. Eighth St., Mio 48647 (989-826-5521)

Kline, Julie (OF)
[UCC Elder] Kalamazoo: First (assoc) (¶346.2) 2019
jkline@umc-kzo.org
(H) 1724 Nichols Rd, Kalamazoo 49006 (269) 330-8502
Kalamazoo: First: 212 S Park St, Kalamazoo 49007-4704 (269) 381-6340

*Klump, Dean Alan (Linda)
[(RE) P 1970; F 1972]. 1971 Plymouth (assoc.); 1974 Lambertville; 1981 Romeo; 1991 Monroe: St. Paul's; 1995 Plymouth: First; **2007 Retired**. Home: 1321 Palmer, Plymouth 48170 (734-927-4762)

*KNAPP, DAVID G (RE) (Jane) – (D-1976, FE-1980, R-2009)
Hopkins/South Monterey 1978; Adamsville 10/16/1982; Jackson: First (Assoc.) 1986; Appointed in Other Annual Conferences (¶331.8, ¶346.1) Waterman/ Preston, Detroit Conf 1989; Transferred to Detroit Conf 1990; Transferred From Detroit Conf 1992; Grand Rapids: Pawating Magedwin And Salem/Bradley Indian Mission 1992; Benton Harbor: Peace Temple 1995; Climax/Scotts 2003; Retired 2009; Mendon/West Mendon (Interim) (LTFT ¼) 1/1/-6/30/2013
dgkcreations@outlook.com
(H) 7792 Kilowatt Dr, Kalamazoo 49048 (269) 775-1387

Kobler, Timothy L timkobler@umichwesley.org
[(OE) OE 2018, Holston Conference] **2018 UM Connectional Structures (¶344.1a,c) Director, University of Michigan Wesley Foundation**. 602 E Huron, Ann Arbor 48104 (734-668-6881). H: 2884 Sorrento Ave, Ann Arbor 48104 (276-614-8141).

*Kohlmann, Kenneth Arlan (Barbara) kakohlmann@msn.com
[(RE) P 1972; F 1975]. 1974 Flint: Court Street (assoc.); 1977 Mt. Clemens (assoc.); 1981 Detroit: Messiah; Sep 1, 1985 Detroit: Redford (assoc.); 1988 Utica: Hope, Mt. Vernon; 1992 Marine City; 1996 Midland: Homer; **2001 Retired**. Home: 50525 Abbey Dr., New Baltimore 48047 (586-716-0262)

*KOHNS, NORMAN C (RE) (Carole) – (D-1967, FE-1969, R-2005)
Transferred from Detroit Conf 1974; Grand Rapids: Aldersgate 01/01/1974; Grand Rapids: Aldersgate/Westgate 1977; Grand Rapids: Aldersgate 1978; Kalamazoo: Sunnyside 1981; Appointed to Extension Ministries (¶344.1b,c) Resident Therapist, Care and Counseling, Eden Theological Seminary, St. Louis, MO 1986; Appointed to Extension Ministries (¶344.1b,c) Samaritan Counseling Center of South Bend, IN 1988; Riverside/Scottdale 11/16/1992; Appointed to Extension Ministries (¶344.1b,c) Director Of Pastoral Counseling, Hospice of Greater Kalamazoo 1993; Caledonia 1996; Retired 2005
normankohns@yahoo.com
(H) 5845 Lyn Haven Dr SE, Kentwood 49512-9497 (616) 554-1244

Koivula, Laurie lkoivula@ymail.com
[(PL) PL Dec 1, 2014, FL-2016, PL-2018]. Dec 1, 2014 West Goodland; 2016 Harrietta, Mesick, Brethren: Epworth, (W. MI Conf.); 2018 Mesick, Brethren: Epworth (LTFT ½); 2019 Pontiac: Grace and Peace Cmnty (LTFT ½). GP: 451 W Kennett, Pontiac 48340 (248- 334-3280). Home: 1851 Birchcrest Dr, Waterford 48328 (231) 557-8131

Kolder, Sandra J. skolder@att.net
[(PL) PL Dec, 2005]. Dec 4, 2005 God's Country Cooperative Parish: Paradise/Hulbert: Tahquamenon; 2011 Munising, Trenary; **2017 Retired**. Home: PO Box 130, W18394 H-42 Rd., Curtis 49820 (906-586-9696)

*KORNOWSKI, SUZANNE P. (RL) (James Ferguson) – (PL-2002, FL-2004, RL-2011)
Oakwood (DSA) (LTFT PT) 06/01/2000-12/1/2002; Oshtemo (DSA) (LTFT PT) 2000; Oshtemo (PTLP 12/1/02-3/21/04) 12/01/2002; Retired 2011
(H) 252 Bobwhite Dr, Pensacola, FL 32514-2714

KRAUS, JAMES W (FD) (Lorie) – (DM-1998, FD-2001)
Director of Music and Director of Leadership Development, Diaconal Minister, St Joseph First 1998; St Joseph First (Deacon) 05/31/2001
jameskrausjr@hotmail.com
(H) 2820 Willa Dr, Saint Joseph 49085-2555 (269) 983-5798
St Joseph First: 2950 Lakeview Ave, Saint Joseph 49085-2317 (269) 983-3929

Krauss, Julie A juliekrauss@hotmail.com
[(PL) PL Jan 1, 2019]. 2018 Jeddo, Avoca (DSA); Jan 1, 2019, Jeddo, Avoca (LTFT ¾); **July 1, 2019 Jeddo, Avoca (LTFT ½).** (J) 8533 Wildcat Rd, PO Box 7, Jeddo 48032-0007 (810-327-6644), (A) 8905 Avoca Rd, Avoca 48006 (810-327-6100). Home: 7864 Wildcat Rd, Grant Twp 48032 (810-327-6144)

*Kreger, Robert Ivan (Karen) rkdataman@aol.com
[(RL) PL Dec 1, 2002]. Dec 1, 2002 Avoca, Ruby; 2003 Ruby; 2008 Sterling Heights; **2013 Retired**. Home: 4747 Lakeshore Rd., Fort Gratiot 48059 (810-327-6016)

KREH, MATTHEW D (FL) (Lori Lou) – (FL-2015)
Bath/Gunnisonville (DSA) 2015; Bath/Gunnisonville 12/01/2015
mattkreh@gmail.com
(H) 2025 Cumberland Rd, Lansing 48906-3771 (517) 449-8178
Bath: PO Box 308, 13777 Main St, Bath 48808-0308 (517) 641-6551
Gunnisonville: PO Box 308, 2031 Clark Rd, Bath 48808-0308 (517) 482-7987

*Kummer, James Philip (Pamela) jkummer@humc.us
[(RE) P 1980; F 1983]. Dec. 1980 Port Sanilac, Forester, McGregor; 1985 Elkton; Apr. 15, 1989 Flint: Calvary (assoc.); Feb. 1, 1992 Livonia: Clarenceville; 1995 Highland; **2016 Retired**. Home: 2864 Bullard Rd., Hartland 48353 (810-632-9026)

*KURSCH, KATHLEEN S (RE) – (D-1999, FE-2003, R-2017)
Waterloo First/Waterloo Village 1998; Grand Ledge: First (Assoc) 02/01/2000; Grand Ledge: First (Assoc) (LTFT ½) / Delta Mills (LTFT ½) 2003; Grand Rapids: South 09/01/2004; Shepherd 2007; Retired 2017
kskursch@juno.com
(H) 11134 Barnsley, Lowell 49331-9001 (989) 506-4601

*LAFRANCE, SALLY J (RE) (David) – (D-1995, FE-1997, R-2005)
Transferred from West Ohio Conf 1999; Climax/Scotts 10/01/1999; Old Mission Peninsula (Ogdensburg) 2001; Twin Lake 2002; Retired 10/01/2004
davidsally@chartermi.net
(H) 15132 Snowberry Ct, Spring Lake 49456-2814 (616) 850-2157

*LAIDLER, D KEITH (RE) (Judy) – (D-1957, FE-1961, R-1997)
Coleman Supply (EUB) 1956; Coleman (EUB) 1957; Petoskey (EUB) 1961; Brown City (EUB) 1964; Buchanan: Faith 1968; Leighton 1972; St Johns: First 10/15/1977; Paw Paw 1984; Lake Odessa: Central 1989; Montague 1992; Retired 1997; Delta Mills 01/01/1999-06/30/1999; Delta Mills 2005-2007
dklaid50@gmail.com
(H) 3335 Starboard Dr, Holland 49424-5425 (616) 786-2774

*LAIMON, JEANNE (RL) (John W.) – (PL-2008, FL-2013, RL-2015)
Williamston: Wheatfield (DSA) (LTFT PT) 2007; Williamston: Wheatfield (LTFT ¼) 12/01/2007; Munith (¼ Time) 2012; Waterloo First (¼ Time) 2013-2/16/2014; Pleasant Lake (¼ Time) 2013; Stockbridge (¼ Time) 2013; Not Appointed 2014; Retired 2015
jeannelaimon@yahoo.com
(H) 6701 Hawkins Rd., Jackson 49201-9579 (517) 769-6570

Lamb, Marcel (Michelle) revmarcel@msn.com
[(FE) OF Wesleyan; PE 2010, FE 2011]. Sep 16, 2005 Mio; 2012 AuGres, Twining: Trinity; **2013 Imlay City**. 210 North Almont Ave., Imlay City 48444 (810-724-0687). Home: 280 Bancroft St., Imlay City 48444 (810-721-7149)

*LaMere, Frederick   falamere@charter.net
[(RE) P 1991, VA]. 1991 Potts Valley Charge; 1993 trans to Detroit Conf, Republic, Woodland; 1996 disability leave; Aug 1, 2000 Beaverton: First, Dale; **2002 Retired**. Home: 3578 W. Riley Rd., Gladwin 48624

*Lancaster, Bonny Joy
[(RL) FL 1992]. Sep 1, 1992 Mayville, Fostoria, Silverwood; Feb 1, 1997 Mayville; 1999 Macon; 2001 West Vienna; **Oct 1, 2006 Retired**. Home: 4134 N State Rd, PO Box 476, Davison 48423 (810-240-1257)

LANCASTER, JANICE T (FD) – (PD-2010, FD-2013)
Holland Hospital, Psychiatric Nurse/Holland: First (Deacon – Assoc Congregational Care LTFT ¼ unpaid) 2010; Deacons Appointed Beyond the Local Church(¶331.1a) Emmanuel Hospice of Grand Rapids, Clinical Nurse/ Northlawn (Assoc Congregational Care LTFT ¼ unpaid) 02/01/2014; Deacons Appointed Beyond the Local Church(¶331.1a) Emmanuel Hospice of Grand Rapids, Clinical Nurse/Northlawn (Assoc Congregational Care LTFT ¼ paid) 01/01/2015; Leave of Absence 03/31/2017

lantock@yahoo.com
(H) 0-660 Krystal Kove, Grand Rapids 49534 (616) 784-5662

*Landis, John David (Carolyn)   jlandis902@gmail.com
[(RE) P 1982; F 1988; RE 2019]. 1980 Buel, Peck, Melvin; 1986 school (United Theological Seminary), Ashland, OH: Trinity; 1987 Romulus: Community; 1994 Detroit: Metropolitan (assoc); 2000 Swartz Creek; 2011 Midland: First; **2019 Retired**. Home: 9535 Hill Rd., Swartz Creek 48473 (989-948-9838)

LANE, M CHRISTOPHER (FE) (Jane Lippert) – (D-1982, FE-1988)
Transferred from Holston Conf 1986; Winn/Blanchard-Pine River/Coomer 1986; Muskegon: Crestwood 1990; Grand Rapids: Genesis (Co-Pastor) 1995; Martin/ Shelbyville 2007; Traverse City: Central (Assoc) 2009

chris@tccentralumc.org
(H) 10160 E. Pickwick Ct, Traverse City 49684 (231) 947-5594
Traverse City: Central: 222 Cass St, Traverse City 49684-5734 (231) 946-5191

*Large, Wayne Thomas (Joy)   wlarge@up.net
[(RE) T 1964; F 1969]. 1967 Newberry; Sep. 1970 Midland: First (assoc.); 1974 Gladstone; 1981 Director, Wesley Foundation, University of Michigan; 1995 Farmington: First; Jun 1, 2001 incapacity leave (para 355); 2002 Royal Oak: First (assoc); **2003 Retired**. Home: 8504 Old Wilsey Bay 12 Lane, Rapid River 49878

Larner, Janet (Peter J. Sivia)
[(FE) P 1979; F 1984]. 1981 Sterling, Alger, Bentley; Oct. 1982 Sutton- Sunshine, Bethel; 1986 Beaverton: First, Dale; 1991 Bay City: First (assoc.) (LTFT ½); Aug 1994 Wagarville; Sep 1, 1994 Gordonville; 2002 sabbatical leave; 2003 Sanford; 2011 voluntary leave of absence; 2011 Churchill; 2013 Corunna; 2017 Shepherd, Blanchard-Pine River

jmlarner@gmail.com
(H) 175 North Dr, Shepherd 48883-9070 (989) 245-8846
Shepherd: PO Box 309, 107 W Wright Ave, Shepherd 48883 (989) 828-5866
Blanchard-Pine River: 7655 W Blanchard Rd, Blanchard 49310 (989) 561-2864

*Larson, Jean M. (Warren) bjtools@charter.net
[(RE) PL 1988; P 1995; F 1998]. 1988 Painesdale: Albert Paine; 1990 Wesley Foundation, Northern Michigan University; school; Jun 16, 1996 Owosso: Burton, Carland; Jan 1, 2000 Stephenson, Hermansville: First; Nov 16, 2001 leave of absence; 2002 Plover Charge (WI conf); 2003 Reese; Jan 1, 2008 leave of absence; **2010 Retired**. Home: 1633 River St., Niagara, WI 54151 (989-863-0148)

Lass, William
[(PL) DSA 2018; PL 2019]. Jan 15, 2018 Lulu (DAS) (LTFT ¼); **Jan 1, 2019 Lulu (LTFT ¼)**. 12810 Lulu Rd, PO Box 299, Lulu 48140-0299 (734-269-9076). Home: 5423 N Stoney Creek Rd, Monroe 48162 (734-289-3510)

*Laub, Mary Grace revlaub@dsnet.us
[(RE) PL 1990; FL 1992; Deacon, AM 1998; FE 2000]. 1990 Painesdale: Albert Paine Memorial; Feb. 15, 1992 God's Country Cooperative Parish: Grand Marais, Germfask; 1998 Heritage; 2001 Escanaba: First; **2010 Retired**. Home: 204 W. Douglass Ave., Houghton 49931 (906-483-2363)

*LAWTON, GEORGE W (RL) (Beverly) – (PL-2001, RL-2007)
Berrien County: Lakeside 09/01/1999; Retired 2007; Berrien County: Lakeside (¼ Time) 2007

geolawton@csinet.net
(H) 8000 Warren Woods Rd #79, Three Oaks 49128-8519 (269) 469-8468
Lakeside: PO Box 402, Union Pier 49129 (269) 469-8468

LAWTON, GREGORY W (FD) – (PD-2007, FD-2010)
Deacons Appointed Within UM Connectional Structure (¶331.1b) Resolution Services Center of CMU (½ Time) / Grand Ledge: First (Deacon) (½ Time) 2007; Grand Ledge First (Deacon) (LTFT ½) and Deacons Appointed Within UM Connectional Structure (¶331.1b) Interim Director of Campus Ministry, Wesley Foundation at MSU (LTFT ½) 12/05/2010; UM Connectional Structures (¶344.1a,c) Director, Campus Ministry Wesley Fellowship Grand Valley State University (LTFT ¾) 2011; Deacons Appointed Beyond the Local Church (¶331.1a) Director, Wesley Fellowship at Grand Valley State University (Full-Time) 2012; Deacons Appointed Beyond the Local Church (¶331.1a) Director, Wesley Fellowship at Grand Valley State University (¼ Time) 04/01/2017; Deacons Appointed Beyond the Local Church (¶331.1a) Assoc Dean of Students, Lithuania Christian College International University 08/10/2017 and Georgetown (Missional) 12/1/2018; Transitional Leave 01/01/2019

gregorywlawton@gmail.com
(H) 8000 Warren Woods Rd, Lot 79, Three Oaks 49128-8526 (616) 805-5407

*Leach, Melvin L. (Judy) pastormel48@gmail.com
[(RE) P 1973; F 1975]. 1973 West Vienna; 1981 Davisburg; Jan 1, 1995 Eastside Covenant Cooperative Parish: Fraser: Christ; 2002 Parish Director; **2015 Retired; Set 1, 2017 Hale: First**. 201 W Main, PO Box 46 Hale 48739-0046 (989-728-9522) Home: 7540 O'Connor, Box 334, Hale 48739

Lee, Andrew H. (Grace) leeandr5@gmail.com
[(FE) FL 2013; PE 2014; FE 2017]. 2013 Ann Arbor: Calvary; **2019 Commerce**. 1155 N. Commerce Rd., Commerce Twp. 48382-2608 (248-363-3935). Home: 840 Morella St., Commerce Twp. 48382-2623 (248-977-0400)

456 MICHIGAN ANNUAL CONFERENCE 2019

Lee, Chul-Goo   eglee1320@yesu.org
[(FE) Korean Methodist Church, PE 2008; FE 2009]. Mar 1, 2004 Madison
Heights: Korean First Central (May 17, 2007 trans to Detroit Conf. from Korean
Methodist Church; **2013 Korean American UMC of South Florida** 4905 W.
Prospect Rd., Ft. Lauderdale, FL 33309 (954-739-8581)

*LEE, DONALD (RLA) – (DSA-2002, PL-2003, R-2010, RLA-2017)
Frontier/Osseo (DSA) 2002; Frontier/Osseo (PTLP) 2003; Discontinued 2010;
Readmitted 2017; Frontier PTLP (¼) (¶357.1) 2017

                                                          donlee@dmcibb.net
(H) PO Box 127, 106 E Maple St, Camden 49232-0127 (517) 398-3082
Frontier: PO Box 120, 9925 Short St, Frontier 49239-0120 (269) 223-0631

*Lee, Hoon Kyong (Kyong Ja)   hklee722@yahoo.com
[(RE) P MN, 1980; F MN, 1983]. 1980 S. NJ Conf., Mays Landing: Korean; Sep
1, 1985 S. NJ Conf., Cherry Hill: First Korean; Jan 1, 1995 Troy: Korean (transfer
to Detroit Conference); **2013 Retired**. Chicago, IL (NCJ Korean Missions)

*LEE, JANET A (RD) – (D-1997, PL-2000, RD-2002)
Transferred from Detroit Conf 1986; Hillsdale: First, Minister of Music and Arts
and Hillsdale Daily News, Religion and Lifestyles Editor 1988; Retired 2002;
Hillsdale First, Minister of Music and Arts 2002-12/31/2012

                                                        Janet_lee@comcast.net
(H) 4300 W Bacon Rd, Hillsdale 49242-8205 (517) 437-4949

*Lee, John Hyung (Jae Hyang)   mgmxbop@aol.com
[(RE) P E. Annual Conf. of Korea, 1977; F E. Annual Conf. of Korea, 1979]. 1974-
79 Jung-gu, Korea: Zion UMC (assoc.); 1975-77 Assistant Professor, Christian
Social Ethics, Methodist Theological Seminary, Seoul, Korea; 1978-79 Professor
of Christian Social Ethics, Methodist Theological Seminary, Seoul, Korea; 1980
Trans. to Western NC Conf., Greensboro: Korean; Sep. 1, 1988 Trans. to Detroit
Conf., Ann Arbor: Korean; 1992 Madison Heights: Korean First Central; Feb 1,
2004 Detroit West District Superintendent; **2011 Retired**. Home: 2064 Christopher Ct., West Bloomfield 48324 (248-366-1948)

*LEE, JUNG KEE (RE) (Eun Su) – (D-1989, FE-1991, R-2013)
Transferred from East Ohio Conf 1998; Lansing: Korean 1998; Other Valid Ministries (¶344.1d) Seoul Theological University 01/01/2004; Retired 02/28/2013
                        (H) 808 N Springs St, Apt 702, Los Angeles, CA 90012-4416

*Leffler, Stephen Douglas (Marilyn)
[(RE) T IN, 1955; F IN, 1958]. 1958 Vincennes; 1961 Merom; 1963 Carrollton;
1966 Indianapolis: Union Chapel (assoc.); 1968 Chaplain, VA Medical Center,
Butler, PA; 1981 Trans. to W. PA Conf.; 1981 Chaplain, VA Medical Center, Saginaw; 1988 Trans. to Detroit Conf.; 1988 Chaplain, VA Medical Center, Saginaw;
Jan., 11, 1992 sabbatical leave; 1992 Bay Port, Hayes; **1994 Retired**. Home:
4392 Ann Street, Saginaw 48603

Leitelt, Betty Kay   pastor.kay@live.com
[(FL) PL 2006; FL 2010]. 2006 Corunna: Northwest Venice; **2010 Caring
Covenant Group Ministry: Otisville, Fostoria, West Deerfield**. (O) Box 125,
200 W. Main St., Otisville 48463 (810-631-2911), (F) Box 67, Fostoria 48435.
Home: 9622 Hammil Rd., PO Box 125, Otisville 48463 (810-631-8395)

LeMoine, Peter hdrider2@chartermi.net
[(PL) PL 208]. **2018 Republic, Michigamme: Woodland** (LTFT ½). (R) 216 Front, PO Box 395 Republic 49879, (906-376-2389), (MW) HCR 1 US 41 East, Michigamme 49861, PO Box 395 Republic 49879 (906-323-6151). Home: 356 Maple S, Republic 49879 (906-376-2085)

Lenard, Jr., Keith A. k19redice@aol.com
[(FL) PL Mar, 2014; FL 2016]. Mar 1, 2014 Wyandotte: Glenwood; Jan 1, 2016 Melvindale: New Hope, Downriver (assoc); 2016 Riverview, Downriver (assoc); **2017 Grosse Pointe (assoc)**. 211 Moross Rd., Grosse Pointe 48326 (313-886-2363). Home: 414 Champine, Grosse Pointe 48236

Leslie, Kristen Jane (Michael Boddy) keslie@eden.edu
[(FE) P, E. OH, 1986; F, E. OH, 1988]. 1988 Westlake (assoc.), (E. OH Conf.); 1989 Chaplain: Adrian College; 1990 Trans. to Detroit Conf., Chaplain: Adrian College; Jul 1, 1993 school (School of Theology of Claremont); Jan 1, 1998 Professor of Pastoral Theology, Yale Divinity School; **2010 Professor of Pastoral Theology and Care,** Eden Theological Seminary, 475 Lockwood Ave., St. Louis, MO 63119 (314-918-2513). Home: 540 Lee Ave. St. Louis, MO 63119 (203-376-4537)

*LESTER, BEN B (RE) (Linda) – (D-1990, FE-1993, R-2011)
Howard City First/Amble/Coral 1988; Cedar Springs/East Nelson 1995; Hart 2003; Retired 2011
hesslakeben@yahoo.com
(H) 1575 Hess Lake Dr, Grant 49327-9395 (231) 834-8868

*Lewis, Alger T. (Ruth) revatl@airadv.net
[(RE) FL 1986; AM 1991; FM 1998]. 1986 Bay Port, Hayes; 1992 North Street; **1999 Retired**. Home: 9906 Lakeside Dr., Bay Port 48720 (989-656-3151)

*Lewis, Bradford K. (Deborah) bklewis2105@charter.net
[(RE) LP 1992; P 1993; F 1996]. Sep 1, 1992 Wellsville; 1994 Romulus: Community; 1998 Roscommon: Good Shepherd of the North; **2010 Retired**. Home: 1980 Teton Ave., Monroe 48162 (989-906-5213)

*LEWIS, EUGENE A (RE) (Marilyn) – (D-1965, FE-1967, R-2003)
Glenn-Pearl 1963; Glenn/Pearl/Casco 1965; Hanover/Horton/Hillside 12/01/1966; Belding/Orleans 07/15/1972; Grand Rapids: Faith 1977; Wacousta Community 1984; Clare 1986; Stevensville 1994; Retired 2003
ealewis25080@gmail.com
(H) 25080 27 1/2 St, Gobles 49055-9231 (269) 628-1482

Lewis, George Henry (Sherry Parker-Lewis) revgeorgelewis@hotmail.com
[(FE) P 1989; F 1992]. 1990 Kilmanagh, Unionville; 1993 Carleton; 1998 Cheboygan: St. Paul's; **2010 Howell: First**. 1230 Bower St., Howell 48843 (517-546-2730). Home: 7608 Brookview Ct., Brighton 48116 (810-229-7831)

*LEWIS, KENDALL A (RE) (Doris) – (D-1970, FE-1974, R-1990)
Transferred from Detroit Conf 1973; Banfield/Briggs/Dowling-South Maple Grove 1973; Country Chapel/Banfield 1975; Marion/ Cadillac: South Community 1977; White Pigeon 1981; Mendon 01/01/1985; Big Rapids: Third Avenue/Paris/ Rodney 1986; Retired 1990
lewiskendall2803@yahoo.com
(H) 179 Summer Street, Battle Creek 49015-2166 (269) 441-1921

*Lewis-Lakin, Barbara (Shawn)   blewislakin@gmail.com
[(RE) P 1980; F 1983]. 1981 Detroit: Aldersgate (assoc.); 1985 Melvindale; 1986 Detroit: Central (assoc.); 1990 school; 1997 Pastoral Counselor, Samaritan Counseling Center; 2004 Pastoral Psychotherapist, Samaritan Counseling Center of Southeastern Michigan (LTFT ½), Chelsea: First (assoc) (LTFT ½). 2010 Samaritan Counseling Center of S. E. Michigan; **Sep 1, 2015 Retired**. Home: 154 S. Cranbrook Cross Road, Bloomfield Hills 48301 (248-629-6232)

Lewis-Lakin, Shawn Patrick (Barbara)   slewis-lakin@fumcbirmingham.org
[(FE) P 1987; F 1990]. 1988 Pontiac: St. James. 1990 Dearborn: First (assoc.); 1994 Trenton: First; 1997 leave of absence; **2017 Birmingham: First (senior assoc) (2019 LTFT ¾)**. 1589 W. Maple, Birmingham 48009 (248-646-1200). Home: 2221 Maplewood, Royal Oak 48073 (734-717-8947)

LEYDORF-KECK, KATHRYN L (PL) (Roger Keck) – (FL-2012, PL-2014)
Salem/Lowe/Maple Rapids (DSA) 2007; Salem/Lowe/Maple Rapids 11/10/2007; Lowe/Maple Rapids (¾ Time) 5/1/2014

kathyleydorf@gmail.com
(H) 10886 S Woodbridge Rd, Bannister 48807-9765 (517) 282-4446
Lowe: 5485 W Lowe Rd, Saint Johns 48879-9789 (989) 224-4460
Maple Rapids: 330 S Maple Ave, Maple Rapids 48853 (989) 224-4460

*Lichtenfelt, Donald Lloyd   donlichtenfelt@yahoo.com
[(RE) T N. Iowa, 1955; F N. Iowa, 1959]. 1954 Calamus, Ground Mound; Dec. 1961 Trans. to Detroit Conf, Fraser; 1967 Mayville, Clifford, Silverwood; 1969 Mayville; 1970 Sabbatical; 1971 Honorable Location; 1974 reinstated; 1974 Utica: Hope, Meade, New Haven; 1980 Harper Woods; 1988 Royal Oak: St. John's; **1994 Retired**. Home: 1417 Copper Glen Dr., Lexington, KY 40519 (859-224-3236)

*Lidums, Olaf R. (Susan)   slidums@aol.com
[(RE) PL Apr, 1998; FL 1998; recognition from ELCA, 1999; FE 2001]. Apr 1, 1998 Detroit: Ford Memorial, Waterman-Preston; Apr 16, 1999 Ford Memorial, Director, New Creations Ministries; 2000 New Lothrop, Juddville; 2003 Flint: Bristol, Dimond; **Apr 1, 2007 Retired**. Home: 4103 Lapeer Rd., Burton 48509 (810-742-3480)

*Liles, Johnny S. (Lynda)   JLiles1208@aol.com
[(RE) P 1989, on recognition of orders, General Baptist Convention; F 1991]. 1988 Warren: First (assoc.); Mar. 16, 1990 Rochester Hills: St. Luke's; **2004 Retired**. Home: 434 Taylor Ave., Rochester 48307 (248-601-3369)

Liles, Lynda B. (Johnny)   liles731@wowway.com
[(FD) CON (SM) 1999; FD 2002] 1986 Howarth, 1975 Paint Creek, 1999 Rochester: St. Luke's; Jun 15, 2006 transitional leave of absence (para. 357); Sep 1, 2006 Troy Fellowship (deacon); **2011 leave of absence**. Home: 434 Taylor Ave., Rochester 48307 (248-601-3369)

*Lim, Paul Byungioo (Susie)
[(RE) P C. IL, 19 ;F C. IL, 19]. 1983 Korean Church; 1985 Korean, North Detroit; 1986 Gwinn; 1987 Hazel Park; 1992 Freeland; Apr 1, 1996 Kum Ran Methodist Church, Seoul, Korea; 1998 Henderson, Chapin; **2000 Retired**. 23480 Lahser Rd., Southfield 48034 (248-356-4677)

Lim, Seok Nam (Soon-Shil)
[(FE) PE 2015; 2018 FE]. (2015 serving in West Michigan Conference). 2016 Dearborn: Good Shepherd; **2018 Alpena: First**. 167 S. Ripley, Alpena 49707 (989-354-2490). Home: 1320 Hobbs Dr., Alpena 49707

*Lindberg, Donna Jeanne (Elwood Berkompas)   djlind@charter.net
[(RE) T 1967; F 1971]. 1970 Beverly Hills (assoc.); 1972 Port Huron: First (assoc.); 1973 Livonia: Newburg (assoc.); Mar. 1974 Detroit: Rice Memorial; Apr. 1979 Hazel Park; 1983 Gaylord; 1989 Ann Arbor District Superintendent; 1993 Ishpeming: Wesley; 1997 Manistique: First (LTFT 2/3); Marquette district, project director; **2004 Retired**. Home: 1530 W. Ridge St., Apt. #47, Marquette 49855 (906-273-1026)

Lindenberg, Scott Paul (Jill)   pastor.scott@ameschurch.org
[(FE) PE 2006; FE 2009]. 2006 Ishpeming: Wesley; 2014 Saginaw: Ames; **2016 Hancock: First**. 401 Quincy, Box 458, Hancock 49930 (906-482-4190). Home: 1631 Portage Dr., Hancock 49930 (906-482-1404)

Lindsey, Duane A   dualind@yahoo.com
[(PL) PL Jan 1, 2019]. 2018 Lennon, Duffield (DSA); Jan 1, 2019 Lennon, Duffield (LTFT ½); **2019 Lake Fenton, Lennon, Duffield**. (LF) 2581 N Long Lake Rd, Fenton 48430 (810-629-5161). (L) 1014 Oak St, PO Box 19, Lennon 48449-0019 (810-621-3676). (D) 7001 Duffield, Swartz Creek 48473 (989-271-9131). Home: 11494 Torrey Rd, Fenton 48430 (810-635-2304)

*Line Yencer, Deborah A. (Ron Yencer)
[(RE) PE 1999; FE 2002; RE 2018]. 1999 Seymour Lake; 2009 Caring Covenant Group Ministry: Davison. 2013 Davison; 2014 Flushing; 2018 Retired; 2018 Mt. Pleasant: Leaton (LTFT ½)

revdebiline@gmail.com
(H) 17429 Summit Ct, Barryton 49305 (248) 425-4684
Leaton: 6890 E Beal City Rd, Mt Pleasant 48858 (989) 773-3838

LIPPERT, JANE R (FE) (Christopher Lane) – (D-1984, FE-1988)
Riverdale: Lincoln Road 1986; Muskegon: Unity (LTFT ½) 1990; Grand Rapids: Genesis (Co-Pastor) (LTFT ½) 1995; Leave of Absence 2007; Traverse Bay 2009; Personal Leave 09/01/2015

janerobertalippert@gmail.com
(H) 10160 E Pickwick Ct, Traverse City 49684-5219 (231) 947-5594

*Liscomb, David M. (Arlene)   dliscomb@cox.net
[(RE) T 1965; F 1968]. 1955 Disco; 1956 (without appointment at his request); 1957 Paint Creek; 1958 Paint Creek, Howarth; 1964 Gambier, Hopewell (NE OH Conf.); 1967 Clinton; 1969 Escanaba: First, Bark River; 1973 Iron Mountain: Trinity; 1982 Troy: First; 1986 Mt. Clemens: First; 1992 Sault Ste. Marie: Central, Algonquin; 1993 disability leave; **1998 Retired**. Home: 600 Marquette, Crystal Falls 49920 (906-875-6140)

PASTORAL RECORDS

LISKE, JULIE A (FD) – (D-1994, FE-1996, FD-2008)
Transferred from Detroit Conf 1994; Portage: Chapel Hill (Assoc) 1994; Appointed to Extension Ministries (¶344.1b,c) Chaplain, Clark Retirement Home 12/01/1997; Wayland 08/01/2001; Leave of Absence 2003; Other Valid Ministries (¶335.1d) Chaplain, Spectrum Health (LTFT) 2004; Leave of Absence 03/08/2005; Kalamazoo: First (Assoc) 2006; Deacons Appointed w/in UM Connectional Structure (¶331.1b) Executive Director, United Methodist Metropolitan Ministry of Greater Grand Rapids (LTFT ¾) and Grand Rapids: Trinity (Deacon, Assoc) (¼ Time) 11/08/2010; Deacons Appointed w/in UM Connectional Structure (¶331.1b) Executive Director, United Methodist Metropolitan Ministry of Greater Grand Rapids (¾ Time) and Chapter Director Of Circles Grand Rapids (LTFT ¼) 2015; Deacons Appointed Beyond the Local Church (¶331.1a) Director, Circles Grand Rapids 03/01/2016
jliske@circlesgr.org
(H) 1323 Suncrest Dr NE, Grand Rapids 49525-4561 (616) 299-0115
(O) 920 Cherry St SE, Grand Rapids 49506-1472

*LITCHFIELD, CARL Q (RE) (Geri) – (D-1985, FE-1988, R-2017)
Brooks Corners/Sears 1986; Barry County: Woodland/Hastings: Welcome Corners 1991; Boyne City/Boyne Falls 2000; Litchfield 2005; Bellaire: Community 2009; Kingsley 2013; Retired 2017; Colon/Burr Oak 02/15/2018; Mendon 2018; Mendon, Burr Oak 10/01/2018
litch2revdup@hotmail.com
(H) 27435 Michigan Ave, Mendon 49072 (269) 275-5296
Mendon: 320 W Main St, PO Box 308, Mendon 49072 (269) 496-4295

*LITCHFIELD, DAVID L (RE) (Vera) – (D-1966, FE-1969, R-2006)
Scottdale (EUB) 1966; West Mendon 12/15/1968; Mendon/West Mendon 1969; Elsie/Duplain 11/15/1970; Niles: Grace 1976; Bellaire: Community 01/15/1981; Kalamazoo Oakwood/Oshtemo 1987; Keeler/Silver Creek 1992; Springport/Lee Center 1998; Battle Creek: Convis Union 2001; Retired 2006
daveralit@tds.net
(H) 103 Hubbard Dr, New Carlisle, IN 46552 (574) 654-2297

*LITCHFIELD, GERALDINE M (RA) (Carl) – (FL-2000, AM-2001, RA-2014)
Barry County: Woodland/Hastings: Welcome Corners (Assoc) 01/01/1993-1994; Brookfield (½ Time) 1995; Horton Bay/Charlevoix: Greensky Hill 2000; Leave of Absence 07/01-08/31/2005; Somerset Center 09/01/2005; Quincy 2007; Williamsburg/Elk Rapids 2009; Retired 2014
revgmlitchfield@yahoo.com
(H) 27435 Michigan Ave, Mendon 49072 (269) 275-5239

*LITCHFIELD, GLENN C (RE) (Dorie) – (D-1981, FE-1985, R-2016)
Vermontville/Gresham 1983; Ashley/Bannister 1990; Kent City: Chapel Hill 1996; Cassopolis 2005; Climax/Scotts 2009; Retired 2016; Kendall 2019
glennlitchfield52@gmail.com
(H) 61470 CR 657, Lawton 49065 (269) 436-0023
Kendall: 26718 Cnty Rd 388, Gobles 49055; PO Box 6, Kendall 49062
(269) 628-2303

Lobb, Grant Richard (Debra) revgrant9@gmail.com
[(FE) P 1983; F 1986]. 1984 LaSalle: Zion; 1988 Croswell: First; 1996 Owosso: First; 2005 Marquette District Superintendent; **2012 Lapeer: Trinity**. 1310 North Main St., Lapeer 48446 (810-664-9941). Home: 804 Fourth St., Lapeer 48446 (810-660-7386)

LOGSTON, JANE D (FE) (Russell) – (D-1988, FE-1991)
Transferred from West Virginia Conf 1994; Quincy 1994; Mason: First (Assoc) 1996; Family Leave 1998; Appointed in Other Annual Conferences (¶337.1) Newberry, Detroit Conf 2001; Lawrence 2003; Hinchman/Oronoko 2006; Berrien Springs/Hinchman/Oronoko 2012; Bear Lake/Arcadia 2014; Medical Leave 09/01/2018
jdlogston@yahoo.com
(H) 133 N Park St, Lake City 49651-9702 (231) 970-2048

LOGSTON, RUSSELL K (FE) (Jane) – (D-1986, FE-1991)
Transferred from West Virginia Conf 1994; Camden/Montgomery/Stokes Chapel 1994; Dansville/Vantown 1996; Constantine 1998; Family Leave 2001; Riverside (LTFT ¼) 01/01/2005; Riverside (LTFT ½) 01/01/2006; Galien/Olive Branch 2006; Sodus: Chapel Hill 2011; Empire 2014; Lake City and St. John's Lutheran Church (¶345) 2019
lcumc301@gmail.com
(H) 133 N Park St, Lake City 49651-9702 (231) 839-7542
Lake City: 301 E John St, PO Box Drawer P, Lake City 49651 (231) 839-2123

*Long, Calvin D. (Beth) calvin-long@hotmail.com
[(RE) P 1983; F 1985; R 2018]. 1980-81 Albany Circuit (Louisville Conf.); 1983 Saginaw: Ames (assoc.); Mar. 1, 1987 Saginaw: Swan Valley; Apr. 1, 1991 Monroe: Frenchtown; Jun 1, 1995 Pigeon: Salem; 2000 Houghton Lake; 2009 Owosso: First; **2018 Retired**. Home: 5531 Timothy Ln, Bath Wwp 48808 (989-954-5485)

Long, Shelly Ann (Steven) pastorshellyrumc@comcast.net
[(PL) PL 2017]. **Nov 15, 2016 Richfield**. 10090 E. Coldwater, PO Box 307, Davison 48423 (810-653-3644). Home: 11564 Kings Coach Road, Grand Blanc 48439

*LONGDEN, LEICESTER R (RE) (Linda) – (D-1973, FE-1976, R-2013)
Transferred from Oregon-Idaho Conf 1992; Lansing: Trinity 1992; Other Valid Ministries (¶335.1a) Assoc Professor of Evangelism & Discipleship, University of Dubuque Theological Seminary 2001; Retired 2013
LLongden@dbq.edu
(H) 3549 Polonaise Dr, Muskegon 49442-1775 (563) 5647274

LOOMIS, SCOTT R (FL) (Kimberly) – (FL-2012)
Pine River Parish: Ashton/Leroy (DSA) 2012; Pine River Parish: Ashton/Leroy 11/10/2012; Pine River Parish: Ashton/Leroy/Luther 06/01/2015
srloomis1@gmail.com
(H) PO Box 234, 400 W Gilbert St, Leroy 49655-0234 (231) 768-4512
Ashton: PO Box 38, 20862 11 Mile Rd, Leroy 49655-8596 (231) 832-8347
Leroy: PO Box 38, 310 West Gilbert St, Leroy 49655-0038 (231) 768-4512
Luther: PO Box 175, 315 State St, Luther 49656-0175 (231) 797-0073

LORING, MARY K (PE) (Mark) – (PL-2010, PE-2015)
Twin Lake (PTLP ½) 2010; Appointed to Extension Ministries (¶344.1b,c) Chaplain, Clark Retirement Community 2013; Appointed to Extension Ministries (¶344.1b,c) Coordinator Of Pastoral Care, Clark Retirement Community (FTLP) 06/01/2014; Jackson: Calvary and Jackson: First (Assoc) 2017; Ann Arbor: Calvary 2019

mkloring23@gmail.com
(H) 700 Newport Place, Ann Arbor 48103-3648 (616) 307-0369
Ann Arbor: Calvary: 1415 Miller Ave, Ann Arbor 48103-3758 (734) 769-0869

LOVER, JOHN D (RE) (Grace) – (D-1960, FE-1963, R-2000)
Transferred from Nebraska Conf 1994; Indian River/Pellston 1994; Indian River Indian River 09/01/1997; Retired 2000

gracie08@charter.net
(H) 725 Highland Terrace, Sheboygan, WI 53083 (920) 395-2055

Low Edwardson, Elise Rodgers (Ryan)   reveliselowedwardson@gmail.com
[(PE) FL 2016; PE 2017]. **2016 Escanaba: Central**. 322 S. Lincoln, Escanaba 49829 (906-786-0643). Home: 1814 22nd Ave., Escanaba 49829 (906-789-1874)

Low Edwardson. Ryan Casey (Elise)
[(PL) FL 2016; PL 2019]. 2016 Escanaba: First, Menominee: First; **2019 Escanaba: First** (LTFT ½). 302 S. Sixth St., Escanaba 49829 (906-786-3713. Home: 1801 17th Ave., Menominee 49858 (906-789-1874)

LOWLEY, PAUL E (RE) (Marjan) – (D-1960, FE-1963, R-2000)
Transferred from Northern Illinois Conf 1991; Ludington United 1991; Retired 2000
(H) 211 Bear Creek Lane, Georgetown, TX 48633-4125 (231) 347-9373

Luce, Michael W.   fathermikeusa@hotmail.com
[(RA) PL 1995; AM 2006]. 1995 Garfield; 2001 Poseyville; **2012 Retired**. 2950 E. Nold, Midland 48640 (989-631-2359)

Luck, Bradley S. (Aimee)   blucky33@comcast.net
[(FE) PL 2011; PE 2014; FE 2017]. 2011 Troy: Fellowship; **2013 Hudson: First; 2018 Dundee**. 645 Franklin St, Dundee 48131 (734-529-3535). Home: 241 Sidney St., Dundee 48131

Ludwig, Brenda L (RL) – (RL-2018)
[Indiana Conference, Retired Local Pastor] Three Oaks (LTFT ¾) 2018
(H) 8000 Warren Woods Rd #81, Three Oaks 49128 (812) 508-5780
Three Oaks: 2 Sycamore St E, Three Oaks 49128 (269) 756-2053

LYMAN, CAROLE STROBE (RE) (Frank) – (D-1985, FE-1989, R-2010)
Muskegon: Lake Harbor (Assoc LTFT ½) 11/01/1984; Muskegon: Lake Harbor (Assoc LTFT ¾) 01/01/1991; Plainwell: First (Co-Pastor) 1991; East Lansing: University (Co-Pastor) 1996; Grand Rapids: Trinity 2006; Retired 2010

carolelyma@aol.com
(H) 29543 Seahorse Cove, Laguna Niguel, CA 92677-1668 (616) 558-1924

LYMAN, FRANK W (RE) (Carole) – (D-1976, FE-1980, R-2010)
Transferred from Detroit Conf 1981; Muskegon: Lake Harbor 1981; Plainwell: First (Co-Pastor) 1991; East Lansing: University (Co-Pastor) 1996; Grand Rapids: Trinity 2006; Retired 2010

franklyma@aol.com
(H) 29543 Seahorse Cove, Laguna Niguel, CA 92677-1668 (616) 558-1924

LYNCH, ROBERT K (FE) (Leslie) – (D-1993, FE-1995)
Mason: First (Assoc) 1992; Paw Paw 1995; Kalamazoo: Milwood 1999; N
Muskegon: Community 2006; Allegan 2012
blynch4551@gmail.com
(H) 1310 South M 40, Allegan 49010 (269) 673-2512
Allegan: 409 Trowbridge St, Allegan 49010-9010 (269) 673-4236

Lynn, Nancy S. nancy@fumc-2a.org
[(FE) PE 2010; FE 2013]. 2010 Ann Arbor: First (assoc.); **2018 Ann Arbor: First**.
120 S. State, Ann Arbor 48104 (734-662-4536). Home: 3475 Glazier Way, Ann
Arbor 48105 (734-730-2421)

*LYONS, GARY V (RE) – (D-1972, FE-1975, R-1996)
Transferred from Detroit Conf 1972; Vermontville/Gresham 1972; Other Valid
Ministries (¶344.1d) Chaplain, US Navy 04/05/1976; Retired 1996
(H) 522 Albion Circle, Gallatin, TN 37066 (615) 230-9754

*Macaulay, Elizabeth Ann Pastorbeth0528@gmail.com
[(RE) PE 1999; FE 2002; RE 2018]. Jun 16, 1999 Sterling Heights; 2008 Trenton:
First; Apr 15, 2013 medical leave; **2018 Retired**. Home: 250 McDougall St, Apt
425, Detroit 48207

*Macaulay, Thomas Paul (Mary) tommac223@aol.com
[(RE) P 1972; F 1975]. 1973 Detroit: Boulevard Temple; 1974 Birmingham: Em-
bury (assoc.); Jan. 1977 Detroit: Waterman, Preston; 1979 Carleton; Jul. 15,
1984 Lincoln Park: First; Jul. 1, 1990 Warren: First; 1997 Lake Orion; 2004 Ann
Arbor District Superintendent; **2010 Retired**. Home: 624 Maple Oaks Court,
Saline 48176 (734-730-1742)

*MacCanon, Francis Richard
[(RE) P Iowa, EUB, 1947; F Iowa, EUB, 1952]. 1947 Laurel; 1949 Seminary;
1952 Center Point; 1957 Located; 1969 Readmitted, Mich. Conf., EUB, Dearborn: First (assoc.); 1974 Detroit: Thoburn; Mar. 1978 Detroit: Zion; Dec. 1978
River Rouge: Epworth, Detroit: Woodmere; Apr. 1983 Oscoda, Oscoda Indian
Mission; **1988 Retired**. Home: 1001 Carpenters Way #G-207, Lakeland, FL
33809

Magner, Eric Lee (PL) (Amy) – (CC-2017, DSA-2017, PL-2017)
Newaygo (DSA) (LTFT ¾) 2017; Newaygo (LP) (LTFT ¾) 12/01/2017
e1972magner@gmail.com
(H) 104 State Rd., Newaygo 49337-8134 (231) 750-3488
Newaygo: 101 State Rd., Newaygo 49337-8135 (231) 652-6581

Malicoat, Bruce W. Bruce.malicoat@gmail.com
[(PL) PL Nov, 2006; FL 2010]. Nov 1, 2006 Arbela (¼); Jan 1, 2008 Arbela (½);
2010 Arbela, West Forest; **2016 West Forest**. 7297 E. Farrand Rd., Millington
48746 (989-871-3456). Home: 129 E. Vates, Frankenmuth 48734 (989-860-
7378)

*Mallory, Mary Lynch revmlm05@yahoo.com
[(RE) P N. Ill, 1979; F Cent. IL, 1986]. 1982 Carthage-Burnside; 1984 Minonk-
Dana; 1988 Piper City; Jul 1, 1993 trans to Detroit Conf, Iron River: Wesley; Feb
1, 2001 Birmingham: Embury; 2006 West Branch: First; **2009 Retired**. Home:
#10 Penny Lane, St. Helen 48656 (989-387-0372)

*Mallory, Paul J. (Kathy)   thevicar@yahoo.com
[(RE) P Cent. IL, 1980; F Cent. IL, 1984; FL 2006; FE 2008]. 1981 Coluse-Dallas City-Nauvoo; 1984 Streator: First (Assoc); 1988 Chastsworth; Jul 1, 1993 trans to Detroit Conf, Crystal Falls-Amasa: Grace; [Nov 1, 1993 surrender of credentials]; 2006 reinstated; 2006 God's Country Cooperative Parish (Parish Director): Grand Marais, Germfask, McMillan; 2011 Iron Mountain: Trinity; **2014 Retired.** Home: 305 S. Steele, Ontonagon 49953

Mancier, Cheryl L. (Carl)   skiinggrammy@hotmail.com
[(PL) PL 2007]. 2007 Washington; 2011 Bentley; **Nov 1, 2016 Harrison: The Gathering** (W. MI). P.O. Box 86, 426 N. First, Suite 106, Harrison 48625. Home: 4338 Bay Rd., Gladwin 48624 (989-426-9886)

Mangum, Lester (Tina)   stjohnpontiac@sbcglobal.net
[(FE) P NY, 1983; F 1986]. 1983 New York City: Willis Avenue; 1985 Trans. to Detroit Conf., Detroit: Central (assoc.); 1986 Director, Young Adult Housing Project of Metropolitan Community Church, NYC (NY Conf., under par. 425.1); 1988 Detroit Human Services; 1989 River Rouge: John Wesley; 1992 Detroit: People's; Jan 1, 2003 Detroit: St. Timothy, West Outer Drive; 2005 Detroit: St. Timothy; Oct 18, 2012 medical leave; **Oct 1, 2013 Pontiac: St. John**. 620 University Dr., Pontiac 48342 (248-338-8933). Home: 622 University Dr., Pontiac 48342 (248-335-7093)

MANNING, JOSHUA (FL) – (FL-2017)
Lake Ann 2017

alpacacries@yahoo.com
(H) 6596 First St, Lake Ann 49650-9549 (334) 320-9603
Lake Ann: 6583 First St, Lake Ann 49650-9549 (231) 275-7236

MANNING, SCOTT E (FE) – (FL-2005, PE-2007, FE-2011)
Middleville/Freeport 2004; Middleville 2006; Constantine/White Pigeon 2009; Rochester Hills: St. Luke 2016

revscottemanning@gmail.com
(H) 59180 Hamilton Circle, Washington Township 48094 (586) 371-4950
Rochester Hills: St. Luke: 3980 Walton Blvd, Rochester Hills 48309-1110
(248) 373-6960

Mannschreck, Jack Lester (Ruth)   jmannschreck@waterfordcumc.org
[(FE) P 1983; F 1986]. 1984 Grosse Pointe (assoc.); 1992 Oxford; 2002 Troy: Big Beaver; **2013 Waterford: Central**. 3882 Highland Rd., Waterford 48328 (248-681-0040). Home: 3720 Shaddick, Waterford 48328 (248-683-2986)

Mannschreck, Jeremiah J. (Sara)
[(FE) FL 2014; PE 2015; FE 2019]. 2014 Ishpeming: Wesley; **2018 Flushing**. 413 E. Main St., Flushing 48433 (810-659-5172). Home: 1159 Clearview Dr., Flushing 48472 (810-659-6231)

MANSKAR, STEVEN W (OE) – (OE-2018)
[Minnestoa Conference, Elder] Grand Rapids: Trinity 2018
steven.manskar@gmail.com
(H) 2128 Monroe Ave NW, Grand Rapids 49505 (615) 948-0650
Grand Rapids: Trinity: 1100 Lake Dr SE, Grand Rapids 49506 (616) 456-7168

*Marble, Charles Robert (Janice)
[(RE) T 1961; F 1963]. 1961 school; Feb. 1963 Detroit: Westlawn (assoc.); 1965 Flint: Central (assoc.); 1967 Inkster: Christ; 1971 Bay City: Fremont Avenue; Jan. 1978 Burton: Atherton; 1985 Dixboro; 1992 Houghton Lake; **2000 Retired**. 2129 Knights Circle, Gladwin 48624 (989-426-4580)

Mariona, Ernesto   netomariona@gmail.com
[(FE) FL May 16, 2008, American Baptist Convention; FE 2011]. 2008-Sept 30, 2017 St. Charles, 2008-2015 Brant; **Oct 1, 2017 Midland: Homer, Gordonville**. (MH) 507 S Homer Rd, Midland 48640 (989-835-5050). (G) 76 E Gordonville Rd, Midland 48640 (989-486-10640. Home: 8225 Beaver Rd, Saint Charles 48655 (248) 760-9590.

*Marr, Beverly Louise (Fred)   revbevmarr@hotmail.com
[(RE) PE 2003; FE 2006]. 2003 Lincoln Community; 2010 Seven Churches United Group Ministry: Durand: First (Parish Director); **2017 Retired**. Home: 3910 Norton Road, Howell 48843 (810-923-6860)

Marsh, Scott W (Meagan)   smarsh3386@gmail.com
[(FL) FL 2019]. **2019 Coleman: Faith**. 310 N 5th St, Coleman 48618-8336 (989-465-6181). Home: 209 Jefferson St, Coleman 48618-9310 (231-760-0601)

Marshall, Murphy C.
[(LP) LP 2015]. **2017 Harper Woods: Redeemer**. 20571 Vernier Rd., Harper Woods 48225 (313-884-2035). Home: 20572 Anita, Harper Woods 48225

Marshall-Smith, June M.   junesmith48124@yahoo.com
[(FE) PL 2006; PE 2007; FE 2011]. 2006 Dearborn: Mt. Olivet; **2007 Novi**. 41671 W. Ten Mile Rd., Novi 48375 (248-349-2652). Home: 49755 Oakwood Dr., Novi 48375 (248-349-6117)

*Martinez-Ventour, Margaret A   pastormmv@comcast.net
[(RL) PL 9/1/03, PE 2004, LP 2012, RL 2019]. Sep 1, 2003 Detroit: Jefferson Avenue; 2005 Detroit: Mt. Hope; 2010 Detroit: Resurrection; **2019 Retired**. Home: 7623 Danbury Cir, W Bloomfield 48322-3569 (313-342-3027)

*Mater, Douglas E. (Margaret)   spamd5@aol.com
[(RE) FL 2003; PE 2004; FE 2007; RE 2019]. 2003 Bay Port, Hayes; 2010 Negaunee: Mitchell; 2016 Saginaw: Ames; **Retired 2019**. Home: 6061 Foxwood Ct, Saginaw 48638 (989-906-1463)

*Mathews, James M. (Coryn)   revmathews@yahoo.com
[(RA) FL 1981; LD, AM 1986; RA 2003]. 1981 Republic, Woodland; Jun. 1, 1984 Iron Mountain: First, Quinnesec; Dec. 1, 1989 Leave of Absence; 1990 L'Anse, Sidnow, Zeba; 1993 Pickford; 1996 Leave of Absence; Aug 1, 1997 Seven Churches United Group Ministry: Vernon, Bancroft; Oct 1, 2001 Roseville: Trinity, Warren: Wesley; 2002 incapacity leave; **2003 Retired;** 2003 Stephenson: Firs (LTFT ½)t; **2019 Keweenaw Parish: Calumet, Lake Linden (LTFT ½)**. (C) 57235 Calumet Ave., Calumet 49913-3015 (906-337-2720), (LL) 53237 N. Hecla, Lake Linden 49945 (906-296-0148). Home: 26350 Wyandotte St., Laurium 49913-2696 (906-337-0539)

*MATHIEU, PAMELA J (RD) – (D-1997, RD-2012)
Transferred from Detroit Conf 1995; Lansing: Mount Hope, Director of Visitation and Adult Ministries 1995; Transitional Leave 12/31/2005; Medical Leave 03/01/2006; Retired 2012

pmath2@gmail.com
(H) 5824 Merritt Rd, Ypsilanti 48197-6602 (517) 214-4441

*MAURER, EDRYE A EASTMAN (RE) – (FL-2000, PE-2003, FE-2006, R-2017)
Lake City 2000; Jackson Calvary 09/01/2010; Jackson Calvary/Zion 2013; Coldwater 2015; Retired 2017

edryemaurer@gmail.com
(H) 10101 Jackson Square, Decatur, GA 30030 (269) 459-5223

*Maxwell, Jeffrey R. (Janet)   jffmxwll@yahoo.com
[(RE) LP 1982; P 1986; F 1989]. 1982 Garfield; 1987 Kilmanagh, Unionville; Jan. 15, 1990 Holly: Calvary; 2001 Farmington: First; 2010 Saginaw Bay District Superintendent; **2016 Retired**. Home: 304 Meadow Lane, Midland 48640 (989-750-7035)

*May, Judith Ann   judymay1947@yahoo.com
[(RE) P 1990; F 1993]. 1989 Four Towns (LTFT); Jan. 1 1991 Four Towns. 1992 Pontiac Cooperative Parish, Parish Director: Four Towns; Feb 1, 1996 Dearborn: First (assoc); 1998 Walled Lake; 2003 Warren: First; 2008 Grosse Pointe; **2016 Retired**. Home: 52843 Sable Drive, Macomb 48042 (586-242-1555

Mayberry, Gregory Mark   gmayberry@bbumc.org [7/15/16]
[(FE) P 1984; F 1986]. 1984 Iron River; 1990 Caseville; May 1, 1998 Milford; 2011 Caro; **2016 Troy: Big Beaver**. 3753 John R, Troy 48083 (248-689-1932). Home: 2050 Fairfield, Troy 48085 (248-689-2839)

*Maynard, William Robert (Janis)   RevBill02@aol,com
[(RE) P 1972; F 1980]. Sep. 1978 Kilmanagh; 1980 Flint: Eastwood; 1986 Mayville, Fostoria, Silverwood; Sep 1, 1992 Mt. Morris; 1996 Corunna; 2001 Davisburg; Jan 1, 2004 incapacity leave; **2009 Retired**. Home: PO Box 163, East Tawas 48730

*Mayo, Judith Y. (James)   jymayo1@comcast.net
[(RD) CE CRT 1990; CON 1992; DFM 1997; RD 2014]. 1984 Livonia: Newburg; 1998 Detroit: Christ; 1999 East Side Covenant Cooperative Parish, parish deacon; Jan 1, 2001 leave of absence; 2001 Ypsilanti: First (deacon); Jan 1, 2007 Ypsilanti: First (deacon); Dec 5, 2007 incapacity leave. **2014 Retired**. Home: 6065 Vista Dr., Ypsilanti 48197 (734-482-0776)

*MAYO, ROBERT J (RE) (Sharon) – (D-1980, FE-1983, R-2013)
Transferred from Northern Indiana Conf 1981; Marcellus/Wakelee 1981; Hastings: Hope 04/01/1986; Traverse City Emmanuel 1992; Grand Rapids: Saint Paul 1999; UM Connectional Structures (¶344.1a,c) District Superintendent, Grand Traverse District 2005; Battle Creek: Chapel Hill 2011; Retired 2013

rmayo777@yahoo.com
(H) 4651 Springmont Dr SE, Kentwood 49512-5470 (616) 228-3075

Mayo-Moyle, Amy E. (Michael) AMayomoyle@yahoo.com
[(FE) PE 2000; FE 2003]. 2000 Detroit: Metropolitan (assoc); 2002 Britton: Grace; Sep 16, 2007 Britton: Grace (LTFT ½); Jan 1, 2009 Britton: Grace (LTFT ¾);2010 Clarkston (assoc.); **2015 Farmington: Orchard**. 30450 Farmington, Farmington Hills 48334 (248-626-3620). Home: 32979 Thorndyke Court, Farmington Hills 48334 (517-918-2215)

Mayo-Moyle, Michael James (Amy) mmayomoyle@michiganumc.org
[(FE) FL 2001; PE 2002; FE 2005]. 2001 Ann Arbor: First (assoc) Feb 1, 2003 Blissfield: First; 2010 Seven Churches United Group Ministry: Byron: First; 2012 Voluntary leave of absence; **2017 Michigan UMC IT Specialist**. 1161 E Clark Rd, Ste 212, DeWitt 48820 (517-347-4030 ext. 4136). Home: 32979 Thorndyke Court, Farmington Hills 48334 (517-918-2215)

MAYS, JONATHAN D (PL) – (PL-2015)
Charlevoix: Greensky Hill (DSA) (½ Time) 2012; Charlevoix: Greensky Hill (PTLP ½) 2015

jonmays7@gmail.com
(H) 409 Prospect St, Charlevoix 49720-1020 (231) 459-8067
Greensky Hill: 8484 Green Sky Hill Rd, Charlevoix 49720-9686 (231) 547-2028

*MAZUR, PAUL D (RE) (Margaret) – (D-1968, FE-1971, R-1990)
Frontier 1963; Girard 1966; Battle Creek: Baseline 1969; Hillside 09/15/1972; Climax/Scotts 09/01/1974; Carson City/Hubbardston 1978; Buchanan: First 1985; Frankfort/Elberta 1987; Coopersville 04/01/1989; Retired 1990

paulmazur12@att.net
(H) 536 Harwood Ct, Eaton Rapids 48827-1686 (517) 663-2687

MCBRIDE, DAVID L (FE) (Bonnie) – (D-1985, FE-1987)
Holton/Sitka 1983; Holton 01/01/1985; Marshall (Assoc) 1988; Ithaca/Beebe 1991; Leighton 2006

office@leightonchurch.org
(H) (616) 891-1646
Leighton: 4180 2nd St, Caledonia 49316-9220 (616) 891-8028

*McBride, William Parker mbill@shianet.org
[(RE) P 1975; F 1981]. 1978 Owendale, Gagetown; 1980 Flint: Faith; 1985 Monroe: Calvary; 1995 Seven Churches United Group Ministry (Parish Director): Durand: First; 2002 North Street; Nov 1, 2014 disability leave; **2016 Retired**. 3900 Aspen Dr., #316, Port Huron 48060 (810-434-3494)

*McCallum, Marvin H. (Joyce) joyce.mccallum@gmail.com
[(RE) T 1959; F 1961]. 1961 Pigeon; 1966 Oxford; 1972 Manistique; Nov. 1975 Chelsea; 1983 Monroe: St. Paul's; 1991 Royal Oak: First; 1995 Port Huron District Superintendent; **2002 Retired**. Home: 5385 Burtch Rd., Jeddo 48032 (810-327-2691)

*MCCOY, J PATRICK (RE) (Susan) – (D-1977, FE-1982, R-2014)
Three Rivers: First/Ninth Street (Assoc) 10/01/1980; Other Valid Ministries (¶344.1d) Resident Supervisory CPE, North Carolina Memorial Hospital 1983; Other Valid Ministries (¶344.1d) Director of Clinical Chaplaincy Iowa Methodist Medical Center 10/15/1985; Other Valid Ministries (¶344.1d) Director of Chaplaincy, Dartmouth-Hitchcock Medical Center, Lebanon NH 11/01/1993; Retired 09/01/2014

(H) 32 Sargent St, Norwich, VT 05055-9407 (802) 649-3736

McCoy, Steven E. (Deborah)
[(FE) PE 1999; FE 2002]. 1999 Midland: First (assoc); 2006 Marquette: First; **2013 Livonia: Newburg**. 36500 Ann Arbor Trail, Livonia 48150 (734-422-0149). Home: 33652 Trillium Court, Livonia 48150 (734-424-4593)

*MCCREEDY, ALLEN D (RE) (Mina Ann) – (D-1965, FE-1970, R-2000)
Kalamazoo: Sunnyside 1967; Kalamazoo: Westwood 1973; Reed City 1977; Cadillac 1990; Retired 2000

2015kaylyn@gmail.com
(H) 2015 Kaylynn Dr, Cadillac 49601-8210 (231) 775-8254

*McCully, Ruth Alida　　　　　　　　　　　ruthmccully@live.com
[(RL) FL 1998]. 1998 Samaria: Grace, Lulu; 2001 Lulu; 2003 Retired; Nov 1, 2007 Azalia, London. **Oct 30, 2009 Retired**. Home: 510 E. Monroe, Dundee 48131 (734-529-5130).

*McCumons, Brent Lee (Marlene)　　　　　　bmccumons@aol.com
[(RE) P 1976; F 1980]. Jan 1, 1975 Second Creek, Edenton, OH (WOH Conf.); 1978 Royal Oak: First (assoc.); 1981 Caseville; 1986 Chesaning: Trinity; 1993 Ann Arbor District Superintendent; 1998 Midland: First **2011 Retired**. Home: 909 Ruddy Duck Lane, Chelsea 48118

McDonald, Ian S.
[(FL) FL 2012]. 2012 God's Country Cooperative Parish: Grand Marais, Germfask, McMillian; **Carson City 2019**. 119 E Elm St, PO Box 298, Carson City 48811-0298. Home: 121 S Abbott St, Carson City 48811-9452 (906-322-5318)

McDoniel, Tommy　　　　　　　　　　revmcdoniel@gmail.com
[(FL) FL 2010]. **2010 Flint: Asbury**. 1653 Davison Rd., Flint 48506 (810-235-0016). Home: 2050 Covert Rd., Burton 48509 (810-705-4401)

MCDOUGALL, HEATHER A (PE) – (FL-2011, PE-2014)
Silver Creek/Keeler 2011; Kalamazoo: Milwood 2013; Appointed to Extension Ministries (¶344.1b,c) PRN Chaplain, Bronson Healthcare Group 09/01/2015; Appointed to Extension Ministries (¶344.1b,c) Chaplain, Bronson Methodist Hospital 02/08/2016; Appointed to Extension Ministries (¶344.1b,c) Chaplain Beacon Health System (LTFT ¾) and Three Rivers: First (LTFT ¼)

chaplainheathermcdougall@gmail.com
(H) 61644 Windridge Ct, Centreville 49032-9560 (269) 352-4857
Three Rivers: First: 215 N Main St, Three Rivers 49093-1504 (269) 278-4722

*McDowell, Ginethea D.
[(RE) PL 1989; P 1994; F 1996]. 1989-91 Caring Covenant Group Ministry: West Deerfield. 1992 no appointment; 1994 Yale, Greenwood; Dec 1, 1998 family leave **2002 Retired**. Home: 124 Happy Haven Dr., Lot 46, Osprey, FL 34229

PASTORAL RECORDS

*McEntarfer, Martin A.
[(RE) FL, Erie, 1950; T. MI, 1953; F 1960]. 1950 Franklin Center; 1951 Lyon Lake; 1953 Delton; 1956 Burton Heights (assoc.); Dec. 1956 Trans. to Detroit Conf., Menominee; 1960 Centerline: Bethel; 1966 Chaplain, Plattsburg AFB, NY; 1969 Site Chaplain, Alaskan Air Command; 1970 Chaplain, Kitty Hawk Center, Wright Patterson AFB, Ohio; 1972 Chaplain, Pilot Training Program, Reese AFB, TX; 1973 Chaplain, Utapoa AB, Thailand; 1974 Chaplain, Regional Medical Center, March AFB, CA; 1978 Senior Chaplain, Irakion AB, Crete, Greece; 1980 Senior Chaplain, David Grant Medial Center, Travis AFB, CA; 1984 Senior Chaplain, March AFB, CA; 1986 USAF Retired; 1986 Service Director, American Cancer Society; 1989 Cancer Control Director, American Cancer Society; **1992 Retired**. Home: 20505 Claremont Ave., Riverside, CA 92507 (951-686-5846)

McGee, Ray Thomas (Darlene)   mcgreeray4@gmail.com
[(FE) LP 1995; FL 1998; AM 2000; FE 2003]. Jan 1, 1995 LaSalle: Zion; Aug 15, 2000 Sebewaing: Trinity; 2004 Flint: Calvary; 2011 Detroit: Metropolitan; **2016 Grosse Pointe**. 211 Moross Rd., Grosse Pointe Farms 48236 (313-886-2363). Home: 64 Moross Rd., Grosse Pointe Farms 48236 (313-881-1129)

McGlothin-Eller, April K. (Vincent)   april.mcgel@gmail.com
[(FD) PD 2006; FD 2009]. Jun 1, 2006 Young Leaders Initiative; Jan 31, 2008 leave of absence; Mar 16, 2008 Student Coordinator for Interfaith Worker Justice, Highland Park Presbyterian; Jun 14, 2010 Stewardship Associate, Garrett-Evangelical Seminary; **2018 Church Engagement Manager, Newnan Office of the UM Children's Home (Par 331.1b) North Georgia Conf.** Home: 6572 Oakwood Dr., Douglasville, GA 30135

McGlothin-Eller, Vincent W. (April)   vincemcgel@gmail.com
[(FD) PD 2009; FD 2012]. 2009 Registrar, Garrett Evangelical Theological Seminary; June 1, 2010 Director of Academic Studies and Registrar GETS; 2018 Director: Academic Studies and Registrar GETS; **Jan 1, 2019 Newman: First (N Georgia Conf)**. 33 Greenville St., Newnan, GA 30263 (770-253-7400). Home: 6572 Oakwood Dr., Douglasville, GA 30135

McIlvenna, Lisa M. (Patrick)   lisamcilvenna@yahoo.com
[(FE) P 1990; F 1993]. 1991 Owendale, Gagetown; 1995 Saginaw: Kochville; Sep 1, 1999 Birmingham: First (assoc.); 2004 Rochester Hills: St. Luke's; 2008 Samaritan Couseling Center, Southeast Michigan; **Jan, 2010 Midland: First (assoc) (½), Executive Director/Pastoral Therapist, Samaritan Counseling Center (½)**. 315 W. Larkin, Midland 48640 (989-835-7511). Home: 531 Morningside Dr, Midland 48640 (248-224-4296)

McInnes, Mary G. (Damon)   revmarymcinnes@att.net
[(FE) P 1996; F 1998]. 1996 Grosse Pointe (assoc); Nov 1, 2002 Farmington: Nardin Park (assoc); 2008 Tawas; 2013 Mount Clemens: First; **2017 South Lyon: First**. 640 S. Lafayette, South Lyon 48178 (248-437-0760). Home: 650 S. Lafayette, South Lyon 48178 (586-515-0013)

McKanders, Cherlyn E.   cmckanders@comcast.net
[(PL) PL 2017]. 2017 Mount Vernon (LTFT ½); **2019 Mt Vernon (LTFT ½), Washington (LTFT ¼)**. (MV) 3000 28 Mile Rd., Washington 48094 (248-650-2213), (W) 58430 Van Dyke, PO Box 158, Washington 48094-0158 (586-781-9662). Home: 59989 Whitman N. #D, Washington 48094-2261 (248-881-8541)

MCKENNEY, WAYNE E (FL) (Sally) – (FL-1995)
Chase Barton/Grant Center (DSA) 1995; Chase: Barton/Grant Center 11/16/1995; Webberville 08/01/2002; Boyne City/Boyne Falls 2005; Oshtemo: Lifespring/Lawton: St Paul's 2014; Lawrence/Lawton: St Paul's 2016
skinnypreacher@me.com
(H) 45520 24th St, Mattawan 49071-8769 (269) 669-7062
Lawrence: PO Box 276, 122 S Exchange St, Lawrence 49064-0276
(269) 674-8381
Lawton: St Paul's: PO Box 456, 63855 N M-40, Lawton 49065-0456
(269) 624-1050

*McKinstry, A. Faye (David) fayemckinstry@comcast.com
[(RE) P 1988; F 1992]. 1988 St. Clair Shores: First (assoc.) (LTFT½); 1990 East Detroit: Peace; Jul 1, 1995 Madison Heights; 1999 Manchester; 2005 Clinton; **2014 Retired**. Home: 35 Ridgemont Dr., Adrian 49221 (517-815-1172)

*McKinstry, David Robert (A. Faye) drmckinstry@gmail.com
[(RE) P 1979; F 1982]. 1980 Oregon, Elba; 1988 St. Clair Shores: First; 1999 Tecumseh; **2010 Retired**. Home: 35 Ridgemont Dr., Adrian 49221 (517-815-1172)

McMunn, Douglas Jay (Marianne) doug.mcmunn@gmail.com
[(FE) P 1985; F 1988]. 1986 Plymouth: First (assoc.); Feb. 16, 1990 Iron Mountain: First, Quinnesec: First; Jan 1, 1996 Pinckney: New Church Development (Arise) Sep 28, 2001 Pinckney: Arise; 2006 Oxford; **2011 Milford**. 1200 Atlantic St. Milford 48381 (248-684-2798). Home: 350 Cabinet St., Milford 48381 (248-685-1737)

McMunn, Marianne (Douglas) mariannemcmunn@sbcglobal.net
[(PL) PL 2010]. Nov 14, 2010 Omo: Zion; 2011 Willow. (**2016** no appointment). Home: 350 Cabinet St., Milford 48381 (248-685-1737)

*MCNARY, SANDRA B HOFFMAN (RE) (Charles) – (D-1984, FE-1988, R-2007)
Transferred from Tennessee Conf 1994; Bangor: Simpson 1994; Retired 2007
sandramcnary@live.com (269) 427-0766

*MCNAUGHTON, JOHN W (RE) (Donna Lee) – (D-1971, FE-1974, R-2003)
Transferred from Detroit Conf 1973; Webberville/Bell Oak 1973; Oakwood 1979; Concord 1982; Plainfield 1984; Gobles-Kendall 1986; Other Valid Ministries (¶426.1) Methodist Church, Blackhearth Circuit, England 1987; Frankfort/Elberta 1993; Lane Boulevard 1996; Kalamazoo: Stockbridge/Lane Blvd 1998; Kalamazoo: Stockbridge Ave (LTFT ½) 01/16/2000; Kalamazoo: Stockbridge Ave/Northwest 05/01/2000; Retired 2003; Bloomingdale (Interim Pastor) 12/08-12/31/2008
thecroikazoo@gmail.com
(H) 2910 Bronson Blvd, Kalamazoo 49008-2372 (269) 383-3433

McNees, Zachary D (FL) – (FL 2019)
Grand Rapids: Northlawn (LTFT ½) and Allendale: Valley Church (Assoc) (LTFT ½) 2019
zmcnees@valleychurchallendale.org
(H) 1141 Northlawn St NE, Grand Rapids 49505-3723 (269) 986-0108
Northlawn: 1157 Northlawn St NE, Grand Rapids 49505-3723 (616) 361-8503
Valley Church: 5980 Lake Michigan Dr, Ste B, Allendale 49401-9576
(616) 892-1042

MCPHERSON, ROB A (FE) (Kristi) – (D-1997, FE-2001)
Grandville (Assoc) 1994; Ovid United Church 1999; Buchanan: First 2006; Hillsdale: First 2018

revrobmac@sbcglobal.net
(H) 1079 Markris Dr, Hillsdale 49242 (269) 845-5221
Hillsdale: First: 45 N Manning St, Hillsdale 49242-1633 (517) 437-3681

*MCREYNOLDS, RUSSELL F (RE) – (D-1971, FE-1974, R-2007)
Transferred from Detroit Conf 1991; Battle Creek: Washington Heights 06/16/1991; UM Connectional Structures (¶344.1a,c) District Superintendent, Kalamazoo District 1996; Lansing: Central 2002; Retired 2007; Lansing: Faith & S Lansing Ministries 2008-2015

russellfmcreynolds@comcast.net
(H) 1721 Dover Place, Lansing 48910-1146 (517) 483-2727

*Mehl, John Matthew, Jr. (Terrie) mudbug@cass.net
[(RE) P 1980; F 1984; RE 2019]. 1982 Argentine, Linden; 1989 Ida; 1996 Ida, Petersburg; 2001 Petersburg (LTFT ½); Jan 1, 2010 incapacity leave; **Jun 1, 2019 Retired**. Home: 16645 Dixon Rd., Petersburg 49270 (734-279-2662)

*MEISTER, DAVID W (RE) (Denise) – (D-1977, FE-1980, R-2016)
Transferred from East Ohio Conf 1978; Rosebush/Leaton 1978; Lakeview/Belvidere 1980; Litchfield 1985; Leave of Absence 03/16/1990; Haslett: Aldersgate 1994; Union City 08/01/1995; Centreville 08/16/1997; Buchanan: First 2003; Casco 2006; Retired 2016

revdmeister@gmail.com
(H) 6775 107th Ave, South Haven 49090-9367 (269) 876-7204

*Melrose, Paul J. (Sue Ellis Melrose) paul.melrose@gmail
[(RE) P 1971 NY; F 1974 NY]. 1971 school; 1973 Bristol: Prospect (assoc); 1975 Bronx: City Island; Jan, 1981 school; 1982 Associate Director, Lakeland Counseling Center, FRMH, Dover, NJ; 1986 Co-Director, Lakeland Counseling Center, FRMH, Dover, NJ; 1993 Director, FRMH Counseling Center, NW New Jersey; 1996 Director, FRMH, New Jersey; 1998 Coordinator, Pastoral Psychotherapy, NW Covenant Medical Center, NJ; 1999 Coordinator, Pastoral Psychotherapy, St. Clares Hospital, Boonton, NJ; Feb 2, 2000 Staff Counselor, Samaritan Counseling Center, Southeast Michigan (transferred to Detroit Conf., 2001); 2006 Executive Director, Samaritan Counseling Center, Southeast Michigan; **2011 Retired**. Home: 1624 N. Golf Glen, Unit A, Madison, WI 53704 (248-231-7229)

*MERCER, DOROTHY M D (RD) (David) – (D-1997, RD-2003)
Grand Rapids: Faith, Director of Music 1987; Stanwood (LTFT ¼) 1997; Retired 03/01/2003

(H) 8651 Mohawk Ct, Stanwood 49346-9644 (231) 972-7175

*Mercer, Douglas Keith (Barbara F.) dougbarbmercer@gmail.com
[(RE) T 1966; F 1968]. 1962 Wellsville; Oct. 1963 Rea, Cone, Azalia; 1966 Concord Charge (Peninsula Conf.); 1968 Port Huron: Washington Avenue; 1970 Algonac; 1974 Flint: Court Street (assoc.); 1977 South Lyon; Jan. 15, 1988 Gladstone: Memorial; 1990 Flint District Superintendent; 1996 Frankenmuth; **2000 Retired**. 10117 Hawthorne Lane, Byron 48418 (810-266-5073)

MERCHANT, MICHELLE (PL) – (PL-2016)
New Hope of Emmett County (DSA) 12/01/2015; New Hope of Emmett County (PTLP ½ Time) 11/15/2016

michellekm64@outlook.com
(H) 3224 Hill Road NW, Rapid City 49676-9585 (231) 564-0723
New Hope: PO Box 72, 4516 N US 31, Levering 49755-0072 (231) 537-2000

MESSNER, JOHN D (FL) (Sally) – (FL-2008)
Marcellus/Wakelee (DSA) 2007; Marcellus/Wakelee 01/01/2008

jdmessner@gmail.com
(H) 224 Davis St, Marcellus 49067-9361 (269) 646-7791
Marcellus: PO Box 396, 197 W Main St, Marcellus 49067-0396 (269) 646-5801
Wakelee: 15921 Dutch Settlement Rd, Marcellus 49067-9530 (269) 646-2049

METZER, KIMBERLY S (FL) (Steve) – (FL-2017)
Hastings Hope 2017

pastorkimmetzer@gmail.com
Hastings Hope: PO Box 410, 2920 S M37, Hstings 49058-9364 (269) 945-4995

*Meyers, Patricia A. (Lee Hearn) patbeaches@comcast.net
[(RE) P 1977; F 1979]. 1977 Flint: Central (assoc.); 1978 Dearborn: First (assoc.); 1980 Pontiac: Baldwin Avenue; 1997 Ferndale: First; 1999 Mt. Clemens: First; Aug 1, 2006 incapacity leave; **2014 Retired**. Home: 15821 19 Mile Rd, Apt 309, Clinton Twp 48038 (586-884-6538)

Middel, Carol Ann bmiddel@aol.com
[(PL) PL Jan 1, 2019]. 2017 Thomas (DSA) (LTFT ½); Jan 1, 2019 Thomas (LTFT ½); **2019 Riverview** (LTFT ½). 13199 Colvin, Riverview 48193-6653 (734-284-2721). Home: 42018 Woodbrook Dr, Canton 48188-2612 (734-765-8143)

*Miles, Catherine J. (Kevin) revcjmm7@gmail.com
[(RD) PD 2009; FD 2012]. May 17, 2009 Detroit: Metropolitan (deacon); Aug 1, 2013 Fraser: Christ (deacon); **2017 Retired**. Home: 906 Hollis St., Port Huron 48060 (586-453-7209)

*Miles, Kevin Lee (Catherine) revkevm@gmail.com
[(RE) P 1990; F 1993]. 1991 Plymouth: First (assoc.); 1995 Blissfield: Emmanuel; 2002 Eastside Covenant Cooperative Parish: Roseville: Trinity; 2012 Oxford; 2014 Davison; **2017 Retired**. Home: 906 Hollis St., Port Huron 48060 (586-453-3275)

Milford, Dale
[(LP) LP 2015]. 2015 Waterford: Four Towns; **2019 Southfield: Hope** (assoc) (LTFT ¼). 26275 Northwestern Hwy, Southfield 48076-3926 (248-356-1020). Home: 29229 Utley Rd, Farmington Hills 48334-4177 (248-417-5905)

*MILLER, CLYDE E (RA) (Judith) – (D-1964, E-1966, AM-1973, RA-1987)
Transferred from South Indiana Conf 1973; Pentwater/Smith Corners 1973; Pentwater 1976; Pentwater/Smith Corners 1977; Dowagiac: First 12/01/1979; Lansing Christ 04/16/1983; Leave of Absence 01/31/1987; Retired 1987

clydemiller@chartermi.net
(H) 1117 Park St, Pentwater 49449-9424 (231) 869-2151

*Miller, Dale M. (Susan)   ddmm27@comcast.net
[(RE) P N. IN, 1972; F 1975]. 1974 Trans. to Detroit Conf., Plymouth: First (assoc.); 1976 Stony Creek; 1981 Gladstone: Memorial; Jan. 1, 1988 Flint: Central; 1992 Pontiac Cooperative Parish, Waterford: Central; Oct 1, 2000 Detroit East: District Superintendent; 2006 Farmington: Nardin Park; **2016 Retired**. Home: 129 Chauncey Ct., Marshall 49068 (248-943-0699)

MILLER, DARRYL L (PL) (Shari Ann) – (PL-2007)
Sand Lake/South Ensley (DSA PTLP ½) 01/01/2007; Sand Lake/South Ensley (PTLP ½) 12/01/2007; Sand Lake/South Ensley (PTLP ¼) 2011
                              parsonmiller@charter.net
           (H) 1568 Solon, Cedar Springs 49319-9438 (616) 696-4057
Sand Lake: PO Box 97, 65 W Maple Street, Sand Lake 49343 (676) 636-5673
South Ensley: PO Box 97, 13600 Cypress Ave, Sand Lake 49343 (616) 365-
                                                                5659

*Miller, Duane E. (Diana)   duane@ddmiller.net
[(RE) P 1968; F 1973]. Mar. 1972 Memphis, Lamb; Nov. 1977 Gwinn, Ishpeming: Salisbury; Jan. 1, 1986 Associate Council Director: Evangelism/Stewardship; Jan 1, 1996 Macomb Community Church; Jan 1, 1999 Seymour Lake; 1999 Caro; 2006 Detroit East District Superintendent; **2011 Retired**. Home: 3352 W. River Dr., Gladwin 48624 (989-426-2644)

Miller, Eric John   pastor@davisburgumc.com
[(PL) PL Dec 1, 2014]. Dec 1, 2014 Davisburg; **2018 Port Huron: Gratiot Park, Port Huron: Washington Avenue** (LTFT ½). (GP) 811 Church St., Port Huron 48060 (810-985-6206), (WA) 1217 Washington Ave., Port Huron 48060 (810-982-7812). Home: 48212 Cardinal, Shelby Twp. 48317 (586-206-4527)

Miller, Mark Alan (Sharon)   tecumcpastor@gmail.com
[(FE) PE 2006; FE 2009]. 2006 Romulus: Community; **2010 Tecumseh**. 605 Bishop Reed Dr, Tecumseh 49286 (517-423-2523). Home: 808 Derby Dr., Tecumseh 49286 (517-423-3767)

MILLER, MARK DOUGLAS (Kelly)
[(FE) P 1983; F 1986]. 1984 Blissfield: Emmanuel (assoc.), Wellsville; May 1, 1989 Owosso: Trinity; 1998 West Branch: First; 2006 Midland: Aldersgate; 2013 Muskegon: Central
                              revmarkmiller@yahoo.com
           (H) 1354 Hendrick Rd, Norton Shores 49441-5738 (231) 766-8989
Muskegon Central: 1011 Second Street, Muskegon 49440-1231 (231) 722-6545

Miller, Jr., Robert A. (Rochelle)   pastorbobmiller@comcast.net {5-17-12]
[(FE) PL 2010; PE 2012; FE 2015]. Jan 1, 2010 Livingston Circuit: Plainfield, Trinity; 2013 Milan: Marble Memorial; **2018 Plymouth: First**. 45201 N. Territorial Rd., Plymouth 48170 (734-453-5280). Home: 1401 Palmer St., Plymouth 48170 (810-623-0985)

*Miller, Sylvester, III   PastorSylMil3@aol.com
[(RE) P N. Miss., 1968; F N. Miss., 1977]. 1969--73 Boyd Chapel, Sturgis; 1979 Pleasant Grove, Louisville, MS; 1983 Director, Holmes County Parish; Aug. 1, 1985 Trans. to Detroit Conf., Detroit: Second Grace (assoc.); Mar. 1, 1986 Flint: E.L. Gordon Sr. Memorial; 1988 Leave of Absence; 1990 Flint: Faith; Aug 1, 2002 leave of absence; **2003 Retired**. Home: PO Box 28185, Birmingham, AL 35228 (205-426-8457)

*Miller, Walter Harry (Sandra)
[(RA) FL 1982; Deacon, AM 1987]. Nov. 1, 1981 Clayton, Rollin Center; 1994 Blissfield: First Dec 1, 2002 leave of absence; **Dec 1, 2004 Retired**. Home: 3805 Townley Highway, Manitou Beach 49253 (517-547-4544)

Miller-Black, Christina Lee (see White, Christina M.)

Minarik, Carman John (Donna)
[(FE) P 1997, W. OH; FE 2000]. 1995 Essex (W. OH); 1997 school; 1998 Carleton; Sep 1, 2002 South Lyon (co-pastor); 2007 Mount Clemens: First (co-pastor); 2013 Escanaba: First; 2016 Owosso: Trinity; 2019 Mecosta: New Hope
pastorcarman.newhope@gmail.com
(H) 3955 9 Mile Rd., Remus 49340-9712 (989) 967-8801
Mecosta: New Hope: 7296 9 Mile Rd., Mecosta 49332-9344 (231) 972-2838

Minarik, Donna Jo (Carman)
[(FE) SP 1998, W. OH; PE 2001; FE 2005]. 1996 Richwood Central (W. OH); 1998 Carleton (assoc); Sep 1, 2002 South Lyon (co-pastor); Sep 16, 2006 leave of absence; 2007 Mount Clemens: First (co-pastor); 2013 Escanaba: Central; 2016 Mason: First (W. MI Conf); 2019 Voluntary Leave of Absence
(H) 3955 9 Mile Rd., Remus 49340-9712 (248) 921-2710

*MINGER, DAVID H (RE) – (D-1991, FE-1993, R-2006)
Nottawa (Part Time) 10/01/1983; Athens 09/01/1987; Springport/Lee Center 01/01/1991; Traverse City Emmanuel 1999; Old Mission Peninsula (Ogdensburg) 02/01/2003; Retired 2006; Pleasant Lake/Jackson: Zion 2008; Griffith (LTFT ¼) 2013-10/16/2014
dhminger@yahoo.com
(H) 806 Emmaus Rd, Eaton Rapids 48827-1679 (517) 256-5857

MINGER, STACY R (FE) – (D-1988, FE-1991)
Girard/Ellis Corners 1989; Wayland 1995; Clergy Appointed to Attend School Student, University of Kentucky 08/01/2001; Appointed to Extension Ministries (¶344.1b,c) Associate Professor, Preaching, Asbury Theological Seminary 2004
Stacy.Minger@asburyseminary.edu
(H) 406 Wabarto Way, Nicholasville, KY 40356-2812 (859) 229-0059
(O) Asbury Theo Sem, 204 N Lexington Ave, Wilmore, KY 40390 (859) 858-2000

*MINOR, DANIEL J (RE) (Jolene) – (D-1968, FE-1970, R-2011)
Transferred from East Ohio Conf 1974; East Jordan/Barnard/Norwood 4/15/1974; Shelby 1981; Parchment 1989; Retired 2011; Gobles/Kendall 09/16/2012-2013
(H) 719 Bayberry Ln, Otsego 49078-1580 (269) 491-5168 revdminor@att.net

MITCHELL, MARK E (FL) (Joyce) – (FL-1995)
Howard City First/Amble/Coral 1995; Howard City: Maple Hill/First/Coral (Assoc) 08/01/1999; Homer/Lyon Lake 2000; Evart 2008; Fife Lake Parish: East Boardman/South Boardman 2012; Sodus: Chapel Hill 2014; North Parma/Springport 2018
mjmjumc@gmail.com
(H) 258 Green St, Springport 49284 (517) 414-0180
North Parma: 11970 Devereaux, PO Box 25, Parma 49269-0025 (517) 531-4619
Springport: 127 W Main St, PO Box 1004, Springport 49284-1004 (517) 857-2777

MITCHUM, JAMES P (FE) (Michelle) – (D-1984, FE-1986)
Charlotte (Assoc) 04/16/1983; Robbins 06/01/1987; Petoskey 1997
james.mitchum@petoskeyumc.org
(H) 900 Jennings Ave, Petoskey 49770-3139 (231) 374-4747
Petoskey: 1804 E Mitchell Rd, Petoskey 49770-9686 (231) 347-2733

Mobley, Zelphia　　　　　　　　　　　　　　　　zemobley@gmail.com
[(FL) PL 2014, FL 2015] Pontiac: Grace & Peace Community, Waterford: Trinity;
2019 Old Mission Penisula. 16436 Center Rd. Traverse City 49686 (231-223-
4393). Home: 14432 Peninsula Dr., Traverse City 49686-9734 (248-223-4141)

MOMANY, CHRISTOPHER P (FE) – (D-1986, FE-1989)
Mecosta: New Hope 1987; Pentwater: Centenary 1993; UM Connectional Structures (¶344.1a,c) Chaplain & Director of Church Relations, Adrian College
01/01/1996; Dowagiac: First 2019
christopherpmomany@gmail.com
(H) 207 Michigan Ave, Dowagiac 49047 (248) 462-5317
Dowagiac: First: 326 N Lowe St, PO Box 393, Dowagiac 49047 (269) 782-5167

Mondragon, Rey Carlos Borja　　　　　　mondragonrey2000@yahoo.com
[(FE) PE 2007; FE 2011]. 2007 school; Ypsilanti: First (assoc.); 2014 Hartford
(West Michigan Conference); **2015 Birch Run, Burt**. (BR) 12265 Church St.,
PO Box 277, Birch Run 48415 (989-624-9340), (B) 2799 Nicholas Rd., PO Box
96, Burt 48417 (989-770-9948). Home: 8196 Poellet, Birch Run 48415 (734-
645-8991)

*Montney, James B.　　　　　　　　　　　　　jbja4047@hotmail.com
[(RL) PL Feb 1, 2006]. Feb 1, 2006 Elba; **2012 Retired**. Home: 5033 N. Washburn, Davison 48423 (810-653-1866)

Moon, Anna Mi-Hyun　　　　　　　　　　　inpottershand12@gmail.com
[(FE) PE 2012; FE 2015]. 2012 North Lake; **2016 Troy: Korean (assoc) Hope
Ministry**. 42693 Dequindre, Troy 48085 (248-879-2240)

*Moore, Frederick Boyce, Sr., (Delores)　　　　Fmoore54@comcast.net
[(RE) P 1974; F 1980]. 1976 River Rouge: John Wesley; Mar. 1981 Detroit: People's; 1992 Pontiac: St. John (LTFT ¾); **2008 Retired**. 2897 Onagon Circle, Waterford 48328 (248-681-4748)

*MOORE, JOHN LEWIS (RE) (Ellie) – (FE-1981, R-1995)
Transferred from Free Methodist 1981; Arden 11/01/1980; Kalamazoo: Stock-
bridge Ave 03/16/1988; Galesburg 1992; Retired 1995; Center Park 1995-1997;
Union City 08/16/1997-2004; Portage First (Assoc) 10/01/2006; Portage First
(Assoc ¾ Time) and Kalamazoo Stockbridge Ave (¼ Time) 2007; Portage First
(Assoc ¾ Time) 2010; Portage First (Assoc ½ Time) and Galesburg (½ Time)
2012-2013; Otsego: Trowbridge (LTFT ¼) 2014-2018
johnmoore2924@gmail.com
(H) 10100 Commons St Apt 1007, Lone Tree CO 80124-5646 (269) 501-8181

MOORE, JOY JITTAUN (FE) – (D-1989, FE-1991)

Jackson: First (Assoc) 1988; Battle Creek: Baseline 1990; UM Connectional Structures (¶344.1a,c) Chaplain and Director of Church Relations, Adrian College 08/16/1993; Battle Creek: Trinity 1995; Lansing: Trinity (Assoc) 05/01/1996; Other Valid Ministries (¶344.1d) Director of Women's Ministries and Ethnic Concerns, Asbury Theo Sem 1997; Other Valid Ministries (¶344.1d) Director of Student Life 1998; Other Valid Ministries (¶335.1a) Instructor of Preaching, Asbury 08/16/2000; Other Valid Ministries (¶344.1d) Professor of Preaching, Asbury Asbury Theo Sem 07/01/2003; Greenville: First 2007; UM Connectional Structures (¶344.1a,c) Assoc Dean for Lifelong Learning, Duke Divinity 2008; UM Connectional Structures (¶344.1a,c) Assoc Dean for Black Church Studies and Church Relations 2009; UM Connectional Structures (¶344.1a) Associate Dean for African-American Church Studies and Assistant Professor of Preaching, Fuller Theological Seminary 09/01/2012; UM Connectional Structures (¶344.1b) Associate Professor of Homiletics and Christian Ministry 2017-04/30/2018; Transitional Leave 05/01/2018-06/30/2018; Appointed in Other Annual Conferences (¶331.8, ¶346.1) Detroit Conference, Flint: Bethel 2018; Associate Professor of Biblical Preaching Luther Seminary (¶344.1d) 2019

drjoyjmoore@gmail.com

Luther Seminary: 2481 Como Ave, St Paul, MN 55108-1445 (651) 641-3476

*MOORE, RICHARD D (RE) (Margo) – (D-1988, FE-1992, R-2015)

Howard City Maple Hill 1989; Howard City Maple Hill/First/Coral 08/01/1999; Hastings: Hope 2000; Retired 2015

(H) 930 W Broadway St, Hastings 49058 (269) 908-0210 moore82@att.net

*MOORE-JUMONVILLE, ROBERT S (RE) (Kimberly) – (D-1989, FE-1992, RE-2019)

Transferred from Illinois Great Rivers Conf 2008; Other Valid Ministries (¶344.1d) Assoc Professor of Religion, Spring Arbor Univ 2007; Appointed to Extension Ministries (¶344.1b,c) Associate Professor of Religion, Spring Arbor University and Pope (LTFT ¼) 2010; Appointed to Extension Ministries (¶344.1b,c) Associate Professor of Religion, Spring Arbor University 2018; Retired Apr. 1, 2019

(H) 21 Dickens Street, Spring Arbor 49283 (517) 524-6818 rmooreju@arbor.edu

*MORRISON, DIANNE DOTEN (RL) (Richard) – (PL-1996, NL-12/31/1997-1998, FL-1998, PL-2007, RL-2016)

Sturgis (Assoc) (LTFT PT) 01/01/1996; Not Appointed 12/31/1997; Gull Lake (Assoc) 1998; Dowling: Country Chapel 02/01/2001; Muskegon: Crestwood 2004; Ferry (LTFT PT) 2007; Hesperia (LTFT PT) 2007; Traverse City: Christ 2011-1/1/2015; Retired 01/01/2016

Ddotenmorr@aol.com

(H) 7750 S West Bayshore Dr, Traverse City 49684-9828 (231) 709-2382

*MORRISON, REBECCA K (RE) – (FL-2002, PE-2003, FE-2008, RE-2019)

Potterville 01/16/2002; Big Rapids: First 2011; Retired 2019

bkmorrison2019@gmail.com

(H) 1625 Meijer Dr, Apt 206, Greenville 48838-3550 (517) 712-4508

*MORRISON, RICHARD A (RE) (Dianne Doten) – (D-1967, FE-1969, R-2007)
Jackson: First (Assoc) 1969; Bainbridge Newhope 1971; Appointed in Other Annual Conferences (¶331.8, ¶346.1) Missioner, Alaska Missionary Conference 1972; Transferred to West Ohio Conf 1975; Transferred from West Ohio Conf 1992; Alden/Central Lake 06/01/1992; Sturgis 1995; UM Connectional Structures (¶344.1a,c) District Superintendent, Albion District 01/01/1998; Muskegon: Lake Harbor 2004; Retired 2007; Hesperia/Ferry 2007-2011

adosuper@aol.com
(H) 7750 S West Bayshore Dr, Traverse City 49684-9828 (231) 944-5503

*Morse, Harold S. (Linda)
[(RE) P 1970; F 1973]. 1972 Rochester: St. Luke's; 1979 Chaplain Supervisor, St. Louis Children's Hospital; **2011 Retired**. Home: 703 Muir Kirk Lane, Manchester, MO 63011 (314-394-1663)

*MORSE, JOHN D (RE) (Darleen) – (D-1971, FE-1975, R-2012)
Center Eaton/Brookfield 1973; Sunfield/Sebewa Center 02/01/1976; Frankfort/Elberta 1982; Traverse City: Christ 1987; Jackson: First (Assoc) 1993; Coopersville 1999; Retired 2012; Twin Lake (LTFT ½) 2013; Twin Lake (LTFT 45%) 01/01/2014-2018

jdm14879@gmail.com
(H) 215 Dee Rd, Muskegon 49444-9742 (231) 798-6943

MORT, JAMES J (FE) (Janet) – (PE-2007, FE-2010)
Marion/Cadillac: South Community 2007

jim.mort@sbcglobal.net
(H) 205 Flemming St, Marion 49665-9706 (231) 743-0062
Marion: PO Box C, 216 W Main St, Marion 49665-0703 (231) 743-2834
Cadillac South Community: 11800 47 Mile Rd, Cadillac 49601 (231) 775-3067

*MORTON, DAVID L (RE) (Carrie) – (D-1959, FE-1966, R-2001)
Gilead (EUB) 1961; Scottdale (EUB) 1963; Vicksburg (EUB) 1965; Hillsdale: First (Assoc) 1969; Kent City: Chapel Hill 1970; Delta Mills/Eagle 01/15/1974; Jackson: First (Assoc) 1982; Battle Creek: Maple 1986; Other Valid Ministries (¶344.1d) Chaplain, Battle Creek Health System 05/01/1996; Retired 2001; Battle Creek: First (LTFT ¼) 03/05/2014-6/30/2014; Coldwater 01/01/2017-6/30/2017

RevMorton62@yahoo.com
(H) 4285 E Kirby Rd, Battle Creek 49017-8034 (269) 964-7098

*Moshauer, Meredith T.
[(RE) T W. NY, 1969; F]. 1969 Farmington: Nardin Park (assoc.); 1977 Leave of Absence; Jan. 1981 Livingston Circuit: Plainfield, Trinity; 1982 Leave of Absence; 1984 Durand Cluster: Lennon, Duffield (part- time); 1988 Detroit: West Outer Drive (LTFT ½); 1990 Highland Park: First (LTFT ½); 1995 Detroit: Waterman-Preston (LTFT ¾); **Aug 31, 1997 Retired**. Home: 1740 Nemoke Trail, #1, Haslett 48840

Mukalay, Gertrude Mwadi (John Kabala Ilonga Ngoie)   frenchumc@yahoo.com
[(OE) OE 2017, North Katanga Conf, Democratic Republic of Congo] **2018 Detroit: French** (New Church Start) (LTFT ¾). 1803 E 14 Mile Rd, Birmingham 48009. Home: 1858 Estates Dr, Detroit 48206

*Mulder, David George (Patricia)   dmulder3@yahoo.com
[(RE) P 1987; F 1990; R 2018]. 1988 Flint: Court Street (assoc.); 1992 Fairgrove, Gilford; 1996 Ypsilanti: St. Matthew's; 2001 Fenton (assoc); 2008 Midland: Homer; 2014 Marlette: First; **2018 Retired**. Home: 308 18th Ave NE, Waseca, MN 56093

MULLIGAN ARMSTRONG, CHERYL A (FD) – (PD-2012, FD-2015)
Deacons Appointed Beyond the Local Church (¶331.1a) Respitory Therapist at Helen DeVos Ped Pulmonary Clinic and Grand Rapids: Genesis (Deacon) Pastoral Care Minister 2012; Deacons Appointed Beyond the Local Church (¶331.1a) Respitory Therapist at Helen DeVos Ped Pulmonary Clinic and Missional at Lowell: First (Deacon Unpaid) 01/01/2014; Deacons Appointed Beyond the Local Church (¶331.1a) Respiratory Therapist, Helen DeVos Pediatric Pulmonary Clinic and Lowell: First (Deacon) Pastor of Discipleship (Paid) 10/09/2015; Deacons Appointed Beyond the Local Church (¶331.4a) Field Clinical Specialist for RespirTech Medial and Lowell: First (LTFT ¼ - Missional Service) 2018

mulliganfore@att.net
(H) 3170 Buttrick Ave SE, Ada 49301-9216 (616) 340-7995
(O) 35 Michigan St NE, Suite 3003, Grand Rapids 49503 (616) 267-2200
Lowell: 621 E Main St, Lowell 49331-1719 (616) 897-5936

*Mumbiro, Elias N. (Tapuwa)   gsumc@wowway.com
[(RE) P Zimbabwe 1977; F N. IN 1977]. Jan 1, 1975-Dec 31, 1975 Associate Pastor, School Chaplain, Mutambara United Methodist Mission Center, Mutambara, Cashel, Zimbabwe; Jan 1, 1976-Dec 31, 1977 Missionary to South Indiana Conference; Jan 1, 1978-Aug 31, 1981 Evansville, IN: St. John's and St. Andrews; 1983 to Dec 15, 1983 Itinerant Missioner to Iowa Conference and Southern District, Minnesota Conference; Jan 1, 1983-Dec 31, 1986 Mission Administrator/Chaplain Old Mutare Mission, Mutare, Zimbabwe; Jan 1, 1987-Aug 31, 1992 Mutasa-Makoni District Superintendent; Sep 1, 1992 River Rouge: John Wesley; 1995 transfer to Detroit Conference, Westland: St. James; Nov 1, 1999 Eastside Covenant Cooperative Parish: St. Clair Shores: Good Shepherd; 2009 Saginaw: State Street; **2015 Retired**.

*Mumford, Gerald Edward (Dorothy)
[(RA) LD 1966; LE 1968; AM 1989]. 1964 West Forest, Otter Lake; 1976 West Deerfield; 1989 Mt. Bethel (part-time); **1993 Retired**. Home: 283 Inner Dr., E., Venice, FL 34292 (941-488-4312)

*Munger, Marjorie H. (Dennis)   margemunger@yahoo.com
[(RE) P 1991; F 1993]. 1991 Flint: Bristol, Dimond; 1993 Canton: Cherry Hill; 1998 Troy: Fellowship; 2002 Lake Orion (assoc); **2013 Retired**. 1317 Gemstone Square, E., Westerville, OH 43081 (614-726-5061)

MURPHY, MARSHALL (FL) (Marian) – (PL-2011, FL-2017)
Battle Creek: Washington Heights (PTLP ¼) 2011; Battle Creek: First (PTLP ½) and Washington Heights (PTLP ¼) 2014; Appointed in Other Annual Conference (¶331.8, ¶346.1) Harper Woods Redeemer, Detroit Conf 2017

mmurphy19@comcast.net
(H) 20592 Anita, Harper Woods 48225 (269) 753-8056
Harper Woods Redeemer: 20571 Vernier Rd, Harper Woods 48225 (313) 884-2035

PASTORAL RECORDS

MURRAY, JOHN PAUL (FL) (Linn) – (FL-2014)
Kalkaska 2015; Menominee: First, Stephenson 2019
jmurray16365@gmail.com
(H) 1801 17th Ave, Menominee 49858 (814) 366-0239
Menominee: First: 601 10th Ave, PO Box 323, Menominee 49858 (906) 864-2555
Stephenson: S 111 Railroad St, PO Box 205, Stephenson 49887 (906) 753-6363

*Myers-Cabeen, Nanette D. (James Sterling Cabeen)
[(RE) P 1986; F 1989]. 1987 Royal Oak: First (assoc.); 1991 Flushing (assoc.).
1992 Flushing (assoc.), LTFT ¾); Jan 1, 1997 Flushing (assoc); 1997 school;
2014 Retired (Bay Regional Medical Center). Home: 353 Old Orchard Dr., Essexville 48732 (989-895-8955)

*Naile, John Edmund (Myrna) revjohn@fumcgaylord.org
[(RE) P 1972; F 1974]. 1973 Carsonville, Applegate, Watertown; 1977 St. Ignace;
1985 St. Clair: First; 1998 Gaylord; **2014 Retired**. Home: 2431 Rainswood Dr.,
Gaylord 48734 (989-732-5325)

*NALETT, LARRY W. (RL) (Elaine) – (PL-1993, FL-1998, RL-2004)
Eagle 1993; Vickeryville / Fenwick / Palo 1998; Retired 8/8/2004; Middleton
9/15/2015-11/29/2015; Carson City 2/22/16-6/30/2016; Ionia: Zion 2018
larrynal62@gmail.com
(H) 620 Rich St, Ionia 48846 (616) 527-2025
Ionia: Zion: 423 W Washington St, Ionia 48846 (616) 527-1910

NASH, KENNETH J (FE) (Christine Frances) – (PE-2000, FE-2004)
Transferred from Kentucky Conf 2000; Carson City 2000; Grand Rapids: Cornerstone (Assoc) 2006; Grand Rapids: Cornerstone (Assoc) (LTFT ¼) 2011;
Grand Rapids: Cornerstone (Assoc) 2012; Appointed to Extension Ministries
(¶345) Wesleyan Church Of Hamburg, NY (Appt to Ecumenical Shared Ministries) 2016
pknash@wchamburg.org
(O) 4999 McKinley Parkway, Hamburg, NY 14075 (716) 649-6335

NDUWA, ERIC MULANDA (FE) (Mafo Sonyi Corinne) – (OE-2015, FE-2017)
[SW Katanga Annual Conf, Elder] Greenville First, Turk Lake/Belding Coopera-
tive Parish (Assoc) (LTFT ¼) 02/01/2015-06/30/2015; Greenville: First, Turk
Lake/Belding Cooperative Parish (Assoc) (LTFT ¼) 2015; Lansing: Mount Hope
(Assoc) 08/01/2015; Transferred from South Congo and Zambia 2017
reveric79@gmail.com
(H) 545 N Dexter Dr, Lansing 48910-3410
Lansing: Mount Hope: 501 E Mount Hope Ave, Lansing 48910 (517) 482-1549

NEIHARDT, MICHAEL R. (PL) – (PL-2012, FL-2015, NL-2016, PL-2017)
Horton Bay (PTLP ¼) 2012; Boyne City/Boyne Falls (¾ Time) and Horton Bay
(¼ Time) 2014; Farwell 2015-09/25/2016; LP w/o Appointment 9/25/2016-2017;
Horton Bay (¼ Time) 2017
barneyfife@torchlake.com
(H) 4979 Boyne City Rd, Boyne City 49712 (231) 392-5258
Horton Bay: 4961 Boyne City Rd, Boyne City 49712-9217 (989) 544-4049

Nellist, David (Glenys) pastor@dearbornfirstumc.org
[(OE) OE 2018, British Methodist Conf.] **2018 Dearborn: First**. 22124 Garrison,
Dearborn 48124 (313-563-5200). Home: 301 S. Silvery Lane, Dearborn 48124
(269) 903-8560

*NELSON, DAVID B (RE) (Jean Freeland) – (D-1961, FE-1964, R-1998)
UM Connectional Structures (¶344.1a,c) Director, Mt Pleasant: CMU Wesley Foundation 1959; Camden/Montgomery 1960; Saugatuck/New Richmond 1962; Coopersville/Nunica 01/01/1965; Portage: Chapel Hill 03/01/1968; Ithaca 1972; Ithaca/Beebe 1976; Lansing: Faith 09/16/1980; Hastings: First 1985; Plainwell: First 1989; UM Connectional Structures (¶344.1a,c) West MI Conference Council Director 1991; Retired 1998

dbnelson@iserv.net
(H) 1220 Pine Ave # B, Alma 48801-1241 (989) 297-0257
Mailing: c/o Sarah Kettelhohn, 5469 George St, Saginaw 48603

NELSON, FOREST (BERT) BERTRAN (OF) (Susan Garbarind) – (OF-2005)
[Presbyterian Church USA] Lyons-Muir Church (LTFT ¾) (¶346.2), 1/1/2005-01/01/2016

fbertnelson@charter.net
(H) 1074 Olmstead Road, Muir 48860-9627 (616) 891-8918

Nelson, Jeffrey Scott (Bridget)   detroitnelsons@aol.com
[(FE) PE 2004; FE 2006]. Feb 1, 2004 Birmingham: First (assoc); 2009 Redford: Aldersgate; **2016 Royal Oak: First**. 320 W. Seventh, Royal Oak 48067 (248-541-4100). Home: 3113 Marion Dr., Royal Oak 48073 (248-629-7185)

*Ness, Lance E.   revness1966@gmail.com
[(RE) SPL Peninsula-Delaware 1990; LP 1994; PM 1998; FE 2003; RE 2017]. 1990 East New Market, MD (Peninsula-Delaware Conf.); Jul 1, 1994 Ontonagon, Greenland, Rockland; Jan 1, 2000 Owosso: Burton, Carland; Aug 1, 2004 Brown City; 2007 Macon; **2017 Retired**. Home: 1203 Middle Neck Drive, Salisbury, MD 21804 (517-902-4609)

*Neumann, Fredrick D. (Kay)   fdneumann@yahoo.com
[(RE) LP 1994; P 1995; F 1998; R 2017]. Aug 1, 1994 Ossineke, Hubbard Lake, Wilson; Aug 1, 1994 Ossineke, Hubbard Lake; 1999 North Street; 2002 Bay City: Fremont Avenue; 2006 Wisner; 2010 Hudson: First; 2013 medical leave of absence; **2017 Retired**. 3046 Camino Real, Las Cruces, NM 88001 (989-884-1776)

NEWSOM, TIFFANY M (PE) – (CC-2014, PE-2017)
Constantine/White Pigeon 2017

newsom.tiffany@gmail.com
(H) 265 White Pigeon St, Constantine 49042-1063 (517) 917-5705
Constantine: 265 East Third St, Constantine 49042-1063 (269) 435-8151
White Pigeon: PO Box 518, 204 N Kalamazoo St, White Pigeon 49099-9105
(269) 483-9054

NGUYEN, DANIEL DUNG (FL) (Minh Ha Le) – (FL-2014)
Grand Rapids: Vietnamese 2012
(H) 497 Harp St. SE, Kentwood 49548-4378 (616) 288-3007
Grand Rapids: Vietnamese: 212 Bellevue St SE, Wyoming 49548-3337
(616) 534-6262

Nguyen, Nhan Duc   ducnhan234@yahoo.com
[(PL) DSA Apr 1, 2014; PL Jan 1, 2019]. Apr 1, 2014 Madison Heights: Vietnamese Ministry (DSA); **Jan 1, 2019 Madison Heights: Vietnamese Ministry** (LTFT ¾). 500 W Gardenia Ave, Madison Heights 48071-4508 (248-545-5554). Home: 38108 Charwood Dr, Sterling Heights 48312-1223 (714-501-0323)

PASTORAL RECORDS

*NICHOLS, LAWRENCE A. (RL) – (FL-1979, NL-1988, PL-1994, FL-2003, RL-2016)
Waterloo Village / Waterloo First (DSA) 1978; Waterloo Village / Waterloo First 1979; Not Appointed 1988; Jackson: Zion (LTFT PT) 02/01/1994; Hersey 2003; Byron Center 2010; Retired 2016

nichols.larry64@comcast.net
(H) 921 Roselle Street, Jackson 49201 (517) 745-4224

*NIELSEN, JUDITH A. (RL) – (FL-1998, NL-2000, RL-2007)
Munith 1998; Pleasant Lake 1998; Not Appointed 2000; Retired 2007
(H) 3024 Norwich Rd, Lansing 48911-1537 (517) 882-0608

*NISWENDER, R IVAN (RE) (Phyllis) – (FE-1958, HL-1971, FE-1989, R-1994)
Hersey (EUB) 1958; Hersey/Grant Center (EUB) 1960; Battle Creek: Calvary (EUB) 1962; Grand Rapids: Northlawn (EUB) 1966; Perry/Shaftsburg 1969; Honorable Location 1971; Otsego: Trowbridge 1981; Readmitted 1989; Otsego: Trowbridge (LTFT ¾) 1989; Otsego: Trowbridge 1993; Retired 1994
(H) 191 Grace Village Dr, Winona Lake, IN 46590-5611 (574) 372-6191

*Noel, Karen Y. (Phares)   revdustynoel@msn.com
[(RE) PE 2001; FE 2004; RE 2018]. 2001 Detroit: St. Paul's (LTFT ½), 2010 Pontiac: St. John's; Sep 29, 2013 voluntary leave of absence; Mar 2, 2015 Garden City: First (interim); 2015 Birmingham: Embury (LTFT ¼); 2016 Birmingham Embury, Sterling Heights; **2018 Retired**. Home: 4673 Walnut Glen Ct, W Bloomfield 48323 (313-595-4051)

*NOGGLE, JAMES C (RE) (Karen) – (D-1995, AM-1995, PE-2014, FE-2016, RE-2019)
Nashville Parish: Peace and Quimby 1989; Millville 03/01/1993; Mecosta: New Hope 1997; Harrison: The Gathering (New Church Start) 2004; The Gathering, Wagarville/Wooden Shoe 2009; Grand Rapids: Northlawn 2010; Lake Odessa: Lakewood 2013; Roscommon: Good Shepherd of the North 2015; Retired Apr 1, 2019

jnoggle@macharcc.com
(H) 10290 N Polk Ave, Harrison 48625-8837 (231) 250-8707

Nolen, Heather L (FL) – (CC-2017, DSA-2017, FL-2017)
Gresham / Sunfield (DSA) 2017; Gresham / Sunfield (FL) 12/01/2017
hauble23@gmail.com
(H) PO Box 25, Sunfield 48890-0025 (734) 846-3941
Gresham: 5055 Mulliken Rd, Charlotte 48813
Sunfield: 227 Logan St, Sunfield 48890 (517) 566-8448

*Norris, Arthur Vernon (Evelyn)
[(RE) P Mich., 1959; F Mich., 1964]. 1963 Howe: Lima; 1966 Novi: Willowbrook; 1969 Owosso: First (assoc.); 1971 Millington, Arbela; 1976 Pontiac: First; 1980 Blissfield: First; 1983 Wyandotte: Glenwood; 1991 Iron Mountain: Trinity; Jul 1, 1994 Hemlock, Nelson; **2001 Retired**. Home: 5900 S. Hemlock, Hemlock 48626

Norton, Michael Kent (Susan)   mikenorton@cantonfriendship.org
[(FE) P 1987; F 1992]. 1987 Snover: Moore, Trinity, Elmer. 1992 Heritage; 1994 Sebewaing: Trinity; **1997 Canton: Friendship**. 1240 Beck Rd., Canton 48187 (734-710-9370). Home: 1237 Lotz Rd., Canton 48188 (734-722-0183)

Norton, Stephanie Elaine (FL) – (FL 2019)
(Great Plains Conference) Hartford 2019

stephanie.e.norton@gmail.com
(H) 143 Paras Hill Dr, Hartford 49057-1164 (269) 532-4741
Hartford: 425 E Main St, Hartford 49057-1160 (269) 621-4103

*Nowacek, Bruce L. (Candy)   b_nowacek@yahoo.com
[(RE) FL 2003; PE 2007; FE 2011]. 2003 Genesee-Thedford Center; 2010 Bay
Port, Hayes; 2012 Yale; Feb 1, 2014 Transitional leave; 2014 Menominee: First;
2016 Retired. Home: 1728 Cowan, National City 48748 (906-792-9051)

Nowak, Heather   heathermarienowak@gmail.com
[(FL) DSA Oct 1, 2016; FL 2017]. Oct 1, 2016-Nov 20, 2017 Pinconning, Garfield
(DSA). **Dec 1, 2017 Pinconning, Garfield**. (P) 314 Whyte St, Pinconning 48650
(989-879-3271). (G) 1701 N Garfield Rd., Linwood 48634 (989-879-6992).

Nunn, Penelope R.   peasweet1961@yahoo.com
[(FL) PL Dec 1, 2014; FL 2018]. Dec 1, 2014 Port Huron: Gratiot Park, Port
Huron: Washington Avenue; **2018 Snover: Heritage**. 3329 W. Snover Rd., PO
Box 38, Snover 48472 (810-9101). Home: 1571 N. Main St., PO Box 65, Snover
48472 (810-672-9233)

*Nusz, Gordon Wayne (Shirley)
[(RE) L Mich., 1966; P 1968; F 1971]. 1970 Detroit: St. James (assoc.); 1974
Swan Valley; 1980 Pigeon: First; 1988 West Branch: First; 1993 Marquette: First;
2000 Northville: First (assoc); May 1, 2002 involuntary leave of absence; **May
1, 2003 involuntary retirement**. Home: 2813 Laurel Hill Dr., Flower Mound, TX
75028 (972-691-1335)

NYSTROM, ROBERT D (FE) (Ronda) – (D-1989, FE-1992)
Hopkins/South Monterey 1989; Traverse City: Central 1992; Bronson: First 1994;
St Louis: First 1998; Dimondale and East Lansing Chapel Hill 2002; East Lansing
Chapel Hill (LTFT ½) 01/16/2004; Webberville 2005; Battle Creek: Birchwood
2007; Battle Creek Birchwood (LTFT ¾) and Athens (LTFT ¼) 2011; Three
Rivers: First/Mendon 2013; Ovid United Church 2015; Ovid United Church/Elsie
2016; Appointed in Other Annual Conferences (¶331.8, ¶346.1) Detroit Confer-
ence, Aburn 2018

rnr@comcast.net
(H) 201 S. Auburn, Auburn 48611 (269) 535-2481
Auburn: 207 S. Auburn, PO Box 66, Auburn 48611 (989) 662-6314

Oh, In Boem (Jooyeun Lim)
[(PE) FL 2013; PE 2016]. Apr 1, 2013 Troy: Korean (assoc); **2016 Wisner**. 5375
N. Vassar Rd., Akron 48701 (989-691-5277). Home: 5363 N. Vassar Rd., Akron

*Okray, Dorothy   djokray@comcast.net
[(RE) PE Troy 1997; FE Troy, 2000]. 1997 Newcomb, NY: Newcomb, Calvary,
Long Lake, NY; 2001 Johnstown (NY): First, Gloversville (NY); 2003 Morenci;
2007 Retired. 7318 Kensington Ct., University Park, FL 34201

OLIN, MELODY L (FL) (Denny) – (FL-2006)
Blanchard-Pine River/Coomer/Winn (DSA) 2006; Blanchard-Pine River/Coomer/ Winn (FTLP) 11/16/2006; Old Mission Peninsula 2010; Empire 2019
MelodyOlin@yahoo.com
(H) 10205 Aylsworth Rd, PO Box 261, Empire 49630-0261 (231) 970-2048
Empire: 10050 W Michigan St, PO Box 261, Empire 49630-0261 (231) 326-5510

*Omansiek, William Walter   omansiek@chartermi.net
[(RE) T 1967; F 1971, HL 1986, FL 2005, FE Jan 1, 2006]. Jan, 1970 Flint: Flint Park; 1971 Chaplain, Methodist Children's Home; 1974 Detroit: St. James (assoc.); 1975 Inkster: Christ; 1979 St. Charles, Brant; 1986 Honorable Location; Jan 1, 2005 Harrisville, Lincoln; 2005 Wisner;2006 Bay City: Fremont Avenue; **2010 Retired**. 801 Pendleton Street, Bay City 48708 (989-778-1405)

*ORR, KARIN K (RE) – (PE-2003, FE-2006, R-2014)
Centreville 2003; Retired 2014
pastorrkarin@gmail.com
(H) 4207 Embassy Drive SE, Grand Rapids 49546 (616) 901-4382

Osborne, Matthew L. (Melissa)   matthewlosborne@gmail.com
[(FL) FL 2012]. 2012 Algonac: Trinity, Marine City; 2013 Sandusky: First; **2018 Ishpeming: Wesley**. 801 Hemlock, PO Box 342, Ishpeming 49849 (906-486-4681). Home: 220 shoreline Dr., Negaunee 49866 (906-475-9337)

OSTEMA, DALE P (FE) (Deborah) – (D-1987, FE-1990)
Baldwin: Covenant Cmnty 1988; Charlevoix/Greensky Hill 02/01/1993; Charlevoix 02/01/1998; Cadillac 2000; Traverse City: Central 2007
dale@tccentralumc.org
(H) 1713 Indian Woods Dr, Traverse City 49686-3031 (231) 933-4026
Traverse City: Central: 222 Cass St, Traverse City 49684-5734 (231) 946-5191

*Osterhout, Donna Joan   donnao3928@gmail.com
[(RE) P 1978; F 1981]. 1979 Inkster; Jan. 1983 Taylor: West Mound; Sep. 1, 1987 Lexington, Bethel; 1991 Lincoln Community; 1996 Marine City; Feb 1, 2002 incapacity leave; **2003 Retired**. 801 W Middle St, Apt 470, Chelsea 48118-1388

Osterman, Rhonda
[(PL) PL Nov, 2012]. **Nov 10, 2012 Madison Heights**. 246 E. 11 Mile Rd., Madison Heights 48071 (248-544-3544). Home: 12998 DeCook Dr., Sterling Hts. 48313 (586-243-9240)

OTIS, SCOTT K (FE) (Carolyn) – (D-1988, FE-1991)
Lyons/Muir (Student Appt) 07/16/1988; Lyons/Muir (Full Time) 11/16/1988; Lyons/Muir/Ionia: Easton 1990; Mecosta: New Hope 1993; Portland 1997; Grand Rapids: Cornerstone (Assoc) 2003; Dorr: Crosswind Community (New Church Start)10/01/2004; Edwardsburg: Hope 2017
scott.otis@hope-umc.us
(H) 20624 Starbrick Rd, Edwardsburg 49112-9275 (616) 307-9765
Edwardsburg: Hope: PO Box 624, 69941 Elkhart Rd, Edwardsburg 49112-0624
(269) 663-5321

OYLER-SAYLES, THERESA LITTLE EAGLE (FE) (Ed) – (PE-2000, FE-2006)
Oakdale/Pa Wa Ting Ma Ged Win 2003; Battle Creek: Maple 2006; Niles: Portage Prairie 2008-2009; Medical Leave 4/15/2009
littleeagle77@hotmail.com
(H) 256 Nottingham Rd, Elkton, MD 21921-4431 (269) 967-7145

PAHL, CRAIG A (FL) – (PL-2000, FL-2004)
Jonesville/Allen 2000; Jonesville/Allen/Moscow Plains 2001; Jonesville/Allen/ Moscow Plains (FT) 2004; Jonesville/Allen 2007; Barnard/East Jordan/Norwood 2014; East Jordan/Barnard 2017

cappahl@netzero.net
(H) PO Box 238, 305 Esterly, East Jordan 49727-0238 (231) 536-7596 East Jordan: PO Box 878, 201 4th St, East Jordan 49727-0878 (231) 536-2161 Barnard: PO Box 878 (15645 Klooster Rd, Charlevoix) East Jordan 49727-0878 (231) 547-5269

*Paige, James E., Jr., (Margaret "Peggy")   Revspaige@yahoo.com
[(RE) P 1971; F 1978]. 1974 Stephenson, Hermansville; 1976 Morrice, Bennington, Pittsburg; 1980 Jeddo, Central-Lakeport (Co-Pastor, LTFT ½); 1985 Leave of Absence; 1986 Glennie, Curran, Wilber (LTFT ½); Jan. 1, 1992 Salem Grove; 1998 Caring Covenant Group Ministry: Oregon, Elba (LTFT) 2002 parish director; Oct 1, 2003 incapacity leave; Jan 1, 2007 Capac: First, Zion Community; 2007 Richfield (LTFT ½); **2008 Retired**. Home: N7344 County Road 577, Ingalls 49848 (231-421-4208)

*Paige, Margaret Ann "Peggy" (James)   mapaige49@yahoo.com
[(RE) P 1975; F 1978]. Jan. 1977 Morrice, Bennington, Pittsburg (Co-Pastor); 1980 Jeddo, Central-Lakeport (Co-Pastor, LTFT ½); 1985 Glennnie, Curran, Wilber (LTFT ½); Nov. 15, 1991 Manchester: Sharon; 1998 Caring Covenant Group Ministry: Columbiaville (parish director); 2002 Port Huron District Superintendent; 2009 Iron Mountain: First, Quinnesec; **2012 Retired**. Home: N7344 County Road 577, Ingalls 49848 (231-421-4208 or 906-221-7677)

Pajak, John J. (Connie)   jpajak@palacenet.com
[(PL) PL 2009]. Apr 1, 2009 Redford: New Beginnings; **2016 New Cooperative: Algonac: Trinity**. 424 Smith St., Algonac 48001 (810-794-4379). Home: 1421 Michigan St., Algonac 48001 (810-794-4892)

Palaszeski, James (Nikki)
[(FL) PL Dec 1, 2014; FL 2016]. Dec 1, 2014 Ubly/Shabbona/Argyle; 2016 Keweenaw Parish: Calumet, Mohawk-Ameek, Lake Linden, Laurium. **2018 Union City, Athens**

pastor.ucaumc@gmail.com
(H) 72 Sycamore Bend, Union City 49094 (989) 912-5738 Union City: 200 Ellen St, PO Box 878, Union City 49094-0095 (517) 741-7028 Athens: 123 Clark St, PO Box 267 Athens 49011-0267 (269) 729-9370

*PANSE, WADE S (RE) (Patti) – (D-1978, FE-1980, R-2012)
Burr Oak 1978; Robbins 03/01/1982; Lansing: Mount Hope 05/01/1987; Appointed in Other Annual Conferences (¶331.8, ¶346.1) Director of Alumni, Asbury Theological School 10/16/1992; Mt Pleasant: First 1995; St Joseph First 1997; Retired 01/01/2012; Cassopolis (LTFT ½) 08/23/2015

wadepanse@hotmail.com
(H) 1218 Riverwood Terrace, Saint Joseph 49085-2118 (269) 449-5335 Cassopolis: PO Box 175, 209 South Rowland St, Cassopolis 49031-0175 (269) 445-3107

PAPARELLA, AMEE A (FE) (James) – (PE-2009, FE-2016)
Williamston 2009; Clergy Appointed to Attend School (¶416.6) MSU 2011; UM
Connectional Structures (¶344.1a,c) Director/Organizer for Women's Advocacy,
General Board of Church and Society 08/27/2012; Wacousta Community 2013;
Leave of Absence To Attend School 2016; Grand Rapids First (Assoc) 2017;
Leave of Absence 02/28/2018
(H) 9755 N Division Ave, Sparta 49345 (517) 862-2599 ameeanne@gmail.com

*Park, John G. (Madeline)   Jgpark@aol.com
[(RE) P E.OH., 1970; F 1973]. 1972 Trans. to Detroit Conf., LaSalle: Zion; 1975
Royal Oak: First (assoc.); 1978 Fairgrove, Gilford; May 1981 Commerce; 1992
Berkley; 1996 Flint: Hope; 2006 Dixboro; **2011 Retired**. 2268 Willow Tree Drive,
Brighton 48116 (810-522-5389)

*Parker, Gerald R. (Holly Craig)   ParkerGrld@netscape.net
[(RE) P 1969; F 1973]. 1972 Britton: Grace, Wellsville; 1973 University of Michi-
gan Law School; 1975 Salem Grove; 1978 Ann Arbor: First (assoc.); 1986
Chelsea; July 16, 1992 Saline; **1994 Retired**. Home: 1500 Hillridge Ct., Ann
Arbor 48103 (734-913-4937)

*Parker, James Floyd (Ines)
[(RE) P 1969; F 1972]. 1971 General Board of Pensions; Apr. 1987 General Sec-
retary, General Board of Pension; **1994 Retired**. Home: 1248 Wickie Pl. SE,
Tumwater, WA 98501 (360-754-3384)

*Parker, Roger Allen (Judith)   roger.parker07@comcast.net
[(RE) T 1967; F 1970]. 1969 Livingston Circuit: Plainfield, Trinity; Oct. 1970 Stony
Creek; 1976 Bay City: Madison Avenue; 1983 Flint: Trinity; Feb 1, 1993 Director:
Cooperative Ministry of Northwest Flint, Flint: Trinity; 1998 sabbatical leave; Oct
1, 1998 LaVergne UMC; 1998 Franklin: First (assoc) (TN Conf, para 337.1); **2008
Retired**. Home: 8522 Parkridge Drive, Dexter 48130 (734-580-2134)

Parker-Lewis, Sherry Lynn (George Lewis)   sherry@brightonfumc.org 6-27-08]
[(FE) PL 1991; P 1996; FE 1999] Sep. 1, 1991 Wagarville: Community, Wooden
Shoe (part-time--½); 1994 Hardy, Hartland (assoc); 1995 Ann Arbor: First
(assoc); 1997 Dundee; Aug 1, 2002 Chesaning: Trinity; **2008 Brighton: First**.
400 E. Grand River, Brighton 48116 (810-229-8561). Home: 7608 Brookview
Ct., Brighton 48116 (810-229-7831)

Parkin, Penny
[(PL) PL Sep 1, 2014]. Sep 1, 2014 Fairgrove; **2017 Fairgrove, Sutton-Sunshine.** (F) 5116 W. Center, Box 10, Fairgrove 48733 (989-693-6564). Home:
2024 Liberty, Fairgrove 48733 (989-600-8086)

PARMALEE, CHAD M (FE) (Roschenne) – (FL-2006, PE-2014, FE-2017)
Jackson: Brookside 09/01/2005; Battle Creek: Chapel Hill 2013
                                                    pastorchad@thehillbc.com
                    (H) 192 Brentwood Dr, Battle Creek 49015-4512 (517) 281-0362
Battle Creek: Chapel Hill: 157 Chapel Hill Dr, Battle Creek 49015 (269) 963-0231

*PARSONS, CYNTHIA M (RE) (Jeff) – (D-1988, FE-1992, R-2018)
North East Missaukee Parish 1989; Williamsburg 1993; Kalamazoo: First (Assoc) 1997; Casco 2001; Berrien Springs (LTFT ½) 2006; Appointed in Other Annual Conferences (¶346.1) Owendale (½) / Gagetown (¼) (LTFT ¾) 2012; Sebewaing: Trinity 2014; Retired 2018

RevCindy47@gmail.com
(H) 450 N Miller, PO Box 563, Sebewaing 48759 (989) 883-2350

*PASSENGER, EDWARD L (RE) (Sally) – (D-1959, FE-1962, HL-1971, FE-1987, R-1999)
Northport/Leland/Northport Indian Mission 1962; Alden 09/15/1965; Caledonia/Parmelee 12/01/1966; Hart/Mears 12/01/1969; Honorable Location 06/01/1971; Appointed to Extension Ministries (¶344.1b,c) Chaplain, Ionia Temporary Correctional Facility 1987; Appointed to Extension Ministries (¶344.1b,c) Chaplain, Carson City Temporary Correctional Facility 12/28/1987; Retired 1999
(H) 526 Ferry St, Spring Lake 49456 (616) 566-8833 revedpass@gmail.com

*Passenger, Margaret Ann (Henry) revmarg@gmail.com
[(RE) P 1997; FE 1999]. 1997 Kingston, Deford; 2001 Pigeon: First; **2005 Retired**. Home: 44 E. Elm Ave., Monroe 48162 (734-242-6944)

PATERA, NANCY J (FL) (Greg) – (PL-2007, FL-2014)
Ionia: Easton (PTLP ½) 01/01/2007; Burnips/Monterey Center 2014; Ionia Parish: LeValley/ Berlin Center 2017

nancypatera@mac.com
(H) 6232 Sunset Beach, Lake Odessa 48849 (616) 642-0966
LeValley: 4018 Kelsey Hwy, Ionia 48846-9431 (616) 527-1480
Berlin Center: 3042 Peck Lake Rd, Saranac 48881-9654 (616) 527-1480

*Paterson, John Douglas (Karla) jdpaterson@me.com
[(RE) P 1981; F 1985; R 2018]. Mar. 1983 Seymour Lake; Sep. 15, 1986 Marquette: Grace, Skandia; 1993 Grayling: Michelson Memorial; 1998 Marquette District Superintendent; 2005 Ann Arbor: First; **2018 Retired**. Home: 729 Lakewood Ln, Marquette 49855 (734-474-4100)

*PATTERSON, PAUL E (RE) – (D-1951, FE-1953, R-1990)
Edwardsburg: Hope 10/01/1950; Grand Rapids: First (Assoc) 1955; Wacousta Community 1957; Cedar Springs 1958; Grand Rapids: South 09/07/1960; Ludington 1964; Kalamazoo: Westwood 1967; Sparta 1968; Allegan 1973; Paw Paw 1979; Grand Rapids: Faith 1984; St Johns: First 1987; Barryton/Chippewa Lake 07/01-10/01/1990; Retired 10/01/1990

rgulbranson@sbcglobal.net
(H) Clark Ret Comm, 1551 Franklin SE, Apt 4065, Grand Rapids 49506
(616) 243-2967

Payne, James A. Pastorjimpayne@gmail.com
[(AM) PL 2005; FL 2010; AM 2018]. 2005 Watrousville. Mar 2, 2010 Sterling, Alger, Garfield; Jan 1, 2013 Sterling, Alger, Standish: Community; Apr 1, 2019 Standish: Beacon of Light, Alger; **2019 Standish: Beacon of Light, Arenac Cnty: Christ**. (BOL) 201 S. Forest, Standish 48658 (989-846-6277), (ACC) 3322 E. Huron Rd., PO Box 145, AuGres 48703 (989-876-7449). Home: 124 N. Chestnut, PO Box 167, Sterling 48659 (989-654-9001)

*PAYNE, MARK R (RE) (Nola) – (D-1994, FE-1997, R-2016)
Rosebush 1992; Rosebush (LTFT ½) 1994; Rosebush (LTFT ¾) 01/01/1995; Rosebush (LTFT ¾) and Clare (Assoc) (LTFT ¼) 1995; Rosebush 1996; Oshtemo: Lifespring (New Church Start) 2001; Robbins 2009; Hastings: First 2014; Retired 12/31/2016   markp@broadstripe.net

*PAYNE, WILLIAM V (RE) (Jayne) – (FL-1951, FD-1960, FE-1962, R-1996)
East Osceola Circuit 1951; Middle Branch 1954; Leave of Absence 1955; Dowagiac: First 1957; Decatur 1960; Edmore: Faith 1961; Paw Paw 1965; Hillsdale: First 1979; Sodus: Chapel Hill 1987; Retired 1996
       wvpayne@triton.net
(H) 8000 Warren Woods Rd, Lot 64, Three Oaks 49128-8525 (269) 469-7643

*Peacock, Richard A. (Janis)   rjpeacock@wowway.com.net
[(RE) P 1970; F 1974]. 1973 Utica (assoc.); 1978 Ortonville; Jul. 1982 Lake Orion; 1993 Farmington: Nardin Park; 1997 Troy: First; **2008 Retired**. Home: 40198 Riverbend Dr., Sterling Heights 48310 (248-321-7480)

PEBLEY, PATRICIA A (FL) (Allen D) – (FL-2014)
Jackson: Trinity/Parma (LTFT ½) 2012; Hillside/Somerset Center 2014
       patpebley@gmail.com
(H) 6094 Folks Rd, Horton 49246-9657 (517) 563-8920
Hillside: 6100 Folks Rd, Horton 49246-9657 (517) 563-2835
SC: PO Box 277, 12095 E Chicago Rd, Somerset Center 49282 (517) 688-4330

*PEDERSEN, DOUGLAS L (RE) (Darlene) – (D-1970, FE-1972, R-2005)
Center Park 1970; Transferred from Minnesota Conf 1971; St Joseph First (Assoc) 1971; Saugatuck 10/15/1973; Saugatuck/Ganges 10/15/1973; Turk Lake 08/15/1975; Wyoming: Wesley Park (Assoc) 1979; Wayland 1982; Grand Rapids: Faith 1987; Leland 02/16/1994; Williamsburg 1997; Emmanuel Traverse City 02/01/2003; Traverse Bay/Williamsburg 01/01/2005 (TC Emmanuel Merged w/ Tc Asbury Becoming Traverse Bay); Retired 2005
       PedersenL5@aol.com
(H) PO Box 314, 102 W Terrace LN Commons, Leland 49654 (231) 256-9088

PENNY III, KELLAS D (FL) (Leanne) – (PL-2013, FL-2014)
Harrison: The Gathering (PTLP ½) 2013; Grand Rapids: Rivercrest (New Church Start) 01/01/2014; Dowagiac: First and UM Connectional Structures (¶344.1a,c) WMC New Church Position 02/01/2015; Dowagiac: First 2015; Water's Edge (New Buffalo) 2017
       kel@h2oedge.org (H) 19603 Oak Dr, New Buffalo 49117 (616) 209-2828
Water's Edge: 18732 Harbor Country Dr, New Buffalo 49117 (269) 469-1250

Perez, Joseph Anthony (Joanne)   joeandjo@tc3net.com
[(AF) New York]. Home: 1330 Trenton, Adrian 49221 (517-263-1807)

Perez, Paul David (Anne)   pperez@michiganumc.org
[(FD) PD 2006; FD 2010]. Wesley Theological Seminary. 2006 Director of Youth Ministry, Dulin United Methodist Church; 2008 Livonia: Newburg (deacon); 2013 Conference Director of Mission and Justice Engagement and Leadership Recruitment; **2018 Associate Director for Mission & Ministry**. 1161 E Clark Rd, Ste 212, DeWitt 48820 (517-347-4030 x 4076)

*PERKINS, A EDWARD (RE) (Shirley) – (D-1967, FE-1970, R-2006)
Transferred from Detroit Conf 1981; Bronson: First 1980; Fremont 04/01/1987; UM Connectional Structures (¶344.1a,c) District Superintendent, Lansing District 1990; Grand Rapids: Trinity 1996; Retired 2006; UM Connectional Structures (¶344.1a,c) Interim Conference Director 10/01/2008-12/31/2008
perksperch@gmail.com
(H) 3052 Bonita Dr SE, Grand Rapids 49508-1424 (616) 606-5060

Perrine, Stephen Kendall (Connie)   sperrine@sbcglobal.net
[(FE) P 1974; F 1976]. 1975 Flushing (assoc.); Oct 1977 Honorable Location; 1995 reinstated; 1995 Warren: Wesley (LTFT ¾); 1998 Beverly Hills; 2003 leave of absence; Aug 16, 2006 South Rockwood; **2016 South Rockwood** (LTFT ½), **Monroe: Calvary** (LTFT ½). (SR) 6311 S. Huron River Dr., South Rockwood 48179 (734-379-3131), (MC) 790 Patterson, Monroe 48161 (734-242-0145). Home: 23435 Oak Glen, Southfield 48033 (248-827-7110)

Peters, Jeremy Troy (Jennifer)   revjtp@hotmail.com
[(FE) PE 2003; FE 2006] 2003 Minister of Religion, British Methodist Church Wakefield Circuit (para 336); Sep 1, 2004 Morrice, Bennington, Pittsburg; 2005 Morrice, Pittsburg, Bancroft; 2008 Fenton (assoc); 2012 Fenton (assoc); South Central Cooperative Ministry: Lake Fenton; **2015 Flint: Court Street**. 225 W. Court St., Flint 48502 (810-235-4651). Home: 1827 Overhill, Flint 48503 (810-407-8333)

*PETERSON, GARY L (RL) (Reba) – (FL-2008, RL-2016)
Olivet (DSA) 2006; Fennville/Pearl 2008; Retired 2016; Claybanks (LTFT ¼) 2016

glpeterson32@frontier.com
(H) 6337 Cheyenne Rd, Pentwater 49449-9409 (231) 869-3373
Claybanks: PO Box 104, 9197 S 56th Ave, Montague 49437-9485 (231) 923-0573

Pethoud, Sue Ann (Rick)   spethoud@casscommunity.org
[(FD) PD 2014; FD 2017]. 2014 Detroit: Cass Community (deacon); **2016 Detroit: Cass Community and Social Services Community Relations liaison (deacon)**. (CC) 3901 Cass Ave., Detroit 48201 (313-833-7730), (SSCR) 11745 Rosa Parks Blvd., Detroit 48206 Home: 4529 Pleasant Valley Rd., Brighton 48114 (810-278-1235)

*PETRO, SUSAN M (RE) – (D-1994, FE-1996, R-2014)
Gull Lake (Assoc) 01/01/1994; Portage: Chapel Hill (Assoc) 01/01/1998; Grand Rapids: Genesis 2007; Retired 2014

suempetro@gmail.com
(H) 7799 Glenwood Pond Dr SE, Alto 49302-9301 (616) 550-6850

PETRUCCI, BARRY T (FE) (Lesa) – (D-1984, FE-1988)
Grandville (Assoc) 1986; Olivet 1989; UM Connectional Structures (¶344.1a,c) Executive Director of UM Metro Mininistries, Greater Grand Rapids 01/01/1995; Portage: Chapel Hill 2001

barrypetrucci@pchum.org
(H) 5300 Bronson Blvd, Portage 49024-5746 (269) 276-0482
Portage: Chapel Hill: 7028 Oakland Dr, Portage 49024-4148 (269) 327-6643

*Pettis, Warren Donald warrenpettis@myfairpoint.net
[(RE) T 1963; F 1965]. 1961 Weston; 1962 Samaria, Lulu; 1968 Saginaw: Ames (assoc.); 1971 Brown City: First, Emmanual; Jan. 1977 Caseville; 1980 Essexville; 1987 Monroe: First; 1989 Gaylord; **1998 Retired**. Home: 1202 Cotton Road, Lyndonville, VT 05851 (802-626-3845)

*Petty, Janet Gaston petty65@msn.com
[(RE)].2002 Detroit: Metropolitan (assoc) (para. 337.1); Feb 1, 2004 Commerce (interim); 2004 trans from CA-Pacific conf.; 2004 Southfield: Hope (assoc); **2012 Retired**. Home: 26110 Hendrie, Huntington Woods 48070 (248-546-9749)

Phillips, Andrew R (OE) – (OE-2018)
[North Carolina Conference, Elder] Hopkins/South Monterey 2018
aphillips@nccumc.org
(H) 86 E 13th St #3, Holland 49423 (919) 259-4681
Hopkins: 322 N Maple St, PO Box 356, Hopkins 49328-0356 (269) 793-7323
S Monterey: Corner of 26th St & 127th Ave, PO Box 356, Hopkins 49328
(269) 793-7323

Phillips, Daniel J.W. dan.jw.phillips@gmail.com
[(FL) PL 2013, FL 2019]. 2013 Kalamo; 2015 Felt Plains, Williamston: Wheatfield; 2017 Riverview; **2019 Bellaire: Community**. 401 N. Bridge St., PO Box 235, Bellaire 49615-0235 (231-533-8133). Home: 4046 Grass Lake Rd., Bellaire 49615-9398 (231-533-4228)

Phillips, Harold V. (Kathy) hal.phillips334@gmail.com
[(AM) FL 1994 from Missionary Church; AM 2001]. 1993 Omard/Cole; Aug 1, 1996 Capac: First & Zion; 2006 South Central Cooperative Ministry: Halsey, South Mundy; 2016 Montrose; **Dec 31, 2016 Retired**. Home: 9788 Boucher Rd., Otter Lake, 48464 (810-410-7234)

*Phillips, Kathy M. (Harold) kphillips9788@gmail.com
[(RL) PL 2009]. 2009 Seven Churches United Group Ministry: Lennon; **2016 Retired**. Home: 9788 Boucher Rd., Otter Lake 48464 (989-795-1024)

*Pieper, Ralph Howard, II (Mary) RMPieper@aol.com
[(RE) P 1972; F 1974]. 1972 Genesee, Thetford Center; 1975 Pigeon: Salem; 1983 Blissfield: First; 1989 Flint: Hope; 1996 Port Huron: First; 2003 Lapeer: Trinity; **2012 Retired; 2018 Mt. Morris: First** (LTFT ¼). 808 E. Mt. Morris Rd, Mt Morris 48458 (810-686-3870). Home: 3373 Brookgate Dr., Flint 48507 (586-260-7538)

*Pierce, Robert Bruce (Sandie) rbrucepierce@gmail.com
[(RE) P W. MI, 19 ; F W. MI, 19]. 1974 Trans. to Detroit Conf., Gwinn, Ishpeming, Salisbury; Sep. 1977 Chaplain, Navy, David Adams Memorial Chapel, Naval Station, Norfolk, VA, Group Chaplain, Stop 19, MAG32; 1990 Chaplain, NavSuppAct, Naples, Italy; 1993 Chaplain, Submarine Group 10; 1997 Regional Chaplain; Command Chaplain, Pearl Harbor; 2000 Command Chaplain, US Navy, Keflavik, Iceland; Sep 1, 2004 Eastern US Regional Field Director, Military Youth Ministry; **Feb 1, 2007 Retired**. Home: 45 Longyear Drive, Negaunee 49866 (906-236-2547)

*PIER-FITZGERALD, J LYNN (RE) (Tom) – (D-1977, FE-1980, R-2017)
East Lansing Chapel Hill/Gunnisonville 1978; White Cloud (LTFT ½) 05/16/1984; Wyoming Park (Assoc) (LTFT ½) 1988; Leave of Absence 1989; Plainfield 08/16/1991; UM Connectional Structures (¶344.1a,c) District Superintendent,Grand Traverse District 1999; Holland: First 2005; Retired 2017
lynn.pier.fitzgerald@gmail.com
(H) 83 West 18th St, Holland 49423-4120 (616) 393-6242

*PIER-FITZGERALD, THOMAS M (RE) (Lynn) – (D-1977, FE-1980, R-2016)
East Lansing: University (Assoc) 1978; East Lansing Chapel Hill/Gunnisonville 1982; White Cloud (LTFT ½) 05/16/1984; Grand Rapids: South 1988; Sabbatical Leave 1998; Elk Rapids/Kewadin (LTFT ¾) 1999; Grandville 2005; Retired 2016
tpfitz5169@sbcglobal.net
(H) 83 West 18th St, Holland 49423-4120 (616) 393-6242

Pittenger, Kathryn L. (Richard)   kpittenger@michiganumc.org
[(FD) PD 2008; FD 2011]. 2008 Waterford: Central (deacon); **2018 Children's Initiatives Coordinator, DeWitt: Redeemer (missional)**. 1161 E Clark Rd, Ste 212, DeWitt 48820 (517-347-4030 ext. 4030). Home: 4551 Seneca Dr., Okemos 48864 (248-505-5848)

PLACE, STEVEN C (FL) (Ilse) – (NL-2010, FL-2011)
LP w/o Appointment 2010; Grand Rapids: Mosaic 01/01/2011; Lake Odessa Lakewood 2017

splaceman@gmail.com
(H) 10121 Brown Rd, Lake Odessa 48849-9207 (616) 901-7633
Lake Odessa: Lakewood: 10265 Brown Rd, Lake Odessa 48849 (269) 367-4800

Platt, Susan E.   suseplatt@gmail.com
[(AM) FL 2011; AM 2013]. 2011 Bay City: Fremont Avenue; 2016 Alpena: First; **2018 Sandusky: First**. 68 Lexington St., Sandusky 48471 (810-648-2606). Home: 155 Bella Ave., Sandusky 48471

Plum, Alexander J.
[(PD) PD 2019]. **2019 Director Global Health Initiatives Henry Ford Health Systems, Detroit: Cass Community Missional Charge Conference** (Para 331.4a). 3901 Cass Ave, Detroit 48201-1721 (313-833-7730). Home: 285 Ashland St, Detroit 48215-3108 (810-210-0090)

Plum, Janine L. (Peter)
[(FE) PL 2008; PE 2015; FE 2018]. 2008 Caring Covenant Group Ministry: Richfield; Aug 1, 2012 school (Asbury); **2015 Seymour Lake**. 3050 Sashabaw, Oxford 48371 (248-628-4763). Home: 3191 Clipper Ct., Oxford 48371 (810-624-1404)

Poag, Patrick R.   churchladylisa@aol.com
[(FL) FL Jul 2, 2002]. Hemlock, Nelson; Jul 1, 2002 Hope, Edenville; 2004 Hope, Edenville; **2005 Hope, Edenville, Dale**. (H) 5278 North Hope Rd., Hope 48628 (989-3811), (E) W. State Rd., Box 125, Edenville 48620 (989-689-6250), (D) 4688 S. Freeman Rd, Beaverton 48612 (989-435-4829). Home: 5302 N. Hope Rd., Hope 48628 (989-689-4788)

POHL, JON L (FL) (Diane) – (FL-2006)
Avondale/North Evart/Sylvan (DSA) 01/15/2006; Ashley/Bannister/Greenbush 2006; Ludington: St Paul 2011; Lansing Asbury 2017
jpohl333@gmail.com
(H) 2412 Post Oak Ln, Lansing 48912-3542 (616) 894-4461
Lansing Asbury: 2200 Lake Lansing Rd, Lansing 48912-3614 (517) 484-5794

*****POHL, KEITH I** (RE) (Roberta) – (D-1958, FE-1960, R-1993)
Nashville 1958; Grand Rapids: First (Assoc) 1961; Rockford 1964; UM Connectional Structures (¶344.1a,c) Director, Wesley Foundation, Michigan State University 10/01/1966; UM Connectional Structures (¶344.1a,c) Associate Editor, Michigan Christian Advocate 1972; UM Connectional Structures (¶344.1a,c) Editor, Michigan Christian Advocate 10/01/1973; UM Connectional Structures (¶344.1a,c) Editor-Publisher, Michigan Christian Advocate 1977; East Lansing: University 08/01/1980; Appointed to Extension Ministries (¶344.1b,c) Editor, Circuit Rider 09/01/1986; Retired 12/31/1993
pohlkirj@cs.com
(H) 665 N Aurelius Rd, Mason 48854-9528 (517) 244-0389

*****POHLY, GERALD A** (RE) – (D-1952, FE-1957, R-1996)
Battle Creek: Calvary (EUB) 1956; Magnolia (EUB) 1961; Wyoming Park 04/01/1969; UM Connectional Structures (¶344.1a,c) District Superintendent, Central District 03/01/1973; Church of the Dunes 1978; Grand Rapids: Trinity 1989; Retired 1996
gedu32@att.net
(H) 2529 Grove Bluff Dr SE, Grand Rapids 49546-5619 (616) 308-0071

POMERVILLE, ANDREW (OF) – (OF-2000)
[Presbyterian Church] East Lansing Peoples Church 2000
Peoples Church: 200 W Grand River Ave, 48823-4212 (517) 332-5073

*****Poole, Karen B.** (Gary)   kbpoole@twmi.rr.com
[(RE) P 1983; F 1988]. 1985 school, St. John's Seminary, Plymouth; 1986 Monroe: St. Paul's (assoc.); 1988 Brighton: First (assoc.); 1993 Farmington: Nardin Park (assoc); 1997 Trenton: First 2003 sabbatical leave; 2004 Waterford: Four Towns, Trinity (Intentional Interim ¶329.3); **2006 Retired**. Home: 30029 Barwell, Farmington Hills 48334 (248-471-9586)

Pope, Marva C   marpo0828@yahoo.com
[(PE) PL 2014; PE 2015]. 2014 Detroit: People's; **2018 Wayne: First**. 3 Towne Square St, Wayne 48184 (734-721-4801). Home: 29875 Rambling Rd., Southfield 48076.

*****POSNIK JR, RALPH A** (RL) (Karen) – (FL-2010; RL-2019)
Barnard/East Jordan/Norwood (DSA) 05/15/2009; Barnard/East Jordan/Norwood 11/15/2009; Niles: Portage Prairie 2014; Retired 2019
servant1@reagan.com
(H) 137 Lakeshire Dr, Fairfield Glade, TN 38558 (231) 883-1985

POWERS, JON R (FE) (Susan Speer-Powers) – (D-1972, FE-1975)
East Lansing: University (Assoc) 1974; Portage: Chapel Hill 1978; Hillside 09/16/1978; UM Connectional Structures (¶344.1a,c) Chaplain and Director of Church Relations, Adrian College 08/16/1981; UM Connectional Structures (¶344.1a,c) Chaplain, Ohio Wesleyan University 08/16/1988
jrpowers@owu.edu
(H) 104 W Winter St, Delaware, OH 43015-1910 (614) 369-1709
Ohio Wesleyan University, 40 Rowland Ave, Delaware, OH 43015-2392
(614) 368-3082

*Powers, Linda Jo   lp05@mediacombb.net
[(RE) P 1995; F 1998]. Jun 16, 1996 Whittemore, Prescott; 2000 Lexington; 2002 Beaverton: First, Dale; 2005 Beaverton: First, Wagarville: Community, Wooden Shoe; 2009 Clayton, Rollin Center; 2012 Glennie, Harrisville, Lincoln; Nov 1, 2014 medical leave; **Oct 1, 2015 Retired**. Home: 139 Northbrook Ct., Decatur, IN 46733 (260-301-9222)

POWERS, NANCY G (FE) (Paul) – (PE-2006, FE-2010)
Reading 2006; Battle Creek: Sonoma/Newton 2008; Perry/Shaftsburg 2012
pastornancy@live.com
(H) PO Box 142, 121 S Madison St, Perry 48872-0142 (517) 625-3444
Perry: PO Box 15, 131 Madison St, Perry 48872 (517) 625-3444
Shaftsburg: PO Box 161, 12821 Warner Rd, Shaftsburg 48882 (517) 675-1567

POY, EUN SIK (FE) – (PL-2015, PE-2016; FE-2019)
Boyne City/Boyne Falls/Horton Bay (LTFT ¾) 09/01/2015; Boyne City/Boyne Falls/Epsilon 2016
cloud.sik@asburyseminary.edu
(H) 8204 E Mitchell Rd, Petoskey 49770 (231) 347-5382
Boyne City: 324 S Park St, Boyne City 49712-1528 (231) 582-9776
Boyne Falls: 3057 Mill St, Boyne Falls 49713-5100 (231) 582-9776
Epsilon: 8251 E Mitchell Rd, Petoskey 49770-8831 (231) 347-6608

*Pratt, David Orville
[(RL) PL Nov 16, 1997, FL 2003]. Nov 16, 1997 Clifford; 2003 Heritage; 2013 Ortonville; **Mar 1, 2016 Retired; 2018 Crystal Valley, Walkerville** (LTFT ¼).
(H) 409 Third St, Ludington 49431 (810) 404-0085 gooey@tir.com
Crystal Valley: 1547 E Hammett Rd, Hart 49420 (231) 873-5422
Walkerville: 189 E Main St, PO Box 125, Walkerville 49459 (231) 873-4236

*PRATT, D KAY (RA) (Merlin) – (PL-1992, FL-1996, AM-2002, RA-2016)
Transferred from South Indiana Conf 1992; Dowling: Country Chapel/Banfield (Co-Pastor) (LTFT ¼) 1992; Shepardsville/Price 1996; St Johns: Pilgrim (Assoc) 2004; Leave of Absence 2006; Appointed in Other Annual Conferences (¶331.8, ¶346.1) Detroit Conference, Denton: Faith 08/15/2008; Leave of Absence 2010; Other Valid Ministries (¶344.1d) Vice-President, Pastors and Priests Available for Service (PAPAS), Jamaica 2011; Retired 2016
mpratteumc@juno.com
(H) 9066 Whittaker Rd, Ypsilanti 48197 (812) 498-7147

*PRATT, MERLIN H (RA) (Kay) – (FL-1991, AM-1997, RA-2019)
Waterloo Village/First (DSA) (Part Time) 1988-02/01/1991; Dowling: Country Chapel/Banfield 1991; Elsie 1996; St Johns: Pilgrim 2003; Leave of Absence 2006; Appointed in Other Annual Conferences (¶331.8, ¶346.1) Detroit Conference, Canton Cherry Hill 08/15/2008; Leave of Absence 2011; Other Valid Ministries (¶344.1d) Port Antonio Circuit, Jamaica District of the Methodist Church in the Caribbean and the Americas 09/01/2011; Appointed in Other Annual Conferences (¶331.8, ¶346.1) Detroit Conference, Ypsilanti: Lincoln Community 2016; Retired 2019
cowtownpreacher@hotmail.com
(H) 1857 S Co Rd 50W, Brownstown, IN 47220 (734) 482-4446

PRENTISS, DEAN N (FE) – (D-1998, FE-2000)
Transferred from Detroit Conf 2003; Mt Pleasant: Trinity/Countryside 1995; Williamston 09/15/1999; Big Rapids: First 2008; Wyoming: Wesley Park 2011
deanprentiss1@gmail.com
(H) 2664 Borglum Avenue NE, Grand Rapids 49505-3616 (616) 514-7124
Wyoming: Wesley Park: 1150 32nd St SW, Wyoming 49509 (616) 988-6738

Prewitt, Victoria Irene gooey@tir.com
[(FL) DSA 2018, FL Jan 1, 2019]. 2018 Crystal Fall: Crist, Amasa: Grace (DSA); **Jan 1, 2019 Crystal Fall: Crist, Amasa: Grace**. (CFC) 500 Marquette Ave, PO Box 27, Crystal Falls 49920-0027, (AG) 209 Pine St, Amasa, 49903. Home: 110 Elm Grove, Crystal Falls 49920 (906-362-0460)

*Price, Carl Edwin (Patricia) carl_pat_price@netzero.com
[(RE) T W. VA, 1957; F W. VA, 1959]. 1953 Palestine; 1956 school; 1959 Trenton, NJ: Broad Street; 1960 Allentown; Oct. 1962 Trans. to Detroit Conf., Birmingham: First (assoc.); 1965 Detroit: St. Mark's; 1968 Pontiac: Central; Nov. 1973 Midland: First; **1998 Retired**. Home: 3303 Thornbrook Ct., Midland 48460 (989-832-4419)

PRICE, WAYNE A (FE) (Joy) – (D-1988, FE-1993)
Transferred from North Carolina Conf 2000; Keswick 2000; Shepherd 2004; Kalamazoo: Westwood 2007; Trenton: Faith 2019
pastorwaynewumc@gmail.com
(H) 1641 Edsel Dr, Trenton 48183-1894 (269) 330-6768
Trenton: Faith: 2530 Charlton, Trenton 48183-2439 (734) 671-5211

*Prout, W. Cadman
[(RE) T 1940; F 1942]. 1940 school; 1941 Highland Park: Trinity (assoc.); 1942 Royal Oak: St. John's; 1949 Livonia; 1953 Four Towns; 1955 Attorney, Friend of the Court, Oakland County; 1963 Sabbatical; 1964 Voluntary Location; **1981 Retired**. Home: (Jun.-Nov.) 4216 Chipmunk, Lincoln 48742; (Nov.-Jun.) 618 Deerwood Ave., Englewood, FL 34223

PUCKETT, TIMOTHY R (PL) (Esther) – (PL-2011)
Frontier (PTLP ¼) 2011; Frontier/Osseo (PTLP ½) 01/01/2012; North Adams/Jerome (PTLP ¼) 2014;
timpuckett761@yahoo.com
(H) 10445 Folks Rd, Hanover 49241-9777 (859) 421-8931
North Adams: PO Box 62, 228 E Main St, North Adams 49262-0062
(517) 287-5190
Jerome: 8768 Jerome Rd, Jerome 49249-9696

QUERY, TODD J (FD) – (PD-2003, FD-2008)
Transferred from Detroit Conf 2004; Holland: First (Assoc) 2003; Appointed in Other Annual Conferences (¶331.8, ¶346.1) Virginia Conference, Williamsburg First 2006; Transitional Leave 12/31/2012; Personal Leave 01/01/2014; Deacons Appointed Beyond the Local Church(¶331.1a) Freelance Curriculum Writer/ Contributer, Sparkhouse, Augsburg Fortess Publishers (LTFT ½) and Wellspring UMC, Virginia Conference (LTFT ¼) 2015

deacontodd08@gmail.com
(H) 2620 Sir Thomas Way, Williamsburg, VA 23185 (757) 208-0207

*RADER, BLAINE B (RE) (Sharon) – (D-1958, FE-1964, R-2004)
Transferred from Northern IL Conf 1978; Other Valid Ministries (¶344.1d) Executive Director, Samaritan Counseling Center, Battle Creek 1978; Other Valid Ministries (¶344.1d) Comprehensive Psychological Services, Grand Rapids 1983; Other Valid Ministries (¶344.1d) Clinical Director, Samaritan Counseling Center of Central Michigan 01/01/1987; Other Valid Ministries (¶344.1d) Clinical Director, Samaritan Counseling Center of Central Michigan (LTFT ½) and Pastoral Counseling and Consultation (LTFT ½) 1990; Leave of Absence 09/01/1992; Other Valid Ministries (¶344.1d) Private Practice of Pastoral Counseling 01/27/1993; Other Valid Ministries (¶344.1d) Executive Director, Samaritan Counseling Center of Southern Wisconsin 01/01/1995; Appointed in Other Annual Conferences (¶337.1) Wisconsin Conf, Good Shepherd UMC 1997; Appointed in Other Annual Conferences (¶337.1) Wisconsin Conf, Madison: Bethany 2001; Retired 2004

Raderbb@aol.com
(H) 450 Davis St #362, Evanston, IL 60201 (312) 255-8544

Radtke, Clifford L
[(PL) PL 2018]. **2018 Port Austin, Pinnebog** (LTFT ¾). (PA) 8625 Arch, Box 129, Port Austin 48467 (989-738-5322), (P) 4619 N. Pinnebog Rd., Kinde 48445. Home: 114 Washington, Port Austin 48467 (989-738-6322)

Rafferty, Cathy Lynne   mail4cr@yahoo.com
[(FE) PE 1999; FE 2002; 2010 transfer to Detroit Conference]. 1999 Grandville (assoc); 2001 Chaplain Clark Retirement Community (¶344.1b,c); Feb 24, 2010 Chaplain, Chelsea Retirement Community (¶344.1b,c); Dec 4, 2017 Chaplain, Adrian Dominican Sisters (¶344.1b,c); **2019 Gladstone: Memorial**. 1920 Lake Shore Dr., Gladstone 49837-1249 (906-428-9311). Home: 1006 Lake Shore Dr., Gladstone 49837-1539 (906-420-8449)

Raineri, Jacqueline
[(FL) FL 2012]. 2012 Wisner; 2016 Webberville, Williamston: Crossroads; 2017 Millville, New Church Start; Jan 1, 2018 Millville; **2018 DownRiver.**

pastorjackieumc@gmail.com
(H) 20433 Foxboro St, Riverview 48193 (517) 623-6594
DownRiver: 14400 Beech Daly, Taylor 48180 (734) 442-6100

Ralston, Douglas E. (Sharon)   dougralston@gmail.com
[(FE) PL 2000, PE 2004, FL Aug 1, 2009; PE 2011; FE 2013]. Nov 1, 2000 LaSalle: Zion; 2004 LaSalle: Zion (LTFT ¾), Lambertville (assoc); Apr 1, 2007 discontinued; Aug 1, 2009 reinstated; Aug 1, 2009 East Side Covenant Cooperative Parish: St. Clair Shores: Good Shepherd; 2014 Dearborn: Good Shepherd; 2016 Trenton: Faith; **2019 Retired.** Home: 147 Borgess Ave, Monroe 48162-2702 (734-676-7079)

RAMSEY, MICHAEL J (PL) (Kathy) – (PL-2010, FL-2017)
Carlisle (PTLP ½) 2010; Carlisle (PTLP ¾) 01/01/2011; Kent City Chapel Hill 2017

pastorramsey@att.net
(H) 14555 Fruit Ridge Ave, Kent City 49330-9751 (616) 293-9831
Chapel Hill: 14591 Fruit Ridge Ave, Kent City 49330-9751 (616) 675-7184

*RANDELS, JEANNE M (RE) (Paul Hartman) – (D-1982, FR-1984, R-2014)
Marshall (Assoc) 1981; Plainfield 02/23/1988; Albion: First 08/16/1991; Okemos Community Church 10/16/1998; Retired 01/01/2014; Lansing: Faith & S Lansing Ministries (LTFT ½) 2015-12/31/2015; Potterville (LTFT ½) 2016-08/31/2016
jeannerandels@gmail.com
(H) 3786 Yosemite Dr, Okemos 48864-3837 (517) 349-3595

Ravi, Latha revlatharavi@gmail.com
[(FE) P 1997; FE 1999]. 1997 Ypsilanti: First (assoc); Jan 1, 2001 Flint: Central; 2002 Detroit: Central (assoc); 2005 Canton: Cherry Hill; 2008 Rochester St. Paul's (assoc.); 2017 sabbatical leave; 2018 appoint. to attend school, U of M, School of Social Work (¶338.4); Jan 1, 2019 Transitional Leave; **2019 Detroit: Cass Community** (assoc) (LTFT ¼). 3901 Cass Ave, Detroit 48201-1721 (313-833-7730). Home: 533 Hill St, Rochester 48307-2213 (248-464-4600)

*Ray, David Evans (Janie Marie)
[(RE) P 1985; F 1988]. 1986 Erie; 1991 Livonia: Newburg (assoc.); 1992 Hazel Park: First; 1994 Corunna; 1996 Leave of Absence; Aug 1, 2000 South Central Cooperative Ministry: Halsey/South Mundy; 2006 leave of absence; **2012 Retired**. Home: 840 Georgia St., Williamston 48895

*Ray, Kenneth Bradley (Diane)
[(RE) P 1992, on recognition of orders, Church of God; F 1994]. 1989 North Street; 1992 Cass City: Salem; 1994 Roseville: Trinity; 2000 Alpena; 2003 Waterford: Trinity; 2004 Oxford; 2006 Redford: New Beginnings; 2007 Stony Creek; **2010 Retired**. Home: 186 Murphys Trail, Kalamazoo 49009 (269-348-1089)

*REECE, WAYNE G (RE) (Jo) – (D-1958, FE-1960, R-2000)
Transferred from North Indiana Conf 1963; Appointed to Extension Ministries (¶344.1b,c) Field Worker Conf; Board of Education 1963; Bangor 1966; Appointed to Extension Ministries (¶344.1b,c) General Board of Education 1970; Appointed in Other Annual Conferences (¶331.8, ¶346.1) Board of Discipleship, Section of Curriculum Resources 1973; Appointed in Other Annual Conferences (¶331.8, ¶346.1) Board of Discipleship, Curriculum Resources Committee 1977; Kalamazoo: First (Assoc) 02/15/1979; Big Rapids: First 1985; Mason: First 1992; Retired 2000

wayne.reece@comcast.net
(H) 12 McKendree Circle, Hermitage, TN 37076 (615) 818-0272

Reed, David Allen david.reed68@gmail.com
[(PE) PE 2017 on recognition of orders from Missionary]. **2017 North Street**. 4580 North Rd., Clyde 48049 (810-385-4027). Home: 4584 North Rd., Clyde 48049 (810-385-8366)

Reed, Nathan T.　　　　　　　　　　　　natereed1977@gmail.com
[(FL) FL 2011]. 2011 Crystal Falls: Christ, Amasa: Grace; 2015 Coleman: Faith; **2019 L'Anse, Sidnaw, Zeba**. (L) 304 N. Main, L'Anse 49946 (906-524-7939), (S) S 121 W. Milltown Rd., Sidnaw 49961, (Z) 16024 Zeba Rd., L'Anse 49946 (906-524-6967). Home: 227 N. Front, L'Anse 49946 (906-524-7936)

Rees, Dianna Lynn (Forrest)　　　　　　　diannarees@hotmail.com
[(FE) PE 2003; FE 2006] 2003 Armada, West Berlin; 2011 Imlay City; **2013 Wyandotte: First**. 72 Oak, Wyandotte 48192 (734-282-9222). Home: 2210 20th St., Wyandotte 48192 (734-284-3224)

*REEVES, KENNETH C (RE) (Susanne) – (D-1978, FE-1982, R-2006)
Transferred from Detroit Conf 1995; Riverdale: Lincoln Road 1995; Burnips/Monterey Center 1997; Marion/Cadillac: South Community 2004; Retired 2006; Marion/Cadillac: South Community 2006-2007

　　　　　　　　　　　　　　　　　　kcreeves1@frontier.com
　　　　　　　(H) 201 James Drive, Roscommon 48653-8351 (989) 821-8504

*Regan, Jeffery D. (Linda)　　　　　　　jeffery.regan@me.com
[(RE) P 1974; F 1977]. 1976 Lakeville, Leonard; 1979 Midland: First (assoc.); Sep. 1982 Grayling; 1989 Utica; 1994 Saginaw Bay District Superintendent; 1998 Conference Council Director; Feb 1, 2001 Rochester: St. Paul's; **2013 Retired**. 51781 Colonial Dr., Shelby Twp. 48316 (586-803-0124)

Reichle, Walter P.
[(FL) FL 2012]. **Oct, 2012 Iron Mountain: First, Quinnesec**. (IM)106 Fourth St., Iron Mountain 49801 (906-774-3586), (Q) 677 Division, PO Box 28, Quinnesec 49876 (906-774-7971). Home: 901 Fairbanks St., Iron Mountain 49801 (906-828-1228)

Reinhardt, Keith　　　　　　　　　　　pkrwilber@gmail.com
[(PL) PL Dec 1, 2014]. Dec 1, 2014 Wilber; **Sept 1, 2016 Wilber, Glennie** (LTFT ¼). (W) 3278 N. Sherman Rd., East Tawas 48730 (989-362-7860), (G) 3170 State St., PO Box 189, Glennie 48737-0189. Home: 7620 Spruce, Hale 48739 (989-710-1976)

Reinker, Heidi C.　　　　　　　　　　hcreinker@gmail.com
[(FE) P 1986; F 1988]. Sep 5, 1986 Seymour Lake; 1989 honorable location; 1996 reinstated 1996 Old Mystic United Methodist Church, Old Mystic, CT (LTFT); 2003 leave of absence; Nov 1, 2003 Richford, Troy Conference; 2010 Waterville Union Church, Waterville, VT; **2016 Trenton: First**. 2610 W. Jefferson, Trenton 48183 (734-676-2066. Home: 2604 Lenox Rd., Trenton 48183 (734-676-0041)

*Reisinger, Jaye Annette (Alan)　　　　　　jayealan@tm.net
[(RD) CRT, 1981; CON (CE), 1982; FD 2002; RD 2018]. 1981 Clio: Bethany; 1985 Leave of Absence; 1986 Saginaw Bay District Project Director. 1992 Medical Leave.; 1994 Leave of Absence; 1999 Freeland (LTFT ¼); 2003 Freeland (deacon) (LTFT ½); **2018 Retired**. Home: 7485 N. River Rd., Freeland 48623 (989-239-1820)

*Rencontre, James A. (Jean)　　　　　　revumc@charter.net
[(RA) PL 1989; FL 1990; AM 1995]. 1989 Upper Peninsula Native American Ministry; 1990 Iron River: Wesley; 1993 Decker, Argyle, Shabbona (LTFT ¾); **1997 Retired**. Home: 709 Garvey St., Ironwood 49938 (906-932-0470)

*Rencontre, Jean B. (James) jbrencontre42@gmail.com
[(RL) PL 1993; FL 1997]. 1993 Decker, Argyle, Shabbona (part-time); 1997 Decker, Argyle, Shabbona; 2000 Ironwood: Wesley, Wakefield; **2008 Retired**. Home: 709 Garvey St., Ironwood 49938 (906-932-0470)

REUM, BETH A (PE) – (NL-2002, FL-2009, PE-2011)
LP w/o Appointment 2002; Manton 2009; Silver Creek/Keeler 2013; Silver Creek (LTFT ¾) 2015; Medical Leave 01/15/2016

pastorbeffy@gmail.com
(H) 5667 Orchard Dr, Berrien Springs 49103-9502 (269) 325-0891

Reynolds, Jonathan E. (Lindsey Hall)
[(FE) FL Jan 9, 2014; PE 2015; FE 2019]. Jan 9, 2014 Rochester: St. Paul (assoc); **2018 Detroit: Cass Community (assoc)**. 3901 Cass Ave., Detroit 48201 (313-833-7730). Home: 130 Arlington, Birmingham 48009 (248-891-2788)

*Rhinesmith, James Lyon
[(RE) T Newark, 1946; F NY East, 1951]. 1946 Paterson, NJ: Hamilton Avenue; 1947 school; 1949 Trans. to NY East Conf., Oceanside; 1951 Long Island: Central Islip; 1953 Norwalk: South Norwalk; 1956 Trans. to Detroit Conf., Detroit: Messiah; 1959 Sandusky; 1963 Marine City; 1965 Oak Park: Faith; 1969 Sabbatical; **1969 Retired**. [Jan. 15, 1986-Dec. 1987 Trenton: Faith (assoc.)-LTFT]. Home: 404 Cheswick Place, #252, Rosemont, PA 19010

*Rhoades, Stephen E. (Debra) srhoades@up.net
[(RE) P 1994 on recognition of orders, Wesleyan Church; F 1997; RE 2019]. 1983 Madison, Good Shepherd Wesleyan Church; Feb 16, 1994 transf to Detroit Conf., Crystal Falls, Amasa: Grace; 2000 Marquette: First; 2004 Crystal Falls: Christ, Amasa: Grace; 2011 L'Anse, Sidnaw, Zeba; **2019 Retired**. Home: 126 S Shore Rd, Crystal Falls 49920 (906- 367-4587)

*Rice, Clifford Clifford496@cs.com
[(RE) SP 1993; PE 1998; FE 2002]. 1993 Detroit: West Outer Drive (LTFT); **2002 Retired**. Home: 20539 Woodward, Clinton Twp. 48035 (586-791-4396)

*Rice, Philip A. (Charlene) Ricepc@chartermi.net
[(RE) P 1969; F 1972]. 1971 Hillman, Spratt; May 1975 Homer; 1979 Freeland; 1987 Essexville: St. Luke's; 1997 Cass City; **2002 Retired**. Home: 6074 Old Hickory Dr., Bay City 48706 (989-684-2629)

Richards, Robert Grant robertgrichards@chartermi.net
[(FL) FL 1993]. Dec 16, 1993 Tawas (assoc); 1997 Monroe: East Raisinville Frenchtown; 2001 Saginaw: Swan Valley; 2013 Saginaw: Swan Valley, LaPorte; **2019 Saginaw: Swan Valley, LaPorte, Hemlock, Nelson**. (SV) 9265 Geddes Rd, Saginaw 48609-9522, (L) 3990 Smith's Crossing, Freeland 48623 (989-695-9692), (H) 406 W. Saginaw St., PO Box 138, Hemlock 48626-0138, (N) 5950 S Hemlock Rd., PO Box 138, Hemlock 48626-0138. Home: 16344 Northern Pintail Trail, Hemlock 48626 (989-642-4560)

*RICKARD, O'RYAN (RL) – (PL-2004, PE-2005, RL-2013)
Morris Chapel 2003; Townline/Breedsville 2004; Salem/Greenbush/Lowe 2005; Salem/Lowe/Maple Rapids 2006; Coloma/Watervliet 2007; Niles: Portage Prairie/Arden 2009; PE Discontinued 2013; Retired LP 2013; Niles: Portage Prairie/Arden (LTFT ¼) 2013; Arden (LTFT ¼) 2014

orr6148@aol.com
(H) 6148 Avon St, Portage 49024-2630 (269) 235-1700
Arden: 6891 M 139, Berrien Springs 49103 (269) 429-4931

RIEGLER, ANNE W (FL) (Mike) – (PL-2010, FL-2017, AM-2019)
LP w/o Appointment 2007; Amble (PTLP) 08/15/2009; Mears/Shelby 2017

pastoranne09@gmail.com
(H) 5181 Hancock St, Montague 49437-1617 (231) 631-0573
Mears: PO Box 100, 1990 N Joy St, Mears 49436-0100 (231) 873-0875
Shelby: 68 E 3rd St, Shelby 49455-1166 (231) 861-2020

RIEGLER, MICHAEL A (FE) (Anne) – (FL-2006, AM-2012, PE-2015, FE-2017)
Big Rapids: Third Avenue/Paris/Rodney 09/11/2005; Edmore: Faith 2011; Montague 2017

pastormikeriegler@gmail.com
(H) 5181 Hancock St, Montague 49437-1617 (231) 631-4712
Montague: 8555 Cook St, Montague 49437-1516 (231) 894-5789

*RILEY, RICHARD M (RE) (Janis) – (D-1975, FE-1979, R-2014)
Sturgis (Assoc) 1977; Middleton/Maple Rapids 1980; Kalkaska 1984; Rockford 1993; Retired 2014

dick.riley52@gmail.com
(H) 4307 Rezen Ct, Rockford 49341-9643 (616) 648-4340

*RITTER, JOHN F. (RL) (Delcina) – (FL-1978, PL-1980, FL-1984, RL-2001)
Ashley / Bannister 10/16/1978; Rosebush (LTFT PT) 1980; Edwardsburg: Hope 03/01/1984; Smith Corners / Crystal Valley / Walkerville 1988; Carlisle 09/01/1990; Girard / Ellis Corners 1994; Turk Lake 07/08/1996; Retired 11/01/2001

(H) 2490 E Levering Rd, Levering 49755-9321 (231) 537-2777

*Ritter, William Anthony (Kristine)   billritter65@yahoo.com
[(RE) T 1963; F 1967]. 1965 Dearborn: First (assoc.); 1969 Livonia: Newburg; 1980 Farmington: Nardin Park; 1993 Birmingham: First; **2005 Retired**. Home: 940 Scott Court, Northville 48176 (248-308-3216)

Robbins, Patrick Doyle (Karen)   suttonsunshine@hotmail.com
[(FL) FL 1998]. 1998 Cole, Omard; 2000 Omard; 2001 Sutton-Sunshine, Bethel, Akron; 2011 Grayling: Michelson Memorial; 2014 Yale; **2019 Brown City, Omard**. (BC) 7043 Lincoln, PO Box 39, Brown City 48416 (810-346-2010), (O) 2055 Peck Rd., Brown City 48416-9146 (810-346-3448). Home: 6931 George St., Brown City 48416 (810-346-2555)

*Roberts, Archie Ted
[(RE) T 1961; F 1963]. 1961 school; 1962 Franklin (assoc.); 1963 Dixboro; 1965 Chaplain, Army, Vietnam; 1966 Chaplain, Air Defense, Cleveland, OH; 1968 Chaplain, Alaska; 1971 Chaplain School; 1972 CPE Student, Englewood Federal Prison; 1973 Military Police School Faculty; 1977 Chaplain, Korea; 1978 Division Chaplain, 24th Div., Ft. Stewart, GA; 1982 Chaplain School, Director of Training, Ft. Monmouth, NJ; 1990 Staff Chaplain, Chapel of Four Chaplains, Valley Forge, PA; **1997 Retired.** Home: G-08 Road, W 6555, Wallace 49893

ROBERTS, Mark J (OE) (Jean) – (OE-2018)
[Alabama-West Florida, Elder] Other Valid Ministries (¶344.1d) Borgess Medicat Center (Chaplain) Kalamazoo (¾) and Kalamazoo: Northwest (LTFT ¼)
Markjrob1963@yahoo.com
(H) 22980 64th Ave, Mattawan 49071 (406) 217-2237
Kalamazoo: Northwest: 3140 N 3rd St, Kalamazoo 49009 (269) 290-1312

ROBERTS, RICHARD D (PL) (Lucinda) – (PL-2015)
Fountain 2012; Free Soil-Fountain (DSA) (LTFT ¼) 2013; Free Soil-Fountain (LTFT ¼) 12/01/2015
onchristthesolidrockistandd@gmail.com
(H) 2415 E Michigan St, Free Soil 49411-9679 (231) 233-8954
Free Soil-Fountain: PO Box 173, 2549 E Michigan St, Free Soil 49411
(231) 690-4591

ROBERTSON, JAMES C (PL) (Jean) – (PL-2014)
Townline (LTFT ¼) 2014
jc.robertson@ymail.com
(H) 55130 County Rd 384, Grand Junction 49056-9725 (269) 838-3500
Townline: 41470 24th Ave, Bloomingdale 49026-9760 (269) 521-4559

*Robertson, Stanley Joe (Mary Ellen)   sjmrobertson@charter.net
[(RE) T 1967; F 1970]. 1969 Detroit: Redford (assoc.); 1970 Homer; 1973 school; 1975 Chaplain, CPE Supervisor, Chillicothe Correctional Institution; 1981 Port Huron: Gratiot Park, Washington Avenue; 1985 Cass City: Trinity; Jan. 1, 1990 Tawas; 2001 sabbatical leave; **2002 Retired.** Home: 907 Monument, Tawas City 48763 (989-362-5881)

*ROBINSON, BEATRICE K (RE) – (D-1990, FE-1992, R-2007)
Pokagon (Part Time) 1988; Riverdale: Lincoln Road 1990; Holland: First (Assoc) 1995; Jackson: Trinity 1998; Bath/Gunnisonville 2006; Retired 2007
bearobin@sbcglobal.net
(H) 706 Huntington Blvd, Albion 49224-9404 (517) 629-5881

*Robinson, William T. (Joyce)   TJMROB@aol.com
[(RE) T S. Caro, Central Jurisd., 1964; F S. Caro, Central Jurisd., 1966]. 1966 Forest City; 1968 Trans. to Detroit Conf., Detroit: East Grand Boulevard; 1970 Detroit: East Grand Boulevard, Urban Missioner; 1971 Urban Missioner; 1974 Ann Arbor: Glacier Way; Oct. 1978 General Board of Global Ministries; 1998 Saginaw Bay District Superintendent; **2004 Retired.** Home: 3310 Corvair Lane, Saginaw 48602 (989-792-7552)

*ROBINSON-FISHER, CAROLYN A. (RL) (Don) – (PL-1988, FL-1991, RL-2011)
Williamston: Wheatfield (LTFT ¼) 1988; Middleton / Maple Rapids 1991; Millville
1997; Three Rivers: Ninth Street / Jones 07/14/1998; Battle Creek: Christ 2007;
Retired 2011
(H) 20908 Collier Rd, Battle Creek 49037 (269) 589-6487

Roe, Jacquelyn   jackieroe2@yahoo.com
[(FE) P 1994; F 1997]. 1995 Gwinn; 2006 Gladstone: Memorial; 2010 Cass City;
2018 Milan: Marble Memorial. 8 Park St., Milan 48160 (734-439-2421). Home:
835 Faith Ct., Milan 48160

Roosa, Kayla
[(PE) PL 2015, FL 2017, PE 2019]. Nov 1, 2015 Poseyville; **2017 Freeland**. 205
E. Washington, PO Box 207, Freeland 48623 (989-695-2101). Home: 7801 N.
River Road, Freeland 48623 (989-573-8357)

*ROOSE, RANDALL E (RA) (LaVonna) – (AM-1986, RA-1993)
[Church of the Brethren] Weidman 01/01/1986; Retired 1993; Leaton (DSA)
08/01/1999-2016
rlroose60@gmail.com
(H) 3380 S Genuine Road, Mt Pleasant 48858-7951 (989) 772-1001

*ROSS, EDWARD C (RE) (Monika) – (D-1976, FE-1980, R-2012)
Mt Pleasant: First (Assoc) 1978; Gull Lake 1981; Jackson: First 1994; Retired
2012; Lansing: Christ (Interim) 12/31/2012; Waterloo Village (LTFT ¼) 2013;
Three Rivers Ninth St (LTFT ¼) 2017
(H) 4231 Persian Dr, Kalamazoo 49006 (269) 382-0870
edward.c.ross45@gmail.com
Three Rivers Ninth St: 16621 Morris Ave, Three Rivers 49093 (269) 273-2065

*Roth, Jr., Robert H.   bobjazzrr@gmail.com
[(RE) West Michigan; trans to Detroit Conf Jan 1, 2015]. 2009 Ann Arbor: First
(assoc.), Director of Wesley Foundation (2010 came out of retirement);2014
Chaplain-Director, Wesley Foundation, University of Michigan; **2018 Retired**.
Home: 270 E 14th St, Holland 49423 (734-369-8068)

Rourke, LuAnn L. (Patrick)   luannrourke@yahoo.com
[(FE) FL 2006; PE 2007; FE 2011]. 2006 Swartz Creek (assoc.); 2009 Seymour
Lake; 2015 Clio: Bethany; **2017 Port Huron: First**. 828 Lapeer Ave., Port Huron
48060 (810-985-8107). Home: 3014 E. Woodland Dr., Port Huron 48060 (810-
987-5333)

Rouse, Ronald (Donna)
[(PL) PL Nov 9, 2013]. **Nov 9, 2013 Attica**. 26789 Dayton Rd., Richmond 48062
(810-724-0690). Home: (248-379-2509)

*Rowe, Edwin A. (Nida Donar).   whereisthepastor@yahoo.com
[(RE) P 1968; F 1972]. 1971 Pontiac: Central (assoc.); 1974 Pontiac Ecumenical
Ministry; 1979 Director, Wesley Foundation, Wayne State University; 1981 De-
troit: Cass Avenue; Jul 1, 1994 Detroit: Central; **Dec 31, 2014 Retired**. 2023
Hyde Park, Detroit 48207 (313-268-0068)

*Rowe, Gregory E. (Karen Kay)   revgrowe@gmail.com
[(RE) SP 1984; P 1986; F 1988]. 1984 Spartanburg (N. IN Conf.); 1986 L'Anse, Sidnaw, Zeba; 1990 Macon; 1993 Caring Covenant Group Ministry: Otisville, West Forest; Feb 1, 1995 Redford: Rice Memorial; 2000 Redford: Rice Memorial, Lola Valley; Jan 26, 2005 Redford: New Beginnings; 2006 Bad Axe: First; 2008 Wayne-Westland: First; 2011 Atherton, Phoenix; **2016 Retired**. Home: 9704 Baywood Dr., Plymouth 48170 (734-656-8226)

*RUBINGH, LARRY W (RE) (Linda) – (D-1981, FE-1987, R-2012)
Camden/Montgomery/Stokes Chapel 1983; Stevensville (Assoc) 1987; Holton 1988; Battle Creek: Convis Union 01/01/1992; Jackson Calvary 1997; Grass Lake 1999; Stockbridge/Munith 2007; Munith (LTFT ¼) 10/15/2010; Medical Leave 09/06/2011; Retired 2012; Allen 2017
        (H) 2480 N Portage Rd, Jackson 49201 (517) 812-6636 lsrlwr@aol.com
Allen: PO Box 103; 167 W Chicago Rd, Allen 49227-0103 (517) 200-8416

*Rule, James Lloyd (JoAn)   Freelandumc@sbcglobal.net
[(RE) P 19 ; F 1984]. 1982 Decker, Shabbona, Argyle; 1986 God's Country Co-operative Parish: Newberry; Jun 1, 1996 Freeland; **2012 Retired**. Home: 10955 Carter Rd., Freeland 48623

*Rupe, Meredith   meredithrupe@ballstate.bsu.edu
[(RE) P 1964 W MI; F 1966 W. MI]. 1964 school; 1966 Elkhart-Hillcrest (N. IN); 1968 Keeler, Sliver Creek (N. IN); 1969 transf. from N. IN to W. MI; Nov 1, 1970 Three Oaks; Nov 15, 1975 Chaplain, Marquette Prison/House of Corrections; 1979 Wesley Foundation, Ferris State University; 1998 Iron Mountain: Trinity (2003 transf. to Detroit Conf.); 2006 Retired. **Grant Center** (LTFT ¼) 2018. GC: 15260 21 Mile Rd, Big Rapids 49307 (231) 796-8006. Home: 620 Birch Circle Dr E, Boyne Falls 49713 (231-549-3142)

*Rupert, James Russell
[(RE) P 1972; F 1975]. 1974 Ferndale: First (assoc.); Dec. 1975 Clinton; 1977 Leave of Absence; 1981 Hillman, Spratt; 1984 Pontiac: Aldersgate, Elmwood; Jan. 1985 Pontiac: Aldersgate, Rochester Hills: First; 1987 Rochester Hills: First; 1990 Dryden, Attica; Oct 1, 1995 Birmingham: Embury; 1997 Burton: Emmanuel; 2000 Burton: Emmanuel, Flint: Asbury; Jul 16, 2006 Hancock: First; **2009 Retired**. Home: 3445 Saginaw, National City 48748

Rush, Albert
[(PL) PL Oct 8, 2007]. Oct 8, 2007 Detroit: West Outer Drive; **2012 Eastside Covenant Cooperative Parish – Eastpointe: Immanuel**. 23715 Gratiot, Eastpointe 48021 (586-776-7750). Home: 22839 Linwood, Eastpointe 48021 (586-871-2025)

*Russell, David Alan   golfathr@verizon.net
[(RE) T 1967; F 1969]. 1966 Carleton; Jan. 1971 Ironwood; 1977 Oxford; 1985 St. Ignace; 1987 Garden City: First; 1990 Howell; **1997 Retired**. Home: 730 Pasadena Ave., Owosso 48867 (989-723-8266)

*RUSSELL, DONALD A (RE) – (D-1958, FE-1962, HL-1977, FE-1980, R-1996)
Transferred from Kentucky Conf 1960; Byron Center 1960; Byron Center/Market Street 1964; Lawton/Porter 1966; Watervliet 1971; Sabbatical Leave 1975; Appointed in Other Annual Conferences (¶331.8, ¶346.1) Wellspring Mission Group, Church of the Savior, Washington DC 1976; Honorable Location 1977; Readmitted, Appointed in Other Annual Conferences (¶331.8, ¶346.1) The Church of the Savior, Washington, DC 1980; Retired 1996
        (H) 4651 County Rd 612 NE, Kalkaska 49646-9518 (231) 258-6728

*Sailor-Petit, Deanna M.   thesailorgroup@comcast.net
[(RL) PL Jan 1, 1999]. Jan 1, 1999 Detroit: West Outer Drive (assoc); 2000 Inkster: Christ (LTFT ½); 2005 Inkster: Christ (LTFT ¼); **Oct 11, 2006 Retired**. Home: 2927 Lyndhurst Place, Chester, VA 23831

Sampson, III, Frederick G.   pastorfgsampson@gmail.com
[(OF), National Baptist Convention]. 2013 Bloomfield Hills: St. Paul; **2016 Bloomfield Hills: St. Paul, Hazel Park**. (BH) 165 E. Square Lake Rd., Bloomfield Hills 48302 (248-338-8233), (HP) 315 E. Nine Mile Rd., Hazel Park 48030 (248-546-5955). Home: 208 Barrington Rd., Bloomfield Hills 48302 (248-338-9528)

*SANDERS, WILLIAM P (RE) (Manila) – (D-1980, FE-1985, R-2003)
Transferred from Detroit Conference Bellevue/Kalamo 1988; Buchanan: First 02/02/1996; Retired 2003; Appointed in Other Annual Conferences (¶331.8, ¶346.1) Detroit Conference, Wisner 2010; Appointed in Other Annual Conferences (¶331.8, ¶346.1) Detroit Conference, Standish/Saganing Indian 2012-01/01/2013; Appointed in Other Annual Conferences (¶331.8, ¶346.1) Detroit Conference, Fairgrove/Watrousville 2013

                                        Chaplainbill4msp@aol.com
                (H) 6116 Slocum St, Unionville 48767-9773 (989) 674-2421
        Fairgrove: PO Box 10, 5116 Center St, Fairgrove 48733-9703 (989) 693-6564
        Watrousville: PO Box 56 (4446 W Caro Rd, Caro 48723), Fairgrove 48733
                                        (989) 673-3434

*Sanderson, Gary Lloyd (Caroline)   Garlcarl@aol.com
[(RE) T 1964; F 1968]. 1966 Goodrich; 1970 Durand, Duffield; 1979 Wyandotte: First; 1989 Flushing; 1995 Ann Arbor: West Side; **1999 Retired**. Home: 319 Sunburst, Flushing 48433 (810-659-4523)

SANDLIN, MARGARET K [MALLORY] (FL) – (SP-2017, FL-2018)
Mendon (¶318.3 LTFT) 2017; Battle Creek: Baseline/Bellevue 2018
                                        revmkm2017@gmail.com
                (H) 523 Sherwood Rd, Bellevue 49021 (989) 387-1494
        BC: Baseline: 9617 Baseline Rd, Battle Creek49017 (269) 763-3201
                Bellevue: 122 W Capital Ave, Bellevue 49021 (269) 793-9421

Sawicki, Michael T. (Patricia)   MichaelTSawicki@gmail.com
[(FE) PE 2001; FE 2004]. Asbury Theological Seminary; Jun 1, 2001 Pigeon: Salem; 2009 FaithWay; **2013 Midland: Aldersgate**. 2206 Airfield Lane, Midland 48642 (989-631-1151). Home: 415 Coolidge Dr., Midland 48642 (989-492-4465)

*Sayer, Cecilia Lee   jolee5053@gmail.com
[(RL) PL Nov. 2013, NL 2017, RL 2019]. Nov 19, 2013 New Lothrop; 2017 no appointment; **2019 Retired**. Home: 7404 Cross Creek Dr., Swartz Creek 48473-1707 (810-635-8117)

*Scavella, Sr., Donald Alexander (Freddie)
[(RE) T GA, 1963; F OH W., 1967]. 1965 Inner City Project Director, Cincinnati, OH; 1967 Shepherd; 1969 Trans. to Detroit Conf., Detroit: Scott Memorial; 1977 Detroit East District Superintendent; Oct. 1982 Associate Council Director: Church Extension, New Church Development, United Methodist Union of Greater Detroit; 1993 Executive Director, United Methodist Union of Greater Detroit; **Dec 31, 2005 Retired**. Home: 24040 Roanoke, Oak Park 48237 (313-861-0895)

Schippert, Ellen O. eos@global.us
[(PL) PL 2007; NL 2015; PL 2019]. 2007 Forester; May 18, 2015 no appointment; **Jan 1, 2019 Applegate, Buel, Croswell: First (LTFT ¾).** (A) 4792 Church, Box 1, Applegate 48401, (B) 2165 E. Peck Rd., Croswell 48422, (C) 13 North Howard St., Croswell 48422 (810-679-3595). Home: 7350 N. Lakeshore Rd., Palms 48465 (989-864-3791)

Schleicher, Andrew John (Lilamani) aschleicher93@gmail.com
[(FD) PD 2004; FD 2010]. 2004 Communications Specialist, UMPH; Aug 1, 2007 leave of absence; Jun 15, 2009 Director of CEF Services, Consulting Ministry of Religious Journalism and Communications; **Jan 1, 2015 Project Coordinator, United Methodist Communications**. 810 12th Ave., S, Nashville, TN 37202 (615-742-5145). Home: 594 Huntington Pkwy., Nashville, TN 37211 (615-837-3330)

*Schleicher, John Gordon (Margery) gschleicher1@wowway
[(RE) PL 1983; SP 1985; P 1987; F 1989]. 1983 Willow; 1985 South Lyon (part-time (assoc.); 1987 Carsonville, Applegate, Watertown: Zion; 1991 Fowlerville: First; August 15, 1992, Chaplain, Chelsea Retirement Home; 2000 Sterling, Alger; 2002 Sterling, Garfield, Alger; 2003 Middlebury (LTFT ½); 2005 Middlebury, Bennington; **2006 Retired**. Home: 1586 Hagadorn Road, Mason 48854 (517-833-4988)

*Schleicher, Margery Ann Taber (Gordon) mschleicher@wowway.com
[(RE) P 1981; F 1983]. 1980 (PL) Livonia: Newburg (assoc.); 1981 Romulus: Community, Willow; Sep. 1983 Romulus: Community; 1987 Sandusky; 1991 Livingston Circuit: Plainfield, Trinity; May 16, 1995 Denton: Faith; 2000 AuGres; 2003 St. Johns: First; **2007 Retired**. Home: 1586 Hagadorn Road, Mason 48854 (517-833-4988)

SCHLIMM, MATTHEW R (FE) (Melanie) – (PE-2002, FE-2005)
Clergy Appointed To Attend School, Duke University 2003; Other Valid Ministries (¶344.1d) Asst Professor, Univ Dubuque Theological Seminary 09/01/2008; Appointed to Extension Ministries (¶344.1b,c) Associate Professor, Old Testament, University of Dubuque Theological Seminary 2015
matthew.schlimm@duke.edu
(H) 2130 Fairway Drive, Dubuque, IA 52001 (563) 589-3101
Univ Dubuque Theological Sem: 2000 University Ave, Dubuque, IA 52001
(563) 589-3101

SCHMIDT, MARCUS V (PL) (Jody) – (CC-2015, PL-2016)
Grand Rapids: Cornerstone (Assoc) South Wyoming Campus (LTFT ½) 05/01/2016

marcuss@cornerstonemi.org
(H) 5482 Fieldstone Dr SW, Wyoming 49418 (616) 443-9257
Cornerstone South Wyoming: 2730 56th St SW, Wyoming 49418-8708
(616) 698-3170

Schneider, Jr., John Henry (Debra)   johnhenryschneider@yahoo.com
[(FE) P 1993; F 1995]. 1993 Morrice, Bennington, Pittsburg; 1997 Wisner; Sep 1, 1999 Monroe: First; 2005 Lincoln Park: Dix, Taylor: West Mound; **2013 Hardy**. 6510 E. Highland Rd., Howell 48843 (517-546-1122). Home: 6520 E. Highland Rd., Howell 48843 (517-579-2626)

*SCHNEIDER, TERRILL M (RA) (Linda) – (PL-2000, FL-2001, AM-2004, R-2018)
Scottdale 06/01/1995; Scottdale/Bridgman Faith 05/01/2000; Retired 10/01/2018
schneider4276@comcast.net
(H) 73239 Cinder Ct, South Haven 49090 (269 767-7218

Schoenhals, Robert David (Jill Warren)   rschoenhals@sbcglobal.net
[(FE) P 1973; F 1976]. 1970 Bethel UCC; 1972 Chaplain, Green's Chapel; 1975 Armada, Omo: Zion; 1983 Seven Churches United Group Ministry: Byron; 1990 Parish Director, Seven Churches United Group Ministry: Byron; 1995 Wesley Foundation, University of Michigan; 2002 Indianapolis: Central Avenue; 2004 Grayling: Michelson Memorial; Feb 1, 2006 leave of absence; 2007 Bloomfield Hills: St. Paul; 2010 West Bloomfield; 2012 Lincoln Park: First; **2013 Ferndale: First**. 22331 Woodward Ave., Ferndale 48220 (248-545-4467). Home: 657 W. Oakridge, Ferndale 48220 (248-542-5598)

*SCHOENHERR, LEONARD R (RE) (Janette) – (D-1973, FE-1975, R-2013)
Transferred from North Indiana Conf 1987; Watervliet 06/09/1987; Coloma/Watervliet 02/16/1996; Marshall 1999; Retired 06/30/2013; Galesburg (LTFT ½) 2013; Galesburg (LTFT ¼) 01/01/2014; Galesburg (LTFT 45%) 01/26/2015; Gull Lake (LTFT 45%) (Co-pastor) 2016

schoenherrlen@gmail.com
(H) 4500 Mountain Ash Lane, Kalamazoo 49004-3781 (269) 903-2182
Gull Lake: 8640 Gull Rd, Richland 49083-9647 (269) 629-5137

*Schomaker, W. Thomas (Patricia)   asktherev@mac.com
[(RE) T 1967; F 1969]. 1967 Columbus (OH): Gates, Fourth UMC; 1969 Linden; Jan. 1976 Wesley Foundation, University of Michigan; 1981 Detroit: Jefferson Avenue; 1990 Troy: Fellowship; 1998 St. Clair: First; **Aug 1, 2004 Retired**. Home: 5656 Firethorne Drive, Bay City 48706 (989-450-5291)

*Schoonover, William Dale (Norma)   Schoonover49892@aol.com
[(RE) T 1966; F 1968]. 1959 Brent Creek, West Vienna; 1962 Elba; 1965 school; 1965 Culloden, Yatesville, Rogers (N. GA Conf.); Mar 1, 1968 Norway, Faithorn; 1974 Negaunee, Palmer; 1982 Flint: Asbury; Feb. 16, 1990 Ontonagon, Greenland, Rockland: St. Paul's; **1992 Retired**. <1994-95 Menominee: First, part-time>. Home: (May-Sep) N 15957 Henderson Lane, Vulcan 49892 (906-250-2138); (Oct-Apr) 5591 Goldenrod St, Kalamazoo 49009

*SCHROCK, JEFFREY J. (RL) (Kathi) – (FL-2000, RL-2016)
Marion / Cadillac: South Community 06/04/2000; Sunfield / Sebewa Center 2004; Moorestown-Stittsville / Merritt-Butterfield 2012; Retired 2016
pastorjs@centurytel.net
(H) 7500 E Boon Rd, Cadillac 49601

Schroeder, Clifford James, III (Rachel) cliff.schroeder@gmail.com
[(FE) FL 1999, PE 2004; FE 2009]. Feb 1, 1999 Dryden, Attica; Jan 1, 2001 Attica; 2007 Birch Run; 2010 Birch Run, Burt; **2012 Holly: Calvary**. 15010 N. Holly Rd., Holly 48442 (248-634-9711). Home: 3464 Quick Rd., Holly 48442 (248-245-9125)

Schumann, William revbillnancy@comcast.net
[(PL) PL 2000]. 2000 Melvindale: New Hope; 2007 Allen Park: Trinity, Melvindale: New Hope; **2011 Retired**. Home: 1386 Dulong, Madison Heights 48971 (313-551-4003)

Schwandt, James P. (Yvonne) jpschwandt@yahoo.com
[(FE) P 1975; F 1978]. 1977 Deckerville, Minden City; 1980 Genesee, Thetford Center; 1987 Rochester: St. Paul's (assoc.); 1988 Pigeon: First; Sep 1, 1994 Tecumseh; 1999 Harper Woods: Redeemer; **Feb 15, 2008 incapacity leave**. Home: 2566 Sunny Creek, SE, Kentwood 49508 (616-554-9181)

*Schweizer, Allen F. mom3@mycidco.com
[(RL) FL 1989]. 1989 Ogden; 1992 Whittemore, Prescott; Jun 1, 1996 Pontiac Cooperative Parish: Four Towns; 1998 Ironwood: Wesley, Wakefield; Oct 1, 1999 Deerfield, Wellsville; **Nov 1, 2000 Retired**. Home: 9440 Forestview Circle, Grand Blanc 48439 (810-655-2454)

SCOTT, JOHN A (FE) (Rebecca) – (FL-2000, PE-2001, FE-2004)
Girard/Ellis Corners 2000; Girard/Ellis Corners/Quincy (Co-Pastor) 09/01/2003; Traverse Windward Community New Church Start 2007; Lakeview: New Life 2011; Manistee 2015

jtentmaker@mac.com
(H) 819 Elm St, Manistee 49660-2035 (231) 723-3304
Manistee: 387 1st St, Manistee 49660-1749 (231) 723-6219

*Scott, Sharon G. sharongscott1939@gmail.com
[(RE) P 1989; F 1991]. Jan. 1, 1989 Detroit: Zion; 1992 Warren: First (assoc.); 1995 Detroit: St. Timothy (assoc); 1998 Waterford: Four Towns; **Sep 1, 2001 Retired**. Home: 33133 Orchard St., Farmington 48336 (248-476-1411)

*Scroggins, Nicholas William (Lorna) pscroggins@charter.net
[(RA) SP 1987; FL 1990; AM 1996]. 1988 Painesdale: Albert Paine; 1990 Republic, Woodland; 1993 Henderson, Chapin; 1998 Britton: Grace; 2002 Hemlock, Nelson; 2009 Marquette: Grace, Skanda; **2010 Retired**. Home: 12306 Conde Dr., Brooksville, FL 35213

*SEAVER, HOWARD D (RA) (Judy) – (FL-2000, AM-2001, RA-2012)
Fife Lake/Boardmans Parish (DSA) 1994; Fife Lake/Boardmans Parish 11/16/1994; Retired 2012

seaver@torchlake.com
(H) 3932 Deater Dr NW, Rapid City 49676-9558 (231) 331-6867

*Secrist, Robert B. (Mary Evelyn)
[(RE) T 1952; F 1955]. 1955 Dearborn: First (assoc.); 1956 Southfield; 1962 Standish; 1966 Dearborn: Warren Valley; 1967 Pontiac: St. James; 1971 Pontiac: St. James, Covert; 1973 Hudson; 1980 Burton: Emmanuel; 1985 Blissfield: Emmanuel; 1987 Fowlerville: First; **1991 Retired**. Home: 12612 St Paul Rd, Chambersburg PA 17202 (931-787-7513)

Seitz, William R. (Kristen Coates)   Seitzdavisburg@aol.com
[(FE) FL 1991; P 1992; F 1996]. 1991 Owosso: Burton, Carland; Jun 1, 1996 Iron Mountain: First; Feb 1, 2004 Davisburg; **2011 Sault Ste. Marie, Algonquin**. (S) 111 E. Spruce St., Sault Ste. Marie 49783 (906-632-8672), (A) 1604 W. Fourth Ave., Sault Ste. Marie 49783 (906-632-7657). Home: 1513 Augusta, Sault Ste. Marie 49783 (906-632-2753)

*SELLECK, DAVID A (RE) (Anne) – (D-1972, FE-1975, R-2015)
St Joseph First (Assoc) 1974; Constantine 04/01/1976; Stockbridge 09/16/1979; Hillsdale: First 1987; Leave of Absence 12/01/1988; Honorable Location 1993; Readmitted 2002; Muskegon Lakeside 2002; Martin/Shelbyville 2009; Manistee 2012; Retired 2015

dselleck2000@gmail.com
(H) 13687 Pinewood Dr, Grand Haven 49417-9467 (231) 299-5374

*SELLECK, GERALD L (RE) (Claudia) – (D-1977, FE-1981, R-2018)
Somerset Center/Moscow Plains 1979; Kalamazoo: First (Assoc) 1982; Courtland - Oakfield 12/01/1984; Hartford 1990; Manistee 1998; Leave of Absence 2002; Holton 2006; Retired 2018

jerryselleck@comcast.net
(H) 1121 Kelsey St NE, Grand Rapids 49505 (231) 225-2856

*SELLECK, RICHARD A (RE) (Eloise) – (D-1961, FE-2063, R-1996)
Ogdensburg (Old Mission Peninsula) 1955; Oakdale 1963; Rockford 1966; Muskegon Heights 1970; Appointed to Extension Ministries (¶344.1b,c) District Superintendent, Kalamazoo District 1977; Appointed to Extension Ministries (¶344.1b,c) West MI Conference Council Director 1983; Lansing: Christ 03/01/1987; Sand Lake/South Ensley 1992; Retired 1996

Rselleck0426@yahoo.com
(H) 1551 Franklin St SE, 1024 Terrace, Grand Rapids 49506 (616) 248-7982

*Seward, Edward Charles   tippicanoe90@hotmail.com
[(RL) FL 1985]. 1983 Glennie, Curran and Wilber; 1985 Snover: Trinity, Moore, Elmer; Jul 1, 1987 Berrien Springs (W. MI); Apr 1, 1990 Litchfield (W.MI). 1990 Harrisville, Lincoln; **Dec 31, 2004 Retired**. Home: 6503 N. Towerline Rd., Hale 48739 (989-728-2866)

*Seymour, Merton Wallace   mseym@hotmail.com
[(RE) T 1959; F 1961]. 1960 Norway; 1963 St. Ignace; 1968 St. Clair; 1975 Alpena; 1983 Davison; 1987 Detroit West District Superintendent; 1993 Plymouth: First; 1995 Royal Oak: First; **1999 Retired**. Home: (summer) 11077 Hillman Rd., Lakeview 48850 (989-352-6805); (winter) Country Park 508, 2331 Belleair Rd., Clearwater, FL 33764

*Seymour, Philip Merritt (Julie) thatcounselor@yahoo.com
[(RE) T 1968; F 1972]. 1970 Novi; 1975 Ypsilanti: First (assoc.); 1977 Saginaw: Sheridan Avenue, Warren Avenue; Jan. 1980 Saginaw: Sheridan Avenue, Burt; 1980 Dearborn: Good Shepherd; 1988 Birmingham: Embury; Sep 1, 1995 Escanaba: Central; 1997 Taylor: West Mound, Melvindale: New Hope; 2000 leave of absence; **2011 Retired**. Home: 14272 Greentrees, Riverview 48192 (734-479-2739)

Shabazz, Rahim O. (Cheryl) rcshabazz623@comcast.net
[(FE) PL 2005; PE 2012; FE 2016] 2005 Detroit: Henderson Memorial; 2006 River Rouge: John Wesley; **2012** Poseyville, Saginaw: West Michigan Avenue; 2015 Romulus: Community; 2017 Detroit: St. Timothy, Westland: St. James; **2018 Detroit: Peoples, Westland: St. James**. (DP) 19370 Greenfield Rd, Detroit 48235 (313-342-7868), (W) 30055 Annapolis, Westland 48186 (734-729-1737). Home: 3722 Heritage Parkway, Dearborn 48124 (313-570-6292)

SHAFER, TODD W (FL) (Noreen) – (DSA-2010, FL-2010)
Mancelona/Alba (DSA) 07/15/2010; Mancelona/Alba 11/01/2010; Indian River 2017

tshafer7@gmail.com
(H) 5954 Berry Ln, Indian River 49749-9487 (231) 587-8461
Indian River: PO Box 457, 956 Eagles Nest Rd, Indian River 49749-0457
(231) 238-7764

SHALER, JOSEPH D (FE) (Terri) – (PE-2001, FE-2003)
Otsego 2001

pastorjoe@otsegoumc.org
(H) 411 Walden Dr, Otsego 49078-9652 (269) 806-9087
Otsego: PO Box 553, 223 E Allegan St, Otsego 49078-0443 (269) 694-2939

*SHAPLEY, JANE B (RE) (Allen) – (D-1984, FE-1987, R-1996)
Kalamazoo: First (Assoc) 1985; Oakdale 1987; Retired 1996

ajshap@telus.net
(H) PO Box 345, Malahat, BC V0R 2L0, Canada (250) 743-1199

*Sharai, Maurice DeMont, Jr. (Susan) Msharai@tc3net.com
[(RE) P 1969; F 1972]. 1971 Redford (assoc.); 1977 Manchester; 1980 Flushing; 1989 Adrian: First; **2005 Retired**. Home: 3 Maumee Ct., Adrian 49221

*SHATZ, CONNIE E. (RL) (Eugene) – (PL-1999, RL-2012)
Belding (LTFT < ¼) 06/21/1999; Retired 2012

shatzconnie@yahoo.com
(H) 11448 Heintzelman NE, Rockford 49341-9534 (616) 754-8023

Shaw, Esrom
[(PL) PL Nov, 2013]. **Nov 9, 2013 Detroit: Mt. Hope**. 15400 E. Seven Mile, Detroit 48206 (313-371-8540). Home: 1685 W. Boston, Detroit 48206 (313-868-1352)

*SHEEN, BRIAN K (RA) (Bonnie) – (AM-2000, RA-2004)
St John Pilgrim 1970; Leave of Absence 11/17/1983; Lansing: Central Free Methodist (Assoc.) 1985; Withdrew to Unite with the Free Methodist Church 1987; Davidson Free Methodist 1990; Owosso Free Methodist 1993-1995; Received from Free Methodist 1998; Sunfield 1998; Retired 2004
bonniesheen@gmail.com
(H) 3170 Crudup Rd, Attalla, AL 35954-8543 (989) 224-6181

*Sheffield, Alice Jean   ajsheffield@gmail.com
[(RL) PL 1995; FL 1997]. 1995 Melvindale: New Hope; Dec 1, 1996 Owendale, Gagetown; 2001 North Lake; **2012 Retired**. Home:37505 Barkridge Circle, Westland 48185 (734-649-3749)

Sherrill, Scott Leonard (Deborah)   scott@mtu.edu
[(PE) PE 2016]. **2016 Vassar: First**. 139 N. Main, Box 71, Vassar 48768 (989-823-8811).

*Shin, Isaac Yong-Choel (Ellen)   isaacyshin@yahoo.com
[(RE) P, MN, 1986; F, MN, 1989]. 1987 Jordan: Immanuel; Apr. 1, 1992 Trans. to Detroit Conf., Ann Arbor: Korean; **2010 Retired**. Home: 33333 South River Bend Rd., Black Canyon City, AZ 85324 (734-649-7788)

Shin, Tae Gyu   stg1999@gmail.com
[(PE) FL 2016; PE 2019]. **2016 Troy: Korean (assoc)**. 42693 Dequindre, Troy 48085 (248-879-2240). Home: 1875 Windwood Dr., #102, Rochester Hills 48307 (909-472-7802)

*Shiplett, Gary Ronald (Carol)
[(RE) P, FL 1964; F, FL, 1966]. 1964 Fieldsboro (NJ); 1865 Coronado (FL); 1966 Roscoe (N. IL); 1969 Naperville: Wesley (assoc); 1970 school; 1973 Leland, Suydam (N. IL); 1874 Frankfort; 1980 Woodale Community; 1991 sabbatical; 1992 Munising LTFT (Det. Conf); 1994 Gladstone: Memorial; **2000 Retired**. 4156 12th Rd., Escanaba 49829

*Shipley, Anthony J. (Gwendolyn)   tony5193@msn.com
[(RE) T NY, 1962; F NY, 1964]. 1964 NY: Metropolitan--Duane; 1966 Brooklyn, NY: Union; 1968 Assistant Program Director, NY Conf.; 1971 Trans. to Detroit Conf., Conference Staff, Program Director; 1982 Detroit West District Superintendent; 1987 Detroit: Scott Memorial; Mar. 1, 1992 Deputy General Secretary, National Division, Gen. Bd. of Global Ministries; 1994 Eastside Covenant Cooperative Parish: Detroit: Christ; **2007 Retired**. Home: 23711 Clarkson, Southfield 48033 (313-861-9180)

*SHROUT, LARRY R (RE) (Sheila) – (D-1970, FE-1977, R-1998)
Transferred from Nebraska Conf 1980; Colon 1980; St Johns: Pilgrim 1983; Retired 1998
lrshrout@gmail.com
(H) 237 W Slope Way, Canton, GA 30115 (770) 704-0711

SHUMAKER, ANTHONY C (FL) (Linda) – (PL-2003, FL-2004, PL-2009, FL-2012)
Almena (DSA) 2002; Almena 12/01/2002; LP w/o Appointment 2003; Burnips/ Monterey Center 2004; Otsego: Trowbridge (PTLP ¾) 2008; Middleville/Snow 2012; Middleville 2017

tshu59@gmail.com
(H) 1497 120th Ave, Hopkins 49328-9626 (269) 650-5112
Middleville: PO Box 400, 111 Church St, Middleville 49333-0400
(269) 795-9266

*Sielaff, Robert (Darlene) drk@firstpresnville.org
[(RE) PL Apr. 1998; PM on recognition from Missouri Lutheran, 1999; FE 2001; RE 2018]. Apr 1, 1998 Dearborn Heights: Warren Valley. 1999 Dearborn Heights: Stephens, Warren Valley; 2012 Walled Lake; 2016 New Hudson; **2018 Retired; 2018 Dearborn: Good Shepherd** (LTFT ½). 1570 Mason, Dearborn 48124 (313-278-4350). Home: 42054 Baintree Circle, Northville 48168

SIMMONS, GARY L (FE) (BethAnn Perkins-Simmons) – (FL-2011, PE-2014, FE-2018)
Mulliken (PTLP ¼) / Barry County: Woodland (LTFT ¼) 2011; Barry-Eaton Co-operative Ministry: Nashville (PTLP ½) and Vermontville (PTLP ¼) Barry County: Woodland (PTLP ¼) 2013; Barry-Eaton Cooperative Ministry: Nashville (LTFT ½) and Vermontville (LTFT ¼) Barry County: Woodland (LTFT ¼) 2014; Ithaca/Beebe 2015

pastorgarysimmons@gmail.com
(H) 601 N Union St, Ithaca 48847-1311 (517) 388-2286
Ithaca: 327 E Center St, Ithaca 48847-1501 (989) 875-4313

Simon, Corey M. pastorcoreysimon@gmail.com
[(PE) FL 2016; PE 2018]. 2016 Ida, Samaria: Grace; **2019 Martin, Shelbyville**. (M) 969 E Allegan, PO Box 154, Martin 49070-0154 (269-672-7097), (S) 938 124th Ave, Shelbyville 49344-9745 (269-672-7097). Home: 948 Lee St, Martin 49070-5100 (231-622-2070)

*SIMON, MICHAEL J. (RL) (Beth) – (PL-2006, FL-2013, RL-2017)
Chase: Barton / Grant Center 2006; Harrison: The Gathering 2010; Lake Ann 2013; Retired 2017 (231) 349-1914

*Simpkins, Webley J. (Betty) wsimpkins@cfl.rr.com
[(RE) T NJ, 1957; F Baltimore, 1960]. 1952 Victoria, Colonial Manor; 1954 Aldine; 1956 Sharptown, Hainesneck; 1958 Eldbrooke; 1959 Woodside; 1961 Trans. to NW IN Conf., Grave; 1965 Transf to Detroit Conf., Birmingham: First (assoc.); 1966 Midland: First (assoc.); 1970 Pigeon: First; 1975 Marquette: First; 1980 Marysville; 1985 Trenton: First; **1994 Retired**. Home: 451 Hansar St., SW, Palm Bay, FL 32908

*Six, Jay Kendall (Linda) jsix@onemissionsociety.org
[(RE) P W. VA, 1976; F W. VA, 1979]. Oct. 1979 Trans. to Detroit Conf., Lake Linden, Painesdale; 1981 Controller, OMS International, Inc.; **2016 Retired**. Home: 890 Ironwood Trail, Greenwood, IN 46143 (317-882-5385)

SKUTAR, CYNTHIA A (FE) (Jerry Welborn) – (D-1987, FE-1990)
Hersey 1988; Kalamazoo: First (Assoc) 1992; Three Rivers: First 1997;
Muskegon: Lake Harbor 2000; Coldwater 2004; Mt Pleasant: First 2010; Grand
Ledge: First 2013

glfumc.cindyskutar@comcast.net
(H) 912 E Scott St, Grand Ledge 48837-2053 (517) 627-7347
Grand Ledge: First: 411 Harrison St, Grand Ledge 48837-1575 (517) 627-3256

*SLATE, EDWARD H (RE) (Patsy) – (D-1974, FE-1978, R-2012)
Whitehall/Claybanks 1976; Leave of Absence 04/17/1983; Comstock 1984;
South Haven: First 1989; Stanwood: Northland 1995; Evart 2006; Niles: Wesley
2008; Retired 2012; Buchanan: Faith (LTFT ½) 2012

faithoffice@sbcglobal.net
(H) 1358 Honeysuckle Ln, Niles 49120-4665 (269) 262-0011
Buchanan Faith: 728 N Detroit St, Buchanan 49107-1243 (269) 695-3261

*Slater, Harold Jon (Karen)   HSlatotrailwulf@aol.com
[(RE) T MI, 1963; F 1969]. 1963 Gilead Circuit; 1966 Ebeneezer Presb., OH;
1967 Oran UCC, OH; 1969 Port Huron: Gratiot Park; 1970 Denton: Faith; Jan.
1972 Lola Valley; Oct. 1973 Ecumenical Institute; Feb. 1975 Calumet, Laurium,
Mohawk-Ahmeek; 1978 Jeddo, Lakeport; 1980 Four Towns, Keego Harbor; Aug.
1, 1986 Four Towns (LTFT ¾), Oakland County Jail Ministry (LTFT ¼); 1989
Freeland; 1992 Hope, Edenville; 2002 St. Charles, Brant; Jan 1, 2008 Reese;
Mar 1, 2010 Retired. Home: 3927 Lincoln Woods Dr., Midland 48642

*SLATTERY, DENNIS E (RE) (Karen) – (D-1982, FE-1985, R-2012)
Ravenna 1983; Climax/Scotts 04/01/1987; Appointed to Extension Ministries
(¶344.1b,c) Chaplain, Army Fort Hood, TX 10/01/1988; Keeler/Silver Creek
1990; Marcellus/Wakelee 1992; Marcellus: Wakelee 1995; Ludington: St Paul
1998; LeValley/Berlin Center 2007; Retired 2012; Grass Lake (LTFT ¼) 2012-
2018

den98@juno.com
(H) 9150 Hamilton Circle, Washington 48094 (616) 755-3554

*Slaughter-Titus, Linda J. (Phylemon Titus)   19titus10@gmail.com
[(RE) PL 1987; SP 1988; P 1991; FE 1999]. 1987 Detroit: Thoburn; 1990 Detroit:
Christ, Jefferson Avenue (assoc.); 1991 Oak Park: Faith; 1995 Detroit: Cass
Community (assoc); 1997 Detroit: Henderson Memorial, Ferndale: St. Paul's;
2000 Detroit: Henderson Memorial; 2001 Detroit: Conant Avenue; Jan 1, 2003
incapacity leave; 2005 Highland Park: Berea-St. Paul's; Mar 1, 2007 voluntary
leave of absence; **2010 Retired**. Home: 1108 Suwannee Dr., Waycross, GA
31501

*SMALL, STEPHEN C (RE) (Karen) – (PE-2001, FE-2004, R-2004)
Glenn 11/16/1998; Center Park 2001; Brookfield Eaton 2004; Retired
10/01/2004; Riverside 2009-2014

karesmall@msn.com
(H) 9658 Allen Court, South Haven 49090 (269) 637-1692

Smalls, Benjamin Kevin   kevinsmalls@aol.com
[(OE) Baltimore/Washington Conf.]. **Jun 1, 2016 Southfield: Hope; 2018
Southfield: Hope, Detroit: St. Timothy**. (SH) 26275 Northwestern Hwy., South-
field 48076 (248-356-1020), (ST) 15888 Archdale, Detroit 48227 (313-837-4070).
Home: 5704 N. Pinnacle, West Bloomfield 48322 (301-512-4075)

*SMITH, BETTY A (RE) (Bill Biergans) – (D-1990, FE-1992, R-2004)
Ludington United (Assoc) 1990; Wacousta Community 1992; Coldwater 1998;
Retired 2004; Potter Park (DSA) 10/16/2004-2005; Grand Ledge: First (Interim)
01/01/2013-03/31/2013; Sunfield and Mulliken (LTFT 45%) 2015-2016
revbet@comcast.net
(H) 1822 Willow Creek Dr, Lansing 48917-7807 (517) 323-0278

*SMITH, CHARLES W (RE) (Arlene) – (D-1971, FE-1976, R-2011)
Transferred from North Indiana 1974; Centreville/Nottawa 1974; Centreville
1976; East Lansing Chapel Hill/Gunnisonville 1984; Shepardsville/Price 1988;
Courtland-Oakfield 1996; Ravenna 2008; Retired 2011
smith_chuckw@yahoo.com
(H) 341 Guy St, Cedar Springs 49319-9317 (616) 970-6269

Smith, Devin R. (Brittany)   smith.devinr@gmail.com
[(FE) PE 2014; FE 2019]. **2015 Blissfield: Emmanuel, Lambertville (assoc.).**
(B) 215 E. Jefferson St., Blissfield 49228 (517-486-3020), (L) 8165 Douglas Rd.,
Box 232, Lambertville 48144 (734-847-3944). Home: 302 E. Jefferson St., Bliss-
field 49228 (517-486-2752)

*Smith, James Allen
[(RE) T 1959; F 1962]. 1960 Rockville (assoc.) (Baltimore Conf.); Feb. 1962
Frankenmuth; 1966 Pinconning; 1969 Detroit: Jefferson Avenue; Oct. 1970 Commerce; 1976 Oscoda, Oscoda Indian Mission; Jan. 1983 Birmingham: Embury;
1988 Sanford; **1993 Retired**. Home: 5995 Weiss Rd., #4, Saginaw 48603 (989-
799-3323)

SMITH, JEAN M (AM) (Gary) – (FL-2002, PL-2003, FL-2006, PL-2009, AM-
2010)
Saugatuck (DSA) 2001; Saugatuck 12/01/2001; Saugatuck/Ganges 01/16/2005;
Ganges/Glenn 2005; Lake City 09/01/2010; Evart/Sears 2019
smithjean56@gmail.com
(H) 8543 7 Mile Rd, Evart 49631-8407 (231) 734-2003
Evart: 619 N Cherry St, PO Box 425, Evart 49631-0425 (231) 734-2130
Sears: 4897 Pratt St, Sears 49679-8777 (231) 734-2733

*Smith, Jerome K. (Mary)   jksmi046@yahoo.com
[(RE) P 1969; F 1972]. 1971 Livonia: St. Matthew's (assoc.); 1975 Livingston
Circuit: Plainfield, Trinity; Jan. 1981 Goodrich; Jan. 15, 1986 Detroit: Metropolitan
(assoc.); 1991 West Bloomfield; Sep 1, 1997 Garden City: First; 2006 Caro; **2011
Retired**. 586 Porta Rosa Circle, St. Augustine, FL 32092 (989-670-4524)

*SMITH, KATHLEEN (RL) (Dennis) – (FL-2002, R-2012)
Vermontville/Gresham 2002; Retired 12/31/2012; Lake Odessa: Lakewood
(Assoc) (LTFT ¼) 07/15/2014-2015; Lake Odessa: Lakewood (Assoc) (LTFT ¼)
and Barry County: Woodland (LTFT ¼) 2015
kdsmith868@gmail.com
(H) 7500 Bayne Rd, Woodland 48897-9632 (269) 367-4123
Lakewood: 10265 Brown Rd, Lake Odessa 48849-9207 (269) 367-4800
Woodland: 203 N Main St, Woodland 48897-9638 (269) 367-4061

*Smith, Russell Lawrence (Ruth)   smith.russell962@gmail.com
[(RE) T 1959; F 1963]. 1959 school; 1963 Dearborn: Mt. Olivet (assoc.); 1967 Highland, Clyde; 1974 Dearborn: Good Shepherd; 1980 Houghton Lake; 1986 Ann Arbor: First (assoc.); **1994 Retired**. Home: 801 W. Middle St., #362, Chelsea 48118 (734-433-1435)

SMITH, SCOTT B (FL) (Stacy) – (FL-2013)
Weidman 2013; Niles: Portage Prairie 2019

nilesmando23@live.com
(H) 3310 W Chicago R, Niles 49120-8717
Niles: Portage Prairie: 2450 Orange Rd, Niles 49120-8786 (269) 695-6708

*Smith, William Michael (Janet)   janetandwilliam@gmail.com
[(RE) T 1966; F 1969]. 1968 Detroit: Aldersgate (assoc.); Jan. 1974 Harbor Beach, Port Hope; Nov. 1978 Dundee; 1992 Clinton; **2005 Retired**. Home: 6231 Clinton-Macon Rd., Clinton 49236 (517-423-6480)

Smith, Willie Frank (Dianne Jefferson-Smith)   smittyo48@aol.com
[(FE) PL 2008; PE 2011; FE 2014]. 2008 Westland: St. James; **2015 Detroit: Conant Avenue**. 18600 Conant Ave., Detroit 48234 (313-891-7237). Home: 16876 Braile, Detroit 48219 (313-566-7226)

SMITH-JANG, BARBARA L (FE) (Soo Chan) – (D-1993, FE-1996)
Grand Ledge: First (Assoc) 1994; Family Leave 1997; UM Connectional Structures (¶344.1a,c) GBGM Missionary to Korea 2000; Other Valid Ministries (¶344.1d) Pastoral Counselor, Taejon Christian International School 2003

smithjang@hotmail.com
(H) Yeolmea Apt 802-901, Yusong-gu No-eun-dong 520-1, Taejon City South Korea, 305-325, Republic of Korea

Snedeker, Kathryn Sue (Haldon Ferris)
[(FE) P 1984; F 1987]. 1985 Flushing (assoc.); 1988 Dearborn: Good Shepherd; Jun 16, 1996 Saginaw: First (co-pastor); 2002 Saginaw: First; **2016 Traverse Bay**

queenrev1@aol.com
(H) 7364 Williams Court, Elk Rapids 49629 (989) 239-9267
Traverse Bay: 1200 Ramsdell St, Traverse City 49684-1451 (231) 946-5323

SNODGRASS, ROBERT L (PL) (Kathe) – (PL-2014, FL-2017)
Morris Chapel (DSA ¼ Time) 2014; Morris Chapel (PTLP ¼ Time) 11/10/14; Niles: Grace (LTFT 45%) 2016; Niles Wesley/Morris Chapel/Niles Grace 2017
rsnodgrass72@gmail.com
(H) 16270 Lewis Rd, Vandalia 49095-9555 (574) 261-5139
Niles Wesley: 302 Cedar St, Niles 49120-2612 (269) 683-7250
Morris Chapel: 11721 Pucker St, Niles 49120-8007 (269) 684-5194
Niles Grace: 501 Grant St, Niles 49120-2955 (269) 683-8770

*Snogren, Dorraine S. (Ruth)   drsnogren@coopresources.net
[(RE) T 1955; F 1958]. 1953 Seaford, Long Island (assoc.); 1956 Onaway; 1962 West Branch; 1968 Flint: Calvary; **1990 Retired**. Home: 24 Chapin St., Bethel, ME 04217 (207-595-8087)

SNOOK, EDWIN D (FL) (Ellen) – (FL-2003)
Big Rapids: Third Ave/Paris/Rodney (DSA) 2002; Big Rapids: Third Ave/Paris/Rodney 12/01/2002; Elsie 07/16/2005; White Cloud 2012

snookedwin@yahoo.com
(H) 718 E Pine Hill Ave, White Cloud 49349-9146 (231) 689-6774
White Cloud: PO Box 188, 1125 E Newell St, White Cloud 49349-0188
(231) 689-5911

*Snyder, David Paul pastordave48@yahoo.com
[(RE) P 1986; F 1991]. 1987 Ishpeming: Salisbury, Palmer, Director, Wesley Foundation, Northern Michigan University (LTFT ¼); 1988 Ishpeming, Salisbury, Palmer; 1990 Calumet, Mohawk-Ahmeek; 1993 L'Anse, Sidnaw, Zeba; Oct 1, 2003 leave of absence; Mar 1, 2004 Iron Mountain: First; Aug 1, 2006 Iron Mountain: First, Quinnesec; 2009 Gladwin; 2012 Sebewaing; **2014 Retired**.

*Snyder, Jean R. jeansnyder@ameritech.net
[(RE) P 1997; FE 1999]. 1997 Lexington, Bethel; 2000 Armada; **Sep 1, 2002 Retired; 2018 Birmingham: Embury** (LTFT ¼). 1803 E. 14 Mile Rd., Birmingham 48009 (248-644-5708). Home: 1582 Millecoquins Ct., Rochester 48307 (248-650-5888)

Snyder, Thomas L. (Lizbeth) tomsnyder@dexterumc.org
[(FD) PD 2014; FD 2017]. **2014 Dexter (deacon)**. 7643 Huron River Dr., Dexter 48130 (734-426-8480). Home: 8650 Huron River Dr., Dexter 48130 (734-476-8954)

Song, Jinny Lee (Solomon)
[(PD) PD 2016]. **2016 Troy: Korean**. 42693 Dequindre, Troy 48085 (248-879-2240)

*Sonquist, G. Charles (Jane Parchem) Sonquist@juno.com
[(RE) T 19 ; F 1968]. 1967 Royal Oak: First (assoc.); 1970 Southfield: United; 1980 Troy: Fellowship; 1990 Livonia: St. Matthew's **Sep 1, 2002 Retired**. Home: 1152 Timberview Trail, Bloomfield 48304 (248-844-7178)

SORDEN, KAREN J (FE) – (FL-2005, PE-2007, FE-2012)
Baldwin: Covenant Community/Luther 2005; Lake Odessa: Central 2012; Cedar Springs 2017; St. Charles Dec. 1, 2017

ksorden@sbcglobal.net
(H) 510 Christy Drive, St. Charles 48655 (989) 865-8144
St. Charles: PO Box 87, 301 W. Belle Ave., St. Charles 48655-0087
(989) 865-9091

*Sorensen, Harlan E. (Luann) luannsorensen@rocketmail.com
[(RE) FL 1999; PE 2001; FE 2004]. 1996 Gratis, Somerville, OH (W. OH). 1999 Seven Churches United Group Ministry: Gaines, Duffield; Nov 15, 2004 Blissfield: Emmanuel; Nov 15, 2005 school; Jun 1, 2006 leave of absence; **2006 Retired**. Home: 2109 Magnolia Parkway, Grovetown, GA 30813 (706-447-2441)

SPACHMAN, DONALD E (FE) (SHELLY) – (D-1982, FE-1984)
Grawn 1982; Shepherd/Pleasant Valley 1992; Shepherd 1997; Keswick 2004; Hastings: First 2010; Greenville: First, Turk Lake/Belding Cooperative Parish 2014

dspachman@yahoo.com
(H) 405 W Grant St, Greenville 48838-2209 (616) 712-6024
Greenville: First: 204 W Cass St, Greenville 48838-1758 (616) 754-8532

*SPACKMAN, JOSEPH L (RE) (Nona) – (D-1985, FE-1989, R-2013)
Mulliken (Ad Interim) 1982; Mulliken/Sebewa Center 1987; St Johns Parish: Salem/Greenbush/Lowe 1991; Allegan 1999; Paw Paw 2007; Retired 2013; Delta Mills (LTFT ¼) 2013

nspackman12@gmail.com
(H) 3806 Cornice Falls Dr Apt 6, Holt 48842-8809 (517) 694-8346
Delta Mills: 6809 Delta River Dr, Lansing 48906-9002 (517) 321-8100

*Spafford, Arthur L. (Lois Sommer)   SpffrdA2F@aol.com
[(RE) T Mich., 1947; F Mich., 1951]. 1949 Dayton, OH: Zion; 1951 Caro Circuit; 1954 Grand Rapids: Hope; 1956 Vicksburg; 1965 Sebewaing; 1968 Dearborn (Good Shepherd after 1969); 1974 Ferndale: First; 1983 Farmington: First; **1991 Retired**. [Mar 1, 1992-Aug 31, 1999, Northville: First (assoc.) LTFT]. Home: 47197 Manhattan Circle, Novi 48374 (248-773-8341)

*SPAHR, SANDRA L (RE) (Michael) – (PE-2000, FE-2003, R-2006)
Newaygo 2000; Retired 2006; Jackson Trinity/Parma (DSA) 2006; Webberville (DSA) 2007-12/31/2007; Appointed in Other Annual Conferences (¶385.6) Rocky Mountain Conference, Monte Vista/Bowen (LTFT ½) 2010; Appointed in Other Annual Conferences (¶331.8, ¶346.1) Rocky Mountain Conference, Avondale (LTFT ½) 2013

(H) 3229 Northridge Dr, Pueblo, CO 81008 (719) 568-5858

*SPALENKA, GORDON E (RE) (Nancy) – (D-1957, FE-1960, R-1993)
Griffith (Assoc), Griffith, IN 1957; Holton/Twin Lake 1959; Muskegon: Lake Harbor 1961; Boyne Falls/Boyne City 1964; Ovid United Church 1965; Leslie/ Felt Plains 1969; Bronson/Snow Prairie 10/15/1969; Arden 1972; Bear Lake/Arcadia/Pleasanton 1975; Mt Pleasant: Trinity/Chippewa 1980; Centerville 1984; Bellaire: Community 1987; Mulliken/Sebewa Center 1991; Retired 1993

gnspalenka@sbcglobal.net
(H) 2119 Waldron St SW, Wyoming 49519-2229 (616) 249-0513

Speiran, Laura Crawford (Ross)   lspeiran@clarkstonumc.org
[(FD) PD 2007; FD 2010]. 2007 Saline: First (deacon); **2014 Clarkston (deacon)** (LTFT ¾) 6600 Waldon Rd., Clarkston 48346 (248-625-1611). Home: 7801 Hoffman, Waterford 48327 (248-242-6159)

Spencer, George Raymond (Donna)   Umcgeorge@aol.com
[(FE) FL (recognition of orders, Church of the Nazarene), 1997; AM 1999, PE 2005; FE 2007]. 1987-1995 Warrenton Church of the Nazarene, Warrenton, OR; 1995-1996 Springwater Church of the Nazarene, Springwater, NY; 1996 trans to Detroit conf., Hope, Mount Vernon; 1999 North Central Macomb Regional Ministry: Mount Vernon, New Hope, Washington; Jan 1, 2002 New Hope, Mt. Vernon; Jun 1, 2002 New Hope; Jan 1, 2002 New Hope; 2010 Trenton: Faith; **2016 Houghton Lake**. 7059 W. Houghton Lake Dr., Houghton Lake 48629 (989-422-5622). Home: 316 Superior, Houghton Lake, 48629 (989-422-4365

*Spencer, Mary E.
[(RL) FL 1995]. 1995 Flint: Eastwood; **Jan 1, 2009 Retired**. Home: PO Box 70132, Las Vegas NV 89170

Sperling, Donald R. (Rosalie) lambsway@hotmail.com
[(FE) P Wyo., 19 ; F 19; HL 1996; PL Apr 1, 2008; AM 2009; FE 2009]. 1988 Transf. to Detroit Conf., Port Huron: Gratiot Park, Washington Avenue. 1996 Honorable Location; Apr 1, 2008 (LTFT ¼) (restored to full membership, May 14, 2009). **2010 Livonia: Clarenceville.**20300 Middlebelt, Livonia 48152 (248-474-3444). Home: 34184 Haldane, Livonia 48152 (248-615-1435)

SPERRY, DONNA J (FL) (George) – (DSA-2014, PL-2014, FL-2016)
Ionia: Easton (DSA) 2014; Ionia: Easton (PTLP ½) 11/1/2014; Ionia: Easton (PTLP ½) and Turk Lake/Belding 2016
pastordonnasperry@gmail.com
(H) 319 Pearl St, Ionia 48846-1339 (586) 255-6228
Ionia: Easton: 4970 Potters Rd, Ionia 48846-9541 (616) 527-6529
Turk Lake: 8900 Colby Rd, Greenville 48838-9502 (616) 745-3718
Belding: 301 Pleasant St, Belding 48809-1647 (616) 794-1244

Spina, Stephen 320phenix@gmail.com
[(OF) DSA 2017; OF 2018 Presbyterian USA] 2017-May 2, 2018 Corunna, New Lothrop: First (DSA); **May 3, 2018 Corunna, New Lothrop: First**. (C) 200 W McArthur St, Corunna 48817 (989-743-5050), (NL) 7495 Orchard St, PO Box 247, New Lothrop 48460 (810-638-5702). Home: 225 W Corunna Ave, Corunna 48817 (989-472-3850)

*SPRAGG, CAROLIN S (RE) – (D-1991, FE-1994, R-2013)
Parma/North Parma 1992; Paw Paw 1999; Fremont 2007; Retired 2013
carolinspragg1946@gmail.com
(H) 1063 Gale Rd, Eaton Rapids 48827-9107 (517) 604-0755

*Srock, Robert A. (Barb) rasbas2g@gmail.com
[(RL) PL 1994; FL 2002]. Nov 16, 1994 Ubly; 2000 Minden City, Forester; 2002 Jeddo, Buel; Dec 1. 2003 incapacity leave; **2012 Retired**. Home: 4706 Stone, Deckerville 48427 (810-376-8022)

*Stallworth, Lynnette
[(RE) P 1980; F W.MI, 1984]. 1982 Trans. to W. MI Conf., Muskegon Heights: Temple; 1984 Trans. to Detroit Conf., Detroit: Faith Bethany; 1988 Detroit: Trinity, Faith Bethany; 1989 Director, Wesley Foundation, Wayne State University **Jan 16, 2002 Retired**. Home: 125 Shell Falls Drive, Apollo Beach, FL 33572 (813-641-0565)

Stanley-Hook, Luanne M (PD) – (PD-2019)
Holland First: UMC Director of Community Involvement (Deacon) 2019
luanne@fumcholland.org
(H) 6618 Butternut Dr, West Olive 49460-7501 (616) 994-0085
Holland: First: 57 W 10th St, Holland 49423-3130 (616) 396-5205

*STARK, ROBERT W (RE) (Mary) – (D-1998, FE-2002, R-2008)
North Evart/Sylvan (DSA) 11/01/1990; Pine River Parish (DSA) 1991; Pine River Parish: Leroy/Ashton/Luther 08/01/1991; Pine River Parish: Leroy/Ashton/ Luther 05/01/1993; Girard/Ellis Corners 1996; Kalkaska 2000; Retired 2008; Grant (LTFT ¼) 07/01-11/01/2011
serenityridge61@yahoo.com
(H) 11649 E 14 1/2 Rd, Manton 49663-8598 (231) 824-3294
(S) 8108 Lake Dr, Palmetto, FL 34221 (231) 564-0677

Starkey, Nathaniel pastornatestarkey@gmail.com
[(FL) FL 2017]. **2017 Stony Creek**. 8635 Stony Creek Rd., Ypsilanti 48197 (734-482-0240). Home: 5493 Willis Rd., Ypsilanti 48197 (734-482-8113)

*STEARS, ETHEL Z (RE) (Robert Richards) – (D-1978, FE-1981, R-1999)
Springport/Lee Center 1979; Grand Rapids: Trinity (Assoc) 09/16/1983; Plainfield 1986; Appointed to Extension Ministries (¶344.1b,c) Director of Development, Clark Home 01/01/1988; Appointed to Extension Ministries (¶344.1b,c) Chaplain, M.J. Clark Memorial Home 1989; Sabbatical Leave 01/15/1994; Grand Rapids: Saint Paul 1994; Retired 1999

e.z.stears@gmail.com
(H) 46 Rivertop Dr, Lowell 49331-9127 (616) 897-0162

Steele, Brian besteele@gmail.com
[(PE) West Michigan Conf.]. **2018 New Baltimore: Grace**. 49655 Jefferson, New Baltimore 48047 (586-725-1054). Home: 33840 Hooker Rd., New Baltimore 48047 (586-648-6242)

STEEN, KATHRYN M (FE) – (D-1994, FE-1997)
Big Rapids Third Ave/Paris/Rodney 1994; Mancelona/Alba 2000; Clergy Appointed to Attend School CPE, Bronson Methodist Hospital, Kalamazoo 2007; Leave of Absence 09/01/2008; Other Valid Ministries (¶344.1d) Chaplain, Munson Medical Center 11/10/2008

steenkathy@yahoo.com
(H) 951 Hammond Place S, Traverse City 49686-8009 (231) 499-3652
(O) 1105 Sixth St, Traverse City 49684-2349 (231) 935-7163

*Steinberg, Bruce R. (Patti) ayooper@gmail.com
[(RL) FL 2011; RL 2018]. 2011 Ontonagon, Greenland, Rockland: St. Paul; **2018 Retired**. Home: 142 Indian Lake Dr, Crystal Falls 49855

STEP, GARY G (FE) (Lori) – (PE-2000, FE-2003)
Indian River 2000; UM Connectional Structures (¶344.1a,c) Director of New Church Development and Congregational Transformation, West Michigan Conference 2012; UM Connectional Structures (¶344.1a,c) Michigan Area Director of Congregational Excellence and New Church Development 01/01/2016; UM Connectional Structures (¶344.1a,c) Associate Director for Congregatonal Vibrancy 2018

gstep@michiganumc.org
(H) 6666 Crown Point Drive, Hudsonville 49426-9014 (231) 420-2676
(O) 207 Fulton St E, Ste 6, Grand Rapids 49503 (517) 347-4030 ext. 4093

Stephan, Brittney D bstephan@michiganumc.org
[(PE) Indiana Conference] **2018 Associate Director for Multi-Cultural Vibrancy**. 1161 E Clark Rd, Ste 212, DeWitt 48820 (517-357-4030 ext. 4073). Home: 40703 Long Horn Dr, Sterling Heights 48313

Stephen, Linda J (PE) – (PE-2018)
Williamston 2018

ljstephan@gmail.com
(H) 733 Orchard Dr, Williamston 48895 (616) 617-9419
Williamston: 211 S Putnam St, Williamston 48895 (517) 655-2430

*STERNAMAN, JOHN R. (RL) (Linda) – (FL-1997, RL-2002)
Riverside 12/01/1997; Retired 2002
(H) 5792 Clymer Rd, Coloma 49038-9394 (269) 468-6454

*Stevens, Gary Ian revgstevens@sbcglobal.net
[(ROF) Congregational]. 2000 Republic, Woodland; 2004 Ishpeming: Salisbury;
Jan 1, 2005 Munising (LTFT ½); **Jan 1, 2009 Retired**. Home: 801 Pine St., Marquette 49855 (906-225-1730)

*Stewardson, Jerry Leo (Ardith)
[(RE) P Cent. IL, 19 ; F Cent. IL, 19]. **19** Trans. to Detroit Conf., Professor of
Religion and Philosophy, Adrian College; **2003 Retired**. Home: 1328 University
Ave., Adrian 49221 (517-263-7554)

*Stewart, Carlyle Fielding, III (Jeane) cspirit@cs.com
[(RE) P (on recognition of orders) 1985; F 1987]. 1985 Trans. from Baptist
Church, Southfield: Hope; **2014 Retired**.

Stewart, David Kirk, Sr. (Ellen) PastorDave@pigeonsalemumc.com
[(FE) P 1985; F 1989]. 1986 Peck, Buel, Melvin; Jun. 1, 1990 Plymouth: First
(assoc.); 1991 Beaverton: First, Dale; Aug 1, 2000 Wayne-Westland: First; 2008
Hale: First; **2013 Pigeon: Salem**. 23 Mabel, Box 438, Pigeon 48755 (989-453-
2552). Home: 7065 Clabuesch St., PO Box 438, Pigeon 48755 (989-453-2317)

*STILWELL, JAMES W. (RL) (Pamela) – (PL-2005, FL-2006, RL-2017)
Olivet 3/1/2005; Arden / Benton Harbor Peace Temple 2006; Pleasant Valley
2009-2015; Three Rivers: Ninth Street 2009-2017; Three Rivers: First 2015-
2017; Retired 2017
(H) 4329 William Ave., Celina, OH 45822 (269) 365-7923

*STODDARD, LINDA D (RE) – (D-1970, FE-1973, R-2017)
Oshtemo/Northwest 1972; Bainbridge New Hope/Scottdale 10/15/1976; Battle
Creek: Convis Union 05/16/1983; Leave of Absence 01/01/1992; Other Valid
Ministries (¶335.1d) Staff Chaplain, Battle Creek Health System (LTFT ¼) 2000;
Battle Creek: Maple (LTFT ¼) 2008; Retired 01/01/2017; Battle Creek: Maple
LTFT ¼) 01/01/2017
mapleumc@yahoo.com
(H) 126 Heather Ridge, Battle Creek 49017 (269) 965-1671
Battle Creek: Maple: 342 Capital Ave NE, Battle Creek 49017 (269) 964-1252

STOLL, MATTHEW T (FE) (Amy) – (FL-2002, PE-2003, FE-2006)
Epsilon/Emmett County: New Hope 2003; Lowell: Vergennes 2010; Holton 2018
pastormattstoll@gmail.com
(H) 8670 Ward St, Holton 49425 (231) 821-0374
Holton: 9530 Holton Duck Lake Rd, Holton 49425 (231) 821-2323

*Stone, Arthur R. (Judith) artintroy@wowway.com
[(RE) PL Nov 1, 1996; PE 1999; FE 2002]. Nov 1, 1996 New Haven-Meade:
Faith; 1999 school (Methesco). Nov 1, 1998 Brown City; 2004 Sebewaing: Trinity
(Intentional Interim ¶329.3); **2006 Retired**. 2847 Quincy Dr., Troy 48085 (248-
835-1301)

*STONE, DIANE E. (RL) – (FL-1996, PL-2004, RL-2010)
Camden / Montgomery / Stokes Chapel 11/16/1996; Springport (LTFT PT) / Lee Center (LTFT PT) 2004; Retired 2010
(H) 234 S Clemens Ave, Lansing 48912-3006 (517) 775-0286

Stone, Eric Alan (Sherry Lee)   reveastone@sbcglobal.net
[(FE) P 1993; F 1996]. 1994 Farmington: Orchard (assoc); Feb 1, 1998 Wesley Foundation: University of Illinois; 1999 Waterford: Central (assoc); Dec 1, 2001 Chaplain/Director: Wesley Foundation, Central Michigan University; 2006 Chaplain/Director U of M Wesley Foundation; **2009 Essexville; St. Luke's**. 206 Scheurmann St., Essexville 48732 (989-893-8031). Home: 212 Hart St., Essexville 48732 (989-894-2453)

*Stout, David A. (Ruthanne)   dastout@hughes.net
[(RE) P 1969; F 1971]. 1962 UCC; 1964 school; 1969 Clawson (assoc.); 1971 Clinton; 1974 Bay City: Christ; Sep. 1978 Bad Axe; 1990 Midland: Aldersgate; Oct 1, 2003 incapacity leave; **2007 Retired**. Home: 5790 Raymond Dr., Gladwin 48624

Stover, Colin P. (Annette)   revstover@yahoo.com
[(FE) PE 2002 (on recognition of orders from United Church of Canada), FE 2005]. 1999 Imlay City, West Goodland-Lum; Jan 1, 2002 Imlay City; 2002 Lapeer: Trinity (assoc.); Jun 1, 2005 Sandusky: First; **2011 incapacity leave**. 922 Elizabeth Ct., Lapeer 48446 (810-660-8359)

*STOVER, ROBERT P (RE) (Kathleen) – (D-1975, FE-1977, R-2012)
Camden/Montgomery/Stokes Chapel 1976; Niles: Portage Prairie 1980; Portage Prairie 1982; Cedar Springs/East Nelson 1987; Ludington: St Paul 1989; Grand Rapids: South 1998; Napoleon 2004; Allegan 2007; Retired 2012; Calhoun County: Homer/Lyon Lake (LTFT ¾) 2012
rpstover48@gmail.com
(H) 105 E Adams St, Homer 49245-1101 (517) 568-1126
Calhoun Cnty: Homer: 101 E Adams St, Homer 49245-1101 (517) 568-4001
Lyon Lake: 8493 17 Mile Rd, Marshall 49068 (269) 789-0017

*Strall, Dana Ray (Sandy)   Dstrall@hotmail.com
[(RE) P 1977; F 1979]. 1977 Port Huron: First (assoc.); Oct. 1980 Lakeville, Leonard; 1985 Midland: First (assoc.); 1988 South Rockwood (LTFT ¾), Flat Rock: First (assoc.) (LTFT ¼); 1990 South Rockwood; Aug 1, 1997 Coleman: Faith; 1999 Erie; 2011 Flat Rock: First; **2017 Retired**. Home: 12638 Dixie Hwy, PO Box 1, South Rockwood 48179 (734-379-9680)

STRANGE, MACK C (OF) (Barbara) – (OF-2007, R-2018)
[Southern Baptist Church, Retired] Grand Rapids: South 2007
mack.strange@gmail.com
(H) 5103 Marlowe SE, Grand Rapids 49508 (616) 532-9226
Grand Rapids: South: 4500 Division Ave S, Grand Rapids 49548-4307
(616) 534-8931

*STREEVY, MICHAEL P (RE) – (D-1987, FE-1995, R-2010)
Elk Rapids/Kewadin 04/01/1987; Jonesville/Allen 1988; Battle Creek: Sonoma/Newton 1995; Galesburg 11/16/1999; Parma/North Parma 2003; North Parma (LTFT ¾) 11/01/2005; North Parma 2008; Litchfield/Quincy 2009; Retired 2010
Dad0kkaj@gmail.com
(H) PO Box 89, Sodus, NY 14551 (585) 943-4328

*Strobe, David Randall (Mary)   dstrobe@comcast.net
[(RE) P 1980; F 1984]. 1982 North Lake; May 1, 1984 Farmington: Nardin Park (assoc.); Apr. 15, 1989 Houghton: Grace; 1995 Milford; Dec 1, 1997 disability leave; 1998 Linden, Argentine; Feb 1, 2001 Hartland; Feb 1, 2006 incapacity leave; 2007 Corunna; **2013 Retired**; Oct 31, 2014 (LTFT ¼) Buron: Christ. 4428 Columbine Ave, Burton 48529-2160 (810-743-1770). Home: 5930 Augusta Ln, Grand Blanc 48439 (248-933-3602)

*Strobe, Donald Bovee   Dstrobe925@aol.com
[(RE) T W. MI, 1956; F W. MI, 1959]. 1972 Trans. to Detroit Conf., Ann Arbor: First; **1990 Retired**. Home: 19191 Harvard Ave., #401A, Irvine, CA 92612 (949-679-9900)

*Strong, David Tull (Marcia)   strongdt11@aol.com
[(RE) T 1959; F 1961]. 1960 Dearborn: First (assoc.); 1964 Richmond; 1969 Troy: Fellowship; 1980 Livonia: St. Matthews 1990 Detroit: Central; 1994 Belleville; **1998 Retired**. Home: 21870 River Ridge Trail, Farmington Hills 48335 (248-888-9848)

STULL-LIPPS, LINDA K (FE) (David Lipps) – (FL-2006, PE-2007, FE-2015)
Parma 01/15/2006; Center Park 2006; Potterville 2011; Riverdale: Lincoln Road (LTFT ¾) 2016

pastorlynelr@gmail.com
(H) 9437 W Lincoln Rd, Riverdale 48877
Riverdale: Lincoln Road: 9479 W Lincoln Rd, Riverdale 48877 (989) 463-5704

*Stybert, Stanley Patrick (Janet)   thegoodword1@att.net
[(RL) PL 1992]. Jan 1, 1993 Seven Churches United Group Ministry: Lennon; Jun 1, 1996 Flint: Bristol, Dimond; 2000 Fowlerville: First; 2007 Flint: Asbury, Burton: Emmanuel; **2010 Retired**; 2012 Owosso: Carland; Jul 1-Oct 31, 2018 Oregon, Elba (LTFT ½). Home: 647 Basswood, Flint 48506 (810-715-9331)

Sudduth, Steven T.
[(OF)]. 2016 Crystal Falls: Christ, Amasa: Grace; **Feb 6, 2018 no appointment**. Home: 504 Blossom St, Iron River 49935 (859-329-9371)

*SUMMERS, VERNE C (RE) (Dawn) – (D-1955, FE-1964, R-1992)
Beaverton/Dale 1956; Elk Rapids 1963; Elk Rapids Parish 1965; Jackson: Brookside 1966; Charlotte 09/01/1974; Okemos Community Church 1987; Mason: First 1989; Retired 1992

dvsumm@juno.com
(H) 13119 Farm Ln, DeWitt 48820 (517) 669-2815

Sutton, Tara Renee   angelicspirit8272@gmail.com
[(FE) P (on recognition of orders, AME) 1998; FE 2001]. 1991 Dolton, IL: Holy Trinity AME; 1998 Flint: Oak Park; Dec 1, 2002 Waterford: Central (interm assoc); 2001 Waterford: Central (assoc); 2005 Flint: Bethel; 2012 Crossroads District Superintendent; **2016 Halsey, South Mundy**. (H) 10006 Halsey Rd., Grand Blanc 48439 (810-694-9243), (SM) 10018 S. Linden Rd., Grand Blanc 48439. Home: PO Box 1181, Grand Blanc 48480

Swainston, Jeffrey (PL) – (CC-2017, DSA-2017, PL-2018)
Manton (DSA) (LTFT ½) 2017; Manton (PL) (LTFT ½) 12/01/2017; Manton (LTFT ¾) 2018

jeffswainston@gmail.com
(H) PO Box 77, 102 N. Michigan, Manton 49663-0902 (616) 813-8746
Manton: 102 N. Michigan Ave, PO Box B, Manton 49663 (231) 824-3593

Swanson, Reed P. (Juliana)   lxxmt@yahoo.com
[(FE) P 1995; F 1998]. 1995 Detroit: Metropolitan (assoc); Aug 1, 1998 Richmond: First; 2004 Tawas; 2008 Clarkston (assoc.); 2010 Stony Creek; 2017 Frankenmuth; Feb 7, 2018 Crystal Falls: Christ, Amasa: Grace (LTFT ½); **2018 Pinckney: Arise**. 11211 Dexter-Pinckney Rd., Pinckney 48169 (734-878-1928). Home: 11267 Dexter-Pinckney Rd., Pinckney 48169 (586-202-1894)

SWANSON, SHERRI L (FE) (Brad Bartelmay) – (D-1987, FE-1994)
Transferred from Iowa Conf 1991; Galien/Olive Branch 1991; Galien/Olive Branch (LTFT ¾) 1993; Berrien County: Lakeside (LTFT ¼) 1995; Three Oaks 09/01/1999; Grand Rapids: Faith 2017; Georgetown 2018

sherriswanson61@gmail.com
(H) 6105 Balcom Ln, Allendale 49401 (269) 405-0002
Georgetown: 2766 Baldwin St, Jenison 49428-8701 (616) 669-0730

SWEET, MARY A (PE) (Jeffrey) – (PE-2015)
Harbor Springs/Alanson 2011; Whitehall/Muskegon: Crestwood 2014; Litchfield/ Jonesville 2017; Jonesville/Napoleon 2019

pastormarysweet@aol.com
(H) 10014 Sunset Dr, Jackson 49201-9850 (231) 881-7367
Jonesville: 203 Concord Rd, Jonesville 49250-9824 (517) 849-9565
Napoleon: 210 Nottawasepee, PO Box 337, Napoleon 49261 (517) 536-8609

SYKES, LORI J (FE) (Gary) – (PE-2007, FE-2010)
St Johns: First 2007; Lansing: First 07/15/2012

revlori@lansingfirst.org
(H) 3727 Delta River Dr, Lansing 48906-3476 (517) 721-1676
Lansing: First: 3827 Delta River Dr, Lansing 48906-3477 (517) 321-5187

*SYNWOLT, ROYAL J (RE) (Constance) – (D-1952, FE-1954, R-1997)
Coloma/Riverside 10/01/1951; Portage 1955; Lansing: Mount Hope 1962; Muskegon: Central 1966; Appointed In Other Annual Conferences (¶331.8, ¶346.1) (Director) Staff ProgTransferred to Detroit Conf 1971; Transferred from Detroit Conf 1983; Kalamazoo: First 1983; Retired 1991

consyn@live.com
(H) 11214 Morning Side Dr, Boyne Falls 49713-9699 (231) 549-2547
(S) 870 NW Sarria Ct, Port St Lucie, FL 34986-1755 (772) 873-0949

*TABOR, KENNETH E. (RL) (Eldonna) – (PL-1999, FL-2006, RL-2010)
Free Soil / Fountain 11/1/1999; Walkerville / Crystal Valley 2000; Ludington 2004; Retired 2010; Crystal Valley / Walkerville 12/1/2015-12/1/2016

taborek@charter.net
(H) 1243 Blue Heron Dr., Ludington 49431-1070 (231) 845-6101

PASTORAL RECORDS

*Tarpley, Thomas E., Sr. (Gloria) tthiwayman@att.net
[(RE) PL 1997; PE 2001; FE 2004]. 1997 Detroit: Cass Community (assoc); 2003 Flint: Trinity; Jan 1, 2007 Flint: Trinity (LTFT ¾), Flint: Faith (LTFT ¼); 2007 Fowlerville; **2015 Retired**. Home: 209 Addison Cr., Fowlerville 48836 (313-407-4151)

Taveirne, Edmond G. (Beth) taveirne@att.net
[(FE) P 1970, N IL; F 1984 N IL]. 1982 Lansing (IL): First (assoc.); 1984 Park Hill: Grace; Elmhurst: First; 1996 Wheaton: Gary Memorial; 2007 transfer to Detroit Conference Fenton; Apr 30, 2011 voluntary leave of absence; 2013 Bethany Methodist Communities; 2014 voluntary leave of absence; 2017 personal leave; **Nov. 15, 2018 Retired**. Home: 102 Indian Trail Dr., Westmont, IL 60559 (312-888-6380)

Taylor, Thomas L. (Carmen) Janese28@aol.com
[(FE) P 1996; F 1998]. 1995 Oak Park: Faith; 1998 Saginaw: Calvary; 2000 Pontiac: First (LTFT ½), Pontiac: Baldwin Avenue (assoc) (LTFT ½). 2001 Pontiac: First; 2008 Madison Heights; Feb 15, 2011 incapacity leave; 2011 Harper Woods: Redeemer, Detroit: Henderson Memorial; **Jan 31, 2013 medical leave**.

Terhune, AmyLee Brun (T. Bradley) pastoramy@clergy.net
[(FE) PE 1999; FE 2002]. 1999 Port Huron: First (assoc); 2002 Caring Covenant Group Ministry: Columbiaville; Dec 1, 2006 Caring Covenant Group Ministry: Columbiaville, Parish Director; 2009 Hancock: First; **2016 Saginaw: First**. 4790 Gratiot, Saginaw 48638 (989-799-0131). Home: 4674 Village Drive, Saginaw 48638 (989-793-5880)

Terhune, T. Bradley (AmyLee) tbradley.terhune726@gmail.com
[(FE) PM 1998; FE 2003]. 1999 Algonac: Trinity; 2002 Caring Covenant Group Ministry: Richfield, Otter Lake; Sep 1, 2004 Caring Covenant Group Ministry: Richfield; 2007 voluntary leave of absence; 2014 Painesdale: A. Paine Memorial; 2016 Arbela; Oct 1, 2017 Saginaw: Kochville, Mapleton; **Sept 1, 2018 Medical Leave**. Home: 4674 Village Drive, Saginaw 48638 (906-231-1495)

*TESTOLIN, ROY G (RE) (Sandy) – (D-1974, FE-1976, R-2013)
Battle Creek: First, Staff Pastoral Counselor (¶337.1) 1990; Transferred from Wisconsin Conf 1999; Appointed to Extension Ministries (¶344.1b,c) Pastoral Counselor, Heritage Interfaith Counseling Center, Battle Creek 1999; Retired 11/01/2013; Appointed to Extension Ministries (¶344.1b,c) Pastoral Counselor, Heritage Interfaith Counseling Center, Battle Creek 11/01/2013
rt232@yahoo.com
(H) 12884 E Dr S, Marshall 49068-9267 (269) 781-9257

THOMAS, Crystal C
[(FL) PL Nov. 2013; FL 2014]. 2013 Flint: Dimond; 2014 Linden, Flint: Dimond; 2015 Linden; **2018 Battle Creek: Christ, Battle Creek: Washington Heights**
athisservice2008@gmail.com
(H) 15 N Woodlawn Ave, Battle Creek 49037 (269) 282-0697
Battle Creek: Christ: 65 Bedford Rd N, Battle Creek 49037-1837 (269) 965-3251
Battle Creek: Washington Hts: 153 Wood St N, Battle Creek 49037-2271
(269) 968-8773

THOMAS, DEBORAH S
[(FE) PE 2000; FE 2003]. Jun 1, 2000 Plymouth: First (assoc); 2004 Royal Oak: St. John's; 2006 Iron Mountain: Trinity; 2011 Bay City: First **2013 Alma**
pastordebthomas@gmail.com
(H) 627 Woodworth Ave, Alma 48801-1746 (989) 463-1485
Alma: 501 Gratiot Ave, Alma 48801-1708 (989) 463-4305

*Thomas, James F. (Joyce)   clergyjft@gmail.com
[(RE) P N. IN, 1952; F N.IN, 1958]. 1954 Decatur, IN: Calvary; 1955 Kewanna Circuit, IN; 1958 Wanatah, IN: Zion; 1960 Porter, IN: First; 1964 Parma, OH (Minister of Education), (E OH Conf); 1968 Boardman: First (Minister of Education); 1972 Trans. to Detroit Conf., Farmington Hills: Nardin Park & Orchard (Minister of Education; 1980 Farmington Hills: Orchard (assoc.); 1982 Grand Blanc; Jan. 1, 1990 Saginaw: First; Sep 1, 1994 Swartz Creek; **2000 Retired**. Home: 2000 32nd St., SE, Apt 202, Grand Rapids 49508

*Thomas, Wayne N. (Janet)   orggardner@aol.com
[(RE) P 1973; F 1976]. 1975 Jasper, Weston; 1976 Monroe: St. Paul's (assoc); 1978 Sutton-Sunshine, Bethel; 1982 Rochester: St. Luke's; 1984 leave of absence; 1988 Durham, NC: Trinity (assoc) (NC Conf., para. 426.1); 1989 transf to Holson Conf., Seymour, TN: Seymour (assoc); 1992 Axley's Chapel, Williamson Chapel; 1995 Axley's Chapel, Binfield; 1996 leave of absence; 1997 trans from N. IN Conf. Royal Oak: First (assoc); 2002 Seven Churches United Group Ministry: Durand: First; **2010 Retired**. Home: 1408 Bonita Drive, Knoxville, TN 37918 (248-842-5366)

*Thompson, James M. (Judith)   thompsonfive@hotmail.com
[(RE) P 1970; F 1975]. 1972 Richmondale Charge (W. OH Conf.); 1974 Oregon, Elba; 1976 Davison Area Group Ministry (parish director): Oregon, Elba; 1980 Hardy; Jan 3, 1984 Pinconning; Jan 16, 1990 Midland: Homer; 1996 Eastern Thumb Cooperative Parish: Port Sanilac, Deckerville (parish director); 1999 Marysville; **2006 Retired**. Home: 5975 Mill Point Court, Kentwood 49512 (616-656-3492)

*THOMPSON, JEFFREY TODD (RE) (Jodi) – (D-1989, FE-1992, R-2010)
Alto/Bowne Center 1990; Muskegon Wolf Lake/Unity 1995; Muskegon Wolf Lake 1998; Charlevoix 2000; Retired 2010
(H) 4354 M 66 N, Charlevoix 49720-9516 (231) 675-2135

*THOMPSON, JOHN ROSS (RE) (Ellen Brubaker) – (D-1966, FE-1968, R-2010)
Transferred from Western Pennsylvania Conf 1995; Grandville 1995; UM Connectional Structures (¶344.1a,c) West MI Conference Director 1998; East Lansing: University 2006; Retired 12/31/2010; Grand Rapids: Trinity (Assoc) (LTFT 1/8) 2015-09/01/2016; Grand Rapids Genesis (Part Time) 01/01/2017-2018
johnellen5@comcast.net
(H) 4114 Sawkaw NE, Grand Rapids 49525 (517) 812-9679

THOMPSON, MARK E (FE) – (D-1988, Fe-1990)
Riverside/Scottdale 01/01/1987; Niles: Grace 11/16/1992; Bellevue/Kalamo 1996; Keeler/Silver Creek 2004; Grand Rapids: Faith 2009; Lansing Central 2017

mark757984@gmail.com
(H) 2828 Woodview Dr, Lansing 48911-1727 (269) 591-0731
Lansing Central: 215 N Capitol Ave, Lansing 48993-1372 (517) 485-9477

*THOMPSON, R JOHN (RE) (Sheryl) – (D-1998, FE-2003, R-2010)
Hudsonville 1997; Hudsonville/Holland: First (Assoc) 1998; Litchfield 04/01/2001; Kent City: Chapel Hill 2005; Retired 2010; Muskegon: Unity (LTFT ¼) 11/01/2011-2014

rjohnthompson@gmail.com
(H) 2418 Valleywood Ct, Muskegon 49441-3293 (231) 563-6417

*THOMPSON, RONALD J (RE) (Hope) – (D-1961, FE-1963, R-1995)
Transferred from Detroit Conf 1975; DeWitt: Redeemer 10/15/1975; Marshall 04/05/1983; Mt Pleasant: First 1989; Retired 1995
(H) 707-A McLaughlin St, Eaton Rapids 48827-2306 (989) 506-3225

Thon, Dorothy Jean (Duane) djthon@hotmail.com
[(FE) PE 2002; FE 2005]. 2002 Pinconning; 2007 Mayville; 2011Bethel (BASS), Akron, Sutton-Sunshine. **2017 Retired**. Home: 1514 Kent Dr, Davison 98924-8837 (989-245-8837)

*Thon, Duane G. (Dorothy) dgthon@mailstation.com
[(RE) LP 1997; PM 1998; FE 2000]. 1997 Saginaw: West Michigan Avenue, Sheridan Avenue; Sep 15, 2005 Saginaw: West Michigan Avenue; **2007 Retired**. Home: 1514 Kent Dr, Davison 98924-8837 (989-245-8837)

THURSTON-COX, HILLARY (PE) (Vaughn) – (OE-2014; PE-2019)
[Free Methodist, Elder] Epsilon/New Hope/Harbor Springs/Alanson (Assoc) 2014; Epsilon/Harbor Springs/Alanson (Assoc) (LTFT ¾) 01/01/2015; Wacousta Community 2016

hillary.thurstoncox@gmail.com
(H) 9590 Looking Glass Brook Dr, Grand Ledge 48837-9268 (231) 250-8142
Wacousta Community: 9180 W Herbison Rd, Eagle 48822-9785 (517) 626-6623

THURSTON-COX, VAUGHN W (OE) (Hillary) – (OE-2008)
[Free Methodist, Elder] UM Connectional Structures (¶344.1a,c) Director, Ferris State University Wesley Foundation 2008; Epsilon/New Hope of Emmett County 2010; Epsilon/New Hope/Harbor Springs/Alanson 2014; Epsilon/Harbor Springs/ Alanson (LTFT ¾) 2015; Mulliken/Sunfield 2016; Mulliken 2017

dr.thurstoncox@gmail.com
(H) 9590 Looking Glass Brook Dr, Grand Ledge 48837-9268 (231) 250-3924
Mulliken: 400 Charlotte St, Mulliken 48861-9772 (517) 649-8382

Timm, Paula M. revtimm2011@att.net
[(FE) P 1990; F 1993]. 1990 Hillman, Spratt; 1992 Flint: Court Street (assoc.); Apr 16, 1994 Redford: Lola Valley; Jan 1, 1997 leave of absence; 1997 Grand Blanc: Phoenix; 2001 Royal Oak: St. John's; 2004 Harbor Beach, Port Hope; **2011 Oak Grove**. 6686 Oak Grove Rd., Oak Grove 48855 (517-546-3942). Home: 6893 Sanford Rd., Howell 48855 (989-712-0113)

Timmons, Faith Elizabeth Green (Gregory) fegisme@aol.com
[(FE) PL 2000; PE 2000; FE 2005]. 2000 Southfield: Hope; Sep 1, 2002 school (Yale); Aug 1, 2004 Detroit: Metropolitan (assoc); 2008 Holly: Calvary; 2012 Flint: Bethel; **Apr 1, 2018 medical leave (¶356)**. Home: 2327 Limestone Ln, Flushing 48433

Timmons, Gregory E (Faith Elizabeth Green Timmons)   timmons2c@gmail.com
[(PL) PL Jan 1, 2019]. 2018 Flint: Calvary (DSA) (LTFT ½); **Jan 1, 2019 Flint: Calvary (LTFT ½)**. 2111 Flushing Rd, Flint 48504-4787 (810-238-7685). Home: 2327 Limestone Ln, Flushing 48433 (810-922-2257)

Tipken, Douglas A (FL) (Dana) – (DSA-2018, CLM-2018, FL-2019)
Fennville/ Fennville: Pearl (DSA) 06/01/2018; Fennville/Fennville: Pearl 01/01/2019

dougtipken@live.com
(H) 687 W Fennville St, Fennville 49408 (269) 873-0014
Fennville: 5849 124th Ave, Fennville MI 49408-9428 (269) 561-5048
Fennville: Pearl: 1689 56th St, PO Box 407, Fennville 49408 (269) 561-5048

Titus, Beth D. (Dale)   bdtitus@sbcglobal.net
[(FE) PL 2002, PE 2004; FE 2008]. Sep 1, 2002 Denton: Faith (LTFT ½); 2008 Ann Arbor: Calvary; 2013 Voluntary leave; **Feb 1, 2015 Farmington Hills: Nardin Park (assoc)**. 29887 W. 11 Mile, Farmington Hills 48336 (248-474-6573). Home: 6771 Kestrel Ridge, Brighton 48116 (810-231-6436)

Titus, Christopher G.L. (Tina)
[(FL) PL 2010; FL 2019]. Nov. 2010 Cole, 2011 Cole, Melvin; **2019 Armada, West Berlin**. (A) 23200 E Main St, PO Box 533, Armada 48005–0533 (586-784-5201), (W) 905 Holmes Rd, PO Box 91, Allenton 48002-0091 (810-395-2409). Home: 23234 E Main, Armada 48005 (586-784-9484)

*Titus, Phylemon D. (Linda Slaughter-Titus)   19titus19@gmail.com
[(RE) T GA., 19 ; F GA., 19]. 1969 Trans. to Detroit Conf., Detroit: Fourteenth Avenue; 1971 Detroit: Henderson Memorial; 1974 Conference Staff, Urban Missioner; 1984 Detroit: Conant Avenue; 1988 Detroit East District Superintendent; 1995 Detroit: St. Timothy 2002 Detroit: St. Timothy, West Outer Drive; **Dec 31, 2002 Retired**. Home: 1108 Suwannee Drive, Waycross, GA 31501

To, Karen Hien Thi Vo (Ut VanTo)   Karenvoto@hotmail.com
[(FE) P 1995; F 1998]. 1995 Dearborn Heights: Warren Valley 1996 school; 1997 Detroit: Cass Community (assoc.); 2001 General Board of Global Ministries, Program Director, Vietnam; **2018 Retired**. Home: 15273 Paris St, Allen Park 48101

Tomasino, Anthony J. (Cordelia)   tomasinos4@juno.com
[(FE) P N. IL 19; FE 2001]. 1998 trans to Detroit Conf. from N. IL Conf.; 1998 Flint: Lincoln Park; 2002 Negaunee: Mitchell; 2003 Associate Professor, Bethel College, Mishawaka, IN (para 335.1); **2016 Caro**. 670 Gilford, Caro 48723 (989-673-2246). Home: 208 W. Burnside, Caro 48723 (989-673-4355)

TOMMY, DOMINIC A (FE) (Comfort) – (PL-1997, FL-1999; PE-2000, FE-2003)
Grand Rapids: First (DSA) (Assoc) 1997; Grand Rapids: First (PTLP) (Assoc)11/16/1997-04/13/1999; Olivet (Assoc) 04/16/1999; Alto/Bowne Center 2000; Berrien Springs/Arden 2002; Stanwood: Northland 2006; Hopkins/South Monterey 2014; Lake Odessa Central 2017

pastordominic61@gmail.com
(H) 455 6th Ave, Lake Odessa 48849-1242 (616) 374-8294
LO: Central: PO Box 485, 912 4th Ave, Lake Odessa 48849 (616) 374-8861

*TORREY, WILLIAM J (RE) (Eileen) – (D-1952, FE-1955, R-1993)
Oshtemo 1951; Wayland 1956; Wacousta Community 1960; Battle Creek: Chapel Hill 1964; South Haven: First 1968; Ludington 1974; Jackson: Brookside 09/15/1978; Portage: Chapel Hill 1985; Rockford 1989; Retired 1993; Portage: First (Assoc LTFT) 1993-05/01/1996
(H) 28 Owl Brook Rd, Ashland, NH 03217 (603) 968-6348
eileen@weisshouse.net

*Tosch, Clare M.
[(RE) P Mich., 1948; F Mich., 1956]. 1948 Cloverdaly, Maplegrove Circuit; 1950 Jackson: Francis Street, Zion; 1958 Blissfield, Ogden; 1963 Pigeon: Salem; 1968 Saginaw: West Michigan Avenue; 1973 Milan: Marble Memorial; 1983 Sanford; 1985 Cheboygan; **1988 Retired**. Home: % James Tosch, 8675 N. River Rd., Freeland

*TOSHALIS, GERALD L (RE) (Barbara) – (D-1968, FE-1973, R-2006)
Voluntary Location 1971; Readmitted 1972; Other Valid Ministries (¶344.1d) Personal Growth Ministry, Grand Rapids Community Counseling 1972; Other Valid Ministries (¶344.1d) Director, Samaritan Health and Living Center 1979; Appointed in Other Annual Conferences (¶426.1) First UMC, San Diego, CA 1990; Grand Rapids: Trinity (Assoc) 1992; Grandville 2001; Grand Rapids: Aldersgate (Interim) 2005; Retired 2006
jtoshalis@gmail.com
(H) Stillpoint, 4305 Persianwood Dr, Kalamazoo 49006 (269) 365-0313

Totty, Darryl E. (Anita)   entj2@aol.com [8-201]
[(FE) PL 1998; FL 1999; PE 2002; FE 2008]. 1998 Eastside Covenant Cooperative Parish: Detroit: Christ (assoc), Jefferson Avenue; Sep 1, 2003 Eastside Covenant Cooperative Parish: Detroit: Conant Avenue; **2015 Detroit: Second Grace**. 18700 Joy Rd., Detroit 48228 (313-838-6475). Home: 29193 Northwestern Hwy., Unit #388, Southfield 48034 (313-215-3841)

*Tousley, Kenneth Lee (Doris)
[(RE) T N. IN., 1958; F N. IN., 1960]. 1955 Prairie: Bethel; 1957 Keystone: Blanche Chapel; 1959 Keystone Parish; 1960 Robinson: Wesley; 1965 Trans. to Detroit Conf., Saginaw: Ames (assoc.); 1968 Tawas; 1982 Adrian; 1989 Port Huron District Superintendent; **1995 Retired**. Home: 1235 Wintergreen St., East Tawas 48730 (989-362-6554)

Tousley, Philip (Laurie)   ptousley@new.rr.com
[(FE) P 1993; F 1995]. 1998 transf to Detroit Conf. from Rocky Mountain Conf.; 1998 Menominee: First; 2011 Bad Axe: First; **2019 2011 Bad Axe: First, Minden City, Ubly**. (BA) 216 East Woodworth, Bad Axe 48413 (989-269-7671), (MC) 3346 Main St., PO Box 126, Minden City 48456-0126 (989-864-3418), (U) 4496 Pike St., PO Box 131, Ubly 49475-0131 (810-672-9929). Home: 1165 Thompson Dr., Bad Axe 48413 (989-269-8403)

TOWNLEY, ALICE FLEMING (FE) (Michael) – (D-1997, FE-2000)
Center Park 1997; Family Leave 2001; Williamston 07/15/2008; Family Leave 2009; Other Valid Ministries (¶344.1d) Assoc for Parish Life, Okemos Presbyterian Church 02/01/2010
aftownley@yahoo.com
(H) 1035 Prescott Drive, East Lansing 48823-2445 (517) 324-5432
(O) 2258 Bennett Rd, Okemos 48823 (517) 507-5117

*Townley, Robert Kemp
[(RE) T 1957; F 1959]. 1956 Scottville (Phil. Conf.); 1959 school; 1960 Midland: First (assoc.); 1966 school; 1972 Program Consultant for Religious Affairs, Clinton, Ingham and Eaton County Health Board Drug Program; **1977 Retired**.

*TOWNSEND, RAYMOND J (RE) (Joyce) – (D-1987, FE-1990, R-2009)
Appointed in Other Annual Conferences (¶331.8, ¶346.1) Detroit Conference, Samaria and Lulu 1984; Plainwell: First (Assoc) 1988; Leighton 1991; Sparta 2006; Retired 2009

shamu25revenge@yahoo.com
(H) 7178 Cornerstone Dr SE, Caledonia 49316-7644 (616) 204-3495

*Townsend, Ted Paul　　　　　　　　　　　　　tedrotown@juno.com
[(RE) T 1955; F 1957]. 1956 Raub, IN; 1957 Seward, AK; 1963 Ann Arbor: West Side (assoc.); 1968 Ferndale: First (assoc.); 1969 Board of Missions, World Division, Professor of Old Testament, Leonard Theological Seminary, India; Oct. 1989 Theological Hall, Sierra Leone; 1995 Missionary in Residence, Methodist Theological School in Ohio; 1996 General Board of Global Ministries, Russia; **1998 Retired**. Home: PO Box 1018, Penney Farms, FL 32079 (904-284-8441)

*Trebilcock, Douglas Robert (Catherine Ann)　　　　DRTMidland@aol.com
[(RE) T 1966; F 1969]. 1967 Hardy; 1969 Rochester: St. Paul's (assoc.); Dec. 1972 Bloomfield Hills: St. Paul; 1975 St. Clair; 1985 Clarkston; 2004 Midland: Aldergate; **2006 Retired**. Home: 2212 Cranbrook Drive, Midland 48642 (989-837-7087)

TREMAN, COLLEEN T (FD) (Keith) – (DM-1984, FD-1997)
Transferred from West Ohio Conf 1985; Muskegon: Central, Director of Christian Education 09/01/1985; Muskegon Lakeside, Director of Christian Education 01/01/1990; Kalamazoo: First, Coordinator of Children's Ministries 1990; Leave of Absence 01/15/1998; Sturgis (Deacon) (LTFT ½) 1998; Lansing: Mount Hope (Deacon) Children's Coordinator (LTFT ½) 2008; Transitional Leave 2015

ctreman@yahoo.com
(H) 5393 Woodrush Ave, Kalamazoo 49009 (269) 625-0511

*TREMAN, KEITH R (RE) (Colleen) – (D-1983, FE-1987, R-2015)
Whitehall/Claybanks 1985; Kalamazoo: First (Assoc) 1990; Sturgis 01/15/1998; Portland 2008; Retired 2015

ktreman@fastmail.fm
(H) 5393 Woodrush Ave, Kalamazoo 49009 (269) 358-3966

Triebwasser, Amy
[(PE) PL Jan. 2016; FL 2017; PE 2019]. Jan 1, 2016 Salem Grove; **2017 Flat Rock**. 28400 Evergreen, Flat Rock 48134 (734-782-2565). 29451 Evergreen, Flat Rock 48134

*Trinidad, Saul Camargo　　　　　　　　　　strinidad@juno.com
[(RE) P Costa Rica Conf., 19_; F Costa Rica, 19_]. 1990 Trans. from Methodist Church of Costa Rica; 1990 Detroit: El Buen Pastor; Sep 1, 1998 Consultant on Hispanic Ministries; **2013 Retired**. Home: 1216 Creek Knoll, San Antonio, TX 78253 (210-679-9736)

TROMMATER, TIMOTHY W (FE) (Erin) – (PE-2015, FE-2018)
Jackson: First (Assoc) 2015; DeWitt Redeemer (Assoc) 2017
tim.trommater@gmail.com
(H) 139 W Brunswick Dr, DeWitt 48820-9107 (517) 783-3803
Redeemer: 13980 Schavey Rd, DeWitt 448820-9013 (517) 669-3430

TROWBRIDGE, SUSAN J (FE) (Roger) – (D-1987, FE-1990)
Peace/Quimby (DSA) 04/01/1993; Transferred from Detroit Conf 1994; Peace/Quimby (LTFT ¾) 1994; Peace 1998; Leave of Absence 03/15/2005; Munith and Stockbridge (LTFT ½) 2014; Battle Creek: First (LTFT ½) 2019
suetrowbridgeart744@gmail.com
(H) 329 S Main St, PO Box 151, Vermontville 49096-0151 (517) 667-8414
Battle Creek: First: 111 E Michigan Ave, Battle Creek 49014 (269) 963-5567

*Trudgeon, Theodore A. aa8yf@yahoo.com
[(RA) PL 2004; AM 2019; RA 2019]. 2004 Bergland, Ewen, Wakefield; **2019 Retired**. Home: 20126 Trudgeon Rd, Ewen 49925-9003 (2533)

*TUPPER, MICHAEL J (RE) (Lori) – (D-1983, FE-1986, R-2016)
Transferred from North Indiana Conf 1993; Casco 04/16/1993; Pentwater: Centenary 2001; UM Connectional Structures (¶346.1) Hope UMC, Red Bird Missionary Conference 2006; Parchment 2011; Retired 2016; Gull Lake (Co-pastor) 01/01/2019
michaeljamestupper@yahoo.com
(H) 45554 West Street, Lawrence 49064-9720 (269) 303-3743
Gull Lake: 8640 Gull Rd, Richland 49803-9647 (269) 629-5137

*TURNER, ARTHUR R (RE) (Johncie Palmer Turner) – (D-1968, FE-1972, R-2006)
Scottdale/Bridgman 04/01/1970; Manton/Fife Lake/East Boardman/South Boardman 1971; Potter Park 1976; Battle Creek: Baseline 1981; Ashley/Bannister 1984; Other Valid Ministries (¶344.1d) Handicapper Information Advocate, Handicapper Information Council & Patient Equipment Locker 1990; Honorable Location 1991; Appointed in Other Annual Conferences (¶331.8, ¶346.1) Detroit Conference, Morrice/Bennington/Pittsburg (Ad-Interim) 1998; Appointed in Other Annual Conferences (¶337.1) Detroit Conference, Morrice/Bennington/ Pittsburg 06/02/1999; Munith/Pleasant Lake 2004; Medical Leave 11/15/2005; Retired 2006; North Adams/Jerome (LTFT ¼) 02/01/2012-2014
arthurturn@gmail.com
(H) 1039 Crestwood Ln, Jackson 49203-3647 (517) 769-2329

*Turner, Johncie Kay [Palmer] (Arthur R. Turner) johnciekay@gmail.com
[(RD) Con CE (E. Ohio) 1991; CRT CE (E. Ohio) 1992; FD 1997]. 1990 Church of the Savior, Canton, Ohio; 1993 Goshen, IN: First; 1996 Ypsilanti: First Presbyterian; Jan 15, 1998 transf to Memphis Conference; Dyersburg (TN): First; Sep 1, 1999 transf to Detroit Conf. Chelsea: First, Minister of Christian Education and S.E.N.I.O.R.S. Ministries; **Aug 31, 2008 Retired**. Home: 1039 Crestwood Ln, Jackson 49203 (734-972-7186)

*TURNER, MOLLY C (RE) – (D-1969, FE-1972, R-2012)
Manton/Fife Lake/East Boardman/South Boardman (Assoc) 1971; Lansing: Mount Hope (Assoc) 1976; Vermontville/Gresham 1979; Breckenridge 1983; Appointed to Extension Ministries (¶344.1b,c) District Superintendent, Central District 1990; UM Connectional Structures (¶344.1a,c) Clergy Assistant to the Bishop 1993; Grand Ledge: First 2003; Retired 2012; Grand Ledge First (Interim) 07/01/2012-12/31/2012

mollycturner@gmail.com
(H) 1873 Hamilton Rd, Okemos 48864-1812 (517) 214-6308

*Turner, Richard A. (Mary Lee)
[(RE) T N. IN, 1957; F N. IN., 1960]. 1954 Windsor, Rehobeth; 1957 Losantville, Blountsville; 1960 Trans. to Detroit Conf., Bay Port; 1965 Millington, Arbela; 1971 Pinconning; Dec. 1, 1983 Saginaw: West Michigan Avenue; Mar. 1, 1987 Saginaw: West Michigan Avenue, Sheridan Avenue; 1991 Onaway, Millersburg; **1995 Retired**. Home: H.C.R. 01, Box 285, Bois Blanc Island 49775

*Tuttle, James Edward (Linda)   jet.tuttle@juno.com
[(RE) P 1972; F 1976]. 1972 Calumet; Feb. 1975 Detroit: Metropolitan (assoc.); 1977 Ypsilanti: St. Matthew's; Jan. 15, 1985 Livonia: Clarenceville; 1990 Flint: Calvary; 1999 Saline; **2016 Retired**. Home: 1450 Maplewood Dr., Saline 48176 (734-944-8081)

*VALE, DIANE (DIA) E (RE) (Marc) – (D-1973, FE-1977, R-1990)
Fife Lake/Boardmans Parish 1976; Lawton 10/15/1977; Other Valid Ministries (¶344.1d) Institute for Advanced Pastoral Studies, Bloomfield Hills 05/01/1980; Sabbatical Leave 1983; Weidman 1984; Leave of Absence 07/15/1985; Retired 1990

diavale@juno.com
(H) 17600 Garvey Rd, Chelsea 48118-9772 (734) 475-9526

VanBeek, Craig H (FL) (Laura) – (DSA-2017, CLM-2017, FL-2019)
Burnips/Monterey Center (DSA) 2017; Burnips/Monterey Center 01/01/2019
(H) 4290 Summer Creek Dr., Dorr 49323 (616) 299-6668
Burnips: 4237 30th St, PO Box 30, Burnips 49314 (616) 896-8410
Monterey Center: 3022 130th Ave, Hopkins 49328 (616) 896-8410

*VanConant, Earleen A.   c.vanconant@yahoo.com
[(RL) FL 1988]. 1989 Omard. Jan. 1, 1992 Cole, Omard (LTFT); 1993 White Pine, Bergland, Ewen, Trout Creek Presb (LTFT ½); 1997 Port Austin, Grindstone/Pinnebog; **Jan 1, 2000 Retired**. Home: 55209 Fallbrooke Dr., Macomb 48042 (586-243-6176)

*VANDENBRINK, SANDRA KAY (RL) (Trevor) – (PL-2001, RL-2013)
Hudsonville 5/31/2001; Bradley Indian Mission / Salem Indian Mission 1/16/2005; Bradley Indian Mission / Salem Indian Mission 2013-10/1/2014; Retired 2013; Kewadin Indian Mission 2015-12/31/2016

sandravandenbrink20@gmail.com
(H) 3933 Kerri Ct., Holland 49424 (616) 886-3579

*VANDERBILT, HERBERT J. (RL) (Emmy) – (PL-2004, NL-2016, RL-2017)
East Nelson 2004; Not Appointed 2016; Retired 12/01/2017
hvanderbilt@comcast.net
(H) 2204 Gee Dr, Lowell 49331-9505 (616 460-0997

PASTORAL RECORDS

VanderSande, Ruth A. ruth.irish@asburyseminary.edu
[(PE) PL Sept 7, 2017; PE 2019]. Sept 7, 2017 Macon (LTFT ½); **2019 Britton Grace, Macon**. (BG) 9250 E Monroe, Britton 49229 (517-451-8280). (M) 11964 Macon Hwy, Clinton 49236 (517-423-8270). Home: 7645 Clinton-Macon Rd, Clinton 49236 (810-335-3962)

VanDessel, Joan E (PE) – (PE-2019)
Grand Rapids: First (assocand Director of Mission and Outreach)
joanv@grfumc.org
(H) 2005 Collingwood Ave SW, Wyoming 49519 (616) 818-9295
Grand Rapids: First: 227 Fulton St E, Grand Rapids 49503 (616) 451-2879

VANDOP, JONATHAN D (FE) (Darcie) – (FL-2008, PE-2009, FE-2014)
Rosebush 2008; Ionia: First 2014; Lyons-Muir 01/01/2016; Leave of Absence (¶353.2a) 2017; Appointed to Extension Ministries (¶344.1b) Chaplain, West Texas VA Health Care System 08/19/2018
uscgemt@yahoo.com
(H) 8119 Rustic Park, San Antonio, TX 78240-5238 (989) 954-7099

*VANLENTE, CHARLES R (RA) (Linda) – (SP-1963, FL-1970, AM-1976, RA-2010)
Ashton Charge 09/01/1963; Morris Chapel/Niles 12/01/1964-09/01/1965; St Johns: Salem 01/15/1970; Maple Hill 1972; Honorable Location 08/15/1976; Holton/Sitka/Twin Lake (Ad Interim) 1978; Readmitted 1982; Holton/Sitka/Twin Lake 1982; Cassopolis 1983; Kalkaska 1993; Grand Rapids: Northlawn 1996; Retired 2010
chucksmemo@gmail.com
(H) 2103 Shetland Dr NE, Grand Rapids 49505-7138 (616) 719-1833

VANLENTE, RONALD D (FE) (Kathleen Logsdon) – (D-1991, FE-1998, OE-2011)
Coloma/Watervliet (LTFT ¾) (¶346.1) 2011; (Watervliet Merged w/ Coloma 6/26/2011) Coloma 1/1/2012; Transferred from Western North Carolina Conf 2013; South Haven: First 2018
ronvanlente@gmail.com
(H) 12320 76th St, South Haven 49090 (269) 468-9378
South Haven: First: 429 Michigan Ave, South Haven 49090-1333
(269) 637-2502

*VanMarter, Dianne Helene (Merl) deerev@aol.com
[(RL) PL 2002]. 2001 Omard; 2002 Omard, Peck (LTFT ¾); Jan 1, 2004 Omard, Peck (LTFT ½); 2005 Peck; 2011 New Haven: Faith (LTFT ½), Omo: Zion (LTFT ¼); Jan 1, 2014 New Haven: Faith; **2015 Retired**. Home: 20100 Cushing, Detroit 48205 (810-488-0608)

VanOudheusden, MELODYE SURGEON (FE) (John) – (D-1994, FE-2005)
Family Leave 1996; Marcellus 2002; Jackson Trinity/Parma 2007; Evart 2012; Evart/Sears 2017; Monroe: St. Paul's 2019
pastormelodye@yahoo.com
(H) 212 Hollywood Dr, Monroe 48162-2659 (517) 250-1879
Monroe: St Paul's: 201 S Monroe St, Monroe 48161-2217 (734) 242-3000

Vasey, Bradley R brickvase@yahoo.com
[(PL) PL 2019]. **2019 Deerfield, Wellsville** (LTFT ½). (D) 110 Williams St, Deerfield 49238 (517-447-3420), (W) 2509 S Wellsville Hwy, Blissfield 49228 (517-486-4777). Home: 4322 Corey Hwy, Blissfield 49228 (419-704-1884)

*VENTURA, OSCAR A (RE) (Naomi) – (D-1975, FE-1978, R-2009)
Transferred from Wisconsin Conf 1996; Grand Rapids: La Nueva Esperanza 12/05/1996; Involuntary Leave of Absence 09/25/2002; Grand Rapids: La Nueva Esperanza 03/17/2003; Retired 2009
(H) Calle Carlos Lassy #13, Apartado Postal 97, Barahona 82000, Dominican Republic

Verhelst, Weatherly Burkhead (Craig) revwow@charter.net
[(FE) P 1993; F 1996]. 1994 Flint: Court Street (assoc); 1998 Middlebury; 2003 Saginaw: State Street; Aug 1, 2009 Utica (assoc.); **2015 Troy: First**. 6363 Livernois, Troy 48098 (248-879-6363). Home: 6339 Vernmoor, Troy 48098 (989-598-6506)

*Verhelst, William A. (Suzanne) wsverhelst@centurytel.net
[(RE) T 1966; F 1968]. 1963 Republic Charge; 1966 Wellington (Cent. IL Conf.); 1968 Gladstone; Apr. 1974 Beverly Hills; 1979 Flint: Central; Oct. 15, 1987 Associate Council Director, Parish Development and Global Ministries; 1997 Detroit West District Superintendent; 2004 Detroit: Metropolitan (Intentional Interim, ¶329.3); **2006 Retired**. Home: 14763 W. Brady, Chesaning 48616 (989-845-5007)

*VERNON, DOUGLAS W (RE) (Jane) – (D-1967, FE-1970, R-2010)
Niles Trinity 1969; Kalamazoo: First (Assoc) 1971; Stockbridge 11/01/1974; Transferred to Detroit Conf 1979; Transferred from Detroit Conf 2000; Retired 2010; Kalamazoo: First 2000; Retired 2010; Lawton: St Paul's (LTFT ¼) 2011-2014; Battle Creek: First (Assoc) (LTFT ¼) 2015-2016
dvernon@fumcnorthville.org
(H) 793 Red Maple Lane, Wixom 48393 (248) 859-2986

*Veska, Rony S (Ivor) rveska@yahoo.com
[(RE) P 1997; FE 2000]. 1997: Ann Arbor: First (assoc.); 1998 Poseyville; Mar 1, 2001 Rochester: St. Paul's (assoc); 2008 Ferndale: First; **2013 Retired**. 31 W. Los Reales Rd., #167, Tucson, AZ 85756

*Vincent, Alonzo Elliott (Elmira) esmithvinc@aol.com
[(RE) P W. OH, 1966; F W. OH, 1968]. 1961 McCabe Chapel (N. Little Rock, AR; 1962 Sweet Home, Lone Oak Circuit, AR; 1966 Chicago: St. Matthew's (assoc.); 1967 Evanston, IL: Sherman Avenue; 1968 Cincinnati: Marbly Memorial; 1973 Cincinnati: Marbly, Bond Hill, St. Mark Parish; 1979 Trans. to Wisconsin Conf., Director of Urban Strategy, Milwaukee; 1983 Southcentral District Superintendent; Jul. 1984 Trans. to Detroit Conf., Detroit: Cass Avenue (assoc.); 1986 Highland Park: Berea-St. Paul's; 1991 Flint: Bethel; 2005 Birch Run; 2007 Attica; 2008 Mt. Morris: First; **2013 Retired**. Home: 9197 Liverpool Ct., Grand Blanc 48439 (810-953-9917)

*VITTOZ, IRENE L. (RL) (Gary) – (PL-2005, RL-2018)
Brookfield Eaton (DSA) 10/01/2004; Brookfield Eaton (PTLP) 11/15/2005; Brookfield Eaton (PTLP) and Pope (PTLP) 2008; Brookfield Eaton (PTLP ¼) and Lee Center (PTLP ¼) 2010; Brookfield Eaton (PTLP ¼) 2014; Retired 2018
ilv@vcconsulting.com
(H) 5503 Long Hwy, Eaton Rapids 48827-9016 (517) 543-4225

Vollmer, Michael W. (Sarah)
[(PE) FL 2014; PE 2016]. 2014 Hemlock, Nelson; **2019 Centreville**. 305 E Main St, Centreville 49032-9619 (269-467-8645). Home: 304 E Market St, Centreville 49032-9671 (989-600-6148)

*Wachterhauser, Paul Thomas (Beth)an twachterhauser@yahoo.com
[(RE) P 1969; F W.MI, 1973]. 1971 Burr Oak; 1974 Trans. to Detroit Conf., Midland: First (assoc.); 1979 Cass City; Sep. 1, 1983 Ann Arbor: First (assoc.); 1997 Caring Covenant Group Ministry: Davison; **2009 Retired**. Home: 716 Surfwood, Davison 48423 (810-653-4459)

Waggoner, Katherine
[(FL) PL 2011; FL 2016]. 2011 Monroe: E. Raisinville Frenchtown (became Heritage UMC, 2012); **2013 Heritage (¼), Monroe: First (¾)**. (H) 4010 N. Custer, Monroe 48162 (734-242-9747), (First) 312 Harrison, Monroe 48161 (734-241-6070). Home: 310 Carey St., Deerfield 49238 (517-447-3915)

WAGNER, Charlene (PL) – (DSA-2018, PL 2019)
Carland (DSA) (LTFT ¼) 2018; Carland (LTFT ¼) 01/01/2019
thewagners2@gmail.com
(H) 587 N Baldwin Rd, Owosso 48867-9386 (989) 494-7763
Carland: 4002 N Carland Rd, Elsie 48831-9469

*WAGNER, GLENN M (RE) (Nancy) – (D-1976, FE-1982, R-2017)
Transferred from Northern Illinois Conf 1992; N Muskegon: Community 1992; Holt 2006; Church of The Dunes 2014; Retired 01/01/2017
gnmbwagner@aol.com
(H) 1284 Oakhampton Rd, Holland 49424-2625 (616) 842-3586

*WAGNER, LYNN W (RE) – (D-1965, FE-1970, R-2002)
Hillsdale: First (Assoc) 1966; Niles: Wesley (Assoc) 1969; Howard City Circuit 09/15/1970; Evart Circuit 03/01/1971; Keeler/Silver Creek 10/15/1973; Mulliken/ Grand Ledge: First (Assoc) 1975; Dowling: Country Chapel/Banfield 1977; Nashville 1984; Middleville/Parmelee 1988; Battle Creek: Maple 1996; Lyons-Muir/Ionia: Easton 2001; Retired 09/01/2002
(H) 26685 Elk Run E, New Hudson 48165 (269) 986-2876

WALES, GARY S (FE) (Cynthia Kaye) – (D-1988, FE-1990)
Fife Lake/Boardman 1987; Otsego: Trowbridge 1994; Kingsley 2008; Charlotte: Lawrence Ave 2013
cgwales7@aol.com
(H) 1072 N Stonehill Dr, Charlotte 48813-8791 (517) 231-6775
Lawrence Ave: PO Box 36, 210 E Lawrence Ave, Charlotte 48813 (517) 543-4670

Walker, James J. (Susan)   sermonator2016@hotmail.com
[(FE) P W.MI, 1985; F W.MI, 1987]. 1985 Lansing: Christ (assoc.); 1989 Trans. to Detroit Conf., Brown City: First, Immanuel; 1996 Utica (assoc); 1998 Wyandotte: First; **2007 Belleville: First**. 417 Charles St., Belleville 48111 (734-697-9288). Home: 455 High St., Belleville 48111 (734-697-7398)

Walkup, Kenny Ray, Jr. (Michelle)
[(PL) PL 2015]. **Nov 23, 2015 South Lyon (associate)**. 640 S. Lafayette, South Lyon 48178. (248-437-0760). Home: 1115 Paddock, South Lyon 48178 (248-361-6658)

***Wallace, Daniel James** (Betty)   danwallace@frontier.com
[(RE) T 1956; F 1958]. 1955 school; 1956 Dundalk, MD; 1957 Pasadena, MD: Mt. Carmel; 1958 Pontiac: Central (assoc.); 1961 Port Huron District Field Worker; 1967 Dearborn Heights: Stephens; 1968 Centerline: Bethel; 1970 Dearborn: First (assoc.); 1976 Saline: 1984 Wayne; 1989 Troy: Big Beaver; 1991 Caring Covenant Group Ministry: Davison; **1997 Retired**. Home: 612 East Third St., Davison 48423 (810-653-7499)

***Wallace**, Joyce E.
[(RE) P; F MO W. Conf] Wesley foundation, Lincoln University; 1995 transfer from Missouri West Conference, Detroit: Central (assoc); 1997 Detroit: Conant Avenue; 2001 Detroit: Scott Memorial; 2005 Hardy; **2013 Retired**; 2015-2018 Middlebury, Pittsburg. Home: 9921 Belcrest Blvd., Fenton 48430 (810-208-0648)

Waller, Tom J.   waller0307@yahoo.com
[(FL) FL Jan, 2015]. Jan 1, 2015 Dearborn Heights: Stephens, Warren Valley; **2018 Richomond: First**. 69495 Main St., Box 293, Richmond 48062 (586-727-2622. Home: 35675 Pound Rd., Richmond 48062 (586-727-655

Wallis, David Michael (Lisa)   norev@juno.com
[(FE) SP 1990; P 1994; F 1997]. 1995 Norway: Grace, Faithhorn; **2006 Mackinaw City: Church of the Straits**. PO Box 430, 307 N. Huron, Mackinaw City 49701 (231-436-8682). Home: 309 East Jamet, PO Box 901, Mackinaw City 49701 (231-436-5484)

***Walls, Suzanne B.** (John)   pastorsuew@yahoo.com
[(RE) SP 1994; PE 1999; FE 2003]. Feb 16, 1995 Inkster: Christ; 2000 Ortonville; 2005 Wyandotte: Glenwood; 2013 Berkley: First, Beverly Hills; **2016 Retired**. Home: 225 Munger Rd., Holly 48442 (248-459-6851)

***WALSWORTH, LOWELL F** (RE) (Jessica) – (D-1959, FE-1962, R-2002)
Hastings Parish 1957; Lyon Lake/Marengo 1959; Kalamazoo: First (Assoc) 1962; Bellevue/Kalamo 1966; Grand Rapids: First (Assoc) 1971; Edwardsburg/Niles Trinity 1973; Battle Creek: Trinity 1978; Vicksburg 1981; Sturgis 1993; Other Valid Ministries (¶344.1d) Assoc Professor, Olivet College 1995; Retired 2002

Ljwalsworth@charter.net
(H) 1412 E Hatch St, Sturgis 49091-1220 (269) 659-4688

Walther, Joel L. (Megan)   pastorjoel@charter.net
[(FE) FL 2011; PE 2012; FE 2015]. 2011 Petersburg, LaSalle: Zion; **2017 Goodrich**. 8071 S. State Road, Goodrich 48438 8071 S. State Road, Goodrich 48438 (810-636-2444). Home: 7228 Chapel View Dr., Clarkston 48346 (734-636-2444)

Walther, Megan Jo Crumm (Joel)   rev.megan.walther@gmail.com
[(FE) PE 2011; FE 2014]. 2011 Erie; **2017 Clarkston (assoc)**. 6600 Waldon Rd., Clarkston 48346 (248-625-1611). Home: 7228 Chapel View Dr., Clarkston 48346 (734-751-6836)

*Walton, Robert E. (Alice)
[(RE) P W. OH, 19 ; F W. OH 19]. 1977 Trans. to Detroit Conf., Detroit: Central (assoc.); 1981 Wesley Foundation, Wayne State University; 1986 Program Secretary, United Methodist Volunteer Services, National Division, Gen. Board of Global Ministries; **2002 Retired**. Home: 211 Bergen St., Brooklyn, NY 11217 (718-624-0207)

*WALWORTH, MAURICE E (RE) (Sally) – (D-1985, FE-1989, R-2006)
Transferred from Southwest Texas Conf 1993; Battle Creek: Baseline 11/01/1993; Lansing: Christ 1996; Jackson Calvary 2003; Retired 2006; Munith/Pleasant Lake 2006; Pleasant Lake 2007-09/30/2007; Somerset Center 2008-2009; Munith 09/06/2011-2012

mewjr1@juno.com
(H) PO Box 612, 257 Lake Heights, Grass Lake 49240-0612 (517) 522-3936

*Ward, George F. (Alice)   Gfward@hotmail.com
[(RE) P 1969; F 1971]. 1970 Dearborn: Mt. Olivet (assoc.); 1972 Southfield: Magnolia; Mar. 1976 Clayton, Rollin Center; Nov. 1, 1981 Croswell; 1988 Franklin: Community (assoc.); 1993 Chesaning: Trinity; 2002 Cass City; **2006 Retired**. 995 N. Baywood, Holland 49424

*Ward, Kenneth Edwin (Sue)   ksward@powerc.net
[(RE) P E.OH, 1968; F E.OH, 1970]. 1970 Waynesburg: Centenary; 1973 Ashland: Christ; Mar. 1978 Trans. to Detroit Conf., Director-Manager, Judson Collins Camp; Jan. 1, 1982 Detroit Conference Staff: Outdoor Education. 1992 Marquette District Superintendent; 1998 Dearborn: First; **2005 Retired**. Home: (May-Oct): 18585 Red Pine Dr., Hillman 49746 (989-742-2133), (Nov-Apr): 905 Conway, #18, Las Cruces, NM 88005

*Ward, Robert Paul
[(RE) T 1949; F 1952]. 1952 Detroit: Westlawn (assoc.); 1954 Troy; 1957 Marquette: First; 1961 Ypsilanti: First; 1965 Adrian; 1969 Flint: Court Street; 1972 Ann Arbor District Superintendent; 1978 Grosse Pointe; 1982 Birmingham: First; **1993 Retired**. Home: 42160 Woodward, #27, Bloomfield Hills 48304 (248-334-8770)

*Washburn, Grant A. (Patricia)   gwashburn2@cox.net
[(RE) P 1968; F 1971]. 1970 Port Huron: Gratiot Park; 1972 Flushing (assoc.); 1975 Mio; 1980 Saginaw: Swan Valley; 1983 Bay City: Madison Avenue; Sep. 1, 1987 Burton: Atherton; 1993 Sterling Heights; **Aug 1, 1995 Retired**. 8378 West Bluefield Avenue, Peoria, AZ 85382 (623-215-7849)

*Webster, Brent L. (Mary)   brent1949@live.com
[(RE) P 1974; F 1977]. 1976 Davison Group Ministry: Richfield; Nov. 1978 Harbor Beach, Port Hope; 1983 Washington, Davis; Sep 1, 1997 West Bloomfield; 2010 Carleton; **2012 Retired**; May 1-June 30, 2019 West Bloomfield. Home: 7863 Academy Court E., Waterford 48329 (248-742-1092)

*Webster, Roy LaVere (Zola)   Laverew@aol.com
[(RE) T 1957; F 1963]. 1955 Indian River; 1957 school; 1962 New Hudson; 1966
Birmingham: First (assoc.); 1968 West Branch; 1973 Holly; 1976 Berkley; 1979
Royal Oak: St. John's; 1988 East Detroit: Immanuel; 1991 Belleville: First; Jun
30, 1994 disability leave; **1995 Retired**. Home: 1160 W. South Boulevard,
Rochester Hills 48309 (248-227-7619)

*Weemhoff, Harold E., Jr., (Chris)   drhalw@sbcglobal.net
[(RE) P W. OH, 1970; F W. OH, 1973]. May 1977 Trans. to Detroit Conf., Birmingham: First (assoc.); 1980 Leave of Absence; 1982 Whittemore, Prescott; 1984
Gladwin; 1986 Laingsburg, Middlebury; 1990 Ann Arbor: Glacier Way; Mar. 1,
1992 Taylor: West Mound; Dec 1, 1997 Taylor: West Mound, Melvindale: New
Hope; 1997 Eastpointe: Immanuel; Jan 1, 2000. Rochester: St. Paul's (assoc);
2008 Troy: First; **2015 Retired**. Home: 5800 Thorny Ash, Rochester 48306 (313-
418-2748)

*WEGNER, GLENN R (RE) (Evelyn) – (D-1975, FE-1978, R-2004)
Transferred from Deroit Conf 1984; Woodland/Welcome Corners 1984; Epsilon/
Levering 1987; Appointed in Other Annual Conferences (¶426.1) West Ohio
Conf., Seaman 09/01/1992; Battle Creek: Baseline 1996; Retired 2004
                     (H) 3788 Bass Rd, Williamsburg, OH 45176-9785 (269) 967-3850

WEILER, CARA B A (FD) (Matthew) – (PD-2007, FD-2011)
Portage: Chapel Hill (Deacon) (LTFT ¼) 10/01/2007; Transferred from Northern
Illinois Conf 2008; Kalamazoo: Sunnyside (Deacon) (LTFT ¼) 10/01/2009; Deacons Appointed w/in UM Connectional Structure (¶331.1b) Kalamazoo: Sunnyside (LTFT ¼) and SW MI Children's Trauma Assessment Center (LTFT ½)
11/18/2009

                                     deaconcara@sunnysideumc.com
                               (H) 3090 Vliet Ln, Kalamazoo 49004-3237
                     Kalamazoo: Sunnyside: 2800 Gull Rd, Kalamazoo 49048-1384
                                                        (269) 349-3047

WEILER, JOHN MATTHEW (FE) (Cara) – (FL-2007, PE-2009, FE-2013)
Portage: Chapel Hill (Assoc) 2007; Portage: Chapel Hill (Assoc) (LTFT ½) and
Kalamazoo: Sunnyside (LTFT ½) 2009; Kalamazoo: Sunnyside 2011
                                     pastormatt@sunnysideumc.com
                     (H) 3090 Vliet Ln, Kalamazoo 49004-3237 (269) 599-2274
                     Kalamazoo: Sunnyside: 2800 Gull Rd, Kalamazoo 49048-1384
                                                        (269) 349-3047

*WEINBERGER, STEPHAN (RE) – (D-1985, FE-1987, R-2016)
Indian River/Pellston 1984; St Johns: First 1990; Lansing: First 2000; Other Valid
Ministries (¶344.1d) Oaks Correctional Facility 2004; Lansing Calvary/Potter
Park 2005; Lansing Calvary 2006; Lansing Calvary/Wheatfield 08/01/2006;
Mancelona/Alba 2007; Muskegon: Lakeside/Crestwood 2010; Pierson Heritage
2014; Retired 03/01/2016; Dimondale 02/01/2019; Stockbridge (LTFT ¼), Munith
(LTFT ¼) 2019

                                     revsteve75@hotmail.com
                     (H) 3880 Lone Pine Dr, Apt 03, Holt 48842 (517) 242-5020
             Munith: 224 N Main St, PO Box 189, Munith 49259-0189 (517) 596-2441
             Stockbridge: 219 E Elizabeth St, Stockbridge 49285-9666 (517) 851-7676

*Weiss, Edward C., Jr.
[(RE) LP 1976; FM 1998]. 1968 Wellsville; 1972 Springville; 1974 Crystal Falls, Amasa; 1985 St. Charles, Brant; **Sep 1, 1994 Retired**. Home: 952 W. Maple Ave., Adrian 49221 (517-265-7259)

*Weiss, James Dewey (Sara)   JDEWeiss@comcast.net
[(RE) T 1954; F 1957]. 1955 Rea, Cone; 1956 Samaria; 1958 Stephens; 1963 Dearborn Heights: Stephens; 1966 Berkley; 1969 Lincoln Park: First; Aug. 1975 Detroit: Trinity; Oct. 1982 Lincoln Park: Dix; 1989 St. Clair Shores: Good Shepherd; 1992 Auburn; **1993 Retired**. Home: 56645 Cardinal Dr., Macomb 48042

*Welbaum, Barbara Ellen   bewelbaum@att.net
[(RE) P 1988; F 1991; RE 2019]. 1989 Port Austin, Grindstone City, Pinnebog; Mar. 1, 1992 Ann Arbor: Glacier Way; 1994 Pontiac Cooperative Parish: Aldersgate, St. James; 1997 Detroit: Redford; 2000 Livonia: Newburg (assoc); 2006 Marysville; **Retired 2019**. Home: 4258 Berkshire Dr, Sterling Hts 48314 (586-219-5263)

*Welch, Karen Alayne [Mars]   karen.mars.tc@gmail.com
[(RE) SP 1993; P 1994; F 1997]. Jan 1, 1994 Dearborn Heights: Warren Valley; 1995 Morenci; Nov 1, 2000 Chelsea Retirement Community: Chaplain; Jul 15, 2002 leave of absence; 2003 God's Country Cooperative Parish: Grand Marais, Germfask, McMillan; 2006 Hillman, Spratt; **2008 Retired**. Home: 9099 Pembrook Dr, Davison 48423-8424 (231-590-2551)

*WELSCH, P KAY (AF) – (D-1986, FE-1992, RE-2004, AF-2004)
[Wisconsin Conf, Retired Elder] Turk Lake (DSA LTFT) 7/16/2005-2012
                                                         kwelsch80@gmail.com
        (H) PO Box 318, 9440 Cutler Road, Lakeview 48850-9714 (989) 352-1209

*WELSH, GERALD L (RE) (Martha Gene) – (D-1957, FE-1960, R-1994)
Sand Lake Circuit 1953; Alma (Assoc) 01/01/1960; Carson City 1961; Harbor Springs 09/01/1965; Stevensville 1968; Bellaire: Community 10/15/1969; Martin/Shelbyville 1976; Evart/Avondale 1984; Bronson: First 1990; Retired 1994
                                                         gwelsh449@gmail.com
                (H) 35 Roberts Ct, Coopersville 49404-1121 (616) 837-7157

WENBURG, RYAN L (FE) (Kathleen "Beth") – (PE-2015, FE-2018)
Hartford/Keeler 2015; Hartford 01/01/2017; Frankenmuth 2019
                                         PastorRyanWenburg@gmail.com
                        (H) 326 E Vates St, Frankenmuth 48734
        Frankenmuth: 346 E Vates St, Frankenmuth 48734-1130 (989) 652-6858

*WENDELL, DONALD R. (RL) (Violet) – (PL-1993, FL-2009, RL-2010)
Moscow Plains (DSA) (LTFT PT) 01/01/1993; Moscow Plains (LTFT PT) 1993; Nottawa (LTFT PT) 01/01/1996; Jackson: Zion (LTFT PT) 07/15/2003; Not Appointed 03/15/2006; Bloomingdale (LTFT ¼) 2006; Mt Pleasant: Trinity / Countryside / Leaton 11/30/2008; Retired 11/01/2009
                        (H) 137 W Michigan Ave, Galesburg 49053-9759 (269) 200-5205

*WESSMAN, ROBERT L (FL) – (FL-2018)
Mason: First (Assoc) 1979; Caledonia 1984; Allegan 1990; Retired 1999
                        (H) 6476 Castle Ave, Holland 49423-8988 (616) 335-8983

West, Brian Gregory. (Stephanie) pastorbrianwest@gmail.com
[(FE) PE 2012; FE 2015]. 2012 Laingsburg; **2018 Laingsburg, Pittsburg (¶206.3)**

(H) 214 Crum, St., Laingsburg 48848 (517) 651-5266
Laingsburg: 210 Crum St, Laingsburg 48848 (517) 651-5531
Pittsburg: 2960 W Grand River Rd, Owosso 48867-8704 (810) 208-0648

*West, Charles Henry (Margaret) mqtchaz@gmail.com
[(RE) P 1978; F 1981]. 1979 Richfield, Otter Lake; 1985 Parish Director, Caring Covenant Group Ministry: Richfield, Otter Lake; Mar. 1, 1988 White Pine Circuit: White Pine, Bergland, Ewen (LTFT ½); 1993 Marquette: Grace, Skandia; **2009 Retired**. Home: 440 E. Prospect, Marquette 49855

*West, Margaret Helen Rodgers (Charles) margiewest@earthlink.net
[(RE) P 1982; F 1985]. 1982 Flint: Hope (assoc.); 1983 Dryden, Attica; Mar. 1, 1988 White Pine Circuit: White Pine, Bergland, Ewen (LTFT ½); 1993 family leave; Sep 1, 1993 Director: Wesley Foundation, N. MI University ¼ Time; 1994 family leave 1999 Chaplain/Director, Wesley Foundation, Northern Michigan University; **2009 Retired**. Home: 440 E. Prospect, Marquette 49855

West, Matthew J (FL) (Melissa) – (FL 2018)
Girard 2018

(H) 199 Highfield Rd, Marshall 49068 (269) 967-4444
Girard: 990 Marshall Rd, Coldwater 49036-9603 (517) 279-9418

*WHEAT, KAREN S (RE) (Vincent) – (D-1972, FE-1975, R-2015)
Niles: Wesley (Assoc) 1974; Gobles/Kendall 09/15/1976; Jackson: Trinity 1986; Battle Creek: First 1998; Charlotte: Lawrence Ave 2002; Schoolcraft 2010; Retired 2015

WheatKS@aol.com
(H) 2933 Hunters Pl, Kalamazoo 49048-6154 (269) 743-7637

WHEELER, JENNIFER J (PL) – (PL-2014, NL-2017, PL-2017)
Augusta: Fellowship (DSA) 2013; Augusta: Fellowship (PTLP ¼) 11/09/2013; LP w/o Appointment 01/16/2017; Muskegon Crestwood 2017

j6wheeler.atis@gmail.com
(H) 1510 Calvin Ave, Muskegon 49442-4115
Muskegon Crestwood: 1220 Creston St, Muskegon 49442-4102
(231) 773-9696

*Wheelock, Calvin H. pastorherbw@aol.com
[(RL) PL 1999; RL 2019]. Dec 16, 1999 Caring Covenant Group Ministry: Arbela; Apr 1, 2005 Parish Director, Caring Covenant Group Ministry: Arbela; Nov 1, 2006 Henderson, Chapin; 2011 Henderson, Chapin, Owosso; **2019 Retired**. Home: 14405 Vassar Rd, Millington 48746-9205 (810-624-0795)

*Whitcomb, Randy James (Michelle Gentile) arejayrev@aol.com
[(RE) P MN, 1984; F 1987; RE 2019]. 1985 Trans. to Detroit Conf., Detroit: Aldersgate (assoc.); 1988 Canton: Cherry Hill; 1993 Flint: Bristol, Dimond; Jun 1, 1996 Lake Orion (assoc); Feb 15, 2001 incapacity leave (para 355.1); 2004 leave of absence; Oct 1, 2007 Chaplain, Great Lakes Caring – Hospice; **Jan. 1, 2019 Retired; Jan. 1, 2019 Chaplain, Great Lakes Caring – Hospice**. Home: 2772 Roundtree Drive, Troy 48083 (248-979-6677)

PASTORAL RECORDS

White, Christina M. (Jason Michael White) pastorchristym.b@gmail.com
[(FD) PD 2015; FD 2018]. 2015 Midland: First (deacon); 2017 Flint: Court Street (deacon), Crossroads District (deacon); **Jan 1, 2019 Flint: Court Street (deacon), East Winds District (deacon)**. (FCS) 225 W. Court St., Flint 48502 (810-235-4651), (EW) 624 W Nepessing, Ste 201, Lapeer 48446 (810-396-1362). Home:602 Avon St, Flint 48503 (989-488-3347)

White, Irene R. irene@up.net
[(PL) PL 1997]. 1997 Escanaba: First (assoc); Sep 1, 1997 Escanaba: First (assoc), Trenary; Jan 1, 2000 Trenary; Jan 1, 2009 Munising, Trenary; **2011 Norway: Grace, Faithorn**. (N) 130 O'Dill Dr., Norway 49870 (906-563-8917), (F) W8601 Blum Rd, Vulcan 49892. Home: 725 Norway St., Norway 49870 (906-563-9877)

White, Reggie Allen reggieallenwhite4609@gmail.com
[(OF) Progressive National Baptist Convention, OF 2019**]. 2019 Southfield: Hope (assoc), Detroit: St. Timothy (assoc)** (LTFT ¼). (SH) 26275 Northwestern Hwy., Southfield 48076-3926 (248-356-1020), (DST) 15888 Archdale St., Detroit 48227-1510 (313-837-4070).

*White, Robert Alan bwhite@up.net
[(RE) FE Great Rivers]. 2000 trans. from Illinois Great Rivers, Keweenaw Charge: Calumet, Mohawk-Ahmeek, Lake Linden, Laurium; **2016 Retired**. Home: 311 Eckart St., Antigo, WI 54409 (309-370-7227)

*Whitely, Betty (Theodore) BettyTedWhitely@aol.com
[(RL) PL 2000; RL 2007]. 1998 Southfield: Hope (assoc); 2000 Saginaw: Burt. Appointment ended May 1, 2007; **2017 Retired**. Home: 17156 Shervilla Place, Southfield 48075 (248-557-4688)

*Whitely Sr., Theodore DeLeon (Betty) BettyTedWhitely@aol.com
[(RE) Elder, AME Zion, 1979; P 1986; F 1988]. 1978-83 St. Paul AME Zion, Carnegie, PA; 1984 Trans. to Detroit Conf., Westland: St. James; Mar. 1, 1987 Detroit: Calvary; 1992 Detroit: St. Paul's; 1996 Detroit: Jefferson Ave.; 1998 Southfield: Hope (assoc); 2000 Saginaw: Calvary; 2003 Saginaw: Calvary; 2004 Burton: Christ; 2006 Detroit: Calvary, Henderson Memorial; 2011 Detroit: Calvary; 2013 Birmingham: Embury, Troy: Fellowship, Waterford: Trinity; 2014 Pontiac: Grace and Peace Community, Waterford: Four Towns; **2015 Retired**. Home: 17156 Shervilla Place, Southfield 48075 (248-557-4688)

*WHITLOCK, BOBBY DALE (RE) – (D-1977, FE-1980, R-2009)
Transferred from Oklahoma Conf 1985; Remus/Halls Corners/Mecosta 09/16/1985; Dansville/Vantown 05/16/1987; Caledonia 1990; Scottville 01/06/1996; Big Rapids: First 2004; Robbins 2008; Retired 2009; Wolf Lake (LTFT ½) 2011; Wolf Lake (LTFT 45%) 01/01/2014-9/1/2014
the.whitlocks81@yahoo.com
(H) 4512 S Quarterline Rd, Muskegon 49444-4245 (231) 457-4705

WHITTEMORE, INGE E (PL) – (PL-2016)
East Nelson (PTLP ½) 2016
ingeandray@aol.com
(H) 590 Wildview, Lowell 49331-9675 (616) 897-6525
East Nelson: 9024 18 Mile Rd NE, Cedar Springs 49319-9217 (616) 696-0661

Wichert, David Allen (Janet)   WichertDG@yahoo.com
[(FE) PE 2002; FE 2008]. 2002 Fairgrove, Gilford; 2006 Plymouth: First (assoc.); 2010 Seven Churches United Group Ministry: Gaines, Duffield; 2013 AuGres, Twining: Trinity [AuGres and Twining: Trinity merged in 2015 forming Arenac County: Christ]; **2019 Saginaw: Ames**. 801 State St., Saginaw 48602 (989-754-6373). Home: 1477 Vancouver, Saginaw 48638 (989-876-0148)

WICKS, JEREMY J (FL) (Toinette) – (PL-2011, FL-2013)
Dansville (DSA ¼ Time) 2011; Dansville (PTLP ¼) 11/13/2011; Dansville and Wheatfield (PTLP ½) 2012; M-52 Cooperative Ministry: Millville (½ Time) and Dansville (¼ Time) and Wheatfield 2013; M-52 Cooperative Ministry: Millville (½ Time) and Dansville (¼ Time) and New Church Start (¼ Time) 2014; Millville and New Church Start (FTLP) 01/01/2015-2017; Traverse City Mosaic (New Church Start) 2017

jeremy_wicks@yahoo.com
(H) PO Box 395, 449 N. Brownson St, Kingsley 49649 (517) 851-1494
TC: Mosaic: 1249 Three Mile Rd S, Traverse City 49696-8307 (231) 943-3048

WIELAND, RYAN B (FE) (Stacey MB) – (PE-2007, FE-2010)
Dowling: Country Chapel (LTFT ¾) 2011; Transferred from Iowa Conf 2013; Grandville 2016

grandvillepastor@gmail.com
(H) 2000 Frontier Ct. SW, Wyoming 49519-4926 (616) 258-2001
Grandville: 3140 Wilson Ave SW, Grandville 49418-1273 (616) 538-3070

WIERMAN, COLLEEN A (FL) (Brian) – (FL-2014)
Brethren: Epworth (PTLP ¼) 2011; Brethren: Epworth/Grant (PTLP ½) 11/27/2011; Grawn (PTLP ½) and Grant (PTLP ¼) Kingsley (Assoc) (PTLP ¼) 2014; Kingsley 2017

cawierman1964@gmail.com
(H) 8658 Hency Rd, Kingsley 49649-9736 (231) 263-4145
Kingsley: PO Box 395, 113 W Blair St, Kingsley 49649-0395 (231) 263-5278

*Wik, Carolyn S.   carolyn5@farmingtonfumc.org
[(RD) DM 2000; FD 2003]. 2000 Farmington: First (deacon); **2014 Retired**. Home: 32850 Ten Mile Rd., Farmington Hills 48336 (248-474-2032)

Wik, Lawrence Allen (Jenny)   larry.wik@lakeorionumc.org
[(FE) P 1993; F 1996]. Jul 1, 1994 Detroit: Ford Memorial; 1998 Canton: Cherry Hill; 2005 Manchester; **2012 Lake Orion**. 140 East Flint, Lake Orion 48362 (248-693-6201). Home: 3691 Hi Crest, Lake Orion 48360 (248-732-7739)

*Wiliford, Lawrence J. (Terry)   holytroubador@comcast.net
[(OR) Retired Elder Upper New York Conf., OR 2019]. **2019 Grass Lake (LTFT ¼)**. 449 E Michigan Ave., Grass Lake 49240-9501 (517-522-8040). Home: 4273 Indian Trl., Jackson 49201-9718 (585-409-3546)

*Wiliford, Terry S. (Lawrence)   pastorterryw@gmail.com
[(OR) Retired Elder Upper New York Conf., OR 2019]. **2019 Jackson: Calvary (LTFT ½)**. 925 Backus St., Jackson 49202 (517-782-0543). Home: 4273 Indian Trl., Jackson 49201-9718 (585-645-4554)

William, Monica pastor@westbloomfieldumc.org
[(FE) PE 2005; FE 2008]. 2004 Ashton, IL (Northern Illinois conference); 2009 Birmingham: First (assoc.) (LTFT ½); 2012 Northville: First (assoc) (LTFT ½); **2019 West Bloomfield**. 4100 Walnut Lake Rd., West Bloomfield 48323 (248-851-2330). Home: 5553 Fox Hunt Lane, West Bloomfield 48322 (248-851-0149)

Williams, Alicea Lynn (Chris) alwharpist30@yahoo.com
[(FD) PD 2006; FD 2010]. 2007 Flint: Court Street (deacon); Oct 1, 2007 Port Huron: First (deacon); Oct 25, 2007 family leave; 2016 transitional leave; **Dec 12, 2016 Mount Clemens: First (deacon)**. 57 S.B. Gratiot Ave., Mt. Clemens 48043 (586-468-6464). Home 21515 Bay Hills Rd., Macomb 48044 (586-746-4650)

WILLIAMS, BEVERLEY J (FL) (Harry) – (FL-2012)
Mesick/Harrietta (DSA) 2012; Mesick/Harrietta 11/10/2012; Mesick/Harrietta/Brethren: Epworth 12/01/2015; Climax/Scotts 2016

bvwllm526@gmail.com
(H) 331 Prairie Drive, Climax 49034-9789 (269) 438-1514
Climax: PO Box 125, 133 East Maple, Climax 49034-0125 (269) 746-4023
Scotts: PO Box 112, 8458 Wallene, Scotts 49088-0012 (269) 626-9757

WILLIAMS, CALEB B (FD) (Colleen) – (PD-2015, FD-2018)
Portage: Chapel Hill (Deacon) 2015; Royal Oak: First (Deacon, Minister of Music and Arts) Sept. 1, 2016

caleb.b.williams@gmail.com
(H) 24819 Rensselaer St, Oak Park 48237-1773 (231) 313-9005
Royal Oak: 320 W Seventh St, Royal Oak 48067-2511 (248) 541-4100

WILLIAMS, CHARLES A (FE) – (FD-1995, FE-2000)
Mesick/Harrietta 1992; Belding 02/15/1997; Quincy 01/01/1999; Alden/Central Lake 2003; Keswick 2010; Leave of Absence 2011; Appointed in Other Annual Conferences (¶331.8, ¶346.1) Detroit Conference, Houghton: Grace 2013; Houghton: Grace / Painesdale: Albert Paine Memorial 2019

pastor@houghtongraceumc.org
(H) 807 Oak Grove Pkwy, Houghton 49931-2708 (906) 482-1751
Houghton: Grace: 201 Isle Royale, Houghton 49931-1806 (906) 482-2780
Painesdale: Albert Paine Mem.: 54385 Iroquois, Painesdale 49955
(906) 482-1470

WILLIAMS, JEFFREY C (FE) (Beverly) – (D-1987, FE-1991)
Center Park 08/01/1989; UM Connectional Structures (¶344.1a,c) Director, WMC Wesley Foundation 02/16/1993; New Church Start/Rockford (Assoc) 2002; White Pines New Church Start 2004; White Pines and Courtland-Oakfield 2009; Hartford 2011; Wayland 2014

jeffwrev@gmail.com
(H) 220 Church St, Wayland 49348-1203 (269) 944-9231
Wayland: 200 Church St, Wayland 49348-1203 (269) 792-2208

PASTORAL RECORDS

WILLIAMS, JEREMY P H (FE) (Tamara) – (D-1996, FE-2001)
Arden 1995; Berrien Springs/Arden 1998; Traverse City: Asbury 2002; Traverse Bay 01/01/2005 (Asbury and Emmanuel merged 01/2005); Albion: First 2009; North Muskegon Community 2017

pastorjeremywilliams@gmail.com
(H) 2317 Marquard Ave, North Muskegon 49445-3228 (517) 554-1836
N Muskegon: 1614 Ruddiman Dr, N Muskegon 49445-3040 (231) 744-4491

Williams, Karen B. (H. Lawrence) pastorkaren5@comcast.net
[(FL) PL 2003; FI 2005]. 2003 Mt. Bethel; 2005 Flint: Lincoln Park; 2009 Waterford: Central (assoc.); **2010 Caring Covenant Group Ministry: Genesee, Thetford Center**. (G) 7190 N. Genesee Rd., Box 190, Genesee 48437 (810-640-2280), (TC) G-11394 N. Center Rd., Genesee 48437 (810-687-0190). Home: 7472 Roger Thomas Dr., Mt. Morris 48458 (810-640-3140)

*WILLIAMS, MYRON K (RE) (Maudy) – (D-1953, FE-1956, R-1994)
Ludington (EUB) 1956; Sodus/Chapel Hill (EUB) 1960; Vicksburg 1969; Holt 1972; Hastings: First 1982; Wyoming: Wesley Park 1985; Retired 1994

myronmaudy@hotmail.com
(H) 5430 E Arbor Ave, Mesa, AZ 85206-1416 (517) 896-4788
(S) 1743 S Stebbins Rd, White Cloud 49349-9301 (231) 689-1689

*WILLIAMS, NOLAN R (RA) (Sandra) – (D-1970, RA-2000)
Coral/Amble 1966; Stanwood/Higbe 1967; Stanwood: Northland 1971; Ionia: Zion/Easton 1974; Ithaca/Beebe 10/01/1980; Niles: Wesley 1991; Retired 01/01/2000

nolanraywilliams37@yahoo.com
(H) 4231 Embassy Dr SE, Grand Rapids 49546-2438 (616) 957-3222

WILLIAMS, RICHARD K (RE) (Susan) – (D-1969, FE-1972, HL-1976, FE-1977, R-2001)
Benton Harbor Peace Temple (Assoc) 1971; Constantine 04/01/1973; Honorable Location 1976; Galien/Olive Branch (Ad Interim) 02/01/1977; Wolf Lake 10/01/1979; Lansing: Trinity (Assoc) 11/01/1983; Hesperia/Ferry 1985; Leave of Absence 10/01/1997; Retired 2001

williric@verizon.net
(H) 332 Birch St, Fremont 49412-1308 (231) 854-3005

WILLIAMS, TAMARA S M (FE) (Jeremy) – (D-1987, FE-1990)
Transferred from Baltimore-Washington Conf 1993; Stevensville (Assoc) 1993; Traverse City: Central (Assoc) 2002; UM Connectional Structures (¶344.1a,c) District Superintendent, Albion District 2009; Medical Leave 2017

Pastortamara@hotmail.com
(H) 2317 Marquard Ave, Muskegon 49445-3228 (269) 967-7104

Williamson, Ronald Todd (FL) – (DSA-2016, FL-2017)
Salem: Indian Mission (DSA) (LTFT ½) 01/01/2016; Bradley: Indian Mission (DSA) (LTFT ½) 01/01/2016; Salem: Indian Mission / Bradley: Indian Mission (FL) 12/01/2017

retrtwilliamson@gmail.com
(H) 1146 Nicolson St., Wayland 49348 (616) 460-1918
Salem: Indian Mission: 3644 28th St, Hopkins 49328-9743 (616) 738-9030
Bradley: Indian Mission: 695 128th Ave, Shelbyville 49344-9500
(616) 738-9030

Willingham, Brian Kendall (Rhonda) pastorbkwillingham@gmail.com
[(PL) PL Dec 1, 2014] Dec 1, 2014 Flint: Charity, Dort Oak Park Neighborhood House; 2015 Flint Charity, Faith; 2018 Flint: Bristol (LTFT ¾); **May 1, 2019 Flint: Bristol (LTFT ½), Burton: Christ (LTFT ¼)**. (FB) G-5285 Van Slyke Rd., Flint 48507 (810-238-9244), (BC) 4428 Columbine Ave, Burton 48529-2160 (810-743-1770). Home: 1884 Springfield Street, Flint 48503 (810-513-1407)

*Willobee, Sondra Blanche (Edwin) sondrawillobee@gmail.com
[(RE) P 1979; F 1984]. 1982 Detroit: Whitefield-Grace; 1985 Detroit: Whitefield-Grace ((LTFT ½); Nov. 15, 1985 North Lake (LTFT ½); 1990 North Lake (LTFT ¾); 1991 Editorial Consultant, Ecumenical Theological Seminary; 1994 leave of absence. 1999 Farmington: First (assoc) (LTFT ½); 2007 South Lyon: First; **2017 Retired**. Home: 11553 McGregor Road, Pinckney 48169 (248-915-8364)

*Willson, Roberta randrwillson@charter.net
[(RL) PL 2008]. 2008 Iron River: Wesley; **2014 Retired**. Home: 203 W. Iron St., Bessemer 49911

Wilsey, Melene pastormelene@aol.com
[(FL) DSA 2015; FL 2017]. 2015 Saginaw: West Michigan Avenue (DSA); **2017 Saginaw: New Heart**. 1802 W. Michigan Ave., Saginaw 48602 (989-792-4689). Home: 1304 W. Stewart, Midland 48640 (989-839-4798)

WILSON, Janet S (FL) – (FL-2018)
Battle Creek: Chapel Hill (Assoc.) 01/01/2018
pastorjanet@thehillbc.com
(H) 20515 Bedford Rd N, Battle Creek 49017-8869 (269) 317-5591
Battle Creek: Chapel Hill: 157 Chapel Hill Dr, Battle Creek 49015
(269) 963-0231

*WILSON, MARGARET E HALLS (RE) – (D-1984, FE-1989, R-2009)
Alto/Bowne Center 1985; Niles: Portage Prairie 1989; Marshall (Assoc) 1994; Otsego 1998; Evart 2000; Grawn 2006; Retired 11/01/2009
megarev44@gmail.com
(H) 615 Bay Hill Drive Apt 5, Traverse City 49684-5642 (231) 743-0119

*WILSON, RICHARD D (RE) – (D-1963, FE-1967, R-2008)
Muskegon: Unity/Twin Lake 1965; Cadillac Selma Street/South Community 10/01/1966; Big Rapids Parish 11/01/1968; Howard City/Coral/Maple Hill 03/01/1971; Howard City First/Coral 1972; Lane Boulevard 1975; Muskegon Lakeside 1981; Buchanan: Faith/Morris Chapel 1987; Sodus: Chapel Hill 1996; Battle Creek Sonoma/Newton 2003; Retired 2008; Quincy (½ Time) 2017
PastorMan127@yahoo.com
(H) 548 East Dr, Marshall 49068-1363 (269) 781-4082
Quincy: 32 W Chicago St, Quincy 49082-1144 (517) 639-5035

*WINGEIER, DOUGLAS E (RE) – (D-1951, FE-1954, R-2000)
Transferred from Wisconsin Conf 2000; Retired 2000
dcwing@dnet.net
(H) 266 Merrimon Ave, Asheville, NC 28801-1218 (828) 456-3857

*Winslow, David Allen (Doribell)
[(RE) T 1965; F 1973]. 1969 All Saints Episcopal Church, Millington, NJ; 1970 Marble Collegiate, NY, NY; 1971 Trinity UMC, Jersey City, NJ; 1973 West Side UMC, Patterson, NJ; 1975 Chaplain School, 1st Marine Air Wing FMF Pac, Japan; 1976 Chaplain NTC, San Diego, CA; 1978 Chaplain, USS Worden, CG-18; 1980 Chaplain USS Reeves, CG-24; 1981 Chaplain, 1st Marine Division, FMF Pac; 1981 Chaplain, 3rd Marine Division, FMF Pac; 1982 Chaplain 1st Marine Division, FMF Pac; 1984 Chaplain Navy Station, Long Beach, CA; 1987 Chaplain, 3rd Marine Air Wing, FMF Pac; 1987 Chaplain, 11th Marine Expeditionary Unit FMF Pac; 1988 Chaplain, 3rd Marine Air Wing, El Toro, CA; 1991 Chaplain, USS Wichita AOR-1; 1993 Chaplain, USNS Mercy, TAH-19 and Navy Hospital, Oakland, CA; 1995 USN Retired; 1997 Chaplain and Board Member, Interfaith Ministries, San Jose, CA, San Jose International Airport and Disaster Service Consultant, Church World Service, 1997-2000; **2008 Retired**. Home: 3845 Pleasant Springs Dr., Naples, FL 34119 (408-784-2850)

Wojewski, Donald L.   donaldlouis51@yahoo.com
[(FL) FL Jan 1, 2005]. Dec 1, 2004; Memphis: First, Lamb; Jan 1, 2005 Omo: Zion. 2005 Rose City: Trinity, Churchill; Jan 1, 2008 Rose City: Trinity (LTFT ½); 2008 Rose City: Trinity, Glennie; 2011 Standish: Community, Saganing Indian Church; 2012 Jeddo, Buel; 2013 Avoca, Jeddo, Ruby; Dec 21, 2017 Jeddo, Avoca; **2018 Caseville**. 6490 Main St., Box 1027, Caseville 48725 (989-856-4009). Home: 6474 Main St., Box 1027, Caseville 48725 (989-856-2626)

WOLFGANG, DONALD W (FE) (Jacqueline) – (OE-2016, FE 2018)
Portage: Pathfinder 2016 (Transferred from S. Georgia Conf. 2018)
BroDon@PathfinderChurch.com
(H) 8731 Newhouse St, Portage 49024 (912) 674-8155
Pathfinder: 8740 S Westnedge Ave, Portage 49003-6232 (269) 327-6761

*Won, Chong Youb   pastorjoywon@yahoo.com
[(RE) P 1991; F 1995]. 1992 South Central Cooperative Ministry: Halsey, South Mundy; 1995 Warren: First (assoc); Sep 1, 1998 Lapeer: Trinity (assoc); 2002 Lincoln Park: First; 2005 Oak Grove; 2011 Algonac: Trinity, Marine City; 2012 Dearborn Heights: Stephens, Warren Valley; **Jan 1, 2015 Retired**. Home: 704 S. Brady St., #A, Dearborn 48124

Woo, Yong Choel   mrwoo19@gmail.com
[(FE) Korean Methodist, OF Feb 1,2009, PE 2012, FE 2014]. 2008 Troy: Korean (assoc.) (2012 Transferred to DAC); Jan 15, 2015 Madisonville: Korean (W OH); **2019 Kalkaska**. 2525 Beebe Rd., Kalkaska 49646-8008 (231-258-2820). Home: 2301 Shawn Rd., NW, Kalkaska 49646-9434 (231-258-5995)

*WOOD, GREGORY B (RE) (Beverly) – (D-1980, FE-1984, R-2015)
New Buffalo/Berrien County: Lakeside 02/01/1982; Lansing: Trinity (Assoc) 1985; Manistee 1990; Portage: First 1998; Retired 2015
gwood1950@gmail.com
(H) 1578 Rupal St, Kalamazoo 49009 (269) 365-5101

Woodford, Steven L. (Ann)   skypilot927@gmail.com
[(FE) P 1996; F 1998]. 1996 Reese; 2000 school; 2001 Chaplain, Spiritual Care Coordinator, Heartland Hospice (335.1); May 1, 2002 Vassar: First; [May 1, 2007 called to active duty chaplaincy]; **2008 Readjustment Counselor, Veterans Administration**. 4048 Bay Rd., Saginaw 48603 (989-321-4650). Home: 4658 N. Steel Rd., Hemlock 48626 (989-928-3845)

Woolley, Marsha Marie (Charles)   mwoolley@fumcnorthville.org
[(FE) P W. MI, 1984; F 1987]. 1985 Trans. to Detroit Conf., Ypsilanti: First
(assoc.); Nov. 1, 1991 Manchester; 1994 Ann Arbor: First (assoc); 2006 Livonia:
Newburg; **2013 Northville: First**. 777 W. 8 Mile Rd., Northville 48167 (248-349-
1144). Home: 20490 Lexington, Northville 48167 (734-349-1143)

*WOOLUM, DONALD (RL) – (FL-1997, RL-2003)
Mulliken / Sebewa Center 08/28/1997; Retired 2003
                              (H) 1104 Clark Rd, Lansing 48917-2154 (517) 649-8689

WORLEY, RONALD L (PL) (Shelly) – (PL-2004, FL-2014)
Crystal Valley/Walkerville (PTLP ½) 2004; LP w/o Appointment 12/01/2013;
Muskegon: Unity (PTLP ¼) 2014

                                          revronworley@gmail.com
(H) PO Box 254, 76 W Muskegon St NW, Kent City 49330-0254 (616) 485-4441
        Muskegon: Unity: 1600 N Getty St, Muskegon 49445-2618 (231) 744-1972

Woycik, Timothy S. (Chris Schwind)   pastortim1953@yahoo.com
[(FE) P NY 19 ; F 1986]. Sep. 1, 1983 Whitmore Lake: Wesley; 1993 Ortonville;
1998 Saginaw: State Street; 2003 AuGres, Twining: Trinity; **2012 Chesaning:
Trinity**. 1629 W. Brady, Chesaning 48616 (989-845-3157). Home: 1701 W.
Brady, Chesaning 48616 (989-845-2227)

WRIGHT, CHRISTINA L (FD) – (PD-2009, FD-2012)
Deacons Appointed w/in UM Connectional Structure (¶331.1b) Advance Direc-
tives Coordinator, Cleveland Clinic 06/07/2009; Clergy Appointed to Attend
School (¶326.1) University of West Georgia 08/01/2009; Deacons Appointed
w/in UM Connectional Structure (¶331.1b) University of West Georgia 2015;
Deacons Appointed Beyond the Local Church (¶331.1a) Chaplain, University of
Michigan Health Care Systems and Missional: Royal Oak 08/10/2015; Deacons
Appointed Beyond the Local Church (¶331.1a), Associate Director, Department
of Spiritual Care, Michigan Medicine, University of Michigan and Missional: Royal
Oak 02/01/2019

                                          cwright1223@gmail.com
                  (H) 45677 Spinning Wheel Dt, Canton 48187 (617) 875-6955
                  (O) 1138 Lariat Loop #104, Ann Arbor 48108 (734) 936-4041

*Wright, Robert Denecke (Jenneth)
[(RE) P 1982; F 1985]. 1983 Port Huron: First (assoc.); 1985 Marine City; Feb.
1, 1988 Bay City: Christ. 1992 Cheboygan: St. Paul's; 1994 Rochester: St. Paul's
(assoc); 1999 Grosse Pointe; 2008 Flint: Court Street; **2015 Retired**. 2016 Alto,
Bowne Center (LTFT ½); **Jan. 1, 2019 Bowne Center (LTFT ¼)**
                                          rdwcsumc@gmail.com
                  (H) 10187 Mulberry Dr, Middleville 49333 (269) 205-2609
        Bowne Center: 12051 84th St SE, Box 122, Alto 49302-9664 (616) 868-7306

WRIGHT, TIMOTHY B (FE) (Paula) – (PE-2005, FE-2008)
Horton Bay/Charlevoix: Greensky Hill 2005; Grand Rapids: Northlawn 2013;
Gladstone: Memorial 2018, Lakeview: New Life 2019
                                          wright.tim.b@gmail.com
        (H) 8544 Howard City Edmore Rd, Lakeview 48850-9115 (989) 352-6728
          New Life: 6584 W Howard City Edmore Rd, Six Lakes 48886-9755
                                                          (989) 352-7788

*Wright, William Robert (Dayna)　　　　　　　　justwright54@gmail.com
[(RE) P 1980; F 1983]. 1981 Lake Linden, Painesdale; Jan. 15, 1985 Birmingham: First (assoc.); 1990 Bad Axe: First; 2006 Sebewaing: Trinity; 2012 Port Huron: First; **2017 Retired**. Home: 6094 Jeddo Road, Jeddo 48032 (810-858-7033

*Wyatt, Christine Elizabeth (Robert)　　　　　　deaconchris1@fmail.com
[(RD) CON 1999; FD 2002]. 1993 Grand Blanc; Dec 1, 1999 Director: Skills on Wheels (LTFT ½);1999 Clarkston (deacon) (LTFT ½). 2004 Clarkston (deacon); **2015 Retired**. Home: 8181 Deerwood, Clarkston 48348 (248-625-5326)

Wylie-Kellermann, William A.　　　　　　　　　Bill@scupe.com
[(FE) P 1972; F 1980]. 1975 Greenway Non-Violent Community; 1979 Detroit: Waterman, Preston; 1981 Leave of Absence; Sep. 1, 1981 Detroit: Cass Community (LTFT ½); 1988 Whitaker School of Theology, Detroit; Sep 1, 1997 Director of M.Div Program, Seminary Consortium of Urban Pastoral Education (LTFT ¾); 2006 St. Peter's Episcopal, Detroit; **2017 Retired**. Home: 4691 Larkins, Detroit 48210 (313-841-7554)

Wyllys, Deane Brian (Nancy)　　　　　　　　dwyllys@sbcglobal.net
[(FE) P 1981; F 1985]. 1983 White Pine, Bergland, Ewen; Feb. 15, 1988 Marine City; 1992 Gladwin: First; Sep 2, 2002 family leave; 2004 Commerce; **2018 Owosso: First**. 1500 N. Water St., Owosso 48867 (989-725-2201). Home: 1415 N. Water St., Owosso 48867

Yoo, Joonshik　　　　　　　　　　　　　　joonys@gmail.com
[(PE) OE 2003 Korean Methodist Church; PE 2013]. May 1, 2003 Amen Korean. 2015 Korean Church of Dayton (¶346.1 W OH Conf.); **Aug. 1, 2019 Ann Arbor: Korean**. 1526 Franklin St, Ann Arbor 48103 (734-662-0660). Home: 1811 Avondale, Ann Arbor 48103

*YOUELLS, RICHARD A (RE) (Carol) – (D-1960, FE-1963, R-1995)
Silver Creek 1958; Bridgman 1963; UM Connectional Structures (¶344.1a,c) Director, CMU Wesley Foundation 1965; UM Connectional Structures (¶344.1a,c) Director, Flint Wesley Foundation 1969; Potterville/West Benton/ Dimondale 1970; South Haven: First 1974; Olivet 08/16/1979; Muskegon Heights: Temple 1989; Church of the Dunes (Assoc) 1991; Retired 1995

gryouells@gmail.com
(H) 740 Clark Crossing SE, Grand Rapids 49506-3309 (616) 243-3759

Youmans, Susan (Dennis)　　　　　　　　　smyoumans@gmail.com
[(FE) PE 2005; FE 2008]. 2005 Caring Covenant Group Ministry: Davison (assoc.); 2008 Farmington: Nardin Park (assoc.); 2012 Warren: First; **2018 Lexington**. 5597 Main St, Lexington 48450 (810-359-8215). Home: 7051 Greenbush Ln, Lexington 48050

YOUNG, MELANIE S (FE) – (D-1993, FE-1995)
Weidman 1993; Muskegon: Central (Assoc) 1994; Leave of Absence 1996; Grovenburg 1997; Quincy 1998; UM Connectional Structures (¶344.1a,c) Director, Wesley Foundation Ferris State University 10/01/1998; Burr Oak (LTFT ½) 2003; Clergy Appointed to Attend School 2006; Constantine 2007; Leave of Absence 2009; Pentwater: Centenary 2014; Oivd/Middlebury (LTFT ¾) 2018
msyoung14760@gmail.com
(H) 141 W Front St, Ovid 48866 (231) 301-2055
Ovid: 131 Front St, PO Box 7, Ovid 48866-0007 (989) 834-5958
Middlebury: 8100 W Hibbard Rd, PO Box 7, Ovid 48866-0007 (989) 834-2573

YOUNG, STEVEN R (FE) (Kathy) – (D-1982, FE-1985)
Turk Lake 1982; Muskegon Lakeside 1987; Sparta 1993; Ithaca/Beebe 2006; Coldwater 2010; Hart 2015
SYoung4152@aol.com
(H) 3818 Melody Lane, Hart 49420-9500 (231) 873-4766
Hart: 308 S State St, Hart 49420-1227 (231) 873-3516

*YOUNGS, DAVID L. (RL) (Doris) – (PL-1976, RL-2006)
Townline (LTFT PT) 03/14/1976; Bloomingdale (LTFT PT) 03/14/1976; Retired 2006; Breedsville (LTFT PT) 2007; Townline (LTFT PT) 01/03/2008-6/1/2008
(H) 1108 Barton St, Otsego 49078-1571 (269) 694-9125

Yum, Jung Eun (Somi Nam)   jeyum@hotmail.com
[(FE) FL Jan, 2006; PE 2007; FE 2010]. Jan 1, 2006 Troy: Korean (assoc.); Jan 2, 2011 MN Conf., Woodbury: Christ Korean; **2014 Midland: First (assoc)**. 315 W. Larkin St., Box 466, Midland 48640 (989-835-6797). Home: 1010 Pepperidge Ct., Midland 48640 (989-486-9307)

*ZAAGMAN, GAYLE S. (RL) (John) – (PL-2001, FL-2002, RL-2014)
Muskegon: Unity (DSA) (LTFT PT) 09/16/1999; Muskegon: Unity (LTFT PT) 02/01/2001; Reading 09/01/2001; Claybanks / Whitehall 2006; Retired 2014
booger99@chartermi.net
(H) 3662 Courtland Dr, Muskegon 49441 (231) 780-3119

*ZACHMAN, LEE F (RE) (Barbara) – (D-1974, FE-1981, R-2010)
Eaton Rapids: First (Assoc) 01/15/1977; North Adams/Jerome 1980; Martin/ Shelbyville 1984; Wyoming Park 04/16/1994; Middleville/Parmelee 1996; Parmelee (LTFT ½) 2004; Retired 12/01/2010
revleezachman@charter.net
(H) 3645 Lakeshore Dr, Shelbyville 49344-9732 (269) 397-1243

*Zeigler, Karl L. (Carmen)   zeigler.karl@yahoo.com
[(RE) T 1968; F 1970]. 1964 Wheatfield, Williamston Center; 1967 Columbus, OH: North Broadway (assoc.); 1968 Camden, Montgomery (W. MI Conf.); 1969 Price, Shepardsville (W. MI Conf.); 1970 Detroit: Christ (assoc.); 1972 Allen Park; 1975 Novi; 1979 Executive Director, United Methodist Foundation; Nov. 1, 1988 President, Bethany Methodist Foundation; Sep. 1, 1990 Leave of Absence; 1991 Richmond: First; Aug 1, 1998 Franklin Community; Nov 1, 2000 Goodrich; **2010 Retired**. Home: 33076 Mazara, Fraser 48026 (248-904-8816)

PASTORAL RECORDS

*Zender, Mark E.   revmarkzender@sbcglobal.net
[(RL) PL Jan 1, 2005; FL Jan 1, 2008; RL 2019]. Jan 1, 2005 Willow (LTFT ¾);
Jan 1, 2008 Willow; 2011 Canton: Cherry Hill, Denton: Faith; 2014 Britton: Grace;
2019 Retired. Home: 7962 Selph Rd, Hillsboro, OH 45133-7935 (313-690-7248)

Ziegler, Timothy R. (Lisa)   timothyiegler@gmail.com
[(FE) FL 2003; PE 2006; FE 2010]. 2003 Ann Arbor: First (assoc); 2009 Lexington; **2013 Ann Arbor: West Side**. 900 S. Seventh, Ann Arbor 48103 (734-663-
4164. Home: 3023 Appleridge, Ann Arbor 48103

*ZIENERT, ELLEN K (RE) – (PL-2005, PE-2010, FE-2013, R-2018)
Chapel Hill East Lansing (DSA) 2005; Chapel Hill East Lansing (Part-Time)
11/15/2005; East Lansing Chapel Hill (LTFT ¼) and Williamston: Crossroads
(LTFT ¼) 2010; St Johns: First 07/15/2012; St Johns: First (LTFT ¾) 01/01/2018;
Retired 2018

                                                  ekzienert@gmail.com
              (H) 13015 Cedar St, Charlevoix 49720 (517) 515-9500

Zimmerman, Teresa "Tina" J. (Greg)   tinajzimm@gmail.com
[(FD) PD 2010; FD 2014]. Jan 1, 2012 Manchester: First (deacon); Dec 4, 2017
Manchester: First (deacon), Interim Director of Spiritual Life Chelsea Retirement
Community; **2019 Associate Director of Spiritual Life Chelsea Retirement
Community, Manchester Missional Charge Conference** (Para 331.1a). 805
W. Middle St., Chelsea 48118 (734-433-1000). Home: 5450 Sharon Hollow, Man-
chester 48158 (734-417-3117)

Zimmerman, Thomas Harold (Julie)   lumcpastor@bex.net
[(FE) P 1986; F 1989]. 1987 Ironwood: Wesley, Wakefield; 1991 Royal Oak: First
(assoc.); 1997 Lambertville; **2016 Saline**. 1200 N. Ann Arbor St., Saline 48176
(734-429-4730). Home: 3020 Aspen Lane, Ann Arbor 48108 (419-262-5575)

Zundel, Jill Hardt (Gary)   RevDrJill@hotmail.com
[(FE) P 1991; F 1995]. 1992 Detroit: Zion; 1994 Hazel Park: First; 1999 Clarkston
(assoc); 2006 New Baltimore: Grace; **2014 Detroit: Central**. 23 E. Adams, Detroit 48226 (313-965-5422). Home: 2013 Hyde Park, #33, Detroit 48207
(313-393-8899)

— MAC Photos

CLERGY ON HONORABLE and
ADMINISTRATIVE LOCATION

This Pastoral Record indicates appointments, but is not necessarily a pension record. The date given following each appointment represents the initial year of that appointment, with changes occurring immediately following Annual Conference unless otherwise noted. The record is maintained by the Michigan Conference Ezra Database Specialist. Correspondence can be sent to pstewart@michiganumc.org

HL=Honorable Location
RHL=Retired Honorable Location
AL=Administrative Location

*Boyd, Gordon B.   Taccess4@yahoo.com
[(HLR) trans. from Independent Assemblies of God, 1978; F 1984; HL 2015; HLR 2016]. Aug., 1979 Lapeer: Trinity (assoc.); 1981 Carsonville, Applegate, Watertown; July 15, 1984 Owosso: Trinity; Oct., 15, 1987 Capac: First, Zion; 1991 Springville; Dec 1, 1992 LaPorte, Mapleton; Sep 1, 1994 North American Study Center; 1997 Counselor-Professor, Baker College, North American Study Center; Integrative Mental Health Center; 2015 Honorable Location; **2016 Honorable Location, Retired**
(H) 26110 Nagel, Roseville 48066 (586-774-8293)

*Brady, William Hugh
[(HLR) T 1961 NE OH, F 1963 NE OH; HL 1976]. 1959 Clarksfield; 1961 Vickery; Sep 1963 trans to Detroit Conf, Pontiac: Central (assoc.); 1966 Four Towns; 1967 Genesee; 1970 National Council of Alcoholism, Flint; 1974 Insight, Inc.; 1976 Honorable Location; **2012 Honorable Location, Retired**.

*Carruth, Hayden Kenna, Jr. (Sylvia)   carruth1973@att.net
[(HLR) P 1980; F 1983; HL 1992]. 1981 Decker, Elmer, Shabbona; Apr. 1982 Shabbona, Argyle, Decker; 1982 Owosso: First (Assoc.); 1984 Manchester; 1989 Hardy; Feb 15, 1992 Honorable Location; **2016 Honorable Location, Retired**
(H) 459 Dupont Ave., Ypsilanti 48197 (734-434-4072)

*Clapp, Jon Marvin (Karen)   jkclapp@hotmail.com
[(HLR) T 1961, F 1964; HL 1981; HLR 2002]. 1962 Farmington Hills: Nardin Park (assoc.); 1965 Detroit: Lola Valley; 1972 Counselor, Macomb County Drug Council; 1973 Case Worker, Oakland County Juvenile Court; 1981 Honorable Location; **2002 Honorable Location, Retired**
(H) 2344 Eaton Gate Rd., Lake Orion 48360 (248-391-0391)

*Crossman, Thomas A. (RHL) – (FL-1980, FD-1983, FE-1986, HL-1991, RHL-2016)
Leaton 08/16/1980; Mt Pleasant: First (Assoc) 08/01/1981; Leave of Absence 06/30/1986; Honorable Location 1991; **Honorable Location, Retired 2016**
t_crossman@verizon.net
(H) 687 W 204th Street #6J, New York NY, 10034-1290 (212) 567-0437

*Dempsey, Bruce W. (RHL) (Anne) – (D-1979, FE-1983, HL-1993, RHL-2018)
Edwardsburg: Hope 1981; Wolf Lake 11/01/1983; Leave of Absence 11/01/1988; Honorable Location 1993; Wolf Lake (Ad Interim) 09/01/2017-07/01/2018; **Honorable Location, Retired 2018**

bwdempsey90@gmail.com
(H) 3950 Westbrook Dr, Muskegon MI, 49444-4165 (616) 847-5145

*Draggoo, David L. (RHL) – (D-1962, FE-1966, HL-1986, RHL-2009)
Morris Chapel 1962; Sturgis (Assoc) 11/01/1964; Burr Oak 1967; Shaftsburg 1971; Perry 1971; Personal Leave 1981; Honorable Location 1986; **Honorable Location, Retired 2009**

dldraggoo@wowway.com
(H) 9637 Jason Rd, Laingsburg, MI, 48848-9282 (517) 651-6846

Easlick, Robert James (LuAnn)   bob.easlick@hotmail.com
[(HL) P 1986; F 1989; HL Sep 1, 2004]. 1987 Calumet, Mohawk-Ahmeek; 1990 Laingsburg, Middlebury; 1993 Whitmore Lake: Wesley; 2001 incapacity leave; 2002 Blissfield: Emmanuel; **Sep 1, 2004 Honorable Location**
(H) 701 Tickner, Linden 48451 (810-397-1376)

*Elliott, James Kyle
[(HLR) T 1959, F 1962; HL 1964]. 1954 Highland Park: Trinity (assoc.); 1957 Rochester (assoc.); 1961 Ortonville; 1963 supernumerary; 1964 Honorable Location; **2012 Honorable Location, Retired**
(H) Rocky Ridge Retirement Center, 3517 Lorna Rd., #3, Hoover, AL 35216
(205-989-9230)

*Ellis, Ronald Fred   ellis4445@gmail.com
[(HLR)]. 1971 Honorable Location; **2012 Honorable Location, Retired**
(H) 2516 Middlebridge Lane, Charlotte, NC 28270 (980-819-5824)

*Ford, Harold G.
[(HLR) T 1965 N IN, F 1967 N IN; HL 1974]. 1965 Warsaw: First (assoc.); 1967 trans to Detroit Conf, Franklin (assoc.); 1969 Detroit: Greenfield; 1974 Honorable Location; **2013 Honorable Location, Retired**
(H) 6855 Dublin Fair, Troy 48098 (248-813-0347)

Frost, Mary Elizabeth Isaacs   jib73@aol.com
[(HL) P 1976, F 1980; HL 1989]. 1978 Grosse Pointe (assoc.); 1980 Gaines; Oct, 1982 Midland: First (assoc.); 1986 leave of absence; **1989 Honorable Location**
(H) 827 Guthrie Ct. Winter Park, FL 32792 (407-227-7601)

*Hainer, C. David (RHL) (Rhonda) – (D-1981, FE-1985, HL-1996)
Bainbridge Newhope 1983; Scottdale 1983; Belding 11/01/1983; Kent City: Chapel Hill 10/01/1988; Leave of Absence 03/01/1991; Honorable Location 1996; **Honorable Location, Retired 2019**

david.hainer@yahoo.com
(H) 163 Southmoor Shrs, Saint Marys, OH 45885 (616) 706-4496

Hall, Melvin Foster   mhall520@comcast.net
[(HL) P N IN, F 1981; HL 1986]. 1979 trans to Detroit Conf, Detroit: Cass Avenue; 1984 leave of absence; **1986 Honorable Location**
(H) 1302 Honan Dr, South Bend, IN 46014 (574-532-4935)

*Herndon, Leon William
[(HLR) P 19 , IA; F 19]. 1998 Oak Park: Faith (1999 trans to Detroit); Apr 1, 2004 incapacity leave; 2010 Honorable Location; **2012 Honorable Location, Retired**
(H) 18501 Cherrylawn, Detroit 48221 (313-861-2733)

Hill, Valerie Marie (AL) – (D-1979, FE-1983, AL-1999)
Hinchman 1981; Oronoko 1981; Bear Lake 03/01/1983; Arcadia 03/01/1983; Osseo 1985; Frontier 1985; Comstock 1989; Leave of Absence 1991; Lee Center 1996; Springport 1996; Ashton 1998; Leroy 1998; **Administrative Location 1999**
(H) 1527 West State St. #108, Belding MI, 48809-9267 (616) 808-6100

*Howard, Mary Evelynn   bdiggs@earthlink.net
[(HLR) P 1971, F 1974; HL 1978; HLR 2010]. 1973 Mt. Clemens: First (assoc.); 1974 New Haven: Meade; 1976 Detroit: Waterman, Simpson; 1977 Detroit: Woodmere, Simpson; 1978 Honorable Location; **2010 Honorable Location, Retired**
(H) PO 452541, Garland, TX 75044 (972-530–0197)

*Long, Michael E. (RHL) (Jean) – (PE-1983, FE-1986, HL-1998, RHL-2018)
Rosebush (Rosebush 3/4 Time And Clare 1/4 Time 7/1/84) (LTFT 3/4) 1984; Clare (Assoc) (LTFT 1/4) 1984; Rosebush 1990; Appointed In Other Annual Conferences (¶331.8, ¶346.1) Detroit Conference, Geneva Hope 1990; Grawn 1992; Somerset Center 1996; Honorable Location 1998; **Honorable Location, Retired 2018**
PastorMikeLong@gmail.com
(H) 1303 6th St, Muskegon MI, 49441-1932 (231) 645-9584

*MacArthur, Terry L. (RHL) – (PE-1974, FE-1977, HL-6/15/1985, RHL-2018)
Appointed In Other Annual Conferences (¶331.8, ¶346.1) In School, Sparta/Bloomfield, OH 1974; St Johns: Salem 1976; Lowe 1976; Greenbush 1976; Three Oaks 10/16/1979; Leave of Absence 1984; Honorable Location 06/15/1985; **Honorable Location, Retired 2018**
tmacarthur@bluewin.ch
(H) 17 Chemin Taverney, CH-1218 Grand Saconnex, Switzerland

McKinven-Copus, Clinton E. (HL) (Laurie) – (D-1984, FE-1987, HL-2007)
South Boardman 1985; East Boardman 1985; Fife Lake 1985; West Mendon 1987; Leslie 1990; Felt Plains 1990; Leave of Absence 09/16/1991; Perry 02/01/1992; Shaftsburg 02/01/1992; Olivet 01/01/1995; Other Valid Ministries (¶344.1D) Executive Director Secom Ministries (¶335.1D) 01/01/2001; Leave of Absence 02/15/2005; **Honorable Location 2007**
clintone@outlook.com
(H) 5480 S Lakeshore Dr, Ludington MI, 49431-9751 (231) 723-6201

*McKinven-Copus, Laurie J. (RHL) (Clinton) – (D-1984, FE-1987, HL-2005, RHL-2013)
Manton 1985; Nottawa (LTFT PT) 1987; Leonidas 1987; Pleasant Lake 1990; Munith 1990; Personal Leave 09/16/1991; Other Valid Ministries (¶344.1D) United Methodist Community House, Church & Community Liaison 1996; Honorable Location 04/02/2005; **Honorable Location, Retired 2013**
office@ludingtonumc.org
(H) 5480 S Lakeshore Dr, Ludington MI, 49431-9751 (231) 845-9414

*McNary, Charles D. (RHL) (Sandra Hoffman McNary)
(D-1965, FE-1968, HL-1977, RHL-1995)
Winn 1961; Coomer 1961; Millbrook 1961; Casnovia 1964; Kent City: Chapel Hill 1964; Kent City: Chapel Hill 1967; Bangor: Simpson 1970; Honorable Location 1977; **Honorable Location, Retired 1995;** Morris Chapel (DSA) 2002-2003
charlesdmcnary@live.com
(H) 32054 County Road 687, Bangor MI, 49013-9476 (269) 427-0766

*Meredith, Thurlan E. (RHL) – (D-1966, FE-1969, HL-1993, RHL-2008)
Gladwin Parish 01/01/1960; Courtland-Oakfield 11/01/1963; Martin 1970; Shelbyville 1970; Grand Rapids: Northlawn 1976; Lake Odessa: Central 1984; Medical Leave 1986; Personal Leave 1988; Honorable Location 1993; Lowell: Snow (Ad Interim) 1995; **Honorable Location, Retired 2008**
temric@peoplepc.com
(H) 541 Alles Dr SW, Byron Center, MI 49315-8654 (616) 785-8494

*Myers, Allen C. (RHL) (Janice) – (FE-1970, HL-1980, RHL-2016)
Honorable Location 1980; **Honorable Location, Retired 2016**
amyers@eerdmans.com
(H) 2011 Orville St, SE, Grand Rapids MI, 49506-4535 (616) 452-5339

*Otter II, Louis Ernest
[(HLR) T 1961 NE OH, F 1963; HL 1971; HLR 1994]. 1961 North Canton; 1962 Pavonia; 1963 trans to Detroit Conf., Kochville; 1968 Plymouth: St. Luke's; 1971 Honorable Location; **1994 Honorable Location, Retired**
(H) 14735 Richfield, Livonia 48154 (734-464-3319)

*Otto, Edward F. (RHL) (Nancy) – (PE-1968, FE-1970, HL-1978, RHL-2012)
Gunnisonville (Transferred From Wisconsin Conference 1969) 1969; Chapel Hill East Lansing 1969; Wacousta Community 12/15/1971; Honorable Location 10/01/1978; **Honorable Location, Retired 2012**
ted@tedottogroup.com
(H) 1335 S Prairie Ave Unit #405, Chicago IL, 60605-3121 (312) 945-3966

*Porter, Robert Lewis
[(HLR) P 1969, F 1972; HL 1980; HLR 2003]. 1971 AuGres, Prescott, Turner, Twining; 1973 Britton: Grace, Wellsville; 1976 Dearborn: First (assoc.); 1978 Munising, Trenary; 1980 Honorable Location; **2003 Honorable Location, Retired**
(H) 2345 Oxford, Apt 229, Berkley 48072 (248-548-4016)

Rafferty, Brian F. (HL) (Andrea) – (D-1993, FE-1995, HL-2016)
Burr Oak 1991; Grant 1993; Kingsley 1993; Church of The Dunes (Assoc) West Olive Area New Church Start 1999; New Foundation 2002; Cedar Springs / East Nelson 2003; Cedar Springs 2004; Williamston: Crossroads 2008; Family Leave 2010; **Honorable Location 2016**
brian.f.rafferty@gmail.com
(H) 244 Church Hill Downs Blvd, Williamston MI, 48895-9053 (517) 648-8747

*Rahn, David Philip revdavefwd@yahoo.com
[(HLR) P 1978; F 1980; HL 1988] 1978 Monroe: St. Paul (assoc); 1980 Halsey, Mt. Bethel; 1987 Caring Covenant Group Ministry: Genesee, Theford Center; 1988 honorable location; 2001 Caring Covenant Group Ministry: Fostoria, West Deerfield; **Oct 10, 2007 Honorable Location, Retired**
(H) 425 Old Bridge, Grand Blanc 48439 (810-694-2725)

Rawson, Rodney E. rerawson@aol.com
[(HL) P 1971, F 1974; HL 1979]. 1973, Riley Center, Berville, West Berlin; 1976 River Rouge: Epworth; **1979 Honorable Location**
(H) 3615 Gillia Circle E., Bartlett, TN 38135 (901-373-3785)

Schark, Donald Christian (Rhonda) dschark@new.rr.com
[(HL) LP 1979;P 1983;F 1986 HL 1995]. 1978-82 Whittemore, Prescott, Maple Ridge Presbyterian; 1984 Azalia, London; 1986 Menominee; Nov. 15, 1991 Leave of Absence; **1995 Honorable Location**
(H) 800 11th Ave., Menominee 49858 (906-864-3502)

*Scheibner, Paul K. (RHL) (Elaine) – (D-1959, FE-1963, HL-1983, RHL-1993)
Girard 1959; In School 1960; Concord 1962; Martin 1965; Shelbyville 1965; Dansville 1970; Vantown 1970; Gunnisonville 1974; Chapel Hill East Lansing 1974; Personal Leave 1978; Honorable Location 1983; **Honorable Location, Retired 1993**
paul_scheibner@yahoo.com
(H) 631 Nixon Blvd, Roscommon, MI, 48653-8760 (989) 821-9723

*Silvernail, Carl G. cgsil@centurytel.net
[(HLR) HL 1969; HLR 1994]. 1969 Honorable Location; **1994 Honorable Location, Retired**
(H) 6910 E. Sanilac Rd., Kingston 49741

*Silvis, Donald Roy
[(HLR) P 1964 MI; F 1966 MI; HL 1972; HLR 1996]. 1964 Marcellues Circuit; 1967 Boyne City; 1969 Snover: Moore, Trinity; 1972 Honorable Location; **1996 Honorable Location, Retired**
(H) 230 N. Jefferson, Lowell 49331

*Small, David E. (RHL) (Elaine Lewis-Small) – (D-1982, FE-1985, HL-1999, RHL-2012)
Brandywine Trinity (Niles Trinity Re-Named Brandywine Trinity 1982) 1981; Appointed In Other Annual Conferences (¶331.8, ¶346.1) Northern New Jersey Conf., Morristown Umc (¶425.1); In School, Drew University 1988; Appointed In Other Annual Conferences (¶331.8, ¶346.1) Northern New Jersey Conf: Anderson And Asbury Umcs (¶337.1) 1998; Honorable Location 1999; Appointed In Other Annual Conferences (¶331.8, ¶346.1) Pacific Northwest Conf: Nooksack Valley, Everson, Wa (Ad Interim) 2008; **Honorable Location, Retired 2012**; Paw Paw (Ad Interim) 2016
desmall62@gmail.com
(H) 52333 Ackley Terrace, Paw Paw MI, 49079 (269) 657-7727

*Steele, Philip P. (RHL) – (D-1964, FE-1968, HL-1971, RHL-2006)
Schoolcraft 1961; Sitka 1964; Wolf Lake 1964; Other Valid Ministries (¶344.1D)
Cooper UCC 1965; Portage: Pathfinder (Assoc) 05/03/1966; Coopersville
03/01/1968; Battle Creek: Birchwood 1970; Honorable Location 1971;
Honorable Location, Retired 2006; Lane Boulevard (DSA) 10/08/2006-
1/1/2007

bro.philip.osl2@verizon.net
(H) 5768 Comstock Ave, Kalamazoo MI, 49048-3414 (269) 668-3973

*Strawn, Charles Edward   cstrawn@etrusca.net
[(HLR) T 1964;F 19 ; HL 1979]. 1964 Kingston, Deford; 1966 Flint: Bristol; 1969
Detroit: Bethany; 1979 Honorable Location; **2012 Honorable Location, Retired**
(H) Amsterdam, The Netherlands

*Tallman, Ronald William   ron@denvercounselor.com
[(HLR) T 1966; F 1969; HL 1981; HLR 2005]. 1968 Pontiac: Central (assoc.);
1971 Saginaw: Epworth; 1974 Detroit: St. Andrew's; 1981 Honorable Location;
2005 Honorable Location, Retired
(H) 2914 S. Scranton S. Aurora, CO 80014 (303-369-8877)

Tuthill, Timothy J. (HL) (Susan) – (D-1998, FE-2001, HL-2017)
Mason: First 1993; MSU Wesley Foundation 2006; Clark Retirement
Community, Chaplain, Director of Pastoral Care 2010; Clark Retirement
Community, Director of Life Enrichment 2013; Clark Retirement Community,
Director of Resident Services 2015; Christian Living Services, Manager of Care
Resources 2016; **Honorable Location, Director of Congregational Care at
GR First 2017**

tim.tuthill@gmail.com
(H) 2139 Glen Echo Dr SE, Grand Rapids, MI, 49545 (517) 449-4965
(O) 227 Fulton St E, Grand Rapids, MI 49503-3236 (616) 452-1568

*Vermeulen, Bertram W. (RHL) – (D-1958, FE-1962, HL-1984, RHL-1998)
Bloomingdale 1954; Three Rivers: Ninth Street 1957; Litchfield 1961; Lansing:
Mount Hope (Assoc) 1965; Dewitt: Redeemer 1967; Fremont 10/15/1969;
Leave of Absence 01/01/1979; Honorable Location 1984; **Honorable Location,
Retired 1998**

bvermeulen0910@sbcglobal.net
(H) 4715 Trillium Spring Blvd Apt 112, Fremont, MI 49412-8622 (231) 335-2171

*Versteeg, George William   georgeversteeg@aol.com
[(HLR) T 1960, F 1963; HL 1976]. 1960 school; 1962 Lambertville; 1966 Plymouth: St. Luke's; 1968 Flint: Burton; 1971 University of Detroit; 1976 Honorable Location; **2012 Honorable Location, Retired**
(H) 11460 Wells Rd., Petersburg 49270 (734-854-1928)

*Vostry, Robert Melvin   Mel_Vostry@yahoo.com
[(HLR) P 1974; F 1979; HL 1991]. 1975 school; Aug, 1975 General Board of
Ministries: Alaska Pipeline Chaplaincy; Oct, 1976 school; 1977 Board of Global
Ministries, Alaska National Division; 1981 leave of absence; Feb 1982 Board
of Global Ministries, Alaska Missionary Conference, Ketchikan; 1986 leave of
absence; 1991 Honorable Location; **2018 Honorable Location, Retired**
(H) PO Box 523, Palmer, AK 99645 (907-715-4631)

*Warren, Harvard James
[(HLR) T 1966, F 1964; HL 1972; HLR 1994]. 1966 Imlay City, Attica; 1972 Honorable Location; **1994 Honorable Location, Retired**
(H) 1801 SE 24th Rd, Apt 119, Ocala, FL 34471-6065 (941-747-8948)

*Whited, Harold Vaughn
[(HLR) T IN 1949, F 1951; HL 1964; HLR 1985]. 1947 Cratherville; 1948 Fairview; 1950 trans to Detroit Conference, Clinton; 1956 school; Feb 1, 1957 Ann Arbor: West Side; Sep 1, 1963 sabbatical; 1964 Honorable Location; **1985 Honorable Location, Retired**
(H) 524 SE 14th Ct., Gresham, OR 97080

*Whiting, Lawrence C.
[(HLR) P 1971; F 1973; HL 1981; HLR 1994]. 1972 Sutton; 1976 Otisville, West Forest, Otter Lake; 1977 school, Marquette University; 1981 Honorable Location; **1994 Honorable Location, Retired**
(H) 723 Creekwood Circle, Vassar 48768 (989-823-8677)

*Wightman, Galen Edward   1orin@verizon.net
[(HLR) T 1961, F 1964; HLR 1970]. 1961 Charlestown, Educational Assistant (W VA); 1962 Wolfstown, (PA Conf.); 1964 Munith; 1967 West Bloomfield; **1970 Honorable Location, Retired**
(H) 6005 Brookland Rd., Alexandria, VA 22310 (703-921-9447)

Wisdom-Long, Michelle M. (HL) (Richard Long) – (D-1996, FE-1998, HL-2011) Kalamazoo: First (Assoc) 11/20/1998; Family Leave 2000; Pleasant Valley (LTFT 1/4) 2001; Pleasant Valley (LTFT 1/2) 01/01/2007; Leave of Absence 2008; Kalamazoo: First (Assoc) (LTFT 1/2) 2010; **Honorable Location 2011**
Revshelly@hotmail.com
(H) 6071 Thunder Bluff Rd, Kalamazoo MI, 49009-9127 (269) 808-0279

*Woodside, Kenneth B.   drkwoodsideforum@aol.com
[(HLR) T 1966 NE; F 1968 NE; HL 1991]. 1968 trans to Detroit Conf., Detroit: Christ (assoc.); 1970 Highland Park: Trinity; Nov, 1976 Detroit Industrial Mission; 1978 leave of absence; 1991 Honorable Location; **2012 Honorable Location, Retired**
(H) 6632 Telegraph, # 344, Bloomfield Hills 48301 (248-645-9898)

*Yordy, David   david@yordy.net
[(HLR) T 1964 Rock River, F 1968; HL 1970; HLR 1994]. Trans to Detroit Conf, Wesley Foundation, Flint; 1969 Director, Wesley Foundation, Northern Michigan University; 1970 Honorable Location; **1994 Honorable Location, Retired**
(H) 1257 Grace Dr., Sycamore, IL 60178 (815-991-9313)

DSA SERVICE RECORD

This DSA Service Record indicates assignments by District Superintendents to serve on a weekly basis. The date given following each assignment represents the initial year of that assignment, with changes occurring immediately following Annual Conference unless otherwise noted. The record is maintained by the Michigan Conference Database Manager. Correspondence can be sent to pstewart@michiganumc.org.

DSA = District Superintendent Assignment

Bailey, Connor James (DSA) – (DSA-2019)
Battle Creek: Newton (DSA) (LTFT 1/4) 2019

connor.j.bailey12@gmail.com
(H) 3727 Greenleaf Cir Apt 211, Kalamazoo 49008 (269) 312-3153
Battle Creek: Newton: 8804 F Drive South, Ceresco 49033 (269) 979-2779

Beasley, Donald (DSA) – (DSA-2016)
Detroit: Ford Memorial (DSA) (LTFT 1/4) 2016

revdonaldjbeasley@yahoo.com
(H) 13969 Fielding Street, Detroit 48223 313 475-3411
Detroit: Ford Memorial: 16400 W Warren Ave, Detroit 48228-3705 (313) 584-0035

Brooks, Mary D (DSA) – (DSA-2013)
Paradise/Hulbert: Tahqamenon (DSA) (LTFT 1/2) 2013

marybrooks729@gmail.com
(H) 207 W Ave. B, Newberry 49868 906) 293-1966
Paradise: 7087 N M123, PO Box 193, Paradise 49768-0193 (906) 492-3585
Hulbert: Tahquamenon: 10505 Maple St, PO Box 91, Hulbert 49748-0091

Corey, Cynthia (DSA) – (DSA-2018)
Bear Lake (DSA) (LTFT 1/4) 11/18/2018

pastorcynthia2019@gmail.com
(H) 8340 Zosel St, PO Box 645, Onekama 49675-0645 (231) 645-1244
Bear Lake: 7861 Main St, PO Box 157, Bear Lake 49614 (231) 864-3680

Cousino, Mickey Ann (DSA) – (DSA-2015, CLM-2015)
Hastings: Welcome Corners (CLM/DSA) (LTFT 1/4) 2015; Nashville: Peace (CLM/DSA) (LTFT 1/4) 09/01/2015-12/31/2017; Freeport (CLM/DSA) (LTFT 1/4) 09/01/2015

macousino1@gmail.com
(H) 1713 W Sisson Rd, Hastings 49058-9534 (616) 765-5322
Hastings: Welcome Corners: 3185 N. M43 Hwy, Hastings 49058 (517) 852-1993

Cramer, Julia Ann (DSA) – (DSA-2019)
Yale/Cole/Melvin (assoc) (DSA) (LTFT 1/4) 2019

cramerjuliann@gmail.com
(H) 7656 Melvin Rd, Melvin 48454 (810) 304-2310
Yale: 2 South Main St, Yale 48097-3316 (810) 387-3962
Cole: 7015 Carson Rd, Yale 48097 (810) 387-4400
Melvin: 1171 Main St, Melvin 48454-9775 (810) 376-4581

Davis, Morgan William "Bill" (DSA) – (DSA-2019)
Big Rapids: Third Avenue/Paris/Rodney (DSA) (LTFT 3/4) 2019
wg1billd@gmail.com
(H) 1764 Kettle Lake Rd, Kalkaska 49646 (231)384-0040
Big Rapids: Third Avenue: 226 N Third Ave, Big Rapids 49307 (231) 796-4157
Paris: 109 Lincoln, Paris 49338 (231) 796-4157
Rodney: PO Box 14, 12135 Charles St, Rodney 49342 (231) 796-4157

Francis, Raymond (DSA) – (DSA-2016, CLM-2016)
Coomer / Winn (CLM/DSA) (LTFT 1/4) 2016
drrayfrancis@yahoo.com
(H) 812 W. Center St, Alma 48801-2140 (989) 330-9135
Coomer: 5410 S. Vandecar Rd, Mt. Pleasant 48858-9551 (989) 866-2566

Gillings, Gary (DSA) – (DSA-2019)
Whittemore (DSA) (LTFT 1/4) 07/01/2019
gary338@centurytel.net
(H) 205 W State St, Whittemore 48770 (989) 756-3981
Whittemore: Box 155, 110 North St., Whittemore 48770 (989) 756-2831

Glygoroff, Steffani (DSA) – (DSA-2019)
Henderson/Chapin/Owosso: Trinity (DSA) (LTFT 3/4) 07/01/2019
trinhendchapumc.gmail.com
(H) 302 E Main St, Henderson 48841 (248) 805-3597
Henderson: 218 E. Main, Henderson 48841 (989) 723-5729
Chapin: 19848 S. Chapin Rd., Elsie 48831 (989) 661-2497
Owosso: Trinity: 720 S. Shiawassee St., Owosso 48867 (989) 723-2664

Henderson, Merry (DSA) – (DSA-2019)
Bentley (DSA) (LTFT 1/4) 01/01/2019
merryyankee@aol.com
(H) 10601 Carr Rd, St Charles 48655-8623 (989) 447-1874
Bentley: 7209 Main St, Bentley 48613, PO Box 1, Rhodes 48652-0001

Hofmann, Mary Wava (DSA) – (DSA-2019)
Northport Indian Mission (DSA) (LTFT 1/2) 4/1/2019
mwavahofmann@gmail.com
(H) 4840 E. Golfview Dr, Leland 49654 (231) 994-2159
Northport: PO Box 401, 8626 N Manitou Trl, Northport 49670 (231) 715-1280

Horn, Ashlei Kristin (DSA) – (DSA-2018)
Bridgman: Faith (DSA) (LTFT 1/4) 10/28/2018
AshleiUMC@yahoo.com
(H) 29680 County Road 687, Bangor 49013-9664 (269) 364-8545
Faith: 9156 Red Arrow Hwy, PO Box 414, Bridgman 49106 (269) 465-3696

Kasper, Anika (DSA) – (DSA-2019)
Mesick/Brethren Epworth (DSA) (LTFT 1/4) 7/14/2019
anikakasper@gmail.com
(H) 3851 N 15 Rd, Mesick 49668 (231) 885-1179
Mesick: PO Box 337, 121 S Alvin St, Mesick 49668 (231) 885-1699
Brethren Epworth: PO Box 177, 3939 High Bridge Rd, Brethren 49619
(231) 477-5486

Korlapati, Arthur D (DSA) – (DSA-2018)
Denton: Faith (DSA) (LTFT 1/4) 2018

davidk@friendshipchurchinfo.com
(H) 7338 Talbot Dr, Apt 102, Lansing 48917 (248) 444-6529
Denton: Faith: 6020 Denton Rd, Belleville 48111-1013 (734) 483-2276

LaGuire, Sean (DSA) – (DSA-2019)
Waterford: Four Town (DSA) (LTFT 1/4) 2019

smith3325@live.com
(H) 11318 Sioux, Redford 48239-2372 (313) 926-2498
Waterford: Four Towns: 6451 Cooley Lake Rd, Waterford 48327 (248) 682-0211

Lawrence, Devin T. (DSA) – (DSA-2019)
God's Country Cooperative Parish: Grand Marais, Germfask, McMillian (DSA) 2019

heydevin@hotmail.com
(H) 719 Garden Ave, Manistique 49854 (906) 202-3231
Grand Marais: N 14226 M-77, PO Box 268, Grand Marais 49839 (906) 494-2751
Germfask: 1212 Morrison St, PO Box 135, Germfask 49836 (906) 586-3162
McMillian: 7406 Co Rd 415, PO Box 54, McMillan 49853 (906) 293-8933

Miller, Alexander (DSA) (Sandy) – (DSA-2003)
Nottawa (DSA) (LTFT 1/4) 2003

umcnottawa1893@gmail.com
(H) 61616 Filmore Rd, Sturgis 49091-9318 (269) 467-7134
Nottawa: PO Box 27, 25838 M-86, Nottawa 49075 (269) 467-7134

Molloy, Larry (DSA) – (DSA-2019)
Mohawk Ahmeek (DSA) (LTFT 1/4) 2019

pastormolloy@gmail.com
(H) 226 Fourth St, Eagle Harbor 49950 (906)284-4221
Mohawk Ahmeek: 120 Stanton Ave, PO Box 76, Mohawk 49950 (906) 337-2710

Mullikin, Keith Paul (DSA) – (DSA-2019)
Ironwood: Wesley (DSA) (LTFT 1/4) 10/01/2018; Ironwood: Wesley/Wakefield (DSA) (LTFT 1/2)

mullik81@gmail.com
(H) 600 Garvey, Ironwood 49938 (906) 285-9847
Ironwood: Wesley: 500 E McLeod Ave, PO Box 9, Ironwood 49938 (906) 932-3900
Wakefield: 706 Putnam St, Wakefield 49968-1048 (906) 988-2533

Newman, Carol A (DSA) (Budd) – (PL-1995, FL-1996, DSA-2012)
Almena (Assoc) 1995; Lawton: St Paul's (Assoc) 1995; Almena (Assoc) 11/16/1995; Lawton: St Paul's (Assoc) 11/16/1995; Kalamazoo: Northwest 1996-2000; Almena 1996-2002; Bloomingdale (DSA) (LTFT 1/4) 09/23/2012

revcnewman@gmail.com
(H) 602 W Van Buren St Apt 24, Gobles, MI 49055 (269) 628-2414
Bloomingdale: PO Box 9, Bloomingdale 49026 (269) 521-3323

Obwoge, Douglas Mochama (DSA) – (DSA-2019)
Brooks Corners (DSA) (LTFT ¼) 07/07/2019

dobwoge@mail.smu.edu
(H) 5951 30th Ave, Sears 49679 (231) 734-2733
Brooks Corners: 5951 30th Ave, Sears 49679 (231) 734-2733

Oldenburg, Dawn (DSA) – (DSA-2018)
Hinchman (DSA) (LTFT ½) 2018; Hinchman/Scottdale (DSA) 10/1/2018
zambonidrvr1218@aol.com
(H) 9862 Vineyard St, Bridgman 49106 (269) 208-9673
Hinchman: 8154 Church St, Berrien Springs 49103-9798 (269) 471-5492
Scottdale: 4271 Scottdale Rd, St Joseph 49085-9366 (269) 429-7270

Pamp, George (DSA) – (DSA-1/1/2017)
Kewadin: Indian Mission (DSA) (LTFT 1/4) 01/01/2017
gpamp@live.com
(H) 851 W. Conway Rd, Harbor Springs 49740-9585 (231) 838-9375
Kewadin: Indian Mission: 7250 Carin Hwy, Kewadin 49648-9782 (616) 886-3579

Pease, Christine L. (DSA) – (CLM-2014)
Pleasant Lake (CLM/DSA) (LTFT 1/4) 2014
peasechris@yahoo.com
(H) 340 Pleasant St, Charlotte 48813-1626 (517) 543-5618
Pleasant Lake: PO Box 82, 4815 E Territorial Rd, Pleasant Lake 49272-9745
(517) 543-5618

Perez, Jr, Michael R. (DSA) – (DSA-2019)
Clawson (DSA) (LTFT 1/4) 1/01/2019; Clawson (DSA) (LTFT 1/2) / Waterford:
Trinity (DSA) (LTFT 1/2) 2019
perezm1551@yahoo.com
(H) 442 N Marias Ave, Clawson 48017-1478 (586) 252-7257
Clawson: 500 E McLeod Ave, PO Box 9, Ironwood 49938-0009 (906) 932-3900
Waterford: Trinity: 6440 Maceday Dr, Waterford 48329-2786 (248) 623-6860

Pinto, Michael A. (DSA) (Susan) – (DSA-2006, PL-2007, DSA-2019)
Lacota (DSA) 2006; Lacota (PTLP ¼) 2007; Discontinuned 04/09/2019; Lacota
(DSA) (LTFT ¼) April 9, 2019
m2pinto@hotmail.com
(H) 2321 Tamarack, Kalamazoo 49006-1426 (269) 207-2095
Lacota: PO Box 7, 01160 CR 681, Lacota 49063-0007 (269) 385-4154

Shaffer, Janet (DSA) – (DSA-2019)
Alger (DSA) (LTFT 1/4) 2019
jshaffertumc4842@gmail.com
(H) 120 Anna Dr, Tawas City 48763 (989) 362-6536
Alger: 7786 Newberry St, Alger 48610-9216 (989) 836-2291

Tucker, Marcia A (DSA) – (DSA-2014)
Ganges (DSA) (LTFT 1/4) 2014
friar.tuck2009@live.com
(H) 6948 Colver, Fennville 49408-9619 (269) 857-4797
Ganges: PO Box 511, 2218 68th St, Fennville 49408-9626 (269) 543-3581

VanderLaan, Kenneth D (DSA) (Cynthia) – (DSA-1993)
Mears (DSA) (1/4 Time) 1993; Mears (DSA) (1/2 time), Jan 1, 2009-2017; Shelby
(DSA) (1/4 time) 2016-2017; Arcadia (DSA) May 1-Nov. 1, 2019
pk.tb4t@gmail.com
5763 W 9th St, Mears 49436 (231) 923-6476
Arcadia: PO Box 72, 3378 Division, Arcadia 49613 (231) 864-3680

Veilleux, Cynthia L (DSA) – (PL-2011, FL-2015, DSA-2018)
Frontier/Osseo (DSA) 11/01/2010; Bronson (PTLP ¾) 2011; Union City/Athens 2015; Discontinued 2018; Galien/Olive Branch (DSA) (LTFT ½) 2018

clveilleux@yahoo.com
(H) 201 N. Cleveland Avenue, Galien 49113 (517) 741-9041
Galien: PO Box 95, 200 Ellen St, Union City 49094-0095 (517) 741-7028
Olive Branch: PO Box 267, 123 N Clark St, Athens 49011-5106 (269) 729-9370

Walters, William (DSA) – (DSA-2018)
Pokagon/Berrien Springs (DSA) 2018

wwalters1965@yahoo.com
(H) 609 Rynearson St, Buchanan 49107 (269) 479-5561
Pokagon: 31393 Kansas St, Dowagiac 49047 (269) 683-8515
Berrien Springs: 310 W Mars, Berrien Springs 49103 (269) 471-7220

Williams, Ava (DSA) – (DSA-2018)
Elsie (DSA) (LTFT 1/2) 2018

pastoravarwilliams@gmail.com
(H) 156 W Main St, Elsie 48831(202) 524-9579
Elsie: 160 W Main St, PO Box 189, Elsie 48831-0189 (989) 862-5239

Wisenbaugh, Jeanne Harmon (DSA) – (DSA-2018)
Oregon/Elba (DSA) (LTFT 1/2) Nov. 1, 2018

revjeannemarie@gmail.com
(H) 1457 Westerrace Drive, Flint 48532 (810) 732-8123
Oregon: 2985 German Rd, Columbiaville 48421 (810) 793-6828
Elba: 154 S Elba Rd, Lapeer 48446 (810) 664-5780

Zinger, Gary Melvin (DSA) – (CLM-2017, DSA-2017)
Carlisle (CLM/DSA) (LTFT 3/4)

garyzinger@gmail.com
(H) 6559 Burlingame Ave SW, Byron Center 49315 (616) 890-2744
Carlisle: 1084 76th St SW, Byron Center 49315 (616) 878-1836

DIACONAL MINISTER SERVICE RECORD

(ACE)--Associate in Christian Education; (CCW)--Church and Community Worker; (CE)--Christian Education; (DE)--Deaconess; (SM)--Sacred Music; (WDM)--World Division Missionary; (YM)--Youth Ministry.

Status abbreviations: COM--Commissioned; CON--Consecrated; CRT--Certified.

*Brooks, Barbara Ann
[(DR) CON N GA (DE)]. Oct 14, 1994 trans. to Detroit Conf.; Oct 14, 1994 Co-operative Ministries/Church and Community Worker; 1998 Church and Community Worker/Teacher, Colegio Americano; **2007 Retired**
(H) 1610 Gregory, Ypsilanti 48197 (734-547-9120)

*Caldwell, Janice
[(DR) DE COM W.MI, 1962; CRT W.MI, 1971; CON 1977; reinst (CE), 1987]. 1957 Spartansburg, SC; 1962 Chattanooga, TN; 1969 Hastings, MI; 1975 Trans. to Detroit Conf., Pontiac: Central; 1983 Voluntary Termination; 1986 Director of Christian Education, Waterford: Central; **1999 Retired**
caldwellpresumc@yahoo.com [6-27-08]
(H) 900 N Cass Lake Rd Apt 124, Waterford 48328-2385 (248-499-8272)

*Case, Jane
[(DR) CON June 1995] Organist, Napoleon UMC 1995; Retired 2011
PO Box 146, 113 West, Napoleon, MI 49261 (517) 536-8781

*Childress, Thelma (John)
[(DR) CRT, 1971; CON (CE), 1977]. 1966 Rochester: St. Paul's. **1994 Retired**
(H) 1661 Bedford Square Dr., #101, Rochester Hills 48306 (248-935-7775)
(H) 610 Burgundy Dr, Madison, TN 37115-3502

*Flegal, Daphna (Gary)
[(DR) CON June 1978] Transferred from North Georgia Conf.; Director of Christian Education, Lansing First and East Lansing University, Dec. 1, 1987; Diaconal Minister of Program, Lansing First 1991; Editor of Children's Publications, General Board of Discipleship 1992; Retired 02/18/2018
(H) 610 Burgundy Dr, Madison, TN 37115-3502 (615) 885-6621

*Foster, Margaret L.
[(DR) CON June 1986] Staff Support, Dyslexia Resource Center; Retired 1999
(H) 660 Lake Dr, Altamonte Springs, FL 32701-5412

Gossett, Timothy (Katherine)
[(DM) CRT 1999]

Griffin, Diane Mary-Allen (Kevin)
[(DM) CRT 1996; CON (CE) 1997]. 1996 Director of Program and Interpretation, Board of Outdoor and Retreat Ministries; Jan 1, 1998 leave of absence; Aug 1, 1999 Iglesia Metodista de Costa Rica; Jan 14, 2003 Methodist Church of Peru, trainer of lay persons; **Jan 1, 2006 Howell: First, Director of Educational Ministries**
dianegriffin@ameritech.net [6-28-08]
(O) 1230 Bower St., Howell 48843 (517-546-2730)
(H) 247 S. Mill St., Pinckney 48169 (734-878-9414)

*Gish, George (Yoko)
[(DR) COM GBGM, 1968; CON (WDM)1983]. 1968 Fransiscan School of Japanese Studies, Tokyo; 1970 Naganuma School, Tokyo; 1973 Kyodan Information Center, Tokyo; 1998 Aoyama Gakuin University; **2003 Retired**
gygishjr@iris.ocn,ne.jp [8-30-04]
(H) 6-10-8 Minami Aoyama, Minoto-Ku, Tokyo 107-0062, Japan (03-3486-8353)

Packer, Matthew J. (Kristina)
[(DM) CON W. MI, 1999; PE 2011; DM 2016]. 1986 Farwell; 1987 St. Bartholomew's Episcopal; 1988 Flint: Central; 1990 Clare; Nov 16, 1999 transf to Detroit Conf., Fenton: Director of Music; May 1, 2006 Flushing: Director of Music; Jun 8, 2016 Surrendered Credentials; **Nov 15, 2017 Fenton: Chancel Choir Director, Music Coordinator** (LTFT ¼)
matt@mattpackerlive.com [5-17-12]
(O) 119 S. Leroy St., Fenton 48430 (810-629-2132)
(H) 6020 Creekside Dr., Swartz Creek 48473 (810-610-3692)

*Quick, Mary Levack
> [(DR) CON (SM), 1990]. 1984 Detroit: Metropolitan 1997 Leave of Absence; **2002 Retired**
>> (H) (May-Dec): 1941 Wellesley Dr., Detroit 48203 (313-891-2861)
>> (Jan-June): Duke University Divinity School, 4902 Victoria Dr., Durham, NC, 27713 (919-493-2967)

*Rice, Beverly (Charles)
> [(DR) CRT, 1984; CON (CE), 1989]. Jan 1, 1978 Port Huron District Project Director. Jan 1, 1982 Director Skills on Wheels; **Dec 31, 1997 Retired**
>> (H) 47840 Jefferson, New Baltimore 48047 (586-949-9348)

*Denotes retired person.

DEACONESS SERVICE RECORD

*Brooks, Barbara Ann
> [(DR) CON N GA (DE)]. Oct 14, 1994 trans. to Detroit Conf.; Oct 14, 1994 Cooperative Ministries/Church and Community Worker; 1998 Church and Community Worker/Teacher, Colegio Americano; **2007 Retired**
>> (H) 1610 Gregory, Ypsilanti 48197 (734-547-9120)

*Caldwell, Janice
> [(DR) DE COM W.MI, 1962; CRT W.MI, 1971; CON 1977; reinst (CE), 1987]. 1957 Spartansburg, SC; 1962 Chattanooga, TN; 1969 Hastings, MI; 1975 Trans. to Detroit Conf., Pontiac: Central; 1983 Voluntary Termination; 1986 Director of Christian Education, Waterford: Central; **1999 Retired**
>> (H) 900 N Cass Lake Rd Apt 124, Waterford 48328-2385 (248-499-8272)

Hillman, Anne M.
> Worship and Discipleship Assistant, Grand Rapids: Trinity
>> annem.hillman@gmail.com
>> (H) 128 Maple St, Rockford 49341

Mossman-Celestin, Valerie
> U.S. Executive Director, HAPI (Haitian Artisans for Peace International.
> CC: Grand Rapids: Trinity
>> valeriemcelestin@gmail.com
>> (H) 2828 Keystone Dr, Hudsonville MI 49426-7720

*Reynolds, Phoebe
> Study leave. **Retired**
>> (H) 3095 Ewald Circle, Detroit 48238 (313-934-5047)

*Denotes retired person.

MISSIONARIES

MISSION PERSONNEL WITHIN
THE MICHIGAN ANNUAL CONFERENCE

Sonya Luna
General Advance #3019618

Serving as Michigan Conference Hispanic/Latino(a) Missionary.

Sonya Luna is a missionary with the Board of Global Ministries of The United Methodist Church serving through the National Plan for Hispanic and Latino Ministries (NPHLM) in the Detroit Annual Conference. Native to Michigan, Sonya earned her Bachelor of Arts from Kalamazoo College. She worked as Latino Ministries Coordinator for Ypsilanti First United Methodist Church, her home church, and as a foreign language teacher for the Maple Academy in Oaxaca, Mexico. She began working in the Detroit Annual Conference in her current position in January, 2008, and has recently expanded responsibilities as Michigan Conference Director for Hispanic and Latino Ministries.

Randy Hildebrant
General Advance #982961

Serving God's County Cooperative Parish in Newberry, MI.

Randy Hildebrant is a Church and Community Worker and assigned to God's Country Cooperative Parish in the Michigan Conference Randy has served as a Church and Community worker for 13 years, serving the Rural Revitalization Project of the Elkhorn Valley District in the Nebraska Conference and the Jubilee Project, an Appalachian ministry based in Sneedville, Tennessee in the Holston Annual Conference. He has a strong commitment to rural ministry and a commitment to bring self-esteem, hope and faith to all God's children throughout the vast parish.

GLOBAL MISSION FELLOWS/US-2S

Emily Burns
General Advance #3022426

Serving at Sunnyside UMC in Kalamazoo.

Emily Burns is a Global Mission Fellow with the United Methodist General Board of Global Ministries, engaged in a two-year term of service with the Michigan Annual Conference. She was commissioned in August 2018.

Emily is from Ohio and a member of the Community Methodist Church in Circleville, a congregation of the West Ohio Annual Conference. She holds a Bachelor of Arts degree in economics from Ohio Wesleyan University in Delaware, Ohio. She has worked as a peer mentor at Ohio Wesleyan and a servant leader intern at Freedom Schools of the Church for All People in Columbus.

"My call to mission has not been dramatic; it has become a 'gut feeling' or a sense of the natural next step. It feels more like a thread that has been woven through my classes, jobs, and relationships that has led me toward and into a life of mission."

Jinnia Siironen

General Advance #3022429

Serving at The NOAH Project in Detroit, MI.

Jinnia Siironen is a Global Mission Fellow with the United Methodist General Board of Global Ministries, engaged in a two-year term of service with the Michigan Annual Conference. She was commissioned in August 2018.

Jinnia is from Franklinville, North Carolina, where she is a member of Grays Chapel United Methodist Church in the Western North Carolina Annual Conference. She holds a degree in culinary arts from Guilford Technical Community College in Jamestown, North Carolina and has worked as a cook and in summer camping programs.

A call to mission service came to Jinnia in a "small and quiet voice," and she is excited to see how God will use her in the future.

Asti White

General Advance #3022366

Serving at Wesley Foundation of Kalamazoo.

Asti Nicholas White is a Global Mission Fellow with the United Methodist General Board of Global Ministries, engaged in a two-year term of service with the Michigan Annual Conference. He was commissioned in August 2018.

Asti is from Grayson, Georgia, and is a member of the Trinity on the Hill United Methodist Church in LaGrange, Georgia, in the North George Annual Conference. He holds a Bachelor of Arts degree in nonprofit leadership from LaGrange College where he also traveled to the Philippines and El Salvador for service and sustainability efforts. He has served in several annual conference youth and young adult leadership programs.

His call to mission emerged along with an expanding awareness of world issues and needs that affect daily lives, such as injustice, homelessness, inadequate health care, racial tensions and poverty. "Justice, mercy and love, he says, "are all important, and, as I see the rise of injustice, I have a responsibility to uproot it."

BEYOND THE MICHIGAN ANNUAL CONFERENCE

MISSION PERSONNEL IN AFRICA

Delbert and Sandy Groves
General Advance #12150Z – Delbert
General Advance #12151Z – Sandra

Serving at New Life Center in Kitwe, Zambia.

Delbert and Sandy Groves are United Methodist missionaries with the General Board of Global Ministries based in Kitwe, Zambia since August 2000. They serve at the New Life Center which offers numerous outreach and training ministries within the Provisional Annual Conference of Zambia.

David Paye Guinkpa
General Advance #15089Z

Serving as the Treasurer for the Liberia Annual Conference in Monrovia, Liberia

David Guinkpa is a missionary with the General Board of Global Ministries of The United Methodist Church serving as the mission treasurer for Liberia Annual Conference, based in Monrovia, Liberia. Formerly, he had oversight of finance and audits with church leaders, mission partners and institutions, and Global Ministries personnel in ensuring that funds are distributed and utilized in appropriate ways in Central Africa. Commissioned as a missionary in 2007, Mr. Guinkpa began his mission work in Uganda. "As a Christian, my responsibility is to serve God, the church, and humanity," he says. "I am from a loving family that was very supportive of my work. I believe that 'God's time is the best.' We are all called to be servants and custodian of the Word of God."

Princess Jusu
General Advance #13037Z

Serving at the Women's Leadership Training Center in Monrovia, Liberia.

Princess M. Jusu is a missionary with the Board of Global Ministries of The United Methodist Church serving in Monrovia, Liberia, as an instructor at the United Methodist Women's Leadership Training Center. "I am hopeful and prayerful that my service will be one that contributes to a more positive environment and will be productive for the women and children that I can assist while on assignment."

Pierre Manya
General Advance #15165Z

Serving as coordinator of health and medical services for the Ivory Coast Conference in West Africa.

Pierre Diamba Manya, MD, is a missionary with the United Methodist General Board of Global Ministries currently serving as coordinator of health and medical services in the Ivory Coast, West Africa. His former assignment was in the Central Congo Episcopal Area in the Democratic Republic of Congo (DRC). A gynecologist and surgeon, he has been in medical mission since 1984. "I perceive my work as a ministry," he says. "Physical healing was a key part of Jesus' ministry... So, when I treat people,or do surgery, it is God who helps to heal them. When they are healed, they thank God and sing songs of praise and become followers of Jesus Christ. It is a way of evangelization."

Emmanuel and Florence Ogugua Mefor
General Advance #13990Z – Emmanuel
General Advance #13991Z – Florence

Serving as a medical doctor in Mutambara, Zimbabwe – Emmanuel

Serving as a nurse and midwife in Mutambara, Zimbabwe – Florence

Dr. Emmanuel Ufonna Mefor, a medical doctor, and Florence Ogugua Mefor, a nurse and mid-wife, are missionaries with the Board of Global Ministries of The United Methodist Church currently assigned to Mutambara, Zimbabwe.

Helen Roberts-Evans
General Advance #3021129

Serving as the director of the Department of General Education & Ministry of The United Methodist Church in Liberia.

Helen Roberts-Evans is a missionary of the General Board of Global Ministries of The United Methodist Church, serving as director of the Department of General Education and Ministry of the United Methodist Church in Liberia. Helen's work includes meeting needs in such areas as teacher training, scholarships, resources, new school construction, and school building renovation and repair. "I want to share the love of Christ with each child because I know that His love brings peace and gives strength to overcome life's challenges."

Temba Nkomozepi
General Advance #3022400

Serving at Mujila Falls Argicultural Centre in Kanyama, Zambia.

Temba Nkomozepi is a missionary with the United Methodist General Board of Global Ministries serving as an agriculturalist at Mujila Falls Agriculture Center in Kanyama, Zambia. He was commissioned in October 2017.

The Mujila Falls Center traces its origins to the Musokatanda Agriculture Project, launched in 1995 by Global Ministries missionaries in the southern part of the Democratic Republic of Congo (DRC). Civil conflict there caused the relocation of personnel to Zambia and the reconstitution of a food security ministry at Mujila Falls on 1000 hectares of land donated by Chief Kanyama of the Lunda people. The chief's condition was that the center would teach basic sound agricultural principles to the residents of his chiefdom. It was dedicated in the year 2000 and has steadily grown in scope and importance to the area, also providing outreach to refugees from DRC.

Temba takes part in a range of agricultural, education, and health projects, as well as church growth and development. Mujila Falls raises essential crops, such as corn, and engages in small animal husbandry, cattle and goat milking, fruit culture, tree nurseries, fish culture, and research.

Mary Randall Mantor (Retired)

Mary Randall Mantor retired effective February 2019.
The Michigan Conference is no longer receiving funds for this missionary.
Please select another missionary to support.

MISSION PERSONNEL IN ASIA

Chin Cho

General Advance #3022047

Serving as coordinator of the United Methodist Mission in Mongolia, based in Ulaanbaatar.

Chin Cho is a missionary with the General Board of Global Ministries serving as the coordinator of the United Methodist Mission in Mongolia, based in Ulaanbaatar. He was commissioned in June 2015. As the country coordinator, Chin oversees the several aspects of ministry, working with local Mongolian United Methodist leaders and other missionaries. He engages in the training of indigenous clergy, who study at the Mongolia Trinity Bible College, where he teaches Wesleyan studies.

Debbie and Lester Dornon

General Advance #10920Z – Debbie
General Advance #10919Z – Lester

Serving as coordinator of expatriate service at Tensen Hospital in western Nepal – Debbie

Serving as senior physician at Tensen Hospital in western Nepal – Lester

Deborah Dornon and Lester Dornon, M.D., are missionaries with the General Board of Global Ministries, Tansen Hospital in western Nepal in Asia. Deborah is assigned as coordinator of expatriate services at the hospital. Lester is assigned as senior physician at the hospital. Lester and Deborah returned to Nepal and Tansen as missionaries in mid-2012, having served there from 1990 to 2002.The hospital in Tansen is related to the United Mission to Nepal, established in 1954 as a partnership between the people of Nepal and a coalition of 20 Christian organizations on four continents.

Hyo-Won Park
General Advance #3021822

Serving as a new church planter in St. Petersburg, Russia.

The Rev. Hyo-Won Park is a missionary with the General Board of Global Ministries serving as a new church planter in St. Petersburg, Russia. He was commissioned in June 2013.

Familiar with the area from time previously spent there, Rev. Park is working with the leadership of the St. Petersburg District in identifying opportunities for new congregations. Methodism returned to St. Petersburg, where it had existed prior to the Communist Revolution, with the dissolution of the Soviet Union almost 25 years ago. Likely constituents for new churches are the young people who come to the city looking for jobs and educational opportunities.

MISSION PERSONNEL IN CENTRAL AMERICA

José Roberto Peña-Nazario
General Advance #14026Z

Serving as pastor at Danli Central UMC in Honduras.

The Rev. José Roberto Peña-Nazario is a missionary with the General Board of Global Ministries of The United Methodist Church assigned as Pastorate, United Methodist Mission in Honduras. He serves as pastor at Danli Central UMC and works at developing new churches and new leaders for Christ's ministry.

Mbwizu Ndjungu and Nkemba Ndjungu
General Advance #12909Z – Mbwizu
General Advance #12910Z – Nkemba

Serving the Methodist Church of Belize.

For the past 10 years Nkemba and Mbwizu Ndjungu have provided leadership in the Cameroon Initiative of The United Methodist Church. Now they leave Africa for service in Central America.

Nkemba reports in a recent email: "We have received a new assignment to serve as missionaries in Belize. We arrived September 10. The Methodist Church of Belize is part of The Methodist Church in the Caribbean and the Americas, composed of Belize, Honduras and Haiti. My task is supervising the work in the Stan Creek Circuit, to groom pastors spiritually. Mbwizu will serve as Director of Christian Education. Our prayer and hope is that you will continue to support us in this new adventure."

MISSION PERSONNEL IN THE MIDDLE EAST

Kristen Brown
General Advance #3021280

Serving as coordinator of interpretation, education, and advocacy through the Methodist liaison.

Kristen Brown is a missionary with the General Board of Global Ministries of the United Methodist Church serving as coordinator of interpretation, education, and advocacy through the Methodist liaison office in Jerusalem. This office is a joint project of Global Ministries, the British Methodist Church, and the World Methodist Council. It relates to ecumenical organizations, churches, and church-related institutions in the Holy Land, and it provides educational venues for Methodist pilgrims to the region.

MISSION PERSONNEL IN NORTH AMERICA

Paul Webster
General Advance #11865Z

Serving in agricultural mission work here in the USA and also consulting beyond our borders.

Rev. Paul L. Webster, commissioned in 1992, is a missionary with the Board of Global Ministries of The United Methodist Church who served at the Mujila Falls Agriculture Centre in Kanyama, Zambia until 2018. The projects he developed and oversaw served the needs of the poor, rural people. "As a rural development specialist, I am attacking the root causes of poverty, disease, and hopelessness through education and training in small animal husbandry, cattle and goat milking, animal traction, tree nurseries, fruit culture, gardening and fish culture at our research and demonstration station. The goal is for families who can provide balanced nutrition for themselves and an income from small-scale, family-based production." Now, Paul is applying these basic principles here in the USA. He is based in his home conference in Wisconsin.

— MAC Photos

CHURCH PASTORAL HISTORIES

In Church Pastoral Histories the dates given following each name indicate a pastoral change at the time of Annual Conference unless otherwise noted. These records begin with the pastor serving each church at the time of the 1968 EUB-Methodist merger. Questions and correspondence about Church Pastoral Histories should be directed to Pamela Stewart at pstewart@michiganumc.org. Physical Address (P), Mailing Address (M), Same Address for Physical and Mailing (P/M). The state is MI in the addresses unless otherwise entered. The district the church is in appears as *[District]*.

Adrian: First UMC *[Heritage]*   adrianfumc@adrianfumc.org
(P/M) 1245 W. Maple Ave., Adrian 49221   (517) 265-5689
   Robert P. Ward 1965-1969; Warren S. Webb (assoc) 1966-1970; Robert C. Brubaker 1969-1974; Bruce W. Garner (assoc) 1970-1973; Robert W. Boley 1974-1982; Howard C. Emrick (assoc) 1974-1975; John N. Hamilton (assoc) 1980-1981; Kenneth L. Tousley 1982-1989; Maurice D. Sharai Jr. 1989-2005; Jack R. Lancaster (assoc) 1989-Mar 31, 1992; Robert W. Boley (assoc) Sep 1, 1992-1998; Gary C. Dawes 2005-2014; Wilson (Drew) Hart 2014-

Alanson UMC *[Northern Waters]*   harborspringsumc@gmail.com
(P) 7330 Chicago St, Alanson 49706; (M) 343 E Main St, Harbor Springs 49740   (231) 548-5709
   Phillip Howell 1968-1971; Philip Brown 1971-1977; Milton TenHave 1977-1979; Richard Matson 1979-1987; Catherine Kelsey 1987-1990; Claudette Haney 1990-April 1993; Birt A. Beers May 1993-1995; Lawrence R. Wood 1995-2003; Kathryn S. Cadarette 2003-2011; Mary A. Sweet 2011-2014; Vaughn Thurston-Cox 2014-2016; [Epsilon/New Hope/Harbor Springs/Alanson became a 4-point charge 2014] Hillary Thurston-Cox (Assoc.) 2014-2016; Randall J. Hitts 2016-2017; Susan E. Hitts 2016- [Harbor Springs / Alanson realigned 2016]

Alba UMC *[Northern Waters]*   mance1@mancelonaumc.org
(P) 5991 Barker St, Alba 49611; (M) PO Box 301, Mancelona 49659-0301   (231) 587-8461
   M. Helen Jackson 1968-1972; George Gierman 1972-1975; Curtis Jensen 1975-1983; Timothy Graham 1983-1990; Gary Coates 1990-Aug. 1991; Pulpit Supply Sept.-Oct. 1991; Wayne Gorsline Nov. 1991-June 15, 1992; John W. Boley June 16, 1992-1997; Carolyn C. Floyd 1997-2000; Kathryn M. Steen 2000-2007; Stephan Weinberger 2007-2010; Zawdie K. Abiade July 1-July 4, 2010; Todd Shafer (DSA) July 15, 2010; Todd Shafer Nov. 1, 2010-2017; Bryan K. Kilpatrick 2017-

Albion: First UMC *[Heritage]*   office@albionfumc.org
(P/M) 600 E Michigan Ave, Albion 49224-1849   (517) 629-9425
   Don Baker Jan. 1966-1969; Lynn A. DeMoss 1969-1979; David S. Evans 1979-1985; Randall R. Hansen (Assoc.) 1983-1985; John W. Ellinger 1985-1990; Dean L. Francis 1990-1991; Jeanne M. Randels Aug. 1991-Oct. 15, 1998; Gregory J. Martin Dec. 1, 1998-2002; Dwayne E. Bagley 2002-2009; Jeremy PH Williams 2009-2017; Leslee Fritz 2017-

Alden UMC *[Norther Waters]*   aldenumc@outlook.com
(P) 9015 Helena Street, Alden 49612; (M) PO Box 130, Alden 49612-0130   (231) 331-4132
   Leonard Yarlott 1968-1970; Paul Hartman 1970-1974; Daniel Miles 1974-1976; Chris Schroeder 1976-1982; David Cheyne 1982-1991; Wayne Gorsline (interim) July-Nov. 1991; Peter H. Shumar Nov. 1991-May 1992; Richard A. Morrison 1992-1995; Richard L. Matson 1995-2003; Charles A. Williams 2003-2010; Daniel W. Biteman, Jr. 2010-

Alger UMC *[Central Bay]*   pastorjimpayne@gmail.com
(P) 7786 Newberry St, Alger 48610; (M) PO Box 167, Sterling 48659-0167   (989) 836-2291
   Byron Coleman 1969-1974; Lynn Chappell 1974-1981; Janet Larner 1981-1982; John J. Britt 1982-1990; Zina B. Bennett Jr. 1990-1993; Jan L. Beaderstadt 1993-Feb 15, 2000; J. Gordon Schleicher 2000-2003; Jon W. Gougeon 2003-Feb 28, 2010; James A. Payne Mar 1, 2010-June 30, 2019; Janet Shaffer (DSA) 2019-

Algonac: Trinity UMC *[Greater Detroit]*   tumc@mich1.net
(P/M) 424 Smith St, Algonac 48001   (810) 794-4379
  Bruce W. Garner 1967-1970; Douglas K. Mercer 1970-1974; Gary Beeker 1974-1984; David S.
  Stiles 1984-90; Susan B. Stiles 1986-1990; James E. Britt 1990-1992; Wayne C. Ferrigan 1992-
  1999; T. Bradly Terhune 1999-2002; Dennis E. Irish 2002-2011; Chong Youb Won 2011-2012;
  Matthew Osborne 2012-2013; Carol Floyd 2013-2014; Mary Beth BeeBe 2014-Sep 1, 2014; Donna
  Cartwright Sep 1, 2014-2015; John Pajak 2015-

Algonquin UMC *[Northern Skies]*   centralumc632@sbcglobal.net
(P) 1604 W 4th Ave, Sault Ste Marie 49783; (M) 111 E Spruce St, Sault Ste Marie 49783
                                                                 (906) 632-8672
  Robert L. Brown 1967-1972; Theodore E. Doane 1972-1980; John C. Huhtala, Sr. 1980-1992;
  David M. Liscomb 1992-1993; George A. Luciani 1993-1998; James H. McLaurin 1998-Feb 1,
  2001; John N. Hamilton Jun 16, 2001-2004; Steven A. Miller 2004-Nov 15, 2010; John Huhtala,
  Sr. (Interim) Jan 9, 2011-2011; William R. Seitz 2011-2014; Larry Osweiler 2014-2018; Victoria L
  Hadaway 2018-

Allegan UMC *[Greater Southwest]*   secretary@allumc.org
(P/M) 409 Trowbridge St, Allegan 49010-1230   (269) 673-4236
  Lester Clough 1968-1973; Paul Patterson 1973-1979; Clarence Hutchens 1979-1983; Robert L.
  Pumfery 1983-1990; Robert L. Wessman 1990-1999; Joseph L. Spackman 1999-2007; Robert P.
  Stover 2007-2012; Robert K. Lynch 2012-

Allen UMC *[Heritage]*   allen.umc@aol.com
(P) 167 W Chicago Rd, Allen 49227; (M) PO Box 103, Allen 49227-0103   (517) 200-8416
  Wayne Fleenor 1967-1970; Peter Kunnen 1970-1972; Morris Reinhart 1972-1974; William Johnson
  1974-1977; Derryl Cook 1977-1978; M. John Palmer 1978-1982; Lloyd Walker 1982-1985; Jack
  Kraklan 1985-1988; Michael Baker-Streevy 1988-1995; Reva Hawke 1995-1997; Nelson Ray
  1997-2000; Craig A. Pahl 2000-2014; [Jonesville/Allen became single charges 2014] Eric Iden
  (DSA) 2014-2015; Robert M. Hughes (DSA) 2015-2016; Clare W. Huyck (RLA) 2016-2017; Larry
  W. Rubingh (Ret.) 2017-

Allendale: Valley UMC *[Midwest]*   mbistayi@valleychurchallendale.org
(P/M) 5980 Lake Michigan Dr, Allendale 49401
  [new church start 2009] Matthew Bistayi 2009- [chartered 9-22-2013]

Alma UMC *[Mid-Michigan]*   office@almaumc.com
(P/M) 501 Gratiot Ave, Alma 48801-1708   (989) 463-4305
  George Elliott 1967-Nov. 1975; Donald Scranton Dec. 1975-1981; Charles D. Grauer 1981-1989;
  David S. Yoh 1989-1995; Phillip J. Friedrick 1995-2012; Melanie J. Baker July 15, 2012-2013;
  Deborah S. Thomas 2013- ; Zachary D. McNees (Assoc.) 2019-

Almena UMC *[Greater Southwest]*   office@almenaumc.com
(P/M) 27503 County Road 375, Paw Paw 49079-9425   (269) 668-2811
  Raymond Carpenter 1966-1977; Philip Steele 1977-1980; C. Nesseth 1980-1981; Dean Francis 1981-
  1985; Beverly Gaska 1985-1987; Billie R. Dalton 1987-1995; Claudette K. Haney 1995-1996; Carol
  Newman (Assoc.) 1995-1996; Carol A. Newman 1996-2002; Anthony C. Shumaker 2002-2003; Cindy E.
  Holmquist 2003-Dec. 31, 2005; Donna J. Keyte Jan. 1, 2006-2019; [Goles / Almena fored a circuit
  07/01/2019] Lawrence James French 2019-

Alpena: First UMC [Northern Water]   pastor@alpenafumc.org
  (P/M) 167 S Ripley Blvd, Alpena 49707   (989) 354-2490
  Verle J. Carson 1965-1972; Louis Ellinger 1972-1975; Merton W. Seymour 1975-1983; Clive H.
  Dickins 1983-1995; Kenneth L. Christler 1995-2000; Kenneth E. Ray Aug 1, 2000-2003; David A.
  Diamond 2003-2006; Eugene K. Bacon 2006-2016; Susan E. Platt 2016-2018; Seok Nam Lim 2018

CHURCH HISTORIES

Amasa: Grace UMC *[Northern Skies]* cumc@up.net
(P) 209 Pine St, Amasa 49903; (M) PO Box 27, Crystal Falls 49920-0027 (906) 875-3123
W. Frederick Worth 1961-1971; Frank Bishop 1971-1974; Edward C. Weiss 1974-1985; Nancy G. Sparks 1985-1993; Paul J. Mallory 1993-Jan 1994; Stephen Rhoades Feb 1, 1994-2000; Elbert P. Dulworth 2000-2004; Stephen E. Rhoades 2004-2011; Nathan T. Reed 2011-2015; Steven T. Sudduth 2016-Feb 6, 2018; Reed P. Swanson Feb 7-Jun 30, 2018; Vicky Prewitt (DSA) 2018-

Amble UMC *[Midwest]* andyhollander122@yahoo.com
(P) 15207 Howard City Edmore Rd, Howard City 49329; (M) PO Box 392, Howard City 49329
(231) 580-6304
Albert Rill 1968-Nov. 1971; Larry Dekema Jan. 1972-1975; Joseph Shaw 1975-1979; John Gurney 1979-Nov. 8, 1981; David England Oct. 1, 1982-1984; Ben Lester 1988-1995; Mark Mitchell (DSA) 1995-July 31, 1999; Charles W. Fullmer (DSA) Aug. 1, 1999-Oct. 31, 2001; Bryan Schneider-Thomas Nov. 1, 2001-2009; Anne W. Riegler Aug. 15, 2009-2017; Andrew Benjamin Hollander (DSA) 2017-Nov. 30, 2017; Andrew Benjamin Hollander (LTFT) Dec. 1, 2017-

Ann Arbor: Calvary UMC *[Heritage]* calvary1415@att.net
(P/M) 1415 Miller Ave, Ann Arbor 48103 (734) 769-0869
Robert C. Grigereit 1968-1976; Dwight W. Murphy 1976-1985; Ira L. Fett 1985-1989; Gary R. Glanville 1989-1996; Douglas K. Olsen 1996-2008; Beth D. Titus 2008-2013; Andrew Lee 2013-2019; Mary K. Loring 2019-

Ann Arbor: First UMC *[Heritage]* tina@fumc-a2.org
(P/M) 120 S State St, Ann Arbor 48104 (734) 662-4536
Hoover Rupert 1959-1972; L. Burlin Main (assoc) 1958-1970; Kendall W. Cowing (assoc) 1959-1973; Joseph A. Pia (assoc) 1960-1962; Melbourne Johnson (assoc) 1963-1969; Fred B. Maitland (assoc) 1970-1983; Donald B. Strobe 1972-1990; Kenneth R. Colton (assoc) 1973-1975; E. Jack Lemon (assoc) 1976-1978; Gerald R. Parker (assoc) 1978-1986; P. Thomas Wachterhauser (assoc) 1983-1997; Russell L. Smith (assoc) 1986-1994; Alfred T. Bamsey 1990-2000; Marsha M. Woolley (assoc) 1994-2006; Sherry Parker (assoc) 1995-1997; David A. Eardley (assoc) 1997-2000; Rony S. Hallstrom (assoc) 1997-1998; Stanley McKinnon (assoc) 1998-Nov 30, 1998; John E. Harnish 2000-2005; Michael Mayo-Moyle (assoc) 2001-Jan 31, 2003; Timothy R. Ziegler (assoc) Jul 16, 2003-2009; J. Douglas Paterson 2005-2018; Joanne R. Bartelt (assoc.) 2006-2009; Robert H. Roth, Jr. (assoc.) 2009-2014; Nancy S. Lynn (assoc.) 2010-2018; Nancy S. Lynn 2018- ; Nicolas R Berlanga (assoc.) 2018-

Ann Arbor: First UMC - Green Wood Campus *[Heritage]*
(P) 1001 Green Rd, Ann Arbor 48105; (M) 120 S State St, Ann Arbor 48104
J. Douglas Paterson 2005-2018; Joanne R. Bartelt (assoc.) 2006-2009; Robert H. Roth, Jr. (assoc.) 2009-2014; Nancy S. Lynn (assoc.) 2010-2018; Nancy S. Lynn 2018- ; Nicolas R Berlanga (assoc.) 2018-

Ann Arbor: Korean UMC *[Heritage]* pastor.hjcho@gmail.com
(P/M) 1526 Franklin St, Ann Arbor 48103 (734) 662-0660
Yohan Choi 1980-1981; Woo-Hyun Jung 1981-1988; Jae (John) H. Lee 1988-Mar 15, 1992; Isaac Y. Shin Apr 1, 1992-2010; Steven H. Khang (assoc) 2007-2014; Hyun Jun Cho 2010-July 31, 2019; TBS

Ann Arbor: West Side UMC *[Heritage]* westside@westside-umc.org
(P/M) 900 S 7th St, Ann Arbor 48103-4769 (734) 663-4164
Milton H. Bank 1968-1975; Wallace Robinson (assoc) 1968-1970; King W. Hanna (assoc) 1970-1972; Duane E. Snyder (assoc) 1972-1974; Frank A. Cozadd 1975-1982; W. Cardwell Prout (assoc) 1976-1986; Elwood J. Berkompas 1982-1995; Nancy A. Woycik (assoc) 1987-Jul. 31, 1990; Jacqueline E. Holdsworth (assoc) 1991-1995; Gary L. Sanderson 1995-1999; Eric Hammer (assoc) 1995-1999; Tracy N. Huffman 1999-2013; Frederick P. Cooley (assoc) 2001-2006; W. Vincent McGlothlin-Ellers (assoc) 2006-2008; Wilson (Drew) Hart (assoc) 2008-2014; Timothy R. Ziegler 2013-

Applegate UMC *[East Winds]*   ngenoff@rocketmail.com
(P) 4792 Church St, Applegate 48401; (M)133 W State St, Croswell 48422   (810) 633-9700
Wallace Zinnecker 1969-1971; Max D. Weeks 1971-1973; John E. Naile 1973-1985; Mary F. Neil 1985-1987; J. Gordon Schleicher 1987-1991; Darrel Tallman 1991-1994; Victor L. Studaker 1994-2000; Emerson W. Arntz 2000-2002; Maureen V. Baker 2002-2007; James E. Barnett 2007-2013; Nicholas K. Genoff 2013-Dec 31, 2018; Ellen O. Schippert Jan 1, 2019-

Arbela UMC *[Central Bay]*   bruce.malicoat@gmail.com
(P) 8496 Barnes Rd, Millington 48746; (M) PO Box 252, Millington 48746   (989) 793-5880
Richard A. Turner 1965-1971; Arthur V. Norris 1971-1976; Paul L. Amstutz 1976-1982; Keith B. Colby 1982-1985; Ronald Figgins Iris 1985-Aug. 31, 1991; Max D. Weeks Sept. 1, 1991-1994; Thomas F. Keef 1994-Dec 31, 1995; Kenneth R. Andrews Jan 1, 1996-Dec 1, 1998; David P. Rahn Jan 1, 1999-Dec 1, 1999; Calvin H. Wheelock Dec 16, 1999-2006; Bruce Malicoat Nov 1, 2006-2016; T. Bradley Terhune 2016-Sept 30, 2017; Dainel J. Wallington Nov 1, 2017-2018; Gloria Haynes (Ret.) 2018-

Arcadia UMC *[Northern Waters]*   blumc316@gmail.com
(P) 3378 Division, Arcadia 49613; (M) PO Box 72, Arcadia 49613-0072   (231) 864-3680
Stephen Hubbell 1967-1969; Richard Matson 1969-1971; Ken Curtis 1971-March 1975; Raymond Roe April-June 1975; Gordon Spalenka 1975-1980; Donald Vuurens 1980-1983; Valerie Hill 1983-1985; John Backoff 1985-1989; William Carr 1989-1993; Pulpit Supply July-Nov. 1993; Arthur C. Murphy Dec. 1, 1993-1999; Mark D. Anderson Feb. 1, 2000-2006; William F. Dye 2006-2011; Roberta W. Cabot 2011-2014; Jane D. Logston 2014-Aug. 31, 2018 [Bear Lake / Arcadia became signle point charges 11-1-2018]; Kenneth D. VanderLaan (DSA) May 1-Nov. 1, 2019

Arden UMC *[Greater Southwest]*   orr6148@aol.com
(P) 6891 US Highway 31, Berrien Springs 49103; (M) 6891 M 139, Berrien Springs 49103
                                          (269) 429-4931
Frederick Fischer 1965-1970; Harrison Harnden 1970-1972; Gordon Spalenka 1972-1975; Wayne Gorsline 1975-1980; John Moore 1980-1988; Jesse Schoebell 1988-1995; Jeremy P.H. Williams 1995-2002; Dominic A. Tommy 2002-2006; James W. Stilwell 2006-2009; [Portage Prairie/Arden two-point charge 2009] O'Ryan Rickard (RLA) 2009- [Arden single-point charge 2014]

Arenac Cnty: Christ UMC *[Central Bay]*   arenacchristumc@gmail.com
(P) 3322 E Huron Rd, AuGres 48703; (M) PO Box 145, AuGres 48703   (989) 876-7449
Stephen N. Meeks (w/Twining: Trinity) 1967-1971; Robert Porter (w/Twining: Trinity) 1971-1973; Dale E. Brown (w/Twining: Trinity) 1973-1979; Gilbert James MacDonald (w/Twining: Trinity) 1979-1985; Lillian G. Richards (w/Twining: Trinity) 1985-1993; Lillian G. Richards 1993-1995; Priscilla J. Seward 1995-1996; Douglas Coone 1996-2000; Margery A. Schleicher 2000-2003; Timothy S. Woycik 2003-2012; Marcel Lamb 2012-2013; Donald Wichert 2013-2019; (AuGres merged with Christ and new name.) James A. Payne 2019-

Armada UMC *[East Winds]*   armadaumc@yahoo.com
(P) 23200 E Main St, Armada 48005; (M) PO Box 533, Armada 48005   (586) 784-5201
Edger M. Smith 1965-1970; Donald W. Brown 1970-1972; Elmer J. Snyder 1972-1974; Ira L. Wood 1974-1975; Robert D. Schoenhals 1975-1983; Robert Thornton 1983- 2000; Jean R. Snyder 2000-Sep 1, 2002; Dianna L. Rees 2003-2011; Curtis Clarke Nov 12, 2011-2019; Christopher G.L. Titus 2019-

Ashley UMC *[Mid-Michigan]*   abgumc@gmail.com
(P) 112 N New St, Ashley 48806; (M) PO Box 7, Ashley 48806-0007   (989) 862-4392
Wayne Sparks 1966-1970; William Cox 1970-1972; Marjorie Matthews June-Sept. 1972; Joseph Dudley Sept. 1972-1973; Miriam DeMint 1973-1975; Emmett Kadwell 1975-Oct. 1978; John Ritter Oct. 1978-1980; Mark Johnston 1980-1982; Donald McLellan 1982-1984; Arthur R. Turner 1984-1990; Glenn C. Litchfield 1990-1996; Robert J. Besemer Sept. 1, 1996-1999; Jana L. Jirak 1999-2003; Diane L. Gordon 2003-2006; Jon L. Pohl 2006-2011; Mona J. Dye 2011-Sept. 30, 2017; [Ashley/Bannister realigned with Pompeii to become Ashley/Bannister/Pompeii charge 2016] Zella Marie Daniel (DSA) Oct. 3, 2017-Dec. 31, 2018; Zella Marie Daniel Jan. 1, 2019-

Athens UMC *[Greater Southwest]*   athensumc@att.net
(P) 123 Clark St, Athens 49011; (M) PO Box 267, Athens 49011-0267   (269) 729-9370
   Garold L. Simison Sept. 1965-1969; James Gerhardt 1969-1970; Dwight Benner 1970-1972; John
   Bauer 1972-Jan. 1974; Gary Kintigh Feb. 1974-1977; Walter Rothfuss 1977-1978; Wendy S. Pratt
   1978-Dec. 1979; Terry Howard Dec. 1979-1980; Richard Young Aug. 1980-1986; Robert G.
   Woodring 1986-1987; David Minger Sept. 1987-1991; Sandra J. Gastian 1991-Dec. 31, 2010;
   Allen Pebley (DSA) date?-2011; Robert D. Nystrom (1/4 time) 2011-2012; [Union City / Athens
   became two-point charge 2012] Seung Ho Baek (1/4 time) 2012-2015; Cynthia L. Veilleux 2015-
   2018; James Palaszeski 2018- [Union City and Athens realigned to become UnionCity/Athens
   charge 2018]

Atherton UMC *[East Winds]*   athertonumc@gmail.com
(P/M) 4010 Lippincott Blvd, Burton 48519   (810) 742-5644
   Emil E. Haering 1967-1975; Donald W. Joiner 1975-Dec. 1977; Charles R. Marble Jan. 1978-
   1985; James R. McCallum 1985-Sept. 1, 1987; Grant A. Washburn Sept. 1, 1987-1993; Bruce L.
   Billing 1993-2011; Gregory E. Rowe 2011-2016; Sang Yoon (Abraham) Chun 2016-

Attica UMC *[East Winds]*   atticamethodist@gmail.com
(P/M) 27 Elk Lake Rd, Attica 48412   (810) 724-0690
   Harvard J. Warren 1969-1972; H. Reginald Cattell 1972-1974; Dale L. Vorman 1974-1977; Bufford
   C. Coe 1977-1983; Margaret H. Rodgers-West 1983-1988; Zina Braden Bennett, Jr. 1988-1990;
   James R. Rupert 1990-Sep 30, 1995; Dennis Madill Nov 16, 1995-Sep 8, 1998; Clifford J.
   Schroeder, III Feb 1, 1999-2007; Alonzo Vincent 2007-2008; Margaret E. Bryce Aug 1, 2008-2013;
   Ronald Rouse 2013-2018; Robert D Nystrom 2018-

Auburn UMC *[Central Bay]*   auburnumc@sbcglobal.net
(P/M) 207 S Auburn, Auburn 48611   (989) 662-6314
   Harold D. Dakin 1967-1972; Arthur R.Parkin 1972-1977; John E. Marvin (interim); Phillip D. Miles
   1977-1980; Joseph H. Ablett 1980-1985; Donald P. Haskell 1985-1992; James D. Weiss 1992-
   1993; Lawson D. Crane 1993-2009; Duane M. Harris 2009-2018; Robert D Nystrom 2018-

Augusta: Fellowship UMC *[Greater Southwest]*   augustafellowshipumc@gmail.com
(P) 103 N. Webster, Augusta 49012; (M)PO Box 337, Augusta 49012-0337   (269) 731-4222
   Marvin Rosa 1967-Feb. 1972; Richard Cobb March 1972-1976; Matthew Walkotten Aug. 1976-Sept.
   1977; Herbert Lowes Feb. 1978-Dec. 1983; Robert Tomlinson Feb. 1984-87; Lloyd Hansen 1987-
   1988; Nelson Ray 1988-May 1993; Sue Gay 1993-2007; Nelson Hall 2007-2013; Jennifer J. Wheeler
   2013-Jan. 16, 2017; Scott M. Bouldrey Jan. 18, 2017-

Avoca UMC *[East Winds]*   juliekrauss@hotmail.com
(P) 8905 Avoca Rd, Avoca 48006; (M) PO Box 7, Jeddo 48032-0007   (810) 327-6144
   John Thomas 1969-1972; Stephen Chapko 1972-1977; Merle M. Nichols 1977-1978; Darrel
   Tallman 1978-1988; Victor L. Studaker 1989-1994; Robert D. Chapman 1994-Oct 15, 2000; Robert
   I. Kreger 2001-2003; Donna J. Osterhout 2003-2007; Nicholas J. Genoff 2007-2013; Donald L.
   Wojewski 2013-2018; Julie Krauss 2018-

Avondale UMC *[Northern Waters]*
(P) 6976 14 Mile Rd, Evart 49631; (M) PO Box 388, Evart 49631-0388
   Edward R. Jones 1967-1969; Walter Easton 1969-1971; Daniel L. Reedy 1971-1972; H. Howard
   Fuller 1973-1975; Laurence Waterhouse June-Oct. 1975; Stanley Hayes Oct. 1975-March 1984;
   Gerald Welsh 1984-1990; Donald L. Buege 1990-Jan. 2006; Jon Pohl Jan. 15 - June 30, 2006;
   Jean A. Crabtree (DSA) Nov. 5, 2006-July 2007; Russell Morgan (DSA) July 8, 2007-2012; Kara
   Lynne Burns (CLM) July 22, 2012-2014; TBS

Azalia UMC *[Heritage]*   christopherbutson@live.com
(P) 9855 Azalia Rd, Azalia 48110; (M) PO Box 216, Milan 48160-0216   (734) 529-3731
John McNaughton 1968-1969; Gary R. Imms 1969-1976; John J. Landon 1976-Mar. 1978; James
B. Lumsden - Mar. 1978-Dec. 1978; D. Byron Coleman Dec. 1978-1982; Mildred M. Hiner 1982-
1984; Donald C. Schark 1984-1986; David W. Purdue 1986-1991; William Michael Clemmer
(interim Jun-Aug, 1991); Diana K. Goudie Sep. 1, 1991-Aug 31, 1994; William Michael Clemmer
Sep 1, 1994-Feb 16, 2003; Richard E. Burstall Mar 1, 2003-2007; Edward L. Tam 2007-Oct 31,
2007; Ruth A. McCully Nov 1, 2007-Nov 15, 2009; Courtney D. Williams Nov 16, 2009-Dec 31,
2013; Christopher Butson Jan 1, 2014-2019; Beatrice S. Alghali 2019-

Bad Axe: First UMC *[East Winds]*   office@badaxefumc.org
(P/M) 216 E Woodworth St, Bad Axe 48413   (989) 269-7671
Jack E. Giguere 1969-1971; Byron G. Hatch 1971-1972; Ross N. Nicholson 1972-1977; Kenneth
R. Colton 1977-1978; David A. Stout 1978-1990; William R. Wright 1990-2006; Gregory E. Rowe
2006-2008; Mary Jean Love 2008-Dec 1, 2010; Donna J. Cartwright (interm) Jan 1., 2011-2011;
Philip Tousley 2011- [Ubly Regional Church 2018; Bad Axe: First / Minden City / Ubly formed Bad
Axe Cooperative Parish 07/01/2019]

Baldwin: Covenant Community UMC *[Northern Waters]*   ljball6@hotmail.com
(P) 5330 S M-37, Baldwin 49304; (M) PO Box 250, Baldwin 49304-0250   (231) 745-3232
Rebecca Neal Niese 1984-1988; Dale Peter Ostema 1988-Jan. 1993; Reva Hawke May 1993-
1995; Mary S. Brown 1995-Oct 15, 1998; David A. Cheyne Jan. 16, 1999-June 30, 1999; Nelson
Hall 1999-2005; Karen J. Sorden 2005-2012; James A. Richie 2012-Jan. 31, 2015; [Baldwin:
Covenant Community / Chase-Barton became cross-district circuit 2015] Lyle J. Ball (LTFT) 2015-

Bancroft UMC *[Mid-Michigan]*   bancroftmorricepastor@gmail.com
(P) 101 S Beach St, Bancroft 48414; (M) PO Box 301, Morrice 48857-0301   (989) 634-5291
Lawrence C. Brooks 1969-1970; Meldon E. Crawford 1970-1975; Thomas E. Hart 1975-Aug.
1980; Willard A. King Sept., 1980-March 15, 1985; Raymond D. Field 1985-1988; Katherine J.
Rairick 1988-1990; Philip D. Voss 1990-Jul 31, 1997; James M. Mathews Aug 1, 1997-Sep 30,
2001; Frederic G. Heath Oct 1, 2001-2003; Richard B. Brown 2003-2005; Jeremy T. Peters 2005-
2008; Jeremy P. Benton 2008-2011; Patricia Elliott 2011-2015; Robert Forsyth Dec 1, 2015-Mar
31, 2017; Terry A Euper Apr 1-Jun 30, 2017; Coleen Wilsdon 2017-

Bangor: Simpson UMC *[Greater Southwest]*   simpsonumcbangor@gmail.com
(P/M) 507 Joy St ,Bangor 49013-1123   (269) 427-7725
Wayne C. Reece Oct. 1966-1970; Charles D. McNary 1970-1977; Lawrence D. Higgins 1977-
1981; Robert C. Carson 1981-1984; Morris J. Reinhart 1984-1987; Robert E. Tomlinson
1987-1989; James E. Hodge 1989-1994; Sandra B. Hoffman 1994-2007; Thomas A. Davenport
2007-2016; Mona K. Joslyn 2016-

Bannister UMC *[Mid-Michigan]*   abgumc@gmail.com
(P/M) 103 E Hanvey St, Bannister 48807   (989) 862-4392
Wayne Sparks 1966-1970; William Cox 1970-1972; Marjorie Matthews June-Sept. 1972; Joseph
Dudley Sept. 1972-1973; Miriam DeMint 1973-1975; Emmett Kadwell 1975-Oct. 1978; John Ritter
Oct. 1978-1980; Mark Johnston 1980-1982; Donald McLellan 1982-1984; Arthur R. Turner 1984-
1990; Glenn C. Litchfield 1990-1996; Robert J. Besemer Sept. 1, 1996-1999; Jana L. Jirak
1999-2003; Diane L. Gordon 2003-2006; Jon L. Pohl 2006-2011; Mona J. Dye 2011-Sept. 30,
2017; [Ashley/Bannister realigned with Pompeii to become Ashley/Bannister/Pompeii charge 2016]
Zella Marie Daniel (DSA) Oct. 3, 2017-Dec. 31, 2018; Zella Marie Daniel Jan. 1, 2019-

Bark River UMC *[Northern Skies]*   1chris1cross1@att.net
(P/M) 3716 D Rd, Bark River 49807   (989) 634-5291
David M. Liscomb 1969-1973; Walter David 1973-1978; Jack Lancaster 1978-1980; Michael L.
Peterlin 1980-1991; Christine J. Bergquist 1991-

Barnard UMC *[Northern Waters]*　　　　　　　　　　cappahl@netzero.net
(P) 15645 Klooster Rd, Charlevoix 49720; (M) PO Box 878, East Jordan 49727　　(231) 547-5269
Stanley Hayes 1967-1970; Lester Priest 1970-Jan. 1974; Daniel Minor April 1974-1981; Betty
Burton 1981-1982; Glenn Britton 1982-1983; Supply pastor 1983-Aug. 1985; Robert Bellairs Aug.
1985-1996; Bernard W. Griner (DSA) 1996-1997; Eugene L. Baughan 1997-2002; D. Michael
Maurer 2002-Nov. 10, 2008; Ralph Posnik (DSA) Nov. 23, 2008; Ralph Posnik Nov. 15, 2009-
2014; Craig A. Pahl 2014-

Barry County: Woodland UMC *[Mid-Michigan]*　　　　kdsmith868@gmail.com
(P/M) 203 N Main St, Woodland 48897-9638　　　　　　　　　　　　(269) 367-4061
Claude Ridley 1968-1972; Richard Erickson 1972-1976; Clinton Bradley-Galloway 1976-1981;
Constance Hefflefinger 1981-1984; Glenn Wegner 1984-1987; Robert Kersten 1987-1991; Carl
Litchfield 1991-2000; Geraldine M. Litchfield (Assoc.) Jan. 1993-1994; Soo Han Yoon Aug. 1,
2000-Jan. 31, 2001; Robert E. Smith Feb. 1, 2001-Dec. 31, 2003; Mary Schippers-DeMunter
(DSA) 2004-2008; James E. Fox (DSA) July 22, 2008-2011; Gary L. Simmons (1/4 time) 2011-
2015; [Barry-Eaton Cooperative Ministry 2013] Kathleen Smith (RLA) 2015-

Barryton: Faith UMC *[Midwest]*　　　　　　　　brookscornersparish@gmail.com
(P/M) 95 E Marion Ave, Barryton 49305　　　　　　　　　　　　　(989) 382-5431
Thomas Tarrant 1967-March 1969; Isaac Sayers March 1969-1975; Altha Barnes 1975-1979; Lyle
Heaton 1979-1984; Jean Crabtree 1984-1990; Pulpit Supply 1990-1991; Arthur C. Murphy 1991-
Dec. 1, 1993; William W. Dornbush Jan. 1-June 30, 1994; Timothy J. Miller 1994-1995; Kevin
Parkins 1995-1998; Robert E. Smith July 16, 1998-Feb. 1, 2001; James E. Cook (DSA) 2001-
Feb. 28, 2002; Merged with Chippewa Lake Jan. 1, 2002 (See Barryton-Chippewa Lake for current
listings); Brian R. Bunch Mar. 1, 2002-2005; name changed to Barryton Faith 2005; Ronald
DeGraw Aug. 1, 2005-Nov. 6, 2005; James L. Breithaupt Mar. 15, 2006-Oct. 19, 2009; Joseph
Beavan Jan. 15, 2010-2014; Bryan K. Kilpatrick 2014-2017; Raymond Johnson (DSA) (LTFT 1/4)
Dec. 1, 2017-June 30, 2018; TBS [Barryton: Faith became single station 2017]

Bath UMC *[Mid-Michigan]*　　　　　　　　　　　　pastor@unitedch.com
(P) 13777 Main St, Bath 48808; (M) PO Box 308, Bath 48808-0308　　(517) 641-6551
Alma Glotfelty 1968-1970; Tom Daggy 1970-1971; Clarence Keith 1971-1976; Dan Miles June-
Dec. 1976; Tom Peters Feb. 1977-1993; Raymond D. Field 1993-1998; Nancy L. Besemer
1998-2003; Thomas L. Truby Oct. 15, 2003-2006; Beatrice K. Robinson 2006-2007; Mark G.
Johnson 2007-2015; Matthew D. Kreh 2015-

Battle Creek: Baseline UMC *[Greater Southwest]*　　　baselineum@gmail.com
(P/M) 9617 Baseline Rd, Battle Creek 49017-9766　　　　　　　　(269) 763-3201
Richard Budden 1966-1969; Paul Mazur 1969-Sept. 1972; Charles Grauer Sept.-Dec. 1972;
Marvin Iseminger Jan. 1973-1977; Harold Diepert 1977-1978; Sharon Rader 1978-1981; Arthur
Turner 1981-1984; Gregory J. Martin Sept. 1984-1987; Robert Woodring Sept. 1987-1990; Joy
Jittaun Moore 1990-Aug. 15, 1993; Maurice E. Walworth, Jr. Nov. 1, 1993-1996; Glenn R. Wegner
1996-2004; Virginia L. Heller 2004-2011; Peggy J. Baker 2011-2018; Margaret Mallory Sandlin
2018-

Battle Creek: Chapel Hill UMC *[Greater Southwest]*　　　office@thehillbc.com
(P/M) 157 Chapel Hill Dr, Battle Creek 49015-4631　　　　　　　　(269) 963-0231
Royce Robinson 1968-1973; William J. Richards 1973-May 1976; Heath T. Goodwin May 1976-
1981; Donald Scranton 1981-1985; Joseph J. Bistayi 1985-1993; James M. Gysel 1993-2011;
Robert J. Mayo 2011-2013; Chad M. Parmalee 2013- ; Janet Sue Wilson (Assoc.) Jan. 1, 2018-
[Battle Creek: Birchwood / Battle Creek: Trinity UMC merged with Battle Creek: Chapel Hill 07-
01-2018]

Battle Creek: Christ UMC *[Greater Southwest]*   BCChristUMC@comcast.net
(P/M) 65 Bedford Rd N, Battle Creek 49037-1837   (269) 965-3251
     Gaylord Howell 1966-1973; Chester Erickson 1973-1978; Morris Bauman 1973-Jan. 1983; Kenneth Vaught Jan. 1983-1986; B. James Varner 1986-July 1992; John Charter Nov. 1992-Jan. 1, 1999; Bruce R. Kintigh Jan. 1, 1999-2007; Carolyn A. Robinson-Fisher 2007-2011; Scott M. Bouldrey 2011-2015; Brian Steele 2015-2018; [BC: Christ / BC: Washington Heights became a two-point charge 2017] Crystal C. Thomas 2018-

Battle Creek: Convis Union UMC *[Greater Southwest]*   convisunionumc@gmail.com
(P/M) 18990 12 Mile Rd, Battle Creek 49014   (269) 965-3787
     Howard McDonald 1968-1973; Willard Gilroy 1973-1979; Dennis Paulson 1979-Apr. 1983; Linda D. Stoddard May 1983-Dec. 1991; Larry W. Rubingh Jan. 1992-1997; Lewis A. Buchner 1997-2001; David L. Litchfield 2001-2006; Sueann Hagan 2006-2017; Eric Iden (DSA) Aug. 1, 2017-Dec. 31, 2017; Andrea L Johnson (LTFH 1/2) Jan. 1, 2018-

Battle Creek: First UMC *[Greater Southwest]*   jharveyclark@firstumcbc.org
(P/M) 111 E Michigan Ave, Battle Creek 49014   (269) 963-5567
     John Tennant 1966-Jan. 1973; David Lee Miles (Assoc.) 1967-1971; Charles Fry Jan. 1973-1978; Howard Lyman 1978-1982; Neil Bintz July-Nov. 1982; Merle Broyles (interim) Nov. 1982-Jan. 1983; Dale Brown Jan. 1983-1993; Ron L. Keller 1993-1998; Karen S. Wheat 1998-2002; William P. Myers, Jr. 2002-Apr. 15, 2007; Donald R. Ferris 2007- ; Billie R. Dalton Mar. 1, 2009-Mar. 5, 2014; David L. Morton (Ret.) Mar. 5-June 30, 2014; Marshall Murphy 2014- ; Scott M. Bouldrey 2014-2015; Douglas W. Vernon (Assoc.) (Ret.) 2015-2016; Michael T. Conklin (Ret.) 2016-2018; Linda J. Farmer-Lewis (Ret.) 2018-2019; Susan Jo Arnold Trowbridge 2019-

Battle Creek: Maple UMC *[Greater Southwest]*   mapleumc@yahoo.com
(P/M) 342 Capital Ave NE, Battle Creek 49017   (269) 964-1252
     Donald Sailor 1966-1972; Jack Baumgart 1972-1980; Curtis Strader 1980-1986; David L. Morton 1986-1996; Lynn W. Wagner 1996-2001; Charles D. Farnum 2001-2006; Theresa Little Eagle Sayles 2006-2008; Linda D. Stoddard (Ret.) 2008-

Battle Creek: Newton UMC *[Greater Southwest]*   NewtonChurch@aol.com
(P/M) 8804 F Drive South, Ceresco 49033   (269) 979-2779
     Howard Moore May 1968-1970; Ray Grienke 1970-Jan. 1974; Ray McBratnie Jan. 1974-1976; Kenneth Curtis 1976-1981; Harry Johnson 1981-1985; Gary Kintigh 1985-1993; Charles M. Shields 1993-1995; Michael Baker-Streevy 1995-Nov. 16, 1999; Charles Edward Rothy 2000-2003; Richard Duane Wilson 2003-2008; Nancy G. Powers 2008-2012; Sally Harrington (Ret.) 2012-2016; Robert J. Freysinger 2016-2019; Connor James Bailey (DSA) 2019-

Battle Creek: Washington Heights UMC *[Greater Southwest]*
                           washingtonheightsumc@gmail.com
(P/M) 153 Wood St N, Battle Creek 49037-2271   (269) 968-8773
     Donald Grant 1967-1972; John L. Thompkins Sept. 1972-1975; Pulpit Supply 1975-1976; Clifton Bullock 1976-Feb. 1991; Herbert Griffin (Assoc.) 1990-1993; Russell McReynolds 1991-1996; Howard (Rick) McKire 1996-Feb. 27, 1997; Curnell Graham 1997-2002; James A. Richie 2002-2009; Sandra V. Douglas (1/4 time) 2009-2011; Marshall Murphy 2011-2017; Brian Steele 2017-2018; [BC: Christ / BC: Washington Heights became a two-point charge 2017] Crystal C. Thomas 2018-

Bay City: Grace UMC *[Central Bay]*   office@baycitygracechurch.org
(P/M) 4267 2 Mile Rd, Bay City 48706   (989) 684-1101
     [New Church Start Jul 1, 2013] Leonard Clevenger 2013-2015; Eric Kieb 2015-

Bay City: Grace – East Campus *[Central Bay]*   office@baycitygracechurch.org
(P) 510 Fremont St, Bay City 48708; (M) 4267 2 Mile Rd, Bay City 48706   (989) 684-1101
     [Bay City: Grace merged with Bay City: Fremont Jun 30, 2016] Eric Kieb 2016-

Bay Port UMC *[Central Bay]*   bayporthayesumc@att.net
(P/M) 836 N 2nd St, Bay Port 48720   (989) 656-2151
   Donald W. Brown 1965-1970; Louis E. Reyner 1970-1975; Richard Andrus 1975-1979; Frederick P. Cooley 1979-1984; Randy A. Chemberlin 1984-1986; Alger T. Lewis 1986-1992; S. Douglas Leffler 1992-1994; Norman R. Beckwith 1994-1998; Barbra Franks 1998-2000; Alan W. DeGraw 2000-2003; Douglas E. Mater 2003-2010; Bruce L. Nowacek 2010-2012; Karl L. Zeigler 2012 (interm)-Dec 31, 2012; Brian K. Johnson Jan 1, 2013-2016; Matthew Chapman 2016-

Bear Lake UMC *[Northern Waters]*   blumc316@gmail.com
(P) 7861 Main St, Bear Lake 49614; (M) PO Box 157, Bear Lake 49614   (231) 864-3680
   Stephen Hubbell 1967-1969; Richard Matson 1969-1971; Ken Curtis 1971-March 1975; Raymond Roe April-June 1975; Gordon Spalenka 1975-1980; Donald Vuurens 1980-1983; Valerie Hill 1983-1985; John Backoff 1985-1989; William Carr 1989-1993; Pulpit Supply July-Nov. 1993; Arthur C. Murphy Dec. 1, 1993-1999; Mark D. Anderson Feb. 1, 2000-2006; William F. Dye 2006-2011; Roberta W. Cabot 2011-2014; Jane D. Logston 2014-Aug. 31, 2018; [Bear Lake / Arcadia became single charges 11-1-2018] TBS

Beaverton: First UMC *[Central Bay]*   beavertonumc@gmail.com
(P/M) 150 W Brown St, Beaverton 48612   (989) 435-4322
   A. H. Keesler 1967-1970; Zina B. Bennett Jr. 1970-1975; Vernon Wyllys 1975-1979; Bruce C. Hatch 1979-1986; Janet Larner 1986-1991; David K. Stewart Sr. 1991-Jul 31, 2000; Frederick LaMere Aug 1, 2000-2002; Linda Jo Powers 2002-2009; Lynn F. Chappell 2009-

Beebe UMC *[Mid-Michigan]*   pastorgarysimmons@gmail.com
(P) 2975 N. Baldwin, Ithaca 48847; (M) 327 E Center St, Ithaca 48847
   Wayne Sparks 1968-1970; Larry Uhrig 1970-1971; Ralph Kline 1971-Sept. 1974; Supply pastor Sept. 1974-1976; David Nelson 1976-Sept. 1980; Nolan Williams Oct. 1980-1991; David McBride 1991-2006; Steven R. Young 2006-2010; Cynthia Greene 2010-2015; Gary L. Simmons 2015- [Ithaca / Beebe became a two-point charge 2018]

Belding UMC *[Midwest]*   beldingu@att.net
(P/M) 301 Pleasant St, Belding 48809   (616) 794-1244
   Ross E. Tracy 1966-1972; Eugene A. Lewis 1972-1977; Richard A. Strait 1977-1981; Ellen A. Brubaker 1981-1983; William D. Carr July-Oct. 1983; C. David Hainer Nov. 1983-Oct. 1988; Theodore F. Cole Oct. 1988-1991; Nathaniel W. Johnson 1991-Aug. 31, 1996; Charles A. Williams Feb. 15, 1997-Jan. 1, 1999; Connie Shatz 1999-2012; [Turk Lake / Belding became two-point charge 2012] Kimberly A. DeLong Aug. 15, 2012-2013; [Greenville First, Turk Lake/Belding Cooperative Parish 2013] Kimberly A. DeLong (Deacon) 2013-2015; Stephen MG Charnley 2013-2014; Stephen F. Lindeman 2013-2014; Donald E. Spachman 2014- ; Eric Mulanda Nduwa (Assoc.) Feb. 15-Aug. 1, 2015 [cooperative parish re-named Flat River Cooperative Parish 2015]; Joseph K. Caldwell (CLM/DSA) Aug. 1, 2015-2016; Donna Jean Sperry 2016-

Bellaire: Community UMC *[Northern Waters]*
(P) 401 N. Bridge St, Bellaire 49615; (M) PO Box 235, Bellaire 49615   (231) 533-8133
   James Lavengood Sept. 1965-Sept. 1969; Gerald Welsh Oct. 1969-1976; Alan Volkema 1976-1977; Garth Smith 1977-1981; David Litchfield 1981-1987; Gordon Spalenka 1987-1991; Richard A. Powell 1991-1998; D.S. Assignment 1998; Mary S. Brown Oct. 16, 1998-2009; Carl Q. Litchfield 2009-2013; Peggy A. Boltz 2013-July 16, 2014; Eric M. Falker Sept. 24, 2014-2019; Daniel J.W. Phillips 2019-

Belleville: First UMC *[Heritage]*   bellevilleumc48111@yahoo.com
(P/M) 417 Charles St, Belleville 48111   (734) 697-9288
   Allen B. Rice II 1965-1969; Charles Dibley 1969-1973; Joy E. Arthur 1973-1982; George E. Spencer 1982-1989; Mary E. Hoff (assoc) 1983-1987; Edwin C. Hoff (assoc) 1983-Jan 4, 1999; Richard O. Griffith 1989-1991; R. LaVere Webster 1991-Jun 30, 1994; David Strong Jul 1, 1994-1998; John N. Grenfell, III 1998-2007; James J. Walker 2007-

Bellevue UMC *[Greater Southwest]* office@bellevueumc.org
(P/M) 122 W Capital Ave, Bellevue 49021 (269) 763-9421
Lowell F. Walsworth 1966-1971; Laurence R. Grubaugh 1971-1973; Milton J. Tenhave 1973-1977; David L. Johnston 1977-May 1983; James William Schoettle May 1983-1988; William P. Sanders 1988-Feb. 1996; Mark E. Thompson 1996-2004; Virginia L. Heller 2004-2011; Peggy J. Baker 2011-2018; Margaret Mallory Sandlin 2018-

Bentley UMC *[Central Bay]* bentleyumc@live.com
(P) 7209 Main St, Bentley 48613; (M) PO Box 1, Rhodes 48652-0001
(With Sterling and Alger) Byron Coleman 1969-1974; Lynn Chappell 1974-1981; Janet Larner 1981-1982; John J. Britt 1982-1990; Zina B. Bennett Jr. 1990-1993; Jan L. Beaderstadt 1993-1995; (Single point charge) Charles Cerling 1995-2000; David LaBeau 2001-2009; John Tousiuck Nov 8, 2009-2011; Cheryl L. Mancier 2011-Oct 31, 2016; David LaBeau (DSA) Dec 1, 2016-Dec 31, 2018; Merry Henderson (DSA) Jan 1, 2019-

Bergland UMC *[Northern Skies]* aa8yf@yahoo.com
(P) 108 Birch, Bergland 49910; (M) PO Box 142, Bergland 49910-0142 (906) 988-2533
Zina Bennett 1966-1970; Lloyd Christler 1970-1972; James Hilliard 1970-1971; Lawrence Brooks 1971-1975; Roger Gedcke 1972-1979; Lillian Richards 1971-1976; Wayne E. Sparks 1975-1980; Myra Sparks 1976-1980; Ed Hingelburg 1979-1981; Robert Thorton 1981-1983; Deane Wyllys 1983-1987; Charles H. West 1987-1993; Margaret H. West 1987-1993; Earleen VanConant 1993-1997; Clarence VanConant 1993-1997; Timothy C. Dibble 1997-2000; Cherrie A. Sporleder 2000-Jun 15, 2002; Theodore A. Trudgeon 2003-2019; [White Pine Community / Ewen / Bergland three-point charge 7-1-2019] Rosemary R. DeHut 2019-

Berrien Cnty: Lakeside UMC *[Greater Southwest]* geolawton@csinet.net
(P) 14970 Lakeside Rd, Lakeside 49116; (M) PO Box 402, Union Pier 49129 (269) 469-8468
Robert Carson 1958-1964; Laurence R. Grubaugh 1964-1968; John Bullock 1968-1974; Robert Pumfery 1974-1979; Pulpit Supply 1979-1981; Charles Tooman 1981-1982; Gregory Wood 1982-1985; B. Gordon Barry 1985-1988; Steven Pearson 1988-1990; Ruth Haynes-Merrifield 1990-1995; Sherri L. Swanson 1995-Sept. 1, 1999; George W. Lawton (RLA) Sept. 1, 1999-

Berrien Springs UMC *[Greater Southwest]*
(P/M) 310 W Mars St, Berrien Springs 49103 (269) 471-7220
David Lutz, March 1967-1969; William A. Wurzel 1969-Feb. 1975; Dennis Buwalda March 1975-Sept. 1978; Gaylord Howell Sept. 1978-1983; Curtis Jensen 1983-1987; Edward & Priscilla Seward 1987-March 1990; Ross Bunce Jr. (Interim) 1990-1991; Wayne H. Babcock 1991-1998; Jeremy P.H. Williams 1998-2002; Dominic A. Tommy 2002-2006; Cynthia M. Parsons 2006-2012; [Berrien Springs / Hinchman / Oronoko became three-point charge 2012] Jane D. Logston (part-time) 2012-2014; [Berrien Springs/Pokagon became a 2-point charge 2014] Brenda E. Gordon 2014-2018; William Walters (DSA) 2018-

Beverly Hills UMC *[Greater Detroit]* admin@bhumc.org
(P/M) 20000 W 13 Mile Rd, Beverly Hills 48025 (248) 646-9777
Robert Boley 1961-1970; Howard Childs 1970-1974; William Verhelst 1974-1979; John W. Bray 1979-1989; Scott Wilkinson 1989-1995; Samuel V. White, III 1995-Nov 24, 1996; Juanita J. Ferguson 1997-1998; Stephen K. Perrine 1998-2003; John K. Benissan 2003-Jul 31, 2008; David E. Huseltine Aug 1, 2008-2013; Suzanne Walls 2013-2015; Anthony Ballah 2016-

Big Rapids: First UMC *[Midwest]* bigrapidsfirstumc@gmail.com
(P/M) 304 Elm St, Big Rapids 49307 (231) 796-7771
James E. Leach 1965-1972; J. Leon Andrews 1972-1980; Richard Johns 1980-1985; Wayne G. Reece 1985-1992; Marvin R. Rosa 1992-March 31, 1993; Keith W. Heifner 1993-1996; Robert E. Jones 1996-2004; Bobby Dale Whitlock 2004-2008; Dean N. Prentiss 2008-2011; Rebecca K. Morrison 2011-2019; Devon R. Herrell 2019-

Big Rapids: Third Avenue UMC *[Midwest]*
(P) 226 N Third Ave, Big Rapids 49307; (M) 628 S Warren Ave, Big Rapids 49307   (231) 796-4157
Richard D. Wilson 1968-1971; Lynn Chapel 1971-1979; John Buker 1979-Jan. 1981; Elaine Buker Jan. 1981-1986; Kendall Lewis 1986-1990; J. Robert Collins 1990-Oct. 1991; Albert Frevert (interim) Jan.-June 1992; David Hills 1992-1994; Kathryn M. Steen 1994-2000; Dawn A. Beamish Jan. 1, 2001-2002; Edwin D. Snook 2002-2005; Michael A. Riegler Sept. 11, 2005-2011; Ed Milam (DSA) July 1-Nov. 12, 2011; Ed Milam Nov. 12, 2011-2014; David J. Cadarette Sr. 2014-April 12, 2015; Kimberly A. DeLong 2015-2017; Devon R. Herrell (LTFT 1/2) 2017-2019; Morgan William (Bill) Davis (DSA) 2019-

Birch Run UMC *[Central Bay]*   godopensdoors@gmail.com
(P) 12265 Church St, Birch Run 48415; (M) PO Box 277, Birch Run 48415   (989) 624-9340
Peyton E. Loy 1962-1970; Gordon D. Everett Jan. 1970-1973; Thomas J. Wood 1973-1980; James D. Jacobs 1980-1989; Dale E. Brown 1989-1999; Sang Yoon (Abraham) Chun 1999-2005; Alonzo E. Vincent 2005-2007; Clifford J. Schroeder, III 2007-2013; Paul G. Donalson 2013-2015; Rey C. B. Mondragon 2015-

Birmingham: Embury UMC *[Greater Detroit]*   emburyumc@yahoo.com
(P/M) 1803 E 14 Mile Rd, Birmingham 48009   (248) 644-5708
Albert E. Hartoog 1966-1969; Timothy R. Hickey 1969-1973; James D. Parker 1973-1979; Haxton H. Patterson 1979-Dec 1981; William E. Frayer Jan 1982-Oct 1982; James A. Smith Jan. 1983-1988; Philip Seymour 1988-Sep 1, 1995; James R. Rupert Oct 1, 1995-1997; Linda J. Donelson 1997-Sep 30, 2000; Mary Lynch Mallory Feb 1, 2001-2006; Elizabeth A. Hill 2006-2010; Carter Cortelyou 2010-2013; Theodore Whitely 2013-2014; Jean Snyder 2014-2015; Karen Y. Noel 2015-2018; Jean Snyder 2018-

Birmingham: First UMC *[Greater Detroit]*   office@fumcbirmingham.org
(P/M) 1589 W Maple Rd, Birmingham 48009   (248) 646-1200
G. Ernest Thomas 1962-1972; William Lovejoy (assoc) 1960-1969; James W. Wright 1972-1982; William H. Fraser (assoc) 1967-1969; John Bunce 1968-1978 (assoc); G. Bryn Evans (assoc) 1970-1981; J. Bruce Brown (assoc) 1971-1973; Thomas H. Beaven (assoc) 1973-1979; Hal Weemhoff (assoc) 1977-1980; Douglas Vernon (assoc) 1979-1984; Robert Paul Ward 1982-1993; Evans C. Bentley (assoc) 1980-1983; Charles H. Beynon (assoc) 1983-Dec, 1995; Ronald K. Fulton (assoc) 1983-Feb. 1988; William R. Wright (assoc) 1985-1990; Juanita Ferguson (assoc) 1990-1993; Bruce Denton (assoc) 1988-1995; Bruce Petrick (assoc) 1993-1995; William Ritter 1993-2005; Matthew J. Hook (assoc.) 1995-2002; Melody P. Hurley (assoc.) 1995-1998; Mariane Meir (assoc.) 1995-1997; Linda J. Farmer-Lewis (assoc) Jun 1, 1998-Jan 1, 1999; Lisa M. McIlvenna (assoc) Sep 1, 1999-2004; Scott A. Harmon (assoc) 2002-2003; Taek H. Kim (assoc) 2002-2004; Lynn M. Hasley (assoc) 2004-Oct 1, 2008; Jeffrey S. Nelson (assoc) 2004-2009; Carl T. Gladstone (deacon) 2004-2008; John E. Harnish 2005-2013; Brian William (assoc) 2009-2012; Monica William (assoc) 2009-2012; Gary Haller (co-pastor) 2013-2017; Laurie Haller (co-pastor) 2013-Jul 14, 2016; Lindsey Hall (assoc) 2013-2019; Zack Dunlap (assoc.; Path One Internship) 2015- ; Daniel J.C. Hart (assoc) 2016-2019; Elbert Dulworth Jun 11, 2017- ; Shawn Lewis-Lakin (sr assoc) 2017- ; Susanne E. Hierholzer (assoc) 2019- ; Sarah Nadeau Alexander (deacon) 2019-

Blanchard-Pine River UMC *[Central Bay]*
(P/M) 7655 W Blanchard Rd, Blanchard 49310   (989) 561-2864
Harold E. Arman 1968-1969; Leslie D. Smith 1969-1977; James C. Sabo-Shuler 1977-1980; James W. Burgess 1980-1986; M. Christopher Lane 1986-1990; Paula Jane Duffey 1990-1998; Dale A. Golden 1998-2005; Paulette G. Cheyne 2005-2006; Melody Lane Olin (DSA) 2006; Melody Olin Nov. 15, 2006-2010; Lawrence Wonsey 2010-2014; Russell D. Morgan 2014-2016; [Blanchard-Pine River became a single-point charge 2016; Shepherd / Blanchard-Pine River became 2-point charge 2017] Janet M. Larner 2017- [Blanchard-Pine River / Shepherd became a single-point charges 01/01/2019]

Blissfield: Emmanuel UMC *[Heritage]* pastor@emmanuel-godwithus.org
(P/M) 215 E Jefferson St, Blissfield 49228 (517) 486-3020
Rupert H. Lindley 1961-1974; Robert N. Hicok 1974-1976; Kenneth L. Harris 1976-1981; David J. Hill 1981-1985; Mark D. Miller (assoc) 1984-May 1, 1989; Robert B. Secrist 1985-1987; Lawrence E. Van Slambrook 1987-1990; Thomas A. Davenport (assoc) 1989-Sep. 15, 1990; John N. Hamilton 1990-1995; Kevin Miles 1995-2002; Robert J. Easlick 2002-Aug 31, 2004; James G. Simmons (interm) Sep1, 2004-Nov 14, 2004; Harlan E. Sorensen Nov 15, 2004-Nov 15, 2005; Aaron Kesson 2006-2012; Lawson D. Crane 2012-Dec 31, 2013; Zachary L. Dunlap Jan 1, 2013-2015; Devin Smith 2015-

Blissfield: First UMC *[Heritage]* blissfumc@gmail.com
(P/M) 201 W Adrian St, Blissfield 49228 (517) 486-4040
Floyd A. Ellison 1967-1973; Charles E. Sutton 1973-1980; Arthur V. Norris 1980-1983; Ralph H. Pieper II 1983-1989; Robert P. Garrett 1989-1994; Walter H. Miller 1994-Dec 1, 2002; Michael Mayo-Moyle Feb 1, 2003-2010; Paul G. Donelson 2010-2013; Kristen I. (Parks) Coristine 2013-2019; Gun Soo Jung 2019-

Bloomfield Hills: St. Paul UMC *[Greater Detroit]* st.paul.bh@sbcglobal.net
(P/M) 165 E Square Lake Rd, Bloomfield Hills 48302-0669 (248) 338-8233
Sam Seizert 1965-1970; Harold Diehl 1970-1972; Douglas Trebilcock Dec.1972-1975; Roger Ireson 1975-1979; David Truran 1979-1983; Guenther Branstner 1983-1989; Pauline S. Hart 1989-1995; James E. Greer, II 1995-Nov 15, 2000; Steven Gjerstad Nov 16, 2000-2002; Alan J. Hanson 2002-2007; Robert D. Schoenhals 2007-2010; Leonard Clevenger 2010-2013; Frederick Sampson, III 2013-

Bloomingdale UMC *[Greater Southwest]* revcnewman@frontier.com
(P) 201 E Pine St, Bloomingdale 49026; (M) PO Box 9, Bloomingdale 49026 (269) 521-3323
Wayne Babcock 1969-1971; Gerald Hudlund 1971-1972; Wayne Barrett 1972-1973; Pulpit supply 1973-1976; David L. Youngs 1976-2006; Donald R. Wendell 2006-Nov. 30, 2008; John W. McNaughton Dec. 8-31, 2008; Eugene B. Moore, Jan. 1, 2009, 2012; Carol A. Newman (DSA 1/4), Sept. 23, 2012-

Bowne Center UMC *[Midwest]* rdwcsumc@gmail.com
(P) 12051 84th St SE, Alto 49302; (M) PO Box 122, Alto 49302 (616) 868-7306
Beulah Poe 1962-1971; Carter Miller 1971-1973; John Eversole 1973-1977; Keith Avery June-Oct. 1977; Albert Sprauge Oct. 1977-Jan. 1978; Herb Kinsey Jan. 1978-May 1979; Martin Fox May 1979-Oct. 1982; Herb Kinsey Oct. 1982-1983; Harold Diepert 1983-March 1985; Margaret Peterson 1985-1989; Jill Rose July-Dec. 1989; Lloyd Hansen Dec. 1989-1990; Todd Thompson 1990-1995; Bryan Schneider-Thomas 1995-2000; Dominic A. Tommy 2000-2002; Dean Irwin Bailey (Ret.) 2002-2014; Andrew Jackson (Ret.) 2014- ; Robert D. Wright (Ret.) 2016-

Boyne City UMC *[Northern Waters]* bcbfumc@me.com
(P/M) 324 S Park St, Boyne City 49712 (231) 582-9776
R.J. McBratnie 1965-1970; Bruce Pierce 1970-Dec. 1973; Ray Grienke Jan. 15, 1974-1981; Forest Crum 1981-1983; Michael T. Conklin 1983-1989; John Backoff 1989-April 1991; Max Gladding (retired) April-June 1991; Gary D. Bondarenko 1991-2000; Carl Q. Litchfield 2000-2005; Wayne E. McKenney 2005-2014; Michael Neihardt 2014-2015; Eun Sik Poy Sept. 1, 2015- [Boyne City / Boyne Falls realigned w/ Boyne City / Boyne Falls / Epsilon 2016]

Boyne Falls UMC *[Northern Waters]* bcbfumc@me.com
(P) 3057 Mill St, Boyne Falls 49713; (M) 324 S Park St, Boyne City 49712 (231) 582-9776
R.J. McBratnie 1965-1970; Bruce Pierce 1970-Dec. 1973; Ray Grienke Jan. 15, 1974-1981; Forest Crum 1981-1983; Michael T. Conklin 1983-1989; John Backoff 1989-April 1991; Max Gladding (retired) April-June 1991; Gary D. Bondarenko 1991-2000; Carl Q. Litchfield 2000-2005; Wayne E. McKenney 2005-2014; Michael Neihardt 2014-2015; Eun Sik Poy Sept. 1, 2015- [Boyne City / Boyne Falls realigned w/ Boyne City / Boyne Falls / Epsilon 2016]

Bradley: Indian Mission of the UMC *[Midwest]*   revrtwilliamson@gmail.com
(P) 695 128th Ave, Shelbyville 49344; (M) 1146 Nicolson St, Wayland 49348   (616) 738-9030
Lewis White Eagle Church 1972-1990; Pulpit Supply 1990-1992; David G. Knapp 1992-1995; Timothy J. Miller 1995-1999; John Pesblakal (DSA)1999-Aug. 31, 2001; Calvin Hill Sept. 1, 2001-2003; Wesley S. Rehberg (DSA) 2003-2005; Sandra VandenBrink, Jan. 16, 2005-2013; Sandra VandenBrink, (Ret.) Director, Senior Meals Program 2013- ; Nancy L. Boelens (Ret.) 2013-Dec. 15, 2015; Ronald Todd Williamson (DSA) Jan. 1, 2016-Nov. 30, 2017; Ronald Todd Williamson Dec. 1, 2017

Breckenridge UMC *[Mid-Michigan]*   breckenridgeumc@yahoo.com
(P) 125 3rd St, Breckenridge 48615; (M) PO Box 248, Breckenridge 48615   (989) 842-3632
Allen Wittrup 1966-1969; Gilbert Heaton 1969-1972; Birt Beers 1972-1977; Philip Brown 1977-1983; Molly Turner 1983-1990; Stanley Hayes 1990-1994; David L. Miles 1994-1999; Emilie Forward 1999-2005; Dale A. Golden 2005-2013; Paul W. Thomas 2013-Aug. 3, 2015; William F. Dye Sept. 1, 2015-2017; Mark G. Johnson (Ret.) 2017-2019; Cleoria M. French 2019-

Brethren: Epworth UMC *[Northern Waters]*   anikakasper@gmail.com
(P) 3939 High Bridge Rd, Brethren 49619; (M) PO Box 177, Brethren 49619   (231) 477-5486
Ward Pierce 1967-1971; Floyd Soper 1986-1993; Russell M. Garrigus (Ret) (DSA) 1993-2002; Lemuel O. Granada 2003-2005; Carl Greene (DSA) 2005; Carl Greene, Nov. 12, 2005-2011; Colleen A. Wierman (1/4 time) 2011-2014; [Brethren Epworth / Grant became single-point charges 2014] Judy Coffey (DSA) 2014-Dec. 1, 2015; Beverley J. Williams, Dec. 1, 2015-2016; Laurie M. Koivula 2016-2018; [Mesick /Harrietta/Brethren became a three-point charge 2016] Laurie M. Koivula (LTFT) 2018-2019; [Mesick/Brethren became a two-point charge 2018] Anika Kasper (DSA) July 14, 2019-

Bridgman: Faith UMC *[Greater Southwest]*   schneider4276@comcast.net
9156 Red Arrow Hwy, Bridgman 49106; (M) PO Box 414, Bridgman 49106   (269) 465-3696
Walter Easton 1968-1969; David Lutz 1969-Jan. 1970; Arthur & Molly Turner April 1970-1971; Merritt Edner 1971-1972; Wayne Babcock 1972-Dec. 1974; Stanley Buck Jan. 1975-Dec. 1981; Daniel Graber Jan. 1982-1983; Joan Hamlin 1983-1985; Laura Truby 1985-Jan. 1987; Richard Bates March-Nov. 1987; Ross Bunce Nov. 1987-1988; B. Gordon Barry 1988-1993; Bradley S. Bartelmay 1993-May 1, 2000; Terrill M. Schneider May 1, 2000-October 1, 2018; Ashlei K Horn (DSA) October 28, 2018- [Bridgman became a single point charge 10-1-2018]

Brighton: First UMC *[Heritage]*   wendy@brightonfumc.org
(P/M) 400 E Grand River Ave, Brighton 48116   (810) 229-8561
Robert C. Brubaker 1964-1969; W. Herbert Glenn 1969-1973; Kearney Kirkby 1973-1977; Richard C. Cheatham 1977-1988; Benjamin Bohnsack 1988-1997; Karen D. Poole (assoc) 1988-1993; Patricia A. Green (assoc.) 1993-1995; Kristine J. Sigal (assoc.) 1995-2000; Gilson M. Miller 1997-2008; Adam W. Bissell (assoc) 2000-2003; Jennifer Browne (assoc.) 2003-2006; Scott Crostek (assoc.) 2006-2009; Loretta M. Job (deacon) 2007-2018; Sherry L. Parker-Lewis 2008- ; John W. Ball (assoc) 2009-2013; Paul S. Hahm (assoc.) 2013-2015; Robert F. Fuchs (assoc.) 2017-

Brighton: First - Whitmore Lake: Wesley Campus *[Heritage]*   wumcwhitmorelake@gmail.com
(P) 9318 Main St, Whitmore Lake 48189; (M) PO Box 431, Whitmore Lake 48189-0431
Walter R. Damberg 1968-1970; Robert C. Strobridge 1970-1972; Dwight W. Murphy 1972-1976; Larry J. Peacock 1976-1979; Ronald K. Fulton 1979-1983; Timothy S. Woycik 1983-1993; Robert J. Easlick 1993-2001; Sandra L. Tannery 2001- Aug 15, 2009; Fred Cooley (interim) Aug 16, 2009-Sep 20, 2009; Frederick M. Hatfield Sep 21, 2009-2018;

Britton: Grace UMC *[Heritage]*   brittongraceumc@yahoo.com
(P/M) 9250 E Monroe Rd, Britton 49229   (517) 451-8280
  John D. Lover, 1966-1969; Lauren J. Strait 1969-1972; Gerald R. Parker 1972-1973; Robert L. Porter 1973-1976; John D. Roach 1976-1979; Kenneth C. Reeves 1979-1982; Thomas E. Sumwalt 1982-1985; Martha C. Gregg Ball 1985-Mar. 31, 1991; Stuart L. Proctor May 1, 1991-1993; David A. Eardley 1993-1997; Marianne M. Meier 1997-1998; Nicholas W. Scroggins 1998-2002; Amy Mayo-Moyle 2002-2010; Richard E. Burstall 2010-2014; Mark Zender 2014-2019; [Britton: Grace / Macon two-point charge 7-1-2019] Ruth A. VanderSande 2019-

Bronson: First UMC *[Greater Southwest]*   umcb@frontier.com
(P/M) 312 E Chicago St, Bronson 49028   (517) 369-6555
  Lloyd A. Phillips 1961-Oct. 1969; Gordon E. Spalenka Oct. 1969-1972; Charles W. Richards 1972-1977; Eldon C. Schram 1977-Oct. 1980; Paul Walter Oct.-Dec. 1980; A. Edward Perkins Dec. 1980-April 1987; Marilyn Barney April-May 1987; Milton John Palmer May 1987-1990; Gerald L. Welsh 1990-1994; Robert D. Nystrom 1994-1998; Mona Joslyn 1998-2006; Matthew Bistayi 2006-2009; Shane Chellis (DSA) 2009-2010; Shane Chellis (part-time) May 25, 2010-2011; Cindy Veilleux 2011-2015; Samuel C. Gordy 2015-

Brookfield Eaton UMC *[Mid-Michigan]*   ilv@vcconsulting.com
(P) 7681 Brookfield Rd, Charlotte 48813; (M) PO Box 430, Charlotte 48813   (517) 543-4225
  John H. King, Jr. 1967-1971; Miriam DeMint 1971-1973; John Morse 1973-March 1976; James Allred March 1976-Sept. 1979; Pulpit Supply Sept. 1979-1980; Robert Hundley 1980-1982; Pulpit Supply July-Oct. 1982; Robert Freysinger Oct. 1982-1985; Ronald Brooks 1985-1988; Robert Roth 1988-1990; Isabel Deppe 1990-1991; Charlene Minger 1991-1995; Geraldine M. Litchfield 1995-2000; Kevin E. Hale 2000-2004; Stephen C. Small 2004-Oct. 1, 2004; Irene Vittoz (DSA) Oct. 1, 2004; Irene Vittoz Nov. 15, 2005-

Brooks Corners UMC *[Northern Waters]*   brookscornersparish@gmail.com
(P/M) 5951 30th Ave, Sears 49679   (231) 734-2733
  Carter Miller 1968-March 1971; Lynn Wagner March 1971-Oct. 1973; Pulpit Supply Nov. 1973-1974; Darryl Cook 1974-May 1977; Kenneth Kline 1977-1986; Carl Q. Litchfield 1986-1991; Eugene L. Baughan 1991-1997; Brian R. Bunch 1997-2005; Ronald DeGraw Aug. 1, 2005-Nov. 6, 2005; James L. Breithaupt Mar. 15, 2006-Oct. 19, 2009; Joseph L. Beavan Jan. 15, 2010-2014; Bryan K. Kilpatrick 2014-2017; Irene Elizabeth Starr Jul. 1-Oct. 22, 2017 [Grant Center / Brooks Corners became a two-point charge 2017] Timothy Locker (DSA) Jan. 1 – June 30, 2019; Douglas Mochama Obwoge (DSA) July 7, 2019-

Brown City UMC *[East Winds]*   browncityumc@gmail.com
(P) 7043 Lincoln St, Brown City 48416; (M) PO Box 39, Brown City 48416   (810) 346-2010
  Gloria Haynes 1996-Sep 30, 1998; Arthur R. Stone Nov 1, 1998-2004; Lance E. Ness Aug 1, 2004-2007; Maureen V. Baker 2007-2013; Dennis Irish 2013-2019; Patrick D. Robbins 2019- [Brown City Cooperative Parish: Brown City and Omard formed 07/01/2019]

Buchanan: Faith UMC *[Greater Southwest]*   faithoffice@sbcglobal.net
(P/M) 728 N Detroit St, Buchanan 49107   (269) 695-3261
  D. Keith Laidler 1968-1972; Kenneth L. Snow 1972-1982; Richard C. Kuhn 1982-1987; Richard D. Wilson 1987-1996; Zawdie K. Abiade 1996-2002; Ralph K. Hawkins 2002-2004; Christopher A. Kruchkow 2004-Feb. 15, 2012; [Buchanan Faith UMC became single point charge 2012] Edward H. Slate (Ret.) (1/2 time) 2012-

Buchanan: First UMC *[Greater Southwest]*   fumcbuchanan@att.net
(P/M) 132 S Oak St, Buchanan 49107   (269) 695-3282
  C. Robert Carson 1966-1972; Ronald Entenman 1972-1979; Ward D. Pierce 1979-1985; Paul D. Mazur 1985-1987; Curtis E. Jensen 1987-Jan. 1996; William P. Sanders Feb. 2, 1996-2003; David W. Meister 2003-2006; Rob A. McPherson 2006-2018; Ellen Dannelley Beirlein 2018-

Buel UMC *[East Winds]*
(P) 2165 Peck Rd, Croswell 48422; (M) 133 W State St, Croswell 48422
William J. Burgess 1968-1973; Martin Caudill 1973-1976; Willard A. King 1976-1980; J.D. Landis 1980-1986; David K. Stewart 1986-1990; Louise R. Ott 1990-1992; Michael F. Bossingham 1992-1994; Thomas K. Spencer 1994-1998; David C. Freeland (co-pastor) 1998-2002; Susan K. Freeland (co-pastor) 1998-2000; Robert A. Srock 2002-Dec 1, 2003; Catherine W. J. Hiner 2004-2009; Micheal P. Kelley 2009-2012; Donald L. Wojewski 2012-2013; Nicholas K. Genoff 2013- Dec 31, 2018; Ellen O. Schippert Jan 1, 2019-

Burnips UMC *[Greater Southwest]*   secretary.bumc@gmail.com
(P) 4237 30th St, Burnips 49314; (M) PO Box 30, Burnips 49314-0030   (616) 896-8410
Ron Smith Oct. 1991-1997; Kenneth C. Reeves 1997-2004; Anthony Carrol Shumaker 2004-2008; Richard A. Fritz 2008-2014; Nancy J. Patera 2014-2017; Craig H. VanBeek (DSA) 2017- Dec. 31, 2018; Craig H. VanBeek Jan. 1, 2019-

Burr Oak UMC *[Greater Southwest]*
(P) 105 S. Fourth St, Burr Oak 49030; (M) PO Box 91, Burr Oak 49030   (269) 489-2985
David Draggoo 1967-1971; P.T. Wachterhauser 1971-1974; Larry D. Higgins 1974-1977; Harold Tabor 1977-1978; Wade S. Panse 1978-March 1982; Dan Bennett 1982-1983; Timothy Boal 1983-1986; John Buker 1986-1988; William Bills 1988-1991; Brian Rafferty 1991-1993; Ruth A. Bonser 1993-1994; Emilie Forward 1994-1999; Martin Cobb 1999-2001; William Chu 2001-2003; Melanie S. Young (1/2 time) 2003-2006; Donald J. Graham 2007-2012; John Sterner 2012-2018; Carl Q Litchfield (Ret.) Feb. 15-Jun. 30, 2018; Carl Q Litchfield (Ret.) Oct. 1, 2018-

Burt UMC *[Central Bay]*
(P) 12799 Nichols Rd, Burt 48417; (M) PO Box 96, Burt 48417-0096   (989) 770-9948
Martin G. Seitz 1968-1972; Ronald Brunger 1972-1976; Kyle Ballard 1976-1979; Philip Seymour 1979; Alan Weeks 1979-1982; Martin G. Seitz 1983-1990; Lois E. Glenn 1990-Dec 31, 1994; Sandra Uptegraff Jan 1, 1994-2000; Betty Whitely 2000-2006; Michael P. Kelley 2006-2009; James O. Bowen 2009-Oct, 2009; Clifford J. Schroeder III, 2010-2013; Paul G. Donalson 2013-2015; Rey C. B. Mondragon 2015-

Burton: Christ UMC *[East Winds]*   ChristUMCBurton@att.net
(P/M) 4428 Columbine Ave, Burton 48529   (810) 743-1770
Peyton E. Loy Jan. 1970-1975; Ralph H. Pieper 1975-1982; William B. Cozadd 1982-1988; Thomas F. Keef 1988-1994; Trevor A. Herm 1994-2004; Theodore D. Whitely 2004-2006; Janet M. Engler 2006-Mar 1, 2009; Kenneth C. Bracken 2009-Dec1, 2010; Naylo T. Hopkins 2011-2014; David Leinke 2014-Oct 30, 2014; David R. Strobe (interim) Nov 1, 2014-Apr 30, 2019; Brian Kendall Willingham May 1, 2019- [Flint: Bristol / Buron: Christ became a two-point charge on May 1, 2019]

Byron Center UMC *[Midwest]*   secretary@byroncenterchurch.org
(P/M) 2490 Prescott St SW, Byron Center 49315   (616) 878-1618
Max Gladding 1966-1975; James C. Grant 1975-1985; Fred Hamlin 1985-1987; William H. Doubblestein 1987-2004; Cynthia S.L. Greene 2004-2010; Lawrence A. Nichols 2010-2016; Jeffrey O. Cummings 2016-

Byron: First UMC *[East Winds]*   byronumc@byronumc.com
(P) 101 S Ann St, Byron 48418; (M) PO Box 127, Byron 48418-0127   (810) 266-4976
Lorenz Stahl 1969-1973; Dalton Bishop 1973-1975; Harry R. Weeks 1975-1979; Martin G. Seitz 1979-1983; Robert D. Schoenhals 1983-1995; Marilyn C. DeGraw 1995-Jan 28, 2000; G. Fred Finzer 2000-2006; Jack E. Johnston 2006-2010 Michael Mayo-Moyle 2010-2012; Nathan Jeffords 2012-2016; Barbara S. Benjamin 2016-

Cadillac: South Community UMC *[Northern Waters]* jim.mort@sbcglobal.net
(P/M) 11800 47 Mile Rd, Cadillac 49601 (231) 775-3067
Richard Wilson Nov. 1966-Nov. 1968; Richard Matson Dec. 1968-Oct. 1969; Edward Eidins Oct. 1969-1971; Robert R. Boyer 1971-1977; Kendall A. Lewis 1977-1981; Donald Fry 1981-1994; James C. Grant 1994-1999; Howard H. Harvey 1999-2000; Jeffrey Schrock 2000-2004; Kenneth C. Reeves 2004-2006; Kenneth C. Reeves (DSA) 2006-7; James J. Mort 2007-

Cadillac UMC *[Northern Waters]* umccadillac@gmail.com
(P) 1020 E Division St, Cadillac 49601; (M) PO Box 37, Cadillac 49601 (231) 775-5362
George Grettenberger Nov. 1967-1980; Richard Wilson 1980-1990; Allen D. McCreedy 1990-2000; Dale P. Ostema 2000-2007; Thomas E. Ball 2007- ; Travis Heystek (Assoc.) 09/01/2018-

Caledonia UMC *[Midwest]* office@caledoniaumc.org
(P/M) 250 Vine St SE, Caledonia 49316 (616) 891-8669
Edward D. Passenger 1966-1969; Robert Boyer 1969-1971; Lloyd Van Lente 1971-1976; Adam Chyrowski 1976-1980; Robert Tomlinson 1980-1984; Robert Wessman 1984-1990; Bobby Dale Whitlock 1990-Jan. 1996; Norman C. Kohns 1996-2005; James E. Hodge 2005-2012; Jodie R. Flessner 2012-2019; Elizabeth Ann Hurd 2019-

Calhoun County: Homer UMC *[Heritage]* homlyl@rocketmail.com
(P/M) 101 E Adams St, Homer 49245 (517) 568-4001
Ronald Wise 1968-1969; Orvel Lundberg 1969-1970; E. Lenton Sutcliffe 1970-1971; Daniel D. Corl 1971-1973; John T. Charter 1973-1978; Harold Deipert 1978-1983; Walter Rothfuss 1983-1987; Linda Farmer-Lewis Sept. 1987-Dec. 1992; Claudette Haney Apr. 16, 1993-1995; Nelson Ray 1995-1997; Linda J. Burson 1997-Jan. 1, 2000; Mark Mitchell 2000-2008; Thomas P. Fox 2008-2012; Robert P. Stover (Ret.) 2012-

Calumet UMC *[Northern Skies]* calumc@pasty.net
(P/M) 57235 Calumet Ave, Calumet 49913 (906) 337-2720
Alan DeGraw 1967-1972; James Tuttle 1972-1975; Harold Slater 1975-1978; Wayne Hutson 1978-1983; Dennis N. Paulson 1983-1987; Robert J. Easlick 1987-1990; David P. Snyder 1990-1993; Nancy G. Sparks 1993-2000; Robert A. White 2000-2016; Richard B. Brown (assoc) 2000-2003; James Palaszeski 2016-2018; Gunsoo Jung 2018-2019; [Keweenaw Parish: Calumet / Lake Linden 7-1-2019] James M. Mathews (Ret.) 2019-

Camden UMC *[Heritage]* pastortrevor1@gmail.com
(P) 205 S Main St, Camden 49232; (M) PO Box 155, Camden 49232-0155 (517) 368-5406
Karl L. Zeigler 1968-1969; John H. Gurney 1969-Aug. 1970; Joseph Huston Aug. 1970-1972; Richard Huskey 1972-1974; J. Brian Selleck 1974-Feb. 1976; Robert P. Stover March 1976-1980; Stephen Beech 1980-1983; Larry W. Rubingh 1983-1987; Frederick G. Hamlin 1987-1994; Russell K. Logston 1994-1996; Diane Stone Nov. 16, 1996-2004; Edward Mohr 2004-2010; Trevor McDermont 2010-2013; Frederick G. Cain (Ret.) (part-time) 2013-

Canton: Cherry Hill UMC *[Heritage]* secretarycherryhillumc@yahoo.com
(P/M) 321 S Ridge Rd, Canton 48188-1011 (734) 495-0035
Reinhardt E. Niemann 1961-1969; Dwight W. Murphy 1969-1972; Leonard C. Ritzler 1972-1977; Bert Hosking 1977-1986; John R. Henry 1986-1988; Randy J. Whitcomb 1988-1993; Marjorie H. Munger 1993-1998; Lawrence A. Wik 1998-2005; Latha Ravi 2005-2008; Frederick M. Hatfield 2008-Aug 15, 2008; Merlin H. Pratt Aug 15, 2008-2011; Mark Zender 2011-2014; Naylo T. Hoplkins 2014-2016; Michael Desotell 2016-

Canton: Friendship UMC *[Heritage]* church@firendshipchurchinfo.com
(P/M) 1240 N Beck Rd, Canton 48187 (734) 710-9370
Michael K. Norton 1997-

Canton: Friendship – Shelby Twp Campus UMC *[Heritage]*
(P) 53245 VanDyke, Shelby Twp 48316; (M) 1240 N Beck Rd, Canton 48187 (734) 710-9370
[Satellite of Canton: Friendship stared 01/01/2017] Michael K. Norton Jan. 1, 2017-

Capac UMC *[East Winds]* capacumparish@yahoo.com
(P/M) 14952 Imlay City Rd, Capac 48014 (810) 395-2112
Roy G. Forsyth 1967-1972; Raymond S. Burkett 1972-1981; Otto F. Flachsmann 1981-1984; Donald L. Bates 1984-Oct. 1987; Gordon B. Boyd 1987-1991; Patricia A. Van Wormer 1991-1996; Harold V. Phillips 1996-2006; Lisa J. Clark (assoc) Oct 1, 2000-2008; Steven A. Gjerstad 2006-Dec 7, 2006; James E. Paige, Jr. Jan 1, 2007-2007; Dale E. Brown 2007-2011; Lisa J. Clark 2011-

Carland UMC *[Mid-Michigan]* thegoodword1@att.net
(P) 4002 N Carland Rd, Elsie 48831; (M) 587 N Baldwin, Owosso 48867 (810) 715-9331
Horace N. Freeman 1969-1974; Homer VanBuren 1974-1983; Billy J. McKown 1983-1989; M. Shirley Jones 1989-1991; Howard M. Jones (assoc) 1989-1991; William R. Seitz 1991-Jan 1, 1996; Jean M. Scroggins Jun 16, 1996-Dec 31, 2000; Lance E. Ness Jan 1, 2000-Jul 31, 2004; Michael S. McCoy Aug 1, 2004-2006; Carole A. Brown Aug 1, 2006-2011; Calvin H. Wheelock 2011-2013; Stanley P. Stybert 2013-2018; Charlene Wagner (DSA) 2018-Dec 31, 2018; Charlene Wagner Jan 1, 2019-

Carleton UMC *[Heritage]* carletonumc@carletonumc.com
(P) 11435 Grafton Rd, Carleton 48117; (M) PO Box 327, Carleton 48117 (734) 654-2833
David A. Russell 1966-1971; Albert E. Hartoog 1971-1974; Howard M. Montgomery 1974-1979; Thomas P. Macaulay 1979-1984; James G. Simmons 1984-1986; Martha H. Cargo 1986-1987; Frederick O. Timm 1987-1993; George H. Lewis 1993-1998; Carman J. Minarik 1998-Aug 31, 2002; Donna J. Minarik (assoc) 1998-Aug 31, 2002; Robert D. Brenner Sep 1, 2002-2010; Kathy Charlefour (assoc) Sep 1, 2003-Oct 31, 2005; Brent L. Webster 2010-2012; Taek H. Kim 2012-

Carlisle UMC *[Midwest]* secretary@carlisleumc.com
(P/M) 1084 76th St SW, Byron Center 49315 (616) 878-1836
John Rothfuss 1968-1971; Curtis Cruff 1971-1975; Leonard Yarlott 1975-1979; Timothy Graham 1979-1983; John Buker 1983-1986; Larry Mannino 1986-1990; John Ritter 1990-1994; Andrew Jackson 1994-2006; Craig L Adams 2006-Dec. 1, 2009; Andrew Jackson (DSA) Dec. 1, 2009-2010; Mike Ramsey 2010-2017; Gary M. Zinger (LM/DSA) 2017-

Caro UMC *[Saginaw Bay]* secretarycumc@centurytel.net
(P/M) 670 W Gilford Rd, Caro 48723 (989) 673-2246
Benjamin C. Whaley (Caro: First) 1968-1971; G. Charles Ball (Caro & Fairgrove EUB) 1966-1971; Benjamin C. Whaley & G. Charles Ball (merged) 1971-1972; Ronald Thompson 1972-1975; John Marvin (interim) Clive Dickins 1975-1983; Brian Kundinger (assoc) 1978-1981; Bonnie Welch (assoc) 1981-1983; John Bunce 1983-1988; Calvin Blue 1988-1999; Duane E. Miller 1999-2006; Jerome K. Smith 2006-2011; Gregory M. Mayberry 2011-2016; Anthony J. Tomasino 2016-

Carson City UMC *[Mid-Michigan]* carsoncityumc@gmail.com
(P) 119 E Elm St, Carson City 48811; (M) PO Box 298, Carson City 48811 (989) 584-3797
Raymond D. Flessner 1970-1978; Paul D. Mazur 1978-1985; A. Ray Grienke 1985-Aug. 16, 1999; Richard A. Powell Aug. 16, 1999-Dec. 16, 1999; Robert E. Horton (DSA) Dec. 16, 1999-July 1, 2000; Kenneth J. Nash 2000-2006; Ronald K. Brooks 2006-2008; Andrew L. Croel 2008-2014; Charles Edward Milam 2014-Feb. 17, 2016; Larry W. Nalett (RLA) Feb. 22-June 30, 2016; Charles R. Kaliszewski (Ret.) 2016-Dec. 31, 2017; Patricia L Brook (Ret) (LTFT 1/4) 2018- ; Todd W Butler (DSA) (LTFT 1/4) (Pastoral Assistant) 2018-2019; Ian S. McDonald 2019-

Carsonville UMC *[East Winds]* mcrgegorumc@airadvantage.net
(P) 3953 W Sheldon Rd, Carsonville 48419; (M) 5791 Paldi Rd, Peck 48466
John Edmund Naile Jan 1, 1997-Jan 1, 1077' Gordon B. Boyd Jun 16, 1981-Jul 14, 1984; Jerry D. Griggs 1998-

Casco UMC *[Greater Southwest]*   cascoumcoffice@gmail.com
(P/M) 880 66th St, South Haven 49090   (269) 227-3328
     Lawrence Lee 1968-1970; O.I. Lundberg 1970-1971; Adam Chyrowski 1971-1977; Athel Lynch 1977-1979; Dan Graber 1979-1980; John Fisher 1980-1986; Theodore Cole 1986-Sept. 1988; Willard Gilroy Oct. 1988-April 15, 1993; Michael J. Tupper April 16, 1993-2001; Cynthia M. Parsons 2001-2006; David W. Meister 2006-2016; Donald J. Graham 2016-2019; Jodi M. Cartwright 2019-

Caseville UMC *[Central Bay]*   cumc@airadv.net
(P) 6490 Main St, Caseville 48725; (M) PO Box 1027, Caseville 48725-1027   (989) 856-4009
     G. William Dunstan 1968-1977; Warren D. Pettis 1977-1980; Wayne E. Sparks 1980-1981; Brent L. McCumons 1981-1986; John N. Hamilton 1986-1990; Gregory M. Mayberry 1990-Apr 30, 1998; Michael L. Quayle May 1, 1998-2004; Philip D. Voss 2004-2010; Linda L. Fuller 2010-2018; Donald L. Wojewski 2018-

Cass City UMC *[Central Bay]*   ccumc@airadv.net
(P/M) 5100 Cemetery Rd, Cass City 48726   (989) 872-3422
     Ira L. Wood 1966-1974; Donald Turbin 1968-1970; Elizabeth D.K. Isaacs 1970-1976; Eldred L. Kelly 1974-1983; Byron Hatch 1976-1979; Paul T. Wachterhauser 1979-1983; Clare Patton 1983-1989; James Mc Callum 1983-1985; S. Joe Robertson 1985-Jan. 1990; Donald J. Daws 1989-1992; Kenneth B. Ray 1992-1994; Robert P. Garrett (assoc) 1994-1997; Richard W. Sheppard 1990-1997; Philip A. Rice 1997-2002; George F. Ward 2002-2006; Paul G. Donelson 2006-2010; Jacquelyn Roe 2010-2018; Robert Paul Demyanovich (DSA) 2018-

Cassopolis UMC *[Greater Southwest]*   casscumc@frontier.com
(P) 209 S Rowland St, Cassopolis 49031; (M) PO Box 175, Cassopolis 49031   (269) 445-3107
     Fred W. McNeil 1960-63; Joseph Wood 1966-1976; James G. Crosby 1976-1983; Charles Van Lente 1983-1993; Donald R. Ferris 1993-2000; Claudette Haney 2000-2005; Glenn Litchfield 2005-2009; James A. Richie 2009-2012; Dawn Laupp 2012-Dec, 31, 2012; Benjamin D. Hutchison Jan. 1, 2013-July 15, 2015; Wade S. Panse (Ret.) Aug. 23, 2015-

Cedar Springs UMC *[Midwest]*   office@cedarspringsumc.org
(P) 140 S Main St, Cedar Springs 49319; (M) PO Box K, Cedar Springs 49319   (616) 696-1140
     Leo Bennett 1965-1970; Stanley Hayes 1970-Oct. 1975; Ralph Kallweit Jan. 1976-1980; Lloyd Hansen 1980-1983; Arthur Jackson 1983-1987; Robert Stover 1987-1989; William Haggard 1989-1995; Ben B. Lester 1995-2003; Brian F. Rafferty 2003-2008; Mary Letta-Bement Ivanov 2008-2014; Stephen F. Lindeman 2014-Mar. 14, 2017; Karen J. Sorden 2017-Nov. 30, 2017; William C. Johnson (Ret) (LTFT 1/4) Jan. 1, 2018-

Central Lake UMC *[Northern Waters]*   dbiteman@outlook.com
(P) 8147 W State Rd, Central Lake 49622; (M) PO Box 213, Central Lake 49622-0213
     Leonard Yarlott 1967-1969; Paul Hartman 1970-1974; Daniel Miles 1974-1976; Chris Schroeder 1976-1982; David Cheyne 1982-1991; Celia Hastings, June-Nov. 1991; Peter H. Shumar Nov. 1991-May 1992; Richard A. Morrison June 1992-1995; Richard L. Matson 1995-2003; Charles A. Williams 2003-2010; Daniel W. Biteman, Jr. 2010-

Central Lakeport UMC *[East Winds]*
(P) 3597 Milwaukee Rd, Lakeport 48059; (M) c/o Marysville UMC, 721 W Huron Blvd, Marysville 48040
     Darrel W. Tallman 1967-1973; Mark K. Smith 1973-1976; Daniel R. Fenton 1976-1978; Harold J. Slater 1978-1980; James E. & Peggy Paige 1980-1985; Georg F.W. Gerritsen 1985-1988; Donald H. Francis 1988-1992; Emerson W. Arntz 1992-2000; Jimmy S. Barnet (co-pastor) 2000-2001; Pamela Barnett (co-pastor) 2000-2001; Susan K. Freeland Montenegro 2001-2003; Ralph T. Barteld 2003-2016; [Marysville / Central Lakeport formed Marysville Cooperative Parish 07/01/2019] Curtis B. Clarke 2019-

Centreville UMC *[Greater Southwest]*   cumchurch@comcast.net
(P/M) 305 E Main St, Centreville 49032   (269) 467-8645
Rudy A. Wittenbach 1967-1974; Charles W. Smith 1974-1984; Gordon E. Spalenka 1984-1987; Paul G. Donelson 1987-1989; Michael T. Conklin 1989-Aug. 1, 1997; David W. Meister Aug. 16, 1997-2003; Karin Orr 2003-2014; Emily K. (Beachy) Slavicek Hansson 2014-Dec. 31, 2018; Debra L. Eisenbise (DSA) Feb. 9-Jun. 30, 2019; Michael W. Vollmer 2019-

Chapin UMC *[Mid-Michigan]*   pastorherbw@aol.com
(P) 19848 S Chapin Rd, Elsie 48831; (M) 218 E Main, Henderson 48841-9765   (989) 661-2497
Monroe J. Frederick 1968-1972; T. K. Foo Sep 18, 1972-1976; Wayne A. Rhodes 1976-1978; James B. Lumsden 1978-1982; David S. Stiles 1982-1984; James P. James 1984-1989; J. Robert Anderson 1989-1993; Nicholas W. Scroggins 1993-1998; Paul B. Lim 1998-2000; Billie Lou Gillespie 2000-Oct 14, 2006; Calvin H. Wheelock Nov 1, 2006-2019; [Henderson / Chapin / Owosso: Trinity formed three-point charge 7-1-2019] Steffani Glygoroff (DSA) 2019-

Charlevoix UMC *[Northern Waters]*   chxumc@gmail.com
(P/M) 104 State St, Charlevoix 49720   (231) 547-2654
Leona Winegarden 1965-1969; Elmer J. Faust 1969-1975; Austin Regier 1975-1981; David Yingling 1981-1988; Benton R. Heisler 1988-Nov. 15, 1992; Dale Peter Ostema Feb. 1, 1993-2000; J. Todd Thompson 2000-2010; Gregory P. Culver 2010-2017; [Charlevoix / Horton Bay became a two-point charge 2016; Charlevoix became a single station 2017] Randall J. Hitts (LTFT 1/2) 2017-

Charlevoix: Greensky Hill UMC *[Northern Waters]*   jonmays7@gmail.com
(P/M) 8484 Green Sky Hill Rd, Charlevoix 49720   (231) 547-2028
Leona Winegarden 1965-1969; Elmer J. Faust 1969-1975; Austin Regier 1975-1981; David Yingling 1981-1988; Benton R. Heisler 1988-Nov. 15, 1992; Dale Peter Ostema Feb. 1, 1993-Feb. 1, 1998; Kathryn S. Slaughter Feb. 1, 1998-2000; Geraldine M. Litchfield 2000-2005; Timothy B. Wright 2005-2013; [became single-point charge 2013] Jonathan D. Mays (DSA) 2013-2015; Jonathan D. Mays (LTFT) 2015-

Charlotte: Lawrence Avenue UMC*[Mid-Michigan]*   laumc@ameritech.net
(P) 210 E Lawrence Ave, Charlotte 48813; (M) PO Box 36, Charlotte 48813   (517) 543-4670
Forrest E. Mohr 1966-1970; Lester Bailey 1970-1974; Verne Summers Sept. 1974-1987; James Mitchum (Assoc.) Apr. 1983-May 1987; George W. Fleming 1987-2002; Don Entenman (Assoc.) 1987-1988; Gary Bondarenko (Assoc.) 1988-1991; Edna Fleming (Assoc.) 1995-2002; Karen S. Wheat 2002-2010; Terry Fisher 2010-2013; Gary S. Wales 2013-

Chase: Barton UMC *[Northern Waters]*   ljball6@hotmail.com
(P) 6957 S Depot St, Chase 49623; (M) PO Box 104, Chase 49623-0104   (231) 832-5069
Michael Nicholson 1988-Dec. 1991; Paul Patterson (ret.) Jan.-June 1992; Deborah R. Miller June 1, 1992-1995; Wayne McKinney (DSA) 1995-July 31, 2002; Timothy W. Doubblestein Sept. 1, 2002-Sept. 15, 2003; Sueann K. Hagan Oct. 16, 2003-2006; Michael J. Simon 2006-2010; Lyle J. Ball (LTFT) 2010- [Baldwin: Covenant Community / Chase-Barton became cross-district circuit 2015]

Cheboygan: St. Paul's UMC *[Northern Skies]*   chebstpauls531@att.net
(P/M) 531 E Lincoln Ave, Cheboygan 49721   (231) 627-5262
Carol O. Oswald 1963-1972; R. Edward McCracken 1972-1978; Ralph T. Barteld 1979-1985; Clare M. Tosch 1985-1988; John F. Greer 1988-1992; Robert D. Wright 1992-1994; Jeffry W. Dinner 1994-1998; George H. Lewis 1998-2010; Trevor A. Herm 2010-2017; John D. Bailey 2017-

Chelsea: First UMC *[Heritage]* jbarrett@chelseaumc.org
(P/M) 128 Park St, Chelsea 48118 (734) 475-8119
Robert M. Worgess 1967-1970; Clive H. Dickens 1970-1975; Marvin H. McCallum 1975-1983; David W. Truran 1983-1986; Gerald R. Parker 1986-Jul. 15, 1992; Richard L. Dake Sep. 1 1992-2004 ; Rebecca Foote (assoc.) 1992-1998; Margaret Garrigues-Cortelyou (assoc) 1998-2000; Johncie (Zellers) Palmer (deacon) Sep 1, 1999-2008; Jennifer W. Williams (assoc) 2000-2003; Joy A. Barrett 2004- ; Barbara Lewis-Lakin (assoc) 2004-2010; Annalissa Gray-Lions (deacon) Jan 1, 2007-2010;

Chesaning: Trinity UMC *[East Winds]* cumc@centurytel.net
(P/M) 1629 Brady St, Chesaning 48616 (989) 845-3157
Charles E. Jacobs 1962-1970; Walter T. Ratcliffe 1970-1974; Lewis P. Compton 1974-1986; Brent L. McCumons 1986-1993; George F. Ward 1993-2002; Sherry L. Parker Sep 1, 2002-2008; Mark G. Johnston 2008-2012; Timothy S. Woycik 2012-

Churchill UMC *[Central Bay]* reidr@ziggnet.com
(P) 501 E State Rd, West Branch 48661; (M) Box 620, West Branch 48661 (989) 312-0105
Fred Timm 1965-1975; James R. Balfour II 1975-1982; David Baize 1982-1983; John R. Crotser 1983-1987; Jeffrey Hildebrand 1987-1989; Barbra Franks 1989-1994; Carter Garrigues-Cortelyou Sep 1, 1994-1998; Thomas K. Spencer 1998-2005; Donald J. Wojewski 2005-Dec 31, 2007; Cindy Gibbs Jan 1, 2008-2010; Ronald Cook Sep 20, 2010-2011; Janet Larner 2011-2013; Brenda K. Klacking 2013-

Clare UMC *[Central Bay]* jbailey@clareumc.org
(P/M) 105 E 7th St, Clare 48617 (989) 386-2591
Donald Winegar 1966-Sept. 1973; C. William Martin Oct. 1973-1979; Marvin R. Rosa 1979-1986; Eugene A. Lewis 1986-1994; Gregory R. Wolfe 1994-2003; Mark R. Payne (Assoc. 1/4 time) 1995-1996; Dennis B. Bromley 2003-2013; John G. Kasper 2013-

Clarkston UMC *[East Winds]* cumcoffice@clarkstonumc.org
(P/M) 6600 Waldon Rd, Clarkston 48346 (248) 625-1611
Frank A. Cozadd 1967-1975; Paul M. Cargo 1975-Dec. 1975; James R. Balfour Jan. 1976-1985; Douglas R. Trebilcock 1985-2004; Carole A. Massey (assoc) 1986-1987; Tracy Lynne Huffman (assoc.) 1995-1999; Jill H. Zundel (assoc) 1999-2006; Christine E. Wyatt (deacon) 1999-2014; Richard L. Dake 2004- ; Matthew L. Pierce (assoc.) 2006-Oct 8, 2007; Reed P. Swanson (assoc) 2008-2010; Amy E. Mayo-Moyle (assoc.) 2010-2015; Laura Speiran (deacon) 2014-; Kyle Bucholtz (assoc) 2015-Dec 31, 2015; Megan Walther (assoc) 2017-

Clawson UMC *[Greater Detroit]* clawsonumchurch@wowway.com
(P/M) 205 N Main St, Clawson 48017 (248) 435-9090
Clyde E. Smith 1968-1973; David A. Stout (assoc) 1968-1971; W. Herbert Glenn 1973-1982; Frank A. Cozadd 1982-1985; Archie H. Donigan 1985-Mar.12-1988; Gordon E. Ackerman 1988-2001; Thomas F. Keef 2001-2010; Margaret Garrigues 2010-Sept 1, 2016; Murphy S. Ehlers (deacon) Jan 1, 2016-Dec 30, 2017; Yoo Jin Kim Sept 1, 2016-2018; Harris M. Dunn Jul 1-Nov 30, 2018; Michael R. Perez (DSA) Jan 1, 2019-

Claybanks UMC *[Midwest]* claybanksumc@gmail.com
(P) 9197 S 56th Ave, Montague 49437; (M) PO Box 104, Montague 49437 (231) 923-0573
Charles Dunbar 1965-1971; Richard Matson 1971-1975; Bernard Randolph 1975-1976; Edward Slate 1976-1983; Steve Smith 1983-1985; Keith Treman 1985-1990; Kay B. Bosworth 1990-1998; Anita Hahn 1998-2006; Gayle Berntsen 2006-2014; [Claybanks realigned from Whitehall/Claybanks to Shelby/Claybanks 2014] Terri L. Cummins 2014-2016; Gary L. Peterson (RLA) 2016- [Claybanks became a single-point charge 2016]

Clayton UMC *[Heritage]*   clayton.rollincenter@gmail.com
(P) 3387 State St, Clayton 49235; (M) PO Box 98, Clayton 49235-0098   (517) 445-2641
Lawson D. Crane 1967-1975; Heath T. Goodwin 1975-1976; George F. Ward 1976- 1981; Walter H. Miller Nov 1, 1981-1994; Craig A. Pillow 1994-2009; Linda Jo Powers 2009-2012; Robert W. Dister 2012-

Climax UMC *[Greater Southwest]*   cxssumc@gmail.com
(P) 133 E Maple St, Climax 49034; (M) PO Box 125, Climax 49034-0125   (269) 746-4023
Garth Smith 1965-1971; Pulpit Supply July-Nov. 1971; Wilbur Williams Nov. 1971-Aug. 1973; Paul Mazur Sept. 1973-1978; Pulpit Supply July-Dec. 1978; Donald Robinson Dec. 1978-Aug. 1979; James Allred Sept. 1979-Dec. 1986; Pulpit Supply Jan.-Apr. 1987; Dennis Slattery Apr. 1987-Oct. 1988; Pulpit Supply Oct.-Dec. 1988; Thomas E. Ball Dec. 1988-1994; David F. Hills 1994-Aug. 1, 1999; Sally J. LaFrance Oct. 1, 1999-2001; Thomas L. Truby 2001-March 1, 2003; David G. Knapp 2003-2009; Glenn C. Litchfield 2009-2016; Beverley J. Williams 2016-

Clinton UMC *[Heritage]*   clinltonumc@frontier.net
(P/M) 10990 Tecumseh Clinton Rd, Clinton 49236   (517) 456-4972
David M. Liscomb 1967-1969; Dean W. Parker 1969-1971; David A. Stout 1971-1974; Ronald K. Corl 1974-1975; James R. Rupert 1975-1977; Thomas A. Kruchkow 1977-Dec. 1979; Jack R. Lancaster Jan. 1980-1989; Roy A. Syme 1989-1992; William M. Smith 1992-2005; A. Faye McKinstry 2005-2014; Pamela A. Beedle-Gee 2014-2018; Robert Blanchard 2018-

Clio: Bethany UMC *[East Winds]*   bethanyumcclio@gmail.com
(P) 353 E Vienna St, Clio 48420; (M) PO Box 327, Clio 48420-0327   (810) 686-5151
S. D. Kinde 1968-1976; John D. Rozeboom 1976-1981; Calvin H. Blue 1981-1988; Thomas G. Badley 1988-1997; Roger F. Gedke 1997-2010; John D. Bailey 2010-2015; LuAnn L. Burke 2015-2017; Catherine (Cathi) M Huvaere 2017-

Coldwater UMC *[Greater Southwest]*   coldwaterum@cbpu.com
(P/M) 26 Marshall St, Coldwater 49036   (517) 279-8402
Mark D. Graham 1968-Sept. 1974; Lester C. Bailey Sept. 1974-1982; James M. Morgan 1982-1988; Royce R. Robinson 1988-1989; Charles W. Richards 1989-1988; Betty A. Smith 1998-2004; Mark Babb (Deacon) 2002-2006; Cynthia Ann Skutar 2004-2010; Denise J. Downs (Assoc.) 2007-2008; Steven R. Young 2010-2015; Edrye A. Maurer 2015-Jan. 1, 2017; David L. Morton (Ret.) Jan. 1, 2017-June 30, 2017; Julie Yoder Elmore 2017-

Cole UMC *[East Winds]*
(P/M) 7015 Carson Rd, Yale 48097   (810) 387-4400
Roy C. Forsyth 1969-1972; Harvard Warren 1972-1988; William D. Wood Jan 1989-Jan, 1992; Earleen A. (Hamblen) VanConant 1992-1993; Harold V. Phillips 1993-1996; Patrick D. Robbins 1998-2000; Debra K. Brown 2000-2010; Christopher G.L. Titus 2010-2019; Dennis Eric Irish 2019-; Julia Ann Cramer (assoc) (DSA) 2019- [Yale / Cole / Melvin became a three-point charge 07/01/2019]

Coleman: Faith UMC *[Central Bay]*   colemanfaithumc@sbcglobal.net
(P) 310 N 5th St, Coleman 48618; (M) PO Box 476, Coleman 48618-0476   (989) 465-6181
R. A. Edwards (w/Geneva Hope) 1969-1971; T. H. Bennink (w/Geneva Hope) 1971-1974; James S. Ritchie (w/Geneva Hope) 1976-1980; Roger L. Colby (w/Geneva Hope) 1980-1986; Stephen Cartwright (w/Geneva Hope) 1986-1988; Joy E. Arthur (w/Geneva Hope) 1988-1990; Joy E. Arthur 1991-1992; Donald J. Daws 1992-Jul 31, 1997; Dana R. Strall Aug 1, 1997-1999; David K. Koski 1999-2008; Caroline F. Hart 2008-2015; Nathan T. Reed 2015-2019; Scott W. Marsh 2019-

Coloma UMC *[Greater Southwest]* office.colomaumc@gmail.com
(P) 144 S Church St, Coloma 49038; (M) PO Box 670, Coloma 49038 (269) 468-6062
George W. Chaffee 1968-1971; Carl Hausermann 1971-1977; Elizabeth Perry Nord (Assoc.) 1976-1981; Dwight Benner 1977-Sept. 1981; Timothy Closson Jan. 1982-Oct. 1986; Laura C. Truby Jan. 1987-1991; Richard Rossiter 1992-Feb. 4, 1996; Leonard R. Schoenherr Feb. 16, 1996-1999; David F. Hills Aug. 1, 1999-2007; O'Ryan Rickard 2007-2009; William W. Chu 2009-2011; Ronald D VanLente 2011-2018 [Watervliet UMC merged w/ Coloma UMC 6-26-11]; David L. Haase (assoc.) 2014-2016; Christine Marie Beaudoin 2018-

Colon UMC *[Greater Southwest]* colonumcsecretary19@gmail.com
(P) 224 N Blackstone Ave, Colon 49040; (M) PO Box 646, Colon 49040 (269) 432-2783
Leon Shaffer 1967-Nov. 1, 1973; Larry R. Sachau March 15, 1974-1979; Theodore Bennink 1979-1980; Larry R. Shrout 1980-1983; Jack Kraklan 1983-1985; Lawrence Hubley Nov. 1, 1985-1991; Raymond D. Flesner 1991-1999; Arthur C. Murphy 1999-Jan. 15, 2007; Donald J. Graham 2007-2012; John Sterner 2012-2015; Carl Q. Litchfield (Ret.) Feb. 15-Jun. 30, 2018; Samuel C. Gordy 2018-

Columbiaville UMC *[East Winds]* columc@frontier.net
(P) 4696 Pine St, Columbiaville 48421; (M) PO Box 98, Columbiaville 48421 (810) 793-6363
Theodore H. Bennink 1969-1971; John F. Greer 1971-1982; Lawrence C. Brooks 1982-1985; Stephen E. Wenzel 1985-1993; Frederick O. Timm 1993-1998; Margaret A. Paige 1998-2002; AmyLee Brun Terhune 2002-2009; Kim D. Spencer 2009-2010; Kristen I. Parks 2010-2013; Esther A. Irish 2013-

Commerce UMC *[Heritage]* commerceumc@sbcglobal.net
(P/M) 1155 N Commerce Rd, Commerce Twp 48382 (248) 363-3935
George MacDonald Jones 1963-1969; John W. Smith 1969-1970; James A. Smith 1970-1976; Gary R. Imms 1976-1981; John G. Park 1981-1992; Dwight W. Murphy 1992-Jan 31, 2004; Janet Gaston Petty (interim) Feb 1, 2004-2004; Deane B. Wyllys 2004-2018; Donald S Weatherup 2018-Jan. 31, 2019; Andrew H. Lee 2019-

Concord UMC *[Heritage]* concordumc1@hotmail.com
(P) 119 S Main St, Concord 4923; (M) PO Box 366, Concord 49237-0366 (517) 524-6156
Everett Love 1967-1969; Daniel Miles 1969-Dec. 1971; Pulpit Supply Jan.-June 1972; Joseph Huston 1972-1975; Ronald Grant 1975-1982; John McNaughton 1982-1984; Pulpit Supply 1984-1986; David Hansen 1986-1989; Ed Dahringer (interim) July-Dec. 1989; Barbara M. Flory Jan. 1990-1998; Harris J. Hoekwater 1998-2006; Melany A. Chalker 2006-2013; David Elmore 2013-2016; Robert M. Hughes (DSA) 2016-2019; Robert M. Hughes 2019-

Constantine UMC *[Greater Southwest]* umcconstantine@yahoo.com
(P) 285 White Pigeon St, Constantine 49042; (M) 265 E Third St, Constantine 49042
(269) 435-8151
Adam Chyrowski 1966-1971; Roger Wittrup 1971-April 1973; Richard Williams April 1973-April 1976; David Selleck April 1976-Sept. 1979; R. Paul Doherty Dec. 1979-1987; Walter Rothfuss 1987-1989; Gerald Hagans 1989-Aug. 1991. James W. Barney Sept. 1991-1998; Russell K. Logston 1998-2001; Mark R. Erbes 2001-2007; Melanie Young 2007-2009; Scott E. Manning 2009-2016 [Constantine / White Pigeon became a two-point charge 2009]; Khristian A. McCutchan 2016-2017; Tiffany M. Newsom 2017-

Coomer UMC *[Central Bay]*
(P) 5410 S Vandecar Rd, Mt Pleasant 48858; (M) 8187 S Winn Rd, Mt Pleasant 48858 (989) 866-2566
Harold Armon 1968-1969; Lawrence Smith 1969-1970; Athel Lynch 1970-1973; Joseph Dudley 1973-1974; Kathy Nickerson 1974-1977; James Sabo-Schuler 1977-1980; James Burgess 1980-1986; M. Christopher Lane 1986-1990; Paula Jane Duffey 1990-1998; Dale A. Golden 1998-2005; Paulette G. Cheyne 2005-2006; Melody Lane Olin (DSA) 2006; Melody Olin Nov. 15, 2006-2010; Lawrence Wonsey 2010-2014; Russell D. Morgan 2014-2016; Raymond W. Francis (DSA) (LTFT 1/4) 2016- [Coomer/Winn realigned to a two-point charge 2016; previously w/ Blanchard-Pine River]

Coopersville UMC *[Midwest]*   office@coopersvilleumc.org
(P/M) 105 68th Ave N, Coopersville 49404   (616) 997-9225
   Philip P. Steele 1968-1969; Vernon L. Michael 1970-1980; David L. Flagel 1980-1989; Paul D. Mazur 1989-1990; Martin M. DeBow 1990-1997; Michael T. Conklin Aug. 1, 1997-1999; John D. Morse 1999-2012; Cori Lynn Cypret Conran 2012-

Corunna UMC *[East Winds]*   corunna.mi.umc@gmail.com
(P/M) 200 W McArthur St, Corunna 48817   (989) 743-5050
   J. Paul Pumphrey 1968-1973; John W. Simpson 1973-1982; Leonard W. Gamber 1982-1990; Paul G. Donelson 1990-1992; Donald P. Haskell 1992-1994; David E. Ray 1994-1996; William R. Maynard 1996-2001; Michael L. Peterlin 2001-Oct 1, 2006; Douglas K. Mercer (interm) Jan 1, 2007-2007; David R. Strobe 2007-2013; Janet Larner 2013-2017; Stephen Spina (DSA) 2017-May 2, 2018; Stephen Spina May 3, 2018-

Corunna: Northwest Venice UMC *[East Winds]*   nbeckwithsr@msn.com
(P/M) 6001 Wilkinson Rd, Corunna 48817   (989) 661-2377
   Fred W. Knecht 1969-1972; Charles F. Kitchenmaster Feb., 1972-1981; Keith Rasey 1981-1984; To be supplied-DS Assignment; Harry M. Brakeman 1987-1991; Richard O. Griffith 1991-1992; Donald O. Crumm 1992-2002; Douglas D. Sheperd 2003-2006; Betty Kay Leitelt 2006-2010; Cheryll Warren Aug 1, 2010-2014; Norman R. Beckwith, Sr. Nov 2, 2014-

Croswell: First UMC *[East Winds]*   ngenoff@rocketmail.com
(P/M) 13 N Howard Ave, Croswell 48422   (810) 679-3595
   John Allan 1966-1979; C. William Bollinger 1979-1981; John Tagenhorst Jun-Aug 1981; George F. Ward 1981- 1988; Grant R. Lobb 1988-1996; Leonard W. Gamber 1996-1999; Elmer A. Armijo 1999-2001; Jerry P. Densmore 2001-2009; Nickolas K. Genoff 2009- Dec 31, 2018; Ellen O. Schippert Jan 1, 2019-

Courtland-Oakfield UMC *[Midwest]*   courtland.oakfieldumc@gmail.com
(P/M) 10295 Myers Lake Ave NE, Rockford 49341   (616) 866-4298
   T.E. Meredith 1968-1970; Richard E. Cobb 1970-March 1972; William J. Bildner 1972-1977; Wendell Stine 1977-1983; Forest H. Crum 1983-Sept. 1984; Gerald Selleck Dec. 1984-1990; Charles K. Stanley Nov. 1, 1990-1996; Charles W. Smith 1996-2008; Michael T. Conklin 2008-2009; Jeffrey C. Williams 2009-2011; Robert Eckert 2011-Oct. 21, 2016; William C. Johnson (Ret.) Nov. 8, 2016-June 30, 2017; Kimberly A. DeLong 2017- [Wyoming Park / Courtland-Oakfield became a two-point charge 2017]

Crystal Falls: Christ UMC *[Northern Skies]*   cumc@up.net
(P) 500 Marquette Ave, Crystal Falls 49; (M) PO Box 27, Crystal Falls 49920   (906) 875-3123
   W. Frederick Worth 1961-1971; Frank Bishop 1971-1974; Edward C. Weiss 1974-1985; Nancy G. Sparks 1985-1993; Paul J. Mallory 1993-Jan, 1994; Stephen M. Rhoades Feb 1, 1994-2000; Elbert P. Dulworth 2000-2004; Stephen E. Rhoades 2004-2011; Nathan T. Reed 2011-2015; Steven T. Sudduth 2016- Feb 6, 2018; Reed P. Swanson Feb 7-Jun 30, 2018; Vicky Prewitt (DSA) 2018-

Crystal Valley UMC *[Midwest]*   gooey@tir.com
(P) 1547 E Hammett Rd, Hart 49420; (M) PO Box 125, Walkerville 49459   (231) 873-5422
   Hubert Bengsten 1965-1974; Pulpit supply 1974-1975; Charles Bowman 1975-Jan. 1977; Harry Parker Feb. 1977-1980; Rebecca Neal Niese 1980-1984; Michael Nicholson 1984-1988; John Ritter 1988-Sept. 1990; Max Gladding Sept.-Oct. 1990; A. Ruth Bonser Oct. 1990-1993; Nancy Bugajski 1993-Oct. 1995; Donald J. Vuurens (DSA) 1996-1998; Steven J. Hale 1998-Nov. 8, 1999; Ronald A. Houk (DSA) Nov. 8, 1999-2000; Kenneth E. Tabor 2000-2004; Ronald L. Worley 2004-Nov. 30, 2013; Ronald Iris (Ret.) Dec. 1, 2013-2015; Theresa Fairbanks (DSA) Jun. 1, 2015-Nov. 14, 2016; Kenneth E. Tabor (RLA) Dec. 1, 2015-Dec. 1, 2016; Theresa Fairbanks (LTFT) Nov. 15, 2016-2018; David O Pratt (Ret) (LTFT) 2018

Dale UMC *[Central Bay]* phope000@centuryte.net
(P) 4688 Freeman Rd, Beaverton 48612; (M) PO Box 436, Beaverton 48612 (989) 435-4829
A. H. Keesler 1967-1970; Zina B. Bennett Jr. 1970-1975; Vernon Wyllys 1975-1979; Bruce C. Hatch 1979-1986; Janet Larner 1986-1991; David K. Stewart Sr. 1991-Jul 31, 2000; Frederick LaMere Aug 31, 2000-2002; Linda Jo Powers 2002-2005; Patrick R. Poag 2005-

Davisburg UMC *[East Winds]* davisburgumc803@aol.com
(P/M) 803 Broadway, Davisburg 48350 (248) 634-3373
Henry W. Powell 1969-1972; Charles R. Jacobs 1972-1976; Otto F. Flachsmann 1976-1981; Melvin Leach 1981-Dec 31, 1994; Steven A. Miller Feb 1, 1995-1999; David D. Amstutz 1999-2001; William R. Maynard 2001-Jan 1, 2004; William R. Seitz Feb 1, 2004-2011; David L. Fleming 2011-Feb 15, 2014; Eric J. Miller Feb 16, 2014-2018; Thomas C. Hartley, Sr. (DSA) 2018-2019; Thomas C. Hartley, Sr. 2019-

Davison UMC *[East Winds]* umchurchoffice.davison@;gmail.com
(P/M) 207 E 3rd St, Davison 48423 (810) 653-5272
John W. Bray 1963-1975; Sam E. Yearby, Jr. 1975-1983; Brent Webster (assoc) 1976-Oct. 1978; Merton W. Seymour 1983-1987; Dwayne L. Kelsey 1987-1991; Daniel J. Wallace 1991-1997; P. Thomas Wachterhauser 1997-2009; Susan M. Youmans (assoc.) 2005-2008; Deborah A. Line 2009-2014; Kevin L. Miles 2014-2017; Bo Rin Cho 2017-

Dearborn: First UMC *[Greater Detroit]* fumcod@aol.com
(P/M) 22124 Garrison St, Dearborn 48124 (313) 563-5200
Frederick C. Vosburg 1961-1976; Daniel J. Wallace (assoc) 1970-1976; Richard MacCanon (assoc) 1969-1974; John W. Mulder 1976- 1980; Robert L. Porter 1976-1978; Patricia Meyers (assoc) 1978-1980; Richard L. Myers 1978-1980; William D. Mercer 1980-1986; Michael L. Raymo (assoc) 1980-1985; Ralph W. Janka 1986-1994; Michelle A. Gentile (assoc) 1985-1988; Timothy P. Wohlford (assoc) 1988-1990; Shawn P. Lewis-Lakin (assoc) 1990-1994; Robert L. Selberg 1994-1998; Mary J. Scifres (assoc) 1994-Oct 31, 1995; Judith A. May Feb 5, 1996-1998; Kenneth E. Ward 1998-2005; Pamela S. Kail (assoc) 1998-2001; Julius Del Pino 2005-2008; Marshal G. Dunlap (co-pastor) 2008-2011 ; Susan DeFoe Dunlap (co-pastor) 2008-2011; Susan DeFoe Dunlap 2011-2013; Tracy N. Huffman 2013-2018; David Nellist 2018- ; Carl T. S. Gladstone (deacon) 2019-

Dearborn: Good Shepherd UMC *[Greater Detroit]* gshepherdumc@att.net
(P/M) 1570 Mason St, Dearborn 48124 (313) 278-4350
Arthur L. Spafford 1966-1974; Russell L. Smith 1974-1980; Philip M. Seymour 1980-1988; Kathryn S. Snedeker 1988-Jun 15, 1996; Dwayne L. Kelsey 1996-Dec 31, 1999; Nancy K. Frank 2000-Oct 1, 2005; Kathy R. Charlefour Nov 1, 2005-2014; Douglas Ralston 2014-2016; Seok Nam Lim 2016-2018; Robert J Sielaff 2018-

Deckerville UMC *[East Winds]*
(P/M) 3346 Main St, Deckerville 48427-9798 (810) 376-2029
Alan W. Weeks 1964-1974; Harry M. Brakeman 1974-1977; James P. Schwandt 1977-1980; Basel W. Curtiss 1980-1983; Zinna Braden Bennett 1983-1985; Richard J. Richmond 1985-1991; Max L. Gibbs 1991-1996; James M. Thompson 1996-1999; Catherine W. J. Hiner Jan 1, 1999-2004; John H. Rapson 2004-2010; Monique R. Carpenter 2010-2015; Dale Barber Nov 1, 2015-2016;

Deerfield UMC *[Heritage]* wmclemmer@hotmail.com
(P) 110 Williams St, Deerfield 49238; (M) 2509 S Wellsville Hwy, Blissfield 49228 (517) 447-3420
Philip D. Miles 1967-1970; Donald L. Bates 1971-1976; Basil W. Curtiss 1976-1980; Howard L. Deardorff 1980-1981; William Michael Clemmer 1981-1984; Thomas C. Anderson 1984-Dec. 31, 1989; Max L. Gibbs Feb. 1, 1990-1991; June M. Westgate 1991-1996; Gerald M. Sever, Jr. 1996-1999; Wilson C. Bailey 1999-Aug 31, 1999; Allen F. Schweitzer Oct 1, 1999-Oct 31, 2000; Edward C. Weiss Nov 1, 2000-2005; William Michael Clemmer 2005-Dec 31, 2013; Samuel Pooley 2014-Dec 31, 2016; David R. McKinstry (Ret.) Jan 8-Jun 30, 2017; William T. Kreichbaum 2017-2019; Bradley R. Vasey 2019-

Delta Mills UMC *[Mid-Michigan]*   nspackman12@gmail.com
(P/M) 6809 Delta River Dr, Lansing 48906   (517) 321-8100
   Donald H. Thomson 1963-1969; Bruce Pierce Aug. 1969-1970; Raymond J. McBratnie 1970-
   1973; Dave Morton 1973-1982; William Dornbush 1982-1986; Clarence W. Hutchens Nov.
   1986-Jan. 1987; Janelle E.R. Gerkin Jan. 1987-1990; Lyle D. Heaton 1990-Jan. 1, 1999; D. Keith
   Laidler Jan. 1, 1999-June 30, 1999; Robert J. Besemer 1999-2002; Kathleen S. Kursch 2003-
   Aug. 31, 2004; Keith Laidler 2005-2007; Paulette G. Cheyne 2007-2013; Joseph L. Spackman
   (Ret.) (1/4 time) 2013-

Delton: Faith UMC *[Greater Southwest]*   faithumc@mei.net
(P) 503 S Grove St, Delton 49046; (M) PO Box 467, Delton 49046-0467   (269) 623-5400
   Earl Champlin 1968-1971; Gordon Showers 1971-1975; Elmer Faust 1975-1990; William A. Hertel
   1990-2001; Daniel B. Hofmann 2001-2007; David F. Hills 2007-2010; Gary L. Bekofske 2010-
   2012; Brian R. Bunch 2012-

Denton: Faith UMC *[Ann Arbor]*   faithchur1@sbcglobal.net
(P/M) 6020 Denton Rd, Belleville 48111   (734) 483-2276
   Clive H. Dickens 1963-1970; Harold J. Slater 1970-1972; Norman R. Beckwith 1972-1976; Susan
   K. DeFoe Dunlap 1976-1983; Hoon Hee Wong 1983-1988; Michelle A. Gentile 1988-1990; Gerald
   S. Hunter 1990-May 15, 1995; Margery A. Schleicher May 16, 1995-2000; Robert D. Brenner
   2000-Aug 31, 2002; Beth D. Titus Sep 1, 2002-2008; Michael Rudd 2008-Aug 1, 2008; D. Kay
   Pratt Aug 15, 2008-2010; Merlin H. Pratt 2010-2011; Mark Zender 2011-2014; Naylo T. Hopkins
   2014-2016; Mannah Harris Dunn 206-2018; Arthur D. Korlapati (DSA) 2018-

Detroit: Calvary UMC *[Greater Detroit]*   detroitcalvaryumc@yahoo.com
(P/M) 15050 Hubbell St, Detroit 48227   (313) 835-1317
   Lloyd Houser 1966-1977; Bishop S. Thompson (assoc) 1974-1977; Edmund Millet Aug. 1977-
   1984; Robert C. Williams 1984-1986; Theodore Whitely 1987-1992; Wilfred E. Johnson Sr.
   1992-1997; Hilda L. Harris 1997-Aug 31, 2004; Jennifer Whatley Williams Sep 1, 2004-2006;
   Theodore B. Whitely, Sr. 2006-2013; Bruce D. Johnson (DSA) 2013-2014; Carter Grimmett Nov
   1, 2013-2014; Will Council 2014-

Detroit: Cass Community UMC *[Greater Detroit]*   ccumcac@aol.com
(P) 3901 Cass Ave, Detroit 48201; (M) 11850 Woodrow Wilson St, Detroit 48206   (313) 883-2277
   Lewis L. Redmond 1953-1981; Edwin A. Rowe 1981-Jun 30, 1994; Juanita Ferguson (assoc)
   1972-1973; Melvin Hall (assoc) 1979-1984; Alonzo E. Vincent (assoc) 1984-1986; William A.
   Kellermann (assoc) 1981; Lyle Kett (assoc) 1900-1900; Harry Watson 1989-1990; Gloria Gerald
   (assoc) 1990-1991; Norman Allen, III (assoc) 1991-1993; Bea Soots Fraser (assoc) 1991-1994;
   Lamarr Gibson (assoc) 1993-1995; Faith E. Fowler Jul 1, 1994- ;Linda Slaughter (assoc.) 1995-
   1997; Karen Vo To (assoc) 1997-2001; Thomas E. Tarpley, Sr. (assoc) 1997-Aug 31, 2003; Sue
   Pethoud (deacon) 2014-Jan 1, 2016; Jonathan E. Reynolds (assoc) 2018- ; Latha Ravi 2019-

Detroit: Cass Community – World Bldg Campus UMC *[Greater Detroit]*
(P) 11745 Rosa Parks Blvd, Detroit 48206; (M) 3901 Cass Ave, Detroit 48201-1721
   [Satellite of Dtroit: Cass Community founded 07/01/2017] Faith E. Fowler 2017- ; Jonathan E.
   Reynolds (assoc.) 2018-

Detroit: Central UMC *[Greater Detroit]*   centralumcdetroit@yahoo.com
(P/M) 23 E Adams Ave, Detroit 48226   (313) 965-5422
   Dwight Large 1967-1970; William Mate (assoc) 1968-1971; James Cochran 1968-1969; Richard
   Devor 1971-1979; Daniel Krichbaum (assoc) 1972-1976; Robert Walton (assoc) 1977-1980; David
   Kidd 1980-1985; Lester Mangum (assoc) 1984-1985; Barbara Byers Lewis (assoc) 1986-1990; David
   Strong 1990-Jun 30, 1994; Linda Lee (assoc) 1990-1992; Emmanuel J. Giddings (assoc) 1992-
   1995; Edwin A. Rowe Jul 1, 1994-2014 ;Joyce E. Wallace (assoc.) 1995-1997; Victoria McKenze
   (assoc) 1997-1998; DaVita McCallister (assoc) Jun 16, 2001-2002; Latha Ravi (assoc) 2002-2005;
   Jill Hardt Zundel 2014-

Detroit: Centro Familiar Cristiano UMC (formerly El Buen Pastor) *[Greater Detroit]*
(P/M) 1270 Waterman St, Detroit 48209   (734) 482-8374
　　Eduardo Cartes 1982-1984; Geraldo Silva 1984-1985; Saul C. Trinidad 1985-1998; Marcos A.
　　Gutierrez Sep 1, 1998-Apr 15, 2005; Dora Gutierrez (assoc) Sep 1, 1998-Dec 31, 2004; Luis M.
　　Collazo 2007-2012; Patricia Gandarilla 2012-

Detroit: Conant Avenue UMC *[Greater Detroit]*   conantave@sbcglobal.net
(P/M) 18600 Conant St, Detroit 48234   (313) 891-7237
　　W. E. Teague 1967-1977; Bishop S. Thompson 1977-1984; Phylemon D. Titus 1984-1988; Hydrian
　　Elliott (assoc) 1985-Feb. 1986; James D. Cochran 1988-1992; Linda Lee 1992-1995; Emmanuel
　　J. Giddings, Sr. 1995-1997; Joyce E. Wallace 1997-2001; Linda Slaughter-Titus 2001-Jan 1, 2003;
　　Carter Grimmett Jan 1, 2003-Jun 30, 2003; Darrel E. Totty Sep 2, 2003-2015; Willie F. Smith 2015-

Detroit: French UMC *[Greater Detroit]*   frenchumcd@yahoo.com
(P/M) 1803 E 14 Mile Rd, Birmingham 48009
　　[New Church Start 07/01/2018] Gertrude Mwadi Mukalay 2018- ; John Kabala Ilunga 2018-

Detroit: Ford Memorial UMC *[Greater Detroit]*   office@fordmemorial.org
(P/M) 16400 W Warren Ave, Detroit 48228   (313) 584-0035
　　Edward Fulcher 1965-1974; D. Clyde Carpenter 1974-1978; Juanita J. Ferguson 1978-1986; Faith
　　E. Fowler 1986-Jun 30, 1994; Lawrence A. Wik Jul 1, 1994-1998; Olaf Ludums 1998-Nov 15,
　　1999; Kenneth Bryant, Jr. May 1, 2000-Mar 1, 2016; Donald Beasley (DSA) 2016-

Detroit: Metropolitan UMC *[Greater Detroit]*   serving@metroumc.org
(P/M) 8000 Woodward Ave, Detroit 48202   (313) 875-7407
　　Robert H. Bodine 1962-1973; William K. Quick 1974-1998; Allen B. Rice (assoc) 1966-1967;
　　William L. Stone (assoc) 1968-1969; Arthur E. Smith (assoc) 1970-1971; Carter W. Preston (assoc)
　　Feb. 1972-Dec. 1974; James E. Tuttle (assoc) Feb 1975-1977; Joseph D. Huston (assoc) 1975-
　　Oct. 1977; Gary L. Damon (assoc) 1977-Jan. 1986; Scott Wilkinson (assoc) 1981-1985; Jerome
　　K. Smith (assoc) 1986-1991; William Michael Clemmer (assoc) 1987-Dec, 1987; William Mercer
　　(assoc) 1990-1993; Charles S.G. Boayue (assoc) 1990-1992; Robert L. Selberg (assoc) 1991-
　　1994; John D. Landis (assoc) 1994-2000; Reed Swanson 1995-Aug 31, 1999; Julius E. Del Pino
　　1998-Dec 31, 2003; Demphna Krikorian (assoc) 1998-2000; Terry W. Allen (assoc) 2000-2002 ;
　　Amy Mayo-Moyle (assoc) 1999-2002; Janet Gaston Petty (assoc) 2002-Dec 31, 2003 ; Bonnie J.
　　Light (deacon) Aug 16, 2002-Dec 31, 2003; William A. Verhelst (Intentional interim) Jan 1, 2004-
　　2006 ; Faith E. (Green) Timmons (assoc) Aug 1, 2004-2008; Tonya M. Arnesen 2006-2011;
　　Catherine J. Miles (deacon) May 17, 2009-2013; Ray T. McGee 2011-2016; Janet Gaston Petty
　　(interim) 2016-

Detroit: Mt. Hope UMC *[Greater Detroit]*   mh_methodist@sbcglobal.net
(P/M) 15400 E Seven Mile Rd, Detroit 48205   (313) 371-8540
　　Rudolph H. Boyce 1969; Lloyd O. Houser 1981; John N. Howell 1981; Susan DeFoe Dunlap 1983;
　　John Martin 1989-Feb 28, 1995; Bea B. Soots Mar 1, 1995-Aug 31, 1997; Sanda Sangaza Sep
　　15, 1997-1999; Maurice R. Horne 1999-2004; Margaret Martinez-Ventour 2005-2010; Henry D.
　　Williams, Jr. 2010-2012; Jean Snyder Sep 2, 2012-2013; Esron Shaw Nov 9, 2014-

Detroit: People's UMC *[Greater Detroit]*   peoplesumcdetroit@outlook.com
(P/M) 19370 Greenfield Rd Detroit 48235   (313) 342-7868
　　Andrew A. Allie 1976-1980; Frederick B. Moore 1980-1992; Lester Mangum 1992-Jan 1, 2003;
　　Julius Nelson Jan 1, 2003-Jun 30, 2003; Jennifer W. Williams 2003-2004; Gary A. Williams 2004-
　　2008; Carter M. Grimmett 2008-2014; Marva Pope 2014-2018; Rahim O. Shabazz 2018-

Detroit: Resurrection UMC *[Greater Detroit]*   resurrectionumc@gmail.com
(P) 8150 Schaefer Hwy, Detroit 48228; (M) 15391 Griggs, Detroit 48238   (313) 582-7011
　　Charles Jones 1986-1992; Hydrian Elliott 1992-Jan 1, 1998; Henry Williams Feb 1, 1998-2010;
　　Margaret Martinez-Ventura 2010-2019; Carolyn A. Jones 2019-

Detroit: St. Paul UMC *[Greater Detroit]* StPaulUMCdet@aol.com
(P/M) 8701 W 8 Mile Rd, Detroit 48221 (313) 342-4656
    Thomas Tinsley 1965-1983; Janet Gaston Petty 1983-1989; Wilford Johnson 1989-1992; Theodore Whitely Sr. 1992-1996; Julius A. McKanders 1996-Nov 5, 2000; Victoria McKenze Nov 16, 2000-2001; Karen Y. Noel 2001-2010; Henry D. Williams, Jr., 2010-Aug 1, 2013; William Reese, Jr. 2014-Feb 3, 2015; Anthony Ballah Apr 15, 2016-2018; Kenneth Johnson 2018-

Detroit: St. Timothy UMC *[Greater Detroit]* sttimothysecretary@yahoo.com
(P/M) 15888 Archdale St, Detroit 48227 (313) 837-4070
    Frank R. Leineke 1977-1979; John Hinkle (assoc) 1978-1980; Roger W. Ireson 1979-Jan. 1 1988; William P. Sanders (assoc) 1981-1982; Anthony Cutting (assoc) 1982-1986; Wilfred E. Johnson, Sr. (assoc) 1986-1989; Douglas W. Vernon Jan. 1, 1988-1991; W. Steven Boom (assoc) 1989-1991; Thomas E. Hart 1991-1995; Philip Burks (assoc) 1991-1993; Hilda L. Harris (assoc) 1993-1995; Phylemon D. Titus 1995-Dec 31, 2002; Sharon G. Niefert (assoc.) 1995-1998; Lester Mangum Jan 1, 2003-2013; Christopher M. Grimes 2013-

Detroit: Scott Memorial UMC *[Greater Detroit]* scottumc@yahoo.com
(P/M) 15361 Plymouth Rd, Detroit 48227 (313) 836-6301
    Donald A. Scavella 1969-1977; George E. Rice 1977-1980; Quincy D. Copper July 1980-1987; Anthony J. Shipley 1987-Mar. 1, 1992; Samuel V. White, III (assoc) 1987-1990; Charles Knight (assoc) 1990-1991; Marquis D. Lyles (assoc) 1991-1994; Andrew A. Allie May 1, 1992-2001; Joyce E. Wallace 2001-2005; Anthony R. Hood 2005-2016; Cornelius Davis, Jr. 2016-

Detroit: Second Grace UMC *[Greater Detroit]* secondgraceumc@gmail.com
(P/M) 18700 Joy Rd, Detroit 48228 (313) 838-6475
    Alvin Burton 1958-1971; Henry E. Johnson 1971-1974; Chester Trice, Sr. 1974-1980; George E. Rice 1980-1984; Carroll Felton 1984-1986; Anthony Cutting 1986-1993; Emmanuel F. Bailey 1993-1999; Charles S. G. Boayue, Jr. 1999-2015; Murphy Ehlers (deacon) Oct 1, 2011-Nov 20, 2015; Darryl E. Totty Nov 30, 2015-

Detroit: Trinity-Faith UMC *[Greater Detroit]* trinityfaith@ameritech.com
(P/M) 19750 W McNichols Rd, Detroit 48219 (313) 533-0101
    Sam S. Tatem 1989-1990; Samuel V. White III 1990-1995; Robert G.Williams 1995-Jan 1, 1998; Hydrian Elliott Jan 16, 1998-Apr 30, 2000; Lamarr V. Gibson Jun 1, 2000-2001; Emmanuel F. Bailey 2001-Aug 31, 2006; Janet J. Brown 2007-2018; Markey C Gray 2018-

DeWitt: Redeemer UMC *[Mid-Michigan]* office@dewittredeemer.org
(P/M) 13980 Schavey Rd, Dewitt 48820 (517) 669-3430
    Rodney J. Kalajainen 1988-; Patricia L. Brook (Assoc.) 1999-Jan. 31, 2002; Timothy W. Trommater (Assoc.) 2017-

DeWitt: Redeemer UMC - St Johns: First Campus *[Mid-Michigan]* sjfumc@4wbi.net
(P/M) 200 E State St, Saint Johns 48879 (989) 224-6859
    [St Johns: First was adopted and became a satellite campus of DeWitt: Redeember July 1, 2018]
    Rodney J. Kalajainen 2018-; Timothy W. Trommater (Assoc.) 2018-

Dexter UMC *[Heritage]* secretary@dexterumc.org
(P/M) 7643 Huron River Dr, Dexter 48130 (734) 426-8480
    William J. Rosemurgy 1965-1971; James L. Hynes 1971-1979; John E. Harnish 1979-1990; Leland E. Penzien 1990-Jan. 17, 1993; Eric S. Hammar (interim Jan.-Jun); Jacqueline E. Holdsworth (assoc) 1991-Aug 31, 1992; William R. Donahue Jr. Jun. 1, 1993-2003; Anna Marie Austin (assoc) 1993-1996; G. Fred Finzer (assoc) 1996-2000; Matthew J. Hook 2003- ; Thomas Snyder (deacon) 2014- ;

Dimondale UMC *[Mid-Michigan]*　　　　　dimondaleumc@gmail.com
(P) 6801 Creyts Rd, Dimondale 48821; (M) PO Box 387, Dimondale 48821　　　(517) 646-0641
Tom Peters 1967-1970; Richard Youells 1970-1974; Thomas Weber 1974-Apr. 1978; John Ristow Apr. 1978-1979; Daryl Boyd 1979-May 1981; Heidi Joos 1981-1983; Glenn Herriman 1983-1985; Richard Powell 1985-1988; Bonnie Yost-McBain 1988-Nov. 1990; Donald D. Entenman 1991-Jan. 31, 1994; Joyce DeToni-Hill Feb. 16, 1994-Oct. 15, 1999; Lillian T. French Nov. 16, 1999-2002; Robert David Nystrom 2002-2004; Thomas Peters (DSA) 2004-2005; Andrew L. Croel 2005-2008; Kimberly A. Tallent 2008-2009; Joseph D. Huston (Ret.) (LTFT) 2009-Feb. 1, 2019; [Dimondale became a single point station 2017] Stephan Weinberger (Ret.) (LTFT) Feb. 2, 2019-2019; Linda J. Farmer-Lewis (Ret.) 2019-

Dixboro UMC *[Heritage]*　　　　　dumc@dixborochurch.org
(P/M) 5221 Church Rd, Ann Arbor 48105　　　　　(734) 665-5632
Robert C. Strobridge 1968-1970; Dwayne Summers 1970-1974; Haldon D. Ferris 1974-1985; Charles R. Marble 1985-1992; James D. Cochran 1992-1998; John C. Ferris 1998-2006; John G. Park 2006-2011; Catherine M. Freeman (deacon) 2008-2014; Tonya M. Arneson 2011-2019; Mary Hagley (deacon) 2013- ; E. Jeanne Garza 2019-

Dorr: CrossWind Community UMC *[Midwest]*　　　　　office@crosswindcc.org
(P/M) 1683 142nd Ave, Dorr 49323　　　　　(616) 681-0302
[new church start 2004; chartered 2009] Scott K. Otis, Oct. 1, 2004-2017; Kevin K. Guetschow 2017-

Dowagiac First UMC *[Greater Southwest]*　　　　　fumcdowagiac@gmail.com
(P) 326 N Lowe St, Dowagiac 49047; (M) PO Box 393, Dowagiac 49047　　　(269) 782-5167
John H. Ristow 1966-1978; Dale Benton 1979-1980; Clyde Miller 1980-1983; Claude Ridley 1983-1987; R. Paul Doherty 1987-2004; William H. Doubblestein 2004-2006; John K. Kasper 2006-2013; David A. Price 2013-Jan. 1, 2015; Kellas D. Penny III, Feb. 1, 2015-2017; Jodi M. Cartwright 2017-2019; Christopher P. Momany 2019-

Dowling: Country Chapel UMC *[Greater Southwest]*　　　　　office@mei.net
(P) 9275 S M 37 Hwy, Dowling 49050; (M) PO Box 26, Dowling 49050　　　(269) 721-8077
Marvin Iseminger 1968-1973; Kendall Lewis 1973-1977; Lynn Wagner 1977-1984; Carl Olson 1984-1985; James Cook 1985-1986; Mary Horn (Schippers) 1986-1991; Merlin Pratt 1991-1996; Kay Pratt (co-pastor) 1992-1996; DeAnn J. Dobbs 1996-Oct. 1, 2000; Dianne D. Morrison Feb. 1, 2001-2004; Patricia Anne Harpole 2004-2009; Kimberly A. Tallent 2009-2011; Ryan Wieland 2011-2016; Richard J. Foster 2016-

DownRiver UMC *[Greater Detroit]*　　　　　office@drumc.org
(P/M) 14400 Beech Daly, Taylor 48180　　　　　(734) 442-6100
Margaret E. Bryce 2013-2018; Keith Lenard (assoc) 2016- ; Jaqueline L Raineri 2018-

Dryden UMC *[East Winds]*　　　　　pastorpatty@hughes.net
(P) 5400 Dryden Rd, Dryden 48428; (M) PO Box 98, Dryden 48428-0098　　　(810) 796-3341
Paul Doherty 1966-1970; Lois Glenn 1970-1974; Dale L. Vroman 1974-1977; Bufford C. Coe 1977-1983; Margaret H. Rodgers-West 1983-1988; Zina Braden Bennett, Jr. 1988-1990; James R. Rupert 1990-Sep 30, 1995; Dennis Madill Nov 16, 1995-Sep 8, 1998; Clifford Schroeder III Feb 1, 1999-Dec 31, 2000; Frederick O. Timm Jan 1, 2001-2003; Carol S. Walborn 2003-Sep 15, 2008; Patricia A. Hoppenworth Oct 1, 2008-

Duffield UMC *[East Winds]*
(P) 7001 Duffield, Swartz Creek 48473; (M) PO Box 19, Lennon 48449　　　(989) 271-9131
Donald D. McLellan 1967-1970; Gary L. Sanderson 1970-1979; Paul I. Greer 1979-1981; Meredith T. Moshauer 1981-1988; James R. Allen 1988-1992; Myra Lee Sparks 1992-1995; David L. Fleming 1995-1999; Harlan E. Sorensen 1999-Nov 14, 2004; John D. Bailey 2005-2010; David A. Wichert 2010-2013; Eric L. Johnson 2013-2018; Duane A Lindsey (DSA) 2018-Dec 31, 2019; Duane A Lindsey Jan 1, 2019- [Lake Fenton / Lennon / Duffield three-point charge 7-1-2019]

Dundee UMC *[Heritage]*   office.dundeeumc@comcast.net
(P/M) 645 Franklin St, Dundee 48131   (734) 529-3535
    Richard L. Beemer 1968-1975; Joseph J. Bistayi 1975-1978; William M. Smith 1978-1992; Linda
J. Donelson 1992-1997; Sherry L. Parker 1997-Jul 31, 2002; Kathleen A. Groff Sep 1, 2002-2008;
Douglas K. Olsen 2008-2015; Seung H. (Andy) Baek 2015-2018; Bradley S. Luck 2018-

Durand UMC *[East Winds]*   durandfumc@frontier.com
(P/M) 10016 E Newburg Rd, Durand 48429   (989) 288-3880
    Donald D. McLellan 1967-1970; Gary L. Sanderson 1970-1979; Ronald W. Tallman 1979-1981;
R. Edward McCracken 1981-Dec. 1989; Thomas C. Anderson Jan. 1, 1990-1995; William P.
McBride 1995-2002; Wayne N. Thomas 2002-2010; Beverly L. Marr 2010-2017; Aaron B. Kesson
2017-

East Boardman UMC *[Northern Waters]*   jack49668@gmail.com
(P) 2082 Boardman Rd SW, S Boardman 49680; (M) PO Box 69, S Boardman 49680 (231) 879-6055
    Gerald L. Hedlund 1966-1971; Arthur and Molly Turner (co-pastors) 1971-1976; Diane Vale 1976-
Oct. 1977; Marion Nye Oct. 1977-1985; Clinton McKinven-Copus 1985-1987; Gary Wales
1987-1994; Howard Seaver 1994-2012; Mark E. Mitchell 2012-2014; Donald L. Buege 2014-2017;
[Williamsburg and (Fife Lake Boardman Parish) Fife Lake / East Boardman / South Boardman
became multi-point charge 2017] John J. Conklin 2017- [2018 Williamsburg, Fife Lake, East
Boardman, South Boardman formed the Unified Parish]

East Jordan UMC *[Northern Waters]*   eastjordanumc@gmail.com
(P) 201 4th St, East Jordan 49727; (M) PO Box 878, East Jordan 49727   (231) 536-2161
    Stanley L. Hayes Nov. 1966-1970; Lester E. Priest 1970-Jan. 1974; Daniel J. Minor April 1974-
1981; Phillip W. Simmons Sept. 1981-1984; Brian Secor 1984-1986; Merlin K. Delo 1986-1997,
Eugene L. Baughan 1997-2002; D. Michael Maurer 2002-Nov. 10, 2008; Ralph Posnik (DSA) Nov.
23, 2008; Ralph Posnik Nov. 15, 2009-2014; Craig A. Pahl 2014-

East Lansing: Peoples Church *[Mid-Michigan]*   office@thepeopleschurch.com
(P/M) 200 W Grand River Ave, East Lansing 48823   (517) 332-5073
    Andrew Pomerville 2000-Jun. 18, 2018; [Served by other demoniation.]

East Lansing: University UMC *[Mid-Michigan]*   office@eluumc.org
(P/M) 1120 S Harrison Rd, East Lansing 48823   (517) 351-7030
    Alden Burns 1966-1971; Arno Wallschlaeger (Assoc.) 1968-1977; Donn Doten 1971-1979; Jon
Powers (Assoc.) 1974-1978; Tom Pier-Fitzgerald (Assoc.) 1978-1982; Keith Pohl 1980-1986;
Robert Hundley (Assoc.) 1982-1990; Sharon Z. Rader 1986-1989; Gessel Berry, Jr. 1989-1991;
William Dobbs 1991-1996; Marguerite M. Rivera (Assoc.) April 16, 1995-1996; Frank W. Lyman,
Jr. & Carole S. Lyman (co-pastors) 1996-2006; John Ross Thompson 2006-Dec. 31, 2010;
Kennetha Bigham-Tsai (Assoc.) 2006-2011; Jennifer Browne 2011-2016; William W. Chu (Assoc.)
2011- ; William C. Bills 2016-

East Nelson UMC *[Midwest]*   eastnelsonumc@yahoo.com
(P/M) 9024 18 Mile Rd NE, Cedar Springs 49319   (616) 696-0661
    Leo Bennett 1965-1970; Stanley Hayes 1970-Oct. 1975; Ralph Kallweit Jan. 1976-1980; Lloyd
Hansen 1980-1983; Arthur Jackson 1983-1987; Robert Stover 1987-1989; William Haggard 1989-
1995; Ben B. Lester 1995-2003; Brian F. Rafferty 2003-2004; Herbert VanderBilt 2004-2016; Inge
E. Whittemore (LTFT) 2016-

Eastpointe: Immanuel UMC *[Greater Detroit]*   secretary@ImmanuelEastpointe.org
(P/M) 23715 Gratiot Ave, Eastpointe 48021   (586) 776-7750
    Arthur E. Smith 1960-1970; John N. Howell 1970-1972; Archie H. Donigan 1972-1980; William D.
Rickard 1980-1988; R. LaVere Webster 1988-1991; David Gladstone 1991-1997; Harold E.
Weemhoff 1997-Dec 31, 1999; Demphna Krikorian 2000-2003; Christopher D. Cowdin (assoc)
2001-2003; Adam W. Bissell 2003-2007; Sang C. Park 2007-Sep 1, 2008; Lynn Marie Hasley Oct
1, 2008-Jan 9, 2012; Albert Rush 2012-

Eaton Rapids: First UMC *[Mid-Michigan]* dsfumer@gmail.com
(P/M) 600 S Main St, Eaton Rapids 48827 (517) 663-3524
Ronald A. Houk Oct. 1971-Jan. 1982; Eric S. Beck (Assoc.) Dec. 1980-1983; Robert E. Betts Feb. 1982-1988; Larry W. Mannino (Assoc.) 1983-1986; Larry E. Irvine 1988-Oct. 15, 1993; Howard (Rick) McKire (Assoc.) Jan. 1993-; Thomas J. Evans Feb. 1, 1994-2007; Daniel B. Hofmann 2007-2014; Martin M. DeBow 2014-

Edenville UMC *[Central Bay]* phopeooo@centurytel.net
(P) 455 W Curtis Rd, Edenville 48620; (M) PO Box 125, Edenville 48620 (989) 689-6250
William Cozadd 1965-1980; Cleon Abbott 1980-1985; Donald Crumm 1985-1992; Harold J. Slater 1992-2002; Patrick R. Poag 2002-

Edmore Faith UMC *[Midwest]* churchmouse833@gmail.com
(P/M) 833 S 1st St, Edmore 48829 (989) 427-5575
C. William Martin 1965-1969; Eldon Eldred 1969-1973; Howard McDonald 1973-1976; David Yingling 1976-1981; Stanley Finkbeiner 1981-Feb. 1987; Stephen Charnley (interim) Feb.-April 1987; Joseph Graybill April 1987-1997; Connie R. Bongard 1997-Jan. 1, 2007; Esther R. Barton (DSA) Jan. 1-June 30, 2007; Susan E. Poynter 2007-2011; Michael A. Riegler 2011-2017; Daniel L. Barkholz 2017-

Edwardsburg: Hope UMC *[Greater Southwest]* hopeumc2@hope-umc.us
(P) 69941 Elkhart Rd, Edwardsburg 49112; (M) PO Box 624, Edwardsburg 49112
(269) 663-5321
(Formerly Adamsville and Edwardsburg); Jeffrey L. Reese Dec. 1, 1997-Dec. 31, 2016; Evan Lash Feb. 1-June 30, 2017; Scott K. Otis 2017-

Elba UMC *[East Winds]* jbja4047@hotmail.com
(P/M) 154 S Elba Rd, Lapeer 48446 (810) 664-5780
Emmett E. Coons 1969-1974; James M. Thompson 1974-1980; David R. McKinstry 1980-1988; Georg F. W. Gerritsen 1988-1996; Wayne E. Samson 1996-1998; James E. Paige, Jr. 1998-Oct 1, 2003; James B. Montney 2004-2014; Barbara Benjamin 2014-2016; Marybelle Haynes 2016-2018; Stanley Patrick Stybert Jul 1-Oct 31, 2018; Jeanne Harmon Wisenbaugh (DSA) Nov 1., 2018-

Elberta UMC *[Northern Waters]* feumc@att.net
(P) 555 Lincoln Ave, Elberta 49628; (M) PO Box 405, Elberta 49628-0405 (231) 352-4311
Richard M. Wilson 1967-1971; John Melvin Bricker 1971-1980; Richard C. Kuhn 1980-1982; John D. Morse 1982-1987; Paul D. Mazur 1987-April 1989; Donald R. Ferris April 1989-1993; John W. McNaughton 1993-1996; Marvin R. Rosa 1996-1999; Kathryn M. Coombs 1999-2002; Gregory P. Culver 2002-2010; Barbara J. Fay 2010-

Elkton UMC *[Central Bay]* elktonumc@yahoo.com
(P) 150 S Main St, Elkton 48731; (M) PO Box 9, Elkton 48731-0009 (989) 375-4113
Thomas J. Wood 1965-1970; O. William Cooper 1970-1974; Albert E. Hartoog 1974-1978; Joel W. Hurley 1978-1983; Ronald L. Iris 1983-1985; James P. Kummer 1985-1989; James P. James 1989-1992; Sang Yoon (Abraham) Chun 1992-1996; W. Peter Crawford 1996-2006; David C. Collins 2006-Apr 15, 2009; John W. Ball Apr 15, 2009-2009; Craig A. Pillow 2009-Oct 31, 2016; Won Dong Kim Jan 1, 2017

Elsie UMC *[Mid-Michigan]* elsieumc@mutualdata.com
(P) 160 W Main S,t Elsie 48831; (M) PO Box 189, Elsie 48831-0189 (989) 862-5239
Gordon Showers 1965-1970; David Litchfield 1970-1976; David Miles 1976-1983; Joe Glover 1983-1985; Fred Fischer 1985-1996; Merlin Pratt 1996-2003; David C. Blair 2003-2004; Jayme L. Kendall 2004-2005; Edwin D. Snook July 16, 2005-2012; Mona Kindel (3/4 time) 2012-2013; Donald R. Ferris-McCann (3/4 time) 2013-2016 [Elsie/Salem became a charge 5-1-14]; Robert D. Nystrom 2016-2018; [Elsie / Ovid became a two-point charge 2016] Ara R Williams (DSA) (LTFT 1/2) 2018

Emmett Cnty: New Hope UMC*[Northern Skies]*   newhopeofemmet@gmail.com
(P) 4516 US Highway 31, Levering 49755; (M) PO Box 72, Levering 49755   (231) 537-2000
Matthew Todd Stoll 2003-2010; Vaughn Thurston-Cox 2010-2015; [Epsilon/New Hope/Harbor
Springs/Alanson became a 4-point charge 2014] Hillary Thurston-Cox (Assoc.) 2014-Jan. 1, 2015;
[New Hope UMC of Emmett County became a single-point charge 2015] Everett L. Harpole 2015-
Dec. 1, 2015; Michelle Merchant (DSA) Dec. 1, 2015-Nov. 14, 2016; Michelle Merchant (LTFT)
Nov. 15, 2016-

Empire UMC *[Northern Waters]*   empireumc@centurytel.net
(P) 10050 W Michigan St, Empire 49630; (M) PO Box 261, Empire 49630   (231) 326-5510
Elmer J. Faust 1966-1969; Edward R. Jones 1969-1971; Alvin Doten 1971-1976; Harry R. Johnson
1976-Sept. 1978; Emmett Kadwell Jr. Oct. 1978-1982; Andrew Weeks 1982-1985; Melanie Baker-
Streevy 1985-1988; Kenneth Curtis 1988-1991; Kathryn M. Coombs 1991-1998; William (Will)
McDonald 1998-Jan. 31, 2003; William F. Dye Feb. 1, 2003-2006; Brenda E. Gordon 2006-2014;
Russell K. Logston 2014-2019; Melody L. Olin 2019-

Engadine UMC *[Northern Skies]*   engadineumc@yahoo.com
(P) 13970 Park Ave, Engadine 49827; (M) 110 W Harrie St, Newberry 49868   (906) 477-9989
Vernon D. Wyllys 1969-1975; James Lumsden 1975-1976; Audrey M. Dunlap 1976-1985; Ramona
Cowling 1985-1987; Phillip D. Voss 1987-1991; Bo L. Lange 1991-1997; Ronald O. Piette 1997-
2000; Max D. Weeks 2000-2003; Saundra J. Clark 2003-2013; Timothy G. Callows 2013-

Epsilon UMC *[Northern Waters]*   cloud.sik@asburyseminary.edu
(P/M) 8251 E Mitchell Rd, Petoskey 49770   (231) 347-6608
Norman Crotser 1968-1969; Seward Walton 1969-1976; John Gurney 1976-1979; Marvin
Iseminger 1979-1981; Jerry Jaquish 1981-1987; Glenn Wegner 1987-Aug. 1992; John F. Greer
Sept.-Nov. 1992; Dennis Bromley Jan. 1993-2003; Matthew Todd Stoll 2003-2010; Vaughn
Thurston-Cox 2010-2016; [Epsilon/New Hope/Harbor Springs/Alanson became a 4-point charge
2014] Hillary Thurston-Cox (Assoc.) 2014-2016; Eun Sik Poy 2016- [Epsilon realigned w/ Boyne
City / Boyne Falls / Epsilon 2016]

Erie UMC *[Heritage]*
(P/M) 1100 E Samaria Rd, Erie 48133   (734) 856-1453
James L. Hynes 1968-1971; James A. Wagoner 1971-1972; John D. Roach 1972- 1976; Norman
R. Beckwith, Sr. 1976-1981; Larry J. Werbil 1981-1985; David L. Baize 1985-1986; David E. Ray
1986-1991; Kenneth C. Reeves 1991-1995; Patricia A. Green 1995-1999; Dana R. Strall 1999-
2011; Megan J. Walther 2011-2017; Mary Hyer 2017-2018; Janet J Brown 2018-

Escanaba: Central UMC *[Northern Skies]*   churchoffice@escanabacentral.org
(P/M) 322 S Lincoln Rd, Escanaba 49829-1342   (906) 786-0643
Joseph Ablett 1969-1971; Clem Parr 1971-1980; James Hilliard 1980-1985; Ralph Barteld 1985-
1991; Daniel M. Young 1991-1995; Philip M. Seymour Sep 1, 1996-1997; Bo L. Lange 1997-2003;
Scott A. Harmon 2003-2013; Donna J. Minarik 2013-2016; Elise Rodgers Low Edwardson 2016-

Escanaba: First UMC *[Northern Skies]*   firstmet@escanabafirstumc.com
(P/M) 302 S 6th St, Escanaba 49829-3917   (906) 786-3713
David M. Liscomb 1969-1973; Walter David 1973-1978; Jack Lancaster 1978-1980; Michael L.
Peterlin 1980-2001; Eileen Kuehnl (assoc) 1995-1997; Philip B. Lynch (assoc) 1997-May 15,2000
; Irene R. Peterlin (assoc) 1997-Dec 31,1999; Mary G. Laub 2001-2010; Margaret H. Host 2010-
2013; Carman Minarik 2013-2016; Ryan C. Edwardson 2016- [Single point charge 7-1-2019]

Essexville: St. Luke's UMC *[Central Bay]*   stlukes-umc@sbcglobal.net
(P/M) 206 Scheurmann St, Essexville 48732-1626   (989) 893-8031
Glenn Atchinson 1966-1972; Alan DeGraw 1972-1975; Robert Hastings 1975-1980; Warren Pettis
1980-1987; Philip A. Rice 1987-1997; Duane M. Harris 1997-2005; Juanita J. Ferguson 2005-
2009; Eric A. Stone 2009-

Evart UMC *[Northern Waters]* evartunitedchurch@yahoo.com
(P) 619 N Cherry St, Evart 49631; (M) PO Box 425, Evart 49631-0425 (231) 734-2130
Milton TenHave 1967-1970; Marjorie Matthews Feb.-Oct. 1970; Laurence Waterhouse Oct. 1970-Oct. 1975; Stanley Hayes Oct. 1975-March 1984; Gerald Welsh 1984-1990; Donald Buege 1990-2000; Margaret Halls Wilson 2000-2006; Edward H. Slate, 2006-2008; Mark Mitchell 2008-2012; Melodye Surgeon (Rider) VanOudheusden 2012-2019; [Evart / Sears became a two-point charge 2017] Jean M. Smith 2019-

Ewen UMC *[Northern Skies]* aa8yf@yahoo.com
(P) 621 M 28, Ewen 49925; (M) PO Box 142, Bergland 49910-0142 (906) 988-2533
Zina B. Bennett 1965-1970; James R. Hilliard 1970-1971; Lawrence Brooks 1971-1975; Roger Gedcke 1972-1979; Lillian Richards 1971-1976; Wayne E. Sparks 1975-1980; Myra Sparks 1976-1980; Ed Hingelburg 1979-1981; Robert Thorton 1981-1983; Deane Wyllys 1983-1987; Charles H. West 1987-1993; Margaret H. West 1987-1993; Earleen VanConant 1993-1997; Clarence VanConant 1993-1997; Timothy C. Dibble 1997-2000; Cherrie A. Sporleder 2000-Jun 15, 2002; Theodore A. Trudgeon 2003-2019; [White Pine Community / Ewen / Bergland three-point charge 7-1-2019] Rosemary R. Dehut 2019-

Fairgrove UMC *[Central Bay]* fgumc@att.net
(P) 5116 Center St, Fairgrove 48733; (M) PO Box 10, Fairgrove 48733 (989) 693-6564
David L. Saucier 1965-1972; Donald P. Haskell 1972-1978; John G. Park 1978-1981; C. William Bollinger 1981-1984; Otto Flachsmann 1984-1992; David G. Mulder 1992-1996; Kevin Harbin Jan 1, 1997-1999; Kevin C. Zaborney 1999-Aug 26, 1999; Fredric Heath May 1, 2000-Sep 30, 2001; David A. Wichert 2002-2006; Daniel Gonder 2006-2013; William Sanders 2013-Aug 31, 2014; Penny Parkin Sep 1, 2014-

Faithorn UMC *[Northern Skies]* gumc@norwaymi.com
(P) W8601 Blum Rd, Vulcan 49892; (M) 130 O'Dill Dr, Norway 49870
William D. Schoonover 1967-1974; Emmett Coons 1974-1977; Mark Karls 1977-1983; Ray D. Field 1983-1985; Carl R. Doersch 1985-1991; Nancy K. Frank 1991-Oct 31, 1994; Deborah R. Jones Feb 16, 1995-1996; David M. Wallis 1996-2006; James E. Britt Aug 16, 2006-2011; Irene R. White 2011-

Farmington: First UMC *[Greater Detroit]* ann5@farmingtonfumc.org
(P) 33112 Grand River Ave, Farmington 48336; (M) PO Box 38, Farmington 48332
(248) 474-6573
Hugh C. White 1969-1972; B. Bryce Swiler (assoc) 1967-1971; John N. Howell 1972-1978; R. Howard F. Snell (assoc) 1971-1977; Charles H. Beynon 1978-1983; Arthur L. Spafford 1983-1991; Edward L. Duncan 1991-1995; Wayne T. Large 1995-Jun 1, 2001; Sondra B. Willobee (assoc) 1999-2007; Jeffrey R. Maxwell 2001-2010; Carolyn S. Wik (deacon) 2000-2014; Robert D. Brenner 2010-2013; Marshal G. Dunlap 2013-Feb 1, 2016; Cornelius Davis, Jr., Feb 1, 2016-2016; Anthony R. Hood 2016-

Farmington: Nardin Park UMC *[Greater Detroit]* LMcDoniel@NardinPark.org
(P/M) 29887 W 11 Mile Rd, Farmington Hills 48336 (248) 476-8860
William D. Mercer 1963-1980; Meredith T. Moshauer (assoc) 1969- 1977; Robert C. Laphew (assoc) 1970-1972; James F. Thomas (assoc) 1972-1982; William E. Frayer (assoc) 1977-1982; William A. Ritter 1980-1993; Jeffry W. Dinner (assoc) 1982-Nov. 1983; David Strobe (assoc) 1984-1989; George Kilbourn (R. assoc) 1984-1992; David Penniman (assoc) 1989-1993; Karen D. Poole (assoc) 1993-1997; Richard A. Peacock 1993-1997; Benjamin Bohnsack 1997-2006; Kathleen Groff (assoc) 1997-Aug 31, 2002; Jane A. Berquist (deacon) 1997-2006; Mary Ann Shipley (assoc) Nov 1, 2002-2008; Dale M. Miller 2006-2016; Susan M. Youmans (assoc) 2008-2012; Beth Titus (assoc.) Feb 1, 2015-; Melanie Lee Carey 2016-

Farmington: Orchard UMC *[Greater Detroit]*   info@orchardumc.org
(P/M) 30450 Farmington Rd, Farmington Hills 48334   (248) 626-3620
    Eric S. Hammar 1967-1977; William M. Hughes (assoc) 1967-1972; James F. Thomas (assoc) 1972-1982; Robert L.S. Brown 1977-1985; Nancy A. Woycik (assoc) 1982-1987; Paul F. Blomquist 1985-1996; James E. Greer II (assoc) 1987-1990; David Huseltine (assoc) 1990-1994; Eric A. Stone (assoc) 1994-Feb 1, 1998; Carol J. Johns 1996-2015; Margo B. Dexter (deacon) 1998-Apr, 2012; Suzanne K. Goodwin (deacon) 2008-2019; Amy Mayo-Moyle 2015- ; Nicholas Bonsky (assoc) 2019-

Farwell UMC *[Central Bay]*   office@farwellumc.org
(P) 281 E Ohio St, Farwell 48622; (M) PO Box 709, Farwell 48622-0709   (989) 588-2931
    Leroy Howe 1967-Dec. 1967; Eldon K. Eldred Dec. 1967-1969; George B. Rule 1969-Feb. 1970; Altha M. Barnes Feb. 15-June 1970; Miriam F. DeMint 1970-1971; Chester J. Erickson 1971-1974; John W. Bullock 1974-1978; Dwight J. Burton 1978-1983; David L. Miles 1983-1994; Thomas E. Ball 1994-2000; Jane Ellen Johnson 2000-Jan. 1, 2007; Connie R. Bongard Jan. 1, 2007-2015; Michael Neihardt 2015-Sept. 25, 2016; Martin T. Cobb 2017-

Felt Plains UMC *[Mid-Michigan]*   feltplainsumc@wowway.biz
(P) 3523 Meridian Rd, Leslie 49251; (M) 401 S Main St, Leslie 49251   (517) 589-9211
    William Wurzel 1966-1969; Gordon E. Spalenka June-Oct. 1969; Arthur A. Jackson Oct. 1969-1972; Wayne E. Sparks 1972-1975; James M. Morgan 1975-1982; Max J. Gladding 1982-1990; Clinton McKinven-Copus 1990-Oct. 1991; Reva Hawke Oct. 1991-April 1993; Derek DeToni-Hill 1993-Oct. 15, 1999; Janet Sweet-Richardson Nov. 1, 1999-2003; Carroll Arthur Fowler 2003-Jan. 1, 2006; Donald L. Buege Jan. 15, 2006-2014; Kelly M. Wasnich July 1-Aug. 10, 2014; Frederick H. Fischer (Ret.) Sept. 14, 2014-2015; Daniel J.W. Phillips 2015-2017; [Grovenburg / Jackson: Zion / Felt Plains / Williamston: Wheatfield became multi-point charge 2017] John Kabala Ilunga 2017-2018 ; Gertrude Mwadi Mukalay 2017-2018; Paul A Damkoehler (LTFT) 2018- [Leslie / Felt Plains became a two-point charge 2018]

Fenton UMC *[East Winds]*   kim.chase@fentonumc.com
(P/M) 119 S Leroy St, Fenton 48430   (810) 629-2132
    Eskil H. Fredrickson 1966-1972; G. Russell Nachtrieb 1972-1974; Theodore I. Hastings 1974-Nov. 1979; James L. Hynes Nov. 1979-1985; Keith Rasey (assoc) 1980-1981; Ellis Fenton (assoc) Nov. 1988-1990; David W. Truran 1986-Dec 6, 2006; Zack A. Clayton (assoc) 1990-1992; Margaret R. Garrigues-Cortelyou (assoc) 1992-Aug 31, 1994; Nancy A. Frank (assoc.) Nov 1, 1994-1996; Carol M. (Blair) Bouse (assoc) Oct 1, 1996-2001; David G. Mulder (assoc) 2001-2008; Matthew J. Packer (diaconal) 2000-2006; Edmond G. Taverine 2007-Apr 30, 2011; Jeremy T. Peters (assoc) 2008-2015; William R. Donahue, Jr. 2011-Mar 11, 2014; Terry Euper (interim) Mar 15, 2014-2014; Jeffry J. Jaggers 2014-; Michelle Forsyth (assoc.) 2015-

Fennville UMC *[Greater Southwest]*   fenumc@frontier.com
(P) 5849 124th Ave, Fennville 49408; (M) PO Box 407, Fennville 49408   (269) 561-5048
    Lloyd R. VanLente 1968-1971; Matthew Walkotten 1971-1976; Miriam DeMint 1976-1978; Ronald Hansen 1978-1984; Stanley Hayes 1984-1990; James Fox 1990-1992; Randall R. Hansen 1992-2000; Jane A. Crabtree 2000-2002; Jean Crabtree (DSA) (Assoc.) 2000-2002; Robert L. Hinklin (DSA) 2002-2003; Raymond R. Sundell 2003-2008; Gary L. Peterson 2008-2016; Daniel L. Barkholz 2016-2017; Eric Perry (DSA) 2017-May 30, 2018; Douglas Allan Tipken (DSA) Jun. 1-Dec. 31, 2018; Douglas Allan Tipken Jan. 1, 2019-

Fennville: Pearl UMC *[Greater Southwest]*   fenumc@frontier.com
(P) 1689 56th St, Fennville 49408 (M) PO Box 407, Fennville 49408   (269-)561-5048
    Ronald Wise 1968-1969; Harold Arman 1969-1971; Arthur Beadle 1971-1973; Matthew Walkotten 1973-1976; Miriam DeMint 1976-1978; Ronald Hansen 1978-1984; Stanley Hayes 1984-1990; James Fox 1990-1992; Randall R. Hansen 1992-2000; Jane A. Crabtree 2000-2002; Jean Crabtree (DSA) (Assoc.) 2000-2002; Robert L. Hinklin (DSA) 2002-; Raymond R. Sundell 2003-2008; Gary L. Peterson 2008-2016; Daniel L. Barkholz 2016-2017; Eric Perry (DSA) 2017-May 30, 2018; Douglas Allan Tipken (DSA) Jun. 1-Dec. 31, 2018; Douglas Allan Tipken Jan. 1, 2019-

Fenwick UMC *[Midwest]* fenwickumc@cmsinter.net
(P) 235 W Fenwick Rd, Fenwick 48834; (M) PO Box 241, Sheridan 48884 (989) 291-5547
John H. Gurney 1970-1976; Norman Crotser 1976-Dec. 1978; Daniel R. Bennett 1979-March 1982; Mark G. Johnson March 1982-1986; James E. Cook 1986-1991; Howard H. Harvey 1991-1996; Patrick Glass 1996-1998; Larry W. Nalett 1998-Aug. 9, 2004; Charles E. Cerling Aug. 10, 2004-2009; Jolennda Cole (DSA) 2009-2010; Jolennda Cole 2010-2011; William F. Dye 2011-2012; Russell D. Morgan (CLM) July 15, 2012-2014; Gerald A Erskine 2014-

Ferndale: First UMC *[Greater Detroit]* ferndalefirstumc@ameritech.net
(P/M) 22331 Woodward Ave, Ferndale 48220 (248) 545-4467
William N. Mertz 1965-1969; Joseph T. Edwards 1969-1974; James M. Morgan (assoc) 1969-1970; Arthur L. Spafford 1974-1983; David Stiles (assoc) 1970-1974; James Rupert (assoc) 1974-Dec 1975; Douglas K. Olsen (assoc) 1976-1981; Terry W. Allen 1983-1989; George Spencer 1989-Feb 21, 1997; Patricia A. Meyers 1997-1999; Dennis N. Paulson 1999-2008; Rony Veska 2008-2013; Robert Schoenals 2013-

Ferry UMC *[Midwest]* humchesp@frontier.com
(P) 2215 Main St, Shelby 49455; (M) 187 E South Ave, Hesperia 49421 (231) 854-5345
Merlin Delo 1966-1978; William Bowers 1978-1980; David Dryer 1980-1984; Richard Williams 1984-Oct 1, 1997; Pulpit Supply Oct. 1, 1997 - Dec. 31, 1997; Susan Olsen Jan. 1, 1998-July 1, 1998; Raymond D. Field 1998-1999; James Bradley Brillhart 1999-2007; Dianne D. Morrison 2007-2011; Richard D. Morrison (DSA) 2007-2011; Paul E. Hane 2011-2018; Paul E. Hane (Ret.) (LTFT) 2018

Fife Lake UMC *[Northern Waters]* jack49668@gmail.com
(P) 206 Boyd St, Fife Lake 49633; (M) PO Box 69, Fife Lake 49633-0069 (231) 920-2908
Gerald L. Hedlund 1966-1971; Arthur and Molly Turner (co-pastors) 1971-1976; Diane Vale 1976-Oct. 1977; Marion Nye Dec. 1977-1978; Pulpit Supply 1978-1979; Athel Lynch 1979-1981; Pulpit Supply 1981-1983; Daniel Biteman, Jr. 1983-1985; Clinton McKinven-Copus 1985-1987; Gary Wales 1987-1994; Howard Seaver 1994-2012; Mark E. Mitchell 2012-2014; Donald L. Buege 2014-2017; [Williamsburg and (Fife Lake Boardman Parish) Fife Lake / East Boardman / South Boardman became multi-point charge 2017] John J. Conklin 2017- [2018 Williamsburg, Fife Lake, East Boardman, South Boardman formed the Unified Parish]

Flat Rock: First UMC *[Greater Detroit]* flatrockumc@sbcglobal.net
(P/M) 28400 Evergreen St, Flat Rock 48134 (734) 782-2565
Floyd P. Braun 1967-1970; Ronald D. Carter 1970-1979; Clyde E. Smith 1979-1981; John W. Hinkle 1981-1989; Gary R. Imms 1989-1991; Alan W. DeGraw 1991-1995; Evans C. Bentley 1995-2004; David E. Huseltine 2004-Jul 31, 2008; John K. Benissan Aug 1, 2008-2011; Dana R. Strall 2011-2017; Amy Triebwasser 2017-

Flint: Asbury UMC *[East Winds]* flintasburyumc@gmail.com
(P/M) 1653 Davison Rd, Flint 48506 (810) 235-0016
Paul I. Greer 1969-1971; Albert C. Fennell 1971-1976; Eskil H. Fredrickson 1976-1982; William D. Schoonover 1982-Feb. 16, 1990; Grant Wessel (associate) 1985-1987; Leonard W. Gamber 1990-1996; Gary A. Allward 1996-2000; James R. Rupert 2000-Jul 31, 2006; Michael L. Quayle Aug 1, 2006-2007; S. Patrick Stybert 2007-2010; Tommy McDoniel 2010-

Flint: Bethel UMC *[East Winds]* bchr@att.net
(P/M) 1309 N Ballenger Hwy, Flint 48504 (810) 238-3843
Donald E. Morris 1969-1973; Russell F. McReynolds 1973-1991; Alonzo E. Vincent 1991-2005; Tara R. Sutton 2005-2012; Faith E. Green Timmons 2012-Mar 30, 2018; Andrew Amadu Allie (Ret.) Apr 1-Jun 30, 2018; Joy Jittaun Moore 2018-2019; Andrew Amadu Allie (Ret.) (interim) 2019-

Flint: Bristol UMC *[East Winds]*   bristolchurch2015@gmail.com
(P/M) 5285 Van Slyke Rd, Flint 48507   (810) 238-9244
Nelson D. Cushman 1969-1971; Fred W. Knecht 1971-1973; Robert T. Koch 1973-1981; Gary Imms May, 1981-1982; Eugene K. Bacon 1982-1988; Hoon Hee Wong 1988-1991; Marjorie H. Munger 1991-1993; Randy J. Whitcomb 1993-Apr 30, 1996; S. Patrick Stybert Jun 16, 1996-2000; Elizabeth M. Gamboa 2000-2003; Olaf R. Lidums 2003-2007; Melvin L. Herman Oct 1, 2007-2018; Brian K. Willingham 2018- [Flint: Bristol / Buron: Christ became a two-point charge on May 1, 2019]

Flint: Calvary UMC *[East Winds]*   flintclavary@gmail.com
(P/M) 2111 Flushing Rd, Flint 48504-4722   (810) 238-7685
Dorraine S. Snogren 1968-1990; James P. Kummer (assoc) Apr. 15, 1989-Jan. 31, 1992; James E. Tuttle 1990-1999; Steven A. Miller 1999-2004; Ray T. McGee 2004-2011; James E. Britt 2011-2018; Gregory E. Timmons (DSA) 2018-Dec 31, 2018; Gregory E. Timmons Jan 1, 2019-

Flint: Charity UMC *[East Winds]*   dopnh@gfn.org
(P/M) 4601 Clio Rd, Flint 48504-6012   (810) 789-2961
Emmanuel F. Bailey 1988-1993; Julius A. McKanders 1993-1996; Philip Burks 1996-Dec 6, 1999; Russel Von Sutton Dec 16, 2000-2003; Hydrian Elliott 2003-2011; David Lieneke 2011-2014; Brian Willingham 2014-2018; Frederick Bowden (DSA) 2018-

Flint: Court Street UMC *[East Winds]*   courtstreetumc@comcast.net
(P/M) 225 W Court St, Flint 48502-1130   (810) 235-4651
Robert P. Ward 1969-1972, Jack E. Price (assoc) 1966-1974; Andrew A. Michelson (assoc) 1968-1972; Kenneth R. Callis 1972-1977; H. Emery Hinkston (assoc) 1972-1974; Douglas K. Mercer (assoc) 1974-1977; Kenneth A. Kohlmann (assoc) 1974-1977; Ralph W. Janka 1977-1986; Donald E. Hall (assoc) 1977-1986; Theodore E. Doane 1986-1990; James D. Cochran (assoc) 1986-1988; Horace L. James (assoc) 1985-; David G. Mulder (assoc) 1988-1992; John E. Harnish 1990-1993; Paula M. Timm (assoc) 1992-Apr 15, 1994; Steven J. Buck 1993-2008; Weatherly A. Burkhead Verhelst (assoc) 1994-1998; Shirley A. Cormicle (assoc) 1999-Jan 1, 2003; Murphy S. Ehlers (deacon) Oct 1, 2000-Dec 1, 2002; Margie R. Crawford (assoc.) 2005-2008; Alicea Williams (deacon) 2007-Sep 30, 2008; Robert D. Wright 2008-2015; Jeremy T. Peters 2015-

Flint: Hope UMC *[East Winds]*   flinthopeumc@yahoo.com
(P/M) G-4467 Beecher Rd, Flint 48532-8532   (810) 732-4820
Gerald H. Fisher 1969-Mar. 1974; Howard B. Childs Mar. 1974-1980; M. Clement Parr 1980-1985; Margaret Rodgers West (assoc) 1982-1983; Frank A. Cozadd 1985-1989; Ralph H. Pieper II 1989-1996; John G. Park 1996-2006' John C. Ferris 2006-2012; John H. Amick 2012-2013; Carol Blair Bouse 2013-

Flushing UMC *[East Winds]*   flumc@sbcglobal.net
(P/M) 413 E Main St, Flushing 48433-2029   (810) 659-5172
Thomas F. Jackson 1968-1971; Jack E. Giguere 1971-1980; Grant A. Washburn (assoc) 1972-1975; Stephen K. Perrine (assoc) 1975-Oct. 1977; Eugene K. Bacon (assoc) 1978-1982; Maurice D. Sharai 1980-1989; Cherie R. Boeneman (assoc) 1982-1983; David L. Baize (assoc) 1983-1985; Kathryn S. Snedeker (assoc) 1985-1988; Susan Jo Arnold Word (assoc) 1988-1991; Gary L. Sanderson 1989-1995; Nanette D. Myers (assoc) 1991-Jan 1, 1997; Adam W. Bissell (assoc) 1997-1998; Bruce M. Denton 1995-2004; Donald S. Weatherup (assoc) 2002-2006; Jeffrey L. Jaggers 2004-2014; Matthew Packer (diaconal) 2008- ; Deborah A. Line Yencer 2014-

Forester UMC *[East Winds]*   eos@globali.us
(P) 2481 N Lakeshore Rd, Carsonville 48419; (M) 7209 Main St, Port Sanilac 48469   (810) 366-0369
James B. Lumsden 1969-1973; J. Paul Pumphrey 1973-1977; Glenn R. Wegner 1977-1980; James P. Kummer Dec. 1980-1985; Kenneth C. Reeves 1985-1991; Gloria Haynes 1991-1996; Ellen Burns 1996-2000; Robert A. Srock 2000-2002; John H. Rapson 2002-2004; Clarence W. VanConant 2004-2007; Ellen O. Schippert 2007-2014; Mark Harriman 2016-2018; Anika Bailey 2018-

Fostoria UMC *[East Winds]* pastor.kay@live.com
(P) 9115 Fostoria Rd, Fostoria 48435; (M) PO Box 125, Otisville 48463 (810) 631-8395
Donald L. Lichtenfelt 1969-1970; Ralph T. Barteld 1970-1979; Dale E. Brown 1979-1984; Allen J.
Lewis Inter.; Wayne C. Ferrigan 1984-1986; William J. Maynard 1986-1992; Bonny J. Lancaster
1992-1997; Donald Fairchild Jan 1, 1998-2001; David P. Rahn 2001-2009; Peggy Garrigues-
Cortelyou May 10, 2009-2010; Betty Kay Leitelt 2010-

Fowlerville: First UMC *[Ann Arbor]* fumc201@sbcglobal.net
(P) 201 S 2nd St, Fowlerville 48836; (M) PO Box 344, Fowlerville 48836 (517) 223-8824
Ronald A. Brunger 1965-1971; Ralph A. Edwards 1971-1975; Emil E. Haering 1975-1982; Paul
L. Amstutz 1982-1987; Robert B. Secrist 1987-1991; J. Gordon Schleicher 1991-Aug. 14, 1992;
Donald H. Francis Sep. 15, 1992-2000; S. Patrick Stybert 2000-2007; Thomas E. Tarpley 2007-
2015; Robert Freysinger 2015-2016; Scott Herald 2016-

Fowlerville: Trinity Livingston Circuit UMC *[Heritage]* livcirumc@gmail.com
(P/M) 8201 Iosco Rd, Fowlerville 48836-9265 (517) 223-3803
Harry Gintzer 1966-1969; Roger A. Parker 1969-1970; Thomas E. Hart 1970-1975; Jerome K.
Smith 1975-1981; Meredith T. Moshauer 1981-Dec. 31, 1981; William R. Donahue Jr. Jan. 14,
1982-Dec. 31, 1987; Richard W. Sheppard Jan. 15, 1988-Dec. 31, 1989; Paul F. Bailey Jan. 1,
1990-1991; Margery A. Schleicher 1991-1995; Myra L. Sparks 1995-Aug 31, 1997; Darrel L. Rice
Jan 1, 1998-2003; Malcolm L. Greene 2003-Aug 31, 2004; Steven A Gjerstad Sep 1, 2004-2006;
Judith M. Darling 2006-2009; Alan DeGraw (interim) 2009-Dec 31, 2009; Robert A. Miller Jan 1,
2010-2013; David C. Freeland 2013-2017; Mark Huff Nov 12, 2017-

Frankenmuth UMC *[Central Bay]* fmuthumc@airadv.net
(P/M) 346 E Vates St, Frankenmuth 48734 (989) 652-6858
Gordon E. Ackerman 1969-1983; G. Charles Ball 1983-1996; Douglas K. Mercer 1996-2000;
Kenneth L. Christler 2000-2006; David A. Eardley 2006-2013; Scott Harmon 2013-2017; Reed P.
Swanson 2017-Feb 6, 2018; Mark A Karls (Ret.) Feb 7, 2018-2019; Ryan L. Wenburg 2019-

Frankfort UMC *[Northern Waters]* feumc@att.net
(P) 537 Crystal Ave, Frankfort 49635; (M) PO Box 1010, Frankfort 49635 (231) 352-7427
Richard M. Wilson 1967-1971; John Melvin Bricker 1971-1980; Richard C. Kuhn 1980-1982; John
D. Morse 1982-1987; Paul D. Mazur 1987-April 1989; Donald R. Ferris April 1989-1993; John W.
McNaughton 1993-1996; Marvin R. Rosa 1996-1999; Kathryn M. Coombs 1999-2002; Gregory
P. Culver 2002-2010; Barbara J. Fay 2010-

Franklin: Community UMC *[Greater Detroit]* ffranklincc@aol.com
(P/M) 26425 Wellington Rd, Franklin 48025 (248) 626-6606
Frank B. Cowick 1967-1980; Roger M. Ireson (assoc) 1970-1975; Jack Stubbs (assoc) 1976-
1980; Samuel F. Stout 1980-1988; J. Douglas Parker (R. assoc) 1985-; William P. Sanders (assoc)
1987-1988; Richard C. Cheatham 1988-Aug 31, 1998; George F. Ward (assoc) 1988-1993; Bruce
E. Petrick 1997-1998; Karl L. Zeigler Sep 1, 1998-Oct 31, 2000; Murphy Ehlers (diaconal) Nov 1,
1998-Sep 30, 2000; James E. Greer Nov 16, 2000-2013; Lynn M. Hasley 2013-2016; David
Huseltine 2016-

Fraser: Christ UMC *[Greater Detroit]* cumcfraser@msn.com
(P/M) 34385 Garfield Rd, Fraser 48026 (586) 293-5340
Eric G. Wehrli 1967-1993; Stephen E. Wenzel 1993-Jul 1, 1994; Melvin Leach Jan 1, 1995-2015;
Catherine Miles (deacon) Aug 1, 2013-2015; Kevin J. Harbin 2015-

Freeland UMC *[Central Bay]* freelandumc@gmail.com
(P) 205 E Washington Rd, Freeland 48623; (M) PO Box 207, Freeland 48623 (989) 695-2101
Howard Montgomery 1967-1974; David Truran 1974-1979; Philip A. Rice 1979-1987; Dennis N.
Paulson 1987-1989; Harold J. Slater 1989-1992; Paul B. Lim 1992-Mar 31, 1996; James L. Rule
Jun 1, 1996-2012; Jaye Reisinger (deacon) 1999-; Lynda F. Frazier 2012-Feb 14, 2014; Elizabeth
Librande Feb 15, 2014-2017; Kayla Marie Roosa 2017-

Free Soil - Fountain UMC *[Northern Waters]*   onchristthesolidrockistandd@gmail.com
(P) 2549 E Michigan St, Free Soil 49411; (M) PO Box 173, Free Soil 49411   (231) 690-4591
Viola Norman 1967-1971; Robert Doner June-Dec. 1971; Lewis Buchner Jan. 1972-Aug. 1972; Russell Garrigus Sept. 1972-1993; Warren Wood (DSA) 1993-Nov. 1, 1999; Kenneth E. Tabor Nov. 1, 1999-2000; Janet Lynne O'Brien (DSA) 2001-Nov. 30, 2001; Janet Lynne O'Brien (part-time) Dec. 1, 2001-2009; Mona Dye 2009-2011; Joyce A. Theisen (DSA) 2011-2013; Richard D. Roberts (DSA) 2013-11/30/2015; Richard D. Roberts (PL) 12/01/2015

Free Soil - Fountain UMC – Fountain Campus *[Northern Waters]*
(P) 5043 N Foster St, Fountain 49410; (M) PO Box 173, Free Soil 49411   (231) 690-4591
Viola Norman 1967-1971; Robert Doner June-Dec. 1971; Lewis Buchner Jan. 1972-Aug. 1972; Russell Garrigus Sept. 1972-1993; Warren Wood (DSA) 1993-Nov. 1, 1999; Kenneth E. Tabor Nov. 1, 1999-2000; Janet Lynne O'Brien (DSA) 2001-Nov. 30, 2001; Jan O'Brien (part-time) Dec. 1, 2001-2002; Lemuel O. Granada 2002-2003; Lemuel Granada 2005-Nov. 30, 2007; Mona J. Dye (part-time) Dec. 1, 2007-2011; Joyce A. Theisen (DSA) 2011-2013; Richard D. Roberts (DSA) 2013-11/30/2015; Richard D. Roberts (PL) 12/01/2015

Freeport UMC *[Mid-Michigan]*   macousino1@gmail.com
(P) 193 Cherry St, Freeport 49325; (M) PO Box 142, Freeport 49325-0142   (616) 765-5316
Harold M. Taber 1966-1969; Charles W. Martin 1969-Oct. 1973; Harold R. Simon Nov. 1973-Oct. 1976; Arthur D. Jackson Apr. 1977-1981; Bradley P. Kalajainen Jan. 1981-1985; Gilbert R. Boersma 1985-Jan. 1989; Janet K. Sweet 1989-1991; Carroll A. Fowler 1991-April 15, 1995; Paulette Cheyne June 1, 1995-1999; Richard A. Powell 1999-Aug. 15, 1999; Deborah R. Miller Aug. 16, 1999-Jan. 31, 2002; Paul Peterson (DSA) 2002-2004; Scott E. Manning 2004-2006; Susan D. Olsen 2006-2015; Mickey Ann Cousino (CLM/DSA) Sept. 1, 2015-

Fremont UMC *[Midwest]*   umcfremont@att.net
(P/M) 351 Butterfield St, Fremont 49412   (231) 924-0030
Lynn DeMoss 1966-1969; Bertram Vermeulen 1969-1978; Constance Heffelfinger (Assoc.) 1978-1981; Eldon K. Eldred 1979-1987; A. Edward Perkins 1987-1990; Harold F. Filbrandt 1990-1994; Daniel M. Duncan 1994-2003; Lawrence R. Wood 2003-2007; Carolin S. Spragg 2007-2013; Martin T. Cobb 2013-2017; Julie E. Fairchild 2017-

Frontier UMC *[Heritage]*
(P) 9925 Short St, Frontier 49239; (M) PO Box 120, Frontier 49239-0120   (269) 223-0631
Kenneth Karlzen 1966-1968; Charles D. Grauer 1968-1970; Daniel W. Harris 1970-1971; Robert E. Jones 1971-Nov. 15, 1973; Marion V. Nye Nov. 15, 1973-1976; Daniel R. Bennett Feb. 1, 1977-1979; Leonard J. Yarlott 1979-1982; Gilbert R. Boersma 1982-1985; Valerie M. Hill 1985-1989; Jerry L. Hippensteel 1989-1994; Susan Deason 1994-1998; Kathy L. Nitz 1998-Aug. 15, 1999; Donald Lee (DSA) 2002-2010; Cynthia Veilleux (DSA) Nov. 1, 2010-2011; Timothy R. Puckett (part-time) 2011-2014; Martin Johnston Sept. 1, 2014-2017; Donald Lee 2017-

Gaines UMC *[East Winds]*   dadj@hotmail.com
(P) 117 W. Clinton St, Gaines 48436; (M) PO Box 125, Gaines 48436   (989) 271-9131
John M. Miller 1969-1970; John D. Roach 1970-1972; Verne W. Blankenburg 1972-1977; David S. Stiles 1977-1980; Mary Isaacs Frost 1980-Oct. 1982; Harry R. Weeks Oct. 1982-Feb. 15, 1986; Larry J. Werbil 1986-Aug. 15, 1989; Dorothy Rossman (Interim part-time); Myra Lee Sparks Oct. 16, 1989-1995; David L. Fleming 1995-1999; Harlan E. Sorensen 1999-Nov 14, 2004; John D. Bailey 2005-2010; David A. Wichert 2010-2013; Eric L. Johnson 2013-2018; Barbara Benjamin 2018-

Galesburg UMC *[Greater Southwest]* galesburgumc@att.net
(P) 111 W Battle Creek St, Galesburg 49053; (M) PO Box 518, Galesburg 49053   (269) 665-7952
Laurence R. Lowell 1968-1969; Pulpit Supply 1969-1970; Milton J. TenHave 1970-1973; Jack
Scott 1973-1977; Allan Valkema 1977-1980; Larry Grubaugh 1980-1988; Rochelle Ray 1988-
1992; John L. Moore 1992-1995; Charles M. Shields 1995-1997; Janet Sweet-Richardson
1997-Nov. 1, 1999; Michael Baker-Streevy Nov. 16, 1999-2003; Keith W. Heifner 2003-2006; Mona
K. Joslyn 2006-2010; [Comstock UMC merged w/ Galesburg UMC 04-29-07]; Sally K. Harrington
(DSA) Nov. 1, 2010-2012; John L. Moore (DSA) (1/2 time) 2012-2013; Leonard R. Schoenherr
(Ret.) 2013-2016; Leonard E. Davis 2016-

Galien UMC *[Greater Southwest]* galienandolivebranch@gmail.com
(P) 208 N Cleveland Ave, Galien 49113; (M) PO Box 266, Galien 49113   (269) 665-7952
Lawrence Smith 1967-1969; Willard Gilroy 1969-1973; Arthur Beadle 1973-1976; Gordon Everett
(interim) July-Nov. 1976; Richard Williams Dec. 1976-Oct. 1979; Paul Smith Nov. 1979-March
1980; Joseph Wood (interim) March-June 1980; William Doubblestein 1980-1983; William Carr
1983-April 1986; Joseph Wood (interim) April-June 1986; Phillip Friedrick 1986-1991; Sherri
Swanson 1991-1995; Charlene A. Minger 1995-1999; Valerie Fons 1999-2001; John G. Kasper
2001-2006; Russell K. Logston 2006-2011; Jeffrey O. Cummings Jan. 1, 2012-2016; Clifford L.
Radtke 2016-2018; Cynthia L. Veilleux (DSA) 2018-

Galien: Olive Branch UMC *[Greater Southwest]* galienandolivebranch@gmail.com
(P) 2289 Olive Branch Rd, Galien 49113; (M) PO Box 266, Galien 49113   (269) 545-2275
Leslie Smith 1965-1969; Willard Gilroy 1969-1973; Arthur Beadle 1973-1976; Gordon Everett
(interim) July-Nov. 1976; Richard Williams Dec. 1976-Oct. 1979; Paul Smith Nov. 1979-March
1980; Joseph Wood (interim) March-June 1980; William Doubblestein 1980-1983; William Carr
1983-April 1986; Joseph Wood (interim) April-June 1986; Phillip Friedrick 1986-1991; Sherri
Swanson 1991-1995; Charlene A. Minger 1995-1999; Valerie Fons 1999-2001; John G. Kasper
2001-2006; Russell K. Logston 2006-2011; Jeffrey O. Cummings Jan. 1, 2012-2016; Clifford L.
Radtke 2016-2018; Cynthia L. Veilleux (DSA) 2018-

Ganges UMC *[Greater Southwest]* gangumc@frontier.com
(P) 2218 68th St, Fennville 49408; (M) PO Box 511, Fennville 49408-0511   (269) 543-3581
Lloyd R. Van Lente Jan. 1966-1971; Matthew Walkoton 1971-1973; Douglas L. Pederson 1973-
1975; Richard W. McLain 1975-1979; Craig L. Adams 1979-1984; Constance L. Heffelfinger
1984-Jan. 1990; Aurther D. Jackson Jan. 1990-Jan. 1991; Leonard Coon Jan.-June 1991; John
Burgess 1991-1994; Marcia L. Elders 1994-1997; Barbara Jo Fay 1997-Dec.31, 2004; Jean M.
Smith Jan. 16, 2005-Sept. 1, 2010; Jack E. Balgenorth Sept. 1, 2010-2014; [Ganges/Glenn
became single charges 2014] Marcia A. Tucker (DSA) 2014-

Garden City: First UMC *[Greater Detroit]* fumcgc@hotmail.com
(P/M) 6443 Merriman Rd, Garden City 48135   (734) 421-8628
Glen E. L. Kjellberg 1970-1977; Robert C. Grigereit 1977-1987; David A. Russell 1987-1990; Gary
L. Damon 1990-Jul 31, 1997; Jerome K. Smith Sep 1, 1997-2006; Kenneth C. Bracken 2006-
2009; Pamela Beedle-Gee 2009-2014; Bea Barbara Fraser-Soots 2014-2015; Jonathan Combs
Dec 1, 2016-

Garfield UMC *[Central Bay]*
(P) 1701 N Garfield Rd, Linwood 48634; (M) 314 Whyte St, Pinconning 48650   (989) 879-6992
Byron G. Hatch (w/Pinconning) 1969-1972; Richard A. Turner (w/Pinconning) 1971-1981; Jeffrey
R. Maxwell 1982-1984; Eldon C. Schram 1984-1996; Michael Luce 1996-2001; J. Gordon
Schleicher 2001-2003; Jon W. Gougeon 2003-2010; James A. Payne 2010-2013; John Tousciuk
2013-Aug 3, 2016; Heather Nowak (DSA) Oct 1, 2016-Sept 30, 2017; Heather Nowak Dec 1,
2017-

Gaylord: First UMC *[Northern Waters]*   fumcoffice@winntel.net
(P) 215 S Center Ave, Gaylord 49735; (M) PO Box 617, Gaylord 49734   (989) 732-5380
    Raymond Roe 1968-1971; Dwayne Summers 1971-1978; John H. Bunce 1978-1983; Donna J.
    Lindberg 1983-1989; Warren D. Pettis 1989-1998; John E. Naile 1998-2014; Daniel J. Bowman
    2014-

Genesee UMC *[East Winds]*   geneseethetford@sbcglobal.net
(P) 7190 N Genesee Rd, Genesee 48437; (M) PO Box 190, Genesee 48437   (810) 640-2280
    William H. Brady 1967-1970; John P. Hitchens 1970-1972; Ralph H. Pieper II 1972-1975; Roger L.
    Colby 1975-1980; James P. Schwandt 1980-1987; David P. Rahn 1987-Nov. 1, 1987; Willard A. King
    Nov. 1, 1987-Aug 31, 1994; Lorrie E. Plate Sep 1, 1994-1998; Malcolm L. Greene 1998-2003; Bruce
    L. Nowacek 2003-2010; Karen B. Williams 2010-

Georgetown UMC *[Midwest]*   info@gumonline.org
(P/M) 2766 Baldwin St, Jenison 49428   (616) 669-0730
    Robert Hinklin Feb. 1, 1976-1984; John R. Smith 1984-Feb. 18, 1999; Joseph J. Bistayi Aug.
    16,1999-2005; Joseph D. Huston 2005-2007; William C. Bills 2007-2016; Jennifer Browne 2016-
    2018; Sherri L Swanson 2018-

Germfask UMC *[Northern Skies]*   pastorimcdonald@outlook.com
(P) 1212 Morrison St, Germfask 49836; (M) PO Box 268, Grand Marais 49839   (906) 586-3162
    Vernon D. Wyllys 1969-1975; James Lumsden 1975-1976; Audrey Dunlap 1976-1985; Ramona
    Cowling 1985-1987; John N. Grenfell III 1987-1992; Mary G. Laub 1992-1998; Tracy L. Brooks
    Aug 16, 1998-2003; Karen A. Mars 2003-2006; Paul J. Mallory 2006-2011; Meredith Rupe Oct
    15, 2011-2012; Ian S. McDonald 2012-2019; Devin T. Lawrence (DSA) 2019-

Girard UMC *[Greater Southwest]*   girardumcsecretary@gmail.com
(P/M) 990 Marshall Rd, Coldwater 49036   (517) 279-9418
    C. Jack Scott 1968-1970; William E. Miles 1970-1971; Harold M. Deipert 1971-1973; Norman A.
    Charter 1973-1976; Densel G. Fuller 1976-1981; Jerry L. Hippensteel 1981-1984; Thomas E. Ball
    1984-Nov. 1988; Stanley Fenner Dec. 1988-1989; Stacy R. Minger 1989-1994; John F. Ritter
    1994-1996; Robert Stark 1996-2000; John Scott 2000-Sept. 1, 2003; John A. Scott & Rebecca
    Scott (CoPastors) Sept 2003-2007; Bruce R. Kintigh 2007-2010; Emily (Slavicek) Beachy Sept.
    1, 2010-2014; Cydney Idsinga 2014-2018; Matthew J West 2018-

Gladstone: Memorial UMC *[Northern Skies]*   mumc@uplogon.com
(P/M) 1920 Lake Shore Dr, Gladstone 49837   (906) 428-9311
    William Verhelst 1968-1974; Wayne T. Large 1974-1981; Dale M. Miller 1981-1988; Douglas K.
    Mercer 1988-1990; Jeffry W. Dinner 1990-1994; Gary R. Shiplett 1994-2000; Joanne R. Bartelt
    2000-2006; Jacquelyn Roe 2006-2010; Elizabeth A. Hill 2010-2015; Caroline F. Hart 2015-2018;
    Timothy B. Wright 2018-2019; Cathy L. Rafferty 2019-

Gladwin: First UMC *[Central Bay]*   fumcgladwin@cynergycomm.net
(P/M) 309 S M 18, Gladwin 48624   (989) 426-9619
    John Cermak Sr. 1966-1972; Byron G. Hatch 1972-1976; Donald Bates 1976-1984; Harold
    Weemhoff 1984-1986; Joel W. Hurley 1986-1992; Deane B. Wyllys 1992-Sep 1, 2002; Jill Bair
    (diaconal) 1999-2001; Charles Marble Sep 15, 2002-Apr 30, 2003 (interm); Lynn F. Chappell May
    1, 2003-2009; David P. Snyder 2009-2012; David D. Amstutz 2012-2018; Carmen Cook 2018-

Gladwin: Wagarville Community UMC *[Central Bay]*
(P/M) 2478 Wagarville Rd, Gladwin 48624   (989) 426-2971
    George Saucier & Bob Bryce 1969-1973; Wayne D. Jensen 1973-1985; Wayne D. Jensen
    (w/Wooden Shoe) 1985-1991; Sherry Parker (w/Wooden Shoe) 1991-1994; Janet Larner 1994-
    Aug 31, 1994; Margaret Garrigues-Cortelyou Sep 1, 1994-1995; Donald P. Haskell 1995-Dec 31,
    2004; Kim Spencer Jan 1, 2005-2005; Linda Jo Powers 2005-2009; Jim Noggle 2009-2012;
    Michael J. Simon 2011-2013; Dennis Paulson 2013-2014; Vincent Nader 2014-Sept 1, 2016; Doug
    Hasse (DSA) Sept 1, 2017- Dec 31, 2018; Doug Hasse Jan 1, 2019-

Glenn UMC *[Greater Southwest]* harold77020@comcast.net
(P) 1391 Blue Star Hwy, Glenn 49416; (M) PO Box 46, Glenn 49416-0046 (269) 227-3930
Lloyd Van Lente 1968-1969; Harold Arman 1969-1971; Arthur Beadle 1971-1973; Pulpit Supply 1973-1974; O. Bernard Strother 1974-1998; Stephen Small Nov. 16, 1998-2001; John R. Cantwell (DSA) 2002-2005; Jean A. Smith 2005-Sept. 1, 2010; Jack E. Balgenorth Sept. 1, 2010-2014; [Ganges/Glenn became single charges 2014] Harold F. Filbrandt (Ret.) 2014-Dec. 31, 2018; TBS

Glennie UMC *[Central Bay]*
(P) 3170 State St, Glennie 48737; (M) PO Box 189, Glennie 48737-0189
Donald Daws 1965-1971; James Gerzetich 1971-1974; Byron Coleman 1974-1979; Norman Horton 1979-1983; Priscilla Seward 1983-1985; Margaret A. Paige 1985-1986; Margaret A. Paige (1/2 time) 1986-1991; James E. Paige Jr. (1/2 time) 1986-1991; George H. Morse 1991-2000; Brenda K. Klacking 2000-2008; Donald Wojewski 2008-2012; Linda Jo Powers 2012-2014; Mary Soderhold (DSA) Nov 1, 2014-Sept 30, 2015; Charles Soderholm (DSA) Oct 1, 2015-Sept 30, 2016;

Gobles UMC *[Greater Southwest]* info@goblesumc.org
(P) 210 E Exchange St, Gobles 49055; (M) PO Box 57, Gobles 49055-0057 (269) 628-2263
James Boehm 1967-1970; Allen Valkema 1970-1971; William Miles 1971-1974; Rudolph Wittenback 1974-1976; Karen S. Slager-Wheat 1976-1986; John McNaughton 1986-1987; Judy K. Downing 1987-1998; Susan Olsen 1998-2004; Mary Beth Rhine 2004-2010; Edward Mohr L. 2010-Sept. 11, 2012; Daniel J. Minor (Ret.) Sept. 16, 2012-June 30, 2013; Nelson L. Hall 2013-2015; John M. Brooks 2015-2019; [Goles / Almena fored a circuit 07/01/2019] Lawrence James French 2019-

Goodrich UMC *[East Winds]* office@goodrichumc.org
(P/M) 8071 S State Rd, Goodrich 48438 (810) 636-2444
Gary L. Sanderson 1966-1970; Donald O. Crumm 1970-Jan. 1981; Jerome K. Smith Jan. 1981-Jan. 15, 1986; John W. Elliott Mar. 1, 1986-Jun 30, 1994; Steven A. Gjerstad Jul 1, 1994-Nov 15, 2000; Karl L. Zeigler Nov 16, 2000-2010; Jeremy P. Africa 2010-2015; Won Dong Kim 2015-Dec 31, 2016; Steven J. Buck Jan 1-Jun 30, 2017; Joel L. Walther 2017-

Gordonville UMC *[Central Bay]* gordonvilleumc@parishonline.tv
(P/M) 76 E Gordonville Rd, Midland 48640 (989) 486-1064
H. Emery Hinkston 1969-1972; Robert Moore 1972-1980; Robert Kersten 1980-1982; Paul Riegle 1982-1983; Joy A. Barrett 1983-1988; Charles Keyworth 1988-Aug 31, 1994; Janet Larner Sep 1, 1994-2002; Phillip D. Voss 2002-Apr 15, 2003; Tracy L. Brooks 2003-2005; Lynda F. Frazier 2005-Jun 20, 2011; Thomas W. Schomaker (interm) Jun 21, 2010-2015; Josheua Blanchard 2015-Aug 31, 2017; Ernesto Mariona Oct 1, 2017-

Grand Blanc UMC *[East Winds]* gbumc515@gmail.com
(P/M) 515 Bush Ave, Grand Blanc 48439 (810) 694-9040
James A. Craig 1967-1971; Frank R. Leineke 1971-1977; John S. Jury 1977-1982; James F. Thomas 1982-Jan. 1, 1990; R. Edward McCracken Jan. 1, 1990-1998; Roger L. Colby 1998-2008; Christine E. Wyatt (diaconal) 1999-2002; G. Patrick England 2008-2016; Julius Del Pino 2016-

Grand Blanc: Phoenix UMC *[East Winds]* phoenixumc@att.net
(P/M) 4423 S Genesee Rd, Grand Blanc 48439-7958 (810) 743-3370
George W. Versteeg 1968-1971; Horace L. James 1971-1975; Louis E. Reyner 1975-1978; Steven Gjerstad 1979-1983; Bonnie D. Byadiah 1983-1992; Colon R. Brown 1992-1997; Paula M. Timm 1997-2001; Bruce L. Billing 2001-2011; Gregory E. Rowe 2011-2016; Sang (Abraham) Chun 2016-

Grand Haven Church of the Dunes *[Midwest]*   jblanchard@umcdunes.org
(P/M) 717 Sheldon Rd, Grand Haven 49417   (616) 842-7980
    Albert W. Frevert 1965-1972; David Miles (Assoc.) 1971-1976; Charles F. Garrod 1972-1978; Lawrence Wiliford (Assoc.) 1976-1978; Gerald A. Pohly 1978-1989; Victor Charnley (Assoc.) 1978-1984; Robert Gillette (Assoc.) 1984-1991; Ellen A. Brubaker 1989-1992; Richard Youells (Assoc.) 1991-1995; Eldon K. Eldred 1992-2003; Brian F. Rafferty (Assoc.) 1999-2003; Daniel M. Duncan 2003-2014; Glenn M. Wagner 2014-Dec. 31, 2016; John E. Harnish (Ret.) Jan. 1-June 30, 2017; Louis W. Grettenberger 2017-

Grand Ledge First UMC *[Mid-Michigan]*   glfumc.secretary@comcast.net
(P/M) 411 Harrison St, Grand Ledge 48837   (517) 627-3256
    H. James Birdsall 1967-1973; Royce R. Robinson 1973-1983; Philip L. Brown 1983-1989; Lynn E. Grimes 1989-1993; Robert H. Roth, Jr. (Assoc.) 1991-1994; William J. Amundsen 1993-2003; Barbara Smith Jang (Assoc.) 1994-1997; Jana L. Almeida (Assoc.) 1997-Oct. 15, 1999; Kathleen S. Kursch (Assoc.) Feb. 1, 2000-Aug. 31, 2004; Molly C. Turner 2003-2012; Molly Turner (DSA) July-Dec. 31, 2012; Gregory W. Lawton (Deacon) 2007-2011; Betty A. Smith (Interim) Jan. 1-Mar. 31, 2013; Terry A. Euper Apr. 1-June 30, 2013; Cynthia Skutar 2013-

Grand Marais UMC *[Northern Skies]*   thevicar@jamadots.com
(P) N14226 M 77, Grand Marais 49839; (M) PO Box 34, Grand Marais 49839   (906) 494-2653
    Carl Shamblen 1966-1969; Vernon D. Wyllys 1969-1975; James Lumsden 1975-1976; Audrey Dunlap 1976-1981; John N. Grenfell III 1987-1992; Mary G. Laub 1992-1998; Tracy L. Brooks Aug 16, 1998-2003; Karen A. Mars 2003-2006; Paul J. Mallory 2006-2011; Meredith Rupe Oct 15, 2011-2012; Ian S. McDonald 2012-

Grand Rapids: Aldersgate UMC *[Midwest]*   aumcoffice@gmail.com
(P/M) 4301 Ambrose Ave NE, Grand Rapids 49525   (616) 363-3446
    Clinton Galloway 1967-Dec. 1973; Norman Kohns Jan. 1974-1981; William Johnson 1981-1992; Thomas B. Jones (Assoc.) 1990-Dec. 31, 1995; Ellen A. Brubaker 1992-Jan. 1, 2002; Cathi M. Gowin Feb. 1, 2002-2005; Gerald L. Toshalis 2005-2006; Gregory J. Martin 2006-2012; [Grand Rapids Aldersgate / Plainfield became two-point charge 2012] Laurie A. Haller 2012-2013; [became single-point charge 2013] James E. Hodge 2013-

Grand Rapids: Cornerstone UMC *[Midwest]*   infogroup@cornerstonemi.org
(P/M) 1675 84th St SE, Caledonia 49316   (616) 698-3170
    [new church start 1990] Bradley P. Kalajainen 1990- ; Scott Keith Otis (Assoc.) 2003-Oct. 1, 2004; Kenneth J. Nash (Assoc.) 2006-2016; Alejandro D. Fernandez (Heritage Hill Campus Pastor) Jan. 1, 2015- ; Marcia L. Elders (South Wyoming Campus Pastor) Jan. 1-June 30, 2015 [South Wyoming UMC merged w/ Cornerstone UMC Jan. 1, 2015]; Marcus V. Schmidt (South Wyoming Campus Pastor) May 1, 2016-

Grand Rapids: Cornerstone UMC - Heritage Hill Campus *[Midwest]*
(P) 48 Lafayette Ave SE, Grand Rapids 49503; (M) 1675 84th St SE, Caledonia 49316
    (616) 698-3170
    [Cornerstone UMC - Heritage Hill Campus launched October 2013] Alejandro D. Fernandez Jan. 1, 2015-

Grand Rapids: Cornerstone UMC - South Wyoming Campus *[Midwest]*
(P) 2730 56th St SW, Wyoming 49418; (M) 1675 84th St SE, Caledonia 49316   (616) 698-3170
    Marcus V. Schmidt May 1, 2016-

Grand Rapids: Faith UMC *[Midwest]*   secretary@grfaithumc.org
(P/M) 2600 7th St NW, Grand Rapids 49504   (616) 453-0693
    Second UMC and Valley UMC merged in 1977 to become Faith UMC. Eugene Lewis 1977-1984; Paul Patterson 1984-1987; Douglas Pedersen 1987-Feb. 15, 1994; Kim L. Gladding 1994-1998; Geoffrey L. Hayes 1998-2009; Mark E. Thompson 2009-2017; Sherri L. Swanson 2017-2018; Daniel M Bilkert (Ret.) 2018-

Grand Rapids: First UMC *[Midwest]*   firstchurch@grandrapidsfumc.org
(P/M) 227 Fulton St E, Grand Rapids 49503   (616) 451-2879
Donald B. Strobe 1964-1972; Carl L. Hausermann (Assoc.) 1967-1971; Lowell F. Walsworth
(Assoc.) 1971-1973; John S. Jury 1972-Nov. 1974; Geoffrey L. Hayes (Assoc.) 1973-1978; William
W. DesAutels Dec. 1974-1981; Robert E. Jones (Assoc.) 1978-1983; Robert C. Brubaker 1981-
Nov. 1987; Darwin R. Salisbury (Assoc.) 1983-1985; Bradley P. Kalajainen (Assoc.) 1985-1990;
Lynn A. DeMoss April 1988-1993; Joyce DeToni-Hill (Assoc.) 1990-1991; Derek DeToni-Hill
(Assoc.) 1990-1993; Gary T. Haller (Co-pastor) 1993-2013; Laurie A. Haller (Co-pastor) 1993-
2006; Dominic A. Tommy (Assoc.) 1997-1999; Jennifer Browne (Assoc.) 2006-2011; Kim DeLong
(Deacon - Director of Education)(1/2 time) 2009-2012; Martha Beals (Deacon) (part-time) July 1-
Nov. 20, 2009; Janet Carter (Deacon) (part-time) 2009- ; Letisha Bowman (Assoc.) 2011-2015;
Robert L. Hundley 2013- ; Amee A. Paparella (Assoc.) 2017-Feb. 27, 2018; Joan Van Dessel
(Assoc.) 2019-

Grand Rapids: Genesis UMC *[Midwest]*   info@genesisumc.org
(P/M) 3189 Snow Ave, Lowell 49331   (616) 974-0400
[new church start 1995] M. Christopher Lane & Jane R. Lippert (co-pastors) 1995-2007; Susan
M. Petro 2007-2014; DeAnn J. Dobbs 2014-Dec. 31, 2016; Georgia N. Hale (Deacon) 2015- ;
John Ross Thompson (Ret.) Jan. 1, 2017-

Grand Rapids: Iglesia Metodista Unida La Nueva Esperanza *[Midwest]*
(P/M) 1005 Evergreen St SE, Grand Rapids 49507   (616) 560-4207
Miguel A. Rivera 1983-1986; Francisco Diaz 1986-1991; Juan B. Falcon 1992-Sep. 1995; Oscar
Ventura Sept. 1995-Sept. 2002; Isidro Carrera Sept. 2002-March 16, 2003; Oscar Ventura Mar.
16, 2003-2009; Jorge Rodriguez 2009-2013; Nohemi Ramirez 2013-2018; Laura Feliciano 2018-

Grand Rapids: Northlawn UMC *[Midwest]*   office@northlawnumc.org
(P/M) 1157 Northlawn St NE, Grand Rapids 49505   (616) 361-8503
Ivan Niswender 1966-1969; Leonard Putnam 1969-1973; Carlton Benson 1973-1976; Thurlan
Meredith 1976-1984; Vance Dimmick, Jr. 1984-1992; Stanley Finkbeiner 1992-1996; Charles R.
VanLente 1996-2010; James C. Noggle 2010-2013; Timothy B. Wright 2013-2018; Janice T.
Lancaster (Deacon) Feb. 1, 2014-Mar. 31, 2017; Craig L. Adams (Ret.) 2018-2019; Zachary D.
McNees 2019-

Grand Rapids: Resotration *[Midwest]*   rcchurch20181@yahoo.com
(P/M) 2730 56th St SW, S Wyoming 49418   (616) 589-4793
[new church start 01/01/2018] Banza Mukalay Jan. 1, 2018-

Grand Rapids: South UMC *[Midwest]*   grsouthumc@comcast.net
(P/M) 4500 Division Ave S, Grand Rapids 49548   (616) 534-8931
Donald Cozadd 1967-1969; Kenneth McCaw 1969-1975; Clarence Hutchens 1975-1979; Ray
Burgess 1979-1988; Thomas M. Pier-Fitzgerald 1988-1998; Robert P. Stover 1998-2004; Kathleen
S. Kursch Sept. 1, 2004-2007; Mack C. Strange 2007-

Grand Rapids: St Paul's UMC *[Midwest]*   grstpaulsumc@gmail.com
(P/M) 3334 Breton Rd SE, Grand Rapids 49512   (616) 949-0880
John S. Myette 1964-1969; William A. Hertell 1969-1974; Robert E. Betts 1974-1982; Edward
Trimmer (Assoc.) 1981-1982; Joseph D. Huston 1982-1989; Andrew Jackson (Assoc. part-time)
Sept. 1-1986-1994; Theron E. Bailey 1989-1994; Ethel Z. Stears 1994-1999; Robert J. Mayo 1999-
2005; Cathi M. Huvaere (formerly Catherine M. Gowin) 2005-2012; Erin L. Fitzgerald 2012-2018;
Virginia L. Heller 2018-

Grand Rapids: Trinity UMC *[Midwest]*   office@grtumc.org
(P/M) 1100 Lake Dr SE, Grand Rapids 49506   (616) 456-7168
  Donn P. Doten 1962-1971; Philip A. Carpenter (Assoc.) 1966-1972; Lawrence R. Taylor 1971-
  1978; Marvin R. Rosa (Assoc.) Feb. 1972-1979; Charles F. Garrod 1978-1984; William John
  Amundsen (Assoc.) 1979-1982; Edward A. Trimmer (Assoc.) 1982-1983; Ethel Stears (Assoc.)
  Sept. 1983-1986; Charles Fry 1984-1989; Timothy P. Boal (Assoc.) 1986-1992; Gerald A. Pohly
  1989-1996; Gerald Toshalis (Assoc.) 1992-2001; A. Edward Perkins 1996-2006; Robert Cook
  (Assoc.) 2001-2006; Carole and Frank Lyman (Co-pastors) 2006-2010; David Nellist 2010-2018;
  Julie Dix (Assoc.) Nov. 8, 2010-2015; Ellen A. Brubaker and John Ross Thompson (Assoc.) 2015-
  Sept 1, 2016; Mariel Kay DeMoss 2016- ; Steven W. Manskar 2018-

Grand Rapids: Vietnamese UMC *[Midwest]*   dhfishing@yahoo.com
(P/M) 212 Bellevue St SE, Wyoming 49548   (616) 534-6262
  Vinh Q. Tran Sept.1, 1987-2004; Cuong Nguyen 2004-2008; Sanh Van Tran 2008-2012; Dung Q.
  Nguyen 2012-

Grandville UMC *[Midwest]*   office@grandvilleumc.com
(P/M) 3140 Wilson Ave SW, Grandville 49418   (616) 538-3070
  Dale Brown 1964-Feb. 1973; L. George Babcock (Assoc.) 1967-1972; E. William Wiltse March
  1973-1977; William H. Doubblestein (Assoc.) 1974-Aug. 1977; Charles Fullmer 1977-1986; Leon
  Andrews 1986-1989; Barry Petrucci (Assoc.) 1986-1989; Kim L. Gladding (Assoc.) 1989-1994; J.
  Melvin Bricker 1989-1995; Rob McPherson (Assoc.) 1994-1999; John Ross Thompson 1995-
  1998; Robert L. Hinklin 1998-2001; Cathy Rafferty (Assoc.) 1999-2001; Gerald L. Toshalis 2001-;
  James Edward Hodge (Assoc.) 2001-2005; Thomas M. Pier-Fitzgerald 2005-2016; Ryan B.
  Wieland 2016-

Grant UMC *[Northern Waters]*   grantumcbuckley@gmail.com
(P) 10999 Karlin Rd, Buckley 49620; (M) PO Box 454, Interlochen 49643   (231) 269-3981
  Marion Nye 1966-1970; Silas H. Foltz 1970-1971; Lewis (Bud) Buckner 1972-1978; Wayne
  Babcock 1978-1983; Beverly Prestwood-Taylor 1983-1986; Beverly Prestwood Taylor (3/4 time)
  1986-May 1988; Bruce Prestwood-Taylor (3/4 time) 1986-May 1988; Bruce Kintigh 1988-1993;
  Brian F. Rafferty 1993-1999; Craig South 1999-2002; James L. Breithaupt (1/4 time) 2002-2004;
  James L. Breithaupt (1/2 time) 2004-Mar. 15, 2006; Carl Greene, Mar. 15, 2006-2011; Robert W.
  Stark (DSA) 2011; Colleen A. Wierman (1/4 time) Nov. 27, 2011-2017 [Brethren Epworth / Grant
  became single-point charges 2014]; Sean T. Barton 2017-2018; Daniel L. Gonder 2018-2019;
  TBS

Grant Center UMC *[Midwest]*
(P/M) 15260 21 Mile Rd, Big Rapids 49307   (231) 796-8006
  David A. Cheyne 1977-1982; Wesley E. Smith 1982-Feb.1984; Martin D. Fox May 1984-Sept.
  1986; Nelson Ray Dec. 1986-1988; Michael Nicholson 1988-Dec. 1991; Paul Patterson (ret.) Jan.-
  June 1992; Deborah R. Miller June 1, 1992-1995; Wayne McKinney (DSA) 1995-July 31, 2002;
  Timothy W. Doubblestein Sept. 1, 2002-Sept. 15, 2003; Sueann K. Hagan Oct. 16, 2003-2006;
  Michael J. Simon 2006-2010; Lyle J. Ball 2010-2015 [Grant Center became single-point charge
  2015] Paula Jane Duffey (Ret.) Aug. 1, 2015-2016; Irene Elizabeth Starr 2016- Oct 27, 2017;
  [Grant Center / Brooks Corners became a two-point charge 2017] Meredith Rupe (Ret.) (LTFT ¼)
  Dec. 1, 2017-

Grass Lake UMC *[Heritage]*   glumc@modempool.com
(P/M) 449 E Michigan Ave, Grass Lake 49240   (517) 522-8040
  Kenneth Harris Dec. 1966-1969; Dale Culver 1969-Dec. 1972; Charles Grauer Jan. 1973-1976;
  Howard McDonald 1976-1979; Kenneth Lindland 1979-Sept. 1983; Gregory Wolfe Nov. 1983-
  1994; Stanley L. Hayes 1994-1999; Larry W. Rubingh 1999-2007; D. Gunnar Carlson 2007-2010;
  Esther Barton (DSA) 2010-2012; Dennis E. Slattery (DSA) (1/4 time) 2012-Sept 30, 2018; Gerald
  S. Hunter (Ret.) (LTFT ¼) Oct. 1-29, 2018; David Carlson Dec 1, 2018-2019; Lawrence J, Wiliford
  (Ret.) 2019-

Grawn UMC *[Northern Waters]* grawnumc@gmail.com
(P) 1260 S West Silver Lake Rd, Traverse City 49685; (M) PO Box 62, Grawn 49637
(231) 943-8353
Carter Miller 1968-1969; Richard LaCicero 1969-Nov. 1970; Russell J. Lautner Nov. 1970-1982; Don Spachman 1982-1992; Michael E. Long 1992-1996; Daniel W. Biteman, Jr. 1996-2006; Margaret Halls Wilson 2006-Nov. 1, 2009; Mary S. Brown, Nov. 1, 2009-2014; Colleen A. Wierman (1/2 time) 2014-2017; Sean T. Barton 2017-2018; Sean Thomas Barton 2018-

Grayling: Michelson Memorial UMC *[Northern Waters]* mmumc@12k.net
(P/M) 400 E Michigan Ave, Grayling 49738 (989) 348-2974
Paul C. Frederick 1969-1976; George E. Spencer 1976-1982; Jeffery D. Regan 1982-1989; Dennis N. Paulson 1989-1993; J. Douglas Paterson 1993-1998; Jeffery L. Jaggers 1998-2004; Robert D. Schoenhals 2004-Feb 1, 2006; Ralph W. Janka (interm) Feb 18, 2006-2006; William A. Cargo 2006-2011; Patrick D. Robbins 2011-2014; Richard M. Burstall 2014-

Greenland UMC *[Northern Skies]* ontmeth@jamadots.com
(P) 1002 Ridge Rd, Greenland 49929; (M) PO Box 216, Ontonagon 49953 (906) 883-3141
Lloyd Christler 1968-1972; James Hillard 1970-1971; James Gerzetich 1971; Lawrence Brooks 1971-1975; Roger Gedcke 1972-1979; Lillian Richards 1971-1976; Wayne E. Sparks 1975-1980; Myra Sparks 1976-1980; Ed Hingelburg 1976-1980; Brian Marshall 1980-1984; Donald J. Emmert 1984-Feb 15, 1990; William D. Schoonover Feb 16, 1990-1991; Mel D. Rose 1992-1994; Lance E. Ness Jul 1, 1994-Dec 31, 2000; Christine Bohnsack May 1, 2000-2004; Cherrie A. Sporleder 2004-2010; Bruce R. Steinberg 2010-2018; Nelson L. Hall 2018-

Greenville: First UMC *[Midwest]* office@greenvillefumc.org
(P/M) 204 W Cass St, Greenville 48838 (616) 754-8532
Darwin R. Salisbury 1964-March 1970; Howard A. Smith March 1970-1972; Harold A. Jayne 1972-Sept. 1977; Kenneth W. Karlzen Sept. 1977-March 1982; Harold L. Mann March 1982-1988; Laren J. Strait (Assoc.) 1980-; Harry R. Johnson 1988-2007; Joy Jittaun Moore 2007-2008; Stephen MG Charnley 2008-14; Stephen F. Lindeman 2013-14; Kimberly A. DeLong (Deacon) 2013-2015; [Greenville First, Turk Lake/Belding Cooperative Parish 2013] Donald E. Spachman 2014- ; Eric Mulanda Nduwa (Assoc.) Feb. 15-Aug. 1, 2015 [cooperative parish re-named Flat River Cooperative Parish 2015] ; Joseph K. Caldwell (CLM/DSA) Aug. 1, 2015-2016

Gresham UMC *[Mid-Michigan]* hauble23@gmail.com
(P) 5055 Mulliken Rd, Charlotte 48813; (M) 235 Dunham St, Sunfield 48890
David C. Haney 1967-1969; William R. Tate 1969-1972; Gary V. Lyons 1972-April 1976; Gerald A. Salisbury April 1976-1979; Molly C. Turner 1979-1983; Glenn C. Litchfield 1983-1990; Richard W. Young 1990-1991; Robert L. Kersten 1991-1995; Jeffrey J. Bowman 1995-2002; Kathleen Smith 2002-Dec. 31, 2012; [Vermontville/Gresham no longer two-point charge 2013] [Barry-Eaton Cooperative Ministry 2013] Bryce E. Feighner 2013-2017; [Gresham/Sunfield became two-point charge 2017] Heather L. Nolen (DSA) 2017-

Griffith UMC *[Heritage]* bralembury@myfrontiermail.com
(P/M) 9537 S Clinton Trl, Eaton Rapids 48827 (517) 663-6262
Lambert G. McClintic 1952-1995; Jack Fugate 1995-July 15, 2008; Charlene A. Minger (1/4 time) 2009-2013; David H. Minger (Ret.) (1/4 time) 2013-Oct. 16, 2014; Larry Embury Jan. 1, 2015-

Gull Lake UMC *[Greater Southwest]* gulllakeumc@gmail.com
(P/M) 8640 Gull Rd, Richland 49083 (269) 629-5137
Keith Heifner Sept. 1980-1981; Edward C. Ross 1981-1994; Stephen M.G. Charnley 1994-2008; Susan M. Petro (Assoc.) 1994-Dec. 31, 1997; Dianne Doten Morrison (Assoc.) 1998-Feb. 1, 2001; David Nellist 2008-2010; Mona K. Joslyn 2010-2015; Rebecca L. Wieringa 2015-2016; Leonard R. Schoenherr (Ret.) 2016- ; Michael James Tupper (Assoc.) Jan. 1, 2019-

Gunnisonville UMC *[Mid-Michigan]*　　　　　　　　pastor@unitedch.com
(P/M) 2031 Clark Rd, Bath 48808　　　　　　　　　　　　(517) 482-7987
　　Stephen Beach 1968-1969; Edward F. Otto 1969-Dec. 1972; Daniel Miles Dec. 1972-1974; Paul
　　K. Scheibner 1974-1978; J. Lynn Pier-Fitzgerald 1978-May 1984; Thomas M. Pier-Fitzgerald (co-
　　pastor) 1982-May 1984; Charles W. Smith May 1984-1988; Carl W. Staser 1988-Jan. 1991;
　　Thomas Peters Jan. 1, 1991-1993; Raymond D. Field 1993-1998; Nancy L. Besemer 1998-2003;
　　Thomas L. Truby Oct. 15, 2003-2006; Beatrice K. Robinson 2006-2007; Mark G. Johnson 2007-
　　2015; Matthew D. Kreh 2015-

Grosse Pointe UMC *[Greater Detroit]*　　　　　　　　office@gpumc.org
(P/M) 211 Moross Rd, Grosse Pointe Farms 48236-2950　　　　(313) 886-2363
　　Perry A. Thomas 1966-1978; Robert P. Ward 1978-1982; Mary Frost (assoc) 1978-1980; David
　　Penniman (assoc) 1980-1984; Robert W. Boley 1982-1989; Jack Mannschreck (assoc) 1984-
　　1992; Jack Giguere 1989-1999; David J. Leenhouts (assoc) 1992-1996; Mary Ann Shipley (assoc)
　　1996-Oct 31, 2002; Robert D. Wright 1999-2008; Pamela A. Beedle-Gee (assoc) 2003-2009;
　　Judith A. May 2008-2016; Daniel Hart (assoc) 2012-2016; Ray McGee 2016- ; Sari Brown (assoc)
　　2016-2017; Keith A. Lenard, Jr. (assoc) 2017-

Gwinn UMC *[Northern Skies]*　　　　　　　　gwinnumc@aol.com
(P) 251 W Jasper, Gwinn 49841; (M) PO Box 354, Gwinn 49841-0354　　　(906) 346-6314
　　Konstantine Wipp 1969-1975; Bruce Pierce 1975-1977; Duane E. Miller 1977-1986; Paul Lim
　　1986-1987; Max Weeks 1987-1991; Ronald F. Iris 1991-1995; Jacquelyn Roe 1995-2006;
　　Geraldine G. Hamlen 2006-2014; Robert A. Fike 2014-

Hale: First UMC *[Central Bay]*　　　　　　　　haleumc@gmail.com
(P) 201 W Main, Hale 48739; (M) PO Box 46, Hale 48739-0046　　　(989) 728-9522
　　Arthur R. Parkin 1963-1972; Henry W. Powell 1972-1973; Willis E. Braun 1973-1979; Theodore
　　I. Hastings 1979-1985; Willard A. King 1985-1987; William Donahue Jr. 1988-1993; G. Patrick
　　England 1993-2008; David Stewart 2008-2013; David J. Goudie 2013-Aug 31, 2017; Melvin Leroy
　　Leach Sept 1, 2017

Halsey UMC *[East Winds]*　　　　　　　　halkathphillips@sbcglobal.net
(P/M) 10006 Halsey Rd, Grand Blanc 48439　　　　　　　　(810) 694-9243
　　Dudley C. Mosure 1969-1977; Susan Bennett Stiles 1977-1980; David P. Rahn 1980-1987; Martha
　　H. Cargo 1987-1992; Chong Youb Won 1992-1995; Robin G. Gilshire 1995-Jul 31, 2000; David
　　E. Ray Aug 1, 2000-2006; Harold V. Phillips 2006-2016; Tara R. Sutton 2016-

Hancock: First UMC *[Northern Skies]*　　　　　　　　hfumc@hotmail.com
(P) 401 Quincy St, Hancock 49930; (M) PO Box 458, Hancock 49930　　　(906) 482-1401
　　Nelson Cushman 1967-1968; George A. Luciani 1968-1980; Charles R. Jacobs 1980-1984;
　　Thomas G. Badley 1984-1988; Fredrick P. Cooley 1988-1995; Eugene K. Bacon Jul 1, 1995-2006;
　　James R. Rupert Jul 16, 2006-2009; AmyLee Terhune 2009-2016; Scott Lindenberg 2016-

Harbor Beach UMC *[East Winds]*　　　　　　　　revsaribrown@gmail.com
(P) 253 S. First St, Harbor Beach 48441; (M) PO Box 25, Harbor Beach 48441　　　(989) 479-6053
　　Carl Shamblen 1968-1970; Thomas C. Badley 1970-1973; William M. Smith 1974-1978; Brent L.
　　Webster 1978-1983; Wayne A. Hawley 1983-1991; Kris S. Kappler 1991-1997; Victoria M. Webster
　　1997-1999; Clarence W. VanConant 1999-2004; Paula M. Timm 2004-2011; Donna J. Cartwright
　　Oct 1, 2011-2012; Mark E. Ryan 2012-Sept 18, 2016; Sari Brown 2017-

Harbor Springs UMC *[Northern Waters]*　　　　　　　　harborspringsumc@gmail.com
(P/M) 343 E Main St, Harbor Springs 49740　　　　　　　　(231) 526-2414
　　Phillip Howell 1968-1971; Philip Brown 1971-1977; Milton TenHave 1977-1979; Richard Matson
　　1979-1987; Catherine Kelsey 1987-1990; Claudette Haney 1990-April 1993; Birt A. Beers May
　　1993-1995; Lawrence R. Wood 1995-2003; Kathryn S. Cadarette 2003-2011; Mary A. Sweet 2011-
　　2014; Vaughn Thurston-Cox 2014-2016; [Epsilon/New Hope/Harbor Springs/Alanson became a
　　4-point charge 2014] Hillary Thurston-Cox (Assoc.) 2014-2016; Randall J. Hitts 2016-2017; Susan
　　E. Hitts 2016- [Harbor Springs / Alanson realigned 2016]

Hardy UMC *[Heritage]*   hardyumcsecy@sbcglobal.net
(P/M) 6510 E Highland Rd, Howell 48843   (517) 546-1122
Douglas R. Trebilcock 1967-1969; W. Harold Pailthorpe 1969-1970; William J. Rosemurgy 1970-1973; Benjamin Bohnsack 1973-1980; James M. Thompson 1980-1983; Dale E. Brown 1984-1989; Hayden K. Carruth Jr. 1989-Feb. 14, 1992; James E. McCallum Mar. 1, 1992-1994; Sherry Parker (assoc--Hardy/Hartland) 1994-1995; Ronda L. (Beebe) Hawkins 1995-Jun 1, 2000; Barbra Franks 2000-2005; Joyce E. Wallace 2005-2013; John H. Schneider, Jr. 2013-

Harper Woods: Redeemer UMC *[Greater Detroit]*   hwredeemer@att.net
(P/M) 20571 Vernier Rd, Harper Woods 48225   (313) 884-2035
Ralph Edwards 1967-1969; Jack Lancaster 1969-1976; Charles Jacobs 1976-1980; Donald L. Lichtenfelt 1980-1988; Ronald Corl 1988-1999; James P. Schwandt 1999-Feb 15, 2008; Marshall G. Dunlap 2008-2011; Thomas Taylor 2011-2013; Thomas Priest, Jr. 2013-Feb 1, 2017; Judith A. May (Ret.) Feb 1-Jun 30, 2017; Marshall Murphy 2017-

Harrietta UMC *[Northern Waters]*   harriettaumc@yahoo.com
(P) 116 N Davis St, Harrietta 49638; (M) PO Box 13, Harrietta 49638-0013   (231) 389-0267
Ward Pierce 1967-1972; Bill Amundsen 1972-1979; Jean Crabtree 1979-Aug. 1980; Donald Buege Sept. 1980-Jan. 1984; Bruce Prestwood-Taylor Jan. 1984-1986; Thomas P. Fox 1986-1992; Charles A. Williams 1992-Feb 14, 1997; J. David Thompson Nov. 16, 1997-2001; John J. Conklin (DSA) 2001-Nov. 30, 2001; John J. Conklin Dec. 1, 2001-2009; Mona L. Kindel 2009-2012; Beverley Williams 2012-2016; Laurie M. Koivula 2016-2018; [Mesick/Harrietta/ Brethren became a three-point charge 2016] [Harrietta became a sigle point charge 2018] Travis Heystek 09/01/2018-

Harrison: The Gathering *{Central Bay]*   gatheringumc@gmail.com
(P) 426 First St S Ste 106, Harrison 48625; (M) PO Box 86, Harrison 48625   (989) 539-1445
[new church start 2004; mission congregation 2009; became 3-point charge: The Gathering (WMAC) & Wagarville/Wooden Shoe UMCs (DAC-Saginaw District) 2009] James C. Noggle 2004-2010; Michael J. Simon 2010-2013; Kellas D. Penny (1/2 time) July 1-Dec.31, 2013; Vincent J. Nader May 1, 2014-2016; Cheryl Lynn Mancier Nov. 1, 2016-

Harrisville UMC *[Central Bay]*   UMCinHarrisvilleMI@charter.net
(P/M) 217 N State St, Harrisville 48740   (989) 724-5450
Carl J. Litchfield 1969-1971; G. MacDonald Jones 1971-1972; Luren J. Strait 1972-1978; Bruce M. Denton 1978-1983; William L. Stone 1983-1990; Edward C. Seward 1990-Dec 31, 2004; William P Sanders (interm) Aug 31, 2004-Dec 31, 2004; William Omansiek Jan 1, 2005-2005; Travis DeWitt Sep 1, 2005-2007; Tracy Brooks 2007-2012; Lynda Jo Powers 2012-Oct 31, 2014; Mary Soderholm Nov 1, 2014-Jun 10, 2017; Charles Sheldon (DSA) Sept 1, 2017-2018; Eric Lee Johnson 2018-

Hart UMC *[Midwest]*   hartumc@gmail.com
(P/M) 308 S State St, Hart 49420   (231) 873-3516
Theron Bailey 1966-Dec. 1969; Edward Passenger Dec. 1969-1971; Jack Kraklan 1971-1979; Lloyd Walker 1979-1982; Kenneth Snow 1982-1989; Laurie Haller 1989-1993; Bruce R. Kintigh 1993-Jan. 1, 1999; Harvey Prochnau Feb. 1, 1999-2003; Ben Bill Lester 2003-2011; Rebecca Farrester Wieringa 2011-2015; Steven R. Young 2015-

Hartford UMC *[Greater Southwest]*   hartfordmethodist@gmail.com
425 E Main St, Hartford 49057   (269) 621-4103
Morris Reinhart 1967-1972; Jean Crabtree 1972-1979; John Hice 1979-1987; David L. Crawford 1987-1990; Gerald L. Selleck 1990-1998; Richard A. Powell 1998-1999; Ronald W. Hansen 1999-2011; Jeffrey C. Williams 2011-2014; Rey Mondragon 2014-2015; [Hartford/Keeler became a two-point charge 2015] Ryan L. Wenburg 2015-2019; [Keeler UMC merged with Hartford UMC 12-31-16] Stephanie Elaine Norton 2019-

Hartland UMC *[Heritage]* hartlandumc@sbcglobal.net
(P/M) 10300 Maple Rd, Hartland 48353 (810) 632-7476
 Charles Kitchenmaster 1966-Jan. 1972; Ted P. Townsend (interim) Feb. 1972-Jun. 1972; Ronald L. Figgins Iris 1972-1975; Horace L. James 1975-1979; John R. Crotser 1979-1983; Mark E. Spaw 1983- (as Hardy/Hartland 1994-95) 1999; Gerald S. Hunter 1999-Sep 17, 2000; Gerald R. Parker (interim) Oct 1, 2000-Jan 31, 2001; David R. Strobe Feb 1, 2001-Feb 1, 2006; Thomas Hart (interm) Mar 1, 2006-Jun 30, 2006; G. Fred Finzer 2006-2012; Paul Gruenberg 2012-

Hastings: First UMC *[Mid-Michigan]* hastingsfumc@gmail.com
(P/M) 209 W Green St, Hastings 49058 (269) 945-9574(P)
 Emeral Price 1967-March 1969; Stanley Buck April 1969-Dec. 1972; Sidney Short Jan. 1973-1982; Myron Williams 1982-May 1985; David Nelson 1985-1989; Philip L. Brown 1989-1994; Bufford W. Coe 1994-Oct. 15, 2000; Kathy E. Brown Feb. 1, 2001-2010; Donald E. Spachman 2010-2014; Mark R. Payne 2014-Dec. 31, 2016; Thomas J. Evans Jan. 1, 2017-June 30, 2017; Bryce E. Feighner 2017-

Hastings: Hope UMC *[Mid-Michigan]* hastingshopeumc@gmail.com
(P) 2920 S M 37 Hwy, Hastings 49058; (M) PO Box 410, Hastings 49058-0410
 Kenneth Vaught 1968-January 1983; Jack Bartholomew February 1983-February 1986; Robert Mayo April 1986-1992; James E. Fox 1992-1995; Laurence E. Hubley 1995-2000; Richard D. Moore 2000-2015; Marcia L. Elders 2015-2017; Kimberly S. Metzer 2017-

Hastings: Welcome Corners UMC *[Mid-Michigan]* macousino1@gmail.com
(P/M) 3185 N M 43 Hwy, Hastings 49058 (269) 945-2654
 John Jodersma 1967-Nov. 1968; Stanley Finkbeiner Nov. 1968-1969; Esther Cox 1969-1975; Richard Erickson 1975-1976; Clinton Bradley-Galloway 1976-1981; Constance Heffelfinger 1981-1984; Glenn Wegner 1984-1987; Robert Kersten 1987-1991; Carl Q. Litchfield 1991-2000; Geraldine M. Litchfield (Assoc.) Jan. 1993-1994; Soo Han Yoon Aug. 1, 2000-Jan. 31, 2001; Robert E. Smith Feb. 1, 2001-Dec. 31, 2003; Robert E. Smith (part-time) Dec. 31, 2003-2006; Susan D. Olsen 2006-2015; Mickey Ann Cousino (DSA) 2015-

Hayes UMC *[Central Bay]* bayporthayes@att.net
(P) 7001 Filion Rd, Pigeon 48755; (M) 836 N 2nd St, Bay Port 48720-9630 (989) 656-2151
 Donald W. Brown 1965-1970; Louis E. Reyner 1970-1975; Richard Andrus 1975-1979; Frederick P. Cooley 1979-1984; Randy A. Chemberlin 1984-1986; Alger T. Lewis 1986-1992; S. Douglas Leffler 1992-1994; Norman R. Beckwith 1994-1998; Barbra Franks 1998-2000; Alan W. DeGraw 2000-2003; Douglas E. Mater 2003-2010; Bruce L. Nowacek 2010-2013; Brian K. Johnson 2013-2016; Matthew Chapman 2016-

Hazel Park: First UMC *[Greater Detroit]* hazelparkfirst@wowway.com
(P/M) 315 E 9 Mile Rd, Hazel Park 48030 (248) 546-5955
 Bryn Evans 1961-1970; Sam Yearby 1970-1975; Reginald Cattell 1975-Feb. 1979; Donna Lindberg 1979-Apr.1983; Robert C. Hastings 1983-1987; Paul Lim 1987-1992; David Ray 1992-1994; Jill H. Zundel 1994-1999; James R. McCallum 1999-Apr 30, 2002; Mary Ellen Chapman May 1, 2002-2010; Cherrie A. Sporleder 2010-2013; Rochelle J. Hunter 2013-2015; Frederick G. Sampson, III 2016-

Hemlock UMC *[Central Bay]* hemlockumc@frontier.com
(P) 406 W Saginaw St, Hemlock 48626; (M) PO Box 138, Hemlock 48626 (989) 642-5932
 A. Theodore Halsted 1965-1970; John C. Huhtala 1970-1975; Terry W. Allen 1976-1978; Tom Brown 1978-1984; Steven A. Gjerstad 1984-Jun 30, 1994; Arthur V. Norris Jul 1, 1994-2001; Karen L. Knight 2001-Jan 1, 2002; Nicholas W. Scroggins 2002-2009; Jerry F. Densmore 2009-2014; Michael W. Vollmer 2014-2019; Robert G. Richards 2019- (Swan Valley (lead church) / LaPorte charge and Hemlock / Nelson charge formed new four point charge July 1, 2019)

Henderson UMC *[East Winds]*   pastorherbw@aol.com
(P) 302 E Main St, Henderson 48841; (M) 218 E Main, Henderson 48841   (989) 723-5729
Monroe J. Frederick 1968-1972; T. K. Foo Sep 18, 1972-1976; Wayne A. Rhodes 1976-1978;
James B. Lumsden 1978-1982; David S. Stiles 1982-1984; James P. James 1984-1989; J. Robert
Anderson 1989-1993; Nicholas W. Scroggins 1993-1998; Paul B. Lim 1998-2000; Billie Lou
Gillespie 2000-Oct 14, 2006; Calvin H. Wheelock Nov 1, 2006-2019; [Henderson / Chapin /
Owosso: Triity frmed three-point charge 07/01/2019] Steffani Glygoroff (DSA) 2019-

Hermansville UMC *[Northern Skies]*   1chris1cross1@att.net
(P) W5494 Second S, Hermansville 49847; (M) 3716 D Rd, Bark River 49807
Calvin Rice 1967-1974; James Paige 1974-1975; John Henry 1975-1981; John Hamilton 1981-
1986; David Leenhouts 1986-1992; W. Peter Bartlett 1992-1996; Kenneth C. Dunstone 1996-Dec
15, 1999; Jean M. Larson Jan 1, 2000-Nov 15, 2001; James A. Fegan Dec 1, 2001-May 31, 2002;
Cherrie A. Sporleder Jun 16, 2002-2004; James M. Mathews 2004-2011; Christine J. Berquist
2011-

Hersey UMC *[Northern Waters]*   herseyumc1@outlook.com
(P) 200 W 2nd St, Hersey 49639; (M) PO Box 85, Hersey 49639-0085   (231) 832-5168
Otto Flachsmann 1964-1969; M.K. Matter 1969-1977; David A. Cheyne 1977-1982; Wesley E. Smith
1982-1984; Martin D. Fox 1984-Sept. 1986; Nelson Ray Dec. 1986-1988; Cynthia A. Skutar 1988-
1992; Timothy J. Miller 1992-1994; Pulpit Supply July 1994; John G. Kasper Aug. 1, 1994-2001;
Raymond D. Field 2001-2003; Lawrence A. Nichols 2003-2010; Mary Beth Rhine 2010-2012; Lemuel
O. Granada (1/4 time) July 29, 2012-

Hesperia UMC *[Midwest]*   humchesp@frontier.com
(P/M) 187 E South Ave, Hesperia 49421   (231) 854-5345
Merlin Delo 1966-1978; William Bowers 1978-1980; David Dryer 1980-1984; Richard Williams
1984-Oct. 1, 1997; Pulpit Supply Oct. 1, 1997 - Dec. 31, 1997; Susan Olsen Jan. 1, 1998-July 1,
1998; Raymond D. Field 1998-1999; James Bradley Brillhart 1999-2007; Dianne D. Morrison 2007-
2011; Richard D. Morrison (DSA) 2007-2011; Paul E. Hane 2011-2018; Paul E. Hane (Ret.) (LTFT)
2018

Highland UMC *[Heritage]*   phaskell@humc.us
(P/M) 680 W Livingston Rd, Highland 48357   (248) 887-1311
Russell L. Smith 1967-1974; H. Emery Hinkston 1974-1983; Gilson M. Miller 1983-1992; David
E. Church 1992-1995; James P. Kummer 1995-2016; Thomas Anderson 2016-

Hillman UMC *[Northern Waters]*   hillmanumc@outlook.com
(P) 111 Maple St, Hillman 49746; (M) PO Box 638, Hillman 49746-0638   (989) 742-3014
Howard E. Shaffer 1964-1971; Philip A. Rice 1971-1975; Robert Kersten 1975-1978; Harold F.
Blakely 1978-1981; James R. Rupert 1981-1984; R. Wayne Hutson 1984-1990; Paula Timm 1990-
1992; Jack E. Johnston 1992-Nov 1, 2005; George Morse (interm) Nov 1, 2005-Jun 30, 2006;
Karen A. Mars 2006-2008; Donald R. Derby 2008-2013; Lisa Kelley 2013-

Hillsdale First UMC *[Heritage]*   office.hillsdalefirstumc@gmail.com
(P/M) 45 N Manning St, Hillsdale 49242   (517) 437-3681
John Francis 1968-1971; David S. Evans 1971-1979; William V. Payne 1979-1987; David A.
Selleck 1987-Dec. 1988; Hugh C. White (Interim) Dec. 1988-1989; Gary L. Bekofske 1989-1996;
Mark G. Johnson 1996-2003; Curtis Eugene Jensen 2003-2010; Patricia L. Brook 2010-2018;
Rob A. McPherson 2018-

Hillside UMC *[Heritage]*   hillsideunited1@frontiernet.net
(P/M) 6100 Folks Rd, Horton 49246   (517) 563-2835
Eugene Lewis 1966-1972; Paul Mazur 1972-1974; Tom Jones 74-78; Jon Powers 78-81; Larry
Wiliford 81-83; Lawrence Hodge 1983-1991; Laurence E. Hubley 1991-1995; David A. Cheyne
1995-1998; Marilyn B. Barney 1998-2008; Denise J. Downs 2008-2009; [Hillside/Somerset Center
two-point charge 2009] E. Jeanne Koughns 2009-2014; Patricia A. Pebley 2014-

Hinchman UMC *[Greater Southwest]*   hinchmanumc@hotmail.com
(P/M) 8154 Church St, Berrien Springs 49103   (269) 471-5492
    Robert Strauss 1968-1981; Valerie Hill 1981-March 1983; Leonard Haynes 1983-1986; Leo Bennett 1986-1989; Walter J. Rothfuss 1989-2000; Brenda Gordon 2000-2006; Jane D. Logston (part-time) 2006-14; [Berrien Springs / Hinchman / Oronoko became 3-point charge 2012] [Hinchman / Oronoko became 2-point charge 2014] Linda R. Gordon 2014-2017; Brenda E. Gordon 2017-2018; Dawn Oldenbury (DSA) (LTFT ½) 2018- [Hinchman / Scottdale beacme two-point charge 10-1-2018]

Holland: First UMC *[Midwest]*   office@fumcholland.org
(P/M) 57 W 10th St, Holland 49423   (616) 396-5205
    Hilding W. Kilgren 1963-1970; Paul E. Robinson (Assoc.) 1965-1972; Darwin R. Salisbury 1970-1977; Brent Phillips (Assoc.) 1972-1973; John L. Francis 1977-1987; William C. Johnson (Assoc.) 1977-1981; Heath T. Goodwin (part-time) 1981-1983; Robert S. Treat (part-time) 1983-1988; Harold F. Filbrandt 1987-1990; Susan J. Hagans (Assoc.) 1988-1995; John W. Ellinger 1990-1996; Beatrice K. Rose (Assoc.) 1995-1998; William E. Dobbs 1996-2005; R. John Thompson (Assoc.) 1998-Apr. 1, 2001; Karen A. Tompkins (Assoc.) 1998-2003; Todd J. Query (Deacon) 2003-2006; J. Lynn Pier-Fitzgerald 2005-2017; Janice T. Lancaster (Assoc. Pastor of Congregational Care) 2010-Jan. 30, 2014; Bradley S. Bartelmay 2017- ; Tania J. Dozeman (Assoc.) 2018- ; LuAnne M. Stanley-Hook (Deacon) 2019-

Holly: Calvary UMC *[East Winds]*   hollycalvarychurch@gmail.com
(P/M) 15010 N Holly Rd, Holly 48442   (248) 634-9711
    Robert F. Davis 1968-1973; R. LaVere Webster 1973-1976; Michael Grajcar, Jr. 1976-1982; Harley L. Siders 1982-1990; Jeffrey R. Maxwell 1990-2001; Mary Jean Love 2001-2008; Faith E. Timmons 2008-2012; Clifford J. Schroeder III 2012-

Holly: Mt. Bethel UMC *[East Winds]*   scottclark714@msn.com
(P/M) 3205 Jossman Rd, Holly 48442   (248) 627-6700
    Donald E. Hall 1969-1970; Dudley C. Mosure 1970-1977; Susan Bennett Stiles 1977-1980; David Rahn 1980-1981; David Davenport 1981-Sept., 1986; Scott Harper 1986-1988; Gerald E. Mumford 1988-1993; Donald Woolum 1993-Sep 30, 1996; Robert Watt Oct 1, 1996-2001; Karen B. Williams 2001-2005; Patricia A. Harton Feb 1, 2006-2010; Pam Kail 2010-2012; Scott Clark 2012-2018; Leah Caron 2018-

Holt UMC *[Mid-Michigan]*   holtumc@acd.net
(P) 2321 Aurelius Rd, Holt 48842; (M) PO Box 168, Holt 48842-0168   (517) 694-8168
    Philip R. Glotfelty, Jr. 1964-1970; Douglas A. Smih 1970-1972; Myron K. Williams 1972-1982; Dennis Buwalda 1982-1989; Joseph D. Huston 1989-1999; Barbara J. Flory (Assoc.) 1998-2000; Lynn E. Grimes 1999-2006; Glenn M. Wagner 2006-2014; Mark R. Erbes 2014-

Holton UMC *[Midwest]*   humcoffice@frontier.com
(P/M) 9530 Holton Duck Lake Rd, Holton 49425   (231) 821-2323
    Ira J. Noordhof 1967-1975; Donald Vuurens 1975-Jan. 1978; Pulpit Supply Jan.-June 1978; Charles Van Lente 1978-1983; David McBride 1983-1988; Larry Rubingh 1988-Dec. 1991; Pulpit Supply Jan.-June 1992; Kenneth Bremer 1992-2006; Gerald Selleck 2006-2018; Matthew Todd Stoll 2018-

Hopkins UMC *[Greater Southwest]*   hsmumc@hotmail.com
(P) 322 N Maple St, Hopkins 49328; (M) PO Box 356, Hopkins 49328-0356   (269) 793-7323
    Glenn Britton 1968-Jan. 1970; Stanley Finkbeiner Feb. 1970-1974; Densel Fuller 1974-1976; Brent Phillips 1976-1978; David Knapp 1978-Oct. 15, 1982; Robert J. Stillson Nov. 1982-1989; Robert D. Nystrom 1989-1992; Marjory A. Berkompas 1992-June 13, 1996; David S. Yoh (DSA) 1996-1999; Raymond D. Field 1999-2001; Reva H. Daniel 2001-2005; Linda J. Burton 2005-2014; Dominic A. Tommy 2014-2017; Joel T. Fitzgerald 2017-2018; Andrew Ryan Phillips 2018-

Horton Bay UMC *[Northern Waters]* barneyfife@torchlake.com
(P/M) 4961 Boyne City Rd, Boyne City 49712 (231) 582-9262
Seward Walton 1968-1976; John Gurney 1976-1978; Steve Tower 1978-1979; Carl Staser 1979-1980; Allen Valkema 1980-1982; Martin Fox 1982-1984; Craig Adams 1984-1994; Kathryn S. Slaughter 1994-2000; Geraldine M. Litchfield 2000-2005; Timothy B. Wright 2005-2013; [Horton Bay became single-point charge 2013] Michael R. Neihardt 2013-2015; Eun Sik Poy Sept. 1, 2015-2016; Gregory P. Culver 2016-2017; [Charlevoix / Horton Bay became a two-point charge 2016; Horton Bay became a single station 2017] Michael R. Neihardt 2017-

Houghton: Grace UMC *[Northern Skies]* churchoffice@houghtongraceumc.org
(P/M) 201 Isle Royale St, Houghton 49931 (906) 482-2780
Carter W. Preston 1968-1972; James H. McLaurin 1972-1978; Alan R. George 1978-1987; Ronald K. Fulton 1987-1988; David R. Strobe 1988-1995; Thomas C. Anderson 1995-2009; David J. Goudie Aug 1, 2009-20-13; Charles A. Williams 2013- [Houghton: Grace / Painesdale: Albert Paine Mem. two-point charge 7-1-2019]

Houghton Lake UMC *[Northern Waters]* hlumc@gmail.com
(P/M) 7059 W Houghton Lake Dr, Houghton Lake 48629 (989) 422-5622
Troy Lemmons 1966-1971; James R. Hilliard 1971-1980; Russell L. Smith 1980-1986; Roger L. Colby 1986-1992; Charles R. Marble 1992-2000; Calvin D. Long 2000-2009; Thomas C. Anderson Aug 1, 2009-2016; George R. Spencer 2016-

Howarth UMC *[Greater Detroit]* howarthumc@att.net
(P/M) 550 E Silverbell Rd, Lake Orion 48360 (248) 373-2360
Elmer J. Snyder 1967-1972; Georg Gerritsen 1972-1978; Dwayne Lee Kelsey 1978-1981; Bruce L. Billing 1982-1993; David K. Koski 1993-1998; Sylvia A. Bouvier 1998-2006; Stephen Fraser-Soots 2006-2009; Thomas M. Sayers 2009-2016; Carolyn Jones 2016-2018; Marvin L. Herman 2018-

Howell: First UMC *[Heritage]* fumcwl@ameritech.net
(P/M) 1230 Bower St, Howell 48843 (517) 546-2730
Allan G. Gray 1962-1973; Lewis C. Sutton 1973-1985; Gary L. Damon 1986-1990; Margaret R. Garrigues-Cortelyou (assoc) 1990-1992; David A. Russell 1990-1997; Charles R. Jacobs 1997-2010; Diane Griffin (deacon) Jan 1, 2006- ; George H. Lewis 2010-

Hudson: First UMC *[Heritage]* fdneumann@yahoo.com
(P/M) 420 W Main St, Hudson 49247 (517) 448-5891
Roland F. Liesman 1965-1973; Robert B. Secrist 1973-1980; James G. Simmons 1980-1984; Ralph C. Pratt 1984-1985; Myra L. Sparks 1985-Oct. 14, 1989; Francis F. Anderson Nov. 1, 1989-1991; Melanie L. Carey 1991-1993; Martha C. Ball Jul. 16, 1993-Jan 15, 1996; Benjamin B. Ball (assoc) Jul. 16, 1993-Jan 15, 1996; Mark G. Johnston Feb 1, 1996-2008; Raymond D. Wightman 2008-2010; Fredrick D. Neumann 2010-2013; Bradley S. Luck 2013-2018; Carol J. Abbott 2018-

Hulbert: Taquamenon UMC *[Northern Skies]* marybrooks729@gmail.com
(P) 10505 Maple St, Hulbert 49748; (M) PO Box 91, Hulbert 49748
Wayne T. Large 1967-1970; Vernon D. Wyllys 1970-1975; James Lumsden 1975-1976; Audrey N. Dunlap 1976-1979; David J. Hill 1979-1980; David K. Campbell 1980-1981; J. Douglas Paterson 1981-1982; James W. Robinson 1982-1983; Julaine A. Hays 1983-1984; Ramona E. Cowling 1984-1985; Melinda R. Cree 1985-1986; Ray S. Peterson 1986-1989; Jan L. Beaderstadt 1989-1991; Audrey M. Dunlap 1991-1993; Donald Bates 1993-Sep 30, 1996; Barbra Franks Oct 1, 1996-1998; Donald L. Bates 1998-2001; Virginia B. Bell 2001-Oct 30, 2005; Sandra J. Kolder Dec 4, 2005-2011; Lowell Peterson 2011-2013; Mary D. Brooks (DSA) 2013-

Ida UMC *[Heritage]*   sachun1128@cs.com
(P) 8124 Ida St, Ida 48140; (M) PO Box 28, Ida 48140   (734) 269-6127
    Paul R. Crabtree 1951-1969; Ferris S. Woodruff 1969-1973; Henry W. Powell 1973-1977; Robert E.
    Burkey 1977-1982; Jack Edward Fulcher 1982-1984; J. Robert Anderson 1984-1989; John M. Mehl
    Jr. 1989-2001; Wayne A. Hawley 2001-2007; Sang Yoon (Abraham) Chun 2007-2016; Corey M.
    Simon 2016-2019; Robert J. Freysinger 2019-

Imlay City UMC *[East Winds]*   icumc@yahoo.com
(P/M) 210 N Almont Ave, Imlay City 48444   (810) 724-0687
    Harvard J. Warren 1969-1972; H. Reginald Cattell 1972-1975; Lawrence C. Brooks 1975-1980;
    Donald J. Daws 1980-1989; James A. Govatos 1989-1998; Colin P. Stover 1998-2002; Rodney
    L. Sanderson-Smith (assoc.) 2000-Mar 31, 2002; Jimmy S. Barnett (assoc) 2001-2002; Pamela
    K. Barnett (assoc) 2001-2002; Kevin J. Harbin 2002-2011; Dianna L. Rees 2011-2013; Marcel
    Lamb 2013-

Indian River UMC *[Northern Waters]*   indianriverumc@gmail.com
(P) 956 Eagles Nest Rd, Indian River 49749; (M) PO Box 457, Indian River 49749   (231) 238-7764
    Gerald Janousek 1968-1970; Argle Leesler 1970-1972; Robert Elder 1972-1976; Morris Reinhart
    1976-1984; Steve Weinberger 1984-1990; Larry Mannino 1990-1994; John D. Lover 1994-2000;
    Gary G. Step 2000-2012; O. Jay Kendall (Assoc.) 2007-Aug. 31, 2012; DeAnn J. Dobbs 2012-
    2014; Patricia A. Harpole 2014-2017; Everett L. Harpole (Assoc.) 2016-2017; Todd W. Shafer
    2017- ; Noreen S. Shafer (Assoc.) 2017-

Ionia: Easton UMC *[Midwest]*   eastonoffice@gmail.com
(P/M) 4970 Potters Rd, Ionia 48846   (616) 527-6529
    George W. Chaffee 1971-1974; Nolan Williams 1974-Oct. 1980; Eldon Schram Oct. 1980-Sept.
    1984; Kathryn M. Williams Sept. 1984-Nov. 1986; Kathryn M. Coombs Nov. 1986-1990; Scott K.
    Otis 1990-1993; David J. Blincoe 1993-Aug. 15, 1994; Supplied by Presbyterian Church Sept.
    1994; Don Wells (Presbyterian) 1995-Jan. 6, 1999; Judy K. Downing 1999-2001; Lynn W. Wagner
    2001-Sept. 1, 2002; Paul F. Bailey (DSA) April 13, 2003; Thomas R. Reaume Sept 1, 2004-Jan.
    1, 2007; Nancy J. Patera, Jan. 1, 2007-2014; Donna Jean Sperry 2014-

Ionia: First UMC *[Midwest]*   ioniafirst@gmail.com
(P/M) 105 E Main St, Ionia 48846   (616) 527-1860
    Lester C. Bailey 1964-1970; Charles W. Fullmer 1970-1977; Carl L. Hausermann 1977-1983; John
    F. Sorensen 1983-1985; Keith A. Bovee 1985-1991; Lawrence E. Hodge 1991-2000; Martin H.
    Culver 2000-2006; Lawrence P. Brown 2006-2014; Jonathan D. Van Dop 2014-2017; [Ionia First
    / Lyons-Muir became a two-point charge 2016] Jonathan E. Bratt Carle 2017-

Ionia Parish: Berlin Center UMC *[Midwest]*   levalleybc@gmail.com
(P) 3042 Peck Lake Rd, Saranac 48881; (M) 4018 Kelsey Hwy, Ionia 48846   (616) 527-1480
    Luther Brokaw 1967-1971; Donald Fry 1971-1973; Lloyd Walker 1973-Aug. 1979; Willis Braun
    Aug. 16, 1979-Feb. 1989; David L. Flagel March 1989-2003; Mark G. Johnson 2003-2007; Dennis
    E. Slattery 2007-2012; Raymond R. Sundell 2012-Nov. 30, 2016; Mark G. Johnson (Ret.) Dec. 1,
    2016-June 30, 2017; Nancy J. Patera 2017-

Ionia Parish: LeValley UMC *[Midwest]*   levalleybc@gmail.com
(P/M) 4018 Kelsey Hwy, Ionia 48846   (616) 527-1480
    Luther Brokaw 1967-1971; Donald Fry 1971-1973; Lloyd Walker 1973-Aug. 1979; Willis Braun
    Aug. 16, 1979-Feb. 1989; David L. Flagel March 1989-2003; Mark G. Johnson 2003-2007; Dennis
    E. Slattery 2007-2012; Raymond R. Sundell 2012-Nov. 30, 2016; Mark G. Johnson (Ret.) Dec. 1,
    2016- June 30, 2017; Nancy J. Patera 2017-

Ionia: Zion UMC *[Midwest]*   zionumcsecretary@gmail.com
(P/M) 423 W Washington St, Ionia 48846   (616) 527-1910
    Chester Erickson 1967-1971; George Chaffee 1971-1974; Nolan Williams 1974-Oct. 1980; Eldon Schram Oct. 1980-1984; Kathryn Williams (Coombs) 1984-Sept. 1986; William Dornbush Nov. 1986-Dec. 31, 1993; Pulpit Supply Jan. 1- June 30, 1994; Craig L. Adams 1994-Sept. 15, 1999; Arlo Vandlen (DSA) Jan. 24, 2000-2001; Donald Graham 2001-2007; Cliff Allen (DSA) 2007; Cliff Allen, Nov. 10, 2007-2018; Larry W. Nalett (Ret.) (LTFT ½) 2018-

Iron Mountain: First UMC *[Northern Skies]*   imfirstumc@att.net
(P/M) 106 4th St, Iron Mountain 49801   (906) 774-3586
    Richard Reese 1967-1971; Monroe Fredrick 1971-1976; John Moore 1976-1980; James Hall 1980-1983; Paul Doering 1983-1984; James Mathews 1984-1989; Douglas J. McMunn 1989-Dec 31, 1995; William R. Seitz Jan 1, 1996-Feb 1, 2004; David P. Snyder Feb 15, 2004-2009; Margaret A.W. Paige 2009-2012; Walter P. Reichle 2012-

Iron Mountain: Trinity UMC *[Northern Skies]*   imtrinityumc@gmail.com
(P/M) 808 Carpenter Ave, Iron Mountain 49801   (906) 774-2545
    Tom Brown II 1968-1973; David M. Liscomb 1973-1982; John F. Greer 1982-1986; John C. Stubbs 1986-1991; Arthur V. Norris 1991-Jun 30, 1994; James A. McLaurin Jul 1, 1994-1998; Scott A. Harmon (assoc) 1996-1998; Meredith Rupe 1998-2006; Philip B. Lynch (assoc) Oct 1, 2000-2003; Deborah S. Thomas 2006-2011; Paul J. Mallory 2011-2014; Geraldine G. Hamlin 2014-

Ironwood: Wesley UMC *[Northern Skies]*   iwumc@charter.net
(P) 500 E McLeod Ave, Ironwood 49938; (M) PO Box 158, White Pine 49971   (906) 932-3900
    Thomas H. Beaven 1966-1970; Lillian G. Richards 1970; David A. Russell 1971-1977; Troy Lemmons 1977-1980; Gary A. Allward 1980-1987; Thomas H. Zimmerman 1987-1991; Carl R. Doersch 1991-1995; Pamela S. Kail 1995-1998; Allen F. Schweitzer 1998-Sep 30, 1999; Cherrie A. Sporleder Feb 1, Jun 30, 2000; Jean B. Rencontre 2000-2008; Rosemary R. DeHut 2008-Aug. 31, 2018; Keith Paul Mullikin (DSA) Oct. 1, 2018- [Ironwood Wesley / Wakefield two-pooint charge 7-1-2019]

Ishpeming: Wesley UMC *[Northern Skies]*   church@ishpemingwesley.org
(P) 801 Hemlock St, Ishpeming 49849; (M) PO Box 342, Ishpeming 49849   (906) 486-4681
    Stanley A. Bailey 1967-1976; Paul C. Frederick 1976-1980; Robert Kersten (assoc) 1978-1980; George A. Luciani 1980-1993; Donna J. Lindberg 1993-1997; Lawrence C. Brooks 1997-1999; Bruce C. Hatch 1999-2001; Paul G. Donelson Oct 1, 2001-2006; Scott P. Lindenberg 2006-2014; Jeremiah J. Mannschreck 2014-2018; Matthew Osborne 2018-

Ithaca UMC *[Mid-Michigan]*   office@Ithacaumc.org
(P/M) 327 E Center St, Ithaca 48847   (989) 875-4313
    John F. Sorensen 1967-1972; David B. Nelson, Jr. 1972-1980; Nolan R. Williams 1980-1991; David L. McBride 1991-2006; Steven R. Young 2006-2010; Cynthia Greene 2010-2015; Gary L. Simmons 2015- [Ithica / Beebe became a two-point charge 2018]

Jackson: Brookside UMC *[Heritage]*   brooksideumc@gmail.com
(P/M) 4000 Francis St, Jackson 49203   (517) 782-5167
    Verne Summers 1966-Aug. 1974; Verner Kilgren Sept. 1974-Sept. 15, 1978; William Torrey Sept. 15, 1978-1985; Richard Johns 1985-1992; David L. Johnston 1992-2005; Charles Campbell July 15, 2005-Sept 1, 2005; Chad M. Parmalee Sept 1, 2005-2013; Ronald K. Brooks 2013- [Jackson Brookside/Trinity became a two-point charge 2015]

Jackson: Calvary UMC *[Heritage]*   jaxcalumc@gmail.com
(P/M) 925 Backus St, Jackson 49202   (517) 782-0543
    J. Leon Andrews 1968-1972; Haven UMC merged with Calvary in 1972; Donald P. Sailor 1972-1977; Claude Ridley 1977-1983; Carl L. Hausermann 1983-1989; George R. Grettenberger 1989-1992; Timothy P. Boal 1992-1997; Linda J. Carlson (Assoc.) 1993-Feb. 16, 1999; Michael T. Conklin 1999-2003; Maurice E. Walworth, Jr. 2003-2006; Linda H. Hollies 2006-Aug. 18, 2007; Lillian T. French Jan. 1, 2008-Sept. 1, 2010; Edrye Maurer Sept. 1, 2010-2015; [Jackson Calvary & Zion became two-point charge 2013] Eric Iden (DSA) 2015-2017; [Jackson: Calvary became single station 2017] Mary K. Loring 2017-2019; Terry S. Wiliford (Ret.) 2019-

Jackson: First UMC *[Heritage]*   church@firstumcjackson.org
(P/M) 275 W Michigan Ave, Jackson 49201   (517) 787-6460
    Robert C. Smith 1966-1971; E. Lenten Sutcliffe (Assoc.) 1968-1971; Richard A. Morrison (Assoc.) 1969-1971; Merle D. Broyles 1971-1981; Wilbur A. Williams (Assoc.) 1971-1973; David C. Brown (Assoc.) 1971-1973; Ivon Gonsor (Assoc.) 1973-1974; George Chaffee (Assoc.) 1974-1984; John Ellinger (Assoc.) Jan. 1972-1976; Richard Erickson (Assoc.) 1976-1982; Larry Taylor 1981-1987; David Morton (Assoc.) 1982-1986; Ted Cole (Assoc.) 1984-1986; Linda Farmer-Lewis (Assoc.) 1986-1987; David Knapp (Assoc.) 1986-1989; Joy Moore 1988-1990; John Cermak 1987-1994; Leo E. Bennett (Assoc.) 1989-1993; Donette Bourke (Deacon) 1990- 2003; John D. Morse (Assoc.) 1993-1999; Edward C. Ross 1994-2012; Sanda Sanganza (Assoc.) 1999-2001; Charles Campbell (Assoc.) 2003-2007; Susan Babb (Assoc.) 2004-2015; Mark Babb (Deacon-Spiritual Formation Consultant) June 1, 2010-2015; Eric S. Beck 2012-2019; Timothy W. Trommater (Assoc.) 2015-2017; Mary K. Loring (Assoc.) 2017-2019; Tonay M. Arnesen 2019-

Jackson: Trinity UMC *[Heritage]*   jacksontrinity@sbcglobal.net
(P/M) 1508 Greenwood Ave, Jackson 49203   (517) 782-7937
    (Jackson Trinity is a merged congregation of Greenwood Ave. UMC, Greenwood Park EUB and Francis Street EUB); James Crosby 1968-1969; Harold Kirkenbauer 1968-1969; Harold Taber 1969-1972; Dale Crawford 1972-1977; B. James Varner 1977-1986; Karen Slager Wheat 1986-1998; Beatrice K. Robinson 1998-2006; [Jackson Trinity / Parma became a charge 2006] Sandra L. Spahr (DSA) 2006-2007; Melodye Surgeon Rider 2007-2012; Patricia A. Pebley (1/2 time) 2012-2014; [Jackson Trinity became single-point charge 2014] Robert Q. Bailey (Ret.) 2014-2015; [Jackson Brookside/Trinity became a two-point charge 2015] Ronald K. Brooks 2015-

Jackson: Zion UMC *[Heritage]*   jacksonZionUMC@gmail.com
(P/M) 7498 Cooper St, Jackson 49201   (517) 769-2570
    Amos R. Bogart Jan. 1968-1969; Frederick W. Werth 1969-1971; Charles R. Campbell 1971-1981; D. David Ward 1981-Jan. 7, 1994; Lawrence A. Nichols Feb. 1, 1994-2003; Donald R. Wendell July 15, 2003-Mar. 15, 2006; William Lang (DSA), Oct. 1, 2006-2007; [Pleasant Lake & Jackson Zion became two-point charge 2008] David H. Minger (DSA) 2008-2013; [Jackson Calvary & Zion became two-point charge 2013] Edrye A. Eastman Maurer 2013-2015; Eric Iden (DSA) 2015-2017; [Grovenburg / Jackson: Zion / Felt Plains / Williamston: Wheatfield became multi-point charge 2017] John Kabala 2017-2018; Gertrude Mwadi Mukalay 2017-2018; TBS

Jeddo UMC *[East Winds]*   juliekrauss@hotmail.com
(P) 8533 Wildcat Rd, Jeddo 48032; (M) PO Box 7, Jeddo 48032   (810) 327-6644
    William J. Burgess 1968-1973; Mark K. Smith 1973-1976; Daniel R. Fenton 1976-1978; Harold J. Slater 1978-1980; James E.& Peggy Paige 1980-1985; Georg F.W. Gerritsen 1985-1988; Donald H. Francis 1988-1992; Emerson W. Arntz 1992-2002; Robert A. Srock 2002-Dec 1, 2003; Catherine W. J. Hiner 2004-2009; Micheal P. Kelly 2009-2012; Donald L. Wojewski 2012-2018; Julie Krauss 2018-

Jerome UMC *[Heritage]* najumcs@yahoo.com
(P/M) 8768 Jerome Rd, Jerome 49249
   Kenneth W. Karlzen 1968-1971; Thomas R. Jones 1971-Aug. 1974; David Flagel Sept. 1975-1980; Lee F. Zachman 1980-1984; Donald McLellan 1984-Sept. 1988; Melanie Baker-Streevy Oct. 1988-1995; Rochelle Ray 1995-2000; Tim Doubblestein 2000-Aug. 31, 2002; Charles Richards Sept. 1-Dec. 31, 2002; Paul Hane Jan. 1, 2003-2011; Kimberly A. Metzger July 1-Dec. 19, 2011; Arthur R. Turner (DSA) Feb. 1, 2012-2014; Timothy R. Puckett 2014-

Jonesville UMC *[Heritage]* jonesvilleunitedmethodist@gmail.com
203 Concord Rd, Jonesville 49250 (517) 849-9565
   Densel Fuller 1968-1974; William Johnson 1974-1977; Derryl Cook 1977-1978; M. John Palmer 1978-1982; Lloyd Walker 1982-1985; Jack Kraklan 1985-1988; Michael Baker-Streevy 1988-1995; Reva Hawke 1995-1997; Nelson Ray 1997-2000; Craig Pahl 2000-2014; [Jonesville/Allen became single charges 2014] Jennifer Ward (DSA) 2014-2017; [Litchfield / Jonesville became two-point charge 2017] Mary A. Sweet 2017- [Jonesville / Napoleon became two-point charege 2019]

Juddville UMC *[Mid-Michigan]* juddvilleunitedmethodistchurch@hotmail.com
(P/M) 3907 N Durand Rd, Corunna 48817 (810) 638-7498
   Paul L. Amstutz 1964-1971; Clifford J. Furness 1971-1976; Donald W. Brown 1976-1978; Linda Susan Garment 1978-1980; Verne W. Blankenburg 1980-1983; Robert J. Henning 1983-Jul. 1990; Mary Thoburn Tame Oct. 16, 1990-Aug 31, 1997; James M. Downing Sep 1, 1997-Aug 16, 1999; Olaf Lidums Nov 16, 2000-2003; David L. Fleming 2003-2011; Janet M. Engler 2011-2013; Danny Bledsoe 2013-2015; Dan Wallington 2015-2018; Wallace Peter Crawford (Ret.) 2018-

Kalamazoo: First UMC *[Greater Southwest]* KalamazooFUMC@umc-kzo.org
(P/M) 212 S Park St, Kalamazoo 49007 (269) 381-6340
   James W. Wright 1964-1972; J. Melvin Bricker (Assoc.) 1966-1971; O. Lavern Merritt (Assoc.) 1968-1970; Ray R. Fassett (Assoc.) 1970-1974; Hoover Rupert 1972-1983; Douglas W. Vernon (Assoc.) 1971-1974; Marvin Zimmerman (Assoc.) 1974-1976; Donald Ludman (Assoc.) 1974-1978; William Richards (Assoc.) 1976-1979; Richard Beckett (Assoc.) 1977-1987; Mac Kelly (Assoc.) 1978-1982; Wayne Reece (Assoc.) 1979-1985; Gerald Selleck (Assoc.) 1982-1984; Royal Synwolt 1983-1991; Jane Shapley (Assoc.) 1985-1987; Dean Francis (Assoc.) 1985-1990; Richard Rossiter (Assoc.) 1987-1992; George Hartmann (Assoc.) 1987-1994; Keith Treman (Assoc.) 1990-1998; Kenneth McCaw 1991-Jan. 1, 2000; Cynthia A. Skutar (Assoc.) 1992-1997; Cynthia M. Schaefer (Assoc.) 1997-2001; Michelle Wisdom-Long (Assoc.) 1998-2000; Ron Keller (interim senior pastor) Jan. 1, 2000-July 1, 2000; Douglas W. Vernon 2000-2010; Dale A. Hotelling (Assoc.) July 16, 2000-2004; Matthew J. Bistayi (Assoc.) 2002-2006; Julie Dix (Assoc.) 2006-2010; John W. Boley 2010-2014; Michelle M. Wisdom-Long (Assoc.) 2010-2011; Stephen MG Charnley 2014-; Manohar A. Joshi (assoc) 2019-; Julie A. Kline (assoc) 2019-

Kalamazoo: Milwood UMC *[Greater Southwest]* office@milwoodunitedmethodistchurch.org
(P/M) 3919 Portage St, Kalamazoo 49001 (269) 381-6720
   Richard C. Miles 1966-1970; Heath T. Goodwin 1970-1971; Alden B. Burns 1971-Dec. 1981; John H. Hice (Assoc.) 1977-1979; Ron L. Keller Jan. 1982-1988; James M. Morgan 1988-1999; Robert K. Lynch 1999-2006; Martin H. Culver 2006-2011; Kennetha J. Bigham-Tsai 2011-2013; Heather A. (McDougall) Molner 2013-Feb. 8, 2016; David A. Newhouse (Ret.) Mar. 1, 2016-2017; Bille R. Dalton (Ret.) 2017-

Kalamazoo: Northwest UMC *[Greater Southwest]* markroberts1903@yahoo.com
(P/M) 3140 N 3rd St, Kalamazoo 49009 (269) 290-1312
   Ray Carpenter 1967-1972; Linda Stoddard 1972-1976; Dorcas Lohr 1976-1982; Pulpit supply 1982-1983; Alden B. Burns 1983-1996; Carol A. Newman 1996-2000; John W. McNaughton 2000-2003; Calvin Y. Hill 2003-2007; Sheila F. Baker 2007-2012; Ronald W. Hansen (DSA) (1/4 time) 2012-2013; Samuel C. Gordy (1/4 time) 2013-2015; Nelson L. Hall 2015-2018; Mark Robers (LTFT ¼) 2018-

Kalamazoo: Sunnyside UMC *[Greater Southwest]*　　　office@sunnysideumc.com
(P/M) 2800 Gull Rd, Kalamazoo 49048　　　　　　　　　　　(269) 349-3047
　Allen D. McCreedy 1967-1973; Robert H. Conn 1973-1976; John W. Ellinger 1976-1981; Norman
　C. Kohns 1981-1985; Paul L. Hartman 1985-1992; John W. Fisher 1992-2004; Billie R. Dalton
　2004-Feb. 28, 2009; Linda J. Burson, Mar. 1-July 1, 2009; John Matthew Weiler (1/2 time) 2009-
　; Cara Weiler (deacon 1/4 time) Oct. 1, 2009-

Kalamazoo: Westwood UMC *[Greater Southwest]*　　　info@westwood-umc.org
(P/M) 538 Nichols Rd, Kalamazoo 49006　　　　　　　　　(269) 344-7165
　A.R. Davis 1968-1973; Allen D. McCreedy 1973-1977; E. William Wiltse 1977-1980; Merged with
　Kalamazoo Simpson 1980; Jack H. Baumgart 1980-1984; Larry E. Irvine 1984-1988; Kenneth W.
　Karlzen 1988-July 31, 1995; Eric S. Beck Aug. 1, 1995-2007; Wayne A. Price 2007-2019; Sandra
　Douglas (Deacon) (1/4 time) 2011- ; Sean K. Kidd 2019-

Kalamo UMC *[Mid-Michigan]*　　　　　　　　　　　　office@kalamochurch.org
(P/M) 1475 S Ionia Rd, Vermontville 49096　　　　　　　　(517) 588-8415
　Lowell F. Walsworth 1966-1971; Laurence R. Grubaugh 1971-1973; Milton J. Tenhave 1973-1977;
　David L. Johnston 1977-May 1983; James William Schoettle May 1983-1988; William P. Sanders
　1988-Feb. 1996; Mark E. Thompson 1996-2004; Bryce Feighner 2004-2013; [Barry-Eaton
　Cooperative Ministry 2013] Dan Phillips 2013-2015; Jerry J. Bukoski (LTFT) 2015-

Kalkaska UMC *[Northern Waters]*　　　　　　　　　　KalkaskaUMC@yahoo.com
(P/M) 2525 Beebe Rd NW, Kalkaska 49646　　　　　　　　(231) 258-2820
　Richard M. Riley 1984-1993; Charles R. VanLente 1993-1996; Charles K. Stanley 1996-Oct. 1,
　1999; Stanley Lee Hayes (DSA) Oct. 1, 1999-July 1, 2000; Robert W. Stark 2000-2008; Gregory
　R. Wolfe 2008-2013; Robert J. Freysinger 2013-2015; John Paul Murray 2015-2019; Yong Choel
　Woo 2019-

Kendall UMC *[Greater Southwest]*　　　　　　　　　　info@goblesumc.org
(P) 26718 County Road 388, Gobles 49055; (M) PO Box 6, Kendall 49062　　　(269) 628-2263
　James Boehm 1967-1970; Allen Valkema 1970-1971; William Miles 1971-1974; Rudolph Wittenback
　1974-1976; Karen S. Slager-Wheat 1976-1986; John McNaughton 1986-1987; Judy K. Downing
　1987-1998; Susan Olsen 1998-2004; Mary Beth Rhine 2004-2010; Edward Mohr L. 2010-Sept. 11,
　2012; Daniel J. Minor (Ret.) Sept. 16, 2012-June 30, 2013; Nelson L. Hall 2013-2015; John M. Brooks
　2015-2019; Glenn C Litchfield 2019-

Kent City: Chapel Hill UMC *[Midwest]*　　　　　　　mary.chapelhillkc@gmail.com
(P/M) 14591 Fruit Ridge Ave, Kent City 49330　　　　　　(616) 675-7184
　Charles McNary 1964-1970; David Morton 1970-Jan. 1974; Stanley Finkbeiner 1974-1981; Ray
　Grienke 1981-1985; Willard Gilroy 1985-Oct. 1988; David Hainer Oct. 1988-March 1991; Mark
　Johnson May 1991-1996; Glenn C. Litchfield 1996-2005; R. John Thompson 2005-2010; Kevin
　Guetschow 2010-2017; Michael J. Ramsey 2017-

Keswick UMC *[Northern Waters]*　　　　　　　　　　office@keswickchurch.com
(P/M) 3376 S Center Hwy, Suttons Bay 49682　　　　　　(231) 271-3755
　Dale Crawford 1968-Oct. 1971; Richard Kuhn Oct. 1971-1980; John Myette 1980-1984; Tom
　Evans 1984-1988; Wayne Gorsline 1988-1991; Martin H. Culver 1991-1999; Wayne A. Price 2000-
　2004; Donald E. Spachman 2004-2010; Charles A. Williams 2010-2011; Patricia A. Haas 2011-

Kewadin: Indian Mission UMC *[Northern Waters]*　　　gpamp@live.com
(P) 7250 Cairn Hwy, Kewadin 49648; (M) 851 W Conway Rd, Harbor Springs 49740
　　　　　　　　　　　　　　　　　　　　　　　　　　　(231) 347-9861
　Harry John Sr. Jan. 1975-1993; Owen White-Pigeon (DSA) 1993-1994; Cletus Marshall 1994-
　Feb. 5, 1995; Pulpit Supply Feb. 6-June 1995; Delfred White-Crow (DSA) 1995-Nov. 15, 1997;
　Delfred White-Crow (part-time) Nov. 16, 1997-Apr. 16, 1998; Thomas H. John Jr 1998-2015;
　[Kewadin Indian Mission became single-point charge 2015] Sandra K. VandenBrink (RLA) 2015-
　Dec. 31, 2016; George Pamp (DSA) Jan. 1, 2017-

Kewadin UMC *[Northern Waters]*   kewadinumc@gmail.com
(P) 7234 Cairn Hwy, Kewadin 49648; (M) PO Box 277, Kewadin 49648   (231) 264-9640
    Glenn Loy 1968-Sept. 1970; Russell Lautner (Assoc.) 1968-Oct. 1970; Gordon Showers Oct.
    1970-Nov. 1971; Robert Doner Dec. 1971-1976; Bernard Randolph 1976-1978; Jack Bartholomew
    1978-Feb. 1983; Stephen Beach Feb. 1983-Nov. 1986; Michael Baker-Streevy Dec. 1986-1988;
    Charles M. Shields 1988-1993; Raymond R. Sundell 1993-1998; Kathryn M. Coombs 1998-1999;
    Janilyn McConnell (Deacon) 1998-2003; Thomas M. Pier-Fitzgerald 1999-2005; William W. Chu
    & Julie A. Greyerbiehl (Chu) 2005-2009; Mary S. Brown July 1-Nov. 1, 2009; Eugene L. Baughan
    (Ret.) Nov. 1, 2009-2015; Howard Harvey 2015-

Kilmanagh UMC *[Central Bay]*   pastorbilloumc@outlook.com
(P/M) 2009 S Bay Port Rd, Bay Port 48720   (989) 975-1500
    Harold F. Blakely 1957-1978; William R. Maynard 1978-1980; Donald McLellan 1980-1982; Robert
    L. Kersten 1982-1986; Jeffrey R. Maxwell 1986-1990; George H. Lewis 1990-1993; Nancy Goings
    1993-Dec 31, 1995; Ronald O. Pietta Jan 1, 1996-1997 Clarence VanConant 1997-1999; Alger T.
    Lewis 1999-Mar 1, 2011; Duane G. Thon 2011-2017; William Cleland 2017-

Kingsley UMC *[Northern Waters]*   kumcadmin@kingsleyumcmi.org
(P) 113 Blair St, Kingsley 49649; (M) PO Box 39,5 Kingsley 49649-0395   (231) 263-5278
    Marion Nye 1966-1970; Silas H. Foltz 1970-1971; Lewis (Bud) Buckner 1972-1978; Wayne
    Babcock 1978-1983; Beverly Prestwood-Taylor 1983-1986; Beverly Prestwood Taylor (3/4 time)
    1986-May 1988; Bruce Prestwood-Taylor (3/4 time) 1986-May 1988; Bruce Kintigh 1988-1993;
    Brian F. Rafferty 1993-1999; Charlene A. Minger 1999-2008; Gary S. Wales 2008-2013; Carl Q.
    Litchfield 2013-2017; Colleen A. Wierman (Assoc.)(1/4 time) 2014-2017; Colleen A. Wierman
    2017-

Kingston UMC *[Central Bay]*   kingstonumchurch@gmail.com
(P) 3453 Washington St, Kingston 48741; (M) PO Box 196, Kingston 48741   (989) 683-2832
    Verne W. Blankenburg 1968-1972; Robert Bryce 1972-1973; Joel W. Hurley 1973-1978; Gilson
    M. Miller 1978-1983; Lawrance D. Higgins 1983-1984; C. Wm Bollinger 1984-1989; Lynn F.
    Chappell 1989-1996; Kwang Min Lee 1996-1997; Margaret Pettit Passenger 1997-2001; Terry D.
    Butters 2001-2005; Richard B. Brown 2005-2010; Debra K. Brown 2010-Mar 15 1, 2015; Margaret
    Passenger (interim) Apr 15, 2015-2015; Carol Joan Abbott 2015-2018; Mark Harriman 2018-

L'Anse UMC *[Northern Skies]*   lumc@up.net
(P/M) 304 N Main St, Lanse 49946   (906) 524-7939
    William Kelsey 1968-1970; Lillian Richards 1971; Howard E Shaffer 1971-1981; John R. Henry
    1981-1986; Gregory Rowe 1986-1990; James M. Mathews 1990-1993; David P. Snyder 1993-
    Oct 1, 2003; John R. Henry 2004-2011; Stephen E. Rhoades 2011-2019; Nathan T. Reed 2019-

Lacota UMC *[Greater Southwest]*   m2pinto@hotmail.com
(P) 01160 CR 681, Lacota 49063; (M) PO Box 7, Lacota 49063-0007   (269) 207-2095
    Robert Victor 1966-1969; John Hagans 1969-1974; Pulpit Supply 1974-1977; Joseph Pratt 1977-
    1980; Carl C. Nisbet 1980-Aug. 31, 2003; Donna Jean Keyte Sept. 1, 2003-Jan. 1, 2006; Michael
    A. Pinto (DSA) 2006-2007; Michael A. Pinto 2007-Apr. 8, 2019; Michael A. Pinto (DSA) April 9,
    2019-

Laingsburg UMC *[Mid-Michigan]*   lumc@cablespeed.com
(P/M) 210 Crum St, Laingsburg 48848   (517) 651-5531
    Dale Ferris 1969-1972; Brian D. Kundinger 1972-1977; David K. Koski 1977-1982; L. Michael
    Pearson 1982-1986; Harold E. Weemhoff 1986-1990; Robert J. Easlick 1990-1993; J. Robert
    Anderson 1993-1999; Gerald M. Sever Jr., 1999-2006; Elbert P. Dulworth 2006-2012; Brian West
    2012-

Lake Ann UMC *[Northern Waters]*   church@lakeannumc.com
(P/M) 6583 1st St, Lake Ann 49650   (231) 275-7236
Carter Miller 1966-1969; Richard LoCicero 1969-1970; Russell J. Lautner Oct. 1970-1982; William
E. Haggard 1982-1989; Charles J. Towersey 1989-Apr. 15, 2008; James L. Breithaupt (Assoc.
1/2 time) 2004-Mar. 15, 2006; Devon R. Herrell June 15, 2008-2013; Michael J. Simon 2013-2017;
Joshua Manning 2017-

Lake City UMC *[Northern Waters]*   lcumc301@gmail.com
(P) 301 E John St, Lake City 49651; (M) PO Box - Drawer P, Lake City 49651   (231) 839-2123
J. William Schoettle 1965-Feb. 1970; Leonard J. Yarlott Feb. 1970-1972; Ward D. Pierce 1972-
Aug. 1976; Ross Bunce Aug. 1976-1979; Willard Gilroy 1979-1985; David L. Dryer 1985-1996;
Jane A. Crabtree 1996-2000; Edrye (Eastman-Sealey) Maurer 2000-Sept. 1, 2010; Jean M. Smith
Sept. 1, 2010-2019; Russell K. Logston 2019-

Lake Fenton UMC *[East Winds]*   pastorcshay@gmail.com
(P/M) 2581 N Long Lake Rd, Fenton 48430   (810) 629-5161
Dwight E. Reibling 1968-1970; Donald C. Turbin 1970-1973; David G. Knapp Dec. 1973-1976;
Clifford J. Furness 1976-Sep 30, 1998; Gloria Haynes Oct 1, 1998-2002; Emerson W. Arntz 2002-
2009; Pamela S. Kail 2009-2012; Jeremy Peters 2012-2015; Charmaine Shay 2015-2019; Duane
A. Lindsey 2019- [Lake Fenton / Lennon / Duffield three-point charge 7-1-2019]

Lake Linden UMC *[Northern Skies]*   calumc@up.net
(P/M) 57235 Calumet Ave, Calumet 49913   (906) 337-2720
J. Howard Wallis 1967-1968; Robert Barry 1969-1970; Lillian Richards; 1970; John Moore 1970-
1976; Martin Caudill 1976-1979; Jay Six 1979-1981; William Wright 1981-1985; W. Peter Bartlett
1985-1987; Pamela J. Scott; Jack E. Johnston 1989-1992; Mary L. Rose 1992-1994; Christine F.
Bohnsack 1994-Feb 29, 2000; Robert A. White Mar 16, 2000- ; Richard B. Brown (assoc) Mar 16,
2000-2003; Robert A. White 2000-2016; James Palaszeski 2016-2018; Gun Soo Jung 2018-2019;
[Keweenaw Parish: Calumet / Lake Linden 7-1-2019] James M. Mathews (Ret.) 2019-

Lake Odessa: Central UMC *[Mid-Michigan]*   info@centralchurch-lakeo.org
(P) 912 4th Ave, Lake Odessa 48849; (M) PO Box 485, Lake Odessa 48849   (616) 374-8861
Marvin F. Zimmerman 1967-1974; William A. Hertel 1974-Sept. 1980; Steve Keller 1980-1984;
Thurlan E. Meredith 1984-1986; Charles W. Richards 1986-1989; D. Keith Laidler 1989-1992;
Emmett H. Kadwell, Jr. 1992-Jan. 1, 2000; Charles M. Shields Feb. 1, 2000-July 1, 2000; Donald
R. Ferris 2000-2007; Eric S. Beck 2007-2012; Karen J. Sorden 2012-2017; Dominic A. Tommy
2017-

Lake Odessa: Lakewood UMC *[Mid-Michigan]*   juliew@lakewoodmiumc.org
(P/M) 10265 Brown Rd, Lake Odessa 48849   (269) 367-4800
Wilbur A. Williams 1967-1971; Charles A. Dunbar 1971-1978; James R. Hulett 1978-1985; Ward
D. Pierce 1985-2001; Curtis E. Jensen 2001-2003; David Lee Flagel 2003-2013; James C. Noggle
2013-2015; Kathleen Smith (RLA) (Assoc.) July 15, 2014- ; Cynthia Greene 2015-2017; Steven
C. Place 2017-

Lake Orion UMC *[East Winds]*   loumc1@sbcglobal.net
(P/M) 140 E Flint St, Lake Orion 48362   (248) 693-6201
Robert Hudgins 1962-1971; Edward L. Duncan 1971-1982; W. Harold Pailthorp (assoc) 1973-
1984; Mary Margaret Eckhardt (assoc) 1978-1983, 1985-1990; Richard A Peacock 1982-1993;
Bruce E. Petrick (assoc) 1990-1993; Robert Davis 1993-1997; Wilson Andrew Hart (assoc) 1993-
Apr 30, 1996; Randy J. Whitcomb (assoc) May 1, 1996-Feb 15, 2001; Thomas P. Macaulay
1997-2004; Carol M. Blair Bouse (assoc) 2001-2002; Marjorie H. Munger (assoc) 2002-2013;
Bruce M. Denton 2004-2012; Lawrence A. Wik 2012- ; John Ball (assoc.) 2013-

Lakeview: New Life UMC *[Midwest]* newlifeumc6584@gmail.com
(P/M) 6584 W Howard City Edmore Rd, Six Lakes 48886 (989) 352-7788
Lawrence P. Brown Jan. 1, 1998-2006; Richard J. Duffy (co-pastor) Jan. 1, 1998-June 30, 1998; Anita Hahn 2006-2011; John A. Scott 2011-2015; Susan J. Babb 2015-2019; Mark R. Babb (Deacon) 2016-2019; Timothy B. Wright 2019-

Lamb UMC *[East Winds]* huff1@aol.com
(P) 1209 Cove Rd, Wales 48027; (M) PO Box 29, Memphis 48041-0029 (810) 392-2294
Max Weeks 1965-1971; Duane E. Miller 1972-1977; Paul W. Reigle 1977-1982; Wayne C. Ferrigan 1982-1984; Martin Caudill 1984- 1987; Oct. Donald L. Bates 1987-1991; Douglas M. Choate 1992-1993; Catherine W. Hiner 1993-1999; David L. Fleming 1999-2001; Janet M. Engler 2001-2004; Donald L. Wojewski Nov 1, 2004-Dec 31, 2004; James E. Huff, Jr. Jan 1, 2005-

Lambertville UMC *[Heritage]* office@labertvilleumc.org
(P) 8165 Douglas Rd, Lambertville 48144; (M) PO Box 232, Lambertville 48144 (734) 847-3944
Leonard C. Ritzler 1966-1972; Harry Gintzer (assoc) 1971-1972; A. Edward Perkins 1972-1974; Dean A. Klump 1974-1981; James R. McCallum 1981-1983; Jeffry W. Dinner 1983-1990; David D. Amstutz 1990-1997; Thomas H. Zimmerman 1997-2016; Douglas E. Ralston (assoc) 2004-Mar 28, 2007; King W. Hanna (interim-assoc) May 1, 2007-Jul 31, 2007; James O. Bowen (assoc) Aug 1, 2007-2008; Aaron B. Kesson (assoc) 2008-2012; Zachary Dunlap (assoc.) Jan 1, 2013-2015; Devin Smith (assoc.) 2015- ; Gene Patrick England 2016-2018; James E. Britt 2018-

Lansing: Asbury UMC *[Mid-Michigan]* asburyumclansing@gmail.com
(P/M) 2200 Lake Lansing Rd, Lansing 48912 (517) 484-5794
Douglas A. Smith 1960-1970; John S. Myette 1970-1978; Geoffrey L. Hayes 1978-1987; William A. Hertel 1987-1990; Charles F. Garrod 1990-Oct. 1992; Benton R. Heisler Nov. 1992-1997; Deborah M. Johnson 1997-2008; Martin M. DeBow 2008-2014; Bo Rin Cho 2014-2017; Jon L. Pohl 2017-

Lansing: Central UMC *[Mid-Michigan]* adminassistant@lansingcentralumc.net
(P/M) 215 N Capitol Ave, Lansing 48933 (517) 485-9477
Howard A. Lyman Feb. 1967-1978; Francis F. Anderson (Assoc.) 1966-1970; Peter H. Kunnen (Assoc.) 1968-1970; Robert E. Betts (Assoc.) 1970-1974; Charles Grauer (Assoc.) 1970-1972; Paul L. Hartman (Assoc.) 1974-Jan. 1980; Samuel H. Evans (Assoc.) 1975-1977; Lloyd VanLente (Assoc.) 1977-1982; Neil F. Bintz 1978-1982; Robert H. Roth, Jr. (Assoc.) May 1980-1983; Sidney A. Short 1982-1993; James M. Gysel (Assoc.) 1983-1993; Lynn A. DeMoss 1993-1997; Pegg Ainslie (Assoc.) 1993-1997; John W. Boley 1997-2002; Russell F. McReynolds 2002-2007; Joseph D. Huston 2007-2009; Ronald K. Brooks 2009-2013; Linda J. Farmer-Lewis 2013-2017; Mark E. Thompson 2017-

Lansing: First UMC *[Mid-Michigan]* office@lansingfirst.org
(P/M) 3827 Delta River Dr, Lansing 48906 (517) 321-5187
Francis C. Johannides 1968-1972; John F. Sorensen 1972-Sept. 1978; Theron E. Bailey Sept. 1978-March 1982; Kenneth W. Karlzen March 1982-1988; Mark D. Graham 1988-1996; Robert L. Hundley 1996-2000; Stephan Weinberger 2000-2004; Melanie J. Baker 2004-2012; Lori J. Sykes July 15, 2012-

Lansing: Grace UMC *[Mid-Michigan]* lgraceumc@gmail.com
(P/M) 1900 Boston Blvd, Lansing 48910 (517) 482-5750
Clarence W. Hutchens 1967-1975; Paul F. Albery 1975-1981; John W. Ellinger 1981-1985; David L. Johnston 1985-1992; Richard E. Johns 1992-1996; Gary L. Bekofske 1996-2005; Timothy P. Boal 2005-2006; Jane Ellen Johnson Jan. 1, 2007-2016; Paul SungJoon Hahm 2016- ; Nancy V. Fancher (Deacon) 2017-

Lansing: Mt Hope UMC *[Mid-Michigan]*   office@mounthopeumc.org
(P/M) 501 E Mount Hope Ave, Lansing 48910   (517) 482-1549
Donald Merrill 1967-Oct. 1975; George Elliott Nov. 1975-1979; Lloyd Phillips 1979-1984; Robert
Hinklin 1984-Feb. 1987; Wade Panse May 1987-Oct. 1992; Paul C. Frederick Dec. 1992-1999;
Pamela J. Mathieu (Deacon) 1995- Ronald K. Brooks (Assoc.) 1998-1999; Ronald K. Brooks
1999-2000; Linda H. Hollies 2000-2001; William Earl Haggard 2002-2012; Lansing Calvary UMC
merged w/ Mt. Hope UMC 07-01-07]; Colleen Treman (Deacon, Children's Coordinator) 2008-
2015; Robert B. Cook 2012- ; Eric Mulanda Nduwa Aug. 1, 2015- ; Nancy V. Fancher (Deacon)
(LTFT ½) 2018-

Lansing: Sycamore Creek UMC *[Mid-Michigan]*   office@sycamorecreekchurch.org
(P/M) 1919 S Pennsylvania Ave, Lansing 48910   (517) 394-6100
[new church start 2000] Barbara J. Flory 2000-2009; Thomas F. Arthur 2009- [Potterville UMC
merged w/ Sycamore Creek UMC and became Sycamore Creek Potterville Campus 12-31-16]
Mark Aupperlee (Assoc.) Jan 1, 2018-

Lansing: Sycamore Creek UMC - Potterville Campus *[Mid-Michigan]*
(P) 105 N Church St, Potterville 48876; (M) 1919 S Pennsylvania Ave, Lansing 48910
                    (517) 645-7701
Thomas F. Arthur Dec. 31, 2016- ; [Potterville UMC merged w/ Sycamore Creek UMC and became
Sycamore Creek Potterville Campus 12-31-16] Mark Aupperlee (Assoc.) Jan 1, 2018-

Lapeer: Trinity UMC *[East Winds]*   trinumc@trinitylapeer.org
(P/M) 1310 N Main St, Lapeer 48446   (810) 664-9941
Arthur B. Howard 1968-1973; Norman R. Beckwith (assoc) 1970-1972; Floyd W. Porter (assoc)
1972-1976; Garfield H. Kellermann 1973-1976; James R. Timmons 1976-1994; David J. Hill
(assoc) 1976-1979; Gordon B. Boyd (assoc) 1979-1981; Allen J. Lewis (assoc) 1979-1981; Donald
E. Washburn (assoc) 1981-1984; David C. Dupree (assoc) 1984-1987; Michael O. Pringle (assoc)
1987-1991; W. Steven Boom (assoc) 1991-Nov 1, 1994; Terry A. Euper 1994-2003; Daniel J.
Bowman (assoc) Jan 1, 1995-Aug 31, 1998; Chong Youb Won (assoc) Sep 1, 1998-2002; Colin
P. Stover (assoc) 2002-May 31, 2005; Ralph H. Pieper, II 2003-2012; Gloria Haynes (assoc) 2005-
2009; Grant R. Lobb 2012-

LaPorte UMC *[Central Bay]*   laportepastor@aol.com
(P/M) 3990 Smith's Crossing, Freeland 48623   (989) 695-9692
Karl Patow 1969-1971; Richard Mansfield 1971; John Eversole 1971-1973; Max Weeks 1973-
1977; Leon Smith 1977-1979; Leonard Gamber 1979-1982; Kenneth Reeves 1982-1985; Edwin
M. Collver 1985-1992; Gordon B. Boyd 1993-Aug 31, 1994; Barbra Franks Sep 1, 1994-Sep 30,
1996; Timothy Hastings Dec 1, 1996-Dec 15, 2003; Elin A. Peckham Dec 16, 2003-Jun 30, 2007;
Bonita Davis Sep 16, 2007-2008; L. Cecille Adams Aug 1, 2008-2013; Robert G. Richards 2013-
[Swan Valley (lead church) / LaPorte charge and Hemlock / Nelson charge formed new four point
charge July 1, 2019]

LaSalle: Zion UMC *[Heritage]*   lasallezionumc@yahoo.com
(P) 1603 Yargerville Rd, La Salle 48145; (M) 1607 Yargerville Rd, La Salle 48145
Tony Johnson 1968-1969; Paul W. Hoffmaster 1969-1972; John G. Park 1972-1975; Donald J.
Daws 1975-1980; Stephen E. Wenzel 1980-1982; Robert Worgess 1982-1984; Grant R. Lobb
1984-1988; Craig A. Smith Aug. 1, 1988-Aug. 16, 1990; Daniel J. Bowman Sep. 16, 1990-Dec 31,
1994; Ray T. McGee Jan 1, 1995-Aug 15, 2000; Judy Link Fuller Sep 1, 2000-Oct 31, 2000;
Douglas E. Ralston Nov 1, 2000-Mar 28, 2007; King W. Hanna (interim) May 1, 2007-Jul 31, 2007;
James O. Bowen Aug 1, 2007-2009; Janet L. Luchs 2009-2011; Joel Walther 2011-2017; Daniel
Hyer 2017-2018; Carter Louis Cortelyou 2018-

Lawrence UMC *[Greater Southwest]*   lawrenceunitedmethodist@gmail.com
(P) 122 S Exchange St, Lawrence 49064; (M) PO Box 276, Lawrence 49064   (269) 674-8381
  Kenneth Snow 1967-1972; Norman Crotser 1972-1976; George Gierman 1976-1979; Leo Bennett
  1979-1986; Mark Johnson 1986-Apr. 1991; Ronald K. Brooks May 1991-1998; Wayne H. Babcock
  1998-Dec. 31, 2002; David S. Yoh (DSA) Jan. 1, 2003-July 1, 2003; Jane D. Logston 2003-2006;
  Clifford L. Radtke 2006-2016; Wayne E. McKenney 2016- [Lawrence / Lawton St. Paul's became
  a two-point charge 2016]

Lawton St Paul's UMC *[Greater Southwest]*   st.paulsoffice2018@gmail.com
(P) 63855 N M 40, Lawton 49065; (M) PO Box 456, Lawton 49065-0456   (269) 624-1050
  Donald Russell 1968-1971; Roger Nielson 1971-1974; Al Sprague 1974-1977; Diane Vale 1977-
  1980; Jeff Edwards 1980-1981; Dean Francis 1981-1985; Beverly Gaska 1985-1987; Billie R.
  Dalton 1987-1995; Claudette I. Haney 1995-2000; Ronald K. Brooks 2000-2006; Daniel W.
  Biteman 2006-2010; Peggy A. Boltz 2010-2011; Douglas W. Vernon (DSA) (1/4 time) 2011-2014;
  [LifeSpring/Lawton St. Paul's became 2-point charge 2014] Wayne E. McKenney 2014- [Lawrence
  / Lawton St. Paul's became a two-point charge 2016]

Leaton UMC *[Central Bay]*   fatpastor@cmsinter.net
(P/M) 6890 E Beal City Rd, Mt Pleasant 48858   (989) 773-3838
  Paul Peet 1968-1969; Fred Fischer 1969-1978; David Meister 1978-1979; Pulpit Supply 1979-
  1980; Thomas Crossman 1980-1981; Pulpit Supply 1981-Jan. 1984; Dale Barry Jan.-Aug. 1984;
  Tim Girkin Oct.-Nov. 1984; Byron Coleman Nov. 1984-Jan. 1992; Connie Bongard Jan. 1992-
  1994; Thomas R. Jones (retired) 1994-July 31, 1999; Randall E. Roose (DSA) Aug. 1, 1999-2004;
  Susan D. Olsen July 16, 2004-2006; Sharyn K. Osmond Aug. 1, 2006-Nov. 30, 2008; Donald R.
  Wendell Nov. 30, 2008-Nov. 1, 2009; Craig L. Adams Dec. 1, 2009-2010; David Michael Palmer
  2010-2016; Russell D. Morgan 2016-2018; Deborah A. Line Yencer (Ret.) (LTFT ¼) 2018-

Lee Center UMC *[Heritage]*   lackcv@yahoo.com
(P/M) 23058 21 Mile Rd, Olivet 49076   (517) 857-3447
  Lynn Chapel 1965-March 1971; Beulah Poe March 1971-1976; Robert Doner 1976-1978; Joel
  Campbell 1978-1979; Ethel Stears 1979-Sept. 16, 1983; William Doubblestein Oct. 16, 1983-
  1987; Eugene Baughan 1987-1991; David H. Minger 1991-1995; Wayne Willer 1995-1996; Valerie
  Hill 1996-1998; David L. Litchfield 1998-2001; David Blair 2001-2003; Diane E. Stone 2004-2010;
  Irene L. Vittoz 2010-2014 [Lee Center UMC became single-point charge 7-1-10]; James Gysel
  (Ret.) 2014-

Leighton UMC *[Midwest]*   office@leightonchurch.org
(P/M) 4180 2nd St, Caledonia 49316   (616) 891-8028
  James Sherwood 1965-1972; Keith Laidler 1972-1977; Curtis Cruff July-Dec. 1977; Donald
  Vuurens Jan. 1978-1980; Richard W. McClain 1980-1986; Kenneth Vaught 1986-May 31, 1991;
  Raymond Townsend 1991-2006; David L. McBride 2006-

Leland UMC *[Northern Waters]*   office@lelandcommunityumc.org
(P) 106 N 4th St, Leland 49654; (M) PO Box 602, Leland 49654-0602   (231) 256-9161
  Elmer J. Faust 1966-1969; Edward Jones 1969-1971; Richard Kuhn Nov. 1971-1980; John Myette
  1980-1984; Tom Evans 1984-Jan. 31, 1994; Doug L. Pedersen Feb. 16, 1994-1997; Joseph M.
  Graybill 1997-2011; Linda J. Farmer-Lewis 2011-2013; Virginia L. Heller 2013-2014; Daniel B.
  Hofmann 2014-

Lennon UMC *[East Winds]*   dualind@yahoo.com
(P) 1014 Oak St, Lennon 48449; (M) PO Box 19, Lennon 48449-0019   (810) 621-3676
  Herbert W. Thompson 1969-1978; Ralph C. Pratt 1978-1979; Paul I. Greer 1979-1981; Meredith
  T. Moshauer 1981-1988; James R. Allen 1988-1992; S. Patrick Stybert 1992-1996; Paul L. Amstutz
  1998-2007; Ron Keller 2007-Nov, 2007; Kathy M. Phillips Dec 1, 2007-2016; Barbara S. Benjamin
  2016-2018; Duane A. Lindsey (DSA) 2018-Dec 31, 2018; Duane A. Lindsey Jan 1, 2019- [Lake
  Fenton / Lennon / Duffield three-point charge 7-1-2019]

Leonard UMC *[East Winds]* pastorpatty@att.net
(P) 245 E Elmwood, Leonard 48367; (M) 3645 Grant Ave, Fort Gratiot 48059 (248) 628-7983
Elmer J. Snyder 1974-1976; Jeffery D. Regan 1976-1979; James W. Burgess 1979-1980; Dana R. Strall 1980-1985; Sylvia A. Bouvier 1985-1987; Emerson W. Arntz 1987-1992; Rothwell W. Mc Vety 1992-1996; Harry Brakeman 1996-1997; Ralph Barteld 1997-2002; Ruthmary King (assoc) 1998-2001; Harold C. Nelson (assoc) 2001-Jan 1, 2003; Harold C. Nelson 2003-Apr 1, 2006; Carol S. Walborn Apr 1, 2006-2008; Patricia A. Hoppenworth 2008-

Leslie UMC *[Mid-Michigan]* leslieumc@wowway.biz
(P/M) 401 S Main St, Leslie 49251 (517) 589-9211
William Wurzel 1966-1969; Gordon E. Spalenka June-Oct. 1969; Arthur A. Jackson Oct. 1969-1972; Wayne E. Sparks 1972-1975; James M. Morgan 1975-1982; Max J. Gladding 1982-1990; Clinton McKinven-Copus 1990-Oct. 1991; Reva Hawke Oct. 1991-April 1993; Derek DeToni-Hill 1993-Oct. 15, 1999; Janet Sweet-Richardson Nov. 1, 1999-2003; Carroll Arthur Fowler 2003-Jan. 1, 2006; Donald L. Buege Jan. 15, 2006-2014; Kelly M. Wasnich July 1-Aug. 10, 2014; Frederick H. Fischer (Ret.) Sept. 14, 2014-2015; Paul A. Damkoehler (LTFT) 2015- [Leslie / Felt Plains became a two-point charge 2018]

Lexington UMC *[East Winds]* lexingtonumc@gmail.com
(P/M) 5597 Main St, Lexington 48450 (810) 359-8215
Kenneth L. Harris 1969-1977; John D. Lover 1977-1982; Max D. Weeks Jan. 1983-1987; Donna J. Osterhout 1987-1991; Richard F. Kriesch 1991-1997; Jean R. Snyder 1997-2000; Linda Jo Powers 2000-2002; Betty Montei Blair 2002-Jan 30, 2009; Timothy R. Ziegler 2009-2013; Maureen Baker 2013-2017; David G. Gladstone (Ret.) 2017-2018; Susan M. Youmans 2018-

Lincoln UMC *[Central Bay]* UMCinLincolnMI@charter.net
(P) 101 E Main St, Lincoln 48742; (M) PO Box 204, Lincoln 48742 (989) 736-6910
Carl J. Litchfield 1969-1971; G. MacDonald Jones 1971-1972; Luren J. Strait 1972-1978; Bruce M. Denton 1978-1983; William L. Stone 1983-1990; Edward C. Seward 1990-Dec 31, 2004; William P. Sanders (interm); Travis DeWitt Sep 1, 2005-2007; Tracy Brooks 2007-2012; Linda Jo Powers 2012-Oct 31, 2014; Mary Soderholm Nov 1, 2014-Jun 10, 2017; Charles Sheldon Sept 1, 2017-2018; Eric Lee Johnson 2018-

Linden UMC *[East Winds]* lumc01@aol.com
(P) 201 S Bridge St, Linden 48451; (M) PO Box 488, Linden 48451-0488 (810) 735-5858
W. Thomas Schomaker 1969-Dec. 1975; James G. Simmons 1976-1980; Dale B. Ward 1980-1981; John M. Mehl, Jr. 1981-1989; Linda J. Donelson 1989-1990; Carter Garrigues-Cortelyou 1990-Aug 31, 1994; Shirley A. Cormicle Sep 1, 1994-1998; David R. Strobe 1998-Jan 31, 2001; Janet M. Stybert 2001-2004; Margaret A. Kivisto 2004-2014; Crystal C. Thomas 2014-2018; Michelle N. Forsyth 2018-

Livingston Circuit: Plainfield, Trinity UMC *[Heritage]* livcirumc@gmail.com
(P) 17845 MI State Rd 36, Gregory 48137; (M) 8201 Iosco Rd, Fowlerville 48836 (517) 223-3803
Harry Gintzer 1966-1969; Roger A. Parker 1969-1970; Thomas E. Hart 1970-1975; Jerome K. Smith 1975-1981; Meredith T. Moshauer 1981-Dec. 31, 1981; William R. Donahue Jr. Jan. 14, 1982-Dec. 31, 1987; Richard W. Sheppard Jan. 15, 1988-Dec. 31, 1989; Paul F. Bailey Jan. 1, 1990-1991; Margery A. Schleicher 1991-1995; Myra L. Sparks 1995-Aug 31, 1997; Darrel L. Rice Jan 1, 1998-2003; Malcolm L. Greene 2003-Aug 31, 2004; Steven A Gjerstad Sep 1, 2004-2006; Judith M. Darling 2006-2009; Alan DeGraw (interim) 2009-Dec 31, 2009; Robert A. Miller Jan 1, 2010-2013; David C. Freeland 2013-2017; Mark Huff Nov 12, 2017-

Livonia: Clarenceville UMC *[Greater Detroit]* clarencevillechurch@gmail.com
(P/M) 20300 Middlebelt Rd, Livonia 48152 (248) 474-3444
Elsie A. Johns 1941-1973; Gerald H. Fisher 1973-1985; James E. Tuttle Jan. 15 1985-1990; Lawrence E. VanSlambrook 1990-Feb. 2, 1992; M. Lester McCabe (assoc) 1990-1992; James P. Kummer Feb. 2, 1992-1995; M. Jean Love 1995-2001; James E. Britt 2001-Aug 14, 2006; Elizabeth A. Librande Aug 15, 2007-2010; Donald L. Sperling 2010-

Livonia: Newburg UMC *[Greater Detroit]*　　　judy@newburgumc.org
(P/M) 36500 Ann Arbor Trl, Livonia 48150　　　(734) 422-0149
　　William A. Ritter 1969-1980; Benjamin Bohnsack (assoc) 1970-1973; Donna J. Lindberg (assoc) 1973-March 1974; Duane E. Snyder 1974-1976; John Ferris (assoc) 1976-Apr. 1979; Jack E. Giguere 1980-1984; Roy G. Forsyth (assoc) 1981-1991; Edward C. Coley 1984-1988; David Church 1988-1992; David E. Ray (assoc) 1991-1993; Gilson M. Miller 1992-1997; Melanie L. Carey (assoc) 1993-2000; Thomas G Badley 1997-2002; Barbara E. Welbaum (assoc) 2000-2006; Terry W. Allen 2002-Sep 1, 2005; Marsha M. Woolley 2006-2013; Paul Perez (deacon) 2008-2013; Steven E. McCoy 2013- ; Rebecca Wilson (deacon) 2014-Jan 1, 2105;

Livonia: St. Matthews UMC *[Greater Detroit]*　　　ekemoli@stmatthewslivonia.com
(P/M) 30900 6 Mile Rd, Livonia 48152　　　(734) 422-6038
　　Paul T. Hart 1968-1971; Jerome K. Smith (assoc) 1971-1975; William D. Rickard 1971-1980; David T. Strong 1980-1990; Kearney Kirby (R. assoc) 1989-1992; G. Charles Sonquist 1990-Aug 31, 2002; Mary Margaret Eckhardt Sep 1, 2002-2010; George E. Covintree, Jr. 2010-2015; Jeremy P. Africa 2015-

London UMC *[Heritage]*　　　christopherbutson@live.com
(P/M) 11318 Plank Rd, Milan 48160　　　(734) 439-2680
　　Gary R. Imms 1969-1976; John J. Landon 1976-Mar. 1978; James B. Lumsden Mar. 1978-Dec. 1978; D. Byron Coleman Dec. 1978-1982; Mildred M. Hiner 1982-1984; Donald C. Schark 1984-1986; David W. Purdue 1986-1991; William Michael Clemmer (interim Jun-Aug. 1991); Diana K. Goudie Sep. 1, 1991- Aug 31, 1994; William Michael Clemmer Sep 1, 1994-Feb 16, 2003; Richard E. Burstall 2003-2007; Edward L. Tam 2007-Oct 31, 2007; Ruth A. McCully Nov 1, 2007-Nov 15, 2009; Courtney D. Williams Nov 16, 2009-Dec 31, 2013; Christopher Butson Jan 1, 2014-2019; Beatroce S. Alghali 2019-

Lowell: First UMC *[Midwest]*　　　office@lowellumc.com
(P/M) 621 E Main St, Lowell 49331　　　(616) 897-5936
　　G. Robert Webber 1965-1969; Hartwell Gosney (Assoc.) 1968-Oct. 1972; Dean E. Bailey 1969-1979; Gerald R. Bates 1979-Apr. 1982; Donald L. Buege (Assoc.) 1979-Aug. 1980; Beulah P. Poe (Assoc.) Sept. 1980-1982; William J. Amundsen 1982-1993; B. Gordon Barry 1993-2003; Michael T. Conklin 2003-2008; Richard W. Blunt 2008-2014; Cheryl A. Mulligan (Deacon) Jan. 1, 2014- ; James Bradley Brillhart 2014-

Lowell: Vergennes UMC *[Midwest]*　　　vergennes.secretary@gmail.com
(P/M) 10411 Bailey Dr NE, Lowell 49331　　　(616) 897-6141
　　William Vowell 1968-1969; Phillip Carpenter 1969-1977; Luren Strait 1978-1979; Donald Buege 1979-Sept. 1, 1980; Stanley Forkner Sept. 1, 1980-1986; Daniel Duncan 1986-1989; Tracy Taylor 1989-1990; Lloyd Hansen 1990-1991; Mary Schippers 1991-March 31, 1995; Pulpit Supply April-June 1995; David F. Stout 1995-1996; Nathaniel W. Johnson Sept. 1, 1996-2010; Matthew Stoll 2010-2018; Thomas C. Fifer 2018-

Ludington: St Paul UMC *[Northern Waters]*　　　stpaulumc333@gmail.com
(P/M) 3212 W Kinney Rd, Ludington 49431　　　(231) 843-3275
　　Jack Kraklan 1967-1971; Bernard Randolph 1971-1974; Forest Crum 1974-1981; Ray D. Flessner 1981-1989; Robert P. Stover 1989-1998; Dennis E. Slattery 1998-2007; Robert J. Henning 2007-2011; Jon L. Pohl 2011-2017; Bradley Bunn (DSA) 2017-

Ludington United UMC *[Northern Waters]*　　　office@ludingtonumc.org
(P/M) 5810 Bryant Rd, Ludington 49431　　　(231) 843-8340
　　Harold F. Filbrandt 1967-1974; William J. Torrey 1974-1978; John F. Sorensen Sept. 15, 1978-1983; William D. Dobbs 1983-1991; Laurie A. Haller (Assoc.) 1985-1989; Paul E. Lowley 1991-2000; Betty A. Smith (Assoc.) 1990-1992; Joe D. Elenbaas 2000-Nov 30, 2006; Kenneth E. Tabor (Assoc.) 2004-2010; Thomas J. Evans 2007-2013; Dennis B. Bromley 2013-

Lulu UMC *[Heritage]*   vmoree@msn.com
(P) 12810 Lulu Rd, Ida 48140; (M) PO Box 299, Ida 48140-0299   (734) 269-9076
Ferris S. Woodruff 1967-1973; Harry Gintzer 1973-1974; Keith Rasey 1974-1976; William Michael
Clemmer 1976-1980; J. Robert Anderson 1980-1984; Raymond J. Townsend 1984-1988; Patricia
A. VanWormer 1988-1991; Doris Crocker 1991-1998; Ruth McCully 1998-2003; Judith M. Darling
Sep 16, 2003-2006; Bonnie M. Frey 2006-Jan 7, 2018; William Lass (DSA) Jan 15-Dec 31, 2018;
William Lass Jan 1, 2019-

Lyon Lake UMC *[Heritage]*   homlyl@rocketmail.com
(P) 8493 17 Mile Rd, Marshall 49068; (M) 101 E Adams St, Homer 49245   (269) 789-0017
A. Ray Noland Sept. 1968-1973; John T. Charter 1973-1978; Harold Deipert 1978-1983; Walter
Rothfuss1983-1987; Linda Farmer-Lewis Sept. 1987-Dec. 1992; Claudette Haney April 16, 1993-
1995, Nelson Ray 1995-1997; Linda J. Burson 1997-Jan. 1, 2000; Mark Mitchell 2000-2008;
Thomas P. Fox 2008-2012; Robert P. Stover (Ret.) 2012-

Lyons-Muir Church *[Midwest]*   info@lyonsmuirchurch.com
(P/M) 1074 Olmstead Rd, Muir 48860   (989) 855-2247
Richard Strait 1972-1977; George Matter 1977-1979; Howard McDonald 1979-1982; Byron
Coleman 1982-1984; Bette Dobie 1984-1988; Scott Otis 1988-1993; David J. Blincoe 1993-Aug.
15, 1994; Supplied by Presbyterian Church Sept. 1994; Don Wells (Presbyterian) 1995-Jan. 6,
1999; Judy K. Downing 1999-2001; Lynn W. Wagner 2001-Sept. 1, 2002; Kathy Jean Clark Aug.
1, 2003-?Jan. 1,2005; Forrest B. Nelson Jan. 1, 2005- Jan. 1, 2016; Jonathan D. VanDop, Jan.
1, 2016-2017; [Ionia First / Lyons-Muir became a two-point charge 2016] Jonathan E. Bratt Carle
2017-

Mackinaw City: Church of the Straits UMC *[Northern Skies]*   office@churchofthestaits.com
(P) 307 N Huron, Mackinaw City 49701; (M) PO Box 430, Mackinaw City 49701   (231) 436-8682
Raymond C. Provost (Presb.) 1965-1984; Douglas W. Vernon 1984-1988; William J. McGuinness
(Presb) 1988-Apr 30, 1996; Wilson "Drew" Andrew Hart May 1, 1996-2001; C. Jack Richardson
(Presb) 2001-2002; Maria Rutland Price (Presb) 2002-2006; David M. Wallis 2006-

Macomb: Faith UMC (formerly New Haven Meade) *[Greater Detroit]*   faith_umc@yahoo.com
(P/M) 56370 Fairchild Rd, Macomb 48042   (586) 749-3147
Joan D. Roach 1965-1970; Forrest Pierce 1970-1972; Donald L. Linchtenfelt 1972-1973; Ronald
Leisman 1973; Donald L. Lichtenfelt 1973-1974; Mary Howard (Rawson) 1974-1976; Donald L.
Lichtenfelt 1976-1980; Thomas F. Keef 1980-1982; Mary F. Neil 1982-1984; John J. Rodgers
1984-1991; Marion A. Pohly Jan.1, 1992-1996; Arthur Stone Nov 16, 1996-Oct 31, 1998; Marion
A. Pohly Nov 1, 1998-Apr 28, 2011; Dianna H. Van Marter 2011-

Macon UMC *[Heritage]*   maconumc@frontier.com
(P/M) 11964 Macon Hwy, Clinton 49236   (517) 4238270
Thomas G. Badley 1968-1970; Robert E. Burkey 1970-1973; John W. Vance 1973-1975; Albert
F. Raloff 1975-1979; Martha H. Cargo 1979-1982; Robert C. Strobridge 1982-1983; Robin G.
Gilshire 1983-1990; Gregory E. Rowe 1990-1993; Ramona E. Cowling 1993-Aug 31, 1997; C.
Michael Madison Sep 1, 1997-1999; Bonnie J. Lancaster 1999-2001; Alan J. Hanson 2001-2002;
Dale E. Brown 2002-2007; Lance E. Ness 2007-2017; Ruth A. VanderSande Sept 7, 2017- [Britton:
Grace / Macon two-point charge 7-1-2019]

Madison Heights: First UMC *[Greater Detroit]*   rhonda8776@gmail.com
(P/M) 246 E 11 Mile Rd, Madison Heights 48071   (248) 544-3544
Ross N. Nicholson 1967-1972; Robert H. Bough 1972-1975; Kenneth A. Kohlmann 1981-Sept.
1985; Ronald K. Corl 1975-1988; Eugene K. Bacon 1988-1995; Faye McKinstry Jul 1, 1995-1999;
Patricia A. Green 1999-2008; Thomas L. Taylor 2008-Feb 15, 2011; Juanita J. Ferguson 2011-
Sep 30, 2011; G. Charles Sonquist Oct 17, 2011-2012; Rhonda Osterman 2012-

Madison Heights: Korean First Central UMC *[Greater Detroit]*   gsj0925@yahoo.com
(P/M) 500 W Gardenia Ave, Madison Heights 48071   (248) 545-5554
Mu-Young Kim Nov. 1 1984-1992; Jae H. Lee 1992-Jan 31, 2004; Chul-Goo Lee Mar 1, 2004-2013; Sang Hyu Han (interim) August 1, 2013-Oct 1, 2013; Gunsoo Jung Oct 1, 2013-2018; Yoo Jin Kim (assoc) 2016-2018; Daeki Kim 2018-

Madison Heights: Vietnamese Ministry UMC *[Greater Detroit]*   ducnhan234@yahoo.com
(P) 500 W Gardenia Ave, Madison Heights 48071; (M) 38108 Charwood Dr, Sterling Heights 48312
Nhan Duc Nguyen Apr 1, 2016-

Mancelona UMC *[Northern Waters]*   mance1@mancelonaumc.org
(P) 117 E Hinman St, Mancelona 49659; (M) PO Box 301, Mancelona 49659   (231) 587-8461
M. Helen Jackson 1968-1972; George Gierman 1972-1975; Curtis Jensen 1975-1983; Timothy Graham 1983-1990; Gary Coates 1990-Aug. 1991; Pulpit Supply Sept.-Oct. 1991; Wayne Gorsline Nov. 1991-June 15, 1992; John W. Boley June 16, 1992-1997; Carolyn C. Floyd 1997-2000; Kathryn M. Steen 2000-2007; Stephan Weinberger 2007-2010; Zawdie K. Abiade July 1-July 4, 2010; Todd Shafer (DSA) July 15, 2010; Todd Shafer Nov. 1, 2010-2017; Bryan K. Kilpatrick 2017-

Manchester UMC *[Heritage]*   office@manchesterumchurch.org
(P/M) 501 Ann Arbor St, Manchester 48158   (734) 428-8495
O. William Cooper Jr. 1965-1970; Walter R. Damberg 1970-1977; Maurice D. Sharai Jr. 1977-1980; David A. Spieler 1980-1981; Thomas E. Hart 1981-1984; Hayden K. Carruth Jr. 1984-1989; Peggy Ainslie 1989-Oct. 31, 1991; Marsha M. Woolley Nov. 1, 1991-1994; Thomas Davenport 1994-Dec 1, 1998; Frank Leineke (interim) Jan 1, 1999-Jun 30, 1999; A. Faye McKinstry 1999-2005; Lawrence A. Wik 2005-2012; Tersea Zimmerman (deacon) Jan 1, 2012- ; Aaron B. Kesson 2012-2017; Dillion S. burns 2017-

Manchester: Sharon UMC *[Heritage]*   RevPHarris@aol.com
(P) 19980 Pleasant Lake Rd, Manchester 48158; (M) PO Box 543, Manchester 48158
(734) 428-7714
Charles R. Fox 1967-1969; O. William Cooper Jr. 1969-1970; John C. Huhtala (assoc) 1969-1970; Michael L. Peterlin 1970-1976; Wayne C. Ferrigan 1976-1980; Ronald L. Figgins Iris 1980-1983; Evans C. Bentley 1983-1987; Vernon D. Jones (DSA) Jan-Jun 1988; Erik J. Alsgaard 1988-Sep. 30, 1991; Margaret A. Paige Nov 15, 1991-1998; Carter L. Garrigues-Cortelyou 1998-2007; Peter S. Harris 2007-

Manistee UMC *[Northern Waters]*   mumc@t-one.net
(P/M) 387 1st St, Manistee 49660   (231) 723-6219
Carleton A. Benson Sept. 1968-1971; Richard M. Wilson 1971-1980; Gilbert B. Heaton 1980-1982; Richard R. Erickson 1982-1990; Gregory B. Wood 1990-1998; Gerald L. Selleck 1998-2002; Jerry Lee Jaquish 2002-2012; David A. Selleck 2012-2015; John A. Scott 2015-

Manistique: First UMC *[Northern Skies]*   1stumcmanistique@gmail.com
(P/M) 190 N Cedar St, Manistique 49854   (906) 341-6662
Theodore E. Doane 1968-1972; Marvin McCallum 1972-1975; Audrey Dunlap 1975-1976; Michael Peterlin 1976-1980; Max D. Weeks 1980-1983; Timothy Hastings 1983-1986; Stuart L. Proctor 1986-1991; Raymond D. Wightman 1991-1997; Donna J. Lindberg 1997-2004; Donald E. Bedwell 2004-

Manton UMC *[Northern Waters]*   umcmanton@charter.net
(P) 102 N Michigan Ave, Manton 49663; (M) PO Box B, Manton 49663   (231) 824-3593
Eduard Eidens 1967-1969; J. William Schoette 1969-1970; Leonard J. Yarlott 1970-1971; Arthur R. Turner 1971-1976; Molly C. Turner (Assoc.) 1971-1976; Norman Charter 1976-1977; J.T. Wood 1977-1981; Deborah Johnson 1981-1985; Laurie McKinven-Copus 1985-1987; Louis W. Grettenberger 1987-1993; Richard W. Blunt 1993-Feb. 1, 1999; Linda J. Carlson Feb. 16, 1999-2009; Beth A. Reum 2009-2013; Noreen S. Shafer 2013-2017; Jeff Swainston (DSA) 2017-Nov 30, 2017; Jeff Swainston (LP) Dec 1, 2017-

Maple River Parish: Lowe UMC *[Mid-Michigan]*   mapleriverumccharge@gmail.com
(P/M) 5485 W Lowe Rd, Saint Johns 48879   (989) 224 -4460
    William Tate 1967-1969; Robert Boyer 1969-1970; Charles VanLente 1970-1972; Everett Love June-Dec. 1972; Harold McGuire 1973-1974; Terry MacArthur 1976-Oct. 15, 1979; Robert Gillette Jan. 1980-1984; Merritt Bongard 1984-1991; Joseph Spackman 1991-1999; James Dibbet 1999-2005; O'Ryan Rickard 2005-2007; Kathryn L. Leydorf (DSA) 2007; Kathryn L. Leydorf Nov. 10, 2007- [Salem/Maple Rapids/Lowe charge re-aligned 5-1-14 to Maple Rapids/Lowe charge; Maple Rapids / Lowe became Maple River Parish 2015]

Maple River Parish: Maple Rapids UMC *[Mid-Michigan]*   mapleriverumccharge@gmail.com
(P) 330 S Maple Ave, Maple Rapids 48853; (M) 5485 W Lowe Rd, St. Johns 48879
                                                                    (989) 224 -4460
    William Tate 1967-1969; Robert Boyer 1969-Feb. 1970; Charles VanLente Feb. 1970-May 1972; Abe Caster May 1972-Jan. 1973; Eldon Schram Feb.-June 1973; J. Thomas Churn 1973-1979; Richard Whale 1979-1980; Richard Riley 1980-1984; Lyle Heaton 1984-1990; Tim Wohlford 1990-1991; Carolyn Robinson 1991-1997; Charles D. Farnum 1997-2001; Martin Cobb 2001-2006; O'Ryan Rickard 2006-2007; Kathryn L. Leydorf (DSA) 2007; Kathryn L. Leydorf Nov. 10, 2007- [Salem/Maple Rapids/Lowe charge re-aligned 5-1-14 to Maple Rapids/Lowe charge; Maple Rapids / Lowe became Maple River Parish 2015]

Marcellus UMC *[Greater Southwest]*   jdmessner@gmail.com
(P) 197 W Main St, Marcellus 49067; (M) PO Box 396, Marcellus 49067   (269) 646-5801
    Ira Fett 1968-1969; Donald Ludman 1969-1974; Wayne Babcock 1975-1978; Derryl Cook 1978-1981; Robert Mayo 1981-1986; Kenneth I. Kline 1986-1992; Dennis E. Slattery 1992-1995; Peggy A. Boltz 1995-2002; Melodye Surgeon Rider 2002-2007; John D. Messner (DSA) 2007; John D. Messner Jan. 1, 2008-

Marcellus: Wakelee UMC *[Greater Southwest]*   jdmessner@gmail.com
(P/M) 15921 Dutch Settlement Rd, Marcellus 49067   (269) 646-2049
    Ira Fett 1968-1969; Donald Ludman 1969-1974; Wayne Babcock 1975-1978; Derryl Cook 1978-1981; Robert Mayo 1981-1986; Kenneth I. Kline 1986-1992; Dennis E. Slattery 1992-1998; Gregory L. Buchner (DSA) 1998-Nov. 16, 1999; Gregory L. Buchner Nov. 16, 1999-2005; Nelson L. Hall 2005-2007; John D. Messner (DSA) 2007; John D. Messner Jan. 1, 2008-

Marion UMC *[Northern Waters]*   marionmiumc@yahoo.com
(P) 216 W Main St, Marion 49665; (M) PO Box C, Marion 49665-0703   (231) 743-2834
    Edward R. Jones 1967-1969; Walter S. Easton 1969-1971; Robert R. Boyer 1971-1977; Kendall A. Lewis 1977-1981; Donald R. Fry 1981-1994; James C. Grant 1994-1999; Howard H. Harvey 1999-2000; Jeffrey Schrock 2000-2004; Kenneth C. Reeves 2004-2006; Kenneth C. Reeves (DSA) 2006-2007; James J. Mort 2007-

Marlette: First UMC *[East Winds]*   fumcmarlette@centurytel.net
(P/M) 3155 Main St., Marlette 48453   (989) 635-2075
    Rex M. Dixon 1966-1970; A. Theodore Halsted 1970-1975; Theodore H. Bennink 1975-1979; John R. Allan 1979-Aug 31, 1998; Daniel J. Bowman Sep 1, 1998-2014; David G. Mulder 2014-2018; Larry Osweiler Jul 1-Sept 5, 2018; George Ayoub Oct 1, 2018-

Marne UMC *[Midwest]*   secretary@marneumc.com
(P) 14861 Washington St, Marne 49435; (M) PO Box 85, Marne 49435   (616) 677-3957
    Kenneth E. Curtis 1967-1969; Don W. Eddy 1969-1971; Kenneth W. Karlzen 1971-1973; Donald Fry 1973-1977; Douglas Knight 1977-1980; Vernon Michael 1980-1982; Keith Bovee 1982-1985; Deborah M. Johnson 1985-1990; Timothy W. Graham 1990-1993; Cathi M. Gowin 1993-Jan. 31, 2002; Patricia L. Brook Feb. 1, 2002-2010; James Thomas Boutell 2010-2018; Cydney M. Idsinga 2018-

Marquette: Hope UMC *[Northern Skies]*   office@mqthope.com
(P/M) 111 E Ridge, Marquette 49855   (906) 225-1344
   Ralph Janka 1967-1971; Robert D. Dobson (assoc) 1968-1972; Alan J. Hanson (assoc.) 1972-1973) Samuel F. Stout 1971-1975; Gilson M. Miller (assoc) 1973-1975; Webley Simpkins 1975-1980; John C. Huhtala (assoc) 1976-1980; Lawrence C. Brooks (assoc) 1980-1982; Benjamin Bohnsack 1980-1988; Steven J. Buck 1988-1993; Stanley A. Bailey, Jr. (assoc) 1989-; Gordon S. Nusz 1993-2000; Stephen E. Rhoades 2000-2004; Elbert P Dulworth 2004-2006; Steven E. McCoy 2006-2013; Alan J. Hansen (interim) 2013-2014; Kristine K. Hintz 2014- ; Christopher Hintz 2016-

Marquette: Hope - Connection Center Campus UMC *[Northern Skies]*   office@mqthope.com
(P) 927 W Fair Ave, Marquette 49855; (M) 111 E Ridge, Marquette 49855
   [Formerly Marquette: Hope – Grace Campus. Satellite of Marquette: Hope founded 07/01/2016]
Kristine K. Hintz 2014- ; Christopher Hintz 2016-

Marquette: Hope - Skandia Campus UMC *[Northern Skies]*   office@mqthope.com
(P) 189 Kreiger Dr, Skandia 49885; (M) 111 E Ridge, Marquette 49855
   UMC [Satellite of Marquette: Hope founded 07/01/2016] Kristine K. Hintz 2014- ;Christopher Hintz 2016-

Marshall UMC *[Heritage]*   rah@umcmarshall.org
(P/M) 721 Old US 27N, Marshall 49068   (269) 781-5107
   Charles Manker 1968-1970; Ralph Witmer 1970-1974; Harold Filbrandt 1974-1983; Jeanne Randels (Assoc.) 1981-1988; Ronald Thompson 1983-1989; David McBride (Assoc.) 1988-1991; Leon Andrews 1989-1992; William Bills (Assoc.) 1991-1994; William Johnson 1992-1996; Margaret H. Peterson (Assoc.) 1994-1998 ; Keith W. Heifner 1996-1999; Judy K. Downing (Assoc.) 1998-1999; Leonard R. Schoenherr 1999-2013; Melany A. Chalker 2013-

Martin UMC *[Greater Southwest]*   martinumc@sbcglobal.net
(P) 969 E Allegan St, Martin 49070; (M) PO Box 154, Martin 49070-0154   (269) 672-7097
   Paul Scheibner 1965-1970; Thurlan Meridith 1970-1976; Gerald L. Welsh 1976-1984; Lee F. Zachman 1984-April 15, 1994; William C. Bills 1994-2007; Christopher L. Lane 2007-2009; David A. Selleck 2009-2012; Donald J. Graham 2012-2014; Sean K. Kidd 2014-2019; Corey M. Simon 2019-

Marysville UMC *[East Winds]*   office@umcmarysville.com
(P/M) 721 Huron Blvd, Marysville 48040   (810) 364-7391
   Howard F. Snell 1965-1971; Joseph H. Ablett 1971-1980; Webley J. Simpkins 1980-1985; Cleon F. Abbott Jr. 1985-1991; Ralph T. Barteld 1991-1997; David D. Amstutz 1997-1999; James M. Thompson 1999-2006; Barbara E. Welbaum 2006-2019; [Marysville / Central Lakeport formed Marysville Cooperative Parish 07/01/2019] Curtis B. Clarke 2019-

Mason: First UMC *[Mid-Michigan]*   info@masonfirst.org
(P/M) 201 E Ash St, Mason 48854   (517) 676-9449
   Keith L. Hayes 1966-1980; Robert L. Wessman (Assoc.) 1979-1984; George R. Grettenberger 1980-1989; Donald R. Ferris (Assoc.) 1984-1989; Verne C. Summers 1989-1992; Charles B. Hodges (Assoc.) 1989-March 1991; Wayne G. Reece 1992-2000; Robert K. Lynch (Assoc.) 1992-1995; Jane D. Logston (Assoc.) 1996-1998; Timothy Tuthill (Assoc.) 1998-2006; Robert L. Hundley 2000-2009; Dwayne E. Bagley 2009-2016; Donna Jo Minarik 2016-2019; Suzanne K. Goodwin 2019-

Mayville UMC *[Central Bay]*   mayvilleumc@att.net
(P) 601 E Ohmer Rd, Mayville 48744 (M) PO Box 189, Mayville 48744   (989) 843-6151
   Donald L. Lichtenfelt 1968-1970; Ralph T. Barteld 1970-1979; Dale E. Brown 1979-1984; Allen J. Lewis Inter.; Wayne C. Ferrigan 1984-1986; William J. Maynard 1986-1992; Bonny J. Lancaster 1992-1999; John W. Ball 1999-2007; Dorothy J. Thon 2007-2011; Carole A. Browne 2011-2019; Nathan J. Jeffords 2019-

McGregor UMC *[East Winds]* mcrgegorumc@airadvantage.net
(P) 2230 Forester Rd, Deckerville 48427; (M) 5791 Paldi Rd, Peck 48466 (810) 378-5686
James B. Lumsden 1969-1973; J. Paul Pumphrey 1973-1977; Glenn R. Wegner 1977-1980;
James P. Kummer Dec. 1980-1985; Kenneth C. Reeves 1985-1991; Gloria Haynes 1991-1996;
Malcolm L. Green 1996-1998; Jerry D. Griggs 1998-

McMillan UMC *[Northern Skies]* pastorimcdonald@outlook.com
(P) 7406 Co Rd 415, McMillan 49853; (M) PO Box 268, Grand Marais 49839 (906) 293-8933
Vernon D. Wyllys 1969-1975; James Lumsden 1975-1976; Audrey M. Dunlap 1976-1985; Ramona
Cowling 1985-1987; Phillip D. Voss 1987-1991; Bo L. Lange 1991-1997; Ronald O. Piette 1997-
1998; Tracy L. Brooks 1998-2003; Karen A. Mars 2003-2006; Paul J. Mallory 2006-2012; Ian S.
McDonald 2012-2019; Devin T. Lawrence (DSA) 2019-

Mears UMC *[Midwest]* office@mearsumc.org
(P) 1990 N. Joy St, Mears 49436; (M) PO Box 100, Mears 49436-0100 (231) 873-0875
Kenneth L. Snow 1990-1993; Kenneth Vanderlaan (DSA) 1993-2017; [Mears and Shelby became
a multi-station circuit 2016]; Anne W. Riegler 2017-

Mecosta: New Hope UMC *[Midwest]* newhope.mecosta@gmail.com
(P/M) 7296 9 Mile Rd, Mecosta 49332 (231) 972-2838
Gordon L. Terpening 1968-1971; Norman Charter 1971-1973; Pulpit Supply 1973-1974; Michael
Nickerson 1974-1977; Ilona Sabo-Schuler 1977-1982; B. Gordon Barry 1982-1985; Pulpit Supply
July-Oct. 1985; Bobby Dale Whitlock Oct. 1985-Apr. 1987; Pulpit Supply April-June 1987; Remus,
Mecosta and Halls Corners merged to form New Hope in 1987; Christopher Momany 1987-1993;
Scott K. Otis 1993-1997; James C. Noggle 1997-2004; Victor D. Charnley 2004-2013; Gregory L.
Buchner 2013-2019; Carman J. Minarik 2019-

Melvin UMC *[East Winds]* marlettelawfirm@yahoo.com
(P/M) 1171 E Main St, Melvin 48454 (810) 376-4518
Earl S. Geer 1969-1973; Martin Caudill 1973-1976; Willard A. King 1976-1980; J.D. Landis 1980-
1986; David K. Stewart 1986-1990; Louise R. Ott 1990-1992; Michael F. Bossingham 1992-1994;
Thomas K. Spencer 1994-1998; David C. Freeland (co-pastor) 1998-2002; Susan K. Freeland
(co-pastor) 1998-Dec 31, 1999; Debra K. Brown 2002-2010; Christopher G.L. Titus 2010--2019;
Dennis Eric Irish 2019- ; Julia Ann Cramer (assoc) (DSA) 2019- [Yale / Cole / Melvin became a
three-point charge 07/01/2019]

Memphis: First UMC *[East Winds]* huff11@aol.com
(P) 81265 Church St, Memphis 48041; (M) PO Box 29, Memphis 48041 (810) 392-2294
Max Weeks 1965-1971; Donald L. Lichtenfelt Inter.; Duane E. Miller March 1972-Nov. 1977; Paul
W. Reigle 1977-1982; Wayne C. Ferrigan 1982-1984; Martin Caudill 1984- 1987; Donald L. Bates
Oct. 1987-1991; Douglas M. Choate 1991-1993; Catherine W. Hiner 1993-1999; David L. Fleming
1999-2001; Janet M. Engler 2001-2004; Thomas G. Badley (interm Aug 1, 2004-Oct 31, 2004;
Donald L. Wojewski Nov 1, 2004-Dec 31, 2004; James E. Huff, Jr. Jan 1, 2005-

Mendon UMC *[Greater Southwest]* mendonmethodist@gmail.com
(P) 320 W Main St, Mendon 49072; (M) PO Box 308, Mendon 49072-0308 (269) 496-4295
Marcius Taber 1968-1969; David Litchfield 1969-1970; Harold Simon 1970-Nov. 1973; Robert
Jones Nov. 1973-1978; John Charter 1978-1981; Ira Noordhoff 1981-Jan. 1985; Kendall Lewis
Jan. 1985-1986; Elaine Buker 1986-1992; Rochelle Ray 1992-1995; Thomas L. Truby 1995-2001;
Ward D. Pierce (DSA) 2001-Dec. 2, 2012 (died); David G. Knapp (interim) Jan. 1-June 30, 2013;
[Three Rivers First / Mendon became two-point charge 2013] Robert D. Nystrom 2013-2015;
[Mendon / West Mendon became two-charge 2015] Thoreau May 2015-2017; Margaret K. Mallory
2017-2018; Carl Q. Litchfield (LTFT ¼) 2018-

Menominee: First UMC *[Northern Skies]*   menomineeumc@gmail.com
(P) HCR 1 US 41 E, Michigamme 49861; (M) PO Box 323, Menominee 49858   (906) 864-2555
Everett D. Erickson 1964-1976; Robert D. Dobson 1976-1986; Donald C. Schark 1986-1991; John N. Grenfell III 1991-1994; William D. Schoonover 1994-1995; John N. Grenfell, III 1995-1998; Philip Tousley 1998-2011; Dale E. Brown 2011-2014; Bruce L. Nowacek 2014-2016; Ryan C. Edwardson 2016-2019; [Menominee: First / Stephenson two-point charge 7-1-2019] John R. Murray 2019-

Mesick UMC *[Northern Waters]*   mesickumc@gmail.com
(P) 121 S Alvin St, Mesick 49668; (M) PO Box 337, Mesick 49668-0337   (231) 885-1699
Ward Pierce 1967-1972; Bill Amundsen 1972-1979; Jean Crabtree 1979-Aug. 1980; Donald Buege Sept. 1980-Jan. 1984; Bruce Prestwood-Taylor Jan. 1984-1986; Thomas P. Fox 1986-1992; Charles A. Williams 1992-Feb. 14, 1997; J. David Thompson Nov. 16, 1997-2001; John J. Conklin (DSA) 2001-Nov. 30, 2001; John J. Conklin Dec. 1, 2001-2009; Mona L. Kindel 2009-2012; Beverley Williams 2012-2016; ; [Mesick/Harrietta/ Brethren became a three-point charge 2016] Laurie M. Koivula 2016-2018 [Mesick/Brethren became a two-point charge 2018] Anika Kasper (DSA) July 14, 2019-

Michigamme: Woodland UMC *[Northern Skies]*   woodumc@gmail.com
PO Box 395, Republic 49879   (906) 323-6151
James Mathews 1978-1984; Charles Keyworth 1984-1988; Robert Duggan 1988-1990; Nicholas W. Scroggins 1990-1993; Fred A. LaMere 1993-1996; Terry J. Kordish 1996-2000l; Gary I. Stevens 2000-2004; James A. Fegan 2004-2009; Mark E. Ryan 2009-2012; Terri L. Branstrom 2012-2016; Peter LeMoine 2016-

Middlebury UMC *[Mid-Michigan]*   middleburyunitedmethodist@gmail.com
(P) 8100 W Hibbard Rd, Ovid 48866; (M) PO Box 7, Ovid 48866-0007   (989) 834-2573
Dale Ferris 1969-1972; Brian D. Kundinger 1972-1977; David K. Koski 1977-1982; L. Michael Pearson 1982-1986; Harold E. Weemhoff 1986-1990; Robert J. Easlick 1990-1993; J. Robert Anderson 1993-1996; Nancy L. Bessemer Sep 1, 1996-1998; Weatherly A. Burkehead Verhelst 1998-2003; J. Gordon Schleicher 2003-2006; Carl R. Cooke Jan 1, 2007-Dec 31, 2008; Norman R. Beckwith, Jr., Jan 1, 2009-Apr 10, 2010; Don Wentz May 1, 2010-2015; Joyce Wallace Oct 1, 2015-2016-2018; Melanie S. Young 2018-

Middleville UMC *[Midwest]*   middlevilleumc@gmail.com
(P) 111 Church St, Middleville 49333; (M) PO Box 400, Middleville 49333   (269) 795-9266
Harold M. Taber 1964-1969; C. William Martin 1969-1973; Harold Simon Nov. 1973-Oct. 1976; Arthur Jackson April 1977-Aug. 1983; Bradley Kalajainen (Assoc.) Jan. 1981-1985; Carl Staser Oct. 1983-1988; Lynn W. Wagner 1988-1996; Lee F. Zachman 1996-2004; Scott E. Manning 2004-2009; [Middleville/Snow two-point charge 2009] Michael T. Conklin 2009-2012; Anthony C. Shumaker 2012- [Middleville became single station 2017]

Midland: Aldersgate UMC *[Central Bay]*   admin@aumcmidland.org
(P/M) 2206 Airfield Ln, Midland 48642   (989) 631-1151
Harold W. Diehl 1965-1970; Zack A. Clayton 1970-1990; David A. Stout 1990-Oct 1, 2003; Douglas R. Trebilcock 2004-2006; Mark D. Miller 2006-2013; Michael T. Sawicki 2013- [Poseyville UMC merged with Midland: Aldersgate UMC 08/01/2018]

Midland: Aldersgate - Saginaw: Kochville Campus UMC *[Central Bay]*   office@kumcsag.com
(P) 6030 Bay Rd, Saginaw 48604; (M) 2206 Airfield Ln, Midland 48642   (989) 792-2321
[Satellite of Midland: Aldersgate stared 09/01/2018] Michael T. Sawicki Aug. 1, 2018-

Midland Cnty: Hope UMC *[Central Bay]*   phope000@centurytel.net
(P/M) 5278 N Hope Rd, Hope 48628   (989) 689-3811
William Cozadd 1965-1980; Cleon Abbott 1980-1985; Donald Crumm 1985-1992; Harold J. Slater 1992-2002; Patrick R. Poag 2002-

Midland: First UMC *[Central Bay]*   tsimons@fumcmid.org
(P/M) 315 W Larkin St, Midland 48640   (989) 835-6797
   Wayne E. North 1965-1973; Webley Simpkins (assoc) 1966-1970; Herbert C. Brubaker (assoc)
   1968-1971; S. H. Evans (assoc) 1968-1971; Wayne Large (assoc) 1970-1974; Ira A. Bush (assoc)
   1971-1995; John W. Parrish (assoc) 1973-1985; Carl E. Price 1973-1998; P. Thomas
   Wachterhauser (assoc) 1974-1979; Jeffery D. Regan (assoc) 1979-1982; Arthur B. Howard (assoc)
   1979-1985; Mary Isaacs Frost (assoc) 1982-1986; Dana Strall (assoc) 1985-1988; Robert Grigereit
   (assoc) 1987-1999; Duane M. Harris (assoc) 1988-1997; Kevin C. Zaborney (assoc) 1997-1999;
   Brent L. McCumons 1998-2011;Charles W. Keyworth (assoc) 1999- ; Susan M. Kingsley (assoc)
   Sep 1, 1999-2008; Steven E. McCoy (assoc) 1999-2006; Jeremy P. Africa (assoc.) 2006-2010;
   Pamela Buckholtz (deacon) 2006-2013; Lisa McIlvenna (assoc) 2008-2013;Catherine Christman
   (assoc.) 2010-2013; John D. Landis 2011-2019; Jung Eun Yum (assoc.) 2014-; Christina Miller-
   Black (assoc.) 2015-2017; Anita K. Hahn 2019-

Midland: Homer UMC *[Central Bay]*   homeroffice@gmail.com
(P/M) 507 S Homer Rd, Midland 48640-8369   (989) 835-5050
   Dale Lantz 1967-1970; S. Joe Robertson 1970-1973; Robert Adams 1973-1975; Walter Radcliffe
   (interim); Philip A. Rice 1975-1979; Henry Powell 1979-1982; Donald Goold & Arthur Howard
   (interim); Kenneth Christler 1983-1988; Paul Bailey 1988-1990; James M. Thompson 1990-1996;
   Kenneth A. Kohlmann 1996-2001; Raymond A. Jacques 2001-2008; David G. Mulder 2008-2014;
   Josheua Blanchard 2014-Aug 31, 2017; Ernesto Mariona Oct 1, 2017-

Milan: Marble Memorial UMC *[Heritage]*   marblemumc@sbcglobal.net
(P/M) 8 Park Ln, Milan 48160   (734) 439-2421
   George Q. Woomer 1966-1969; Charles W. Cookingham 1969-1973; Clare M. Tosch 1973-1983;
   Diana K. Goudie (assoc) 1983-Aug. 31, 1991; Robert F. Goudie 1983-Aug 31, 1994; King W.
   Hanna Sep 1, 1994-2003; Kristine J. Sigal 2003-Oct 1, 2007; Thomas E. Hart (interm) Oct 1, 2007-
   2008; Patricia A. Green 2008-2013; Robert A. Miller, Jr. 2013-2018; Jacquelyn A. Roe 2018-

Milford UMC *[Heritage]*   churchoffice@milfordumc.net
(P/M) 1200 Atlantic St, Milford 48381   (248) 684-2798
   Archie H. Donigan 1966-1972; Wayne W. Brookshear 1972-1983; James C. Braid 1983-1995;
   David R. Strobe 1995-Dec 1, 1997; Paul Blomquist (interim) Dec 1, 1997-Apr 30, 1998; Gregory
   M. Mayberry May 1, 1998-2011; Douglas J. McMunn 2011- ; Sherry Foster (deacon) 2008-

Millersburg UMC *[Northern Waters]*   onawayumc@voyager.net
(P) 5484 Main St, Millersburg 49759; (M) PO Box 258, Millersburg 49759   (989) 745-4479
   Charles R Fox (Onaway) 1969-1972; N. Ralph Guilliat (Millersburg) 1967-1972; G. Charles Ball 1972-
   1983; Roy A. Syme 1983-1989; Michael Grajcar Jr. 1989-1991; Richard A. Turner 1991-1995; John
   N. Hamilton 1995-Jun 15, 2001; W. Peter Bartlett 2001-2011; Josheua Blanchard 2011-2014; Carman
   Cook 2014-2018; Yoo Jin Kim 2018-

Millington UMC *[Central Bay]*   millingtonumc@millingtonumc.com
(P) 9020 State Rd, Millington 48746; (M) PO Box 321, Millington 48746   (989) 871-3489
   Richard A. Turner 1965-1971; Arthur V. Norris 1971-1976; Paul L. Amstutz 1976-1982; Keith B.
   Colby 1982-1985; Ronald Figgins Iris 1985-Aug. 31, 1991; Max D. Weeks Sept. 1, 1991-1994;
   Thomas F. Keef 1994-2001; Wilson Andrew Hart 2001-2006; W. Peter Crawford 2006-2015; John
   J. Britt 2015-

Millville UMC *[Mid-Michigan]*   millvillechurch@yahoo.com
(P/M) 1932 N M 52, Stockbridge 49285   (517) 851-7853
   Daniel Harris 1965-1970; Dorr Garrett 1970-1973; Lester Priest Jan. 15, 1974-1980; Robert Stillson
   1980-Nov. 15, 1982; Donald Vuurens Feb. 1983-1986; Richard Young 1986-1990; Jeffrey Wright
   1990-Jan. 1993; James C. Noggle March 1993-1997; Carolyn A. Robinson 1997-1998; Richard
   A. Tester 1998-2004; Robert J. Freysinger 2004-2013; [M-52 Cooperative Ministry 2013; re-named
   Connections Cooperative Ministry 2015] Jeremy J. Wicks (1/2 time) 2013-2017; [Dansville UMC
   merged with Millville UMC 12-31-14] Jaqueline L. Raineri 2017-2018; Theresa Fairbanks 2018-
   - [Millville / Williamston: Wheatfield became multi-point charge 2018]

Minden City UMC *[East Winds]* dcbarber229@att.net
(P) 3346 Main St, Minden City 48456; (M) PO Box 126, Minden City 48456 (810) 648-4155
Alan W. Weeks 1964-1974; Harry M. Brakeman 1974-1977; James P. Schwandt 1977-1980; Basel W. Curtiss 1980-1983; Zina Braden Bennett 1983-1985; Richard J. Richmond 1985-1991; Max L. Gibbs 1991-1996; Ellen Burns Nov, 1996-2000; Robert A. Srock 2000-2002; John H. Rapson 2002-2010; Monique R. Carpenter 2010-2015; Dale Barber Dec 15, 2015-Mar 30, 2019; Philip L. Tousley 2019- [Seperated as a two-point charge from Minden City 07/01/2019; Bad Axe: First / Minden City / Ubly formed Bad Axe Cooperative Parish 07/01/2019]

Mio UMC *[Central Bay]* office@mioumc.org
(P/M) 1101 W 8th St, Mio 48647 (989) 826-5598
Robert Kersten 1969-1975; Grant Washburn 1975-1980; David Diamond 1980-1986; Lois Glenn 1986-1990; John J. Britt 1990-2005; Kenneth Tousley (interm) 2005-Sep 15, 2005; Marcel Lamb, Sep 16, 2005-2012; Tracy Brooks 2012-2014; Brenda K. Klacking 2014-

Mohawk-Ahmeek UMC *[Northern Skies]* calumc@up.net
(P) 120 Stanton, Mohawk 49950; (M) 57235 Calumet Ave, Calumet 49913 (906) 337-2720
Alan DeGraw 1967-1972; James Tuttle 1972-1975; Harold Slater 1975-1978; Wayne Hutson 1978-1983; Dennis N. Paulson 1983-1987; Robert J. Easlick 1987-1990; David P. Snyder 1990-1993; Nancy G. Sparks 1993-2000; Robert A. White 2000-2016; Richard B. Brown (assoc) 2000-2003; James Palaszeski 2016-2018; Gun Soo Jung 2018-2019; Larry Molloy (DSA) 2019-

Monroe: Calvary UMC *[Heritage]* monroecalvaryumc@yahoo.com
(P/M) 790 Patterson Dr, Monroe 48161 (734) 242-0145
Otto F. Hood 1968-1974; J. Edward Fulcher 1974-1977; Gary A. Allward 1977-1980; Georg F. W. Gerritsen 1980-1985; William P. McBride 1985-1995; Paul G. Donalson 1995-1997; James E. Armbrust (co-pastor) 1997-1999; Judith A. Armbrust (co-pastor) 1997-1999; David J. Goudie 1999-2004; Janet M. Engler 2004-2006; William T. Kreichbaum 2006-2016; Steven Perrine 2016-

Monroe: First UMC *[Heritage]* monroefumc@gmail.com
(P/M) 790 Patterson Dr, Monroe 48161 (734) 242-0145
Elwood J. Berkompas 1965-1972; George E. Spencer 1972-1975; Robert F. Goudie 1975-1983; Robert C. Watt 1983-1987; Warren D. Pettis 1987-1989; James D. Jacobs 1989-Aug 31, 1999; John H. Schneider, Jr. Sep 1, 1999-2005; Sang Yoon (Abraham) Chun 2005-2007; Clarence W. VanConant 2007-2010; Phillip D. Voss 2010-2011; Bradford Lewis 2011-2013; Katherine C. Waggoner 2013-

Monroe: Heritage UMC (formerly E. Raisinville Frenchtown) *[Heritage]* katiewaggoner@gmail.com
(P/M) 4010 N Custer Rd, Monroe 48162 (734) 242-9747
Paul R. Crabtree 1951-1969; Otto F. Hood 1969-1974; J. Edward Fulcher 1974-1977; Paul W. Crabtree 1977-1985; Daniel W. Harris 1985-1995; M. Lester McCabe 1988-1990; Mary T. Tame 1990-Oct. 15, 1990; Robert L. S. Brown (interim); Calvin D. Long Apr. 1, 1991-1995; Carolyn Harris (co-pastor) 1995-1997; Daniel W. Harris (co-pastor) 1995-1997; Robert G. Richards 1997-2001; Kathy R. Charlefour 2001-Oc 31, 2005; Margaret A. Passenger Nov 1, 2005-2011; Katherine C. Waggoner 2011-

Monroe: St. Paul's UMC *[Heritage]* stpaulsmonroe@sbcglobal.net
(P/M) 201 S Monroe St, Monroe 48161 (734) 242-3000
Raymond R. Lamb 1966-1969; M. Clement Parr (assoc) 1968-1971; William N. Mertz 1969-1978; Roy A. Syme (assoc) 1971-1973; E. Jack Lemon (assoc) 1973-1976; Wayne N. Thomas (assoc) 1976-1978; Hugh C. White 1978-1983; David Rahn (assoc) 1978-1980; Marvin H. McCallum 1983-1991; Karen D. Poole (assoc) 1986-1988; Claire A. Clingerman (assoc) 1988-1990; Dean A. Klump 1991-1995; Jacqueline E. Holdsworth (co-pastor) 1995-2003; John W. Kershaw (co-pastor) 1995-2003; Jacqueline E. Holdsworth 2003-2004; Evans C. Bentley 2004-2018; Tracy N. Huffman 2018-2019; Melodye Surgeon VanOudheusden 2019-

Montague UMC *[Midwest]*   montagueumc@gmail.com
(P/M) 8555 Cook St, Montague 49437   (231) 894-5789
    Wirth G. Tennant 1965-1972; Gilbert B. Heaton 1972-1977; Birt A. Beers 1977-1983; Robert E. Jones, Jr. 1983-1992; D. Keith Laidler 1992-1997; Timothy P. Boal 1997-2005; Gary Bekofske 2005-2009; Randall R. Hansen 2009-2014; Mary S. Brown 2014-Nov. 30, 2016; David "Gunnar" Carlson Dec. 1, 2016-June 30, 2017 [Whitehall UMC merged with Montague UMC, 6-02-17] Michael A. Riegler 2017-

Monterey Center UMC *[Greater Southwest]*   secretary.bumc@gmail.com
(P) 3022 130th Ave, Hopkins 49328; (M) PO Box 30, Burnips 49314-0030   (616) 896-8410
    Ron Smith Oct. 1991-1997; Kenneth C. Reeves 1997-2004; Anthony Carrol Shumaker 2004-2008; Richard A. Fritz 2008-2014; Nancy J. Patera 2014-2017; Craig H. VanBeek (DSA) 2017-Dec. 31, 2018; Craig H. VanBeek Jan. 1, 2019-

Montgomery UMC *[Heritage]*   pastortrevor1@gmail.com
(P) 218 S Michigan St, Montgomery 49255; (M) PO Box 155, Camden 49232   (517) 269-4232
    Karl L. Zeigler 1968-1969; John H. Gurney 1969-Aug. 1970; Joseph Huston Aug. 1970-1972; Richard Huskey 1972-1974; J. Brian Selleck 1974-Feb. 1976; Robert P. Stover March 1976-1980; Stephen Beech 1980-1983; Larry W. Rubingh 1983-1987; Frederick G. Hamlin 1987-1994; Russell K. Logston 1994-1996; Diane Stone Nov. 16, 1996-2004; Edward Mohr 2004-2010; Trevor McDermont 2010-2013; Frederick G. Cain (Ret.) (part-time) 2013-

Montrose UMC *[East Winds]*   montroseumc1@gmail.com
(P) 158 E State St, Montrose 48457; (M) PO Box 3237, Montrose 48457   (810) 639-6925
    Dalton Bishop 1967-1973; Robert C. Watt 1973-Nov., 1980; Richard L. Beemer Jan., 1981-1993; Dennis N. Paulson 1993-Jan 16, 1997; David C. Collins 1997-2006; Wayne C. Ferrigan 2006-2012; Norman R. Beckwith, Sr. 2012-2013; Susan Bennett Stiles 2013-2016; Harold V. Phillips 2016-

Morenci UMC *[Heritage]*   donagalloway@msn.com
(P) Corner of S Summit & Main, Morenci 49256; (M) 111 E Main St, Morenci 49256   (517) 458-6923
    Emmett E. Coons 1966-1969; Cleon F. Abbott Jr. 1969-1973; Alan J. Hanson 1973-1981; Richard W. Sheppard 1981-Jan 14, 1988; Evans C. Bentley Jan. 15, 1988-1995; Karen A. (Welch) Mars 1995-Oct 31, 2000; Earl Eden (interim) Nov 1, 2000-Jun 15, 2001; Elmer A. Armijo Jun 16, 2001-2003; Dorothy J. Okray 2003-2007; Richard E. Burstall 2007-2010; Donna Galloway 2010-

Morrice UMC *[Mid-Michigan]*   bancroftmorricepastor@gmail.com
(P) 204 Main St, Morrice 48857; (M) PO Box 301, Morrice 48857   (517) 625-7715
    Richard Andrus 1969-1972; Terry A. Euper 1972-1976; James E. Paige, Jr. (co-pastor) 1976-1980; Margaret A. Paige (Co-Pastor) 1977-1980; Charles J. Bamberger 1980-1990; Donald Woolum 1990-1993; John H. Schneider, Jr. 1993-1997; Penney Meints 1997-1998; Arthur R. Turner 1998-2004; Jeremy T. Peters 2004-2008; Jeremy P. Benton 2008-2011; Patricia Elliott 2011-2015; Robert Forsyth 2015-Mar 31, 2017; Terry A. Euper (Ret.) Apr 1, 2017-2017; Coleen Wilsdon (DSA) 2017-Nov 30, 2017; Coleen Wilsdon Dec 1, 2017-

Morris Chapel UMC *[Greater Southwest]*   rsnodgrass72@gmail.com
(P) 11721 Pucker St, Niles 49120; (M) 1730 Holiday Dr, Niles 49120   (269) 684-5194
    Albert O'Rourke 1968-1970; Douglas Vernon 1970-1971; Pulpit Supply 1971-1972; Kenneth L. Snow 1972-1982; Richard C. Kuhn 1982-1987; Richard D. Wilson 1987-1996; Zawdie K. Abiade 1996-2002; Charles D. McNary (DSA) 2002-2003; O'Ryan Rickard 2003-2004; Christopher A. Kruchkow 2004-Feb. 15, 2012; [Morris Chapel UMC became single point charge 2012] Samuel Gordy (1/4 time) Mar. 11, 2012-2013; Rob Snodgrass 2014- [Morris Chapel / Niles Grace became a two-point charge 2016; Niles Wesley / Morris Chapel / Niles Grace became a 3-point charge 2017]

Mount Clemens: First UMC *[Greater Detroit]* office@mountclemensumc.org
(P/M) 57 Southbound Gratiot Ave, Mt Clemens 48043 (586) 468-6464
Ronald Cornwell (assoc) 1963-1971; James R. Balfour 1969-1976; Robert Adams (assoc) 1971-1973; Mary E. Howard (assoc) 1973-1974; John W. Elliott (assoc) 1974-1977; Stanley A. Bailey 1976-1986; Kenneth A. Kohlmann (assoc) 1977-1981; Thomas R. Kinney (assoc) 1981-1984; Frederick P. Cooley (assoc) 1984-1988; David M. Liscomb 1986-1992; Richard C. Andrus 1992-1999; William D. Rickard (assoc) 1991-1993; Patricia A. Meyers 1999-2006; G. Charles Sonquist (interim) 2006-2007; Carman J. Minarik (co-pastor) 2007-2013; Donna J. Minarik (co-pastor) 2007-2013; Mary G. (Gibson) McInnes 2013-2017; Maureen V. Baker 2017-2019; Daniel J.C. Hart 2019-

Mt. Morris: First UMC *[East Winds]* rmpieper@aol.com
(P/M) 808 E Mt Morris Rd, Mt Morris 48458 (810) 686-3870
Ellis A. Hart 1968-1973; Charles C. Cookingham 1973-1976; Jack Lancaster 1976-Aug., 1978; Walter David Aug., 1978-1986; Donald E. Hall 1986-Aug., 1992; William R. Maynard Aug. 1992-1996; Robert E. Burkey 1996-2003; Elizabeth M. Gamboa 2003-2008; Alonzo Vincent 2008-2013; Janet M. Engler 2013-Oct 1, 2015; Bruce Lee Billing (Ret.) Oct 1, 2015-2018; Ralph H Pieper II (Ret.) 2018-

Mt Pleasant: Chippewa Indian UMC *[Central Bay]* CWhite-Pigeon@sagchip.org
(P) 7529 E Tomah Rd, Mount Pleasant 48858; (M) 3490 S Leaton Rd, Mt Pleasant 48858
Joseph Sprague 1974-1986; Maynard Hinman DSA 1986-1987; Joseph Sprague 1984-1986; Chris Cavender DSA 1990-Dec. 31, 1991; James Burgess Jan.1992-June1992; Joseph Sprague June 15, 1992-1994; Carla Sineway (1/3 time) 1994-Nov. 1, 2003; Matthew Sprague (1/3 time) 1994-Nov. 15, 1995; Owen White-Pigeon (1/3 time) 1994; Owen White-Pigeon (DSA) 2011-Aug. 26, 2019

Mt Pleaseant: Countryside UMC *[Central Bay]*
(P) 4264 S Leaton Rd, Mt Pleasant 48858; (M) 202 S Elizabeth St, Mt Pleasant 48858
(989) 773-0359
George Rule 1968-1970; Joseph Dudley 1970-Sept. 1972; Daren C. Durey Oct. 1972-Jan. 1977; Robert E. Tomlinson Feb. 1977-1980; Gordon Spalenka 1980-1984; Janelle Gerken 1984-Jan. 1987; Michael J. Kent May 1987-Jan. 1991; James Cook 1991-1995; Dean Prentiss 1995-Sept. 14, 1999; Susan D. Olsen July 16, 2004-2006; Sharyn K. Osmond Aug. 1, 2006-Nov. 30, 2008; Donald R. Wendell Nov. 30, 2008-Nov. 1, 2009; Craig L. Adams Dec. 1, 2009-2010; David Michael Palmer 2010-2016; Russell D. Morgan 2016-2018; TBS

Mt Pleasant: First UMC *[Central Bay]* office@mtpfumc.org
(P/M) 400 S Main St, Mt Pleasant 48858 (989) 773-6934
Paul Albery 1966-1970; Neil Bintz 1970-1978; Albert W. Frevert 1978-1989; Edward C. Ross (Assoc.) 1978-1981; Rodney J. Kalajainen (Assoc.) 1981-1984; Thomas Crossman (Assoc.) 1984-1986; Steven M. Smith (Assoc.) 1986-1991; Ronald J. Thompson 1989-1995; Janet K. Sweet (Assoc.) 1991-1994; Connie R. Bongard (Assoc.) Aug. 1, 1994-1997; Wade S. Panse 1995-1997; Benton R. Heisler 1997-2002; Mark R. Erbes (Assoc.) 1997-2001; Michelle LaMew (Assoc.) 2001-; John W. Boley 2002-2010; Charles D. Farnum (Assoc.) July 16, 2006-2007; Cynthia A. Skutar 2010-2013; Diane Gordon 2013-2018; Julie A. Greyerbiehl 2018-

Mt Pleasant: Trinity UMC *[Central Bay]*
(P/M) 202 S Elizabeth St, Mt Pleasant 48858 (989) 772-5690
G.B. Rule 1967-1969; J.A. Dudley 1969-1972; Daren C. Durey 1972-1977; Robert E. Tomlinson 1977-1980; Gordon E. Spalenka 1980-1984; Janelle E. Gerken 1984-1987; Michael J. Kent 1987-1991; James Cook 1991-1995; Dean Prentiss 1995-Sept. 14, 1999; Jana Lynn Almeida Oct. 16, 1999-2004; Susan D. Olsen July 16, 2004-2006; Sharyn K. Osmond Aug. 1, 2006-Nov. 30, 2008; Donald R. Wendell Nov. 30, 2008-Nov. 1, 2009; Craig L. Adams Dec. 1, 2009-2010; David Michael Palmer 2010-2016; Russell D. Morgan 2016-2018; TBS

Mt. Vernon UMC (formerly New Beginnings) *[Greater Detroit]*   bwmtvernon@gmail.com
(P/M) 3000 28 Mile Rd, Washington 48094   (248) 650-2213
     [merger of Davis and Mount Vernon, Oct 22, 2009] Douglas J. Shephard 2009-Nov 30, 2011;
     Jacque Hodges Dec 1, 2011-2017; Cherlyn McKanders 2017-

Mulliken UMC *[Mid-Michigan]*   mulliken.church@gmail.com
(P/M) 400 Charlotte St, Mulliken 48861   (517) 649-8382
     Everatt Love 1968-1972; David A. Cheyne 1972-1975; Lynn Wagner 1975-1977; John Eversole
     1977-1982; Joseph Spackman 1982-1983; Ken Lindland 1983-1987; Joseph Spackman 1987-
     1991; Gordon Spalenka 1991-1993; Robert Besemer 1993-Aug. 31, 1996; Donald Woolum Sept.
     16, 1996-2003; Judith Lee Scholten 2003-2011; Gary L. Simmons 2011-2013; [Barry-Eaton
     Cooperative Ministry 2013] Claire W. Huyck 2013-2015; Betty A. Smith (Ret.) 2015-Dec. 31, 2015;
     Lyle D. Heaton Jan. 1-June 30, 2016; Vaughn W. Thurston-Cox 2016- [Mulliken became single
     station 2017]

Munising UMC *[Northern Skies]*   umcmunising@jamadots.com
(P/M) 312 Lynn St, Munising 49862   (906) 387-3394
     Norman C. Kohns 1969-1973; Konstantin Wipp 1974-1978; Robert L. Porter 19778-1980; William F.
     Bowers 1980-1983; Joel W. Hurley 1983-1986; Mary B. Willoughby 1986-1989; Ray S. Peterson
     1989-1991; Gary R. Shiplett 1992-1994; James M. Downing 1994-Aug 31, 1997; Rosemarie O.
     Fahrion 1997-Dec 31, 2004; Gary I. Stevens Jan 1, 2005-Jan 1, 2009; Irene R. White Jan 1, 2009-
     2011; Sandra J. Kolder 2011-

Munith UMC *[Mid-Michigan]*   MunithUMC@gmail.com
(P) 224 N Main St, Munith 49259; (M) PO Box 189, Munith 49259-0189   (517) 596-2441
     Frederick Werth 1967-1971; Bert L. Cole March 1972-1973; Larry Irvine 1973-1975; Thomas
     Adams 1976-1978; James Barney 1979-1983; Linda Farmer-Lewis 1983-1986; Milton TenHave
     1986-1990; Laurie McKinven-Copus 1990-Sept. 1991; Robert Marston Oct. 1991-1998; Judith A.
     Nielson 1998-2000; Charles Cerling 2000-Aug. 9, 2004; Arthur R. Turner 2004-Nov. 15, 2005;
     Kenneth Karlzen (DSA) Dec. 2005-2006; Maurice Walworth (DSA) 2006-2007; Larry W. Rubingh
     2007-Sept. 6, 2011; Maurice E. Walworth, Jr. (pulpit supply) Sept. 6, 2011-2012; Jeanne M. Laimon
     (1/4 time) 2012-2014 [M-52 Cooperative Ministry 2013-2014]; Susan J. Trowbridge 2014-2019;
     Stephan Weinberger (Ret.) 2019-

Muskegon: Central UMC *[Midwest]*   cumc@muskegoncentralumc.org
(P/M) 1011 2nd St, Muskegon 49440   (231) 722-6545
     Royal J. Synwolt 1966-1971; Robert H. Jongeward 1971-1979; Lynn A. DeMoss 1979-1988; Ron
     L. Keller 1988-1993; Daniel M. Duncan (Assoc.) 1989-1994; Ray W. Burgess 1993-2000; Melanie
     S. Young (Assoc.) 1994-1996; Virginia L. Heller (Assoc.) 1996-1998; Gregory P. Culver (Assoc.)
     1998-2002; Randall R. Hansen 2000-2009; M. Kay DeMoss (Deacon) 2003-2015; Gary L.
     Bekofske 2009-2010; Diane Gordon 2010-2013; Mark D. Miller 2013-

Muskegon: Crestwood UMC *[Midwest]*   judyccstk@yahoo.com
(P/M) 1220 Creston St, Muskegon 49442   (231) 773-9696
     Carl B. Strange 1962-1969; John S. Myette 1969-1970; Phillip R. Glotfelty, Jr. 1970-1973; Kenneth
     W. Karlzen 1973-1977; David G. Showers 1977-1980; Lawrence E. Hodge 1980-1983; Birt A.
     Beers 1983-1990; M. Chris Lane 1990-1995; Victor D. Charnley 1995-2004; Dianne D. Morrison
     2004-2007; Diane M Bowden 2007-2008; Dale Hotelling 2008-2010; Stephan Weinberger 2010-
     2014; [Muskegon Crestwood realigned from Lakeside/Crestwood to Whitehall/Crestwood 2014]
     Mary A. Sweet 2014-2017; Jennifer J. Wheeler 2017- [Whitehall and Crestwood became multi-
     station circuit 2014; Crestwood became a single station 2017]

Muskegon Hts: Temple UMC *[Midwest]* templeumcmkht@gmail.com
(P/M) 2500 Jefferson St, Muskegon Heights 49444 (231) 733-1065
Verner Kilgren 1962-1970; Richard Selleck 1970-1977; Dale Crawford 1977-1979; Robert Pumfrey 1979-1983; Don Eddy 1983-1989; Richard Youells 1989-1991; Gerald F. Hagans 1991-Sept. 1, 2006; Robert B. Cook Sept. 1, 2006-2012; Jeffrey J. Bowman, Sr. 2012-

Muskegon: Lake Harbor UMC *[Midwest]* Office@LakeHarborUMC.org
(P/M) 4861 Henry St, Norton Shores 49441
Wayne Speese 1964-1975; Harold Kirchenbauer Oct. 1975-1981; Frank Lyman 1981-1991; Carole Lyman (Assoc.) 1984-1991; Jack Stubbs 1991-1995; Susan J. Hagans 1995-2000; Cynthia Ann Skutar 2000-2004; Richard A. Morrison 2004-2007; Mark R. Erbes 2007-2014; Mary Letta-Bement Ivanov 2014- [Muskegon Lakeside merged w/ Muskegon Lake Harbor 07-01-16]

Muskegon: Unity UMC *[Midwest]* rworley@promed.org
(P/M) 1600 N Getty St, Muskegon 49445 (231) 744-1972
Kenneth McCaw Dec. 1966-1969; Austin Regier 1969-1975; Joseph Glover 1975-1983; Eric Beck 1983-1986; Susan Krill (Hagans) 1986-Nov. 1988; Ronald Carl Robotham Jan. 1989-1990; Jane Lippert 1990-1995; J. Todd Thompson 1995-1998; Kimberly A. DeLong 1998-Sept. 16, 1999; Gayle Berntsen Sept, 16, 1999-Sept. 1, 2001; James Meines Dec. 1, 2001-2005; Brian M. McLellan (DSA) 2005-Feb. 15, 2006; James Meines (DSA) Apr. 15, 2006-Oct. 31, 2006; Nancy L. (Besemer) Boelens Nov. 1, 2006-Dec. 31, 2008; Gilbert R. Boersma (1/4 time) 2009-Oct. 31, 2011; R. John Thompson (DSA) (1/4 time) Nov. 1, 2011-2014; Ronald L. Worley 2014

Napoleon UMC *[Heritage]* napoleonunited@att.net
(P) 210 Nottawasepee, Napoleon 49261; (M) PO Box 337, Napoleon 49261 (517) 536-8609
Robert Kersten 1967-1969; Robert Hinklin 1969-1972; Douglas Smith 1972-1973; Marjorie Matthews 1973-Dec. 1975; J. Brian Selleck March 1976-Sept. 1978; Francis Anderson Sept. 1978-Sept. 1980; Wayne Gorsline Sept. 1980-1988; Robert J. Freysinger 1988-2004; Robert P. Stover 2004-2007; Jennifer Jue 2007-2013; Gregory R. Wolfe (Ret.) 2013-2019; Mary A. Sweet 2019- [Jonesville / Napoleon became two-point charege 2019]

Nashville UMC *[Mid-Michigan]* numcoffice@att.net
(P) 210 Washington St, Nashville 49073; (M) PO Box 370, Nashville 49073 (517) 852-2043
James Crosby 1969-1975; Leonard F. Putnam 1975-1984; Lynn Wagner 1984-1988; Ronald K. Brooks 1988-May 15, 1991; Kenneth Vaught June 1, 1991-1994; James L. Hynes 1994-2000; Gail C. Patterson 2000-Dec. 31, 2001; Dianne M. Bowden January 16, 2002-2007; Cathy M. Christman 2007-2010; Nancy J. Bitterling 2010-2013; Gary L. Simmons 2013-2015; [Barry-Eaton Cooperative Ministry 2013] Nancy V. Fancher (Deacon) 2014-2015; Karen L. Jensen-Kinney 2015-

Nashville: Peace UMC *[Mid-Michigan]* macousino1@gmail.com
(P/M) 6043 E M 79 Hwy, Nashville 49073 (517) 852-1993
Robert E. Boyer 1968-1969; Marion R. Putnam 1969-Jan. 1970; E.F. Rhoades Feb.-July 1970; Michael Williams Aug. 1970-1971; William P. Reynders 1971-Feb. 1972; Thomas Churn March 1972-April 1973; Thomas Peters May 1973-Aug. 1976; Dale D. Spoor Sept. 1976-Dec. 1979; Steven Reid Jan. 1980-Jan. 1984; Mary Curtis March 1984-1989; James Noggle 1989-Feb. 1993; Susan A. Trowbridge March 1993-March 15, 2005; Nancy V. Fancher (DSA) March 16, 2005-March 31, 2006; Susan D. Olsen 2006-2015; Mickey Ann Cousino (CLM/DSA) Sept. 1, 2015-

Negaunee: Mitchell UMC *[Northern Skies]* mitchellumc@sbcglobal.net
(P) 207 N Teal Lake Ave, Negaunee 49866; (M) PO Box 190, Negaunee 49866 (906) 475-4861
Albert F. Roloff 1965-1974; William D. Schoonover 1974-1982; King Wm. Hanna 1982-Aug 31, 1994; John Bunce Sep 1, 1994-1998; Scott A. Harmon 1998-2002; Anthony J. Tomasino 2002-2003; Eric D. Kieb 2003-2010; Douglas E. Mater 2010-2016; J. Albert Barchue 2016-

Nelson UMC *[Northern Water]*   hemlockumc@frontier.net
(P) 5950 S Hemlock Rd, Hemlock 48626; (M) PO Box 138, Hemlock 48626   (989) 642-8285
A. Theodore Halsted 1965-1970; John C. Huhtala 1970-1975; Terry W. Allen 1976-1978; Tom Brown 1978-1984; Steven A. Gjerstad 1984-Jun 30, 1994; Arthur V. Norris Jul 1, 1994-2001; Karen L. Knight 2001-Jan 31, 2002; Nicholas W. Scroggins 2002-2009; Jerry F. Densmore 2009-2014; Michale W. Vollmer 2014-2019; Robert G. Richards 2019- (Swan Valley (lead church) / LaPorte charge and Hemlock / Nelson charge formed new four point charge July 1, 2019)

NE Missaukee Parish: Merritt-Butterfield UMC *[Northern Waters]*   m-mchurches@centurytel.net
(P/M) 428 S Merritt Rd, Merritt 49667   (231) 328-4598
Athel Lynch 1968-1970; Marion Nye 1970-1973; Eugene Baughan 1974-1987; Bernard Griner 1988-1989; Cynthia Schaefer 1989-1993; (Merritt and Butterfield merged on July 1, 1991.) Pulpit Supply July 1-Aug. 31, 1993; O. Jay Kendall Sept. 1, 1993-2005; Brian R Bunch, Aug. 1, 2005-2012; Jeffrey J. Schrock 2012-2016; Joshua Henderson Sept. 1, 2016-July 31, 2019; Hyun-Jun Cho Aug. 1, 2019-

NE Missaukee Parish: Moorestown-Stittsville UMC *[Northern Waters]*
                                                         m-mchurches@centurytel.net
(P/M) 4509 E Moorestown Rd, Lake City 49651   (231) 328-4598
Athel Lynch 1968-1970; Marion Nye 1970-1973; Eugene Baughan 1974-1987; Bernard Griner 1988-1989; Cynthia Schaefer 1989-1993; Stittsville merged with Moorestown in 1993; O. Jay Kendall Sept. 1, 1993-2005; Brian R Bunch, Aug. 1, 2005-2012; Jeffrey J. Schrock 2012-2016; Joshua Henderson Sept. 1, 2016-July 31, 2019; Hyun-Jun Cho Aug. 1, 2019-

New Baltimore: Grace UMC *[Greater Detroit]*   gumcnb@comcast.net
(P/M) 49655 Jefferson Ave, Chesterfield 48047   (586) 725-1054
Robert C. Andrus 1979-1987; David D. Amstutz 1987-1990; James E. Greer II 1990-1995; Donald J. Emmert 1995-May 31, 2000; Tonya M. Arneson Jun 1, 2000-2006; Jill Hardt Zundel 2006-2014; Jean-Pierre Duncan 2014-2018; Brian Steele 2018-

New Buffalo: Water's Edge UMC *[Greater Southwest]*   betty@h2oedge.org
(P/M) 18732 Harbor Country Dr, New Buffalo 49117   (269) 469-1250
John Bullock 1968-1974; Robert Pumfery 1974-1979; Joseph Beattie 1979-1980; Ken Vanderlaan 1980-1981; Charles Tooman 1981-Jan. 1982; Gregory B. Wood Feb. 1, 1982-1985; B. Gordon Barry 1985-1993; Bradley S. Bartelmay 1993-2017; [01/01/12 New Buffalo First UMC renamed New Buffalo: Water's Edge UMC] Kellas D. Penny III 2017-

New Hudson UMC *[Heritage]*   newhudsonumc@sbcglobal.net
(P) 56730 Grand River Ave, New Hudson 48165; (M) PO Box 803, New Hudson 48165
                                                                             (248) 437-6212
Robert A. Mitchinson 1966-2002; Gerald S. Hunter 2002-Oct 15, 2015; Thomas Tarpley Oct 15, 2015-2016; Robert Sielaff 2016-2018; Seung (Andy) Ho Baek 2018-

New Lothrop: First UMC *[Mid-Michigan]*   umc7495@centurytel.net
(P) 7494 Orchard Street, New Lothrop 48460; (M) PO Box 247, New Lothrop 48460
                                                                             (810) 638-5702
Paul L. Amstutz 1964-1971; Clifford J. Furness 1971-1976; Donald W. Brown 1976-1978; Linda Susan Garment 1978-1980; Verne Blankenburg 1980-1983; Robert J. Henning 1983-Jul., 1990; Mary Thoburn Tame 1990-Aug 3, 1997; James M. Downing Sep 1, 1997-Aug 16, 1999; Olaf Lidums Nov 16, 2000-2003; David L. Fleming 2003-2011; Janet M. Engler 2011-2013; Cecillia Lee Sayer 2013-2017; Stephen Spina (DSA) 2017-May 2, 2018; Stephen Spina May 3, 2018- Correct in Ezra

Newaygo UMC *[Midwest]*   umcnew@newaygoumc.com
(P) 101 State Rd, Newaygo 49337; (M) PO Box 366, Newaygo 49337-0366   (231) 652-6581
  Jean Crabtree 1967-1972; Paul E. Robinson 1972-1975; James W. Boehm 1975-1984; John S.
  Myette 1984-1988; Stephen M.G. Charlney 1988-1994; Donald R. Fry 1994-1999; Sandra L. Spahr
  2000-2006; Patricia L. Bromberek 2006-2011; Kathy Groff (Ret.) 2011-2017; Eric L. Magner (DSA)
  2017-Nov 30, 2017; Eric L. Manger (PL) (THFT ¾) Dec 1, 2017-

Newberry UMC *[Northern Skies]*   nbyumc@up.net
(P/M0) 110 W Harrie St, Newberry 49868   (906) 293-5711
  Wayne T. Large 1967-1970; Robert N. Hicok 1970-1974; William E. Miles 1974-1975; Ralph A.
  Edwards 1975-1979; David J. Hill 1979-1981; June M. Westgate 1981-1986; James L. Rule 1986-
  1996; Wm. Peter Bartlett 1996-2001; Jane D. Logston 2001-2003; Saundra J. Clark 2003-2013;
  Timothy G. Callow 2013-

Niles: Grace UMC *[Greater Southwest]*   nilesgraceumc@att.net
(P/M) 501 Grant St, Niles 49120   (269) 683-8770
  Leonard Putnam 1964-1969; Orin M. Bailey 1969-1971; Don Cozadd 1971-1976; David Litchfield
  1976-1981; John Charter 1981-Nov. 1992; Mark E. Thompson Nov. 1992-1996; Glenn McNeil
  1996-2000; Nancy J. Bitterling 2000-2002; Patricia L. Bromberek (SP-DSA) 2002-2004; Anthony
  Tomasino (DSA) Oct. 17, 2004-2016; [Morris Chapel / Niles Grace became a two-point charge
  2016; Niles Wesley / Morris Chapel / Niles Grace became a 3-point charge 2017] Robert L.
  Snodgrass II 2016-

Niles: Portage Prairie UMC *[Greater Southwest]*   ppumcs@aol.com
(P/M) 2450 Orange Rd, Niles 49120   (269) 695-6708
  Darrell Osborn 1968-1970; Robert Welfare 1970-1974; Robert Stillson 1974-1980; Robert Stover
  1980-1987; Morris Reinhart 1987-1989; Margaret Peterson 1989-1994; Larry W. Mannino 1994-
  1995; David H. Minger 1995-1999; Thomas P. Fox 1999-2008; Theresa Little Eagle Sayles
  2008-Apr. 15,2009; [Portage Prairie/Arden two-point charge 2009] O'Ryan Rickard 2009-2014;
  Ralph A. Posnik Jr 2014-2019; [Portage Prairie single-point charge 2014] Scott B. Smith 2019-

Niles: Wesley UMC *[Greater Southwest]*   johnwesley2561@sbcglobal.net
(P/M) 302 Cedar St, Niles 49120   (269) 683-7250
  Robert Trenery 1968-1974; Mark Graham 1974-1984; Lloyd Phillips 1984-1991; Nolan R. Williams
  1991-Jan. 1, 2000; Emmett H. Kadwell, Jr. Jan. 1, 2000-2008; Edward H. Slate 2008-2012; Cathi
  M. Huvaere 2012-2017; [Niles Wesley / Morris Chapel / Niles Grace became a
  3-point charge 2017] Robert L. Snodgrass II 2017-

North Adams UMC *[Heritage]*   najumcs@yahoo.com
228 E Main St, North Adams 49262; (M) PO Box 62, North Adams 49262   (517) 287-5190
  Kenneth W. Karlzen 1968-1971; Thomas R. Jones 1971-Aug. 1974; David Flagel Sept. 1975-
  1980; Lee F. Zachman 1980-1984; Donald McLellan 1984-Sept. 1988; Melanie Baker-Streevy
  Oct. 1988-1995; Rochelle Ray 1995-2000; Tim Doubblestein 2000-Aug. 31, 2002; Charles
  Richards Sept. 1-Dec. 31, 2002; Paul Hane Jan. 1, 2003-2011; Kimberly A. Metzger July 1-Dec.
  19, 2011; Arthur R. Turner (DSA) Feb. 1, 2012-2014 [Osseo UMC merged w/ North Adams UMC
  4-6-14] Timothy R. Puckett 2014-

North Branch UMC *[East Winds]*   nblumc@gmail.com
(P) 4195 Huron St, North Branch 48461; (M) PO Box 156, North Branch 48461-0156   (810) 688-2610
  John D. Lover 1969-1977; Henry W. Powell 1977-1979; Roger F. Gedcke 1979-1997; C. Michael
  Madison 1997-Aug 31, 1997; Mary T. Tame Sep 1, 1997-1999; Wayne C. Ferrigan 1999-2006;
  Michael S. McCoy 2006-Mar 31, 2009; Ronald G. Hutchinson Apr 16, 2009-

North Lake UMC *[Heritage]*   secretary.nlumc@gmail.com
(P/M) 14111 N Territorial Rd, Chelsea 48118   (734) 475-7569
   George T. Nevin 1964-1969; George Q. Woomer 1969 (interim); Frederick Atkinson Oct. 1, 1969-
Feb. 4, 1971; Harry R. Weeks Mar. 1971-1973; John W. Todd 1973-1974; David S. Stiles
1974-1977; John W. Elliott 1977-1982; David R. Strobe 1982-1984; David C. Collins 1984-1985;
Sondra B. Willobee 1985-1991; Wayne A. Hawley 1991-2001; Alice J. Sheffield 2001-2012; Anna
Moon 2012-2016; Todd Wesley Jones 2016-

North Muskegon Community UMC *[Midwest]*   wendy@communitychurchumc.org
(P/M) 1614 Ruddiman Dr, North Muskegon 49445   (231) 744-4491
   David S. Yoh 1968-Sept. 1978; Dennis Buwalda Sept. 1978-1982; Laurence L. Waterhouse 1982-
1986; John W. Fisher 1986-1992; Glenn M. Wagner 1992-2006; Robert K. Lynch 2006-2012;
Phillip J. Friedrick July 15, 2012-2017; Jeremy P.H. Williams 2017-

North Parma UMC *[Heritage]*
(P) 11970 Devereaux, Parma 49269; (M) PO Box 25, Parma 49269-0025   (517) 531-4619
   Edward Dahringer 1968-Sept. 1980; Jean Crabtree Nov. 1980-Jan. 1984; Jerry Hippensteel 1984-
1989; Charlotte Lewis 1989-1992; Carolin S. Spragg 1992-1999; Keith W. Heifner 1999-2003;
Michael P. Baker-Streevy 2003-2009; Melissa Claxton 2009-2018; [North Parma / Springport
became two-point charge 7-1-10] Mark E. Mitchell 2018-

Northport: Indian Mission UMC *[Northern Waters]*   pastor@NorthportIndianumc.org
(P) 8626 N Manitou Trl, Northport 49670; (M) PO Box 401, Northport 49670   (231) 715-1280
   Marshall Collins (DSA) 1991-2001; Kathryn Coombs (DSA) 2003-2005; Thomas H. John Jr. 2005-
2015; [Northport Indian Mission became single-point charge 2015] Terry M. Wildman (DSA)
2015-Nov 30, 2017; Terry M Wildman (PL) (LTFT 1/2) Dec 1, 2017-2019; Mary Wava Hofmann
(DSA) Apr. 1, 2019-

North Street UMC *[East Winds]*   northstreetumc@gmail.com
(P/M) 4580 North Rd, North Street 48049   (810) 385-4027
   Herbert Griffith 1963-1981; David D. Amstutz 1981-1987; David C. Dupree 1987-1989; Kenneth
B. Ray 1989-1992; Alger T. Lewis 1992-1999; Fredrick D. Neumann 1999-2002; William P. McBride
2002-Oct 31, 2014; David A. Reed Dec 12, 2014-

Northville: First UMC *[Heritage]*   fumc777@fumcnorthville.org
(P/M) 777 W 8 Mile Rd, Northville 48167   (248) 349-1144
   Guenther C. Branstner 1968-1983; Eric S. Hammar 1983-1991; Douglas W. Vernon 1991-2000;
Arthur L. Spafford (assoc) Mar. 1, 1992-Aug 31, 1999; Thomas M. Beagan (assoc) 1992-2000;
Cynthia A. Loomis-Abell 1999-2000; John E. Hice 2000-2008; Gordon W. Nusz (assoc) 2000-May
1, 2002; Jennifer L Bixby (assoc) 2000-2004; Lisa L. Cook (assoc) 2004-2009; Steven J. Buck
2008-2013; Stephan A. D'Angelo (assoc) 2009-2012; Monica William (assoc) 2012-2019; Marsha
M. Woolley 2013-

Norway: Grace UMC *[Northern Skies]*   gumc@norwaymi.com
(P/M) 130 O'Dill Dr, Norway 49870   (906) 563-8917
   William D. Schoonover 1967-1974; Emmett Coons 1974-1977; Mark Karls 1977-1983; Ray D.
Field 1983-1985; Carl R. Doersch 1985-1991; Nancy K. Frank 1991-Oc 31, 1994; Deborah R.
Jones Feb 16, 1995-1996; David M. Wallis 1996-2006; James E. Britt Aug 16, 2006-2011; Irene
R. White 2011-

Norwood UMC *[Northern Waters]*
(P/M) 00667 4th St. Norwood Village, Charlevoix 49720
   Stanley Hayes 1967-1970; Lester Priest 1970-Jan. 1974; Daniel Minor April 1974-1981; Betty
Burton 1981-1982; Glenn Britton 1982-1983; Supply pastor 1983-Aug. 1985; Robert Bellairs Aug.
1985-1996; Bernard W. Griner (DSA) 1996-1997; Eugene L. Baughan 1997-2002; D. Michael
Maurer 2002-Nov. 10, 2008; Ralph Posnik (DSA) Nov. 23, 2008; Ralph Posnik Nov. 15, 2009-
2014; Craig A. Pahl 2014-2017; Haldon Dale Ferris 2017-Aug 31, 2017; TBS

Nottawa UMC *[Greater Southwest]* umcnottawa1893@gmail.com
(P) 25838 M 86, Nottawa 49075; (M) PO Box 27, Nottawa 49075-0027 (269) 467-7134
Rudy A. Wittebach 1967-1974; Charles W. Smith 1974-1976; Elanor Carpenter 1976-Nov. 1980; Carl Leth Nov. 1980-Oct. 1983; David H. Minger Oct. 1983-1987; Laurie J. McKinven-Copus 1987-1990; Emilie Forward 1990-1994; Pulpit Supply July-Sept. 1994; Mona Joslyn (DSA) Oct. 1994-1996; Donald R. Wendell Jan. 1996-July 15, 2003; Alexander Miller (DSA) (LTFT ¼) 2003-

Novi UMC *[Heritage]* admin@umcnovi.com
(P/M) 41671 W 10 Mile Rd, Novi 48375 (248) 349-2652
Albert E. Hartoog 1969-1970; Philip M. Seymour 1970-1975; Karl L. Zeigler 1975-1979; Richard O. Griffith 1979-1984; Kearney Kirkby (assoc) 1982-1989; Charles R. Jacobs 1984-1997; Louise R. Ott 1997-2004; Jacqueline E. Holdsworth 2004-Mar 1, 2007; Alan W. DeGraw (interim) Mar 1, 2007-2007; June M. Marshall Smith 2007-

Oak Grove UMC *[Heritage]* oakgrove3395@att.net
(P/M) 6686 Oak Grove Rd, Howell 48855 (517) 546-3942
Robert M. Stoppert 1967-1969; James S. Ritchie 1969-1975; Lawson D. Crane 1975-1986; David A. Diamond 1986-1988; M. Jean Love 1988-1995; Alan W. DeGraw 1995-Jul 31, 2000; Robin G. Gilshire Aug 1, 2000-2001; June M. Westgate 2001-2005; Chong Y. Won 2005-2011; Paula M. Timm 2011-

Okemos: Community Church *[Mid-Michigan]* office@OkemosOCC.org
(P) 4734 Okemos Rd, Okemos 48864; (M) PO Box 680 ,Okemos 48805 (517) 349-4220
John E. Cermak 1966-1987; Lynn E. Grimes (Assoc.) 1983-1986; Verne C. Summers 1987-1989; Richard C. Sneed (Assoc.) 1989-1991; Charles D. Grauer 1989-1996; Pegg Ainslie (Assoc.) 1991-1993; Joyce DeToni-Hill (Assoc.) 1993-Feb. 15, 1994; James W. Boehm 1996-Sept. 1, 1998; Jeanne M. Randels Oct. 16, 1998-Jan. 1, 2014; Richard W. Blunt 2014-

Old Mission Peninsula UMC *[Northern Waters]* melodyolin@yahoo.com
(P/M) 16426 Center Rd, Traverse City 49686 (231) 223-4393
Richard W. Blunt 1986-1993; Orin L. Daniels 1993-1995; Dale Hotelling 1995-July 16, 2000; Sally J. LaFrance 2001-2002; Stanley Lee Hayes (DSA) 2002-Jan. 31, 2003; David H. Minger Feb. 1, 2003-2006 (Church changed name from Ogdensburg to Old Mission Peninsula 2004); Martin Cobb 2006-2010; Melody Lane Olin 2010-2019; Zelphia Mobley 2019-

Omard UMC *[East Winds]* omardumc@yahoo.com
(P/M) 2055 Peck Rd, Brown City 48416 (810) 346-3448
Basil W. Curtiss 1968-1971; Allen J. Lewis 1971-1979; Donald L. Casterline 1979-1986; Milton E. Stahl 1987-1988; Earleen A. (Hamblen) Van Conant 1988-1993; Harold V. Phillips 1993-1996; Rothwell McVety 1996-1997; Patrick D. Robbins May 1, 1998-2001; Dianne H. VanMarter 2001-2005; Marvin H. McCallum (interm) 2005-2007; Peggy A. Katzmark 2007-2014; Daniel William Surbrook (DSA) 2014-2015; Thomas G. Badley (Ret.) Aug 9-Nov 2, 2015; Patrick D. Robbins 2019- [Brown City Cooperative Parish: Brown City and Omard formed 07/01/2019]

Omo: Zion UMC *[Greater Detroit]* omozionumc@hotmail.com
(P) 63020 Omo Rd, Lenox 48050; (M) PO Box 344, Richmond 48062 (586) 428-7988
Edgar M. Smith 1969-1970; Donald W. Brown 1970-1972; Elmer J. Snyder 1972-1974; Ira L. Wood 1974-1975; Robert D. Schoenhals 1975-1983; Robert Thornton 1983-2000; Victor Studaker 2000-Dec 31, 2004; Donald L. Wojewski Jan 1, 2005-2005; Susan K. Montenegro 2005-Oct 7, 2007; Donald R. Sperling Nov 1, 2007-2010; Marianne M. McMunn 2010-2011; Dianna H. Van Marter 2011-Dec 31, 2013; Donna J. Zuhlke Jan 1, 2014-Sept 1, 2018; Mary Ellen Chapman (Ret.) Sep 3, 2018- [Omo: Zion / Washington became signle point charges 7-1-2019]

Onaway UMC *[Northern Waters]*   onawayumc@src-milp.com
(P) 3647 N Lynn St, Onaway 49765; (M) PO Box 762, Onaway 49765   (989) 745-4479
Charles R Fox (Onaway) 1969-1972; N. Ralph Guilliat (Millersburg) 1967-1972; G. Charles Ball 1972-1983; Roy A. Syme 1983-1989; Michael Grajcar Jr. 1989-1991; Richard A. Turner 1991-1995; John N. Hamilton 1995-Jun 15, 2001; W. Peter Bartlett 2001-2011; Josheua Blanchard 2011-2014; Carman Cook 2014-2018; Yoo Jin Kim 2018-

Ontonagon UMC *[Northern Skies]*   ontmeth@jamadots.com
(P) 109 Greenland Rd, Ontonagon 49953; (M) PO Box 216, Ontonagon 49953   (906) 884-4556
Lloyd Christler 1968-1972; James Hillard 1970-1971; Lawrence Brooks 1971-1975; Roger Gedcke 1972-1979; Lillian Richards 1971-1976; Wayne E. Sparks 1975-1980; Myra Sparks 1976-1980; Ed Hingelburg 1976-1980; Brian Marshall 1980-1984; Donald J. Emmert 1984-Feb 1, 1990; William D. Schoonover Feb 16, 1990-1991; Mel D. Rose 1992-1994; Lance E. Ness Sep 1, 1994-Dec 31, 1999; Christine F. Bohnsack Mar 1, 2000-2004; Cherrie A. Sporleder 2004-2010; Bruce R. Steinberg 2010-2018; Nelson L. Hall 2018-

Oregon UMC *[East Winds]*
(P) 2985 German Rd, Columbiaville 48421; (M) 2971 German Rd, Columbiaville 48421
                                                                        (810) 793-6828
Emmett E. Coons 1969-1974; James M. Thompson 1974-1980; David R. McKinstry 1980-1988; Georg F. W. Gerritsen 1988-1996; Wayne E. Samson 1996-1998; James E. Paige, Jr. 1998-Oct 1, 2003; Carole A. Brown Sep 1, 2004-Jul 31, 2006; Marybelle Haynes Aug 1, 2006-2018; Stanley Patrick Stybert (Ret.) Ju 1-Oct 31, 2018; Jeanne Harmon Wisenbaugh (DSA) Nov 1., 2018-

Ortonville UMC *[East Winds]*   ortonvilleumc@gmail.com
(P) 93 N Church St, Ortonville 48462; (M) PO Box 286, Ortonville 48462   (248) 627-3125
Horace Murry 1969-1973; Alan R. George 1973-1978; Richard A. Peacock 1978-Jul., 1982; R. Stanley Sutton Aug., 1982-1984; Daniel M. Young 1984-1991; Gary R. Imms 1991-1993; Timothy S. Woycik 1993-1998; Frederick O. Timm 1998-2000; Suzanne B. Walls 2000-2005; Timothy C. Dibble 2005-2011; Jeremy Benton 2011-2013; David O. Pratt 2013-Mar 1, 2016; W. Peter Crawford mar 1, 2016-2016; Brian K. Johnson 2016-

Oscoda UMC *[Central Bay]*   umcoscoda@gmail.com
(P/M) 120 W Dwight St, Oscoda 48750   (989) 739-8591
William Stone 1969-1976; James A. Smith 1976-1983; F. Richard MacCanon 1983-1988; William A. Cargo 1988-2006; Briony E. Peters-Desotell 2006-2014; William R.Seitz 2014-

Oscoda Indian Church UMC *[Central Bay]*   umcoscoda@gmail.com
(P) 7994 Alvin Rd, Mikado 48745; (M) 120 W Dwight St, Oscoda 48750   (989) 739-8591
William Stone 1969-1976; James A. Smith 1976-1983; F. Richard MacCanon 1983-1988; William A. Cargo 1988-2006; Briony E. Peters-Desotell 2006-2014; William R. Seitz 2014-

Oshtemo: LifeSpring UMC *[Greater Southwest]*   lifespring.churchoffice@gmail.com
(P/M) 1560 S 8th St, Kalamazoo 49009   (269) 353-1303
[new church start 2001] Mark R. Payne 2001-2009; Patricia A. Harpole 2009-2014; [LifeSpring/Lawton St. Paul's became 2-point charge 2014] Wayne E. McKenney 2014-2016; Jason E. Harpole 2016- [LifeSpring became a single-point charge 2016]

Oshtemo UMC *[Greater Southwest]*   oshumc@att.net
(P) 6574 Stadium Dr, Kalamazoo 49009; (M) PO Box 12, Oshtemo 49077   (269) 375-5656
Jay Gunnett Apr. 1968-1971; Laurence Dekema 1971-Jan. 1972; Linda Stoddard 1972-Oct. 1976; Pulpit Supply Oct. 1976-1977; Dorcas Lohr 1977-1982; Kenneth H. Kline 1982-1987; David L. Litchfield 1987-1992; Lewis A. Buchner 1992-1997; Charles M. Shields 1997-Feb. 1, 2000; Suzanne Kornowski 2000-2011 (Kalamazoo: Oakwood merged with Oshtemo on October 27, 2002) Peggy Boltz 2011-2013; John W. Fisher (Ret.) 2013-

Ossineke UMC *[Northern Waters]*   ossinekemiumc@gmail.com
(P) 13095 US Hwy 23 S, Ossineke 49766; (M) 7770 Scott Rd, Hubbard Lake 49747
(989) 471-2334
Kyle Ballard 1968-1970; John Miller 1970-1982; James Lumsden 1982-1988; Stephen Cartwright 1988-1990; Priscilla Seward 1990-1994; Fredrick D. Neumann Aug 1, 1994-1999; John D. Bailey 1999-2005; Stephen T. Euper 2005-2010; Jack E. Johnston 2010-2012; Micheal P. Kelley 2012-

Otisville UMC *[East Winds]*   otisvilleunitedmethodistchurch@yahoo.com
(P) 200 W Main St, Otisville 48463; (M) PO Box 125, Otisville 48463   (810) 631-2911
Beatrice Townsend 1969-1971; Basel W. Curtiss 1971-1976; Lawrence C. Whiting 1976-1977; Bruce L. Billing 1977-1982; Janice I. Martineau 1982-1985; G. Patrick England Sept. 1, 1985-1993; Gregory E. Rowe 1993-Feb 28, 1995; Billy J. McKown Mar 1, 1995-2005; James P. James 2005-2007; Carter Garrigues-Cortelyou 2007-2010; Betty Kay Leitelt 2010-

Otsego UMC *[Greater Southwest]*   office@otsegoumc.org
(P) 223 E. Allegan St, Otsego 49078; (M) PO Box 443, Otsego 49078-0443   (269) 694-2939
Birt Beers 1967-1972; Leonard Yarlott 1972-1975; J. William Schoettle 1975-1983; Robert H. Roth, Jr. 1983-1985; James C. Grant 1985-March 1992; Emerson Minor (interim) March-August 1992; James C. Grant 1992-1994; Philip L. Brown 1994-1998; Margaret H. Peterson 1998-2000; Joseph D. Shaler 2001-

Ovid: United Church *[Mid-Michigan]*   sue@unitedchurchofovid.com
(P) 131 W Front St, Ovid 48866; (M) PO Box 106, Ovid 48866-0106   (989) 834-5958
Claude B. Ridley, Jr. 1972-1977; Gilbert B. Heaton 1977-1980; Carl W. Staser 1980-Oct. 1983; Ronald W. Hansen Feb. 1, 1984-1993; Richard L. Matson 1993-1995; Steven D. Pearson 1995-1997; Robert L. Pumfery 1997-1999; Rob A. McPherson 1999-2006; Donald R. Fry 2006-2008; Gregory L. Buchner 2008-2013; Paul A. Damkoehler 2013-2015; Robert D. Nystrom 2015-2018 [Elsie / Ovid became a two-point charge 2016] Melanie S. Young 2018- [Middlebury / Ovid became a two-point charge 2018]

Owendale UMC *[Central Bay]*   bcleland@comcast.net
(P) 7370 Main St, Owendale 48754; (M) PO Box 98, Owendale 48754   (989) 678-4172
Clifford M. DeVore 1968-1971; Paul L. Amstutz 1971-1976; Carl J. Litchifeld 1976-1978; William P. Mc Bride 1978-1980; Myra L. Sparks 1980-1985; Zina B. Bennett 1985-1988; Mary F. Neil 1988-1991; Lisa M. McIlvenna 1991-1995; Carol M. Blair 1995-Sep 30, 1996; Allice J. Sheffield Dec 1, 1996-2001; John Heim 2001-2012; Cynthia M. Parsons 2012-2014; William C. Cleland 2014-

Owosso: Burton UMC *[Mid-Michigan]*   pastorherbw@aol.com
(P) 510 N Baldwin Rd, Owosso 48867; (M) 218 E Main, Henderson 48841   (989) 723-3981
Horace N. Freeman 1969-1974; Homer VanBuren 1974-1983; Billy J. McKown 1983-1989; M. Shirley Jones 1989-1991; Howard M. Jones (assoc) 1989-1991; William R. Seitz 1991-Jan 1, 1996; Jean M. Scroggins Jun 16, 1996-Dec 31, 1999; Lance E. Ness Jan 1, 2000-Jul 31, 2004; Michael S. McCoy Aug 1, 2004-2006; Carole A. Brown Aug 1, 2006-2011; Calvin H. Wheelock 2011-2019; [Single point charge 07/01/2019]

Owosso: First UMC *[Mid-Michigan]*   firstumc@michonline.net
(P/M) 1500 N Water St, Owosso 48867   (989) 725-2201
Ivan O. Gonser 1968-1972; Arthur V. Norris (assoc) 1969-1971; David G. Knapp (assoc) 1971-Dec. 1973; Paul T. Hart Jan., 1972-1977; Thomas G. Butcher (assoc) Dec. 1975-1977; Norbert W. Smith 1977-1985; J. Michael Pearson (assoc) 1977-1980; Susan Bennett Stiles (assoc) 1980-1982; Hayden K. Carruth (assoc) 1982-1984; Peter S. Harris (assoc) 1984-1986; Carol J. Johns 1985-1996; John W. Simpson (assoc) 1986-1989; Grant R. Lobb 1996-2005; Eric D. Kieb (assoc) 2001-2003; Duane M. Harris 2005-2009; Calvin D. Long 2009-2018; Deane B. Wyllys 2018-

Owosso: Trinity UMC *[Mid-Michigan]*　　　　　　　　　trinityumc@michonline.net
(P/M) 720 S Shiawassee St, Owosso 48867　　　　　　　　　　　　(989) 723-2664
　　Clyde R. Moore 1968-1974; Alan W. Weeks 1974-1980; Ralph C. Pratt 1980-July 15, 1984; Gordon
　　B. Boyd July 15, 1984-1987; Martin R. Caudill Oct. 15, 1987-1988; Mark D. Miller May 1, 1989-
　　1998; Norman R. Beckwith, Sr. 1998-2008; Susan M. Kingsley 2008-2016; Carman J. Minarik
　　2016-2019; [Henderson / Chapin / Owosso: Triity frmed three-point charge 7-1-2019] Steffani
　　Glygoroff (DSA) 2019-

Oxford UMC *[East Winds]*　　　　　　　　　　　　　　oumc.office@sbcglobal.net
(P/M) 21 E Burdick St, Oxford 48371　　　　　　　　　　　　　　(248) 628-1289
　　Marvin H. Mc Callum 1966-1972; J. Edward Cherryholmes 1972-1973; Donald H. Hall 1973-1977;
　　David A. Russell 1977-1985; Dwight W. Murphy 1985-1992; Jack L. Mannschreck 1992-2002;
　　Joseph R. Baunoch 2002-2004; Kenneth B. Ray 2004-2006; Douglas J. McMunn 2006-2011; Jean
　　Snyder 2011-2012; Kevin L. Miles 2012-2014; Jennifer Jue 2014- [Oxford / Thomas two-point
　　charge 07/01/2019]

Painesdale: Albert Paine Mem. UMC *[Northern Skies]*　　　　revlaub@charter.net
(P) 54385 Iroquois, Painesdale 49955; (M) 204 W Douglass, Houghton 49931　　(906) 482-1470
　　A. P. Young 1962-1970; John Moore 1970-1976; Martin Caudill 1976-1979; Jay Six 1979-1981;
　　William Wright 1981-1985; W. Peter Bartlett 1985-1987; Nicholas W. Scroggins 1987-1990; Mary
　　G. Laub 1990-1992; Christine F. Bohnsack 1992-1995; Lillian G. Richards 1995-Oct 15, 2012;
　　Mary G. Laub Nov 1, 2012-2014; T. Bradley Terhune 2014-2016; Mary Laub 2016-2019;
　　[Houghton: Grace / Painesdale: Albert Paine Mem. Two-point charge 7-1-2019] Charles A. Williams
　　2019-

Paint Creek UMC *[Greater Detroit]*　　　　　　　　　　　howarthumc@att.net
(P/M) 4420 Collins Rd, Rochester 48306　　　　　　　　　　　　(248) 373-2360
　　Elmer J. Snyder 1967-1972; Harold S. Morse 1972-1977; Paula Barker 1977-1979; Jeffery W.
　　Dinner 1979-1982; Bruce L. Billing 1982-1993; David K. Koski 1993-1998; Sylvia A. Bouvier 1998-
　　2006; Stephen Fraser-Soots 2006-2009; Thomas M. Sayers 2009-2016; Carolyn Jones
　　2016-2018; Marvin L. Herman 2018-

Palo UMC *[Midwest]*　　　　　　　　　　　　　　　　fenwickumc@cmsinter.net
(P) 8445 Division St, Palo 48870; (M) PO Box 241, Sheridan 48884-0241　　　(989) 291-5547
　　John H. Gurney 1970-1976; Norman Crotser 1976-Dec. 1978; Daniel R. Bennett 1979-March
　　1982; Mark G. Johnson March 1982-1986; James E. Cook 1986-1991; Howard H. Harvey 1991-
　　1996; Patrick Glass 1996-1998; Larry W. Nalett 1998-Aug. 9, 2004; Charles E. Cerling Aug. 10,
　　2004-2009; Jolennda Cole (DSA) 2009-2010; Jolennda Cole 2010-2011; William F. Dye 2011-
　　2012; Russell D. Morgan (CLM) July 15, 2012-2014; Gerald A Erskine (DSA) 2014-Nov. 9, 2014;
　　Gerald A Erskine Nov. 10, 2014-

Paradise UMC *[Northern Skies]*　　　　　　　　　　marybrooks729@gmail.com
(P) 7087 N M123, Paradise 49768; (M) PO Box 193, Paradise 49768　　　　(906) 492-3585
　　Wayne T. Large 1968-1970; Robert N. Hicok 1970-1974; William E. Miles 1974-1975; Ralph A.
　　Edwards 1975-1979; David J. Hill 1979-1980; David K. Campbell 1980-1981; Douglas Paterson
　　1981-1982; James W. Robinson 1982-1983; Julaine A. Hays 1983-1984; Ramona E. Cowling
　　1984-1985; Melinda R. Cree 1985-1986; Ray S. Peterson 1986-1989; Jan L. Beaderstadt 1989-
　　1991; Audrey M. Dunlap 1991-1993; Donald Bates 1993-Sep 30, 1996; Barbra Franks Oct 1,
　　1996-1998; Donald L. Bates 1998-2001; Virginia B. Bell 2001-Oct 30, 2005; Sandra J. Kolder Dec
　　4, 2005-2011; Lowell Peterson 2011-2013; Mary D. Brooks (DSA) 2013-

Parchment UMC *[Greater Southwest]*　　　　　　　　　　parchmentumc@tds.net
(P/M) 225 Glendale Blvd, Parchment 49004　　　　　　　　　　(269) 234-40125
　　Wayne Groat Feb. 1968-Feb. 1969; James W. Dempsey March 1969-1973; Gaylord D. Howell
　　1973-1978; David S. Yoh Sept. 1978-1989; Daniel J. Minor 1989-2011; Michael J. Tupper 2011-
　　2016; Thomas A. Davenport 2016-

Paris UMC *[Midwest]*

(P) 109 Lincoln, Paris 49338; (M) 226 N Third Ave, Big Rapids 49307   (231) 796-4157
Richard Wilson 1968-1971; Lynn Chapel 1971-1979; John Buker 1979-1981; Elaine Buker 1981-1986; Kendall Lewis 1986-1990; J. Robert Collins 1990-Oct. 1991; David F. Hills 1992-1994; Kathryn M. Steen 1994-2000; Dawn A. Beamish Jan. 1, 2001-2002; Edwin D. Snook 2002-2005; Michael A. Riegler Sept. 11, 2005-2011; Ed Milam (DSA) July 1-Nov. 12, 2011; Ed Milam Nov. 12, 2011-2014; David J. Cadarette Sr. 2014-April 12, 2015; Kimberly A. DeLong 2015-2017; Devon R. Herrell 2017-2019; Morgan William (Bill) Davis (DSA) 2019-

Parmelee UMC *[Midwest]*   wvcleggjr@gmail.com

(P) 9266 W Parmalee Rd, Middleville 49333; (M) PO Box 237, Middleville 49333   (269) 795-8816
Edward D. Passenger 1966-1969; Robert Boyer 1969-1971; Lloyd Van Lente 1971-1976; Adam Chyrowski 1976-1980; Robert Tomlinson 1980-1981; Arthur Jackson 1981-Aug. 1983; Carl Staser Oct. 1983-1988; Lynn W. Wagner 1988-1996; Lee F. Zachman 1996-2004; Lee F. Zachman (1/2 time) 2004-Nov. 30, 2010; Vance Dimmick (DSA) (1/4 time) Nov. 28, 2010-Nov. 5, 2012; William V. Clegg, Jr (Ret.) (1/4 time) Nov. 11, 2012-

Paw Paw UMC *[Greater Southwest]*   pawpawunitedmethodistchurch@gmail.com

(P/M) 420 W Michigan Ave, Paw Paw 49079   (269) 657-7727
William Payne 1965-1979; Paul Patterson 1979-1984; Keith Laidler 1984-1989; Ward N. Scovel 1989-1995; Robert K. Lynch 1995-1999; Carolin S. Spragg 1999-2007; Joseph L. Spackman 2007-2013; Trevor J. McDermont 2013-2016; David E. Small 2016-

Pentwater Centenary UMC *[Midwest]*   pentwaterumc@gmail.com

(P) 82 S Hancock, Pentwater 49449; (M) PO Box 111, Pentwater 49449   (231) 869-5900
W. Jackson 1967-1970; Glenn B. Britton 1970-1973; Clyde Miller 1973-1979; Charles M. Johnson 1979-1982; Milton John Palmer 1982-1985; Gary T. Haller 1985-1993; Christopher P. Momany 1993-Dec. 31, 1996; Curtis E. Jensen Jan. 16, 1996-2001; Michael J. Tupper 2001-2006; Harris J. Hoekwater 2006-2012; Gary L. Bekofske 2012-2014; Melanie S. Young 2014-2018; William E. Haggard 2018-

Perry UMC *[Mid-Michigan]*   pastornancy@live.com

(P) 131 Madison St, Perry 48872; (M) PO Box 15, Perry 48872-0015   (517) 625-3444
Karl W. Patow 1962-1969; Ivan Niswender 1969-1971; David Draggoo 1971-1981; Jeff Siker-Giesler 1981-1983; Harris Hoekwater 1983-Jan. 1992; Clinton McKinven-Copus Feb. 1992-Dec. 31, 1994; Pulpit Supply Jan. 1-April 15, 1995; Carroll A. Fowler April 16, 1995-2003; Carolyn C. Floyd 2003-2008; Raymond R. Sundell 2008-2012; Nancy G. Powers 2012-

Petersburg UMC *[Heritage]*   pastor@petersburgumc.org

(P) 152 Saline St, Petersburg 49270; (M) PO Box 85, Petersburg 49270   (734) 279-1118
Philip D. Miles 1967-1970; Donald L. Bates 1971-1976; Basil W. Curtiss 1976-1980; Howard L. Deardorff 1980-1981; William Michael Clemmer 1981-1984; Thomas C. Anderson 1984-Dec. 31, 1989; Max L. Gibbs Feb. 1, 1990-1991; June M. Westgate 1991-1996; John M. Mehl, Jr. 1996-Oct 1, 2008; King W. Hanna (interim) Oct 15, 2008-Jan 15, 2009; Robert Dister (interim) Jan 28, 2009-Mar 1, 2009; King W. Hanna Mar 1, 2009-Dec 31, 2009; Janet L. Luchs Jan 1, 2010-2011; Joel Walther 2011-2017; Daniel Hyer 2017-2018; Carter Louis Cortelyou 2018

Petoskey UMC *[Northern Waters]*   info@petoskeyumc.org

(P/M) 1804 E Mitchell Rd, Petoskey 49770   (231) 347-2733
Ralph P. Witmer 1964-Sept. 1970; Charles L. Manker Sept. 1970-Oct. 15, 1975; Donald H. Merrill Oct. 15, 1975-1986; Charles W. Fullmer 1986-April 30, 1994; Don W. Eddy March 1, 1994-Dec. 1996; James P. Mitchum 1997-

Pickford UMC *[Northern Skies]*   pickfordumc@gmail.com
(P) 115 E Church St, Pickford 49774; (M) PO Box 128, Pickford 49774   (906) 647-6195
Ralph H. Pieper 1969-1975; Richard Beemer 1975-1981; Howard Shaffer 1981-1986; Lawson D. Crane 1986-1993; James M. Mathews 1993-1996; Lynn F. Chappell 1996-May 1, 2003; Paul Gruenberg 2003-2012; Larry D. Osweiler 2012-2014; Timothy Bashore 2014-

Pierson: Heritage UMC *[Midwest]*   church.heritageumc@gmail.com
(P/M) 19931 W Kendaville Rd, Pierson 49339   (231) 937-4310
Richard D. Moore Aug. 1 1999-2000; Mark Mitchell (Assoc.) Aug. 1, 1999-2000; Thomas E. Ball 2000-2007; James Bradley Brillhart, 2007-2014; Stephan Weinberger 2014-Mar. 1, 2016; Charles R. Kaliszewski (DSA) Mar. 1-June 30, 2016; Terri L. Cummins 2016-

Pigeon: First UMC *[Central Bay]*   pigeonfirstumc@gmail.com
(P) 7102 Michigan Ave, Pigeon 48755; (M) PO Box 377, Pigeon 48755   (989) 453-2475
Meldon E. Crawford 1966-1970; Webley J. Simpkins 1970-1975; Martin G. Seitz 1975-1979; Ralph C. Pratt 1979-1980; Gordon Wayne Nusz 1980-1988; James P. Schwandt 1988-Aug 31, 1994; Willard A. King Sep 31, 1994-1998; Karen L. Knight 1998-2001; Margaret A. Passenger 2001-2005; John J. Britt 2005-2015; Cindy Gibbs 2015-

Pigeon: Salem UMC *[Central Bay]*   salemumc@avci.net
(P) 23 Mabel St, Pigeon 48755; (M) PO Box 438, Pigeon 48755-0438   (989) 453-2552
Raymond F. Roe 1968-1971; Sam H. Evans 1971-1975; Ralph H. Pieper II 1975-1983; Mark A. Karls 1983-1986; Timothy S. Hastings 1986-1990; Steven A. Miller 1990-Jan 31, 1995; Calvin Long Jun 1, 1995-2000; Gary A. Allward 2000-Nov 30, 2000; Michael T. Sawicki 2001-2009; Gloria Haynes 2009-2012; John K. Benissan 2012-2013; David K. Stewart, Sr. 2013-

Pinckney: Arise UMC *[Heritage]*   arise@arisechurch.org
(P/M) 11211 Dexter Pinckney Rd, Pinckney 48169   (734) 878-1928
Douglas J. McMunn Jan 1, 1996-2006; Donald S. Weatherup 2006-2018; Reed P. Swanson 2018-

Pinconning UMC *[Central Bay]*   pumchurch@centurytel.net
(P/M) 314 Whyte St, Pinconning 48650-8606   (989) 879-3271
Byron G. Hatch (w/Garfield) 1969-1971; Richard Turner (w/Garfield) 1971-1981; Richard Turner 1981-1983; James M. Thompson 1983-1990; Donald Emmert Feb 16, 1990-1995; Gerald S. Hunter 1995-1999; Lawrence C., Brooks 1999-2002; Dorothy J. Thon 2002-2007; Charles Marble (interim) 2007-2008; Donald Mosher 2008-2010; John Tousciuk 2011- Agu 31, 2016; Heather Nowak (DSA) Oct 1, 2016 - Nov 30, 2017; Heather Nowak Dec 1, 2017-

Pine River Parish: Ashton UMC *[Northern Waters]*   srloomis1@gmail.com
(P) 20862 11 Mile Rd, Leroy 49655; (M) PO Box 38, Leroy 49655-0038   (231) 832-8347
David Dryer April 1968-1974; Ilona Sabo-Schuler 1974-1977; Robert Boyer 1977-1979; Harold R. Simon 1979-1983; Mark Gaylord-Miles 1983-Jan. 1985; Pulpit Supply Jan.-June 1985; Douglas Kokx 1985-1991; Robert W. Stark 1991-1996; Valerie M. Sisson Sept. 16, 1996-1998; Valerie M. Hill 1998-1999; David A. Cheyne 1999-2003; Jodie R. Flessner 2003-2012; Scott R. Loomis 2012-

Pine River Parish: LeRoy UMC *[Northern Waters]*   srloomis1@gmail.com
(P) 310 West Gilbert St, LeRoy 49655; (M) PO Box 38, Leroy 49655-0038   (231) 768-4512
David Dryer 1968-1974; Ilona Sabo-Schuler 1974-1977; Robert Boyer 1977-1979; Harold R. Simon 1979-1983 Mark Gaylord-Miles 1983-Jan. 1985; Pulpit Supply Jan.-June 1985; Douglas Kokx 1985-1991; Robert Stark 1991-1996; Valerie M. Sisson Sept. 16, 1996-1998; Valerie M. Hill 1998-1999; David A. Cheyne 1999-2003; Jodie R. Flessner 2003-2012; Scott R. Loomis 2012-

Pine River Parish: Luther UMC *[Northern Waters]* srloomis1@gmail.com
(P) 315 State St, Luther 49656; (M) PO Box 175, Luther 49656-0175 (231) 797-0073
David Dryer 1968-1974; Ilona Sabo-Schuler 1974-1977; Robert Boyer 1977-1979; Harold Simon 1979-1983; Mark Gaylord-Miles 1983-Dec. 1984; Pulpit Supply Jan.-June 1985; Douglas Kokx 1985-1991; Robert Stark 1991-April 1993; Reva Hawke May 1993-1995; Mary S. Brown 1995-Oct. 15, 1998; David A. Cheyne Jan. 16, 1999-June 30, 1999; Nelson Hall 1999-2005; Karen J. Sorden 2005-2012; James A. Richie 2012-Jan. 31, 2015; [Luther was added to Pine River Parish: Ashton/Leroy/Luther 2015] Scott R. Loomis 2015-

Pinnebog UMC *[Central Bay]* pacharge@hotmail.com
(P/M) 4619 Pinnebog Rd, Kinde 48445 (989) 738-5322
Elizabeth D.K. Isaacs 1969-1970; Robert P. Garrett 1970-1989; Barbara E. Welbaum 1989-1992; Raymond A Jacques 1992-1997; Earleen VanConant 1997-Dec 31, 1999; Robert P. Garrett 2000-2002; David C. Freeland 2002-2013; Nancy J. Bitterling 2013-2018; Clifford L. Radtke 2018-

Pittsburg UMC *[East Winds]* heiligj@michonline.net
(P) 2960 W Grand River Rd, Owosso 48867; (M) c/o Janet Demerly, Treasurer, 3888 W Brewer Rd, Owosso 48867 (810) 208-0648
Lawrence C. Brooks 1969-1972; Terry A. Euper 1972-1976; James E. Paige, Jr. 1976-1980; Margaret A. Paige (Co-Pastor) 1977-1980; Charles J. Bamberger 1980-1990; Donald Woolum 1990-1993; John H. Schneider, Jr. 1993-1997; Penney Meints 1997-1998; Arthur R. Turner 1998-2004; Jeremy T. Peters 2004-2008; Jeremy P. Benton 2008-2011; Don Wentz 2011-2015; Joyce Wallace Oct 1, 2015-2018; Brian G. West 2018-

Plainwell First UMC *[Greater Southwest]* plainwellumc@gmail.com
(P) 200 Park St, Plainwell 49080; (M) PO Box 85, Plainwell 49080-0085 (269) 685-5113
Emerson B. Minor 1964-1984; James W. Boehm 1984-1989; Raymond Townsend (Assoc.) 1988-1991; David B. Nelson, Jr. 1989-1991; Frank W. Lyman, Jr. and Carole Strobe Lyman (co-pastors) 1991-1996; Charles D. Grauer 1996-2003; Cindy E. Holmquist (Assoc.) 2001-June 30, 2003; Harvey K. Prochnau 2003-2010; Barbara Jo Fay (Assoc.) 2007-2010; Kathy E. Brown 2010-

Pleasant Lake UMC *[Heritage]* peasechris@yahoo.com
(P) 4815 E Territorial Rd, Pleasant Lake 49272; (M) PO Box 83, Pleasant Lake 49272
(517) 543-5618
Frederick Werth 1967-1971; Bert L. Cole March 1972-1973; Larry Irvine 1973-1975; Thomas Adams 1976-1978; James Barney 1979-1983; Linda Farmer-Lewis 1983-1986; Milton TenHave 1986-1990; Laurie McKinven-Copus 1990-Sept. 1991; Robert Marston Oct. 1991-1998; Judith A. Nielson 1998-2000; Charles E. Cerling 2000-Aug. 9, 2004; Arthur R. Turner 2004-Nov. 15, 2005; Kenneth Karlzen (DSA) Dec. 2005-2006; Maurice Walworth (DSA) 2006-Sept. 30, 2007; Thomas Peters (DSA) Oct. 1, 2007-Apr. 23, 2008; [Pleasant Lake & Jackson Zion became two-point charge 2008] David H. Minger (DSA) 2008-2013; [Pleasant Lake became single-point charge 2013] [M-52 Cooperative Ministry 2013-2014] Jeanne M. Laimon (1/4 time) 2013-2014; Christine L. Pease (DSA) 2014-

Pleasant Valley UMC *[Heritage]* jrhumenik@gmail.com
(P) 9300 West XY Ave, Schoolcraft 49087; (M) PO Box 517, Schoolcraft 49087 (269) 679-5352
Robert J. Stillson 1963-1969; Vern Michael 1969-1970; Roger Nielson 1970-1971; Lay Speakers 1971-1972; Dale Benton 1972-1978; John W. Fisher 1978-1980; Dale Crawford 1980-1983; Dwight J. Burton 1983-1992; Laura Truby 1992-1996; Ronald S. Scholte 1996-2000; Larry Reeves 2000; Michelle Wisdom-Long 2001-2008; [Schoolcraft Pleasant Valley / White Pigeon became a two-point charge 2008] Janet Luchs 2008-2009; [Three Rivers Ninth / Schoolcraft Pleasant Valley became a two-point charge 2009] James W. Stilwell 2009-2015; [Schoolcraft/Pleasant Valley became a charge 2015] Julia R. Humenik 2015-

Plymouth: First UMC *[Heritage]*   liz@pfumc.org
(P/M) 45201 N Territorial Rd, Plymouth 48170   (734) 453-5280
  Ronald K. Corl (assoc) 1967-1971; Paul M. Cargo 1968-1975; Dean A. Klump (assoc) 1971-1974;
  Samuel F. Stout 1975-1980; Dale M. Miller (assoc) 1974-1976; Dwayne L. Kelsey (assoc) 1976-
  1978; Frederick C. Vosburg (assoc) 1976-1993; Frank W. Lyman Jr. (assoc) 1978-1981; John N.
  Grenfell Jr. 1980-1993; Thomas E. Sumwalt (assoc) 1980-1982; Stephen E. Wenzel (assoc) 1982-
  1985; Larry J. Werbil (assoc) 1985-1986; Douglas J. McMunn (assoc) 1986-Feb. 1990; David K.
  Stewart Sr. (assoc) 1990-1991; Kevin L. Miles (assoc) 1991-1995; Merton W. Seymour 1993-
  1995; Dean A. Klump 1995-2007; Tonya M. Arnesen (assoc.) 1995-May 31, 2000; Deborah S.
  Thomas (assoc) Jun 1, 2000-2004; Jeremy P. Africa (assoc.) Jun 1, 2005-2006; David Allen
  Wichert (assoc.) 2006-2010; John N. Grenfell, III 2007-2018; Elizabeth A. Librande (assoc.) 2010-
  Feb 15, 2014; Nicholas R. Berlanga Feb 15, 2014-2018; Robert A. Miller Jr. 2018- ; Suzanne L.
  Hutchison (assoc.) 2018-

Pokagon UMC *[Greater Southwest]*   PokagonUMC@aol.com
(P/M) 31393 Kansas St, Dowagiac 49047   (269) 683-8515
  Albert A. O'Rourke 1962-1974; Harold Deipert 1974-1977; Gary D. Kintigh 1977-1981; Michael
  Conklin 1981-1983; Theodore H. Bennink (retired, part-time) 1983-1984; Reva Hawke 1984-1988;
  Beatrice Rose 1988-1990; Claude Ridley (retired) May 1-Nov. 1, 1990; Theodore Bennink (retired)
  Nov. 1, 1990-April 30, 1991; Claude Ridley (retired May 1-Nov. 1, 1991; Richard Muessig (DSA)
  Nov. 1, 1991-April 30, 1992; Claude Ridley (retired) May 1-Aug. 30, 1992; Richard Muessig Sept.
  1992-2001; Valerie Fons 2001-2003; Patrica Ann Haas 2003-2011; Sean K. Kidd (DSA) (1/2 time)
  2011-2014; [Berrien Springs/Pokagon became a 2-point charge 2014] Brenda E. Gordon 2014-
  2018; William Walters (DSA) 2018-

Pompeii UMC *[Mid-Michigan]*   billmona3@gmail.com
(P) 135 Burton St, Pompeii 48874; (M) PO Box 125, Pompeii 48874-0125   (989) 838-4159
  Robert E. Tomlinson 1974-Jan. 1977; Donald L. Warmouth Feb. 1977-1978; Glenn Britton 1978-
  1979; Lois H. Gremban 1979-1981; Dale F. Jaquette Aug. 1981-April 1990; T. Ried Martin
  1990-1993; Karen E. Nesius 1993-1994; Jodie Flessner 1994-2003; William F. Foldesi Nov. 16,
  2003-Apr. 7, 2007; Clare Huyck (DSA) 2007; Clare Huyck Nov. 10, 2007-2012; William F. Dye
  July 15, 2012-Sept. 1, 2015 ; Mona J. Dye 2011-Sept. 30, 2017; [Ashley/Bannister realigned with
  Pompeii to become Ashley/Bannister/Pompeii charge 2016] Zella Marie Daniel (DSA) Oct. 3, 2017-
  Dec. 31, 2018; Zella Marie Daniel Jan. 1, 2019-

Pontiac: Grace & Peace Cmnty UMC *[Greater Detroit]*   lward@graceandpeace.comcastbiz.net
(P/M) 451 W Kennett Rd, Pontiac 48340   (248) 334-3280
  Dudley Mosure 1967-1969; Donald Bates 1969-1970; John Kershaw 1970-1975; Thomas Badley
  1975-1978; Donald McClennan 1978-1979; Martin Caudill 1979-1984; James R. Rupert 1984-
  1987; Sylvia Bouvier 1987-1992; James Allen 1992-1994; Barbara E. Welbaum 1994-1997;
  Kenneth L. Bracken 1997-2006; Bea Barbara Fraser-Soots 2006-2014; Theodore D. Whitely, Sr.
  2014-2015; Zelphia Mobley 2015-2019; Laurie M. Koivula 2019-

Pontiac: St. John UMC *[Greater Detroit]*   st.johnpontiac@sbcglobal.net
(P/M) 620 University Dr, Pontiac 48342   (248) 338-8933
  C.R. Trice 1968-1974; Henry Johnson 1975-1980; Andrew Allie 1981- May 1991; Frederick Moore,
  Sr. 1992-2008; Johnnie L. Dyer (assoc) 2000-2004; Gary A. Williams 2008-2009; Andrew Allie
  2009-2010; Karel Y. Noel 2010-Sep 15, 2013; Lester Mangum Oct 1, 2013-

Pope UMC *[Heritage]*
(P) 10025 N Parma Rd, Springport 49284; (M) 10401 Townley Rd, Springport 49284 (517) 857-3655
  Lambert G. McClintic 1952-1995; Jack Fugate 1995-July 15, 2008; Irene Vittoz (part-time) 2009-
  2010; Robert S. Moore-Jumonville 2010-2018; Lawrence J. Embury 2018-

Portage: Chapel Hill UMC *[Greater Southwest]* office@pchum.org
(P/M) 7028 Oakland Dr, Portage 49024 (269) 327-6643
David Nelson 1968-1972; Dow Chamberlain 1972-1978; Jon Powers July-August 1978; Joseph Bistayi Sept. 1978-1985; William Torrey 1985-1989; Carl Hausermann 1989-2001; Julie A. Liske (Assoc.) 1994-Nov. 30, 1997; Susan M. Petro (Assoc.) Jan. 1, 1998-2007; Barry Thayer Petrucci 2001- ; John M. Weiler (Assoc.) 2007-2011; Cara Weiler (deacon 1/4 time) Oct. 1, 2007-Oct. 1, 2009; Virginia L. Heller (Assoc.) 2011-2013; Caleb B. Williams (Deacon) 2015-Sept. 1, 2016; Patricia L. Catellier (Deacon) Jan. 1, 2016-

Portage: Pathfinder UMC *[Greater Southwest]* office@pathfinderchurch.com
(P/M) 8740 S Westnedge Ave, Portage 49002 (269) 327-6761
Donald Scranton 1967-1970; Paul Albery 1970-1975; Kenneth McCaw 1975-1983; Logan Weaver (Assoc.) Oct. 1, 1980; Royce Robinson 1983-Dec. 1986; Robert Hinklin March 1987-1998; Logan Weaver (Pastor Emeritus, Assoc.) Jan. 1, 1988; William J. Torrey (Ret. Assoc.) 1993-1995; Gregory B. Wood 1998-2015; John L. Moore (Ret. Assoc.) (DSA), Oct. 1, 2006-2013; Ronald W. Hansen (Ret.) 2015-2016; Donald W. Wolfgang 2016-

Portland UMC *[Mid-Michigan]* portlandmiumc@gmail.com
(P/M) 310 E Bridge St, Portland 48875 (517) 647-4649
Raymond Norton 1967-1969; Donald Cozadd 1969-1971; Carlton Benson 1971-1973; Harold Homer 1973-1978; C. Dow Chamberlain 1978-Nov. 1985; David Evans (interim) Nov. 1985-Feb. 1986; Dale Crawford Feb.-Oct. 1986; David Evans (interim) Oct. 1986-Feb. 1987; Stanley Finkbiener 1987-1992; Elaine M. Buker 1992-1997; Scott K. Otis 1997-2003; Gregory Ryan Wolfe 2003-2008; Keith R. Treman 2008-2015; Letisha M. Bowman 2015-

Port Austin U.P.C. UMC *[Central Bay]* pacharge@hotmail.com
(P) 8625 Arch; Port Austin 48467; (M) PO Box 129, Port Austin 48467 (989) 738-5322
William Small 1967-1968; Robert P. Garrett 1968-1989; Barbara E. Welbaum 1989-1992; Raymond A Jacques 1992-1997; Earleen VanConant 1997-Dec 31, 1999; Robert P. Garrett 2000-2002; David C. Freeland 2002-2013; Nancy J. Bitterling 2013-2018; Clifford L. Radtke 2018-

Port Hope UMC *[East Winds]*
(P) 4521 Main St, Port Hope 48468; (M) PO Box 25, Harbor Beach 48441 (989) 479-6053
Robert P. Garrett 1968-1970; Thomas G. Badley 1970-1973; William M. Smith 1974-1978; Brent L. Webster 1978-1983; Wayne A. Hawley 1983-1991; Kris S. Kappler 1991- 1997; Victoria M. Webster 1997-1999; Clarence W. VanConant 1999-2004; Paula M. Timm 2004-2011; Mark E. Ryan 2012-Sept 18, 2016; Sari Brown 2017-

Port Huron: First UMC *[East Winds]* phfumc@advnet.net
(P/M) 828 Lapeer Ave, Port Huron 48060 (810) 985-8107
John N. Grenfell Jr. 1968-1974; William Schlitts (assoc) 1968-1972; Donna J. Lindberg (assoc) 1972-1973; Harry R. Weeks (assoc) 1973-1975; O. William Cooper Jr. 1974-1979; James D. Jacobs (assoc) 1975-1977; Dana R. Strall (assoc) 1977-1980; Paul F. Blomquist 1979-1985; William G. Wager (assoc) 1980-1984; Jacqueline E. Holdsworth (assoc) 1981-1983; Robert D. Wright (assoc) 1983-1985; Richard D. Lobb 1985-1992; Trevor A. Herm (assoc) Jan. 1 1986-1989; Jeffery L. Jaggers (assoc) Jan 1 1990-1994; John C. Huhtala 1992-1996; Kevin C. Zaborney (assoc) 1994-1997; Ralph H. Pieper, II 1996-2003;Connie S. Porter (assoc) 1997-Nov 1, 1998; AmyLee Brun Terhune (assoc) 1999-2002; David G. Gladstone 2003-2012; Alicea L. Williams (deacon) Oct 1, 2007-Oct 25, 2011; William R. Wright 2012-2017; LuAnn Lee Rourke 2017-

Port Huron: Gratiot Park UMC *[East Winds]*
(P/M) 811 Church St, Port Huron 48060 (810) 985-6206
Harold J. Slater 1969-1970; Grant A. Washburn 1970-1973; Lloyd E. Christler 1973-1978; John N. Howell 1978-1981; S. Joe Robertson 1981-1985; Robert E. Burkey 1985-1988; Donald R. Sperling 1988-1996; Georg F. W. Gerritsen 1996-Dec 31, 1999; Susan K. Freeland Jan 1, 2000-2001; Robert D. Chapman 2001-2014; Penelope P. Nunn 2014-2018; [Port Huron: Wasihton Ave. UMC merged with Port Huron: Gratiot Park 07/01/2018] Eric J. Miller-2018

Port Sanilac UMC *[East Winds]*
(P) 7225 Main St, Port Sanilac 48469; (M) 7209 Main St, Port Sanilac 48469   (810) 622-0001
James B. Lumsden 1969-1973; J. Paul Pumphrey 1973-1977; Glenn R. Wegner 1977-1980;
James P. Kummer Dec. 1980-1985; Kenneth C. Reeves 1985-1991; Gloria Haynes 1991-1996;
James M. Thompson 1996-1999; Catherine W. J. Hiner 1999-2004; Clarence W. VanConant 2004-
2007; Eric L. Johnson 2007-2012; Ellen Burns 2013-2016; Mark Harriman 2016-2018; Anika Bailey
2018-

Quincy UMC *[Heritage]*   umcquincy@gmail.com
(P/M) 32 W Chicago St, Quincy 49082   (517) 639-5035
W. Ernest Combellack 1967-1969; Jack Bartholomew 1969-1974; Bruce Keegstra 1974-1977;
Kay Williams 1977-1979; Jim Gysel 1979-1983; James Barney 1983-1987; Joan Hamlin 1987-
1994; Jane D. Logston 1994-1996; John Knowlton 1996-1998; Melanie S. Young 1998-Oct. 1,
1998; Charles A. Williams Jan. 1, 1999-2003; John A. Scott & Rebecca Scott (CoPastors) Sept.
2003-2007; Geraldine M. Litchfield 2007-2009; [Litchfield/Quincy two-point charge 2009] Michael
P. Baker-Streevy 2009-2010; Martin T. Cobb 2010-2013; Julie Elmore 2013-2017; [Quincy UMC
became single station 2017] Richard D. Wilson (Ret.) 2017-

Quinnesec: First UMC *[Northern Skies]*   QuinnesecUMC@yahoo.com
(P) 677 Division, Quinnesec 49876; (M) PO Box 28, Quinnesec 49876   (906) 774-7971
Richard Reese 1967-1971; Monroe Fredrick 1971-1976; John Moore 1976-1980; James Hall
1980-1983; Paul Doering 1983-1984; James Mathews 1984-1989; Douglas J. McMunn 1989-Dec
31, 1995; Scott A. Harmon 1996-1998; Pauline E. Rupe Aug 16,1998-2006; David P. Snyder Aug
1, 2006-2009; Margaret A.W. Paige 2009-2012; Walter P. Reichle 2012-

Ravenna UMC *[Midwest]*   ravennaumc@gmail.com
(P) 12348 Stafford St, Ravenna 49451; (M) PO Box 191, Ravenna 49451   (231) 853-6688
Harry R. Johnson 1967-Dec. 1968; William Foster Dec. 1968-1973; William Bowers 1973-1978;
Lewis Buchner 1978-1983; Dennis Slattery 1983-1987; Kenneth Curtis 1987-1988; Rick Powell
1988-1991; Pamela Kail 1991-1994; Daniel B. Hofmann 1994-2001; Mary Bement Ivanov 2001-
2008; Charles W. Smith 2008-2011; Carleton R. Black (DSA) 2011; Carleton R. Black Nov. 12,
2011-

Reading UMC *[Heritage]*   office@readingumc.com
(P) 312 E Michigan St, Reading 49274; (M) PO Box 457, Reading 49274-0457
Harold Cox 1968-Sept. 1969; William Bowers Sept. 1969-1972; Eric Johnson 1972-1975; Dennis
Paulson 1975-1979; Altha M. Barnes 1979-1983; Harold R. Simon 1983-March 1990; Dale F.
Jaquette April 1990-1992; Thomas P. Fox 1992-1999; Kathy L. Nitz Aug. 16, 1999-July 31, 2001;
Gayle Berntsen Sept. 1, 2001-2006; Nancy G. Powers 2006-2008; DeAnn J. Dobbs 2008-2012;
Robert M. Hughes 2012-2014; Deborah S. Cole Sept. 1, 2014-

Redford: Aldersgate UMC *[Greater Detroit]*   redfordaldersgatge@sbcglobal.net
(P/M) 10000 Beech Daly Rd, Redford 48239   (313) 937-3170
William G. Wager 1966-1980; William W. Smith (assoc) 1968-1974; David K. Koski (assoc) 1974-
1977; Thomas F. Keef (assoc.) 1977-1980; Archie H. Donigan 1980-1985; Barbara J. Byers Lewis
(assoc) 1981-1985; Randy J. Whitcomb (assoc) 1985-1988; M. Clement Parr 1985-Aug 31, 1994;
Troy Douthit (assoc) 1988-1990; Bufford Coe (assoc) 1990-1994; Diana Goudie (co-pastor) Sep
1, 1994-2003; Robert Goudie co-pastor Sep 1, 1994-2003; Diana Goudie 2003-2009; [merged
with Redford: Redford, 2005]; Jeffrey S. Nelson 2009-2016; Jonathan Combs (assoc) 2015- ;
Benjamin Bower 2016-

Redford: Aldersgate - Brightmoore Campus UMC *[Greater Detroit]*
(P) 12065 W Outer Dr, Detroit 48223; (M) 10000 Beech Daly Rd, Redford 48239   (313) 937-3170
[Satellite of Redford: Aldersgate] Jonathan Combs (assoc) 2015-

Redford: New Beginnings UMC *[Greater Detroit]*   newbeginningsumc@sbcglobal.net
(P/M) 16175 Deleware Ave, Redford 48240   (313) 255-6330
   Gregory E. Rowe Jan 1, 2005-2006; Kenneth B. Ray 2006-2007; John H. Amick 2007-2008;
   Ronald L.F. Iris 2008-Apr 1, 2009; John J. Pajak Apr 1, 2009-2015; Diane Covington 2015-

Reed City UMC *[Heritage]*   office@readingumc.com
(P/M) 503 S Chestnut St, Reed City 49677   (231) 832-9441
   Charles W. Fullmer 1966-1970; Forrest E. Mohr 1970-1977; Allen D. McCreedy 1977-1990;
   Richard L. Matson 1990-1993; Gregory J. Martin 1993-Dec. 1, 1998; Jennifer Browne (Assoc.)
   Jan. 15, 1997-Dec. 1, 1998; Richard W. Blunt Feb. 1, 1999-2008; Emmett H. Kadwell, Jr. 2008-
   2011; Kathryn S. Cadarette 2011-2019; Kristen I. Coristine 2019-

Reese UMC *[Central Bay]*   pastorgougeon@gmail.com
(P) 1968 Rhodes St, Reese 48757; (M) PO Box 7, Reese 48757-0007   (989) 868-9957
   Donald Pinner 1968-1970; Edgar M. Smith 1970-1976; Monroe J. Frederick 1976-1988; Sang
   Yoon (Abraham) Chun 1988-1992; James P. James 1992-1996; Steven J. Woodford 1996-2000;
   Raymond D. Wightman 2000-2003; Jean M. Larson 2003-Dec 31, 2007; Harold J. Slater 2008-
   Feb 28, 2010; Jon W. Gougeon Mar 1, 2010-

Republic UMC *[Northern Skies]*   hdrider2@chartermi.net
(P) 216 Front, Republic 49879; (M) PO Box 395, Republic 49879   (906) 376-2389
   Michael Peterlin 1969-1970; Ronald Lindner 1970-1972; Alden Thomas 1972-1974; Alan Larsen
   1974-1978; James Mathews 1978-1984; Charles Keyworth 1984-1988; Robert Duggan 1988-
   1990; Nicholas W. Scroggins 1990-1993; Fred A. LaMere 1993-1996; Terry J. Kordish 1996-2000;
   Gary I. Stevens 2000-2004; James A. Fegan 2004-2009; Mark E. Ryan 2009-2012; Terri L.
   Branstrom 2012-2016; Peter LeMoine 2016-

Richfield UMC *[East Winds]*   pastorshellyRUMC@comcast.net
(P) 10090 E Coldwater Rd, Davison 48423; (M) PO Box 307, Davison 48423   (248) 417-1196
   Beatrice Townsend 1969-1971; Basel W. Curtiss 1971-1976; Brent Webster 1976-1979; Charles
   H. West 1979-Mar. 1988; Dennis Norris 1988-1989; Paul G. Donelson 1989-1990; Robert D.
   Harvey 1990-1994; Dorothy J. Rossman Nov 16, 1994-2002; T. Bradly Terhune 2002-2007; James
   E. Paige, Jr. 2007-2008; Jannie L. Plum 2008-2012; Barbara Benjamin Aug 1, 2012-2012; Barbara
   Benjamin 2012-2016; Shelly Ann Long 2016-

Richmond: First UMC *[East Winds]*   fumc@methodist.comcastbiz.net
(P) 69495 N Main St, Richmond 48062; (M) PO Box 293, Richmond 48062   (586) 727-2622
   Richard L. Myers 1969-1973; Roy Syme 1973-1983; Steven Gjerstad 1983-1984; Gary Beeker 1984-
   1991; Karl L. Zeigler 1991-Aug 31, 1998; Reed P. Swanson Sep 1, 1998-2004; Trevor A. Herm
   2004-2010; Thomas F. Keef 2010-2014; Suzanne L. Hutchison 2014-2018; Thomas Waller 2018-

Riverdale: Lincoln Road UMC *[Mid-Michigan]*   lincolnroadumc@casair.net
(P/M) 9479 W Lincoln Rd, Riverdale 48877   (989) 463-5704
   John Buckner 1966-1972; Eldon Schram 1973-1977; Marvin Iseminger 1977-1979; Milton TenHave
   1979-1986; Jane Lippert 1986-1990; Beatrice Rose 1990-1995; Kenneth C. Reeves 1995-1997;
   Lois M. Munn 1997-2000; Charles M. Shields 2000-2002; Nancy J. Bitterling 2002-2010; Jana
   Lynn Almeida 2010-2016; Linda (Lyne) K. Stull-Lipps 2016-

Riverside UMC *[Greater Southwest]*   riverside_umc@att.net
(P) 4401 Fikes Rd, Benton Harbor 49022; (M) PO Box 152, Riverside 49084   (269) 849-1131
   George Chaffee 1968-1971; Carl L. Hausermann 1971-1977; Elizabeth Perry Nord 1976-Oct.
   1986; Mark Thompson Jan. 1987-Nov. 15, 1992; Norman C. Kohns Nov. 16, 1992-1993; Jackie
   Bralick 1993-Feb. 1, 1995; Pulpit Supply Feb.-April 1995; Alan D. Stover May 1, 1995-Sept. 25,
   1997; John Sternaman Dec. 1, 1997-2002; Michael R. Bohms 2002-Dec. 31, 2003; Thomas Meyer
   (DSA) Feb. 1, 2004-June 30, 2004; Sheila F. Baker 2004-2005; Russell K. Logston 2005-2006;
   Walter G. Gerstung (DSA) July 1, 2006; David S. Yoh (DSA), Oct. 4, 2006-2009; Stephen C. Small
   (DSA) 2009-2014; David L. Haase 2014-

Riverview UMC *[Greater Detroit]*   TheRiverviewUMC@att.net
(P/M) 13199 Colvin St, Riverview 48193   (734) 284-2721
     Robert C. Watt 1968-1973; J. Bruce Brown 1973-1981; William A. Cargo 1981-1988; Michael Grajcar 1988-1989; Gary A. Allward 1989-1996; June M. Westgate 1996-2001; David D. Amstutz 2001-2012; Gloria Haynes 2012-Aug 1, 2015; Alan Hansen Aug 1, 2015-2016; Keith Lenard 2016-2017; Daniel J.W. Phillips 2017-2019; Carol Ann Middel 2019-

Robbins UMC *[Mid-Michigan]*   robbins@robbinsumc.org
(P/M) 6419 Bunker Rd, Eaton Rapids 48827   (517) 663-5226
     Maurice Glasgow 1966-1977; Joseph Huston 1977-1982; Wade Panse 1982-1987; James P. Mitchum 1987-1997; Martin M. DeBow 1997-2008; Bobby Dale Whitlock 2008-2009; Mark R. Payne 2009-2014; Peggy A. Katzmark 2014-

Rochester Hills: St. Luke's UMC *[Greater Detroit]*   stlukesrh@gmail.com
(P/M) 3980 Walton Blvd, Rochester Hills 48309   (248) 373-6960
     David E. Church 1968-1970; Daniel Krichbaum 1970-1972; Harold Morse 1972-1977; R. Stantley Sutton 1977- Aug. 1982; Wayne N. Thomas Oct. 1982-Jan. 1984; David B. Penniman May 1, 1984-1989; Jeffrey B. Hildebrand 1989-1990; Johnny S. Liles Mar. 1990-2004; Sharyn K. Osmond (assoc) Jan 16, 1999-2002; Lynda B. Hamilton (deacon) 1999- ; Murphy S. Ehlers (deacon) 2002-Dec 1, 2002; Lisa M. McIlvenna 2004-2008; Julius Del Pino 2008-2016; Scott E. Manning 2016-

Rochester: St. Paul's UMC *[Greater Detorit]*   rachel@stpaulsrochester.org
(P) 620 Romeo Rd, Rochester 48307; (M) PO Box 80307, Rochester 48308   (248) 651-9361
     William Richards 1967-1973; Timothy Hickey 1973-Sep 30, 2000; Athanasius P. Rickard (assoc) 1963-1975; Howard Short (assoc) 1967-1968; Loren Strait (assoc) 1968-1969; Douglas Trebilcock (assoc) 1969-1973; Dale Lindsey (assoc) 1973; Thomas Badley (assoc) 1973-1975; Gilson Miller (assoc) 1975-1978; Ronald Brunger (assoc) 1975-1979; Duane J. Hicks (assoc) 1978-1981; Ralph A. Edwards (assoc) 1979-1985; Devin S. Chisholm (assoc) 1981-1983; James E. Greer, II (assoc) 1983-1987; James R. Hilliard (assoc)1985-1988; James P. Schwandt (assoc) 1987-1988; David A. Diamond (assoc) 1988-1994; Samuel Stout (assoc) 1988-1990; Robert D. Wright (assoc) 1994-1999; Joanne Bartelt (assoc) 1996-2000; Harold E. Weemhoff, Jr. (assoc) Jan 1, 2000-2008; Jeffrey D. Regan Feb 1, 2001-2013; Rony S. (Hallstrom) Veska (assoc) Mar 1, 2001-2008; John Amick (assoc) 2008-2012; Latha Ravi (assoc) 2008-2017; David A. Eardley 2013- ; Jon Reynolds (assoc.) Jan 9, 2014-2018; Carter M. Grimmett (assoc.) 2017- ; Erin L. Fitzgerald (assoc.) 2018-

Rockford UMC *[Midwest]*   office@rockfordumc.org
(P/M) 159 Maple St, Rockford 49341   (616) 866-9515
     Richard A. Selleck 1966-1970; Ron L. Keller 1970-1973; George A. Belknap 1973-1978; John S. Myette 1978-1980; J. Melvin Bricker 1980-1989; Leonard F. Putnam (Assoc. part-time) 1984-1994; William J. Torrey 1989-1993; Richard M. Riley 1993-2014; Jeffrey Charles Williams (Assoc.) 2002-2004; Kenneth J. Bremer 2014-2017; Cynthia S.L. Greene 2017-2019; Gregory L. Buchner 2019-

Rockland: St. Paul UMC *[Northern Skies]*   ontmeth@jamadots.com
(P) 50 National Ave, Rockland 49960; (M) PO Box 216, Ontonagon 49953   (906) 886-2851
     Lloyd Christler 1968-1972; James Hillard 1970-1971; James Gerzetich 1971; Lawrence Brooks 1971-1975; Roger Gedcke 1972-1979; Lillian Richards 1971-1976; Wayne E. Sparks 1975-1980; Myra Sparks 1976-1980; Ed Hingelburg 1976-1980; Brian Marshall 1980-1984; Donald J. Emmert 1984-Feb 15, 1990; William D. Schoonover Feb 16, 1990-1991; Mel D. Rose 1992-1994; Lance E. Ness Sep 1, 1994-Dec 31, 1999; Christine F. Bohnsack Mar 1, 2000-2004; Cherrie A. Sporleder 2004-2010; Bruce R. Steinberg 2010-2018; Nelson L. Hall 2018-

Rodney UMC *[Midwest]*
(P) 12135 Charles St, Rodney 49342; (M) PO Box 14, Rodney 49342-0014   (231) 796-4157
   Richard Wilson 1968-1971; Lynn Chapel 1971-1979; John Buker 1979-1981; Elaine Buker 1981-1986; Kendall Lewis 1986-1990; J. Robert Collins 1990-Oct. 1991; David F. Hills 1992-1994; Kathryn M. Steen 1994-2000; Dawn A. Beamish Jan. 1, 2001-2002; Edwin D. Snook 2002-2005; Michael A. Riegler Sept. 11, 2005-2011; Ed Milam (DSA) July 1-Nov. 12, 2011; Ed Milam Nov. 12, 2011-2014; David J. Cadarette Sr. 2014-April 12, 2015; Kimberly A. DeLong 2015-2017; Devon R. Herrell 2017-2019; Morgan William (Bill) Davis (DSA) 2019-

Rollin Center UMC *[Heritage]*   clayton.rollincenter@gmail.com
(P) 3988 Townley Hwy, Manitou Beach 49253; (M) PO Box 98, Clayton 49235   (517) 445-2641
   Lawson D. Crane 1967-1975; Heath T. Goodwin 1975-1976; George F. Ward 1976- 1981; Walter H. Miller Nov 1, 1981-1994; Craig A. Pillow 1994-2009; Linda Jo Powers 2009-2012; Robert W. Dister 2012-

Romeo UMC *[East Winds]*   romeounited@sbcglobal.net
(P/M) 280 N Main St, Romeo 48065   (586) 752-9132
   J. Douglas Parker 1969-1973; Calvin Blue 1973-1981; Dean A. Klump 1981-1991; Dwayne L. Kelsey 1991-1996; Gary R. Glanville 1996-2015; John D. Bailey 2015-2017; Trevor A. Herm 2017-

Romulus: Community UMC *[Greater Detroit]*   office@communityunited.comcastbiz.net
(P/M) 11160 Olive St, Romulus 48174   (734) 941-0736
   Frank R. Lieneke 1966-1971; Haldon D. Ferris 1971-1974; Paul I. Greer 1974-1977; Floyd A. Ellison 1977-1981; Margery A. Schleicher 1981-1987; John D. Landis 1987-1994; Bradford K. Lewis 1994-1998; William Kren 1998-2006; Mark A. Miller 2006-2010; Cindy Gibbs 2010-2015; Rahim O. Shabazz 2015-2017; Rochelle J. Hunter 2017-Feb 28, 2018; James Reinker Mar 1, 2018-

Roscommon: Good Shepherd UMC *[Nothern Waters]*   office@gsumc-roscommon.com
(P/M) 149 W Robinson Lake Rd, Roscommon 48653   (989) 275-5577
   Kenneth L. Christler 1988-1995; Joel W. Hurley 1995-1998; Bradford K. Lewis 1998-2010; Eric D. Kieb 2010-2015; James C. Noggle 2015-Mar 31, 2019; Thomas Leo Hoffmyer Apr 1, 2019-

Rosebush UMC *[Central Bay]*   rosebushumc@gmail.com
(P) 3805 School Rd, Rosebush 48878; (M) PO Box 187, Rosebush 48878   (989) 433-2957
   Paul Peet 1968-1969; Fred Fischer 1969-1978; David Meister 1978-1980; John Ritter 1980-1984; Michael Long 1984-1992; Mark R. Payne 1992-2001; Brian Charles LaMew 2001-May 1, 2005; Gregory L. Buchner 2005-2008; Jonathan D. Van Dop 2008-2014; Joseph L. Beavan 2014-

Rose City: Trinity UMC *[Central Bay]*   N_Jeffords@yahoo.com
(P) 125 West Main St, Rose City 48654; (M) PO Box 130, Rose City 48654   (989) 685-2350
   Fred Timm 1965-1975; James R. Balfour II 1975-1982; David Baize 1982-1983; John R. Crotser 1983-1987; Jeffrey Hildebrand 1987-1989; Barbra Franks 1989-Aug 31, 1994; Carter Garrigues-Cortelyou Sep 1, 1994-1998; Thomas K. Spencer 1998-2005; Donald J. Wojewski 2005-2011; Joseph Coon 2011-2016; Nathan J. Jeffords 2016-2019; Helen Alford (DSA) 2019-

Roseville: Trinity UMC *[Greater Detroit]*   rosevilletrinity@gmail.com
(P/M) 18303 Common Rd, Roseville 48066   (586) 776-8828
   James W. Deeg 1967-1973; Tom Brown II 1973-1978; Thomas G. Badley 1978-1984; Sam Yearby Jr. 1984-1994; Kenneth B. Ray 1994-2000; Paul G. Donelson 2000-Sep 30, 2001; James A. Mathews Oct 1, 2001-2002; Kevin L. Miles 2002-2012; Stephen Euper 2012-

Royal Oak: First UMC *[Greater Detroit]* office@rofum.org
(P/M) 320 W 7th St, Royal Oak 48067 (248) 541-4100
Everett Seymour 1963-1974; Charles Songquist (assoc) 1967-1969; David W. Truran (assoc) 1970-1972; Samuel Seizert (assoc) 1970- 1981; James R. Balfour, II (assoc) 1972-1975; John G. Park (assoc) 1975-1978; Brent L. McCumons (assoc) 1978-1981; Gerald Fuller (assoc) 1981-1984; Steven J. Buck (assoc) 1982-1988; Thomas Rousseau (assoc.) 1984-1987; Raymond R. Lamb 1974-1987; Edward L. Duncan July 1987-1991; Nanette Myers (assoc) 1987-1992; Thomas H. Zimmerman (assoc) 1991-1997; Marvin H. McCallum 1991-1995; Merton W. Seymour 1995-1999; Wayne N. Thomas (assoc) 1997-2002; Marshall Dunlap (co-pastor) 1999-2008; Susan K. Defoe Dunlap (co-pastor) 1999-2008; Wayne T. Large (assoc) 2002-2003; John H. Hice 2008-2016; Jeffrey S. Nelson 2016- ; Caleb Williams (deacon) Sep 1, 2016- ; Myra Moreland Jan 1, 2018-

Saginaw: Ames UMC *[Central Bay]* office@ameschurch.org
(P/M) 801 State St, Saginaw 48602 (989) 754-6373
Richard D. Lobb 1967-1985; Warren Pettis (assoc) 1968-1971; Eldred Kelley (assoc) 1971-1974; Steve Patton (assoc) 1974-1977; Richard Sheppard (assoc) 1977-1981; Gary Glanville (assoc) 1981-1983; Calvin Long (assoc) 1981-1987; O. William Cooper Jr. 1985-1989; Steven Miller (assoc) 1987-1990; John Hinkle 1989-1994; Timothy Hastings (assoc) 1990-1994; Lawrence C. Brooks 1994-1997; Mark A. Karls 1997-2014; Scott P. Lindenberg 2014-2016; Douglas E. Mater 2016-2019; David A. Wichert 2019-

Saginaw: First UMC *[Central Bay]* firstumsag@aol.com
(P/M) 4790 Gratiot Rd, Saginaw 48638 (989) 799-0131
Norbert W. Smith 1967-1972; Lois Glenn (assoc) 1966-1970; A. Edward Perkins (assoc) 1970-1972; Robert L. S. Brown 1972-1977; Carol J. Johns (assoc) 1972-1978; Paul T. Hart 1977-1980; Gary W. Bell (assoc) 1978-1980; Frank B. Cowick 1980-1990; Tim Hastings (assoc) 1980-1983; Gary Dawes (assoc) 1983-1987; Steven E. Poole (assoc) 1988-1990; Karen Knight Ott (assoc) 1990-1993; James F. Thomas 1990-Aug 31, 1994; M. Clement Parr Sep 1, 1994-Dec 26, 1995; Walter David (interim) Jan 1, 1996-Jun 14, 1996; Haldon D. Ferris (co-pastor) Jun 16, 1996-2002; Kathryn S. Snedeker (co-pastor) Jun 16, 1996-2002; Kathryn S. Snedeker 2002-2016; Amylee B. Terhune 2016-

Saginaw: New Heart UMC (formerly Saginaw: West Michigan Ave) *[Central Bay]*
wmaumc@yahoo.com
(P/M) 1802 W Michigan Ave, Saginaw 48602 (989) 792-4689
Clare M. Tosch 1968-1973; A. Claire Wolfe 1973-1975; Donald W. Pinner 1975-1978; Georg Gerritsen 1978-1980; Troy Lemmons 1980-1983; Richard Turner 1983-1987; Richard Turner 1987-1991; David C. Collins 1991-1997; Duane G. Thon 1997-2007; Micheal P. Kelley 2007-2009; George A. Dorado 2009-2010; Rahim O. Shabazz 2012-2015; Melene Wilsey (DSA) 2015-2017; Melene Wilsey 2017-

Saginaw: Swan Valley UMC *[Central Bay]* svumc_48609@yahoo.com
(P/M) 9265 Geddes Rd, Saginaw 48609 (989) 781-0860
Charles Kolb (org. 1969) 1969-1974; Gordon Nusz 1974-1980, Grant Washburn 1980-1983; Gary Glanville 1983-1987; Calvin Long 1987-1991; W. Peter Crawford 1991-1996; Nancy K. Frank 1996-2000; Robert Harvey (interim) 2000-2001; Robert G. Richards 2001- (Swan Valley (lead church) / LaPorte charge and Hemlock / Nelson charge formed new four point charge July 1, 2019)

Salem Grove UMC *[Heritage]* cmbeau81@aol.com
(P/M) 3320 Notten Rd, Grass Lake 49240 (734) 475-2370
George T. Nevin 1964-1969; George Q. Woomer 1969 (interim); Frederick Atkinson Oct. 1, 1969-Feb. 4, 1971; Harry R. Weeks Mar. 1971-1973; John W. Todd 1973-1974; Richard C. Stoddard 1974-1975; Gerald R. Parker 1975-1978; Ferris S. Woodruff 1978-1979; Ronald A. Brunger 1979-1981; Dale B. Ward 1981-1984; David C. Collins 1984-1985; Donald Woolum 1985-1990; Michael F. Bossingham 1990-Dec. 31, 1991; James E. Paige Jr. Jan. 1, 1992-1998; Carolyn G. Harris (co-pastor) 1998-2003; Daniel W. Harris (co-pastor) 1998-2003; Carolyn G. Harris 2003-2013; Christine Beaudoin 2013-2015; Amy Triebwasser 2015-2017; Mary J. Barrett 2017-

Salem: Indian Mission of the UMC *[Midwest]* revrtwilliamson@gmail.com
(P) 3644 28th St, Hopkins 49328; (M) 103 Mason St SW, Byron Center 49315 (616) 738-9030
Lewis White Eagle Church 1948-1990; Pulpit Supply 1990-1992; David G. Knapp 1992-1995; Timothy J. Miller 1995-1999; John Pesblakal (DSA)1999-Aug. 31, 2001; Calvin Hill Sept. 1, 2001-2003; Wesley S. Rehberg (DSA) 2003-2005; Sandra VandenBrink, Jan. 16, 2005-2013; Sandra VandenBrink, (Ret.) Director, Senior Meals Program 2013- ; Nancy L. Boelens (Ret.) 2013-Dec. 15, 2015; Ronald Todd Williamson (DSA) Jan. 1, 2016-Nov. 30, 2017; Ronald Todd Williamson Dec. 1, 2017-

Saline: First UMC *[Heritage]* office@fumc-salinle.org
(P/M) 1200 N Ann Arbor St, Saline 48176 (734) 429-4730
George Saucier 1967-1969; Ira L. Fett 1969-1976; Daniel J. Wallace 1976-1984; Lloyd E. Christler 1984-Jul. 15, 1992; Eric S. Hammar (interim); Paul G. Donelson (assoc) 1992-1995; Gerald R. Parker Jul. 16, 1992-1994; John Hinkel 1994-1999; James E. Tuttle 1999-2016; Tyson G. Ferguson (assoc) 2002-2004; Laura C. Speiran (deacon) 2007-2014; Thomas H. Zimmerman 2016-

Samaria: Grace UMC *[Heritage]* sachun1128@cs.com
(P) 1463 Samaria, Samaria 48177; (M) PO Box 28, Ida 48140-0028 (734) 856-6430
John C. Huhtala 1968-1969; James L. Hynes 1969-1971; Ronald K. Corl 1971-1974; Thomas G. Butcher 1974-1976; Willilam Michael Clemmer 1976-1980; J. Robert Anderson 1980-1984; Raymond J. Townsend 1984-1988; Patricia A. VanWormer 1988-1991; Doris Crocker 1991-1998; Ruth A. McCully 1998-2001; Wayne A. Hawley 2001-2007; Sang Yoon (Abraham) Chun 2007-2016; Corey M. Simon 2016-2019; Robert J. Freysinger 2019-

Sand Lake UMC *[Midwest]* seumc@charter.net
(P) 65 W Maple St, Sand Lake 49343; (M) PO Box 97, Sand Lake 49343 (616) 636-5673
Jerry L. Hippensteel 1977-1981; Richard Strait 1981-1984; Richard Fairbrother 1984-1989; Mary Curtis 1989-91; Richard Sneed 1991-1992; Richard A. Selleck 1992-1996; Howard H. Harvey 1996-1999; Nathan D. Junius 1999-Feb. 1, 2002; Lloyd R. Hansen Feb. 1, 2002-June 30, 2002; Donald Turkelson (DSA)(part-time) 2002 - Nov. 30, 2007; Darryl Miller (DSA) (1/2 time) Jan. 1, 2007; Darryl Miller (part-time) Dec. 1, 2007-

Sandusky: First UMC *[East Winds]* sfumc@avci.net
(P/M) 68 Lexington St, Sandusky 48471 (810) 648-2606
Horace James 1966-1971; Clifford M. De Vore 1971-1975; Frederick O. Timm 1975-1987; Margery A. Schleicher 1987-1991; Michael O. Pringle 1991-1997; Donald D. Gotham 1997-Aug 31, 2004; Georg F. W. Gerritsen (interim) Sep 1-15, 2004; John N. Grenfell, Jr. (interim) Sep 16, 2004-Jan 1, 2005; Marvin H. McCallum (interim) Jan 1, 2005-Feb 28, 2005; John N. Grenfell, Jr. (interim) Mar 1, 2005-May 31, 2005; Colin P. Stover Jun 1, 2005-Jan 1, 2011; Ellen Burns Jan 1, 2011-2012- Eric L. Johnson 2012-2013; Matthew Osborne 2013-2018; Susan E. Platt 2018-

Sanford UMC *[Central Bay]* sanumc@tds.net
(P/M) 2560 N West River Rd, Sanford 48657 (989) 687-5353
James C. Braid 1969-1983; Clare M. Tosch 1983-1985; Haldon D. Ferris 1985-1988; James A. Smith 1988-1993; Bruce C. Hatch 1993-1999; J. Robert Anderson 1999-Oct 15, 2002; Ronald G. Cook Oct 16, 2002-Jun 30, 2003 (interm); Janet Larner 2003-2011; Anthony Cutting 2011-2014; Lisa Cook 2014-

Saugatuck UMC *[Greater Southwest]* saugatuckmc@i2k.com
(P) 250 Mason St, Saugatuck 49453; (M) PO Box 647, Saugatuck 49453 (269) 857-2295
C. Dow Chamberlain 1967-1969; Harold Arman 1969-1971; Arthur Beadle 1971-1973; Douglas L. Pedersen Oct. 1973-Aug. 1975; Richard W. McClain Aug. 1975-1979; Craig L. Adams 1979-1984; Constance L. Heffelfinger 1984-1996; Fred & Joan Hamlin (DSA) 1996-1998; Karen A. Tompkins 1998-2001; Jean Smith (DSA) 2001; Jean Smith Dec. 1, 2001-2005; Letisha Bowman (DSA) 2005-2007; Letisha Bowman (part-time) 2007-2011; John Huenink July 1-Aug. 31, 2011; Emmett H. Kadwell, Jr. (Ret.) (1/4 time) Sept. 1, 2011-

Sault Ste. Marie: Central UMC *[Nothern Skies]*   centralumc632@sbcvglobal.net
(P/M) 111 E Spruce St, Sault Sainte Marie 49783   (906) 632-8672
     Robert L. Brown 1967-1972; Theodore E. Doane 1972-1980; John Huhtala, Sr. 1980-1992; David
M. Liscomb 1992-1993; George A. Luciani 1993-1998; James H. McLaurin 1998-Feb 1, 2001;
John N. Hamilton Jun 16, 2001-2004; Steven A. Miller 2004-Nov 15, 2011; John Huhtala, Sr.,
(interim) Jan 9, 2011-2011; William R. Seitz 2011-2014; Larry D. Osweiler 2014-2018; Victoria L.
Hadaway 2018-

Schoolcraft UMC *[Greater Southwest]*   office@schoolcraftumc.com
(P) 342 N Grand Ave, Schoolcraft 49087; (M) PO Box 336, Schoolcraft 49087-0336
     (269) 679-4845
     Robert J. Stillson 1963-1969; Vern Michael 1969-1970; Roger Nielson 1970-1971; Lay Speakers
1971-1972; Dale Benton 1972-1978; John W. Fisher 1978-1980; Dale Crawford 1980-1983; Dwight
J. Burton 1983-1992; Laura C. Truby 1992-1998; Marilyn M. Sanders 1998-Jan. 16, 2000; Pete
Love (DSA) 2000-; David Nellist 2000-2008; Seung Ho "Andy" Baek 2008-2010; Karen S. Wheat
2010-2015; [Schoolcraft/Pleasant Valley became a charge 2015] Julia R. Humenik 2015-

Scottdale UMC *[Greater Southwest]*   schneider4276@comcast.net
(P) 4271 Scottdale Rd, St Joseph 49085; (M) 4276 Scottdale Rd, St Joseph 49085   (269) 429-7270
     David Litchfield 1966-1969; David Lutz 1969-1970; Arthur Turner 1970-1971; Merritt Edner 1971-
1972; Wayne Babcock 1972-1975; Ross Bunce 1975-1977; Linda Stoddard 1977-1983; C. David
Hainer 1983-1984; Elizabeth Perry Nord 1984-Oct. 1986; Mark Thompson Jan. 1987-Nov. 15,
1992; Norman C. Kohns Nov. 16, 1992-1993; Jackie Bralick 1993-Feb. 1, 1995; Pulpit Supply
Feb.-May 1995; Terrill M. Schneider June 1, 1995-Oct. 1, 2018; Dawn Marie Oldenburg (DSA)
Oct. 1, 2019- [Hinchman / Scottdale beacme two-point charge 10-1-2018]

Scotts UMC *[Greater Southwest]*   cxssumc@ctsmail.net
(P) 8458 Wallene, Scotts 49088; (M) PO Box 112, Scotts, 49088-0112   (269) 626-9757
     Garth Smith 1965-1971; Pulpit Supply July-Nov. 1971; Wilbur Williams Nov. 1971-Aug. 1973; Paul
Mazur Sept. 1973-1978; Pulpit Supply July-Dec. 1978; Donald Robinson Dec. 1978-Aug. 1979;
James Allred Sept. 1979-Dec. 1986; Pulpit Supply Jan.-Apr. 1987; Dennis Slattery Apr. 1987-Oct.
1988; Pulpit Supply Oct.-Dec. 1988; Thomas E. Ball Dec. 1988-1994; David F. Hills 1994-Aug. 1,
1999; Sally J. LaFrance Oct. 1, 1999-2001; Thomas L. Truby 2001-March 1, 2003; David G. Knapp
2003-2009; Glenn C. Litchfield 2009-2016; Beverley J. Williams 2016-

Scottville UMC *[Northern Waters]*   secretary@thesumc.com
(P/M) 114 W State St, Scottville 49454   (231) 757-3567
     Bernard Fetty 1964-Jan. 1970; J. William Schoettle Feb. 1970-1975; Harold Taber 1975-Jan. 1976;
Lloyd R. Hansen Feb. 1976-Oct. 1980; William Mathae Nov. 1980-Dec. 1983; D. Hubert Lowes
Jan. 1984-1993; Merritt F. Bongard 1993-Aug. 16, 1995; Pulpit Supply Aug. 1995-Jan. 1996;
Bobbie Dale Whitlock Jan. 1996-2004; Robert Ellery Jones 2004-2009; John J. Conklin 2009-
2017; Richard Hodgeson 2017-

Sears UMC *[Northern Waters]*   brookscornersparish@gmail.com
(P) 4897 Pratt St, Sears 49679; (M) PO Box 425, Evart 49631-0425   (231) 734-2733
     Dan Reedy 1968-1969; Carter Miller 1969-March 1971; Lynn Wagner March 1971-Oct. 1973;
Eugene Baughn Oct. 1973-March 1974; Daryl Cook 1974-1977; Kenneth Kline 1977-1986; Carl
Litchfield 1986-1991; Eugene L. Baughan 1991-1997; Brian R. Bunch 1997-2005; Ronald DeGraw
Aug. 1, 2005-Nov. 6, 2005; James L. Breithaupt Mar. 15, 2006-Oct. 19, 2009; Joseph L. Beavan
Jan. 15, 2010-2014; Bryan K. Kilpatrick 2014-2017; Melodye Surgeon (Rider) VanOudheusden
2017-2019; [Evart / Sears became a two-point charge 2017] Jean M. Smith 2019-

Sebewaing: Trinity UMC *[Central Bay]* tumc.sebewaing@gmail.com
(P/M) 513 Washington St, Sebewaing 48759 (989) 883-3350
Conrad Lee Higdon 1968- Dec. 1969; Robert Worgess 1970-1976; Elizabeth D.K. Isaacs 1976-1980; Donald O. Crumm Jan. 1981-1985; Lawrence C. Brooks 1985-1994; Michael K. Norton 1994-1997; Richard F. Kriesch 1997-2000; Ray T. McGee Aug 15, 2000-2004; Arthur R. Stone 2004-2006; William R. Wright 2006-2012; Daniel P. Snyder 2012-2014; Cynthia M. Parson 2014-2018; Pamela A. Beedle-Gee 2018-

Seymour Lake UMC *[East Winds]* office@seymourlakeumc.org
(P) 3050 S Sashabaw Rd, Oxford 48371; (M) 3100 S Sashabaw Rd, Oxford 48371 (248) 572-4200
W. Howard Nichols 1969-1975; Lorenz Stahl 1975-1979; Kenneth L. Christler 1979-Jan. 1983; J. Douglas Paterson 1983-Sept. 15, 1986; Heidi C. Reinker Sept. 15, 1986-1988; Karen L. Knight Apr. 15, 1989-1990; R. Wayne Hutson 1990-1991; Erik J. Alsgaard Oct. 1, 1991-Dec 31, 1994; John Martin Mar 1, 1995-Aug 4, 1998; Duane E. Miller Jan 1, 1999-Jun 30, 1999; Deborah A. Line 1999-2009; LuAnn Lee Rourke 2009-2014; Danny Bledsoe (assoc.) Jan 9, 2014-2015; Janine Plum 2015-

Shabbona UMC *[East Winds]* dcbarber229@att.net
(P/M) 4455 Decker Rd, Decker 48426 (989) 872-8094
Stephen Chapko 1968-1972; Carl Shamblen 1972-1973; Carl Silvernail (interim); William J. Burgess (interim); Wayne A. Rhodes 1974-1976; John E. Tatgenhorst 1976-1981; Hayden K. Carruth 1981-1982; James L. Rule 1982-1986; Wallace Peter Crawford 1986-1991; Jan L. Beaderstadt 1991-1993; James A. Rencontre 1993-1997; Jean B. Rencontre 1993-2000; Ellen Burns 2000-2010; John Heim (assoc) 2000-2001; Frederick J. McDowell (assoc) 2001-2003; Pamela K. Barnett 2010-2014; James Palaszecki 2014-2016; Dale Barber 2016-Mar 30, 2019; [Seperated as a two-point charge from Minden City 2019] Nancy J. Bitterling 2019-

Shaftsburg UMC *[Mid-Michigan]* pastornancy@live.com
(P) 12821 Warner Rd, Shaftsburg 48882; (M) PO Box 161, Shaftsburg 48882-0161 (517) 675-1567
Karl Patow 1962-1969; Ivan Niswender 1969-1971; David Draggoo 1971-1981; Jeff Siker-Geisler 1981-1983; Harris Hoekwater 1983-Jan. 1992; Clinton McKinven-Copus Feb. 1992-Dec. 31, 1994; Pulpit Supply Jan. 1-April 15, 1995; Carroll A. Fowler April 16, 1995-2003; Carolyn C. Floyd 2003-2008; Raymond R. Sundell 2008-2012; Nancy G. Powers 2012-

Shelby UMC *[Midwest]* shelbyumc@gmail.com
(P/M) 68 E 3rd St, Shelby 49455 (231) 861-2020
Ronald Houk Jan. 1966-Oct. 1971; James Fox Nov. 1971-Aug. 1977; Robert Carson Sept. 1977-1981; Daniel Minor 1981-1989; Ray Flessner 1989-1991; Keith Bovee 1991-1994; James E. Hodge 1994-2001; Lewis A. Buchner 2001-Feb. 1, 2002; Peggy A. Boltz 2002-2010; Terri Cummins 2010-2016 [Shelby became a two-point charge Shelby/Claybanks 2014]; Kenneth D. Vanderlaan (DSA) 2016-2017 [Mears and Shelby became a multi-station circuit 2016]; Anne W. Riegler 2017-

Shelbyville UMC *[Greater Southwest]* martinumc@sbcglobal.net
(P) 938 124th Ave, Shelbyville 49344; (M) PO Box 154, Martin 49070-0154 (269) 672-7097
Paul Scheibner 1965-1970; Thurlan Meridith 1970-1976; Gerald L. Welsh 1976-1984; Lee F. Zachman 1984-April 15, 1994; William C. Bills 1994-2007; Christopher L. Lane 2007-2009; David A. Selleck 2009-2012; Donald J. Graham 2012-2014; Sean K. Kidd 2014-2019; Corey M. Simon 2019-

Shepardsville UMC *[Mid-Michigan]* pastorjudy777@gmail.com
(P/M) 6990 Winfield Rd, Ovid 48866 (989) 834-5104
Leroy Howe 1968-1969; Karl Ziegler 1969-1970; Roger Wittrup 1970-1971; Darold Boyd 1971-1978; Rodney Kalajainen 1979-1981; Bruce Kintigh 1981-1988; Charles Smith 1988-1996; D. Kay Pratt 1996-2004; Rob McPherson (Administrative Pastor) 2005; Gordon Schleicher (Administrative Pastor) 2006; Cheryll Warren (DSA) 2007; Cheryll Warren Nov. 10, 2007-June 30, 2009; Judy A. Hazle (DSA) Aug. 1, 2009-

Shepherd UMC *[Central Bay]* office@shepherdumcmi.org
(P) 107 W Wright Ave, Shepherd 48883; (M) PO Box 309, Shepherd 48883 (989) 828-5866
G. Albert Rill 1971-1976; Joseph Dudley 1976-Aug. 1979; Michael L. Selleck Aug. 1979-1986; Leonard B. Haynes 1986-1992; Donald E. Spachman 1992-2004; Wayne Allen Price 2004-2007; Kathleen S. Kursch 2007- 2017 [Shepherd / Blanchard-Pine River became 2-point charge 2017] Janet M. Larner 2017- [Blanchard-Pine River / Shepherd became a single-point charges 01/01/2019]

Sidnaw UMC *[Nothern Skies]* lumc@up.net
(P) 6071 W Milltown Rd, Sidnaw 49961; (M) 304 N Main St, Lanse 49946
Zina B. Bennett, Jr. 1966-1971; William Kelsey 1970; Howard E Shaffer 1971-1981; John R. Henry 1981-1986; Gregory Rowe 1986-1990; James M. Mathews 1990-1993; David P. Snyder 1993-Oct 1, 2003; John R. Henry 2004-2011; Stephen E. Rhoades 2011-2019; Nathan T. Reed 2019-

Silver Creek UMC *[Greater Southwest]* silvercreekumc@gmail.com
(P/M) 31994 Middle Crossing Rd, Dowagiac 49047 (269) 782-7061
Meredith Rupe 1968-Nov. 1970; Gary Gamble Nov. 1970-May 1973; Supply pastor June-Oct. 1973; Lynn Wagner Oct. 1973-1975; Daniel Barker 1975-Sept. 1978; Gregory Wolfe Oct. 1978-Nov. 1983; Donald Buege Jan. 1984-1990; Dennis Slattery 1990-1992; David L. Litchfield 1992-1988; Virginia L. Heller 1998-2004; Mark E. Thompson 2004-2009; Julie A. Greyerbiehl 2009-2011; Heather McDougall 2011-2013; Beth A. Reum 2013-Jan. 15, 2016 [Silver Creek became single-point charge 2015]; Sara Louise Carlson Feb. 2, 2016-

Silverwood UMC *[East Winds]* ronhutchinson50@aol.com
(P) 2750 Clifford Rd, Silverwood 48760; (M) PO Box 556, Mayville 48744 (989) 761-7599
Donald L. Lichtenfelt 1968-1970; Ralph T. Barteld 1970-1979; Dale E. Brown 1979-1984; Allen J. Lewis Inter.; Wayne C. Ferrigan 1984-1986; William J. Maynard 1986-1992; Bonny J. Lancaster 1992-1998; Ronald G. Hutchinson 1998-Apr 15, 2009-

Sitka UMC *[Midwest]* francis1491@aol.com
(P/M) 9606 Dickinson Rd, Holton 49425 (231) 744-1767
Kenneth D. McCaw 1967-1968; Austin W. Regier 1969; Ira J. Noordhof 1971-1975; Donald J. Vuurens, Oct. 15, 1975-Dec. 31, 1977; Wayne Speese (Pulpit Supply) Jan. 1, 1978-June 1978; Charles R. VanLente 1978-1983; Steven D. Pearson 1983-1988; Kathryn B. Robotham 1988-1990; Michael A. Van Horn 1990-1991; Leonard Coon 1991-Nov. 1, 1999; Milton Stahl (interim) Nov. 1, 1999-July 1, 2000; Patrick Cameron 2000-Nov. 30, 2001; James Meines December 1, 2001-2005; Brian M. McLellan (DSA) 2005-Feb. 15, 2006; James Meines (DSA) Apr. 15, 2006-Oct. 31, 2006; Nancy L. (Besemer) Boelens Nov. 1, 2006-2008; Paul Lynn (part-time) 2008-Nov. 15, 2009; Gerald F. Hagans (DSA) (1/4 time) Nov. 15, 2009-2019; TBS

Snover: Heritage UMC *[East Winds]* heritageumchurch@gmail.com
(P) 3329 W Snover Rd, Snover 48472; (M) PO Box 38, Snover 48472 (810) 672-9101
Michael K. Norton 1990-1994; Jeffery L. Jaggers 1994-1998; Mary G. Laub 1998-2001; David L. Fleming 2001-2003; David O. Pratt 2003-2013; Donald R. Derby 2013-2018; Penelope R. Nunn 2018-

Sodus: Chapel Hill UMC *[Greater Southwest]* chumcsodus@comcast.net
(P/M) 4071 Naomi Rd, Sodus 49126 (269) 927-3454
Myron Kent Williams 1960-1969; B. James Varner 1969-1973; Leonard Putnam 1973-1975; George Fleming 1975-1987; William V. Payne 1987-1996; Richard D. Wilson 1996-2003; David A. Cheyne 2003-2005; James A. Dibbet 2005-2011; Russell K. Logston 2011-2014; Mark E. Mitchell 2014-2018; Brenda E. Gordon 2018-

Somerset Center UMC *[Heritage]*   somersetcentermethodist@frontiernet.net
(P) 12095 E. Chicago Rd, Somerset Center 49282; (M) PO Box 277, Somerset Center 49282
(517) 688-4330
Richard Stoddard 1968-1974; David Showers 1974-1976; Martin Fox 1976-1979; Gerald Selleck 1979-1982; Mark Kelly 1982-1983; Dr. Campbell 1983-1984; Jim Hodge 1984-1989; Lawrence P. Brown 1989-1996; Michael E. Long 1996-1998; James W. Barney 1998-2005; Geraldine M. Litchfield 2005-2007; Denise J. Downs 2007-2008; Maurice Walworth Jr. (DSA) 2008-2009; [Hillside/Somerset Center two-point charge 2009] E. Jeanne Koughns 2009-2014; Patricia A. Pebley 2014-

South Boardman UMC *[Northern Waters]*   jack49668@gmail.com
(P) 5488 Dagle St SW, S Boardman 49680; (M) PO Box 112, S Boardman 49680   (231) 879-6055
Gerald L. Hedlund 1966-1971; Arthur and Molly Turner (co-pastors) 1971-1976; Diane Vale 1976-Oct. 1977; Marion Nye Dec. 1977-1978; Pulpit Supply 1978-1979; Athel Lynch 1979-1981; Pulpit Supply 1981-1983; Daniel Biteman, Jr. 1983-1985; Clinton McKinven-Copus 1985-1987; Gary Wales 1987-1994; Howard Seaver 1994-2012; Mark E. Mitchell 2012-2014; Donald L. Buege 2014-2017; [Williamsburg and (Fife Lake Boardman Parish) Fife Lake / East Boardman / South Boardman became multi-point charge 2017] John J. Conklin 2017- [2018 Williamsburg, Fife Lake, East Boardman, South Boardman formed the Unified Parish]

South Ensley UMC *[Midwest]*   seumc@charter.net
(P) 13600 Cypress Ave, Sand Lake 49343; (M) PO Box 97, Sand Lake 49343   (616) 636-5659
Jerry L. Hippensteel 1977-1981; Richard Strait 1981-1984; Richard Fairbrother 1984-1989; Mary Curtis 1989-91; Richard Sneed 1991-1992; Richard A. Selleck 1992-1996; Howard H. Harvey 1996-1999; Nathan D. Junius 1999-Feb. 1, 2002; Lloyd R. Hansen Feb. 1, 2002-June 30, 2002; Donald Turkelson (DSA)(part-time) 2002-Nov. 30, 2007; Darryl Miller (DSA) (1/2 time) Jan. 1, 2007; Darryl L. Miller (part-time) Dec. 1, 2007-

South Haven: First UMC *[Greater Southwest]*   southhavenmethodist@gmail.com
(P/M) 429 Michigan Ave, South Haven 49090   (269) 637-2502
William Torrey 1968-1974; Richard Youells 1974-Aug. 15, 1979; Larry Irvine Sept. 16, 1979-1984; C. William Martin 1984-1989; Edward Slate 1989-1995; Billie R. Dalton 1995-2004; John W. Fisher 2004-2013; Devon R. Herrell 2013-2014; Virginia L. Heller 2014-2018; Ronald D. VanLente 2018-

South Lyon: First UMC *[Heritage]*   slfumc@sbcglobal.net
(P/M) 640 S Lafayette St, South Lyon 48178   (248) 437-0760
Roger W. Merrell 1966-1970; Donald D. McLellan 1970-1975; Milton H. Bank 1975-1977; Douglas K. Mercer 1977-1988; J. Gordon Schleicher (assoc) 1985-1987; Ralph A. Edwards (assoc) 1987-1991; Alan R. George 1988-1995; Nina C. Weaver (assoc) Sep. 1, 1992-1995; Pauline S. Hart (co-pastor) 1995-2002; Thomas E. Hart (co-pastor) 1995-Aug 31, 2002; Carman J. Minarik (co-pastor) Sep 1, 2002-2007; Donna J. Minarik (co-pastor) Sep 1, 2002-Sep 15, 2006; Sondra B. Willobee 2007-2017; Kenny Walkup (assoc) Nov 23, 2016- ; Mary G. McInnes 2017-

South Monterey UMC *[Greater Southwest]*   crowemitzi@yahoo.com
(P) Corner of 26th St & 127th Ave, Hopkins 49328; (M) PO Box 356, Hopkins 49328
(269) 793-7323
Glenn Britton 1968-Jan. 1970; Stanley Finkbeiner Feb. 1970-1974; Densel Fuller 1974-1976; Brent Phillips 1976-1978; David Knapp 1978-Oct. 15, 1982; Robert J. Stillson Nov. 1982-1989; Robert D. Nystrom 1989-1992; Marjory A. Berkompas 1992-June 13, 1996; David S. Yoh (DSA) 1996-1999; Raymond D. Field 1999-2001; Reva H. Daniel 2001-2005; Linda J. Burton 2005-2014; Dominic A. Tommy 2014-2017; Joel T. Fitzgerald 2017-2018; Andrew R. Phillips 2018-

South Mundy UMC *[East Winds]* smhumc01@gmail.com
(P) 10018 Linden Rd, Grand Blanc 48439; (M) 10006 Halsey Rd, Grand Blanc 48439
(810) 655-4184
T. Thornley Eddy 1962-1978; Ralph C. Pratt 1978-1979; Stephen K. Perrine 1979-1980; David P. Rahn 1980-1987; Martha H. Cargo 1987-1992; Chong Youb Won 1992-1995; Robin G. Gilshire 1995-Jul 31, 2000; David E. Ray Aug 1, 2000-2006; Harold V. Phillips 2006-2016; Tara R. Sutton 2016-

South Rockwood UMC *[Heritage]* sperrine@sbcglobal.net
(P) 6311 S Huron Rvr Dr, S Rockwood 48179; (M) 23435 Oak Glen Dr, Southfield 48033
(734) 379-3131
Zina B. Bennett, Jr. 1975-1983; Robert C. Strobridge 1983-1988; Dana R. Strall 1988-Jul 31, 1997; Philip D. Voss Aug 31, 1997-2002; Elizabeth A. Librande 2002-Aug 14, 2006; Stephen K. Perrine Aug 15, 2006-

Southfield: Hope UMC *[Greater Detroit]* kevinsmalls@aol.com
(P/M) 26275 Northwestern Hwy, Southfield 48076 (248) 356-1020
G. Charles Sonquist 1970-1980; Terry W. Allen 1980-1983; Carlyle F. Stewart, III 1983-2014; Hilda L. Harris (assoc.) 1995-1997; Lamarr V. Gibson (assoc) 1997-May 30, 2000; Vivian C. Bryant (assoc) 1997-2003; Theodore D. Whitely (assoc) 1998-2000; Betty Whitely (assoc) 1998-2000; Troy M. Benton (assoc) 2000-2003; Faith Green (assoc) 2000-Sep 1, 2002; Anthony R. Hood (assoc) Oct 1, 1999-2002; Gary A. Williams (assoc) 2000-2004; Kenny J. Waldon (assoc) 2003-2005; Janet Gaston Petty (assoc) 2004-2012; Cornelius Davis, Jr. 2014-Sep 22, 2015; Benjamin K. Smalls 2016- ; Christopher Michael Grimes (assoc) 2017- ; Rosaline D. Green (Ret. 2019) Dec 1, 2017- ; Dale R. Milford (assoc) 2019- ; Reggie Allen White (assoc) 2019-

Sparta UMC *[Midwest]* spartaumc@spartaumc.com
(P/M) 54 E Division St, Sparta 49345 (616) 887-8255
Paul Patterson 1968-1973; Eldon K. Eldred 1973-April 1979; Ronald Entenman 1979-1985; James R. Hulett 1985-1993; Steven R. Young 1993-2006; Raymond J. Townsend 2006-2009; Louis W. Grettenberger 2009-2017; Phillip J. Friedrick 2017-

Spratt UMC *[Nothern Waters]* pastorlisakelley@outlook.com
(P) 7440 M 65 S, Lachine 49753; (M) PO Box 323, Lachine 49753 (989) 742-4372
Howard E. Shaffer 1964-1971; Philip A. Rice 1971-1975; Robert Kersten 1975-1978; Harold F. Blakely 1978-1981; James R. Rupert 1981-1984; R. Wayne Hutson 1984-1990; Paula Timm 1990-1992; Jack E. Johnston 1992-Oct 30, 2005; George Morse (interm) Nov 1, 2005-Jun 30, 2006; Karen A. Mars 2006-2008; Donald R. Derby 2008-2013; Lisa Kelley 2013-

Springport UMC *[Heritage]*
(P) 127 W Main St, Springport 49284 (517) 857-2777
Lynn Chapel 1965-March 1971; Beulah Poe March 1971-1976; Robert Doner 1976-1978; Joel Campbell 1978-1979; Ethel Stears 1979-Sept. 16, 1983; William Doubblestein Oct. 16, 1983-1987; Eugene Baughan 1987-1991; David H. Minger 1991-1995; Wayne Willer 1995-1996; Valerie Hill 1996-1998; David L. Litchfield 1998-2001; David Blair 2001-2003; Diane E. Stone 2004-2010; Melissa Claxton 2010-2018; [North Parma / Springport became two-point charge 7-1-10] Mark E. Mitchell 2018-

Springville UMC *[Heritage]* sumchurch@springvilleumc.us
(P/M) 10341 Springville Hwy, Onsted 49265 (517) 467-4471
Ford Baker 1968-1969; Harold R. Krieg 1969-1971; Edward C. Weiss Jr. 1972-1973; Juanita J. Ferguson 1973-1978; Donald W. Brown 1978-1980; Richard L. Dake 1980-1985; William P. McKnight 1985-1991; Gordon B. Boyd 1991-Nov. 30, 1992; James G. Simmons (interim); C. Earl Eden Jr. Mar. 1, 1993-1999; Victoria M. Webster 1999-May 19, 2000; Melany A. Chalker 2000-2006; Margery H. Host 2006-2010; Ronald A. Fike 2010-2014; Julius Nagy 2014-2018; Evans C. Bentley (Ret.) 2018-

St. Charles UMC *[Central Bay]* stcharlesumc@att.net
(P) 301 W Belle Ave, Saint Charles 48655; (M) PO BOX 87, Saint Charles 48655 (989) 865-9091
George Jones 1966-1971; John Crotser 1971-1979; William Omansiek 1979-1985; Edward C.
Weiss Jr. 1985-Aug 31 1, 1994; Charles W. Keyworth Sep 1, 1994-1999; Kevin J. Harbin 1999-
2002; Harold J. Slater 2002-2008; Ernesto Mariona 2008-Sept 30, 2017; Karen J. Sorden Dec 1,
2017-

St. Clair: First UMC *[East Winds]* scfumc@sbcglobal.net
(P/M) 415 N 3rd St, Saint Clair 48079 (810) 329-7186
Merton W. Seymour 1968-1975; Douglas R. Trebilcock 1975-1985; John E. Naile 1985-1998; W.
Thomas Schomaker 1998-Jul 31, 2004; Marvin H. McCallum (interim) Aug 1-31, 2004; Donald D.
Gotham Sep 1, 2004-2011; Margie R. Crawford 2011-2018; John Nicholas Grenfell III 2018-

St. Ignace UMC *[Nothern Skies]* umethstig@att.net
(P) 615 W US Highway 2, St Ignace 49781; (M) PO Box 155, St Ignace 49781 (906) 643-8088
Howard R. Higgins 1968-1973; Dale Lantz 1973-1977; John E. Naile 1977-1985; David A. Russell
1985-1987; Robert C. Watt 1987-Jun 30, 1994; John Elliott Jul 1, 1994-Apr 15, 2002; James R.
Balfour II 2002-2010; Erik J. Alsgaard 2010-2013; Susanne E. Hierholzer 2013-2019; Eric M.
Falker 2019-

St Johns: Pilgrim UMC *[Mid-Michigan]* office@pilgrimumchurch.com
(P/M) 2965 W Parks Rd, Saint Johns 48879 (989) 224-6865
Eugene Friesen 1966-1970; Brian K. Sheen 1970-1983; Larry R. Shrout 1983-1998; Raymond
R. Sundell1998-2003; Merlin H. Pratt 2003-2006; D. Kay Pratt (Assoc.) 2004-2006; Price UMC
merged with St Johns Pilgrim 2005; Kenneth J. Bremer 2006-2014; Andrew L. Croel 2014-

St Joseph: First UMC *[Greater Southwest]* office@sjfirstumc.org
(P/M) 2950 Lakeview Ave, St Joseph 49085 (269) 983-3929
Sidney A. Short Feb. 1968-Jan. 1973; Richard E. Johns (Assoc.) Apr. 1968-Apr. 1969; Gary
Gamble (Assoc.) 1969-1971; Douglas L. Pedersen (Assoc.) 1971-Oct.1973; Dale D. Brown Feb.
1973-Dec. 1982; David A. Selleck (Assoc.) 1974-Mar. 1976; Harold F. Filbrandt Feb. 1983-Mar.
1987; Benton R. Heisler (Assoc.) 1986-Aug. 1988; Ronald A. Houk 1987-1997; Charles K. Stanley
(Assoc.) Oct. 1988-Oct. 1990; Shelley L. Caulder (Assoc.) Dec. 1991-1996; Thomas C. Nikkel
(Assoc.) 1996-2000; Wade S. Panse 1997-Jan. 1, 2012; James W. Kraus, Jr. (Deacon) 2001- ;
Terry Euper (DSA) Jan. 1, 2012; Harris J. Hoekwater 2012-2018; Daniel R. Colthorp (Deacon)
2016-2018; Daniel R. Colthopr 2018-

St Louis: First UMC *[Mid-Michigan]* stlouisfumc@yahoo.com
(P/M) 116 S Franklin St, Saint Louis 48880 (989) 681-3320
Harold L. Mann 1972-March 1982; Gerald R. Bates April 1982-1987; Richard C. Kuhn 1987-1998;
Robert D. Nystrom 1998-2002; Lillian T. French 2002-Dec. 31, 2007; [Pleasant Valley UMC merged
w/ St. Louis UMC 01-01-08] Terri L. Bentley Feb. 1, 2008-

Standish: Beacon of Light UMC (formerly Standish: Community) *[Central Bay]* cumcch@att.net
(P) 201 S Forest St, Standish 48658; (M) PO Box 186, Standish 48658 (989) 846-6277
Albert Johns, 1967-1972; C. William Bollinger 1972-1977; Paul Greer 1977-1979; Byron G. Hatch
1979-1983; Devin S. Chisholm 1983-2011; Donald J. Wojewski 2011-2012; William P. Sanders
2012-2013; James A. Payne 2013- [Sterling UMC merged into Standish: Community UMC
04/01/2019 to become Standish: Beacon of Light]

Stanwood: Northland UMC *[Midwest]* secretary@northlandumc.org
(P) 6842 Northland Dr, Stanwood 49346; (M) PO Box 26, Stanwood 49346 (231) 823 -2300
Nolan Williams 1967-1974; Bernard Randolph 1974-March 1975; Max Gladding March 1975-
1982; Emmett Kadwell 1982-1992; Jack Bartholomew 1992-1995; Edward H. Slate 1995-2006;
Dominic A. Tommy 2006-2014; Gary D. Bondarenko 2014-

Stephenson UMC *[Northern Skies]* sumc111@att.net
(P) S 111 Railroad St, Stephenson 49887; (M) PO Box 205, Stephenson 49887 (906) 753-6363
Calvin Rice 1967-1974; James Paige 1974-1975; John Henry 1975-1981; John Hamilton 1981-1986; David Leenhouts 1986-1992; W. Peter Bartlett 1992-1996; Kenneth C. Dunstone 1996-Dec 15, 1999; Jean M. Larson Jan 1, 2000-Nov 15, 2001; James A. Fegan Dec 1, 2001-May 31, 2002; Cherrie A. Sporleder Jun 16, 2002-2004; James M. Mathews 2004-2019; John P. Murray 2019-

Sterling Heights UMC *[Greater Detroit]* shumc@wowway.com
(P/M) 11333 16 1/2 Mile Rd, Sterling Heights 48312 (586) 268-3130
Walter David 1967-1973; Richard L. Myers 1973-1978; Donald P. Haskell 1978-1985; Michael L. Raymo 1985-1988; Joy A. Barrett 1988-1993; Grant A. Washburn 1993-Aug 1, 1995; Kwang M. Lee Aug 1, 1995-1996; David J. Leenhouts 1996-Sep 19, 1998; Elizabeth A. Macaulay Jun 16, 1999-2008; Robert I. Kreger 2008-2013; Norma Taylor 2013-Mar 1, 2016; Karen Y. Noel 2016-2018; Joel Thomas Fitzgerald 2018-

Stevensville UMC *[Greater Southwest]* office@stevensvilleumc.org
(P/M) 5506 Ridge Rd, Stevensville 49127 (269) 429-5911
Gerald Welsh 1968-Oct. 1969; Lloyd Phillips Oct. 1969-1979; Dean Bailey 1979-1987; Steve Emery (Assoc.) 1981-1987; Geoffrey Hayes 1987-March 23, 1994; Larry Rubingh (Assoc.) 1987-1988; Jeffrey Wright (Assoc.) 1988-1990; Bradley Bartelmay (Assoc.) 1990-1993; Tamara S.M. Williams (Assoc.) 1993-2002; Eugene A. Lewis 1994-2003; Terri L. Bentley (Assoc.) 2002-Feb. 1, 2008; Beryl Gordon Barry 2003-2015; David F. Hills Aug. 1, 2015-

Stockbridge UMC *[Mid-Michigan]* sumcaa@aol.com
(P/M) 219 E Elizabeth St, Stockbridge 49285 (517) 851-7676
William Frayer 1965-1969; Raymond Norton 1969-1971; Dale Spoor 1971-Sept. 1974; Douglas Vernon Oct. 1974-Sept. 1979; David Selleck Oct. 1979-1987; Richard Matson 1987-1990; Birt Beers 1990-1993; Stuart L. Proctor 1993-Sept. 1995; Robert J. Henning 1996-2007; Larry W. Rubingh 2007-Oct. 15, 2010; Galen L. Goodwin (Retired Elder, Greater New Jersey Conf), Interim Pastor, Oct. 24, 2010-July 1, 2011; Robert J. Freysinger 2011-2013; [M-52 Cooperative Ministry 2013-2014] Jeanne M. Laimon (1/4 time) 2013-2014; Susan J. Trowbridge 2014-2019; Stephan Weinberger (Ret.) 2019-

Stokes Chapel UMC *[Heritage]* revfgcain@yahoo.com
(P) 201 Main St, Montgomery 49255; (M) PO Box 155, Camden 49232 (517) 368-5406
Karl L. Zeigler 1968-1969; John H. Gurney 1969-Aug. 1970; Joseph Huston Aug. 1970-1972; Richard Huskey 1972-1974; J. Brian Selleck 1974-Feb. 1976; Robert P. Stover March 1976-1980; Stephen Beech 1980-1983; Larry W. Rubingh 1983-1987; Frederick G. Hamlin 1987-1994; Russell K. Logston 1994-1996; Diane Stone Nov. 16, 1996-2004; Edward Mohr 2004-2010; Trevor McDermont 2010-2013; Frederick G. Cain (Ret.) (part-time) 2013-

Stony Creek UMC *[Heritage]* SCumc8635@gmail.com
(P/M) 8635 Stony Creek Rd, Ypsilanti 48197 (586) 202-1894
Robert N. Hicok 1967-Sep 30, 1970; Roger A. Parker Oct 1, 1970-1976; Dale M. Miller 1976-1981; Douglas K. Olsen 1981-1996; Peter S. Harris 1996-2007; Kenneth B. Ray 2007-2010; Reed P. Swanson 2010-2017; Nathaniel R. Starkey 2017-

Sturgis UMC *[Greater Southwest]* fumcsturgis@gmail.com
(P/M) 200 Pleasant St, Sturgis 49091 (269) 651-5990
Charles B. Hahn 1966-1970; Hilding Kilgren 1970-1977; Miriam DeMint (Assoc.) 1969-1970; David Dunn (Assoc.) 1970-1973; Dennis Paulsen (Assoc.) 1973-1975; Edward Boase (Assoc.) 1975-1977; George Hartmann 1977-1987; Richard Riley (Assoc.) 1977-1980; Mark Graham 1987-1988; Susan Adsmond Fox July-Sept. 1987; Ray W. Burgess 1988-1993; Lowell F. Walsworth 1993-1995; Richard A. Morrison 1995-Jan. 1, 1998; Dianne Morrison (Assoc.) Jan. 1996-Jan. 1, 1998; Keith R. Treman Jan. 15, 1998-2008; Colleen T. Treman (Deacon) 1998-2008; J. Robert Keim (Assoc.) Dec. 16, 1999-Dec. 31, 2011; Deborah M. Johnson 2008-2014; E. Jeanne Koughn 2014-2019; Susan J. Babb 2019- ; Mark R. Babb (deacon) 2019-

Sunfield UMC *[Mid-Michigan]*   sumcoffice@centurytel.net
(P) 227 Logan St, Sunfield 48890; (M) PO Box 25, Sunfield 48890-0025   (517) 566-8448
   Marjorie S. Matthews June-Sept. 1968; Robert Keith Sept. 1968-1971; Ralph G. Kallweit 1971-
   Jan. 1976; John Morse Feb. 1976-1982; J. Chris Schroeder 1982-Jan. 1992; Harris J. Hoekwater
   Jan. 1992-1998; Brian K. Sheen 1998-2004; Jeffrey J. Schrock 2004-2012; Clare W. Huyck 2012-
   2015 [Sunfield/Sebewa Center no longer two-point charge 2013] [Barry-Eaton Cooperative Ministry
   2013] Betty A. Smith (Ret.) 2015-Dec. 31, 2015; Lyle D. Heaton Jan. 1-June 30, 2016; Vaughn W.
   Thurston-Cox 2016-2017; [Gresham and Sunfield became two-point charge 2017] Heather L.
   Nolen (DSA) 2017; Heather L. Nolen (FL) Dec 1, 2017-

Sutton Sunshine UMC *[Central Bay]*   pastorpennyparkin@gmail.com
(P) 2996 Colwood Rd, Caro 48723; (M) 2988 Colwood Rd, Caro 48723   (989) 673-6695
   Wallis E. Braum 1964-1970; Carl Shamblen 1970-1972; Lawrence C. Whiting 1972-1975; Peyton
   E. Loy 1975-1978; Wayne N. Thomas 1978-1982; Janet Larner 1982-1986; Duane M. Harris 1986-
   Nov. 1988; Billy J. McKown 1989-Feb 28, 1995; Donald D. Gotham Oct 1, 1996-1997; Raymond
   A. Jacques 1997-2001; Patrick D. Robbins 2001-2011; Dorothy J. Thon 2011-2017; Penny Parkin
   2017-

Swartz Creek UMC *[East Winds]*   office@umc-sc.org
(P/M) 7400 Miller Rd, Swartz Creek 48473   (810) 635-4555
   Harold A. Nessel 1970-1974; John W. Murbach 1974-Oct., 1983; H. Reginald Cattell Nov. 1, 1983-
   Aug 31, 1994; Emil E. Haering (assoc) 1990-1991; James F. Thomas Sep 1, 1994-2000; John D.
   Landis 2000-2011; LuAnn L. Rourke (assoc.) 2006-2009; Matthew Packer (deacon) May 1,2006-
   2008; Kevin J. Harbin 2011-2015; Gary R. Glanville 2015-

Tawas UMC *[Central Bay]*   tawasumc@sbcglobal.net
(P/M) 20 E M 55, Tawas City 48763   (989) 362-4288
   Kenneth L. Tousley 1968-1982; Ralph D. Churchill 1982-1984; Ronald D. Carter 1984-1990; S.
   Joe Robertson 1990-2001; Robert Richards (assoc) Jan 1, 1994-1997; Lisa L. (Okrie) Cook
   (assoc) 1997-Apr 30, 2000; David E. Huseltine 2001-2004; Reed P. Swanson 2004-2008; Mary
   Ann Gibson 2008-2013; Daniel Gonder 2013-2018; Kris Stewart Kappler 2018-

Tecumseh UMC *[Heritage]*   tumc@tc3net.com
(P/M) 605 Bishop Reed Dr, Tecumseh 49286   (517) 423-2523
   Donald C. Porteous 1962-1973; Allan G. Gray 1973-1983; Gordon E. Ackerman 1983-1988; Stuart
   L. Proctor (assoc) 1984-1986; John H. Bunce 1988-Aug 31, 1994; James Schwandt Sep 1, 1994-
   1999; David R. McKinstry 1999-2010; Mark A. Miller 2010-

Thetford Center UMC *[East Winds]*   geneseethetford@sbcglobal.net
(P) G-11394 North Center Rd, Clio 48420; (M) PO Box 190, Genesee 48437   (810) 640-2280
   Fred E. Wager 1969-1970; John P. Hitchens 1970-1972; Ralph H. Pieper II 1972-1975; Roger L.
   Colby 1975-1980; James P. Schwandt 1980-1987; David P. Rahn 1887; Willard A. King Nov 1,
   1987-Aug 31, 1994; Lorrie E. Plate Sept 1, 1995-1998; Malcom L. Greene 1998- 2003; Bruce L.
   Nowacek 2004-2010; Karen B. Williams 2010-

Thomas UMC *[East Winds]*   thomasumc504@gmail.com
(P) 504 First St, Oxford 48371; (M) PO Box 399, Oxford 48371-0399   (248) 628-7636
   Fred Clark 1954-1972; George F. W. Gerritsen 1972-1978; Dwayne L. Kelsey 1978-Oct. 1981;
   Donald H. Francis 1981-1988; Mary Margaret Eckhardt 1988-2002; Gloria Haynes 2002-2005;
   Thomas K. Spencer 2005-Dec 1, 2006; Donald H. Francis (interim) Dec 1, 2006-Dec 31, 2006;
   Carla Ann Jepson Jan 1, 2007-2016; Mark Huff (DSA) 2016-2017; Carol Ann Middel (DSA) 2017-
   2019; [Oxford / Thomas two-point charge 07/01/2019] Jennifer J. Jue 2019-

Three Oaks UMC *[Greater Southwest]*   toumc@att.net
(P/M) 2 Sycamore St E, Three Oaks 49128   (269) 756-2053
   Larry Waterhouse Apr. 1966-Oct. 1970; Meredith Rupe Nov. 1970-Nov. 1975; Larry Irvine Nov.
   1975-Sept. 1979; Terry MacArthur Sept. 1979-1983; Ross Bunce 1983-1985; Lloyd Walker 1985-
   1988; Steven Pearson 1988-1995; Orin L. Daniels 1995-1998; David A. Cheyne 1998-Jan. 16,
   1999; Sherri L. Swanson Sept. 1, 1999-2017; Susan D. Martin 2017-2018; Brenda Lee Ludwig
   (LTFT ¾) 2018-

Three Rivers: Center Park UMC *[Greater Southwest]*   officemcp@gmail.com
(P/M) 18662 Moorepark Rd, Three Rivers 49093   (269) 279-9109
   Richard Darhing 1969-1970; Douglas Pederson 1970-1971; Luther Brokaw 1971-1975; Logan
   Weaver 1975-1978; Albert O'Rourke Sept. 1978-April 1982; Jesse Schwoebell 1982-1988; Dwight
   Stoner 1988-1989; Jeffrey Williams August 1989-Feb. 1993; Nelson Ray June 1993-1995; John
   L. Moore 1995-1997; Alice Fleming Townley 1997-2001; Stephen C. Small 2001-2004; Patricia L.
   Bromberek 2004-2006; Linda K. Stull-Lipps 2006-2011; Martin Culver (RLA) 2011-2019; [Center
   Park and Three Rivers First became multi station circuit 2017] Derl G. Keefer 2019-

Three Rivers: First UMC *[Greater Southwest]*   trfumc@live.com
(P/M) 215 N Main St, Three Rivers 49093   (269) 278-4722
   Richard H. Beckett 1968-1976; Charles D. Grauer 1976-1981; Raymond McBratnie (Assoc.) 1976-
   1980; James Patrick McCoy (Assoc.) Oct. 1980-1983; Frank B. Closson 1981-April 1985; John
   A. Backoff (Assoc.) 1983-1985; James E. Fox May 1985-1990; Robert L. Pumphery 1990-1997;
   Cynthia A. Skutar 1997-2000; Donald R. Fry 2000-2006; Maria L. Rutland Nov. 1, 2006-2012;
   Robert D. Nystrom (1/2 time) 2012-2015; [Three Rivers First / Mendon became two-point charge
   2013; Three Rivers First / Ninth Street became two-point charge 2015] James W. Stilwell 2015-
   2017; [Center Park and Three Rivers First became multi station circuit 2017] Martin H. Culver
   (RLA) 2017-2018; Derl Keefer 2018-2019; Heather Ann McGougall 2019-

Three Rivers: Ninth Street UMC *[Greater Southwest]*
(P) 700 9th St, Three Rivers 49093; (M) 16621 Morris Ave, Three Rivers 49093   (269) 273-2065
   Eugene Moore 1968-1972; Helen Jackson 1972-Jan. 1974; Albert A. O'Rourke Nov. 1974-1976;
   Charles Grauer 1976-1981; Raymond McBratnie (Assoc.) 1976-Aug. 1980; James Patrick McCoy
   (Assoc.) Oct. 1980-1983; Frank Closson 1981-April 1985; John A. Backoff (Assoc.) 1983-1985;
   Phillip Simmons 1985-1988; Reva Hawke 1988-Oct. 1991; Marilyn B. Barney Oct. 1991-1998;
   Carolyn A. Robinson 1998-2007; Thomas R. Reaume (part-time) 2007-2009; [Three Rivers Ninth
   / Schoolcraft Pleasant Valley became a two-point charge 2009] James W. Stilwell 2009-2017
   [Three Rivers First / Ninth Street became two-point charge 2015; Three Rivers Ninth Street became
   single station 2017]; Edward C. Ross (Ret.) 2017-

Townline UMC *[Greater Southwest]*   townlineumc@gmail.com
(P/M) 41470 24th Ave, Bloomingdale 49026   (269) 521-4559
   John Gurney 1965-1969; Wayne Babcock 1969-1971; Gerald Hudlund 1971-1972; Wayne Barrett
   1972-1974; Pulpit Supply 1974-1976; David Youngs 1976-1978; Lloyd Bronson 1978-1985; Dwight
   Stoner 1985-1988; Donald Williams 1988-1990; William Brady 1990-1991; Kenneth J. Littke 1991-
   1998; D.S. Assignment 1998; Jana Jirak Sept. 16, 1998-1999; Robert L. Pumfery 1999-October
   31, 2002; Patricia Anne Harpole November 1, 2002-2004; O'Ryan Rickard 2004-2005; Sheila F.
   Baker 2005-Jan. 3, 2008; David L. Youngs Jan. 3, 2008 - June 2008; David L. Haase (DSA) (1/4
   time) Jan. 3, 2008; David L. Haase (1/4 time) July 1, 2008-2014; James C. Robertson (1/4 time)
   2014-

Traverse Bay UMC *[Northern Waters]* tbumc@traversebaychurch.org
(P/M) 1200 Ramsdell St, Traverse City 49684 (231) 946-5323
Traverse City Asbury & Emmanuel merged to become Traverse Bay UMC January 2005;
[ASBURY: Dale E. Crawford 1967-Oct. 1971; Wilson Tennant Nov. 1971-May 1976; Richard E.
Cobb 1976-Aug. 1980; Wirth G. Tennant (Assoc.) 1978-Sept. 1983; William A. Hertel Sept. 1980-
1987; John H. Hice 1987-1995; William E. Haggard 1995-2002; Jeremy P.H. Williams 2002- ;]
[Emmanuel: George Belknap 1966-1973; B. James Varner 1973-1977; Kenneth A.O. Lindland
1977-1979; Jack Kraklan 1979-1983; Steven Averill 1983-April 1989; Lewis Buchner 1989-1992;
Robert J. Mayo 1992-1999; David H. Minger 1999-Jan. 31, 2003; Douglas L. Pedersen Feb. 1,
2003- ;] Jeremy P.H. Williams 2002-2009; Douglas L. Pedersen Feb. 1, 2003-2005; Devon R.
Herrell (Assoc.) 2005-2008; Jeanne E. Koughn (Assoc.) 2008-2009; Jane R. Lippert 2009-Sept.
1, 2015; John E. Harnish Sept. 1, 2015-2016; Kathryn Sue Snedeker 2016-

Traverse City: Central UMC *[Northern Waters]* office@tccentralumc.org
(P/M) 222 Cass St, Traverse City 49684 (231) 946-5191
William N. DesAutels 1968-Nov. 1974; Robert C. Brubaker Dec. 1974-1981; Ellen A. Brubaker
(Assoc.) 1975-1981; Joanne Parshall (Assoc.) 1981-Sept. 1982; David L. Crawford 1981-1987;
Gary T. Haller (Assoc.) 1981-1985; Kathy E. Brown (Assoc.) 1985-1990; Dean I. Bailey 1987-
2002; Steven R. Emery-Wright (Assoc.) Aug. 1990-May 1992; Robert D. Nystrom (Assoc.) 1992-
1994; John W. Ellinger 2002-2007; Tamara S.M. Williams (Assoc.) 2002-2009; Dale Ostema 2007-
; Christopher M. Lane (Assoc.) 2009-

Traverse City: Mosaic *[Northern Waters]* jeremy_wicks@yahoo.com
(P/M) 1249 Three Mile Rd S, Traverse City 49696 (231) 946-3048
[New Church Start Jul 1, 2017] Jeremy J. Wicks 2017-

Trenary UMC *[Nothern Skies]* skolder@att.net
(P) N1133 ET Rd, Trenary 49891; (M) PO Box 201, Trenary 49891 (906) 446-3599
Norman Kohns 1969-1973; William Verhelst 1973-1974; Wayne Large 1974-1977; Robert Porter
1977-1979; William Bowers 1979-1983; George Thompson 1983-1985; James Ritchie 1985-1992;
Gail P. Baughman 1993-1994; James M. Downing 1994-1997; Irene R. White Sep 1, 1997-2011;
Sandra J. Kolder 2011-

Trenton: Faith UMC *[Greater Detroit]* trentonfaithumc@sbcglobal.net
(P/M) 2530 Charlton Rd, Trenton 48183 (734) 671-5211
Robert L. Selberg 1969-1978; Edward C. Coley 1978-1984; Richard O. Griffith 1984-1989; James
L. Rhinesmith (assoc) 1984-1988; Marshall G. Dunlap (co-pastor) 1989-1999; Susan K. DeFoe
Dunlap (co-pastor) 1989-1999; Mark E. Spaw 1999-2010; George R. Spencer 2010-2016; Douglas
E. Ralston 2016-2019; Wayne A. Price 2019-

Trenton: First UMC *[Greater Detroit]* trentonfumc@gmail.com
(P/M) 2610 W Jefferson Ave, Trenton 48183 (734) 676-2066
Walter C. B. Saxman 1962-1971; Robert J. Hudgins 1971-1976; Ira L. Fett 1976-1985; Webley J.
Simpkins 1985-1994; Shawn P. Lewis-Lakin 1994-1997; Karen D. Poole 1997-2003; Raymond D.
Wightman 2003-2008; Elizabeth A. Macaulay 2008-Apr 1, 2013; Mary Beth Beebe Apr 15, 2013-
2013; Benjamin Bower 2013-2016; Heidi C. Reinker 2016-

Troy: Big Beaver UMC *[Greater Detroit]* bbumc@bbumchurch.org
(P/M) 3753 John R Rd, Troy 48083 (248) 689-1932
Michael Grajcar Jr. 1969-1976; Terry Euper 1976-1989; Daniel J. Wallace 1989-1991; Edwin
Hingelberg 1991-Feb 26, 1997; H. Emory Hinkston 1997-2002; Jack L. Mannschreck 2002-2013-
David E. Huseltine 2013-2016; Gregory M. Mayberry 2016-

Troy: First UMC *[Greater Detroit]*   troyfirst@sbcglobal.net
(P/M) 6363 Livernois Rd, Troy 48098   (248) 879-6363
    Robert M. Clune 1967-1969; Alfred T. Bamsey 1969-1976; Elwood J. Berkompas 1976-1982; David M. Liscomb 1982-1986; William D. Mercer 1986-1990; Terry Allen 1990-1997; Richard A. Peacock 1997-2008; Harold E. Weemhoff, Jr. 2008-2015; Weatherly Burkhead Verhelst 2015-

Troy: Korean UMC *[Greater Detroit]*   bibisisi@gmail.com
(P/M) 42693 Dequindre Rd, Troy 48085   (248) 879-2240
    Young B. Yoon 1978-Dec 31, 1994; Kwang Min Lee (assoc) Dec. 1989-1991; Paul Lee (assoc) 1992-1994; Dongil Chang (assoc) 1994-1997; Hoon K. Lee Jan 1, 1995-2013; Sang K. Choi (assoc) 1996-Mar 31, 2001; Jin Young Oh (assoc) Jan 1, 1998-Aug 1, 2002; Min Hyuk Woo (assoc) Jun 1, 2001-2011; S. David Ryn (assoc.) Jul 12, 2004-2006; Jung Eun Yum (assoc.) Jan 1, 2006-2011; Youngchoel Woo (assoc) 2008-Jan 15, 2015; David Inho Kim (assoc) 2008-2016; Chan Joung Jang 2013-Jan 31, 2018; In Boem Oh (assoc.) 2013-2016; Se Jin Bae (assoc.) Mar 1, 2015- ; Tae Gyu Shin (assoc) 2016- ; Anna Mi-Hyun Moon (assoc) 2016- ; Jinny L. Song (deacon) 2016- ; Kyunglim Shin Lee Feb 9, 2018- Dec 31, 2018; Eung Yong Kim Jan 1, 2019-

Troy: Korean – Hope Campus UMC *[Greater Detroit]*   troyhopeministry@gmail.com
(P/M) 42693 Dequindre Rd, Troy 48085   (248) 879-2240
    [New Church Start] Anna Mi-Hyun Moon (assoc) 2016-

Turk Lake UMC *[Midwest]*   pastordonnasperry@gmail.com
(P/M) 8900 Colby Rd, Greenville 48838   (616) 754-3718
    George Fleming 1965-1975; Douglas Pedersen 1975-1979; Jim Hartman 1979-1982; Steven Young 1982-1987; Joyce DeToni-Hill 1987-1990; Jane Crabtree 1990-1996; John F. Ritter 1996-Nov. 1, 2001; Ronald W. DeGraw Nov. 1, 2001-2005; Kay Welsch (DSA) July 16, 2005-2012; [Turk Lake / Belding became two-point charge 2012] Kimberly A. DeLong Aug. 15, 2012-2013; [Greenville First, Turk Lake/Belding Cooperative Parish 2013] Kimberly A. DeLong (Deacon) 2013-2015; Stephen MG Charnley 2013-14; Stephen F. Lindeman 2013-14; Donald E. Spachman 2014- ; Eric Mulanda Nduwa (Assoc.) Feb. 15-Aug. 1, 2015 [cooperative parish re-named Flat River Cooperative Parish 2015] ; Joseph K. Caldwell (CLM/DSA) Aug. 1, 2015-2016; Donna Jean Sperry 2016-

Twin Lake UMC *[Midwest]*   jdm14879@gmail.com
(P) 5940 S Main St, Twin Lake 49457; (M) PO Box 352, Twin Lake 49457   (231) 828-4083
    Kenneth D. McCaw 1967-1968; Austin W. Regier 1969; Alma H. Glotfelty 1970; Ira J. Noordhof 1971-1975; Donald J. Vuurens, Oct. 15, 1975-Dec. 31, 1977; Wayne Speese (Pulpit Supply) Jan. 1, 1978-June 1978; Charles R. VanLente 1978-1983; Steven D. Pearson 1983-1988; Kathryn B. Robotham 1988-1990; Michael A. Van Horn 1990-1991; Leonard Coon 1991-Oct. 31, 1999; Milton Stahl (interim) Nov. 1, 1999-July 1, 2000; Patrick Cameron 2000-2002; Sally J. LaFrance 2002-Oct. 1, 2004; Paul R. Doherty (DSA) Nov. 1, 2004-2010; Mary Loring 2010-2013; John D. Morse (Ret.) 2013-2018; William F. Dye

Ubly UMC *[East Winds]*   goja@speednetllc.com
(P) 4496 Pike St, Ubly 49475; (M) PO Box 131, Ubly 49475-9560   (810) 672-9929
    Maynard Q. Kent 1964-1977; Emerson W. Arntz 1977-1982; Carl A. Renter 1982-1987; Earleen A. VanConant 1987-1989; Rothwell McVety 1989-1991; Catherine W. Hiner 1991-1993; Robert A. Srock 1993-2000; Ellen Burns 2000-2010; John Heim (assoc) 2000-2001; Fredrick J. McDowell (assoc) 2001-2001; Pamela K. Barnett 2010-2014; James Palaszeski 2014-2016; Philip L. Tousley 2019- [Bad Axe: First / Minden City / Ubly formed Bad Axe Cooperative Parish 07/01/2019]

Union City UMC *[Greater Southwest]*   unioncityumc@frontier.com
(P) 200 Ellen St, Union City 49094; (M) PO Box 95, Union City 49094-0095   (517) 741-7028
    Philip L. Brown 1966-1971; Walter J. Rothfuss 1971-1973; Larry Grubaugh 1973-1980; Adam Chyrowski 1980-1986; Eric S. Beck 1986-July 31, 1995; David W. Meister Aug. 1, 1995-Aug. 15, 1997; D.S. Assignment Aug. 16, 1997; John L. Moore (DSA) Aug. 17, 1997-2004; Robert M. Hughes 2004-2012; [Union City / Athens became two-point charge 2012] Seung Ho Baek (3/4 time) 2012-2015; Cynthia L. Veilleux 2015-2018; James Palaszeski 2018-

Utica UMC *[Greater Detroit]*   charlotte@uticaumc.org
(P/M) 8650 Canal Rd, Sterling Heights 48314   (586) 731-7667
Samuel F. Stout 1966-1971; Paul S. Durham (assoc) 1969-1971; Robert E. Horton 1971-1977;
Kenneth R. Callis 1977-1989; Richard A. Peacock (assoc) 1973-1978; William R. Donahue (assoc)
1979-1982; John R. Walters (assoc) 1982-1983; Thomas M. Beagan (assoc) 1983-1987; Gary R.
Glanville (assoc) 1987-1989; Christopher D. Cowdin (assoc) 1989-1996; Jeffery D. Regan 1989-
1994; David Diamond 1994-2003; James J. Walker (assoc) 1996-1998; Vincent P. Facione (assoc)
1998- Nov 30, 1999; William R. Donahue, Jr. 2003-2011; David J. Goudie (assoc) 2004-2009;
Weatherly Burkhead Verhelst (assoc) 2009-2015; Donald D. Gotham 2011-

Vassar: First UMC *[Central Bay]*   vassarfumc@sbcglobal.net
(P) 139 N Main St, Vassar 48768; (M) PO Box 71, Vassar 48768-0071   (989) 823-8811
Robert Bough 1968-1972; Clare Patton 1972-1983; Alan DeGraw 1983-1991; Charles Knight
1991-Dec 31, 1996; Richard W. Sheppard 1997-Oct 26, 2001; Steven L. Woodford May 1, 2002-
2010; William Sanders (interim) May 1, 2007-2008; Tyson G. Ferguson 2010-2013; Catherine
Christman 2013-2016; Scott Sherrill 2016-

Vernon UMC *[East Winds]*   nbeckwithsr@msn.com
(P) 202 E Main St, Vernon 48476; (M) PO Box 155, Vernon 48476   (989) 288-4187
Ralph D. Harper 1968-1970; Meldon E. Crawford 1970-1975; Thomas E. Hart 1975-1980; Willard
A. King Sept., 1980-Mar. 15, 1985; Raymond D. Field 1985-1988; Katherine J. Rairick 1988-1991;
Philip D. Voss 1991-Jul 31, 1997; James M. Mathews Aug 1, 1997-Sep 30, 2001; Frederic G.
Heath Oct 1, 2001-2003; Richard B. Brown 2003-2006; Billy J. McKown 2006-Jun 6, 2007; Gerald
M. Sever, Jr., 2007-2015; Norman R. Beckwith, Sr. 2016-

Vickeryville UMC *[Midwest]*   fenwickumc@cmsinter.net
(P) 6850 S Vickeryville Rd, Sheridan 48884; (M) PO Box 241, Sheridan 48884-0241
     (989) 291-5547
John H. Gurney 1970-1976; Norman Crotser 1976-Dec. 1978; Daniel R. Bennett 1979-March
1982; Mark G. Johnson March 1982-1986; James E. Cook 1986-1991; Howard H. Harvey 1991-
1996; Patrick Glass 1996-1998; Larry W. Nalett 1998-Aug. 9, 2004; Charles E. Cerling Aug. 10,
2004-2009; Jolennda Cole (DSA) 2009-2010; Jolennda Cole 2010-2011; William F. Dye 2011-
2012; Russell D. Morgan (CLM) July 15, 2012-2014; ;Gerald A Erskine (DSA) 2014-Nov. 9, 2014;
Gerald A Erskine Nov. 10, 2014-

Vicksburg UMC *[Greater Southwest]*   reception@vicksburgumc.org
(P/M) 217 S Main St, Vicksburg 49097   (269) 649-2343
Dean Bailey (Methodist) 1966-1969; David Morton (EUB) 1965-1969; Myron K. Williams 1969-
1972; C. Robert Carson 1972-Oct. 1977; Francis C. Johannides Oct. 1977-1981; Lowell F.
Walsworth; 1981-1993; Lawrence R. Wood (Assoc.) 1991-1995; James R. Hulett 1993-1997; Jana
Lynn Almeida (Assoc.) 1995-1997; Isabell M. Deppe 1998-Sept. 2000; Bufford W. Coe, Oct. 15,
2000-2017; Gregory P. Culver 2017-

Wacousta: Community UMC *[Mid-Michigan]*   office@wacoustaumc.org
(P/M) 9180 W Herbison Rd, Eagle 48822   (517) 626-6623
Dale Spoor 1967-1971; Edward Otto 1971-1977; John R. Smith 1977-1984; Eugene Lewis 1984-
1986; James Hynes 1986-1992; Betty A. Smith 1992-1998; D.S. Assignment 1998; Lyle D. Heaton
Jan. 1, 1999-2013; Amee A. Paparella 2013-2016; Hillary Thurston-Cox 2016-

Wakefield UMC *[Nothern Skies]*   aa8yf@yahoo.com
(P/M) 706 Putnam St, Wakefield 49968   (906) 988-2533
J. Harold Wallis 1971-1976; Lillian G. Richards 1976-1984; Gary A. Allward 1984-1987; Thomas
H. Zimmerman 1987-1991; Carl R. Doersch 1991-1995; Pamela S. Kail 1995-1998; Allen F.
Schweitzer 1998-Sep 30, 1999; Cherrie A. Sporleder Feb 1, 2000-Jun 30, 2000; Jean B. Rencontre
2000-2008; Theodore A. Trudgeon 2008-2019; [Ironwood Wesley / Wakefield two-pooint charge
7-1-2019] Keith Paul Mullikin (DSA) 2019-

Walkerville UMC *[Midwest]* gooey@tir.com
(P) 189 E Main St, Walkerville 49459; (M) PO Box 125, Walkerville 49459 (231) 873-4236
A. Ruth Bonser Oct. 1990-1993; Nancy Bugajski 1993-1996; Donald J. Vuurens (DSA) 1996-1998; Steven J. Hale 1998-Nov. 8, 1999; Ronald A. Houk (DSA) Nov. 8, 1999-2000; Kenneth E. Tabor 2000-2004; Ronald L. Worley 2004-Nov. 30, 2013; Ronald Iris (Ret.) Dec. 1, 2013-2015; Theresa Fairbanks (DSA) Jun. 1, 2015-Nov. 14, 2016; Kenneth E. Tabor (RLA) Dec. 1, 2015-Dec. 1, 2016; Theresa Fairbanks Nov. 15, 2016-2018; David O Pratt (Ret) (LTFT) 2018-

Walled Lake UMC *[Heritage]* walledlakeumc@sbcglobal.net
(P/M) 313 Northport St, Walled Lake 48390 (248) 624-2405
Horace G. Thurston 1968-1970; David E. Church 1970-1978; Lloyd E. Christler 1978-1984; Leland E. Penzien 1984-1990; John R. Crotser (assoc) 1987-1990; Tat-Khean Foo 1990-1997; Samuel D. Fry, Jr. 1997-1998; Judith A. May 1998-2003; Demphna R. Krikorian 2003-Aug 1, 2003; Gordon Ackerman (interm) Aug 1, 2003-2004; Taek H. Kim 2004-2012; Robert Sielaff 2012-2016; Ian Boley 2016-

Warren: First UMC *[Greater Detroit]* contact@warrenfirstumc.org
(P/M) 5005 Chicago Rd, Warren 48092 (586) 264-4701
Douglas Parker 1968-1969; Harold Johnson (assoc) 1967-1968; Paul F. Blomquist 1969-1973; Robert Davis 1973-1979; Randall Vinson (assoc) 1980 Mar 1982; John Britt (assoc) 1982-Nov 1982; M. Jean Love (assoc) 1984; O. William Cooper 1979-1985; Norbert W. Smith 1985-1990; Johnny S. Liles (assoc) 1988-Mar 1990; Richard Andrus (assoc) Jan. 1990-1992; Thomas P. Macaulay July 1990-1997; Sharon G. Scott-Niefert (assoc) 1992-1995; Chong Yaub Won (assoc.) 1995-Aug 31, 1998; David G. Gladstone 1997-2003; Carolyn F. Hart (assoc) 1999- ; Murphy Ehlers (deacon) Dec 1, 2002-2003; Judith A. May 2003-2008; Dennis N. Paulson 2008-2012; Susan M. Youmans 2012-2018; Melissa J. Claxton 2018-

Washington UMC *[Greater Detroit]*
(P) 58430 Van Dyke Rd, Washington 48094; (M) PO Box 158, Washington 48094 (586) 781-9662
Harry M. Brakeman 1968-1974; John E. Harnish 1974-1979; John C. Stubbs 1979-1983; Brent L. Webster 1983-Aug 31, 1997; Bea B. Soots Sep 1, 1997-Dec 31, 1998; George R. Spencer Jan 1, 1999-2002; James E. Barnett (assoc) 2000-Jun 1, 2002; James E. Barnett Jun 1, 2002-Feb 1, 2007; Arthur R. Stone (interim) Jan 14, 2007-Feb 28, 2007; Jean R. Snyder (interim) Mar 1, 2007-2007; Cheryl Mancier 2007-2011; William C. Schumann 2011-2014; Donna J. Zuhlke 2014-Sept 1, 2018; Mary Ellen Chapman (Ret.) Sep 3, 2018-2019; [Omo: Zion / Washington became signle point charges 7-1-2019] Cherlyn E. McKanders 2019-

Waterford: Central UMC *[Greater Detroit]* info@waterfordcumc.org
(P/M) 3882 Highland Rd, Waterford 48328 (248) 681-0040
(Previously: Pontiac: Central)--Carl E. Price 1968-1973; Richard L. Clemans (assoc) 1963-1969; James H. McLaurin (assoc) 1966-1968; Ronald Tallman (assoc) 1968- 1971; Edwin A. Rowe (assoc) 1971-1974; Alan DeGraw (assoc) 1975-1978; Max L. Gibbs (assoc) 1978-1980; Richard L. Myers (assoc) 1980-1989; Ralph D. Churchill 1973-1982; W. Herbert Glenn 1982-1992 (changed church to Waterford: Central 1992); W. Herbert Glenn 1982-1992; George Covintree (assoc.) 1989-1993; Dale Miller 1992-Sep 30, 2000; Susan Bennett Stiles (assoc) Apr 15, 1994-May 1, 1999; Eric A. Stone (assoc) 1999-Nov 30, 2001; James G. Kellermann Nov 1, 2000-2013; Tara R. Sutton (assoc) Dec 31, 2001-2005; Wendy Lyons Chrostek (assoc.) 2006-2009; Kathryn L. Pittenger (deacon) 2008-2018; Karen B. Williams (assoc) 2009-2010; Jack L. Mannschreck 2013- ;

Waterford: Four Towns UMC *[Greater Detroit]* fourtownsumc@gmail.com
(P/M) 6451 Cooley Lake Rd, Waterford 48327 (248) 682-0211
Daniel L. Rial 1968-1969; Frank Dennis 1969-1971; Troy Lemmons 1971-1977; Dale Ferris 1977-1979; Leroy E. Philbrook 1979-1980; Harold Slater 1980-1989; Judith A. May 1989-Jan 1, 1996; Allen F. Schweizer Jun 1, 1996-1998; Sharon S. Niefert 1998-Aug 31, 2001; Cynthia Loomis-Able Sep 1, 2001-2004; Karen D. Poole 2004-2006; Bea Barbara Fraser-Soots 2006-2014; Theodore D. Whitely, Sr. 2014-2015; Dale R. Milford (DSA) 2015-2019; Sean LaGuire (DSA) 2019-

Waterford: Trinity UMC *[Greater Detroit]*   wtrinityumc@juno.com
(P/M) 6440 Maceday Dr, Waterford 48329   (248) 623-6860
    Timothy Hickey 1967-1969; Don Crumm 1969-1970; Bob Goudie 1970- 1976; Tat-Khean Foo
    1976-1990; John C. Ferris 1990-1998; Juanita J. Ferguson 1998-2003; Kenneth B. Ray 2003-
    2004; Karen D. Poole 2004-2006; Kim D. Spencer 2006-2009; Carter Cortelyou 2010-2013;
    Theodore Whitely, Sr. 2013-2015; Zelphia Mobley 2015-2019; Michael R. Perez, Jr. (DSA) 2019-

Waterloo Village UMC *[Heritage]*   waterloovillageumc@gmail.com
(P/M) 8110 Washington St, Grass Lake 49240   (734) 475-1171
    Wilbur Silvernail 1960-1969; Donald R. Fry 1969-1970; Altha M. Barnes 1970-1975; Richard M.
    Young 1975-1976; Glenn Kjellburg 1976-1978; Pulpit Supply 1978-1979; L. A. Nichols 1979-1988;
    Merlin Pratt 1988-1991; Wayne Willer 1991-1995; Pulpit Supply 1995; Kathleen A. Groff Dec.
    1995-July 31, 1997; Mona Joslyn Aug. 1, 1997-1998; Kathleen S. Kursch 1998-Feb. 1, 2000;
    Georgiana M. Dack (1/4 time) Feb. 1, 2000-2013; [Waterloo Village/First no longer two-point charge
    2013] Edward C. Ross (Ret.) (1/4 time) 2013-2016; Mary J. Barrett 2016-

Watrousville UMC *[Central Bay]*   chaplainbill4msp@aol.com
(P) 4446 W Caro Rd, Caro 48723; (M) 2076 1st St, Vassar 48768   (989) 673-3434
    Donald Pinner 1968-1970; Edgar M. Smith 1970-1976; Monroe J. Frederick 1976-1988; Sang
    Yoon (Abraham) Chun 1988-1992; James P. James 1992-1996; Martin G. Seitz 1996-1998; Wayne
    C. Samson 1998-2005; James A. Payne 2005-Feb 28, 2010; Daniel Gonder Mar 1, 2010-2013;
    William Sanders 2013-

Wayland UMC *[Midwest]*   office@waylandumc.org
(P/M) 200 Church St, Wayland 49348   (269) 792-2208
    H. Forest Crum, 1960-66; Bernard R. Randolph 1966-1970; Leo E. Bennett 1970-1979; Richard
    W. Barker 1979-1982; Douglas L. Pedersen 1982-1987; James W. Barney 1987-Sept. 1991;
    Wendell R. Stine Sept. 1991-1995; Stacy R. Minger 1995-Jul. 31, 2001; Julie A. Dix Aug. 1, 2001-
    2003; Nancy L. Besemer 2003-Nov. 1, 2006; Gary D. Bondarenko Nov. 15, 2006-2014; Jeffrey C.
    Williams 2014-

Wayne-Westland: First UMC *[Greater Detroit]*   fumcww@yahoo.com
(P/M) 3 Towne Square St, Wayne 48184   (734) 721-4801
    Russell W. Sursaw 1966-1970; Charles E. Jacobs 1970-1984; Daniel J. Wallace 1984-1989;
    Martha C. Gregg (Ball) (assoc) 1984-1985; John W. Kershaw 1989-1995; Fredrick P. Cooley 1995-
    Jul 31, 2000; David K. Stewart Sr. Aug 1, 2000-2008; Gregory E. Rowe 2008-2011; Paul S. Hahm
    2011-2013; Jennifer Jue 2013-2014; Carter L. Cortelyou 2014-2018; Marva Pope 2018-

Webberville UMC *[Mid-Michigan]*   webbervillechurch@gmail.com
(P/M) 4215 E Holt Rd, Webberville 48892   (517) 521-3631
    Gary Lyons 1968-1969; Milford Bowen 1969-1973; John McNaughton 1973-1979; Ross Bunce
    1979-1983; Wayne Babcock 1983-1991; David Cheyne 1991-1995; Dwayne E. Bagley 1995-2002;
    Wayne E. McKenney Aug. 1, 2002-2005; Robert D. Nystrom 2005-2007; Sandra L. Spahr (DSA)
    2007-Dec. 31, 2007; Paul A. Damkoehler, Jan. 1, 2008-2013; [M-52 Cooperative Ministry 2013;
    re-named Connections Cooperative Ministry 2015] Richard J. Foster (3/4 time) 2013-2016;
    Jacqueline Raineri 2016-2017; Martin A. Johnston 2017-

Weidman UMC *[Central Bay]*   weidmanumc@yahoo.com
(P) 3200 N Woodruff Rd, Weidman 48893; (M) PO Box 98, Weidman 48893   (989) 644-3148
    James Linton 1967-1969; Lawrence R. Smith 1969-1970; Athel J. Lynch 1970-1977; Vance M.
    Dimmick, Jr. 1977-1984; Diane E. Vale 1984-1985; Pulpit supply July 1985-Jan. 1986; Randall E.
    Roose Jan. 1986-1993; Melanie S. Young 1993-1994; Jerry L. Hippensteel 1994-March 26, 1995;
    Pulpit Supply April-June 1995; James H.K. Lawrence 1995-May 10, 1999; Craig L. Adams Sept.
    16, 1999-2006; David Price (DSA) 2006-Nov. 15, 2006; David Price Nov. 15, 2006-2013; Scott B.
    Smith 2013-2019; Cynthia S.L. Greene 2019-

Wellsville UMC *[Heritage]*   wmclemmer@hotmail.com
(P/M) 2509 S Wellsville Hwy, Blissfield 49228-9554   (517) 486-4777
    Edward C. Weiss 1968-1972; Gerald R. Parker 1972-1973; Robert L. Porter 1973-1976; John D. Roach 1976-1979; Kenneth C. Reeves 1979-1982; Thomas C. Sumwalt 1982-1984; Mark D. Miller 1984-1989; Thomas A. Davenport 1989-Sep. 15, 1990; Benjamin B. Ball Sep. 16, 1990-1991; Kimberly A. Barker 1991-May 31, 1992; Bradford K. Lewis Jun. 1, 1992-1994; Gerald M. Sever, Jr. 1994-1999; Wilson C. Bailey 1999-Aug 31, 1999; Allen W. Schweitzer Oct 1, 1999-Oct 31, 2000; Edward C. Weiss Nov 1, 2000-2005; William Michael Clemmer 2005-Dec 31, 2013; Samuel Pooley 2014-Dec 31, 2014; David R McKinstry Jan 8-Jun 30, 2017; William T. Kreichbaum 2017-2019; Bradley R. Vasey 2019-

West Berlin UMC *[East Winds]*   cbclarke95@gmail.com
(P) 905 Holmes Rd, Allenton 48002; (M) PO Box 533, Armada 48005   (810) 395-2409
    Paul Jarvis 1967-1970; Victor L. Studaker 1970-1973; Rodney E. Rawson 1973-1976; James B. Limsden 1976-1978; David D. Amstutz 1978-1981; Emerson W. Arntz 1982-1991; Rothwell W. McVety 1991-1997; Ralph Barteld 1997-2003; Ruthmary King (assoc) 1998-2001; Harold Nelson (assoc) 2001-2003; Dianna L. Rees 2003-2011; Curtis Clarke (DSA) Jul 1,-Nov 11, 2011-Curtis Clarke Nov 12, 2011-2019; Christopher G.L. Titus 2019-

West Bloomfield UMC *[Greater Detroit]*   wbumc@sbcglobal.net
(P/M) 4100 Walnut Lake Rd, West Bloomfield 48323   (248) 851-2330
    Leland E. Penzien 1969-1984; Thomas E. Hart 1984-1991; Jerome K. Smith 1991-Jul 31, 1997; Brent L. Webster Sep 1, 1997-2010; Robert D. Schoenals 2010-2012; Brian K. William 2012-Apr 16, 2019; Brent L. Webster (Ret.) May 1-Jun30, 2019; Monica L. William 2019-

West Branch: First UMC *[Central Bay]*   office@westbranchfumc.org
(P/M) 2490 W State Rd, West Branch 48661   (989) 345-0210
    R. LaVere Webster 1968-1973; Howard R. Higgins 1973-1977; Walter R. Damberg 1977-1983; Bruce M. Denton 1983-1988; Gordon W. Nusz 1988-1993; David Penniman 1993-Dec 17, 1997; Kenneth Tousley (interim) Dec 18, 1997-1998; Mark D. Miller 1998-2006; Mary Lynch Mallory 2006-2009; Lisa L. Cook 2009-2014; Timothy C. Dibble 2014-

West Deerfield UMC *[East Winds]*   pastor.kay@live.com
(P) 383 Otter Lake Rd, Fostoria 48435; (M) PO Box 185, Fostoria 48435
    John F. Greer 1971-1976; Gerald E. Mumford 1976-1989; Ginethea D. McDowell 1989-1992; Nobel R. Joseph 1992-Dec 31, 1996; David M. Fairchild Jan 1, 1997-2001; David P. Rahn 2001-May 1, 2009; Peggy Garrigues-Cortelyou 2009-2010; Betty Kay Leitelt 2010-

West Forest UMC *[East Winds]*   smithsk1962@gmail.com
(P) 7297 Farrand Rd, Millington 48746; (M) 129 E Vates, Frankenmuth 48734   (989) 860-7378
    Gerald E. Mumford 1964-1976; Lawrence C. Whiting 1976-1977; Bruce L. Billing 1977-1982; Janice I. Martineau 1982-1985; G. Patrick England Sept. 1, 1985-1993; Gregory E. Rowe 1993-Feb 28, 1995; Billy J. McKown Mar 1, 1995-2005; James P. James 2005-2007; Carter L. Garrigues-Cortelyou 2007-2010; Bruce E. Malicoat 2010-

West Vienna UMC *[East Winds]*   westviennaumc@gmail.com
(P/M) 5485 W Wilson Rd, Clio 48420   (810) 686-7480
    John N. Grenfell, Sr. 1968-1973; Melvin Leach 1973-1981; William B. Cozadd 1981-1982; David K. Koski 1982-1986; Wayne C. Ferrigan 1986-1992; James E. Britt 1992-2001; Bonny J. Lancaster 2001-2006; Billie Lou Gillespie Oct 15, 2006-

Westland: St. James UMC *[Greater Detroit]*   stsjamesumcwestland@att.net
(P/M) 30055 Annapolis Rd, Westland 48186-5372   (734) 729-1737
    Bradley F. Watkins 1968-1971; Clarence Acklin 1971-1974; Charles A. Talbert (part-time R) 1974-1979; Janet Gaston Petty 1980-1984; Theodore Whitely 1984-1986; Robert G. Williams 1986-1995; Elias Mumbiro 1995-Oct 31, 1999; Cheryl Myhand Nov 16, 1999-Apr 30, 2000; Hydrian Elliott May 1, 2000-2003; Carter M. Grimmett Sep 1, 2003-2008; Willie Frank Smith 2008-2015; Christopher M. Grimes 2015-2017; Rahim O. Shabazz 2017-

Weston UMC *[Heritage]*   donagalloway@msn.com
(P) 4193 Weston Rd, Weston 49289; (M) PO Box 96, Weston 49289   (517) 436-3492
Robert Hinklin 1968-1969; John F. Price 1969-1971; Ronald Hart 1971-1972; Richard C. Andrus 1972-1975; Wayne N. Thomas 1975-1976; Donald A. Wittbrodt 1977-1978; Mark K. Smith 1978-2012; David McKinstry 2012-2014; Lawson Crane 2014-2015; Tyler Kleeberger 2015-2016; Dona Galloway 2016-

White Cloud UMC *[Midwest]*   whitecloudumc@att.net
(P/M) 1125 E Newell St, White Cloud 49349   (231) 689-5911
William A. Hertel 1966-1969; Kenneth E. Curtis 1969-1971; Allan R. Valkema 1971-1976; Peter H. Kunnen 1976-Jan. 1984; Thomas and Lynn Pier-Fitzgerald (co-pastors) May 1984-1988; Jerry L. Jaquish 1988-2002, Jeffrey J. Bowman 2002-2012; Edwin D. Snook 2012-

White Pigeon UMC *[Greater Southwest]*
(P) 204 N Kalamazoo St, White Pigeon 49099; (M) PO Box 518, White Pigeon 49099
                                                                      (269) 483-9054
Lyle Chapman 1965-1969; Robert Stillson 1969-1975; Daniel Wolcott 1975-Sept. 1977; Donald Fry Nov. 1977-1981; Kendall Lewis 1981-Jan. 1985; Wesley Smith Jan. 1985-Sept. 1990; Charles Vizthum Nov. 1990-July 31, 1995; Mary Pieh 1996-1998; Patrick Glass 1998-Sept. 15, 2001; Linda J. Burton (DSA) 2001-2002; Linda J. Burton 2002-2005; Ronna L. Swartz 2005-2007; Janet L. Luchs (part-time) 2007-2009 [Schoolcraft Pleasant Valley / White Pigeon became a two-point charge 2008]; Scott E. Manning 2009-2016 [Constantine / White Pigeon became a two-point charge 2009]; Khristian A. McCutchan 2016-2017; Tiffany M. Newsom 2017-

White Pine UMC Community *[Northern Skies]*   wpcumc@yahoo.com
(P) 9 Tamarack, White Pine 49971; (M) PO Box 158, White Pine 49971   (906) 885-5419
Lloyd E. Christler 1968-1972; James Hilliard 1970-1971; Lawrence Brooks 1971-1975; Roger Gedcke 1972-1979; Lillian Richards 1971-1976; Wayne E. Sparks 1975-1980; Myra Sparks 1976-1980; Ed Hingelberg 1979-1981; Robert Thornton 1981-1983; Deane Wyllys 1983-1987; Charles H. West 1987-1993; Margaret H. West 1987-1993; Earleen VanConant 1993-1997; Clarence VanConant 1993-1997; Timothy C. Dibble 1997-2000; Cherrie A. Sporleder 2000-Jun 15, 2002; Rosemary R. DeHut Aug 1, 2002- [White Pine Community / Ironwood: Wesley became single point charges 9-1-2018] [White Pine Community / Ironwood: Wesley became single point charges 9-1-2018] [White Pine Community / Ewen / Bergland three-point charge 7-1-2019]

Whittemore UMC *[Central Bay]*   whittemoreumc@yahoo.com
(P) 110 North St, Whittemore 48770; (M) PO Box 155, Whittemore 48770   (989) 756-2831
Arthur Parkin (Whittemore) 1963-1972; Henry Powell (Whittemore) 1972-1973; Stephen Meeks (Prescott) 1967-1971; Robert L. Porter (Prescott) 1971-1973; Merle Nichols 1973-1978; Donald Shark 1978-1982; Harold Weemhoff 1982-1984; Lynn Chappell 1984-1989; Donald Milano 1989-1992; Allen Schweizer 1992-May 31, 1996; Linda Jo Powers Jun 16, 1996-2000; Kim Spencer 2000-Aug 31, 2002; Donald R. Derby Nov 1, 2002-2005; Bruce A. Mitchell 2005-2008; Brenda K. Klacking 2008-2014; Joseph Coon 2014-2016; Nathan J. Jeffords 2016-2019; Gary Gillings (DSA) 2019-

Wilber UMC *[Central Bay]*   pkrwilber@gmail.com
(P) 3278 Sherman Rd, East Tawas 48730; (M) 7620 Spruce St, Hale 48739   (989) 362-7860
Charles Hanley 1969-1974; L. Susan Garment 1974-1975; Clifford DeVore 1975-1980; William Stone 1980-1983; Priscilla Seward (w/Glennie, Curran) 1983-1985; Margaret A. Paige (w/Glennie, Curran) 1985-1986; Margaret A. Paige (w/Glennie, Curran) (1/2 time) 1986-1991; James E Paige Jr. (w/Glennie, Curran) (1/2 time) 1986-1991; Charles Bamberger 1991-1992; Deborah Lewis 1992-1993; Thomas Spencer 1993-1994; Charles J. Bamberger Oct 1, 1994-2008; Brenda K. Klacking 2008-2014; Keith Reinhardt 2014-

Williamsburg UMC *[Northern Waters]*   wumctoday@gmail.com
(P) 5750 Williamsburg Rd, Williamsburg 49690; (M) PO Box 40, Williamsburg 49690
(231) 267-5792
Merritt F. Bongard 1991-1993; Cynthia W. Schaefer 1993-1997; Douglas L. Pedersen 1997-2005; William W. Chu & Julie A. Greyerbiehl (Chu) 2005-2009; Geraldine M. Litchfield 2009-2014 [Elk Rapids UMC merged w/ Williamsburg UMC 4-1-11] Nathaniel R. Starkey 2014-2017; [Williamsburg and (Fife Lake Boardman Parish) Fife Lake / East Boardman / South Boardman became multi-point charge 2017] John J. Conklin 2017- [2018 Williamsburg, Fife Lake, East Boardman, South Boardman formed the Unified Parish]

Williamston Crossroads UMC *[Mid-Michigan]*   office.umccrossroads@gmail.com
(P/M) 5491 Zimmer Rd, Williamston 48895   (517) 655-1466
Williamston: Center and Bell Oak merged to become Williamston: Crossroads UMC June 14, 2000; Patricia A. Skinner June 14, 2000-2002; DeAnn J. Dobbs 2002-2008; Brian F. Rafferty 2008-2010; Ellen K. Zienert 2010-2012; Richard J. Foster (1/4 time) Aug. 1, 2012- [M-52 Cooperative Ministry 2013-2016; re-named Connections Cooperative Ministry 2015] Jacqueline Raineri 2016-2017; Martin A. Johnston 2017-

Williamston UMC *[Mid-Michigan]*   julie@williamstonumc.org
(P/M) 211 S Putnam St, Williamston 48895   (517) 655-2430
Ferris S. Woodruff 1966-1979; Harold A. Kirchenbauer 1969-Oct. 1975; Laurence L. Waterhouse Oct. 1975-1982; Ilona R. Sabo-Shuler 1982-1994; Robert H. Roth, Jr. 1994-1999; Dean Prentiss Sept. 15, 1999-2008; Alice Fleming Townley (3-6 months interim, para. 338.3b) July 15, 2008-2009; Amee Anne Miller 2009-2011; Julie A. Greyerbiehl 2011-2018; Linda J. Stephan 2018-

Williamston: Wheatfield UMC *[Mid-Michigan]*
(P/M) 520 Holt Rd, Williamston 48895   (517) 851-7853
Eugene Tate Oct.-Dec. 1968; Dennis Ferris Dec. 1968-April 1969; Wayne Gorsline April 1969-1975; Millard Wilson 1975-1977; Marcel Elliott 1977-Jan. 1978; Thomas Butcher Jan. 1978-Oct. 1979; Dennis Demond Oct. 1979-1980; Fred Fischer 1980-1985; Susan Adsmand 1985-1987; David Wendland 1987-1988; Carolyn Hare Robinson 1988-1991; Paulette Cheyne 1991-1995; Valerie Fons 1995-1999; Stephen F. Ezop 1999-June 30, 2002; Sharyn K. Osmond 2002-2006; Stephan Weinberger Aug. 1, 2006-2007; Jeanne Laimon (DSA) 2007; Jeanne Laimon (1/4 time) Dec. 1, 2007-2012; Jeremy J. Wicks (1/4 time) 2012-2014 [M-52 Cooperative Ministry 2013-2014]; Richard J. Ahti (DSA) 2014-2015; Daniel J.W. Phillips 2015-2017; [Grovenburg / Jackson: Zion / Felt Plains / Williamston: Wheatfield became multi-point charge 2017] John Kabala 2017-2018 ; Gertrude Mwadi Mukalay 2017-2018;Teresa Fair banks 2018- [Millville / Williamston: Wheatfield became multi-point charge 2018]

Willow UMC *[Heritage]*   willowumc@gmail.com
(P) 36925 Willow Rd, New Boston 48164; (M) PO Box 281, New Boston 48164   (734) 654-9020
David A. Russell 1965-1969; Harry Gintzer 1969-1971; Keith C. Chappell 1971-1973; Richard F. Venus-Madden 1973-1976; John W. Walter 1976-1977; Norman A. Charter 1977-1979; Dale M. Miller 1979-1981; Margery A. Schleicher 1981- Aug. 31, 1983; J. Gordon Schleicher Sep. 1, 1983-Dec. 31, 1984; Fred B. Maitland (interim) Jan - Jun 1985; Jack Edward Fulcher 1985-1989; Charles W. Booth 1989-Feb. 1991; Edward Coley (interim) Mar-Jun 1991; Hoon Hee Wong 1991-Nov 1, 1994; Otto Hood Nov 1, 1994-2000; Elizabeth A. Librande 2000-2004; Mark E. Zender 2004-2011; Marianne M. McMunn 2011-Feb 1, 2016; Bradford K. Lewis (Ret.) Feb 1, 2016-2017; Kelly Vergowven (DSA) Jul 1-Nov 11, 2017; Kelly Vergowven Nov 12, 2017-

Winn UMC *[Central Bay]* wumc8187@yahoo.com
(P/M) 8187 S. Winn Rd, Mt Pleasant 48858 (989) 866-2440
Harold Arman 1968-1969; Lawrence Smith 1969-1970; Athel J. Lynch 1970-1973; Joseph A. Dudley 1973-1974; Kathy Nickerson 1974-1977; James C. Sabo-Schuler 1977-1980; James W. Burgess 1980-1986; M. Christopher Lane 1986-1990; Paula Jane Duffey 1990-1994; Philip Bacon 1994-1997; Ron Smith 1997-1999; Paulette Cheyne 1999-2006; Melody Lane Olin (DSA) 2006; Melody Olin Nov. 15, 2006-2010; Lawrence Wonsey 2010-2014; Russell D. Morgan 2014-2016; Raymond W. Francis (DSA) 2016- [Coomer/Winn realigned to a two-point charge 2016; previously w/ Blanchard-Pine River]

Wisner UMC *[Central Bay]* wisnerumc@wisnerumc.com
(P/M) 5375 Vassar Rd, Akron 48701 (989) 691-5277
Clare Patton 1967-1972; E. Neil Sheridan 1972-1981; Lynn Chappell 1981-1984; Shirley & Howard Jones 1984-1986; Mark Karls 1986-1997; John H. Schneider, Jr. 1997-Aug 31, 1999; Wilson C. Bailey Sep 1, 1999-2005; William W. Omansiek 2005-2006; Frederick D. Neumann 2006-2010; William Sanders 2010-2012; Jacqueline Raineri 2012-2016; In Boem Oh 2016-

Wolf Lake UMC *[Midwest]* secretarywolflakeumc@frontier.com
(P/M) 378 Vista Terrace, Muskegon 49442 (231) 788-3663
Kenneth McCaw Nov. 1966-1969; Austin Reiger 1969-1975; Craig Adams 1975-Aug. 1979; Richard Williams Sept. 1979-Nov. 1983; Bruce Dempsey Nov. 1983-Nov. 1988; Gilbert Boersma Jan. 1989-Jan. 31, 1995; Pulpit Supply Feb.-June 1995; J. Todd Thompson 1995-2000; Laurence E. Hubley 2000-Nov. 15, 2001; Roberta W. Cabot Nov. 16, 2001-2011; Bobby Dale Whitlock (Ret.) 2011-Sept. 1, 2014; Susan J. Hagans (Ret.) Sept. 1, 2014-2018; Mona Joann Dye (Ret.) (LTFT ½) 2018-

Worth: Twp Bethel UMC (Worth Twp.) *[East Winds]*
(P) 8020 Babcock Rd, Croswell 48422; (M) PO Box 143, Croswell 48422 (810) 327-1440
Kenneth L. Harris 1969-1977; John D. Lover 1977-1982; Max D. Weeks Jan. 1983-1987; Donna J. Osterhout 1987-1991; Richard F. Kriesch 1991-1997; Jean R. Snyder 1997-1999; Linda L. Fuller, 1999-2010; Kevin Fick Apr 26, 2011-Jan, 2013; Tim Bashore Nov 9, 2013-2014; Mark Harriman 2014-2018; Donald Derby 2018-

Wyandotte: First UMC *[Greater Detroit]* fumcoffice@sbcglobal.net
(P/M) 72 Oak St, Wyandotte 48192 (734) 282-9222
James R. Timmons 1970-1976; H. H. Patterson 1976-1979; Gary Sanderson 1979-1988; Otto F. Hood (assoc) 1988-1994; Richard L. Myers 1988-1998; James J. Walker 1998-2007; Alan J. Hanson 2007-2013; Dianna L. Rees 2013-

Wyoming Park UMC *[Midwest]* wyomingparkumc@gmail.com
(P/M) 2244 Porter St SW, Wyoming 4951 (616) 532-7624
James W. Dempsey 1965-1969; Gerald A. Pohly 1969-Feb. 1973; John P. Hitchens (Assoc.) 1972-1985; Stanley H. Forkner March 1, 1973-1979; C. William Martin 1979-1984; Ward N. Scovel 1984-1989; Don Eddy 1989-Feb. 28, 1994; Lee F. Zachman April 16, 1994-1996; William C. Johnson 1996-2012; Robert Eckert (Assoc.) Apr. 1, 2006-2008; Joel T. Fitzgerald 2012-2017; Kimberly A. DeLong 2017- [Wyoming Park / Courtland-Oakfield became a two-point charge 2017]

Wyoming: Wesley Park UMC *[Midwest]* info@wesleypark.org
(P/M) 1150 32nd St SW, Wyoming 49509 (616) 988-6738
Kenneth Lindland 1968-Dec. 1969; Theron Bailey Dec. 1969-Sept. 1977; James E. Fox Sept. 1977-April 1985; (Griggs St. UMC merged with Wesley Park in Jan. 1979. Ward Pierce was pastor of Griggs St.)Ward Pierce Jan.-March 1979; Douglas Pedersen (Assoc.) 1979-1982; Myron K. Williams 1985-1994; William V. Clegg 1994-2011; Dean N. Prentiss 2011-

Yale UMC *[East Winds]*   office@yaleumc.org
(P/M) 2 S Main St, Yale 48097   (810) 387-3962
   D. Olney White 1969-1972; Charles R. Fox 1972-1977; Steven J. Buck 1977-1982; Charles R. Vinson 1982-1986; Donald Milano 1986-1989; Trevor A. Herm 1989-1994; Ginethea D. McDowell 1994-Dec 1, 1998; John R. Allan Jan 1, 1999-2008; Marvin H. McCallum (interm) Jan 1, 2009-2009; Bernadine Wormley-Daniels 2009-2012; Bruce L. Nowacek 2012-Feb 1, 2014; John C. Huhtala, Sr. Feb 15, 2014-2014; Patrick D. Robbins 2014--2019; Dennis Eric Irish 2019- ; Julia Ann Cramer (assoc) (DSA) 2019- [Yale / Cole / Melvin became a three-point charge 07/01/2019]

Ypsilanti: First UMC *[Heritage]*   fumcypsi@fumcypsi.org
(P/M) 209 Washtenaw Rd, Ypsilanti 48197   (734) 482-8374
   Kenneth R. Callis 1965-1972; Timothy R. Hickey (assoc) 1965-1967; Charles R. Kishpaugh (assoc) 1967-1969; Charles R. Jacobs (assoc) 1969-1972; L. LaVerne Finch (assoc) 1969-1971; Hugh C. White 1972-1978; Joseph J. Bistayi (assoc) 1972-1975; Philip M. Seymour (assoc) 1975-1977; Tom G. Burdette (assoc) 1977-1983; Perry A. Thomas 1978-1990; William P. McKnight (assoc) 1983-1985; Marsha M. Woolley (assoc) 1985-Oct. 31, 1991; David E. Kidd 1990-1997; Louise R. Ott (assoc) Jan 1, 1992-1997; Terry W. Allen 1997-2000; Latha Ravi (assoc) 1997-Dec 31, 2000 ; Melanie L. Carey 2000-2011; Judith Y. Mayo (deacon) 2001-Dec 5, 2007; Ventra Asana (deacon), 2001-Jan 25, 2003; Rey Carlos Mondragon (assoc) 2008-2013; Timothy C. Dibble 2011-2014; Briony Desotell 2014- ; Patricia Ganderilla (assoc.) 2015-2017

Ypsilanti: Lincoln Community UMC *[Heritage]*   pastormaryellen@wowway.com
(P/M) 9074 Whittaker Rd, Ypsilanti 48197   (734) 482-4446
   Bernard Hearl 1964-1977; C. William Bollinger 1977-1979; Howard M. Montgomery 1979-1983; Tom G. Burdette 1983-1985; David C. Collins 1985-1991; Donna J. Osterhout 1991-1996; Walter B. Fenton 1996-2003; Beverly L. Marr 2003-2010; Mary Ellen Chapman 2010-2016; Merlin H. Pratt 2016-2019; Christopher A. Butson 2019-

Ypsilanti: St. Matthew's UMC *[Heritage]*   saintmattsumc@gmail.com
(P/M) 1344 Borgstrom Ave, Ypsilanti 48198   (734) 483-5876
   William A. Kendall 1967-1969; Thomas H. Beaven 1969-1973; P. Glen Trembath 1973-1977; James E. Tuttle 1977-1984; Richard L. Dake 1984-Aug. 31, 1992; Ronald K. Fulton (interim) Sept 1, 1992-Nov 30, 1992; Gary C. Dawes Dec 1, 1992-1996; David G. Mulder 1996-2001; Pamela S. Kail 2001-2009; Steven H. Khang 2009-2014; Michael Desotell 2014-

Zeba UMC *[Northern Skies]*   lumc@up.net
(P) Zeba Rd, L'anse 49946; (M) 304 N Main St, Lanse 49946   (906) 524-6967
   William Kelsey 1968-1970; Lillian Richards 1971; Howard E Shaffer 1971-1981; John R. Henry 1981-1986; Gregory Rowe 1986-1990; James M. Mathews 1990-1993; David P. Snyder 1993-Oct 1, 2003; John R. Henry 2004-2011; Stephen E. Rhoades 2011-2019; Nathan T. Reed 2019-

MERGED CHURCHES

Battle Creek: Birchwood UMC *[Greater Southwest]*
(P/M) 3003 Gethering Rd, Battle Creek 49015
   Ron L. Keller 1966-1970; Philip P. Steele 1970-1971; Lawrence E. Hodge 1971-1980; Ward N. Scovel 1980-1984; Rodney J. Kalajainen 1984-1988; David W. Yingling 1988-1991; Phillip J. Friedrick 1991-1995; Melanie J. Baker-Streevy 1995-2003; Karen A. Tompkins 2003-Jan. 1, 2007; David Dryer Jan. 1-June 30, 2007; Robert D. Nystrom 2007-2011; Robert D. Nystrom (3/4 time) 2011-2012; [Battle Creek Birchwood / Trinity became two-point charge 2012] Bruce R. Kintigh (1/2 time) 2012-2018; [Battle Creek: Birchwood / Battle Creek: Trinity UMC merged with Battle Creek: Chapel Hill 07-01-2018]

Battle Creek: Trinity UMC *[Greater Southwest]*
Harold L. Mann 1968-1973; Wirth G. Tennant 1973-1978; Lowell Walsworth 1978-1981; Lloyd M. Schloop 1981-1984; Victor Charnley 1984-1995; Joy Jittaun Moore 1995-1996; David L. Dryer 1996-2006; Diane Gordon 2006-2010; Bruce R. Kintigh 2010-2012; [Battle Creek Birchwood / Trinity became two-point charge 2012] Bruce R. Kintigh (1/2 time) 2012-2018; [Battle Creek: Birchwood / Battle Creek: Trinity UMC merged with Battle Creek: Chapel Hill 07-01-2018]

Comstock UMC *[Kalamazoo]*
Wilbur Courter 1967-Jan. 1973; David Dunn Jan. 1973-Dec. 1973; David Charter Feb. 1974-Feb. 1976; Thomas Evans 1976-1984; Edward Slate 1984-1989; Valerie Hill 1989-1991; Mary Curtis 1991-1998; Peggy J. Baker 1998-2006; Paulette G. Cheyne 2006-Nov. 15, 2006; [Comstock UMC merged w/ Galesburg UMC 04-29-07]

Dansville UMC *[Lansing]*
Silas Foltz 1968-1970; Paul Schreibner 1970-1974; David Dryer 1974-1980; Joseph Graybill 1980-May 1987; Bobby Dale Whitlock 1987-May 1990; Clyde Miller (interim) May-Sept. 1990; Genevieve DeHoog Oct. 1990-1994; Pulpit Supply July-Aug. 1994; DeAnn J. Dobbs Sept. 1, 1994-1996; Russell K. Logston 1996-1998; DSA 1998-1999; Stephen F. Ezop 1999-June 30, 2002; Sharyn K. Osmond 2002-2006; Kimberly A. Tallent Aug. 1, 2006-2008; Donald R. Fry (DSA) (1/4 time) 2008-2011; Jeremy J. Wicks (1/4 time) 2011-Dec, 31, 2014 [M-52 Cooperative Ministry 2013] [Dansville UMC merged with Millville UMC 12-31-14]

Elk Rapids UMC *[Grand Traverse]*
Lawrence Hodge 1966-Nov. 1968; Glen Loy Oct. 1968-Oct. 1970; A.J. Lynch (Assoc.) June-Oct. 1968; R.J. Lautner (Assoc.) 1968-Oct. 1970; Gordon Showers Oct. 1970-Oct. 1971; Robert Doner Dec. 1971-1976; Bernard Randolph 1976-1978; Jack Barthlomew 1978-Feb. 1983; Stephen Beach April 1983-Nov. 1986; Michael Baker-Streevy Dec. 1986-1988; Charles Shields 1988-1993; Raymond R. Sundell 1993-1998; Kathryn M. Coombs 1998-1999; Thomas M. Pier-Fitzgerald 1999-2005; William W. Chu & Julie A. Greyerbiehl (Chu) 2005-2009; Geraldine M. Litchfield 2009- [Elk Rapids UMC merged w/ Williamsburg UMC 04-01-11]

Keeler UMC *[Kalamazoo]*
Meredith Rupe 1968-Nov. 1970; Gary E. Gamble Nov. 1970-1973; Supply pastor June-Oct. 1973; Lynn W. Wagner Oct. 1973-1975; Daniel R. Barker 1975-Sept. 1978; Gregory R. Wolfe Oct. 1978-Nov. 1983; Donald L. Buege Jan. 1984-1990; Dennis E. Slattery 1990-1992; David L. Litchfield 1992-1998; Virginia L. Heller 1998-2004; Mark E. Thompson 2004-2009; Julie A. Greyerbiehl 2009-2011; Heather McDougall 2011-2013; Beth A. Reum 2013-2015; [Hartford/Keeler became a two-point charge 2015] Ryan L. Wenburg 2015- [Keeler UMC merged with Hartford UMC 12-31-16]

Lansing Calvary UMC *[Lansing]*
Morris Bauman 1965-1973; H. James Birdsall 1973-1978; William Dobbs 1978-1983; Dale Crawford 1983-Feb. 1986; Jack M. Bartholomew Feb. 1986-1992; Leonard B. Haynes 1992-1998; Paula Jane Duffey 1998-2005; Stephan Weinberger 2005-2007; [Lansing Calvary UMC merged w/ Mt. Hope UMC 07-01-07]

Muskegon Lakeside UMC *[Midwest]*
Robert Treat 1967-1981; Richard D. Wilson 1981-1987; Steven R. Young 1987-1993; William P. Myers, Jr. 1993-2002; David A. Selleck 2002-2009; Zawdie K. Abiade 2009-2010; Stephan Weinberger 2010-2014; [Lakeside became a single-point charge 2014] Donald J. Graham 2014-2016 [Muskegon Lakeside merged w/ Muskegon Lake Harbor 07-01-16]

Osseo UMC *[Albion]*
William F. Bowers 1966-Sept. 15, 1969; Charles D. Grauer Sept. 15, 1969-1970; Daniel W. Harris 1970-1971; Robert E. Jones 1971-Nov. 15, 1973; Marion V. Nye Nov. 15, 1973-1976; Daniel R. Bennett Feb. 1, 1977-1979; Leonard J. Yarlott 1979-1982; Gilbert R. Boersma 1982-1985; Valerie M. Hill 1985-1989; Jerry L. Hippensteel 1989-1994; Susan Deason 1994-1998; Kathy L. Nitz 1998-Aug. 15, 1999; Clarence Able (DSA) 2001-2002; Donald E. Lee 2003-2010; Cynthia Veilleux (DSA) Nov. 1, 2010-2011; Kimberly A. Metzger July 1-Dec. 19, 2011; Timothy Puckett (part-time) Jan. 1, 2012- [Osseo UMC merged w/ North Adams UMC 04-06-14]

Pleasant Valley UMC *[Heartland]*
G. Albert Rill 1971-1976; Joseph Dudley 1976-Aug. 1979; Michael L. Selleck Aug. 1979-1986; Leonard B. Haynes 1986-1992; Donald E. Spachman 1992-1997; Doris Lyon 1997-Jan. 1, 2008 [Pleasant Valley UMC merged w/ St. Louis UMC 01-01-08]

Port Huron: Washington Avenue UMC *[East Winds]*
Douglas K. Mercer 1968-1970; Richard C. North 1970-1972; Lloyd E. Christler 1972-1978; John N. Howell 1978-1981; S. Joe Robertson 1981-1985; Robert E. Burkey 1985-1988; Donald R. Sperling 1988-1996; Georg F. W. Gerritsen 1996-Dec 31, 1999; Susan K. Freeland Montenegro Jan 1, 2000-Dec 1, 2003; Nickolas K. Genoff Jan 1, 2004-2009; Robert D. Chapman 2009-2014; Penelope P. Nunn 2014-2018; [Port Huron: Washington Ave. UMC merged with Port Huron: Gratiot Park 07/01/2018]

Poseyville UMC *[Central Bay]*
H. Emery Hinkston 1969-1972; Robert Moore 1971-1980; Robert Kersten 1980-1982; Paul Riegle 1981-1983; John W. Elliott 1981-1986; Bruce C. Hatch 1986-1993; Karen L. Knight 1993-1998; Rony S. Hallstrom 1998-Feb 29, 2001; Michael W. Luce 2001-2012; Rahim O. Shabazz 2012-2015; Karen Knight Price 2015-Nov 1, 2015; Kayla Marie Roosa Nov 1,2015-2017; Lynda F. Frazier 2017-July 31, 2018 [Poseyville UMC merged with Midland: Aldersgate UMC 08/01/2018]

Potterville UMC *[Lansing]*
Thomas Peters 1967-1970; Richard Youells 1970-1974; Gregory Wolfe 1974-Oct. 1978; J. Thomas Churn Oct. 1978-1982; Austin Regier 1982-1987; Beverly Gaska 1987-Jan. 1991; Charles B. Hodges March 1991-March 1992; Milton J. TenHave (interim) March-July 1992; John Buker 1992-1995; Paul F. Bailey 1995-May 1, 2001; Rebecca K. Morrison Jan. 16, 2002-2011; Lyne Stull-Lipps 2011-2016; Jeanne M. Randels (Ret.) July 1-Sept. 1, 2016; [Potterville UMC merged w/ Sycamore Creek UMC 6/21/2017 and became Sycamore Creek Potterville Campus 12-31-16]

South Wyoming UMC *[Midwest]*
Walter Rothfus 1968-1971; Curtis Cruff 1971-1975; Leonard Yarlott 1975-1979; Edward Trimmer 1979-1981; Ben Chapman 1981-1982; Howard Harvey 1982-1988; John Myette 1988-March 15, 1991; Arthur D. Jackson March 15, 1991-Dec. 31, 1993; John Myette Jan. 1, 1994-1995; Lois M. Munn 1995-1997; Donald D. Entenman 1997-Sept. 30, 1997; Rhonda J. Prater Nov. 16, 1997-2003; Marcia L. Elders (part-time) 2003-2015 [merged with Cornerstone UMC 1-1-15; re-named Cornerstone UMC-South Wyoming Campus, building temporarily closed May 31, 2015 to re-open in fall 2015]

Sterling UMC *[Central Bay]*
Byron Coleman 1969-1974; Lynn Chappell 1974-1981; Janet Larner 1981-1982; John J. Britt 1982-1990; Zina B. Bennett Jr. 1990-1993; Jan L. Beaderstadt 1993-Feb 15, 2000; J. Gordon Schleicher 2000-2003; Jon W. Gougeon 2003-2010; James A. Payne 2010-Apr. 1, 2019; [Sterling UMC merged into Standish: Community UMC 04/01/2019 to become Standish: Beacon of Light]

St Johns: First UMC *[Heartland]*
Harold Homer 1968-1972; Francis Johannides 1972-1977; Keith Laidler 1977-1984; Mark Graham 1984-1987; Paul Patterson 1987-1990; Stephan Weinberger 1990-2000; Carolyn C. Floyd 2000-2003; Margery A. Schleicher 2003-2007; Lori J. Sykes 2007-2012; Ellen K. Zienert July 15, 2012-2018 [merged with DeWitt: Redeemer and became DeWitt: Redeemer – St. Johns: First Campus 07-01-18]

Watervliet UMC *[Kalamazoo]*
Lawrence Grubaugh 1968-1971; Donald Russell 1971-1975; Joseph Wood 1975-1978; Lawrence Wiliford 1978-Sept. 1981; Katherine Williams (Coombs) Dec. 1981-Sept. 1984; Fred Hamlin Nov. 1984-1985; Kenneth Curtis 1985-May 1987; Len Schoenherr 1987-1999; David F. Hills Aug. 1, 1999-2007; O'Ryan Rickard 2007-2009; William W. Chu 2009-2011; Ron Van Lente 2011- [Watervliet UMC merged w/ Coloma UMC 06-26-11]

Whitehall UMC *[Midwest]*
Charles Dunbar 1965-1971; Richard Matson 1971-1975; Bernard Randolph 1975-1976; Edward Slate 1976-1983; Steve Smith 1983-1985; Keith Treman 1985-1990; Kay B. Bosworth 1990-1998; Anita Hahn 1998-2006; Gayle Berntsen 2006-2014; [Whitehall realigned from Whitehall/Claybanks to Whitehall/Crestwood 2014] Mary A. Sweet 2014-2017 [Whitehall and Crestwood became multi-station circuit 2014] [Whitehall UMC merged with Montague UMC, 07-01-17]

CLOSED CHURCHES
Congregations closed in accordance with ¶2549 of *The Book of Discipline, 2016*.

Alto UMC *[Midwest]*
Beulah Poe 1962-1971; Carter Miller 1971-1973; John Eversole 1973-1977; Keith Avery June-Oct. 1977; Albert Sprauge Oct. 1977-Jan. 1978; Herb Kinsey Jan. 1978-May 1979; Martin Fox May 1979-Oct. 1982; Herb Kinsey Oct. 1982-1983; Harold Diepert 1983-March 1985; Margaret Peterson 1985-1989; Jill Rose July-Dec. 1989; Lloyd Hansen Dec. 1989-1990; Todd Thompson 1990-1995; Bryan Schneider-Thomas 1995-2000; Dominic A. Tommy 2000-2002; Dean Irwin Bailey (Ret.) 2002-2014; Andrew Jackson (Ret.) 2014-2016; Robert D. Wright (Ret.) 2016-Dec 31, 2018. [Alto UMC closed 12-31-2018]

Battle Creek: Sonoma UMC *[Albion]*
Howard Moore May 1968-1970; Ray Grienke 1970-Jan. 1974; Ray McBratnie Jan. 1974-1976; Kenneth Curtis 1976-1981; Harry Johnson 1981-1985; Gary Kintigh 1985-1993; Charles M. Shields 1993-1995; Michael Baker-Streevy 1995-Nov. 16, 1999; Charles Edward Rothy 2000-2003; Richard Duane Wilson 2003-2008; Nancy G. Powers 2008-2012; Sally Harrington (Ret.) 2012- [Sonoma UMC discontinued 06-30-14]

Benton Harbor Peace Temple UMC *[Kalamazoo]*
George Hartman 1966-1971; Carlos Page 1971-1989; Dow Chamberlain 1989-Nov. 30, 1993; Donald Entenman Feb. 1, 1994-1995; David G. Knapp 1995-2003; Deborah R. Miller 2003-Nov. 14, 2003; David S. Yoh (DSA) Nov. 15, 2003-2006; James W. Stilwell 2006-2009; Sandra V. Douglas (Deacon) (1/4 time) 2008-2009 [Benton Harbor: Peace Temple UMC discontinued 06-30-09]

Brandywine: Trinity UMC *[Kalamazoo]*
Vernon L. Michaels 1967-1969; Douglas Vernon 1969-1971; Robert Wellfare 1971-1973; Lowell F. Walsworth 1973-1978; Raymond D. Flessnor 1978-1981; David E. Small 1981-1987; Arthur C. Murphy Aug. 1987-1991; Edward A. Friesen 1991-1993; Patricia A. Myles 1993-Apr. 17, 1994; Richard L. Eslinger 1994-Nov. 1, 1998; Matthew Bistayi Jan. 1, 1999-2002; Allen J. Duyck 2002-Sept. 22, 2003; Carl Harrison Feb. 1, 2004-2008; Christopher A Kruchkow (DSA) 2008-2009 [Brandywine: Trinity UMC discontinued 08-30-08]

Breedsville UMC *[Kalamazoo]*
Lloyd Bronson 1967-1978; Lloyd Bronson 1978-1981; Charles McNary 1981-1991; James Hodge 1991-1992; Kenneth J. Littke 1992-1998; D.S. Assignment 1998; Jana Jirak Sept. 16, 1998-1999; Robert L. Pumfery 1999-October 31, 2002; Patricia Anne Harpole November 1, 2002-2004; O'Ryan Rickard 2004-2005; Sheila F. Baker 2005-2007; David L. Youngs 2007-2008; David L. Haase (DSA) (1/4 time) Jan. 3, 2008; David L. Haase (1/4 time) July 1, 2008-2014; Jason E. Harpole (1/4 time) 2014-2016 [Breedsville UMC discontinued 11-12-16]

Dearborn Heights: Stephens UMC *[Detroit Renaissance; Greater Detroit]*
Charles F. Davenport 1968-1977; Roy G. Forsyth 1977-1981; Edwin C. Hingelberg 1981-1988; Robert C. Hastings 1988-1994; James R. McCallum 1994-1999; Robert Sielaff 1999-2012; Chong Yuob Won 2012-Dec 31, 2014; Tom Waller Jan 1, 2015-2018; Carolyn A. Jones Jul 1-Dec 31, 2018. [Dearbon Heights: Stephens UMC closed 12-31-2018]

Eagle UMC *[Lansing]*
William Cox 1968-1970; Raymond J. McBratnie 1970-1974; David Morton 1974-1982; William Dornbush 1982-Nov. 1986; Janell E.R. Gerken Jan. 1987-1988; Raymond D. Field 1988-1993; Larry W. Nalott 1993-1998; Stephen F. Ezop 1998-1999; D. Michael Maurer Aug. 16, 1999-2002; Judith Lee Scholten 2003-2011 [Eagle UMC discontinued 10-15-11]

East Lansing Aldersgate UMC *[Lansing]*
William Clegg 1984-1994; David W. Meister 1994-July 31, 1995; Kenneth W. Karlzen Aug. 1, 1995-2000; Gary D. Bondarenko 2000-Nov. 15, 2006; Paulette G. Cheyne Nov. 15, 2006-Apr. 1, 2008 [East Lansing Aldersgate UMC discontinued 04-01-08]

East Lansing Chapel Hill UMC *[Lansing]*
Stephen Beach 1968-1969; Edward F. Otto 1969-Dec. 1972; Daniel Miles Dec. 1972-1974; Paul K. Scheibner 1974-1978; J. Lynn Pier-Fitzgerald 1978-May 1984; Thomas M. Pier-Fitzgerald (co-pastor) 1982-May 1984; Charles W. Smith May 1984-1988; Carl W. Staser 1988-Jan. 1991; Beverly E. Gaska Jan. 1991-July 31, 1995; D. Michael Maurer Aug. 1, 1995-2002; Robert David Nystrom 2002-Jan. 15, 2004; Robert David Nystrom (1/2 time) Jan. 16, 2004-2005; Ellen K. Zienert 2005-2012; [East Lansing Chapel Hill discontinued 06-24-12]

Ellis Corners UMC *[Albion]*
Logan Weaver 1968-1976; Densel G. Fuller 1976-1981; Jerry L. Hippensteel 1981-1984; Thomas E. Ball 1984-Nov. 1988; Stanley Fenner Dec. 1988-1989; Stacy R. Minger 1989-1994; John F. Ritter 1994-1996; Robert Stark 1996-2000; John Scott 2000-Sept. 1, 2003; John A. Scott & Rebecca Scott (CoPastors) Sept. 2003-2007; Bruce R. Kintigh 2007- ; [Ellis Corners UMC discontinued 12-31-07]

Grand Rapids Mosaic UMC *[Grand Rapids]*
[new church start 1997; "Michigan Suhbu Korean UMC" re-named "Church of All Nations", 2006; renamed "Mosaic UMC" 2012] Seung Ho Baek July 16, 1997-2008; Robert Eckert (part-time) 2008-2009; Trevor McDermont 2009-2010; Steven C. Place Jan. 1, 2011-2017 [Mosaic UMC closed 07-01-17]

Grand Rapids Oakdale UMC *[Grand Rapids]*
Arthur Jackson 1966-Oct. 1969; Kenneth Lindland Dec. 1969-1973; Brent Phillips 1973-1976; Douglas Knight 1976-1978; Charles Dunbar 1978-1979; Ed Trimmer 1979-1982; Cathy Kelsey 1982-1987; Jane Shapley 1987-1996; Marguerite R. Bermann 1996-1999; Calvin Hill Aug. 16, 1999-2003; Theresa Little Eagle Oyler-Sayles 2003-2006; Andy Baek 2006-2008 [Oakdale UMC discontinued 06-30-08]

Grand Rapids Olivet UMC *[Grand Rapids]*
Grand Orin Bailey 1964-1969; Allen Wittrup 1969-1977; C. Jack Scott 1977-1979; Richard Youells Aug. 1979-1989; Barry T. Petrucci 1989-Dec. 31, 1994; Clinton McKinven-Copus Jan. 1, 1995-Jan. 1, 2001; Dominic A. Tommy (Assoc.) Apr. 16, 1999-2000.; Robert Eckert (DSA) 2001-2005; James Stilwell March 1, 2005-2006; Gary Peterson (DSA) 2006-2008; James Thomas Boutell (part-time) 2008-2010; Jean & Jane Crabtree (DSA) 2010- [discontinued 12-12-10]

Grand Rapids Plainfield UMC *[Grand Rapids]*
K.C. Downing 1967-1969; C. Dow Chamberlain 1969-1972; Don W. Eddy (Assoc.) 1971-1979; Robert L. Hinklin 1972-1976; Marvin F. Zimmerman 1976-1978; Wayne C. Barrett 1978-1982; Neal M. Kelly 1982-1984; John McNaughton 1984-1986; Ethel Z. Stears 1986-1988; Jeanne Randels 1988-1991; Lynn Pier-Fitzgerald 1991-1999; Neil Davis 1999-2002; Robert R. Cornelison 2002-2005; Joyce F. Gackler June 1, 2005-2012; [Grand Rapids Aldersgate / Plainfield became two-point charge 2012] Laurie A. Haller 2012-2013 [Plainfield UMC discontinued 06-30-13]

Greenbush UMC *[Heartland]*
William Tate 1967-1969; Robert Boyer 1969-1970; Charles VanLente 1970-1972; Everett Love June-Dec. 1972; Norman Wood 1973-1976; Terry MacArthur 1976-Oct. 15, 1979; Robert Gillette Jan. 1980-1984; Merritt Bongard 1984-1991; Joseph Spackman 1991-1999; James Dibbet 1999-2005; O'Ryan Rickard 2005-2006; Jon L. Pohl 2006-2011; Mona J. Dye 2011-2015 [Greenbush UMC discontinued 09-28-15]

Grovenburg UMC *[Lansing]*
Maurice Glasgow 1966-1978; Paul Mergener (Assoc.) 1976-Oct. 1978; Joseph Huston Oct. 1978-Oct. 1981; Paul Wehner Oct. 1981-1986; Marty DeBow 1986-1990; Kyewoon Choi 1990-1997; Melanie S. Young 1997-1998; Richard J. Duffey 1998-2005; Andrew L. Croel 2005-2008; Kimberly A. Tallent 2008-2009; Joseph D. Huston (Ret.) 2009-2017; [Grovenburg / Jackson: Zion / Felt Plains / Williamston: Wheatfield became multi-point charge 2017] John Kabala 2017- ; Gertrude Mwadi Mukalay 2017-2018; [Grovernbury UMC discontinunted 06-30-2018]

Hudsonville UMC *[Grand Rapids]*
Deborah Johnson Sept. 1990-1997; R. John Thompson 1997-Apr. 1, 2001; Sandra K. VandenBrink 2001-Jan. 1, 2005; [Hudsonville UMC discontinued 01-01-05]

Jones UMC *[Albion]*
Reva Hawke 1988-Oct. 1991; Marilyn B. Barney Oct. 1991-1998; Carolyn A. Robinson 1998-2007; Thomas R. Reaume (part-time) 2007-2009; Jack Balgenorth 2009-Sept. 1, 2010 [discontinued 09-01-10]

Kalamazoo Lane Blvd UMC *[Kalamazoo]*
Marion Burkett 1966-1969; James Lavengood 1969-1972; Harold Taber 1972-1975; Richard D. Wilson 1975-1981; Gary Kintigh 1981-1985; Robert Freysinger 1985-1988; Daniel Biteman 1988-1996; John W. McNaughton 1996-Jan. 16, 2000; James Dyke (DSA) 2000-2006; David S. Yoh (DSA), July 1, 2006-Oct. 4, 2006; Philip P. Steele (DSA), Oct. 8, 2006; Kevin E. Hale (DSA), Jan. 1, 2007; Martin H. Culver (DSA), Mar. 18, 2007-Mar. 25, 2008 [Lane Boulevard UMC discontinued 03-25-08]

Kalamazoo Stockbridge Avenue UMC *[Kalamazoo]*
Lloyd Schloop 1968-1973; Kenneth O. Lindland 1973-1977; Charles W. Richards 1977-1986; Curtis Strader 1986-1988; John Moore 1988-1992; Dwight J. Burton 1992-1998; John W. McNaughton 1998-2003; Calvin Y. Hill 2003-2007; John L. Moore (DSA) 2007-2010; Ronald D. Slager 2010-2015; Sara L. Carlson 2015-Jan. 31, 2016 [Stockbridge Avenue UMC discontinued 07-01-16]

Lansing Christ UMC [Lansing]

Wilson Tennant 1966-1969; Meinte Schuurmans (Assoc) 1966-1980; David L. Crawford 1969-1977; Thomas L. Weber (Assoc) 1974-1978; Donald P. Sailor 1977-February 1983; Clyde E. Miller April 1983-March 1987; Eric Burrows (Assoc) 1983-1984; Philip Simmons (Assoc) 1984-1985; James J. Walker (Assoc) 1985-1989; Richard A. Selleck March 1987-1992; Rebecca N. Niese (Assoc) 1991-October 31, 1994; Robert E. Jones 1992-1996; Maurice E. Walworth, Jr. 1996-2003; Charles David Grauer 2003-Dec. 31, 2012; Edward C. Ross (Interim), Jan. 1-June 30, 2013; Lyle D. Heaton 2013-Dec. 31, 2015 [Lansing Christ UMC discontinued 12-31-15]

Lansing Faith UMC [Lansing]

J. Edward Cherryholmes Apr. 1964-Apr. 1969; Richard E. Johns Apr. 1969-1980; David B. Nelson Jr. 1980-1985; John Palmer 1985-May 1987; Kenneth W. Bensen May 1987-2003; James A. Richie (Assoc.) 2000-2002; Cornelius Davis (Assoc. 1/4 time) 2003-2008; (Lansing Faith merged with South Lansing Ministries 2005); Russell F. McReynolds (Ret.) 2008-2015; Jeanne M. Randels (Ret.) July 1-Dec. 31, 2015 [Lansing Faith UMC discontinued 12-31-15]

Lansing: Korean UMC [Lansing]

Young Ho Ahn 1984-Sept. 1985; Chung Soon Chang Sept. 1985-1988; Hyo Nam Hwang Oct. 1988-1998; Jung Kee Lee 1998-Dec. 31, 2003; Bo Rin Cho Mar. 1, 2004-2014; Seok Nam Lin 2014-2016 [Lansing: Korean UMC discontinued 07-01-16]

Lansing Potter Park UMC [Lansing]

Ronald Entenman 1967-1972; Peter Kunnen 1972-1976; Arthur Turner 1976-1981; Clinton Bradley-Galloway 1981-1983; Lewis Buchner 1983-1986; Zawdie Abiade 1986-1988; Donald Entenman 1988-1991; Isabell Deppe 1991-Dec. 31, 1997; D. Michael Maurer (Pastor Interim, part time) Jan. 1, 1998-June 30, 1998; Grace Kathleen O'Connor 1998-2001; Lamarr V. Gibson 2001-2004; Betty A. Smith (DSA) October 16, 2004-2005; Stephan Weinberger 2005-2006; [Potter Park UMC discontinued 06-30-06]

Lansing: Trinity UMC [Lansing]

James E. Fox 1968-1971; Gerald R. Bates 1971-1979; Larry Sachua 1979-1989; Richard Williams (Assoc.) 1983-1985; Gregory Wood (Assoc.) 1985-1990; Dennis Buwalda 1989-1992; Paul C. Frederick (Assoc.) 1990-Dec. 1992; Leicester Longden 1992-2001; Linda J. Farmer-Lewis (Assoc.) Jan. 1993-1994; Joy J. Moore (Assoc.) 1995-1997; Cynthia S.L. Green (Assoc.) May 1, 1998-2004; Rae L. Franke (Deacon) 1998-2003; William Beachy 2001-2014; Steve J. Buck 2014-2015 [Lansing Trinity UMC discontinued 07-01-15]

Lansing: Vietnamese UMC [Mid-Michigan]

Vinh Q. Tran, Jan. 1, 1986 - 2004; Cuong M. Nguyen 2004-2008; Tho Van Phan (DSA) 2009-Oct. 15, 2009 [Lansing: Vietnamese UMC discontinued 10-15-2009]

Litchfield UMC [Heritage]

Dorr Garrett 1968-1970; Peter Kunnen 1970-1972; Morris Reinhart 1972-1976; Stephen Keller 1976-Dec. 1979; Paul Hartman Jan. 1980-1985; David Meister 1985-March 1990; Kathy Brown 1990-Feb. 1, 2001; R. John Thompson Apr. 1, 2001-2005; Carl Q. Litchfield 2005-2009; [Litchfield/Quincy two-point charge 2009] Michael P. Baker-Streevy 2009-2010; Martin T. Cobb 2010-2013; Julie Elmore 2013-2017; [Litchfield / Jonesville became two-point charge 2017] Mary A. Sweet 2017-2019 [Litchfield closed 06-30-2019]

Mapleton UMC [Central Bay]

Karl Patow 1969-1971; Richard Mansfield 1971; John Eversole 1971-1973; Max Weeks 1973-1977; Leon Smith 1977-1979; Leonard Gamber 1979-1982; Kenneth Reeves 1982-1985; Edwin M. Collver 1985-1992; Gordon B. Boyd 1993-Aug 31, 1994; Barbra Franks Sep 1, 1994-Sep 30, 1996; Timothy Hastings Dec 1, 1996-2004; Michael P. Kelley 2004-2007; Leonard Clevenger 2007-2010; L. Cecile Adams 2010-2013; Richard Hodgeson 2013-2017; T. Bradley Terhune Oct 1, 2017-Aug 31, 2018; Leonard Clevenger Oct 1, 2018-2019 [Mapleton UMC closed 06-30-2019]

Marengo UMC *[Albion]*
Stanley Fenner 1989-Aug. 8, 2000; Gerry Retzloff (DSA) Jan. 1, 2010- [Marengo UMC discontinued 07-01-16]

Middleton UMC *[Heartland]*
De Layne Hersey 1967-1969; Herald Cox Sept. 1969-Sept. 1971; Lloyd Hansen Sept. 1971-May 1972; Abe Caster May 1972-Jan. 1973; Eldon Schram Feb.-June 1973; J. Thomas Churn 1973-1979; Richard Whale 1979-1980; Richard Riley 1980-1984; Lyle Heaton 1984-1990; Tim Wohlford 1990-1991; Carolyn A. Robinson 1991-1997; Charles D. Farnum 1997-2001; Martin Cobb 2001-2006; William F. Foldesi 2006-Apr. 7, 2007; Clare Huyck (DSA) 2007; Clare Huyck Nov. 10, 2007-2012; William F. Dye July 15, 2012-Aug. 31, 2015; Larry W. Nalett (RLA) Sept. 15-Nov. 29, 2015 [Middleton UMC discontinued 12-01-15]

Moscow Plains UMC *[Albion]*
Densel Fuller Feb. 1969-1974; David Showers 1974-1976; Martin Fox 1976-1979; Gerald Selleck 1979-1982; Mark Kelly 1982-1983; Dr. Campbell 1983-1984; Jim Hodge 1984-1989; Lawrence P. Brown 1989-Dec. 1992; Donald R. Wendell Jan 1, 1993-Dec. 31, 1995; Bernice Taylor-Alley (DSA) 1996-2001; Craig Pahl 2001-2007; [Moscow Plains UMC discontinued 06-30-07]

North Evart UMC *[Heartland]*
Carter Miller 1968-March 1971; Lynn Wagner March. 1971-Oct. 1973; Pulpit Supply Nov. 1973-1974; Darryl Cook 1974-May 1977; Kenneth Kline 1977-1981; Pulpit Supply June-Aug. 1981; Dwight Benner Sept. 1981-1983; Purlin Wesseling Aug. 1983-1986; Frank Closson 1986-Jan. 1988; Jane Crabtree Jan. 1988-1990; Pulpit Supply July-Nov. 1991; Robert Stark Nov. 1990-Aug. 1991; Carol Lynn Bourns Sept. 1991-Dec. 31, 1994; Pulpit Supply Jan. 1995-1996; Jean Crabtree (DSA) 1996-2000; Donald L. Buege 2000-Jan. 2006; Jon Pohl Jan. 15 - June 30, 2006; Jean A. Crabtree (DSA) Nov. 5, 2006-July 2007; Russell Morgan (DSA) July 8, 2007-2012; Kara Lynne Burns (CLM) July 22, 2012- [North Evart UMC discontinued 07-01-14]

North Star UMC *[Heartland]*
Robert E. Tomlinson 1974-Jan. 1977; Donald L. Warmouth Feb. 1977-1978; Glenn Britton 1978-1979; Lois H. Gremban 1979-1981; Dale F. Jaquette Aug. 1981-April 1990; T. Ried Martin 1990-1993; Karen E. Nesius 1993-1994; Jodie Flessner 1994-2003; William F. Foldesi Nov. 16, 2003-Apr. 7, 2007; Clare Huyck (DSA) 2007; Clare Huyck Nov. 10, 2007-2012; William F. Dye July 15, 2012- [North Star UMC discontinued 07-01-15]

Oronoko UMC *[Kalamazoo]*
Robert Strauss 1968-1981; Valerie Hill 1981-March 1983; Leonard Haynes 1983-1986; Leo Bennett 1986-1989; Walter J. Rothfuss 1989-2000; Brenda Gordon 2000-2006; Jane D. Logston (part-time) 2006-14; [Berrien Springs/Hinchman/Oronoko became 3-point charge 2012] [Hinchman/Oronoko became 2-point charge 2014] Linda R. Gordon 2014-2017; Brenda E. Gordon Jul 1-Dec 27, 2017. [Oronoko UMC discontinued 12-27-17]

Otsego: Trowbridge UMC *[Greater Southwest]*
Henry Houseman 1962-1974; Leon Shaffer 1974-1981; R. Ivan Niswender 1981-1994; Gary S. Wales 1994-2008; Anthony C. Shumaker (part-time) 2008-2012; Sheila F. Baker (1/2 time) 2012-Feb. 2, 2014; John L. Moore (Ret.) 2014-2017 [Otsego: Trowbridge UMC closed 12-31-2018]

Outland *[Albion]*
[new church start 2006] Peggy J. Baker 2006-2011; Stacy Caballero 2011-Mar. 1, 2012 [Outland discontinued 02-29-12]

Parma UMC *[Albion]*
Edward Dahringer 1968-Sept. 1980; Jean Crabtree Nov. 1980-Jan. 1984; Jerry Hippensteel 1984-1989; Charlotte Lewis 1989-1992; Carolin S. Spragg 1992-1999; Keith W. Heifner 1999-2003; Michael P. Baker-Streevy 2003-Nov. 1, 2005; Lynn Stull-Lipps Jan. 15-June 30, 2006; [Jackson Trinity / Parma became a charge 2006] Sandra L. Spahr (DSA) 2006-2007; Melodye Surgeon Rider 2007-2012; Patricia A. Pebley (1/2 time) 2012-2014 [Parma UMC discontinued 07-01-14]

Pawating Magedwin UMC *[Grand Rapids]*
David G. Knapp 1992-1995; Timothy J. Miller 1995-Jan. 31, 2002; Deborah R. Miller Feb. 1, 2002-2003; Theresa Little Eagle Oyler-Sayles 2003-2006; [Pawating Magedwin UMC discontinued 07-01-06]

Perrinton UMC *[Heartland]*
Robert E. Tomlinson 1974-Jan. 1977; Donald L. Warmouth Feb. 1977-1978; Glenn Britton 1978-1979; Lois H. Gremban 1979-1981; Dale F. Jaquette Aug. 1981-April 1990; T. Ried Martin 1990-1993; Karen E. Nesius 1993-1994; Jodie Flessner 1994; William F. Foldesi Nov. 16, 2003-Apr. 7, 2007; Clare Huyck (DSA) 2007; Clare Huyck Nov. 10, 2007-2012; William F. Dye July 15, 2012-Aug. 31, 2015 [Perrinton UMC discontinued 09-02-15]

Quimby UMC *[Lansing]*
John Joldersma 1965-1970; Esther Cox 1970-1971; William P. Reynders 1971-Feb. 1972; Thomas Churn March 1972-April 1973; Thomas Peters May 1973-Aug. 1976; Dale D. Spoor Sept. 1976-Dec. 1979; Steven Reid Jan. 1980-Jan. 1984; Mary Curtis March 1984-1989; James Noggle 1989-Feb. 1993; Susan A. Trowbridge, March 1993-1998; Kenneth R. Vaught (DSA) 1998-2011; Bryce E. Feighner 2011-2013; [Barry-Eaton Cooperative Ministry 2013] Jerry Bukoski 2013-2018 [Quimby UMc discontinued 06-30-18]

Saginaw: State Street UMC *[Central Bay]*
Kearney Kirkby 1967-1973; Donald C. Porteous 1973-1983; H. Emery Hinkston 1983-1988; Phillip Miles 1988-1993; Joy A. Barrett 1993-1998; Timothy Woycik 1998-2003; Weatherly Burkhead Verhelst 2003-2009; Elias N. Mumbrio Aug 1,2009-2015; Monique Tuner 2015-2019 [Closed 06-30-2019]

Salem UMC *[Heartland]*
William Tate 1967-1969; Robert Boyer 1969-1970; Charles VanLente 1970-1972; Everett Love June-Dec. 1972; Paul Jones 1973-1975; Douglas Jones 1975-1976; Terry MacArthur 1976-Oct. 15, 1979; Robert Gillette Jan. 1980-1984; Merritt Bongard 1984-1991; Joseph Spackman 1991-1999; James Dibbet 1999-2005; O'Ryan Rickard 2005-2007; Kathryn L. Leydorf (DSA) 2007; Kathryn L. Leydorf Nov. 10, 2007-2014; [Elsie/Salem became a charge 5-1-14] Donald R. Ferris-McCann May 1, 2014-Aug. 2, 2015 [Salem UMC discontinued 12-31-15]

Sebewa Center UMC *[Lansing]*
Marjorie Matthews June-Sept. 1968; Robert D. Keith Sept. 1968-1971; Ralph Kallweit 1971-Jan. 1976; John Morse Feb. 1976-1982; Chris Schroeder 1982-Nov. 1984; Kenneth A.O. Lindland Nov. 1984-1987; Joseph L. Spackman 1987-1991; Gordon Spalenka 1991-1993; Robert Besemer 1993-Aug. 31, 1996; Donald Woolum Sept. 16, 1996-2003; Judith Lee Scholten 2003-2004; Jeffrey J. Schrock 2004-2012; Clare W. Huyck 2012-2013 [Sunfield/Sebewa Center no longer two-point charge 2013] [Barry-Eaton Cooperative Ministry 2013] [Sebewa Center UMC discontinued 12-31-14]

Snow UMC *[Grand Rapids]*
Ralph Tweedy 1967-1969; Wayne Barrett 1969-1972; Steven Beach 1972-1974; Ed Passenger 1974-1977; Allen Wittrup 1977-1985; Richard Strait 1985-1986; Dan Duncan 1986-1989; Tracey Taylor 1989-1990; Lloyd Hansen 1990-1991; Mary (Horn) Schippers 1991-March 31, 1995; Pulpit Supply April-June 1995; Thurland Meredith (ad interim) 1995-2008; Vance Dimmick (DSA) 2008-2009; [Middleville/Snow two-point charge 2009] Michael T. Conklin 2009-2012; Anthony C. Shumaker 2012-2017 [Snow UMC closed 07-01-17]

Sylvan UMC *[Heartland]*
Kenneth I. Kline 1977-1981; Pulpit Supply June-Aug. 1981; Dwight Benner Sept. 1981-1983; Purlin Wesseling Aug. 1983-1986; Frank Closson 1986-Jan. 1988; Jane Crabtree Jan. 1988-1990; Pulpit Supply July-Nov. 1991; Robert Stark Nov. 1990-Aug. 1991; Carol L. Bourns Sept. 1991-Dec. 31, 1994; Pulpit Supply Jan. 1995-1996; Jean Crabtree (DSA) 1996-2000; Donald L. Buege 2000-Jan. 2006; Jon Pohl Jan. 15 - June 30, 2006; Jean A. Crabtree (DSA) Nov. 5, 2006-July 2007; Russell Morgan (DSA) July 8, 2007-Nov. 9, 2009; Pat Robinson (DSA) Nov. 9, 2009 [Sylvan UMC became single-point charge Nov. 9, 2009] [discontinued 12-31-11]

Traverse City: Christ UMC *[Grand Traverse]*
John D. Morse 1987-1993; Louis W. Grettenberger 1993-2009; Mary S. Brown July 1-Nov. 1, 2009; Hal Ferris (DSA) Nov. 1-30, 2009; John W. Ellinger (DSA) Dec. 1, 2009-June 1, 2010; Kathryn M. Coombs (DSA) 2010-2011; Dianne Doten Morrison 2011- Jan. 1, 2016; Paul Cole (DSA) Oct. 1, 2015-Mar. 11, 2016 [Traverse City: Christ UMC discontinued 06-30-17]

Traverse City Windward *[Grand Traverse]*
[new church start 2007] John A. Scott 2007-2011; Rebecca Scott (Assoc.) Nov. 1, 2008-2010 [Windward new church start discontinued 05-15-11]

Vermontville UMC *[Lansing]*
David C. Haney 1967-1969; William R. Tate 1969-1972; Gary V. Lyons 1972-April 1976; Gerald A. Salisbury April 1976-1979; Molly C. Turner 1979-1983; Glenn C. Litchfield 1983-1990; Richard W. Young 1990-1991; Robert L. Kersten 1991-1995; Jeffrey J. Bowman 1995-2002; Kathleen Smith 2002-Dec. 31, 2012; [Vermontville/Gresham no longer two-point charge 2013] [Barry-Eaton Cooperative Ministry 2013] Gary L. Simmons (1/4 time) 2013-2015; Nancy V. Fancher (Deacon) 2014-2015; Karen L. Jensen-Kinney 2015-Dec 31, 2017 [Vermontville UMC discontinued 12-31-17]

Village Church (New Church Start) *[Lansing]*
[M-52 Cooperative Ministry 2014; re-named Connections Cooperative Ministry 2015] Jeremy J. Wicks 2014-2017; Jaqueline L. Raineri 2017-2018 [Millville: Village Church Campus discontinued 10-31-17]

Waterloo First UMC *[Lansing]*
Wilbur Silvernail 1960-1969; Donald R. Fry 1969-1970; Altha M. Barnes 1970-1975; Richard M. Young 1975-1976; Glenn Kjellburg 1976-1978; Pulpit Supply 1978-1979; L. A. Nichols 1979-1988; Merlin Pratt 1988-1991; Wayne Willer 1991-1995; Pulpit Supply 1995; Kathleen A. Groff Dec. 1995-July 31, 1997; Mona Joslyn Aug. 1, 1997-1998; Kathleen S. Kursch 1998-Feb. 1, 2000; Georgiana M. Dack (1/4 time) Feb. 1, 2000-2013; [Waterloo Village/First no longer two-point charge 2013] [M-52 Cooperative Ministry 2013] Jeanne M. Laimon (1/4 time) 2013-2014 [Waterloo First UMC was discontinued 07-01-14]

West Mendon UMC *[Albion]*
William Foster 1965-Dec. 1968; David Litchfield Dec. 15, 1968-1971; Harold Simon 1971-1973; William Dobbs 1973-1978; Frank Closson 1978-1981; Larry Higgins 1981-1983; Lloyd Hansen 1983-1987; Clinton McKinven-Copus 1987-1990; Carolyn Floyd 1990-1997; Reva Hawke 1997-2001; Ward D. Pierce (DSA) 2001-Dec. 2, 2012 (died); David G. Knapp (interim) Jan. 1, 2013-June 30, 2013; [West Mendon became single-point charge 2013] Thoreau May 2013-2017; [Mendon / West Mendon became a multi-charge 2015] [West Mendon UMC discontinued 07-01-2017]

White Pines UMC *[Grand Rapids]*
[new church start 2004] Jeffrey C. Williams 2004-2011; Dale A. Hotelling 2011-Aug. 31, 2012 [White Pines new church start discontinued 08-31-12]

— MAC Photos

MICHIGAN ANNUAL CONFERENCE
OF THE
UNITED METHODIST CHURCH
THE 1ˢᵗ SESSION
May 30 - June 2, 2019
2018 LOCAL CHURCH DATA
STATISTICIAN'S AND TREASURER'S REPORT

Mr. David Dobbs, CONFERENCE TREASURER
Rev. Ron Iris, CONFERENCE STATISTICIAN
Rev. Tom Fox, ASSISTANT STATISTICIAN

Format for Journal 2018 Statistics Report of the Michigan Annual Conference

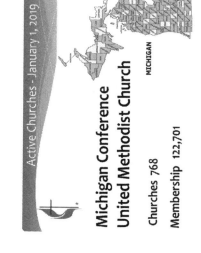

Active Churches - January 1, 2019

Michigan Conference
United Methodist Church

MICHIGAN

Churches 768

Membership 122,701

Shepherds
Counting Sheep!

Striving for
Perfection!

The report contains the following lines:

1	Membership 12.31.2018
4	Membership 12.31.2019
7	Average Worship Attend.
9	Baptized Members/ Not Professing
10	Constituents
11	Total members in Christian Formation Groups
13	Ave. Weekly Sunday School Attendance
18a	Membership in U.M.M.
19a	Membership in U.M.W.
20b	Number of person sent out on other mission teams
21	Number of community ministries for outreach, justice, mercy
24 & 25	Value of church assets and buildings
26 & 27	Church Debt
28a	Ministry Shares Budget Apportioned
29a	Ministry Shares Paid
28b	District Ministry Shares Budget Apportioned
29b	District Ministry Shares Paid
30 - 38	Church Benevolence Giving
39a	Pension Apportioned
39b	Pension Paid
41a	Pastor's Base Compensation
41b	Assoc. Pastor's Base Compensation
40, 42a, 42b, 43, 44	Pastoral Benefits
41c & 42c	Deacons salary/benefits
45	Other Church Staff and Diaconal salary/benefits
46	Local Church program expenses
47	Local Church operating expenses
48 & 49	Local Church capital expenses
50	Grand Total Local Church expenses
51	Number of households giving to the church
52	Total income for annual budget (52a—g)
53	Total dedicated income (53a—d)
54	Total Assistance Income (54a—c)

We covet your feedback. Is there any information you look for in the Journal Statistics Report that is not listed above? Please contact the Statistician and give your suggestions.

If a line number is missing from the chart above and you need that information, i.e. Conference ethnic or gender composition, a specific Special Sunday offering total, please contact either the Treasurer's office or the Database Specialist or the Statistician to download it for you.

Complete spreadsheets with all lines in the Local Church Reports for the last decade are available upon request of statistician@michiganumc.org; 517-347-4030 ext. 4161.

CONFERENCE Number	Church Name	Total professing members reported at the close of last year (1)	TOTAL PROFESSING MEMBERS reported at the close of this year (4)	Average attendance at all weekly worship services (7)	Total Baptized Members who have not become Professing Members (9)	Number of other constituents of the church (10)	TOTAL Christian Formation Group Participants (Total of lines 11a-d) (11)	Average weekly attendance (all ages) in Sunday Church School or other weekly education classes (13)	Membership in United Methodist Men (18a)	Membership in United Methodist Women (19a)	Number of persons sent out on UMVIM teams from this local church (20b)	Total Number of community ministries for outreach, justice, and mercy offered by this local church (21)	Value of church assets and buildings (24 & 25)	Church Debt (26 & 27)	Amount APPORTIONED to the local church by the CONFERENCE (28a)	Amount PAID by the local church to the CONFERENCE for all apportioned causes (28a)	Amount APPORTIONED to the local church by the DISTRICT (if applicable) (28b)
CLOSED	WEST MENDON	101	0	56	0	0	16	10	0	0	0	0	0	0	12,548	0	519
CLOSED	FLINT: EASTWOOD	49	0	17	0	10	0	3	0	0	0	0	0	0	6,605	0	0
CLOSED	WHITMORE LAKE: WESLEY	89	0	31	0	10	20	3	0	14	0	0	1,900,368	0	7,762	0	221
CLOSED	LAURIUM	65	0	10	0	0	1	1	0	2	0	0	0	0	3,565	0	589
CLOSED	GROVENBURG	33	0	12	0	0	0	0	0	0	0	0	0	0	7,019	630	257
CLOSED	QUIMBY	20	0	1	0	16	0	0	0	0	0	0	0	0	2,393	1,197	144
CLOSED	DEARBORN HTS: WARREN VALLEY	46	0	19	0	5	3	2	0	0	0	0	0	1,631	3,901	0	262
CLOSED	MELVINDALE: NEW HOPE	38	0	12	0	41	21	19	4	5	0	0	0	0	5,414	0	363
		441	0	158	0	41	61	19	4	21	0	0	1,900,368	1,631	49,207	1,827	2,355
	NORTHERN SKIES DISTRICT																
31,001	ALGONQUIN	56	54	23	0	0	6	0	0	9	0	0	260,000	532	4,869	4,869	805
31,002	AMASA: GRACE	23	25	15	0	3	28	20	0	0	0	0	57,000	0	2,022	2,022	335
31,003	BARK RIVER	75	77	19	0	15	26	19	0	0	0	3	192,045	0	2,858	2,858	473
31,004	BERGLAND	14	14	20	0	33	3	0	0	0	0	0	229,292	0	2,668	0	442
31,005	CALUMET	99	99	42	0	0	7	6	0	25	0	1	689,500	0	5,731	5,731	947
31,006	CHEBOYGAN: ST PAUL'S	261	249	104	0	147	72	20	10	40	0	0	3,132,506	4,851	21,110	17,045	3,489
31,007	CRYSTAL FALLS: CHRIST	127	125	46	0	39	35	15	0	15	0	8	1,632,126	0	9,665	6,766	1,502
31,008	EMMETT CNTY: NEW HOPE	59	45	50	0	54	41	4	0	0	0	5	1,006,282	0	9,905	9,905	530
31,009	ENGADINE	37	41	32	0	54	44	5	0	15	1	5	633,159	0	5,496	5,496	909

STATISTICAL INFORMATION

CONFERENCE Number	29b	30-38	39a	39b	41a	41b	40, 42a-44	41c & 42c	45	46	47	48 & 49	50	51	52	53	54
CLOSED	0	5,031	0	0	8,000	0	2,150	0	8,000	500	11,000	0	34,681	35	55,000	100	0
CLOSED	0	0	1,940	0	0	0	0	0	0	0	1	0	1	0	0	0	0
CLOSED	0	0	1,710	1,710	17,600	0	0	0	0	57	12,709	0	32,076	40	21,462	0	0
CLOSED	371	0	1,120	0	0	0	0	0	0	0	1	0	372	30	12,000	0	0
CLOSED	200	723	2,697	2,697	0	0	0	0	0	0	0	0	4,251	0	0	0	0
CLOSED	72	1,069	1,830	0	0	0	0	0	0	0	0	0	2,339	36	10,017	0	0
CLOSED	262	25	1,060	0	7,418	0	2,994	0	1,595	1	3,777	1,631	17,703	20	12,800	0	0
CLOSED	0	0	0	0	4,500	0	0	0	0	151	2,000	1,500	8,151	0	0	0	0
CLOSED	905	6,848	10,357	4,407	37,518	0	5,144	0	9,595	709	29,490	3,131	99,574	161	111,279	100	0
31001	805	2,018	940	940	5,032	0	2,219	0	5,747	500	11,202	0	33,332	17	28,986	4,575	0
31002	335	400	650	650	3,947	0	1,200	0	0	200	5,000	2,258	13,754	23	16,176	0	0
31003	473	1,513	1,320	1,320	12	0	4,341	0	0	1,075	3,367	0	17,217	28	25,615	9,823	0
31004	442	100	960	960	10,002	0	1,200	0	150	200	3,624	0	16,678	12	15,076	942	0
31005	947	1,014	1,120	1,120	8,841	0	7,978	0	6,828	200	32,942	20,000	85,601	56	86,432	5,000	0
31006	2,816	3,223	6,170	6,170	50,500	0	25,846	0	32,381	4,495	27,478	9,849	179,803	153	167,812	14,507	0
31007	1,502	251	3,660	2,562	28,750	0	11,429	0	6,744	0	12,865	0	70,869	62	89,264	595	0
31008	530	4,191	3,744	3,744	21,632	0	33,571	0	0	1,156	17,950	2,282	94,961	33	78,474	10,919	0
31009	907	8,991	2,070	2,070	19,853	0	5,178	0	0	6,915	7,574	18,048	75,032	48	60,511	1,140	100

Column line descriptions:
- 29b: Amount PAID by the local church to the DISTRICT for all apportioned causes (if applicable)
- 30-38: Church Benevolence Giving
- 39a: Total ASKED for clergy pension
- 39b: Total PAID for clergy pension
- 41a: Base compensation paid to/for the Senior Pastor or other person assigned or appointed in the lead pastoral role to the church
- 41b: Base compensation paid to/for all Associate Pastor(s) and other pastoral staff assigned or appointed to the church, include deacons and other clergy in this role.
- 40, 42a-44: Pastoral Benefits
- 41c & 42c: Deacons salary/benefits
- 45: Total amount paid in salary and benefits for all other church staff and diaconal ministers
- 46: Total amount spent for local church program expenses
- 47: Total amount spent for other local church operating expenses
- 48 & 49: Local church capital expenses
- 50: TOTAL CHURCH EXPENSES (Sum of lines 29a through 49)
- 51: Number of giving units
- 52: Total income for annual budget/spending plan
- 53: Total income for designated causes including capital campaign and other special projects
- 54: Total income from connectional and other institutional sources outside the local church

STATISTICAL INFORMATION

CONFERENCE Number	Church Name	Total professing members reported at the close of last year (1)	TOTAL PROFESSING MEMBERS reported at the close of this year (4)	Average attendance at all weekly worship services (7)	Total Baptized Members who have not become Professing Members (9)	Number of other constituents of the church (10)	TOTAL Christian Formation Group Participants (Total of lines) (11a-d)	Average weekly attendance (all ages) in Sunday Church School or other weekly education classes (13)	Membership in United Methodist Men (18a)	Membership in United Methodist Women (19a)	Number of persons sent out on UMVIM teams from this local church (20b)	Total Number of community ministries for outreach, justice, and mercy offered by this local church (21)	Value of church assets and buildings (24 & 25)	Church Debt (26 & 27)	Amount APPORTIONED to the local church by the CONFERENCE (28a)	Amount PAID by the local church to the CONFERENCE for all apportioned causes (29a)	Amount APPORTIONED to the local church by the DISTRICT (if applicable) (28b)
31010	ESCANABA: CENTRAL	180	176	67	22	38	55	40	0	0	0	5	2,981,831	0	18,396	18,396	3,041
31011	ESCANABA: FIRST	109	107	46	23	45	16	8	0	0	0	4	1,954,916	0	12,698	0	2,099
31012	EWEN	22	23	18	7	22	8	1	0	0	0	3	186,000	192	1,999	1,599	328
31013	FAITHORN	30	30	25	5	20	0	0	0	0	0	3	93,500	0	1,414	1,414	234
31014	GERMFASK	22	24	20	0	0	45	0	0	0	0	3	513,852	0	2,487	0	412
31015	GLADSTONE: MEMORIAL	296	277	100	45	66	45	31	0	0	0	20	3,446,144	0	21,630	12,762	3,575
31016	GRAND MARAIS	111	11	10	0	32	3	0	0	0	0	0	816,015	0	2,837	0	469
31017	GREENLAND	43	41	21	0	16	5	25	0	11	0	0	382,000	0	2,039	2,039	337
31018	GWINN	223	225	88	38	184	171	0	0	31	0	3	2,795,000	5,000	16,274	16,274	2,690
31019	HANCOCK: FIRST	280	298	81	44	49	90	42	0	27	0	21	4,264,000	2,291	20,874	20,874	3,451
31020	HERMANSVILLE: FIRST	64	65	24	0	5	0	4	0	0	0	0	173,295	0	4,014	2,360	663
31021	HOUGHTON: GRACE	250	254	96	2	0	59	14	0	0	0	0	1,695,940	0	18,381	0	4,517
31022	HULBERT: TAHQUAMENON	8	7	10	0	35	6	6	0	0	0	17	376,332	100	1,034	1,034	171
31023	IRON MOUNTAIN: FIRST	67	66	34	24	33	27	16	0	18	0	4	1,043,870	64,514	9,285	9,285	1,535
31024	IRON MOUNTAIN: TRINITY	318	304	113	34	143	76	18	0	38	21	2	4,374,213	0	26,750	26,750	4,195
31025	IRONWOOD: WESLEY	127	126	45	0	0	8	8	0	21	0	5	103,376	183,000	8,357	8,357	1,381
31026	ISHPEMING: WESLEY	548	550	151	0	0	86	17	0	0	0	5	5,298,273	0	27,313	27,313	4,515
31027	LAKE LINDEN	120	122	42	0	0	14	5	0	13	0	0	630,000	0	4,261	4,261	704
31028	L'ANSE	197	196	55	52	51	42	22	0	30	0	1	1,427,693	0	12,832	8,982	2,122

NS

STATISTICAL INFORMATION

CONFERENCE Number	29b — Amount PAID by the local church to the DISTRICT for all apportioned causes (if applicable)	30-38 — Church Benevolence Giving	39a — Total ASKED for clergy pension	39b — Total PAID for clergy pension	41a — Base compensation paid to/for the Senior Pastor or other person assigned or appointed in the lead pastoral role to the church	41b — Base compensation paid to/for all Associate Pastor(s) and other pastoral staff assigned or appointed to the church; and include deacons and other clergy in this role.	40, 42a-44 — Pastoral Benefits	41c & 42c — Deacons salary/benefits	45 — Total amount paid in salary and benefits for all other church staff and diaconal ministers	46 — Total amount spent for local church program expenses	47 — Total amount spent for other local church operating expenses	48 & 49 — Local Church capital expenses	50 — TOTAL CHURCH EXPENSES (Sum of Lines 29a through 49)	51 — Number of giving units	52 — Total income for annual budget/spending plan	53 — Total income for designated causes including capital campaign and other special projects	54 — Total income from connectional and other institutional sources outside the local church
31010	3,087	1,545	5,030	5,030	41,228	0	15,958	0	24,573	7,382	37,406	0	154,605	83	155,013	11,076	0
31011	2,099	21,578	2,400	2,400	20,022	0	9,916	0	9,951	2,592	19,374	891	88,823	42	83,635	24,627	0
31012	328	1,296	960	768	10,002	0	0	0	775	450	3,500	2,800	21,518	26	15,646	447	0
31013	234	4,400	620	620	4,653	0	2,700	0	0	429	4,412	0	18,862	10	32,258	1,650	0
31014	412	735	1,520	1,520	12,970	0	13,079	0	0	0	5,100	40,356	33,816	20	27,000	0	0
31015	2,188	14,592	6,300	6,300	50,750	0	34,019	0	41,586	7,272	35,300	1,500	245,125	113	193,998	69,534	0
31016	472	830	1,520	1,520	12,970	0	2,651	0	0	80	5,353	5,106	25,376	5	17,000	1,000	0
31017	337	2,599	950	950	0	0	0	0	50	0	3,950	3,222	15,031	16	26,712	1,641	0
31018	2,690	2,240	5,270	5,270	43,077	0	1,264	0	14,000	13,106	39,662	0	140,795	118	157,934	5,370	300
31019	3,451	14,216	5,850	5,850	48,311	0	31,338	0	23,143	5,363	43,332	750	195,878	83	187,079	9,577	0
31020	663	4,438	1,590	1,590	12,205	0	5,155	0	0	106	8,514	0	35,781	22	43,821	820	0
31021	4,517	30,718	5,760	5,760	52,017	0	25,344	0	12,640	3,282	41,799	0	176,077	83	142,154	4,419	0
31022	1,710	3,334	100	100	3,522	0	387	0	0	501	3,559	9,302	14,147	20	7,491	3,329	0
31023	1,535	3,193	3,090	3,090	18,469	0	9,704	0	7,368	4,726	12,981	19,128	79,653	31	77,393	8,971	0
31024	3,851	15,372	5,670	5,670	47,338	0	28,559	0	60,791	5,880	40,949	10,796	254,288	155	252,201	18,231	1,700
31025	1,381	4,237	3,270	3,270	12,022	1,100	2,764	0	4,949	645	18,592	28,637	68,113	50	59,144	29,504	800
31026	4,515	15,638	5,120	5,120	43,993	0	35,588	0	57,563	15,183	58,906	358	292,456	209	271,154	12,018	0
31027	704	655	1,120	1,120	8,527	2,057	8,153	0	2,218	1	6,536	0	34,590	42	38,427	812	0
31028	2,122	4,556	4,670	4,670	38,773	0	14,778	0	9,857	3,444	10,364	7,025	104,571	45	102,054	3,630	0

NS

CONFERENCE Number	Church Name	Total professing members reported at the close of last year (1)	TOTAL PROFESSING MEMBERS reported at the close of this year (4)	Average attendance at all weekly worship services (7)	Total Baptized Members who have not become Professing Members (9)	Number of other constituents of the church (10)	TOTAL Christian Formation Group Participants (Total of lines 11a-d) (11)	Average weekly attendance (all ages) in Sunday Church School or other weekly education classes (13)	Membership in United Methodist Men (18)	Membership in United Methodist Women (19a)	Number of persons sent out on UMVIM teams from this local church (20b)	Total Number of community ministries for outreach, justice, and mercy offered by this local church (21)	Value of church assets and buildings (24 & 25)	Church Debt (26 & 27)	Amount APPORTIONED to the local church by the CONFERENCE (28a)	Amount PAID by the local church to the CONFERENCE for all apportioned causes (29a)	Amount APPORTIONED to the local church by the DISTRICT (if applicable) (28b)
31029	MACKINAW CITY: CHURCH OF THE STRAITS	112	112	120	20	20	78	20	20	0	0	2	1,428,739	0	10,394	10,394	1,718
31030	MANISTIQUE: FIRST	147	154	54	2	0	22	16	0	24	0	0	30,614	0	9,835	9,835	1,626
31031	MARQUETTE: HOPE	309	314	140	37	102	141	15	16	38	0	5	9,470,483	0	15,312	15,312	3,609
31032	MCMILLAN	18	14	13	0	16	0	8	0	8	0	4	657,712	0	2,876	2,876	476
31033	MENOMINEE: FIRST	87	86	57	0	2	37	10	10	29	0	1	1,496,103	309,322	14,415	10,813	2,383
31034	MICHIGAMME: WOODLAND	29	22	13	1	14	1	0	0	0	0	0	546,392	2,155	3,326	3,326	550
31035	MOHAWK AHMEEK	24	27	14	1	0	1	1	0	0	0	0	125,000	0	3,662	0	605
31036	MUNISING	83	71	35	3	25	42	6	0	21	0	11	1,075,520	0	6,844	6,844	1,132
31037	NEGAUNEE: MITCHELL	233	213	60	53	17	48	14	10	0	0	0	4,668,376	0	21,418	8,329	3,540
31038	NEWBERRY	90	90	35	0	0	25	10	0	14	0	5	1,119,500	0	9,138	9,138	1,510
31039	NORWAY: GRACE	145	148	68	34	38	23	8	0	0	0	0	836,000	0	10,050	10,050	1,661
31040	ONTONAGON	145	131	27	1	3	8	0	0	19	0	2	1,196,824	0	5,734	5,734	947
31041	PAINESDALE: ALBERT PAINE MEM.	36	42	17	0	26	10	11	0	0	0	2	29,761	770	1,981	1,981	327
31042	PARADISE	31	31	20	1	11	9	35	0	0	0	0	744,000	0	3,388	3,388	560
31043	PICKFORD	196	209	162	42	75	22	4	3	0	0	0	2,211,846	0	16,285	10,000	2,692
31044	QUINNESEC	55	56	29	20	23	25	4	0	0	0	4	638,000	0	5,068	5,068	838
31045	REPUBLIC	46	43	18	20	18	7	0	0	17	0	7	250,000	462	5,411	5,411	895
31046	ROCKLAND: ST PAUL'S	66	66	27	4	21	0	0	0	11	0	1	1,092,285	0	3,487	3,487	576
31047	SAULT ST MARIE: CENTRAL	175	162	82	66	55	80	23	0	30	0	1	6,778,401	0	22,556	22,556	3,800

STATISTICAL INFORMATION

CONFERENCE Number	29b Amount PAID by the local church to the DISTRICT for all apportioned causes (if applicable)	30-38 Church Benevolence Giving	39a Total ASKED for clergy pension	39b Total PAID for clergy pension	41a Base compensation paid to/for the Senior Pastor or other person assigned or appointed in the lead pastoral role to the church	41b Base compensation paid to/for all Associate Pastor(s) and other pastoral staff assigned or appointed to the church, include deacons and other clergy in this role.	40, 42a-44 Pastoral Benefits	41c & 42c Deacons salary/benefits	45 Total amount paid in salary and benefits for all other church staff and diaconal ministers.	46 Total amount spent for local church program expenses	47 Total amount spent for other local church operating expenses	48 & 49 Local Church capital expenses	50 TOTAL CHURCH EXPENSES (Sum of lines 29a through 49)	51 Number of giving units	52 Total income for annual budget/spending plan	53 Total income for designated causes including capital campaign and other special projects	54 Total income from connectional and other institutional sources outside the local church
31029	1,718	27,926	7,120	7,120	59,950	0	30,471	0	37,923	5,204	36,111	0	216,817	130	226,170	1,150	0
31030	1,681	7,683	2,120	2,120	26,543	0	14,509	0	11,379	915	26,678	16,980	118,323	51	101,695	17,056	1,020
31031	3,609	6,545	12,740	12,740	53,500	53,500	27,502	0	71,012	9,069	89,627	25,933	368,349	126	271,140	34,679	65,000
31032	476	3,314	1,520	1,520	12,970	0	3,351	0	0	350	4,652	0	29,509	12	19,790	800	0
31033	2,383	3,000	2,400	2,400	20,020	0	8,179	0	17,942	3,125	20,754	26,051	114,667	55	106,608	10,899	0
31034	550	4,268	540	540	8,881	0	4,911	0	0	965	7,654	2,326	33,421	20	31,459	0	0
31035	277	0	1,120	1,120	12,000	0	2,000	0	3,023	500	3,461	0	22,381	12	12,190	0	1,307
31036	1,132	8,566	1,670	1,670	24,620	0	5,092	0	7,536	2,883	11,947	0	70,290	66	60,193	4,177	0
31037	2,350	3,880	5,620	6,192	47,380	0	27,775	0	41,619	2,666	31,801	36,385	208,377	90	146,200	11,153	0
31038	1,510	4,933	3,110	3,110	24,546	0	8,662	0	4,377	1,497	21,063	0	78,836	50	75,393	3,974	0
31039	1,661	3,564	4,120	4,120	34,640	0	11,058	0	5,600	1,910	16,150	0	88,753	60	89,999	0	0
31040	947	2,782	2,300	2,300	30,970	0	0	0	1,614	500	14,000	19,255	78,102	35	73,138	2,139	0
31041	351	2,025	670	670	10,440	0	410	0	710	250	5,371	1,400	23,608	22	32,499	125	7,000
31042	560	181	370	370	9,400	0	0	0	792	1,753	8,932	0	25,376	30	33,845	0	0
31043	2,692	39,102	4,750	4,750	43,200	0	27,529	0	28,050	9,964	31,229	49,117	245,633	110	221,560	43,099	1,000
31044	838	4,783	1,460	1,460	14,592	0	5,318	0	4,005	793	8,697	12,150	57,704	29	40,852	7,968	0
31045	895	1,856	540	540	8,881	0	4,041	0	4,154	1,356	5,540	1,197	33,870	30	33,330	0	0
31046	576	1,340	1,750	1,750	0	0	0	0	22,015	1,014	6,192	0	36,374	26	34,712	3,991	0
31047	3,800	4,857	4,920	4,920	31,443	0	20,510	0	30,595	8,625	46,529	0	173,835	69	160,263	6,105	0

NS

CONFERENCE Number	Church Name	Total professing members reported at the close of last year (1)	TOTAL PROFESSING MEMBERS reported at the close of this year (4)	Average attendance at all weekly worship services (7)	Total Baptized Members who have not become Professing Members (9)	Number of other constituents of the church (10)	TOTAL Christian Formation Group Participants (Total of lines 11a-d) (11)	Average weekly attendance (all ages) in Sunday Church School or other weekly education classes (13)	Membership in United Methodist Men (18a)	Membership in United Methodist Women (19a)	Number of persons sent out on UMVIM teams from this local church (20b)	Total Number of community ministries for outreach, justice, and mercy offered by this local church (21)	Value of church assets and buildings (24 & 25)	Church Debt (26 & 27)	Amount APPORTIONED to the local church by the CONFERENCE (28a)	Amount PAID by the local church to the CONFERENCE for all apportioned causes (29a)	Amount APPORTIONED to the local church by the DISTRICT (if applicable) (28b)
31048	SIDNAW	15	16	13	0	7	0	0	0	0	0	0	138,939	0	2,177	2,177	360
31049	ST IGNACE	171	171	76	10	77	62	12	0	30	0	4	1,596,591	0	17,512	17,512	2,895
31050	STEPHENSON	72	62	35	13	10	9	7	0	17	0	1	827,533	0	8,077	8,077	1,334
31051	TRENARY	21	21	15	0	6	8	1	0	0	0	3	643,843	0	2,377	2,377	394
31052	WAKEFIELD	28	28	24	6	13	8	5	0	0	7	0	266,000	0	2,529	2,529	418
31053	WHITE PINE COMMUNITY	72	72	40	9	19	19	13	0	17	7	2	920,779	0	4,309	4,309	713
31054	ZEBA	29	29	20	0	19	0	0	0	0	0	0	387,365	0	3,077	3,077	509
	NORTHERN SKIES DISTRICT TOTALS	6,101	6,021	2,611	618	1,648	1,657	550	79	568	29	159	79,554,766	573,189	488,437	400,992	81,939
	NORTHERN WATERS DISTRICT																
32001	ALANSON	36	34	22	0	0	0	0	0	0	0	0	509,264	23,334	8,374	0	211
32002	ALBA	27	25	25	15	48	14	4	0	0	0	0	111,000	0	4,056	0	203
32003	ALDEN	59	59	39	8	26	6	5	0	24	9	2	1,478,000	0	10,154	10,154	428
32004	ALPENA: FIRST	248	241	98	0	47	78	15	13	22	0	2	4,350,663	0	25,077	0	2,474
32005	ARCADIA	17	17	18	0	21	6	0	13	12	0	1	160,000	0	2,681	2,092	109
32006	ASHTON	37	34	21	0	0	5	1	0	0	0	0	668,491	0	4,622	1,702	283
32007	AVONDALE	8	8	14	0	0	0	0	0	0	0	0	128,256	0	1,198	1,198	46
32008	BALDWIN: COVENANT CMNTY	49	37	40	0	28	27	3	0	0	0	4	735,000	0	7,582	7,583	341
32009	BARNARD	63	65	45	0	35	13	1	0	18	0	0	501,158	0	3,936	3,936	356

STATISTICAL INFORMATION

NW

CONFERENCE Number	29b Amount PAID by the local church to the DISTRICT for all apportioned causes (if applicable)	30-38 Church Benevolence Giving	39a Total ASKED for clergy pension	39b Total PAID for clergy pension	41a Base compensation paid to/for the Senior Pastor or other person in lead pastoral role	41b Base compensation paid to/for all Associate Pastor(s) and other pastoral staff	40, 42a-44 Pastoral Benefits	41c & 42c Deacons salary/benefits	45 Total amount paid in salary and benefits for all other church staff and diaconal ministers	46 Total amount spent for local church program expenses	47 Total amount spent for other local church operating expenses	48 & 49 Local church capital expenses	50 TOTAL CHURCH EXPENSES (Sum of Lines 29a through 49)	51 Number of giving units	52 Total income for annual budget/spending plan	53 Total income for designated causes including capital campaign and other special projects	54 Total income from connectional and other institutional sources outside the local church
31048	360	2,168	320	320	2,585	0	1,060	0	955	1,234	6,837	4,500	22,196	7	24,291	243	0
31049	2,899	3,656	5,170	5,170	38,384	0	34,210	0	18,671	4,794	23,860	18,510	167,666	93	168,130	5,360	800
31050	1,334	4,964	1,980	1,980	25,160	0	9,073	0	5,206	739	15,030	0	71,563	30	62,819	9,466	0
31051	165	912	640	640	9,448	0	2,269	0	0	0	6,352	856	23,019	24	21,527	2,468	0
31052	418	9,875	1,090	1,090	10,002	0	6,282	0	4,000	1,200	6,928	1,000	37,042	37	46,478	3,950	0
31053	713	5,051	2,070	2,070	16,250	0	7,181	0	2,156	7,330	9,888	7,754	61,803	82	44,815	19,393	0
31054	509	415	1,250	1,250	10,340	0		0	840	2,561	5,451	1,395	33,019	23	34,223	415	0
	79,457	325,518	152,804	152,086	1,215,563	56,657	595,712	0	645,488	156,380	992,315	407,117	5,027,285	2,924	4,631,779	442,767	79,027
32001	0	406	0	0	12,462	0	4,403	0	10,940	1,919	9,493	1,050	40,693	1	29,896	3,162	0
32002	428	0	0	0	11,283	0	5,447	0	1,000	200	5,000	0	22,930	10	30,500	0	0
32003	0	9,586	8,363	8,363	33,450	0	20,463	0	7,438	578	22,867	0	113,327	44	94,034	20,027	0
32004	147	787	5,260	5,260	43,255	0	31,315	0	47,299	4,728	29,339	0	161,983	70	150,177	11,095	0
32005	104	850	0	0	8,737	0	2,768	0	1,817	556	4,033	0	21,000	18	24,226	1,862	0
32006	46	1,638	0	0	10,250	0	7,040	0	720	171	12,352	0	33,977	25	34,166	1,882	0
32007		304			0	0	0	0		69	3,462	1,077	8,631	12	10,650	153	0
32008	341	6,053	4,478	4,478	19,177	0	32,236	0	2,475	5,947	12,232	0	88,047	32	61,463	4,908	5,000
32009	356	4,928	8,348	8,348	11,575	0	8,286	0	1,524	701	5,526	0	45,180	49	39,075	5,387	0

STATISTICAL INFORMATION

NW

CONF. No.	Church Name	(1) Total professing members reported at the close of last year	(4) TOTAL PROFESSING MEMBERS reported at the close of this year	(7) Average attendance at all weekly worship services	(9) Total Baptized Members who have not become Professing Members	(10) Number of other constituents of the church	(11a-d) TOTAL Christian Formation Group Participants (Total of lines 11a-d)	(13) Average weekly attendance (all ages) in Sunday Church School or other weekly education classes	(18a) Membership in United Methodist Men	(19a) Membership in United Methodist Women	(20b) Number of persons sent out on UMVIM teams from this local church	(21) Total Number of community ministries for outreach, justice, and mercy offered by this local church	(24 & 25) Value of church assets and buildings	(26 & 27) Church Debt	(28a) Amount APPORTIONED to the local church by the CONFERENCE	(29a) Amount PAID by the local church to the CONFERENCE for all apportioned causes	(28b) Amount APPORTIONED to the local church by the DISTRICT (if applicable)
32010	BEAR LAKE	92	74	40	3	20	26	0	6	12	0	1	1,388,155	7,432	12,769	504	653
32011	BELLAIRE: COMMUNITY	180	150	100	10	124	80	16	0	0	0	1	481,960	0	19,918	19,918	1,494
32012	BOYNE CITY	60	60	48	0	0	26	2	0	0	0	2	973,991	24,314	10,760	6,941	472
32013	BOYNE FALLS	25	25	16	0	0	9	1	0	1	0	1	273,180	0	3,386	1,685	203
32014	BRETHREN: EPWORTH	38	36	15	144	22	23	12	10	0	0	0	1,033,510	0	3,998	1,999	283
32015	CADILLAC	389	383	127	0	60	48	18	0	82	0	11	3,254,608	0	40,117	29,194	2,951
32016	CADILLAC: SOUTH COMMUNITY	34	34	34	0	0		10	0	0	0	0	747,659	0	6,072	6,071	247
32017	CENTRAL LAKE	28	25	13	9	1	8	0	16	0	0	0	826,000	0	4,666	4,666	211
32018	CHARLEVOIX	87	86	53	0	0	28	49	0	15	0	7	3,461,403	0	11,837	11,837	638
32019	CHARLEVOIX: GREENSKY HILL	103	103	46	0	40	28	8	0	7	0	0	670,000	33,000	5,346	0	776
32020	CHASE: BARTON	12	12	14	0	20	13	0	0	0	0	0	770,000	0	5,891	5,891	182
32021	EAST BOARDMAN	28	26	35	61	0	23	14	0	0	0	2	541,000	0	6,829	0	254
32022	EAST JORDAN	116	112	54	28	38	26	6	18	10	0	1	1,446,140	0	12,430	8,287	856
32023	ELBERTA	27	27	32	5	0	0	0	0	0	0	3	577,819	0	5,218	5,218	203
32024	EMPIRE	83	79	50	0	51	47	10	0	45	0	0	1,087,142	0	15,824	15,825	624
32025	EPSILON	43	42	41	1	17	23	6	0	0	0	0	430,488	0	5,719	5,719	305
32026	EVART	81	80	54	0	60	14	3	0	20	0	3	467,602	0	17,557	0	535
32027	FIFE LAKE	32	36	50	54	33	13	10	0	8	0	1	800,001	0	9,838	10,658	254
32028	FRANKFORT	109	106	75	0	0	0	0	0	75	0	0	2,050,399	0	23,240	23,241	762

STATISTICAL INFORMATION

NW

CONFERENCE Number	Amount PAID by the local church to the DISTRICT for all apportioned causes (if applicable) (29b)	Church Benevolence Giving (30-38)	Total ASKED for clergy pension (39a)	Total PAID for clergy pension (39b)	Base compensation paid to/for the Senior Pastor or other person assigned or appointed in the lead pastoral role to the church (41a)	Base compensation paid to/for all Associate Pastor(s) and other pastoral staff assigned or appointed to the church. Include deacons and other clergy in this role. (41b)	Pastoral Benefits (40, 42a-44)	Deacons salary/benefits (41c & 42c)	Total amount paid in salary and benefits for all other church staff and diaconal ministers (45)	Total amount spent for local church program expenses (46)	Total amount spent for other local church operating expenses (47)	Local Church capital expenses (48 & 49)	TOTAL CHURCH EXPENSES (Sum of lines 29a through 49) (50)	Number of giving units (51)	Total income for annual budget/spending plan (52)	Total income for designated causes including capital campaign and other special projects (53)	Total income from connectional and other institutional sources outside the local church (54)
32010	16	1,321	8,886	6,665	21,896	5,600	12,264	0	12,816	700	18,776	0	80,558	73	86,122	0	400
32011	1,494	6,144	6,938	6,938	37,000	0	31,624	0	19,640	10,088	29,325	4,067	166,238	129	153,243	14,291	0
32012	311	6,780	7,611	7,611	16,237	0	11,487	0	21,679	6,799	15,926	3,106	96,877	45	76,342	8,291	0
32013	55	720	7,611	7,611	8,118	0	5,176	0	5,782	334	4,562	3,162	29,594	13	29,394	795	0
32014	141	400	0	0	9,568	0	6,549	0	3,975	970	7,273	11,217	30,875	37	38,949	0	0
32015	2,197	18,968	13,667	13,527	59,990	6,063	30,583	0	51,687	10,826	66,845	180	301,097	267	274,138	56,241	3,000
32016	247	3,835	0	0	20,873	0	4,102	0	1,500	2,146	9,026	10,000	47,980	22	42,851	5,047	0
32017	211	621	3,093	3,093	11,425	0	10,952	0	0	200	6,179	3,577	44,254	10	39,800	0	16,500
32018	638	668	3,701	0	20,623	0	21,343	0	19,048	1,010	23,693	0	105,530	30	83,253	8,596	17,217
32019	0	0	0	0	12,200	0	23,200	0	7,000	2,000	10,000	0	54,400	98	46,700	0	0
32020	182	1,756	0	0	9,593	0	9,616	0	1,200	1,546	22,807	10,000	52,591	12	46,447	1,256	0
32021	0	1,200	1,438	1,438	15,598	0	8,096	0	1,158	1,244	7,814	2,609	46,548	35	49,150	1,500	0
32022	856	8,154	0	1,791	32,946	0	25,545	0	18,831	3,263	15,295	1,521	117,577	52	112,193	20,799	0
32023	203	2,972	0	0	9,864	0	2,313	0	10,053	892	11,915	0	44,951	43	55,349	8,911	0
32024	624	7,239	8,527	8,527	45,480	0	22,938	0	17,317	6,501	16,465	0	140,916	52	125,981	2,760	7,920
32025	0	7,430	0	0	16,236	0	3,248	0	5,400	778	13,251	0	46,343	26	44,744	13,588	0
32026	275	0	8,734	8,734	51,131	0	28,626	0	21,085	3,983	31,319	6,000	144,878	43	131,586	3,635	3,500
32027	761	5,496	1,438	1,438	6,778	2,232	6,234	0	1,475	2,370	4,502	0	49,458	40	84,881	0	0
32028		8,374	9,248	9,248	39,457	0	18,128	0	44,329	11,089	47,845	0	202,472	98	194,276	33,295	0

CONFERENCE Number	Church Name	Total professing members reported at the close of last year (1)	TOTAL PROFESSING MEMBERS reported at the close of this year (4)	Average attendance at all weekly worship services (7)	Total Baptized Members who have not become Professing Members (9)	Number of other constituents of the church (10)	TOTAL Christian Formation Group Participants (11)	Average weekly attendance (all ages) in Sunday Church School or other weekly education classes (13)	Membership in United Methodist Men (18a)	Membership in United Methodist Women (19a)	Number of persons sent out on UMVIM teams from this local church (20b)	Total Number of community ministries for outreach, justice, and mercy offered by this local church (21)	Value of church assets and buildings (24 & 25)	Church Debt (26 & 27)	Amount APPORTIONED to the local church by the CONFERENCE (28a)	Amount PAID by the local church to the CONFERENCE for all apportioned causes (29a)	Amount APPORTIONED to the local church by the DISTRICT (if applicable) (28b)
32029	FREE SOIL - FOUNTAIN	30	30	15	5	35	12	0				13	909,000	6,200	1,845	0	232
32030	GAYLORD: FIRST	578	579	272	205	142	211	43	17	62	0	4	4,159,321	0	36,841	36,841	3,635
32031	GRANT	70	61	32	2	15	34	5	0	0	0	2	618,947	0	6,410	5,876	508
32032	GRAWN	97	98	75	0	38	46	16	0	0	0	0	1,071,666	0	11,227	11,228	704
32033	GRAYLING: MICHELSON MEM.	237	226	143	0	149	22	14	0	42	42	5	2,417,332	0	19,362	0	1,910
32034	HARBOR SPRINGS	68	72	48	0	0	8	3	0	0	0	1	2,686,269	38,702	9,343	2,268	493
32035	HARRIETTA	62	52	32	12	23	37	10	0	0	0	1	668,000	0	6,130	4,456	450
32036	HERSEY	74	76	35	24	35	60	12	0	5	0	10	500,800	0	6,951	6,951	488
32037	HILLMAN	116	101	59	0	0	10	9	0	0	0	4	516,088	0	8,357	8,357	825
32038	HORTON BAY	35	32	29	2	160	105	36	16	29	3	4	423,510	3,600	5,499	5,040	254
32039	HOUGHTON LAKE	447	426	187	1	349	162	40	0	0	42	10	2,525,000	187,671	31,630	26,806	3,627
32040	INDIAN RIVER	278	267	203	2		57	9	0	0	0	12	1,565,112	270,018	23,334	19,495	2,335
32041	KALKASKA	126	125	78	1	77	55	35	11	20	0	9	476,663	107,616	20,577	9,987	1,066
32042	KESWICK	61	60	58	7	31	0	3	1	2	0	0	968,410	0	14,093	14,093	450
32043	KEWADIN	45	43	32	7	0	75	0	0	22	0	0	1,123,636	0	6,785	6,785	327
32044	KEWADIN: INDIAN MISSION	29	20	10	0	48	101	25	0	0	0	5	500,500	0	1,461	1,461	218
32045	KINGSLEY	119	142	126	35	150	43	38	0	12	0	10	1,449,845	0	8,213	8,216	878
32046	LAKE ANN	164	165	125	4			38	22	12	0	2	1,803,053	161,436	21,151	4,375	1,189
32047	LAKE CITY	163	162	67		92	43	16	0	44	0		774,227	87,251	14,894	14,894	1,197

STATISTICAL INFORMATION

NW

CONFERENCE Number	29b Amount PAID by the local church to the DISTRICT for all apportioned causes (if applicable)	30-38 Church Benevolence Giving	39a Total ASKED for clergy pension	39b Total PAID for clergy pension	41a Base compensation paid to/for the Senior Pastor or other person assigned or appointed in the lead pastoral role to the church	41b Base compensation paid to/for all Associate Pastor(s) and other pastoral staff assigned or appointed to the church, include deacons and other clergy in this role.	40, 42a-44 Pastoral Benefits	41c & 42c Deacons salary/benefits	45 Total amount paid in salary and benefits for all other church staff and diaconal ministers	46 Total amount spent for local church program expenses	47 Total amount spent for other local church operating expenses	48 & 49 Local church capital expenses	50 TOTAL CHURCH EXPENSES (Sum of Lines 29a through 49)	51 Number of giving units	52 Total income for annual budget/spending plan	53 Total income for designated causes including capital campaign and other special projects	54 Total income from connectional and other institutional sources outside the local church
32029	0	0	0	0	4,000	0	0	0	0	5,149	8,351	1,881	19,381	18	17,188	0	0
32030	3,685	22,250	9,400	9,400	74,255	55,735	51,811	0	49,358	25,038	111,578	6,700	446,651	310	455,661	24,941	0
32031	466	1,416	0	0	7,051	4,618	4,466	0	2,400	5,002	12,617	0	43,912	30	39,376	320	0
32032	704	10,164	6,754	6,754	30,016	0	20,127	0	0	464	27,648	13,602	120,707	56	93,636	217,599	0
32033	0	1,516	5,230	5,230	43,099	0	15,424	0	26,542	4,568	26,320	1,938	124,637	138	127,632	26,395	4,500
32034	114	1,422	6,687	2,472	23,180	0	9,005	0	14,428	5,197	28,961	8,777	95,824	87	88,410	1,968	0
32035	327	0	0	0	9,994	0	4,347	0	0	2,111	11,047	0	32,282	29	49,577	0	0
32036	488	2,484	0	2,200	18,692	0	3,000	0	6,255	1,713	9,761	1,787	49,344	41	54,205	3,194	0
32037	825	8,441	2,200	2,200	18,300	0	9,995	0	13,084	1,045	16,626	0	80,660	48	72,833	9,262	1,500
32038	233	0	0	0	16,261	0	2,566	0	225	2,107	13,743	6,790	40,175	24	43,428	2,315	0
32039	3,300	700	7,160	7,160	59,761	0	32,615	0	61,692	5,427	56,230	38,714	260,481	176	262,912	1,700	5,000
32040	1,946	21,493	9,516	9,516	41,249	16,666	31,016	0	58,708	14,918	55,577	43,255	309,298	130	133,898	105,083	0
32041	1,066	8,018	6,821	6,252	36,376	0	26,656	0	10,400	5,835	33,062	27,622	180,907	36	149,070	18,218	300
32042	450	457	8,124	8,124	39,327	0	32,604	0	5,558	756	22,359		151,350	47	146,966	4,295	0
32043	327	5,116	0	0	20,000	0	1,343	0	12,443	951	16,728	179,037	242,730	43	39,163	164,589	0
32044	392	0	0	0	10,000	0	1,200	0	0	50	4,000		17,103	0	0		23,500
32045	878	4,850	7,171	2,295	37,804	0	39,120	0	18,633	3,330	13,370	3,449	131,945	60	136,784	800	8,000
32046	1,189	2,452	7,500	7,500	40,000	0	21,120	0	20,684	5,270	32,574	31,200	166,364	97	197,741	0	0
32047	1,197	5,415	7,864	7,864	41,942	0	37,775	0	12,239	8,202	22,455	30,000	181,983	55	111,168	3,739	33,051

STATISTICAL INFORMATION

NW

Conf. No.	Church Name	1 Total professing members reported at the close of last year	4 TOTAL PROFESSING MEMBERS reported at the close of this year	7 Average attendance at all weekly worship services	9 Total Baptized Members who have not become Professing Members	10 Number of other constituents of the church	11 (11a-d) TOTAL Christian Formation Group Participants	13 Average weekly attendance (all ages) in Sunday Church School or other weekly education classes	18a Membership in United Methodist Men	19a Membership in United Methodist Women	20b Number of persons sent out on UMVIM teams from this local church	21 Total Number of community ministries for outreach, justice, and mercy offered by this local church	24 & 25 Value of church assets and buildings	26 & 27 Church Debt	28a Amount APPORTIONED to the local church by the CONFERENCE	29a Amount PAID by the local church to the CONFERENCE for all apportioned causes	28b Amount APPORTIONED to the local church by the DISTRICT (if applicable)
32048	LELAND	302	315	120	0	175	182	35	0	0	0	0	2,726,822	166,381	37,958	37,958	2,190
32049	LEROY	86	83	41	0	154	6	2	0	0	0	3	878,902	0	9,105	8,097	631
32050	LUDINGTON: ST PAUL	144	142	71	50	48	26	20	0	0	0	6	1,980,000	0	18,287	11,284	1,037
32051	LUDINGTON: UNITED	383	316	208	0	330	132	37	0	143	22	9	4,561,554	162,903	44,423	44,422	3,147
32052	LUTHER	27	25	21	0	29	26	0	0	0	0	1	242,000	44,135	2,664	1,554	211
32053	MANCELONA	100	97	48	19	127	15	5	0	27	0	1	580,073	0	11,646	11,646	754
32054	MANISTEE	310	323	170	4	209	90	30	0	75	0	0	3,111,976	111,976	41,910	38,418	2,328
32055	MANTON	118	123	79	0	35	14	8	0	0	0	0	1,337,000	5	12,367	9,688	856
32056	MARION	100	94	35	0	0	0	7	0	9	0	0	921,272	0	6,467	4,645	733
32057	MERRITT-BUTTERFIELD	57	55	66	0	80	22	22	0	0	0	6	1,229,080	0	9,096	9,097	464
32058	MESICK	59	57	20	0	0	5	4	0	0	0	2	291,761	5,049	5,127	1,769	421
32059	MILLERSBURG	60	61	27	0	16	5	0	0	0	0	2	125,000	0	4,390	2,195	252
32060	MOORESTOWN-STITTSVILLE	44	43	45	0	50	20	5	0	0	0	0	458,606	0	6,280	6,279	319
32061	NORTHPORT: INDIAN MISSION	41	50	25	0	3	10	4	0	0	0	0	415,000	0	1,595	1,595	290
32062	NORWOOD	9	8	5	0	35	4	4	0	0	0	4	300,400	0	1,724	0	80
32063	OLD MISSION PENINSULA	95	95	35	0	62	56	33	0	45	0	0	1,063,556	0	14,209	11,225	725
32064	ONAWAY	198	200	78	2	30	106	15	8	9	0	3	509,560	608	15,275	2,360	1,507
32065	OSSINEKE	108	101	51	15		34	13	0		0	5	1,145,961	4,800	12,390	12,390	1,222
32066	PETOSKEY	483	469	143	85	193	86	6	0	64	21	4	1,682,395	235,097	48,451	48,462	3,625

STATISTICAL INFORMATION

NW

CONFERENCE Number	29b	30-38	39a	39b	41a	41b	40, 42a-44	41c & 42c	45	46	47	48 & 49	50	51	52	53	54
32048	2,190	58,740	13,305	13,305	65,500	0	23,803	0	104,059	10,068	65,687	12,487	393,797	185	329,264	52,083	0
32049	612	1,887	7,088	7,088	21,924	0	15,124	0	4,243	1,474	10,340	10,660	81,449	30	71,571	14,134	0
32050	640	2,880	7,253	7,253	38,685	0	22,578	0	27,082	2,200	24,300	12,710	149,612	60	149,922	17,990	0
32051	3,147	41,184	12,409	12,409	66,019	0	31,366	0	79,238	20,834	107,280	379,516	785,417	228	344,791	302,348	0
32052	211	985	7,172	7,172	5,670	0	3,911	0	6,932	289	8,455	23,585	44,660	14	23,047	13,246	0
32053	754	8,388	10,313	8,594	26,775	0	19,040	0		1,884	23,434	2,934	108,959	83	98,354	22,677	0
32054	2,134	11,101			55,300	0	22,081	0	127,263	20,196	45,489	14,336	344,912	167	333,769	42,378	0
32055	647	1,934	1,688	1,688	23,507	0	11,321	0	12,530	2,000	17,000	22,000	102,315	56	103,534	130	0
32056	544	5,627	8,697	8,697	23,911	0	750	0	3,477	1,013	11,895	205	60,764	24	68,529	13,757	0
32057	464	3,826	7,252	7,252	20,156	0	17,708	0	7,112	5,070	15,563	11,539	97,787	48	77,404	9,931	0
32058	145	197	4,617	4,617	9,589	0	15,482	0	0	3,989	9,060	6,924	51,772	28	41,877	103	0
32059	252	608	1,310	1,310	10,708	0	9,987	0	2,229	1,101	6,048	863	35,301	27	30,993	18,058	0
32060	319	19,738	3,340	3,061	15,837	0	13,849	0	1,887	653	7,765	1,909	66,327	29	52,994	4,343	0
32061	290	0			34,000	0	2,940	0	0	3,242	13,150		60,187	40	15,891	100	34,000
32062	0	200			3,000	0	1,000	0		200	4,000	0	8,400	5	10,300	7,236	0
32063	573	7,170	7,727	7,727	41,208	0	28,441	0	5,027	982	20,025	6,111	122,378	39	120,351	225	0
32064	2,360	4,722	3,040	3,040	25,410	0	23,558	0	13,949	4,624	19,015		105,149	70	96,743	8,667	0
32065	1,222	5,869	4,830	4,830	40,490	0	16,989	0	13,707	5,353	19,411	0	120,261	58	102,084		424
32066	3,625	31,736	13,584	13,584	72,448	0	29,635	0	130,996	13,558	80,223	75,207	499,464	241	363,907	93,228	0

Column descriptions:
- 29b: Amount PAID by the local church to the DISTRICT for all apportioned causes (if applicable)
- 30-38: Church Benevolence Giving
- 39a: Total ASKED for clergy pension
- 39b: Total PAID for clergy pension
- 41a: Base compensation paid to/for the Senior Pastor or other person assigned or appointed in the lead pastoral role to the church
- 41b: Base compensation paid to/for all Associate Pastor(s) and other pastoral staff assigned or appointed to the church, include deacons and other clergy in this role
- 40, 42a-44: Pastoral Benefits
- 41c & 42c: Deacons salary/benefits
- 45: Total amount paid in salary and benefits for all other church staff and diaconal ministers
- 46: Total amount spent for local church program expenses
- 47: Total amount spent for other local church operating expenses
- 48 & 49: Local church capital expenses
- 50: TOTAL CHURCH EXPENSES (Sum of Lines 29a through 49)
- 51: Number of giving units
- 52: Total income for annual budget/spending plan
- 53: Total income for designated causes including capital campaign and other special projects
- 54: Total income from connectional and other institutional sources outside the local church

STATISTICAL INFORMATION

CONFERENCE Number	Church Name	Total professing members reported at the close of last year (1)	TOTAL PROFESSING MEMBERS reported at the close of this year (4)	Average attendance at all weekly worship services (7)	Total Baptized Members who have not become Professing Members (9)	Number of other constituents of the church (10)	TOTAL Christian Formation Group Participants (Total of lines 11a-d) (11)	Average weekly attendance (all ages) in Sunday Church School or other weekly education classes (13)	Membership in United Methodist Men (18a)	Membership in United Methodist Women (13a)	Number of persons sent out on UMVIM teams from this local church (20b)	Total Number of community ministries for outreach, justice, and mercy offered by this local church (21)	Value of church assets and buildings (24 & 25)	Church Debt (26 & 27)	Amount APPORTIONED to the local church by the CONFERENCE (28a)	Amount PAID by the local church to the CONFERENCE for all apportioned causes (29a)	Amount APPORTIONED to the local church by the DISTRICT (if applicable) (28b)
32067	REED CITY	303	285	96	18	151	49	10	0	0	0	4	3,060,000	0	26,061	2,874	2,017
32068	ROSCOMMON: GOOD SHEPHERD	220	220	158	0	82	50	8	0	28	0	4	3,345,000	430,355	28,985	28,985	2,860
32069	SCOTTVILLE	123	123	86	9	46	39	30	0	76	0	4	3,260,500	55,106	19,557	3,137	914
32070	SEARS	7	11	14	0	20	16	3	0	0	0	0	59,000	0	1,803	0	72
32071	SOUTH BOARDMAN	10	10	18	0	31	21	6	0	0	0	1	509,292	0	999	999	73
32072	SPRATT	97	70	38	1	21	0	0	0	15	0	0	737,472	0	6,506	6,506	642
32073	TRAVERSE BAY	223	191	134	240	67	65	48	0	0	5	12	990,000	0	32,157	32,157	1,566
32074	TRAVERSE CITY: CENTRAL	1,067	1,070	497	240	321	769	43	0	93	0	0	5,150,066	0	131,031	131,031	7,446
32075	TRAVERSE CITY: MOSAIC	0	0	1	0	45	7	7	0	0	0	0	1,100,000	268,497	0	0	0
32076	WILLIAMSBURG	71	63	42	0	45	7	7	0	0	0	2	663,589	0	12,448	10,373	522
	NORTHERN WATERS DISTRICT TOTALS	9,755	9,453	5,217	1,085	4,395	3,455	919	138	1,173	102	210	97,516,105	2,435,486	1,104,768	844,865	74,044
	CENTRAL BAY DISTRICT																
33001	ALGER	20	20	12	0	3	10	12	0	1	0	3	206,591	0	3,509	3,509	346
33002	ARBELA	59	61	20	0	0	13	0	0	0	0	0	111,000	295	3,921	3,137	308
33003	ARENAC CNTY: CHRIST	81	74	41	21	71	30	8	6	10	2	1	2,080,700	0	13,267	13,267	1,309
33004	AUBURN	179	172	94	21	61	50	41	7	49	5	2	3,064,856	23,292	26,208	8,475	2,474
33005	BAY CITY: GRACE	452	444	377	46	248	282	34	51	108	0	20	5,337,232	0	34,865	34,865	3,439
33006	BAY PORT	79	78	37	1	20	26	8	0	0	0	0	994,000	0	5,673	0	650

NW   CB

STATISTICAL INFORMATION

CB

CONFERENCE Number	29b Amount PAID by the local church to the DISTRICT for all apportioned causes (if applicable)	30-38 Church Benevolence Giving	39a Total ASKED for clergy pension	39b Total PAID for clergy pension	41a Base compensation paid to/for the Senior Pastor or other person assigned or appointed in the lead pastoral role to the church	41b Base compensation paid to/for all Associate Pastor(s) and other pastoral staff assigned or appointed to the church, include deacons and other clergy in this role.	40, 42a-44 Pastoral Benefits	41c & 42c Deacons salary/benefits	45 Total amount paid in salary and benefits for all other church staff and diaconal ministers	46 Total amount spent for local church program expenses	47 Total amount spent for other local church operating expenses	48 & 49 Local Church capital expenses	50 TOTAL CHURCH EXPENSES (Sum of lines 29a through 49)	51 Number of giving units	52 Total income for annual budget/spending plan	53 Total income for designated causes including capital campaign and other special projects	54 Total income from connectional and other institutional sources outside the local church
32067	1,176	5,996	9,896	9,896	52,776	0	31,483	0	37,004	1,947	63,739	0	206,891	124	173,428	12,948	0
32068	2,860	12,747	7,330	7,330	55,550	0	30,290	0	71,899	9,313	42,013	87,551	348,538	171	243,634	62,298	0
32069	147	1,000	6,728	6,728	35,880	0	29,905	0	13,460	7,085	41,198	18,095	156,635	76	134,201	995	0
32070	0		0	0	9,282	697	4,207	0	70	250	2,180	0	15,989	8	13,808	0	158
32071	73	3,645	1,438	1,438	2,742	0	2,385	0	92	0	3,633	495	16,199	17	16,477	0	0
32072	642	3,733	2,260	2,260	19,500	0	12,190	0	6,917	454	11,051	9,225	72,478	30	58,325	765	0
32073	1,566	1,434	10,191	10,191	49,939	0	9,304	0	100,697	5,042	48,539	132,038	258,869	100	236,892	69,203	0
32074	7,446	146,795	28,322	28,322	85,142	63,672	96,300	0	426,245	62,994	184,529	0	1,366,514	345	1,093,302	0	18,800
32075	522	0	7,806	7,806	0	0	0	0	0		1	0	7,807	0	0	39,943	0
32076	522	2,478	4,313	4,313	23,000	4,600	16,144	0	17,494	3,949	20,287	1,488	104,648	45	103,268	1,618,685	182,770
	61,781	589,444	376,066	360,137	2,102,477	159,883	1,279,945		1,863,446	368,505	1,915,439	1,282,196	10,828,118	5,159	8,917,894		
33001	300	0	810	810	6,851	0	2,285	0	0	1,256	18,369	5,000	38,380	20	20,915	100	0
33002	0	0	1,470	1,176	12,000	0		0	0	897	5,940	0	23,150	10	28,172	400	0
33003	1,309	1,116	5,490	5,490	40,145	0	25,016	0	3,468	1,152	15,155	0	106,118	35	84,501	1,610	0
33004	2,474	6,065	6,840	5,548	34,762	0	29,127	0	40,596	4,393	56,937	62,262	250,639	121	218,069	22,820	0
33005	3,439	10,957	6,600	6,600	50,580	0	37,336	0	183,016	52,315	99,539	23,089	501,736	313	379,150	33,062	0
33006	500	836	2,140	2,140	16,270	0	13,247	0	2,027	1,245	8,425	0	44,690	35	40,072	5,792	0

CONFERENCE Number	Church Name	Total professing members reported at the close of last year (1)	TOTAL PROFESSING MEMBERS reported at the close of this year (4)	Average attendance at all weekly worship services (7)	Total Baptized Members who have not become Professing Members (9)	Number of other constituents of the church (10)	TOTAL Christian Formation Group Participants (11)	Average weekly attendance (all ages) in Sunday Church School or other weekly education classes (13)	Membership in United Methodist Men (18a)	Membership in United Methodist Women (19a)	Number of persons sent out on UMVIM teams from this local church (20b)	Total Number of community ministries for outreach, justice, and mercy offered by this local church (21)	Value of church assets and buildings (24 & 25)	Church Debt (26 & 27)	Amount APPORTIONED to the local church by the CONFERENCE (28a)	Amount PAID by the local church to the CONFERENCE for all apportioned causes (29a)	Amount APPORTIONED to the local church by the DISTRICT (if applicable) (28b)
33007	BEAVERTON: FIRST	60	61	43	2	39	10	9	0	15	0	3	1,098,500	0	6,608	6,608	652
33008	BENTLEY	41	39	20	13	30	14	4	0	0	0	0	966,000	10,000	3,687	3,687	364
33009	BIRCH RUN	96	97	40	0	0	6	5	0	0	0	5	778,621	346	9,081	9,081	713
33010	BLANCHARD-PINE RIVER	31	24	10	0	1	1	0	2	10	0	0	0	277	2,550	0	208
33011	BURT	49	49	17	10	33	11	3	0	0	4	5	200,000	0	3,689	3,689	289
33012	CARO	327	325	122	2	33	86	33	13	14	0	2	2,633,736	0	24,640	24,640	2,431
33013	CASEVILLE	140	147	54	22	50	12	0	0	53	0	0	2,138,000	1,104	14,024	11,219	1,490
33014	CASS CITY	181	180	70	6	29	65	30	0	0	0	2	2,145,190	121,076	17,230	0	1,722
33015	CHURCHILL	92	92	33	0	45	12	4	0	16	0	8	401,320	0	6,662	6,662	657
33016	CLARE	285	270	109	2	123	184	60	0	25	15	13	3,304,250	240,000	30,783	10,261	1,924
33017	COLEMAN: FAITH	152	137	114	0	0	82	33	15	11	0	0	2,561,782	0	17,695	17,695	1,746
33018	COOMER	30	21	15	0	20	0	0	0	0	0	0	210,000	0	1,818	1,818	215
33019	DALE	24	23	22	14	3	25	2	0	12	0	2	1,008,000	0	4,046	4,046	652
33020	EDENVILLE	29	27	15	2	14	5	5	0	0	0	0	336,500	0	3,845	3,845	379
33021	ELKTON	179	174	80	52	65	26	12	0	10	0	4	230,000	0	16,302	13,961	1,867
33022	ESSEXVILLE: ST LUKE'S	258	256	82	22	26	108	22	0	41	0	1	3,603,309	154,149	24,633	10,493	2,430
33023	FAIRGROVE	66	54	28	0	53	5	5	0	0	0	2	1,602,860	6,100	7,113	7,113	702
33024	FARWELL	118	120	65	0	84	46	12	12	10	0	0	194,000	101,000	13,033	1,500	780
33025	FRANKENMUTH	495	483	153	0	84	102	28	0	36	0	0	4,481,854	0	42,460	42,460	4,189

STATISTICAL INFORMATION

CB

CONFERENCE Number	29b. Amount PAID by the local church to the DISTRICT for all apportioned causes (if applicable)	30-38 Church Benevolence Giving	39a. Total ASKED for clergy pension	39b. Total PAID for clergy pension	41a. Base compensation paid to/for the Senior Pastor or other person assigned or appointed in the lead pastoral role to the church	41b. Base compensation paid to/for all Associate Pastor(s) and other pastoral staff assigned or appointed to the church, include deacons and other clergy in this role.	40, 42a-44 Pastoral Benefits	41c & 42c Deacons salary/benefits	45 Total amount paid in salary and benefits for all other church staff and diaconal ministers	46 Total amount spent for local church program expenses	47 Total amount spent for other local church operating expenses	48 & 49 Local church capital expenses	50 TOTAL CHURCH EXPENSES (Sum of Lines 29a through 49)	51 Number of giving units	52 Total income for annual budget/spending plan	53 Total income for designated causes including capital campaign and other special projects	54 Total income from connectional and other institutional sources outside the local church
33007	652	4,553	1,060	1,060	16,562	0	6,301	0	3,023	4,687	15,049	1,926	60,421	45	70,770	1,308	0
33008	364	2,061	620	620	7,000	0	4,000	0	0	500	10,000	3,500	31,732	15	29,000	3,500	0
33009	713	1,912	4,080	4,080	45,361	0	16,322	0	10,000	1,045	24,371	2,167	115,052	40	94,042	605	16,959
33010	0	330	770	770	4,200	0	0	0	960	335	8,779	2,184	17,558	9	17,525	5,700	0
33011	290	124	1,360	1,360	16,959	0	3,809	0	0	1,000	7,400	2,000	36,631	20	28,832	11	0
33012	2,441	19,075	5,780	5,780	50,400	0	11,911	0	61,910	13,945	40,909	29,091	260,102	135	239,232	53,024	0
33013	1,490	14,129	5,520	4,416	38,911	0	9,251	0	29,478	7,500	29,999	13,496	159,889	58	99,329	615	0
33014	1,986	1,427	5,660	5,660	23,132	18,000	19,224	0	11,440	1,500	29,000	13,452	124,821	100	128,900	0	0
33015	657	547	1,680	1,680	17,480	0	4,453	1,453	4,747	4,557	13,199	845	56,280	46	54,786	0	0
33016	716	19,050	9,364	9,364	49,939	0	36,109	0	95,403	3,333	56,655	15,548	296,378	219	240,733	36,525	6,830
33017	1,746	23,597	4,520	4,520	38,085	0	26,032	0	26,329	6,555	48,076	51,002	242,637	89	186,247	101,657	2,000
33018	215				3,500	0	0	0	2,000	80	5,000	0	12,613	10	14,100	0	0
33019	652	4,386	1,260	1,260	10,403	0	3,940	0	0	763	13,061	0	38,511	17	44,437	495	0
33020	400	183	1,240	1,240	10,175	0	7,162	0	1,505	230	5,887	10,432	41,059	17	26,716	10,300	2,000
33021	524	1,427	4,850	4,850	42,500	0	26,496	0	20,403	1,602	24,034	6,692	142,474	58	152,470	3,590	3,590
33022	2,430	6,644	6,110	6,110	51,112	0	30,781	0	25,976	6,871	51,518	13,420	205,355	126	157,551	39,400	0
33023	702	1,576	2,170	2,170	17,939	0	4,824	0	6,076	4,756	15,355	18,344	78,855	24	50,826	5,607	500
33024	135	1,112	7,688	7,688	41,000	0	7,959	0	10,924	1,096	63,626	9,883	144,923	58	117,199	34,622	400
33025	3,189	22,426	3,060	3,060	53,208	0	29,651	0	68,876	35,082	77,520	22,026	367,498	158	369,173	41,903	

STATISTICAL INFORMATION

CONFERENCE Number	Church Name	Total professing members reported at the close of last year (1)	TOTAL PROFESSING MEMBERS reported at the close of this year (4)	Average attendance at all weekly worship services (7)	Total Baptized Members who have not become Professing Members (9)	Number of other constituents of the church (10)	TOTAL Christian Formation Group Participants (Total of lines 11a-d) (11)	Average weekly attendance (all ages) in Sunday Church School or other weekly education classes (13)	Membership in United Methodist Men (16a)	Membership in United Methodist Women (19a)	Number of persons sent out on UMVIM teams from this local church (20b)	Total Number of community ministries for outreach, justice, and mercy offered by this local church (21)	Value of church assets and buildings (24 & 25)	Church Debt (26 & 27)	Amount APPORTIONED to the local church by the CONFERENCE (28a)	Amount PAID by the local church to the CONFERENCE for all apportioned causes (29a)	Amount APPORTIONED to the local church by the DISTRICT (if applicable) (28b)
33026	FREELAND	212	184	83	0	80	42	15	0	0	0	2	2,220,402	1,908	25,322	15,193	2,498
33027	GARFIELD	47	46	15	0	0	10	6	0	0	0	0	231,710	0	3,017	3,017	298
33028	GLADWIN: FIRST	149	141	104	0	63	80	35	14	40	0	13	2,664,779	2,181	20,463	20,463	2,018
33029	GLENNIE	23	22	16	0	22	6	0	0	7	0	1	181,698	45,000	1,610	1,610	159
33030	GORDONVILLE	115	113	56	182	38	33	15	0	20	1	9	723,140	0	12,226	12,226	1,258
33031	HALE: FIRST	196	184	117	1	191	117	28	0	33	0	3	2,375,463	29,000	24,176	24,176	2,385
33032	HARRISON: THE GATHERING	48	47	28	0	4	17	4	0	4	0	1	0	0	0	0	0
33033	HARRISVILLE	56	56	28	0	0	10	10	12	31	0	3	1,445,300	0	6,211	5,663	0
33034	HAYES	79	76	28	36	41	50	6	0	15	0	0	545,823	0	7,444	7,444	852
33035	HEMLOCK	132	136	40	0	23	8	4	20	0	0	0	2,800,000	15,402	13,683	2,737	1,350
33036	KILMANAGH	32	31	17	0	6	0	0	0	30	0	0	258,874	0	3,257	3,257	250
33037	KINGSTON	121	121	60	26	12	43	25	0	0	0	4	1,530,000	0	10,201	10,201	1,163
33038	LAPORTE	40	36	28	11	14	27	14	0	7	0	0	919,597	0	3,486	3,486	344
33039	LEATON	42	40	25	0	24	15	12	6	10	0	2	1,116,500	0	5,423	5,423	280
33040	LINCOLN	74	65	49	0	17	25	12	0	0	0	7	1,036,500	0	4,276	4,276	422
33041	MAPLETON	17	18	12	0	99	18	9	16	0	0	0	570,000	0	3,375	3,375	333
33042	MAYVILLE	206	187	97	79	10	22	22	0	36	0	0	2,886,425	172,514	16,599	16,599	1,901
33043	MIDLAND CNTY: HOPE	92	68	42	10	10	16	7	0	6	0	26	490,218	0	9,242	9,242	912
33044	MIDLAND: ALDERSGATE	283	427	189	21	125	103	41	0	0	38	42	3,640,293	0	35,375	35,375	3,490

CB

STATISTICAL INFORMATION

CB

CONFERENCE Number	29b Amount PAID by the local church to the DISTRICT for all apportioned causes (if applicable)	30-38 Church Benevolence Giving	39a Total ASKED for clergy pension	39b Total PAID for clergy pension	41a Base compensation paid to/for the Senior Pastor or other person assigned or appointed in the lead pastoral role to the church	41b Base compensation paid to/for all Associate Pastor(s) and other pastoral staff assigned or appointed to the church, include deacons and other clergy in this role.	40, 42a-44 Pastoral Benefits	41c & 42c Deacons salary/benefits	45 Total amount paid in salary and benefits for all other church staff and diaconal ministers	46 Total amount spent for local church program expenses	47 Total amount spent for other local church operating expenses	48 & 49 local church capital expenses	50 TOTAL CHURCH EXPENSES (Sum of Lines 29a through 49)	51 Number of giving units	52 Total income for annual budget/spending plan	53 Total income for designated causes including capital campaign and other special projects	54 Total income from connectional and other institutional sources outside the local church
33026	2,498	2,316	4,770	2,862	39,350	0	21,152	0	25,926	12,667	44,959	0	166,923	130	158,959	1,950	0
33027	298	486	1,410	1,410	11,892	0	2,856	0	0	454	3,962	0	24,375	20	21,700	1,067	0
33028	2,018	13,894	6,710	6,710	46,723	0	31,407	0	24,906	12,017	39,464	31,069	228,671	126	211,393	39,205	0
33029	159	482	760	760	7,752	80	2,122	0	0	744	9,091	60,102	82,902	25	47,217	842	45,000
33030	1,258	8,232	2,320	2,320	19,200	0	15,379	0	8,833	4,166	25,894	1,519	99,027	45	77,679	2,285	2,000
33031	2,385	5,617	5,440	5,440	8,400	0	19,778	0	49,566	8,321	22,985	34,988	181,656	96	238,589	6,097	0
33032	0	0	0	0	0	0	0	0	0	0	1	0	1	0			0
33033	731	699	730	730	6,250	0	13,116	0	6,250	400	12,000	1,769	33,761	36	49,930	769	0
33034	1,281	3,587	2,620	2,620	20,314	0	19,628	0	2,028	1,104	18,344	0	69,288	32	65,206	14,999	0
33035	250	255	3,260	3,260	27,203	0	5,053	0	20,000	3,000	25,000	6,500	108,864	48	131,920	0	0
33036	1,168	804	880	880	9,150	0	0	0	0	45	1	2,527	21,967	10	29,068	349	0
33037	344	2,684	4,400	4,400	36,320	0	18,294	0	3,569	2,500	9,109	3,569	91,814	50	86,269	4,736	0
33038	280	4,505	1,180	1,180	10,200	0	3,000	0	1,382	2,885	12,163	0	37,763	24	37,202	1,729	2,000
33039	422	5,741	1,988	1,988	9,925	0	2,456	0	9,620	205	13,980	5,742	41,380	16	40,800	1,245	400
33040	378	5,995	510	510	9,850	0	978	0	725	491	13,589	0	51,473	62	55,172	4,515	0
33041	1,901	2,661	1,080	1,080	9,300	0	730	0		3,481	11,500		33,230	10	35,500		800
33042	912	9,037	4,660	4,660	38,468	0	16,112	0	30,884	9,531	26,493	46,290	199,975	69	171,797	4,385	0
33043	0	6,103	3,760	3,760	31,011	0	19,092	0	2,800	914	15,000	8,000	96,834	46	94,824	5,711	2,000
33044		36,646	7,260	7,260	53,017	0	53,533	0	126,380	39,939	41,003	82,152	475,305	189	461,773	100,100	2,000

STATISTICAL INFORMATION

CB

Conference Number	Church Name	1 Total professing members reported at the close of last year	4 TOTAL PROFESSING MEMBERS reported at the close of this year	7 Average attendance at all weekly worship services	9 Total Baptized Members who have not become Professing Members	10 Number of other constituents of the church	11a-d TOTAL Christian Formation Group Participants	13 Average weekly attendance (all ages) in Sunday Church School or other weekly education classes	18a Membership in United Methodist Men	19a Membership in United Methodist Women	20b Number of persons sent out on UMVIM teams from this local church	21 Total Number of community ministries for outreach, justice, and mercy offered by this local church	24 & 25 Value of church assets and buildings	26 & 27 Church Debt	28a Amount APPORTIONED to the local church by the CONFERENCE	29a Amount PAID by the local church to the CONFERENCE for all apportioned causes	28b Amount APPORTIONED to the local church by the DISTRICT (if applicable)
33045	MIDLAND: HOMER	129	125	62	12	20	72	35	0	0	0	4	1,775,130	1,228	19,538	3,775	1,927
33046	MIDLAND: FIRST	1,885	1,869	532	12	0	525	212	30	40	16	9	25,819,212	0	181,560	181,560	18,899
33047	MILLINGTON	234	234	88	4	119	124	35	10	28	0	11	3,240,057	0	20,813	20,813	1,633
33048	MIO	114	101	38	0	53	19	8	25	18	0	2	1,529,830	11,238	11,136	11,136	1,099
33050	MT PLEASANT: COUNTRYSIDE	53	53	25	0	0	15	22	0	10	0	6	489,200	240,000	5,155	5,155	345
33051	MT PLEASANT: FIRST	345	342	161	7	124	199	35	0	78	0	9	4,139,881	17,054	46,446	46,446	2,243
33052	MT PLEASANT: TRINITY	40	39	20	0	0	19	10	0	0	0	0	575,000	0	4,023	0	260
33053	NELSON	71	91	45	21	30	10	10	0	15	0	1	593,707	0	6,052	6,052	597
33054	OSCODA	213	211	88	0	75	62	25	25	0	0	0	1,537,952	0	18,401	2,000	1,815
33055	OSCODA: INDIAN MISSION	71	87	8	1	0	11	7	0	0	0	0	40,553	0	1,617	1,617	160
33056	OWENDALE	70	69	40	0	42	22	19	0	31	0	0	70,700	149,245	4,522	4,522	518
33057	PIGEON: FIRST	179	172	59	21	29	83	40	19	19	0	4	1,629,750	0	15,754	15,754	1,804
33058	PIGEON: SALEM	153	153	94	19	14	171	6	1	21	0	2	695,000	0	23,875	23,875	2,734
33059	PINCONNING	120	92	25	0	10	6	1	0	0	0	0	1,124,000	2,658	8,364	8,364	825
33060	PINNEBOG	15	15	18	0	9	1		0	11	0	5	351,000	4,110	3,231	3,231	370
33061	PORT AUSTIN UPC	35	39	30	2	24	12	5	0	25	0	0	500,982	546	5,391	5,391	617
33062	POSEYVILLE	82	0	35	35	24			0	0	0	0	0	0	10,826	3,609	1,068
33063	REESE	157	135	70	3	63	37	24	24	16	0	0	1,027,000	0	12,216	12,216	1,205
33064	ROSE CITY: TRINITY	96	98	60		40	37	24	24	22	0	9	998,986	27,347	8,904	4,952	878

STATISTICAL INFORMATION

CB

CONFERENCE Number	29b	30-38	39a	39b	41a	41b	40, 42a-44	41c & 42c	45	46	47	48 & 49	50	51	52	53	54
33045	1,927	2,833	3,530	3,530	28,800	0	23,476	0	21,457	1,580	24,512	8,772	120,662	50	101,688	12,076	7,000
33046	18,898	253,306	18,300	18,300	102,322	48,370	58,953	0	789,221	161,599	252,629	124,105	2,009,263	2,500	1,877,075	72,330	3,289
33047	1,633	16,909	6,360	6,360	52,050	0	27,035	0	27,999	9,475	28,776	39,972	230,972	64	218,955	23,833	2,000
33048	1,099	4,186	3,150	3,150	24,288	0	6,308	0	983	1,536	16,625	19,816	69,311	42	79,014	2,454	0
33050	345	5,129	10,679	10,679	7,701	0	2,908	0	1,300	2,646	31,785	74,702	76,785	20	41,711	2,615	0
33051	2,243	38,683	0		56,739	0	17,257	0	155,757	9,534	50,412	11,782	462,452	340	378,007	110,622	0
33052	0	1,672	1,630	1,630	9,060	0	4,785	0	0	800	14,300	15,000	42,399	9	34,274	1,250	0
33053	550	2,323	5,050	5,050	13,601	0	9,164	0	6,000	300	5,000	60,304	59,620	32	63,000	1,500	0
33054	1,815	2,410	390	390	41,646	0	31,223	0	17,698	11,019	33,996	0	207,161	120	183,568	2,182	0
33055	160	465	3,590	3,590	3,000	0	0	0	0	1,311	5,567	181,938	12,510	0	11,369	0	0
33056	518	1,922	5,090	5,090	22,875	0	17,068	0	0	990	9,741	10,791	243,164	25	58,258	64,661	500
33057	1,804	4,208	6,040	6,040	42,700	0	27,802	0	24,705	4,151	20,337	7,006	157,342	86	165,702	10,237	0
33058	2,734	38,905	2,810	2,810	51,885	0	37,143	0	40,446	33,351	25,445	0	266,830	83	229,661	0	5,000
33059	825	2,622	1,340	1,340	23,682	0	6,695	0	11,553	1,794	14,087	2,500	72,432	27	68,127	1,345	0
33060	370	1,323	2,690	2,690	9,990	0	12,996	0	0	50	4,836	0	34,136	8	28,771	2,971	0
33061	617	2,129	770	224	18,078	0	15,963	0	0	221	8,400		55,989	46	70,621	500	11,000
33062	620	10,963	5,720	5,720	4,153	0	0	0	3,660	840	15,100	28,164	39,169	50	18,206	21,357	0
33063	1,205	3,260	2,690	2,690	45,000	0	24,374	0	0	7,099	18,480	22,406	145,518	70	134,272	1,646	0
33064	878	2,069			22,402	0	23,669	0	0	4,287	30,580		113,933	49	104,716		0

Column key:
- 29b: Amount Paid by the local church to the DISTRICT for all apportioned causes (if applicable)
- 30-38: Church Benevolence Giving
- 39a: Total ASKED for clergy pension
- 39b: Total PAID for clergy pension
- 41a: Base compensation paid to/for the Senior Pastor or other person assigned or appointed in the lead pastoral role to the church
- 41b: Base compensation paid to/for all Associate Pastor(s) and other pastoral staff assigned or appointed to the church, include deacons and other clergy in this role.
- 40, 42a-44: Pastoral Benefits
- 41c & 42c: Deacons salary/benefits
- 45: Total amount paid in salary and benefits for all other church staff and diaconal ministers
- 46: Total amount spent for local church program expenses
- 47: Total amount spent for other local church operating expenses
- 48 & 49: Local Church capital expenses
- 50: TOTAL CHURCH EXPENSES (Sum of Lines 29a through 49)
- 51: Number of giving units
- 52: Total income for annual budget/spending plan
- 53: Total income for designated causes including capital campaign and other special projects
- 54: Total income from connectional and other institutional sources outside the local church

STATISTICAL INFORMATION

Conference Number	Church Name	1 Total professing members reported at the close of last year	4 TOTAL PROFESSING MEMBERS reported at the close of this year	7 Average attendance at all weekly worship services	9 Total Baptized Members who have not become Professing Members	10 Number of other constituents of the church	11a-b TOTAL Christian Formation Group Participants (Total of lines 11a-d)	13 Average weekly attendance (all ages) in Sunday Church School or other weekly education classes	18b Membership in United Methodist Men	19a Membership in United Methodist Women	20b Number of persons sent out on UMVIM teams from this local church	21 Total Number of community ministries for outreach, justice, and mercy offered by this local church	24 & 25 Value of church assets and buildings	26 & 27 Church Debt	28a Amount APPORTIONED to the local church by the CONFERENCE	29a Amount PAID by the local church to the CONFERENCE for all apportioned causes	28b Amount APPORTIONED to the local church by the DISTRICT (if applicable)
33065	ROSEBUSH	98	110	100	0	151	39	6	10	10	0	1	1,255,000	0	20,140	20,140	696
33066	SAGINAW: AMES	274	254	152	24	14	158	115		40	0	11	3,357,874	648	43,064	10,375	4,248
33067	SAGINAW: FIRST	384	353	121	38	73	88	12	15	62	8	5	9,852,200	0	40,234	40,234	3,969
33068	SAGINAW: KOCHVILLE	105	94	37	0	11	57	14	0	0	0	7	2,342,801	0	12,391	12,391	1,222
33069	SAGINAW: NEW HEART	58	58	43	12	7	97	0	0	6	0	12	438,000	0	10,507	0	1,037
33070	SAGINAW: STATE STREET	147	156	70	0	60	72	14	10	9	0	2	2,829,138	247,384	20,734	8,970	2,045
33071	SAGINAW: SWAN VALLEY	125	124	58	36	24	66	5	11	20	0	9	1,503,500	0	16,715	0	1,649
33072	SANFORD	177	172	67	21	58	22	8		11	0		1,725,443	0	17,648	17,648	1,741
33073	SEBEWAING: TRINITY	194	197	73	50	41	102	27		0	0	17	8,293,147	0	18,068	1,816	2,069
33074	SHEPHERD	84	84	43	6	18	36	10	8		0	3	509,725	0	17,588	17,588	618
33075	ST CHARLES	161	139	71	21	28	24	8	0	15	0	1	3,229,834	16,713	15,926	15,926	1,571
33076	STANDISH: COMMUNITY	53	51	24	7	2	16	6	0	14	0	5	1,513,000	29,545	4,968	360	490
33077	STERLING	92	96	30	5	9	19	5	12	0	0	0	434,125	0	6,542	300	645
33078	SUTTON-SUNSHINE	72	78	38	3	9	12	3		12	0	5	1,063,179	0	5,170	5,170	592
33079	TAWAS	222	226	120	0	113	91	52		34	0	16	3,404,735	670,535	22,501	22,501	2,220
33080	VASSAR: FIRST	169	182	84	1	143	93	23		0	0	2	2,755,931	1,425	20,914	0	2,063
33081	WAGARVILLE: COMMUNITY	59	59	50	0	30	24	0		17	2	1	744,190	0	7,875	7,875	777
33082	WATROUSVILLE	119	119	50	18	0	12	12	7	42	2	0	512,751	8,641	4,508	4,508	445
33083	WEIDMAN	112	108	70	0	0	7	36	12	15	0	0	1,050,000	0	14,303	2,686	717

CB

STATISTICAL INFORMATION

CB

CONFERENCE Number	29b	30-38	39a	39b	41a	41b	40, 42a-44	41c & 42d	45	46	47	48 & 49	50	51	52	53	54
	Amount PAID by the local church to the DISTRICT for all apportioned causes (if applicable)	Church Benevolence Giving	Total ASKED for clergy pension	Total PAID for clergy pension	Base compensation paid to/for the Senior Pastor or other person assigned or appointed in the lead pastoral role to the church	Base compensation paid to/for all Associate Pastor(s) and other pastoral staff assigned or appointed to the church; include deacons and other clergy in this role.	Pastoral Benefits	Deacons salary/benefits	Total amount paid in salary and benefits for all other church staff and diaconal ministers	Total amount spent for local church program expenses	Total amount spent for other local church operating expenses	Local Church capital expenses	TOTAL CHURCH EXPENSES (Sum of Lines 29a through 49)	Number of giving units	Total income for annual budget/spending plan	Total income for designated causes including capital campaign and other special projects	Total income from connectional and other institutional sources outside the local church
33065	696	5,327	7,222	7,222	45,000	0	30,373	0	22,587	3,214	22,608	47,435	204,602	116	154,007	25,046	0
33066	4,248	1,465	6,380	6,380	52,225	0	31,926	0	92,491	98,317	43,873	0	341,300	77	290,047	17,520	0
33067	3,969	26,064	7,620	7,620	64,767	0	35,321	0	110,699	10,513	73,103	0	372,290	119	398,452	59,607	0
33068		472	3,230	3,230	0	0	0	0	0	1,118	22,013	8,751	47,975	0	0	0	0
33069	1,037	3,250	4,610		37,104	0	14,218	0	13,700	11,858	31,181	0	98,130	60	68,606	18,000	0
33070	2,045	2,141	4,430	4,430	36,967	0	16,132	0	28,152	7,264	55,595	33,726	193,508	64	161,504	2,714	800
33071	1,741	3,593	6,550	6,550	50,000	0	40,253	0	34,543	9,437	16,178	6,562	142,995	68	156,712	1,660	0
33072	2,069	5,261	5,980	5,980	49,386	0	7,904	0	37,230	1,399	35,260	7,274	194,158	95	183,725	4,460	2,000
33073	618	4,153	4,700	4,700	48,000	0	25,244	0	20,481	5,664	47,152	0	149,213	90	141,940	13,057	0
33074	1,571	13,046	9,225	9,225	45,000	0	17,646	0	11,328	2,334	30,911	4,800	155,294	53	141,042	0	2,851
33075	490	13,061	5,330	5,330	46,000	0	3,540	0	32,682	5,546	27,709	0	170,271	86	139,890	61,671	3,150
33076	592	400	1,260	360	15,499	0	0	0	0	324	18,529	0	39,502	25	39,975	14,181	0
33077	2,220	0	2,970	2,970	22,542	0	2,617	0	0	523	14,560	12,828	40,895	46	47,812	127	0
33078	2,063	7,761	2,450	2,450	20,000	0	19,606	0	700	2,500	19,719		74,337	43	74,979	13,257	0
33079	777	1,613	5,410	5,410	44,654	0	26,485	0	36,954	2,746	66,350	666,184	868,238	133	308,909	7,927	0
33080	445	3,716	4,710	4,710	40,440	0	300	0	20,100	9,822	39,494	11,947	158,777	71	145,395	8,393	700
33081	66	3,930	2,440	2,440	10,800	0	1,180	0	5,800	2,070	7,800	38,593	80,385	38	80,036	35,035	0
33082		3,643	1,380	1,380	22,080	0	20,600	0	3,120	452	8,684	16,839	62,331	57	39,580	1,520	0
33083		13,300	7,459	7,459	39,780	0		0	9,686	1,023	19,000	0	113,600	50	72,439		0

STATISTICAL INFORMATION

CONFERENCE Number	Church Name	Total professing members reported at the close of last year (1)	TOTAL PROFESSING MEMBERS reported at the close of this year (4)	Average attendance at all weekly worship services (7)	Total Baptized Members who have not become Professing Members (9)	Number of other constituents of the church (10)	TOTAL Christian Formation Group Participants (Total of lines 11a-d) (11)	Average weekly attendance (all ages) in Sunday Church School or other weekly education classes (13)	Membership in United Methodist Men (18a)	Membership in United Methodist Women (19a)	Number of persons sent out on UMVIM teams from this local church (20b)	Total Number of community ministries for outreach, justice, and mercy offered by this local church (21)	Value of church assets and buildings (24 & 25)	Church Debt (26 & 27)	Amount APPORTIONED to the local church by the CONFERENCE (28a)	Amount PAID by the local church to the CONFERENCE for all apportioned causes (29a)	Amount APPORTIONED to the local church by the DISTRICT (if applicable) (28b)
33084	WEST BRANCH: FIRST	244	213	81	0	56	352	25	15	15	0	16	1,364,800	0	24,406	24,406	2,408
33085	WHITTEMORE	60	64	40	37	8	21	15	0	12	0	3	975,400	0	5,473	5,473	540
33086	WILBER	30	24	18	0	15	17	15	0	8	0	0	450,000	0	2,875	2,875	284
33087	WINN	44	40	19	0	0	0	0	0	0	0	0	320,950	0	4,003	4,003	286
33088	WISNER	167	163	81	57	103	74	27	0	0	7	1	2,348,151	0	15,549	15,549	1,534
	CENTRAL BAY DISTRICT TOTALS	12,799	12,515	5,745	1,061	3,498	4,777	1,591	376	1,351	98	366	163,735,837	2,351,961	1,322,654	1,027,056	124,717
	MIDWEST DISTRICT																
34001	ALLENDALE: VALLEY CHURCH	102	129	155	0	0	221	35	0	0	0	4	590,000	70,000	28,211	17,208	2,266
34002	ALTO	68	0	30	0	0	23	10	0	0	0	1	0	0	5,614	0	892
34003	AMBLE	64	63	47	0	40	38	10	0	0	0	2	400,000	0	9,157	9,157	364
34004	BARRYTON: FAITH	24	23	15	0	10	11	2	0	8	0	0	380,053	0	2,371	37	163
34094	BERLIN CENTER	48	48	24	3	16	10	0	0	12	0	0	145,094	0	5,618	0	319
34005	BELDING	46	35	14	8	21	11	10	0	4	0	4	1,200,000	0	2,889	1,022	306
34007	BIG RAPIDS: FIRST	286	276	131	46	142	90	48	0	0	0	2	1,097,157	0	38,458	38,458	1,950
34008	BIG RAPIDS: THIRD AVENUE	57	51	38	3	27	11	2	0	0	0	2	206,679	0	4,181	4,181	397
34009	BOWNE CENTER	92	94	48	0	20	20	8	0	0	0	0	928,212	0	6,197	4,128	1,180
34010	BRADLEY: INDIAN MISSION	28	28	22	0	5	6	3	0	0	0	0	373,500	0	2,763	2,763	380
34011	BROOKS CORNERS	25	25	28	0	35	0	19	0	0	0	0	560,000	0	8,490	8,490	163

MW

CB

STATISTICAL INFORMATION

MW

CONFERENCE Number	29b — Amount PAID by the local church to the DISTRICT for all apportioned causes (if applicable)	30-38 — Church Benevolence Giving	39a — Total ASKED for clergy pension	39b — Total PAID for clergy pension	41a — Base compensation paid to/for the person assigned or appointed in the Senior Pastor or other lead pastoral role to the church	41b — Base compensation paid to/for all Associate Pastor(s) and other pastoral staff assigned or appointed to the church. Include deacons and other clergy in this role	40, 42a-44 — Pastoral Benefits	41c & 42c — Deacons salary/benefits	45 — Total amount paid in salary and benefits for all other church staff and diaconal ministers	46 — Total amount spent for local church program expenses	47 — Total amount spent for other local church operating expenses	48 & 49 — Local Church capital expenses	50 — TOTAL CHURCH EXPENSES (Sum of lines 29a through 49)	51 — Number of giving units	52 — Total income for annual budget/spending plan	53 — Total income for designated causes including capital campaign and other special projects	54 — Total income from connectional and other institutional sources outside the local church
33084	2,408	7,464	6,040	6,040	46,593	0	21,996	0	54,888	21,110	36,086	0	220,991	147	201,724	14,725	0
33085	540	610	1,790	1,790	14,787	0	16,073	0	0	765	12,231	841	53,110	40	43,687	47,059	0
33086	286	48	760	760	8,500	0	0	0	0	500	7,000	0	19,683	10	33,000	400	0
33087	1,534	128	5,120	5,120	8,944	0	3,218	0	4,847	877	13,667	5,125	35,970	10	39,209	205	0
33088		12,560			43,147	0	34,492	1,453	19,416	18,966	31,910	5,125	187,819	66	159,138	13,346	0
	111,263	781,600	330,775	320,121	2,484,936	66,450	1,315,865	1,453	2,580,209	730,484	2,399,562	2,058,749	13,877,733	7,997	11,896,547	1,284,119	124,769
34001	1,382	5,000	8,738	8,738	46,600	0	6,400	0	76,596	31,500	28,000	11,648	233,072	95	231,294	78,332	5,000
34002	364	173,000	0	0	10,703	0	2,297	0	2,200	889	21,357	344,550	554,996	29	33,009	257,044	0
34003	63	5,925	3,107	3,107	24,877	0	19,391	0	1,210	3,269	12,224	0	79,524	38	68,854	16,128	1,000
34004	319	40	0	0	3,250	0	15,306	0	4,585	280	7,930	0	16,185	10	12,277	1,305	0
34005	90	2,629	1,349	1,349	2,050	0	2,117	0	9,793	321	10,429	9,733	50,580	21	65,932	2,295	0
34006	1,950	558	9,563	9,563	9,000	0	27,746	0	0	869	24,164	0	39,169	18	25,707	255	0
34007	397	27,075	0	0	51,000	0	6,356	0	79,853	32,680	70,532	64,390	403,247	133	290,439	55,878	0
34008	789	1,220	0	0	7,958	0	2,624	0	560	1,333	6,122	850	28,977	42	32,930	1,819	0
34009	380	395	0	0	12,500	0	0	0	5,150	1,225	10,932	5,015	42,758	45	46,924	0	0
34010	163	1,200	0	0	31,500	0	0	0	2,640	50	6,478	500	45,511	6	25,000	17,108	0
34011		17,404	0	0	11,825	0	0	0	0	1,314	15,671	0	54,867	16	54,390		0

STATISTICAL INFORMATION

CONFERENCE Number	Church Name	1 Total professing members reported at the close of last year	4 TOTAL PROFESSING MEMBERS reported at the close of this year	7 Average attendance at all weekly worship services	9 Total Baptized Members who have not become Professing Members	10 Number of other constituents of the church	11 TOTAL Christian Formation Group Participants (Total of lines 11a-d)	13 Average weekly attendance (all ages) in Sunday Church School or other weekly education classes	18a Membership in United Methodist Men	19a Membership in United Methodist Women	20b Number of persons sent out on UMVIM teams from this local church	21 Total Number of community ministries for outreach, justice, and mercy offered by this local church	24 & 25 Value of church assets and buildings	26 & 27 Church Debt	28a Amount APPORTIONED to the local church by the CONFERENCE	29a Amount PAID by the local church to the CONFERENCE for all apportioned causes	28b Amount APPORTIONED to the local church by the DISTRICT (if applicable)
34012	BYRON CENTER	161	159	73	2	0	54	21	0	0	0	0	1,024,390	105,000	19,131	8,828	2,125
34013	CALEDONIA	169	169	83	0	218	94	26	0	6	0	20	1,130,769	0	23,300	1,014	2,255
34014	CARLISLE	102	91	65	0	55	14	0	0	0	0	0	790,000	33,975	15,529	15,529	1,338
34015	CEDAR SPRINGS	159	154	106	0	178	23	23	0	12	0	2	3,359,897	0	26,138	26,138	2,189
34016	CLAYBANKS	57	49	45	2	47	18	20	0	13	0	0	1,374,505	0	5,280	5,280	856
34017	COOPERSVILLE	89	96	95	0	98	104	18	0	0	0	15	510,000	245,981	14,484	2,000	1,193
34018	COURTLAND-OAKFIELD	111	102	65	0	62	37	13	0	16	0	1	798,791	0	16,435	16,435	1,482
34019	CRYSTAL VALLEY	26	21	9	35	20	8	0	0	5	0	6	451,532	0	1,786	1,786	240
34020	DORR: CROSSWIND CMNTY	67	67	129	0	191	94	30	0	0	0	3	420,985	280,947	16,392	2,563	530
34021	EAST NELSON	123	105	77	0	40	43	5	0	0	0	1	1,016,000	0	17,150	17,150	1,521
34022	EDMORE: FAITH	162	157	86	0	42	38	19	0	13	0	0	1,538,636	0	17,251	17,251	1,066
34023	FENWICK	11	11	16	0	19	4	4	0	8	0	0	694,621	0	1,891	1,891	72
34024	FERRY	39	39	28	0	8	20	0	0	0	0	3	154,000	0	5,579	5,579	563
34025	FREMONT	353	350	107	135	185	257	35	0	55	0	14	4,014,686	0	31,839	31,839	4,694
34026	GEORGETOWN	474	426	254	114	283	245	79	0	48	6	17	3,491,993	0	62,692	62,692	9,454
34027	GRAND HAVEN: CHURCH OF THE DUNES	596	555	283	34	122	302	70	0	80	8	6	7,470,781	143,395	75,930	75,930	7,984
34028	GRAND RAPIDS: ALDERSGATE	157	170	93	82	75	163	30	30	0	0	3	2,112,225	0	26,683	26,683	3,892
34029	GRAND RAPIDS: CORNERSTONE	1,586	1,651	2,016	82	2,500	3,750	2,199	0	0	65	18	17,090,946	896,924	329,386	329,386	32,214
34030	GRAND RAPIDS: FAITH	151	147	69	4	41	35	15	0	0	0	0	3,170,474	0	22,950	22,950	4,448

MW

STATISTICAL INFORMATION

MW

CONFERENCE Number	Amount PAID by the local church to the DISTRICT for all apportioned causes (if applicable) 29b	Church Benevolence Giving 30-38	Total ASKED for clergy pension 39a	Total PAID for clergy pension 39b	Base compensation paid to/for the Senior Pastor or other person assigned or appointed in the lead pastoral role to the church 41a	Base compensation paid to/for all Associate Pastor(s) and other pastoral staff assigned or appointed to the church, include deacons and other clergy in this role 41b	Pastoral Benefits 40, 42a-44	Deacons salary/benefits 41c & 42c	Total amount paid in salary and benefits for all other church staff and diaconal ministers 45	Total amount spent for local church program expenses 46	Total amount spent for other local church operating expenses 47	Local Church capital expenses 48 & 49	TOTAL CHURCH EXPENSES (Sum of lines 29a through 49) 50	Number of giving units 51	Total income for annual budget/spending plan 52	Total income for designated causes including capital campaign and other special projects 53	Total income from connectional and other institutional sources outside the local church 34
34012	969	1,327	7,728	7,728	41,216	0	29,631	0	15,527	11,979	36,367	25,081	178,653	70	136,848	28,028	0
34013	88	3,342	9,818	9,818	51,600	0	29,241	0	45,365	2,842	30,733	15,667	189,710	101	180,401	25,504	0
34014	1,338	5,680	703	703	0	0	537	0	19,131	3,071	24,081	206,393	275,760	67	111,024	68,057	0
34015	2,189	17,855	0	0	25,000	0	1,687	0	32,515	14,630	44,527	0	165,244	172	178,669	24,614	0
34016	856	18,279	8,124	8,124	12,000	0	3,838	0	5,320	1,534	8,277	11,288	66,672	38	167,187	16,639	1,395
34017	0	5,144	0	0	39,744	0	30,708	0	20,606	3,498	11,754	34,934	156,512	62	119,995	36,576	0
34018	1,482	12,995	0	0	22,838	0	11,646	0	22,158	6,579	29,267	35,024	158,424	58	118,866	11,578	0
34019	240	1,303	0	0	4,905	0	4,154	0		1,439	6,775	1,000	21,602	10	12,216	328	0
34020	83	1,057	9,900	9,900	46,000	0	42,523	0	34,182	6,457	21,408	21,401	185,574	70	182,998	3,489	0
34021	1,521	10,769	2,640	2,640	17,000	0	28,412	0	23,091	11,827	30,087	1,656	144,153	71	142,484	8,673	0
34022	1,249	8,572	7,219	7,219	31,539	2,980	28,111	0	25,790	1,790	18,794	0	140,315	69	141,125	7,835	0
34023	72	686	0	0	4,000	0	557	0	5,042	104	6,686	154	14,150	12	12,964	359	0
34024	563	3,338	0	0	9,865	0	5,276	0		12,357	10,036		39,699	22	38,671	1,256	0
34025	4,694	7,247	7,500	7,500	36,000	0	18,838	0	61,386	22,891	46,949	11,919	238,729	112	250,175	24,428	0
34026	10,324	48,879	12,646	12,646	66,700	0	34,918	0	179,658	52,897	98,447	30,840	567,995	287	595,993	15,262	0
34027	7,984	92,456	12,694	12,694	67,700	0	26,133	0	207,929	4,909	137,811	59,494	744,008	312	535,510	225,173	0
34028	3,894	8,881	10,737	10,737	58,756	0	5,563	0	51,562	306,023	44,245	107,164	322,394	65	227,883	68,262	0
34029	32,214	178,006	29,823	27,338	113,900	60,177	84,569	0	1,297,502	581	370,903	332,396	3,132,414	1,467	2,377,408	1,233,622	0
34030	4,448	3,288	5,006	12,086	36,814	0	26,248	0	43,257		44,260	0	193,932	135	157,261	15,919	0

STATISTICAL INFORMATION

MW

CONFERENCE Number	Church Name	Total professing members reported at the close of last year (1)	TOTAL PROFESSING MEMBERS reported at the close of this year (4)	Average attendance at all weekly worship services (7)	Total Baptized Members who have not become Professing Members (9)	Number of other constituents of the church (10)	TOTAL Christian Formation Group Participants (Total of lines) (11a-d)	Average weekly attendance (all ages) in Sunday Church School or other weekly education classes (13)	Membership in United Methodist Men (18a)	Membership in United Methodist Women (19a)	Number of persons sent out on UMVIM teams from this local church (20b)	Total Number of community ministries for outreach, justice, and mercy offered by this local church (21)	Value of church assets and buildings (24 & 25)	Church Debt (26 & 27)	Amount APPORTIONED to the local church by the CONFERENCE (28a)	Amount PAID by the local church to the CONFERENCE for all apportioned causes (29a)	Amount APPORTIONED to the local church by the DISTRICT (if applicable) (28b)
34031	GRAND RAPIDS: FIRST	912	914	460	149	70	631	204	0	0	0	0	39,720,409	0	137,373	137,239	18,450
34032	GRAND RAPIDS: GENESIS	206	170	49	3	0	58	16	0	0	28	0	684,095	235,774	25,541	5,282	3,575
34033	GRAND RAPIDS: LA NUEVA ESPERANZA	73	70	90	10	20	70	28	0	18	0	0	1,131,001	36,026	2,639	0	1,271
34034	GRAND RAPIDS: NORTHLAWN	182	182	74	2	79	45	40	16	0	0	0	2,590,599	193,909	18,623	26,675	3,755
34036	GRAND RAPIDS: SAINT PAUL'S	184	176	89	2	26	51	35	15	0	0	6	2,065,515	65,700	26,675	26,675	4,151
34037	GRAND RAPIDS: SOUTH	124	120	63	8	24	88	24	15	12	0	6	1,215,223	0	20,417	20,417	2,324
34038	GRAND RAPIDS: TRINITY	524	502	170	115	75	197	50	27	100	25	8	7,750,613	0	67,477	16,869	10,606
34039	GRAND RAPIDS: VIETNAMESE	125	120	110	2	12	82	60	0	35	2	2	305,000	0	8,098	8,243	205
34040	GRANDVILLE	250	248	163	0	56	95	17	5	49	0	1	4,738,667	0	35,446	35,446	4,886
34041	GRANT CENTER	22	21	21	71	20	7	7	5	15	0	15	654,673	0	4,236	4,236	150
34042	GREENVILLE: FIRST	625	580	105	50	105	56	54	0	65	0	10	3,845,460	1,205,916	29,897	100	4,063
34043	HART	126	123	59	65	186	99	8	22	21	0	10	2,481,958	50,000	19,159	14,842	849
34044	HESPERIA	71	69	55	1	53	16	9	0	14	0	0	557,200	0	10,074	10,069	984
34045	HOLLAND: FIRST	597	592	324	0	551	280	142	0	137	0	16	11,850,776	24,952	75,070	75,070	7,853
34046	HOLTON	219	209	174	0	201	154	101	0	0	0	2	2,344,870	0	31,821	31,071	4,055
34047	IONIA: EASTON	85	78	41	0	37	28	0	0	16	0	2	1,240,559	0	7,173	7,173	566
34048	IONIA: FIRST	112	101	57	0	34	54	11	0	19	0	3	3,607,498	0	17,816	0	728
34049	IONIA: ZION	81	78	45	0	10	13	15	0	0	0	0	2,375,753	0	12,126	0	527
34050	KENT CITY: CHAPEL HILL	141	144	53	1	12	38	22	0	0	10	1	1,944,024	8,179	15,870	908	1,862

STATISTICAL INFORMATION

MW

CONFERENCE Number	29b – Amount PAID by the local church to the DISTRICT for all apportioned causes (if applicable)	30-38 – Church Benevolence Giving	39a – Total ASKED for clergy pension	39b – Total PAID for clergy pension	41a – Base compensation paid to/for the Senior Pastor or other person assigned or appointed in the lead pastoral role to the church	41b – Base compensation paid to/for all Associate Pastor(s) and other pastoral staff assigned or appointed to the church. Include deacons and other clergy in this role.	40, 42a-44 – Pastoral Benefits	41c & 42c – Deacons salary/benefits	45 – Total amount paid in salary and benefits for all other church staff and diaconal ministers	46 – Total amount spent for local church program expenses	47 – Total amount spent for other local church operating expenses	48 & 49 – Local Church capital expenses	50 – TOTAL CHURCH EXPENSES (Sum of Lines 29a through 49)	51 – Number of giving units	52 – Total income for annual budget/spending plan	53 – Total income for designated causes including capital campaign and other special projects	54 – Total income from connectional and other institutional sources outside the local church
34031	18,450	71,278	15,495	18,245	83,400	9,692	65,774	0	569,264	65,037	197,143	0	1,235,522	242	1,164,417	24,829	0
34032	718	1,818	4,500	3,757	34,500	0	10,430	0	59,651	6,450	33,445	21,636	177,687	73	166,792	1,000	0
34033	0	0	0	0	34,600	0	15,480	0	12,375	3,000	23,000	0	76,080	20	21,000	62,981	31,290
34034	4,151	5,368	4,263	4,263	28,457	0	41,287	0	40,622	9,104	57,461	55,018	213,333	78	157,630	19,260	13,000
34035	2,324	12,567	9,249	9,249	42,168	0	24,078	0	28,004	2,739	51,948	30,099	244,296	75	210,286	20,243	0
34036	2,652	12,698	4,378	4,378	49,700	0	17,311	0		25,370	38,267	13,541	212,010	69	162,975		37,078
34037	209	35,945	14,114	14,114	65,304	0	51,239	0	245,740	39,050	93,615	90,005	654,533	137	462,713	201,482	45,000
34038	6,886	4,200	7,664	7,664	36,363	0	31,120	0	0	42,000	33,000	4,500	167,299	37	77,000	7,200	0
34039	133	20,424	9,675	9,675	46,967	0	35,836	0	62,502	15,207	64,298	45,833	343,074	164	307,317	59,044	0
34040	658	6,065		0	10,000	0	0	0	4,250	1,523	6,765	0	32,972	21	39,258	3,310	0
34041	989	18,073	11,719	11,719	59,000	0	21,120	0	57,779	1,553	49,579	125,885	344,808	130	170,834	94,370	0
34042	7,853	18,424	8,625	8,625	46,000	0	29,844	0	40,278	9,477	23,533	7,277	198,958	56	156,802	55,770	0
34043	3,962	4,705	3,645	3,645	18,320	0	9,798	0	12,684	1,806	18,807	0	80,823	57	77,697	2,812	0
34044	566	31,446	16,785	15,062	71,070	19,989	54,235	0	235,286	37,027	148,550	116,399	811,987	320	710,634	109,903	0
34045	0	10,445	10,421	10,421	55,581	0	30,440	0	34,431	17,174	57,830	0	251,355	140	234,588	18,796	0
34046	92	2,485	3,531	3,531	18,540	0	8,867	0	7,127	1,368	8,831	3,200	61,688	40	54,115	11,575	2,500
34047		9,201	7,500	7,500	40,000	0	19,825	0	32,955	24,155	33,530	7,170	174,336	59	163,695	9,770	0
34048		150	1,217	1,217	14,004	0	4,535	0	1,345	120	14,709	0	36,080	20	85,093	0	0
34049		406	7,734	6,488	38,161	0	22,917	0	9,984	1,405	18,662	1,916	100,939	70	90,708	3,448	0
34050																	

STATISTICAL INFORMATION

MW

CONFERENCE Number	Church Name	Total professing members reported at the close of last year (1)	TOTAL PROFESSING MEMBERS reported at the close of this year (4)	Average attendance at all weekly worship services (7)	Total Baptized Members who have not become Professing Members (9)	Number of other constituents of the church (10)	TOTAL Christian Formation Group Participants (Total of lines 11a-d) (11)	Average weekly attendance (all ages) in Sunday Church School or other weekly education classes (13)	Membership in United Methodist Men (18a)	Membership in United Methodist Women (19a)	Number of persons sent out on UMVIM teams from this local church (20b)	Total Number of community ministries for outreach, justice, and mercy offered by this local church (21)	Value of church assets and buildings (24 & 25)	Church Debt (26 & 27)	Amount APPORTIONED to the local church by the CONFERENCE (28a)	Amount PAID by the local church to the CONFERENCE for all apportioned causes (29a)	Amount APPORTIONED to the local church by the DISTRICT (if applicable) (28b)
34051	LAKEVIEW: NEW LIFE	224	215	88	0	67	41	25	15	25	0	4	2,645,548	0	27,546	27,546	1,456
34052	LEIGHTON	152	135	125	52	50	211	67	0	0	0	18	4,295,849	0	30,012	22,337	1,967
34053	LEVALLEY	149	148	98	27	130	36	13	0	12	0	1	496,707		18,543	18,543	988
34054	LOWELL: FIRST	345	350	166	1	166	172	9	0	67	0	3	4,767,514	9,363	42,783	43,114	4,484
34055	LOWELL: VERGENNES	107	106	81	0	138	111	27	0	0	0	5	502,329		26,160	19,823	1,324
34056	LYONS-MUIR	68	64	41	0	19	24	13	0	6	0	3	1,415,128	0	8,548	9,677	449
34057	MARNE	94	94	90	0	0	0	12	5	10	0	2	780,008	0	12,903	594	1,063
34058	MEARS	85	91	70	3	18	17	2	20	15	0	0	858,000	0	13,178	13,178	646
34059	MECOSTA: NEW HOPE	447	226	118	2	70	212	5	32	32	0	4	762,534	269,579	25,859	15,340	2,971
34060	MIDDLEVILLE	209	222	167	0	100	68	30	2	18	0	6	1,285,362	365,224	28,440	17,448	2,530
34061	MONTAGUE	357	367	127	8	25	68	30	8	0	0	9	6,585,043	15,244	24,513	24,513	5,013
34062	MUSKEGON HEIGHTS: TEMPLE	125	126	60	0	58	46	7	0	0	0	6	390,750	0	27,499	27,455	2,173
34063	MUSKEGON: CENTRAL	229	218	100	0	41	29	0	0	30	0	1	3,382,312	10,000	49,167	6,585	4,415
34064	MUSKEGON: CRESTWOOD	76	67	38	0	27	29	7	0	0	0	4	2,312,000	19,500	8,286	0	1,318
34065	MUSKEGON: LAKE HARBOR	394	393	189	44	72	105	36	0	0	0	4	3,253,252	0	42,023	42,023	6,810
34066	MUSKEGON: UNITY	26	24	16	8	4	7	0	0	12	0	0	502,000	0	5,336	5,336	616
34067	NEWAYGO	79	83	63	19	132	42	40	10	32	0	1	1,158,751	7,716	15,104	15,104	1,115
34068	NORTH MUSKEGON: COMMUNITY	351	355	128	0	70	167	65	0	25	30	2	1,045,000	0	30,976	30,976	6,023
34069	PALO	12	12	9	0	5	9	9	0	0	0	0	466,608	0	1,026	0	98

STATISTICAL INFORMATION

MW

CONFERENCE Number	Amount PAID by the local church to the DISTRICT for all apportioned causes (if applicable) 29b	Church Benevolence Giving 30-38	Total ASKED for clergy pension 39a	Total PAID for clergy pension 39b	Base compensation paid to/for the Senior Pastor or other person assigned or appointed in the lead pastoral role to the church 41a	Base compensation paid to/for all Associate Pastor(s) and other pastoral staff assigned or appointed to the church include deacons and other clergy in this role 41b	Pastoral Benefits 40, 42a-44	Deacons salary/benefits 41c & 42c	Total amount paid in salary and benefits for all other church staff and diaconal ministers 45	Total amount spent for local church program expenses 46	Total amount spent for other local church operating expenses 47	Local Church capital expenses 48 & 49	TOTAL CHURCH EXPENSES (Sum of Lines 29a through 49) 50	Number of giving units 51	Total income for annual budget/spending plan 52	Total income for designated causes including capital campaign and other special projects 53	Total income from connectional and other institutional sources outside the local church 54
34051	1,456	7,547	6,678	6,678	40,445	12,405	30,821	0	46,569	5,963	116,393	1,410	297,233	100	205,309	18,825	0
34052	1,967	28,117	12,988	12,988	61,726	0	29,251	0	33,034	11,738	60,185	18,933	280,276	89	249,765	46,721	0
34053	988	34,149	7,291	7,291	8,885	0	47,929	0	22,827	5,854	43,031	27,846	217,343	51	164,351	53,334	0
34054	5,153	18,674	10,429	7,822	54,276	6,400	36,631	0	60,089	73,961	84,823	21,938	412,881	100	340,420	93,808	0
34055	1,128	7,045	9,528	9,528	43,447	0	44,472	0	34,642	4,106	27,398	6,673	198,262	63	186,836	34,999	0
34056	31	2,289	0	0	9,000	0	13,998	0	13,366	6,834	28,216	0	74,328	32	58,036	0	0
34057	797	164	8,120	8,120	42,000	0	5,490	0	26,953	3,123	22,275	15,528	134,127	60	132,663	7,810	0
34058	646	13,700	7,875	7,875	15,800	0	23,410	0	8,550	13,526	27,000	0	123,685	39	134,945	325	0
34059	1,220	14,460	9,892	9,892	52,755	0	23,484	0	55,119	32,274	73,866	115,854	394,264	94	234,892	68,972	4,000
34060	1,552	15,795	8,698	8,698	43,684	0	20,100	0	25,563	7,300	37,000	53,170	230,310	146	283,023	38,009	0
34061	5,013	10,101	9,848	9,848	53,040	0	22,523	0	58,824	20,589	75,584	91,768	371,803	175	247,378	20,400	0
34062	2,170	6,072	9,242	9,242	49,289	0	32,353	0	52,000	4,959	33,862	2,450	219,852	73	209,607	10,900	0
34063	4,415	17,221	11,858	11,858	58,650	0	46,057	0	120,509	26,412	141,702	97,630	531,039	109	310,463	79,380	0
34064	0	600	0	0	15,312	0	0	0	7,220	500	21,195	7,546	52,373	35	57,050	2,500	0
34065	6,810	30,029	12,577	12,577	67,077	0	11,828	0	120,706	20,509	52,945	55,831	420,335	185	373,811	15,326	500
34066	616	1,039	0	0	12,780	0	1,411	0	6,033	498	8,800	0	36,513	10	44,898	0	0
34067	1,115	6,914	5,905	1,551	29,592	0	7,192	0	24,343	1,595	41,899	2,594	131,899	83	106,229	3,290	0
34068	6,023	15,313	11,250	11,250	60,000	0	13,368	0	42,955	8,693	41,690	2,971	233,239	112	237,050	8,510	0
34069	0	5	0	0	4,000	0	557	0	0	104	4,886	0	9,552	7	9,099	0	0

STATISTICAL INFORMATION

CONFERENCE Number	Church Name	1	4	7	9	10	11	13	18a	19a	20b	21	24 & 25	26 & 27	28a	29a	28b
34070	PARIS	39	36	30	0	30	0	0	0	0	0	1	230,240	0	5,161	5,161	260
34071	PARMELEE	50	50	25	0	0	0	0	0	0	0	0	239,611	0	4,369	4,369	643
34072	PENTWATER: CENTENARY	145	141	67	51	53	29	12	12	17	0	4	2,541,459	0	21,780	21,780	1,073
34073	PIERSON: HERITAGE	216	211	88	9	94	70	12	12	0	0	5	923,332	128,720	16,594	16,594	1,372
34074	RAVENNA	72	62	43	0	33	33	9	0	0	0	4	508,000	11,338	14,304	82	1,318
34075	ROCKFORD	440	415	234	0	0	216	49	3	0	0	4	6,618,607	620,989	68,896	68,896	6,005
34076	RODNEY	17	16	10	6	4	13	6	0	0	0	1	142,483	0	1,993	1,993	119
34077	SALEM: INDIAN MISSION	25	24	12	0	15	66	6	0	0	0	0	358,795	9,150	2,658	1,551	342
34078	SAND LAKE	17	14	22	0	61	19	18	0	14	0	34	42,849	0	2,998	2,998	119
34079	SHELBY	69	66	47	3	14	21	6	0	5	0	0	1,775,000	77,636	8,871	3,414	931
34080	SITKA	21	26	15	0	15	26	9	0	0	0	0	433,000	0	1,898	1,898	360
34081	SOUTH ENSLEY	42	47	38	10	0	33	9	20	8	0	0	127,100	0	5,959	5,959	267
34082	SPARTA	215	190	129	6	109	122	32	0	44	0	3	1,366,230	0	30,773	7,694	3,094
34083	STANWOOD: NORTHLAND	131	126	93	19	126	17	64	0	20	0	3	2,196,075	0	20,235	20,235	910
34084	TURK LAKE	35	35	24	0	8	22	17	0	0	0	4	1,394,001	0	4,284	4,284	228
34085	TWIN LAKE	90	87	55	3	0	0	5	0	0	0	2	1,608,208	0	6,975	6,975	1,505
34086	VICKERYVILLE	13	12	6	0	5	0	0	0	0	0	0	494,631	0	1,590	1,590	93
34087	WALKERVILLE	11	11	26	5	30	0	8	0	0	0	4	465,384	0	3,210	3,210	131
34088	WAYLAND	114	113	53	99	65	69	25	0	0	0	0	3,107,082	0	15,091	6,835	1,548

Column headers:
- 1: Total professing members reported at the close of last year
- 4: TOTAL PROFESSING MEMBERS reported at the close of this year
- 7: Average attendance at all weekly worship services
- 9: Total Baptized Members who have not become Professing Members
- 10: Number of other constituents of the church
- 11: TOTAL Christian Formation Group Participants (Total of lines 11a-d)
- 13: Average weekly attendance (all ages) in Sunday Church School or other weekly education classes
- 18a: Membership in United Methodist Men
- 19a: Membership in United Methodist Women
- 20b: Number of persons sent out on UMVIM teams from this local church
- 21: Total Number of community ministries for outreach, justice, and mercy offered by this local church
- 24 & 25: Value of church assets and buildings
- 26 & 27: Church Debt
- 28a: Amount APPORTIONED to the local church by the CONFERENCE
- 29a: Amount PAID by the local church to the CONFERENCE for all apportioned causes
- 28b: Amount APPORTIONED to the local church by the DISTRICT (if applicable)

MW

CONFERENCE Number	Amount PAID by the local church to the DISTRICT for all apportioned causes (if applicable) [29b]	Church Benevolence Giving [30-38]	Total ASKED for clergy pension [39a]	Total PAID for clergy pension [39b]	Base compensation paid to/for the Senior Pastor or other person assigned or appointed in the lead pastoral role to the church [41a]	Base compensation paid to/for all Associate Pastor(s) and other pastoral staff assigned or appointed to the church. Include deacons and other clergy in this role. [41b]	Pastoral Benefits [40, 42a-44]	Deacons salary/benefits [41c & 42c]	Total amount paid in salary and benefits for all other church staff and diaconal ministers [45]	Total amount spent for local church program expenses [46]	Total amount spent for other local church operating expenses [47]	Local Church capital expenses [48 & 49]	TOTAL CHURCH EXPENSES (Sum of Lines 29a through 49) [50]	Number of giving units [51]	Total income for annual budget/spending plan [52]	Total income for designated causes including capital campaign and other special projects [53]	Total income from connectional and other institutional sources outside the local church [54]
34070	260	5,165	0	0	11,596	1,020	9,077	0	816	82	5,709	0	38,886	36	46,054	3,210	0
34071	643	603	0	0	19,136	0	187	0	0	357	10,827	0	36,122	28	38,513	0	0
34072	1,073	9,584	4,313	4,313	53,229	0	15,454	0	15,960	15,048	44,177	972	181,590	119	154,400	41,504	0
34073	1,372	2,787	7,303	7,303	38,950	0	34,168	0	13,684	8,777	35,822	20,622	180,079	60	143,303	26,532	0
34074	1,318	5,951	6,785	6,506	36,188	0	17,584	0	10,593	3,235	17,831	12,270	111,558	58	89,193	21,543	0
34075	6,005	55,936	11,820	11,820	59,975	0	41,394	0	209,879	32,166	91,856	129,750	707,676	300	512,300	49,293	0
34076	119	530	8,010	2,031	3,183	0	1,544	0	280	1,090	3,197	1,000	11,936	15	10,190	939	0
34077	199	2,000	0	0	10,700	0	2,500	0	2,000	200	5,000	12,135	27,181	5	11,950	1,229	500
34078	119	1,667	0	0	1,793	0	5,796	0	575	1,996	9,536	56,275	36,615	16	28,383	22,114	0
34079	621	3,252	0	0	21,000	0	0	0	7,391	3,471	18,172	0	113,596	49	66,910	300	0
34080	360		0	0	7,500	0	188	0	0	2,400	5,251	0	17,597	13	16,000	5,439	0
34081	267	5,916	12,622	12,622	3,586	0	7,511	0	4,180	4,180	10,762	0	42,361	48	50,645	2,831	0
34082	772	5,888	9,375	9,375	69,751	0	34,413	0	57,445	8,636	39,680	0	236,901	115	238,624	25,979	0
34083	910	8,753	1,688	1,688	50,000	0	23,958	0	33,666	2,661	20,189	3,151	172,898	87	152,814	1,888	0
34084	228	4,097	0	0	9,000	0	1,439	0	3,825	5,040	10,615	0	40,216	15	33,426	1,308	3,000
34085	1,505	2,097	0	0	10,000	0	17,327	0	3,675	2,060	17,038	12,000	72,677	47	69,887	728	0
34086	93	221	0	0	4,000	0	557	0	0	104	6,240	1,010	13,815	6	12,668	0	0
34087	131		0	0	6,773	0	5,323	0	0	230	8,447	0	24,114	15	32,358		0
34088	1,548	1,514	9,844	9,844	58,100	0	14,440	0	17,526	4,330	20,953	0	135,090	47	123,406	9,860	37

Column codes: (1) Total professing members reported at the close of last year; (4) TOTAL PROFESSING MEMBERS reported at the close of this year; (7) Average attendance at all weekly worship services; (9) Total Baptized Members who have not become Professing Members; (10) Number of other constituents of the church; (11) TOTAL Christian Formation Group Participants (Total of lines 11a-d); (13) Average weekly attendance (all ages) in Sunday Church School or other weekly education classes; (18a) Membership in United Methodist Men; (19a) Membership in United Methodist Women; (20b) Number of persons sent out on UMVIM teams from this local church; (21) Total Number of community ministries for outreach, justice, and mercy offered by this local church; (24 & 25) Value of church assets and buildings; (26 & 27) Church Debt; (28a) Amount APPORTIONED to the local church by the CONFERENCE; (29a) Amount PAID by the local church to the CONFERENCE for all apportioned causes; (28b) Amount APPORTIONED to the local church by the DISTRICT (if applicable)

Conf. No.	Church Name	1	4	7	9	10	11	13	18a	19a	20b	21	24 & 25	26 & 27	28a	29a	28b
34089	WHITE CLOUD	124	126	106	55	70	99	45	10	0	0	1	2,827,000	0	22,396	22,396	1,495
34090	WOLF LAKE	105	102	45	45	20	50	18	0	0	0	6	2,412,064	0	11,615	9,288	1,814
34091	WYOMING PARK	125	116	62	0	100	77	60	0	0	0	4	3,053,000	268,349	18,317	10,726	2,522
34092	WYOMING: WESLEY PARK	271	283	176	124	120	56	50	0	15	174	7	4,999,740	540,447	45,716	26,668	5,620
	MIDWEST DISTRICT TOTALS	16,008	15,393	9,633	1,501	8,214	10,238	4,438	252	1,194	174	360	222,368,405	5,949,933	2,182,181	1,744,196	234,584
	MID-MICHIGAN DISTRICT																
35001	ALMA	216	217	125	1	65	95	30	22	40	0	2	3,964,907	39,668	27,366	27,679	1,419
35002	ASHLEY	31	28	18	0	12	20	9	0	7	6	0	155,000	0	6,050	6,050	208
35003	BANCROFT	70	61	27	0	11	18	3	5	11	0	5	483,019	0	4,192	4,192	329
35004	BANNISTER	44	43	25	0	0	15	13	0	17	8	6	388,256	0	5,692	5,692	293
35005	BARRY COUNTY: WOODLAND	54	58	25	0	35	12	18	0	10	0	0	118,000	0	4,920	4,920	433
35006	BATH	93	90	56	0	68	123	13	0	4	5	5	1,240,818	53,457	9,753	9,753	698
35007	BEEBE	10	10	17	16	10	0	0	0	11	0	0	468,266	0	1,505	1,505	67
35008	BRECKENRIDGE	136	128	55	0	31	28	14	11	0	0	0	2,426,673	0	12,748	3,762	891
35009	BROOKFIELD EATON	29	31	22	0	35	5	2	0	0	0	0	149,610	0	5,175	5,175	209
35010	CARLAND	20	18	25	0	7	4	2	0	0	0	0	274,869	2,838	2,308	2,308	181
35011	CARSON CITY	276	286	102	3	130	75	41	0	25	0	0	1,262,219	216,604	24,254	24,254	1,835
35012	CHAPIN	73	73	42	14	50	28	12	0	18	0	6	218,401	0	4,921	4,921	386

STATISTICAL INFORMATION

MM

CONFERENCE Number	29b Amount PAID by the local church to the DISTRICT for all apportioned causes (if applicable)	30-38 Church Benevolence Giving	39a Total ASKED for clergy pension	39b Total PAID for clergy pension	41a Base compensation paid to/for the Senior Pastor or other person assigned or appointed in the lead pastoral role to the church	41b Base compensation paid to/for all Associate Pastor(s) and other pastoral staff assigned or appointed to the church. Include deacons and other clergy in this role	40, 42a-44 Pastoral Benefits	41c & 42c Deacons salary/benefits	45 Total amount paid in salary and benefits for all other church staff and diaconal ministers	46 Total amount spent for local church program expenses	47 Total amount spent for other local church operating expenses	48 & 49 Local Church capital expenses	50 TOTAL CHURCH EXPENSES (Sum of Lines 29a through 49)	51 Number of giving units	52 Total income for annual budget/spending plan	53 Total income for designated causes including capital campaign and other special projects	54 Total income from connectional and other institutional sources outside the local church
34089	1,495	4,219	8,906	8,906	41,832	0	30,245	0	27,295	6,126	39,567	0	182,081	60	186,097	2,985	0
34090	1,455	976	0	0	4,976	0	14,956	0	22,987	5,871	33,578	0	94,087	38	112,792	365	0
34091	2,522	8,934	8,152	8,152	22,838	0	12,313	0	19,143	1,796	33,841	53,317	173,582	43	138,741	23,148	0
34092	3,278	5,013	11,885	11,885	60,694	0	43,529	0	122,011	14,088	86,152	162,552	535,870	133	430,073	32,471	144,300
	197,141	1,293,585	530,692	521,106	3,015,533	112,663	1,733,741	0	5,059,118	1,215,184	3,725,409	2,840,772	21,458,448	8,377	17,372,540	3,728,334	
35001	1,433	11,263	10,281	10,281	56,000	0	22,112	0	48,255	28,800	44,994	106,719	357,536	127	206,297	206,231	0
35002	208	2,236	790	790	12,600	0	2,497	0	1,900	1,000	10,000	300	37,581	0	42,807	2,200	0
35003	330	8,737	430	430	8,794	0	2,346	0	8,771	724	11,223	7,112	52,669	0	66,149	1,918	0
35004	293	6,529	0	0	6,127	0	1,617	0	2,333	2,653	7,841	0	33,085	29	43,181	3,301	0
35005	487	1,397	7,076	7,076	0	0	10,413	0	3,990	1,090	14,255	7,390	43,942	23	37,333	523	0
35006	698	4,175	0	0	14,934	0	17,216	0	8,729	5,125	9,485	27,239	104,430	62	65,513	23,391	18,000
35007	67	538	0	0	2,075	0		0	7,620	1,240	7,620	7,537	13,045	15	12,648	0	0
35008	238	728	3,186	3,186	36,241	0	23,196	0	15,402	3,333	29,838	1,085	123,461	64	111,136	22,366	0
35009	209	2,585	740	740	7,110	0	10,551	0	2,985	1,870	4,757		36,327	25	31,040	1,474	0
35010	181	1,692	0	0	10,340	0	3,359	0	300	439	3,322		22,681	17	20,860	1,010	0
35011	1,835	18,212	1,520	1,520	12,618	3,601	989	0	19,628	4,678	47,657	80,399	213,871	70	202,928	8,814	0
35012	382	4,005			12,024	0	1,600	0	0	3,600	10,629	5,500	44,181	50	43,653	3,115	0

CONFERENCE Number	Church Name	1 – Total professing members reported at the close of last year	4 – TOTAL PROFESSING MEMBERS reported at the close of this year	7 – Average attendance at all weekly worship services	9 – Total Baptized Members who have not become Professing Members	10 – Number of other constituents of the church	11a-d – TOTAL Christian Formation Group Participants (Total of lines 11a-d)	13 – Average weekly attendance (all ages) in Sunday Church School or other weekly education classes	18a – Membership in United Methodist Men	19a – Membership in United Methodist Women	20b – Number of persons sent out on UMVIM teams from this local church	21 – Total Number of community ministries for outreach, justice, and mercy offered by this local church	24 & 25 – Value of church assets and buildings	26 & 27 – Church Debt	28a – Amount APPORTIONED to the local church by the CONFERENCE	29a – Amount PAID by the local church to the CONFERENCE for all apportioned causes	28b – Amount APPORTIONED to the local church by the DISTRICT (if applicable)
35013	CHARLOTTE: LAWRENCE AVE	236	227	110	1	0	0	35	10	36	0	3	1,664,391	0	32,663	24,497	1,909
35014	CHESANING: TRINITY	322	313	132	0	0	142	52	12	33	0	0	3,357,000	0	23,917	23,917	1,877
35015	CORUNNA	75	73	40	0	10	0	0	0	0	0	1	2,830,164	20,899	14,784	1,800	1,160
35016	CORUNNA: NORTHWEST VENICE	17	15	14	5	10	12	9	0	8	0	0	310,000	0	1,868	1,868	147
35017	DELTA MILLS	70	57	36	0	11	21	14	0	16	0	19	941,216	0	7,297	7,297	521
35018	DEWITT: REDEEMER	744	848	489	259	1,264	1,047	265	0	0	0	14	5,242,496	0	137,996	137,996	6,199
35018a	DEWITT: REDEEMER - St Johns: First Campus	105	0	60	33	60	18	8	7	30	0	1	3,417,216	2,884	18,530	18,530	761
35019	DIMONDALE	62	61	56	0	40	5	0	0	6	0	3	2,200,158	12,816	13,432	13,432	505
35020	EAST LANSING: THE PEOPLES CHURCH	270	270	90	0	0	75	20	39	36	0	0	1,150,000	0	0	2,440	3,786
35021	EAST LANSING: UNIVERSITY	452	459	231	22	65	321	40	14	40	8	4	4,327,777	834,566	74,047	80,218	3,015
35022	EATON RAPIDS: FIRST	317	312	237	0	270	172	30	0	0	0	2	6,798,649	244,763	55,182	20,039	832
35023	ELSIE	115	109	60	0	107	22	7	0	20	0	3	1,081,500	0	13,589	6,596	144
35024	FELT PLAINS	16	14	14	41	0	7	0	0	0	0	0	665,001	0	3,256	3,256	576
35025	FOWLERVILLE: FIRST	124	120	54	0	40	70	21	8	20	0	6	3,605,740	0	20,193	13,317	234
35026	FOWLERVILLE: TRINITY	79	68	30	10	57	22	6	10	11	0	0	1,174,000	0	8,226	8,226	64
35027	FREEPORT	8	7	7	32	0	76	0	0	0	0	0	987,375	0	3,129	3,129	2,486
35028	GRAND LEDGE: FIRST	292	275	130	30	88	22	22	121	170	2	0	5,316,316	0	38,245	38,245	529
35029	GRESHAM	67	62	57	0	35	22	10	0	14	0	2	194,500	0	6,229	6,229	537
35031	GUNNISONVILLE	64	58	54	0	31	61	3	0	0	0	4	831,000	0	12,268	12,268	

STATISTICAL INFORMATION

MM

CONFERENCE Number	Amount PAID to DISTRICT for apportioned causes (29b)	Church Benevolence Giving (30-38)	Total ASKED for clergy pension (39a)	Total PAID for clergy pension (39b)	Base comp. Senior Pastor (41a)	Base comp. Associate Pastor(s)/other (41b)	Pastoral Benefits (40, 42a-44)	Deacons salary/benefits (41c & 42c)	Salary/benefits other staff (45)	Local church program expenses (46)	Other local church operating expenses (47)	Local Church capital expenses (48 & 49)	TOTAL CHURCH EXPENSES (50)	Number of giving units (51)	Income for annual budget/spending plan (52)	Income for designated causes (53)	Income from connectional/other sources (54)
35013	1,432	10,159	10,631	10,631	56,700	0	35,038	0	39,356	6,962	65,104	22,319	272,198	106	248,913	81,660	0
35014	1,877	14,407	6,420	6,420	52,500	0	20,612	0	51,540	9,462	34,721	32,499	247,955	84	249,999	94,867	0
35015	0	717	1,130	1,130	18,685	0	9,153	0	15,071	1,053	42,840	0	90,449	50	104,000	800	0
35016	521	312	560	560	8,808	0	1,200	0	600	700	3,000	0	17,048	8	16,000	0	0
35017	6,199	5,205	26,530	26,530	18,528	45,787	2,927	0	7,247	5,035	14,332	74,348	135,440	40	52,200	626,365	13,000
35018	761	219,410	3,328	3,328	91,080	0	94,913	0	499,024	72,001	234,875	188,335	1,616,150	707	1,374,794	200,850	35,000
35018a	505	5,806	0	0	33,986	0	10,020	0	49,328	2,579	30,076	37,212	191,626	69	193,438	165,652	0
35019	60	7,586	0	0	19,488	0	28,154	0	20,349	2,266	20,409	41,280	153,469	45	111,469	13,326	0
35020	4,101	6,000	13,159	13,159	0	0	0	0	0	1	1	0	8,502	1	1	0	0
35021	1,508	19,791	10,868	10,868	61,228	0	32,734	0	211,725	20,134	108,072	277,620	828,782	223	584,149	146,923	0
35022	404	44,087	0	0	52,861	0	32,256	0	176,432	44,956	99,411	84,949	567,367	249	453,007	158,922	0
35023	144	0	0	0	20,557	0	12,726	0	18,529	2,888	27,163	19,771	108,634	38	88,856	9,255	0
35024	576	927	4,250	4,250	12,539	0	2,750	0	2,455	412	8,530	0	31,013	11	26,279	169	2,066
35025	234	4,568	660	660	39,341	0	5,695	0	35,109	3,461	27,061	18,835	152,213	62	125,297	2,621	0
35026	64	939	0	0	22,200	0	0	0	16,316	711	18,518	0	67,804	17	71,735	1,367	0
35027	2,466	3,593	12,000	12,000	6,395	0	396	0	0	5,762	7,537	9,131	36,007	8	20,856	17,432	1,925
35028	529	24,778	0	0	64,000	0	30,434	0	87,120	5,525	43,311	1,582	309,481	162	274,218	94,883	864
35029	537	581	0	0	13,265	0	19,229	0	1,435	2,546	11,517	7,694	63,025	44	58,554	6,743	0
35031		4,179			22,418	0	19,374	0	9,179	9,967	15,236	675	93,833	45	83,793	10,243	0

STATISTICAL INFORMATION

CONFERENCE Number	Church Name	Total professing members reported at the close of last year (1)	TOTAL PROFESSING MEMBERS reported at the close of this year (4)	Average attendance at all weekly worship services (7)	Total Baptized Members who have not become Professing Members (9)	Number of other constituents of the church (10)	TOTAL Christian Formation Group Participants (Total of lines 11a-d) (11)	Average weekly attendance (all ages) in Sunday Church School or other weekly education classes (13)	Membership in United Methodist Men (18a)	Membership in United Methodist Women (19a)	Number of persons sent out on UMVIM teams from this local church (20b)	Total Number of community ministries for outreach, justice, and mercy offered by this local church (21)	Value of church assets and buildings (24 & 25)	Church Debt (26 & 27)	Amount APPORTIONED to the local church by the CONFERENCE (28a)	Amount PAID by the local church to the CONFERENCE for all apportioned causes (29a)	Amount APPORTIONED to the local church by the DISTRICT (if applicable) (28b)
35032	HASTINGS: FIRST	311	201	144	42	41	146	52	0	10	0	3	7,922,291	0	31,403	31,403	2,414
35033	HASTINGS: HOPE	133	70	60	0	33	36	34	0	0	0	1	1,634,275	200,000	15,680	7,840	1,067
35034	HASTINGS: WELCOME CORNERS	26	25	17	0	19	0	0	0	0	0	0	56,000	0	4,455	5,046	217
35035	HENDERSON	50	53	28	4	42	17	17	0	0	0	0	613,192	0	4,905	4,905	385
35036	HOLT	410	388	243	0	348	241	63	0	75	0	11	5,017,662	0	57,002	57,005	3,465
35037	ITHACA	130	129	85	3	67	23	12	0	16	0	3	395,000	0	20,009	16,674	899
35038	JUDDVILLE	38	40	23	4	12	5	0	0	16	0	1	3,002,595	0	4,939	4,939	388
35039	KALAMO	55	53	29		32	17	0	4	9	0	3	116,969	0	4,198	4,198	529
35040	LAINGSBURG	194	116	85	34	54	65	20	0	12	0	6	2,194,250	154,086	15,042	15,042	1,180
35041	LAKE ODESSA: CENTRAL	140	130	68	23	42	54	21	0	36	0	3	4,743,954	0	22,695	22,721	1,187
35042	LAKE ODESSA: LAKEWOOD	265	235	170	1	188	638	130	0	0	0	33	5,473,800	499,906	42,544	31,908	2,213
35043	LANSING: ASBURY	150	143	65	0	8	44	5	0	0	0	1	4,668,647	0	22,276	11,238	1,204
35044	LANSING: CENTRAL	307	307	97	3	200	209	54	0	12	0	3	21,215,000	0	42,211	8,862	2,205
35045	LANSING: FIRST	138	128	72	9	42	41	0	6	12	1	2	4,216,000	52,059	24,389	16,259	1,163
35046	LANSING: GRACE	207	215	125	32	93	146	70	0	25	0	0	1,073,093	0	27,154	27,185	1,636
35047	LANSING: MOUNT HOPE	288	284	237	123	96	315	118	0	31	0	5	4,455,152	0	64,610	59,468	2,245
35048	LANSING: SYCAMORE CRK	294	290	259		85	59	51	0	8	3	0	4,074,356	87,405	33,211	21,587	2,408
35049	LESLIE	57	55	26	0	18	9	0	0	13	0	9	1,476,435	0	8,051	8,287	658
35050	LIVINGSTON CIRCUIT: PLAINFIELD	55	41	26	0	58	0	0	0	12	0	0	1,043,040	1,250	6,597	0	188

MM

STATISTICAL INFORMATION

MM

CONFERENCE Number	29b Amount PAID by the local church to the DISTRICT for all apportioned causes (if applicable)	30-38 Church Benevolence Giving	39a Total ASKED for clergy pension	39b Total PAID for clergy pension	41a Base compensation paid to/for the Senior Pastor or other person in the lead pastoral role	41b Base compensation paid to/for all Associate Pastor(s) and other pastoral staff	40, 42a-44 Pastoral Benefits	41c & 42c Deacons salary/benefits	45 Total amount paid in salary and benefits for all other church staff and diaconal ministers	46 Total amount spent for local church program expenses	47 Total amount spent for other local church operating expenses	48 & 49 Local Church capital expenses	50 TOTAL CHURCH EXPENSES (Sum of lines 29a through 49)	51 Number of giving units	52 Total income for annual budget/spending plan	53 Total income for designated causes including capital campaign and other special projects	51 Total income from connectional and other institutional sources outside the local church
35032	2,414	34,686	12,000	12,000	64,000	0	12,961	0	64,099	9,965	73,137	72,311	376,976	183	213,286	144,466	0
35033	533	1,043	6,687	6,687	35,603	0	11,729	0	15,005	677	44,393	52,631	176,141	65	169,407	14,970	0
35034	217	1,494	0	0	12,881	0		0		423	10,555	7,100	37,716	14	26,371	700	0
35035	385	1,875	1,520	1,520	12,024	0	1,019	0	4,745	289	11,602	6,940	45,304	32	47,670	28,386	0
35036	3,465	52,307	12,614	12,614	67,275	0	33,390	0	178,322	16,778	103,555	3,112	527,823	215	445,830	64,753	0
35037	749	2,100	8,128	8,128	40,071	0	37,456	0	17,390	4,559	19,060		146,187	86	154,929	25,463	0
35038	388	11,134	580	580	12,000	0		0	9,501	11,017	17,053	62,432	129,044	31	112,106	97	0
35039	529	12,361	0	0	9,740	0	8,318	0	4,952	3,151	9,624	3,870	56,743	23	39,768	3,142	6,194
35040	1,180	4,132	5,720	5,720	44,880	0	31,038	0	21,713	2,760	24,853	118,307	269,625	93	141,977	118,480	0
35041	1,200	13,915	8,527	8,527	38,208	0	28,209	0	39,590	2,817	42,821	48,504	246,512	83	184,950	81,237	0
35042	1,660	16,464	8,691	8,691	47,181	0	34,183	0	68,773	12,459	82,833	118,303	422,455	133	400,945	43,783	0
35043	602	6,187	7,500	7,500	41,240	0	30,650	0	46,422	3,112	24,829	3,459	174,239	90	135,536	49,405	300
35044	463	7,393	10,125	10,125	52,000	0	27,000	0	137,000	16,000	162,000	14,000	434,843	85	329,600	10,000	0
35045	775	2,507	9,281	9,281	49,500	0	24,439	0	39,070	22,887	40,332	7,558	212,608	86	187,314	6,925	0
35046	1,636	10,787	8,466	8,466	48,000	0	30,023	0	70,804	12,884	59,584	91,737	361,106	112	216,596	57,581	0
35047	2,074	29,093	13,480	12,248	61,200	35,662	46,120	16,890	141,006	24,276	88,972	25,480	481,347	182	510,984	24,380	23,000
35048	1,566	14,686	15,031	15,031	47,636	0	40,499	0	114,412	8,937	53,006	9,487	378,502	298	256,644	233,375	0
35049	676	2,246	0	0	12,822	0	5,938	0	10,188	2,139	15,537		67,320	30	44,841	2,791	0
35050	188	838	660	660	22,200	0	0	0	16,316	150	7,728	0	48,080	20	42,302	270	0

STATISTICAL INFORMATION

CONFERENCE Number	Church Name	Total professing members reported at the close of last year (1)	TOTAL PROFESSING MEMBERS reported at the close of this year (4)	Average attendance at all weekly worship services (7)	Total Baptized Members who have not become Professing Members (9)	Number of other constituents of the church (10)	TOTAL Christian Formation Group Participants (Total of lines 11a-d) (11)	Average weekly attendance (all ages) in Sunday Church School or other weekly education classes (13)	Membership in United Methodist Men (18a)	Membership in United Methodist Women (19a)	Number of persons sent out on UMVIM teams from this local church (20b)	Total Number of community ministries for outreach, justice, and mercy offered by this local church (21)	Value of church assets and buildings (24 & 25)	Church Debt (26 & 27)	Amount APPORTIONED to the local church by the CONFERENCE (28a)	Amount PAID by the local church to the CONFERENCE for all apportioned causes (29a)	Amount APPORTIONED to the local church by the DISTRICT (if applicable) (28b)
35051	LOWE	70	70	60	1	0	0	12	0	0	0	0	810,000	0	9,113	9,113	416
35052	MAPLE RAPIDS	35	34	29	0	25	0	0	0	0	0	0	445,000	0	6,879	6,879	228
35053	MASON: FIRST	440	433	134	96	329	123	23	0	84	0	0	5,450,064	338,294	48,276	34,101	3,617
35054	MIDDLEBURY	42	38	15	0	0	0	0	0	0	0	3	634,236	0	3,151	3,151	247
35055	MILLVILLE	114	113	58	0	53	21	16	4	12	0	6	2,571,372	0	14,550	10,915	938
35056	MORRICE	76	70	19	0	6	10	0	4	5	0	2	881,033	0	4,367	4,367	343
35057	MULLIKEN	30	29	24	0	35	22	6	0	0	0	4	220,000	14,028	5,078	2,330	209
35058	MUNITH	37	39	33	1	8	83	12	4	0	0	1	1,041,000	0	5,407	5,407	297
35059	NASHVILLE	104	95	55	1	29	0	0	0	10	0	0	715,308	0	10,059	10,184	946
35060	NASHVILLE: PEACE	26	24	22	0	0	25	6	10	23	0	8	442,000	5,257	2,913	2,913	217
35061	NEW LOTHROP: FIRST	77	75	33	3	135	212	28	35	30	3	15	988,543	0	7,965	7,965	625
35062	OKEMOS: COMMUNITY CHURCH	448	448	145	58	0	36	5	0	0	0	0	6,312,113	35,500	61,914	41,383	3,617
35063	OVID UNITED CHURCH	93	83	62	43	0	7	0	0	0	0	0	2,076,000	0	8,381	4,969	613
35064	OWOSSO: BURTON	27	25	9	5	0	0	0	0	0	0	0	1,002,000	0	3,251	3,251	255
35065	OWOSSO: FIRST	271	268	134	0	138	120	36	8	73	2	8	7,635,039	0	33,610	33,610	2,637
35066	OWOSSO: TRINITY	121	122	49	0	27	18	14	0	20	0	2	2,052,000	0	14,231	1,272	1,117
35067	PERRY	47	47	37	0	44	37	0	0	7	0	4	1,600,610	0	7,424	7,424	393
35068	PITTSBURG	36	27	12	0	30	31	6	0	7	0	0	257,900	8,120	1,860	1,860	146
35069	POMPEII	37	36	29	0	0	0	0	0	15	0	7	1,152,700	3,715	5,880	5,880	254

MM

STATISTICAL INFORMATION

MM

Column key:
- **29b** — Amount PAID by the local church to the DISTRICT for all apportioned causes (if applicable)
- **30-38** — Church Benevolence Giving
- **39a** — Total ASKED for clergy pension
- **39b** — Total PAID for clergy pension
- **41a** — Base compensation paid to/for the Senior Pastor or other person assigned or appointed in the lead pastoral role to the church
- **41b** — Base compensation paid to/for all Associate Pastor(s) and other pastoral staff assigned or appointed to the church, include deacons and other clergy in this role
- **40, 42a-44** — Pastoral Benefits
- **41c & 42c** — Deacons salary/benefits
- **45** — Total amount paid in salary and benefits for all other church staff and diaconal ministers
- **46** — Total amount spent for local church program expenses
- **47** — Total amount spent for other local church operating expenses
- **48 & 49** — Local Church capital expenses
- **50** — TOTAL CHURCH EXPENSES (Sum of Lines 29a through 49)
- **51** — Number of giving units
- **52** — Total income for annual budget/spending plan
- **53** — Total income for designated causes including capital campaign and other special projects
- **54** — Total income from connectional and other institutional sources outside the local church

CONFERENCE Number	29b	30-38	39a	39b	41a	41b	40, 42a-44	41c & 42c	45	46	47	48 & 49	50	51	52	53	54
35051	416	8,084	0	0	18,250	0	8,625	0	3,726	5,894	8,509	9,796	72,413	45	78,147	7,463	0
35052	228	2,165	4,473	4,473	18,250	0	7,125	0	4,260	500	7,733	0	51,613	25	48,027	1,000	0
35053	2,555	5,984	11,250	11,250	60,000	0	20,912	0	128,823	5,246	68,917	178,765	516,553	164	438,632	73,991	0
35054	247	164	810	810	11,176	0	1,375	0	1,122	28	17,454	86,679	35,527	17	26,758	0	1,637
35055	704	1,700	10,783	10,783	34,852	0	28,747	0	18,766	4,856	53,426	870	251,428	25	137,230	89,643	21,250
35056	343	5,704	430	430	8,794	0	2,345	0	0	1,158	10,732	0	34,743	28	31,454	7,076	0
35057	76	0	5,546	765	29,576	0	8,354	0	0	1,175	14,460	0	56,736	34	34,501	1,325	7,047
35058	297	1,200	4,579	4,579	17,801	0	13,724	0	4,927	330	10,178	8,110	58,443	25	36,625	13,232	0
35059	946	6,335	6,659	6,659	36,376	0	28,054	0	4,881	9,495	25,304	4,862	136,344	40	110,936	11,920	1,666
35060	217	2,300	1,130	1,130	11,424	0	9,338	0	6,967	7,598	5,760	1,687	27,476	20	23,074	1,349	0
35061	625	2,017			18,685	0		0			25,465		81,477	25	78,537	4,771	0
35062	3,617	64,186	13,500	13,500	61,608	0	58,722	0	161,656	23,459	79,266	12,785	520,182	160	452,816	25,773	0
35063	331	12,312	8,486	8,486	25,298	0	16,027	0	24,507	5,978	32,801	8,020	138,729	68	118,337	43,072	0
35064		1,419	1,520	1,520	10,021	0	0	0	0	2,000	10,000	0	28,111	10	53,100	4,000	0
35065	2,637	36,416	7,870	7,870	62,582	0	25,895	0	84,029	8,776	66,938	50,456	379,309	130	294,816	24,852	24,400
35066	0	888	6,060	6,060	49,171	0	12,363	0	18,915	6,900	19,900	0	115,469	72	103,034	5,096	0
35067	393	3,019	4,453	4,453	23,748	0	15,522	0	4,789	4,327	7,785	3,996	75,456	27	69,954	3,294	0
35068		1,089	430	430	6,700	0	400	0	1,500	500	5,000	0	17,479	15	17,005	600	0
35069	254	1,160	0	0	2,512	0	7,799	0	2,334	1,000	8,593	1,639	31,171	38	51,267	1,080	0

STATISTICAL INFORMATION

Conference Number	Church Name	Total professing members reported at the close of last year (1)	TOTAL PROFESSING MEMBERS reported at the close of this year (4)	Average attendance at all weekly worship services (7)	Total Baptized Members who have not become Professing Members (9)	Number of other constituents of the church (10)	TOTAL Christian Formation Group Participants (Total of lines 11a-d)	Average weekly attendance (all ages) in Sunday Church School or other weekly education classes (13)	Membership in United Methodist Men (18a)	Membership in United Methodist Women (19a)	Number of persons sent out on UMVIM teams from this local church (20b)	Total Number of community ministries for outreach, justice, and mercy offered by this local church (21)	Value of church assets and buildings (24 & 25)	Church Debt (26 & 27)	Amount APPORTIONED to the local church by the CONFERENCE (28a)	Amount PAID by the local church to the CONFERENCE for all apportioned causes (29a)	Amount APPORTIONED to the local church by the DISTRICT (if applicable) (28b)
35070	PORTLAND	227	228	105	0	32	51	25	0	25	0	4	2,528,638	0	33,613	26,890	2,534
35072	RIVERDALE: LINCOLN ROAD	123	117	54	0	51	40	14	0	8	0	5	997,662	0	16,702	16,702	795
35073	ROBBINS	121	121	57	26	36	68	23	0	0	2	6	1,832,896	0	16,364	7,501	1,034
35074	SHAFTSBURG	50	50	40	31	55	41	23	0	0	0	5	841,659	0	7,542	7,542	409
35075	SHEPARDSVILLE	33	34	22	10	23	26	4	0	8	0	14	313,000	0	3,441	3,437	223
35076	ST JOHNS: PILGRIM	231	236	233	10	179	205	83	0	40	0	0	2,452,929	0	42,701	42,701	1,456
35077	ST LOUIS: FIRST	220	207	98	0	82	78	5	16	12	0	0	3,027,481	0	18,591	13,891	1,411
35078	STOCKBRIDGE	38	39	45	0	0	45	15	0	0	0	0	660,000	0	5,716	10,595	289
35079	SUNFIELD	49	46	42	0	50	40	15	0	5	0	0	1,185,000	0	13,451	1,401	474
35080	VERNON	28	25	15	0	16	6	3	0	0	0	0	1,120,000	5,765	2,407	0	189
35081	WACOUSTA COMMUNITY	263	258	103	0	310	84	20	0	20	0	6	2,899,817	46,526	22,479	15,735	2,078
35082	WEBBERVILLE	118	114	75	1	42	54	32	8	33	0	8	2,328,342	146,958	15,749	4,014	971
35083	WILLIAMSTON	144	153	64	0	49	43	5	0	0	0	15	4,210,565	0	18,915	18,915	1,146
35084	WILLIAMSTON: CROSSROADS	40	38	35	0	0	29	17	0	24	0	5	2,166,000	0	9,093	9,091	449
35085	WILLIAMSTON: WHEATFIELD	46	46	16	0	14	0	4	0	0	0	0	259,853	0	4,915	4,915	385
	MID-MICHIGAN DISTRICT TOTALS	11,597	11,080	6,262	1,032	5,818	6,136	1,805	347	1,317	37	296	193,737,008	3,027,364	1,531,594	1,258,382	88,840
	EAST WINDS DISTRICT																
36001	APPLEGATE	89	93	26	0	0	11	3	9	12	0	5	646,910	0	3,746	3,746	429

EW

MM

STATISTICAL INFORMATION

EW

CONFERENCE Number	29b Amount PAID by the local church to the DISTRICT for all apportioned causes (if applicable)	30-38 Church Benevolence Giving	39a Total ASKED for clergy pension	39b Total PAID for clergy pension	41a Base compensation paid to/for the Senior Pastor or other person assigned or appointed in the lead pastoral role to the church	41b Base compensation paid to/for all Associate Pastor(s) and other pastoral staff assigned or appointed to the church, include deacons and other clergy in this role.	40,42a-44 Pastoral Benefits	41c & 42c Deacons salary/benefits	45 Total amount paid in salary and benefits for all other church staff and diaconal ministers	46 Total amount spent for local church program expenses	47 Total amount spent for other local church operating expenses	48 & 49 local Church capital expenses	50 TOTAL CHURCH EXPENSES (Sum of Lines 29a through 49)	51 Number of giving units	52 Total Income for annual budget/spending plan	53 Total income for designated causes including capital campaign and other special projects	54 Total Income from connectional and other institutional sources outside the local church
35070	2,027	1,285	11,078	11,078	59,085	0	30,785	0	45,711	4,618	43,554	35,870	260,903	120	230,027	83,774	0
35072	795	9,999	5,796	5,796	38,643	0	7,779	0	17,542	2,272	46,238	2,170	147,936	45	125,966	14,098	1,950
35073	460	11,759	7,265	7,265	38,744	0	25,928	0	18,652	1,882	22,104	11,062	145,357	45	126,338	27,248	570
35074	409	3,474	4,453	4,453	23,748	0	19,579	0	4,430	6,123	12,128	0	81,886	37	82,039	17,636	0
35075	223	7,345	0	0	10,080	0	0	0	1,329	2,229	10,385	0	35,028	19	27,278	445	0
35076	1,456	36,009	10,238	10,238	44,630	0	32,774	0	97,889	42,583	50,906	28,367	387,553	207	378,465	8,135	0
35077	1,411	5,181	7,581	7,581	33,231	0	14,816	0	27,123	4,379	37,538	1,190	146,341	107	161,646	8,188	0
35078	489	50	2,181	2,181	13,920	0	15,883	150	8,640	3,626	14,781	0	70,315	35	63,961	3,432	0
35079	38	5,358	1,380	1,380	17,931	0	10,560	0	24,335	4,439	18,141	0	83,583	50	91,780	8,241	0
35080		1,400	760		12,000	0	1,400	0	1,500	300	1,500	0	18,100	20	35,000	50	0
35081	1,455	8,908	8,124	8,124	43,327	0	21,891	0	39,228	3,536	35,707	29,209	207,120	114	205,892	11,531	0
35082	486	1,073	6,791	6,791	7,464	0	21,132	0	16,334	1,937	47,656	24,351	131,238	50	129,020	24,781	0
35083	1,146	7,173	8,501	8,501	45,339	0	24,837	0	31,132	4,568	45,535	10,536	197,682	67	180,878	154,327	5,000
35084	449	5,074	0	0	3,720	0	22,573	0	6,003	4,855	17,284	0	69,049	29	62,797	9,315	0
35085	385	980	0	0	8,148	85,050	6,007	0	3,710	870	9,762	268	35,045	20	33,061	920	375
	74,114	921,600	404,696	397,923	2,418,837	85,050	1,377,750	17,040	3,166,176	583,690	2,796,259	2,215,450	15,312,171	6,245	12,820,557	3,508,283	164,244
36001	429	10	1,240	1,240	10,201	0	7,263	0	0	100	9,116	0	32,105	0	37,935	50	0

CONFERENCE Number	Church Name	Total professing members reported at the close of last year (1)	TOTAL PROFESSING MEMBERS reported at the close of this year (4)	Average attendance at all weekly worship services (7)	Total Baptized Members who have not become Professing Members (9)	Number of other constituents of the church (10)	TOTAL Christian Formation Group Participants (Total of lines 11a-d) (11)	Average weekly attendance (all ages) in Sunday Church School or other weekly education classes (13)	Membership in United Methodist Men (18a)	Membership in United Methodist Women (19a)	Number of persons sent out on UMVIM teams from this local church (20b)	Total Number of community ministries for outreach, justice, and mercy offered by this local church (21)	Value of church assets and buildings (24 & 25)	Church Debt (26 & 27)	Amount APPORTIONED to the local church by the CONFERENCE (28a)	Amount PAID by the local church to the CONFERENCE for all apportioned causes (29a)	Amount APPORTIONED to the local church by the DISTRICT (if applicable) (28b)
36002	ARMADA	107	119	57	61	22	70	26	0	10	0	2	998,740	0	12,664	12,664	1,450
36003	ATHERTON	136	180	47	2	19	21	25	9	6	0	2	2,956,386	0	12,964	4,033	1,017
36004	ATTICA	80	78	53	1	12	29	29	12	19	0	3	882,500	45,618	10,708	10,708	1,226
36005	AVOCA	38	44	40	47	13	0	10	0	14	0	8	673,383	0	4,223	3,801	484
36006	BAD AXE: FIRST	256	236	97	23	13	45	15	15	30	0	1	3,945,015	0	19,894	19,894	2,278
36007	BROWN CITY	126	120	53	0	33	74	22	8	29	0	2	2,976,100	3,875	12,351	12,351	1,414
36008	BUEL	64	63	32	17	6	24	20	12	12	0	5	275,000	1,842	3,657	3,657	419
36009	BURTON: CHRIST	92	71	31	0	33	35	14	0	12	0	0	1,441,203	27,421	9,194	342	722
36010	BYRON: FIRST	105	100	72	18	51	53	26	6	18	0	12	3,053,290	0	15,639	15,639	1,227
36011	CAPAC	119	109	46	2	18	36	14	6	0	0	3	750,000	0	11,162	6,346	1,280
36012	CARSONVILLE	12	12	10	15	0	0	0	0	0	0	0	30,368	0	2,651	2,651	304
36013	CENTRAL LAKEPORT	41	40	22	2	10	4	3	0	12	0	1	1,079,892	0	4,544	3,181	520
36014	CLARKSTON	1,580	1,609	521	272	691	1,200	220	75	50	9	1	13,662,942	4,575,000	128,683	128,683	10,098
36015	CLIO: BETHANY	288	269	130	73	4	76	48	6	52	0	7	5,348,843	0	34,683	34,683	2,722
36016	COLE	89	89	80	0	208	41	28	5	12	0	1	170,000	0	7,815	7,815	895
36017	COLUMBIAVILLE	175	175	57	12	13	13	10	12	12	0	8	1,927,500	0	11,927	500	935
36018	CROSWELL: FIRST	66	63	43	31	28	19	10	7	16	0	10	1,882,000	45,401	7,517	7,517	861
36019	DAVISBURG	61	53	22	0	13	10	8	0	0	0	1	2,032,000	0	11,859	4,584	931
36020	DAVISON	255	241	138	0	42	60	35	10	104	0	6	5,429,562	27,403	40,702	40,702	3,189

Column headings:

- 29b — Amount PAID by the local church to the DISTRICT for all apportioned causes (if applicable)
- 30-38 — Church Benevolence Giving
- 39a — Total ASKED for clergy pension
- 39b — Total PAID for clergy pension
- 41a — Base compensation paid to/for the lead pastoral role to the church person assigned or appointed to the Senior Pastor or other
- 41b — Base compensation paid to/for all Associate Pastor(s) and other pastoral staff assigned or appointed to the church. Include deacons and other clergy in this role
- 40, 42a-44 — Pastoral benefits
- 41c & 42c — Deacons salary/benefits
- 45 — Total amount paid in salary and benefits for all other church staff and diaconal ministers
- 46 — Total amount spent for local church program expenses
- 47 — Total amount spent for other local church operating expenses
- 48 & 49 — Local church capital expenses
- 50 — TOTAL CHURCH EXPENSES (Sum of Lines 29a through 49)
- 51 — Number of giving units
- 52 — Total income for annual budget/spending plan
- 53 — Total income for designated causes including capital campaign and other special projects
- 54 — Total income from connectional and other institutional sources outside the local church

CONF No	29b	30-38	39a	39b	41a	41b	40, 42a-44	41c & 42c	45	46	47	48 & 49	50	51	52	53	54
36002	1,450	3,625	3,450	3,450	29,890	0	26,839	0	10,077	5,700	7,818	16,550	118,063	86	99,355	16,983	5,931
36003	1,017	685	4,490	4,490	34,643	0	24,006	0	14,292	2,299	31,555	1,225	118,245	157	113,216	34,432	1,020
36004	0	6,217	2,950	2,950	27,500	0	7,480	0	0	1,285	25,612	31,993	113,745	28	99,864	16,360	5,000
36005	484	2,674	1,400	1,260	10,782	0	10,353	0	0	845	14,340	3,290	47,829	21	34,233	1,590	0
36006	2,278	1,039	6,950	6,950	56,818	0	20,115	0	33,047	14,177	36,379	73,338	264,035	113	177,585	39,558	0
36007	1,414	156	6,660	6,660	48,500	0	10,301	0	6,641	2,155	15,209	6,000	109,387	93	144,589	2,446	0
36008	419	13,281	1,240	1,240	10,200	0	4,195	0	2,241	534	12,800	6,050	46,326	30	32,459	0	0
36009	772	180	1,400	1,400	25,008	0	1,001	0	39,275	1,500	25,310		63,804	40	50,121	180	0
36010	1,227	5,680	2,990	2,990	22,508	0	3,221	0	6,910	13,853	29,657	10,354	144,404	40	108,840	4,286	2,200
36011	1,280	1,941	4,890	4,890	41,000	0	10,000	0		2,736	17,230	0	92,333	47	85,331	350	375
36012	0	240	1,020	1,020	10,482	0	3,620	0	7,828	410	5,776	0	24,199	12	25,389	0	0
36013	520	4,307	600	600	6,000	0	0	0		3,273	16,895		42,604	20	32,979	2,673	0
36014	10,906	89,149	22,800	22,800	109,601	48,960	39,150	36,864	567,829	69,049	228,327	2,889,638	4,240,958	517	1,340,418	591,132	0
36015	2,722	10,987	6,800	6,800	55,620	0	13,696	0	70,590	8,210	60,806	36,950	301,064	130	293,636	8,962	0
36016	895	1,118	2,200	2,200	26,944	0	21,250	0		3,469	11,909	3,568	79,168	0	75,003	0	0
36017	935	630	4,520	4,520	39,389	0	750	0	12,435	366	19,803	35,086	79,328	58	91,593	180	1,000
36018	861	4,045	1,240	1,240	10,201	0	4,101	0	6,717	464	17,048	13,622	87,280	35	70,314	8,836	0
36019	200	497	2,450	2,450	5,000	0	5,579	0	16,600	1,103	38,980		88,615	22	74,472	906	0
36020	3,189	32,837	6,450	6,450	54,335	0	34,690	0	101,746	8,815	62,996	55,694	401,454	180	379,963	38,435	0

STATISTICAL INFORMATION

EW

CONFERENCE Number	Church Name	Total professing members reported at the close of last year (1)	TOTAL PROFESSING MEMBERS reported at the close of this year (4)	Average attendance at all weekly worship services (7)	Total Baptized Members who have not become Professing Members (9)	Number of other constituents of the church (10)	TOTAL Christian Formation Group Participants (Total of lines 11a-d) (11)	Average weekly attendance (all ages) in Sunday Church School or other weekly education classes (13)	Membership in United Methodist Men (18a)	Membership in United Methodist Women (19a)	Number of persons sent out on UMVIM teams from this local church (20b)	Total Number of community ministries for outreach, justice, and mercy offered by this local church (21)	Value of church assets and buildings (24 & 25)	Church Debt (26 & 27)	Amount APPORTIONED to the local church by the CONFERENCE (28a)	Amount PAID by the local church to the CONFERENCE for all apportioned causes (29a)	Amount APPORTIONED to the local church by the DISTRICT (if applicable) (28b)
36021	DECKERVILLE	41	24	21	0	11	9	5	4	0	0	13	284,429	0	3,332	3,332	382
36022	DRYDEN	72	70	29	5	26	14	12	0	0	0	0	2,499,000	486	11,446	9,157	1,311
36023	DUFFIELD	47	47	37	0	0	0	0	0	8	0	0	1,204,800	16,000	4,040	4,040	317
36024	DURAND: FIRST	129	128	72	40	140	68	10	21	15	0	5	3,469,400	372,000	16,227	1,268	1,273
36025	ELBA	30	30	20	0	0	12	1	0	7	0	2	64,126	0	3,306	3,306	259
36026	FENTON	877	867	273	219	396	263	75	16	76	0	20	18,270,919	757,102	69,565	69,565	5,459
36027	FLINT: ASBURY	132	136	32	36	0	33	7	6	11	0	8	545,418	0	15,932	3,985	1,250
36028	FLINT: BETHEL	262	260	125	0	0	260	75	15	33	0	0	6,717,170	0	33,176	33,176	2,603
36029	FLINT: BRISTOL	60	60	31	0	13	3	15	0	10	0	0	870,000	0	9,552	955	750
36030	FLINT: CALVARY	115	101	58	0	25	37	6	7	0	0	4	725,515	1,768	37,936	2,125	2,977
36031	FLINT: CHARITY	69	78	34	0	4	18	71	20	11	0	2	6,828,967	53,003	4,953	4,953	389
36032	FLINT: COURT STREET	439	501	160	122	67	199	0	0	69	85	12	6,715,400	0	59,839	59,839	4,696
36033	FLINT: FAITH	32	32	12	0	32	12	5	14	9	0	0	4,092,000	68,705	3,112	0	244
36034	FLINT: HOPE	169	160	62	6	297	51	61	10	0	0	2	3,983,963	0	23,918	2,751	1,877
36035	FLUSHING	345	313	166	0	0	61	0	0	90	0	10	4,489,663	0	39,478	39,478	3,098
36036	FORESTER	51	51	15	0	32	0	0	0	10	0	0	310,000	0	3,819	3,819	437
36036	FOSTORIA	39	39	27	0	10	13	10	25	8	0	1	701,167	54,106	3,681	3,681	289
36038	GAINES	68	63	35	5	28	24	7	9	14	0	4	1,458,209	0	9,619	9,619	755
36039	GENESEE	70	71	27	0	0	51	14	12	12	1	6	1,537,081	0	6,144	6,144	482

CONFERENCE Number	29b Amount PAID by the local church to the DISTRICT for all apportioned causes (if applicable)	30-38 Church Benevolence Giving	39a Total ASKED for clergy pension	39b Total PAID for clergy pension	41a Base compensation paid to/for the lead pastoral role	41b Base compensation paid to/for all Associate Pastor(s) and other pastoral staff	40, 42a-44 Pastoral Benefits	41c & 42c Deacons salary/benefits	45 Total amount paid in salary and benefits for all other church staff and diaconal ministers	46 Total amount spent for local church program expenses	47 Total amount spent for other local church operating expenses	48 & 49 Local church capital expenses	50 TOTAL CHURCH EXPENSES (Sum of lines 29a through 49)	51 Number of giving units	52 Total income for annual budget/spending plan	53 Total income for designated causes including capital campaign and other special projects	54 Total income from connectional and other institutional sources outside the local church
36021	382	10,413	600	600	6,000	0	0	0	0	290	12,354	0	33,371	19	22,703	12,068	0
36022	0	182	2,430	1,944	22,640	0	5,071	0	4,962	100	16,953	0	61,009	20	76,174	0	0
36023	0	600	1,630	1,630	16,666	0	0	0	975	75	5,635	7,662	37,283	19	42,965	710	1,000
36024	1,273	1,954	2,940	2,940	49,440	0	26,352	0	8,622	2,500	31,766	45,500	171,615	71	133,118	3,621	0
36025	259	1,234	940	940	9,713	0		0	2,500	919	7,122		25,993	18	29,744	43,069	0
36026	5,459	36,265	15,470	15,470	92,635	39,252	35,740	0	171,575	19,905	136,953	240,805	863,624	304	739,632	3,372	5,000
36027	2,603	783	4,520	4,520	38,086	0	14,949	0	11,000	7,399	71,469	112,325	264,516	32	167,036	432	0
36028	0	1,548	5,930	5,930	55,514	12,000	19,331	0	93,000	10,000	47,000	10,000	290,077	143	190,084	3,000	1,650
36029	2,977	3,000	3,470	1,041	24,550	0	4,200	0	15,000	840	21,000	4,000	74,586	29	77,540	54,413	59,392
36030	0	69,411	3,875	3,875	35,286	0	20,680	0	60,607	7,972	68,014	23,288	294,235	51	192,721	1,832	0
36031	389	461	880	880	9,488	0	2,609	0	1,680	600	30,000	7,328	58,386	15	57,700	61,968	0
36032	4,696	38,213	13,580	13,580	69,653	28,206	56,168	9,790	209,212	24,773	163,065	285,000	962,195	160	603,646	500	3,000
36033			840		8,970	0		0		1,000	17,000		26,970	10	26,000		
36034	3,096	4,603	5,930	5,930	48,500	0	35,175	0	26,155	3,644	72,201	27,485	226,444	52	184,250	25,005	0
36035	0	12,934	7,640	7,640	55,975	0	21,433	0	80,823	11,377	71,950	7,740	304,708	201	300,432	41,745	800
36036	289	626	860	860	9,485	0	6,559	0	50	2,000	8,000	12,225	31,399	20	33,264	0	0
36037	755	1,077	1,360	1,360	11,313	0	4,386	0	5,490	744	11,175	1,689	41,765	31	40,007	3,937	200
36038		12,924	3,160	3,160	23,777	0	11,936	0	5,718	2,475	23,591		105,952	37	86,808	7,024	600
36039	482	1,022	2,420	2,420	19,932	0	8,544	0		1,885	7,822		55,633	28	55,308	1,244	1,250

STATISTICAL INFORMATION

EW

CONFERENCE Number	Church Name	1 — Total professing members reported at the close of last year	4 — TOTAL PROFESSING MEMBERS reported at the close of this year	7 — Average attendance at all weekly worship services	9 — Total Baptized Members who have not become Professing Members	10 — Number of other constituents of the church	11 (11a-d) — TOTAL Christian Formation Group Participants	13 — Average weekly attendance (all ages) in Sunday Church School or other weekly education classes	18a — Membership in United Methodist Men	19a — Membership in United Methodist Women	20b — Number of persons sent out on UMVIM teams from this local church	21 — Total Number of community ministries for outreach, justice, and mercy offered by this local church	24 & 25 — Value of church assets and buildings	26 & 27 — Church Debt	28a — Amount APPORTIONED to the local church by the CONFERENCE	29a — Amount PAID by the local church to the CONFERENCE for all apportioned causes	28b — Amount APPORTIONED to the local church by the DISTRICT (if applicable)
36040	GOODRICH	271	355	124	84	53	148	36	10	49	0	0	6,966,954	637,257	31,906	10,595	2,504
36041	GRAND BLANC	355	329	152	117	0	153	35	25	52	0	0	3,807,188	138,329	32,699	32,699	2,566
36042	GRAND BLANC: PHOENIX	38	34	20	9	14	22	6	0	8	0	2	1,993,133	0	6,127	6,127	481
36043	HALSEY	94	91	52	20	49	30	13	0	34	0	3	1,418,727	0	8,617	8,617	676
36044	HARBOR BEACH	41	42	33	0	20	7	10	0	0	0	0	967,788	1,756	7,317	7,317	838
36045	HOLLY: CALVARY	150	148	121	0	120	69	40	0	21	0	12	3,287,329	302,852	25,622	25,622	2,011
36046	HOLLY: MT BETHEL	54	57	30	21	0	18	9	0	0	0	5	166,000	277	4,150	3,113	326
36047	IMLAY CITY	104	95	82	0	68	89	20	16	16	0	10	2,226,217	105,593	15,792	15,792	1,808
36048	JEDDO	128	107	30	0	10	24	10	11	11	0	22	1,066,600	11,972	7,466	7,466	855
36049	LAKE FENTON	186	182	39	21	22	25	0	16	16	0	0	1,522,533	68,738	9,314	9,314	731
36050	LAKE ORION	615	595	186	355	513	284	30	0	32	0	15	5,676,800	1,388,000	68,476	30,814	7,842
36051	LAMB	39	41	27	0	16	0	1	20	8	0	4	639,000	0	4,043	4,043	463
36052	LAPEER: TRINITY	476	469	338	80	257	242	28	20	150	34	2	6,299,474	0	49,017	49,017	5,613
36053	LENNON	70	66	12	24	0	10	10	0	8	0	0	640,000	0	5,779	5,779	454
36054	LEONARD	31	34	136	0	12	10	4	0	0	0	0	450,702	0	2,237	2,237	256
36055	LEXINGTON	143	142	54	19	70	123	38	27	34	0	15	2,536,454	0	17,664	17,664	2,023
36056	LINDEN	117	113	75	1	33	37	5	0	20	0	2	1,371,428	0	11,116	9,000	872
36057	MARLETTE: FIRST	174	161	86	0	152	104	20	7	11	0	4	2,360,230	0	25,172	0	0
36058	MARYSVILLE	285	273	86	68	73	141	36	0	8	0	12	3,319,310	0	24,899	0	2,851

STATISTICAL INFORMATION

EW

CONFERENCE Number	29b Amount PAID by the local church to the DISTRICT for all apportioned causes (if applicable)	30-38 Church Benevolence Giving	39a Total ASKED for clergy pension	39b Total PAID for clergy pension	41a Base compensation paid to/for the Senior Pastor or other person assigned or appointed in the lead pastoral role to the church	41b Base compensation paid to/for all Associate Pastor(s) and other pastoral staff assigned or appointed to the church. Include deacons and other clergy in this role.	40, 42a-44 Pastoral Benefits	41c & 42c Deacons salary/benefits	45 Total amount paid in salary and benefits for all other church staff and diaconal ministers	46 Total amount spent for local church program expenses	47 Total amount spent for other local church operating expenses	48 & 49 Local Church capital expenses	50 TOTAL CHURCH EXPENSES (Sum of lines 29a through 49)	51 Number of giving units	52 Total income for annual budget/spending plan	53 Total income for designated causes including capital campaign and other special projects	54 Total income from connectional and other institutional sources outside the local church
36040	2,504	16,605	5,620	5,620	46,000	0	25,679	0	56,919	28,098	61,749	147,867	401,636	191	253,569	123,975	0
36041	2,566	23,330	7,820	7,820	63,975	0	22,565	0	88,920	5,472	58,819	49,425	355,591	176	297,888	33,190	0
36042	481	9,181	1,500	1,500	14,847	0	10,809	0	10,428	2,352	22,647	36,117	114,489	15	59,183	31,404	0
36043	3,108	2,446	3,060	3,060	22,248	0	14,906	0	11,224	2,838	12,018	1,610	82,075	50	79,534	600	320
36044	838	1,197	2,160	2,160	17,840	0	12,385	0	3,090	1,748	10,385	16,500	73,460	25	67,558	5,093	8,500
36045	0	1,516	6,800	6,800	58,941	0	38,087	0	44,971	10,858	42,300	32,844	261,939	93	265,678	16,045	0
36046	499	6,869	1,110	833	10,840	0		0	1,950	429	8,913	0	33,426	21	33,695	109	0
36047	1,808	8,734	5,630	5,630	47,173	0	4,978	0	19,322	934	11,332	10,043	125,746	74	135,240	8,151	0
36048	844	2,894	2,330	2,330	20,731	0	13,204	0	1,014	7	14,589	2,300	65,379	37	64,239	6,308	1,250
36049	731	1,728	1,740	1,740	16,087	0	0	0	8,027	2,399	31,690	6,990	78,626	60	68,721	6,337	0
36050	7,842	30,027	14,750	14,750	69,800	50,900	67,498	0	142,677	23,492	104,796	208,326	750,922	338	737,718	94,971	0
36051	463	1,091	1,640	1,640	9,720	0	3,222	0	900	637	22,705	0	44,421	24	31,152	0	0
36052	5,613	28,657	8,810	8,810	74,263	0	25,250	0	193,405	34,140	82,954	0	502,109	248	467,356	28,947	0
36053	454	6,140	1,500	1,500	11,223	0	1,965	0	975	3,989	13,838	1,712	47,575	20	40,212	828	0
36054	0	0	1,100	1,100	11,009	0	0	0	0	100	5,902	0	18,111	11	15,555	0	0
36055	2,037	15,393	4,050	4,050	62,603	5,000	18,133	0	18,663	26,039	10,616	36,063	211,261	90	154,471	64,620	0
36056	1,531	634	3,290	3,290	18,632	0	10,457	0	23,262	0	19,030	1,000	91,836	74	85,872	3,200	0
36057	0	7,308	7,980	7,980	53,244	0	34,369	0	36,412	2,464	33,577	24,750	200,104	145	186,524	12,355	0
36058	2,851	8,377	7,010	7,010	57,371	0	17,124	0	49,356	10,102	34,148	0	186,339	100	171,309	21,289	0

STATISTICAL INFORMATION

EW

CONFERENCE Number	Church Name	Total professing members reported at the close of last year (1)	TOTAL PROFESSING MEMBERS reported at the close of this year (4)	Average attendance at all weekly worship services (7)	Total Baptized Members who have not become Professing Members (9)	Number of other constituents of the church (10)	TOTAL Christian Formation Group Participants (Total of lines 11a-d) (11)	Average weekly attendance (all ages) in Sunday Church School or other weekly education classes (13)	Membership in United Methodist Men (18a)	Membership in United Methodist Women (19a)	Number of persons sent out on UMVIM teams from this local church (20b)	Total Number of community ministries for outreach, justice, and mercy offered by this local church (21)	Value of church assets and buildings (24 & 25)	Church Debt (26 & 27)	Amount APPORTIONED to the local church by the CONFERENCE (28a)	Amount PAID by the local church to the CONFERENCE for all apportioned causes (29a)	Amount APPORTIONED to the local church by the DISTRICT (if applicable) (28b)
36059	MCGREGOR	78	80	91	12	95	51	16	0	13	0	0	238,753	0	4,673	4,673	535
36060	MELVIN	27	27	40	0	82	0	0	0	0	0	0	37,042	0	3,972	3,972	455
36061	MEMPHIS: FIRST	45	45	31	16	29	20	6	0	0	0	2	1,483,876	0	4,556	4,556	522
36062	MINDEN CITY	24	24	17	0	65	24	0	0	0	0	0	101,300	0	1,557	1,557	178
36063	MONTROSE	132	138	100	2	68	9	30	0	0	0	3	2,760,228	0	16,120	16,120	1,265
36064	MT MORRIS: FIRST	128	126	39	0	40	19	9	0	12	0	0	849,000	52,867	12,823	3,294	1,006
36065	NORTH BRANCH: FIRST	126	121	54	26	76	16	0	0	10	0	0	1,731,924	0	8,376	8,376	959
36066	NORTH STREET	143	136	53	0	14	46	7	0	32	0	0	1,975,260	161,718	14,486	1,272	1,659
36067	OMARD	71	70	41	0	12	47	17	10	14	2	5	55,214	0	2,597	2,597	297
36068	OREGON	96	96	43	21	64	62	6	0	7	0	2	554,343	0	4,288	4,288	336
36069	ORTONVILLE	145	129	75	0	62	15	17	10	31	0	4	840,639	66,700	16,060	25	1,260
36070	OTISVILLE	67	67	39	95	52	31	7	8	26	0	7	1,795,000	0	6,256	6,256	491
36071	OXFORD	149	135	50	6	52	25	8	8	10	0	6	3,683,435	0	17,111	250	1,959
36072	PORT HOPE	48	53	45				13	0	10	0	1	546,004	0	5,705	5,705	653
36073	PORT HURON: FIRST	687	637	178	115	102	136	35	42	120	3	12	7,286,974	0	50,985	50,985	5,839
36074	PORT HURON: GRATIOT PK	54	58	29	0	3	15	4	0	11	0	0	765,270	0	6,277	3,766	719
36075	PORT HURON: WASHINGTON AVE	38	0	8	0	1	7	0	0	0	0	0	0	0	3,143	314	360
36076	PORT SANILAC	56	56	37	2	20	13	10	0	10	0	0	850,000	0	4,489	0	514
36077	RICHFIELD	61	65	40	4	10	45	22	0	11	0	0	731,691	0	5,445	5,445	427

CONFERENCE Number	Amount PAID by the local church to the DISTRICT for all apportioned causes (if applicable) 29b	Church Benevolence Giving 30-38	Total ASKED for clergy pension 39a	Total PAID for clergy pension 39b	Base compensation paid to/for the Senior Pastor or other person assigned or appointed in the lead pastoral role to the church 41a	Base compensation paid to/for all Associate Pastor(s) and other pastoral staff assigned or appointed to the church. Include deacons and other clergy in this role 41b	Pastoral Benefits 40, 42a-44	Deacons salary/benefits 41c & 42c	Total amount paid in salary and benefits for all other church staff and diaconal ministers 45	Total amount spent for local church program expenses 46	Total amount spent for other local church operating expenses 47	Local Church capital expenses 48 & 49	TOTAL CHURCH EXPENSES (Sum of Lines 29a through 49) 50	Number of giving units 51	Total income for annual budget/spending plan 52	Total income for designated causes including capital campaign and other special projects 53	Total income from connectional and other institutional sources outside the local church 54
36059	0	8,340	3,010	3,010	20,965	0	12,299	0	0	5,443	10,307	0	65,037	64	80,860	0	0
36060	455	0	1,110	1,110	8,558	0	500	0	0	200	23,622	0	38,417	0	30,865	0	0
36061	522	8,227	1,640	1,640	13,016	0	2,885	0	2,700	643	8,513	0	42,702	25	37,340	11,411	0
36062	178	4,146	940	940	8,970	0	140	0	0	738	2,460	10,987	19,129	11	18,491	104	3,000
36063	1,265	8,735	3,540	3,540	20,508	0	10,774	0	28,387	8,753	26,541	2,350	135,610	96	147,489	3,544	4,800
36064	1,006	1,128	1,790	1,790	19,527	0	0	0	14,817	1,691	28,154	13,076	73,757	26	73,749	3,058	0
36065	969	3,386	2,230	2,230	23,250	0	14,320	0	21,709	2,264	19,318	54,908	94,568	63	75,207	11,668	10,000
36066	1,659	2,094	5,020	5,020	41,087	0	0	0	8,680	4,932	33,205	11,726	167,177	62	124,725	28,762	0
36067	297	1,496	600	600	6,000	0	0	0	0	3,048	7,984	13,268	33,748	23	41,221	1,930	0
36068	0	1,739	1,870	1,870	9,683	0	9,715	0	1,384	1,233	11,262	13,524	54,442	39	42,996	7,771	600
36069	1,260	8,486	4,710	4,710	40,425	0	25,934	0	14,363	8,906	23,516	11,993	141,149	81	170,932	2,465	175
36070	491	5,080	2,040	2,040	16,969	0	7,079	0	8,397	1,129	13,867	2,518	73,201	63	49,239	2,750	2,917
36071	250	5,250	5,620	5,620	44,000	0	29,391	0	26,160	3,033	24,292		140,744	85	122,428	2,542	8,000
36072	653	7,042	2,640	2,640	21,804	0	15,138	0	3,030	3,029	15,767		74,808	45	84,830	11,285	10,724
36073	5,839	17,290	7,950	7,950	65,000	0	9,114	0	143,775	42,567	80,155	81,300	503,975	239	420,159	111,345	0
36074	718	1,805	1,290	1,290	4,630	0	13,000	0	3,000	989	15,600	275	45,073	19	44,708	6,568	0
36075	360	0	870	522	4,530	0	0	0	2,255	150	4,000	3,893	16,024	8	16,000	0	0
36076	0	1,200	860	860	4,350	0	0	0	0	800	11,000	0	18,210	27	21,510	450	0
36077	427	4,659	1,790	1,790	18,821	0	3,356	0	2,950	339	15,038	29,586	82,411	25	46,647	15,826	10,000

EW

CONFERENCE Number	Church Name	1. Total professing members reported at the close of last year	4. TOTAL PROFESSING MEMBERS reported at the close of this year	7. Average attendance at all weekly worship services	9. Total Baptized Members who have not become Professing Members	10. Number of other constituents of the church	11. TOTAL Christian Formation Group Participants (Total of lines 11a-d)	13. Average weekly attendance (all ages) in Sunday Church School or other weekly education classes	18a. Membership in United Methodist Men	19a. Membership in United Methodist Women	20b. Number of persons sent out on UMVIM teams from this local church	21. Total Number of community ministries for outreach, justice, and mercy offered by this local church	24 & 25. Value of church assets and buildings	26 & 27. Church Debt	28a. Amount APPORTIONED to the local church by the CONFERENCE	29a. Amount PAID by the local church to the CONFERENCE for all apportioned causes	28b. Amount APPORTIONED to the local church by the DISTRICT (if applicable)
36078	RICHMOND: FIRST	208	211	71	30	75	18		11	30	11	1	1,963,000	0	16,667	16,667	1,909
36079	ROMEO	301	254	141	77	109	130	5	8	45	0	30	4,493,373	599,588	35,071	35,071	4,016
36080	ST CLAIR: FIRST	346	311	80	32	67	69	18	0	25	1	1	4,103,605	3,090	24,570	24,570	2,814
36081	SANDUSKY: FIRST	202	196	93	0	0	75	40	8	8	0	0	861,209	0	18,294	18,294	2,095
36082	SEYMOUR LAKE	149	125	81	49	2	64	23	8	0	0	1	1,616,597	319,670	20,335	20,335	1,596
36083	SHABBONA	85	86	40	0	20	40	25	5	20	0	0	1,553,000	21,655	5,987	3,000	607
36084	SILVERWOOD	40	38	18	0	8	0	30	10	16	0	0	549,839	0	2,854	2,854	327
36085	SNOVER: HERITAGE	106	112	77	76	56	52	37	10	0	0	2	2,693,570	0	20,256	6,000	2,320
36086	SOUTH MUNDY	113	110	53	38	52	63	30	0	0	0	8	1,585,693	0	8,564	8,564	672
36087	SWARTZ CREEK	590	561	296	47	77	135	101	40	30	0	0	6,982,109	56,842	66,973	66,973	5,256
36088	THETFORD CENTER	64	63	24	9	51	47	16	0	16	1	5	893,210	0	5,667	5,667	445
36089	THOMAS	39	31	22	0	11	16	4	0	0	0	0	467,085	0	4,932	4,932	565
36090	UBLY	27	28	14	0	0	0	3	0	5	0	0	233,337	60	1,992	1,793	228
36091	WEST BERLIN	47	45	25	5	12	5	5	0	14	0	2	659,256	0	4,469	4,469	512
36092	WEST DEERFIELD	49	52	47	4	85	19	9	14	11	0	8	514,500	0	2,503	2,503	196
36093	WEST FOREST	78	77	48	45	104	54	8	0	0	0	15	793,385	0	4,674	4,674	367
36094	WEST VIENNA	87	84	66	15	40	56	24	14	36	0	19	2,724,685	0	14,641	4,707	1,149
36095	WORTH TWP: BETHEL	64	66	19	0	26	4	3	5	14	0	0	425,000	0	4,557	608	522
36096	YALE	95	94	58	0	9	35	9	15	15	0	1	300,000	0	18,029	0	2,065

STATISTICAL INFORMATION

EW

CONFERENCE Number	Amount PAID by the local church to the DISTRICT for all apportioned causes (if applicable) 29b	Church Benevolence Giving 30-38	Total ASKED for clergy pension 39a	Total PAID for clergy pension 39b	Base compensation paid to/for the Senior Pastor or other person assigned or appointed in the lead pastoral role to the church 41a	Base compensation paid to/for all Associate Pastor(s) and other pastoral staff assigned or appointed to the church, include deacons and other clergy in this role. 41b	Pastoral Benefits 40, 42a-44	Deacons salary/benefits 41c & 42c	Total amount paid in salary and benefits for all other church staff and diaconal ministers 45	Total amount spent for local church program expenses 46	Total amount spent for other local church operating expenses 47	local Church capital expenses 48 & 49	TOTAL CHURCH EXPENSES (Sum of Lines 29a through 49) 50	Number of giving units 51	Total income for annual budget/spending plan 52	Total income for designated causes including capital campaign and other special projects 53	Total income from connectional and other institutional sources outside the local church 54
36078	1,909	16,512	4,890	4,890	35,376	0	26,937	0	26,476	2,717	35,743	2,142	169,369	105	138,818	14,169	0
36079	4,016	12,943	7,330	7,330	60,000	0	17,106	0	69,521	5,643	75,678	337,378	624,686	173	361,163	242,308	0
36080	2,814	8,564	6,000	6,000	46,681	0	40,420	0	50,343	3,220	31,718	19,452	233,782	101	208,495	4,780	0
36081	2,095	5,961	5,380	5,380	45,100	0	33,060	0	17,415	11,853	26,476	0	165,634	107	157,917	19,827	15,503
36082	1,596	14,584	5,200	5,200	41,500	0	11,667	0	33,478	20,204	54,205	52,473	255,242	92	219,379	4,333	0
36083	607	123	1,910	1,910	17,940	0	2,963	0	0	738	15,140	43,222	85,643	29	72,002	8,970	0
36084	327	1,795	2,270	2,270	10,138	0	1,400	0	0	150	7,700	0	26,634	19	9,185	220	0
36085	2,320	14,575	5,160	5,160	39,513	0	27,274	0	13,639	6,100	35,139	1,290	151,010	83	147,090	22,339	3,000
36086	672	5,303	3,060	3,060	25,229	0	19,306	0	12,170	2,212	12,431	2,305	91,252	67	88,978	1,258	525
36087	5,256	21,828	13,450	13,450	73,942	49,272	19,385	0	181,507	16,707	117,730	153,752	719,802	271	545,054	127,244	0
36088	446	409	2,420	2,420	19,932	0	8,481	0	5,872	449	7,830	1,776	53,282	21	52,943	4,061	500
36089	0	19	880	880	18,000	0	1,250	0	3,885	1,312	12,038	0	37,365	12	40,011	1,663	0
36090	228		600	540	6,000	0		0	0	3,517	4,402	12,974	16,499	7	21,940	0	0
36091	512	3,038	1,380	1,380	11,090	0	11,613	0	0	525	9,707	800	55,308	31	38,975	15,616	0
36092	196	905	1,130	1,130	9,428	0	3,655	0	1,800	549	4,224		25,190	32	42,761	16,420	175
36093	367	5,436	3,960	3,960	39,238	0		0	0	6,282	10,449	2,900	70,406	57	78,010	565	0
36094	3,700	8,167	5,390	5,390	44,526	0	12,896	0	22,000	7,000	26,035		137,321	60	132,166	11,451	500
36095	522	525	860	860	9,007	0	4,484	0	0	1,620	12,319	0	29,945	16	22,718	543	0
36096	2,065	2,745	5,270	5,270	44,268	0	27,903	0	15,950	1,500	22,877	15,000	137,578	25	77,262	0	10,000

STATISTICAL INFORMATION

GS

EW

CONFERENCE Number	Church Name	1 Total professing members reported at the close of last year	4 TOTAL PROFESSING MEMBERS reported at the close of this year	7 Average attendance at all weekly worship services	9 Total Baptized Members who have not become Professing Members	10 Number of other constituents of the church	11a-d TOTAL Christian Formation Group Participants (Total of lines 11a-d)	13 Average weekly attendance (all ages) in Sunday Church School or other weekly education classes	18a Membership in United Methodist Men	19a Membership in United Methodist Women	20b Number of persons sent out on UMVIM teams from this local church	21 Total Number of community ministries for outreach, justice, and mercy offered by this local church	24 & 25 Value of church assets and buildings	26 & 27 Church Debt	28a Amount APPORTIONED to the local church by the CONFERENCE	29a Amount PAID by the local church to the CONFERENCE for all apportioned causes	28b Amount APPORTIONED to the local church by the DISTRICT (if applicable)
	EAST WINDS DISTRICT TOTALS	15,062	14,704	6,737	2,509	5,430	5,938	1,888	630	1,879	147	410	221,253,134	9,986,694	1,553,025	1,177,869	141,514
	GREATER SOUTHWEST DISTRICT																
37001	ALLEGAN	302	302	97	2	750	81	23	12	70	0	3	2,738,000	0	24,754	6,964	2,858
37002	ALMENA	89	92	57	2	23	16	17	10	0	0	77	1,550,968	0	9,166	9,166	974
37003	ARDEN	17	16	13	24	8	8	7	0	5	0	0	557,900	0	4,458	0	158
37004	ATHENS	30	32	25	24	30	11	5	0	0	0	0	785,070	0	4,628	4,628	171
37005	AUGUSTA: FELLOWSHIP	56	46	31	1	26	15	0	0	5	0	5	835,395	0	4,675	4,675	231
37006	BANGOR: SIMPSON	160	147	50	49	21	3	12	12	19	0	8	2,156,000	391,004	17,371	3,603	1,512
37007	BATTLE CREEK: BASELINE	82	81	90	0	105	119	42	0	0	0	2	1,723,944	0	12,687	12,500	378
37008	BATTLE CREEK: BIRCHWOOD	89	0	89	2	0	0	0	0	0	0	0	250,000	0	11,912	5,956	484
37009	BATTLE CREEK: CHAPEL HILL	324	435	191	0	212	431	56	0	0	33	1	6,051,185	5,899	53,165	62,925	1,678
37010	BATTLE CREEK: CHRIST	90	87	46	0	10	38	3	0	9	0	5	289,122	0	12,560	0	474
37011	BATTLE CREEK: CONVIS UNION	61	54	32	3	15	0	0	0	0	0	0	1,670,883	0	11,524	11,524	318
37012	BATTLE CREEK: FIRST	197	166	71	26	30	65	25	0	0	0	3	4,852,000	0	23,777	0	1,028
37013	BATTLE CREEK: MAPLE	69	67	48	0	54	29	10	0	0	0	7	3,223,771	0	10,390	10,454	413
37014	BATTLE CREEK: NEWTON	80	78	42	0	13	22	6	0	7	0	2	1,045,602	0	10,796	4,018	454
37015	BATTLE CREEK: TRINITY	66	0	31	0	0	0	0	0	0	0	0	0	0	7,608	3,804	363
37016	BATTLE CREEK: WASHINGTON HTS	24	24	7	0	0	8	0	0	5	0	2	2,013,625	0	5,921	4,326	186

STATISTICAL INFORMATION

GS

Column key:
- 29b — Amount PAID by the local church to the DISTRICT for all apportioned causes (if applicable)
- 30-38 — Church Benevolence Giving
- 39a — Total ASKED for clergy pension
- 39b — Total PAID for clergy pension
- 41a — Base compensation paid to/for the Senior Pastor or other person assigned or appointed in the lead pastoral role to the church
- 41b — Base compensation paid to/for all Associate Pastor(s); and other pastoral staff assigned or appointed to the church, include deacons and other clergy in this role
- 40, 42a-44 — Pastoral Benefits
- 41c & 42c — Deacons salary/benefits
- 45 — Total amount paid in salary and benefits for all other church staff and diaconal ministers
- 46 — Total amount spent for local church program expenses
- 47 — Total amount spent for other local church operating expenses
- 48 & 49 — Local Church capital expenses
- 50 — TOTAL CHURCH EXPENSES (Sum of lines 29a through 49)
- 51 — Number of living units
- 52 — Total income for annual budget/spending plan
- 53 — Total income for designated causes including capital campaign and other special projects
- 54 — Total income from connectional and other institutional sources outside the local church

CONF. No.	29b	30-38	39a	39b	41a	41b	40, 42a-44	41c & 42c	45	46	47	48 & 49	50	51	52	53	54
Total	133,819	762,190	378,175	373,595	2,917,793	233,590	1,264,819	46,654	3,040,755	577,124	3,009,086	5,438,820	18,975,884	6,990	13,746,164	2,205,967	178,907
37001	2,858	11,374	10,821	10,821	57,710	0	31,027	0	72,704	25,000	48,000	50,000	316,458	110	194,400	34,400	0
37002	974	10,363	3,840	3,840	19,000	0	19,914	0	8,685	6,076	15,567	0	93,585	51	83,099	19,749	0
37003	0	515	0	0	16,250	0		0	6,664	577	6,954	1,617	32,577	9	32,999	8,235	0
37004	171	363	0	0	9,590	0	6,967	0	4,625	2,342	13,405	390	37,856	29	41,401	2,175	0
37005	231	1,377	8,547	7,204	12,000	0	4,282	0	4,278	793	12,333	0	40,316	23	38,766	912	0
37006	314	704	8,820	8,820	41,904	0	31,361	0	33,570	340	21,197	35,196	146,101	46	129,209	990	1,600
37007	373	2,102	4,733	4,733	19,933	0	10,755	0	5,639	10,816	16,807	1,910	117,586	41	106,963	978	0
37008	242	874	14,093	14,093	11,923	0	1,050	0	23,917	0	12,476	1,103	43,996	54	36,019	132,346	0
37009	2,262	102,626	7,064	7,064	48,600	32,622	46,277	0	20,138	38,661	87,802	14,364	574,149	237	478,864	403,858	8,800
37010	318	1,507	0	0	25,372	0	23,191	0	10,409	1,527	31,078	9,650	119,527	44	87,068	31,663	0
37011	0	3,319	0	0	17,831	0	6,464	0	81,388	2,444	14,455	3,395	70,159	28	73,140	1,736	0
37012	417	0	0	0	10,500	0	26,000	0	16,058	1,302	67,516	0	185,404	75	168,487	12,890	0
37013	22	433	0	0	5,872	0	15,386	0	3,684	1,086	33,780	17,687	101,389	50	81,656	3,040	0
37014	182	367	0	0	19,800	0	0	0	4,919	488	7,718	0	36,695	30	42,417	0	0
37015	124	1,206	0	0	11,923	0	1,050	0	15,500	300	6,420	0	29,992	21	24,031		0
37016		3,500	0	0	8,457	0	1,625	0			27,500	15,000	76,332	18	31,300	27,000	24,800

STATISTICAL INFORMATION

GS

CONFERENCE Number	Church Name	Total professing members reported at the close of last year (1)	TOTAL PROFESSING MEMBERS reported at the close of this year (4)	Average attendance at all weekly worship services (7)	Total Baptized Members who have not become Professing Members (9)	Number of other constituents of the church (10)	TOTAL Christian Formation Group Participants (Total of lines 11a-d) (11)	Average weekly attendance (all ages) in Sunday Church School or other weekly education classes (13)	Membership in United Methodist Men (18a)	Membership in United Methodist Women (19a)	Number of persons sent out on UMW/UMVIM teams from this local church (20b)	Total Number of community ministries for outreach, justice, and mercy offered by this local church (21)	Value of church assets and buildings (24 & 25)	Church Debt (26 & 27)	Amount APPORTIONED to the local church by the CONFERENCE (28a)	Amount PAID by the local church to the CONFERENCE for all apportioned causes (29a)	Amount APPORTIONED to the local church by the DISTRICT (if applicable) (28b)
37017	BELLEVUE	126	124	55	23	130	53	18	12	14	0	0	2,915,306	0	12,509	12,509	635
37018	BERRIEN CNTY: LAKESIDE	32	35	16	0	20	9	0	0	0	0	0	752,300	0	5,494	5,494	315
37019	BERRIEN SPRINGS	30	29	12	5	0	13	15	0	0	0	0	3,734,000	0	7,849	5,649	306
37020	BLOOMINGDALE	22	21	12	0	21	11	4	0	0	0	2	392,000	0	2,299	363	222
37021	BRIDGMAN: FAITH	45	39	13	0	3	0	0	0	0	0	0	382,700	0	6,005	6,000	437
37022	BRONSON: FIRST	58	60	38	31	22	21	16	0	0	0	4	2,292,001	0	11,006	11,006	358
37023	BUCHANAN: FAITH	120	122	77	24	28	0	29	0	10	0	0	2,853,000	0	12,440	5,777	1,076
37024	BUCHANAN: FIRST	163	149	70	2	35	28	13	0	0	0	1	3,061,068	0	19,659	15,504	1,642
37025	BURNIPS	57	61	61	0	29	48	13	0	12	0	0	1,070,000	0	9,346	6,780	510
37026	BURR OAK	37	32	10	0	0	5	0	0	0	0	0	302,000	0	3,926	0	196
37027	CASCO	178	152	80	59	150	69	30	6	25	0	2	3,407,725	0	15,756	15,756	1,661
37028	CASSOPOLIS	77	60	59	0	49	52	5	0	0	0	8	311,531	0	9,358	3,358	743
37029	CENTREVILLE	180	191	71	93	28	58	54	0	0	0	9	985,000	0	20,293	20,293	988
37030	CLIMAX	93	92	63	0	43	24	18	0	20	0	1	708,852	1,600	15,486	15,486	464
37031	COLDWATER	244	243	132	55	83	99	30	26	68	5	6	6,998,435	0	28,621	28,621	1,432
37032	COLOMA	162	156	72	14	22	25	14	0	0	0	6	933,585	0	21,728	12,906	1,550
37033	COLON	63	67	39	0	36	10	3	0	0	0	2	842,453	0	9,918	9,918	328
37034	CONSTANTINE	137	133	35	31	10	18	9	0	0	0	0	2,886,397	0	12,835	12,884	700
37035	DELTON: FAITH	170	174	108	0	74	125	49	0	0	15	3	1,215,266	0	20,928	16,847	837

STATISTICAL INFORMATION

GS

Line item legend:
- 29b — Amount PAID by the local church to the DISTRICT for all apportioned causes (if applicable)
- 30-38 — Church Benevolence Giving
- 39a — Total ASKED for clergy pension
- 39b — Total PAID for clergy pension
- 41a — Base compensation paid to/for the Senior Pastor or other person assigned or appointed in the lead pastoral role to the church
- 41b — Base compensation paid to/for all Associate Pastor(s) and other pastoral staff assigned or appointed to the church. Include deacons and other clergy in this role
- 40, 42a-44 — Pastoral Benefits
- 41c & 42c — Deacons salary/benefits
- 45 — Total amount paid in salary and benefits for all other church staff and diaconal ministers
- 46 — Total amount spent for local church program expenses
- 47 — Total amount spent for other local church operating expenses
- 48 & 49 — Local church capital expenses
- 50 — TOTAL CHURCH EXPENSES (Sum of Lines 29a through 49)
- 51 — Number of giving units
- 52 — Total income for annual budget/spending plan
- 53 — Total income for designated causes including capital campaign and other special projects
- 54 — Total income from connectional and other institutional sources outside the local church

CONFERENCE Number	29b	30-38	39a	39b	41a	41b	40,42a-44	41c&42c	45	46	47	48&49	50	51	52	53	54
37017	635	731	0	0	19,932	0	11,477	0	15,021	0	19,491	0	79,796	60	102,610	391	0
37018	315	6,560	0	0	1,440	0	17,119	0	6,060	969	16,398	0	54,355	18	40,404	7,122	0
37019	37	1,126	0	0	19,076	7,535	7,865	0	8,836	927	33,885	1,600	86,501	16	75,597	5,547	3,600
37020		125	0	0	8,311	0		0	210	100	9,327	0	18,493	15	22,553	0	0
37021	437	5,082	0	0	18,088	0	0	0		298	10,096	0	40,001		45,819	7,173	0
37022	358	3,481	0	0	22,672	0	7,519	0	10,753	1,810	19,411	4,251	86,768	30	85,167	5,243	0
37023		6,841	0	0	16,210	0	13,540	0	0	1,897	38,508	13,120	95,893	51	100,392	5,221	0
37024	1,642	8,197	0	0	36,000	0	30,274	0	29,368	3,272	23,724	23,922	179,464	81	179,100	14,720	0
37025	370	2,265	5,507	5,507	20,075	0	6,080	0	6,754	5,000	7,500	3,932	58,756	88	95,503	5,515	0
37026		28,404	7,561	7,561	9,500	0	1,500	0	2,500	600	14,500	0	28,600	22	29,500	0	0
37027	1,661	2,387	0	0	40,543	0	17,181	0	30,398	2,682	47,523	0	192,312	98	127,666	44,071	0
37028	743	20,834	8,164	8,164	26,337	0	1,530	0	23,986	4,761	29,171	25,927	118,200	58	76,601	13,367	0
37029	988	2,316	6,435	6,435	43,887	0	31,451	0	28,679	4,830	21,952	714	180,063	70	155,512	24,783	0
37030	464	28,791	7,059	7,059	23,719	0	23,880	0	11,342	151	32,639	11,891	128,947	29	53,762	28,667	0
37031	1,432	11,345	9,000	9,000	48,000	0	23,619	0	36,824	10,159	84,865	41,143	312,454	156	247,591	67,135	3,195
37032	1,694	4,639	10,448	10,448	46,520	0	24,087	0	43,756	5,414	25,889	14,127	196,186	73	175,851	16,272	0
37033	328	3,848	0	0	22,810	0	9,422	0	12,113	1,064	23,115	0	83,409	44	79,132	11,382	0
37034	700		7,499	7,499	26,798	0	19,509	0	2,059	1,456	14,328	29,690	118,771	40	73,336	29,604	0
37035	674	31,438	8,813	8,078	43,833	0	31,588	0	17,052	52,481	42,469	8,770	253,230	100	59,057	73,545	0

STATISTICAL INFORMATION

GS

CONFERENCE Number	Church Name	Total professing members reported at the close of last year (1)	TOTAL PROFESSING MEMBERS reported at the close of this year (4)	Average attendance at all weekly worship services (7)	Total Baptized Members who have not become Professing Members (9)	Number of other constituents of the church (10)	TOTAL Christian Formation Group Participants (Total of lines 11a-d) (11)	Average weekly attendance (all ages) in Sunday Church School or other weekly education classes (13)	Membership in United Methodist Men (18a)	Membership in United Methodist Women (19a)	Number of persons sent out on UMVIM teams from this local church (20b)	Total Number of community ministries for outreach, justice, and mercy offered by this local church (21)	Value of church assets and buildings (24 & 25)	Church Debt (26 & 27)	Amount APPORTIONED to the local church by the CONFERENCE (28a)	Amount PAID by the local church to the CONFERENCE for all apportioned causes (29a)	Amount APPORTIONED to the local church by the DISTRICT (if applicable) (28b)
37036	DOWAGIAC: FIRST	182	165	77	0	52	0	12	0	0	0	0	1,197,834	0	19,482	19,482	1,698
37037	DOWLING: COUNTRY CHAPEL	163	172	98	0	60	83	28	0	0	0	0	1,507,913	0	14,263	0	1,107
37038	EDWARDSBURG: HOPE	463	456	141	148	373	54	38	0	21	0	33	1,434,164	194,573	35,515	35,515	4,835
37039	FENNVILLE	82	73	40	0	0	26	4	0	0	0	3	1,977,400	17,440	12,557	8,350	789
37040	FENNVILLE: PEARL	30	30	28	0	13	10	4	0	0	0	2	348,900	0	3,730	3,730	287
37041	GALESBURG	80	76	48	0	0	0	0	0	10	0	0	637,441	0	9,766	9,766	403
37042	GALIEN	53	49	22	0	5	9	3	0	0	0	0	600,500	0	6,706	977	520
37043	GALIEN: OLIVE BRANCH	78	75	23	36	10	4	4	0	0	0	1	555,556	0	5,762	4,802	649
37044	GANGES	82	83	33	5	40	20	11	0	30	0	0	561,000	0	3,762	2,307	752
37045	GIRARD	96	84	56	1	7	25	6	11	20	0	6	1,050,000	0	12,677	12,677	494
37046	GLENN	17	17	29	0	0	8	3	0	10	0	1	974,394	0	4,286	1,432	204
37047	GOBLES	58	57	42	0	35	14	9	0	12	0	10	481,172	0	10,336	10,336	510
37048	GULL LAKE	294	265	117	2	48	117	32	0	0	18	5	2,063,685	300,000	29,363	29,381	2,979
37049	HARTFORD	240	253	118	12	120	78	33	0	21	1	4	2,611,202	0	23,350	23,350	1,986
37050	HINCHMAN	79	59	16	0	8	0	0	0	0	0	3	863,128	0	2,954	2,708	510
37051	HOPKINS	64	65	37	3	15	26	16	0	12	0	7	3,750,000	0	9,605	9,605	603
37052	KALAMAZOO: FIRST	836	861	288	172	222	695	70	0	100	16	13	27,500,000	0	113,603	113,603	7,739
37053	KALAMAZOO: MILWOOD	161	142	115	4	54	62	6	0	0	0	6	3,657,342	392,994	21,101	21,101	1,652
37054	KALAMAZOO: NORTHWEST	23	23	21	0	0	8	0	0	0	0	0	686,550	0	3,159	3,159	204

STATISTICAL INFORMATION

GS

CONFERENCE Number	29b Amount PAID by the local church to the DISTRICT for all apportioned causes (if applicable)	30-38 Church Benevolence Giving	39a Total ASKED for clergy pension	39b Total PAID for clergy pension	41a Base compensation paid to/for the Senior Pastor or other person assigned or appointed in the lead pastoral role to the church	41b Base compensation paid to/for all Associate Pastor(s) and other pastoral staff assigned or appointed to the church. Include deacons and other clergy in this role.	40, 42a-44 Pastoral Benefits	41c & 42c Deacons salary/benefits	45 Total amount paid in salary and benefits for all other church staff and diaconal ministers	46 Total amount spent for local church program expenses	47 Total amount spent for other local church operating expenses	48 & 49 Local Church capital expenses	50 TOTAL CHURCH EXPENSES (Sum of Lines 29a through 49)	51 Number of giving units	52 Total income for annual budget/spending plan	53 Total income for designated causes including capital campaign and other special projects	54 Total income from connectional and other institutional sources outside the local church
37036	1,698	644	5,015	5,454	26,747	0	22,601	0	23,096	968	40,473	71,438	212,600	63	148,760	46,756	0
37037	4,835	13,897	7,111	7,111	37,934	0	31,146	0	10,260	9,004	27,668	8,423	145,443	82	119,614	0	0
37038	790	9,730	12,255	12,255	63,697	0	41,949	0	60,984	19,616	40,224	111,322	400,127	160	258,701	69,554	0
37039	287	6,131	0	0	29,003	0	1,125	0	14,666	3,197	17,822	34,269	115,353	40	88,229	19,349	0
37040	403	175	0	0	10,250	0	2,299	0	4,946	550	5,072	800	27,622	25	30,707		0
37041	22	681	1,800	1,800	11,500	0	7,996	0	20,153	63	21,616	0	72,665	45	90,592	3,712	0
37042	541	892	0	0	14,000	0	10,800	0	3,350	100	6,500	0	38,441	45	43,000	2,994	0
37043	461	5,641	0	0	12,000	0	0	0	6,760	200	6,125	3,105	36,069	43	31,501	1,254	0
37044	494	1,340	7,282	7,282	5,000	0	0	0	13,055	713	24,501	1,076	50,482	13	34,293	2,550	0
37045	68	1,000	0	0	38,764	0	3,936	0	4,295	500	28,560	4,500	98,584	51	113,191	1,541	0
37046	510	980	6,821	6,821	13,200	0	188	0		7,274	9,664	3,798	30,032	35	26,476	4,789	0
37047	2,979	4,064	0	0	15,000	0	12,334	0	1,560	4,349	16,044	31,487	91,478	43	81,240	38,555	0
37048	1,986	26,082	7,957	7,957	43,718	0	11,915	0	72,280	25,943	66,997	5,934	260,470	100	287,654	20,866	0
37049	467	9,715	0	0	18,982	0	37,346	0	27,389	3,956	12,024	34,415	195,362	181	199,984	81,924	0
37050	603	5,200	6,821	6,821	28,213	0	4,899	0	3,388	5,741	12,204	2,000	86,219	14	55,407	475	0
37051	7,739	765	14,588	14,588	77,250	0	6,320	0	9,840	146,114	19,519	125,588	89,427	42	73,669	229,048	15,300
37052	1,652	191,775	0	0	7,000	91,845	36,197	0	441,902	2,468	174,520	69,010	1,421,121	350	938,374	1,180	0
37053	204	2,580	0	0	5,637	0	25,014	0	57,563	537	60,819	1,695	247,207	106	183,269	0	4,300
37054		5,254	0	0		0	19,290	0	0		12,710		48,486	22	29,308	0	0

CONFERENCE Number	Church Name	Total professing members reported at the close of last year (1)	TOTAL PROFESSING MEMBERS reported at the close of this year (4)	Average attendance at all weekly worship services (7)	Total Baptized Members who have not become Professing Members (9)	Number of other constituents of the church (10)	TOTAL Christian Formation Group Participants (Total of lines 11a–d) (11)	Average weekly attendance (all ages) in Sunday Church School or other weekly education classes (13)	Membership in United Methodist Men (18a)	Membership in United Methodist Women (19a)	Number of persons sent out on UMVIM teams from this local church (20b)	Total Number of community ministries for outreach, justice, and mercy offered by this local church (21)	Value of church assets and buildings (24 & 25)	Church Debt (26 & 27)	Amount APPORTIONED to the local church by the CONFERENCE (28a)	Amount PAID by the local church to the CONFERENCE for all apportioned causes (29a)	Amount APPORTIONED to the local church by the DISTRICT (if applicable) (28b)
37055	KALAMAZOO: SUNNYSIDE	111	106	92	23	79	142	15	0	0	0	4	1,595,376	0	20,724	3,497	1,002
37056	KALAMAZOO: WESTWOOD	251	201	150	36	82	98	40	20	35	0	9	5,070,000	400,000	43,688	22,787	2,440
37057	KENDALL	22	22	12	2	4	4	1	0	3	0	7	281,000	0	4,453	4,453	241
37058	LACOTA	28	30	28	1	0	2	16	0	0	0	0	366,600	0	3,496	0	241
37059	LAWRENCE	113	110	35	16	20	35	10	0	5	0	3	766,000	74,786	8,002	0	1,132
37060	LAWTON: ST PAUL'S	102	85	64	0	73	56	20	0	15	0	4	1,639,163	0	15,260	15,260	854
37061	MARCELLUS	76	68	30	0	28	30	10	0	4	0	0	900,000	0	7,334	483	724
37062	MARCELLUS: WAKELEE	80	77	45	0	15	0	8	0	0	0	0	350,000	0	8,626	7,031	760
37063	MARTIN	115	117	61	0	36	37	13	0	0	0	1	1,203,180	0	14,433	1,443	1,548
37064	MENDON	80	73	34	0	0	20	12	0	0	0	5	1,054,999	0	10,523	10,523	429
37065	MONTEREY CENTER	47	47	47	0	18	20	18	4	0	0	0	585,000	0	7,115	1,170	418
37066	MORRIS CHAPEL	20	23	23	0	10	0	0	0	0	0	0	355,001	0	4,298	4,298	185
37067	NEW BUFFALO: WATER'S EDGE	179	182	96	0	161	63	15	0	0	0	5	3,036,615	0	37,808	37,808	1,615
37068	NILES: GRACE	43	58	23	0	0	7	3	0	0	0	1	2,211,000	0	4,455	2,473	418
37069	NILES: PORTAGE PRAIRIE	161	157	69	0	29	48	47	0	0	0	0	2,455,001	0	12,822	10,685	1,484
37070	NILES: WESLEY	168	150	56	0	26	24	24	0	15	0	6	4,659,771	0	20,192	16,827	1,763
37071	NOTTAWA	11	11	10	0	25	11	11	0	0	0	2	40,001	0	2,617	2,617	55
37072	OSHTEMO	111	104	60	1	54	10	18	0	20	0	4	504,001	3,260	11,834	4,128	1,067
37073	OSHTEMO: LIFESPRING	53	55	31	0	0	16	4	0	0	0	0	0	507,848	0	0	0

STATISTICAL INFORMATION

GS

CONFERENCE Number	29b Amount PAID by the local church to the DISTRICT for all apportioned causes (if applicable)	30-38 Church Benevolence Giving	39g Total ASKED for clergy pension	39h Total PAID for clergy pension	41a Base compensation paid to/for the Senior Pastor or other person assigned or appointed in the lead pastoral role to the church	41b Base compensation paid to/for all Associate Pastor(s) and other pastoral staff assigned or appointed to the church, include deacons and other clergy in this role.	40, 42a-44 Pastoral Benefits	41c & 42c & 44 Deacons salary/benefits	45 Total amount paid in salary and benefits for all other church staff and diaconal ministers	46 Total amount spent for local church program expenses	47 Total amount spent for other local church operating expenses	48 & 49 Local Church capital expenses	50 TOTAL CHURCH EXPENSES (Sum of Lines 29a through 49)	51 Number of giving units	52 Total Income for annual budget/spending plan	53 Total income for designated causes including capital campaign and other special projects	54 Total income from connectional and other institutional sources outside the local church
37055	169	7,272	8,007	8,007	43,000	0	41,500	0	36,000	400	26,000	85,000	250,845	0	0	0	0
37056	1,273	28,155	10,866	9,622	54,000	2,500	35,000	0	85,000	23,000	76,000	266,000	603,337	90	348,300	197,000	0
37057	241	1,982	0	0	7,639	0	2,871	0	1,530	344	7,905	167	27,132	9	28,569	1,502	0
37058	0	2,560	0	0	8,000	0	0	0	0	356	12,670	0	23,586	16	37,255	2,950	0
37059	854	2,310	5,100	5,100	22,216	0	19,038	0	15,724	5,943	28,239	14,373	94,909	31	82,965	11,012	0
37060	48	0	5,280	5,280	25,000	0	22,790	0	3,500	4,647	24,188	2,349	118,402	64	111,716	29,630	0
37061	619	364	6,907	6,907	37,400	0	9,500	0	5,000	800	34,000	0	92,638	38	60,000	0	0
37062	155	8,302	7,618	7,618	17,350	0	300	0	21,993	1,000	23,000	5,127	54,664	15	70,000	11,282	4,262
37063	429	22,235	0	0	28,442	0	24,898	0	15,252	4,541	21,714	0	124,233	55	96,965	1,742	0
37064	10	1,313	0	0	20,167	0	3,971	0	6,636	1,053	18,073	729	91,703	28	82,854	0	0
37065	185	27,335	10,350	10,350	16,425	0	4,501	0		300	7,500	0	38,583	47	57,452	10,000	796
37066	1,615	2,932	7,984	7,984	10,000	0	5,478	0	57,999	1,325	24,212	7,352	55,848	17	36,789	38,225	0
37067	527	7,587	0	0	36,248	0	27,539	0	12,371	17,417	96,772	0	318,069	61	267,876	650	0
37068	1,237	4,768	7,689	7,689	13,000	0	884	0	14,758	200	7,879	0	40,266	17	28,857	0	0
37069	1,469	2,043	0	0	41,010	0	0	0	24,827	2,227	32,298	5,000	117,491	157	102,896	19,078	0
37070	0	7,719	0	0	20,000	0	17,232	0	0	2,199	39,680	0	132,002	68	138,657	1,768	0
37071	372	0	0	0	6,500	0	1,470	0	15,361	25	9,906	12,295	19,944	8	9,283	16,592	0
37072	0				5,002	0	39,053	0		13,401	26,068	41,448	123,399	65	91,238	0	0
37073					15,002	0	203	0		110	22,890		79,653	12	76,902		0

STATISTICAL INFORMATION

GS

CONFERENCE Number	Church Name	Total professing members reported at the close of last year	TOTAL PROFESSING MEMBERS reported at the close of this year	Average attendance at all weekly worship services	Total Baptized Members who have not become Professing Members	Number of other constituents of the church	TOTAL Christian Formation Group Participants (Total of lines 11a-d)	Average weekly attendance (all ages) in Sunday Church School or other weekly education classes	Membership in United Methodist Men	Membership in United Methodist Women	Number of persons sent out on UMVIM teams from this local church	Total Number of community ministries for outreach, justice, and mercy offered by this local church	Value of church assets and buildings	Church Debt	Amount APPORTIONED to the local church by the CONFERENCE	Amount PAID by the local church to the CONFERENCE for all apportioned causes	Amount APPORTIONED to the local church by the DISTRICT (if applicable)
		1	4	7	9	10	11	13	18a	19a	20b	21	24 & 25	26 & 27	28a	29a	28b
37074	OTSEGO	356	360	307	4	276	240	112	8	26	42	4	3,299,949	51,137	27,676	27,676	3,192
37075	OTSEGO: TROWBRIDGE	52		35	0	14	14	10	0	0	0	4	1,682,149	0	6,194	0	455
37076	PARCHMENT	245	241	73	2	63	30	20	14	49	0	2	4,928,000	0	23,296	23,372	2,255
37077	PAW PAW	119	111	50	0	51	29	14	0	0	0	0	3,725,480	42,291	15,285	0	1,290
37078	PLAINWELL: FIRST	177	172	109	74	112	75	7	0	0	0	7	4,825,800	475,928	26,197	22,175	1,735
37079	PLEASANT VALLEY	62	55	27	10	38	7	7	0	15	0	0	650,402	0	6,162	5,649	288
37080	POKAGON	97	96	52	0	30	54	24	0	0	0	0	100,000	0	10,028	7,774	900
37081	PORTAGE: CHAPEL HILL	499	507	226	172	291	267	110	20	31	0	15	5,476,159	455,853	91,958	92,258	4,705
37082	PORTAGE: PATHFINDER	415	385	241	75	304	390	65	0	0	0	14	5,630,918	789,531	60,182	60,182	3,758
37083	RIVERSIDE	72	69	42	0	40	11	5	0	0	0	4	2,122,400	0	6,300	6,300	667
37084	SAUGATUCK	52	51	25	0	5	15	13	0	0	0	0	576,889	0	7,986	7,986	682
37085	SCHOOLCRAFT	91	95	54	5	22	64	25	0	21	0	5	2,953,753	43,124	12,501	6,978	2,181
37086	SCOTTDALE	58	52	30	2	12	20	12	0	29	0	0	808,178	12,150	6,932	0	548
37087	SCOTTS	37	31	29	0	43	11	1	0	11	0	1	305,000	940	6,130	3,950	196
37088	SHELBYVILLE	58	60	41	5	41	14	2	0	15	0	2	1,036,000	4,000	7,639	7,639	773
37089	SILVER CREEK	91	86	45	0	0	0	0	0	0	0	0	743,046	0	11,593	11,596	863
37090	SODUS: CHAPEL HILL	178	176	67	61	76	51	10	0	0	0	0	518,799	0	19,228	3,829	1,595
37091	SOUTH HAVEN: FIRST	128	125	71	1	1	48	37	7	5	0	2	908,000	0	24,103	13,559	1,207
37092	SOUTH MONTEREY	34	34	10	3	1	6	0	0	2	0	1	221,000	0	5,192	5,192	315

STATISTICAL INFORMATION

GS

CONFERENCE Number	Amount PAID by the local church to the DISTRICT for all apportioned causes (if applicable) (29b)	Church Benevolence Giving (30-38)	Total ASKED for clergy pension (39a)	Total PAID for clergy pension (39b)	Base compensation paid to/for the Senior Pastor or other person assigned or appointed in the lead pastoral role to the church (41a)	Base compensation paid to/for all Associate Pastor(s) and other pastoral staff... Include deacons and other clergy in this role. (41b)	Pastoral Benefits (40, 42a-44)	Deacons salary/benefits (41c & 42c)	Total amount paid in salary and benefits for all other church staff and diaconal ministers (45)	Total amount spent for local church program expenses (46)	Total amount spent for other local church operating expenses (47)	Local church capital expenses (48 & 49)	TOTAL CHURCH EXPENSES (Sum of Lines 29a through 49) (50)	Number of giving units (51)	Total income for annual budget/spending plan (52)	Total income for designated causes including capital campaign and other special projects (53)	Total income from connectional and other institutional sources outside the local church (54)
37074	3,192	4,898	10,875	10,875	52,000	0	33,382	0	78,289	13,316	57,390	48,223	329,241	233	207,174	18,997	0
37075	0	3,182	0	0	27,544	0	0	0	0	2,489	10,463	0	43,678	29	59,148	0	0
37076	2,264	3,958	11,025	11,025	56,000	0	22,450	0	33,500	1,580	48,521	3,500	206,170	44	164,229	16,107	0
37077	0	2,500	11,119	11,119	45,000	0	443	0	42,308	1,335	41,161	0	132,747	50	115,958	0	0
37078	1,500	4,853	0	0	59,303	0	28,187	0	56,734	5,251	49,104	87,233	325,459	103	233,649	86,412	1,700
37079	264	4,620	4,763	4,763	12,191	0	7,850	0	2,475	408	10,097	560	44,114	21	41,772	1,220	0
37080	696	11,185	13,931	13,931	19,814	0	17,436	0	8,530	12,467	11,274	2,082	96,021	52	83,736	3,427	0
37081	4,705	19,894	0	0	73,031	14,183	50,393	0	160,442	20,182	211,830	149,677	810,526	262	723,008	9,940	0
37082	3,758	18,156	11,250	11,250	60,000	20,000	15,250	0	162,866	14,571	117,000	566,735	1,049,768	200	409,468	267,809	0
37083	667	3,678	0	0	8,470	0	8,226	0	9,320	979	21,428	0	59,068	39	56,032	450	0
37084	682	2,400	0	0	0	0	21,640	0	4,749	5,430	6,687	5,200	54,774	28	53,934	5,755	0
37085	2,181	6,509	6,858	6,858	23,719	0	17,233	0	15,071	1,698	20,735	11,996	112,978	49	101,752	49,535	0
37086	0	1,880	6,988	6,988	22,185	0	2,501	0	0	700	7,000	3,000	44,254	40	46,000	3,400	0
37087	196	1,274	0	0	13,929	0	15,762	0	4,632	260	9,504	3,653	53,160	34	49,783	2,275	0
37088	773	2,981	0	0	12,189	0	9,849	0	11,725	3,925	6,252	1,104	56,437	33	59,038	18,957	0
37089	862	6,933	0	0	3,773	0	13,603	0	16,861	4,095	16,106	16,052	89,881	33	84,383	15,308	0
37090	317	39,196	9,121	9,871	48,643	0	30,805	0	23,323	3,941	44,148	58,903	262,876	114	178,071	25,689	0
37091	679	8,083	8,857	8,784	47,238	0	26,663	0	34,783	2,282	47,299	14,035	203,425	70	179,435	8,675	0
37092	315	3,076	0	0	15,742	0	3,280	0	3,488	1,979	13,889	535	47,496	10	44,354	0	0

STATISTICAL INFORMATION

CONFERENCE Number	Church Name	Total professing members reported at the close of last year (1)	TOTAL PROFESSING MEMBERS reported at the close of this year (4)	Average attendance at all weekly worship services (7)	Total Baptized Members who have not become Professing Members (9)	Number of other constituents of the church (10)	TOTAL Christian Formation Group Participants (Total of lines 11a-d) (11)	Average weekly attendance (all ages) in Sunday Church School or other weekly education classes (13)	Membership in United Methodist Men (18a)	Membership in United Methodist Women (19a)	Number of persons sent out on UMVIM teams from this local church (20b)	Total Number of community ministries for outreach, justice, and mercy offered by this local church (21)	Value of church assets and buildings (24 & 25)	Church Debt (26 & 27)	Amount APPORTIONED to the local church by the CONFERENCE (28a)	Amount PAID by the local church to the CONFERENCE for all apportioned causes (29a)	Amount APPORTIONED to the local church by the DISTRICT (if applicable) (28b)
37093	ST JOSEPH: FIRST	382	343	122	0	62	139	138	0	0	0	8	5,695,136	0	56,677	17,119	4,046
37094	STEVENSVILLE	456	434	170	6	350	226	21	0	100	0	0	6,483,700		45,682	45,682	4,315
37095	STURGIS	316	316	97	16	25	57	34	0	0	0	16	8,130,548		35,850	35,850	1,810
37096	THREE OAKS	127	124	72	26	44	35	4	0	0	0	0	423,211		14,752	15,981	1,262
37097	THREE RIVERS: CENTER PARK	126	127	87	47	81	74	50	0	0	0	5	2,221,500		13,665	13,665	650
37098	THREE RIVERS: FIRST	135	135	51	51	56	21	0	6	32	0	9	4,301,619	16,042	12,388	8,003	715
37099	THREE RIVERS: NINTH STREET	52	52	24	24	20	49	2	4	8	0	0	829,824		5,320	5,320	253
37100	TOWNLINE	66	67	49	40	45	39	8	0	0	0	4	856,673		3,929	3,929	510
37101	UNION CITY	106	92	67	0	61		15	4	44	0	3	2,001,114		14,027	0	524
37102	VICKSBURG	305	280	132	0	96	174	35	0	97	0	6	1,853,572	613,657	34,211	18,522	3,063
37103	WHITE PIGEON	49	45	19	0	38	13	4	0	8	0	0	1,954,540		6,065	6,065	283
	GREATER SOUTHWEST DISTRICT TOTALS	13,523	12,969	6,682	1,503	6,102	5,549	1,868	172	1,090	130	416	220,581,332	4,794,057	1,667,653	1,281,112	115,413
	HERITAGE DISTRICT																
38001	ADRIAN: FIRST	486	462	127	130	100	44	25	25	110	0	5	9,930,422	0	56,123	56,123	1,599
38002	ALBION: FIRST	241	231	69	4	41	48	23	0	37	0	4	8,445,808	14,298	27,868	12,331	1,229
38003	ALLEN	42	46	38	10	24	24	0	0	6	0	5	574,000	0	4,847	4,861	226
38004	ANN ARBOR: CALVARY	75	64	28	0	8	0	3	0	0	0	1	2,171,112	1,536	13,077	9,154	373
38005	ANN ARBOR: FIRST	1,095	1,009	552	125	230	899	258	0	233	83	10	19,459,700	839,970	157,425	157,425	4,398

HG

GS

STATISTICAL INFORMATION

HG

CONFERENCE Number	29b Amount PAID by the local church to the DISTRICT for all apportioned causes (if applicable)	30-38 Church Benevolence Giving	39a Total ASKED for clergy pension	39b Total PAID for clergy pension	41a Base compensation paid to/for the Senior Pastor or other person assigned or appointed in the lead pastoral role to the church	41b Base compensation paid to/for all Associate Pastor(s) and other pastoral staff assigned or appointed to the church, include deacons and other clergy in this role.	40, 42a-44 Pastoral Benefits	41c & 42c Deacons salary/benefits	45 Total amount paid in salary and benefits for all other church staff and diaconal ministers	46 Total amount spent for local church program expenses	47 Total amount spent for other local church operating expenses	48 & 49 Local church capital expenses	50 TOTAL CHURCH EXPENSES (Sum of Lines 29a through 49)	51 Number of giving units	52 Total income for annual budget/spending plan	53 Total income for designated causes including capital campaign and other special projects	54 Total income from connectional and other institutional sources outside the local church
37093	1,222	18,943	19,371	18,439	51,443	0	67,653	68,796	91,901	70,636	66,754	21,602	494,508	170	445,294	63,654	0
37094	4,615	21,833	13,098	13,098	69,855	0	33,638	0	98,218	13,888	73,901	29,513	404,241	169	342,114	43,743	0
37095	1,810	23,019	9,656	9,656	51,500	0	41,424	0	67,939	6,293	48,068	16,427	301,986	136	257,539	26,206	0
37096	1,367	1,688	4,741	4,741	41,002	0	15,464	0	7,009	1,776	16,789	0	105,817	83	109,197	11,607	0
37097	650	6,657	0	0	4,164	0	21,434	0	20,856	1,882	31,646		100,954	68	112,396	7,981	0
37098	462	3,023	0	0	26,042	0	2,894	0	24,528	4,065	30,242	63,242	163,501	66	110,894	26,871	0
37099	253	1,284	0	0	0	1,000	10,553	0	2,700	751	10,809	8,432	40,102	27	35,637	14,634	0
37100	510	1,138	7,253	7,253	0	0	9,838	0		7,842	14,667	6,390	44,314	36	38,666	13,707	0
37101	0	500	10,575	10,575	38,680	0	21,120	0	13,563	4,862	30,715	66,641	183,334	35	87,330	2,309	0
37102	1,663	11,602	248	248	52,500	0	45,070	0	138,262	9,351	81,475	59,257	428,277	134	267,017	5,815	0
37103	283	797			13,178	0	11,922	0		3,862	13,514	29,045	78,914	26	51,400	18,462	0
	91,794	962,203	427,584	424,446	2,692,586	169,685	1,640,556	68,796	2,923,397	722,300	3,248,323	2,551,036	16,776,234	6,567	12,785,903	2,674,653	68,353
38001	1,599	19,690	7,170	7,170	59,798	0	31,881	0	205,824	37,851	120,236	0	540,172	183	504,831	140,222	750
38002	544	14,258	5,438	5,438	29,000	0	29,082	0	48,643	5,012	37,944	15,613	197,865	86	197,721	60,846	0
38003	227	5,525		0	19,200	0	0	0	3,300	1,239	6,500	1,818	42,670	25	40,905	5,363	0
38004	300	2,166	5,120	3,584	43,992	0	25,892	0	10,400	3,000	37,000	0	135,488	22	133,415	25,000	0
38005	5,898	159,558	18,300	18,300	97,527	53,645	71,223	0	619,513	100,132	195,760	264,179	1,743,160	513	1,472,581	344,477	0

STATISTICAL INFORMATION

CONFERENCE Number	Church Name	1. Total professing members reported at the close of last year	4. TOTAL PROFESSING MEMBERS reported at the close of this year	7. Average attendance at all weekly worship services	9. Total Baptized Members who have not become Professing Members	10. Number of other constituents of the church	11a-b-d. TOTAL Christian Formation Group Participants (Total of lines)	13. Average weekly attendance (all ages) in Sunday Church School or other weekly education classes	18a. Membership in United Methodist Men	19a. Membership in United Methodist Women	20b. Number of persons sent out on UMVIM teams from this local church	21. Total Number of community ministries for outreach, justice, and mercy offered by this local church	24 & 25. Value of church assets and buildings	26 & 27. Church Debt	28a. Amount APPORTIONED to the local church by the CONFERENCE	29a. Amount PAID by the local church to the CONFERENCE for all apportioned causes	28b. Amount APPORTIONED to the local church by the DISTRICT (if applicable)
38006	ANN ARBOR: KOREAN	211	210	180	0	0	236	60	80	76	0	0	1,530,097	824,651	28,554	0	814
38007	ANN ARBOR: WEST SIDE	280	260	118	62	65	109	50	0	50	10	0	4,887,082	352,999	50,295	50,295	1,433
38008	AZALIA	27	26	14	6	8	9	0	0	0	0	0	973,943	0	3,722	3,722	106
38009	BELLEVILLE: FIRST	311	298	158	4	78	161	40	90	87	6	8	8,111,846	56,000	34,804	34,804	992
38010	BLISSFIELD: EMMANUEL	51	50	43	27	42	80	24	0	0	0	3	756,500	0	13,384	13,384	457
38011	BLISSFIELD: FIRST	148	143	48	48	74	32	6	0	0	0	3	1,937,000	0	12,869	0	367
38012	BRIGHTON: FIRST	718	764	385	164	226	674	19	0	157	2	8	9,310,916	403,709	71,078	71,078	2,026
38013	BRITTON: GRACE	185	150	50	35	20	18	25	6	15	0	3	990,000	8,769	12,878	0	370
38014	CALHOUN COUNTY: HOMER	54	45	37	14	18	31	14	0	5	0	0	2,285,954	0	7,648	0	273
38015	CAMDEN	21	11	8	0	0	0	5	6	5	0	4	590,001	0	3,672	0	106
38016	CANTON: CHERRY HILL	67	66	33	77	172	12	11	0	0	0	12	1,125,711	0	14,975	2,647	492
38017	CANTON FRIENDSHIP	269	270	258	89	200	401	37	10	8	30	0	2,820,000	730,000	43,478	43,478	1,239
38018	CARLETON	258	267	112	0	209	66	51	15	12	0	17	3,180,102	0	22,059	22,059	628
38019	CHELSEA: FIRST	651	649	259	0	32	441	157	9	0	0	2	1,895,341	306,206	63,615	63,615	1,813
38020	CLAYTON	36	36	29	0	15	10	10	15	12	0	2	1,138,727	0	6,633	6,633	189
38021	CLINTON	118	118	65	1	245	12	12	9	0	0	2	3,115,289	331,653	14,832	1,000	423
38022	COMMERCE	640	639	241	0	78	385	120	15	70	0	0	3,025,439	1,204,363	51,629	7,835	1,471
38023	CONCORD	102	100	68	10	0	111	20	18	15	0	8	1,990,533	246,843	15,091	15,091	620
38024	DEERFIELD	14	14	15			8	5	0	0	0	0	230,000	0	2,480	0	71

HG

STATISTICAL INFORMATION

HG

CONFERENCE Number	29b Amount PAID by the local church to the DISTRICT for all apportioned causes (if applicable)	30-38 Church Benevolence Giving	39a Total ASKED for clergy pension	39b Total PAID for clergy pension	41a Base compensation paid to/for the Senior Pastor or other person assigned or appointed in the lead pastoral role to the church	41b Base compensation paid to/for all Associate Pastor(s) and other pastoral staff assigned or appointed to the church, include deacons and other clergy in this role	40, 42a-44 Pastoral Benefits	41c & 42c Deacons salary/benefits	45 Total amount paid in salary and benefits for all other church staff and diaconal ministers	46 Total amount spent for local church program expenses	47 Total amount spent for other local church operating expenses	48 & 49 Local Church capital expenses	50 TOTAL CHURCH EXPENSES (Sum of lines 29a through 49)	51 Number of giving units	52 Total income for annual budget/spending plan	53 Total income for designated causes including capital campaign and other special projects	54 Total income from connectional and other institutional sources outside the local church
38006	814	16,175	11,270	11,270	47,275	38,920	43,015	0	0	54,099	33,833	72,328	317,729	85	328,897	18,529	0
38007	1,760	35,707	6,800	6,800	49,615	0	22,069	35,963	115,518	38,583	121,199	36,596	514,105	168	411,250	285,774	4,084
38008	0	3,005	1,050	1,050	9,960	0	1,200	0	0	300	5,700	0	24,937	19	21,566	0	0
38009	992	8,755	8,950	8,950	73,264	0	29,146	0	86,129	10,475	45,985	6,755	305,255	165	277,529	6,800	0
38010	457	113	2,490	2,490	21,000	0	20,594	0	18,610	5,939	36,196	1,420	118,783	42	88,736	10,099	1,000
38011	367	0	5,040	5,040	41,976	45,449	16,159	9,023	10,122	3,056	23,531		101,671	74	98,951	3,172	0
38012	2,026	87,980	16,790	16,790	81,991	0	49,164	0	169,699	66,555	64,730	166,967	831,452	466	743,806	76,524	60,000
38013	370	2,000	5,240	5,240	44,137	0	20,600	0	2,800	1,000	20,000	2,000	98,147	55	74,000	13,000	0
38014	0	2,077	0	0	14,610	0	17,358	0	10,521	2,958	17,051	0	64,575	25	55,418	2,711	0
38015	0	0	0	0	9,000	0	900	0	0	603	11,590	350	22,443	8	0	0	0
38016	1,239	1,070	2,630	2,630	21,500	0	2,135	0	14,528	1,425	4,026	6,687	56,648	25	79,177	245	1,000
38017	628	7,860	8,000	8,000	54,419	0	50,592	0	79,196	92,915	100,050	83,400	526,149	152	9,175	92,705	0
38018	1,813	4,101	6,170	6,170	51,984	0	33,011	0	34,306	9,383	33,369	2,643	197,654	147	204,881	17,156	0
38019	189	32,099	8,690	8,690	77,723	0	23,072	0	296,243	28,286	102,374	76,316	710,231	336	639,355	134,869	0
38020	422	7,250	2,260	2,260	18,500	0	14,104	0	4,995	3,778	13,876		71,585	21	73,292	4,888	800
38021	1,471	49	5,560	5,560	40,956	0	27,918	0	206	1,159	31,125	70,455	178,850	94	129,100	43,212	0
38022	620	11,927	8,710	8,710	71,851	0	18,770	0	102,325	119,848	70,620	135,305	548,662	245	526,576	142,741	0
38023	0	2,206	0	0	37,691	0	2,607	0	43,818	3,022	40,117	132,374	277,548	47	107,077	52,812	0
38024	0	211	580	0	6,730	0	1,300	0	0	0	4,744	0	12,985	10	10,432	0	0

STATISTICAL INFORMATION

HG

CONFERENCE Number	Church Name	Total professing members reported at the close of last year (1)	TOTAL PROFESSING MEMBERS reported at the close of this year (4)	Average attendance at all weekly worship services (7)	Total Baptized Members who have not become Professing Members (9)	Number of other constituents of the church (10)	TOTAL Christian Formation Group Participants (Total of lines 11a-d) (11)	Average weekly attendance (all ages) in Sunday Church School or other weekly education classes (13)	Membership in United Methodist Men (18a)	Membership in United Methodist Women (19a)	Number of persons sent out on UMVIM teams from this local church (20b)	Total Number of community ministries for outreach, justice, and mercy offered by this local church (21)	Value of church assets and buildings (24 & 25)	Church Debt (26 & 27)	Amount APPORTIONED to the local church by the CONFERENCE (28a)	Amount PAID by the local church to the CONFERENCE for all apportioned causes (29a)	Amount APPORTIONED to the local church by the DISTRICT (if applicable) (28b)
38025	DENTON: FAITH	42	19	16	0	1	7	0	0	0	0	5	1,608,232	10,000	6,630	1,688	189
38026	DEXTER	1,165	1,218	556	153	2	835	175	140	0	0	6	10,042,866	3,800,000	120,456	120,456	3,433
38027	DIXBORO	216	214	85	27	74	102	25	7	30	0	25	537,571	0	24,073	24,073	686
38028	DUNDEE	260	262	97	66	112	53	34	7	12	0	1	4,251,207	41,534	17,646	17,646	503
38029	ERIE	142	144	51	20	0	57	36	12	20	0	6	1,726,606	5,415	10,604	897	302
38030	FRONTIER	41	38	24	2	24	11	0	7	0	0	4	385,357	0	3,683	3,683	231
38031	GRASS LAKE	127	126	72	20	37	20	15	0	0	0	2	2,159,610	0	14,633	14,637	615
38032	GRIFFITH	43	39	31	0	13	17	9	15	0	0	3	682,000	257,604	4,828	402	268
38033	HARDY	105	115	45	0	80	20	3	18	20	0	0	2,818,808	0	14,953	7,495	491
38034	HARTLAND	119	119	60	0	58	27	8	18	17	0	8	3,007,601	186,104	20,713	4,848	481
38035	HIGHLAND	445	444	221	0	249	214	54	2	0	0	17	3,780,438	471,409	60,374	60,374	1,721
38036	HILLSDALE: FIRST	147	151	90	0	80	24	3	0	0	0	5	7,626,124	368,818	16,842	16,842	772
38037	HILLSIDE	112	115	47	36	36	22	6	7	4	0	9	642,475	0	15,659	15,659	574
38038	HOWELL: FIRST	534	526	249	55	58	445	175	19	125	50	1	9,625,828	1,235,720	53,729	53,729	1,531
38039	HUDSON: FIRST	130	123	50	25	71	68	25	0	49	2	5	4,243,000	0	12,901	1,852	368
38040	IDA	83	86	22	36	0	42	2	0	24	0	2	470,556	0	11,556	11,556	329
38041	JACKSON: BROOKSIDE	143	145	82	36	29	30	33	0	0	0	3	2,578,603	0	20,865	16,692	797
38042	JACKSON: CALVARY	109	107	55	43	39	96	8	0	10	0	21	4,934,234	11,800	17,517	2,813	559
38043	JACKSON: FIRST	676	650	206	299	249	313	28	0	112	70	4	6,637,621	0	76,424	76,424	3,453

CONFERENCE Number	Amount PAID by the local church to the DISTRICT for all apportioned causes (if applicable) 29b	Church Benevolence Giving 30-38	Total ASKED for clergy pension 39a	Total PAID for clergy pension 39b	Base compensation paid to/for the Senior Pastor or other person assigned or appointed in the lead pastoral role to the church 41a	Base compensation paid to/for all Associate Pastor(s) and other pastoral staff assigned or appointed to the church; include deacons and other clergy in this role. 41b	Pastoral Benefits 40, 42a-44	Deacons salary/benefits 41c & 42c	Total amount paid in salary and benefits for all other church staff and diaconal ministers 45	Total amount spent for local church program expenses 46	Total amount spent for other local church operating expenses 47	Local Church capital expenses 48 & 49	TOTAL CHURCH EXPENSES (Sum of Lines 29a through 49) 50	Number of giving units 51	Total income for annual budget/spending plan 52	Total income for designated causes including capital campaign and other special projects 53	Total income from connectional and other institutional sources outside the local church 54
38025	189	0	1,060	1,060	8,625	0	4,141	0	9,174	1,914	20,158	0	46,949	0	49,755	20,000	0
38026	3,433	168,260	16,940	16,940	92,190	34,356	75,020	0	624,604	82,663	142,551	3,984,314	5,344,787	476	1,496,667	445,886	2,000
38027	686	8,314	8,330	8,330	67,915	21,671	19,677	0	25,600	6,108	42,290		224,664	114	229,958	10,269	1,900
38028	503	4,072	6,450	6,450	43,138	0	24,455	0	31,156	5,475	37,822	30,552	201,269	100	184,743	28,555	15,265
38029	302	5,743	4,750	575	39,322	0	10,180	0	3,300	470	27,452	2,400	90,641	61	76,823	17,830	52,189
38030	231	1,190	0	0	5,600	0	14,640	0		100	8,069	43,181	33,513	25	27,439	8,483	0
38031	615	8,694	0	0	14,124	0	19,209	0	12,334	2,702	35,476	29,806	150,972	71	130,176	23,665	5,100
38032	22	1,166			0	0	10,000	0		2,000	20,474	76,293	63,870	34	57,283	2,623	
38033	5,210	279	6,260	6,260	52,098	0	10,896	0	22,630	4,210	38,400	22,182	223,771	40	69,000	0	0
38034	481	6,537	6,090	6,090	51,000	0	33,064	0	29,128	786	33,024	995,636	187,140	70	191,366	1,165	0
38035	1,721	25,811	7,460	7,460	55,537	0	34,409	0	188,458	90,874	76,776	819,788	1,537,056	165	464,188	445,578	0
38036	772	33,977	10,428	10,428	55,615	0	22,072	0	213,294	32,736	138,009	11,167	1,343,533	68	143,134	599,900	0
38037	574	6,682	5,244	5,244	27,968	0	24,141	0	15,855	4,725	24,002	183,884	136,017	46	123,757	12,227	0
38038	1,532	18,534	9,070	9,070	64,635	0	17,635	0	217,692	25,110	92,573	15,000	684,394	268	495,206	298,105	21,000
38039	300	1,304	4,850	4,850	36,137	0	21,382	0	3,190	11,008	21,044	11,436	116,067	59	140,316	23,055	600
38040	0	3,014	2,140	2,140	16,023	0	13,623	0	11,451	5,000	16,902	0	91,145	33	98,587	6,137	0
38041	638	5,811	9,753	9,753	31,064	0	14,580	0	38,233	4,477	46,670	31,942	167,918	51	140,442	8,364	0
38042	91	5,711	0	0	17,600	0	19,930	0	52,506	483	50,239	174,233	181,315	75	118,196	45,882	0
38043	3,453	29,811	21,317	21,317	64,215	21,512	66,066	0	222,474	11,255	146,828		837,588	427	615,598	17,843	21,490

CONFERENCE Number	Church Name	Total professing members reported at the close of last year (1)	TOTAL PROFESSING MEMBERS reported at the close of this year (4)	Average attendance at all weekly worship services (7)	Total Baptized Members who have not become Professing Members (9)	Number of other constituents of the church (10)	TOTAL Christian Formation Group Participants (Total of lines 11a-d) (11)	Average weekly attendance (all ages) in Sunday Church School or other weekly education classes (13)	Membership in United Methodist Men (18a)	Membership in United Methodist Women (19a)	Number of persons sent out on UMVIM teams from this local church (20b)	Total Number of community ministries for outreach, justice, and mercy offered by this local church (21)	Value of church assets and buildings (24 & 25)	Church Debt (26 & 27)	Amount APPORTIONED to the local church by the CONFERENCE (28a)	Amount PAID by the local church to the CONFERENCE for all apportioned causes (29a)	Amount APPORTIONED to the local church by the DISTRICT (if applicable) (28b)
38044	JACKSON: TRINITY	50	48	33	3	10	22	16	9	0	0	0	4,024,415	0	7,856	6,547	298
38045	JACKSON: ZION	13	13	14	0	30	8	5	0	7	0	0	264,047	0	1,897	1,897	70
38046	JEROME	24	23	16	0	19	5	0	2	10	0	6	117,824	0	3,494	3,494	131
38047	JONESVILLE	118	112	52	0	20	23	15	0	0	0	4	818,703	0	10,378	946	640
38048	LAMBERTVILLE	420	408	141	24	250	66	4	0	0	0	2	4,135,481	0	29,901	29,901	852
38049	LA SALLE: ZION	76	76	35	18	0	0	11	0	15	0	4	1,810,000	0	5,246	5,246	150
38050	LEE CENTER	56	58	36	10	50	27	5	0	0	0	4	153,146	0	4,994	4,993	278
38051	LITCHFIELD	114	107	37	10	100	42	6	0	6	0	7	1,753,405	3,664	10,103	2,527	615
38052	LONDON	80	78	35	5	32	17	10	0	20	0	0	348,400	1,294	4,248	4,248	121
38053	LULU	34	32	11	0	0	6	2	0	0	0	1	672,905	0	2,377	2,377	68
38054	LYON LAKE	44	38	32	6	10	4	2	4	0	0	0	1,090,000	0	7,369	7,369	221
38055	MACON	84	59	40	20	11	0	8	15	0	0	4	1,180,000	0	9,571	9,571	273
38056	MANCHESTER: FIRST	174	172	69	56	22	52	13	0	25	0	11	1,058,145	132,460	21,236	21,236	605
38057	MANCHESTER: SHARON	132	129	48	17	40	42	12	0	15	1	16	584,290	0	15,908	13,522	453
38058	MARSHALL	456	451	278	2	220	252	26	0	0	10	21	10,696,700	596,906	42,158	42,158	2,349
38059	MILAN: MARBLE MEMORIAL	292	288	86	46	56	61	18	0	55	0	4	3,129,406	0	18,969	18,969	541
38060	MILFORD	269	242	99	105	122	40	4	0	35	1	3	1,261,098	177,554	31,450	31,450	896
38061	MONROE: CALVARY	58	57	31	4	8	8	8	0	0	0	0	1,775,950	0	9,755	9,755	278
38062	MONROE: FIRST	80	75	28	16	40	31	5	0	0	0	0	1,737,000	0	9,492	7,900	271

STATISTICAL INFORMATION

HG

CONFERENCE Number	29b Amount PAID to DISTRICT	30.38 Church Benevolence Giving	39a Total ASKED for clergy pension	39b Total PAID for clergy pension	41a Base comp Senior Pastor	41b Base comp Associate Pastors	40,42a-44 Pastoral Benefits	41c&42c Deacons salary/benefits	45 Salary/benefits all other staff	46 Local church program expenses	47 Other operating expenses	48&49 Local Church capital expenses	50 TOTAL CHURCH EXPENSES	51 Number of giving units	52 Total income annual budget	53 Total income designated causes	54 Total income connectional
38044	248	0	0	0	28,632	0	0	0	8,737	3,187	28,680	0	76,031	28	70,452	0	0
38045	70	1,570	0	0	6,172	0	47	0	0	418	12,619	0	22,793	14	14,334	4,575	0
38046	131	1,473	0	0	7,201	0	9,733	0	0	2,516	12,882	0	37,430	20	28,696	1,973	0
38047	54	370	0	0	20,196	0	13,262	0	14,880	1,625	20,664	0	71,997	62	75,849	3,503	0
38048	852	24,122	9,890	9,890	58,899	22,427	11,834	0	49,185	28,111	59,309	15,208	309,738	228	285,008	25,480	1,000
38049	150	22	2,380	2,380	19,341	0	5,375	0	2,970	865	12,488	0	48,837	27	47,031	12,952	0
38050	278	6,820	7,574	7,574	18,000	0	809	0	0	8,595	4,925	3,749	48,169	23	43,550	6,600	1,900
38051	153	870	0	0	14,135	0	22,446	0	14,212	3,312	23,067	7,037	95,333	41	100,670	32,602	0
38052	121	1,852	600	600	9,796	0	3,155	0	2,080	1,600	12,000	0	34,852	36	35,637	4,220	0
38053	68	234	0	0	9,400	0	600	0	0	75	5,000	0	18,354	12	18,488	1,015	0
38054	221	3,680	1,230	1,230	14,610	0	15,455	0	5,505	2,198	8,649	30,050	87,687	16	84,883	7,315	8,100
38055	285	3,493	4,750	4,750	20,000	0	6,931	0	0	564	15,292	2,512	59,878	51	73,747	4,102	0
38056	605	12,133	5,540	5,540	39,835	0	27,442	0	45,726	7,835	34,590	39,534	233,686	69	213,494	28,088	0
38057	453	8,653	10,041	10,041	51,639	0	8,518	0	17,686	4,812	31,040	49,504	191,367	81	188,901	193,078	0
38058	2,349	75,670	5,650	5,650	53,550	0	36,863	0	192,965	51,057	122,116	108,070	694,839	257	526,562	141,177	0
38059	541	5,265	7,250	7,250	47,600	0	26,101	0	29,175	2,950	46,681	14,667	197,599	122	163,263	16,346	0
38060	896	24,831	3,180	3,180	50,685	0	21,793	0	44,152	5,381	68,503	63,175	318,116	160	273,640	66,896	0
38061	278	2,427	2,660	2,660	25,500	0	8,150	0	11,930	1,025	30,782	0	93,027	29	98,902	1,835	2,250
38062	0	5,086	0	0	9,403	0	2	0	20,480	0	22,578	0	68,109	40	87,732	3,254	1,000

CONFERENCE Number	Church Name	Total professing members reported at the close of last year (1)	TOTAL PROFESSING MEMBERS reported at the close of this year (4)	Average attendance at all weekly worship services (7)	Total Baptized Members who have not become Professing Members (9)	Number of other constituents of the church (10)	TOTAL Christian Formation Group Participants (Total of lines 11a-d) (11)	Average weekly attendance (all ages) in Sunday Church School or other weekly education classes (13)	Membership in United Methodist Men (18a)	Membership in United Methodist Women (19a)	Number of persons sent out on UMVIM teams from this local church (20b)	Total Number of community ministries for outreach, justice, and mercy offered by this local church (21)	Value of church assets and buildings (24 & 25)	Church Debt (26 & 27)	Amount APPORTIONED to the local church by the CONFERENCE (28a)	Amount PAID by the local church to the CONFERENCE for all apportioned causes (29a)	Amount APPORTIONED to the local church by the DISTRICT (if applicable) (28b)
38063	MONROE: HERITAGE	41	44	34	23	18	31	10	0	0	0	0	594,300	178	3,637	1,910	104
38064	MONROE: ST PAUL'S	543	541	150	3	134	108	53	0	22	0	0	11,151,100	9,752	38,816	38,816	1,106
38065	MONTGOMERY	22	21	12	0	0	0	0	0	4	0	0	1,151,364	0	2,573	2,577	111
38066	MORENCI	87	90	45	0	11	34	20	0	0	0	5	3,025,620	32,387	8,923	0	254
38067	NAPOLEON	98	92	51	11	20	18	16	0	9	0	4	1,698,718	0	12,836	962	499
38068	NEW HUDSON	79	86	52	1	30	24	12	0	12	0	0	1,241,696	0	14,997	0	427
38069	NORTH ADAMS	48	47	24	24	42	43	4	10	8	0	0	183,030	13,799	6,375	3,721	231
38070	NORTH LAKE	115	114	50	0	39	26	10	26	41	15	5	1,428,028	0	12,016	12,016	342
38071	NORTH PARMA	79	75	20	24	10	26	16	45	0	0	0	539,710	0	6,798	3,399	403
38072	NORTHVILLE: FIRST	1,036	1,028	428	108	447	753	221	15	0	38	15	12,447,062	835,604	107,504	107,504	3,064
38073	NOVI	138	129	66	0	20	54	40	2	0	0	2	1,285,948	518,787	24,684	15,515	703
38074	OAK GROVE	95	93	47	17	23	96	19	10	53	0	8	1,610,719	0	12,091	0	345
38075	PETERSBURG	84	84	35	8	0	7	7	0	9	0	0	1,944,690	0	6,332	6,332	180
38076	PINCKNEY: ARISE	94	92	94	0	0	7	0	0	0	0	0	1,221,108	78,254	15,613	9,368	445
38077	PLEASANT LAKE	37	30	10	0	4	0	4	0	0	0	0	532,902	0	1,816	2,275	312
38078	PLYMOUTH: FIRST	625	596	272	43	97	324	66	0	0	0	8	11,491,657	0	111,730	111,730	3,185
38079	POPE	24	24	29	11	55	13	4	0	0	0	0	515,152	0	2,392	2,392	121
38080	QUINCY	56	53	53	0	51	30	14	0	0	0	0	674,130	0	10,362	10,362	323
38081	READING	111	111	73	22	56	50	34	0	26	0	11	2,913,398	0	13,676	13,676	574

STATISTICAL INFORMATION

HG

CONFERENCE Number	29b Amount PAID by the local church to the DISTRICT for all apportioned causes (if applicable)	30-38 Church Benevolence Giving	39a Total ASKED for clergy pension	39b Total PAID for clergy pension	41a Base compensation paid to/for the Senior Pastor or other person assigned or appointed in the lead pastoral role to the church	41b Base compensation paid to/for all Associate Pastor(s) and other pastoral staff assigned or appointed to the church, Include deacons and other clergy in this role	40, 42a-44 Pastoral Benefits	41c & 42c Deacons salary/benefits	45 Total amount paid in salary and benefits for all other church staff and diaconal ministers	46 Total amount spent for local church program expenses	47 Total amount spent for other local church operating expenses	48 & 49 Local Church capital expenses	50 TOTAL CHURCH EXPENSES (Sum of lines 29a through 49)	51 Number of giving units	52 Total income for annual budget/spending plan	53 Total income for designated causes including capital campaign and other special projects	54 Total income from connectional and other institutional sources outside the local church
38063	103	22	890	712	9,334	0	1,500	0	4,440	199	10,022	0	28,242	16	33,328	0	0
38064	1,106	15,204	6,490	6,490	47,332	0	31,494	0	109,790	10,080	85,832	73,887	420,031	182	312,791	119,155	0
38065	114	55,547	0	0	8,947	0	4,265	0	0	0	11,426	67,766	150,642	12	13,545	1,120,090	0
38066	254	460	2,020	1,414	16,940	0	14,926	0	10,443	437	15,043	3,894	63,811	20	55,770	465	7,873
38067	38	4,921	5,930	5,930	35,166	0	13,817	0	12,892	3,317	21,732	1,029	93,874	48	87,617	100,217	0
38068	427	361			53,768	0	19,339	0	16,948	258	31,332	5,903	134,266	85	126,395	19,652	850
38069	135	4,732			7,201	0	9,733	0	1,575	613	9,814	28,419	65,943	24	44,686	3,514	1,999
38070	0	8,859	4,780	4,780	40,637	0	7,038	0	10,827	4,844	17,040	172	106,213	73	115,307	23,072	21,500
38071	202	0	9,167	9,167	16,400	0	0	0	3,029	82	9,539	2,142	43,960	27	68,728	25	0
38072	3,064	50,565	15,100	15,100	101,900	32,750	26,472	0	494,267	67,694	198,902	223,135	1,321,353	505	1,194,295	185,171	35,500
38073	703	12,228	5,560	5,560	47,540	0	30,604	0	45,651	19,649	57,805	83,066	318,321	81	241,277	33,602	700
38074	345	5,029	5,740	5,740	38,983	0	13,930	0	8,606	1,023	20,728	632	95,016	35	105,157	5,227	0
38075	180	6,240	2,380	2,380	21,990	0	24,950	0	850	3,795	18,975	20,174	85,692	37	61,679	10,523	0
38076	530	2,877	6,850	6,850	49,881	0	0	0	19,649	6,200	22,140	0	137,669	108	133,240	1,713	0
38077	391	354	0	0	12,984	0	0	0	0	921	10,979	0	27,904	8	15,183	456	0
38078	3,185	43,216	17,090	17,090	84,523	45,379	52,180	0	287,052	54,570	156,770	44,561	900,256	302	925,478	37,287	15,136
38079	121	220	0	0	0	0	9,675	0	0	408	11,511	15,000	39,327	28	25,082	0	0
38080	323	9,102	0	0	2,000	0	20,952	0	21,128	5,503	10,664	50,880	130,914	92	60,922	44,623	0
38081	574	6,349	6,887	6,887	36,732	0	33,020	0	13,833	2,554	20,517	28,140	162,282	79	109,051	28,167	0

CONFERENCE Number	Church Name	1. Total professing members reported at the close of last year	4. TOTAL PROFESSING MEMBERS reported at the close of this year	7. Average attendance at all weekly worship services	9. Total Baptized Members who have not become Professing Members	10. Number of other constituents of the church	11a-b. TOTAL Christian Formation Group Participants (Total of lines)	12. Average weekly attendance (all ages) in Sunday Church School or other weekly education classes	18a. Membership in United Methodist Men	19a. Membership in United Methodist Women	20b. Number of persons sent out on UMVIM teams from this local church	21. Total Number of community ministries for outreach, justice, and mercy offered by this local church	24 & 25. Value of church assets and buildings	26 & 27. Church Debt	28a. Amount APPORTIONED to the local church by the CONFERENCE	29a. Amount PAID by the local church to the CONFERENCE for all apportioned causes	28b. Amount APPORTIONED to the local church by the DISTRICT (if applicable)
38082	ROLLIN CENTER	44	44	24	0	25	14	0	0	4	0	5	425,568	0	5,913	0	169
38083	SALEM GROVE	32	35	17	0	14	0	0	0	7	0	5	340,000	0	4,676	4,676	133
38084	SALINE: FIRST	704	706	329	105	647	449	162	0	30	29	29	10,386,385	0	86,198	86,198	2,457
38085	SAMARIA: GRACE	35	36	17	0	16	12	1	0	7	0	0	491,302	5,653	4,965	0	141
38086	SOMERSET CENTER	39	38	20	0	0	10	0	0	6	0	5	1,025,404	0	3,643	3,643	206
38087	SOUTH LYON: FIRST	593	614	253	127	206	477	142	79	74	26	23	5,610,459	341,149	49,939	49,939	1,423
38088	SOUTH ROCKWOOD	124	119	60	13	28	38	10	0	22	0	5	742,370	0	8,905	8,905	254
38089	SPRINGPORT	64	63	36	1	15	29	6	0	0	0	3	484,160	1,155	7,350	7,350	328
38090	SPRINGVILLE	145	142	35	40	56	10	5	0	15	0	0	919,533	0	5,759	5,468	164
38091	STOKES CHAPEL	18	18	29	0	0	0	11	0	14	0	0	427,572	0	4,193	4,193	96
38092	STONY CREEK	138	139	55	16	36	17	0	0	0	0	5	1,956,000	9,000	15,460	1,471	441
38093	TECUMSEH	260	269	61	0	12	16	12	0	0	0	0	6,468,946	174,575	21,036	8,964	600
38094	WALLED LAKE	156	145	59	19	30	33	16	0	8	16	2	1,578,000	0	26,523	4,095	756
38095	WATERLOO VILLAGE	53	56	17	0	30	7	5	0	0	0	6	511,227	0	3,937	3,937	425
38096	WELLSVILLE	38	38	25	6	15	0	12	0	6	0	0	275,000	0	4,216	0	120
38097	WESTON	106	104	50	4	20	36	20	0	43	0	1	738,905	0	6,334	6,334	180
38098	WILLOW	87	93	54	0	12	42	9	0	78	0	5	1,365,600	0	7,133	7,133	203
38099	YPSILANTI: FIRST	403	351	107	4	27	120	42	0	0	0	4	10,749,141	0	45,066	45,066	1,330
38100	YPSILANTI: LINCOLN CMNTY	63	58	44		23	37	13	0	0	4	3	3,421,490	0	10,334	10,334	295

STATISTICAL INFORMATION

HG

Column legend:
- 29b: Amount PAID by the local church to the DISTRICT for all apportioned causes (if applicable)
- 30-38: Church Benevolence Giving
- 39a: Total ASKED for clergy pension
- 39b: Total PAID for clergy pension
- 41a: Base compensation paid to/for the Senior Pastor or other person assigned or appointed in the lead pastoral role to the church
- 41b: Base compensation paid to/for all Associate Pastor(s) and other pastoral staff assigned or appointed to the church, include deacons and other clergy in this role.
- 40, 42a-44: Pastoral Benefits
- 41c & 42c: Deacons salary/benefits
- 45: Total amount paid in salary and benefits for all other church staff and diaconal ministers
- 46: Total amount spent for local church program expenses
- 47: Total amount spent for other local church operating expenses
- 48 & 49: local church capital expenses
- 50: TOTAL CHURCH EXPENSES (Sum of Lines 29a through 49)
- 51: Number of giving units
- 52: Total income for annual budget/spending plan
- 53: Total income for designated causes including capital campaign and other special projects
- 54: Total income from connectional and other institutional sources outside the local church

CONFERENCE Number	29b	30-38	39a	39b	41a	41b	40, 42a-44	41c & 42c	45	46	47	48 & 49	50	51	52	53	54
38082	169	508	2,260	2,260	18,500	0	14,104	0	2,380	2,390	5,990	0	46,301	27	46,023	2,528	0
38083	133	720	2,150	2,150	23,615	0	3,000	0	575	700	7,340	1,000	43,909	20	53,430	6,000	0
38084	2,457	58,023	8,310	8,310	63,075	0	29,786	0	310,369	58,679	159,792	31,239	807,928	421	740,318	106,872	2,500
38085	141	219	2,140	440	18,792	0	2,628	0	390	535	6,032	358	29,535	16	27,008	678	0
38086	206	305	1,748	1,748	9,322	28,202	8,920	0	6,457	32,250	20,562	8,798	59,461	21	27,115	0	20,000
38087	1,424	36,784	11,320	11,320	60,976	0	59,620	7,000	207,307	8,752	87,472	78,723	654,017	302	571,843	117,087	5,500
38088	254	692	3,180	3,180	25,500	0	1,150	0	3,000	90	9,220	8,248	75,901	37	74,818	53,157	0
38089	328	7,005	0	0	23,215	0	21,120	0	2,550	329	12,957	0	74,615	30	68,928	3,895	0
38090	0	1,236	2,330	2,330	18,985	0	1,100	0	0	350	9,850	1,739	41,037	51	39,365	0	0
38091	96	2,190	0	0	8,976	0	4,028	0		7,047	7,805	5,577	33,215	17	41,803	3,250	0
38092	540	1,599	4,770	4,770	39,000	0	31,039	0	12,451	3,766	42,434	45,089	186,440	48	123,695	34,869	43,250
38093	600	1,847	5,730	5,730	46,904	0	17,593	0	47,222	2,176	46,149	202,540	381,315	95	173,556	66,097	1,000
38094	756	9,341	4,320	4,320	36,136	0	30,765	0	52,241	180	44,967	34,518	219,315	75	180,946	1,935	0
38095	496	317	0	0	0	0	11,973	0	0	418	12,246	0	29,149	20	25,427	361	0
38096	0	24	580	580	11,172	0	1,300	0	5,340	12,171	13,650	13,676	27,144	22	43,088	270	0
38097	180	10,615	2,020	2,020	19,232	0	9,046	0	3,000	1,000	12,802	3,000	91,416	40	87,821	7,221	0
38098	248	16	740	740	27,720	0	3,300	0		33,139	8,000	10,111	54,157	30	67,000	500	0
38099	1,330	24,313	6,190	6,190	51,150	0	10,282	0	95,733	2,038	95,519	0	372,833	155	363,128	97,559	0
38100	295	2,040	4,890	4,890	40,181	0	11,461	0	10,084		46,335		127,658	41	117,414	10,615	0

CONFERENCE Number	Church Name	Total professing members reported at the close of last year (1)	TOTAL PROFESSING MEMBERS reported at the close of this year (4)	Average attendance at all weekly worship services (7)	Total Baptized Members who have not become Professing Members (9)	Number of other constituents of the church (10)	TOTAL Christian Formation Group Participants (Total of lines 11a-11d) (11)	Average weekly attendance (all ages) in Sunday Church School or other weekly education classes (13)	Membership in United Methodist Men (18a)	Membership in United Methodist Women (19a)	Number of persons sent out on UMVIM teams from this local church (20b)	Total Number of community ministries for outreach, justice, and mercy offered by this local church (21)	Value of church assets and buildings (24 & 25)	Church Debt (26 & 27)	Amount APPORTIONED to the local church by the CONFERENCE (28a)	Amount PAID by the local church to the CONFERENCE for all apportioned causes (29a)	Amount APPORTIONED to the local church by the DISTRICT (if applicable) (28b)
38101	YPSILANTI: ST MATTHEW'S	104	109	30	0	14	14	14	0	0	0	0	965,842	0	7,390	6,651	211
	HERITAGE DISTRICT TOTALS	19,931	19,562	8,981	2,526	6,416	9,909	2,814	710	1,995	393	461	299,598,411	14,641,572	2,245,665	1,858,319	70,789
	GREATER DETROIT DISTRICT																
39001	ALGONAC: TRINITY	89	83	45	1	22	11	2	10	10	0	2	2,706,280	9,770	8,218	1,282	972
39002	BEVERLY HILLS	70	72	37	0	26	20	5	0	11	1	1	2,551,000	0	12,106	12,106	813
39003	BIRMINGHAM: EMBURY	46	43	26	11	10	16	2	0	0	0	3	2,760,612	36,666	14,069	14,069	945
39004	BIRMINGHAM: FIRST	2,903	2,816	928	517	931	1,840	227	81	146	15	70	54,428,255	0	354,198	354,198	23,800
39005	BLOOMFIELD HLS: ST PAUL	69	68	37	10	26	17	11	12	12	0	0	4,572,995	0	16,510	1,995	1,110
39006	CLAWSON	107	79	30	0	27	34	8	0	18	0	3	2,262,962	0	23,406	5,313	1,572
39007	DEARBORN HTS: STEPHEN'S	61	0	28	0	14	13	0	0	0	0	0	0	7,073	8,897	0	598
39008	DEARBORN: FIRST	368	369	113	65	38	108	20	0	25	0	0	6,563,207	0	43,942	6,373	2,953
39009	DEARBORN: GOOD SHEPHERD	158	136	47	39	66	27	7	13	0	0	2	4,268,431	0	21,242	21,242	1,427
39010	DETROIT: CALVARY	156	140	49	0	0	4	6	0	8	0	4	4,612,300	30,183	11,854	686	796
39011	DETROIT: CASS CMNTY	100	97	77	11	10	48	14	8	7	0	0	7,729,400	233,862	15,887	15,887	1,067
39012	DETROIT: CENTRAL	277	273	86	3	46	71	17	8	24	0	0	13,722,749	183,501	60,481	0	4,064
39013	DETROIT: CENTRO FAMILIAR CRISTIANO	1	25	30	3	160	27	12	0	0	0	8	86,001	19,249	0	0	0
39014	DETROIT: CONANT AVE	138	129	56	0	0	87	59	13	45	0	0	955,000	18,423	28,449	2,200	1,911
39015	DETROIT: FORD MEM.	29	21	22	8	15	16	10	0	0	0	1	814,100	111,874	15,791	0	1,061

STATISTICAL INFORMATION

GD

CONFERENCE Number	29b Amount PAID by the local church to the DISTRICT for all apportioned causes (if applicable)	30-38 Church Benevolence Giving	39a Total ASKED for clergy pension	39b Total PAID for clergy pension	41a Base compensation paid to/for the Senior Pastor or other person assigned or appointed in the lead pastoral role to the church	41b Base compensation paid to/for all Associate Pastor(s) and other pastoral staff assigned or appointed to the church. Include deacons and other clergy in this role.	40, 42a-44 Pastoral Benefits	41c & 42c Deacons salary/benefits	45 Total amount paid in salary and benefits for all other church staff and diaconal ministers	46 Total amount spent for local church program expenses	47 Total amount spent for other local church operating expenses	48 & 49 Local Church capital expenses	50 TOTAL CHURCH EXPENSES (sum of lines 29a through 49)	51 Number of giving units	52 Total income for annual budget/spending plan	53 Total income for designated causes including capital campaign and other special projects	54 Total income from connectional and other institutional sources outside the local church
38101	211	3,086	2,750	2,475	22,468	0	6,637	51,986	11,168	2,211	23,353	1,830	80,090	60	75,798	7,241	2,500
	71,901	1,324,431	471,457	462,407	3,468,276	344,311	1,818,175	51,986	5,888,705	1,359,208	4,181,426	8,940,222	29,769,367	9,802	20,190,199	6,304,817	359,736
39001	972	1,154	2,310	2,310	19,043	0	2,868		8,444	1,114	13,607	18,640	69,434	37	54,835	984	0
39002	813	3,602	3,575	3,575	30,044	0	26,714		34,692	500	30,607	0	142,653	72	100,405	22,405	0
39003	945	1,156	1,110	1,110	13,187	0	2,484		41,304	2,293	39,754	5,955	122,257	25	126,694	966	0
39004	23,800	407,699	38,010	38,000	126,875	216,031	136,392		1,609,113	493,044	527,316	186,495	4,118,973	1,080	2,765,714	642,244	0
39005	1,110	762	2,200	2,200	16,479	500	20,019		33,654	3,660	36,269	9,000	125,148	33	119,774	6,306	0
39006	1,540	1,384	2,140	2,140	14,395	0	12,324		64,694	2,150	25,617	8,202	138,259	45	132,156	1,522	0
39007	0	35	3,390	2,448	20,641	0	7,650		8,300	500	18,000	0	57,574	48	49,994	2,185	0
39008	0	14,660	7,300	7,300	61,145	0	32,492		130,189	10,749	107,693	29,181	399,782	180	338,529	53,110	11,749
39009	1,427	12,901	4,750	4,750	38,391	0	11,547		26,959	15,287	49,211	4,288	186,003	54	131,938	30,907	0
39010	1,067	520	1,860	254	19,000	22,750	0		16,632	2,910	62,000	3,856	105,858	40	93,450	1,795	1,777
39011	1,064	3,618	8,280	8,280	47,791	0	34,284	2,400	51,760	250	47,791	55,748	291,626	41	146,557	75	57,500
39012	4,064	628	8,450	8,450	68,500	0	40,426	0	126,312	1,825	161,830	15,639	427,674	55	331,904	1,119	0
39013	0	0	4,840	3,872	3	0	12	0	3	3	3	3,423	3,896	3	15	12	10,055
39014	1,851	1,956	6,550	6,550	51,400	0	12,000	2,000	43,829	5,000	40,480	5,500	168,689	51	148,537	0	5,000
39015	0	0	440	0	9,000	0	2,000		8,943	200	48,414		76,057	12	30,214	15,153	4,500

STATISTICAL INFORMATION

GD

CONFERENCE Number	Church Name	Total professing members reported at the close of last year (1)	TOTAL PROFESSING MEMBERS reported at the close of this year (4)	Average attendance at all weekly worship services (7)	Total Baptized Members who have not become Professing Members (9)	Number of other constituents of the church (10)	TOTAL Christian Formation Group Participants (Total of lines 11a-d)	Average weekly attendance (all ages) in Sunday Church School or other weekly education classes (13)	Membership in United Methodist Men (18a)	Membership in United Methodist Women (19a)	Number of persons sent out on UMVIM teams from this local church (20b)	Total Number of community ministries for outreach, justice, and mercy offered by this local church (21)	Value of church assets and buildings (24 & 25)	Church Debt (26 & 27)	Amount APPORTIONED to the local church by the CONFERENCE (28a)	Amount PAID by the local church to the CONFERENCE for all apportioned causes (29a)	Amount APPORTIONED to the local church by the DISTRICT (if applicable) (28b)
39016	DETROIT: METROPOLITAN	355	356	235	37	91	77	39	6	43	3	17	33,824,984	228,000	67,052	3,000	4,505
39017	DETROIT: MT HOPE	56	56	31	0	2	23	12	0	6	0	6	80,000	32,695	12,345	0	830
39018	DETROIT: PEOPLE'S	101	71	31	0	4	19	10	0	20	0	2	456,000	82,409	22,920	0	1,540
39019	DETROIT: RESURRECTION	115	114	40	0	0	33	20	0	0	0	0	2,010,000	12,493	9,364	0	629
39020	DETROIT: SCOTT MEMORIAL	367	327	160	4	135	78	30	47	70	0	5	1,055,000	179,602	38,305	6,961	2,588
39021	DETROIT: SECOND GRACE	425	367	146	4	7	364	57	52	43	0	3	5,658,280	760,366	29,944	6,000	2,012
39022	DETROIT: ST PAUL	100	98	43	0	0	16	8	9	19	0	3	550,000	54,581	8,617	1,394	579
39023	DETROIT: ST TIMOTHY	79	76	38	0	0	0	8	5	19	0	0	305,214	48,786	20,980	2,500	1,409
39024	DETROIT: TRINITY-FAITH	149	155	56	3	25	40	13	20	27	0	7	2,437,800	137,564	21,224	17,220	1,426
39025	DOWNRIVER	267	234	95	0	60	45	15	0	16	0	0	3,292,428	500,000	22,960	16,603	1,543
39026	EASTPOINTE: IMMANUEL	140	135	90	2	41	22	10	0	0	0	3	2,750,000	60,000	16,603	16,603	1,115
39027	FARMINGTON: FIRST	375	366	163	45	23	83	40	40	51	11	34	4,339,592	231,707	50,123	26,626	3,367
39028	FARMINGTON: NARDIN PARK	803	792	195	39	158	282	21	0	0	0	0	8,313,570	0	75,796	34,000	3,589
39029	FARMINGTON: ORCHARD	635	645	267	171	262	370	101	0	0	0	13	7,376,392	452,601	75,288	75,288	3,565
39030	FERNDALE: FIRST	165	158	56	130	70	76	14	0	40	0	24	7,758,067	0	28,450	6,056	1,911
39031	FLAT ROCK: FIRST	167	168	80	18	38	74	31	14	27	0	7	3,861,903	0	20,107	20,107	1,351
39032	FRANKLIN: COMMUNITY	233	207	77	19	24	50	10	0	30	0	1	5,075,063	0	39,707	15,000	2,668
39033	FRASER: CHRIST	204	194	158	65	50	107	70	0	25	0	10	3,960,200	0	36,197	0	2,432
39034	GARDEN CITY: FIRST	134	132	70	0	25	19	8	12	24	0	0	3,103,873	180,888	16,469	2,650	1,107

Column key:
- 29b: Amount PAID by the local church to the DISTRICT for all apportioned causes (if applicable)
- 30–38: Church Benevolence Giving
- 39a: Total ASKED for clergy pension
- 39b: Total PAID for clergy pension
- 41a: Base compensation paid to/for the Senior Pastor or other person assigned or appointed in the lead pastoral role to the church
- 41b: Base compensation paid to/for all Associate Pastor(s) and other pastoral staff assigned or appointed to the church. Include deacons and other clergy in this role.
- 40, 42a–44: Pastoral Benefits
- 41c & 42c: Deacons salary/benefits
- 45: Total amount paid in salary and benefits for all other church staff and diaconal ministers
- 46: Total amount spent for local church program expenses
- 47: Total amount spent for other local church operating expenses
- 48 & 49: Local Church capital expenses
- 50: TOTAL CHURCH EXPENSES (Sum of Lines 29a through 49)
- 51: Number of giving units
- 52: Total income for annual budget/spending plan
- 53: Total income for designated causes including capital campaign and other special projects
- 54: Total income from connectional and other institutional sources outside the local church

CONFERENCE Number	29b	30–38	39a	39b	41a	41b	40,42a–44	41c&42c	45	46	47	48&49	50	51	52	53	54
39016	4,505	37,479	5,320	5,320	78,373	0	14,984	0	196,787	15,272	295,331	133,400	784,451	70	384,806	316,939	0
39017	0	0	860		9,000	0	0	0	22,000	300	40,000	3,000	74,300	30	67,969	838	0
39018	651	200	2,270	2,270	21,692	0	9,307	0	11,050	18,944	51,738	4,129	119,781	35	115,670	0	0
39019	0	1,510	1,930		19,708	0	0	0	14,000	3,225	18,600	8,000	63,733	1	86,800	0	0
39020	2,588	14,027	7,330	7,330	60,000	0	29,854	0	102,322	4,207	88,456	15,992	319,220	150	271,882	50,125	2,500
39021	2,012	92	10,310	10,310	85,643	0	13,718	0	35,485	38,241	80,980	50,160	336,576	151	291,146	16,700	16,523
39022	1,872	827	1,490	1,189	11,000	0	1,500	0	18,300	650	24,661	0	59,264	63	69,041	173	0
39023	497	1,544	2,180	109	16,429	0	0	0	20,629	413	36,769	0	77,067	110	66,405	3,544	821
39024	1,426	2,214	5,020	5,020	42,047	0	16,153	0	38,328	10,486	48,040	7,200	172,744	72	167,720	62,946	2,001
39025	1,543	616	7,150	7,150	48,025	0	17,597	0	45,479	12,728	41,104	13,750	206,810	110	157,814	0	10,000
39026	1,115	19,416	4,480	4,480	37,337	0	20,268	0	23,127	2,389	36,584	0	142,519	135	133,561	7,165	0
39027	2,973	19,588	7,950	7,155	65,000	30,110	38,594	0	198,832	14,960	129,466	91,436	594,458	200	413,577	2,107,721	0
39028	5,093	21,283	12,690	12,690	80,000	29,881	26,227	0	232,454	35,680	200,948	167,045	843,835	341	651,480	152,635	0
39029	3,565	4,735	12,710	12,710	68,943	0	53,114	0	200,622	60,141	168,813	145,564	839,924	328	677,284	18,890	0
39030	1,947	11,839	7,150	6,435	59,698	0	24,305	0	45,193	4,171	91,111	23,470	267,121	55	204,041	14,937	0
39031	1,351	6,002	4,280	4,280	36,400	0	6,819	0	29,259	9,311	66,009	41,530	226,905	134	216,279	6,128	0
39032	2,668	22,935	6,140	6,140	51,500	0	23,596	0	129,281	5,745	70,038	8,789	318,759	98	320,120	3,880	0
39033	2,431	0	7,110	7,110	61,753	0	28,128	0	88,559	7,033	56,686	43,500	318,135	195	361,231	2,000	20,000
39034	795		4,210	3,810	28,676	0	24,000	0	30,800	2,725	40,000	35,000	168,456	98	145,000		0

STATISTICAL INFORMATION

GD

CONFERENCE Number	Church Name	1. Total professing members reported at the close of last year	4. TOTAL PROFESSING MEMBERS reported at the close of this year	7. Average attendance at all weekly worship services	9. Total Baptized Members who have not become Professing Members	10. Number of other constituents of the church	11a-d. TOTAL Christian Formation Group Participants (Total of lines 11a-d)	13. Average weekly attendance (all ages) in Sunday Church School or other weekly education classes	18a. Membership in United Methodist Men	19a. Membership in United Methodist Women	20b. Number of persons sent out on UMVIM teams from this local church	21. Total Number of community ministries for outreach, justice, and mercy offered by this local church	24 & 25. Value of church assets and buildings	26 & 27. Church Debt	28a. Amount APPORTIONED to the local church by the CONFERENCE	29a. Amount PAID by the local church to the CONFERENCE for all apportioned causes	29b. Amount APPORTIONED to the local church by the DISTRICT (if applicable)
39035	GROSSE POINTE	556	570	171	71	77	224	56	6	118	81	1	6,039,606	0	67,060	67,060	4,505
39036	HARPER WOODS: REDEEMER	71	60	41	0	17	5	10	0	0	0	16	2,841,272	0	18,525	18,525	1,245
39037	HAZEL PARK: FIRST	61	54	34	16	20	15	14	0	0	0	2	1,515,000	0	8,136	8,136	546
39038	HOWARTH	43	41	31	8	38	8	4	0	8	0	2	109,220	0	6,321	6,321	724
39039	LIVONIA: CLARENCEVILLE	117	111	73	8	39	99	54	0	0	0	10	7,525,424	3,150	33,410	0	2,245
39040	LIVONIA: NEWBURG	557	560	210	109	132	493	107	0	4	95	27	8,595,919	57,732	47,830	38,188	2,265
39041	LIVONIA: ST MATTHEW'S	421	419	91	57	0	136	50	0	63	0	4	4,850,000	19,500	30,084	30,084	2,021
39042	MACOMB: FAITH	52	50	34	0	9	62	6	0	14	0	0	1,475,234	0	4,556	4,556	522
39043	MADISON HTS	61	58	45	0	13	24	18	5	0	0	5	1,719,000	28,724	9,149	5,934	615
39044	MADISON HTS: KOREAN FIRST CENTRAL	184	176	107	0	0	196	15	0	0	0	1	3,390,000	1,019,395	32,568	13,250	2,188
39045	MADISON HTS: VIETNAMESE MINISTRY	29	38	15	0	152	13	0	0	14	16	0	1,200	0	0	0	0
39046	MT CLEMENS: FIRST	308	277	120	0	5	92	8	0	14	0	5	1,150,000	383,821	32,427	18,491	4,481
39047	MT VERNON	61	59	20	58	32	11	3	5	0	0	2	1,148,668	174,500	9,278	9,278	1,062
39048	NEW BALTIMORE: GRACE	199	193	121	0	0	140	55	15	9	0	4	2,164,083	266,000	28,075	10,748	3,215
39049	OMO: ZION	74	74	28	0	10	0	0	1	2	0	4	140,000	0	1,952	1,952	224
39050	PAINT CREEK	60	54	34	0	48	14	5	0	10	0	0	880,700	0	5,491	5,491	629
39051	PONTIAC: GRACE AND PEACE CMNTY	113	111	25	18	34	33	7	37	32	0	2	1,844,800	0	10,631	0	834
39052	PONTIAC: ST JOHN	118	107	57	5	900	134	53	0	56	0	13	1,513,222	1,400	23,309	7,700	1,829
39053	REDFORD: ALDERSGATE	378	341	219	0	0	0	0	0	0	0	28	7,159,987	0	55,644	4,500	3,739

STATISTICAL INFORMATION

GD

CONFERENCE Number	29b Amount Paid by the local church to the DISTRICT for all apportioned causes (if applicable)	30-38 Church Benevolence Giving	39a Total ASKED for clergy pension	39b Total PAID for clergy pension	41a Base compensation paid to/for the Senior Pastor or other person assigned or appointed in the lead pastoral role to the church	41b Base compensation paid to/for all Associate Pastor(s) and other pastoral staff assigned or appointed to the church, include deacons and other clergy in this role.	40, 42a-44 Pastoral Benefits	41c & 42c Deacons salary/benefits	45 Total amount paid in salary and benefits for all other church staff and diaconal ministers	46 Total amount spent for local church program expenses	47 Total amount spent for other local church operating expenses	48 & 49 Local church capital expenses	50 TOTAL CHURCH EXPENSES (Sum of Lines 29a through 49)	51 Number of giving units	52 Total income for annual budget/spending plan	53 Total income for designated causes including capital campaign and other special projects	54 Total income from connectional and other institutional sources outside the local church
39035	4,505	37,330	13,590	13,590	74,800	41,000	24,539	0	133,234	21,368	175,106	113,012	705,544	187	603,616	159,233	2,000
39036	1,245	4,223	4,650	4,650	38,140	0	6,418	0	44,980	2,955	56,031	46,100	223,267	39	191,046	24,574	0
39037	546	251	2,200	2,200	18,479	0	8,085	0	19,114	3,517	19,686	26,972	103,469	35	85,694	710	0
39038	724	2,494	1,720	1,720	17,940	0	480	0	9,908		20,422	26,469	89,995	23	54,247	118,261	0
39039	2,245	6,111	5,710	5,710	48,523	0	29,799	25,847	39,966	41,616	76,155	25,843	275,968	66	207,514	63,173	0
39040	2,265	51,201	8,860	8,860	64,288	0	35,322	0	154,893	9,014	81,156	89,640	560,674	307	432,972	66,779	0
39041	2,021	10,629	6,270	6,270	52,813	0	30,131	0	55,364	8,717	89,204	7,770	293,003	134	285,407	1,930	0
39042	522	238	1,290	1,290	20,580	0	930	0	0	987	12,783	0	41,886	17	35,928	8,568	0
39043	477	1,119	2,220	2,220	18,484	0	2,000	0	12,762	4,000	25,000	5,114	77,110	50	82,050	2,600	0
39044	0	10,669	7,830	7,830	46,500	26,392	35,281	0	31,119	62,270	71,884	46,295	351,490	0	372,016	0	45,000
39045	0	0	0	0	26,643	0	14,800	0	0	8,600	1	3,600	53,644	15	13,464	0	17,000
39046	4,481	62,392	8,900	8,900	56,000	20,991	24,003	0	45,036	25,481	87,278	128,915	481,968	203	371,559	119,109	1,500
39047	0	3,877	2,640	2,640	17,760	0	9,850	0	5,420	675	18,300	500	68,300	38	75,806	16,037	0
39048	3,880	7,511	6,360	6,360	48,010	0	15,757	0	66,841	6,210	34,309	39,340	238,966	121	232,734	6,703	0
39049	224	134	880	880	9,000	0		0	0	2,414	2,672	0	14,862	17	11,350	0	0
39050	629	6,284	1,720	1,720	17,945	0	605	0	10,528	30,208	15,409	58,626	119,651	40	47,933	20,291	0
39051	0	1,080	2,150	215	10,310	0	4,482	0	1,128	5,653	36,098	1,501	85,022	27	62,954	876	21,000
39052	2,326	1,484	5,670	5,670	45,720	0	16,565	0	47,937	7,917	37,495	78,780	249,305	87	123,287	54,580	0
39053	2,898	0	6,970	6,970	45,000	15,000	20,130	0	123,935		71,877	1,902	300,129	232	234,344	6,565	0

STATISTICAL INFORMATION

GD

CONFERENCE Number	Church Name	1 — Total professing members reported at the close of last year	4 — TOTAL PROFESSING MEMBERS reported at the close of this year	7 — Average attendance at all weekly worship services	9 — Total Baptized Members who have not become Professing Members	10 — Number of other constituents of the church	11a-d — TOTAL Christian Formation Group Participants (Total of lines)	13 — Average weekly attendance (all ages) in Sunday Church School or other weekly education classes	18a — Membership in United Methodist Men	19a — Membership in United Methodist Women	20b — Number of persons sent out on UMVIM teams from this local church	21 — Total Number of community ministries for outreach, justice, and mercy offered by this local church	24 & 25 — Value of church assets and buildings	26 & 27 — Church Debt	28a — Amount APPORTIONED to the local church by the CONFERENCE	29a — Amount PAID by the local church to the CONFERENCE for all apportioned causes	28b — Amount APPORTIONED to the local church by the DISTRICT (if applicable)
39054	REDFORD: NEW BEGINNINGS	25	23	20	0	15	17	15	0	0	0	0	2,027,000	4,972	10,772	0	724
39055	RIVERVIEW	87	84	28	9	20	9	9	0	0	0	0	1,084,000	0	9,745	7,309	654
39056	ROCHESTER HLS: ST LUKE'S	156	143	59	16	50	4	6	10	7	0	0	2,932,768	0	33,234	0	2,233
39057	ROCHESTER: ST PAUL'S	2,207	2,182	544	453	444	798	53	75	186	21	2	13,044,630	0	159,888	91,516	10,743
39058	ROMULUS: COMMUNITY	74	72	35	0	16	7	7	0	0	0	0	2,603,500	15,032	16,195	5,000	1,088
39059	ROSEVILLE: TRINITY	179	173	104	44	22	54	60	8	45	0	3	3,381,039	1,626,242	29,730	20,838	1,998
39060	ROYAL OAK: FIRST	665	771	399	156	526	341	32	241	61	0	1	9,162,096	4,544,481	72,484	36,242	4,870
39061	SOUTHFIELD: HOPE	960	1,018	431	0	0	121	45	3	429	27	50	14,594,602	23,343	225,528	30,000	15,153
39062	STERLING HEIGHTS: FIRST	66	66	23	148	24	10	6	0	14	0	3	1,333,999	306,572	10,980	2,000	738
39063	TRENTON: FAITH	546	442	199	21	217	139	24	0	232	0	2	2,293,857	0	34,809	34,809	2,339
39064	TRENTON: FIRST	101	105	46	61	67	32	8	10	51	0	4	2,830,000	0	15,191	12,153	1,020
39065	TROY: BIG BEAVER	360	350	177	2	89	143	41	32	71	0	10	3,400,400	1,685,000	39,406	39,406	2,648
39066	TROY: FIRST	407	402	166	0	66	235	71	474	575	0	25	10,348,284	2,191,738	43,901	31,050	2,078
39067	TROY: KOREAN	1,090	1,111	1,340	123	0	1,101	360	26	41	38	7	9,690,165	20,081	123,593	123,593	8,304
39068	UTICA	304	281	186	32	73	181	160	0	78	0	17	9,357,240	0	59,448	59,448	3,994
39069	WARREN: FIRST	264	265	107	0	19	111	19	0	0	0	0	4,698,000	0	34,558	34,558	2,322
39070	WASHINGTON	36	37	26	0	27	0	0	0	0	0	0	115,000	0	3,668	3,668	420
39071	WATERFORD: CENTRAL	482	454	169	95	791	218	40	0	0	0	15	17,205,402	15,207	74,172	34,171	7,575
39072	WATERFORD: FOUR TOWNS	36	20	20	0	37	0	0	0	8	0	0	861,590		4,043	2,830	317

CONFERENCE Number	29b Amount PAID to DISTRICT for all apportioned causes	30-38 Church Benevolence Giving	39a Total ASKED for clergy pension	39b Total PAID for clergy pension	41a Base compensation lead Pastor	41b Base compensation Associate Pastor(s)/other pastoral staff	40,42a-44 Pastoral Benefits	41c & 42c Deacons salary/benefits	45 Salary & benefits all other church staff/diaconal	46 Local church program expenses	47 Other local church operating expenses	48 & 49 Local church capital expenses	50 TOTAL CHURCH EXPENSES	51 Number of giving units	52 Income annual budget/spending plan	53 Income designated causes/capital campaign	54 Income connectional/other institutional
39054	720	360	2,470	0	25,964	0	26	0	5,200	1,200	30,002	6,500	69,972	28	67,253	0	0
39055	461	234	2,400	2,400	20,000	0	2,908	0	10,000	800	12,000	0	56,112	40	70,100	700	0
39056	0	0	5,870	5,870	51,000	0	48,377	0	44,989	600	43,266	940	195,042	122	15,019	6,102	0
39057	0	64,072	22,720	22,720	95,543	96,092	114,690	0	561,403	145,264	281,502	152,262	1,625,064	738	1,349,373	383,206	0
39058	1,090	274	2,550	2,550	20,766	0	2,665	0	20,466	7,965	30,480	30,202	119,768	59	135,439	831	0
39059	4,870	3,649	5,620	5,620	45,204	0	18,233	0	41,536	4,103	43,094	5,356	188,723	422	185,414	49,465	0
39060	0	23,122	12,670	12,670	65,100	71,534	49,852	70,415	280,615	49,229	371,260	1,050,202	2,013,577	800	1,145,102	97,334	20,000
39061	738	11,416	17,110	11,625	95,275	0	501,782	0	404,577	150,000	400,000	485,302	2,161,511	28	1,565,958	2,205	0
39062	2,339	331	3,310	3,310	38,557	0	15,272	0	13,370	1,316	21,827	4,485	101,206	199	89,869	64,951	0
39063	1,020	16,147	5,990	5,990	49,939	0	16,246	0	102,049	14,410	66,736	62,115	370,780	64	363,867	6,629	0
39064	2,648	3,330	7,090	4,080	33,695	0	23,764	0	35,912	3,594	22,576	0	140,124	164	144,453	70,842	0
39065	2,950	21,713	7,090	7,090	61,000	0	19,247	0	112,597	18,013	76,320	79,137	437,171	178	336,993	30,877	0
39066	8,304	14,805	7,110	7,110	59,303	165,682	44,029	0	125,499	24,076	158,469	135,358	602,649		513,936	0	0
39067	3,994	21,038	27,650	27,650	53,000	0	315,997	0	77,773	279,765	208,437	200,360	1,481,599	603	1,592,268	0	0
39068	2,322	41,489	8,540	8,540	69,870	0	16,718	0	121,330	26,524	133,489	51,929	533,331	229	468,931	35,068	6,253
39069	420	11,418	6,300	6,300	51,028	0	19,467	0	88,598	5,630	73,952	23,800	317,073	124	246,214	15,747	10,000
39070	6,576	716	980	980	10,000	0	0	0	3,369	0	10,224	0	29,377	17	36,060	0	0
39071	0	28,110	14,830	14,830	75,084	0	51,302	44,859	233,436	11,445	191,478	77,317	768,608	301	630,891	79,900	0
39072	0	2,008	860	860	10,000	0	4,133	0	12,935	300	23,190	0	56,256	20	23,326	0	0

STATISTICAL INFORMATION

GD

CONFERENCE Number	Church Name	Total professing members reported at the close of last year (1)	TOTAL PROFESSING MEMBERS reported at the close of this year (4)	Average attendance at all weekly worship services (7)	Total Baptized Members who have not become Professing Members (9)	Number of other constituents of the church (10)	TOTAL Christian Formation Group Participants (Total of lines 11a-d) (11)	Average weekly attendance (all ages) in Sunday Church School or other weekly education classes (13)	Membership in United Methodist Men (16a)	Membership in United Methodist Women (19a)	Number of persons sent out on UMVIM teams from this local church (20b)	Total Number of community ministries for outreach, justice, and mercy offered by this local church (21)	Value of church assets and buildings (24 & 25)	Church Debt (26 & 27)	Amount APPORTIONED to the local church by the CONFERENCE (28a)	Amount PAID by the local church to the CONFERENCE for all apportioned causes (29a)	Amount APPORTIONED to the local church by the DISTRICT (if applicable) (29b)
39073	WATERFORD: TRINITY	41	41	41	6	10	10	2	0	0	0	3	804,000	0	7,388	7,388	755
39074	WAYNE-WESTLAND: FIRST	134	78	39	22	51	8	4	0	43	0	0	1,860,000	0	19,666	5,000	1,321
39075	WEST BLOOMFIELD	153	154	65	19	75	78	20	19	0	7	5	3,023,547	32,532	18,512	18,512	1,244
39076	WESTLAND: ST JAMES	79	80	35	0	21	32	4	0	19	0	3	444,118	51,116	9,556	600	642
39077	WYANDOTTE: FIRST	315	297	143	0	56	123	36	0	54	0	48	5,997,017	0	34,895	34,895	2,344
	GREATER DETROIT DISTRICT TOTALS	21,672	21,004	9,501	2,754	6,643	9,588	2,395	1,304	3,024	317	557	381,397,247	16,082,781	2,763,309	1,553,956	189,668
Closed	MICHIGAN CONFERENCE	441	0	158	0	41	61	19	4	21	0	0	1,900,368	1,631	49,207	1,827	2,355
NS	NORTHERN SKIES DISTRICT TOTALS	6,101	6,021	2,611	618	1,648	1,657	550	79	568	29	159	79,554,766	573,189	488,437	400,992	81,939
NW	NORTHERN WATERS DISTRICT TOTALS	9,755	9,453	5,217	1,085	4,395	3,455	919	138	1,173	102	210	97,516,105	2,435,486	1,104,768	844,865	74,044
CB	CENTRAL BAY DISTRICT TOTALS	12,799	12,515	5,745	1,061	3,498	4,777	1,591	376	1,351	98	366	163,735,837	2,351,961	1,322,654	1,027,056	124,717
MW	MIDWEST DISTRICT TOTALS	16,008	15,393	9,633	1,501	8,214	10,238	4,438	252	1,194	174	360	222,368,405	5,949,933	2,182,181	1,744,196	234,584
MM	MID-MICHIGAN DISTRICT TOTALS	11,597	11,080	6,262	1,032	5,818	6,136	1,805	347	1,317	37	296	193,737,008	3,027,364	1,531,594	1,258,382	88,840
EW	EAST WINDS DISTRICT TOTALS	15,062	14,704	6,737	2,509	5,430	5,938	1,888	630	1,879	147	410	221,253,134	9,986,694	1,553,025	1,177,869	141,514
GS	GREATER SOUTHWEST DISTRICT TOTALS	13,523	12,969	6,682	1,503	6,102	5,549	1,868	172	1,090	130	416	220,581,332	4,794,057	1,667,653	1,281,112	115,413
HG	HERITAGE DISTRICT TOTALS	19,931	19,562	8,981	2,526	6,416	9,909	2,814	710	1,995	393	461	299,598,411	14,641,572	2,245,666	1,858,319	70,789
GD	GREATER DETROIT DISTRICT TOTALS	21,672	21,004	9,501	2,754	6,643	9,588	2,395	1,304	3,024	317	557	381,397,247	16,082,781	2,763,309	1,553,956	189,668
Totals	MICHIGAN CONFERENCE TOTALS	126,889	122,701	61,527	14,589	48,205	57,308	18,287	4,012	13,612	1,427	3,235	1,881,642,613	59,844,668	14,908,493	11,148,574	1,123,863

CONFERENCE Number	29b Amount PAID by the local church to the DISTRICT for all apportioned causes (if applicable)	30-38 Church Benevolence Giving	39a Total ASKED for clergy pension	39b Total PAID for clergy pension	41a Base compensation paid to/for the Senior Pastor or other person assigned or appointed in the lead pastoral role to the church	41b Base compensation paid to/for all Associate Pastor(s) and other pastoral staff assigned or appointed to the church. Include deacons and other clergy in this role.	40, 42a-44 Pastoral Benefits	41c & 42c Deacons salary/benefits	45 Total amount paid in salary and benefits for all other church staff and diaconal ministers	46 Total amount spent for local church program expenses	47 Total amount spent for other local church operating expenses	48 & 49 Local Church capital expenses	50 TOTAL CHURCH EXPENSES (Sum of Lines 29a through 49)	51 Number of giving units	52 Total income for annual budget/spending plan	53 Total income for designated causes including capital campaign and other special projects	54 Total income from connectional and other institutional sources outside the local church
39073	755	2,795	2,150	2,150	18,120	0	9,162	0	10,200	3,345	16,426	9,050	79,391	36	68,213	1,331	1,500
39074	0	2,679	4,120	4,120	29,832	0	14,733	0	21,192	9,000	54,979	0	141,535	91	125,064	41,708	0
39075	1,244	15,256	5,690	5,690	47,158	0	24,027	0	28,014	12,563	23,712	3,948	180,124	82	167,296	12,615	0
39076	452	95	2,180	900	21,850	0	3,180	0	0	7,243	20,341	700	55,361	29	53,323	49	5,000
39077	2,344	15,567	6,450	6,450	55,428	735,963	35,698	145,521	124,243	19,926	56,900	58,620	410,071	149	319,239	21,067	0
	146,856	1,122,033	474,155	451,957	3,196,769	735,963	2,319,461	145,521	6,968,803	1,824,019	6,095,452	4,275,854	28,836,619	10,313	22,610,064	5,134,020	271,679
Closed	905	6,848	10,357	4,407	37,518	0	5,144	0	9,595	709	29,490	3,131	99,574	161	111,279	100	0
NS	79,457	325,518	152,804	152,086	1,215,463	56,657	595,712	0	645,488	156,380	992,315	407,117	5,027,285	2,924	4,631,779	442,767	79,027
NW	61,781	589,444	376,066	360,137	2,102,477	159,883	1,279,864	0	1,863,446	368,505	1,915,439	1,282,196	10,828,118	5,159	8,917,894	1,618,685	182,770
CB	111,263	781,600	330,775	320,121	2,484,936	66,450	1,315,865	1,453	2,580,209	730,484	2,399,562	2,058,749	13,877,733	7,997	11,896,547	1,284,119	124,769
MW	197,141	1,293,585	530,692	521,106	3,015,533	112,663	1,733,741	0	5,059,118	1,215,184	3,725,409	2,840,772	21,458,448	8,377	17,372,540	3,728,334	144,300
MM	74,114	921,600	404,696	397,923	2,418,837	85,050	1,377,750	17,040	3,166,176	583,690	2,796,259	2,215,450	15,312,171	6,245	12,820,557	3,508,283	164,244
EW	133,819	762,190	378,175	373,595	2,917,793	233,590	1,264,819	46,654	3,040,755	577,124	3,009,086	5,438,820	18,975,884	6,990	13,746,164	2,205,967	178,907
GS	91,794	962,203	427,584	424,446	2,692,586	169,685	1,640,556	68,796	2,923,397	722,300	3,248,323	2,551,036	16,776,234	6,567	12,785,903	2,674,653	68,353
HG	71,901	1,324,431	471,457	462,407	3,468,276	344,311	1,818,175	51,986	5,888,705	1,359,208	4,181,426	8,940,222	29,769,367	9,802	20,190,199	6,304,817	359,736
GD	146,856	1,122,033	474,155	451,957	3,196,769	735,963	2,319,461	145,521	6,968,803	1,824,019	6,095,452	4,275,854	28,836,619	10,313	22,610,064	5,134,020	271,679
Totals	969,031	8,089,452	3,556,761	3,468,185	23,550,288	1,964,252	13,351,168	331,450	32,145,692	7,537,603	28,392,761	30,013,347	160,961,433	64,535	125,082,926	26,901,745	1,573,785

MICHIGAN CONFERENCE PLAN OF ORGANIZATION

The Michigan Conference equips and connects through:
Christ-Centered Mission and Ministry;
Bold and Effective Leaders;
Vibrant Congregations.

§ 1   AGENCIES RELATING TO CHRIST-CENTERED MISSION AND MINISTRY

1.1   COMMISSION ON THE ANNUAL CONFERENCE SESSION
    1.1.1   Purpose – Arrange and plan the annual conference session.
    1.1.2   Duties.
        1.1.2.1   Manage the order and flow of the entire annual conference session,
including business/plenary sessions, for all matters.
        1.1.2.2   Facilitate the business sessions of the annual conference.
        1.1.2.3   Coordinate the daily schedule of the annual conference business sessions.
        1.1.2.4   Plan, coordinate, and implement the worship and program content of the annual conference session.
        1.1.2.5   Appoint the following for the annual conference session:
            1.1.2.5.1   Worship planning task force in consultation with the Worship Coordinator.
            1.1.2.5.2   Any other people or task forces as the commission may deem necessary.
        1.1.2.6   Ensure the Committee on the Journal (§ 1.3, below), which is amenable to it, is fulfilling its responsibilities pursuant to *The Book of Discipline* and the Plan of Organization and direction of the annual conference.
        1.1.2.7   Executive Committee duties: implement the actions of the full commission between sessions of the full commission; interface with all vendors; establish and monitor annual budget; assist chairperson as requested in setting agenda for full commission.
    1.1.3   Membership.
        1.1.3.1   Eight voting members shall be nominated by the Committee on Nominations, in consultation with the Executive Team, who shall be either clergy members of the annual conference or lay people who are members of a local church within the annual conference.
        1.1.3.2   Annual Conference Coordinator/Coordinator for Event Planning.
            1.1.3.2.1   Gives project management assistance to the Commission.
            1.1.3.2.2   Creates systems for event planning an assists conference-sponsored event planning teams in setting up their event registration processes.
            1.1.3.2.3   Negotiates venue terms and options.
            1.1.3.2.4   Reports directly to the Director of Connectional Ministries (see *The Book of Discipline*, ¶ 608).
        1.1.3.3   *Ex officio* with vote.
            1.1.3.3.1   Resident bishop (or representative).
            1.1.3.3.2   Conference lay leader (or representative).

1.1.3.3.3   Conference secretary.

1.1.3.3.4   Chair of the Committee on Rules.

1.1.3.3.5   A district superintendent designated by the cabinet.

1.1.3.3.6   Legislative Coordinator.

1.1.3.3.7   Conference facilitator.

1.1.3.3.8   A representative of the Board of Ordained Ministry.

1.1.3.4   *Ex officio* with vote, but no vote.

1.1.3.4.1   Director of Connectional Ministries (see *The Book of Discipline*, ¶ 608).

1.1.3.4.2   Director of Communications (see *The Book of Discipline*, ¶ 609).

1.1.4   Organization.

1.1.4.1   The Commission shall elect from among its membership the following:

1.1.4.1.1   Chairperson.

1.1.4.1.2   Vice chairperson.

1.1.4.1.3   Head Usher.

1.1.4.1.4   Worship Coordinator.

1.1.4.2   The Legislative Coordinator shall have the following duties:

1.1.3.2.1   Receive new business in accordance with the rules of order (§ 5, below).

1.1.3.2.2   Assign business to legislative committees as appropriate in consultation with the Executive Team.

1.1.3.2.3   Maintain and revise (as necessary) the schedule of legislative process for the annual conference session in consultation with the rest of the Executive Committee (see § 1.1.4.5, below).

1.1.3.2.4   Manage the flow of the legislative work of the annual conference session in consultation with the Executive Team.

1.1.4.3   The conference secretary shall serve as the secretary of the commission.

1.1.4.4   Members shall serve four-year terms, renewable twice, in annually staggered classes.

1.1.4.5   The Executive Committee shall be composed of the persons serving in the following capacities:

1.1.4.5.1   Bishop.

1.1.4.5.2   Clergy Assistant to the Bishop.

1.1.4.5.3   Chairperson.

1.1.4.5.4   Worship Coordinator.

1.1.4.5.5   Director of Connectional Ministries (see *The Book of Discipline*, ¶ 608).

1.1.4.5.6   Legislative Coordinator.

1.1.4.5.7   Director of Communications (see *The Book of Discipline*, ¶ 609).

1.1.4.5.8   Conference Secretary.

1.1.4.5.9   Annual Conference Coordinator.

1.2   COMMISSION ON COMMUNICATIONS

1.2.1   Purpose – Assist the conference Director of Communications (see *The Book of Discipline*, ¶ 609) in communicating (via various forms of media) news and information about the annual conference and its ministries to the local churches of the conference and to the wider world.

    1.2.2   Duties.

           1.2.2.1   As determined by the conference director of communications.

           1.2.2.2   Fulfill all other responsibilities enumerated in ¶ 650 of *The Book of Discipline*.

    1.2.3   Membership.

           1.2.3.1   Four persons who shall be clergy members or local pastors of the annual conference (if clergy) or professing members of a local church within the annual conference (if laity).

           1.2.3.2   Members shall serve four-year terms, renewable once, in annually staggered classes.

           1.2.3.3   *Ex officio* with vote.

                 1.2.3.3.1   Bishop or clergy assistant to the Bishop (at the Bishop's discretion).

                 1.2.3.3.2   Conference lay leader.

                 1.2.3.3.3   Any board member of United Methodist Communications residing within the bounds of the annual conference.

           1.2.3.4   *Ex officio* with voice, but no vote.

                 1.2.3.4.1   Senior editor of conference communications.

                 1.2.3.4.2   I.T. data manager (or representative).

                 1.2.3.4.3   Conference Director of Communications (see *The Book of Discipline*, ¶ 609).

                 1.2.3.4.4   Director of Connectional Ministries (see *The Book of Discipline*, ¶ 608).

           1.2.3.5   Members shall be nominated by the Committee on Nominations, in consultation with the director of communications.

    1.2.4   Organization – The Conference Director of Communications (see *The Book of Discipline*, ¶ 609) shall chair the commission.

    1.2.5   Amenability – The commission shall be amenable to the Conference Leadership Council (§ 2.1, below).

    1.2.6   Relationship – The board shall relate to United Methodist Communications.

  1.3 COMMITTEE ON THE JOURNAL

    1.3.1   Purpose – Compile and cause to be published the journal of the annual conference.

    1.3.2   Duties.

           1.3.2.1   Review the format and content of the conference journal, ensuring compliance with *The Book of Discipline*.

           1.3.2.2   Prepare a report for inclusion in the conference journal reviewing that legislation that requires follow-up or implementation by the conference or any agency thereof.

           1.3.2.3   Cause the conference journal to be printed and distributed to all members (clergy and lay) of the annual conference and all local churches of the annual conference.

    1.3.3   Membership.

           1.3.3.1   Four people who shall be members of the annual conference (if clergy) or professing members of a local church within the annual conference (if laity).

1.3.3.2   Members shall serve four-year terms, renewable once, in annually staggered classes.

1.3.3.3   Members shall be nominated by the Committee on Nominations.

1.3.3.4   *Ex officio* with vote – Conference secretary.

1.3.3.5   *Ex officio with voice, but no vote* – Conference Director of Communications (see *The Book of Discipline*, ¶ 609).

1.3.4   Organization.

     1.3.4.1   The conference secretary shall serve as chairperson and secretary.

     1.3.4.2   The committee shall elect from among its members a vice chairperson.

1.3.5   Amenability – The committee shall be amenable to the Commission on the Annual Conference Session (§ 1.1, above).

1.4   BOARD OF JUSTICE

1.4.1   Purpose.

     1.4.1.1   Relate the gospel to the world by showing that the reconciliation of humans to God effected through Jesus Christ involves personal, social, and civic righteousness.

     1.4.1.2   Challenge and equip the agencies of the annual conference to a full and equal participation of racial and ethnic constituencies in the total life and mission of the church.

     1.4.1.3   Challenge the annual conference and its local churches and agencies to a continuing commitment to the full and equal responsibility and participation of women in the total life and mission of the church.

     1.4.1.4   Advocate for the role of persons with disabilities in ministry and the leadership of the annual conference.

1.4.2   Duties.

     1.4.2.1   Division of Church and Society.

         1.4.2.1.1   Implement the Social Principles and the annual conference's policy statements on social issues within the annual conference.

         1.4.2.1.2   Provide forthright witness and action on issues of human well-being, justice, peace, and the integrity of creation.

         1.4.2.1.3   Develop, promote, and distribute resources to inform, motivate, train, and organize people toward issues of social justice.

         1.4.2.1.4   Fulfill all other responsibilities enumerated in ¶ 629 of *The Book of Discipline*.

     1.4.2.2   Division on Religion and Race.

         1.4.2.2.1   Review and make appropriate recommendations for racial and ethnic inclusiveness and equity within the annual conference staff and on all annual conference agencies.

             1.4.2.2.1.1   Review and make appropriate recommendations for total inclusiveness an equity among conference staff and on all conferences agencies, reporting annually to the annual conference.

PLAN OF ORGANIZATION

1.4.2.2.1.2 Provide resources through collaboration and training to enable the work of the local church ministry area of religion and race, with particular emphasis placed on pastors and congregations involved in cross-racial/cross-cultural ministry.

1.4.2.2.2 Consult with the Board of Ordained Ministry and the cabinet to ensure racial/ethnic inclusion and equity in the recruitment, credentialing, and itineracy processes of the annual conference. The executive committee of the Board of Ordained Ministry and cabinet shall meet at least once per year in joint sessions with the Commission on Religion and Race to create and assess long-term plans for identifying and developing clergy leaders who will serve the growing racial and ethnic populations of the church.

1.4.2.2.3 Consult with local churches of the annual conference whose neighborhoods are experiencing changing racial/ethnic demographics in their neighborhoods and that desire to be in ministry with those changing neighborhoods, but coordinating conference leadership in support of racial and social justice movements impacting local communities, in consultation and partnership with other entities within and outside the boundaries of the annual conference.

1.4.2.2.4 Support and provide programs of education in areas of cultural competency and racial justice and reconciliation.

1.4.2.2.4.1 Support and provide programs of education in areas of intercultural competency, institutional equity, and vital conversation at every level of the conference.

1.4.2.2.4.2 Partner with the Board of Justice and other agencies as they seek to develop vital conversations, programs, and policies of racial/institutional equity and intercultural competency.

1.4.2.2.5 Partner with appropriate agencies and entities, and denominational bodies to assist in the resolution of complaints of racial/ethnic discrimination made by clergy or laity.

1.4.2.2.6 Fulfill all other responsibilities enumerated in ¶ 643 of *The Book of Discipline.*

1.4.2.3 Division on the Status and Role of Women.

1.4.2.3.1 Be informed about the status and role of all women in the total life of the annual conference.

1.4.2.3.2 Assist the resident bishop and cabinet in focusing on issues related to women such as sexual harassment.

1.4.2.3.3 Fulfill all other responsibilities enumerated in ¶ 644 of *The Book of Discipline.*

1.4.2.4 Division on Disability Concerns.

1.4.2.4.1 Develop programs that meet the needs of persons with disabilities.

1.4.2.4.2 Assist the resident bishop and cabinet in focusing on issues important to persons with disabilities.

1.4.2.4.3 Provide resources to local churches seeking to develop ministries that are attitudinally and architecturally accessible.

1.4.2.4.4 Fulfill all other responsibilities enumerated in ¶ 653 of *The Book of Discipline*.

1.4.3 Membership.

1.4.3.1 Division of Church and Society.

1.4.3.1.1 Four people who shall be members of the annual conference (if clergy) or professing members of a local church within the annual conference (if laity).

1.4.3.1.2 Members shall serve four-year terms, renewable once, in annually staggered classes.

1.4.3.1.3 Members shall be nominated by the Committee on Nominations.

1.4.3.1.4 *Ex officio* with vote:

1.4.3.1.4.1 The mission coordinator for social action of the conference United Methodist Women.

1.4.3.1.4.2 Any member of the General Board of Church and Society residing within the bounds of the annual conference.

1.4.3.1.4.3 The conference peace with justice coordinator, who shall be named by the Division of Church and Society and shall serve at the division's pleasure for up to eight years.

1.4.3.2 Division on Religion and Race.

1.4.3.2.1 Two clergy members of the annual conference.

1.4.3.2.2 Two laymen who shall be professing members of a local church within the annual conference.

1.4.3.2.3 Two laywomen who shall be professing members of a local church within the annual conference.

1.4.3.2.4 Members shall serve four-year terms, renewable once, in annually staggered classes.

1.4.3.2.5 Members shall be nominated by the Committee on Nominations.

1.4.3.2.6 *Ex officio* with vote – Any member of the General Commission on Religion and Race residing within the bounds of the annual conference.

1.4.3.3 Division on the Status and Role of Women.

1.4.3.3.1 Two clergy women who shall be members of the annual conference.

1.4.3.3.2 A clergyman who shall be a member of the annual conference.

1.4.3.3.3 Three laymen who shall be professing members of a local church within the annual conference.

1.4.3.3.4 Three laywomen who shall be professing members of a local church within the annual conference.

1.4.3.3.5   Members shall serve four-year terms, renewable once, in annually staggered classes.

1.4.3.3.6   Members shall be nominated by the Committee on Nominations.

1.4.3.3.7   *Ex officio* with vote – Any member of the General Commission on the Status and Role of Women residing within the bounds of the annual conference.

1.4.3.4   Division on Disability Concerns.

1.4.3.4.1   Four people who shall be members of the annual conference (if clergy) or professing members of a local church within the annual conference (if laity).

1.4.3.4.2   Members shall serve four-year terms, renewable once, in annually staggered classes.

1.4.3.4.3   Members shall be nominated by the Committee on Nominations.

1.4.3.4.4   At least one member of the division shall have a physical disability.

1.4.3.4.5   At least one member of the division shall have a mental disability.

1.4.4   Organization.

1.4.4.1   The board shall be organized in four divisions as enumerated above.

1.4.4.2   Each division shall elect from among its members a convener.

1.4.4.2.1   The convener of the Division on the Status and Role of Women shall be a woman.

1.4.4.2.2   One of the conveners shall serve as vice chairperson of the board. The conveners shall decide amongst themselves who this shall be.

1.4.4.3   In addition to the members enumerated above, an additional person, nominated by the Committee on Nominations, shall serve as the chairperson of the board. This chairperson shall be a member of the annual conference (if clergy) or a professing member of a local church within the annual conference (if laity).

1.4.5   Amenability – The board shall be amenable to the Conference Leadership Council (§ 2.1, below).

1.4.6   Relationship – The board shall relate to the following general agencies:

1.4.6.1   General Board of Church and Society.

1.4.6.2   General Commission on Religion and Race.

1.4.6.3   General Commission on the Status and Role of Women.

1.5   BOARD OF GLOBAL MINISTRIES

1.5.1   Purpose – Engage the annual conference and its local churches in ministry with persons and in places around the world.

1.5.2   Duties.

1.5.2.1   Act as a conduit for interpretation, support, and programming between the annual conference and the General Board of Global Ministries.

1.5.2.2   Plan, promote, and develop a spirit of global ministry within the annual conference and its local churches.

1.5.2.3   Encourage and support specialized urban and town and country ministries.

1.5.2.4   Envision and develop new forms of mission appropriate to the changing needs of the world.

1.5.2.5   Appoint and train conference disaster relief coordinators.

1.5.2.6   Recruit and support missionaries.

1.5.2.7   Promote Christian, financial, and professional standards in health and welfare ministries within the annual conference.

1.5.2.8   Fulfill all other responsibilities enumerated in ¶ 633 of *The Book of Discipline*.

1.5.3   Membership.

     1.5.3.1   Twelve people who shall be members of the annual conference (if clergy) or professing members of a local church within the annual conference (if laity).

     1.5.3.2   Members shall serve four-year terms, renewable once, in annually staggered classes.

     1.5.3.3   Members shall be nominated by the Committee on Nominations.

     1.5.3.4   *Ex officio* with vote:

         1.5.3.4.1   Mission coordinator for education and interpretation of the conference United Methodist Women.

         1.5.3.4.2   The conference secretary of global ministries, who shall be appointed by the board and shall serve at its pleasure for up to eight years.

         1.5.3.4.3   Conference disaster response coordinator (selected by the Board of Global Ministries).

         1.5.3.4.4   Any member of the General Board of Global Ministries residing within the bounds of the annual conference.

         1.5.3.4.5   Conference VIM coordinator.

1.5.4   Organization – The board shall elect the following officers from among its members:

     1.5.4.1   Chairperson.

     1.5.4.2   Vice chairperson.

1.5.5   Amenability – The board shall be amenable to the Conference Leadership Council (§ 2.1, below).

1.5.6   Relationship – The board shall relate to the General Board of Global Ministries.

1.6   COMMISSION ON ARCHIVES AND HISTORY

1.6.1   Purpose – Collect and preserve the records and historical data of the annual conference.

1.6.2   Duties.

     1.6.2.1   Maintain a fire-safe historical and archival depository for the records and items of historical nature of the annual conference.

     1.6.2.2   Liaise with shrines, landmarks, and historical sites related to the annual conference and its churches and ministries.

     1.6.2.3   Work with the Commission on the Annual Conference Session in the planning of historical observances at the annual conference session.

     1.6.2.4   Encourage and assist local churches in the preservation and compilation of records and history.

     1.6.2.5   Fulfill all other responsibilities enumerated in ¶ 641 of *The Book of Discipline*.

1.6.3   Membership.

       1.6.3.1   Four clergy members of the annual conference.

       1.6.3.2   Four lay persons who shall be professing members of a church within the annual conference.

       1.6.3.3   Members shall be nominated by the Committee on Nominations.

       1.6.3.4   Members shall serve four-year terms, renewable once, in annually staggered classes.

       1.6.3.5   The archivists of the conference archives shall serve as ex-officio members with voice and vote.

       1.6.3.6   The president of the Michigan Area United Methodist Church Historical Society shall serve as an ex-officio member with voice and vote.

       1.6.3.7   Any member of the General Commission on Archives and History shall serve as an ex officio member with voice and vote.

1.6.4   Organization – The commission shall elect from among its members the following officers:

       1.6.4.1   Chairperson.

       1.6.4.2   Vice chairperson.

       1.6.4.3   Secretary.

       1.6.4.4   Treasurer.

1.6.5   Amenability – The commission shall be amenable to the Conference Leadership Council (§ 2.1, below).

1.6.6   Relationship – The commission shall relate to the General Commission on Archives and History and the Michigan Area United Methodist Church Historical Society.

§ 2   AGENCIES RELATING TO BOLD AND EFFECTIVE LEADERS

2.1   CONFERENCE LEADERSHIP COUNCIL.

    2.1.1.   Purpose – The basic governing council of the annual conference.

    2.1.2.   Duties.

       2.1.2.1.   Implementation of the vision and direction of the annual conference.

       2.1.2.2.   Ensuring that the following agencies, which are amenable to it, are fulfilling their responsibilities pursuant to *The Book of Discipline* and the Plan of Organization and direction of the annual conference:

          2.1.2.2.1   Board of Congregational Life (§ 3.5, below).

          2.1.2.2.2   Board of Global Ministries (§ 1.5, above).

          2.1.2.2.3   Board of Justice (§ 1.4, above).

          2.1.2.2.4   Board of Laity (§ 3.3, below).

          2.1.2.2.5   Board of Young People's Ministries (§ 3.4, below).

          2.1.2.2.6   Commission on Archives and History (§ 1.6, above).

          2.1.2.2.7   Commission on Communications (§ 1.2, above).

          2.1.2.2.8   Committee on African-American Ministry (§ 3.9, below).

          2.1.2.2.9   Committee on Asian-American Ministry (§ 3.7, below).

          2.1.2.2.10 Committee on the Episcopacy (§ 2.4, below).

          2.1.2.2.11 Committee on Hispanic/Latino Ministry (§ 3.6, below).

          2.1.2.2.12 Committee on Human Resources (§ 2.5, below).

          2.1.2.2.13 Committee on Native American Ministry (§ 3.8, below).

          2.1.2.2.14 Protection Policy Implementation Team (§ 2.6, below).

2.1.2.3   Ensuring that all agencies amenable to it (see § 2.1.2.2, above)
are functioning with values and goals that are aligned with the vision for ministry set by the annual conference.

2.1.2.4   Evaluation of the fruitfulness and effectiveness of the work
of all agencies amenable to it (see § 2.1.2.2, above).

2.1.2.5   Ensuring that all agencies amenable to it (see § 2.1.2.2, above)
compile a list (that shall be published in the conference journal) of
all non-conference entities to which they have provided funding
(and which are thereby responsible for ensuring the appropriate
use of such funding).

2.1.2.6   At its discretion, the council may create and define the positions
of additional conference directors (beyond those defined in *The
Book of Discipline*).

2.1.2.7   The council may create task forces, work groups, and *ad
hoc* committees as needed in order to ensure that its work
is being done.

2.1.3   Membership.

    2.1.3.1   With voice and vote.

        2.1.3.1.1   Four clergy members of the annual conference, at
least one of whom shall be a member of the Board of
Ordained Ministry.

        2.1.3.1.2   Five lay people who are professing members of a con-
gregation within the annual conference.

    2.1.3.2   *Ex officio* with voice and vote.

        2.1.3.2.1   Conference lay leader.

        2.1.3.2.2   President of the Council on Finance and Administra-
tion.

        2.1.3.2.3   A representative of the Division on Religion and Race
of the Board of Justice.

        2.1.3.2.4   Any member of the Connectional Table residing within
the bounds of the Annual Conference.

    2.1.3.3   *Ex officio* with voice only.

        2.1.3.3.1   Director of Administrative Services and Conference
Treasurer (see *The Book of Discipline*, ¶ 619).

        2.1.3.3.2   Director of Connectional Ministries (see *The Book of
Discipline*, ¶ 608).

        2.1.3.3.3   Director of Communications (see *The Book of Disci-
pline*, ¶ 609).

        2.1.3.3.4   Bishop or clergy assistant to the Bishop (at the
Bishop's discretion).

        2.1.3.3.5   Dean of the appointive cabinet.

        2.1.3.3.6   Director of Benefits and Human Resources.

        2.1.3.3.7   Any other directors whose position may be created by
the Conference Leadership Council (see § 2.1.2.6,
above).

    2.1.3.4   Members shall be nominated by the Committee on Nominations.

    2.1.3.5   Members shall serve three-year terms, renewable thrice, in annu-
ally staggered classes.

    2.1.3.6   Except for *ex officio* members listed hereinabove, chairpersons of
conference agencies and employees of conference agencies shall
be ineligible for membership on the council.

2.1.4   Organization.

     2.1.4.1   The council, in consultation with the Bishop, shall elect from among its voting members a president, vice president, and secretary.

     2.1.4.2   The Director of Administrative Services and Conference Treasurer (see *The Book of Discipline*, ¶ 619) shall be the council treasurer.

2.2 BOARD OF ORDAINED MINISTRY.

2.2.1   Purpose – To counsel and guide the equipping and qualification of candidates for ordained ministry and conference membership.

2.2.2.   Duties.

     2.2.2.1   Assume the primary responsibility for the enlistment and recruitment of ordained clergy by working in consultation with the cabinet and the General Board of Higher Education and Ministry to study and interpret the clergy needs and resources of the annual conference.

     2.2.2.2   Renew a culture of call in the church by giving strategic leadership to the annual conference, local churches, and other ministry settings.

     2.2.2.3   Seek from schools of theology information about the personal and professional qualities of candidates for ministry.

     2.2.2.4   Appoint and train clergy mentors.

     2.2.2.5   Examine all applicants as to their qualification and fitness for the following:

         2.2.2.5.1   Annual election as local pastor.

         2.2.2.5.2   Election to associate membership.

         2.2.2.5.3   Election to provisional membership.

         2.2.2.5.4   Election to full membership.

     2.2.2.6   Interview and make recommendations for applicants/those formally recommended for a change in conference relationship.

     2.2.2.7   Provide support services for the career development, continuing education, morale, and preparation for retirement of clergy.

     2.2.2.8   Provide means of evaluating the effectiveness of clergy in the annual conference.

     2.2.2.9   Provide continuing support and management of diaconal ministers.

     2.2.2.10   Administer the conference ministerial education fund.

     2.2.2.11   Collaborate with the director of clergy excellence in the development of bold and effective leaders.

     2.2.2.12   Fulfill all other responsibilities enumerated in ¶ 635 of *The Book of Discipline*.

2.2.3   Membership.

     2.2.3.1   With voice and vote.

         2.2.3.1.1   At least twenty-five full (*i.e.*, ordained) clergy members of the annual conference.

             2.2.3.1.1.1   At least one of whom shall be engaged in extension ministry.

             2.2.3.1.1.2   At least one of whom shall be age thirty-five or younger.

             2.2.3.1.1.3   At least two-thirds of whom shall be graduates of theological schools listed by the University Senate.

             2.2.3.1.1.4   At least one of whom shall be retired.

2.2.3.1.2 At least three clergy persons who are either associate members or local pastors who have completed course of study.

2.2.3.1.3 At least twelve lay people who are professing members of a local church within the annual conference.

2.2.3.2 *Ex officio* with voice and vote.

2.2.3.2.1 Chairpersons of the following:

2.2.3.2.1.1 Order of Elders.

2.2.3.2.1.2 Order of Deacons.

2.2.3.2.1.3 Fellowship of Local Pastors and Associate Members.

2.2.3.2.2 A district superintendent named by the Bishop.

2.2.3.2.3 Director of Clergy Excellence.

2.2.3.3 Members shall be nominated by the Bishop.

2.2.3.4 Members shall serve four-year terms (starting at the close of the annual conference session following General Conference), renewable twice, with quadrennially staggered classes.

2.2.4 Organization.

2.2.4.1 The board shall elect from among its members the following officers:

2.2.4.1.1 Chairperson.

2.2.4.1.2 Vice chairperson.

2.2.4.1.3 Secretary.

2.2.4.1.4 At least one registrar.

2.2.4.2 The conference relations committee of the board shall be chaired by the vice chairperson of the board and shall be composed of as many members as the board shall decide. District superintendents may not serve on the conference relations committee.

2.2.4.3 The board may establish further committees of itself as it may deem necessary.

2.3 COMMITTEE ON NOMINATIONS

2.3.1 Purpose – Preparation and presentation to the annual conference a slate of nominees for the conference agencies, giving careful consideration to racial/ethnic, geographic, demographic, age, and gender balance.

2.3.2 Duties.

2.3.2.1 Preparation of a slate of nominees for presentation to the annual conference. The committee shall have the duty, whenever necessary, to assign nominees to specific classes within an agency.

2.3.2.2 Assist other agencies with the following:

2.3.2.2.1 Identifying the skill sets and perspectives needed to perform the agency's work.

2.3.2.2.2 Auditing the skill sets of current and prospective members.

2.3.2.3 Except as otherwise provided by *The Book of Discipline*, filling agency vacancies that occur between sessions of the annual conference.

2.3.2.4 By a three-fourths vote, the committee may remove from office any member of an agency for whose nominations it is responsible should that member fail to perform the duties required.

2.3.3 Membership.

2.3.3.1 Two persons nominated by the annual conference session.

2.3.3.2 Ten persons nominated by the Conference Leadership Council.

2.3.3.3 *Ex officio* with vote.

    2.3.3.2.1 A district superintendent designated by the cabinet.

    2.3.3.2.2 Conference lay leader (or designated representative).

    2.3.3.2.3 Chairperson (or representative) of the Committee on Rules.

    2.3.3.2.4 Secretary of the annual conference.

2.3.3.4 *Ex officio* with voice, but no vote – Director of Connectional Ministries (see *The Book of Discipline*, ¶ 608).

2.3.3.5 Members shall serve four-year terms, renewable once, staggered annually.

2.3.4 Organization – The committee shall elect the following officers from among its members:

2.3.4.1 Chairperson.

2.3.4.2 Vice chairperson.

2.3.4.3 Secretary.

2.4 COMMITTEE ON THE EPISCOPACY

2.4.1 Purpose – Provide personal support and counsel to the resident bishop.

2.4.2 Duties.

2.4.2.1 Support the resident bishop in the oversight of the spiritual and temporal affairs of the church, with special reference to areas in which the bishop has presidential responsibility.

2.4.2.2 Be available to provide counsel to the resident bishop.

2.4.2.3 Make determinations and appropriate recommendations concerning the episcopal needs of the conference.

2.4.2.4 Advise the bishop as to conditions within the annual conference.

2.4.2.5 Interpret the nature and function of the episcopal office to the annual conference.

2.4.2.6 Engage in annual consultation and appraisal concerning the balance of the resident bishop's relationship to and responsibilities within the annual conference and its agencies.

2.4.2.7 Report the annual conference's needs concerning episcopal leadership to the jurisdictional committee on the episcopacy via the committee's representatives thereto. The committee's representatives to the jurisdictional committee on the episcopacy shall ensure that this report includes profiles of the annual conference's assets, limits, and strengths, and that it shall be used when the jurisdictional committee assigns bishops to episcopal areas.

2.4.2.8 Ensuring that the Committee on the Episcopal Residence (§ 4.7, below), which is amenable to it, is fulfilling its responsibilities pursuant to *The Book of Discipline* and the Plan of Organization and direction and of the annual conference.

2.4.2.9 Fulfill all other responsibilities enumerated in ¶ 637 of *The Book of Discipline*.

2.4.3 Membership.

2.4.3.1 Members nominated by the Committee on Nominations.

    2.4.3.1.1 Six clergy members of the conference.

    2.4.3.1.2 Six lay persons who shall be professing members of a local church within the conference, one of whom shall be the conference lay leader.

2.4.3.2 Three members appointed by the resident bishop who, if laity, shall be professing members of a local church within the conference and, if clergy, shall be members of the annual conference.

2.4.3.3 Members of the jurisdictional committee on the episcopacy who reside within the bounds of the conference shall be *ex officio* members with vote.

2.4.3.4 No staff person of the annual conference or any agency thereof, nor an immediate family member of such staff person shall serve as a member of the committee, except that this prohibition shall not apply to the conference lay leader nor to members of the jurisdictional committee on the episcopacy residing within the bounds of the conference.

2.4.3.5 Members shall serve four-year terms, renewable once, in annually staggered classes.

2.4.3 Organization – The committee shall elect from among its members the following officers:

    2.4.3.1 Chairperson.

    2.4.3.2 Vice chairperson.

    2.4.3.3 Secretary.

2.4.4 Amenability – The committee shall be amenable to the Conference Leadership Council (§ 2.1, above).

2.5 PROTECTION POLICY IMPLEMENTATION TEAM

2.5.1 Purpose – Train and certify those who will work with children, youth, or vulnerable adults at conference events.

2.5.2 Duties.

    2.5.2.1 Propose changes to the conference protection policy (§ 8, below) as needed.

    2.5.2.2 In accordance with the policies and procedures of the conference protection policy (§ 8, below), train and certify volunteers to work with children, youth, and vulnerable adults at conference events.

    2.5.2.3 In accordance with the policies and procedures of the conference protection policy (§ 8, below), train volunteer certification trainers.

    2.5.2.4 In accordance with the policies and procedures of the conference protection policy (§ 8, below), process and certify (or decline, as appropriate) applications for protection policy certification.

2.5.3 Membership.

    2.5.3.1 Eight adults (at least 18 years of age) who shall be members of the annual conference (if clergy) or professing members of a local church within the annual conference (if laity).

    2.5.3.2 Members shall serve four-year terms, renewable once, in annually staggered classes.

    2.5.3.3 Members shall be nominated by the Committee on Nominations.

2.5.4 Organization – The committee shall elect the following officers from among its members:

    2.5.4.1 Chairperson.

    2.5.4.2 Vice chairperson.

2.5.5 Amenability – The committee shall be amenable to the Conference Leadership Council (§ 2.1, above).

§ 3   AGENCIES RELATING TO VIBRANT CONGREGATIONS

3.1   UNITED METHODIST WOMEN

    3.1.1.   Purpose – To know God and to experience freedom as whole persons through Jesus Christ; to develop a creative, supportive fellowship; and to expand concepts of mission through participation in the global ministries of the church.

    3.1.2.   Duties.

        3.1.2.1   Work with the district and local units of United Methodist Women in developing programs to meet the needs and interests of women and the concerns and responsibilities of the global church.

        3.1.2.2   Promote the plans and responsibilities of the national office of United Methodist Women.

        3.1.2.3   Fulfill all other responsibilities enumerated in ¶ 647 of *The Book of Discipline.*

    3.1.3   Membership.

        3.1.3.1   The membership shall be composed of all of the members of the local United Methodist Women units existing within the bounds of the conference.

        3.1.3.2   *Ex officio* with vote

            3.1.3.2.1   Resident bishop.

            3.1.3.2.2   Members of the board of directors of the national office of United Methodist Women residing within the bounds of the conference.

            3.1.3.2.3   Members of the United Methodist Women Program Advisory Group residing within the bounds of the conference.

            3.1.3.2.4   Members of the North Central Jurisdiction United Methodist Women leadership team residing within the bounds of the conference.

    3.1.4   Organization – The United Methodist Women shall elect from among its members the following positions:

        3.1.4.1   President.

        3.1.4.2   Treasurer.

        3.1.4.3   Secretary.

        3.1.4.4   A committee on nominations whose membership shall be determined by the membership of the United Methodist Women.

        3.1.4.5   Any other committees that the membership may create.

    3.1.5   Relationship – The conference United Methodist Women shall relate to the national organization of United Methodist Women.

3.2.   UNITED METHODIST MEN

    3.2.1   Purpose – A creative, supportive fellowship of men who seek to know God and Jesus Christ that meets the inspirational needs of men in evangelism, mission, and spiritual discipline.

    3.2.2   Duties.

        3.2.2.1   Promote the objectives and responsibilities of the General Commission on United Methodist Men.

        3.2.2.2   Establish, support, and maintain local church units of United Methodist Men.

        3.2.2.3   Empower personal witness and evangelism in men.

PLAN OF ORGANIZATION

3.2.2.4   Encourage the involvement of men in mission.

3.2.2.5   Promote the scouting movement and other youth organizations recognized by the General Commission on United Methodist Men.

3.2.2.6   Fulfill all other responsibilities enumerated in ¶ 648 of *The Book of Discipline*.

3.2.3   Membership.

3.2.3.1   The membership of the United Methodist Men shall be made up of all men who are professing members of local churches within the bounds of the annual conference.

3.2.3.2   *Ex officio* members.

3.2.3.2.1   Any member of the North Central Jurisdiction United Methodist Men residing within the bounds of the conference.

3.2.3.2.2   Any member of the General Commission on United Methodist Men residing within the bounds of the annual conference.

3.2.3.2.3   Conference lay leader (or designated representative).

3.2.3.2.4   Resident bishop.

3.2.4   Organization.

3.2.4.1   The organization shall elect the following officers from among its members:

3.2.4.1.1   President.

3.2.4.1.2   Vice-president.

3.2.4.1.3   Secretary.

3.2.4.1.4   Treasurer.

3.2.4.2   The resident bishop shall serve as the honorary president.

3.2.4.3   The organization may elect additional officers and committees as its members may direct.

3.2.5   Relationship – The conference United Methodist Men shall relate to the General Commission on United Methodist Men.

3.3 BOARD OF LAITY

3.3.1   Purpose.

3.3.1.1   Foster an awareness of the role of laity in the church.

3.3.1.2   Develop and promote stewardship within the annual conference.

3.3.1.3   Provide for the training of lay members of the annual conference.

3.3.1.4   Provide support and direction for the ministry of the laity at all levels of the church.

3.3.1.5   Provide organization and support for the development of local church leaders.

3.3.2   Duties.

3.3.2.1   Develop and promote programs to cultivate the further understanding of the theological and biblical basis for the ministry of the laity.

3.3.2.2   Give direction and guidance to lay programs within the conference.

3.3.2.3   Give support and direction to the conference for local church leadership development.

3.3.2.4   Advocate for the needs of lay people within all levels of the church.

              3.3.2.5   Organize a conference committee on lay servant ministries in accordance with ¶¶ 266-268 of *The Book of Discipline*.

              3.3.2.6   Fulfill all other responsibilities enumerated in ¶ 631 of *The Book of Discipline*.

3.3.3   Membership.

              3.3.3.1   Conference lay leader.

              3.3.3.2   Conference associate lay leader.

              3.3.3.3   The district lay leaders.

              3.3.3.4   The associate district lay leaders.

              3.3.3.5   Conference director of lay servant ministries.

              3.3.3.6   President of the United Methodist Men (or representative).

              3.3.3.7   President of the United Methodist Women (or representative).

              3.3.3.8   Convener of the Division of Young Adult Ministry of the Board of Young People's Ministries.

              3.3.3.9   Convener of the Division of Youth Ministry of the Board of Young People's Ministries.

              3.3.3.10   Conference scouting coordinator.

              3.3.3.11   Director of Connectional Ministries (see *The Book of Discipline*, ¶ 608).

              3.3.3.12   A district superintendent designated by the cabinet.

3.3.4   Organization.

              3.3.4.1   The conference lay leader shall be the chairperson of the board.

              3.3.4.2   The conference associate lay leader shall be the vice chairperson of the board.

3.3.5   Amenability – The board shall be amenable to the Conference Leadership Council (§ 2.1, above).

3.4 BOARD OF YOUNG PEOPLE'S MINISTRIES

3.4.1   Purpose.

              3.4.1.1   Strengthen youth ministry in the local churches of the annual conference.

              3.4.1.2   Strengthen young adult ministry in the local churches of the annual conference.

              3.4.1.3   Interpret and promote United Methodist ministries in higher education.

3.4.2   Duties.

              3.4.2.1   Division of Youth Ministry.

                      3.4.2.1.1   Initiate and support plans, activities, and projects that are of particular interest to youth.

                      3.4.2.1.2   Support and facilitate the formation of youth caucuses.

                      3.4.2.1.3   Recommend to the Committee on Nominations qualified youth for conference agency membership.

                      3.4.2.1.4   Elect representatives to jurisdictional youth events.

                      3.4.2.1.5   Assist graduating youth entering college with transition to campus ministries.

                      3.4.2.1.6   Set policy and give direction for the conference Youth Service Fund.

                      3.4.2.1.7   Recommend to the General and Jurisdictional Conference delegation qualified youth for general and jurisdictional agency membership.

3.4.2.1.8 Facilitate an Adult Workers network for designing training for workers with youth ministries in local churches.

3.4.2.1.9 Fulfill all other responsibilities enumerated in ¶ 649 of *The Book of Discipline.*

3.4.2.2 Division of Young Adult Ministry.

3.4.2.2.1 Initiate and support plans, activities, and projects that are of particular interest to young adults (age 18-30).

3.4.2.2.2 Support and facilitate the formation of young adult caucuses.

3.4.2.2.3 Recommend to the Committee on Nominations qualified young adults for conference agency membership.

3.4.2.2.4 Assist graduating college students with transition to adult congregational life.

3.4.2.2.5 Recommend to the General and Jurisdictional Conference delegation qualified young adults for general and jurisdictional agency membership.

3.4.2.2.6 Fulfill all other responsibilities enumerated in ¶ 650 of *The Book of Discipline.*

3.4.2.3 Division of Higher Education and Campus Ministry.

3.4.2.3.1 Make recommendations concerning annual conference policies in the area of higher education.

3.4.2.3.2 Train and provide resources for the local churches of the annual conference in them areas of higher education and campus ministry.

3.4.2.3.3 Evaluate schools, colleges, universities, and campus ministries related to the annual conference, with concern for the quality of their performance, the integrity of their mission, and their response to the missional goals of the annual conference.

3.4.2.3.4 Advocate for the financial needs of conference-related schools, colleges, universities, and campus ministries.

3.4.2.3.5 Monitor the annual conference's fiduciary and legal relationships with United Methodist-related schools, colleges, universities, and campus ministries.

3.4.2.3.6 Assist colleges and universities affiliated with the annual conference in raising funds and attracting students.

3.4.2.3.7 Encourage participation in campus ministries.

3.4.2.3.8 Provide resources and training for campus ministries.

3.4.2.3.9 Fulfill all other responsibilities enumerated in ¶ 634 of *The Book of Discipline.*

3.4.3 Membership.

3.4.3.1 Division of Youth Ministry.

3.4.3.1.1 Two clergy persons appointed in the annual conference, who shall serve four year terms, renewable once, in biennially staggered classes.

3.4.3.1.2 Two adult (*i.e.*, age 18 or older) laypersons who shall be professing members of a local church within the annual conference, who shall serve four-year terms, renewable once, in biennially staggered classes.

3.4.3.1.3 Ten youth (age 13-17), who shall be professing members of a local church within the annual conference, who shall serve one-year terms, renewable as long as they are under age 18 at the start of a new term.

3.4.3.1.4 Members shall be nominated by the Committee on Nominations.

3.4.3.2 Division of young adult ministry.

3.4.3.2.1 Two young adult (age 18-30) clergy persons of the annual conference who shall be nominated by the committee on nominations.

3.4.3.2.2 Four young adult lay persons (age 18-30) who shall be nominated by the committee on nominations and who shall be professing members of a local church within the annual conference.

3.4.3.2.3 Members shall serve one-year terms, renewable as long as they are age 30 or under at the start of the new term.

3.4.3.3 Division of Higher Education and Campus Ministry.

3.4.3.3.1 Six people who shall be members of the annual conference (if clergy) or professing members of a local church within the annual conference (if laity).

3.4.3.3.2 Members shall serve four-year terms, renewable once, in annually staggered classes.

3.4.3.3.3 Members shall be nominated by the Committee on Nominations.

3.4.3.3.4 *Ex officio* with vote – any member of the General Board of Higher Education and Ministry residing within the bounds of the annual conference.

3.4.4 Organization.

3.4.4.1 The board shall be organized in three divisions as enumerated above.

3.4.4.2 Each division shall elect from among its members a convener.

3.4.4.3 One of the conveners shall serve as vice chairperson of the board. The conveners shall decide amongst themselves who this shall be.

3.4.4.4 In addition to the members enumerated above, an additional person, nominated by the Committee on Nominations, shall serve as the chairperson of the board. This chairperson shall be a member of the annual conference (if clergy) or a profession member of a local church within the annual conference (if laity).

3.4.4.5 *Ex officio* with voice, but no vote – A representative of the Michigan Area Board of Christian Camping.

3.4.5 Amenability – The board shall be amenable to the Conference Leadership Council (§ 2.1, above).

3.4.6 Relationship – The board shall relate to the following general agencies.

3.4.6.1 General Board of Higher Education and Ministry.

3.4.6.2 Discipleship Ministries.

3.5   BOARD OF CONGREGATIONAL LIFE
   3.5.1   Purpose.
      3.5.1.1   Lead and assist the local churches of the annual conference in their efforts to communicate and celebrate the redeeming love of God as revealed in Jesus Christ and to invite persons into discipleship through this love.
      3.5.1.2   Inform the conference and its agencies of the needs an opportunities of small membership churches.
      3.5.1.3   Interpret and advocate for the unity of the Christian church, while encouraging dialog and cooperate with persons of other religions, starting at the local church level.
      3.5.1.4   Promote and interpret ethnic local church concerns to the annual conference.
      3.5.1.5   Collaborate with the director of congregational vibrancy in overseeing any staff and processes related to the development of vital congregations and new church development.
   3.5.2   Duties.
      3.5.2.1   Division of Congregational Vibrancy.
         3.5.2.1.1   Develop a unified and comprehensive program for leadership training to serve all age groups in the home, church, and community.
         3.5.2.1.2   Develop and promote a comprehensive program of Christian education for all ages.
         3.5.2.1.3   Provide training for local church confirmation leaders.
         3.5.2.1.4   Plan and promote an effective, comprehensive ministry of evangelism for persons of all ages.
         3.5.2.1.5   Promote the use of *The United Methodist Hymnal* and *The United Methodist Book of Worship* in all local churches of the conference.
         3.5.2.1.6   Promote seminars and training events in the area of worship, including music and other arts.
         3.5.2.1.7   Plan and promote a comprehensive program of stewardship for all age groups.
         3.5.2.1.8   Develop programming for the local church regarding ecology and the environment.
         3.5.2.1.9   Promote and provide training regarding spiritual formation and devotional life for persons of all ages.
         3.5.2.1.10 Fulfill all other responsibilities enumerated in ¶ 630 of *The Book of Discipline*.
      3.5.2.2   Division on the Small-Membership Church.
         3.5.2.2.1   Assist the Committee on Nominations in ensuring that laity and clergy from small-membership churches are included in the decision-making agencies of the annual conference.
         3.5.2.2.2   Assist the resident bishop and cabinet in focusing on issues related to small membership churches.
         3.5.2.2.3   Fulfill all other responsibilities enumerated in ¶ 645 of *The Book of Discipline*.
      3.5.2.3   Division on Christian Unity and Interreligious Relationships.
         3.5.2.3.1   Recommend to the annual conference goals, objectives, and strategies for the development of ecumenical relationships.

3.5.2.3.2   Encourage participation by the local churches of the annual conference in ecumenical ministries and missions.

3.5.2.3.3   Fulfill all other responsibilities enumerated in ¶ 642 of *The Book of Discipline.*

3.5.3   Membership.

      3.5.3.1   Division of Congregational Vibrancy.

           3.5.3.1.1   Four people who shall be members of the annual conference (if clergy) or professing members of a local church within the annual conference (if laity).

           3.5.3.1.2   Members shall serve four-year terms, renewable once, in annually staggered classes.

           3.5.3.1.3   Members shall be nominated by the Committee on Nominations.

           3.5.3.1.4   *Ex officio* with vote – any member of Discipleship Ministries residing within the bounds of the annual conference.

      3.5.3.2   Division on the Small-Membership Church.

           3.5.3.2.1   Four people who shall be members of the annual conference (if clergy) or professing members of a local church within the annual conference (if laity).

           3.5.3.2.2   Members shall serve four-year terms, renewable once, in annually staggered classes.

           3.5.3.2.3   Members shall be nominated by the Committee on Nominations.

      3.5.3.3   Division on Christian Unity and Interreligious Relationships.

           3.5.3.3.1   Six persons who shall be members of the annual conference (if clergy) or professing members of a local church within the annual conference (if laity), one of whom shall serve as the district coordinator for Christian unity and interreligious relationships.

           3.5.3.3.2   Members shall serve four-year terms, renewable once, in annually staggered classes.

           3.5.3.3.3   Members shall be nominated by the Committee on Nominations.

           3.5.3.3.4   *Ex officio* with vote – any United Methodists residing within the bounds of the annual conference who are members of the following:

               3.5.3.3.4.1   The Office of Christian Unity and Interreligious Relationships of the Council of Bishops.

               3.5.3.3.4.2   The governing board of the National Council of the Churches of Christ in the U.S.A.

               3.5.3.3.4.3   The World Methodist Council.

               3.5.3.3.4.4   The United Methodist delegation to the most recent World Council of Churches Assembly.

               3.5.3.3.4.5   The United Methodist delegation to the most recent plenary meeting of Churches Uniting in Christ.

3.5.4   Organization.

3.5.4.1   The board shall be organized in four divisions as enumerated above.

3.5.4.2   Each division shall elect from among its members a convener. One of the conveners shall serve as vice chairperson of the board; the conveners shall decide amongst themselves who this shall be.

3.5.4.3   In addition to the members enumerated above, an additional person, nominated by the Committee on Nominations, shall serve as the chairperson of the board. This chairperson shall be a member of the annual conference (if clergy) or a professing member of a local church within the annual conference (if laity).

3.5.4.4   The director of congregational vibrancy shall be an *ex officio* member of the board with vote.

3.5.5   Amenability – The board shall be amenable to the Conference Leadership Council (§ 2.1, above).

3.5.6   Relationship – The board shall relate to Discipleship Ministries.

3.6   COMMITTEE ON HISPANIC/LATINO MINISTRY

3.6.1   Purpose.

3.6.1.1   Implement the National Plan for Hispanic Ministry within the bounds of the conference.

3.6.1.2   Provide direction and leadership for Hispanic/Latino ministries within the conference.

3.6.2   Duties – The committee shall, in keeping with its purpose (as set forth in § 3.6.1, above), define its duties in any way it sees fit, subject to the approval of the Conference Leadership Council.

3.6.3   Membership – The committee shall define its membership in any way it sees fit, subject to the approval of the Conference Leadership Council.

3.6.4   Organization – The committee shall organize itself in any way it sees fit, subject to the approval of the Conference Leadership Council.

3.6.5   Amenability – The committee shall be amenable to the Conference Leadership Council (§ 2.1, above).

3.7   COMMITTEE ON ASIAN-AMERICAN MINISTRY

3.7.1   Purpose.

3.7.1.1   Develop and support leadership for Asian-American churches and communities within the annual conference.

3.7.1.2   Train, support, and empower Asian-American clergy and lay leadership for effective ministry in their churches, their communities, and the world.

3.7.2   Duties – The committee shall, in keeping with its purpose (as set forth in § 3.7.1, above), define its duties in any way it sees fit, subject to the approval of the Conference Leadership Council.

3.7.3   Membership – The committee shall define its membership in any way it sees fit, subject to the approval of the Conference Leadership Council.

3.7.4   Organization – The committee shall organize itself in any way it sees fit, subject to the approval of the Conference Leadership Council.

3.7.5   Amenability – The committee shall be amenable to the Conference Leadership Council (§ 2.1, above).

PLAN OF ORGANIZATION

3.8   COMMITTEE ON NATIVE AMERICAN MINISTRY
   3.8.1   Purpose – Monitor and promote Native American ministries within the annual conference.
   3.8.2   Duties.
           3.8.2.1   Manage the distribution of the Native American Ministries Sunday offering.
           3.8.2.2   Fulfill all other responsibilities enumerated in ¶ 654 of *The Book of Discipline*.
           3.8.2.3   The committee shall, in keeping with its purpose (as set forth in § 3.8.1, above), define any other duties in any way it sees fit, subject to the approval of the Conference Leadership Council.
   3.8.3   Membership.
           3.8.3.1   Insofar as possible, the majority of the committee's members should be Native Americans.
           3.8.3.2   Taking into account the mandate of § 3.8.3.1, above, the committee shall define its membership in any way it sees fit, subject to the approval of the Conference Leadership Council.
   3.8.4   Organization – The committee shall organize itself in any way it sees fit, subject to the approval of the Conference Leadership Council.
   3.8.5   Amenability – The committee shall be amenable to the Conference Leadership Council (§ 2.1, above).

3.9   COMMITTEE ON AFRICAN-AMERICAN MINISTRY
   3.9.1   Purpose.
           3.9.1.1   Develop and support leadership for African-American churches and communities within the annual conference.
           3.9.1.2   Train, support, and empower African-American clergy and lay leadership for effective ministry in their churches, their communities, and the world.
   3.9.2   Duties – The committee shall, in keeping with its purpose (as set forth in § 3.9.1, above), define its duties in any way it sees fit, subject to the approval of the Conference Leadership Council.
   3.9.3   Membership – The committee shall define its membership in any way it sees fit, subject to the approval of the Conference Leadership Council.
   3.9.4   Organization – The committee shall organize itself in any way it sees fit, subject to the approval of the Conference Leadership Council.
   3.9.5   Amenability – The committee shall be amenable to the Conference Leadership Council (§ 2.1, above).

§ 4   ADMINISTRATIVE AGENCIES

4.1   COUNCIL ON FINANCE AND ADMINISTRATION.
   4.1.1   Purpose – To develop, maintain, and administer a comprehensive and coordinated plan of fiscal and administrative policies, procedures, and management services for the annual conference.
   4.1.2.   Duties.
           4.1.2.1.   Cooperation with the Conference Leadership Council in the development of the conference benevolences budget pursuant to ¶ 612.7 of *The Book of Discipline*.
           4.1.2.2.   Presentation to the annual conference of a budget, developed in conjunction with the recommendations of the Conference Leadership Council.

PLAN OF ORGANIZATION

4.1.2.3. Development of a ministry share formula for approval by the annual conference.

4.1.2.4. Ensure that appropriate compensation is provided for Clergy Assistant to the Bishop, the district superintendents, and the director of connectional ministries.

4.1.2.5. Develop policies for clergy moves undertaken in connection with a change in appointment.

4.1.2.6. Make a recommendation to the annual conference regarding any request for a conference-wide financial appeal.

4.1.2.7. Ensuring that the Commission on Equitable Compensation (§ 2.14, below), is fulfilling its responsibilities pursuant to *The Book of Discipline* and the direction of the annual conference.

4.1.2.7.1. Create and define, in consultation with the Committee on Human Resources, the position of Director of Conference Benefits and Human Resources.

4.1.2.8. Fulfill all other responsibilities enumerated in ¶¶ 613-618 of *The Book of Discipline*.

4.1.3. Membership.

4.1.3.1. With voice and vote.

4.1.3.1.1 Six clergy members of the annual conference.

4.1.3.1.2 Seven lay people who are professing members of a local church within the annual conference.

4.1.3.1.3 At least one of the thirteen members enumerated above shall be appointed to (in the case of a clergy person) or a member of (in the case of a lay person) a church with fewer than two hundred members.

4.1.3.2 *Ex officio* with voice and vote – Any member of the General Council on Finance and Administration who resides within the bounds of the annual conference.

4.1.3.3 *Ex officio* with voice only.

4.1.3.3.1 Director of Administrative Services and Conference Treasurer (see *The Book of Discipline*, ¶ 619).

4.1.3.3.2 Resident Bishop or clergy assistant to the Bishop (at the Bishop's discretion).

4.1.3.3.3 A district superintendent chosen by the Cabinet.

4.1.3.3.4 Director of Connectional Ministries (see *The Book of Discipline*, ¶ 608).

4.1.3.3.5 Director of Benefits and Human Resources.

4.1.3.3.6 Any other conference directors as the Conference Leadership Council shall designate.

4.1.3.3.7 Any director level benefits officer as determined by the Board of Pension and Health Benefits.

4.1.3.4 Members shall be nominated by the Committee on Nominations.

4.1.3.5 Members shall serve four-year terms (starting at the close of the annual conference session following General Conference), renewable once, with quadrennially staggered classes.

4.1.4 Organization.

4.1.4.1 The council shall elect from among its voting members a president, a vice president, and a secretary.

4.1.4.2   The Director of Administrative Services and Conference Treasurer (see *The Book of Discipline,* ¶ 619) shall be the council treasurer.

4.1.5   Relationship – The council shall relate to the General Council on Finance and Administration.

4.2   BOARD OF PENSION AND HEALTH BENEFITS

4.2.1   Purpose – Have charge of the interests and work of providing pension benefits and health insurance coverage to the clergy and eligible lay employees of the annual conference.

4.2.2   Duties.

4.2.2.1   Provide retirement, disability, and death benefits for all clergy members of the annual conference, their surviving spouses, and their dependent children.

4.2.2.2   Work with the Clergy Retirement Security Program of the General Board of Pension and Health Benefits.

4.2.2.3   Provide health insurance coverage for all clergy members, full-time local pastors, and full-time lay employees of the annual conference.

4.2.2.4   Continuously evaluate the quality and cost of the conference health insurance plan.

4.2.2.5   Provide information regarding conference health insurance benefits to all persons upon request.

4.2.2.6   Fulfill all other responsibilities enumerated in ¶ 639 of *The Book of Discipline.*

4.2.3   Membership.

4.2.3.1   Six clergy members of the annual conference.

4.2.3.2   Six lay persons who shall be professing members of a local church within the annual conference.

4.2.3.3   Members shall be nominated by the Committee on Nominations.

4.2.3.4   Members shall serve one non-renewable eight-year term, in annually staggered classes.

4.2.3.5   *Ex officio* with vote.

4.2.3.5.1   Any board member of Wespath Benefits and Investments residing within the bounds of the annual conference.

4.2.3.5.2   A district superintendent designated by the cabinet.

4.2.3.6   *Ex officio* with voice, but no vote.

4.2.3.6.1   Director of Administrative Services and Conference Treasurer (see *The Book of Discipline,* ¶ 619).

4.2.3.6.2   Director of Benefits and Human Resources.

4.2.3.6.3   Any other conference directors as the Conference Leadership Council shall designate.

4.2.3.6.4   Any director level benefits officer as determined by the Board.

4.2.4   Organization.

4.2.4.1   The committee shall elect from among its members the following officers:

4.2.4.1.1   Chairperson.

4.2.4.1.2   Vice chairperson.

4.2.4.1.3   Secretary.

4.2.4.2   The Director of Administrative Services and Conference Treasurer (see *The Book of Discipline,* ¶ 619) shall serve as the treasurer of the board.

4.2.4.3   The executive committee of the board shall be composed of the four officers enumerated above.

4.2.5   Relationship – The board shall relate to Wespath Benefits and Investments.

4.3 ADMINISTRATIVE REVIEW COMMITTEE

4.3.1.   Purpose – To ensure that the disciplinary procedures for involuntary changes in conference relationship are followed.

4.3.2.   Duties.

4.3.2.1   Review the entire administrative process leading to the action for a change in conference relationship.

4.3.2.2   Report to the clergy session on the finding of its review.

4.3.2.3   Fulfill all other responsibilities enumerated in ¶ 636 of *The Book of Discipline.*

4.3.3   Membership.

4.3.3.1   Three full clergy members of the annual conference.

4.3.3.2   Two additional full clergy members of the annual conference who shall serve as alternate committee members.

4.3.3.3   None of the foregoing shall be a district superintendent (or a relative thereof) or a member of the Board of Ordained Ministry (or a relative thereof).

4.3.3.4   Members shall be nominated by the Bishop.

4.3.3.5.   Members shall serve four-year terms, renewable once.

4.4. BOARD OF TRUSTEES

4.4.1.   Purpose – Management of property owned by the annual conference.

4.4.2   Duties.

4.4.2.1   Receive and hold in trust for the benefit of the annual conference all donations and bequests of real property and tangible personal property made to the annual conference.

4.4.2.2   Maintain all conference property.

4.4.2.3   Sell any conference property as may be directed by the annual conference or allowed by *The Book of Discipline.*

4.4.2.4   In conjunction with the conference chancellor, manage any legal affairs related to any conference property.

4.4.2.5   The Board of Trustees shall serve as the Board of Directors of the Michigan Conference of The United Methodist Church, a Michigan ecclesiastical corporation.

4.4.2.5   Fulfill all other responsibilities enumerated in ¶ 2512 of *The Book of Discipline.*

4.4.3   Membership.

4.4.3.1   Six clergy members of the annual conference.

4.4.3.2   Six lay persons who are professing members of a local church within the annual conference.

4.4.3.3   *Ex officio* with voice, but not vote.

4.4.3.3.1   Director of Administrative Services and Conference Treasurer (see *The Book of Discipline,* ¶ 619).

4.4.3.3.2   Director of Connectional Ministries (see *The Book of Discipline,* ¶ 608).

4.4.3.4   All board members must be at least eighteen years of age.

4.4.3.5   All board members must fulfill any other criteria for serving on the board of directors of a corporation that the laws of the State of Michigan may require.

4.4.3.6   Members shall be nominated by the Committee on Nominations.

4.4.3.7   Except as otherwise required by law, members shall be elected to four-year terms, renewable once, with annually staggered classes.

4.4.4   Organization.

4.4.4.1   Except as otherwise required by law, the board shall elect the following from among its members:

1.5.4.1.1   Chairperson.

1.5.4.1.2   Vice chairperson.

1.5.4.1.3   Secretary.

4.4.4.2   Except as otherwise required by law, the Director of Administrative Services and Conference Treasurer (see *The Book of Discipline*, ¶ 619) shall serve as the board treasurer.

4.5 COMMITTEE ON INVESTIGATION

4.5.1   Purpose – Consideration of judicial complaints against clergy members of the annual conference, clergy on location within the bounds of the annual conference, local pastors, and diaconal ministers.

4.5.2   Duties.

4.5.2.1   Conduct an investigation into the allegations made in a judicial complaint made against any of the persons enumerated above.

4.5.2.2   Issue a bill of charges and specifications against the respondent to a judicial complaint upon a finding of reasonable grounds.

4.5.2.3   Fulfill all other responsibilities enumerated in ¶¶ 2703-2706 of *The Book of Discipline*.

4.5.3   Membership.

4.5.3.1   Four ordained clergy members of the annual conference.

4.5.3.2   Three lay people who are professing members of a local church within the annual conference.

4.5.3.3   Three ordained clergy members of the annual conference shall serve as alternate members.

4.5.3.4   Six lay people – three of whom, if possible, shall be diaconal ministers – who are professing members of a local church within the annual conference shall serve as alternate members.

4.5.3.5   Members shall be nominated by the resident bishop.

4.5.3.6   Members shall serve a one-quadrennium term.

4.5.3.7   Members of the following entities and their immediate family members shall be ineligible for membership of the committee:

4.5.3.7.1   Cabinet.

4.5.3.7.2   Board of Ordained Ministry.

4.5.4   Organization.

4.5.4.1   The committee shall elect a chairperson from among its membership.

4.5.4.2   Seven members (or alternate members seated as members) shall constitute a quorum.

4.5.4.3   For the investigation of complaints against a diaconal minister, two alternate lay members shall be seated (bringing the total of lay members to five).

4.6 COMMITTEE ON RULES

    4.6.1   Purpose.

        4.6.1.1   In consultation with the Conference Leadership Council, maintain the efficient functionality and disciplinary compliance of the annual conference plan of organization.

        4.6.1.2   Consult with the Commission on the Annual Conference Session to ensure the efficient and orderly flow of the legislative process in preparation for and at the annual conference session.

    4.6.2   Duties.

        4.6.2.1   Initiate and propose revisions of the annual conference plan of organization as appropriate.

        4.6.2.2   Initiate and propose revisions of the rules of order (§ 5, below) as appropriate.

        4.6.2.3   Assign and train legislative committee chairs and recorders.

    4.6.3   Membership.

        4.6.3.1   Eight voting members who shall be either clergy members of the annual conference or lay people who are members of a local church within the annual conference.

        4.6.3.2   *Ex officio* with vote.

            4.6.3.2.1   Legislative Coordinator (Selected by the Commission on the Annual Conference Session)

            4.6.3.2.2   Annual Conference Facilitator.

            4.6.3.2.3   A district superintendent designated by the cabinet.

            4.6.3.2.4   Annual Conference Secretary.

            4.6.3.2.5   Conference parliamentarian (if one is appointed by the bishop).

        4.6.3.3   *Ex officio* with voice, but no vote – Director of Connectional Ministries (see *The Book of Discipline*, ¶ 608).

        4.6.3.4   Members shall be nominated by the Committee on Nominations.

        4.6.3.5   Members shall serve four-year terms, renewable twice, in annually staggered classes.

    4.6.4   Organization.

        4.6.4.1   The committee shall elect from among its members the following officers:

            4.6.4.1.1   Chairperson.

            4.6.4.1.2   Vice-chairperson.

            4.6.4.1.3   Secretary.

4.7 EPISCOPAL RESIDENCE COMMITTEE

    4.7.1   Purpose – Give oversight in matters of upkeep, maintenance, improvements, and insurance for the episcopal residence.

    4.7.2   Duties.

        4.7.2.1   Make recommendations regarding the purchase or sale of an episcopal residence.

        4.7.2.2   Prepare a proposed annual budget for the cost of providing the episcopal residence.

        4.7.2.3   Supervise the expenditure of funds related to the maintenance and upkeep of the episcopal residence.

        4.7.2.4   Fulfill all other responsibilities enumerated in ¶ 638 of *The Book of Discipline*.

4.7.3 Membership.

    4.7.3.1 Chairperson of the Committee on the Episcopacy (or representative).

    4.7.3.2 President of the Council on Finance and Administration (or representative).

    4.7.3.3 Chairperson of the Board of Trustees (or representative).

    4.7.3.4 Others may be co-opted, with voice but without vote, as needed.

4.7.4 Amenability – The committee shall be amenable to the Committee on the Episcopacy (§ 2.10, above).

4.8 COMMISSION ON EQUITABLE COMPENSATION

4.8.1 Purpose – Recommend conference standards for pastoral support and administer funds used to supplement pastoral support in instances where a charge is unable to meet its support requirements.

4.8.2 Duties.

    4.8.2.1 Submit to the annual conference session a recommended schedule of the required minimum salary for appointed pastors.

    4.8.2.2 Recommend to the annual conference standards and guidelines to be used in determining whether a charge qualifies for equitable compensation support.

    4.8.2.3 Administer the equitable compensation fund in accordance with the standards and guidelines adopted by the annual conference.

    4.8.2.4 Fulfill all other responsibilities enumerated in ¶ 625 of *The Book of Discipline*.

4.8.3 Membership.

    4.8.3.1 Four clergy members of the annual conference, at least one of whom shall be appointed to a church with fewer than 200 members.

    4.8.3.2 Four lay persons who shall be professing members of a church within the annual conference, at least one of whom shall be a member of a church with fewer than 200 members.

    4.8.3.3 Members shall serve four-year terms, renewable once, in annually staggered classes.

    4.8.3.4 Members shall be nominated by the Committee on Nominations.

    4.8.3.5 *Ex officio* with vote.

        4.8.3.5.1 A district superintendent appointed by the cabinet.

        4.8.3.5.2 A member of the Council on Finance and Administration.

    4.8.3.6 *Ex officio* with voice, but no vote – Director of Administrative Services and Conference Treasurer (see *The Book of Discipline*, ¶ 619).

4.8.4 Organization.

    4.8.4.1 The commission shall elect from among its members the following officers:

        4.8.4.1.1 Chairperson.

        4.8.4.1.2 Vice chairperson.

        4.8.4.1.3 Secretary.

    4.8.4.2 The Director of Administrative Services and Conference Treasurer (see *The Book of Discipline*, ¶ 619) shall serve as the treasurer of the commission.

4.8.5   Amenability – The board shall be amenable to the Council on Finance and Administration (§ 4.1, above).

4.9 COMMITTEE ON HUMAN RESOURCES

4.9.1   Purpose – Provide adequate program and support staff to carry out the purposes, goals, and responsibilities of the annual conference.

4.9.2   Duties.

    4.9.2.1   The committee shall be amenable to the Council on Finance and Administration with respect to administrative human resources policies and procedures. While the committee is primarily an administrative committee, it has a critical role in the programming functions of the conference. It is the responsibility of the committee to constantly evaluate the conference's staffing needs vis-à-vis the vision and mission of the conference.

    4.9.2.2   The committee shall also be amenable to the Conference Leadership Council, having input and taking direction on conference staffing as it relates to the mission and vision of the conference.

    4.9.2.3   Consult and collaborate with director level staff and the appointive cabinet (as needed) on the hiring, evaluation, support, training, and termination of non-exempt and exempt staff.

    4.9.2.4   Guide the annual evaluation of director level staff.

    4.9.2.5   Oversee the implementation of conference human resources policies and procedures handbook.

    4.9.2.6   Oversee the editing and maintenance of the conference employee handbook.

    4.9.2.7   Defines the role and functions of the Director of Benefits and Human Resources in consultation with the Council on Finance and Administration.

4.9.3   Membership.

    4.9.3.1   Eight people who shall be members of the annual conference (if clergy) or professing members of a local church within the annual conference (if laity).

    4.9.3.2   Members shall serve four-year terms, renewable once, in annually staggered classes.

    4.9.3.3   Members shall be nominated by the Committee on Nominations.

    4.9.3.4   *Ex officio* with vote.

        4.9.3.4.1   Bishop or clergy assistant to the Bishop (at the Bishop's discretion).

        4.9.3.4.2   A district superintendent chosen by the cabinet.

    4.9.3.5   *Ex officio* with voice, but no vote.

        4.9.3.5.1   Director of Connectional Ministries (see *The Book of Discipline*, ¶ 608).

        4.9.3.5.2   Director of Administrative Services and Conference Treasurer (see *The Book of Discipline*, ¶ 609).

        4.9.3.5.3   Director of Benefits and Human Resources.

        4.9.3.5.4   Chair of the personnel committee of the Council on Finance and Administration.

4.9.4   Organization.

    4.9.4.1   A chairperson chosen by the Committee on Nominations from among the members.

    4.9.4.2   A vice-chairperson chosen by the Committee on Human Resources from among its membership.

    4.9.4.3   A secretary chosen by the Committee on Human Resources from among its membership.

4.9.5   Amenability – The committee shall be amenable to the Council on Finance and Administration (§ 4.1., above) and the Conference Leadership Council (§ 2.1, above) as expounded in §§ 4.9.2.1 and 4.9.2.2, above.

§ 5   RULES OF ORDER

5.1   PRE-CONFERENCE

    5.1.1   Reports.

        5.1.1.1   All agencies that are directly amenable to the annual conference (enumerated hereinabove) and director-level staff of the annual conference are required to submit an annual report to the conference secretary no later than February 15. These reports shall be available on the conference website no later than April 1 and shall be included in the conference journal. Each agency's report shall include the report of any agencies amenable to it. (See § 5.1.1.4, below.)

        5.1.1.2   Notwithstanding § 5.1.1.1, the Board of Pension and Health Benefits and the Director of Administrative Services and Conference Treasurer shall submit an annual report no later than March 31.

        5.1.1.3   Notwithstanding § 5.1.1.1, the Committee on Nominations shall submit an annual report no later than the start of the annual conference session.

        5.1.1.4   All agencies not directly amenable to the annual conference (enumerated hereinabove) shall submit a report to the agency to which they are amenable no later than January 20. These reports shall be included in the reports of those supervising agencies as specified in § 5.1.1.1, above.

        5.1.1.5   The report of the conference statistician shall be available on the conference website no later than March 31 and shall be printed in the Journal.

        5.1.1.6   The proposed plan of organization of the annual conference shall be made available on the conference website no later than April 15 and shall be printed in the Journal.

    5.1.2   Resolutions.

        5.1.2.1   A resolution – a motion to initiate new business in the annual conference session – may be submitted by any of the following:

            5.1.2.1.1   A clergy member of the annual conference.

            5.1.2.1.2   A professing member of a local church within the annual conference.

            5.1.2.1.3   A specific person on behalf of an agency or other subdivision of the annual conference.

            5.1.2.1.4   A specific person on behalf of a local church or ministry setting of the annual conference or a committee thereof.

        5.1.2.2   All resolutions, upon being introduced in the annual conference session, must be presented by a member (clergy or lay) of the annual conference. The presenter of the resolution need not be the author of the resolution.

5.1.2.3   All resolutions must be submitted in writing to the Legislative Co-ordinator no later than February 15.

5.1.2.4   A copy of any resolution that would require an expenditure of more than $1000 must be sent to the Council on Finance and Administration, along with a five-year cost projection, no later than February 1.

5.1.2.5   If a resolution is submitted by multiple persons or entities, only the name of the person(s) actually signing it shall be published as the submitter. If more than two people actually sign a resolution, only the first two names will be published, along with the total number of additional signers.

5.1.2.6   Resolutions may be accompanied by a rationale, which shall not exceed 300 words.

5.1.2.7   The Committee on Rules reserves the right to edit any resolution for grammar, spelling, and clarity. The committee's edits shall not substantively alter the resolution.

5.1.2.8   Anyone submitting a resolution that affects other people or other entities is strongly encouraged to consult with the affected parties before submitting the resolution.

5.1.2.9   Anyone wishing to introduce a resolution (that was not timely submitted) directly in the plenary at the Annual Conference session must (in addition to requesting a suspension of the rules [§ 5.1.2.3]) have brought the following:

      5.1.2.9.1   At least 1700 paper copies of the resolution.

      5.1.2.9.2   A copy of the resolution on a thumb drive.

5.1.3   All resolutions and other items that must be voted or acted upon by the annual conference shall be posted to the conference website no later than April 15.

5.1.4   All requests for presentation time at the annual conference session must be made to the Commission on the Annual Conference Session no later than February 15. The granting of such requests shall be at the discretion of the Commission on the Annual Conference Session.

5.2 MEMBERSHIP

5.2.1   The annual conference membership shall be composed of the following:

5.2.1.1   Clergy members as defined in ¶¶ 32 and 602 of *The Book of Discipline*.

5.2.1.2   At least one lay person elected by each charge.

      5.2.1.2.1   A charge that has more than one church with 101 or more professing members shall elect one lay member for each church with 101 or more professing members.

      5.2.1.2.2   Each charge with more than one clergy person under episcopal appointment shall be entitled to as many lay members as it has clergy under episcopal appointment.

      5.2.1.2.3   Churches with more than 167 professing members shall be entitled to at least one lay member for every 167 professing members or major fraction thereof.

      5.2.1.2.4   Lay members shall have been professing members of The United Methodist Church for at least two years and shall have been active participants in The United Methodist Church for at least four years.

5.2.1.2.5   The rule that lay members shall have been professing members of The United Methodist Church for at least two years (§ 5.2.1.2.4, above) shall not apply in the case of youth (under age 18).

5.2.1.3   Deaconesses and home missioners under episcopal appointment within the bounds of the annual conference.

5.2.1.4   Diaconal ministers who are members of a local church within the annual conference.

5.2.1.5   Presidents of the conference United Methodist Women and United Methodist Men.

5.2.1.6   Conference lay leader.

5.2.1.7   District lay leaders.

5.2.1.8   Convener of the Division of Youth Ministry of the Board of Young People's Ministries.

5.2.1.9   Convener of the Division of Young Adult Ministry of the Board of Young People's Ministries.

5.2.1.10   One person between the ages of 12 and 18, inclusive, from each district.

5.2.1.11   One person between the ages of 18 and 30, inclusive, from each district.

5.2.1.12   Conference director of lay servant ministries.

5.2.1.13   Conference secretary of global ministries.

5.2.2   In order to equalize lay and clergy membership as required by ¶¶ 32 and 602.4 of *The Book of Discipline*, the following persons, when laity, shall be members of the annual conference in the order listed below.

5.2.2.1   Conference secretary.

5.2.2.2   Conference chancellor.

5.2.2.3   Annual Conference Coordinator.

5.2.2.4   Director of Administrative Services/Conference Treasurer (see *The Book of Discipline*, ¶ 619).

5.2.2.5   Conference parliamentarian.

5.2.2.6   Associate conference lay leader.

5.2.2.7   Director of Connectional Ministries (see *The Book of Discipline*, ¶ 608).

5.2.2.8   Any other conference director.

5.2.2.9   Any conference associate director.

5.2.2.10   Chairperson of the Committee on the Episcopacy.

5.2.2.11   Persons serving on general or jurisdictional agencies or the Connectional Table.

5.2.2.12   Delegates to General and Jurisdictional Conferences for the four Annual Conference sessions following their election.

5.2.2.13   Conference statistician.

5.2.2.14   Members of the Committee on Rules.

5.2.2.15   Members of the Conference Leadership Council.

5.2.2.16   Members of the Council on Finance and Administration.

5.2.2.17   Trustees of the annual conference.

5.2.2.18   Legislative coordinator.

5.2.2.19   Conference facilitator.

5.2.2.18   Members of the Commission on the Annual Conference Session.

5.2.2.19   Members of the Committee on the Journal.

5.2.2.20   Members of the Board of Ordained Ministry.

5.2.2.21   Chairpersons of other conference agencies (enumerated in §§ 1-4, above).

5.2.3   Any remaining lay members necessary for equalization shall be selected by the Board of Laity.

5.2.4   The following, if laity, shall be granted voice but not vote:

5.2.4.1   A representative from each of the affiliate entities enumerated in § 10, below.

5.2.4.2   Affiliate clergypersons.

5.3   RESPONSIBILITY FOR THE COST OF ATTENDANCE

5.3.1   Active clergy – The local church or ministry to which clergy are appointed shall pay for registration, room, and board.

5.3.2   Retired clergy (except as stated in § 5.3.7, below).

5.3.2.1   The annual conference shall pay for registration.

5.3.2.2   Retired clergy shall pay for their own room and board.

5.3.3   Laity representing charges – The charge shall pay for registration, room, and board.

5.3.4   Laity attending by virtue of office (enumerated in §§ 5.2.1.3 through 5.2.1.13 and 5.2.2, above) – The annual conference shall pay for registration, room, and board.

5.3.5   Laity selected by the Board of Laity (as per § 5.2.3, above) – The annual conference shall pay for registration, room, and board.

5.3.6   Those who are being received into provisional membership and who are not currently serving as local pastors – the Board of Ordained Ministry shall pay for registration, room, and board.

5.3.7   Notwithstanding § 5.3.2, above, the Board of Ordained Ministry shall pay for registration, room, and board for retired clergy serving on the Board of Ordained Ministry.

5.4   THE ANNUAL CONFERENCE SESSION

5.4.1   In accordance with ¶ 603.2 of *The Book of Discipline*, the Bishop shall determine the time of the annual conference session.

5.4.2   The Commission on the Annual Conference Session shall determine the place and the program for the annual conference session.

5.4.3   In addition to the business (plenary) sessions of the annual conference, the following sessions shall also be held:

5.4.3.1   An orientation session for lay members of the annual conference shall be held early in the conference session. It is recommended that this be done as early as possible.

5.4.3.2   Clergy session.

5.4.3.2.1   A clergy session shall be held at which questions relating to matters of ordination, character, and conference relations of clergy shall be attended to.

5.4.3.2.2   Ordained clergy and lay members of the Board of Ordained Ministry shall have voice and vote in the clergy session.

5.4.3.2.3   Non-ordained clergy shall have voice, but no vote in the clergy session.

5.4.3.2.4   Lay persons, other than those serving on the Board of Ordained Ministry, shall not be admitted to the clergy session unless the clergy session shall expressly authorize otherwise.

5.4.3.3 Corporate session.

    5.4.3.3.1 A corporate session shall be held to handle any corporate matters that may be required by the laws of the State of Michigan and any other business specified by the Board of Trustees.

    5.4.3.3.2 The chair of the Board of Trustees shall preside at the corporate session.

5.4.4 All materials distributed by the ushers at the annual conference session must be approved by either the Commission on the Annual Conference Session or the Committee on Rules.

5.4.5 Voting area.

    5.4.5.1 At the first business session of the annual conference session, a voting bar shall be fixed. All members of the annual conference, lay and clergy, must display a membership badge in order to be admitted to the bar of the conference.

    5.4.5.2 Except for volunteers assisting with the functioning of the annual conference session (*e.g.*, ushers and pages), paid personnel acting within the course of their duties (*e.g.*, audio-visual technicians and facilities staff), area office staff, and anyone entitled to voice but not vote in the annual conference session (as enumerated in § 5.2.4, above), no one who is not a voting member of the annual conference shall be allowed in the bar of the conference when the conference is in session.

    5.4.5.3 Except by leave of the annual conference, no member who is not within the bar of the conference at the time a question is called for shall be allowed to vote.

5.4.6 Accessibility – Handicap accessible seating areas shall be clearly marked at all Annual Conference business sessions.

5.4.7 Voting procedure.

    5.4.7.1 All voting shall be by show of colored placards unless otherwise directed by the presiding officer. A division of the house shall occur upon motion for same, supported by at least one-fifth of the members present and voting.

    5.4.7.2 Except as otherwise directed by *The Book of Discipline* or by these rules, all questions shall be decided by a simple majority of those present and voting.

5.4.8 No later than 11:00 a.m., the minutes of the previous day's proceedings shall be made publicly available for viewing, by posting in a conspicuous place at the site of the conference session, posting to the conference website, or e-mailing to conference members.

5.4.9 Reports timely submitted for approval need not be read aloud or read into the record before being voted upon.

5.4.10 Introductions of speakers shall be limited to two minutes.

5.4.11 Opportunity shall be given for announcements to be read by the conference secretary at the close of each business session.

5.4.12 Procedures governing speeches from the floor of the business session.

    5.4.12.1 Microphones shall be placed around the conference floor so that members may speak from near their seats.

    5.4.12.2 Any member desiring to speak in debate, present any matter, or make any motion shall raise the provided colored placard while seated and wait to be recognized by the chair.

5.4.12.3   Upon being recognized by the chair, members shall proceed to the microphone to which they were directed and before saying anything else shall give their name and the church or extension ministry to which they are appointed (in the case of active clergy), church (in the case of laity representing their local church pursuant to § 5.2.1.2, above), agency or position (in the case of laity who are members by virtue of office pursuant to § 5.2.2, above), equalization status (in the case of laity selected by the Board of Laity pursuant to § 5.2.3, above), or retired status (in the case of retired clergy).

5.4.12.4   After identifying themselves, members speaking to a motion shall state whether they are speaking for or against said motion.

5.4.12.5   Any member desiring to speak on a question of privilege shall, upon being recognized by the chair, briefly state the question but shall proceed only when the chair has decided it to be a privileged question.

5.4.12.6   No member shall speak more than twice as to the same motion.

5.4.12.7   Speeches shall be no longer than three minutes in duration. This time period shall begin after a speaker has been properly recognized by the Chair and has properly introduced himself/herself.

5.4.12.8   Except for non-debatable motions, no resolution, report, or motion shall be adopted or a question relating thereto decided without opportunity having been given for at least three speeches in favor thereof and three speeches against.

5.4.12.9   Before debate on any resolution begins, the presenter or his/her representative shall have the opportunity to speak for up to three minutes.

5.4.12.10 At the conclusion of debate on any main motion, the presenter of said motion or his/her representative shall be entitled to speak up to one minute even after the previous question has been called.

5.4.13   Legislative committees.

5.4.13.1   The Committee on Rules shall, in consultation with the Commission on the Annual Conference Session, decide the number of legislative committees into which the annual conference will be divided.

5.4.13.2   The conference registrar shall randomly assign all members to a legislative committee, with care being given to make certain that members with disabilities be assigned to a committee meeting in a room with barrier-free access.

5.4.13.3   All resolutions to come before the annual conference shall be assigned by the Committee on Rules to any of the legislative committees. The Committee on Rules may, at its discretion assign resolutions directly to the plenary, by-passing legislative committees. Such an action should only be taken in cases where a resolution is non-controversial and/or highly technical in nature.

5.4.13.4   All resolutions, upon initially being brought to the floor (whether in a legislative committee or in the plenary) shall be introduced by a presenter who must be a member of the annual conference. The presenter shall have up to three minutes to speak to the resolution before debate begins. At the conclusion of debate, the presenter of said motion shall be entitled to speak up to three minutes even after the previous question has been called. No resolution shall be considered by its assigned committee unless a presenter is present at the committee session. In the event no presenter for a resolution is present, no one may designate himself/herself as a presenter.

5.4.13.5   All rules governing debate in the plenary session shall govern debate in legislative committees.

5.4.13.6   Notwithstanding § 5.4.13.2, the chairperson and recorder of a given legislative committee shall be members (with all privileges appertaining thereto) of that committee only.

5.4.13.7   Notwithstanding § 5.4.13.2, the presenter of a resolution being considered by a given legislative committee shall be a member of that committee only.

5.4.13.8   If a resolution has more than one presenter, only one of those presenters shall be entitled to voice and vote in the committee (except for presenters who were originally selected by the registrar as members of that committee).

5.4.13.9   When a legislative committee votes in favor of a resolution, the resolution shall come before the plenary as perfected for ordinary debate and discussion in accordance with all applicable rules.

5.4.13.10   When a legislative committee votes against a resolution, the question of whether to consider that resolution notwithstanding the vote of the legislative committee shall be brought to the plenary. Only in the event that at least 20% of the plenary votes in favor of consideration shall the resolution then be considered by the plenary.

5.4.13.11   When the question of consideration of a resolution notwithstanding the vote of the legislative committee is brought before the plenary in accordance with § 5.4.13.11, the presenter of the resolution shall not have the opportunity to speak before the vote on whether to consider the resolution is taken. Should the plenary vote to consider a resolution notwithstanding the vote of the legislative committee, the presenter shall then have the opportunity to speak for up to three minutes before debate begins and shall have the right to give a concluding speech (§ 5.4.12.10).

5.4.13.12   A legislative committee may only consider business assigned to it by the Committee on Rules, except that any substitute resolution duly moved by a member of the legislative committee shall be considered by the committee.

5.4.13.13   At the discretion of the Commission on the Annual Conference Session, a non-legislative discussion item may be assigned to the several legislative committees provided that such discussion advances a clearly defined purpose.

5.4.13.14   After the legislative committees have concluded their business, the Legislative Coordinator shall compile a written report of their work, to be presented to the plenary as soon as possible. The report shall contain the following:

5.4.13.14.1   Editorial corrections to any resolutions.

5.4.13.14.2   Proposed amendments (to any resolutions or substitute resolutions), including the results of the votes thereon.

5.4.13.14.3   Proposed secondary amendments (to any resolutions or substitute resolutions), including the results of the votes thereon.

5.4.13.14.4   Proposed substitute resolutions, including the results of the votes thereon.

5.4.13.14.5   The results of the final votes taken on all resolutions (or substitutes thereto).

5.4.13.14.6   The names of the committee chairs and recorders.

5.4.13.14.7   A listing of which resolutions have been placed on the consent calendar (see § 5.4.14, below).

5.4.13.15   Once adopted, all resolutions shall be valid until the close of the Annual Conference session eight years thence (unless otherwise prohibited by *The Book of Discipline*).

5.4.14   Consent calendar.

5.4.14.1   Any resolution (or substitute resolution) that sustains a vote of concurrence by at least nine-tenths of its legislative committee shall be placed on the conference consent calendar.

5.4.14.2   All resolutions placed on the conference consent calendar shall be considered *en masse* by the plenary, whose consideration of the consent calendar shall not be subject to debate, amendment, or substitution.

5.4.14.3   Notwithstanding § 5.4.14.2, any resolution may be removed from the consent calendar by a vote of at least two-fifths of the plenary. Any resolution, upon being removed from the consent calendar, shall be considered as an ordinary item of business.

5.4.14.4   The consent calendar shall not be brought to a vote until at least two hours after it has been distributed to the members of the conference.

5.4.15   Adopted resolutions.

5.4.15.1   All adopted resolutions shall be published on the conference website as soon as is practical.

5.4.15.2   The conference secretary shall determine which resolutions require action by an agency, officer, or employee of the annual conference and shall, as soon as is practical after the close of the annual conference session, submit the relevant resolution(s) to the parties of whom action is required.

5.4.15.3   Any resolution or any portion of a resolution subsequently ruled by a bishop's decision of law to be null, void, and/or of no effect shall immediately be removed from the conference website, and all conference action thereon shall immediately cease. In the event that the Judicial Council fails to sustain the ruling of the Bishop in whole or in part, any reinstated portion of the resolution shall immediately be returned to the conference website, and all conference action thereon shall immediately resume.

5.4.15.4   Except as otherwise specified either therein or by *The Book of Discipline*, all resolutions adopted by the annual conference shall be valid from the close of the annual conference session until the close of the following annual conference session.

5.5   NOMINATIONS

5.5.1   Each agency shall annually review its membership to identify members who have not functioned. After consultation with the person(s) so identified, a written request for replacement shall be sent to the Committee on Nominations no later than January 10, with a copy of such request sent to the person(s) so identified.

5.5.2   Any agency wishing to suggest nominees may do so by submitting the request in writing to the Committee on Nominations no later than January 10.

5.5.3   Except as otherwise required by *The Book of Discipline,* all terms of office shall begin at the close of the annual conference session.

5.5.4   Aside from *ex officio* membership, no one may serve on more than two agencies at once.

5.5.5   The Committee on Nominations, when nominating persons for agency membership, shall give primary consideration to aptness, experience, diversity, inclusiveness, and efficiency.

5.5.6   Aside from *ex officio* membership, no employee of the annual conference shall be eligible to serve on an agency that has supervisory responsibility over the area of that employee's work.

5.5.7   Except as otherwise provided herein, no district superintendent shall serve on a conference agency.

5.5.8   At the annual conference session immediately following General Conference, the annual conference shall elect people – nominated by the Committee on Nominations in consultation with the Conference Leadership Council – to the following positions:

  5.5.8.1   Secretary.

  5.5.8.2   Director of Administrative Services and Conference Treasurer (see *The Book of Discipline,* ¶ 619).

  5.5.8.3   Statistician.

5.6   DEPENDENT CARE

5.6.1   While carrying out the responsibilities of the annual conference or any agency thereof, members may be reimbursed for dependent care provided in their homes. Such reimbursement shall not exceed ten hours per day and shall not exceed minimum wage.

5.6.2   Each agency shall be responsible for budgeting for appropriate dependent care expenses when considering its membership and time requirements.

5.6.3   Dependent care expenses shall be vouchered and reimbursed.

5.6.4   Local churches are encouraged to support members in need of dependent care for conference responsibilities by volunteering to provide dependent care whenever possible.

5.6.5   Agency members are encouraged to enlist family members and friends for dependent care whenever possible.

5.6.6   Conference agencies may choose to provide on-site childcare. In such cases, parents shall be responsible for bringing necessary items (*e.g.*, toys, lunches) for their children. The conference protection policy (§ 8, below) shall be strictly followed.

5.7   GENERAL AND JURISDICTIONAL CONFERENCES

5.7.1   Nomination of candidates for General and Jurisdictional Conference delegation.

  5.7.1.1   Nomination forms designed by the Committee on Rules and the Order of Business shall be made available on the conference website no later than October 15 of the calendar year preceding delegate elections.

5.7.1.2   Candidates may be nominated by themselves or by another clergy member of the annual conference (in the case of clergy) or by another professing member of a local church within the annual conference (in the case of laity).

5.7.1.3   The names of the candidates and the information on their nomination forms shall be posted to the conference website no later than April 1.

5.7.2   Election of delegates.

5.7.2.1   Elections shall occur at the annual conference session in the calendar year immediately preceding General Conference.

5.7.2.2   The Commission on the Annual Conference Session shall appoint a group of tellers, who shall be composed of people ineligible (as per ¶¶ 35-36 of *The Book of Discipline*) and/or unwilling to serve as delegates.

5.7.2.3   The election of General Conference delegates and Jurisdictional Conference delegates shall constitute a single process, with General Conference delegates being elected first.

5.7.2.4   Eligible voters may vote for as many different people as are being elected on a particular ballot.

5.7.2.5   In order to be elected, a candidate must receive a vote on a simple majority of valid (*i.e.*, non-defective) ballots cast.

5.7.2.6   Clergy and laity ballots shall be taken separately, alternating between the two.

5.7.2.7   After the designated number of delegates for General Conference has been elected, the election of Jurisdictional Conference delegates shall begin on the following ballot.

5.7.2.8   The Jurisdictional Conference delegates shall serve as reserve delegates to General Conference in the order elected.

5.7.2.9   After the designated number of delegates for Jurisdictional Conference has been elected, an additional ballot shall be taken, on which the two highest vote-getters (regardless of whether their vote totals constitute a majority) shall be elected as reserve delegates to Jurisdictional Conference.

5.7.2.10   Ties shall be broken by the casting of lots.

5.7.2.11   All conference members must be seated in the bar of the conference at the time a vote is taken in order to vote.

5.7.2.12   A ballot that includes more votes than people being elected on that ballot shall be invalid and shall not be counted in the vote total.

5.7.2.13   After each vote, the secretary of the conference (or a person designated by him/her) shall announce the number of votes received by all candidates who received at least 10 votes.

5.7.2.14   Write-in votes shall be allowed on any ballot, provided the name being written in meets the requirements set forth in ¶¶ 35-36 of *The Book of Discipline*.

5.7.2.15   Candidates' names need not be spelled correctly on a ballot. Any ballot on which the intent of the voter can be reasonably discerned will be counted.

5.7.3   Petitions to General and Jurisdictional Conferences.

5.7.3.1   Anyone eligible to submit a resolution to the annual conference may submit a proposed petition to General or Jurisdictional Conferences for endorsement by the annual conference.

5.7.3.2 Petitions to General or Jurisdictional Conferences shall be treated like resolutions except that they shall not be subject to amendment (although they shall be subject to substitution, and substitute motions shall be subject to amendment).

5.7.4 Endorsement of episcopal nominees.

5.7.4.1 At the session of the annual conference immediately prior to Jurisdictional Conference, the annual conference may endorse any number of episcopal nominees, up to the number of bishops being elected.

5.7.4.2 The Jurisdictional Conference delegation, at its discretion, may nominate candidates for endorsement.

5.7.4.3 Immediately following the presentation of the candidates for endorsement recommended by the Jurisdictional Conference delegation, any conference member may make a nomination from the floor.

5.7.4.4 Any full elder eligible for the office of bishop may be endorsed for election. A full elder need not be a member of the annual conference or a declared candidate for the episcopacy in order to be endorsed.

5.7.4.5 A ballot shall be taken no less than four hours after nominations are made.

5.7.4.6 Members may vote for up to the number of episcopal vacancies in the jurisdiction or the number of nominations, whichever is fewer. Provision shall be made on each ballot for a vote of no endorsement.

5.7.4.7 A nominee must receive a vote on at least 60% of the valid (*i.e.*, non-defective) ballots in order to receive the endorsement of the annual conference.

5.7.4.8 The number of ballots taken shall be equal to the number of episcopal vacancies, except that no further ballots shall be taken if either of the following occurs:

5.7.4.8.1 The number of candidates who have received the endorsement of the annual conference has reached the number of episcopal vacancies.

5.7.4.8.2 At least 60% of the valid (*i.e.*, non-defective) ballots cast are for a vote of no endorsement.

5.8 PARLIAMENTARY AUTHORITY

5.8.1 The proceedings of the annual conference shall be governed by the following in order of priority and precedence:

5.8.1.1 *The Book of Discipline.*

5.8.1.2 The acts of the preceding North Central Jurisdictional Conference.

5.8.1.3 The Plan of Organization of the Michigan Annual Conference.

5.8.1.4 *Robert's Rules of Order Newly Revised* (11th edition).

5.8.2 The Plan of Organization of the Michigan Annual Conference shall remain in force and effect until repealed, amended, or superseded by a vote of at least two-thirds of the annual conference.

5.8.3 Notwithstanding § 5.8.2, if any portion of the Plan of Organization of the Michigan Annual Conference be invalidated, either directly or indirectly, by General Conference, the Judicial Council, or an episcopal ruling of law, the remaining portions of the Plan of Organization shall remain in effect.

§ 6 OFFICERS OF THE ANNUAL CONFERENCE

6.1 SECRETARY

   6.1.1   Election.

        6.1.1.1   At the first session of the annual conference following General Conference, the annual conference shall elect a secretary, nominated by the Committee on Nominations in consultation with the Bishop, who shall take office immediately following the adjournment of that session of the annual conference.

        6.1.1.2   Notwithstanding the foregoing, the outgoing secretary shall still be responsible for the completion of that year's conference journal.

        6.1.1.3   The secretary shall serve a four-year term, renewable once.

        6.1.1.4   If the secretary wishes to retire after one term, he/she must notify the Committee on Nominations and the Bishop by January 1 of the year preceding General Conference.

   6.1.2   The secretary, after certifying the number of lay members necessary for equalization with clergy members, shall determine the distribution of lay members (in accordance with the rules hereinabove) and shall notify the proper persons no later than January 10.

   6.1.3   Duties.

        6.1.3.1   Serve as the chair of the Committee on the Journal.

        6.1.3.2   Receive all required agency annual reports and shall ensure that they contain no action items or budget proposals.

        6.1.3.3   Keep a fair and accurate record of the proceedings of the annual conference session.

        6.1.3.4   Preserve the journals and papers of the annual conference.

        6.1.3.5   Receive and review any written notices of corrections and additions to the conference journal as published, incorporating them into the permanent records of the annual conference as appropriate.

        6.1.3.6   Serve *ex officio* on the Commission on the Annual Conference Session and the Committee on Rules and the Order of Business.

6.2 STATISTICIAN

   6.2.1   The statistician shall be elected, upon nomination of the Committee on Nominations in consultation with the Bishop and Conference Treasurer, at the session of the annual conference immediately preceding General Conference.

   6.2.2   The statistician shall report directly to the conference treasurer.

   6.2.3   The statistician shall serve a four-year term, renewable once.

6.3 FACILITATOR

   6.3.1   The conference shall elect, upon nomination of the Committee on Nominations, a layperson to serve as facilitator.

   6.3.2   The facilitator shall serve a four-year term, renewable once.

   6.3.3   The facilitator shall be seated at an announced location on the floor of the annual conference session and shall have the duties of assisting anyone who needs assistance in understanding and using procedures and resources of the conference session.

   6.3.4   The facilitator shall serve as an *ex officio* member of the Commission on the Annual Conference Session and the Committee on Rules.

6.3.5   Nominated by the Committee on Nominations and elected by the annual conference for a four-year term, renewable once.

6.4 PARLIAMENTARIAN

6.4.1   The Bishop may, at his or her discretion, appoint a conference parliamentarian.

6.4.2   The parliamentarian shall assist the Bishop in ensuring that the annual conference session is run in accordance with the rules of order set forth hereinabove.

6.4.3   The parliamentarian, should one be chosen, shall serve at the Bishop's pleasure.

6.5 CHANCELLOR

6.5.1   The conference shall designate a chancellor, who shall be nominated by the Bishop and elected quadrennially by the annual conference.

6.5.2   The chancellor shall be a member of a local church within the annual conference and shall also be a member in good standing of the State Bar of Michigan.

6.5.3   Except as prohibited by the Michigan Rules of Professional Conduct, the chancellor shall serve as legal advisor to the Bishop and to the annual conference.

6.6 DIRECTOR OF ADMINISTRATIVE SERVICES AND CONFERENCE TREASURER

6.6.1   Coordinates and collaborates with the Council on Finance and Administration regarding the conference budget process and the oversight of the treasury staff.

6.6.2   Coordinates with the Board of Trustees regarding facility contracts and concerns.

6.6.3   Oversees information technology (I.T.) contracts in consultation with the director of communications.

6.6.4   Elected by the annual conference at the first session following each General Conference.

6.6.5   Directly amenable to the Council on Finance and Administration (§ 1.2, above).

6.6.6   Fulfills all other responsibilities enumerated in ¶ 619 of *The Book of Discipline*.

6.7 LAY LEADER

6.7.1   Fosters awareness of the role of the laity within the congregation and through their ministries in the home, workplace, community, and world.

6.7.2   Advocates for the role of the laity in the life of the church, encouraging laypersons in the general ministry of the church.

6.7.3   Meets with the cabinet when matters relating to the coordination, implementation, or administration of the conference program, or other matters as the cabinet may determine.

6.7.4   Fulfills all other responsibilities enumerated in ¶ 607 of *The Book of Discipline*.

6.7.5   Nominated by the Bishop in consultation with the Board of Laity, and elected for one four-year term.

§ 7 FINANCIAL POLICIES

[*To be supplied by the Council on Finance and Administration.*]

§ 8 PROTECTION POLICY

[*To be supplied by the Protection Policy Implementation Team.*]

§ 9 HUMAN RESOURCES POLICIES

[*To be supplied by the Committee on Human Resources.*]

§ 10 AFFILIATE ENTITIES OF THE ANNUAL CONFERENCE

10.1 AFFILIATED VIA THE BOARD OF GLOBAL MINISTRIES
10.1.1   Bronson Health Group.
10.1.2   Clark Retirement Community.
10.1.3   Methodist Children's Home Society.
10.1.4   United Methodist Community House.
10.1.5   United Methodist Retirement Communities, Inc.

10.2 AFFILIATED VIA THE BOARD OF YOUNG PEOPLE'S MINISTRIES
10.2.1   Adrian College.
10.2.2   Albion College.
10.2.3   Bay Shore Evangelical Association.
10.2.4   Michigan Area Board of Christian Camping.
10.2.5   Lake Louise Christian Community.

10.3 AFFILIATED VIA THE COMMISSION ON ARCHIVES AND HISTORY – Michigan Area United Methodist Church Historical Society, Inc.

10.4 AFFILIATED VIA THE COUNCIL ON FINANCE AND ADMINISTRATION
10.4.1   Michigan Area Loan Funds.
10.4.2   United Methodist Foundation of Michigan.

§ 11 DISTRICTS

11.1. Nine Districts. There shall be nine (9) Districts in the Michigan Conference. The boundaries shall be determined from time to time by the Bishop. (2016 Discipline ¶ 415.4)

11.2 *Book of Discipline.* At all times, operation of the Districts in the Michigan Conference shall be subject to the *Book of Discipline*, as amended from time to time, and this Plan of Organization.

11.3. Incorporation. All Districts shall be separately incorporated and shall comply with the Michigan Non-Profit Corporation Act. (*Book of Discipline* ¶ 2518.2). The bylaws shall describe the duties of the Officers and Directors. The District Leadership Team shall be the Board of Directors of the corporation. The officers of the District Leadership Team shall be the officers of the corporation.

11.4. Basic District Structure. The following shall be the basic structure of each District.

11.4.1 District Conference. Each District shall hold a District Conference at least annually at a time and place selected by the District superintendent in consultation with the District Leadership Team and in a manner consistent with the Discipline. (2016 Discipline ¶ 658-659). Membership of the District Conference shall be all clergy members of the Michigan Conference appointed or residing in the District, and the professing members of all congregations located in the District. No congregation shall be represented by more than ten (10) professing members.

11.4.2 District Leadership Team. Each District shall have a District Leadership Team.

    11.4.2.1. Membership. The team shall consist of between six (6) and fifteen (15) members as nominated by the District Nominating Committee and as elected by the District Conference. The members shall serve for three (3) year terms, and no member may serve for more than three consecutive terms. The District Conference may stagger the terms in its discretion. The District Superintendent and the Lay Leader shall be members with voice and vote. The District Leadership Team shall elect its own officers; a Chair, Secretary and Treasurer, who shall also be the officers of the Corporation. It may elect such additional officers as it deems appropriate.

    11.4.2.2. Vision Team. Prior to and at the commencement of each new District, and for a reasonable time thereafter, in the discretion of the District Superintendent, a Vision Team may be organized to do visioning for the District. The members shall be appointed by the District Superintendent. This Vision Team will disband after it has done its initial visioning work and a District Leadership Team is properly elected by the District Conference. The Vision Team shall perform the functions of the District Leadership Team until the District Leadership Team is properly elected by the District Conference.

    11.4.2.3. Roles and Responsibilities. The District Leadership Team shall be the primary programmatic, fiduciary and administrative agency of District. It may create such subcommittees as it deems appropriate.

        11.4.2.3.1. The District Leadership Team officers shall serve as the Board of Trustees for the District and perform all functions inherent in a Board of Trustees, including the owning of any District real estate and being the party to any legal contracts. (*Book of Discipline* ¶2518). Unless the District Leadership Team is directed by the Annual Conference Board of Trustees, the Annual Conference Board of Trustees shall be responsible for the sale of all closed church buildings and parsonages in the District or owned by the District.

        11.4.2.3.2. The District Leadership Team shall serve as the District Board of Missions. It shall receive and manage all invested and budgeted funds held by the District. Invested funds shall consist of funds currently held by District Boards of Mission and Church Extension, or their equivalent, prior to January 1, 2019. Additional invested funds may be received through gift, fundraising, or the receipt of the proceeds of the sale of closed church property, as determined by the Annual Conference. With the advice of the District Superintendent and the Conference Leadership Council, the District Leadership Team shall make all decisions regarding the use of invested and budgeted funds in the mission and ministry of the District.

11.4.2.3.3. Exception. The United Methodist Union of Greater Detroit shall serve as the Board of Missions for the District(s) which includes the City of Detroit.

11.4.3   Committees Required by Discipline. All Districts shall have a District Committee on the Superintendency, District Committee on Ministry, and District Committee on Church Location and Building. The makeup, meetings, and authority of these committees shall be as required by the Discipline. They shall report regularly to the District Conference and District Leadership Team.

11.4.4   Nominating Committee. There shall be a District Nominating Committee to make recommendations to the District Conference. It shall consist of between four (4) and ten (10) members. The District Superintendent shall be the chair of the Committee and the Lay Leader shall be a member. Members shall be elected to three (3) year terms, with no member serving more than three consecutive terms. Members shall be elected by the District Conference and may be in staggered classes as directed by the District Conference. In making nominations for all District agencies, care shall be taken to have an inclusive membership and that is otherwise representative of the District

11.4.5   Reporting and Accountability. The District Leadership Team shall make oral and written annual reports to the District Conference and such reports as requested to the Michigan Conference of all of its activities, including the receipt, investment, management and disbursement of assets. The District Leadership Team shall also be amenable to the Conference Leadership Council, and shall be amenable to the Conference Board of Trustees for property related matters and to the Conference Council on Finance and Administration for all financial matters.

11.5 Other Agencies. The District may have such other agencies as the District Conference may determine from time to time not inconsistent with the Discipline or this Plan of Organization.

INDEX – PLAN OF ORGANIZATION

— MAC Photos

INDEX – GENERAL

Made in the USA
Monee, IL
02 December 2019

17787240R00455